# SAUNDERS
# AN INTRODUCTION TO CRIMINAL LAW IN CONTEXT

## Cases, Notes and Materials

*Third Edition*

*edited by*
## R.P. Saunders
*Professor of Law, Carleton University*

*with the assistance of*
## J. McMunagle
*B.A., LL.B.*

*co-editor of 1st and 2nd editions*
## C.N. Mitchell

Thomson Professional Publishing

©1996 by Thomson Canada Limited.

All rights reserved. No part of this publication covered by the publisher's copyright may be reproduced, stored in a retrieval system, or transmitted, in any form or by any means, electronic, mechanical, photocopying, recording, or otherwise, without the prior written permission of the publisher.

The publisher is not engaged in rendering legal, accounting or other professional advice. If legal advice or other expert assistance is required, the services of a competent professional should be sought. The analysis contained herein represents the opinions of the authors and should in no way be construed as being official or unofficial policy of any governmental body.

This work reproduces official English language versions of federal and provincial statutes and regulations. As the federal material, and many of the provincial statutes and regulations also have official French versions, the reader is advised that reference to the official French language material may be warranted in appropriate circumstances.

**Canadian Cataloguing in Publication Data**

An Introduction to criminal law in context.

(A Carswell student edition)
3rd ed.
At head of title: Saunders & Mitchell.
Includes bibliographical references.
ISBN 0-459-55440-9

1. Criminal law — Canada.   2. Criminal law — Canada — Cases.   I. Mitchell, Chet N.
II. Saunders, Ron P.   III. Series: Carswell student editions

KE8808.2.I58 1996      345'.71      C96-931622-4
KF9220.ZA2158 1996

The acid-free paper used in this publication meets the minimum requirements of American National Standard for Information Sciences — Permanence of Paper for Printed Library Materials, ANSI Z39.48-1984.

Thomson Professional Publishing

One Corporate Plaza, 2075 Kennedy Road, Scarborough, Ontario M1T 3V4
Customer Service:
Toronto 1-416-609-3800
Elsewhere in Canada/U.S. 1-800-387-5164
Fax 1-416-298-5094

*For Emma, Katie and Patrick, with love*
*— R.P.S.*

*For my entire family, especially Ann and the children for their unfailing support and for the many students with whom I have had the privilege of learning the criminal law.*
*— J.A.M.*

# EDITOR'S NOTE

The editors gratefully acknowledge the authors and publishers who have granted permission to reproduce their work in this book. It should be noted that the footnotes and bibliographies of most of the readings have been removed in the interest of space and cost, and readers are directed to the original readings in order to find them.

The editors also acknowledge the valuable contributions of Professor Ross Hastings of the Department of Criminology, University of Ottawa, and Professor Barry Wright of the Department of Law, Carleton University, who wrote original selections for this text and who commented on the materials chosen and topics covered.

The editors would also like to thank Lisa Bruneau for her clerical assistance and for her patience.

Unfortunately, my friend and colleague, Chet Mitchell, who co-edited the first two editions of this text, died in January, 1991, soon after the publication of the second edition. Much of this text continues to owe its content and direction to his efforts and contributions. His intellect, warmth, originality and generosity of spirit are greatly missed both in Carleton University and in the wider academic community.

R.P. Saunders
July, 1996

# Copyright/Acknowledgements

The publishers and the authors gratefully acknowledge the authors, publishers and organizations listed below for their permission to reproduce the following excerpts. Every effort was made to locate the authors of materials contained herein and to obtain permissions, and the Publishers apologize for any errors or omissions.

**The Role of Law in Social Transformation: Is a Jurisprudence of Insurgency Possible?**
*Stephen Brickey & Elizabeth Comack*
Appearing in (1987), 2 Canadian Journal of Law and Society 97. Reprinted by Permission of Canadian Journal of Law and Society.

**Models of Justice: Portia or Persephone? Some Thoughts on Equality, Fairness and Gender in the Field of Criminal Justice**
*Frances M. Heidensohn*
Appearing in (1986), 14 International Journal of Sociology of Law 287. Reprinted by Permission of Academic Press Inc. (London) Ltd.

**Criminal Legislation**
*E.G. Ewaschuk*
Appearing in (1983-84), 26 Criminal Law Quarterly 97. Reprinted by Permission of E.G. Ewaschuk and Canada Law Book Inc., 240 Edward Street, Aurora, Ontario L4G 3S9.

**Ideology in the Work of the Law Reform Commission of Canada: The Case of the Working Paper on the General Part**
*R.P. Saunders & Ross Hastings*
Appearing in (1983), 25 Criminal Law Quarterly 206. Reprinted by Permission of R.P. Saunders, R. Hastings and Canada Law Book Inc., 240 Edward Street, Aurora, Ontario L4G 3S9.

**S.C.C. Judge Supports Task Forces to Probe Gender Bias in Courts**
*Cristin Schmitz*
Copyright 1990, The Lawyers Weekly, reprinted by permission.

**Ambiguity and Vagueness in the Criminal Law**
*Stephen Kloepfer*
Appearing in (1984-85), 27 Criminal Law Quarterly 94. Reprinted by Permission of Canada Law Book Inc., 240 Edward Street, Aurora, Ontario L4G 3S9.

**S.C.C. Has Always Had Policy-Making Role, Justice Says**
*Julia Gulej*
Copyright 1990, The Lawyers Weekly, reprinted by permission.

**Controlling the Trial Process: The Judge and the Conduct of Trial**
*Stanley A. Cohen*
Appearing in (1977), 36 C.R.N.S. 15. Reprinted by Permission of Stanley Cohen.

**Drug Enforcement Powers and the Canadian Charter of Rights and Freedoms**
*R. Solomon*
Appearing in (1983), 21 University of Western Ontario Law Review 220. Reprinted by Permission of University of Western Ontario Law Review.

**Battered Women: Definition, Models and Prosecutorial Policy**
*A. McGillivray*
Appearing in (1987), 6 Canadian Journal of Family Law 15. Reprinted by Permission of Canadian Journal of Family Law.

**The Trial Judge: Pilot, Participant, or Umpire?**
*H.W. Silverman*
Appearing in (1973), 11 Alberta Law Review 40. Reprinted by Permission of H.W. Silverman and the Alberta Law Review.

**Dispensing Justice in Courtroom 121**
*Michael Valpy*
Reprinted by Permission of the Globe & Mail.

**Osgoode Dean Answers Report's Discrimination Charges**
*Cristin Schmitz*
Copyright 1990, The Lawyers Weekly, reprinted by permission.

**Is There a Place for the Victim in the Prosecution Process?**
*Patricia Clarke*
Appearing in (1986), 8 Canadian Criminology Forum 31. Reprinted by Permission of Canadian Criminology Forum.

**Toward a Revised Sentencing Structure for Canada**
*Keith Jobson & Gerry Ferguson*
Appearing in (1987), 66 Canadian Bar Review 1. Reprinted by Permission of Keith Jobson, Gerry Ferguson and the Canadian Bar Review.

**Democracy, Class and the National Parole Board**
*M. Mandel*
Appearing in (1985), 27 Criminal Law Quarterly 159. Reprinted by Permission of M. Mandel and Canada Law Book Inc., 240 Edward Street, Aurora, Ontario L4G 3S9.

**State, Civil Society and Total Institutions: A Critique of Recent Social Histories of Punishment**
*M. Ignatieff*
Appearing in (1981), 3 Crime and Justice 153. Reprinted by Permission of University of Chicago Press.

**Recklessness and the Limits of Mens Rea: Beyond Orthodox Subjectivism**
*Earl Fruchtman*
Appearing in (1987), 29 Criminal Law Quarterly 315. Reprinted by Permission of Canada Law Book Inc., 240 Edward Street, Aurora, Ontario L4G 3S9.

**'Can George Fletcher Help Solve the Problem of Criminal Negligence?'**
*Anne Stalker*
Appearing in (1982), 7 Queen's Law Journal 274. Reprinted by Permission of Anne Stalker.

**"Th' Attempt, and not the Deed, Confounds Us": Section 24 and Impossible Attempts**
*Barry Brown*
Appearing in (1981), 19-20 University of Western Ontario Law Review 226. Reprinted by Permission of University of Western Ontario Law Review.

**The Political Use of Criminal Conspiracy**
*Wes Wilson*
Appearing in (1984), 42 University of Toronto Faculty Law Review 60. Reprinted by Permission of the University of Toronto Faculty Law Review.

**A New Crime in Old Battles: Definitional Problems with Sexual Assault**
*S.J. Usprich*
Appearing in (1987), 29 Criminal Law Quarterly 200. Reprinted by Permission of S.J. Usprich and Canada Law Book Inc., 240 Edward Street, Aurora, Ontario L4G 3S9.

**How Society Whitewashes Corporate Crime**
*M. Cash Mathews*
Appearing in (1988), 65 Business and Society Review 48. Reprinted by Permission of Business and Society Review.

**Law, Ideology and Corporate Crime: A Critique of Instrumentalism**
*Neil Surgent*
Appearing in (1989), Canadian Journal of Law and Society 39. Reprinted by Permission of Canadian Journal of Law and Society.

**Assumptions and Implications of New Canadian Legislation for Young Offenders**
*Susan A. Reid & Marge Reitsma-Street*
Appearing in (1984), 7 Canadian Criminology Forum 1. Reprinted by Permission of Canadian Criminology Forum.

**Prostitution: A Critical Analysis of Three Policy Approaches**
*Frances M. Shaver*
Appearing in (1985), XI Canadian Public Policy 493. Reprinted by Permission of Canadian Public Policy.

# Table of Contents

**CHAPTER 1 CRIMINAL LAW AND GOVERNMENT REGULATION IN PERSPECTIVE** .................... 1
Crime and the Criminal Law System
*C. Mitchell* .................... 1
Roher v. The Queen .................... 3
Questions .................... 37
Discussion .................... 38
Further Reading .................... 39

**CHAPTER 2 PERSPECTIVES ON CRIMINAL LAW** .................... 41
Introduction
*R.P. Saunders* .................... 41

**2.1 Traditional Legal Perspectives**
*R.P. Saunders* .................... 43

**2.2 Law in the Social Sciences**
*Ross Hastings* .................... 45

**2.3 The Critical Perspective on Criminal Law**
*Ross Hastings* .................... 49
The Role of Law in Social Transformation:
Is a Jurisprudence of Insurgency Possible?
*Stephen Brickey & Elizabeth Comack* .................... 57

**2.4 Feminist Perspectives on Criminal Law** .................... 64
Personal Autonomy and the Criminal Law: Emerging Issues for Women
*Elizabeth A. Sheehy* .................... 64
Models of Justice: Portia or Persephone?
Some Thoughts on Equality, Fairness and Gender in the Field of Criminal Justice
*Frances M. Heidensohn* .................... 68

**2.5 Historical Perspectives on Criminal Law**
*Barry Wright* .................... 78
Questions/Discussion .................... 82
Further Reading .................... 82

**CHAPTER 3 THE PRODUCTION OF CRIMINAL LAW** .................... 85
General Introduction .................... 85

**3.1 Legislation and the Role of Parliament** .................... 90
Introduction .................... 90
The Constitutional Basis of the Criminal Law Power
*P.W. Hogg* .................... 92

Re Nova Scotia Board of Censors and MacNeil .................. 94
Rio Hotel Ltd. v. Liquor Licensing Board ...................... 102
Criminal Legislation
*E.G. Ewaschuk, Q.C* ...................................... 104
Ideology in the Work of the Law Reform Commission of Canada:
The Case of the Working Paper on the General Part
*Ross Hastings & R.P. Saunders* ............................. 119
Criminal Law in Canadian Society ............................ 128
Questions/Discussion ...................................... 135
Further Reading .......................................... 135

## 3.2 The Role of the Courts ............................... 136
Introduction ............................................. 136
Ambiguity and Vagueness in the Criminal Law: An Analysis of Types
*Stephen Kloepfer* ........................................ 138
R. v. Paré ............................................... 146
S.C.C. Has Always Had Policy-Making Role, Justice Says
*Julia Gulej* ............................................. 154
Law Society of Upper Canada v. Skapinker .................... 157
Hunter v. Southam Inc. .................................... 159
Controlling the Trial Process: The Judge and the Conduct of Trial
*Stanley A. Cohen* ........................................ 163
Questions/Discussion ..................................... 171
Further Reading .......................................... 172

## CHAPTER 4 CRIMINAL LAW — PERSONNEL, PARTICIPANTS, AND POWERS ........................................ 173

### 4.1 Police .............................................. 173
Historical Development
*C. Mitchell* ............................................. 173
Regulating Professional Police
*C. Mitchell* ............................................. 179
Introduction
*R.P. Saunders* .......................................... 184
Drug Enforcement Powers and the Canadian Charter of Rights and Freedoms
*R. Solomon* ............................................ 184
Strategies for Police Accountability and Community Empowerment
*Ross Hastings and R.P. Saunders* .......................... 187
Questions ............................................... 194
Discussion .............................................. 194
Further Reading ......................................... 194

### 4.2 Defence/Prosecutor .................................. 195
The Criminal Prosecution ................................. 195
Background and Issues
*Barry Wright and Chet Mitchell* ........................... 195

Some Consequences of Public Prosecutorial Power: The Decision to
    Proceed with a Prosecution
*Barry Wright* . . . . . . . . . . . . . . . . . . . . . . . . . . . . . . . . . . 198
Battered Women: Definition, Models and Prosecutorial Policy
*A. McGillivray* . . . . . . . . . . . . . . . . . . . . . . . . . . . . . . . . 202
Other Discretionary Powers of the Prosecutor . . . . . . . . . . . . . . . 210
Regina v. Romeo . . . . . . . . . . . . . . . . . . . . . . . . . . . . . . . 211
Conway v. The Queen . . . . . . . . . . . . . . . . . . . . . . . . . . . . 214
The Role of Defence Counsel . . . . . . . . . . . . . . . . . . . . . . . . 222
Regina v. Rockwood . . . . . . . . . . . . . . . . . . . . . . . . . . . . . 223
Questions/Discussion . . . . . . . . . . . . . . . . . . . . . . . . . . . . . 227
Further Reading . . . . . . . . . . . . . . . . . . . . . . . . . . . . . . . . 227

**4.3 Judges** . . . . . . . . . . . . . . . . . . . . . . . . . . . . . . . . . . . **228**
Introduction . . . . . . . . . . . . . . . . . . . . . . . . . . . . . . . . . . 228
The Trial Judge: Pilot, Participant, or Umpire?
*H. Silverman* . . . . . . . . . . . . . . . . . . . . . . . . . . . . . . . . . 228
Dispensing Justice in Courtroom 121
*M. Valpy* . . . . . . . . . . . . . . . . . . . . . . . . . . . . . . . . . . . 236
MacKeigan v. Hickman . . . . . . . . . . . . . . . . . . . . . . . . . . . . 238
Questions/Discussion . . . . . . . . . . . . . . . . . . . . . . . . . . . . . 239
Further Reading . . . . . . . . . . . . . . . . . . . . . . . . . . . . . . . . 240

**4.4 Victims** . . . . . . . . . . . . . . . . . . . . . . . . . . . . . . . . . . **240**
Introduction
*Ross Hastings* . . . . . . . . . . . . . . . . . . . . . . . . . . . . . . . . . 240
Report of the Canadian Federal-Provincial Task Force on Justice for
    Victims of Crime
*Ministry of Supply and Services* . . . . . . . . . . . . . . . . . . . . . . 244
Is There a Place for the Victim in the Prosecution Process?
*Patricia Clarke* . . . . . . . . . . . . . . . . . . . . . . . . . . . . . . . . 255
Questions/Discussion . . . . . . . . . . . . . . . . . . . . . . . . . . . . . 269
Further Reading . . . . . . . . . . . . . . . . . . . . . . . . . . . . . . . . 269

**4.5 The Accused** . . . . . . . . . . . . . . . . . . . . . . . . . . . . . . **270**
Selecting Accused: Characteristics of the Offender
*C. Mitchell* . . . . . . . . . . . . . . . . . . . . . . . . . . . . . . . . . . 270
Questions/Discussion . . . . . . . . . . . . . . . . . . . . . . . . . . . . . 277
Further Reading . . . . . . . . . . . . . . . . . . . . . . . . . . . . . . . . 277

**4.6 Criminal Penalizers** . . . . . . . . . . . . . . . . . . . . . . . . . . **278**
Introduction . . . . . . . . . . . . . . . . . . . . . . . . . . . . . . . . . . 278
A Framework for the Correctional Law Review, Working Paper No. 2
*Solicitor General of Canada* . . . . . . . . . . . . . . . . . . . . . . . . 280
Correctional Philosophy, Working Paper No. 1
*Solicitor General of Canada* . . . . . . . . . . . . . . . . . . . . . . . . 285
A Framework for the Correctional Law Review, Working Paper No. 2
*Solicitor General of Canada* . . . . . . . . . . . . . . . . . . . . . . . . 288

Creating Choices or Repeating History: Canadian Female Offenders and
  Correctional Reform
*K. Moffatt* . . . . . . . . . . . . . . . . . . . . . . . . . . . . . . . . . . . 291
Questions/Discussion . . . . . . . . . . . . . . . . . . . . . . . . . . . . 301
Further Reading . . . . . . . . . . . . . . . . . . . . . . . . . . . . . . . 301

## CHAPTER 5  SENTENCING AND PAROLE . . . . . . . . . . . . . . . 303
Introduction . . . . . . . . . . . . . . . . . . . . . . . . . . . . . . . . . 303

**5.1 Sentencing** . . . . . . . . . . . . . . . . . . . . . . . . . . . . . . . 304
Toward a Revised Sentencing Structure for Canada
*Keith Jobson & Gerry Ferguson* . . . . . . . . . . . . . . . . . . . . . . 304
Statutory Sentencing Reform: The Purpose and Principles of Sentencing
*J. Roberts and A. von Hirsch* . . . . . . . . . . . . . . . . . . . . . . . 314
R. v. Hollinsky . . . . . . . . . . . . . . . . . . . . . . . . . . . . . . . . 324
R. v. Shropshire . . . . . . . . . . . . . . . . . . . . . . . . . . . . . . . 328
R. v. Morin . . . . . . . . . . . . . . . . . . . . . . . . . . . . . . . . . . 334

**5.2 Parole** . . . . . . . . . . . . . . . . . . . . . . . . . . . . . . . . . . 338
Protecting Society Through Community Corrections
*Correctional Service of Canada* . . . . . . . . . . . . . . . . . . . . . . 338
Democracy, Class and the National Parole Board
*M. Mandel* . . . . . . . . . . . . . . . . . . . . . . . . . . . . . . . . . . 340
Cunningham v. Canada . . . . . . . . . . . . . . . . . . . . . . . . . . . 352
Gallichon v. Canada (Commissioner of Corrections) . . . . . . . . . . . 356
Questions . . . . . . . . . . . . . . . . . . . . . . . . . . . . . . . . . . . 365
Further Reading . . . . . . . . . . . . . . . . . . . . . . . . . . . . . . . 365

## CHAPTER 6  CRIMINAL LAW LIABILITY . . . . . . . . . . . . . . . 367
Introduction . . . . . . . . . . . . . . . . . . . . . . . . . . . . . . . . . 367

**6.1  Elements of an Offence** . . . . . . . . . . . . . . . . . . . . . . . 368
   **6.1.1  Actus Reus** . . . . . . . . . . . . . . . . . . . . . . . . . . 368
Introduction . . . . . . . . . . . . . . . . . . . . . . . . . . . . . . . . . 368
Regina v. Jordan . . . . . . . . . . . . . . . . . . . . . . . . . . . . . . . 369
Regina v. Smith . . . . . . . . . . . . . . . . . . . . . . . . . . . . . . . 372
People v. Beardsley . . . . . . . . . . . . . . . . . . . . . . . . . . . . . 375
Regina v. Lavin . . . . . . . . . . . . . . . . . . . . . . . . . . . . . . . 378
Regina v. Thornton . . . . . . . . . . . . . . . . . . . . . . . . . . . . . 381
Fagan v. Commissioner of Metropolitan Police . . . . . . . . . . . . . . 386
Regina v. Cooper . . . . . . . . . . . . . . . . . . . . . . . . . . . . . . 389
Questions/Discussion . . . . . . . . . . . . . . . . . . . . . . . . . . . . 395
Further Reading . . . . . . . . . . . . . . . . . . . . . . . . . . . . . . . 396
   **6.1.2  Mens Rea** . . . . . . . . . . . . . . . . . . . . . . . . . . 396
Introduction . . . . . . . . . . . . . . . . . . . . . . . . . . . . . . . . . 398
Beaver v. The Queen . . . . . . . . . . . . . . . . . . . . . . . . . . . . 398
Regina v. King . . . . . . . . . . . . . . . . . . . . . . . . . . . . . . . . 403

Regina v. Ladue . . . . . . . . . . . . . . . . . . . . . . . . . . . . . . 407
Regina v. Droste . . . . . . . . . . . . . . . . . . . . . . . . . . . . . 409
Recklessness and the Limits of Mens Rea: Beyond Orthodox
   Subjectivism
*Earl Fruchtman* . . . . . . . . . . . . . . . . . . . . . . . . . . . . . . 412
R. v. Tutton . . . . . . . . . . . . . . . . . . . . . . . . . . . . . . . 421
Regina v. Hundal . . . . . . . . . . . . . . . . . . . . . . . . . . . . . 428
Regina v. Creighton . . . . . . . . . . . . . . . . . . . . . . . . . . . 434
Questions/Discussion . . . . . . . . . . . . . . . . . . . . . . . . . . 447
Further Reading . . . . . . . . . . . . . . . . . . . . . . . . . . . . . 448
  **6.1.3 Strict and Absolute Liability** . . . . . . . . . . . . . . . 448
Introduction . . . . . . . . . . . . . . . . . . . . . . . . . . . . . . . 448
Rex v. Ping Yuen . . . . . . . . . . . . . . . . . . . . . . . . . . . . 449
R. v. Sault Ste. Marie . . . . . . . . . . . . . . . . . . . . . . . . . . 450
Regina v. Burt . . . . . . . . . . . . . . . . . . . . . . . . . . . . . . 457
Wholesale Travel Group Inc. v. The Queen . . . . . . . . . . . . 461
Questions/Discussion . . . . . . . . . . . . . . . . . . . . . . . . . . 476
Further Reading . . . . . . . . . . . . . . . . . . . . . . . . . . . . . 476

**6.2 Incomplete Offences** . . . . . . . . . . . . . . . . . . . . . . . **477**
  **6.2.1 Attempts** . . . . . . . . . . . . . . . . . . . . . . . . . . . . 477
Introduction . . . . . . . . . . . . . . . . . . . . . . . . . . . . . . . 477
R. v. Deutsch . . . . . . . . . . . . . . . . . . . . . . . . . . . . . . 478
R. v. Sorrell and Bondett . . . . . . . . . . . . . . . . . . . . . . . . 483
"Th' Attempt, and not the Deed, Confounds Us":
   Section 24 and Impossible Attempts
*Barry Brown* . . . . . . . . . . . . . . . . . . . . . . . . . . . . . . 486
Regina v. Scott . . . . . . . . . . . . . . . . . . . . . . . . . . . . . 490
Regina v. Smith . . . . . . . . . . . . . . . . . . . . . . . . . . . . . 492
Regina v. Ancio . . . . . . . . . . . . . . . . . . . . . . . . . . . . . 496
Questions/Discussion . . . . . . . . . . . . . . . . . . . . . . . . . . 500
Further Reading . . . . . . . . . . . . . . . . . . . . . . . . . . . . . 500
  **6.2.2 Counselling** . . . . . . . . . . . . . . . . . . . . . . . . . 501
Introduction . . . . . . . . . . . . . . . . . . . . . . . . . . . . . . . 501
Regina v. McLeod . . . . . . . . . . . . . . . . . . . . . . . . . . . 501
Questions/Discussion . . . . . . . . . . . . . . . . . . . . . . . . . . 504
Further Reading . . . . . . . . . . . . . . . . . . . . . . . . . . . . . 504
  **6.2.3 Conspiracy** . . . . . . . . . . . . . . . . . . . . . . . . . . 504
Introduction . . . . . . . . . . . . . . . . . . . . . . . . . . . . . . . 504
The Queen v. O'Brien . . . . . . . . . . . . . . . . . . . . . . . . . 505
The Political Use of Criminal Conspiracy
*Wes Wilson* . . . . . . . . . . . . . . . . . . . . . . . . . . . . . . . 509
Questions/Discussion . . . . . . . . . . . . . . . . . . . . . . . . . . 515
Further Reading . . . . . . . . . . . . . . . . . . . . . . . . . . . . . 515

**6.3 Attaching Liability: The Limits of Liability** . . . . . . . . **515**
Introduction . . . . . . . . . . . . . . . . . . . . . . . . . . . . . . . 515

Regina v. Kulbacki ............................. 517
Regina v. Salajko .............................. 519
Regina v. Madigan ............................. 520
Henderson v. The King ......................... 522
The Queen v. Trinneer ......................... 526
Questions/Discussion ........................... 530
Further Reading ............................... 530

## CHAPTER 7 DEFENCES AND DENIALS ........ 531
Introduction .................................. 531

### 7.1 Justifications ......................... 532
#### 7.1.1 Duress ............................. 532
The Queen v. Carker (No. 2) ................... 533
Pacquette v. The Queen ........................ 536
Hibbert v. The Queen .......................... 539
Questions/Discussion ........................... 552
Further Reading ............................... 552
#### 7.1.2 Necessity .......................... 553
Perka v. The Queen ............................ 553
R. v. Roberts ................................. 562
MacMillan Bloedel Ltd. v. Simpson .............. 564
Questions/Discussion ........................... 568
Further Reading ............................... 569
#### 7.1.3 Self Defence ....................... 569
Introduction .................................. 569
Regina v. Cadwallader ......................... 570
Regina v. Breau ............................... 574
Brisson v. The Queen .......................... 576
R. v. Whynot (Stafford) ....................... 578
R. v. Lavallée ................................ 582
Questions/Discussion ........................... 593
Further Reading ............................... 594
#### 7.1.4 Defence of Property ................. 594
Introduction .................................. 594
Regina v. Stanley ............................. 595
R. v. Born With a Tooth ....................... 600
Questions/Discussion ........................... 606
Further Reading ............................... 607
#### 7.1.5 Consent ............................ 607
Introduction .................................. 607
Regina v. Maki ................................ 608
Regina v. Jobidon ............................. 611
Questions/Discussion ........................... 615
Further Reading ............................... 615

**7.2 Absence of Intent or Knowledge** . . . . . . . . . . . . . . . . . . . . . . . **615**
   **7.2.1 Mistake of Fact** . . . . . . . . . . . . . . . . . . . . . . . . . . . . 615
Introduction . . . . . . . . . . . . . . . . . . . . . . . . . . . . . . . . . . . . 615
R. v. Williams . . . . . . . . . . . . . . . . . . . . . . . . . . . . . . . . . . 616
The Queen v. Kundeus . . . . . . . . . . . . . . . . . . . . . . . . . . . . 619
Pappajohn v. The Queen . . . . . . . . . . . . . . . . . . . . . . . . . . . 624
Laybourn, Bulmer and Illingworth v. R. . . . . . . . . . . . . . . . . . . 629
Questions/Discussion . . . . . . . . . . . . . . . . . . . . . . . . . . . . . 634
Further Reading . . . . . . . . . . . . . . . . . . . . . . . . . . . . . . . . 635
   **7.2.2 Ignorance of the Law** . . . . . . . . . . . . . . . . . . . . . . . . . 635
Introduction . . . . . . . . . . . . . . . . . . . . . . . . . . . . . . . . . . . 635
Regina v. Shymkowich . . . . . . . . . . . . . . . . . . . . . . . . . . . . 636
Regina v. Howson . . . . . . . . . . . . . . . . . . . . . . . . . . . . . . . 637
Regina v. Campbell and Mlynarchuk . . . . . . . . . . . . . . . . . . . . 640
Regina v. Cancoil Thermal Corporation and Parkinson . . . . . . . . . 643
Forster v. The Queen . . . . . . . . . . . . . . . . . . . . . . . . . . . . . 648
Questions/Discussion . . . . . . . . . . . . . . . . . . . . . . . . . . . . . 651
Further Reading . . . . . . . . . . . . . . . . . . . . . . . . . . . . . . . . 652

**7.3 Policy Defences** . . . . . . . . . . . . . . . . . . . . . . . . . . . . . . . . **652**
   **7.3.1 Entrapment** . . . . . . . . . . . . . . . . . . . . . . . . . . . . . . . 652
Introduction . . . . . . . . . . . . . . . . . . . . . . . . . . . . . . . . . . . 652
Mack v. R. . . . . . . . . . . . . . . . . . . . . . . . . . . . . . . . . . . . . 652
Showman v. R. . . . . . . . . . . . . . . . . . . . . . . . . . . . . . . . . . 665
Barnes v. R. . . . . . . . . . . . . . . . . . . . . . . . . . . . . . . . . . . . 669
Questions/Discussion . . . . . . . . . . . . . . . . . . . . . . . . . . . . . 672
Further Reading . . . . . . . . . . . . . . . . . . . . . . . . . . . . . . . . 673
   **7.3.2 Charter Protections** . . . . . . . . . . . . . . . . . . . . . . . . . . 674
Regina v. Oakes . . . . . . . . . . . . . . . . . . . . . . . . . . . . . . . . 674
Smith v. The Queen . . . . . . . . . . . . . . . . . . . . . . . . . . . . . . 685
Vaillancourt v. R. and Attorney General of Ontario . . . . . . . . . . . 690
Regina v. Mellenthin . . . . . . . . . . . . . . . . . . . . . . . . . . . . . 699
Bartle v. The Queen . . . . . . . . . . . . . . . . . . . . . . . . . . . . . . 704
Questions/Discussion . . . . . . . . . . . . . . . . . . . . . . . . . . . . . 713
Further Reading . . . . . . . . . . . . . . . . . . . . . . . . . . . . . . . . 713

**7.4 Incapacity** . . . . . . . . . . . . . . . . . . . . . . . . . . . . . . . . . . . . **714**
General Introduction . . . . . . . . . . . . . . . . . . . . . . . . . . . . . . . 714
   **7.4.1 Provocation or Heat of Passion** . . . . . . . . . . . . . . . . . . . 715
Introduction . . . . . . . . . . . . . . . . . . . . . . . . . . . . . . . . . . . 715
R. v. Hill . . . . . . . . . . . . . . . . . . . . . . . . . . . . . . . . . . . . . 716
   **7.4.2 Defence of Mental Disorder and Diminished Responsibility** . . . . 723
Introduction . . . . . . . . . . . . . . . . . . . . . . . . . . . . . . . . . . . 723
Insanity . . . . . . . . . . . . . . . . . . . . . . . . . . . . . . . . . . . . . 723
Diminished Responsibility . . . . . . . . . . . . . . . . . . . . . . . . . . 727

Hadfield to Swain: The Criminal Code Amendments Dealing with the
  Mentally Disordered Accused
*A.J.C. O'Mara* . . . . . . . . . . . . . . . . . . . . . . . . . . . . . . . 729
R. v. Worth . . . . . . . . . . . . . . . . . . . . . . . . . . . . . . . . . 740
### 7.4.3 Intoxication . . . . . . . . . . . . . . . . . . . . . . . . . 743
Introduction . . . . . . . . . . . . . . . . . . . . . . . . . . . . . . . . 743
R. v. Daviault . . . . . . . . . . . . . . . . . . . . . . . . . . . . . . . 749
### 7.4.4 Automatism . . . . . . . . . . . . . . . . . . . . . . . . . 762
Introduction . . . . . . . . . . . . . . . . . . . . . . . . . . . . . . . . 762
Rabey v. The Queen . . . . . . . . . . . . . . . . . . . . . . . . . . . 765
R. v. Parks . . . . . . . . . . . . . . . . . . . . . . . . . . . . . . . . . 779
Questions . . . . . . . . . . . . . . . . . . . . . . . . . . . . . . . . . . 788

## CHAPTER 8  CURRENT ISSUES IN CRIMINAL JUSTICE . . . . . . 789

### 8.1 Sexual Assault . . . . . . . . . . . . . . . . . . . . . . . . . . . 789
Issues in Sexual Assault
*R.P. Saunders* . . . . . . . . . . . . . . . . . . . . . . . . . . . . . . 789
R. v. McCraw . . . . . . . . . . . . . . . . . . . . . . . . . . . . . . . 796
Sexual Assault: Substantive Issues Before and After Bill C-49
*Don Stuart* . . . . . . . . . . . . . . . . . . . . . . . . . . . . . . . . 800
R. v. Livermore . . . . . . . . . . . . . . . . . . . . . . . . . . . . . . 812
Questions/Discussion . . . . . . . . . . . . . . . . . . . . . . . . . . 816
Further Reading . . . . . . . . . . . . . . . . . . . . . . . . . . . . . 817

### 8.2 Racism and the Criminal Justice System . . . . . . . . . . . . . . 818
Introduction . . . . . . . . . . . . . . . . . . . . . . . . . . . . . . . . 818
Royal Commission on the Donald Marshall, Jr., Prosecution
*Volume One: Commissioners' Report* . . . . . . . . . . . . . . . 819
Questions/Discussion . . . . . . . . . . . . . . . . . . . . . . . . . . 840
Further Reading . . . . . . . . . . . . . . . . . . . . . . . . . . . . . 841

### 8.3 Crime in the Workplace . . . . . . . . . . . . . . . . . . . . . 842
Introduction . . . . . . . . . . . . . . . . . . . . . . . . . . . . . . . . 842
How Society Whitewashes Corporate Crime
*M. Cash Mathews* . . . . . . . . . . . . . . . . . . . . . . . . . . . 842
Law, Ideology and Corporate Crime: A Critique of Instrumentalism
*Neil Sargent* . . . . . . . . . . . . . . . . . . . . . . . . . . . . . . . 846
Questions/Discussion . . . . . . . . . . . . . . . . . . . . . . . . . . 864
Further Reading . . . . . . . . . . . . . . . . . . . . . . . . . . . . . 864

### 8.4 Young Offenders . . . . . . . . . . . . . . . . . . . . . . . . . 865
Introduction . . . . . . . . . . . . . . . . . . . . . . . . . . . . . . . . 865
The 1995 Young Offenders Act Amendments: Compromise or Confusion?
*Nicolas Bala* . . . . . . . . . . . . . . . . . . . . . . . . . . . . . . . 866
Questions/Discussion . . . . . . . . . . . . . . . . . . . . . . . . . . 892
Further Reading . . . . . . . . . . . . . . . . . . . . . . . . . . . . . 892

# 1

# CRIMINAL LAW AND GOVERNMENT REGULATION IN PERSPECTIVE

## Crime and The Criminal Law System
### C. Mitchell

DEFINING CRIME

**The Legal Definition**

Crime can be defined from at least three perspectives: the legal, ethical and contractual. It is natural in a book on criminal law to begin with the legal definition of crime but an informed understanding of crime requires an equal consideration of other definitions.

To lawyers and judges working within the criminal law system, a crime is any act prohibited or punishable by law or, more specifically, is "any form of human behaviour designated by law makers as criminal and subject to penal to penal sanctions." (Parker, 1987). Legalistic definitions of crime are also employed by some criminologists. Michael and Adler (1933:2,5) assert that "the most precise and least ambiguous definition of crime is that which defines it as behaviour which is prohibited by the criminal code" and thus, logically, "if crime is merely an instance of conduct which is proscribed by the criminal code it follows that the criminal law is the formal cause of crime." Quinney (1970) likewise defines "crime" as "a legal category that is assigned to conduct by authorized agents of a politically organized society". The legal definition of crime is simultaneously broad and narrow. It is broad because it means that any form of behaviour can be designated a "crime". Behaviour that is commonplace today, like drinking coffee and smoking tobacco in cafés, was once a serious crime. Centuries ago in some European countries tobacco was declared a dangerous drug and its users were subject to prohibitions and harsh penalties (seldom inflicted) such as flogging, amputation of hands and execution. Similarly, when the coffee drinking habit first developed in Arabia around the 15th century, some municipal governments prohibited both coffee houses and the public sale of the drug. Conversely, behaviour now regarded as criminal was at other times widely accepted. Canadian apothecaries, physicians and pharmaceutical producers in 1900 offered the public a large and varied supply of opiate-based concoctions. Tonics, medicines and "remedies" based on cocaine were also popular. *Vin Mariana*, a mixture of red wine and cocaine, sold especially well, perhaps because it was endorsed by a Roman Catholic Pope and an American President among other celebrities. Anyone selling the exact same products today in Canada faces lengthy imprisonment. Trading in certain chemicals has been designated a "crime". The list of activities that can be designated criminal is endless. The Iranian government has waged a "war" against rock music and has outlawed the wearing by women of certain types of clothes and adornments. Traditionally, many occupations (money lenders, prostitutes, boxers, gamblers), religions (Jews, Christians, Hugenots) and even ideologies have been designated as crimes. There may a core of "real crimes" that are criminal in every society but there are also behaviours or statuses that are criminalized in one jurisdiction while being ignored, accepted or rated as no more than mild vices in another.

The narrowness of the legal definition of crime stems from the requirement that only behaviour designated by law makers as criminal will count as crime. No matter how harmful or immoral an activity might be, it is not a "crime" unless law makers so designate. If authorized law makers do not exist, a situation prevailing in primitive cultures, then "crime" as we know it will be lacking. McGinley's definition of crime (1981:283) highlights the state's role and the state's interest in crime: "criminal conduct is that conduct which challenges the authority of the state by contravening a categorical imperative wherein the state demands obedience on the basis that the state itself has commanded obedience". The key to the legal definition of crime is therefore the activities of the "law makers". Who are the law makers? The legal answer is those persons authorized by law to make, or create or "designate" law. The most obvious law makers are the municipal, provincial and federal legislators who are authorized by constitutional laws and conventions to create laws within their allotted jurisdiction. Federal legislators have authority to create "criminal" laws and many of these are contained in the Criminal Code. Two examples of federally created crimes are section 151 (repealed R.S. 1985, c. 19) and section 163 of the Code:

> **151.** Every male person who, being eighteen years of age or more, seduces a female person of previously chaste character who is sixteen years of age is guilty of an indictable offence and is liable to imprisonment for two years.

> **163.**(1)(b) Everyone commits an offence who makes, prints, publishes, distributes, sells or has in his possession for the purpose of publication, distribution or circulation, a crime comic.

It is not clear why Parliament created either of these crimes. The sections have been rarely, if ever, enforced and citizens rarely, if ever, bring complaints regarding these crimes to the attention of the police. But while there may be no pressing need or popular support for Parliament's creation of former section 151 and section 163(1)(b), the behaviour so described is nonetheless a "crime" and remains a crime until amended or removed by legislative or judicial action. McGinnis (1987) found seven cases involving the crime comics sections. The case of *Roher v. The Queen* (1953), 107 C.C.C. 103, is extracted here to provide an example of how legislators, police and judges can, in all earnestness, make the selling of *Dick Tracy* comics a "crime". According to McGinnis, in 1940 a New York psychiatrist, Federic Wertham, launched the first public campaign against crime comics. Wertham claimed these comics caused their readers to become juvenile delinquents and he was particularly critical of *Wonder Woman*. Wertham's war on comics was picked up and promoted by Parent-Teacher Associations (PTA) in Canada and the U.S. British Columbia PTAs recruited E. Davie Fulton, the P.C. member for Kamloops, (and later a federal Minister of Justice and Justice of the B.C. Supreme Court) to champion their cause in Parliament. On the basis of anecdotal horror stories about teenage murders inspired by stacks of crime comics,

Fulton and his supporters asserted a direct, indisputable link between comics and real-life crime. In the Parliamentary debates of 1949 no one demanded actual proof that comics caused harm and the Criminal Code was amended solely on the basis of unsubstantiated, unverified and unscientific claims. As the following decision of the Manitoba Court of Appeal illustrates, the issue of actual harm to society is even more remote in the courts than it was in Parliament.

## Roher v. The Queen
### (1953), 107 C.C.C. 103 (Man. C.A.).

Appeal from conviction by Police Magistrate respecting sale of a crime comic. Affirmed.

*F.J. Turner*, Q.C., and *Keith Turner*, for appellant, Roher *C.W. Tupper* Q.C., for the Crown.

McPHERSON C.J.M.: — This is an appeal from a conviction by Maris H. Garton, Esq., Police Magistrate, at the City of Winnipeg, on April 29, 1953, for "that the appellant did unlawfully have in his possession for sale a crime comic contrary to the provisions of section 207, subsections (1)(b) and (3) of the Criminal Code". The appellant was sentenced to pay a fine of $5 and costs or in default thereof to imprisonment for a term of 5 days in common gaol for the Eastern Judicial District. The prosecution was brought as a test case under said section and the appeal is against both conviction and sentence.

The matter is one of considerable importance to the citizens of this country and for the purpose of informing the public of the views of the Court in relation to such prosecution it is advisable to deal with the matter at length and in detail both as to the law and the facts. The difficulty with which administration of the law is faced in prosecuting under said section is that each individual case must necessarily depend entirely upon the publication objected to and its contents.

Section 207 of the *Criminal Code* was amended by 1949 (2nd Sess), c. 13. That amendment consisted of the repeal of the previous s. 207 and enactment of an entirely new section, portions of which, so far as this prosecution is concerned, are as follows:

> 207(1) Every one is guilty of an indictable offence and liable to two years' imprisonment who
> (b) makes, prints, publishes, distributes, sells or has in possession for any such purpose, any crime comic.

"Crime Comic" is defined in s. 207(3) as follows:

> 207(3) 'Crime Comic' means in this section any magazine, periodical or book which exclusively or substantially comprises matter depicting pictorially the commission of crimes, real or fictitious.

The following provisions of s. 207 are also relevant to a charge of this nature:

> 207(4) No one shall be convicted of any offence in this section mentioned if he proves that the public good was served by the acts alleged to have been done, and that there was no excess in the acts alleged beyond what the public good required.
>
> (6) The motives of the accused shall in all cases be irrelevant.
>
> (7) It shall be no defence to a charge under subsection one that the accused was ignorant of the nature or presence of the matter, picture, model, crime comic or other thing.

The publication upon which the prosecution was based is "No. 62, April, 'Dick Tracey' ", and the appeal is on the ground that the said exhibit "does not exclusively or substantially comprise matter depicting pictorially the commission of crime, real or fictitious". No submission was made that s. 207(4) was a further defence available to the appellant. The exhibit consisted of 34 pages, including the cover, of printed and pictorial contents, of which 10 pages were advertising matter. The appellant admitted that in addition to that on the front cover there were seven pictures in the first story actually depicting the commission of a crime. In answer to a question that I put to appellant's counsel: whether he was submitting that where in any picture there was shown a man firing a revolver and, in the next picture, a man dropping dead from the effects of the shot, that only the second picture would be one depicting crime, he stated that such was his submission. I cannot agree with that interpretation and will briefly describe the first story in the publication:

The book is illustrated by a series of panel pictures — usually 12 to a page — describing the stories. On the first page is shown an "ice-house" set on a pneumatic pontoon, in which an officer of the law has been caught by an electric device set in operation by the would-be murderer, the latter hauling the victim into another room where he applies the "murder mask" in an attempt at murder. The next page shows continuation of the attempted murder: the policeman struggling free and chasing the criminal, who opens a valve in the pontoon for the purpose of sinking it and drowning the policeman inside the building and another on the pontoon outside the building. The following pictures show the policeman struggling to avoid drowning and endeavouring to escape. While they are doing this the criminal goes to another place, commits a murder, then leaves the body and disappears. The pictures then return to the two officers trying to escape from drowning and the next 27 panels depict their struggles and the efforts of other police officers trying to break into the building and rescue them. The illustrations then revert to the previous murder and devote 5 panels to it, showing elimination by the murderer of what might be clues involving him. Returning again to the house on the raft, 7 pictures are allotted to showing the eventual rescue of the two officers from drowning. The next 41 panels depict the criminal's actions in his endeavour to elude police, and their efforts to apprehend him. The ensuing picture shows the criminal arriving to commit a further murder, which he attempts in the third panel on the following page but finds he has mistaken the identity of the would-be victim. For the next 2 pages he proceeds in again attempting to murder the hero of the story but is finally shot by the police in time to rescue the hero. The balance of the story of 15 pictures describes the method in which the murder mask operated and the reasons for the criminal acting as he did.

It is my considered opinion that the whole story as published consists of the depicting of crime in its various phases: namely, preparations for the commission of crime, action taken in accordance with those preparations, and steps taken by the authorities for arrest of the criminal.

The next story is not quite so bloodthirsty. It shows robbery being committed and the knocking down of a child by the robbers' car in their endeavours to escape, the rescue of the child, destruction of clues by the criminals, commission of a second robbery and the get-away of the robbers, and the commission of a further robbery and chase of the criminals by the police. The outcome is unknown, as it is a continued story which at this phase ends in an advertisement to buy the next issue of the paper.

The third story depicts the reporting of a murder to the police, the finding of the body, and evidence leading to the arrest of the guilty party.

The fourth story — on a single page — depicts a murder and the arrest of the murderer.

I cannot arrive at any other conclusion than that the whole pictorial part of the exhibit depicts crime in its various phases, and I by no means eliminate those pictures which are explanatory of preparations made to commit the actual crime from being part of the crime itself.

In *R. v. Alberta News Ltd.* (1951), 101 Can. C.C. 219, the publication before the Court was an entirely different style of publication to the one in this case and on the facts stated in the judgment it would appear to have been a proper decision; but I am not commenting on the interpretation of the law in that case although I do agree with the trial Magistrate's adoption of Maxwell on Interpretation of Statutes, 9th ed., p. 280, as follows: 'Among them is the rule that that sense of the words is to be adopted which best harmonises with the context and promotes in the fullest manner the policy and object of the Legislature. The paramount object, in construing penal as well as other statutes, is to ascertain the legislative intent, and the rule of strict construction is not violated by permitting the words to have their full meaning, or the more extensive of two meanings, when best effectuating the intention.' [pp. 221-2]

My interpretation of the section dealing with "crime comics" is that the Legislature wished to enact laws to protect the children of this country from the evil effects of being subjected to publications dealing with crime, and that the word "commission" in the section is not restricted to the actual instantaneous act constituting the crime but includes the preparations for same and all factors which naturally arise in connection with such crime.

The sentence — a fine of $5 or, in default, 5 days' imprisonment — was also appealed against and this Court has the power, if it sees fit, to increase that sentence. In the present case I am not in favour of so doing, because this is a "test" case taken against one of many-hundred vendors of comic books in this city. There have been rumours, and I have been told by people whose statements I would accept, that the system of distribution of these books is such that if a small dealer wishes to procure certain comics which are clean and proper, he can only do so by also purchasing certain additional books designated by the distributors. If this is the existing condition I think it might be worth the attention of the authorities with a view to investigating the facts of the situation which apparently faces the small dealer, whereby he has to buy material he does not require in order to obtain other material he does require for his customers and also to meet business competition in his area.

I might also add what I stated shortly at the end of the hearing in this case: that my personal opinion is that when crimes are committed on a commercial scale for the purpose of making profit a fine is not the proper punishment, as that means only the equivalent of a tax, the severity of which depends upon the profit made by the offender on his whole business. A term in gaol or penitentiary to those who are primarily responsible for commission of the offences would not only be more just and appropriate but also more effective. In the present case the publication is published in St.

Louis under management in New York and apparently is imported into Canada, so that original vendors in Canada are the distributors. It is at that point where the most effective restrictive action could be taken.

There is a defence available under s-s. (4), above quoted, if it can be shown that the publication is for the public good. The only defence under this section I have ever heard suggested is that by reading these publications the child acquires a desire to read. To me it is a strange basis upon which to start child education and, logically considered, could be quite easily adapted to other phases of training; for instance, by starting children on "home-brew" they might connoisseurs of fine liquors and whisky and eventually experiment with a drink of milk!

I am aware that in submitting this judgment it is entirely different to those which are usually delivered by this Court, but I do so because in the first place this is a test case in reference to a matter that is definitely harmful to the children of this country; also because many similar cases may arise before Police Magistrates and other Courts and I feel it my responsibility to place clearly before them my views of what constitutes an offence under the section of the Code now before us, not overlooking the basic fact that each publication has to be considered on its own individual merits or demerits.

COYNE J.A.: — I agree with the conclusion of the Chief Justice and his reasons in support. The appeal should be dismissed.

BEAUBIEN J.A.: — I have had the privilege of reading and considering the reasons for judgment of the Chief Justice and I agree with him that the appeal should be dismissed.

*The appeal is dismissed.*

. . .

Within Canada the authority to define criminal law is closely tied to the power to enforce that definition. This power consists of both physical and psychological components. The physical components include the army, police, judges, public prosecutors, prison personnel and government ministries. Armed forces are under direct political control in Canada and are usually assigned the task of dealing with external threats. Under vaguely defined "emergencies", however, Parliament can use the army to put down revolts, rebellions, insurrections and internal security threats. *The War Measures Act*, R.S., c. W-2, s. 1, was employed in 1971 during the FLQ affair, for example, to temporarily increase the fire power available to the federal government. Political authority is also backed by more than 50,000 public police in Canada in federal, provincial and municipal agencies. Police authority is supported by the court system comprised of bailiffs, clerks, sheriffs, Justices of the Peace (J.P.s), lawyers, prosecutors and judges. In addition, criminal law matters are overseen by federal agencies such as the departments of Justice, Revenue Canada, Citizenship & Immigration and the Solicitor-General. Finally, wardens, guards, parole officers and forensic psychiatrists are authorized to exercise coercive state control.

Physical force is not omnipotent and even a modern bureaucratic government constitutes a small elite. Moreover, soldiers and police will not obey every order or enforce every law. Both within and without the government there is significant scope for resistance and revolt. All governments, therefore, attempt to bolster their law creating authority by instilling in citizens a tradition of wilful submission to authority. Legitimation is the process whereby government justifies its coercive apparatus by reference to divine right, historical inevitability or allegedly democratic choice. Legitimation's object is to develop a general sense that political authority is just, good and right. It is important to note here the evident propensity of most people to obey authoritative figures even when ordered to inflict apparently painful penalties on innocent victims (Milgram, 1974). Ironically, this uncritical willingness to obey orders can cause greater social damage than the rebellious acts of a small anti-establishment minority.

One of the standard methods of legitimation is propaganda and the political manipulation of names and titles. Examples include the "Criminal Justice System", "Ministry of Justice" and "Corrections Canada". American police form "Benevolent Associations". Other manipulative titles worth mentioning are "Peace Officers" and honorariums for judges and politicians such as "Your Honour", "Justice Smith", "Right Honourable" and "Your Worship". Calling members of Parliament "Honourable" does not make them so, just as calling a criminal law system a "Justice System" does not make it just. However, the power to define criminal law is held by the same people with the power to bestow propagandistic titles on themselves and their bureaucracies. By calling a certain branch of the state bureaucracy "Justice", the hope is that most people will accept the name at face value. In this text we will attempt to avoid such titles unless quoting from specific sources or mentioning specific names. Where possible, neutral terms such as Criminal Law System will be substituted for biased terms such as the Criminal Justice System.

The legal definition of crime, according to Parker, contains two other elements. One is that the forbidden behaviour be "subject to penal sanctions". As we will suggest below, there are a number of procedural features that distinguish "criminal" law from other varieties of law. The second element mentioned is that criminal law only deals with "human behaviour". In fact, criminal law does not extend to all humans. Many jurisdictions, including Canada, exempt youngsters below a certain age from any criminal liability. This and other exemptions will be discussed below. Suffice it to say now that an exemption from criminal law does not necessarily mean lenient treatment. Dogs are exempt from criminal liability but a dog that bites two people or seriously injures a child will usually be taken into custody and killed by government agents whereas a human who bites two people will not be executed and may not even be incarcerated. In the same way, ten year old children are exempt from criminal law but they are subject to laws forcing school attendance and granting parents or other legal guardians near dictatorial powers.

**Ethical Definition of Crime**

The legal definition of crime is a positivist definition; it focuses on describing the law accurately and its critical faculty extends only to questioning whether a given criminal law is properly authorized. In contrast, ethical definitions import a normative aspect and attempt to describe what the criminal law should be. Ethical and legal definitions are readily distinguished: everything that deserves to be declared a crime by some ethical rule is not designated a crime by the legal authorities and all crimes do not deserve to be regarded as unethical. In mapping the intersection of criminal law and morality Wexler (1976:356-9) observes that:

> In modern societies, a great deal of the criminal and quasi-criminal law has nothing to do with moral values; many acts are illegal which are not bad... A great many immoral acts which even [John Stuart] Mill would say that the law could prohibit are not illegal. Our criminal law ignores a great many acts which obviously cause harm to people... Finally, the private morality which the law does embody is often not the morality of the society... [thus] in the face of serious social evil the law seems either to be impotent or to be allied with what is wrong rather than what is right.

A legal definition of crime has unlimited content — "any form of human behaviour" — whereas all ethical definitions limit what should and should not be crimes. The most familiar ethical limit is that only wrongful acts should be made crimes. An ethicist would argue that designating helpful, positive behaviour like charity, working, gift giving and child producing, as criminal will lead to perverse results. The difficulty, of course, is in determining which behaviour is wrongful and which is helpful. When the human population was much smaller and tribal survival depended on a steady production of children, procreation tended to be encouraged and obstacles to procreation, like homosexuality, were often regarded as wrongful. Now, when continued population growth can possibly thwart human survival, some people argue that "excessive" procreation is selfish, shortsighted and unethical.

The key to an ethical definition of crime is the possession of a normative system or set of criteria measuring the degree of wrongness. Most ethicists insist that "crimes" should consist of serious wrongs only. How then can one go about measuring and identifying wrongfulness? There exist three general methods which, for our purposes, we will label the traditional, the intuitional and the consequential.

The traditional method of ethical judgment can be usefully compared to the formation of language. Every human language follows certain rules according to which words, letters, sounds or sentences are right or wrong. The sentence — "Sins be after should all crimes all? — is "wrong" because the word order does not follow the rules of the English language (After all, should all sins be crimes?) Language rules develop over a long period and arise through the trial-and-error use of language by many people. There is no centralized rule maker who handed down language laws carved in stone tablets. Similarly, in early cultures the perception of wrongful behaviour was based on custom, taboos and traditions rather than explicit laws. In ancient Greece, circa 1200 BC, the words that come closest to law are "dike" and "tyemis" but they actually mean "custom". Under a purely traditional system of ethical determination, acts like hunting deer in the spring, eating pork or collecting interest on loans are judged wrongful because of the dictates of custom. Wrongfulness is thus determined by consulting tribal elders, reviewing ancient stories and, where written records exist, by reading about earlier customs. One of the earliest recordings of customs is the so-called Code of Hammurabi, carved in 2 metre black basalt columns and erected around 1750 B.C. Hammurabi was perhaps the world's first literate king but his Code does not correspond with modern legislative dictates of a ruler. Instead, the 282 pronouncements on the stele merely recorded practices which by that time were already customary in Babylon. Equivalent social orders are investigated by modern anthropologists who typically find that among customary societies "the use of force is minimal...there are leaders rather than rules, and...cohesion is achieved by rules rather than by laws and by consensus rather than by dictation". (Uchendu, 1965:46) For the most part, custom provides primitive cultures with a full set of judgments about right and wrong. Interestingly, people who live according to a set of customs will usually be unable to explain the custom in objective or consequential terms. Taboos about hunting will not be explained in terms of sustaining an optimal ratio of prey to predator yet it is likely that the taboo developed precisely to prevent over-hunting. Custom and tradition are still important in contemporary cultures. One example is the traditional judgment that having more than one marriage partner at a time is wrongful behaviour. This judgment is reflected in sections 290 and 293 of the Code which prohibit bigamy and polygamy. While certain cultures in the Islamic and Oriental tradition accepted polygamy, monogamy has long been the custom in the Hellenic and European cultures. Over time matrimonial custom became matrimonial law, church law and finally criminal law when, by an Act of 1603, English law-makers classified bigamy as a capital offence and "felony". When asked to explain why bigamy or polygamy are "wrongful" most Canadians would be hard-pressed to supply a cogent rationale. This by no means suggests that good reasons for condemning polygamy in our social context do not exist, it merely illustrates that traditional judgments about right and wrong are not based on people's awareness of the original or continuing reasons behind the judgment. This process introduces what is probably the greatest weakness of the traditionalist method, namely the incapacity to adapt quickly to altered social conditions. If we do not know the reasons why polygamy was regarded as wrongful it will be difficult to change our customs if the justifying conditions cease to exist. Still, the traditionalist method has its strengths. In a trial-and-error process, customs that did not maintain or improve a people's survival capacity would not tend to be passed on. Certainly, traditional judgments about wrongness should not be dismissed merely because proponents cannot explain their custom. After all, one can use a language quite effectively without conscious awareness of its rules of grammar.

While some custom evolved into or was taken up by law, it is a mistake to regard custom as the natural precursor to law, as a sort of quasi-law. Diamond (1971:45) explains:

> "[L]aw is not definite and certain while custom is vague and uncertain. Rather the converse holds. Customary rules must be clearly known; they are not sanctioned by organized political force, hence serious disputes about the nature of custom would destroy the integrity of society — But laws may always be invented, and stand a good chance of being enforced... In fascist Germany, customs did not become laws... Rather, repressive laws conjured up in the interests of the Nazi Party and its supporters, cannibalized the institutions of German society... 'The absolute reign of law' has been synonymous with the absolute reign of lawlessness.

Custom is decentralized, organic and mostly unconscious, and being thus is uniform and egalitarian. Law is centralized, contrived and conscious and for the most part is non-uniform and elitist. State-sponsored efforts by elite French academics to outlaw new words and expressions used by millions of francophones illustrates one of the prime relationships between custom and law. Law is the product of organized, and usually narrow, force. Perhaps the ultimate challenge is to reproduce at a complex legal level the degree of assent and consensus typical of all customary orders.

The intuitional basis for ethical judgment is personal feeling rather than knowledge of tradition. Intuitionalists determine that a certain practice is right or wrong according to their own response. If they are distressed, disgusted, annoyed, disturbed, dissatisfied or repelled then they will tend to regard the behaviour in question as wrongful. Lord Devlin, a British jurist who favoured linking criminal law with moral judgment, was a traditionalist when he referred to Church of England rules as a basis for judgment but he was an intuitionalist when he appealed to the 'feelings of right-thinking men and women' (Devlin, 1965). For Devlin, using the criminal law to punish homosexual acts was justified, 'If it is the genuine feeling of our society that homosexuality is a vice so abominable that its mere presence is an offence'. One, however, wonders how the judicial members of the House of Lords ascertain what are society's "genuine" feelings or, indeed, how a reified concept like "society" can have feelings.

Feelings or intuitive conclusions may seem a rather unreliable and insubstantial basis for deciding criminal law's content but the method should not be dismissed too hastily. A primary source of feeling is conditioning or inculturation. Conditioning is the process whereby parents train their children to develop a conscience. Guilt and embarrassment probably govern human behaviour far more effectively than do legal penalties. Without conditioning humans will not feel that theft or assault or eating without utensils or defecating in public are "wrong". Since children in a given culture are conditioned to accept a common language and a common set of behaviours, most people's feeling about right and wrong will be in general harmony. This will be most true in stable, insular societies but even among cosmopolitan or ethnically diverse cultures, a broad ethical consensus will exist. This consensus, however, may be overlooked because, psychologically, people's attention is naturally drawn to contrast and change rather than to constant, unvarying norms (Garan, 1982).

Intuitional ethical judgment also includes unconscious assessments. When one stands on a hill top and surveys the surrounding forest, streams and fields one's judgment of beauty is not based on a conscious, point-by-point deliberation but rather on a more complex and largely automatic assessment. The limited role played by conscious thought in governing human behaviour is discussed at length in *The Origin of Consciousness in the Breakdown of the Bicameral Mind* (Jaynes, 1976). Jaynes' psychological and historical research suggests that self-consciousness is a learned process that evolved only 3,000 years ago and that early civilizations were populated by people with a less evolved, split or "bicameral" consciousness. According to Jaynes, bicameral people were regulated by conditioned and intuitive responses from the brain's right hemisphere which were communicated to the left hemisphere as auditory or visual hallucinations. Furthermore, this guidance was interpreted as directives from "gods", seen initially as the "spirits" of deceased parents and tribal elders. While this system prevailed, laws and police were unnecessary; in ancient Egypt and Sumer there are few if any scenes of brutality or harshness (Wilson, 1984:108). As Jaynes remarks, "Within each bicameral state...the people were probably more peaceful and friendly than in any civilization since". This purely intuitive customary system, however, was apparently unable to cope with the larger more complex civilizations coming into existence some 4,000 years ago.

The final method for judging wrongness can be broadly termed "consequentialist" because the ethical verdict depends on the consequences of the behaviour in question.

In simplest terms, an act is wrong if it results in net social harm. The utilitarian version of this method uses happiness or satisfaction as the basis for measuring a harmful result. In the original arguments of Priestly and Bentham, behaviour was right if it contributed to the greatest happiness of the greatest number. Happiness, however, proved to be a problematic criterion by which to measure ethical value. Despite considerable ingenuity, utilitarians could not make happiness a workable guide so, gradually, happiness was replaced by social welfare goals (Mitchell, 1986). Representative of this trend is the economic analysis that judges behaviour good or bad depending on whether it aids or impairs a society's total wealth. Bad behaviour is "diseconomic" and criminal behaviour should, by this theory, be restricted to that which is extremely diseconomic.

Taking things from unconsenting persons, for example, is generally harmful. This harmfulness may not be obvious looking only at the perpetrator and victim because while the victim loses the perpetrator enjoys an offsetting gain. More important, however, are the responses of the millions of potential victims who, in order to avoid being victimized, invest in locks, guns, alarms, guard dogs and security services and who experience anxiety and increased distrust of other people. The key to a consequentialist analysis is a full and thorough accounting of *all* the relevant consequences of a given act. Since a full accounting is difficult, time consuming and expensive, many consequential analysts tend to draw unwarranted conclusions based on insufficient data. It is instructive to compare the three normative systems on this point. A traditionalist has little difficulty identifying theft as wrongful since theft is condemned in ancient texts and even older customs. Theft is also readily judged as wrong intuitionally. Ironically, consequentialists have the most difficulty deciding that theft is wrong because they must actually identify and tabulate the results of theft, a task of immense challenge, so it is not surprising that the consequentialist method is the last to be employed.

**Contractual Definitions of Crime**

Contractual definitions of crime are generated along two different strands. One is based on analysis of a hypothetical social contract while the other concerns the practical question of democratic choice.

The social contract is a familiar concept found in the philosophies of Locke, Rosseau, Kant and Rawls. The idea of a social contract is that government and law should be the result of mutual determination between equal contractors. By this measure "crime" will consist only of those behaviours designated as crimes by all the parties to the contract. If all the contractors were artificially rendered equal then Rawls argues that the result must be fair rules (Rawls, 1971:12). The key to a genuine contractual definition of crime is thus mutual forbearance which prevents any contractor exploiting any other. In the "original position" contrived by Rawls, every contractor would in effect be asked—what criminal laws will you impose on yourself in order to protect yourself other people committing the same acts against you? Will you, for example, agree to prohibit theft knowing that by doing so you permit everyone else to punish you if you commit theft? Under these conditions, a crime is essentially a breach of a term of the social contract.

Mutual restraint and agreement is also a central component of Posner's economic theory of criminal law (Posner, 1985). Posner praises the market exchange of goods and services because each party voluntarily gives up their labour to receive something in trade. If this voluntary exchange is rejected by one party who simply takes what she wants at gun point, then the result is crime. Posner, therefore, defines "crime" as "market by-passing". This definition is easy to understand where an explicit market in goods and services exists. But Posner extends the definition beyond acquisitive crimes like theft, fraud, robbery and embezzlement to include the allegedly more personal crimes of violence and passion. This extension is based on the existence of "implicit" markets for fighting, sexual outlet and the like, a point the following fictional examples illustrate. Arnie and Chris both like fighting. Arnie joins a martial arts club and takes up boxing so he has access to others who will voluntarily fight with him. Chris, on the other hand, attacks unsuspecting people who have not agreed to fight. This is criminal assault because it by-passes an implicit market. The same is true for sexual outlet. Both Bert and Jason seek sexual partners but while Bert dates others and engages in consensual acts only, Jason attacks women and obtains his goal by means of coercion.

It is even possible to conceive of implicit markets for killing other people as a logical extension of duels and war games. In Robert Sheckley's futuristic novel *The 10th Victim* (1965), a few especially adventurous people join in an annual contest whereby participants are alternatively hunter and victim. The object of the game is to kill your opponent (the victims are not told who their hunters are) and the prize is the acquisition of your opponent's property. While this sport obviously results in death, consider in what ways it differs from such dangerous games as mountain climbing, boxing, and All Terrain Vehicle (ATV) riding (which has killed hundreds of Americans since 1982).

The second strand of the contractual definition of crime involves direct democratic choice where "crime" is defined as those acts so designated by some plurality of citizens. On this point Nettler (1982:27) reports that:

> Criminal law is one arm of coercive control. What is at issue in democracies is how the citizenry wishes that force to be used and against which people and which acts. There are no adequate studies addressing this issue. We have no measures of the balance of demands for the manufacture or reduction of criminal law. Surveys have questioned samples of the population about particular questions...but we lack comprehensive investigation of public conceptions of wrongs to be pursued as crimes... Lacking information about the full roster of wrongs citizens believe should be crimes, attention is advisably limited to the so-called 'classical crimes'...(Crimes *mala in se*)...which have received general condemnation. There seems to be nearly universal agreement in defining as crimes such perennial wrongs as murder, burglary, arson, and a variety of larcenies.

Commentators on criminal law issues frequently make reference to laws which reflect "society's disapproval", which result from "society's demands" or which allegedly flow from the "public's concerns". Two objections must be lodged against such statements. First, one should not personify "society" or "the state" as if there existed some monolithic, animated creature or some collective unconscious that has feelings or opinions. Public opinion, if carefully canvassed, will always be diverse. Second, one should not presume that criminal law reflects a general public or democratic consensus or results from general demands unless one has direct, verifiable and relevant evidence. Politicians creating or supporting a law tend to justify their actions by claiming that the law is in answer to public demand. This appeal to democratic sensibilities should not be accepted on faith since, in fact, there are many instances of criminal law creation that ignore or even contradict broad majoritarian interests.

According to orthodox liberal theory, a free vote in a representative democracy naturally leads to laws that reflect the "will of the people". The concrete formulation of this concept in the U.S. occurs when criminal law prosecutions are entitled *The People v. Smith*. The case title's obvious inference is that all citizens implicity consent to and benefit from such legal actions. If inappropriate behaviours are made crimes or if serious wrongdoing is ignored then a critical electorate will supposedly vote the offending government out of office and set up a reform regime. Logically, if the Criminal Code is not revised it must mean that no substantial majority wants revision. There are a number of substantial problems or fallacies in the standard liberal theory. First, voters do not exercise much control over their elected representatives. Voters merely choose between a few party candidates; the preliminary and probably more important competition occurs at the nomination stage. After election, party discipline prevails because party support is the key to promotion, appointments and renomination. Election costs also limit voter control. Few politicians or even parties can afford to finance their own election campaigns so they must seek outside assistance. Such assistance, often from concentrated interest groups like businesses, unions and professions, does not come without conditions and expectations. According to some research, voters' control over elected representatives has declined since the early 1800s. Earlier conditions entailing small governments, part-time legislators, weak political parties, strong political customs and low election expenses have changed. Free elections remain but other political circumstances have altered in ways that permit modern government to be less democratic (Buchanan, 1978, 1984).

The suggestion that criminal laws are selected by the public also presupposes that most people know enough about the *Criminal Code* to have opinions about it. As Downs (1957:255) explains:

> Clearly, the cost of acquiring information and communicating opinions to government determines the structure of political influence. Only those who can afford to bear this cost are in a position to be influential... Yet without such knowledge [voters] cannot have policy preferences for the government to pay attention to.

Government agents allege that the modern drug prohibitions set out in the *Narcotic Control Act* and the *Food and Drug Act* are, for example, a response to an initiating and continuing public demand. Historical evidence indicates that the drug laws sparked widespread interest rather than being the result of popular interest (Boyd, 1984; Comack, 1985; Green, 1979; Mitchell, 1986). Contemporary evidence suggests that voters remain ill-informed about the drug laws. Voters do not know how much the laws cost to enforce, what effects the laws have on police or judicial procedures or what social consequences are attributable to the laws. Voters do not know the identity of drug-related lobbyists nor do they know of the links that exist between politicians on one hand and drug producers on the other. The connections between alcohol and tobacco producers and legislators are particularly well-developed but still remain publicly obscure. Arguably, voters are ignorant of these and many other criminal law matters because the cost of informing themselves is greater than any benefit that will follow from being well-informed. In short, voters are "rationally ignorant". This situation is exacerbated either by government making information difficult and expensive to acquire or by government obstructing democratic choice so that even well-informed voters cannot have much impact on legislation.

Democratic input can be increased by a number of means including direct referenda, voter initiatives, special constitutional assemblies, limits on campaign expenses and contributions and, finally, the extension of voting selection to previously appointed positions such as judges, police chiefs, regulatory board members, prison wardens, parole officers, public prosecutors, heads of public corporations and ambassadors. Ensuring maximum democratic input, however, does not in itself guarantee a fair and just result. If voters are unconstrained by constitutional limits, it is probable that the majority will vote for criminal laws that favour themselves even at the expense of persecuted minorities. A country 90% Christian may vote a law prohibiting Islamic practices or a predominantly alcohol-using majority may outlaw a minority practice like cocaine use. The ethical response to this tyranny of the majority is that whether laws are passed by a dictator, a representative body or by direct voter choice, the law makers should be restricted to fair choices.

## THE OBJECTIVE OF GOVERNMENT REGULATION

Criminal law is one method of government regulation. Before considering the methodological characteristics of criminal law in section 3 of this Chapter we begin here with the more substantive question of what activities government should regulate. According to the Canadian Committee on Corrections, the protection of society is not merely the basic purpose, it is "the only justifiable purpose of the criminal process in contemporary Canada". While correct as far as it goes, this statement cannot explain the unique features of criminal law since societal protection is the alleged purpose of almost all government regulation. A genuine need for public safety may justify some government response but that response need not take the form of criminal law. Criminal law is merely one type of legal intervention. In solving a given problem there may be other legal methods that are safer, less expensive, more effective and more respectful of human rights than criminal law. Modern legislators are widely and properly criticized for overusing criminal law, for asking criminal law institutions to solve problems beyond or outside their capabilities. To formulate criminal law policy, it is imperative that one understand both how criminal law works and what criminal law should work at. The following material considers the type of threats faced by contemporary society.

### Protecting the Environment

One of the gravest long term threats is the modern assault on the earth's biosphere. All facets of the environment are experiencing damage (Howard, 1980). Water supplies are harmed by agricultural by-products, inadequate sewage processing, industrial chemicals and effluent discharges. Polluted water imposes costs on everyone. There are direct physiological costs caused by water-borne diseases like cholera or dysentery or by water-borne toxic chemicals like dioxin. Mercury at a few hundred parts per billion can cause nerve disorders, impaired vision, paralysis and death. There are also financial costs in treating water to eliminate pollutants or in acquiring clean water from more remote sources. The atmosphere is a dumping ground for millions of tons of pollutants. Airborne contaminants including hydrocarbons, sulphur dioxide, oxides of nitrogen, carbon monoxide and lead impose on the public a staggering array of costs (Taylor, et al., 1971). Pollutants eat away at fabrics, metals and the bricks, mortar and stone of buildings causing billions of dollars in damage each year. Acid rain is allegedly defoliating and destroying entire forests of maple, beech, ash and oak. Pollutants also cause direct personal damage ranging from bothersome odours and eye irritation to bronchial disease, premature death and birth defects.

Environmental damage to soil and landscape is another contemporary concern. Pesticides, chemicals, improper land use, and badly designed irrigation can erode, impair or destroy the soil. Soil destruction, in turn, leads to the loss of forests from which the world derives much of its oxygen. Besides deforestation and the advance of deserts, species' habitats are damaged, their migration routes are disrupted and their food sources wiped out. Rare species are hunted, often illegally, for trophies. On the topic of killing animals, livestock can be lawfully killed by human owners and wildlife can be hunted in season. Even where a total ban exists, for example whooping cranes are never in season, wrongful killing of animals is not murder, it is merely a regulatory infraction. This tradition may be changing. Certain species, like giant pandas are so rare that penalties for killing them are likely to escalate. Since the Chinese number a billion and the giant pandas in China only about 600, on the basis of scarcity value some may view pandas as more worthy of protection than humans. Certain other species, like whales, porpoises and apes, are intelligent enough that rare or not, killing them is increasingly seen as seriously wrongful. What, in principle, is the difference between intentionally killing a severely retarded human and killing a chimpanzee with a sign language vocabulary of 200 words? Should murder be contingent on a species-based test or is such a test chauvinistic and in need of being replaced by an objective test based on intelligence, brain capacity or some other measure of evolutionary development?

Other environmental threats can be briefly noted. Some, like excess radiation, are entirely tasteless, odourless and intangible. Excess radiation may result from atomic fission power plant malfunctions, like the meltdown of a reactor in Chernobyl, in the then USSR, that contaminated crops and animals thousands of kilometres away in Norway and France. Excess radiation may also stem from pollution-related damage to the protective ozone layer that shields life on the planet's surface from ultra-violet radiation. In contrast to radiation, noise is very noticeable pollutant. Excessive noise, mostly from vehicles, construction equipment and amplifiers, now plagues all modern cities. Noise impairs health, lowers the quality of life and devalues real estate. Excessive noise naturally damages hearing but increased noise is also associated with high blood pressure, ulcers, fatigue and anxiety (Turk, et al. 1972).

How do wrongs against the environment compare to ordinary crimes such as theft, murder and robbery? Environmental damage is probably more of a threat. Acid rain appears to be stealing more value from property than direct theft, while air and water pollutants likely cause more physical damage than all muggings and assaults. The monetary value of environmental damage is largely unknown, nor are there good estimates of crime-related costs. This paucity of data makes it difficult to rationally order law enforcement resources. Government cannot concentrate preventive efforts on the leading sources of social damage unless some sort of accounting of damages is conducted.

Even where ordinary crimes and environmental assaults cause equal damage they differ in other respects. One difference is the causal complexity typical of environmental damage. Systems and methods must be invented to identify and detect pollutants, trace their sources and learn their effects. This will almost always be difficult. For example, lead poisoning may be due to lead from gasoline, lead from water pipes or lead from smelters. What constitutes a "safe level" of lead in the blood has been periodically lowered over the years. Moreover, lead-related ailments may parallel symptoms from other diseases. Thus it is a daunting task for a lead-poisoning victim to diagnose the condition or to attribute the injury to a specific source of lead. In comparison, the causal issues in ordinary crimes are relatively easy. Victims either witness the crime being committed themselves or witness the immediate consequences when they return, for instance, to discover their apartment ransacked.

A second difference is the scale of harm caused by individual wrongs. With ordinary crimes like assault and robbery, each offence tends to be significantly and acutely damaging. Even at the low end, the average break and either causes over $1000 worth of damage to the victim. Graffiti removal costs the New York City Transit Authority millions of dollars annually. Vandalism can also result in extreme damage such as the case where the removal of a stop sign caused the deaths of four people in a car-truck collision (Francis, 1983). Environmental damage follows quite a different pattern. The damage caused by a specific motorist on a given day is usually very minor. One motorist, like one termite or one army ant, is not a significant threat. However, if we total the effect of millions of motorists aggregated over years, the negative impact is considerable. Prior to 1973, the automobile was the single largest source of air pollution in North America. In addition, the automobile's impact on cities, public safety, economics and culture has been widespread and substantially negative. The different pattern affects people's perception of danger. Acute, easily understood dangers like theft are much more visible than chronic, subtle and aggregated dangers like pollution.

**Regulating the Regulators**

Laws are not self-executing. People must be appointed, hired and given power to administer regulations and that power can be abused. Behind the institutional trappings and ceremonies, government is merely an assortment of people paid from the public treasury (McGinley, 1981). A perennial problem with government personnel is who will regulate the regulators. Modern societies have not solved this problem. Government agents from clerks to the highest elected officials routinely break both domestic and international laws (Lieberman, 1972). Government agents may also cause considerable damage by not enforcing laws or by creating laws that abuse citizens. The American Friends Service Committee (1971:10-11) summed up the matter of government wrongdoing:

Actions that clearly ought to be labelled "criminal" because they bring the greatest harm to the greatest number, are in fact accomplished officially by agencies of government... Hundreds of unlawful killings by police go unprosecuted each year. The largest forceful acquisitions of property...has been the theft of lands guaranteed by treaty to Indian tribes, thefts sponsored by the government. The largest number of dislocations, tantamount to kidnapping—the evacuation and internment of Japanese-Americans during World War II—was carried out by government with the approval of the courts.

A familiar species of government wrongdoing includes bribe taking, nepotism, improper use of public property and embezzlement for personal gain. Such acquisitive misbehaviour is often regarded as relatively harmless. Indeed, some Third World regimes pay bureaucrats low salaries with the expectation that income earned from bribery and kickbacks will augment their official remuneration. Bureaucrats may also seek out and promote such entrepreneurial bribery schemes because a bribery-based system gives far greater power and discretion to individual bureaucrats than does a rule-based system. Furthermore, acquisitive corruption is not always a matter of small bribes among minor functionaries. Ferdinand Marcos, when he was President of the Philippines, is reported to have diverted billions of dollars of public funds to his personal use. Similar if less extensive theft of public money was evidenced by Argentina's military government in the 1970's and 1980's, by the Duvalier regimes in Haiti, and by a number of other American and African governments. It is not unusual to find that citizens suffer most at the hands of those who are supposedly entrusted to protect public welfare.

A second type of government abuse entails systematic abuses perpetrated not by deviant individuals or personally corrupt leaders but by governing groups establishing wrongful policies. Lieberman cites cases of protectors and police using false evidence to secure convictions, of department heads violating regulations intended to minimize wasteful expenditures and of bureaus engaged in approved but illegal operations. Perhaps most dangerous are abuses accomplished through legitimate channels, policies that are both wrongful and legal. Since some people are prone to regard all lawful edicts as ethically right and all illicit acts as ethically wrong, juxtaposition of the legal with the unethical causes considerable confusion, paralysis and inappropriate response. Examples of legal-unethical policies include the anti-semitic regulations duly passed by the National Socialists in Germany 1933-1945, the racist laws familiar to many regimes and the legal witch hunts against illicit drug users pursued avidly by the Canadian and American governments. The damage done by such policies often far surpasses the damage wrought by ordinary criminals. While the Nazi government proclaimed that Jews were the major threat to German citizens, the actual threat to Germans was the Nazi government (Shirer, 1960).

In the case of the Third Reich, the legitimation of unethical practices was aided and abetted by the German courts. Although opponents of the regime were generally denied a fair trial and although defence lawyers were afraid to raise procedural challenges, judges co-operated with the government. This co-operation extended to collusion between some judges and the Gestapo in the persecution of German jews and to sentencing at least 30,000 people to death between 1942-45 for crimes such as a Jew having sexual intercourse with an "Aryan". Reifner (1986:104) traces the effect of judicial acquiesence:

In the eyes of the public, the court system—its personnel and structures as well as its traditional habits—had not changed since the regime of the last German Kaiser. The legitimizing effects of the judiciary's involvement in fascist political activity were probably more significant in their impact on the conscience of participants in Nazi terrorism...than in their immediate and actual results. If the courts legitimated the system, giving racism a seemingly rational image and making murderous intentions legally realizable, how could ordinary citizens know what was right and wrong, what was criminal and what was patriotic?

A financial example of legal-unethical regulations is the official debasement of currency. At various times in antiquity government treasuries cheated citizens by debasing the official metal coinage. Debasement occurred when the silver and gold content was diluted with brass and copper yet citizens were ordered to accept the new coinage at the original face value. In 100 A.D. a pure silver Roman denarius purchased one bushel of wheat. Two centuries later the denarius was pure copper and it took 3000 of them to buy the same amount of wheat. While spectacular, this rate of inflation pales in comparison with the debasement of paper money which can accomplish the same effect in a single year. When government debases the nation's currency the change affects a transfer of wealth similar to the way that theft transfers wealth from victims to thieves. With currency debasement, the persons most damaged are the elderly on pensions or fixed incomes and the financially unsophisticated. Their wealth is shifted to borrowers, to government and to skilled or lucky speculators. Losing half the value of a pension through currency debasement is equivalent to losing the same amount through fraud or theft. Actually, in some respects, losses through theft are preferable because at least the thief might be apprehended, convicted and ordered to pay restitution or to undergo punishment. The likelihood of government authorities being held responsible for, in effect, counterfeiting their nation's currency is almost nil.

Government-initiated damage reaches its zenith in the waging of war. Casualties in World War I came to about 9 million people. The war squandered Europe's human and material resources to an unprecedented extent. Unfortunately, the amazing amount of war damage in 1914-18 was exceeded in 1939-45. In this second major conflict about 15 million military persons and 35 million civilians perished. The Soviet Union was hardest hit losing 20 million dead and leaving another 25 million homeless. In 1984 Goode estimated that the total number of deaths in legal combat during the 20th century stood at 80 million (Goode, 1984:226). Furthermore, 17 million people had died in wars since 1945, with 25% of the fatalities occurring in just two areas: Korea and Indochina. An optimistic trend to note is the decline in war deaths into the 1970s and 80s. Most war deaths now come about through close range killing by machine gun, mortars and small artillery; glamorous and expensive weapons like tanks and airplanes mostly just destroy other tanks and airplanes. There are of course numerous exceptions to this, notably found in the fighting in the former Yugoslavia and in Rwanda.

War killing is usually distinguished from crime or wrongful acts on the grounds that war is authorized and legitimated whereas murder is unauthorized. While the distinction is clear in principle, things are not so straightforward in practice. The U.S. involvement in Vietnam illustrates the point. America's military excursion in Vietnam was implemented by a small number of people in the armed forces and the federal government. The question of war was never put directly to the voters nor was Congress instrumental in the early stages of military escalation. Furthermore, a large portion of the soldiers sent into combat were involuntarily drafted and compelled to kill other people under threat of court martial. Labelling such a war "legitimate" raises grave concerns about the political process and about the objective value of legitimation. This skeptical view does not deny the possibility of a democratically sanctioned war fought by volunteers or draftees raised by universal conscription. The Swiss defence against Austria in 1315 and 1388, the Greeks at Marathon against the Persians, the Israelis in 1967, the liberation of Kuwait in 1991——these are examples perhaps of justified wars. But such wars may be the exception, not the rule. Even amongst the supposedly militaristic Germans, a sizeable majority in 1939 would probably have voted against attacking Poland or any other major state. The Nazi regime never put the issue to the voters but then most modern democratic governments do not seek or permit direct voter input on war issues either.

**Regulating the Marketplace**

Business abuses involve more than white collar crimes. Certain minor abuses are scarcely regulated. These include legal but irksome practices such as telephone soliciting, junk mailings, distribution of throwaway flyers and advertising on billboards. More problematic is the prevalence of legal but misleading advertising. Such advertising is not false but vital information is left out and false expectations are created. Pharmaceutical promotions of painkillers or analgesics are a prime example. Advertisement for these drugs mention only their initial, short term effects of symptom alleviation. Never mentioned are the long term results or the risks of repeated consumption. Tobacco advertising follows the same pattern. The entire focus is on the immediate gratification users can obtain from taking tobacco. Not mentioned is the probability of cancer, addiction, health impairment and death. Tobacco products now bear certain warnings but only because government ordered producers to make the addition. Similar and more extensive warnings are warranted for a large number of drug products.

Businesses may attempt to defraud customers, suppliers and competitors. Business crime in Canada is estimated to cost billions of dollars annually. Such crimes includes physicians submitting false claims to medical insurance plans, stock manipulation by inside traders, collusion by firms bidding on government contracts, pyramid sales schemes and a host of other deceitful practices (Croft, 1975). Some cases involve large losses to a few victims. Alberta lawyer Peter Petrasuk stole $2.3 million from his clients, some of whom entrusted him with their life savings. Petrasuk received a 10-year prison term and indirectly spawned a consumer-volunteer organization in 1981 called the Victims of Law Dilemma made up initially of his former clients. A real estate fraud perpetrated by Argosy Financial Group of Canada Ltd. and its president in the 1980's cost a thousand investors about $24 million. Other trust company scams involved Astra Trust Co., Dominion Trust Co., and the Toronto real estate fraud by Greymac Trust Co. and Seaway Trust Co.

In other cases, the losses are spread very thinly over a large group of victims. In the 1980's, the stockbroking firm of E.F. Hutton was fined $2 million (U.S.) for a cheque-kiting operation that ultimately hurt a number of banks and their shareholders.

Ivan Boesky was fined the record amount of 138.5 million (U.S.) in 1987 for using insider information to speculate on corporate takeovers. The victims of Boesky's offence were all other buyers and sellers of the affected stock. Boesky, who also received a 3 year jail term, garnered much of his illegal information from Dennis Levine, a New York investment banker who was convicted and fined $362,000. Price fixing is also an excellent example of how businesses can make large illicit gains by stealing small sums from millions of customers. For over forty years General Electric, Westinghouse and two other U.S. corporations conducted a rigged bidding system in order to extract high, non-competitive prices on government products. They also conspired to exclude new competitors, fix the price of products such as lightbulbs and divide the market between them. The result was higher prices for a range of electrical appliances and services and the blockage of new products like lightbulbs that would last longer and use less electricity. Blocking innovation may hurt society more in the long run than fixing prices. In Canada, price-fixing, bid-rigging and other illegal trade practices are regulated federally under various sections of the Competition Act, R.S., 1985, c. C-34.

Businesses or professions that achieve monopolistic market positions gain the power to abuse the public interest. Electric streetcars were the dominant form of urban transit by the 1920s yet they survived in only a few cities thereafter, Toronto being a principal exception. What happened to the trolley car? General Motors joined with Standard Oil and Firestone Tire Company to buy out transit companies in the Depression and replace streetcars with GM buses riding on Firestone tires and fuelled by Standard Oil's diesel fuel. While the three corporations were convicted in 1949 of criminal conspiracy over this matter they received only token penalties (Solomon, 1980). Similar costs are imposed on society by professions. A study by the then Consumer and Corporate Affairs Canada investigated 13 major professions including law, medicine and accounting. The report concluded that mandatory fee schedules, advertising restrictions and barriers to inter-provincial competition cost customers about $700 million per year (Dewees, 1983).

An important avenue of business abuse is the manufacture, sale and distribution of defective products. Some of these defects are the result of inadvertent or accidental mishaps. Michigan Chemical Corporation in 1973 mistakenly mixed livestock feed with PBBs (polybrominated biphenyls) and thereby contaminated thousands of people, pigs and cattle and millions of chickens. Other defects are less accidental. The Ford Pinto, for example, was a poorly engineered car whose defects were known to Ford Motor Company. Indeed, all motor vehicles produced in the 1950s and 1960s suffered from known and correctable defects such as lack of seat belts, unpadded dashboards, poor brakes, obstructed view and high pollution output. These defects were not accidental or the result of ignorance. Finally, some defective products are marketed in direct violation of the law. Pharmaceutical firms have been convicted in a number of cases of doctoring test results and altering data in order to gain approval for new drugs (Mintz, 1965; Silverman & Lee, 1974).

Businesses can also abuse their employees by ignoring safety regulations, by not warning of or alleviating occupational hazards and by deceiving employees about such hazards. Naturally, all activities and all occupations entail some degree of risk. Particularly dangerous occupations include mining, construction, smelting and logging. Interestingly, police work is not a very dangerous occupation. In any case, a risk level above what is reasonably necessary amounts to employee abuse. While this formula is simple in theory, assessing risk levels and attributing causal relationships is difficult in practice, particularly in the case of long term disabilities from dust, pollutants, asbestos, noise and radiation. Connecting this type of disability to employment conditions is daunting partly because other causal agents, like tobacco smoking or viral cancers, may be partly or wholly responsible for an individual's impaired health.

So far we have considered businesses which engage in wrongful practices in the context of conducting a legitimate enterprise. There also exist businesses whose primary activities are illegitimate and which are other referred to as "organized crime". The standard view of organized crime is one in which criminal gangs or mobs, usually of south European extraction, prey on a helpless public. A vicious army of thugs is seen to be at war with decent society. This war involves bribing officials, extorting protection money, murder for hire, kidnapping, car theft rings and the infiltration of unions and legitimate businesses. "Crime fighters" stress the enormous financial impact of organized crime but do not question the legal framework responsible for generating the illegal profits (Government of B.C., 1980). An alternate theory of organized crime adds to or disagrees with the orthodox model. In the alternate view, organized crime centres around illicit marketing opportunities created by government. Here organized crime does not victimize the public, rather it exists to provide popular services like drugs, gambling, risky loans and commercial sex that government has wrongfully prohibited.

A case in point is "loansharking" involving loans at "usurious" rates of interest. Some people cannot acquire legitimate loans because they are poor credit risks or want the money for unapproved or illegal purposes. Such creditors must pay high rates of interest to lenders but the law interferes by making it illegal to make or collect such loans. Specifically, section 347 of the Code makes it an offence to advance anyone credit at an annual interest rate exceeding 60 percent. Legitimate lenders therefore cannot serve the high risk market which, by elimination, falls into the hands of those willing to break the law and to use coercive means to enforce their loan agreements. Police emphasize the assaults and extortion sometimes committed by such lenders but coercive behaviour of that sort is criminal quite apart from special rules about high rate loans. Furthermore, section 347 does not accommodate those situations where through defaults or bonuses an ordinary business deal can exceed the "criminal rate" of interest. Interestingly, while the police testify that loansharks typically charge interest rates of 80 percent a month, the police asked Parliament to fix the "criminal rate" much lower at 5 percent a month (60 percent expressed annually).

Service crime garners wide support from its customers and from opponents of prohibition. Far from being viewed as "evil", smugglers and purveyors of illicit goods are frequently portrayed as folk heroes engaged in principled opposition to government oppression. Furthermore, organized criminals are not limited to any specific ethnic group. Rather, successive waves of immigrants to North America pursue illicit business partly because established forces block their access to licit businesses and professions. Thus at different periods, historians identify Irish gangs, Jewish gangs, Chinese gangs and, far enough back, even English gangs. This type of organized "crime" is the direct result of law and would disappear immediately with changes in the law. The same is not true for crimes such as robbery or sale of stolen goods. We can see how the "problem" of cigarette smuggling in 1993-4 was largely "solved" by lowering the domestic taxes on these products.

**Regulating Individuals**

Human resourcefulness and creativity are not directed solely to beneficial ends. The same talents also appear in the exploitation and harming of other people. Some forms of exploitation are more readily resorted to than others. For example, while wrongdoers stole 160,000 automobiles in Canada in 1994 — a figure which represents 1 in every 10 households in the country — and there were 388,000 incidents of breaking and entering, only 596 murders took place. This latter statistic represents a 25-year low in the homicide rate.

Direct or personal wrongs include much of the substantive content of every jurisdiction's criminal law. They include wrongful killings, unprovoked assault, beating, torture, intimidation, sexual abuse, kidnapping and wrongful detention. While some of these misbehaviours are quite rare, others are relatively common. Murder can be contrasted in this regard with assault or with sexual harassment. Of offences reported by police in Canada, 1 in 10 is a violent crime, and 4 out of 10 violent crimes involve a weapon. Of the 3 million crimes reported in 1994, over half were property related.

The exploitation and maltreatment of other people appears throughout recorded history in every complex human society. Such basic continuity should raise some doubts about explanations of violent crimes that focus entirely on the specifics of current political, economic or social conditions. Still, the historically consistent presence of some crime does not deny the possibility of change. Both the rate of wrongdoing and the style of crime may alter dramatically. Since the late 1950's in Canada the official rate of crime has increased significantly over a broad range of fences. While violent crime has increased dramatically in the 1970's and 80's, recent years have seen a slight drop in the rates of both violent crime and crime in general. Similarly in the U.S., there have been large increases in the rate of violent crime in the decades leading up to the 1990's. The U.S. murder rate doubled in the period 1950-1985, and remains four times the Canadian homicide rate (9.03 per 100,000 versus 2.04 in Canada).

Besides more crime, the U.S. statistics also record more offences between strangers. But these official figures must be carefully analyzed and hasty conclusions avoided. Official statistics only approximate the real crime rate for a number of reasons including changing definitions of crime, new reporting methods, new police procedures or initiatives and variations in victim reporting. Besides rates of offences, styles of abuse may also change. At one period, murder may be predominantly an acquisitive activity practised by bandits, robbers and highwaymen. At other times, murder may tend to involve sexual motives, religious intolerance, racial tensions or social rebellion. Interestingly, in Canada the greatest risk of being murdered occurs during one's first year of life. Of 27 children under the age of one killed in 1994, 20 were killed by a parent while 3 were killed by another family member.

Personal wrongs often inflict physical damage such as injury, maiming, loss of faculties, pain and death. In addition, psychological and emotional harm may accompany the more visible injuries. Damage of this type includes anxiety, sleep disturbance, and loss of self-esteem. Moreover, psychological harm is suffered both by actual victims and by potential victims.

Wrongs directed against others' property comprise over half of officially reported offences. The relative risks of suffering from the traditional wrongs are well documented. If the Canadian rate of theft in 1990 was taken as 1 then other rates are as follows: murder (0.035), robbery (0.14), motor vehicle theft (5) and break and enter (17). Burglary is not only common, it is costly to the victim (average loss between $1,000 and $3,000 per incident); but the cost of property crime must also include the effort, expense and social impact of pursuing property protection measures such as alarm systems, locks, fences, guard dogs, self-defence courses, firearms and private security personnel. Tucker (1985:47) estimated that Americans spend $15 billion on public policing and another $18 billion on all private security employment. Paying 400,000 people to guard old wealth means those human resources cannot be employed in creating new wealth. We should also note the existence of secondary costs. For example, the mere locking of doors is a social cost, one that most people now take for granted but also one that is noticed and resented by people who migrate from remote communities where a locked door is an affront to the integrity of one's neighbours. A society that needs locks everywhere has a higher cost of living than an equal but lock-free society. Economist Gordon Tullock (1981) estimated the consequences of repealing the laws against theft and concluded that such a repeal would cause more theft, more self-defense, a personal arms race and a large decline in productive activity. According to Tucker (1985:181) crime "is a negative-sum game, creating distrust and causing people to cooperate less. It injures the whole society...[because] poverty does not cause crime, crime causes poverty". Even minor abuse of private property can be demoralizing; vandalism in particular is a form of social sabotage (Francis, 1983). To function effectively, humans require a certain degree of control over their personal and social environment. Where that personal control is seriously threatened, as is the case now in many decaying urban centres in the U.S., morale suffers. British Telecom's pay phones provide another case study. In 1987 BT recorded 500,000 serious attacks on its 79,000 public telephones with repair costs at $45 million. Poorer areas where people most need the phones suffer the highest rate of vandalism. Revealingly, BT is replacing traditional glassed call boxes because of their vulnerability to vandalism but when such booths were introduced sixty years ago neither theft nor vandalism were problems.

Business-oriented wrongdoings have been mentioned. Businesses themselves, however, are victimized by their employees who, because of their inside knowledge and position of trust, have the opportunity to exploit their employers. Losses through employee theft and pilfering are reported to exceed losses through shoplifting and burglary. Businesses hire security firms to supervise employee behaviour, a task that often entails undercover operations. Particularly vulnerable are financial service business whose employees must handle money and other commercial paper. Brian Molony, an assistant manager of the Toronto branch of the Canadian Imperial Bank of Commerce, was convicted in 1984 of stealing $10.2 million from the bank and served less than half of his 6 year sentence. By comparison, bank robbers who come in armed through the front door escape with about $3,000 on the average.

Employee misbehaviour also includes the violence and vandalism associated with some union activities. Reynolds (1987:135) reports on the incidence and style of union crime in the U.S.:

> From 1977 to 1979...incidents of labour violence by bombing alone caused $3.8 million in property damage. Between 1975 and 1983, there were 3,157 violent union incidents reported in the popular press.... Haggard and Thieblot (1983) analyzed the data on the 2,598 incidents for 1975-81 [and]...found 49 deaths attributable to labour violence; $15.2 million in damage to company plant and equipment; 2,732 instances of damage to automobiles; 133 cases of managers' and non-strikers' homes being firebombed, shot at or vandalized; hundreds of cases of sabotage and vandalism; and thousands of shots having been fired. Based on the evidence, the authors' conclusions seemed warranted; labour violence is substantial, systematically applied, and not diminishing, and much of the law enforcement community tacitly allows unions wide latitude to use intimidation and coercive techniques.

Frederic Hayek (1960:267) argues a legal reversal occurred with unions, whereby in the space of a century or so, unions progressed from outlaw status to a privileged place above the general rules of criminal law.

Besides their property and themselves, citizens possess certain rights. Rights, however, are counter-balanced by obligations. A legal right to vote means that government is burdened with a legal obligation to provide the means and opportunity to vote. A legal right to privacy means that others have a legal obligation not to intrude. All rights, legal or moral, have meaning only in light of opposite obligations. These obligations are frequently avoided, which is to say individuals abuse the rights of others. Take the use of public conveniences. People share sidewalks, public transit vehicles, parks and other common areas. Any person's right to use and enjoy these common areas is contingent on the behaviour of others. When individuals behave rudely or obnoxiously in public they infringe on everyone else's rights. The damage may be minor compared to physical assault, yet ill-mannered behaviour has a corrosive effect on the social structure. Such behaviour includes littering, jumping queues, foul language, lack of personal hygiene, excessive noise making, racial or sexual slurs, disrespect for persons with disabilities and unwarranted insults. Citizens also possess certain rights to privacy which are abused through telephone pranks, indecent exposure or high-pressure sales tactics in door-to-door selling.

## METHODS OF GOVERNMENT REGULATION

Many of the threats to public safety described above are counteracted in part by social, cultural and private mechanisms. In his *A Criminal History of Mankind* (1984), Wilson comments that people now have difficulty conceiving of how powerful were the religious and moral codes of a few centuries ago when the "faithful" actually believed that a powerful, vengeful god was always watching them, ready to condemn any transgression (Wilson, 1985:648). Customs are also important non-legal regulators. People generally refrain from appearing in public in a sordid condition not because body odour is illegal but because they are conditioned to be embarrassed by a certain level of uncleanliness. While Europeans of the 14th century viewed bathing with great suspicion, our social standards now require daily personal cleansing.

Cultural conditioning is a powerful source of regulation so one might hope that social standards about environmental damage are increasing. A century from now driving an internal combustion vehicle may be viewed with the same distaste which now greets defecating in public. Unfortunately, conditioned conscience, peer pressure and social disincentives do not always provide a satisfactory level of protection. Furthermore, social regulations are primarily preventive. Such regulation lacks the full capacity to compensate victims or to apprehend and punish wrongdoers. Where social regulation fails or is incomplete, some level of government intervention is required.

Some forms of government intervention are less coercive than others. Tax controls and subsidy policies are relatively non-coercive because they merely create incentives to act in certain ways. A tax on alcoholic beverages discourages consumption while a subsidy on pollution-control equipment encourages installation of that equipment. With either the tax or the subsidy, no specific course of action is compelled. Most regulation takes a more coercive form. Standards are set that must be met or certain actions are prohibited. Laws against the use of leaded gasoline or against "underage" alcohol use are examples of direct command-type regulation. All criminal laws are command-type regulations.

Regulation methods vary according to the roles assigned private persons as opposed to the state. Criminal law is primarily a public system. In contrast, tort law is dominated by private initiative. Regulations also vary according to the extent of the coverage. Some regulatory schemes are individualistic, like criminal law, while some involve mass coverage through bureaucratic rather than police controls. In this section, we consider the varieties of public regulation as well as the characteristics of private law schemes.

## Public Law Regulation

### Tax and Subsidy

Punitive or sumptuary taxes such as those levied on tobacco or alcohol products are fault-based and designed to regulate behaviour. As Lon Fuller explained, taxes are "close cousins to the criminal law [when] their principal object is...not merely to raise revenue, but to shape human conduct in ways thought desirable by the legislator" (Fuller, 1969:60). The theory behind sumptuary tax regulation is simple. If the use of certain goods or services is generating social harm, that harm can be reduced if use of the offending products is reduced. Economic experiments indicate that as the price of a commercial product increases, purchases of that product decrease. Thus a tax on alcohol should cause a decrease in alcohol consumption and, in fact, such decreases are observed when taxes increase the real price of alcohol (Mitchell, 1983).

Note how a tax control mechanism functions. There is no absolute standard of alcohol-related behaviour established. Citizens are not forced to buy alcohol nor are they compelled to purchase any specific amount. The tax is not individualistic. Instead, the tax regulation is administered impersonally and on a mass scale. No information is gathered about the individual alcohol taxpayer. There is no court, no investigation, no finding of guilt required before the penalty is assessed. The tax penalty is paid merely on the grounds that commercial alcohol is being purchased for consumption.

No special allowances need be made or individual cases considered. The cost of the regulatory tax per person affected is extremely low, perhaps pennies per case. This is because the tax is impersonal, because millions of people are penalized and because the regulatory work involved is not labour intensive.

A sumptuary tax scheme usually imposes a very small penalty. The scale of the penalty is optional, however. In theory, the tax could be set at any level whatsoever. The tax on a litre of rum could be set at $5,000. Two objections are possible to that level of tax. First, such an extreme penalty is not deserved. Second, an excessive tax will have an effect similar to a prohibition on all commercial sales of alcohol. The higher the tax the more incentive is provided to illicit sellers of the taxed product. At a tax rate of $5,000 per litre of liquor there would be almost no taxed sales of the drug. Instead, sales would occur through the blackmarket where the official price would be easily undercut. Insensitivity to tolerable tax levels is apparent in many regimes where government tax or price controls are subverted by underground traders. As noted above, a good example here is the flood of cigarette smuggling into Canada in 1993-4 and the government's response of dramatically reducing domestic taxes in order to curb the activity.

Tax penalties serve as disincentives to discourage certain behaviours. In contrast, subsidies use a carrot approach to reward certain actions. Both approaches focus on preventing wrong doing. Take, for example, the question of vulnerability to crime. Muggers tend to prey on the weakest people—small women, the aged, the intoxicated. Subsidies for women to take self-defense courses, to buy and learn about protective devices (mace, sirens, guns) or to organize mutual protection societies might be a cost effective way to prevent victimization. Defensive measures, as noted, involve investment in human or physical capital. Government subsidies are capable of encouraging such investment or of directing it toward specific goals. Some types of housing arrangements are more conducive to occupant safety than others. If government can identify the superior architectural methods of reducing misbehaviour, then government agencies could subsidize and thus encourage the reproduction of those safer forms of housing or urban design.

To some extent tax and subsidy methods are symmetrical. Unsafe work conditions or defective products could be taxed or subsidies could be awarded to safe work conditions and products. Polluters could be taxed or subsidies given for pollution reduction. But, overall, tax controls are more versatile than the subsidy approach. In many cases a tax limitation could not be reproduced by a positive incentive scheme. A tax on recreational drugs like alcohol cannot be paired against a subsidy scheme achieving the same effect. With tax there will also be fewer administrative decisions needed to identify who qualifies for the penalty.

*Rationing, Zoning and Licensing*

Direct command-type regulations tend to impose universal standards or blanket prohibitions. Section 210 of the Code prohibits the operation of a "bawdy house" anywhere in Canada at any time. Similarly, theft is everywhere prohibited. In contrast, rationing permits some amount of the targeted activity to be conducted while zoning permits the regulated behaviour to occur but only in specified places and usually only at certain times. Rationing is primarily employed in the regulation of minor misbehaviour, the so-called "vices" such as gambling, prostitution and drugs. In 1919 the U.S. government instituted a national prohibition against the sale or manufacture of beverage alcohol while, in contrast, Sweden chose to ration alcohol rather than outlaw it. Men received a more generous ration than women, alcohol offences could result in the loss of one's ration cards and, at one point, married women were not permitted their own ration card. Logan proposes a marijuana rationing scheme for Britain. Under this plan licensed sellers, perhaps pharmacists, would distribute a maximum amount of the drug to each customer per week. Customers would be compelled to restrict their purchases of cannabis to the one supplier with whom they would be registered (Mitchell, 1983).

Like tax controls, rationing systems are a mass-oriented regulatory method. However, unlike taxes, a ration system raises no revenue and tends to be more complicated to administer. The complexity increases as the rationing plan attempts to affect specific individuals. A cannabis tax following the tobacco model would be totally impersonal. In contrast, Logan's cannabis rationing proposal requires a very personal relationship between regulator, seller and customer. The medical prescription of controlled drugs illustrates the level of complexity rationing schemes often attain. An additional problem with rationing is enforcement. Ration cards, like food stamps, are forged, counterfeited or circulated illegally as a form of currency. Large amounts of the rationed product are also diverted from legal to illegal distributors. With popular prescription drugs like the tranquillizers or amphetamine, sometimes most of a legal production run is eventually diverted to illicit sellers. Illicit producers also go into business to supply the artificially restricted demand.

Services as well as products can be rationed. Access to commercial suppliers of sex could be restricted to ration card holders. Such a scheme might also entail a qualification test for those requiring "therapeutic" sex or tourists or members of the armed forces would be permitted sex ration cards by the government. Outside the rationing system, all prostitution would be banned. In some ancient cultures the ritual sale of temple sex by priestesses duplicated many aspects of a rationing system. On a more topical note, countries like the Bahamas ration casino gambling by permitting only tourists, not citizens, to place wagers. A related form of rationing restricts the form of vice available rather than the quantity purchased. Many state and provincial governments now permit citizens to wager unlimited sums through government lotteries and in approved casinos while at the same time prohibiting other forms of gambling.

Zoning controls limits the geographical placement of socially disruptive activities. Under zoning controls, taverns, casinos, bawdy houses, pornography stores, chemical dumps and smelters are not illegal *per se*, they are just restricted to certain locations. Theoretically, there is no limit to what can be permitted in a given zone. A certain zone could be designated an assault centre where people wishing to fight one another would go in search of adventure. In certain respects, such a zone might not differ much from some physical contact sports like martial arts, football or hockey. We will consider below the issue of consent and whether one should be free to consent to assault or homicide.

Licensing controls generally do not restrict quantity or location; rather they affect quality. Licensing arises ostensibly when government is concerned that because the wrong people are dispensing product X the public is endangered. Thus licensing controls exist to ensure that only duly licensed and authorized persons operate taverns, sell lottery tickets, run bawdy houses or prescribe drugs. Again, there is no theoretical limit to what a license holder might be permitted. Ian Fleming's fictional creation James Bond was often referred to as "007", the number on his "license to kill".

Licensing schemes are extremely commonplace in Canada. Most relate to professional or commercial controls whereby only licensed persons can operate taxi cabs, give legal advice, perform surgery, issue warrants or detain certain criminal suspects. Other license schemes are broad based and control activities such as hunting, flying, and driving motor vehicles. Actually, hunting licences are usually just ration cards which control the specific animal population. However, rationing and licensing are readily combined. Drivers in Ontario are licensed under a point program that, in effect, rations traffic infractions. Each offence is worth a specific number of points. Within a two year period drivers that use up their total point allotment lose their license to drive. This scheme may purport to measure a driver's qualifications but it is more readily understood as a ration system. Since the majority of drivers exceed legal speed limits and commit a host of other offences, the loss of points in many cases may be due more to bad luck than to unsafe or especially incompetent driving.

*Direct Command Regulations*

This type of regulation establishes certain legal standards and then prohibits any departure from those standards unless specific exemptions are granted. The criminal law prohibition of robbery is an example of this regulatory method but so is the forced schooling of all persons under a specified age (usually 15 or 16 years of age is the statutory standard enforced by the truancy law). While criminal law is probably the most familiar member of the direct command genre of regulation, there are a number of other regulations worth considering.

Three leading examples of mass coverage command regulation are compulsory schooling, compulsory auto insurance and traffic laws. Accepting that mass education is a valuable social objective does not necessarily lead to a legal prohibition against not attending school, which is the offence of truancy. Government could instead pay children directly for attending school or tax them for not attending. Either method might achieve a higher attendance rate than the present method of simply forbidding non-attendance. Truancy rates in some Canadian and U.S. high schools indicate that when a significant portion of students refuse to attend regularly, enforcement resources fail to cope adequately with the challenge. In some New York city schools the truancy rate exceeds 20% of all students and school boards lose permanent track of thousands of students every year. With the present compulsory system there is also the danger of creating harmful incentives. If school is compulsory then students must attend whether or not the school experience is valuable, educational or safe. These dangers may be magnified where the state has a total monopoly on schooling. In that situation, youngsters are forced not only to attend a school but to attend a specific school chosen by the government. Since such schools face little real competition and deal with a captive audience, incentives to deliver a high standard, popularly valued education may well decline over time. From 1966 to 1981 average test scores on the Scholastic Aptitude Test given to American college bound high school seniors declined. Verbal scores fell 11% and math scores fell 7% with the greatest declines occurring at the top of the score distribution (Thurow, 1985).

Most forms of insurance are not compulsory. One is not forced to insure one's life, personal possessions or house. Such was originally the case for automobile users. Individuals could buy auto insurance or not as they wished. Without insurance, however, motorists faced the possibility of having to directly pay for collision damage and for injuries caused to other persons. The first type of damage is of no public concern because it is limited to the motorists themselves. Damage to other people is a different matter. If an uninsured motorist seriously injured some one and was sued in tort law for damages, the likelihood of non-payment was substantial. Wanting to avoid bankruptcy and financial ruin most people willingly purchase insurance to cover claims made against them. Some motorists, though, are judgment proof. They have no significant assets or income hence the threat of liability is of little concern. For this group, insurance must be mandatory. So, as a result of some people's failure to insure against auto-accident liability, all motorists in most jurisdictions are prohibited from driving without such insurance (Ontario has had compulsory insurance since 1979, England since 1930). This rule is coercive but has little impact on the majority of motorists who willingly insure themselves. Interestingly, the same analysis could be applied to criminal law. At present, citizens and foreign guests in Canada are not obliged to carry criminal liability insurance. If someone commits sexual assault their victim can sue them in civil court for money compensation. Unfortunately, many wrongdoers lack the resources to pay such damages. Their victims therefore go uncompensated in tort law while victims of auto-related injuries are guaranteed insured coverage.

Traffic laws, the third example of mass coverage command regulation, constitute the major source of recorded offences. Abolish the automobile and we immediately abolish most criminal or quasi-criminal convictions. According to the Ouimet Report (1969) traffic offences represented almost 90% of the increased crime rate since 1901. Of individuals charged with a legal offence today about 8 out of 10 are guilty of some driving-related offence. Motor vehicle collisions are clearly a major social threat: between 1945 and 1995 in Canada over 200,000 persons were killed in accidents, a number greater than Canadian fatalities in WW I (60,661) and WW II (42,042). What is not at all clear is whether criminal law regulations help reduce vehicular collisions and mishaps. In seeking to promote auto safety, legislators have relied primarily on prohibitory regulations with an attendant focus on driver error. Other regulatory methods are seldom exploited. For example, some European governments approach speed control much differently than North American regimes. In some residential-pedestrian areas, cars are either excluded or controlled by speed bumps. Called "sleeping policemen" by the British, speed bumps are the most effective device available to reduce vehicular velocity. On major highways in Germany no maximum speed limits are dictated. Both policies reduce the need for direct enforcement. Indirect regulatory schemes of a less coercive nature are also possible. Motor vehicle safety can be promoted by reducing dependence on automobiles, by subsidizing high density habitation and taxing suburbs, by rationing motor car owners, by changing automobile design or by subsidizing public transit. Another preventive strategy would be to raise the initial standard for driver's licences. Originally, no tests were required to obtain a driver's licence; now some standards are set but these are significantly below the level demanded of private pilots. Reward systems are also possible. Good drivers, however defined, could be rewarded with lower insurance costs, free licence renewal, special licence plate stickers, gasoline tax rebates or similar incentives. A few of these methods have been employed by modern legislators but numerous methods that would seriously curtail automobiles have not been used.

Although traffic offence convictions play a central role in the criminal law system, it is not known whether citizens approve of such laws or whether the laws are worth enforcing. Canadian and American studies indicate that from 60-85 percent of all drivers violate the speed limit laws. There is good evidence to suggest that speed contributes little to explaining the death rate of car occupants (Friedland, 1989). Variance in speed between drivers seems a more important factor since accidents increase with the amount of overtaking and passing that occurs and these increase with speed variance. Apparently, it is safest to drive at the 85th percentile speed. At its best, traffic law enforcement is sporadic: for every on duty patrol officer in the U.S. there is 190 miles of highway. At its worst, enforcement is irrational: speed limits are most vigorously enforced on open, uncrowded highways where danger is minimal and least enforced in cities and on congested roads. It is instructive to note that lawmakers decided to rely heavily on criminal law regulation of traffic safety without supporting evidence that their choice was popular or effective.

Another fertile field of command-type regulation relates to business standards and practices. Businesses operate under an array of obligatory commands such as those affecting food product quality, metric measures, packaging, weigh scales, minimum wages, rent control, fire safety requirements and building codes. Despite considerable diversity, these regulatory schemes share important common elements. First, such schemes are the modern product of recent legislation. Second, the behaviour being prohibited is usually not regarded as morally reprehensible. Indeed, in certain cases the forbidden activity is regarded by many citizens as proper and right. Such opinions attach to forced metrification, minimum wage laws and rent controls. Third, the penalties directed against regulatory infractions are usually limited, mild and impersonal. Landlords charging more than rent control regulations permit are not imprisoned or treated "like criminals". Instead, they are subject to financial penalties which, at most, will force them to cease their business operations.

Some offences, particularly traffic violations, follow this pattern. Traditional crimes are a different matter. They are not the product of recent law making but rather are inherited from a long line of historical legal intervention and custom. In part because of their customary foundation, traditional crimes tend to be viewed as repugnant. Finally, the penalties inflicted against perpetrators of these wrongs are often severe and highly personal. convicted criminals are not merely put out of business, they are frequently removed altogether from society. Partly because criminal law is older and partly because it usually involves serious offences, it tends to be more formal, individualistic and professionalized than other direct command regulations. Complex rules, often the result of historical circumstances no longer in effect, govern who can arrest criminal offenders, who can prosecute and by what procedures, what evidence is admissible in court and what type of penalty is inflicted. To a greater extent than most other regulatory areas, criminal law is dominated by lawyers, judges and common law developments. To understand criminal law's historic roots it will be helpful to examine its private law forerunner.

**Private Law Regulation**

*The Development of Tort Law*

Victims who suffer financial or personal loss at the hands of a wrongdoer may seek redress through purely private means. Such self-help may consist of searching for stolen property and taking the property back into possession or of confronting the wrongdoer and through negotiation arranging some form of compensation. This compensation could include return of property, money payment, or personal service by the perpetrator. Finally, victims may retaliate against wrongdoers by doing them counteracting harm. This last form of self-help is still an important feature of international affairs between nation states. Military battles, civil wars, trade embargoes, divestitures and boycotts are examples of methods governments use in response to real or perceived wrongdoings. Why do governments still pursue extra-legal self-help methods of retaliation? The simple answer is the lack of a global government. When Iraq invaded Iran in 1981, the Iranian government could not dial 911 and ask the international police to stop the invasion and arrest the Iraqi leaders.

Without a developed law enforcement apparatus there can be no public law. Since human society evolved from stateless origins, it is natural that community protection began as self-help and then evolved into private law. It was only after the advent of the central state that public law could play an important role. In the early Ionian Greek communities of Ithaca, Pylos and Mycenae (c. 1200 B.C.) the state's only function was defence against foreign invaders. Indeed, even the Trojan "war" was largely a personal vendetta by certain Greeks against the family of Paris over his abduction of Helen. Theft, murder and assault were not public offences. No courts, police or lawyers existed. The tribal or city leader functioned as part-time priest, military commander and judge. There were no organized priesthoods or temples. No large temples appeared in Greece until 800 B.C. By necessity, most people did everything for themselves including farming, hunting, craft making and trade. Odysseus, though king of Ithaca, built his own house. Metal work and prophecy existed as occupational specialties but law did not (Posner, 1981:127-38).

Murder as described in Homer's *Iliad* is a private affair. The murderer faced retaliation by the victim's family who would either kill the murderer or accept a payment in compensation instead. Even the killing of the king Agamemnon was a personal offence against his family or clan, not a crime of treason. At this level of social development, the family dominates. The state was mostly just a loose conglomeration of large families; the kin unit was also the economic, social and judicial unit. Priam, the king of Troy, resided with 50 sons and 12 sons-in-law. Such a family could itself function as a small military unit, and in Homer's saga family loyalties almost always take priority over the common interest. Priam, the father of Paris, champions his son's cause although Paris has offended customs, the other Trojans despise Helen and the entire city of Troy is besieged. Legally, the family was dominant because responsibility and enforcement were collective and they needed to be collective in the absence of public enforcement. Imagine the plight of a single victim of theft. To help themselves they needed to discover the wrongdoer and either retaliate directly or force payment in compensation. They were very unlikely to accomplish those goals without support. A credible threat of retaliation would be needed to prompt the wrongdoer to make amends. Larger families thus provided preventive security and a force capable of retaliating against wrongdoers. Urban street gangs today probably develop for similar reasons.

Like a solitary victim, a single wrongdoer was also in a vulnerable position, given a choice of being killed in retaliation or paying compensation in appeasement. Since single persons would rarely be able to pay sufficient compensation for serious offences like killing, they would need the support of their family. This collective responsibility provided strong incentives for families to police their members very closely. Since everyone would suffer if anyone committed a harmful act, family members endeavoured to prevent wrongdoing. In some cases, families would banish potential troublemakers to avoid retaliation from a victim's clan.

To sum up primitive legal systems, self-help evolves at first into private law where the family, not the state, is the enforcement mechanism. Enforcement begins with direct retaliation, which often leads to feuds, but as wealth increases, retaliation is replaced by compensation. Compensation is socially superior because feuds are minimized and property is merely transferred not destroyed. Compensation schedules in customary law usually set out in fixed detail a schedule of payments where, for example, a killing is worth forty head of cattle or injury to a leg is worth two head. Finally, liability for compensation is strict. Whether one kills another accidentally or intentionally, compensation for the harm is still obligatory. Payment for accidental harms is sometimes less but is not absent altogether.

Since tort law continues today to encompass misbehaviours ("tortious" acts) that also tend to be the most traditional crimes, an obvious puzzle is the existence of two overlapping legal fields. If conversion could be dealt with in civil court why did the state create the most equal offence of theft to be prosecuted in a different court? The first part of the answer is the rise of centralized, bureaucratic "states" which are a prerequisite of public law. Various theories explain the state's origin: that it originated from conquest and defence against conquest, or that it arose from large-scale projects (irrigation, bridges), or that it developed through concentrations of wealth permitting specific families to hire retainers (private soldiers) to protect their property. The second part of the answer deals with benefits derived from centralized control and taxation. By reframing a private wrong as a "public" wrong, the compensation is converted into a "fine" payable to the ruler. At the same time, in a centralized state the ruler collectivizes the public loss not covered in a system of private compensation. When a knight was killed, the knight's family suffered a loss but the king was also injured insofar as the knight's military services and other public obligations could not be fulfilled. This analysis suggests that a centralized state expands the scope of public prosecution over time. In the next section the rise of criminal law in England is examined as a test of this hypothesis.

*Private and Public Law in English History*

Prior to the Norman conquest of 1066, England had no criminal law, no legislature and no permanent judiciary. Baker explains that the earliest written codes of Anglo-Saxon "law" dealt with custom and focused on fixing the scale of "blood-money" or compensation in lieu of feuding (Baker, 1979:3). Even prior to 1066, however, some police functions had shifted from the kin group to the king's court and the incentives behind this change are worth considering. The traditional justification for developing a centralized, public prosecution system was the king's need to promote peace and discourage outlaws, bandits and rebels. Baker speaks of the "king's peace" and the expansion of "royal justice" as being "necessary to preserve law and order" but he admits that "royal justice" was "beneficial to the king's purse" because the "fiscal profits of punishment fell into the coffers of powerful individuals or of the Crown by right of jurisdiction" (*ibid*:413).

How could the king or other government personnel profit from inventing criminal law? The two primary sources of revenue were confiscation of property and fines. So-called "Pleas of the Crown" first involved wrongs personal to the king. Breaches of the "King's peace" were met by fines and over time kings increased the scope of their "peace" because the fines "were a source of revenue" (Kiralty, 1965:349). Davidson (1966:78) argues that:

> The fine continued its popularity even after the Norman conquests in 1066, but the real reason behind its popularity now was that it was one of the best ways of financing the Crown and filling the royal coffers. Thus to some extent the fine forestalled and replaced the taxes of later generations. The amercement of minor offences was looked upon as a logical auxiliary to the forfeiture of the estates of convicted felons.

Under the Saxons, all homicide cases were civil actions whereas under the Normans they became crimes for which a "murder fine" was exacted. According to Baker (Id., 15) early Norman legal efforts arose because:

> [T]he pursuit of law and order was profitable. Some pleas of the Crown were purely fiscal, but all criminal justice bore golden fruit in fines and forfeitures. The pipe rolls of the Exchequer testify to the steady revenue from judicature, and in 1301 it was recorded that Edward I 'gained great treasure' to pay his military campaigns by 'causing justice to be done on malefactors'.

Initially, the king's peace was limited to specific public acts, such as neglect of military service, for which no private suit was possible. Special "Peaces" were also applied to specific locations, like highways, and to specific times, like Easter. Eventually, the King's Peace grew to cover all England at all times. Diamond (1971:53) asserts that "every conceivable occasion was utilized for the creation of law in support of bureaucracy and sovereign. We observe no abstract principle, no impartial justice...only the spontaneous opportunism of a new class designing the edifice of its power... 'it was mainly for the sake of the profits that early justice was administered at all [by the Norman Kings]' ". In Maitland's memorable phrase, 'the king has a peace that devours all others'.

Besides fining wrongdoers, the king's judges were in some instances empowered to confiscate a felon's property. Felonies were "unemendable" wrongs for which one could not simply pay compensation. Originally, these were confined to matters within the king's obvious jurisdiction and included offences such as treason and cowardice in battle, but eventually "treason" came to include private killings and other serious torts. Convicted felons forfeited their lives, their land was returned to their feudal lords and their personal goods or chattels were given over to the king. With lesser wrongs the court ordered both a fine to the king and damages to the victim but no personal compensation was ordered in a felony case.

The law on felonies illustrates the conflict between the traditional, private tort law and the newer, government sponsored criminal law. Since felony victims were not compensated by the king's court, such victims preferred to settle with offenders privately. This became an offence against "royal justice" and was termed "compounding a felony" (Baker 1979:414). Victims then sought other means of avoiding the king's interference. The resulting lack of criminal prosecutions in the 12th and 13th centuries led the king to develop means for compelling subjects to present and prosecute felonies. One means was the creation of the royal office of the "coroner". Coroners, as the king's agents, travelled out to investigate every violent or suspicious death. This was not done out of curiosity but to produce felony convictions. If the coroner suspected foul play then the local community leaders were ordered to identify and produce the guilty parties.

The king also faced internal opposition. The 1352 *Statute of Treason* limited the types of wrongs that could be characterized as "treason" and was passed at the insistence of the barons. Apparently, the barons complained because with every new treason offence created by the king's judges, the king acquired more offenders' property instead of the property going to the barons or their immediate subjects (Kiralfy, 1958:365). There may also have been some concern on the barons' part that a king with unchecked power to create treasons would eventually reclassify their own political opposition, which led to the *Magna Carta*, as treason.

The same social conditions permitting the rise of centralized kingdoms also contributed to the creation of "crime control" problems. Private tort systems depend in primitive cultures or kin group of collective responsibility. By 1066 individualism was beginning to replace the customary notions of collective liability. Combined with greater mobility and cultural diversity, the weakening of kin group policing and compensating meant that more wrongs went uncompensated. "Outlaws" were people unable to pay fines or compensations or who lived as bandits outside towns, villages or feudal manors. These bandits or outlaws were usually gangs centred around a core of brothers or other close relatives and while some outlaw bands were in business for themselves, others operated on behalf of magnates or religious houses (Bellamy, 1973:69-73). Since outlaws were immune from tort restrictions they could only be dealt with by a public group which naturally tended to be organized by the king. Kiralfy, for example, notes that Henry II (1154-1189) took over the job of ridding the community of its worst offenders. Criminal-type or "afflictive" punishments like banishment, execution or maiming arose in connection with the battle against outlaws. In tort law, of course, it made little sense to banish or kill the person from whom you expected compensation.

Still, if satisfactory compensation was not paid the next best solution was pure afflictive punishment and the threat of such penalties must always be in the background for a primitive private law system to be effective. A social dilemma seems to evolve, however, in that a move toward greater flexibility, privacy and personal initiative confounds the conditions necessary for effective tort law enforcement. Fragmented families and independent persons escape the strictures of kin group customs but they render themselves vulnerable to predatory behaviour. In answer to this vulnerability, law enforcement shifts from amateurs to professionals, from private citizens to the king's agents. As to the fundamental cause of criminal law, it may be that kings exploited the opportunities presented by the failure of private law more than they engineered the eclipse of tort law by contrived design. Conquests, kings, soldiers and personal ambition are rather constant factors in any historical equation so the centralizing objectives of the Norman kings cannot, in themselves, explain the rise of public law. Moreover, the same trends are observable in other historical contexts and in other occupations besides government.

Kiralfy observes that the historical distinction between tort and crime "was essentially procedural in its origins" (id., 359). These procedural distinctions remain today and are responsible for the particular features of criminal law. Tort defendants, if found liable, paid damages whereas criminals were fined or subject to afflictive punishments. Tort defendants faced their alleged victims whereas criminal defendants faced the king (the Crown). Naturally since the king controlled the judges and the court, criminal law procedure was stacked against the accused, sometimes to an extreme degree. In tort law, a plaintiff must prove damages and can only extract a monetary penalty proportionate to the harm caused or intended. Since criminal law penalties are fixed by the government and administered by government agents (the judges and prosecutors) there is usually no requirement that damages be proved or that the penalty be justified. A person convicted of possessing LSD in Canada can be fined $5,000 and sentenced to 3 years in prison [Section 47 of the *Food and Drugs Act*] without the prosecutor showing or being able to show any damages at all. Tort law is self-enforcing as victims seek personal compensation whereas criminal law offers very little to individual victims and therefore comes to rely on a professional cadre of law enforcers paid by the king or government. In turn, this professional police force rearranges criminal procedure regarding arrest, search, interrogation and identification of suspects to suit its own bureaucratic interests. Similarly, criminal law transforms the tort plaintiff's independent legal counsel into a bureaucratic Crown Prosecutor. (See Section 4.2)

McGinley (1981:281-2) explains that the state is much more concerned with enforcing criminal rather than civil laws because criminal conduct "challenges the institutional supremacy of the state by questioning its authority". Since obedience is the primary concern, the state prosecutes a law breaker even when the accused's conduct is not morally wrong. Harm to the state occurs, after all, merely through the act of disobedience. Attempted crimes, as attempts at disobedience, leave defendants liable to serious penalties, whereas the concept of attempted tort is sketchy and undeveloped.

## Bibliography
- American Friends Service Committee, *Struggle for Justice* (New York: Hill and Wang, 1971).
- Baker, J.H., *An Introduction to English Legal History* (Toronto: Butterworths, 1979).
- Beauchamp, D.E., *Beyond Alcoholism—Alcohol and Public Health Policy* (Philadelphia: Temple University Press, 1980).

- Bellamy, J., *Crime and Public Order in England in the Later Middle Ages* (Toronto: University of Toronto Press, 1973).
- Boyd, N., "The Origins of Canadian Narcotics Legislation: The Process of Criminalization in Historical Context" (1984), 8 Dalhousie Law Journal 102.
- Buchanan, J., "From Private Preferences to Public Philosophy: The Development of Public Choice", in J. Buchanan, ed., *The Economics of Politics* (London: Institute of Economic Affairs, 1978).
- Buchanan, J., "The Limits of Taxation", in *Taxation: An International Perspective* (Vancouver: The Fraser Institute, 1984).
- Comack, E., "The Origins of Canadian Drug Legislation: Labelling versus Class Analysis", in T. Fleming, ed., *The New Criminologies in Canada* (Toronto: Oxford University Press, 1985).
- Croft, R., *Swindle—A Decade of Canadian Stock Frauds* (Toronto: Gage Publishers, 1975).
- Davidson, R., "The Promiscuous Fire" (1965), 8 Criminal Law Quarterly 74.
- Devlin, P., *The Enforcement of Morals* (London: Oxford University Press, 1965).
- Dewees, D., ed., *The Regulation of Quality* (Toronto: Butterworths, 1983).
- Diamond, J.S., "The Rule of Law Versus the Order of Custom" (1971), 38 Social Research 42.
- Downs, A., *An Economic Theory of Democracy* (New York: Harper & Row, 1957).
- Ericson, R., *Reproducing Order* (Toronto: University of Toronto Press, 1982).
- Francis, D.B., *Vandalism—The Crime of Immaturity* (New York: Lodestar Books, 1983).
- Friedland, M., *Sanctions and Rewards in the Legal System: A Multidisciplinary Approach* (Toronto: University of Toronto Press, 1989).
- Fuller, Lon, *The Morality of Law* (New Haven: Yale University Press, 1969).
- Garan, D.G., *Against Ourselves: Disorders from Improvements under the Organic Limitedness of Man* (New York: Philosophical Library, 1979).
- Goode, E., *Drugs in American Society*, 2nd ed. (New York: Alfred A. Knopf, 1984).
- Government of British Columbia, The Business of Crime (1980).
- Government of Canada, *The Criminal Law in Canadian Society* (1982).
- Green, M., "The History of Canadian Narcotics Control" (1979), 37 University of Toronto Faculty of Law Review 42.
- Hayek, F., *The Constitution of Liberty* (Chicago: University of Chicago Press, 1960).
- Hills, S.L., *Crime, Power and Morality* (New York: Dodd, Mead & Co., 1971).
- Howard, R., *Poisons in Public—Case Studies of Environmental Pollution in Canada* (Toronto: James Lorimer, 1980).
- Jaynes, J., *The Origins of Consciousness in the Breakdown of the Bicameral Mind* (Boston: Houghton Mifflin, 1976).
- Kiralfy, A.K., *Potter's Historical Introduction to English Law* (London: Sweet & Maxwell, 1958).
- Lieberman, J.K., *How the Government Breaks the Law* (New York: Stein & Day, 1972).
- McGinley, G.P., "An Inquiry into the Nature of the State and its Relation to the Criminal Law" (1981), 19 Osgoode Hall Law Journal 267.
- McGinnis, J., "Bogeman and the Law: Crime, Comics and Pornography" (1988), 20 Ottawa Law Review 3.
- Michael, J. and Adler, M., *Crime, Law and Social Science* (New York: Harcourt Brace, 1933).
- Milgram, S., *Obedience to Authority* (London: Tavistock, 1974).
- Mintz, *The Therapeutic Nightmare* (Boston: Houghton Mifflin, 1965).
- Mitchell, C., "A Comparative Analysis of Cannabis Regulation" (1983), 9 Queen's Law Journal 110.

- Mitchell, C., "The Mispursuit of Happiness: Divorcing Normative Legal Theory from Utilitarianism" (1986), 16 Manitoba Law Journal 123.
- Nettler, G., *Responding to Crime* (Cincinnati: Anderson Publishing, 1982).
- Parker, G., *An Introduction to Criminal Law* (Toronto: Methuen, 1987).
- Posner, R., *The Economics of Justice* (Cambridge: Harvard University Press, 1981).
- Posner, R., "An Economic Theory of the Criminal Law" (1985), 85 Columbia Law Review 1193.
- Quinney, R., *The Problem of Crime* (New York: Dodd, Mead & Co., 1970).
- Rawls, J., *A Theory of Justice* (Cambridge: Harvard University Press, 1971).
- Reifner, U., "The Bar in the Third Reich: Anti-Semitism and the Decline of Liberal Advocacy" (1986), 32 McGill Law Journal 96.
- Reynolds, M.O., *Making America Poorer— The Cost of Labor Law* (Washington: Cato Institute, 1987).
- Sheckley, R., *The 10th Victim* (New York: Ace Books, 1965).
- Silverman, M. & Lee, P., *Pitts, Profits and Politics* (Berkeley: University of California Press, 1974).
- Shirer, W.L., *The Rise and Fall of the Third Reich* (New York: Simon & Schuster, 1960).
- Solicitor General of Canada, "Report of the Canadian Committee on Corrections—Toward Unity: Criminal Justice and Corrections (The Ouimet Report)" (Ottawa: Canada, 1969).
- Solomon, L., *Energy Shock* (Toronto: Pollution Probe Foundation, 1980).
- Taylor, F., Kettle, P., Putnam, R., *Pollution: The Effluence of Affluence* (Toronto: Methuen, 1971).
- Thurow, G., *Rhetoric and American Statesmanship* (Durham: Carolina Academic Press, 1985).
- Tucker, W., *Vigilante—The Backlash Against Crime in America* (New York: Stein & Day, 1985).
- Tullock, G., "The Welfare Costs of Monopolies, Tariffs, and Theft: in Tullock, Buchanan & Tullison, eds., *Towards A Theory of the Rent-Seeking Society* (Texas: A & M University Press, 1981).
- Turk, A., Turk, J., Wittes, J., *Ecology, Pollution, Environment* (Philadelphia: W.B. Saunders, 1972).
- Uchendu, V., *Igbo of Southeast* (London: Holt, Rinehart & Winston, 1965).
- Wexler, S., "The Intersection of Law and Morals" (1976), 54 Canadian Bar Review 351.
- Wilson, C., *A Criminal History of Mankind* (New York: G.P. Putnam's 1984).

## Questions

1. What crimes are likely to be dropped in the 21st century? What new crimes will probably be created?
2. Under what social conditions do criminal law controls expand? Conversely, under what imaginable social conditions would criminal law "wither away"?
3. Certain factions want abortion (or prostitution, loan sharking, crime comics, narcotics) to be a criminal offence under almost any circumstances, whereas some others want matters concerning abortion, etc., kept entirely out of the Criminal Code. Using the three different ethical systems described above, analyse the issue of abortion's criminality.
4. If suicide is legal, should competent adults be free to consent to their own death in blood sports like survival games with real ammunition and attractive prizes?
5. Conduct an informal survey to determine what threats to personal and social security most people regard as paramount. As a secondary matter, determine what solutions people favour to meet these threats. What proportion rely on legal solutions?

6. Over the last twenty years, in which countries have governments been more of a threat to society than so-called criminals? In what countries has the reverse been true? In your opinion, what significant features distinguish conditions in these two groups of nations?
7. Should all Canadians over a certain age be compelled to purchase criminal liability insurance in order that all victims of crime would be compensated in civil law, at least where the offender is identified? Would such compulsory criminal insurance be enforceable?
8. Given limited police resources how would you design a law enforcement program to minimize traffic mishaps.
9. Why did tort law precede criminal law and what social factors led to the development of criminal law?

**Discussion**
1. Source: D. Koontz, "The Undercity" in R. Elwood, ed., *Future City* (Trident Press, 1973).
   In this short story an old soldier in the former criminal "underworld" talks to his daughter about all the criminal opportunities he once enjoyed:

   > Nearly all forms of gambling were illegal back then. An enterprising young man could step in, buck the law, and clean up a tidy sum with a minimal financial outlay and with almost no personal risk at all. Cops and judges were on the take; clandestine casinos, street games and storefront betting shops thrived. No longer. They legalized it, and they gave us bank clerks for casino managers, CPA's instead of bouncers. The made gambling respectable—and boring.
   >
   > Drugs were illegal then, too. Grass, hash, skag, speed ... God, an enterprising young kid like yourself could make a fortune in a year. But now grass and hash are traded on the open market, and all the harder drugs are available to all who will sign a health waiver and buy them from the government. Where's the thrill now? Gone. And where's the profit? Gone, too.
   >
   > Sex. Oh, kid, the money to be made on sex, back then. It was *all* illegal: prostitution, dirty movies, picture postcards, erotic dancing, adultery, you name it! Now the government licenses the brothels... Hell, kid, even murder was illegal in those days.

   Note: This story is predictive and may not be accurate but it did anticipate the rapid rise of legal and government sponsored gambling over the last two decades. How was gambling transformed from a vice to a virtue? Consider also the morality of governments commercially promoting lotteries and casinos when the ads do not mention the remote odds of winning or warn people about the habit forming dangers of gambling.
2. How would people behave if unencumbered by normal legal restrictions?
   The behaviour of diplomats provides a partial answer to this question because by international law and convention, diplomats (and their families, employees and assistants) are immune from the law of the host nation. In Ottawa for 1983, 4,323 traffic tickets were issued to diplomatic plates. Only 184 were paid, which constitutes 4.2%. The worst offenders were, in order, Nigerians, Algerians, Somalians and the French. The Vatican paid both its tickets. American diplomats paid 31 out of 146 tickets. See C. Ashman & P. Trescott, *Diplomatic Crime* (Washington: Acropolis Books, 1987).
3. The Ontario *Ticket Speculation Act*, makes it illegal for anyone to sell or purchase tickets "at a higher price than that at which they are advertised or announced to be for sale by the owner or proprietor" of a sports, theatre or amusement show. Despite this law, some ticket scalpers working high price venues like Maple Leaf Gardens in Toronto earn over $100,000 annually (Toronto Star, Oct. 29, 1989, A10). Fines under the Act range from $5 to $50. (In March 1990, the Ontario government increased fines under many Acts including this one: ticket speculators now risk fines up to $5,000.) Who would want such a law passed? What dangers, if any, would attend a free market in re-sale tickets?

4. Source: K. Finsterbusch & H. Greisman, "The Unprofitably of Warfare in the Twentieth Century" (1974-75), 22 Social Problems 450.

War and crime have much in common. But war in the 20th century, with over 80 million deaths, has probably been far more destructive than ordinary crime. Many people oppose warfare but pacifist arguments have been made for thousands of years without having permanent or significant impact. Others argue that, like crime, war flows from material conditions and will only cease when it is no longer "profitable". While some 19th century wars of imperialism, such as the U.S. seizure of the Philippines from Spain in 1898, achieved considerable gains at little cost, 20th century wars generally achieved very little at enormous cost. This is because conditions changed. Vulnerable, unarmed areas no longer exist for colonization. Fewer weak empires exist to fight over. War technology has rendered war far more destructive. The 1.9 million battle deaths in the Korean War alone outnumber all the battle deaths in the 34 international wars between the time of Napoleon (1800) and 1914. Some theorists also argue that the spread of liberal-democratic states, as in Eastern Europe in 1989-90, will reduce warfare because the political composition of liberal-democracies makes them reluctant to start wars but difficult to defeat if they are the victims of aggression. What other conditions will alter the prospects of war?

For a critical assessment of Canada's wars see G. Dyer and T. Vijoen, *The Defence of Canada: In the Arms of Empire 1760-1939* (Toronto: McClelland and Stewart, 1990).

## Further Reading

Some readers may want to learn more about the substantive criminal law in Canada at this stage of the course. A number of texts are available including the following:

- Simon Verdun-Jones, *Criminal Law in Canada: Cases, Questions & The Code* (Toronto: Harcourt Brace Jovanovich, 1989). This text describes many of the basic features of Canadian criminal law, and is written for undergraduates not planning to enter the legal profession.
- Don Stuart and R. Delisle, *Learning Canadian Criminal Law, 5th ed.* (Toronto: Carswell, 1995). A thorough and detailed statement of the law primarily for law students and practitioners.
- Alan Mewett and M. Manning, *Mewett and Manning on Criminal Law, 3rd ed.* (Toronto: Butterworths, 1994). The standard text on criminal law.
- Augustine Brannigan, *Crimes, Courts and Corrections: An Introduction to Crime and Social Control in Canada* (Toronto: Holt, Rinehart and Winston, 1984). A useful, broad-ranging book and one that is probably widely available on the used-book market.
- Simon Verdun-Jones and C. Griffiths, *Canadian Criminal Justice, 2nd ed.* (Toronto: Butterworths, 1994).

# 2

# PERSPECTIVES ON CRIMINAL LAW

## Introduction

*R.P. Saunders*

The approaches to and theoretical perspectives on criminal law and criminal justice are many and varied, yet one's approach or perspective colours the way one sees criminal law in a very fundamental way. It is both ironic and puzzling that legal professionals have for so long been one-dimensional in their orientation and ignored the value of alternative approaches in understanding and formulating criminal law. Criminal law, contrary to what some traditional, legalistic approaches to it might claim, is not a "thing" derived from heaven, from the past, from custom, or from nature; it is a reflection of the views and perspectives of policy-makers on what they want the law, and specifically criminal law, to accomplish. It is also a reflection of their views on human nature and human activity, as well as a statement about the potential of the state to interfere in social conflicts and to control human behaviour in a meaningful and effective manner.

The difficulty is, of course, the definition of what it is one is talking about when the term "law" is used. Are we referring to the actual rules or laws which make up a body we collectively call "law", or are we talking about something wider than this, something that would encompass broader and more ambiguous principles, or rights such as those encompassed in the "Rule of Law" or those found in so-called "natural law" doctrines? We shall see that how writers define law and its institutions is an important factor in determining the scope and method of their inquiry into an understanding of law and reform.

There is also the problem of the use of terminology generally in looking at approaches to law and criminal law. To begin, there are conflicting definitions and terms within law itself, depending upon the particular school of thought one adopts. In addition, there is also the challenge of communicating across disciplines and of understanding the terminology and methodology of other fields of expertise and study. Law as a discipline has done particularly poorly in this regard. For the most part, the mainstream of legal studies has maintained an unhealthy and even anti-intellectual insularity as to the other disciplines' approaches to law.

The result has been a lack of rigour and of depth in the work and research which is produced in legal academia, notably when comparisons are made to the body of knowledge and writing in other disciplines. This is especially true in the area of criminal law, where the traditional doctrinal approach of lawyers and legal writers has too often been limited to a narrow analysis of the cases, legislation and processes related to criminal justice. This approach has been criticised as sterile, circular and self-contained, and as having very little to offer in the way of substantive policy choices and effective, meaningful critiques. We shall return to this criticism below and in Chapter 3 in our discussion on the production of criminal law.

In discussing various theories and approaches, there is always the danger of not giving enough credence to one particular perspective versus another. This is not to say that legal writers should strive to be neutral in their presentation, for this is the very criticism one can make of the pretenses of traditional legal theories: they tend toward neutrality and detachment. For example, we are not neutral in our approach: we adopt an explicitly critical perspective. However, that said, an explanation of other approaches is in order to allow the reader to be exposed to the various perspectives, and thus to become an aware and knowledgeable reader in the area of criminal justice, particularly in understanding the (often undisclosed and unacknowledged) biases and slants others bring to the field. Hopefully, the reader will adopt certain priorities and principles, and ultimately become more fully aware of her or his perspective, the grounds for it, and most importantly, the value of being self-conscious about one's perspective in any examination of criminal law. Such a recognition can only lead to a fuller understanding of the operation of the criminal law and ultimately to better, more progressive and more effective criminal justice policies.

The problem of prioritizing perspectives, of course, need not lead to an exclusionary or insulated approach to criminal law. Depending on how we define our approach, there is usually room to borrow or adapt or subsume other views. The value and worth of different concerns must be emphasized (in some contexts) in a way which gives them more than the perfunctory lip-service often found in traditional legal writings. Each reader should attempt to address the issue of perspective individually and to incorporate and refine what is most valuable and important in the various perspectives.

The remaining sections of this chapter describe and discuss several of the approaches to the analyses of law which are or have been in vogue. In the section immediately following, the traditional orthodox legal view is examined and critiqued. This view is found wanting. The gaps and shortcomings which are discussed have formed part of the impetus behind the development of an alternative or critical perspective; this perspective is described in the third section of this chapter. The second section looks at the contributions of other disciplines to the study and development of criminal law. It describes how disciplines such as sociology, political science, economics and psychology have provided new understandings of criminal law, and have acted as a spur to the development of innovative and challenging perspectives within the discipline of law itself. Finally, it is important to note that none of the sections attempts to be all-inclusive as to the respective perspectives, but rather each is deliberately selective in its approach to the topic. This is because the purpose of this chapter is not a detailed exposition of the myriad of views which exist. On the contrary, we wish to focus on a selective presentation of the principal themes and directions which have influenced, continue to guide or might in the future contribute to the formulation and implementation of criminal justice policy in Canada. For a good overview of the issues and developments, see Chapters 14 and 20 of M. Fitzgerald, *et al.* under "Further Reading" below.

In the last fifteen years, feminist writers and researchers have made an enormous contribution to our theoretical understanding of law and to the design and implementation of strategies of resistance and reform. There are many variants of feminism (as can be seen in the Sheehy excerpt). However, these are linked by the common themes of the inequality of power, and of gender bias, discrimination and injustice in the values and practices of the criminal law. Heidensohn's article is a critique of male-centred approaches and an attempt to set out an alternative feminist model for a criminal justice system, one that would address the real needs and experiences of women. In addition to these articles, there are several attempts throughout the text to highlight feminist perspectives in the context of specific topics, for example in regard to the male-controlled production of criminal law (in Chapter 3), the issue of the battered woman's syndrome both in self defence (in Chapter 7) and in prosecutorial policy (in Chapter 4), and sexual assault (in Chapter 8). In sum, it is important to not only be aware of but also to incorporate the values and concerns of feminism in the development of the theoretical models of and practical strategies for criminal justice.

The final section introduces the reader to historical perspectives on criminal law and their importance in any examination of criminal justice. The law has evolved over a long period of time and has gone through many incarnations in different cultures and eras, yet there is a tendency to ignore the past and the lessons (both positive and negative) we can learn from it.

The section also provides a capsule view of the history of criminal law in Canada and prepares the reader for the readings on the production of criminal law (Chapter 3) and on the status of the defence and prosecutor (Chapter 4).

## 2.1 TRADITIONAL LEGAL PERSPECTIVES
*R. P. Saunders*

In looking at traditional orthodox approaches to law in general and criminal law in particular, we can identify several common themes and positions, even though there are many variants and schools within the traditional approaches. Rather than examining and comparing in detail these various schools of thought, it is more useful for our purposes to identify some of these common features and to situate their general approach in the overall range of criminal law perspectives. What then are these common features, and how and why are they important?

The traditional approach within law is one which takes the law as given and fails to explore the social or political dimensions of the institutions, agents, processes and activities of law. It is an approach that concentrates on the written, formal aspects of law and that assumes that the law is a neutral force to be used and manipulated (usually for good) by the state and by individual, legally constituted agents. It is "law-centred" in that law is seen as a good in and of itself to be put to a myriad of uses and purposes which can bring about social change and real progress. While there are differences within the various schools of liberal and conservative thought, the essential approach is one which is formalistic and rule and process-oriented. It assumes a high degree of social consensus and argues that these rules and processes reflect shared values and concerns. It also assumes that law operates primarily for the benefit of the system as opposed to the interests of any of particular individual or group.

Numerous examples of this approach can be found in legal literature and in the policy responses of the state to social problems. These responses of the state are discussed in more detail in Chapter 3, where the book deals with the difficulties inherent in a criminal justice policy formation process which is largely controlled by legal professionals. Specific examples are discussed in Chapter 8, notably where the issues in the area of sexual assault are addressed. There, we will argue that the response of the state has been limited to a technical "re-formation" or revision of the criminal law to make it better, more efficient and more accommodating. While the criminal law should fulfill these demands, the state must not ignore or avoid other, more social (and often more costly) responses to the problems represented by the sexual assault. What we see again and again on the part of the state is the use of criminal law to provide a full "answer" to a social problem in a manner which allows the state to silence or manage complaints and to avoid dealing with the root causes of a situation. For example, in the area of sexual assault, we have to look beyond changes in the criminal law, and attempt to rid society of sexist and patriarchal structures, relations and attitudes, both within the criminal justice system and in society as a whole. Numerous other examples exist to illustrate this issue, including prostitution (where the legal changes in the law simply tend to make it easier to arrest and convict prostitutes), drunk driving (where the penalties have become more and more harsh in recent years), and victims of crime (where as we shall see in Chapter 4 the state response has been "cheap" and largely symbolic). The point to remember is that the complex social dimensions of the problems surrounding criminal law must not and cannot be forgotten, yet they often are in a traditional legal approach which focuses almost exclusively on notions of individual guilt and responsibility (see Chapter 6), on the formal aspects of the process and rights which allegedly attach to the individual, and on the rules and regulations that make up the criminal law in its most basic sense, though arguably not its most important.

A term which has been used to describe this orthodox approach is "doctrinal", a term that emphasizes the self-contained and tautological nature of the enterprise. The focus is on what the doctrine and institutions of law are, not the contradictions and debates which are inherent in the formation and implementation of law. This approach ignores the social process of producing and reproducing social structures and social relations. Another term that might be used is "legal fetishism" (Collins, 1982), a term which accurately describes the intellectual orientation of and emotional attachment to the approach. This term, while it can be employed to indicate and delineate Marxist criticisms of law, is used here in a more restricted manner (and only for the purposes of this text) to set out the boundaries of the conventional approach.

The essence of the traditional perspectives is that law is seen as representing a value consensus in society, that law in its formal manifestations, both substantively and in its processes, represents the shared values that society holds collectively. Within this view, the law is seen as fundamental to social order. A legal order is held to be a necessary component of a civilized social order: it serves to mark the acceptable limits of behaviour, to express society's unwillingness to tolerate threats to order, and to mobilize legitimate state institutions in response to these threats. Central to this idea is the belief that "legal rules are at the centre of social life" (Collins, p. 11) and that they satisfy social wants.

Another important feature of the traditional approach is the idea that "law is a unique phenomenon which constitutes a discrete focus of study" (*ibid.*). It reflects the argument that the discipline is "special" due to its unique patterns of institutions and relationships, its possession of a "mode of discourse" used only by lawyers, and the fact that "legal rules also function as normative guides to behaviour" (*ibid.*) and as such are different from other modes of control, such as brute force. Of course, these notions can be, and often are criticized. The idea of law as a necessary is criticized on the grounds that it is much too simplistic and ignores the important role that informal modes of control and non-legal rules can play in shaping and determining the formation and direction of behaviour. The argument is that rather than being law-centred, it is much more valuable to adopt an integrative approach that seeks to study and understand law principally in the context both of the social and political functions that it fulfills, and of the social structures and processes within which it emerges.

The essential criticism of traditional legal approaches is that they are overarchingly oriented toward the formal manifestations of law and the institutions and processes that surround those manifestations. Law school study is still focused on the courts, the cases, and the formal rules, in spite of the calls in the last two decades for more interdisciplinary and socialized approaches to the study of law.[1] It is a technical,

---

[1] See Consultative Group on Research and Education in Law, *Law and Learning: Report to the Social*

professional training which teaches students how to argue, manipulate, and use the rules, and not necessarily to understand the reality and impact of the rules in their social setting. Yet surely this is the most important dimension to legal rules from a policy perspective: such an understanding is a precondition to the development of a criminal justice system which has any potential of meeting the needs of today's society.

This is not to deny that cases, trials and interpretations of the legislation hold a very strong attraction. One need only look to the law schools, or to the entertainment industry with its many lawyers' shows (though most bear little resemblance to the reality of everyday practice). But one has to be careful to resist the seduction of this limited but comforting approach to the criminal justice system: we must look deeper. We have to understand that the dilemmas and contradictions in the law and its stated ideals are very real; that equality is often there in rhetoric but not in practice; that who you are, the colour of your skin, your income, your class background and other social, gender and ethnic factors can all combine to play an important part in the nature and outcome of one's interaction with the criminal justice system. How we incorporate and give meaning and weight to these factors can change our focus and give us new, more progressive insights into criminal law. We will discuss the nature of an alternative to this approach in the third section of this chapter. First, however, we will turn to a brief discussion of the types of questions and issues in the study of law which have been raised by researchers from other social sciences.

## 2.2 LAW IN THE SOCIAL SCIENCES
*Ross Hastings*

The traditional legal perspective is clearly a narrow and one-dimensional approach to the study of the emergence, maintenance and reform of the criminal law. This is unfortunate, given the importance of criminal law to the welfare of society in general and of individuals. It is also surprising, because the criminal law has long been a topic of interest within other disciplines, and is at the centre of some of the most important contemporary debates within the social sciences.

Sociology, psychology, political science and economics have all had something to say about the crucial issues of the origin and the impact of criminal law, and about the orientation and purpose of legal reform. More recently, the inter-disciplinary fields of criminology and of socio-legal studies have become focal points for attempts to formulate an alternative to the traditional legal perspective.

To this point, neither the discipline of criminology nor the field of socio-legal studies has produced a magical answer. For that matter, their biggest contribution to date may lie in the demonstration that the pursuit of a single, all-encompassing theory of criminal law may be the social science equivalent to a child's fantasy of grabbing the pot of gold at the end of a rainbow. Nevertheless, progress has been made. The key lies in the willingness of both criminology and socio-legal studies to accept and

---

Sciences and Humanities Research Council of Canada (Ottawa: Social Science and Humanities Research Council of Canada, 1983). For a review of the report, see (1984), 16 Ottawa Law Review 218.

value the enormous and bewildering complexity of the criminal law, and to recognize the contributions that other approaches and disciplines have made to our ability to come to grips with this phenomenon.

The purpose of this section is to review briefly the contribution of each of these approaches to the study of criminal law. It will begin with a discussion of what the social sciences of sociology, psychology, political science and economics have made of the law. The focus will be on the different kinds of questions one might ask in attempting to make sense of law, and on the competing approaches one might use in attempting to answer these questions. This will prepare the ground for our discussion on how criminology and socio-legal studies are attempting to formulate an alternative and more critical, analytical perspective.

The issue of the origin and consequences of criminal law has been featured prominently within the field of sociology. The classic sociological authors of the 19th century were concerned with the general issue of how social order was possible in a complex and dynamic society, especially in the light of the dizzying rate of change that marked the transition to so-called modern times, and of the increasing competition and conflict which accompanied the transition to capitalism. Obviously, authors such as Karl Marx, Emile Durkheim and Max Weber developed very different answers to this question, but each focused on the social role of law as a critical dimension of any useful explanatory approach. Marx, for example, emphasized the role of criminal law in smoothing the transition to capitalism by "educating" people to the new idea of the value of private property and by eliminating or restricting the notion of common or collective rights from the criminal law. The legal basis of feudalism, with (for example) its notion of the rights of serfs to have access to common lands was inconsistent with the needs of capitalism, with its notion of private property and individual rights and responsibilities. The transition from one economic system to another required a shift to a legal system which was better adapted to the requirements of the pursuit of profit. Marx also argued that the criminal law, both in terms of content and enforcement served to protect and legitimate the interests of the more politically and economically powerful groups in society.

Durkheim was concerned with the issue of the relationship of law and social change. In his view, social order in modern society was characterized by a transition in the basis of social solidarity. Modern society was too complex, heterogeneous and differentiated to regulate conflicts through the traditional forms of negotiation and separation or restitution which characterized simpler societies. Such procedures reflect an informal and interpersonal world that no longer exists. The impersonal nature of modern social relations means that people deal with each other in a much more limited and specialized way. This requires a legal mechanism that will serve to regulate this process and to assure all participants that their rights and concerns will be protected. The formal criminal law is just such a tool.

Weber focused on law as an aspect of the emerging emphasis on rationality which characterized the modern world. His view was that social order, and the ability of the state to manage society, was based less and less on the direct exercise of power and increasingly on the formal legal authority of the state. People accept the law because they see the state as the legitimate representative of the collective interests. The threat to order, then, is less from invading armies from other countries, and more the inability of the state to generate a consensus on its behalf. The law plays a crucial role in both socializing the law-abiding citizen and controlling those who pose a threat. There are a number of other early sociologists who have made significant contributions to the sociology of law. The common threat to the sociological approach is an insistence on the social character of law. The criminal law does not emerge out of a set of abstract ideals. It reflects a strategic response by some individuals to very real and very situated conflicts, and it has very real consequences for the outcome of these same conflicts. The result is that the analyses of criminal law cannot be disconnected from the social situation within which it emerges and upon which it acts.

This theme is very much a part of those approaches to law which have characterized the fields of political science and economics. However, each has had a different emphasis, and has made a different kind of contribution to our understanding of the causes and consequences of the criminal law. In the case of political science, the emphasis has tended to be on the formal institutional mechanisms where the processes of the creation and reform of the criminal law actually occur. Political scientists begin with the fact that the criminal law is created by the state, and direct their attention to the formal procedures which are involved, and the informal exercise of power and influence that is at the heart of making or changing law. Thus, for example, there is a debate within political science over whether power is legitimately distributed among a plurality of social groups, or is centralized within a relatively small and very powerful elite. This has obvious implications for any understanding of why our society has the law it does. In practical terms, we will want to scrutinize the criminal law to see what its content reflects. For example, our laws on homicide and child abuse probably come as close as any to being a reflection of a consensus over the kinds of protection from violence we all want and expect in a "civilized" society. In such cases, the pluralist approach offers a reasonable explanation of why we have the law we do (though it is less satisfactory as an explanation of the selective application or enforcement of the law among different classes or ethnic groups). On the other hand, the pluralist notion of a neutral state which arbitrates conflicts among relatively equal groups provides a less satisfactory explanation of the content and enforcement of our laws on sexual assault (see Chapter 8 for a full discussion on this issue). It is becoming increasingly clear that the reform of the criminal law may be necessary but far from sufficient in order to improve significantly the protection of women from violence. A number of feminist authors have quite convincingly argued that the criminal law only focuses on individual rights (such as the right to private property), but it is not designed to address collective rights, nor is it able to redress collective inequality or exploitation (cf. Snider, 1988). A more convincing explanation of the situation of women can be found in the critical legal approach to the analysis of the relationship of the state to the legitimation and reproduction of class relations, and in the feminists' contributions to our understanding of the impact of patriarchy and sexism in the production and reform of law. We will return to these themes in the next section.

The field of economics has taken a quite different approach to the law. For the most part, economists interested in the criminal law have been concerned with the issue of efficiency. Their focus is on whether existing laws and practices are effectively serving their presumed roles of deterring criminal acts and preventing recidivism. For example, many of the authors within this approach have focused on the impact of our laws and practices in the area of sentencing. One debate is over the issue of judicial discretion in the sentencing of convicted offenders. On one side, there are those (usually of a more psychological or sociological orientation) who argue that judges must have the leeway to tailor sentences in such a way as to adapt them to the particular situation of the offender. This is necessary to maximize the ability of the criminal justice system to rehabilitate and reintegrate offenders. One might argue, for example, that an upper class corporate criminal does not have to be sent to jail, both because there is less danger to society in letting this person stay free and because this individual is a better prospect for rehabilitation.

However, a number of economists have been very critical of this approach. To begin, there is the obvious problem of discrimination: people guilty of the same act, and who presumably have caused similar degrees of harm to their victims, are treated in very different ways. This is not fair, and it is hard to reconcile this with our society's avowed commitment to the principle of equality before the law. More importantly though, for these economists, there is the very real question of whether this practice may actually contribute to more crime. Economists tend to adopt a classical or utilitarian view of behaviour. This means that they assume individuals rationally assess the potential costs and benefits of behavioural options before proceeding to act. If this is the case, the prevention of crime is largely a matter of making the perceived costs of crime higher than its perceived benefits. Indications are that the most effective way of doing this is by increasing the perceived *certainty* of being caught and punished. On this basis, judicial discretion and the resultant disparity in sentencing is counterproductive, for it reduces people's perception of the likelihood of having to pay for their crimes. In practical terms, this approach provides a fairly convincing explanation of why police roadside checks are a better deterrent to drinking and driving than admonitions by brewers to "drink responsibly" or than the rare (even if severe) sentencing of a convicted impaired driver.

The field of psychology has had relatively little impact on traditional legal approaches. This is somewhat astounding, given the contributions of psychology to our understanding of human perception and social behaviour. For example, the fundamental definitional component of a crime is the notion of individual responsibility (see Chapter 6). Psychologists have made enormous contributions to the explanation of the biological and interactional determinants of social behaviour, yet little of this work has penetrated the traditional approach (or, for that matter, the training of lawyers). Perhaps more importantly, it is psychologists and psychiatrists who are asked to determine those situations when individuals cannot or should not be held responsible for their behaviour. The area of defences and excuses for criminal acts is a major part of the Criminal Code (see Chapter 7). On a more practical level, psychologists have much to tell us about perception and memory which is of enormous relevance to the credibility of victims and witnesses of crime. Yet, it is difficult to detect in the Code, in the cases, or in most traditional legal scholarship, a sophisticated understanding of the debates in psychology over the extent to which individuals are relatively free to control their behaviour or determined by biological or psychological influences which they are relatively powerless to control.

It is clear, then, that the criminal law has been little more that the almost exclusive preserve of lawyers and the courts. It should be equally clear that it is impossible to develop an adequate critical understanding of the creation, application or reform of criminal law without acknowledging and integrating the contributions of other disciplines. More specifically, a critical legal approach must deal with the following issues:

1. How is law created? When do individuals or groups turn to the law to solve their problems or advance their interests?
2. What is the role of the state in this process? Does the state serve as a neutral manager of conflicts in a pluralist society, or does it serve or advance the interests of the more powerful sectors of society?
3. What are the consequences of law? Does the law serve the purposes for which we claim it was intended, or are there hidden agendas buried in the justifications and legitimations which are provided?
4. Where does the law fit in our everyday lives? Does it help to manage relations and resolve conflicts, or does it actually complicate and obfuscate social relations?

We will attempt to provide a brief version of what we think a critical legal studies approach to these issues would look like in the next section of this chapter

## 2.3 THE CRITICAL PERSPECTIVE ON CRIMINAL LAW
*Ross Hastings*

In essence, the critical perspective seeks to overcome the limitations of the traditional legal approaches by providing a fully social perspective on the creation and application of the criminal law and on the process of legal reform. It rejects the limited and exclusionist orientation of the traditional approaches, and the monopoly of legalists in the field of law, in favour of a broader appreciation of the social production and legitimation of law, and of its impact on social relations.

Now, in an ideal world, we would be able to present a fully articulated and universally agreed upon version of the critical perspective. Unfortunately, the development of critical legal approaches has not yet reached this stage, and there are a number of areas and issues over which there is considerable disagreement and debate among individuals who nevertheless consider themselves (and their "opponents") to be critical legal scholars. We will address some of the main points of contention in a moment. For now, suffice it to say that the term "critical approach" is an umbrella concept which groups together a range of conceptual and theoretical options, some of which are very closely related and others which are competing if not contradictory.

There is, however, a general agreement on the goal of a fully social theory of law and reform, and on the necessity of adopting a dialectical approach if we are to be able to construct such a theory. The notion of a dialectical approach is, at one and the same time, one of the most complex and one of the simplest ideas in the social sciences. In its complexity, it harkens back to a complex web of ontological, epistemological and theoretical debates which are well beyond the scope or purpose of this text. In its simplicity, the notion of dialectic warns us against the adoption of any simplistic causal approaches to explanation. It is, in other words, the opposite of what is proposed in the traditional view of law as emerging and existing in a pure state, as some kind of neutral reflection of natural order and social consensus.

Instead, the critical perspective argues that the law must be analyzed and understood dialectically: the law is *both* a social product (it reflects and expresses the outcome of a specific, historically located set of social relations), and *at the same time*, the law has an impact on these same social relations (the law is, in a very real sense, a producer of social relations). The study of law must therefore be situated within the specific time and place, and in the context of specific struggles. This view of the law as both product and producer, as both outcome and active agent, is at the heart of the critical approach.

The remainder of this section will focus on how the critical approach has emerged and developed over the last twenty-five years. It will begin with a discussion of the emergence of the early conflict approaches, and the subsequent rejection of the traditional pluralist/consensus approaches to the creation and enforcement of law. It will then go on to discuss the main conceptual and theoretical options within the critical approach, and attempt to synthesize some of the key points of the critical perspective.

## A. THE PLURALIST APPROACH TO LAW

The traditional legal approaches to the question of the creation and enforcement of the law are usually grouped under the heading of the pluralist or consensus perspective on social order and the role of the state. In this perspective, it is argued that the law reflects and encodes the consensual values which are most important for the integration and survival of society. Thus, we have laws against homicide because this type of behaviour represents a grave threat to our collective ability to sustain orderly and predictable social relations: such acts go beyond the tolerance limits of our society. On the other hand, we seldom bother to encode less significant social norms, such as the injunction not to eat with one's fingers or not to put one's elbows on the table. The law, then, is reserved for the embodiment and the protection of the most important of our consensually shared social values.

This, however, raises the question as to who decides when a value is important enough to require codification and enforcement. No one is naive enough to believe that this process occurs automatically or spontaneously. The pluralists recognize that it occurs within the social institutions of the state, and reflects the outcomes of the processes that characterize the modern state. To this point, there is little to distinguish this view of the state from most others. The differences are to be found in the pluralist view of how the state works. For the pluralists, the fundamental role of the state is to contribute to the survival of the social system by acting as a site and a mechanism for the resolution, or at least the management and control, of social conflicts. The state is considered to be relatively neutral in this process: its concern is not to take sides, but rather to guarantee that conflicts are managed in such a way that they will not threaten the overall welfare of the system. Pluralists argue it does this by assuring that conflicts are fought out according to consensually agreed upon rules and processes. The state thus functions as a referee or an arbitrator — it does not care who wins, it is only concerned that all parties play by the rules of the game. This approach tends to see the state as relatively open and accessible. This is not to say that power is equally distributed, or that all sectors of society have the same access to or impact on the state. It is rather that the state itself is not seen as having any particular axe of its own to grind. It is there to serve the common good, and to balance competing interests in a manner that will assure and advance the interests of society in general, rather than the interests of any specific group. Moreover, no one argues that the actions of the state always serve an absolute good. There is no doubt that certain laws, or certain patterns of enforcement, have differential impacts on different individuals or groups. The argument is rather that this situation is acceptable, perhaps even necessary, because it represents the best the state can do for the common good given the resources which it has at its disposal and the problems with which it has to cope.

## B. ALTERNATIVES TO PLURALISM: CONFLICT THEORY

The pluralists thus see the state as operating relatively independently of the competition and conflicts which tend to characterize political and economic relations within a modern capitalist state. The early versions of conflict theory were essentially an attempt to "take on" the pluralists on this point, and to offer an alternative vision of the role of the state and the function of law. The conflict approach argues that society is socially constructed — it is produced and reproduced by individuals and groups engaged in social relations of competition and conflict over the allocation and control of scarce resources. Attention is thus shifted away from the notion of social consensus and towards the analysis of the competing interests of these groups and of their differential access to the kinds of political, economic and ideological power which are necessary if they are to "win" their way.

In this view, the state is an instrument: it serves the interests of the dominant social classes or the elites in our society. The pluralist notion of a neutral state that serves the common good is rejected as a theoretical explanation — the state is rather seen as an agent or tool of the ruling elites and as a legitimating devise that helps them mask their use of the state to advance their economic interests or to control the underclasses in our society. In this view, the law is the iron fist hidden with the velvet glove of this appearance of benign neutrality. It serves to patrol and police the borders of social relations in order to maintain the domination of the ruling classes and guarantee the safety of their investments and the advancement of their interests.

This is an attractive approach at a gut level. The problem is that it is as naive and oversimplified as the pluralist view which it is intended to replace. It has the advantage of alerting us to those situations of conflicts of interest and power which the pluralist approaches fail to recognize, much less explain. By the same token, it fails to account for those situations where there may actually be a degree of consensus, or at least where the state cannot be said to be serving the direct interests of the ruling elite. For example, while conflict theory helps us understand our laws on theft or rape, it would be more difficult to argue that our current law on bestiality is an instrument that makes a significant contribution to advancing the economic interests of the ruling elite. More importantly, conflict theory fails to provide a convincing theoretical explanation of the advances which have been made by the underclasses, or of the ability of certain minority groups to use the mechanism of the state to advance their interests, sometimes at the expense of the so-called ruling elite.

The point is that a simplistic conspiracy theory is not an adequate replacement for the pluralists' faith in consensus and the detached neutrality of the state. The conflict approaches did, however, have the enormous benefit of alerting us to the political, economic and ideological realities which underlie and shape social relations. The challenge for critical approaches is to integrate this awareness without falling prey to simple-minded conspiracy theories about the working of the state.

## C. THE EMERGENCE OF THE CRITICAL PERSPECTIVE

The challenge to critical approaches is to come up with a theoretical explanation capable of providing a convincing answer to the following two questions:

1. How do social structures contextualize and limit social relations and human potential?
   A critical approach to the analysis of law and legal reform must be able to appreciate the realities of class relations within modern societies, and to analyze the role of the state in sustaining and reproducing these relations. More specifically, it must address the issue of how the creation and enforcement of the law contribute in a strategic manner to these wider social processes.
2. What can be done to challenge the existing situation, and to contribute to the reduction and elimination of all forms of inequality?
   The problem with both the pluralist and the instrumentalist approaches is that they provide little guidance for social reform. We need a theory which can be translated into realistic goals and workable strategies for social reform.

In other words, we need a theoretical explanation of law which will provide both an analysis of the creation and impact of the law, and some guidance as to the types of reforms which will contribute to social equality and the welfare of society.

The beginnings of such an explanation are to be found in the structuralist response to the limitations of the instrumentalist approach. The structuralists reject the instrumentalist view of the state. They argue that the idea that the state always acts at the behest of the ruling class is both overly simplistic and historically inaccurate. It fails to recognize that the so-called ruling class is not homogeneous, but rather is characterized by internal conflicts of interests which make it unlikely (to say the least) that it will always and everywhere speak with "one voice". Moreover, it recognizes that social power is not the exclusive property of the ruling classes. There is no doubt that power is not distributed equally in our society, or that the dominant classes are much more likely to possess or control the kinds of economic or ideological resources which will give them a better chance of "getting their way" in most situations of social conflict. Nevertheless, it is also true that the subordinate classes are not without power or influence of their own. The failure to recognize this reality leaves us unable to provide any kind of explanation for social changes which actually do recognize and advance the interests of subordinate or minority groups in our own society.

For the structuralists, the beginning of a more complex and more accurate explanation of these phenomena is a reformulated model of the state. The key to this new model lies in the rejection of the simplistic notion of the state as a mere instrument in the hands of those who have economic power, and in the shift to a view of the state as a site for the production and reproduction of class relations under capitalism. The approach begins with the common sense idea that the groups in power, or at least those groups who benefit from current social arrangements, will obviously wish to preserve and reproduce things much the way they are now — people are not likely to simply give away their power, resources and influence simply because somebody else feels that the current situation is "unfair". This brings us to the strategic question of how best to do this. The argument is that the state is the site where this work is accomplished.

The production and reproduction of social relations are complex and difficult. It involves two tasks, and part of the problem is that these tasks can often be contradictory. The first task or function of the state is to foster the conditions which will facilitate the accumulation of capital. For example, the Free Trade Agreement can be seen as an attempt by the Canadian state to make Canada more attractive to investors; their ability to pursue and increase profits is supposed to result in increased benefits for all. This accumulation task is not a simple one, given the complexity of modern capitalist economies and the internal contradictions in the interests of the dominant economic groups in our society. One need only look to the debates over free trade in Canada, or to the difficulties that Finance Ministers have in proposing budgets which will please all sectors of economic interests to realize that the role of the state is neither simple nor one-dimensional. In most cases, the policies and programmes of the state advance the interests of some at the expense of others. In this sense, the function of the state is not to serve as an instrument of some hypothetical homogeneous capitalist class. Rather, the state is seen as serving the more disembodied and long term interests of the accumulation of capital. This often means that the short run interests of certain groups of capitalists may have to be compromised or sacrificed. To this extent, the structuralists argue that the state in modern capitalism possesses a degree of *relative autonomy* — it is not merely an instrument, but has a sphere of power, influence and interests which set it apart, and sometimes in conflict, with the immediate interests of capitalists.

To this point, we still have a fairly economistic theory of the role of the state: in a sense, all that has been accomplished is to shift the emphasis from the state as an instrument of the ruling elite to the state as an instrument of capitalist accumulation. This is where the structuralists introduce the second role or function of the state. In their view, the state cannot foster accumulation unless it can also assure the role or function of legitimation. On this level, the task of the state is to create and maintain conditions that will foster social cohesion. The logic behind this notion is that capitalist accumulation is impossible unless society is well-ordered. The process of economic production is threatened by labour unrest or social instability; such situations reduce the likelihood that an investor will obtain a profitable return on an investment. In simple terms, investors will be scared off. This not only threatens the profit margins of the economic elite, but it also has consequences for the levels and types of employment in a society, and the quality of life of its citizens. In practical terms, one might try to imagine whether one would be more likely to invest one's money in a stable economy (like Canada, Japan or the United States), or in a society marked by high levels of instability or unrest (like some of the countries in Eastern Europe). Without denying that there are some of us who are altruistic enough to invest our money where it might do other people the most good, the structuralists argue that the capitalists' pursuit of profit will generally result in a tendency to put the money where it is likely to be safest and to extract the greatest return in terms of financial profit.

This legitimation function puts enormous pressure on the state to manufacture public consent to its policies and programmes. One might think, for example, of the massive selling job done on behalf of the free trade agreement in the late 1980's and early 1990's, or of the enormous investments governments now make in what is clearly a selling job on their behalf. The basic strategy of the state to accomplish this legitimation function is to attempt to universalize social interests, to create and foster the impression that the interests of the state in the process of accumulation are actually the interests of the society as a whole. There are two approaches to accomplishing this task. On the one hand, the state engages in the process of education, where it takes on the ideological work of convincing people of where their real interests lie. On the other hand, the state backs up this educational work with a network of coercive institutions. These are the institutions which patrol the limits of society: their task is to rehabilitate and reintegrate those who have gone wrong, and to control those whose unwillingness or inability to play by the socially constructed rules in force constitute a threat to the processes of accumulation or legitimation. Those who are unable to get along are usually treated through medical or psychiatric institutions, while those who are unwilling to play along usually fall under the purview of the criminal justice system.

The law has a crucial role to play in both the educational and the coercive phases of the legitimation process. The educational phase of the process can only "work" to the extent that people believe that their interests are being served. The state must create the impression that it is neutral, and that its policies and programmes are for the general welfare of all, otherwise its ability to advance the interests of accumulation will be compromised. One component of this attempt to create an appearance of equality is the notion of the rule of law. The idea of the rule of law is that everyone will be treated the same by the state, that we all have the same rights and responsibilities. This democratic principle creates the illusion that the state treats us all the same: we are legal equals, with equivalent rights and responsibilities. However, this apparent legal equality masks the very real social inequalities of resources, power and opportunity which underlie it. We are educated to the belief that this legal equality is all the state can and should provide; the state should not be expected to resolve collective problems. The implication is that social inequalities of class or reward are legitimate, because they are the "fair" (and thus legitimate) result of a competition among individuals who had a relatively equal opportunity to succeed. The results of class competition thus are seen to reflect, for the most part, the ability and hard work of the individuals in question. Social situations of inequality, such as disparities on the basis of gender, race or ethnicity are recognized as problematic, but are usually treated through some relatively minor form of tinkering with the system (such as a public awareness programme or some commitment to a policy of affirmative action on behalf of the minority group in question). The argument is the system may not be perfect, but its blemishes and warts do not require major social surgery. To the extent that the law succeeds in convincing us that rights, responsibilities, and outcomes are individual affairs, the state is able to foster the legitimation of the current realities of inequality and class disparity, and thus to maintain conditions which are propitious for accumulation.

The second, and more obvious, impact of the law is in the sphere of coercion. If the "rule of law" is designed to educate and convince, the enforcement of law is intended to discipline and control. Once again, though, the law can only perform this function efficiently and effectively to the extent that it is generally perceived to be fair, or to treat everyone the same. Thus, the state must convince us that there are no hidden interests being served and that the law works the same for everyone. The typical response to this problem is a legal system which formally excludes certain behaviours for all members of society, but which in practice selectively enforces this formal code in order to serve its primary concern with the tasks of legitimation and accumulation. This is not a simple conspiracy notion of the workings of the law, nor does it assume that all the people who work within the criminal justice system are dupes. One can readily assume good will and good intentions on the part of all involved. This does not change the fact that the operation of the law is selective. Seemingly similar behaviours, such as theft by a poor youth and tax evasion by a rich individual are dealt with quite differently. The inappropriate behaviours of different social classes, such as drug use and abuse among the disadvantaged or among the rich, are not responded to in the same manner or with the same intensity. This is not to say that the rich are immune. For that matter, the appearance of equality is preserved through the occasional ritual sacrifice of some member of the elite who has overstepped the limits of tolerance (although a cynic might argue that the sin usually lies less in the actual behaviour and more in the incipient threat of a failure of the legal system to respond to the maintenance of the appearance of legal equality).

The point is that the state, in part through the mechanism of the law, tries to organize civil and social life in a manner that sustains and reproduces current social and class arrangements. The law serves the cause by locating rights and responsibilities at the level of the individual rather than at the level of the collectivity (in technical terms, the individual is the juridical object), and in so doing contributes to the legitimating and masking of the real class interests that underlie social relations. The theoretical problem with the model, to this point, is that it tends to overstate the functional relation of law and the state to the abstract requirements of capitalist economies. Law and the state have a tendency to be reduced to structural necessity, and the real struggles which are engaged in by real agents sometimes get lost in the shuffle.

However, this is not a valid criticism of all critical approaches to the analysis of law. The theoretical solution to the problem lies in part in the concept of the rule of law, and in the related requirement for the state to appear neutral if it is to serve the role of fostering accumulation and legitimation within current social arrangements. The very functions which the state must serve, and the necessary tensions and even contradictions in these functions, result in the state possessing a degree of relative autonomy from capital. Its responsibility to manage civil and social life make it a site for social and political conflict. Class conflicts that might have been fought out in purely economic terms in earlier stages of capitalism are now displaced into the "arena" of the state — the state is the place where these conflicts are resolved, but its relative autonomy makes it an active participant (with its own interests and concerns) in the process of constructing resolutions to these conflicts.

The state can only carry on this activity to the extent that it is actually perceived to work, at least to some extent, for most sectors of society (events in the latter part of the last decade and the early part of this one in Eastern Europe provide an illustration of what happens when the state can no longer convince or coerce people into going along). In practical terms, this means that the requirement to appear neutral will sometimes require the state to act in a manner which is inimical to the accumulation of capital (at least for certain groups) or the legitimation of current social arrangements. Examples of such situations in Canada might be found in the institutionalization of medicare in the 1960s, or perhaps, in the ability of French-Canadian Nationalists to exert greater control over the government of Quebec. In both these cases, real changes have occurred from below, so to speak, as the result of the space that the tension in the roles of the state creates for the possibility of social reform.

What does all of this mean for students who wish to make some sense of the law in their everyday lives? The answer is in a series of injunctions about how we should study law. In our view, the law is a reflection and a result of historically situated practices and struggles. To the extent that this is true, it makes little or no sense to approach the law as if it were disconnected from these struggles. In this sense, the traditional approaches to law are clearly unsatisfactory. Their willingness to disconnect the law from social, political and economic realities leaves us with a sterile and dehumanized explanation of law. The critical view is based on the contention that real people make laws under social circumstances which they can influence, though not necessarily control. Any reasonable analysis of law must therefore start with an analysis of the social processes of constructing and applying laws, and of the historically specific social structures and social contexts which limit (but do not determine) the outcomes in question. The law is part of the wider repertoire of social and class struggles. Like any of these struggles, it must be understood as the emergent product of the structures which contextualize its construction, and of the agents who are responsible for the constructive work itself.

In simpler terms, we must see the law as both a product of social relations, and yet as having an impact on these same social relations. This dialectical appreciation of the nature of law means that our theories and explanations must always be specific to the workings of the law in a specific time and a specific place. The critical perspective, with its insistence on the roles and functions of the state, and on the place that the state provides for waging and winning struggles from both above and below, seems to us to hold the greatest promise for constructing the kind of theoretical explanation we have in mind.

The Brickey and Comack article that follows provides a provocative discussion of the strategic implications of a critical approach and attempts to outline the possibilities and potential that particular struggles may hold for leading to meaningful legal and social reform. It is a seminal effort to overcome the negativism of earlier approaches and to chart a more positive, progressive course for the future.

## The Role of Law in Social Transformation: is a Jurisprudence of Insurgency Possible?*
*Stephen Brickey & Elizabeth Comack*

* Excerpt from (1987), 2 Canadian Journal of Law and Society 907 at 106-119

In approaching the task of assessing the role of law in social transformation, we start from the premise, documented in Tigar and Levy's analysis of European society between the eleventh and nineteenth centuries, that legal change did not simply go through a single stage of transformation in the movement from feudalism to capitalism. Rather, the process was one of an increasing number of small, incremental legal changes that gave increasing power and legitimacy to the fledgling capitalist class. Consistent with this premise, we do not expect law to be either the vanguard or the consequence of the transformation from capitalist to socialist society. We would argue, instead, that it will be one of many strategic areas where existing tension within the system can be used to push the contradictions that result from the structure of capitalism.

Before delineating those legal activities that best represent a jurisprudence of insurgency, we readily admit the difficulty in attempting to predict what will be the most 'progressive' avenues of legal reform. The advantage of retrospective analysis — like that conducted by Tigar and Levy — is that one can discern the significance of small legal changes over historical periods by examining the diverse consequences these changes had over time. When trying to forecast how current legal changes may facilitate future substantive changes in society, one is blind to all of the potential consequences these changes may produce. If, however, historical analysis has any value, it is in the extent to which it enables us to make prescriptive statements, even tentative ones, on how to transform the existing system.

The central issue to be addressed is one of specifying the criteria by which legal reforms are to be evaluated. More specifically, what kinds of legal reform could be defined as insurgent in terms of their orientation or consequence? How do we distinguish, for example, between reforms which aim only for a greater participation of individuals within the capitalist order (i.e., demanding a "bigger share" of the capitalist pie) from those which aim to transform the very basis of that order?

Structuralists have premised their skepticism about law on the observation that equality is limited to the legal sphere (i.e., it does not extend to the economic sphere of capitalist society). It is in this respect that principles like "equality of all before the law" or "blind justice" are viewed as a major source of legitimation for the system of structured or economic inequality. However, several writers have argued that this position with its ritual invocation of the Anatole France quote, lets the law off too lightly since the law is applied in anything but an equal manner. This recognition of the inequalities in the legal order has led to a number of suggestions for reform.

Mandel, for example, in his analysis of Canadian sentencing law, notes that a central feature of sentencing practices is the recognition of varying punishment according to the offenders 'character,' in particular, the offender's relation to the productive apparatus. By taking into account such factors as educational attainment, employment record and one's "good standing in the community" in the determination of sentence, the law operates to the advantage of one class over another. High status offenders, by virtue of their class position, are perceived as requiring (even deserving) less punishment to ensure their continued conformity. Hence, by varying punishment according to class, the law has the net effect of preserving the status quo of inequality dominance and subordination. In light of this analysis, Mandel suggests that if sentencing was based solely on the utilitarian principle of general deterrence, that is, the protection of individuals from the harmful effects of crime at the least social cost, punishment would then be based entirely on the conduct sought to be prevented, and not on the "character" (i.e., class) of the offender.

What would be the effect of such a reform? Mandel suggests that it would represent a move in the direction of the 'neutral' state which liberals claim exists in modern democratic societies, that is, the system would be more 'just' in the sense that punishment would no longer vary by class. In this respect, such a reform strategy is laudable to the extent that it would mitigate the unequal treatment to which members of the subordinate classes are subjected by the legal system.

Yet, what of the structuralist argument that equality in sentencing practices would only reinforce the system of economic inequality and hence further legitimate that system? On the one hand, removing the class-based nature of punishment (i.e., viewing dominant class members as 'deserving' of lesser punishment) would eliminate one of the means by which class relations are strengthened and reinforced by the legal order. On the other hand, not taking class differences into account could be viewed as a way of ignoring and/or denying the class differences that do exist. Although punishment would no longer vary by class, crime would continue to vary by class. In this respect Mandel's reform proposal has its advantages, but it is limited. It would only take us part way toward the development of a 'jurisprudence of insurgencgency.' Such a reform is not insurgent to the extent that it fails to call into question class relations.

Other writers have focused their attention on the content of law. While the criminal law defines certain acts as 'socially injurious' or 'harmful,' it does not tend to define other acts — which are potentially more serious and harmful — as criminal and hence worthy of severe sanctions. For instance, violence against individuals occurs regularly in the workplace of capitalist societies. This typically takes the form of unsafe or hazardous working conditions, exposure to carcinogenic substances and the like. The result has been the loss of life and health for a substantial number of workers. Yet, while such occurrences meet the requirements normally associated with crime (for example, the intentional failure to provide safety equipment or the flagrant violation of safety regulations by owners in order to cut costs and increase profits), they are seldom defined or sanctioned as such. Reiman, therefore, has suggested that the criminal law be redrawn to more accurately reflect the real dangers that individuals pose to society:

> Avoidable acts where the actor had reason to know that his or her acts were likely to lead to someone's death should be counted as forms of murder. Avoidable acts where the actor had reason to believe that his or her acts were likely to lead to someone's injury should be counted as forms of assault and battery. Acts that illegitimately deprive people of their money or possessions should be treated as forms of theft regardless of the color of the thief's collar. Crime in the suites should be prosecuted and punished as vigorously as crime in the streets.

Glasbeek and Rowland have taken this issue one step further. They suggest that there already exist provisions in the criminal law which, although not initially designed for the purpose, could be applied to employer violations of workplace health and safety. This approach is essentially one which advocates the use of criminal law as a vehicle for highlighting the class conflicts inherent in the productive process. By criminalizing employer practices which result in worker injury and death, the severity of the problem would be reinforced. In effect, the strategy proposed by Glasbeek and Rowland is one which aims at using the assumptions of the governing class to the advantage of the working class. To quote the authors:

> Because of the assumptions of the liberal state, the ideology of law requires it to claim that it punishes behaviour which has been judged unacceptable by society no matter who the perpetrator of the offensive behaviour is. It will be interesting to see how the administrators of the legal justice system respond when it is argued that entrepreneurs offend against the criminal process in much the same way as do robbers of private property and people.

In this respect, such a reform strategy would advance the development of a jurisprudence of insurgency in that it endeavours to push the rule of law to its full limit and extent. Defining the violence which occurs in the workplace of capitalist societies as criminal would have the potential of not only holding employers more accountable for their actions but of raising the consciousness of workers as well.

On another level a jurisprudence of insurgency must also be capable of addressing the *manner* in which legal issues are handled by the courts. To elaborate, the law adheres to the principle of 'blind justice'. In so doing, it responds not to the "why" of an act, but to whether or not the act was committed. The race, class or sex of the accused is deemed irrelevant, as the primary criterion for judging cases is the empirical question of whether a formally proscribed act was committed. In short, the issue becomes a matter of "legally relevant facts" and, in the process of resolving this issue, the case is both *individualized* and *depoliticized*. As Grau explains:

> Cases are tried only between legal parties with defined legal interests that conflict over narrowly drawn legal issues. Collective needs are denied. The specificity of the rights and the narrowness of the legal issues combine to preclude the introduction of broader, though relevant, social questions. This restriction effectively depoliticizes the case.

This feature of the legal order contributes to one of the main legitimizing effects of the rule of law, that is, the idea that society is composed, almost exclusively, of individuals and not groups, aggregates or classes. Equally significant is the related belief that legal struggles and political struggles are separate and distinct activities. We would argue, therefore, that a jurisprudence of insurgency must alter this artificial distinction between legal and political issues. This will encompass a two-sided dialectical process. The one side involves attempting to bring the collective nature of the problem into the legal arena while the other side involves broadening the definition of the situation to encompass the political nature of the problem.

## *"Collectivizing" and "Politicizing" Legal Battles*

One way in which the law is being pushed to deal with problems that are more than individual concerns is the strategic use of law by groups to address collective problems. Historically, the labour movement was one of the first to view the problems of workers as a condition common to all individuals whose work placed them in a subordinated position to capital. Because of the blatant nature of this subordination and the fact that workers could readily interact with other co-workers who were experiencing the same consequences of subordination, craft workers are quicker than other groups to approach their problems as collective in nature.

Before describing how some collectivities are currently attempting to use the law and assessing the insurgent nature of these efforts, it is important to note the dynamic interplay that appears to exist between groups defining their problems as collective problems and the concomitant recognition of the political nature of their problems. The consistency with which groups redefine their problems as political issues suggests that politicization is a typical — if not inevitable — consequence of recognizing the collective nature of the problem. By the very act of sharing their problem with others in a similar condition, people come to realize that approaching the problem as a narrow legal issue is unrealistic and often ineffective.

Of greater significance, however, is the tendency for groups not to rely solely on the courts to resolve their problems. By recognizing the political nature of their problems, activist groups also attempt to put pressure directly on the state by engaging in legislative and lobbying activities, which has traditionally been the almost exclusive domain of the major economic interests in society. The use of lobbying by farmworkers, tenants, environmental groups, women, Indians, the handicapped and the elderly is an indication of the extent to which collectivities are broadening the scope of their struggles beyond the traditional locus of the courts.

Although the lobbying efforts of the above groups may not be successful, they are an indication of how the groups view their difficulties as political problems and not simply legal problems. Billings describes this difference in her assessment on the use of advocacy by women's organizations:

> More and more, therefore, lobbying...has become a familiar tool of the women's movement. Although largely unproductive in proportion to the amount of energy expanded *lobbying has at least familiarized women with the corridors of power*, created networks across the country and...created lengthy policy agendas that are agreed to nation-wide as the action priorities.

Although we will argue that the strategies utilized by some groups are more "insurgent" than other strategies, it is important to recognize that the very act of subordinate groups approaching the law as a collective is of value to the extent that it results in politicizing the manner in which the problem is defined.

## *Collectivities Using the Law*

There appears to be a growing awareness among activist groups of the limitations and constraints of approaching the law as individuals. One way in which groups have attempted to increase their power in using the law is to develop strategies that increase the chances that cases heard before the courts represent the collective interests of the group (given the structural limitation that these collective interests must be fought on an individual basis since collectivities are not recognized as legal actors). Some of these strategies continue to use the courts as the arena for battle but expand the techniques by which groups gain access to the courts. The methods used include class action suits, test cases, judicial reviews, standing as *amicus curiae* and private prosecution.

There are a number of current examples of individuals in Canada forming groups with the sole purpose of fighting legal issues from a collective rather than an individual base. One of the most recent examples of this is the organization of women fighting for a range of issues that address the many consequences of the systemic subordination of women in capitalist society. These issues include affirmative action, equal pay for work of equal value, the handling of sexual offenses by the criminal justice system and the way in which wife battering is dealt with by the police and the courts. One of the consequences of women defining the legal battle as a collective battle is the shift in strategies that will increase the ability of women to influence the types of cases that should be emphasized in the legal arena. A report by the Canadian Advisory Council on the Status of Women, for example, suggests taking a systematic approach to litigation that would further the collective interests of women. The approach would involve the following four steps:

1. defining a goal in terms of the desired principle of law to be established;
2. plotting how the principle of law can be established from case to case in incremental, logical and clear steps;
3. selecting winnable cases suitable for each stage taken to achieve the goal;
4. consolidating wins at each stage by bringing similar cases to create a cluster of cases in support of the principle established.

It is true that some of the above issues (such as affirmative action) simply strive for women to gain a larger piece of the pie within the existing system. Nonetheless, the importance is in the fact that the state is being asked to recognize that it is *not* the problem of a few individuals but a condition of a large segment of the population that has been adversely affected by the economic system. This demand for the recognition of problems as more than individual problems is also evident in the development of anti-poverty organizations, Indian groups fighting for aboriginal land claims and victims' groups demanding greater participation in the criminal justice system. The presumption that legal battles, particularly those in the area of civil law, are exclusively conflicts between individuals and the state or individuals against corporations is becoming less and less tenable.

Although the above strategies used by groups in approaching the law have a number of advantages over traditional approaches, the fact that the law forces these groups to fight their battles through cases of specific individuals in court limits the ability to use the law to redress collective problems. As long as the state is allowed to approach problems of inequality on an individual, case by case basis, there is little likelihood of the law being an effective tool for redressing the collective problems of subordinate groups.

## Collective Rights

We would argue that one way in which the law could be used to promote substantive change is to have collectivities recognized as legal actors in society. In other words, to establish the legal principle that, in addition to individual rights in law, there are or should be collective rights that would acknowledge the existence of subordinate groups and provide them, analogically, with the same rights and freedoms that individuals currently have, in principle if not in practice. The recognition of collective rights enables groups to move away from the narrowly defined manner in which current legal ideology defines conflicts in society.

One subject which immediately comes to mind when discussing collective rights is the *Canadian Charter of Rights and Freedoms*. The passage of the *Constitution Act, 1982* has been lauded by some commentators, as a means of providing the legal rights and guarantees that would mitigate against the discrimination of minorities in Canada. However, as Rush has argued, while the *Charter* protects individual rights, collective rights are either ill-protected or disregarded altogether. Rush suggests two ways in which collective rights can be perceived constitutionally:

> First, collective rights are those rights which accrue to individuals because of their placement or membership in an identifiable group. In this sense, the realization of the right for each individual depends on its realisation for everyone in the group. These are the right of cultural communities, ethnic and minority groups.... Second, collective rights are also rights which accrue to groups as groups. These include: the right of Indian people to title to and jurisdiction over their aboriginal land; and the right of women to affirmative action programmes in the workplace.

Following this, Rush notes that "working class rights," full aboriginal rights and the rights of women have not been recognized. In this regard, we would argue, alongside Rush, that continued pressure from working people, women, and ethnic and minority groups for greater recognition of collective rights in the *Charter* is needed.

It should be noted that not every instance of the demand for, or recognition of, collective rights represents explicit insurgent activity. For example, the current legislation in Canada regarding hate literature gives groups the legal ability to prohibit the broadcast or publication of material that has the express purpose of producing hatred toward the group. It is the collective analogy to the law of libel that affords an individual the right to protection from malicious material. While this law recognizes the existence of groups as legal actors, there is nothing within the law that directly addresses the relationship of groups to the state or to the economic base of the system. Similarly, what has historically been recognized as the collective right of management to determine the conditions of work, rates of productivity and the like would obviously fall outside the boundaries of a jurisprudence of insurgency. What this highlights is the need to question "collective right to what?" and establish the criteria and principles on which collective rights should be based.

### *Legal Recognition of Structural Inequality*

To what extent is the demand for collective rights and the politicization of collectivities in their legal struggles indicative of a jurisprudence of insurgency? We would argue that, in addition to the obvious value of individuals no longer viewing their problems as isolated, non-political problems, there has been limited success by collectivities in demanding that the legal system *not* approach all citizens as equals. That is, groups are contending that it is unjust to start from the premise that all individuals are equal legally.

The current emphasis on affirmative action programs by the government could be interpreted as a recognition by the state that there is *structural* and *systemic* inequality in capitalist society. Women, minority groups, the handicapped and other groups who have been at the economic margins have been successful in getting the state at least to acknowledge the problem (even if the remedies to the problem have not been forthcoming). In a similar manner, the current efforts to establish the principle of equal-pay-for-work-of-equal-value is an attempt to pressure the government to acknowledge the structural inequality that has resulted from a segmented labour market.

Both affirmative action and the principle of equal-pay-for-work-of-equal-value are *potentially* insurgent because they use a contradiction within legal ideology to push the law and the state past the limits established by the legal system. By groups bringing public attention to the inconsistency that the law is premised on all citizens being equal, yet large segments of the society have been placed in a position of structural inequality, the state is placed in a position of either admitting that all citizens are not equal or making adjustments to provide greater equality. Although the state may attempt to coopt movement toward greater equality, the public focus on the contradiction requires that the state take some form of ameliorative action.

## CONCLUSION

The purpose of this paper has been to open up debate on and interest in the role of law in social transformation. If one accepts that a socialist society is not going to emerge in a full-blown manner, then one must assess how the existing system — including law — can be used to push capitalist society along the path toward socialism. The jurisprudence of insurgency is based on the idea that to abandon law as an agent of change is to negate one method that can be used to challenge the present system. The insurgent role of law is to identify the existing contradictions within legal ideology and to use those contradictions to pit that ideology against itself.

Although it has been argued in this paper that the area of collective rights is one avenue that has the potential of bringing the issue of systemic inequality to the forefront, it must also be admitted that the demand for collective rights has the potential of producing divisions within the working class. These divisions are most likely to occur where some segments of the working class perceive a threat from the collective rights won by other segments of that class. A current example of this is affirmative action policy and the negative reaction to this initiative by individuals who do not fit into one of the target groups identified in the policy. The nature of the conflict is often expressed in the form of collective rights versus individual rights. While there will undoubtedly be instances where collective and individual rights will come into conflict, one should also note that capitalists have in the past facilitated this view of the inherent incompatibility of collective rights and individual rights to suit their own interests.

It must also be admitted that there is a danger in groups using the law in the attempt to achieve their aims. Chief among these dangers is the likelihood that groups will start to define their struggles as ones to be fought exclusively within the legal arena. The consequence of this is that a loss in the courts is seen as the end of the struggle. Several authors have written on the difficulties encountered when a group places all of its energies in legal struggles. In fact, Glasbeek has taken the position that groups should avoid using the *Charter* as a political tool. While recognizing the difficulties in using law in a progressive manner, we would continue to argue, for the reasons stated earlier, that the law should not be abandoned as an arena for social struggle.

Finally, a jurisprudence of insurgency has implications for the role that social scientists and legal practitioners play in legal struggles. For the social scientist, perhaps the most important role is to perform the task originally explicated by C. Wright Mills: to demonstrate the linkage between private troubles and public issues. Applying Mills's dictum to the area of law, the task of the social scientist is to show the commonality of individuals' legal problems and the commonality of interests individuals have in collectively addressing these problems.

For the legal practitioner, the traditional approach to the practice of law and the lawyer-client relationship would be inadequate in developing collective struggles in law. In an article written on the subject of poverty law, Wexler describes the inadequacies of approaching social problems from a narrow legal perspective and suggests that conventional legal training does not equip lawyers for the problems that are systemic in nature:

> Traditional practice hurts poor people by isolating them from each other, and fails to meet their need for a lawyer by completely misunderstanding that need. Poor people have few individual legal problems in the traditional sense; their problems are the product of poverty, and are common to all poor people.... In this setting the object of practicing poverty law must be to organize poor people, rather than to solve their legal problems. The proper job for a poor people's lawyer is helping poor people to organize themselves to change things so that either no one is poor or (less radically) so that poverty does not entail misery.

By defining legal problems in a larger economic and social context, the lawyer is more likely to adopt an approach to litigation and other legal activities that would best benefit the group. Just as importantly, a lawyer who views the problem in the above manner will, one hopes, also see the value of other kinds of insurgent activities that fall outside of the traditional boundaries of adversarial law, such as confrontations, rent strikes, boycotts and other actions that, while not always legal, can produce effective results for economically subordinate groups.

## 2.4 FEMINIST PERSPECTIVES ON CRIMINAL LAW

### Personal Autonomy and The Criminal Law:
### Emerging Issues for Women*
*Elizabeth A. Sheehy*

* Excerpt from Background Paper to Canadian Advisory Council on Status of Women, (Ottawa: Canadian Advisory Council on Status of Women, September 1987), pp. 3-8.

### EQUALITY THEORIES

Many possible equality theories could be used to guide development of policies on women's justice issues. Four such models are described briefly here and their relative advantages and disadvantages noted. This section of the paper concludes by observing that objectives need to be clarified by the Council before a specific approach can be adopted.

## *Strict Identical Treatment*

This equality model is usually identified as a liberal or egalitarian approach. It denies that there are any important, immutable differences between women and men, and is premised on the idea that if real equality of opportunity exists, women will eventually be on an equal footing socially, politically, and economically with men in our society. This theory calls for the elimination of legal or other distinctions between the sexes and promotes gender-neutral, strictly identical treatment of women and men.

The advantages of this model are that it has a simple and clear application to many issues (i.e., statutory rape laws limited to the protection of young women would violate this model); it is politically feasible in that it is entirely consistent with a liberal political framework; and it carries an important message that women should not be distinguished as "Other' by our society.

These advantages do not compensate for the disadvantages of this model. One serious disadvantage is that the model assumes the continued existence of the current social and political structure and necessarily measures "equal treatment" by prevailing norms and values. These norms have been shaped by a society that has historically oppressed women, and the norms are therefore male-defined. Thus women can advance and attain equal treatment and rewards only to the extent that they can mimic male career patterns and values. Women risk losing further ground under this model because when they fail to achieve equal "success" under the rule of identical treatment, it may be considered that women really are inferior!

A second disadvantage of the identical treatment approach is that the judiciary in both Canada and the United States, while willing to apply this model for the benefit of male litigants, has thus far demonstrated intransigence when asked to guarantee strictly identical treatment for women. A third and related problem is that the model has nothing to offer women when there is no analogous male experience by which to claim women's right to identical treatment. Consequently, this model can be used to deny women any rights or protections with respect to pregnancy and abortion.

A fourth and final failure of the identical treatment model is that its emphasis on gender neutrality and formal equality further entrenches inequality by obscuring real social and economic inequalities. While it is true that some amount of statutory sex stereotyping can be eliminated by framing all criminal offences in gender-neutral terms, what is lost is an appreciation of who does what to whom and of the significance of gender in our conceptualization and policing of criminal offences. The result is that unequal gender relations thrive when the rhetoric of gender neutrality denies their existence. For these reasons, the identical treatment model should be rejected as incapable of promoting any significant advancement of women's autonomy interests.

## *Identical Treatment with Biological Exceptions*

This model uses many of the same premises and applications as the strict identical treatment approach. Proponents of this approach argue, however that to ignore women's actual and immutable biological differences — pregnancy and lactation —

and to require that the different social and economic needs generated by these functions be addressed only to the extent that men are comparably situated means that women will inevitably be severely disadvantaged in practice. Other "differences" between women and men are viewed as social or economic constructs that will atrophy as we approach a society that faithfully uses an identical treatment approach. Pregnancy and lactation as differences are not about to disappear, and substantive equality would be blocked by a refusal to take these differences into account in policy and law making. This model would therefore require that women's specific needs in relation to these biological differences be met so that they can participate in all activities in our society.

One advantage of this model is that it is aimed more carefully at producing short-term equal results for women. It is also respectful of women's childbearing function and avoids minimizing its social and economic significance. The other advantage is that the model clearly limits the bases on which women and men can be treated differently.

One disadvantage of this model is that judges might not be able to distinguish invidious from beneficial treatment accorded to pregnant or lactating women. As a result, judges might end up approving of policies that in fact stereotype or disadvantage women on the basis of these biological differences. Further, the model is rather weak in that it does little to alter women's disadvantaged position: the theory supports the current political structure, and it legitimizes the inequality of power between men and women as a group by denying that the other disadvantages experienced by women (e.g., vulnerability to rape) are real or deserving of recognition. The major failure of this model is that it assumes that such a principle could radically alter women's disadvantaged position. Thus it hides the pervasiveness of sexism.

## *Treatment According to All Differences*

This theory asserts that since women are different from men, physically, socially, psychologically, economically, and politically, all policies and laws must be designed to take these differences into account, which would eventually result in substantive equality for women. This model does not assume that these differences will or will not disappear over time. Instead, it acknowledges that some of the differences are positive and that others, while perhaps negative, have been created and maintained by the political structure and thus are not about to disappear quickly or without further struggle.

This model has the advantage of exposing and accounting for all the ways women are disadvantaged; it also affirms women's values and realities by respecting those differences regardless of their source. The model also has the important advantage of illustrating the need for structural change and for re-evaluating the rules for determining the meaning and legitimacy of identical treatment as a social policy.

The model also carries certain disadvantages. One is that the model might further entrench differences between men and women that serve to disempower women. Thus, one author has argued that the "female characteristics" that will be rewarded are those that have been developed in women for the purpose of survival under conditions of inequality. This model, like the models discussed previously, might also be used to justify policies that actually oppress women further, e.g., one of excluding women from jobs as prison guards because of the special vulnerability to rape. A final problem with this model is that it focuses on "differences", which is essentially a legalistic construct, instead of on the question of women's systemic subordination.

## *Subordination Principle*

This model defines women's inequality in terms of subordination to men rather than differences between the two groups. Practices, policies, and laws are evaluated to assess whether they operate to maintain women in a subordinate position. If these laws and policies are purportedly justifiable on the basis of women's differences, then the differences themselves must also be examined to ascertain whether they are a consequence of social or economic oppression. The assessment of whether a practice or policy subordinates women is made with regard to its historical origins, its social and economic effects, and its real meaning as understood by women. This model then requires affirmative steps toward eliminating the subordinate status, inducing, for example, a "redistribution of historical burdens and benefits".

The important advantage of the subordination principle, is that it avoids legalistic analysis of what differences are not valid bases for disparate treatment, focusing instead on women's experience of the effect of such practices. It thus asks the law to pronounce on the reasons for gender differences. Do they work to the benefit of the male gender? Do they result in reduced autonomy, self-esteem, employment options, etc., for women? This model is also significant in that it demands practical and immediate remedial action as opposed to formal vindication of abstract rights.

The subordination principle is sufficiently wide that it can encompass all previously discussed models as possible solutions to subordinating laws or policies. This model also appears to be superior to the "treatment according to all differences" approach. First, it would not approve of and entrench differences produced by conditions of inequality. Second, it provides a clearer and more articulate standard for judges to employ in assessing whether a given policy ought to be supported or sanctioned and reversed.

One disadvantage of the model is that it presents the same opportunity for perversion by decision-makers who will not or cannot discern the subordinating effect of certain policies. The other problem is that the model has such potential to alter the social, political, and economic structures of our society that it is likely to be opposed vehemently and vigorously in the political arena.

These four equality models can be used in several ways. They can be invoked individually for different issues; one model can be isolated as a guiding principle for all or most issues; or new models can be created by combining or altering these theories. For instance, the National Association of Women and the Law (NAWL) has adopted a mix of models B and C: it advocates a modified identical treatment approach except with respect to pregnancy issues. NAWL has modified the identical treatment approach because it recognizes the disadvantages of this approach. It therefore employs a gender-neutral, identical treatment model that is, however, sensitive to the differences between men and women and that is designed to achieve substantive equality for women. For instance, laws mandating parental leave would be geared to women's specific physical and economic needs but would be framed in gender-neutral terms.

## Models of Justice: Portia or Persephone?
## Some Thoughts on Equality, Fairness and Gender
## in the Field of Criminal Justice*
*Frances M. Heindensohn*

* (1986), 14 International Journal of the Sociology of Law 287.

## INTRODUCTION

Questions about gender and justice are firmly on both academic and public agendas at present. What are, however, much less clear, are the basic assumptions which underpin these discussions. When, for example, courts are criticised for being 'unfair' or 'unjust', to women what, in feminist terms, does this mean? Do we have a benchmark against which justice for women can be measured? If not, can we construct one? How is this to be done? These seem to me to be quite fundamental questions which are often skimmed over or ignored. In this paper, I propose to examine what justice for women in the context of criminal justice may mean, what now exists, and what possible alternatives there might be to our present 'system'.

## JUSTICE

Criminal justice can be seen as a series of institutions and systems: (a) as a *moral* or value system where social norms are expressed, supported by penal sanctions and (b) as an *administrative* process, or processes, and also (c) as part of a system of *social control*; which has informal as well as formal structure and sanctions. In practice, of course, all these interact.

When we look at feminist critiques of criminal justice, the importance of stressing these interactions becomes apparent. Most criticisms focus initially on administrative practices: however, these are almost invariably linked to deep-seated assumptions about the roles of men and women and gender-appropriate behaviour. Often, there is a further crucial, socio-economic or other major dimension.

Several writers have criticized the operations of the police and the judiciary in relation to prostitution. McLeod's concept of injustice in the treatment of prostitutes has three levels. First she compares their legal and social status with that of their male clients who are neither charged nor stigmatized (McLeod, 1982, p.22). She then notes that the unique system of charging and cautioning prostitutes threatens their civil liberties and infringes basic rights (p. 24). Finally, she points to the gender inequalities inherent in our society which make selling sex for gain a relatively attractive occupation for some poor women. (p. 146).

Edwards focuses on rather different aspects of injustice in the treatment of prostitutes. She too notes their uniquely stigmatizing court treatment and cites instances of their clients' reputations being preserved, even though kerb crawling by men may be more of an actual nuisance than soliciting or loitering. She emphasises that the legal treatment of prostitutes: "has had a much greater and more profound influence on the criminal justice system than to be merely *discriminatory*" (Edwards, 1984, p. 68, emphasis added).

In her view, it strikes at the heart of justice and renders justice for the prostitute, as defendant, witness or victim in criminal proceedings almost unattainable. In her general discussion of women before the courts, Edwards emphasises the harm caused by the use of individualised and medicalised treatments for women. These approaches because they lead to harsher sentences, to greater paternalism and interference in women's lives or to an imposition of sexist stereotypes upon deviant women she sees as unjust. "Women defendants are on trial both for their legal infractions and for their defiance of appropriate femininity and gender roles" (Edwards, 1984, p. 216).

This is very close to Pat Carlsen's conclusion from her study of women sentenced to Cornton Vale Prison in Scotland:

> "Women's imprisonment is a very specific form of social control especially tailored for the disciplining of women. For the majority of these imprisoned women have not merely broken the law. As women, mothers and wives they have, also, some how stepped out of place" (Carlsen, 1983, p. 59).

Similar analyses of criminal injustice to women have been offered in relation to juveniles. Harris suggests that girls receive supervision orders for lesser offences than boys (Harris 1985) and Chesney-Lind that they are punished for sexual misdemeanours which go unpunished in boys (Chelsey Lind 1973) while Casburn and Parker *et al.* noted that the comparative rarity of girls appearing before juvenile courts led to them being handled as "doubly deviant" and thus waiting longer for decisions, experiencing more invasion of privacy, etc. (Casburn, 1979; Parker *et al.*, 1981).

We can then, I would suggest, summarise modern criticisms of criminal injustice to women as having three main aspects. These are:

(a) that girls or women are not treated *equally* with men and boys — when they are prostitutes, for example, or receive harsher sentences for the same offence;
(b) that females are *unfairly* or unjustly treated in relation to a concept such as 'natural justice' or 'human rights' as in the stigmatising of 'common prostitutes';
(c) that girls or women are *inappropriately* treated in relation to their offence and degree of blame — when their treatment is medicalised, for example.

Now such criticisms seem to me to be located well within the traditional framework of criminal jurisprudence. Indeed the principles they imply correspond closely to those of the 'classical' school.

I suggest calling this model 'Portia' because Shakespeare's heroine in *The Merchant of Venice* neatly encapsulates so many aspects of it. The focus of the 'Portia' model is clearly male and a rational, clear-thinking, procedurally competent male at that. The means of achieving justice are through laws and courts, in the present system, and there is only one world-view which is ultimately valid, that of white middle-class males. The concept of justice is one of legal equity.

Although feminist views on injustice have taken this rational-legal form, I think there are also deeper issues involved, a more profound 'hidden agenda' which we also need to explore. In both academic accounts and even more noticeably, in the views of women defendants and victims in the criminal justice system there is a sense of outrage greater than that which the violation of rational principles would justify (see e.g. Peckham, 1985; Hayes, 1985; Carlen, 1985). Are we then justified in saying that there is a particular female or feminist concept of justice which the criminal justice system of patriarchal society violates? If this is so, what would be special and distinctive about feminist justice: a just treatment of women?

## JUSTICE FOR WOMEN

"Women suffer from systematic social injustice because of their sex...that proposition...(is) the essence of feminism and...anyone who accepts it (is)...a feminist" argues Radcliffe Richards (1980), p. 14).

Radcliffe Richards following the American philosopher John Rawls (1972), defines justice as fairness and tries in her book to lay down principles of sexual justice and practical rules derived from these. She is almost entirely concerned with *distributive* rather than *retributive* justice, i.e. with how resources are shared out in society, but she observes that: "questions of retributive justice actually reduce to questions of distributive justice" (Radcliffe Richards, 1980, p. 354).

In the course of her discussion of justice, she argues that: "a just society is one in which the least well off groups is as well off as possible" and that 'justice' in "this definition does not entail equality on average between men and women" (pp. 124-125).

As we have noted, much even of the feminist criticism of criminal injustice to women is based on assumptions about equality: women are unfairly treated when they are more harshly punished than comparable men, for the same offence. This is very much in accord with a long lineage of criminological and socio-legal thinking which assesses criminal justice within fairly narrow criteria. Baldwin & Bottomley for instance, define justice in terms of the rightness of objectives and the fairness and accountability of the procedures involved. (Baldwin & Bottomley, 1978, p. 5).

Even if the police, the courts and prisons operated with total fairness to women in their own terms (and I do not think that they do) they would still be part of a society which has fundamental injustices based on sex at its core. Three particular aspects are crucial: sexual inequality, the narrow stereotyping of women's behaviour and the distribution of power. Sex should not, in theory, need to be any women's destiny today. In practice, being born a woman is likely to mean being poorer, less well-educated, having a more routine job, carrying a double burden of work in and out of the home; above all having far less autonomy and far fewer real choices in life than being born to manhood.

Within the smaller social space and the lesser share of resources available to them, women are also confined to a narrow range of conventionally acceptable behaviour. 'Wives', 'mothers' and 'typical women' are alleged and supposed to act in certain ways. Some of the key assumptions behind sexual stereotypes are particularly relevant to criminality: thus males are said to be aggressive, females passive; women are thought of as 'naturally' devious and manipulative. Both these features of the social context in which justice is effected depend on a third: the power dimension. Ours is a society in which men are dominant and women subordinate in both private and public spheres — from Parliament to public houses, from the boardroom to the bedroom, power and control are vested in men and largely denied to women.

These features of society cannot be left outside the police station or courtroom when women confront the apparatus of criminal justice. Indeed, it is clear that they are present and pressing in many such situations. Carlen, for example, has pointed out the impossibility of fair and equal treatment for women offenders in her Scottish study because of the poverty, domestic violence and profoundly chauvinistic society they inhabit (Carlen, 1983), while Eaton has shown in London and Kruttschnitt in America that courts may take into account women's 'conventional' feminine behaviour and the informal social control which binds them in considering the sentencing tariff (Eaton, 1985).

Women who have been involved in crime do seem often to react to their experiences in distinctive ways which say a great deal about their perceptions of the 'fairness' of the system. Very few women offenders glory in their misdemeanours in the way some of the male colleagues do by, for example, writing self-justifying accounts of them. When women do recount their experiences, they are much more likely to deny their deviance and stress their virtues and conformity (see Heidensohn, 1985 for an analysis). Joannes Hayes, the central figure in the so-called "Kerry Babies" case declares: "I'd been verbally bullied in the cause of justice, and now the women of Ireland were demanding an unwritten element of law — Fair Play" (Hayes, 1985, p. 20).

Audrey Peckham feels that she was ill at the time of her alleged offence and found her experiences of arrest and charge bewildering and grotesque:

> "I was merely, it seemed to me, a middle-aged woman, feeling my age, about to be charged with an offence I had not committed and totally unworthy of the drama and histrionics that the police had displayed with that elaborate stake out. I felt very angry about it, and hoped sincerely that the police felt as foolish as they jolly well ought to have done — after all the painstaking preparation, to have only caught a little teacher having a breakdown" (Peckham, 1985, pp 21-22).

I have already suggested that justice for women cannot simply be measured in terms of fair, open and rational treatment for them in the courts (i.e. the Portia model), although these are important dimensions, and our present arrangements do not always do women justice even on these terms. In addition, procedural justice has to be seen in its wider social context and in particular for women, in relation to the disadvantages they experience in society which makes them unequal to men even before they encounter the law. Now it can of course be argued that women are not the only social group to be so disadvantaged. Indeed it is very clear, for instance, that members of ethnic minorities, or unskilled workers or young people can often be in similarly disadvantaged positions. There have been protests and campaigns about injustice and bias, especially as these affect black people. There is however, I believe, a further and very specific way in which women are likely to experience and perceive the criminal justice system as unjust and that is because it is to them a peculiarly alien and unfamiliar world.

Few parts of our social world are quite so notably male than those of crime and its controlling agencies. Crime, according to official records and various other surveys and studies is overwhelmingly a male activity: over 80% of all serious offences are committed by men or boys. Females commit few serious offences and recidivism is far less common. Court appearances by girls and women are even less frequent: 90% of delinquent girls are cautioned even for serious offences. Men, too, predominate in the staffing and manning of the police and the courts. Women also have experience of the police and courts as victims as well as offenders and over several crimes are likely to feel some alienation and ambiguity. Thus in cases of rape and of domestic violence, police responses especially have been highly criticised as being unfair and unfeeling (Toner, 1982).

Women in general are not familiar with the criminal justice system, nor it with them. Indeed criminologists have coined the term "doubly deviant" to describe courts' view of women offenders since they transgress two codes: legal rules about crime and society's approved pattern for proper, conforming womanhood. There is also evidence to suggest that women find their penal treatment unfair for similar reasons (Carlen, 1985), but also too because their lower crime rates do actually lead not to better prisons but to poorer: women are incarcerated further from home, there can be little segregation of offenders, or specialised programmes. Women clearly find prison a harsh punishment: their disciplinary offences and their intake of medicinal drugs are both high (Heidensohn, 1985). The penal system is designed to deal with male delinquencies and women fit uneasily into its patterns.

There is considerable support for the view that prison is a harsher and more unusual punishment for women than it is for men (Heidensohn, 1969, 1975; Giallombardo, 1966; Carlen, 1983, 1985; Expenditure Committee, 1978-1970). Among the reasons for this are that women lose more by imprisonment because their family lives are disrupted, their children separated from them and profoundly damaging stigma acquired. Regimes in women's prisons, while sometimes superficially 'softened' with cosmetic coverings of say choice of clothing, are often: "much more rigid than those imposed in the men's prisons" (Carlen, 1985, p.182).

In particular, a form of repressive resocialisation appears to be attempted in some women's prisons, emphasising the need for conformity to good behaviour and conventional femininity, yet in the setting of a corrective institution. Carlen (1985) has pointed out how confusing this is: "Women who have already rejected conventional and (for them) debilitating female roles are constantly enjoined 'to be feminine'".

Player (in press) has observed, in studying the use of youth custody for women that there is a clear reversal of the usual (for men) practice of segregating adult and youthful offenders. She suggests that this is because of an implicit expectation that: "adult women would perform a 'maternal role' towards the younger inmates".

Again, the emphasis is on a double resocialisation to women in prison: as conventional 'mature', 'maternal' and 'responsible' adults and as reformed offenders (Player, in press).

Perhaps the reason women are most likely to find the formal machinery of criminal justice harsh and unfair is that most of them, unlike most men, are subject to elaborate and subtle informal social control. I have described elsewhere (Heidensohn, 1985) how pervasively this operates, with women being confined and controlled by their domestic ties, by patriarchal authority, by the division of public and private domains. In addition to this comprehensive and effective network of silken bonds, our society exhorts and prescribes good behaviour and conformity in women through magazines, films and television programmes, as well as the less ephemeral media of folk myth and legend, organised religion and popular culture. Women who confront the abstract system of formal justice are not only treated as 'doubly deviant' as women and offenders, they also experience 'double jeopardy' — they are likely already to have experienced the narrow confines and the informal, but formidable, system of sanctions which penalise deviant women.

Criminal justice is not only a matter of procedural propriety and fairness of tariff (although these are important); it also involves issues of social justice. This is true for all accused persons who may be disadvantaged by adverse social circumstances, but women experience two distinctive sorts of disadvantages, which markedly affect their rights and their treatment: they are greatly *over*represented among the poor and the least powerful in our society while at the same time being rarely found to be officially criminal or as crime-control officials. Criminal injustice to women is, then, a compound of legal and administrative inequalities, such as in the treatment of prostitutes and of women who are role-deviant, and of social and sexual injustice. I am still measuring these on the scales derived earlier from traditional philosophical and legal notions, namely equality, fairness and appropriateness, the assumed comparison always being with men. Now I want to look at whether this takes us far enough and answers the questions with which I began.

When men campaign for improvements in their rights whether political, social or economic, their object has always been to achieve parity with other, more privileged *men*. It is rather surprising that arguments about equal treatment with women have hardly ever been used by men seeking redress of grievances. The case made in the 1960s against the criminalizing of private male homosexual activities was based on the concepts of privacy and lack of a victim. Comparisons were made with tolerance to adultery but not in terms of the rights of males and females. A few men have tried to use the Sex Discrimination Act in Britain, to equalise times for leaving work, for example. Women, too, have generally seen the rights of *man* to which they have aspired as being the same rights as *men* have had. This is the first, or 'Portia' model of rights and justice. There are other possibilities. One is to improve women's lot in *relation to their present position* but in a narrow and usually stereotyping fashion.

I suggest calling this the 'essentially feminine', or 'Persephone' approach, because it presupposes that women have certain inherent feminine characteristics different and requiring different treatment from the characteristics of men.

**Table 1**
*Models of Justice*

| Model | Values and Characteristics | System | Concept of Justice | Features |
|---|---|---|---|---|
| Portia | Masculine Rationality Individualism | Civic rights Rule of law | Legal,, Equality,, Procedural | Norm is male |
| Persephone | Feminine Caring and personal | Networks Informal | Responsibility Co-operation | Norm is female |

## PORTIA

Almost every feminist movement has sought to achieve the same rights for women as men enjoy. This is only realistic, for two major reasons. Firstly, as it is clear that men are the dominant, powerful group in all known societies, then obviously equality with the strongest is what anyone would seek. Secondly, domestically privatised and isolated as they are, women need access to the public sphere of politics and the market before they can achieve anything and this means access through and alongside men.

Even today, our judicial system is built around males, so that women who encounter it have to measure up to male-based norms and rules which may ignore for instance women's dependency on men or children's dependency on their mothers. Much recent public concern has focused on the sense of injustice felt by men who have to support their former wives, and English law has even been changed in response to this.

Yet many women also have such feelings even if they have not been as fully articulated. Scutt, for example, writing of her study of marriage and divorce in Australia notes:

> "Women have a sense that they are being treated unfairly because they cannot quantify the efforts that they have made, and think at times 'but I did do something that was worthwhile, didn't I?' 'Surely my efforts should be given some recognition in terms of property division?' " (Scutt, pers. comm. and see Scutt & Graham, 1984).

Alternatively, women may be tested against norms about proper female behaviour which are derived from (man-made) stereotypes of femininity. Thus the definition of some forms of murder as infanticide by the mother, or the recent establishment of a defence plea based on premenstrual tension may give some relative leniency to some women, but at considerable cost in paternalism and loss of autonomy to them and many others. Thus *if some women* are impelled to irrational behaviour by their hormonal urges, so the argument goes, then no women can be trusted to be rational and make major decisions. All female deviance can be then regarded as pathological, its source literally within the deviant herself. This was clearly the thinking behind the plans for the new Holloway prison when they were first mooted in 1968 (Faulkner, 1971). Although these plans have long since been overtaken by other ideas about women's criminality, generations of women prisoners have had to suffer their consequences (Heidensohn, 1975; Carlen, 1985).

The alternative for women to the strict rationality of this model is likely to be the use of narrow stereotypes of femininity. Certain actions may be interpreted as explicable because of assumed female characteristics and punishment may be accordingly less (though it will probably be paternalistic and may still be stigmatising).

However, women who fail to conform to expectations of appropriate female behaviours may be treated very much more severely, because of their failure to weep or to show maternal love or even to look 'feminine'. (Such allegations have been made about, for example, the cases of Ruth Ellis (Delaney, 1985), of Christine Villemin (Smyth, 1985), the 'Dingo baby case' and of Karen Tyler (Toynbee, 1986). The 'Portia' model is the most familiar and the most widely accepted model of justice. It is the one that most feminists take for granted in measuring and pointing out deficiencies in present provision and practices. Its flaws are admirably summed up by Scutt:

"Women confront a legal system that professes to be attuned to the rights of all. It professes the ideals of fairness and equality. Many legal writers, judges and lawyers have concocted a jurisprudence that bolsters that false notion. Yet, as some men have recognised, 'fairness' is accorded only to those (that is, men) having the means to pay, and having the rights deemed worthy of protection. 'Equality' is judged according to the rule that 'some [men] are more equal than others'. It has taken women to press home the place patriarchal notions have in law" (Scutt, 1985).

## PERSEPHONE

If we reject the 'Portia' model and search for alternatives, we come of course into speculative realms. Modern feminist psychologists have proposed important changes in thinking about moral development. Several writers have worked particularly on new psychologies which could offer at least the basis of a new and better moral order. Miller, for example, argues that our present civilisation is built upon the historic subordination of women who become the 'carriers' of all the things: sexuality, emotion, creativity, managing bodily functions which men wished to repress and be dissociated from. In her 'new psychology' women have to recognise these qualities and functions as real strengths and add to them power and self-determination (Miller, 1978, p. 129). What is significant for our purposes in seeking new or alternative models in Miller's work is that she starts from a position of (re)valuing women and their experience and as a base for making moral judgments. As Eisenstein puts it:

"the goal for women... should by no means be to learn to act like, think like and adopt the values of, men and the male-dominant culture. Rather, concepts such as autonomy, power, authenticity, self-determination — all of these should be re-examined and redefined by women...(Miller takes) the condition of women as potentially normative for all human beings" (Eisenstein, 1984, pp. 66-68).

Gilligan too seeks to redress the balance in studies of moral development by adding women back in. She describes men and women as having different maturing experiences. Men become detached, autonomous and individualised and take a: "rights conception of morality...geared to arriving at an objectively fair or just resolution to moral dilemmas upon which all rational persons could agree" (Gilligan, 1982, p. 21-22)

Women, on the other hand, take part in a different cycle of growth and attachment as soon as they are adult, they become responsible for the care of others and help them in turn to mature, thus perpetuating a cyclical pattern. In consequence, women see moral problems differently (she uses empirical studies to demonstrate this) and thus: "the psychology of women that has consistently been described as distinctive in its greater orientation toward relationships and interdependence implies a *more contextual mode of judgement and a different moral understanding*" (Gilligan, 1982, p. 22).

Gilligan calls this approach Demeter/Persephone after the Homeric myth of mother and daughter whose story exemplifies the cycle of fertility of sowing and reaping, conception and birth. She goes on to stress that men have a 'justice' model of morality, based on rights while women have a 'caring' model. Both, she argues, must be recognised because the:

"two disparate modes of experience...are in the end connected. While an ethic of justice proceeds from the premise of equality — that everyone should be treated the same — an ethic of care rests on the premise of non-violence that no one should be hurt".

How might this translate into a new model of justice?

While women-centered approaches are obviously attractive and one can, on the basis of these writers' work begin to construct notions of justice and even practices, there are difficulties and dangers. The dangers, I think, lie partly in producing a version of justice which is welfare-based and individualised with the problems attendant upon it. However, the central problem is essentially one of *power*: it is possible, just, to envisage a separate, gentler, more sympathetic justice system exclusively reserved for women. That is, after all, what we already have broadly for juveniles: anonymity, informality, an emphasis on familial relationships and emotional maturity rather than strict notions of guilt. But just as adults control the juvenile court so would men still be in charge of female courts. Moreover, it strains credibility to believe that *men* would allow themselves or their peers to be subjected to a new, feminine morality and judgement. Women would thus, I am afraid, be two-fold losers; they might be 'infantilised' and they would also probably see what little influence they can exert over male behaviour through the courts lost. There are interesting avenues still to be explored within this model. It has also to be said that some recent developments in the criminal justice system do have Persephone aspects: community service orders for instance, exemplify an attachment and reparation approach, making the offender literally refurbish the social fabric. Again ideas of conciliation and of victim-offender contact and support schemes are 'outwith' traditional ideas of justice and stress 'caring' rather than 'rights' values.

## CONCLUSION

I have tried in this paper to explore some of the ideas about gender and criminal justice which feminists have increasingly offered us. Most relate to a traditional concept of justice as equality or as fairness, but there was clear evidence of a deep-seated dissatisfaction with such notions, since they ignore huge stretches of women's experiences and their discontent. However, the central problem of alternative, women-centred models lies in patriarchy — the male control of power and resources in our (and every other) society. Nevertheless, they can provide us with heuristic devices to explore and criticise.

There are in everyday practice, many questions faced by professionals, by policy makers, by lawyers and clients which may, I hope be a little illuminated by this discussion. Is it fair for example, for non-delinquent girls to join Intermediate Treatment programmes? Is it fair for them not to? Should rape victim and accused both be anonymous? Should adult female offenders mix with youth custody cases for their own good?

There is also a list of sensible items to be considered when we face the real, sad everyday world:

1. Even in its own narrow terms, the 'Portia' model can be criticised and evaluated, procedurally and in principle. Courts, for example, have been imprisoning prostitutes for not paying fines. Edwards has criticised defence barristers whose questioning of rape victims is doubtful and seems designed to destroy the victim's character and, in her view, breaks the Bar's code of conduct.

2. A certain amount can be achieved by education and politics — 'consciousness raising' has clearly helped the introduction of different approaches to rape.
3. Any new criminal justice or penal measure should, as a matter of routine, be examined for its impact on gender.
4. While a separate *judicial* system for women is not feasible, and probably not viable, a separate and very different *penal* system is. This might involve small, well-scattered houses or hostels, with good community links and support.

Criminal justice for women involves, as it does for men, social justice too. Whichever model we take needs power and resources to make it work. What an exercise like this reminds us of is that women in our courts, police stations, etc. experience the stigma of 'double deviance' and risk the penalties of double jeopardy. They are fairly helpless before these hazards since they are not of their making or choosing. Little by little, grain of sand by grain of sand things may be changing. Nevertheless, while this is a man's world it will be his concept of justice which will prevail and his will be the one women have to use.

## References
- Baldwin, J. & Bottomley, A.K. (1978) *Criminal Justice*. Martin Robertson: London.
- Carlen, P. (1983) *Women's Imprisonment*. Routledge and Kegan Paul. London.
- Carlen, P. (Ed.), (1985) *Criminal Women*. Polity Press: Oxford.
- Casburn, M. (1979) *Girls Will be Girls*. W.R.R.C.; London.
- Chesney-Lind, M. (1973) Judicial enforcement of the female sex role. *Issues in Criminology* 51-69.
- Delaney, S. (1985) *Observer*, 3 March 1985.
- Eaton, M. (1985) Documenting the defendant: placing women in social inquiry reports. In *Women in Law* (Brophy J. & Smart, C., Eds). Routledge and Kegan Paul: London.
- Edwards, S. (1981) *Women on Trial*. Manchester University Press; Manchester.
- Eisenstein, H. (1984) *Contemporary Feminist Thought*. Unwin: London.
- Expenditure Committee (1978-1979) *Education, Arts and Home Affairs Sub-Committee of the Expenditure Committee; Women and the Penal System*. Evidence in Vols 61-i to 611-xiv.
- Faulkner D.E.R. (1971) The redevelopment of Holloway Prison. *Howard Journal of Penology and Crime Prevention* 13(2).
- Giallombardo, R. (1966) *Society of Women: a study of a Women's Prison*. Wiley: Chichester.
- Gilligan, C. (1982) *In a Different Voice*. Harvard University Press: Cambridge.
- Harris, R. (1985) Towards just welfare. *British Journal of Criminology*, 25.
- Hayes, J. (1985) *My Story*. Brandon: Kerry.
- Heidensohn, F. (1969) Prison for women. Howard Journal.
- Heidensohn, F. (1975) The imprisonment of females. In *The Use of Imprisonment* (McConville, S.: Ed.) Routledge and Kegan Paul: London pp. 43-56.
- Heidensohn, F. (1985) *Women and Crime*. Macmillan: London.
- McLeod, E. (1982) *Women Working: Prostitution Now*. Croom Helm: London.
- Parker, H., Casburn, M. & Turnbull, D. (1981) *Receiving Juvenile Justice*. Blackwell: Oxford.
- Peckham, A. (1985) *A Woman in Custody*. Fontana: London.
- Player, E. (1986) Women's imprisonment: the effects of youth custody. *British Journal of Criminology* (in press).
- Rawls, J. (1972) *A Theory of Justice*. Oxford University Press.
- Radcliffe Richards, J. (1980) *The Sceptical Feminist*. Pelican: Harmondsworth.

- Scutt, J. & Graham, D. (1984) *For Richer, For Poorer: Money, Marriage and Property Rights*. Penguin: Ringwood.
- Scutt, J. (1985) In pursuit of equality: women and legal thought 1788-1984. In *Women, Social Science and Public Policy* (Goodnow, J. & Pateman, C. Eds) Academy of Social Sciences: Australia.
- Smyth, R. (1985) *Observer*, 11 August 1985.
- Toner, B. (1982) *The Facts of Rape*. Arrow Books: London.
- Toynbee, P. (1986) *Guardian*, 17 March 1986.

## 2.5 HISTORICAL PERSPECTIVES ON CRIMINAL LAW
*Barry Wright*

Careful and rigorous historical inquiry tends to confirm many of the suggestions made by scholars doing critical research on modern crime, criminal law and its administration. History, first of all, underlines the relativity of what is defined as crime. The types of behaviour considered criminal, especially when it comes to property offences, have changed considerably over time. The industrial revolution, for instance, transformed property interests, exchange relationships and ways of doing business. New crimes emerged to secure the changing economic realities (Linebaugh, 1985). There has been less change in the definition of violent offences, although there are notable examples such as the ending of the spousal immunity rule in cases of rape in 1983. For all offences there have been important transformations in how they have been administered, reflecting the impact of prevailing cultural, patriarchal and socio-economic influences on power.

History reveals interesting transitions and developments in criminal law institutions. Despite the medieval origins of the public adversarial jury trial, many people are surprised to discover that the basic institutions at the beginning and end of the modern "criminal justice system" — the police and the penitentiary — are relatively recent additions to the system. Law enforcement, including detection, apprehension and prosecution depended largely on private initiative until the early nineteenth century and the controversial establishment of trained "professional" police, which increased the state's surveillance and crime prevention functions enormously (Storch, 1975; Emsley, 1987). Until this period as well, capital punishment governed most serious offences known as felonies, although it was often mitigated by jury verdicts and more importantly, official discretionary pardons made conditional on secondary punishments such as transportation. Minor offences known as misdemeanours were punished by a variety of corporal punishments, fines and occasionally, time in "houses of correction". There were also "gaols" for accused persons awaiting trial but imprisonment was not considered a penal option for convicted serious offenders. In a remarkably short period of time, in the early nineteenth century, capital penalties were repealed and the penitentiary transformed the administration of punishment (Ignatieff, 1985). Discretionary physical punishment and examplary public hangings became less important than the effective disciplinary "processing" of convicted offenders, justified in terms of certain punishment (which for utilitarian reformers was more effective for deterrence than severity of punishment) and the possibilities of rehabilitation.

Transformation, although at a somewhat slower pace, also took place in the criminal trial that lay in between these new disciplinary mechanisms. Prosecutorial authority increasingly became public, as the Crown extended control over the management of routine criminal prosecutions, displacing the private prosecutor by the mid 19th century. Lawyers "colonized" the criminal trial increasingly after the mid 18th century, reducing the victim and the accused to a passive role. The emergence of lawyers as the "motor force" of the trial resulted in the elaboration of procedural and evidentiary rules. Despite the traditional popular assumptions, not to mention those of the legal profession, these innovations did not evolve over centuries through some sort of gradual internal innovation and improvement. Nor did they have much to do with some sort of response to "moral decline." They were tied up with dramatic social change, political crises and ambitious new strategies of power.

These are obviously very broad brush-strokes and those who research the history of crime and criminal law present accounts which are much more complex and detailed. And it should be stressed that there is much contentious historical debate and a variety of interpretations concerning the details of these developments. This reflects the nature of the historical enterprise. It is not an objective science. It is subject to the research limits of the archival records and the interpretative limits of the historian. A variety of interpretations result, some of which are more compelling and rigorous than others. Despite this variety, most serious historians agree that the criminal law and its administration cannot be understood in isolation from social forces and political and economic context. It is not surprising that most of the impetus for the recent proliferation of historical research on criminal law comes not so much from legal scholarship (with its preoccupation with technical doctrine) but from social history, political economy and criminology.

With these *caveats* in mind about over-generalization and related concerns about teleological presentism (judging past events from present day standards rather than those of the period), a brief chronological sketch of developments in criminal law may be set out in terms of the medieval and early modern period, the seventeenth and eighteenth centuries, and finally the nineteenth century when the system as we know it today took shape. It should be noted that the focus is necessarily English criminal law. Canadian provinces "received" English criminal law and English institutional models in the colonial period and our *Criminal Code* which was later developed by the federal government was significantly influenced by Stephen's Draft English Code. The Canadian "content" of our criminal law did not so much arise out of creative innovation but out of necessities of particular Canadian conditions.

After the Norman conquest of 1066 criminal law played an important role in consolidating the power of the new state. Very quickly criminal law came to be regarded as something more than involving the victim or the peace of the local community. Crimes came to be seen as violations of an ambitious new notion, the King's peace. Doctrinally, this led to the separation between torts and those harms seen as breaches of the King's peace — the felony and misdemeanour offences. These criminal offences were tried in royal courts set up in the counties, supervised by the King's local agent — the justice of the peace, who also presided over trials for misdemeanours and organized felony proceedings to be presided over by royal justices on the assize circuits. Trials proceeded adversarially and to deal with the weighing of proof, the jury of local upstanding citizens was devised with the responsibility of delivering the verdict. The political dimensions of these developments are difficult to ignore: the King's peace represented the hegemony of royal power and matters that threatened disorder, the apparatus of the royal courts and the justice of the peace extended administrative presence throughout the countryside, and even the jury may be seen as a way of co-opting local power by involving it in the processes of royal justice.

Arguably, the elaboration of the criminal law system was more important than armed occupation in ensuring long term order and stability. However, over the centuries the formal claims of the law and the personnel in the system sometimes became obstacles, especially as royal rule became more arbitrary. Juries, for instance, would use their power on the verdict to give decisions according to conscience, thereby nullifying the law and indirectly voicing popular protest against oppressive laws or prosecutions. The Court of Star Chamber, originally a mechanism to bring order to common law, was used to by-pass the political inconveniences of regular criminal trials by jury. The political conflicts that led to the English Revolution, the constitutional resolutions of 1689 and later the Act of Settlement had important implications on the administration of criminal law. All citizens had the right to trial by jury, the crown prerogatives on prosecutions were to be exercised circumspectly and judicial tenure was placed on good behaviour rather than royal pleasure.

As a result of these advances the overtly political uses of the criminal law could indeed be increasingly contested using the formal claims derived from constitutional advances which further secured the rule of law. The emergence of a defence bar, notably lawyers such as Thomas Erskine and William Garrow, successfully battled political prosecutions to support political liberties and won important advances for the rights of the accused. Nonetheless, the 18th century saw the criminal law employed in new ways to reinforce the authority of the ruling classes. The administration of criminal law became an important site where ideological functions of the state were developed and refined. Douglas Hay's remarkable synthesis of this period underlines the important role of criminal proceedings in shaping the climate of popular thought. Hay's complex analysis demonstrates how the majesty of the assizes and the claims of justice were balanced with the wide exercise of discretion (mercy through the conditional pardon) in a manner which masked the material interests of the powerful and helped legitimate their authority (Hay, 1975; see also Langbein, 1983 and Linebaugh, 1985). It was an approach which could not survive the pressures created by the industrial revolution. The creation of new property offences and the vast increase in the number of offences punishable by death created huge pressures on the criminal courts. The new definitions of crime were compounded by objective increases in crime caused by the socio-economic dislocations of urbanization, the uncertainties of wage labour and the increased criminal opportunities of city existence. There was an increasing gulf between the terrifying claims of the law (wide ranging capital offences) and its inconsistent application (although felony convictions increased tremendously, not all could be hanged and ever greater numbers of convicts were transported to a penal colony after receiving a conditional pardon.)

As suggested at the outset, the early nineteenth century saw a transformation in criminal law doctrine and its administration. Law enforcement was professionalized, capital offences were radically reduced and punishment became more certain and proportional to the gravity of the offences. Obstensibly utilitarian or humanitarian reforms swept through the system, reaching from the creation of the professional police, changes to prosecutions and trial procedures, through to the creation of the penitentiary for serious offenders. Although in whig accounts the early nineteenth century in England was an era of rational criminal law reform in the name of efficiency and humanitarianism, the progress was not entirely benevolent. The social discipline of criminal law, with new institutions such as police and the penitentiary, reached greater numbers more effectively than was ever possible before (McGowan, 1983).

It is at this point that we can finally shift to Canada. English criminal law and its institutional models were adopted in Canada during the early part of these reforms in England. The British North American colonies obviously had different social problems that an England pre-occupied with urban difficulties and an industrial working class. They nonetheless continued to slavishly follow English developments. When the provinces first developed their own legislatures and courts they formally received English law as the core of their own laws. Thereafter, they could amend or elaborate this core doctrine according to local conditions. This took place in Upper Canada, for instance, in 1792. In 1833 the province adopted forty years' worth of wide-ranging English doctrinal innovations in a single legislative package and construction was commenced on the Kingston penitentiary despite the fact that there was no serious crime problem. The province's ruling elite seemed to embrace the ambitious new criminal law strategies in an attempt to bolster its power (Taylor, 1979). After the Dominion of Canada was established in 1867, consolidation of provincial criminal laws into a national criminal code became part of Sir John A. Macdonald's "national policy" (along with the creation of the North West Mounted Police and an array of economic measures to help secure the vast north west previously governed by the Hudson Bay Company). Canada eventually developed a criminal code in 1892, unlike England, but according to colonial form our code was based on a bill drafted by James Fitzjames Stephen for an English code which failed to get a majority at Westminster (Parker, 1981, Brown, 1989).

There are, of course, important Canadian stories based on a diverse population's particular experiences with the criminal law. The imperial imposition of a system of British law over both the indigenous approaches of native peoples and a pre-existing French legal system, and the resulting uses of criminal law to subjugate diverse groups perceived to stand in the way of national development, is an important theme here (Phillips, Loo and Lewthwaite, 1994). Canadian governments have frequently used the criminal law to deal with perceived national security threats, reflecting loyalist anxieties in the colonial period, anxieties which after confederation were articulated in the form of the Dominion government's powers over "peace, order and good government". The historical record suggests that our governments have apprehended insurrection all too easily, rarely coming under critical scrutiny, perhaps because of Canadians' traditional "deference to authority" (Greenwood and Wright, 1996).

Historical perspectives on the criminal law illustrate the true complexity of the role of criminal law in the exercise of power. History provides us with empirical evidence to support a skepticism which causes us to question assertions that the criminal law comes into being according to consensus and is administered in a democratically accountable manner. It also supports a skepticism towards opposite assertions which reduce the criminal law to an instrument manipulated according to class-interested ends. The uses of criminal law cannot be reduced to the same thing as resorting to state sanctioned violence or military intervention. The state may favour criminal law over brute coercion in order to lend legitimacy to its perceptions and interventions. Such legitimacy is lost if the law is too blatantly manipulated for partisan ends. For this reason criminal proceedings can sometimes be a site of "counter-hegemonic' struggle against authority. History demonstrates both the importance and the complex role of criminal law in the exercise of power.

**Bibliography**
- D.H. Brown, The Genesis of the Canadian Criminal Code of 1892 (Toronto, 1989)
- D.O. Carrigan, *Crime and Punishment in Canada: A History* (Toronto, 1991)
- F.M. Greenwood and B. Wright eds., *Canadian State Trials Volume One: Law, Politics and Security Measures, 1607-1837* (Toronto, 1996)
- D. Hay, "Property, Authority and the Criminal Law" in Hay, Linebaugh, Thompson *et al, Albion's Fatal Tree* (New York, 1975)
- M. Ignatieff, "State, Civil Society and Total Institutions: A Critique of Recent Social History of Punishment" in Sugarman ed., *Legality, Ideology and the State* (New York, 1985)
- J. Langbein, "Albion's Fatal Flaws" (1983) 98 *Past and Present*, 96
- P. Linebaugh, "(Marxist) Social History and (Conservative) Legal History: A Reply to Professor Langbein" (1985) 60 *New York L.R.* 242.
- R. McGowan, "The Image of Justice and Reform of the Criminal Law in Early Nineteenth Century England" (1983) 32 *Buffalo Law Review*, 89
- R.C. MacLeod ed., *Lawful Authority: Readings on the History of Criminal Justice in Canada* (Toronto, 1988)
- G. Parker, "The Origins of the Canadian Criminal Code" in D.H. Flaherty ed., *Essays in the History of Canadian Law Volume 1* (Toronto, 1981)
- J. Phillips, T. Loo, and S. Lewthwaite eds, *Essays in the History of Canadian Law Volume V: Crime and Criminal Justice* (Toronto, 1994)
- W. Pue and B. Wright eds., *Canadian Perspectives on Law and Society: Issues in Legal History* (Ottawa, 1988)
- M. Storch, "The Plague of Blue Locusts" (1975) 20 *International Review of Social History*, 61
- C.J. Taylor, "The Kingston Ontario Penitentiary and Moral Architecture" (1979) 12 *Histoire sociale/Social History*, 385

**Questions/Discussion**
1. How would a pluralist, a conflict theorist or a critical theorist view the content and enforcement of criminal law? What would be the major points of debate in their respective analyses of the criminal law in the areas of theft, homicide and industrial pollution?
2. How would a pluralist and a critical theorist differ in their approaches to the reform of the laws which regulate behaviours in the area of morality (for example, homosexuality or drugs)?
3. What are the contributions of feminist approaches to the analysis and reform of the criminal law? How do these approaches differ from traditional legal approaches to criminal law?
4. What is the relevance of historical perspectives on criminal law and reform? Is it useful to be informed by the past when we consider changes to the present system?

## References and Further Reading
- Abella, R., "Equality, Human Rights, Women and the Justice System" (1994), 39 McGill Law Journal 489.
- Bierne, P. and R. Quinney, eds., *Marxism and Law*. (Toronto: Wiley, 1979).
- Boyd, S. and E. Sheehy, "Feminist Perspectives on Law: Canadian Theory and Practice" (1986), 2 Canadian Journal of Women and the Law 1.
- Boyle, C., *et al. A Feminist Review of Criminal Law* (Ottawa: Supply and Services, 1985).
- Brockman, J., " 'Resistance by the Club' to the Feminization of the Legal Profession" (1992), 7 Canadian Journal of Law and Society 47.
- Collins, H. *Marxism and Law* (Toronto: Oxford University Press, 1982).
- Currie, D., "Feminist Encounters with Postmodernism: Exploring the Impasse of Patriarchy and Law" (1992), 5 Canadian Journal of Women and the Law 63.
- Currie, E., "Crime and the Conservatives" (Fall 1985) *Dissent* 427.
- Fitzgerald, M., *et al., Crime and Society: Readings in History and Theory* (London: RKP and Oxford University Press, 1981).
- Fudge, J., "What Do We Mean By Law and Social Transformation?" (1990), 5 Canadian Journal of Law and Society 47.
- Hall, S., *et al., Policing the Crisis* (London: Macmillan, 1978).
- Jessop, B., *The Capitalist State* (Oxford: Martin Robertson, 1981).
- Nelken, D., "Critical Criminal Law" (1987), 14 Journal of Law and Society 105.
- Panitch, L., ed., *The Canadian State* (Toronto: University of Toronto Press, 1977)
- Reiman, J., *The Rich Get Richer and the Poor Get Prison* (Toronto: Wiley, 1979).
- Russell, M., "A Feminist Analysis of the Criminal Trial Process" (1989/90), 3 Canadian Journal of Women and the Law 552.
- Smart, C., "Feminism and Law: Some Problems of Analysis and Strategy" (1986), 14 International Journal of the Sociology of Law 109.
- Smart, C., *Women, Crime and Criminology: A Feminist Critique* (London: Routledge, 1967).
- Snider, L., "Feminism, Punishment and the Potential of Empowerment" (1994), 9 Canadian Journal of Law and Society 75,
- Snider, L., "The Potential of the Criminal Justice System to Promote Feminist Concerns." Paper presented to the American Society of Criminology (Chicago: November, 1988).

# 3

# THE PRODUCTION OF CRIMINAL LAW

**General Introduction**
*R.P. Saunders*

This chapter examines the authoritative sources of criminal law and the problems, issues and concerns associated with both the evolution and the current production of criminal law in Canada. The history of the development of criminal legislation and criminal common law is not a particularly illustrious one in this country and we will examine some of the continuing issues and factors which have led to and continue to create various problems in the area. The focus throughout the chapter is on the processes and the institutions which produce criminal law. In this regard, it should be stressed that we are not exhaustive in our approach to the production of criminal law, for while we focus on two of the principal sources of criminal law — Parliament and the courts — we largely ignore (at least for the moment) another important source in the development of criminal law, that is, administrative law. A fourth source, constitutional law is examined within the specific context of the role and powers of the courts to make criminal law, and again in Chapter 7 in reference to the developing area of Charter defences.

In regard to administrative law, the effect of the multitude of administrative regulations, internal guidelines, bureaucratic procedures and employee manuals is important and often determining, and should not be forgotten when looking at the more traditional and often more formal aspects of the production of criminal law. This is particularly true in the areas of probation, parole, and prisoners' rights, some of which we examine later in this text (for example, when issues surrounding parole are looked at in Chapter 5.) In a similar vein, we must not forget the effects of the exercise of an individual agent's discretion on the operation and enforcement of the law, and we must keep in mind that although the criminal law often appears "neat", self-contained and discrete in its formal manifestations such as legislation and court pronouncements, the reality for the individual involved in the criminal justice system, whether as an accused, a victim, a witness or an agent of the system, can be something very different. Also, such realities can be coloured by the status, gender, class, ethnicity, sexual orientation, language, education and/or past relationship of the individuals involved. We return to many of these issues surrounding the exercise of discretion when the problems associated with police enforcement of the law and the exercise of prosecutorial duties are examined in Chapter 4.

As for the question of why the *process* of producing criminal law is important, it is imperative to be aware that how we proceed with change can be very important as to a reform measure's ultimate worth and success. In this regard, there are various issues that should be kept in mind as we look both at the different ways in which criminal law is produced and at the differing attributes of the responsible institutions. These issues can be used as standards or reference points as the reader proceeds through the chapter in order to evaluate the effectiveness and validity of the various reform mechanisms.

The first issue to keep in mind throughout the chapter is that of "input". Input has several aspects to it which relate to the production of criminal law. "Who" it is who produces the criminal law and their qualifications is a question which was not addressed in traditional legal writings. If the traditional assumptions are that law is representative of society as a whole, that law is merely reflective of widely held and shared values and perspectives, and that the law is neutral in its formulation, the question of "who" the producer is is not especially important. If, however, a more critical or socio-legal stance is taken, then the question takes on an important dimension. In this light, one would want to examine the class, gender, and ethnicity of the state agents as a group and question whether such factors have significant consequences for the criminal law which is produced, enforced and applied. For example, judges as a group are not representative of society as a whole, and women and visible minorities in particular are greatly underrepresented in the judiciary.[1] As a result, can we see any effects of this lack of balance in the criminal law in areas such as sexual assault[2] or domestic violence,[3] or generally in the treatment of native people or visible minorities in the criminal justice system.[4] The same types of questions can also be raised in regard to legislators, police officers and Crown prosecutors.

In the articles in this chapter it is apparent that the production of criminal law is for the most part controlled by legal professionals. On the one hand, this might seem perfectly natural given the issues, concerns and rights involved and considering what is at stake in the outcome of criminal matters. But if we shift our focus away from traditional legalistic questions, then our response might be different and more critical. If we look at the criminal law as a matter which affects us all in society, as a device which can be seen as only one instrument of social control (albeit an intrusive one) among many, then the argument must be for the widest possible input into its production and enforcement. Choices must be made as to what is to be brought within the ambit of the criminal justice system and alternatives must be examined as to their suitability or superiority, and these decisions must not be left up to any one group of interests, particularly one as narrowly based as the legal profession.[5] But it is not only the lack of participation of a variety of groups in society which creates problems, it is also the type of approach and expertise which legal professionals bring to the job of criminal law reform.

Lawyers are by training and practice process-oriented, concentrating on the rules and procedures by which disputes are taken through the system. The substantive policy issues and choices which lie at the heart of the process, that is, what activities the criminal law is meant to encompass or what it is the criminal law ought to be accomplishing, are not within that area of expertise. Also, by virtue of their common law traditions and reasoning processes — traditions and processes which consistently look backward to precedent and established practice, and

---

[1] According to *Touchstones for Change: Equality, Diversity and Accountability — The Report on Gender Equality in the Legal Profession* prepared by the Task Force on Gender Equality (Ottawa: The Canadian Bar Association, 1993), women represented approximately 12% of federally appointed judges and 13% of provincially appointed judges in 1993.

[2] This issue is dealt with extensively in Chapter 8.

[3] See, for example, Tim Quigley, "Battered Women and the Defence of Provocation" (1991), 55(2) Saskatchewan Law Review 223-261, Martha Shaffer, "R. v. Lavallée: A Review Essay" (1990), 22 Ottawa Law Review 607-624, Anne McGillvray, "Battered Women: Definition, Models and Prosecutorial Policy" (1987), 6 Canadian Journal of Family Law 15, excerpted in Chapter 4, Section 2; and D. Brodsky, "Educating Juries: The Battered Woman Defence in Canada" (1987), 25 Alberta Law Review 461; E. Comack, "Justice For Battered Women?" (1988), 22 Canadian Dimension 8; and *R. v. Lavallée*, excerpted in Chapter 7.

[4] See, for example, the recent *Report of the Commission on Systemic Racism in the Ontario Criminal Justice System* (Toronto: Queen's Printer for Ontario, 1995); the *Report of the Aboriginal Justice Inquiry of Manitoba* (Winnipeg: Aboriginal Justice Inquiry, 1991); The *Report of the Royal Commission on the Donald Marshall, Jr., Prosecution: Findings and Recommendations, Volume One* (Halifax: The Commission, 1989); and Michael Harris, *Justice Denied: The Law versus Donald Marshall* (Toronto: Totem Books, 1986). Excerpts from the Marshall inquiry report are reproduced in Chapter 8, section 2.

[5] See Chapter 3 of Olsen's *The State Elite*, under Further Reading, as to the narrowness of the representation (though published in 1980, the book remains a valuable contribution to the literature in this area), as well as various articles given in the reading list of section 2 of this chapter.

which defend the status quo — lawyers tend be quite limited and conservative in their vision.[6] These tendencies are important if we consider the need for forward-looking, flexible and adaptable processes in achieving progressive criminal law reform.

In the work and focus of legal professionals, one also sees a concentration on the formal aspects of the criminal justice system, notably in regard to the centrality which they give to the trial process and the work of judges. The trial process cannot be dismissed as meaningless or unimportant, but the focus must shift to other segments of the system. Not only do the overwhelming number of people charged plead guilty and thereby forgo their right to trial, but such an approach ignores questions of why and how those people arrived in the criminal justice system, as result of whose actions, and just as importantly, who did not make it there, who was weeded out and by what process or according to what criteria. For example, can one see factors such as income status gender or ethnicity at work in the enforcement and prosecution process? These are the types of concerns that are missed if we concentrate on the more formal aspects of the criminal process.

Given the quickly changing nature of society and the consequent nature of the required responses on the part of the criminal law, regressive, formalistic, and legalistic approaches do not serve well the production of criminal law. What *is* needed is the input on criminal justice and social policy experts, experts both in "society" and in the appropriate policy responses required. Of course, this is an idealized view, for such experts can be wrong or the reforms can be distorted in practice, but recognizing such problems does not deny the potential benefits of opening up the production process to the diversity of views and insights that are too often denied a voice now.

A good example of the closed nature of the process can be found in the former Law Reform Commission of Canada, a federal body which, until 1992, advised the government on, among other things, criminal law reform. The make-up of the LRCC's criminal law project team was almost exclusively legal professionals, and the consultation process was similarly restricted to groups like the defence bar, the chiefs of police, the judiciary, and Crown prosecutors.[7] What could be expected and what did occur was a relatively sterile, legalistic, technocratic approach to criminal law reform, an approach which focused on form over substance. This approach is not exclusive to the work of the Commission, but rather is found generally in the work of the criminal justice bureaucracy itself. How to broaden the input effectively and consistently remains one of the crucial problems facing the criminal justice system. Even with this enhanced input there would be no guarantee that all the resulting policies would be the "right" ones, but at a minimum the increased potential for success would be there along with an increased acceptability of those policies. Interestingly, a new Law Commission of Canada is currently (1996) being set up with, according to the Department of Justice's news release of October, 1995, a promise to adopt "a new approach to law reform, governed by several principles [including] ... responsiveness; innovation; inclusiveness; a multi-displinary approach and openness".

The point of acceptability brings in another and final aspect of the issues surrounding input, that of what we can broadly call "democracy" or accountability. Those who make policy that affects all of society should be accountable and responsible in some manner to those who are affected by the policy. Since the advent of the Canadian Charter of Rights and Freedoms in 1982, we have been faced with the growing intervention by an appointed, tenured judiciary in the production of criminal law. Judicial intervention did occur in the era before the Charter but it was largely restricted to issues surrounding the division of powers, the interpretation of statute

---

[6] See generally, E. S. Robinson, *Law and The Lawyers* (Toronto: MacMillan, 1973).
[7] For a discussion of many of these issues surrounding the work of the former Law Reform Commission of Canada, see the Hastings and Saunders article reproduced in section 1 of this chapter.

law and the control of the process (which affects the content and operation of the law in practice). These issues, along with Charter issues, are addressed in section 2 of this chapter. The point to be kept in mind is the judiciary's lack of accountability to the public which the judiciary allegedly serves. This is particularly important when the lack of representation and the politics and secrecy surrounding the appointment process within the judicial branch are addressed.[8]

Of course, it is not only the judicial branch where the absence of accountability is evident. Criticisms can be raised about the reality of accountability and responsibility in regard to the federal parliament and the provincial legislatures, but at a minimum there is an argument that the "potential" for accountability exists even though it may not often be attained (for good or for bad[9]). Furthermore, concerns surround the lack of accountability that exists in the exercise of discretion by many criminal justice agents. The exercise of discretion can have a very great impact on the way criminal law in practice is produced and on its real effects on individuals coming in contact with the criminal law. Too often the exercise of discretion is part of a hidden, non-reviewable process over which little or no control is exercised. Good examples of the (often unfettered) exercise of discretion can be found in the work of the Crown Prosecutors and of the police, both of which are discussed in Chapter 4.

Input and its various facets are not the only issues to keep in mind, however, as one proceeds through the readings. Another is that of certainty, the idea that the law should be "knowable" and understandable for all citizens, that the law should be readily accessible. While there is a self-evident sense of fairness in this notion, unfortunately the goal is too often not fulfilled. Criminal law remains the preserve of legal professionals with its arcane language and rituals that allow those professionals to maintain their control. The question to keep in mind is which production process might best accomplish this goal of certainty? Which process is more likely to result in policies accessible to, understood by, and accepted by the greatest number? For example, an argument can be made that statute law is inherently easier to find and to comprehend than case law, which often encompasses a series of cases and requires the ability to distinguish, delineate, and comprehend the various fact situations and rulings. Judicial decisions are largely inaccessible to the layperson because those judgments are written for other lawyers and not the general population that is subject to the rules expounded in the cases. It is not that statute law necessarily or automatically fulfills standards of certainty, but again it is the potential which might exist in one forum versus the other. One of the basic premises of our legal system is that citizens are subject to rules which are set out in advance and therefore, presumably, "knowable". How true is this in practice given the need for lawyers' expertise in criminal cases today, and what is the potential for fulfilling this goal?

Consistency of approach and purpose is another important issue to keep in mind. As we will see in the readings, legislative responses have proven to be haphazard and uneven. In addition, there is a call for the establishment and use of general principles to guide the development of criminal justice policy and to avoid piecemeal reform measures that respond to short term, expedient, political concerns. The present Criminal Code has yet to provide these principles, though we can see numerous versions of them proposed in various reports, notably in the

---

[8] See, for example, J. S. Zeigel, "Appointments to the Supreme Court of Canada" (1994), 5 Constitutional Forum 10-15, Peter Russell and J.S. Zeigel, "Federal Judicial Appointments: An Appraisal of the First Mulroney Government's Appointments and the New Judicial Advisory Committees" (1991), 41 University of Toronto Law Journal 4-37, J.S. Zeigel, "Federal Judicial Appointments: The Time is Ripe for Change" (1987), 37 University of Toronto Law Review 1-24, and Carl Baar, "Judicial Appointments and the Quality of Adjudication: The American Experience in a Canadian Perspective" (1986). 20 Thémis 1-26.

[9] A good example in this regard is the issue of capital punishment which has been abolished as a penalty in the Criminal Code even though surveys of the general population consistently indicate strong support for such a measure.

government's *Criminal Law in Canadian Society* (which is excerpted below), which stated (p. 38):

> The basic problem confronting criminal law and the criminal justice system ... is not the variety of specific concerns and complaints about particular phenomena — which are mere symptoms — but rather a debilitating confusion at the most basic level, concerning what the criminal law ought to be doing.[10]

The problem of the lack of consistency can be seen not only internally within the individual units of the criminal justice system, but also between different components of the system. The courts often have different goals or principles in mind from those of the legislature, correctional authorities may be attempting to accomplish different goals again, and the same can hold true for the police, Crown prosecutors, parole officers, and probation agencies. The failure to develop a comprehensive set of principles to guide the development and operation of the criminal law both within and between criminal justice institutions is a major problem that continues to cause disharmony and inconsistency.

A final point in this regard is that the process should possess a degree of flexibility so as to allow the criminal law to adapt and adjust readily to changing social conventions and perspectives. The judicial system has often been criticised for the slow development of the law that occurs in the courts. It is a process not particularly well suited to speedy, comprehensive changes in the law, yet under the Charter it is becoming a popular forum for the resolution of criminal justice policy issues. Given the time it takes for a matter to work its way through the court system and the focused and narrow nature of most cases, broad-based policy movement is generally not seen in the courts except over a long period of time.

In sum, the reader should approach an examination of the processes and structures that produce criminal law with a critical and questioning eye. It is important to keep in mind these issues that are germane to the production of criminal law and to be wary of the claims that are made by the producers. The questions of input, certainty, consistency, and flexibility cannot be overlooked in the search for a critical understanding of the origins and substance of criminal law. Criminal law is not a given or a constant from heaven; it expresses real values, and choices have been made by real people who have been influenced by concrete structures and perceptions. To understand the potential, limitations and deficiencies of criminal law, we must understand the dynamics of the relationships and processes which produce it. And such an understanding presupposes that we have in mind certain qualities or standards important in regard to both the processes and the final product.

A final point to make is that the relationship between processes can often be a problematic one in the sense that the failure of one institution or system to adequately deal with a problem can lead to change emanating from another group. One of the arguments about matters such as abortion or many common law defences being dealt with by the courts is that the legislative authorities have themselves failed to act sufficiently and responsibly. And there is the argument that parliament is sometimes pressured to move on matters such as sexual assault due to the inability and/or sensitivity of the courts in handling the issues involved. The relationship between the processes is, therefore, often an interactive and reflexive one and, though they are presented as compartmentalized subjects, the individual processes are neither isolated nor self-contained.

---

[10] See also the Law Reform Commission's *Our Criminal Law* (Report 3), 1976, or the report of the Canadian Sentencing Commission, *Sentencing Reform. A Canadian Approach* (1987).

## 3.1 LEGISLATION AND THE ROLE OF PARLIAMENT

**Introduction**

*R.P. Saunders*

The role of parliament in the production of criminal law is an important one: this section addresses the issues and problems that arise in the context of fulfilling that role. There are several dimensions to the role which require examination, including the nature and history of the process, the inherent problems of the current process, the reform mechanisms that attach to the process, the role of the provinces and the constitutional issues surrounding the creation of criminal law. In regard to the latter, this section begins with a basic definition of criminal law from a constitutional perspective, that is, which level of government has the authority under the constitution to make criminal law.

As is obvious from the readings, only the federal parliament has the exclusive power to make acts criminal by virtue of paragraph 27 of section 91 of the Constitution Act, 1867, which gives the federal government authority in regard to "The Criminal Law, except the Constitution of Courts of Criminal Jurisdiction, but including the Procedure in Criminal Matters".[1] This does not mean that the provinces have no role to play, for not only do they enact many laws that carry with them penal sanctions (and are usually referred to as "quasi-criminal laws"),[2] but the provinces also have an important role to play in the implementation and enforcement of the criminal law.[3]

As for the provinces' role in regard to the former, the provinces enact a wide range of laws within their jurisdiction that carry varying types of penalties, including fines and imprisonment. These offenses are generally considered less serious than federal offenses and the penalties which attach are usually less onerous. This perception can be deceptive, however, for these provincial offences often serve important regulatory functions and the breaking of them can have serious consequences, if not immediately, then in the long term. For example, individual hunting law violations may not be especially serious and the same is true for the breaking of parking regulations, but if these rules were not there or were continually and uniformly ignored, then wildlife or the free movement of traffic might be endangered. Furthermore, effective environmental regulation is a matter that is increasingly seen as imperative, even though the cumulative damage from pollution is sometimes not seen until years in the future. Also, convictions for these types of offences can have important effects on individuals through the loss of liberty, loss of employment, or the loss of money in the form of fines.

As for the implementation role played by the provinces, how the law is enforced and in what areas (both geographically and topically) have a very real effect on the meaning and experience of the criminal law for all citizens.[4] For example, if police forces are instructed not to lay charges in regard to certain types of crimes, this changes the complexion and substance of the law (see Chapter 4, section 1). Even before the relevant section on abortion in the Criminal Code was

---

1 See also s. 91(28) Where the federal government is given control over "The Establishment, Maintenance, and Management of Penitentiaries".
2 See s. 92(15) of the Constitution Act, 1867, which gives the provinces authority over "The Imposition of Punishment by Fine, Penalty, or Imprisonment for enforcing any Law of the Province made in relation to any Matter coming within any of the Classes of Subjects enumerated in this Section", that is, within the powers of the provinces as set out in s. 92.
3 See s. 92(14) of the Constitution Act, 1982, which gives the provinces authority in regard to "The Administration of Justice in the Province, including the Constitution, Maintenance, and Organization of Provincial Courts, both of Civil and of Criminal Jurisdiction ... "
4 The role of municipal authorities can be important in this regard as well in fulfilling their provincially mandated responsibilities, but their role will not be considered separately.

ruled invalid and of no effect, the Quebec government had refused to prosecute under the section due to the unwillingness of juries to convict. In the corrections sector, if the provinces do not commit funds to treatment facilities and programmes, the provisions for such in the Criminal Code or the Young Offenders Act will themselves be of little value to those who were targeted by the drafters of those sections.[5] Therefore, while a great deal of attention may not be focused explicitly on the roles which the provinces play, those roles and responsibilities should be recognized as important and at times determining.

Fortunately, in the last decade, there has been an increasing amount of consultation, co-operation, and co-ordination between the two levels of government. In the area of criminal law reform, this has at times meant in practice the federal government seeking the agreement of the provinces before any reform is designed and implemented. This is often regarded as necessary if the reforms are to be effectively instituted by provincially appointed prosecutors, police and correctional agents. For our limited purposes here, however, we concentrate on the federal power to enact criminal law, although we recognize that this arena represents only one, albeit important, facet of the production process.

The constitutional division of responsibilities between the two levels of government means that the courts are called upon to decide if a government is acting within its sphere of power, and to do that the courts have developed tests when deciding if a particular subject matter properly falls within the criminal power or not. These tests are quite vague and open, and criticisms have been raised that it often comes down to the eye of any particular "beholding" court. In the readings by Hogg and Ewaschuk and in the two cases of *Rio Hotel* and *MacNeil*, note what the tests and important factors are as to determining criminal legislation and subject matter, and ask yourself how certain and helpful these tests really are.

In regard to the historical development of the criminal law in Canada, one of the original problems was the lack of a consistent and comprehensive set of principles, and a consequent lack of direction to guide the evolution of criminal law. At its origin, we can witness this in the adoption of the first Criminal Code in 1892, a code which was not a truly comprehensive code but rather a compilation of the criminal common law and criminal legislation up to that point in time. It was a reflection of not only indigenous case law and legislation, but also (and more importantly) English law in the area. What this means, on the one hand, of course, is that the Criminal Code at the outset was not a break with the past and a new beginning, but rather was a continuation of laws and rules reflecting older conceptions of society, values, and morality, and enshrining "scientific" facts and knowledge from earlier periods. The Code, therefore, in one sense was outdated from its very birth. On the other hand, there was no overarching set of principles and goals with which to not only implement and enforce the code, but also guide the evolution and development of the code.

The problems found with the enactment of the original code can be seen in the course of its development through the years. It was a haphazard and piecemeal development that responded to a series of crises and issues (both real and perceived), political responses that resulted in various add-ons to the code and to criminal legislation in general. The changes were for the most part political and expedient reactions, lacking a commitment to longer term goals of the criminal justice system. The need to remove politics from the process, or at least the need to introduce independent policy advice to the process has been recognized for a long time and was one of the reasons behind the establishment of the now disbanded Law Reform Commission of Canada (LRCC) in 1971. Many of the same problems remain today, however, in regard to the

---

[5] For example, s. 255 of the Criminal Code provides for the possibility of treatment as an alternative to imprisonment and/or fines for those convicted under s. 253, the breathalizer offence, and who have alcohol or drug problems. Yet not all the provisions have been proclaimed in force in all the provinces and are therefore not available to all offenders across the country.

political, short term nature of the criminal law reform process. While it can be argued that expedient concerns will always be there in some form or another, such concerns should only emphasize the need for independent, principled planning in regard to the long term development of criminal law in Canada. As for the work of the LRCC in this area, the Hastings and Saunders article raises various concerns about the worth of this work, of the approach taken and of the process used, and is generally pessimistic as to the overall value of the LRCC and its contributions to the production of criminal law. More importantly, the article also addresses the issues related to approaches to criminal law reform generally, and the need for fully social approaches to such reform rather than narrow, legalistic, technical approaches. As noted in the "General Introduction" above, this need appears to be recognized in the announcement of the government's latest initiative in creating a new "Law Commission of Canada".

Other problems or issues to keep in mind throughout the readings are those related to input, as noted above in the introduction of this Chapter. Ask yourself who has input into the system and how effective is that input? What type of expertise is being employed in the production of criminal law in this arena and what are the prospects of meaningfully opening up the process to other interests and types of knowledge? The parliamentary process is very often a secretive process with the "real" decisions being made behind closed doors. Many of these concerns are fully addressed only in courses on political decision-making, but they are important to the type of criminal law ultimately produced. Even with its faults, it might be argued that the legislative route is still the most democratic and the one that holds the greatest potential for better and wider input, particularly when we contrast it with the production of criminal law within the judicial process?

Currently, there is an on-going criminal law reform project involving several criminal justice agencies, a project whose goal is the development of an all-new, comprehensive criminal code for Canada. The preliminary findings and conclusions of this project, following closely on some of the work of the Law Reform Commission, are found in the 1982 document, *Criminal Law in Canadian Society*, which is reproduced in part in this chapter and which, though published in 1982, continues to inform and influence government activity in criminal law reform. The document, not surprisingly, explicitly reflects a consensus perspective on the foundations underlying criminal law and its enforcement.

## The Constitutional Basis of the Criminal Law Power*
### P.W. Hogg

* Excerpt from Hogg, Peter W., "The Constitutional Basis of the Criminal Law Power" in *Constitutional Law of Canada*

**Definition of Criminal Law**

The federal Parliament's power to enact "criminal law" has proved very difficult to define. In the *Board of Commerce* case (1922) Viscount Haldane held that the power was applicable only "where the subject matter is one which by its very nature belongs to the domain of criminal jurisprudence". Like Viscount Haldane's definitions of the peace, order, and good government power and the trade and commerce power, this definition of criminal law appeared to be too narrow. Although Viscount Haldane did not spell out what he meant by a "domain of criminal jurisprudence", the phrase could be read as freezing the criminal law into a mould established at some earlier time, presumably 1867.

After Viscount Haldane's death (in 1928), Lord Atkin in the *P.A.T.A.* case (1931) repudiated the domain of criminal jurisprudence theory and made clear that the federal power was "not confined to what was criminal by the law of England or of any Province in 1867", and that "the power may extend to legislation to make new crimes". Lord Atkin in the *P.A.T.A.* case offered a rival definition of criminal law:

> The criminal quality of an act cannot be discerned by intuition; nor can it be discovered by reference to any standard but one: Is the act prohibited with penal consequences?

This definition appeared to be too wide in that it would enable the federal Parliament to expand its jurisdiction indefinitely, simply by framing its legislation in the form of a prohibition coupled with a penalty. Nor was this definition sufficiently qualified when Lord Atkin later said that "the only limitation on the plenary power of the Dominion to determine what shall or shall not be criminal is the condition that Parliament shall not in the guise of enacting criminal legislation in truth and in substance encroach on any of the classes of subjects enumerated in s. 92". This says no more than the trite proposition that a law must be properly classifiable as in relation to the criminal law, and it no doubt contemplates the possibility of a statute in which the prohibition and penalty are unimportant appendages to provisions which really seek to accomplish the legislative goal by other means. Even setting aside this kind of "colourable" statute, which no-one would seriously seek to uphold as criminal, the *P.A.T.A.* definition is still too wide because it would uphold any federal law which employs a prohibition and penalty as its primary mode of operation. If the only characteristics of the criminal law are the formal ones of a prohibition and a penalty, then there is no principled basis for denying to a law with those characteristics the criminal classification.

It is clear that a proper balance in the distribution of legislative powers requires some third ingredient in the definition of criminal law. This was demonstrated in the *Margarine Reference* (1951), where the law in issue simply prohibited the manufacture, importation or sale of margarine. It was common ground that the purpose of this law was to protect the dairy industry. The Privy Council held that, although the law perfectly fitted the criminal form of a prohibition coupled with a penalty, the economic object of protecting an industry from its competitors made the law in pith and substance in relation to property and civil rights in the province.

It follows from the *Margarine Reference* that the elusive third ingredient of a criminal law is typically criminal public purpose. In the Supreme Court of Canada, Rand J., whose reasoning was adopted by the Privy Council, said that a prohibition was not criminal unless it served "a public purpose which can support it as being in relation to the criminal law". And what were the public purposes which would qualify? "Public peace, order, security, health, morality" these are the ordinary though not exclusive ends served by that law ... ". It will be noticed that Rand J. was careful not to give an exhaustive definition of the purpose of the criminal law. It was enough for him to be confident that the protection of the dairy industry was not a qualifying purpose. But while he characterized that purpose as "to benefit one group of persons as against competitors in business", no doubt the proponents of such protective legislation would deny that such a narrow definition was appropriate and would define the purpose in terms of national economic policy of benefit to all Canadians. Rand

J.'s tendentious description of the margarine law, and his failure to provide a test for the identification of a typically criminal public purpose, detract from the value of his much-quoted opinion. Indeed, it is fair to say that the requirement of a typically public purpose is really only a slightly more sophisticated formulation of Viscount Haldane's "domain of criminal jurisprudence".

. . . .

The *Margarine Reference* should not be read as denying that the criminal law can serve economic ends. A large part of the criminal law is devoted to the protection of private property — a purpose, one might add, which confers a larger benefit on those who own property than on those who do not. But, apart from the traditional crimes of theft and its many variants, various forms of economic regulation have been upheld as criminal law. The *P.A.T.A.* case itself upheld anti-combines (competition) laws under the criminal power, and under this general rubric a variety of federal laws have been upheld, including prohibitions on price discriminations and resale price maintenance and a judicial power to enjoin some of the prohibited practices. The false prospectus provisions of the Criminal Code have been upheld as criminal law, establishing that securities regulation — at least in crude form — is within the criminal law. In short, there is abundant support for Laskin's assertion that "resort to the criminal law power to proscribe undesirable commercial practices is today as characteristic of its exercise as has been resort thereto to curb violence or immoral conduct".

## Re Nova Scotia Board of Censors and MacNeil
(1978), 44 C.C.C. (2d) 316 at 335 (S.C.C.).

Appeal by the Nova Scotia Board of Censors and the Attorney-General of Nova Scotia from a judgment of the Nova Scotia Supreme Court, Appeal Division, 78 D.L.R. (3d) 46, 36 C.C.C. (2d) 45, *sub nom. MacNeil v. The Queen*, 14 N.S.R. (2d) 225 *sub nom. McNeil v. A.-G. N.S.*, declaring certain sections of the *Theatres and Amusements Act*, R.S.N.S. 1967, c. 304, as amended, and certain Regulations made thereunder *ultra vires*.

[Excerpts from the judgment of Ritchie J. are reproduced below.]

RITCHIE J.: — This is an appeal brought with leave of this Court from a judgment of the Appeal Division of the Supreme Court of Nova Scotia rendered pursuant to an application made at the instance of the respondent McNeil whose standing to initiate the proceedings in a representative capacity on behalf of other Nova Scotians was confirmed by order of this Court (see 55 D.L.R. (3d) 632, [1976] 2 S.C.R. 265, 12 N.S.R. (2d) 85, 5 N.R. 48 [affg 46 D.L.R. (3d) 259, 9 N.S.R. (2d) 506]).

The respondent's application was for a declaration that certain sections of the *Theatres and Amusements Act*, R.S.N.S. 1967 c. 304, as amended, and certain Regulations made thereunder were *ultra vires* and beyond the legislative competence of the Province of Nova Scotia.

The exciting cause of the application appears to have been the exercise by the Nova Scotia Amusements Regulation Board (hereinafter referred to as "the Board") of the authority which the Act purports to confer on it, to prevent a film entitled "Last Tango in Paris" from being exhibited in the theatres of Nova Scotia.

It is the statutory provisions purporting to authorize the Board to regulate and control the film industry within the Province of Nova Scotia according to standards fixed by it, which are challenged by the respondent on the ground that the citizens of Nova Scotia are thereby denied, on moral grounds, their right to exercise their freedom of choice in the viewing of films and theatre performances which might otherwise be available to them, and it is further alleged that the legislation constitutes an invasion of fundamental freedoms.

The questions raised by the application were reserved for the consideration of the Appeal Division by order of Mr. Justice Hart made pursuant to s. 30(3) of the *Judicature Act*, 1972 (NS), c. 2, and that Division having reserved its decision, granted the following order:

> It is Hereby Declared that the words 'prohibiting' in sections 2(1)(b) and 2(1)(g) and subsections (2) and (3) of Section 3 of the *Theatres and Amusements Act* are null and void and of no effect being ultra vires the legislature of Nova Scotia.
> It is further declared that regulations 4, 5(1), 13, 18 and 32 made pursuant to the *Theatres and Amusements Act* are null and void and of no effect being ultra vires the legislature of Nova Scotia;

. . . .

In all such cases the Court cannot ignore the rule implicit in the proposition stated as clearly as 1878 by Mr. Justice Strong in *Severn v. The Queen*, 2 S.C.R. 70 at p. 103, that any question as to the validity of provincial legislation is to be approached on the assumption that it was validly enacted. As was said by Fauteux, J., as he then was, in the *Reference re Farm Products Marketing Act* (1957), 7 D.L.R. (2d) 257 at p. 311, [1957] S.C.R. 198 at p. 255:

> There is a *presumptio juris* as to the existence of the *bona fide* intention of a legislative body to confine itself to its own sphere and a presumption of similar nature that general words in a statute are not intended to extend its operation beyond the territorial authority of the Legislature.

When the Act and the Regulations are read as a whole, I find that to be primarily directed to the regulation, supervision and control of the film business within the Province of Nova Scotia, including the use and exhibition of films in that Province. To this end the impugned provisions are, in my view, enacted for the purpose of reinforcing the authority vested in a provincially appointed Board to perform the task of regulation which includes the authority to prevent the exhibition of films which the Board, applying its own local standards, has rejected as unsuitable for viewing by provincial audiences. This legislation is concerned with dealings in and the use of property (i.e., films) which take place wholly within the Province and in my opinion it is subject to the same considerations as those which were held to be applicable in such cases as *Shannon et al. v. Lower Mainland Dairy Products Board et al.*, [1938] 4 D.L.R. 81, [1938] A.C. 708, [1938] 2 W.W.R. 604; *Home Oil Distributors Ltd. et al. v. A.-G.B.C.*, [1940] 2 D.L.R. 609, [1940] S.C.R. 444, and *Caloil Inc. v. A.-G. Can. et al.* (1971), 20 D.L.R. (3d) 472, [1971] S.C.R. 543, [1971] 4 W.W.R. 37.

In the *Shannon* case, the Natural Products Marketing legislation was put in issue as constituting an encroachment on "the regulation of trade and commerce", a subject assigned exclusively to the Parliament of Canada by s. 91(2), and in the course of delivering the opinion of the Judicial Committee, Lord Atkin had occasion to say of this ground [at p. 84 D.L.R., p. 718 A.C.]:

> It is sufficient to say upon the first ground that it is apparent that the legislation in question in confined to regulating transactions that take place wholly within the Province, and are therefore within the sovereign powers granted to the legislature in that respect by s. 92 of the British North America Act.

More recently, in commenting on that case and the *Home Oil* case, *supra*, Mr. Justice Pigeon had occasion to say in *Caloil Inc. v. A.-G. Can., supra*, at p. 477 D.L.R., p. 549 S.C.R.:

> It is to be noted that the *Shannon* and *Home Oil* cases both dealt with the validity of provincial regulation of local trades. They hold that provincial authority over transactions taking place wholly within the Province is, as a rule, applicable to products imported from another country, or brought in from another Province, as well as to local products. However, it must be borne in mind that the division of constitutional authority under the Canadian Constitution often results in overlapping legislation.

It will be seen that, in my opinion, the impugned legislation constitutes nothing more than the exercise of provincial authority over transactions taking place wholly within the Province and it applies to the "regulating, exhibition, sale and exchange of films" whether those films have been imported from another country or not.

We are concerned, however, in this appeal with a decision of the Appeal Division of the Supreme Court of Nova Scotia in which the majority quite clearly struck down the legislation as *ultra vires* on the sole ground that it was concerned with morality and as such constituted an invasion of the criminal law field reserved to the exclusive legislative authority of Parliament under s. 91(27) of the *British North America Act, 1867*.

The following passage from the reasons of judgment of the Judges concerned serve to indicate the narrow basis on which they proceeded [78 D.L.R. (3d) 46, 36 C.C.C. (2d) 45, *sub nom. McNeil v. The Queen*, 14 N.S.R. (2d) 255 [*sub nom. McNeil v. A.-G. N.S.*]. In my view this is most clearly stated by Mr. Justice Cooper when he says [at pp. 50-1 D.L.R., p. 49 C.C.C.]:

> Although the Amusements Regulation Board gave no reasons for placing "Last Tango in Paris" in the so-called rejected classification and thus prohibiting the showing of this film in theatres in this Province I think it clear from the material before us that this action was taken because the film was considered by the Board to offend against acceptable standards of morality.
>
> This leads me to what in my opinion is the sole issue before us in this appeal, namely, has the Legislature of this Province power to enact legislation under which a board or any other body or person may, in the interests of public morality, be authorized to prohibit the showing of a film or is the power to enact such legislation solely reserved for the Parliament of Canada? The short answer to this question is that the field of public morals is an aspect of criminal law which falls within the exclusive jurisdiction of the Parliament of Canada under s. 91(27) of the *British North America Act, 1867* ...

The same question was answered by Chief Justice MacKeigan in the following in the following terms [at p. 48 D.L.R., p. 47 C.C.C.]:

> Censorship of this type is obviously directed at obscenity and other immoral exhibitions. Provincial legislation purporting to make such exhibitions offences punishable by prosecution would indisputably be a direct and invalid invasion of the federal criminal field.

Mr. Justice Coffin expressed himself to the same effect saying [at p. 50 D.L.R., p. 49 C.C.C.]:

> I am limiting my conclusions to the jurisdictional point that the legislation is valid criminal law and I am not entering the field of fundamental freedoms.

Mr. Justice Macdonald on the other hand, while agreeing with the other members of the Court, expressed the view that the legislation was *ultra vires* on the further ground, which had been advanced by the applicant, that it was potentially offensive as constituting " an unwarranted and illegal intrusion upon the fundamental freedoms of the citizens of Canada and in particular the Province of Nova Scotia".

As the latter ground formed no part of the reasoning upon which the judgment appealed from is based, I think it more satisfactory to proceed first to a consideration of the morality issue.

Although no reasons were given by the board for the rejection of "Last Tango in Paris", all members of the Appeal Division were satisfied that its exhibition was prohibited on moral grounds and under all the circumstances I think it to be apparent that this was the case. In any event, I am satisfied that the Board is clothed with authority to fix its own local standards of morality in deciding whether a film is to be rejected or not for local viewing.

Simply put, the issued raised by the majority opinion in the Appeal Divisions is whether the Province is clothed with authority under s. 92 of the *British North America Act, 1867* to regulate the exhibition and distribution of films within its own boundaries which are considered unsuitable for local viewing by a local board on grounds of morality or whether this is a matter of criminal law reserved to Parliament under s. 91(27).

In the present context, the question of whether or not the impugned legislation encroaches on the criminal law authority is, in my opinion, best approached in light of the statement made by Kerwin, C.J.C., in the course of his reasons for judgment in *Lord's Day Alliance of Canada v. A.-G. B.C. et al.* (1959), 19 D.L.R. (2d) 97 at p. 102, 123 C.C.C. 81 at p. 87, [1959] S.C.R. 497 at p. 503, where he said:

> In constitutional matters there is no general area of criminal law and in every case the pith and substance of the legislation in question must be looked at.

Under the authority assigned to it by s. 92(27), the Parliament of Canada has enacted the *Criminal Code*, a penal statute the end purpose of which is the definition and punishment of crime when it has been proved to have been committed.

On the other hand, the *Theatres and Amusements Act* is not concerned with creating a criminal offence or providing for its punishment, but rather in so regulating a business within the Province as to prevent the exhibition in its theatres of performances which do not comply with the standards of propriety established by the Board.

The areas of operation of the two statutes are therefore fundamentally different on dual grounds. In the first place, one is directed to regulating a trade or business where the other is concerned with the definition and punishment of crime; and in the second place, one is preventive while the other is penal.

As the decision of the Appeal Division depends upon equating morality with criminality, I think it desirable at this stage to refer to the definitive statement made by Lord Atkin in this regard in the course of his reasons for judgment in *Proprietary*

*Articles Trade Ass'n v. A.-G. Can.*, [1931] 2 D.L.R. 1 at pp. 9-10, 55 C.C.C. 241 at p. 250, [1931] A.C. 310 at p. 324, where he said:

> Morality and criminality are far from co-extensive; nor is the sphere of criminality necessarily part of a more extensive field covered by morality — unless the moral code necessarily disapproves all acts prohibited by the State, in which case the argument moves in a circle. It appears to their Lordships to be of little value to seek to confine crimes to a category of acts which by their very nature belong to the domain of "criminal jurisprudence" ...

I share the opinion expressed in this passage that morality and criminality are far from co-extensive and it follows in my view that legislation which authorizes the establishment and enforcement of a local standard of morality in the exhibition of films is not necessarily "an invasion of the federal criminal field" as Chief Justice Mackeigan thought it to be in this case.

Even if I accepted the view that the impugned legislation is concerned with criminal morality, it would still have to be noted that it is preventive rather than penal and the authority of the Province to pass legislation directed towards prevention of crime is illustrated by the case of *Bedard v. Dawson et al.*, [1923] 4 D.L.R. 293, 40 C.C.C. 404, [1923] S.C.R. 681, which was concerned with the validity of a statute of the Province of Quebec entitled "An Act respecting the owners of houses used as disorderly houses", by which the Judge was authorized to order the closing of a disorderly house. The legislation was held to be *intra vires* on the ground that it was concerned with property within the Province and Mr. Justice Anglin said, at p. 297 D.L.R., p. 408 C.C.C. p. 685 S.C.R.:

> ... I am of the opinion that this statute in no [way] impinges on the domain of criminal law but is concerned exclusively with the control and enjoyment of property and the safeguarding of the community from the consequences of an illegal and injurious use being made of it — a pure matter of civil right. In my opinion in enacting the statute now under consideration the Legislature exercised the power which it undoubtedly possesses to provide for the suppression of a nuisance and the prevention of its recurrence by civil process.

The law of nuisance was undoubtedly a factor in the reasoning of some of the Judges in this Court and in the Court of King's Bench of Quebec, but in my view the matter was not too broadly stated by Duff, J., as he then was, at p. 297 D.L.R., pp. 407-8 C.C.C., p. 684 S.C.R. where he said:

> The legislation impugned seems to be aimed at suppressing conditions calculated to favour the development of crime rather than at the punishment of crime. This is an aspect of the subject in respect of which the Provinces seem to be free to legislate. I think the legislation is not invalid.

As I have already said, however, I take the view that the impugned legislation is not concerned with criminality. The rejection of films by the Board is based on a failure to conform to the standards of propriety which it has itself adopted and this failure cannot be said to be "an act prohibited with penal consequences" by the Parliament of Canada either in enacting the *Criminal Code* or otherwise. This is not to say that Parliament is in any way restricted in its authority to pass laws penalizing immoral acts or conduct, but simply that the provincial Government in regulating a local trade may set its own standards which in no sense exclude the operation of the federal law.

There is, in my view, no constitutional barrier preventing the Board from rejecting a film for exhibition in Nova Scotia on the sole ground that it fails to conform to standards of morality which the Board itself has fixed notwithstanding the fact that the film is not offensive to any provision of the *Criminal Code*; and, equally, there is no constitutional reason why a prosecution cannot be brought under s. 163 of the *Criminal Code* in respect of the exhibition of a film which the Board of Censors has approved as conforming to its standards of propriety.

. . . .

It will be seen that in my view the impugned legislation "has for its true object, purpose, nature and character" the regulation and control of a local trade and that it is therefore valid provincial legislation.

I now turn to a consideration of the specific section declared to be *ultra vires* by the Appeal Division of Nova Scotia, the validity of which is the subject of the constitutional question directed by order of the Chief Justice. In this regard it is noteworthy that the 1st paragraph of the order of the Appeal Division expressly declares that the word "prohibiting" in s. 2(1)(b) and (g) and s-ss. (2) and (3) of s. 3 are null and void and the use of this word in these sections of the statute forms the basis of the Court's declaration that they are *ultra vires* The Legislature of Nova Scotia. As I find the legislation to have a valid provincial purpose, I take the view that at least the first paragraph of the order made by the Appeal Division is inconsistent with the judgment of this Court in *Quong Wing v. The King* (1914), 18 D.L.R. 121, 23 C.C.C. 113, 49 S.C.R. 440. In that case the legislation prohibited the employment of white women by Chinese and provided a penalty of $100 for its contravention. In the course of his reasons for judgment at pp. 124-5 D.L.R., p. 116 C.C.C., p. 444 S.C.R., Sir Charles Fitzpatrick, C.J., explained the legislation as follows:

> In terms the section purports merely to regulate places of business and resorts owned and managed by Chinese, independent of nationality, in the interest of the morals of women and girls in Saskatchewan.

And in upholding the validity of the legislation he observed that [p. 117 C.C.C.]:

> This legislation may affect the civil rights of Chinamen, but it is primarily directed to the protection of children and girls.

In the same case, Duff, J., as he then was, had this to say at p. 138 D.L.R., p. 130 C.C.C., p. 462 S.C.R.:

> The enactment is not necessarily brought within the category of "criminal law," as that phrase is used in sec. 91 of the B.N.A. Act, 1867, by the fact merely that it consists simply of a prohibition and of clauses prescribing penalties for the non-observance of the substantive provisions. The decisions in *Hodge v. The Queen*, 9 App. Cas. 117 and in the *Attorney-General for Ontario v. The Attorney-General for the Dominion*, [1896] A.C. 248, as well as in the *Attorney-General of Manitoba v. The Manitoba Licence-Holders' Association*, [1902] A.C. 73, already mentioned, established that the provinces may, under sec. 92(16) of the B.N.A. Act, 1867, suppress a provincial evil by prohibiting *simpliciter* the doing of the acts which constitute the evil or the maintaining of conditions affording a favourable *milieu* for it, under the sanction of penalties authorized by sec. 92(15).

In conformity with this authority, Judson, J., stated in *O'Grady v. Sparling, supra*, at p. 159 D.L.R., p. 15 C.C.C., p. 819 S.C.R.:

> What meaning can one attach to such phrases as "an area of criminal law" or "domain of criminal law" in relation to such a subject-matter? A provincial enactment does not become a matter of

criminal law merely because it consists of a prohibition and makes it an offence for failure to observe the prohibition ...

I conclude from these decisions that if the legislation is found to have been enacted for a valid provincial purpose the prohibition is equally valid. Much the same considerations apply to the Regulations declared to be *ultra vires* by the second paragraph of the order of the Appeal Division. Regulations 4 and 5(1) simply provide that no theatre owner shall permit the use for exhibition in his theatre of any film which has not been authorized under the Regulations. These provisions are of the same character as those considered by the Court in the *Quong Wing* case where the first section of the challenged legislation provided that [at p. 124 D.L.R., p. 116 C.C.C., p. 444 S.C.R.]:

> "1. No person shall employ in any capacity any white woman or girl or permit any white woman or girl ... to frequent any restaurant, laundry or other place of business or amusement owned, kept or managed by any Chinaman."

and, as I have said, if the Act is for a valid provincial purpose, the Regulations made thereunder may validly preclude theatre owners from producing performances or exhibiting films which are not authorized by the Board. Regulation 13 is to the same effect providing as it does that:

> 13. No person shall advertise any performance unless the permission of the Board has first been obtained.

Regulation 18 is, in my opinion, similarly valid, but I consider it of interest to reproduce s-s. (5) of that Regulation as it appears to me to illustrate the fact that the legislation has been enacted to regulate not only the exhibition of films in theatres, but the whole film business as conducted by film exchanges within the Province. The subsection reads:

> 18(5) No film exchange shall use, exhibit, sell, lease or exchange any film unless a certificate of the Board has been issued in respect thereof and any film which is used, exhibited, sold, leased or exchanged in violation of this regulation may be confiscated by the Board.

Regulation 32 reads as follows:

> 32(1) No theatre owner or amusement owner shall permit any indecent or improper performance in his theatre or place of amusement.
>
> (2) No performer shall take part in any indecent or improper performance.
>
> (3) The Board may from time to time define what constitutes an indecent or improper performance within the meaning of these Regulations.

In my view the provisions of this Regulation are in their effect and purpose indistinguishable from s. 159(2) of the *Criminal Code* which provides, in part:

> 159(2) Every one commits an offence who knowingly, without lawful justification or excuse,
>
> . . . .
>
> (b) publicly exhibits ... an indecent show,

The use of the word "indecent" in both s-ss. (1) and (2) of the Regulation and in the *Criminal Code* is the common factor making the two enactments virtually identical, and the judgment of this Court in *Johnson v. A.G. Alta*, [1954] 2 D.L.R. 625,

108 C.C.C. 1, [1954] S.C.R. 127, constitutes conclusive authority against the validity of such a provincial enactment.

The authority purported to be conferred on the Board by Regulation 32(3) is not an independent enactment and cannot stand alone, nor is it within the legislative authority of the Province to authorize a provincial authority to define what constitutes an offence prescribed by the *Criminal Code*.

Unlike the other provisions of the statute and Regulations to which I have referred, this Regulation is not governed by the decision in *O'Grady v. Sparling, supra; Stephens v. The Queen, supra*, and *Mann v. The Queen, supra*, where the offences created by provincial legislation were of a different character to those enacted by the *Criminal Code*.

In view of the above I find that Regulation 32 is invalid as being indistinguishable from the like provisions of the *Criminal Code*. I am, however, of opinion that this Regulation is clearly severable from the balance of the Regulations and the statute and that it in no way detracts from, varies or curtails the authority vested in the Board under the statute itself.

As I have said, I take the view that the legislation here in question is, in pith and substance, directed to property and civil rights and therefore valid under s. 92(13) of the *British North America Act, 1867* but there is a further and different ground on which its validity might be sustained. In a country as vast and diverse as Canada, where tastes and standards may vary from one area to another, the determination of what is and what is not acceptable for public exhibition on moral grounds may be viewed as a matter of a "local and private nature in the Province" within the meaning of s. 92(1) of the *British North America Act, 1867*, and as it is not a matter coming within any of the classes of subject enumerated in s. 91, this is a field in which the Legislature is free to act.

In the Reference as to the validity of "An Act to amend the *Supreme Court Act*", *Reference re Privy Council Appeals*, [1940] 1 D.L.R. 289, [1940] S.C.R. 49 [affd [1947] 1 D.L.R. 801, [1947] A.C. 127, [1947] 1 W.W.R. 305], Chief Justice Duff had occasion to say at pp. 296-7 D.L.R., pp. 58-9 S.C.R.:

> The legislative powers of the Provinces are strictly confined in their ambit by the territorial limits of the Provinces. The matters to which that authority extends are matters which are local in the provincial sense. This principle was stated in two passages in the judgment in the *Local Option case (A.-G. Ont. v. A.-G. Can)*, [1896] A.C. 348 delivered by Lord Watson speaking for a very powerful Board at pp. 359 and 365, respectively. I quote them ...

The second passage to which the Chief Justice referred reads as follows:

> "It is not necessary for the purposes of the present appeal to determine whether provincial legislation for the suppression of the liquor traffic, confined to matters which are provincial or local within the meaning of Nos. 13 and 16, is authorized by the one or by the other of these heads. It cannot, in their Lordships' opinion, be logically held to fall within both of them. In s. 92, No. 16 appears to them to have the same office which the general enactment of Canada, so far as supplementary of the enumerated subject, fulfills in s. 91. It assigns to the provincial legislature all matters in a provincial sense local or private which have been omitted from the preceding enumeration, and, although its terms are wide enough to cover, they were obviously not meant to include, provincial legislation in relation to the classes of subjects already enumerated."

As I indicated at the outset, I have taken note of the lengthy judgment of Mr. Justice Macdonald in the Appeal Division in which he finds that the impugned legislation is *ultra vires* as infringing on the fundamental freedoms to which he refers, which include freedom of association; of assembly; of speech; of the press; of other media in the dissemination of news and opinion; of conscience and of religion.

Mr. Justice Macdonald's approach appears to me to be illustrated by the following comment which he makes after referring to censorship legislation relating to morals in other Provinces [at p. 55]:

> The foregoing criteria are of the usual "sex, morals and violence" type that are normally associated with film censorship. In the present case, however, the censorship criterion, being left to the *Board* to determine, *could* be much wider and encompass political, religious and other matters. In my opinion censorship relating to party politics cannot be tolerated in a free society where unfettered debate on political issues is a necessity, subject, of course, to the criminal law, particularly those provisions of the *Criminal Code*, relating to sedition, treason and incitement to crime.

(The emphasis is added.)

It is true that no limitations on the authority of the board are spelled out in the Act and that it might be inferred that it *could* possibly affect some of the rights listed by Macdonald, J.A., but having regard to the presumption of constitutional validity to which I have already referred, it appears to me that this does not afford justifications for concluding that the purpose of the Act was directed to the infringement of one or more of those rights. With the greatest respect, this conclusion appears to me to involve speculation as to the intention of the Legislature and the placing of a construction on the statute which is nowhere made manifest by the language employed in enacting it.

For all these reasons, I would allow this appeal, set aside the judgment of the Appeal Division of Nova Scotia and substitute for the declaration made thereunder a declaration that Regulation 32 made pursuant to the *Theatre and Amusements Act* of Nova Scotia is null and void.

This does not appear to me to be a case in which costs should be awarded.

*Appeal allowed in part.*

## Rio Hotel Ltd. v. Liquor Licensing Board
(1987), 58 C.R. (3d) 387 (S.C.C.).

[Only the judgment of Dickson C.J.C. is reproduced below.]

DICKSON C.J.C.: — The issue in this appeal [from 29 D.L.R. (4th) 662, 69 N.B.R. (2d) 20, 177 A.P.R. 20] is whether a province has legislative authority to prevent "nude entertainment" as one aspect of a legislative scheme regulating the sale of liquor in the province. I have had the benefit of reading the reason for judgment prepared by my colleague Estey J. and, although I am in full accord with his disposition of the appeal, I prefer to reach that conclusion by a different route. I am happy to adopt Estey J.'s recitation of the facts and judicial history of this case.

It has long been settled that under s. 92(13) and (16) or the Constitution Act, 1867, the provinces are vested with legislative authority to regulate the conditions for the sale and consumption of alcohol within the province: see *Ont. (A.G.) v. Can. (A.G.)*, [1986] A.C. 348, 5 Cart. 295 (P.C.) and *Man. (A.G.) v. Man. Licence Holders' Assn.*, [1902] A.C. 73 (P.C.). It is also well settled that in regulating the distribution of alcohol a province may attach conditions to any licence with a view to providing for the "good government" of liquor outlets: see *Hodge v. R.* (1883), 9 App. Cas. 117 at 131 (P.C.). It seems clear therefore that s. 63.01(5) of the Liquor Control Act, R.S.N.B. 1973, c. L-10, which permits the provincial Liquor Licensing Board to attach conditions to a liquor license prohibiting "specified kinds of live entertainment" in licensed premises, is prima facie within the legislative competence of the New Brunswick Legislature.

The difficulty in this case, however, arises because, in granting entertainment license 5199E to Rio Hotel Ltd., the Liquor Licensing Board imposed a condition preventing all "nude entertainment". The appellant contends that this condition relates to public morality and therefore falls within the exclusive jurisdiction of the federal Parliament under the criminal law power of s. 91(27) of the Constitution Act, 1867. Parliament has indeed enacted legislation which relates directly or indirectly to public nudity (ss. 159(2)(b), 163, 169 and 170 of the Criminal Code). It is common ground that these Criminal Code provisions are intra vires the Parliament of Canada. The dispute therefore resolves itself into the following question: Can a provincial prohibition of nude entertainment attached to a liquor licensing scheme operate notwithstanding the more general but related prohibitions contained in the Criminal Code?

The Attorney General of New Brunswick submits that the impugned licence condition is part of a legislative scheme which "has a purpose entirely different from that sought to be served by the criminal law". While the criminal law addresses nudity and obscenity, the license condition is simply directed toward the types of entertainment available as a marketing device for the sale of liquor within the province. This submission clearly calls into play the "aspect doctrine" first articulated by the Privy Council in the late 19th century. The doctrine was summarized neatly by Their Lordships in *Hodge v. R.*, supra, at p. 130: "subjects which in one aspect and for one purpose fall within sect. 92, may in another aspect and for another purpose fall within sect. 91". The inverse proposition is equally true: see also *Russell v. R.* (1982), 7 App. Cas. 829, 2 Cart. 12 (P.C.), and *Citizens Ins. Co. of Can. v. Parsons; Queens Ins. Co. v. Parsons* (1881), 7 App. Cas. 96, 1 Cart. 265 (P.C.).

The operation of the aspect doctrine was discussed fully by this court in *Multiple Access Ltd. v. McCutcheon*, [1982] 2. S.C.R. 161, 18 B.L.R. 138 D.L.R. (3d) 1, 44 N.R. 181 [Ont.], and the relationship between federal legislative paramountcy and the aspect doctrine was explained in some detail. It is unnecessary to here reiterate the analysis. Suffice it to say that when a particular legislative subject matter can be said to have a "double aspect", so that, viewed in one light, the subject falls within the legislative competence of Parliament and, viewed in another light, it falls within the legislative competence of a provincial legislature, federal legislation will be paramount only when there is a direct conflict with the relevant provincial legislation. Mere duplication does not constitute a "direct conflict". Rather, the phrase suggests that, for federal paramountcy to operate, the related federal and provincial legislation must be contradictory. Relying upon the holding of Martland J. in *Smith v. R.*, [1960] S.C.R. 776, 33 C.R. 318, 128 C.C.C. 145, 25 D.L.R. (2d) 225 [Ont.], the majority in *Multiple Access Ltd.* held, at p. 191 [S.C.R.]:

> In principle, there would seem to be no good reasons to speak of paramountcy and preclusion except where there is actual conflict in operation as where one enactment says "yes" and the other says "no" ...

The double aspect doctrine will apply whenever the contrast between the relative importance of the federal and provincial characteristics of a particular subject matter is not sharp.

Applying these principles to the circumstances of the case at bar, I conclude that the provincial legislation which authorizes the impugned licence condition is intra vires the legislature of New Brunswick. The legislation is, as I have stated, prima facie related to property and civil rights within the province and to matters of a purely local nature. The legislature seeks only to regulate the forms of entertainment that may be used as marketing tools by the owners of licensed premises to boost sales of alcohol. Although there is some overlap between the licence condition precluding nude entertainment and various provisions of the Criminal Code, there is no direct conflict. It is perfectly possible to comply with both the provincial and the federal legislation. Moreover, the sanction for breach of the provincially-imposed licence conditions is suspension or cancellation of the liquor licence. No penal consequences ensue for the nude entertainer or for the holder of the licence. Under the relevant Criminal Code provisions, the primary object is obviously to punish entertainers and proprietors who breach the prohibitions on public nudity. I cannot say that the federal characteristics of this subject matter are palpably more important than the provincial characteristics. The provincial regulatory scheme relating to the sale of liquor in the province can, without difficulty, operate concurrently with the federal Criminal Code provisions.

I should point out that the instant case is distinguishable from the situation discussed in *Westendorp v R.*, [1983] 1 S.C.R. 43, 32 C.R. (3d) 97, [1983] 2 W.W.R. 385, 23 Alta. L.R. (2d) 289, 20 M.P.L.R. 267, 2 C.C.C. (3d) 330, 144 D.L.R. (3d) 259, 41 A.R. 306, 46 N.R. 30. In that case, the city of Calgary enacted a by-law purportedly in relation to the use of city streets. In fact, one selection of the by-law was a blatant and colourable attempt to punish prostitution. That section was held by this court to be an "intruded provision" that bore no relation, either in subject matter or in the scale of penalties, to the remainder of the by-law. In other words, the prostitution provision could not be said to relate to any head of provincial jurisdiction; it was not truly part of a regulatory scheme authorized under s. 92(13) or 92(16) of the Constitution Act, 1867. The licence conditions in the instant case are only part of a comprehensive scheme regulating the sale of liquor in New Brunswick. There is no colourable intrusion upon a federal head of jurisdiction.

Finally, I agree with Estey J. that this is not an appropriate case in which to deal with freedom of expression as guaranteed by s. 2(*b*) of the Canadian Charter of Rights and Freedoms.

I would dismiss the appeal with costs.

## Criminal Legislation*
*E.G. Ewaschuk, Q.C.*

- (1983-84), 26 Criminal Law Quarterly 97.

Criminal legislation covers a broad range of powers, conduct and procedures relating to the general subject-matter of crime. It is legislation which defines which acts or omissions constitute criminal offences, defines who are parties to the offences and prescribes the process by which accused persons may be brought to court, convicted and sentenced or acquitted. It thus involves police powers, court proceedings and corrections. The purpose of this article is to inform the reader of the parameters of criminal legislation in its most general sense. An historical background of criminal legislation in Britain as well as Canada, will be canvassed as will the present system of enacting criminal legislation in Canada. Finally, the future of criminal law in Canada will also be discussed in describing a present federal initiative termed, "The Criminal Law Review."

## CRIMINAL LEGISLATION IN GENERAL

Under the Constitution Act, 1867, the federal Parliament in Canada has exclusive authority to legislate with respect to criminal law and procedure. Thus, the federal government, since 1867, has enacted various federal criminal Acts, for example: the Criminal Code, the Juvenile Delinquents Act, the Narcotic Control Act, the Food and Drugs Act, the Combines Investigation Act, etc. In so stating, it is clear that not all crimes are found within the Criminal Code, as is commonly believed, and, by definition, provincial governments have no constitutional power to enact criminal legislation. Of course, provincial Legislatures, however, have power to create offences passed in relation to their specific legislative powers. Therefore provincial Legislatures may enact offences in relation to regulation of the highways; *e.g.*, careless driving, speeding, etc.

A threshold question to be determined is: what is the proper legislative subject-matter of criminal law? At one time it was thought that the subject-matter of criminal law was unlimited and that the criminal nature of an act was determined solely by the fact that it was an act "prohibited with penal consequences". That pragmatic definition suffices for a unitary state like Britain but proved unacceptable for a political federation like Canada.

The present acceptable definition of criminal legislation requires the legislation to serve a public purpose and to generally relate to public peace, order, security, health or morality. That criterion was arrived at by the Supreme Court of Canada, and adopted on appeal by the Judicial Committee of the Privy Council, in considering whether federal legislation prohibiting the manufacture, importation or sale of margarine was valid criminal legislation. In striking down this legislation designed to protect the dairy industry, the court decided that the legislation was constitutionally invalid ("colourable") since it could not be justified as the proper subject-matter of criminal law. Consequently, not all types of misconduct may be validly characterized as criminal in nature.

Another important and new factor in considering the validity of criminal legislation is whether the legislation contravenes the Charter of Rights and Freedoms which came into force on April 17, 1982. The Charter displaces the former constitutional doctrine of parliamentary sovereignty by specifically empowering the judiciary to strike down any law inconsistent with a right or freedom guaranteed by the Charter.

A further and most controversial question dealing with criminal law lies in the domain of policy and not legality. It relates to the question of what type of conduct may the state prohibit. In that regard, the philosopher John Stuart Mill, in the 19th century, proffered his criterion which, in effect, held that the state may not prohibit conduct which does not result in substantial harm.

Many agree with him and firmly hold that the state has no business prohibiting moral conduct, especially conduct which is victimless, *e.g.* conduct which involves consenting adults. However, most states do not adhere to that dictum and do in fact prohibit such victimless conduct as gross indecency between consulting adults, gambling and smoking marihuana. The question, as stated, lies in the area of acceptable social policy and values and not pure law.

In the domain of enacted legislation, the Criminal Code, by s. 8, now specifically provides that no person shall be convicted of an offence at common law. That reference is important in so far as the Criminal Code now requires criminal offences to be found in legislative enactments. At common law, crimes were divided into treasons, felonies, misdemeanours and petty offences. A great number of these offences were defined by custom, *i.e.*, by judicial precedent, and not by legislative enactment. For example, under the common law of England, the felonies of murder, manslaughter, mayhem, arson, rape, robbery, burglary, prison breach and rescue of felon were not found in legislative enactments. While some of those offences still remain common law offences in England, no common law offences survive in Canada since the coming into force of s. 8 in 1955. Instead, as stated, the offences must be found in some specific federal enactment.

The Criminal Code is obviously the most important federal enactment relating to criminal legislation. It is roughly composed of three major divisions — that pertaining to the general part, that pertaining to criminal offences and that pertaining to various procedures related to police, courts and corrections. A cursory examination of the Code is important in that it reveals what the Code, with its some 773 sections, does and does not contain. Section 1 relates the title of the enactment while s. 2 is a general interpretation section defining various terms found in several places in the Code itself. Part I contains ss. 3 to 45 and is general in nature. It makes specific reference to various defences which exculpate an accused from a crime. But not all defences are found in the Criminal Code. Some common law defences, unlike common law offences, have escaped being legislated, but continue to afford an accused a justification or excuse not specifically found in the Criminal Code.

Part II of the Criminal Code contains ss. 46 through 106 and is entitled "Offences Against Public Order", *e.g.*, treason. Part III contains ss. 107 to 137 and is entitled "Offences Against the Administration of Law and Justice", *e.g.*, perjury. Part IV contains ss. 138 to 178 and is entitled "Sexual Offences, Public Morals and Disorderly Conduct", *e.g.*, rape. Part V contains ss. 179 to 195 and is entitled "Disorderly Houses, Gaming and Betting", *e.g.*, keeping a common bawdy house. Part VI contains ss. 196 to 281.3 and is entitled "Offences Against the Person and Reputation", *e.g.*, murder. Part VII contains ss. 282 to 336 and is entitled, "Offences Against Rights of Property". *e.g.*, theft. Part VIII contains ss. 337 to 384 and is entitled "Fraudulent Transactions Relating to Contracts and Trade", *e.g.*, fraud. Part IX contains ss. 385 to 405 and is entitled "Wilful and Forbidden Acts in Respect of Certain Property", *e.g.*, arson. Part X contains ss. 406 to 420 and is entitled, "Offences Relating to Currency", *e.g.*, counterfeit money.

The procedural parts of the Criminal Code begin with Part XI containing ss. 421 to 425, entitled "Attempts — Conspiracies — Accessories". It defines the punishment for these crimes. Part XII contains ss. 425 to 438 and is entitled, "Jurisdiction". It defines the jurisdiction of a court in relation to territory as well as subject-matter. It should be noted that not all courts are empowered to try all offences. Part XIII contains ss. 439 to 447 and is entitled "Special Procedure and Powers". Part XIV contains ss. 448 to 462 and is entitled "Compelling Appearance of Accused Before a Justice and Interim Release" and deals with summonses, warrants and bail, etc. Part XV contains ss. 463 to 481 and is entitled, "Procedure on Preliminary Inquiry". Part XVI contains ss. 482 to 502 and is entitled, "Indictable Offences — Trial Without Jury". Part XVII contains ss. 403 to 600 and is entitled, "Procedure by Indictment" and relates to jury trials. Part XVIII contains ss. 601 to 624, and is entitled, "Appeals — Indictable Offences". Part XIX contains ss. 625 to 643 and is entitled, "Procuring Attendance of Witnesses", *e.g.*, by subpoena or warrant. Part XX contains ss. 644 to 686 and is entitled, "Punishments, Fines, Forfeitures, Costs and Restitution of Property" and relates to sentencing powers. Part XXI containing ss. 687 to 695 is entitled, "Dangerous Offenders". Part XXII contains ss. 696 to 707 and is entitled, "Effect and Enforcement of Recognizances", relating to bail. Part XXIII contains ss. 708 to 719 and is entitled, "Extraordinary Remedies", *e.g., certiorari*, prohibition, and *mandamus* relating to jurisdictional questions. Part XXIV contains ss. 720 to 772 and is entitled, "Summary Convictions", *i.e.*, trials of minor criminal offences without a preceding preliminary inquiry and without the option of a jury trial.

Finally, Part XXV contains only s. 773, making reference to the drafting of various forms of documentation referred to in the Criminal Code.

More particularly, the Criminal Code in part defines various crimes and their constitutive elements, *e.g.*, sexual assault. It then specifies the type of offence sexual assault is, *i.e.*, an indictable or summary conviction offence. An indictable offence is more serious and entails maximum punishments of 2, 5, 10 or 14 years' imprisonment or life. A summary conviction offence, on the other hand, entails a maximum of 6 months' imprisonment but in practice usually involves a fine or discharge. The Code then specifies in what circumstances a peace officer or civilian has the power to arrest an accused. It further defines, assuming an arrest for sexual assault, whether or not the accused should be released on bail and under what terms and conditions. It also defines what type of court located in what territorial jurisdiction shall hear the trial of the accused. The Code further defines under what circumstances a preliminary inquiry preceding a trial is required for a charge of sexual assault. However, the Code does not define what evidence is admissible at a preliminary inquiry or trial on a charge of sexual assault. Instead, the common law rules of evidence apply as may the Canada Evidence Act. However, the Criminal Code does define the punishment for the crime of sexual assault, assuming a conviction. It further defines to what court an appeal may be brought by either the accused or the Crown.

It also should be noted that the procedures outline in the Code for processing various types of indictable and summary conviction offences apply as well to criminal offences found in other federal statutes. Thus, the Narcotic Control Act makes it an offence to possess heroin, a narcotic, and defines the punishment for committing that offence. But it does not, to any great extent, define the applicable court procedures for the processing of a charge of possessing heroin. Instead, the Criminal Code procedures for the most part apply. Thus Criminal Code procedures apply to the processing of most federal criminal offences found in other federal enactments.

## HISTORICAL BACKGROUND TO THE CRIMINAL CODE

As earlier stated, the common law in England divided crime into three major groups: (1) treason, (2) felony, (3) misdemeanours. As well, there were petty offences tried in local, as opposed to royal, courts. Prior to the invention of the printing press in the 15th century, crime, for the most part, tended to be defined by custom. In other words, judges would refer to past precedents as constituting definitional authority of what conduct was and was not criminal in nature.

However, that is not to say the Parliament did not start to enact criminal legislation at an early date. Indeed as early as 1350, the British Parliament enacted the Statute of Treasons which specified exactly what conduct constituted high treason including, amongst various other matters, demonstrating a manifest intent to kill the King, levying war against the King, adhering to the King's enemy, and giving his enemies aid and comfort. However, for the most part, criminal legislation was minimal until the 19th century.

At the turn of the 19th century, there were over a hundred criminal offences in England punishable by hanging or some more barbaric form of death. Indeed, for most felonies, the only two punishments were death or transportation to the colonies. In fact no power existed to imprison a convicted felon. However, that is not to deny that many convicts were in fact pardoned prior to their scheduled hangings and then shipped from England to do slave labour in the United States or later, in Australia.

With the development of various schools of criminological theory on the European continent, a movement arose demanding widespread reform to criminal punishment and specifically to abolish death as the general punishment for most serious crimes. That movement also took hold in England. Commencing with legislation in the 1830's, mandatory hangings as the fixed punishment for various felonies was progressively abolished.

In the same vein, as the result of eight Royal Commissions' reports on crime, a number of general criminal statutes were enacted in 1861. Although since altered to some degree in name and form, these reform laws have survived in substance until the present. So well received were these criminal statutes that a further Royal Commission was subsequently struck to study the desirability of one Criminal Code for Britain. As a result of many years of study, the Royal Commission in 1879 proposed a self-contained draft Criminal Code. However, due probably to the British love of tradition and history, the proposed Criminal Code was never enacted. Indeed, to this day Britain struggles with more than 200 statutes containing criminal legislation. In many instances, five, six, or even seven statutes creating various criminal offences may apply in respect of the same conduct.

Starting in the early 1960's the Criminal Law Revision Committee was struck by the British Home Secretary to advise him on proposed criminal legislation. That Committee has made various reports, the majority of which have found their way into enacted legislation. As well, the English Law Reform Commission has also published various reports relating to criminal law. Its reports have also found their way into various enacted legislation. Indeed, within the last few years a Standing Committee has been struck by the Home Secretary to study the feasibility and the means of enacting one Criminal Code to apply to all criminal legislation in Britain. If successful, the British will have a Criminal Code more than 100 years after Canada adopted its Criminal Code in response to the English draft Criminal Code of 1879.

The Canadian legal system is divided obviously into the common law and the civil law traditions. Whereas the common law tradition is empirical in nature and tends to evolve on a case by case basis, the civil law tradition is *"a priori"* in nature and favours legislation in respect of all legal subject-matter. Given the blend of the Canadian legal systems, it is little wonder that in 1892 Canada enacted its own Criminal Code without much difficulty, contrary to what took place in Britain.

Prior to 1867, each province enacted its own criminal legislation; however, that legislation generally related to criminal procedure and evidence rather than to criminal offences. Instead, the common law offences, as well as British statutory offences, applied generally to the provinces in Canada. But just two years after Confederation, the federal Parliament enacted several Bills relating to criminal legislation which dealt with offences relating to forgery, larceny, malicious damage to property, offences against the person and coinage, and with respect to criminal procedure, legislation dealing with juvenile offenders, summary conviction, indictable offences and a separate Criminal Procedure Act.

In 1886 those statutes were consolidated although, for the most part, left unchanged. Around this time, work had already reached Canada that Britain was contemplating the need for the passage of one Criminal Code, *i.e.*, one statute containing all criminal law. That need was considered in Canada and response proved generally favourable to the idea of the passage of a self-contained Criminal Code. As a result, the federal Department of Justice began to study the matter.

Finally, in 1892, the federal Parliament enacted the first Criminal Code which came into force on January 1st, 1893, together with a Canada Evidence Act. At that time, Sir John Thompson, the Minister of Justice, stated that the Criminal Code was founded on the draft Code prepared by the British Royal Commission, on Stephen's *Digest of the Criminal Law*, Burbridge's *Digest of the Canadian Criminal Law* of 1889 and various Canadian statutes.

It can be stated fairly that the Criminal Code of Canada was, to a great extent, lifted from the draft Criminal Code proposed by the British Royal Commission. Many of those proposed offences simply duplicated previous English common law or criminal legislation. Indeed, many offences found in the 1892 Criminal Code (Canada) were merely a distillation of offences as defined by judicial precedent. But unlike the uncertainty that continued in Britain, the Criminal Code (Canada) proved invaluable to the judiciary and the legal profession, as well as the police and general public, in readily determining what the elements of various criminal conduct were and the applicable criminal procedures. However, not all common law offences were defined in the Criminal Code and, as earlier stated, it was not until the 1955 Code that common law offences were finally abolished in Canada.

In relation to criminal procedure, very little of the Criminal Code of 1892 duplicated the draft Criminal Code of the Royal Commissioners. Instead, the criminal procedure prescribed by the 1892 Code reflected a hodgepodge of various legislation already passed in Canada as well as a distillation of practice as found in various Canadian texts. The procedure tended to be somewhat uniquely Canadian in flavour. Indeed, the felony-misdemeanour distinction fashioned at common law had already been abolished and replaced by the present classification of indictable and summary conviction offences. All references to the word "malicious" were also deleted from the Criminal Code. Furthermore, the common law distinction between accessories before the fact and principals in the first degree and principals in the second degree were also abolished and replaced by the concept of "parties" to the offence. In other words, as at present, there were principal parties to criminal offences, as well as secondary parties, but all were guilty in equal degree.

For the most part, the 1892 Code was well received by the Canadian legal profession and gave some semblance of logical order to Canadian criminal law and procedure. Various revisions followed the 1892 Code. Indeed, in 1906 major amendments were enacted to the criminal law. However, the 1927 consolidation was simply that, a consolidation and not a revision of the 1892 and 1906 Codes.

Later it became quite apparent that the Criminal Code contained various anomalies and antiquated terminology requiring excision, rewording and consolidation. Thus in 1947 a Criminal Code Revision Committee was struck to rearrange, simplify and revise the Criminal Code. That Committee reported in 1953 with the result that major amendments came into force on April 1st, 1955, to what has been called the 1955 Code. While the Committee made substantive changes to the Criminal Code, those changes related in many instances to merely form and drafting style and were aimed at putting the Criminal Code into 20th century, as opposed to 19th century, wording.

As a result, many of the offences in the present Code are still based on 19th century morality and value judgments. Indeed, the present Code continues to be a melange of the British Royal Commission's draft Criminal Code, pre-1892 Canadian legislation and indigenous legal treatises, as well as substantive *ad-hoc* amendments passed in more recent times.

Twentieth century amendments have related to such pieces of legislation as those referring to drunk and impaired driving, the breathalyser, therapeutic abortion committees, morality offences by consenting adults, wiretap legislation, dangerous offenders and the firearms acquisition scheme — a regulatory scheme relating to long-arm weapons. Indeed the Criminal Code, with its patchwork of various amendments enacted over the span of nearly 100 years, does not strike even the initiated reader as reflecting a consistent or logical scheme. Instead, it reflects disparate reasoning and drafting styles and does not reflect the values of the 1980s, nor a consistent and intelligible writing style for the present era.

## PRESENT SYSTEM OF ENACTING CRIMINAL LEGISLATION

### *Sources of Legislation*

Sources of government criminal legislation are many. On a daily basis, the Minister of Justice receives dozens of letters from various lawyers, judges, government officials as well as from general members of the public complaining about various provisions of the Criminal Code or some other problems that exists with respect to the criminal justice system. Examining and responding to ministerial correspondence occupies a great deal of Department of Justice officials' time. In the Department, ministerial letters are enclosed in yellow dossiers, affectionately known as "yellow daffodils". Over the course of the year, many of these letters point out discrepancies in the Criminal Code between various provisions, discrepancies between the English and French versions of criminal statutes, as well as general deficiencies in law. In addition, other Ministers, federal or provincial, and federal or provincial officials correspond with the Minister of Justice asking that various modifications with respect to the criminal justice system be considered.

As a result, many of these complaints are formally considered at a conference termed, "The Uniform Law Conference of Canada", which sits on an annual basis Members of this conference are called "Commissioners" and come generally from government departments, such as the federal Department of Justice as well as various provincial Attorneys-General Departments. In addition, each province, together with the federal government, generally appoints a member of the private bar to represent the interests of the accused at the criminal side of the conference.

In addition to outside resolutions, each province generally submits its own resolutions for consideration by commissioners on the criminal side.

A resolution will generally state the problem, will relate the background of the problem as well as the current law interpreting the problem, and then set out various alternative solutions to the problem. Finally, the resolution will recommend a solution to the problem. Most resolutions are set forth in a three to four-page format.

During the one-week conference, as many as 50 to 60 resolutions may be considered with a rate of passed resolutions ranging anywhere from 20 to 80%, depending on the nature of the resolution and the nature of the membership in the particular year. Further time may be spent by Commissioners in considering Law Reform Commission reports, as well as federal legislation currently before Parliament.

As a general observation, it is fair to say that the majority of successful resolutions passed at a Uniform Law Conference eventually find their way into enacted federal legislation. For that reason the Conference is perhaps the single most important source of criminal legislation. However, approval of a resolution generally constitutes but the end of a first-stage process which began as a complaint to a particular Minister pointing out some deficiency in the criminal justice system.

Attorneys-General meetings are another important source of criminal legislation. Often Attorneys-General meet at a provincial level in the absence of the federal Minister of Justice. However, when the federal Minister of Justice is invited to meet with his provincial colleagues, then matters of general importance and broad implications to the criminal justice system are often discussed. Sometimes resolutions are considered which deal with policy matters not requiring legislation. However, matters involving broad change to the criminal law are also considered. Where there is general consensus that legislation is required, then obviously the federal Minister of Justice is usually favourably disposed to enact legislation on the recommendation of his provincial counterparts.

The federal Solicitor-General usually attends the Attorneys-General meetings and has an important though secondary voice at these meetings. When, however, police, penitentiary or parole matters are discussed, he discharges the primary federal role in dealing with such matters.

Perhaps the most striking feature of these meetings is the voluminous, well-indexed black briefing books prepared for all Ministers by their officials, be they provincial or federal. The co-ordinating effort that goes into scheduling and running the meetings of Attorneys-General is nothing short of colossal. From these mammoth briefing books, legislation and much lesser dimensions may eventually be enacted.

The Law Reform Commission of Canada is a further source of criminal legislation. The Law Reform Commission was set by the statute in 1972 by the then Minister of Justice, the Honourable John Turner. It was Mr. Turner's wish that the Law Reform Commission, through study papers, working papers and reports, would eventually give the Canadian public a new and modern Criminal Code reflecting present-day values and needs. In fact, in 1970, Mr. Turner had already announced that "the Commission should have a complete rewriting of the Criminal Law as one of its first projects". However, that wish has not as yet come to pass.

Although the Law Reform Commission has published a great number of papers on criminal law, very few of their recommendations have yet found their way into the statute books. But that is not to deny these papers have generated a great deal of study and interest. The papers, in other words, have proved educational and have, to a great extent, changed the way the Canadian legal profession views the criminal justice system.

Little change, as stated, has resulted from the Law Reform Commission recommendations as to how the criminal justice system functions on a technical basis. However, the federal Department of Justice is charged with the responsibility of responding to Law Reform Commission reports with a view to recommending possible legislation. It may therefor be expected that future federal legislation will, in fact, reflect various recommendations of the Law Reform Commission of Canada.

## *The Cabinet Process*

Criminal legislation is generally enacted through public as opposed to private members' Bills. In other words, criminal legislation is usually proposed by the government of the day and not by private members. To be sponsored by the government, the proposals must go through what is termed a Cabinet process.

The Cabinet process begins with a recommendation from the Minister in charge of the particular legislation. In fact, each federal Minister is assigned various Acts for which he is responsible. For example, the Minister of Justice is responsible for the Criminal Code; the Solicitor-General is responsible for the Juvenile Delinquents Act; the Minister of Health and Welfare is responsible for the Narcotic Control Act and the Food and Drugs Act; and the Minister of Consumer and Corporate Affairs is responsible for the Combines Investigation Act. Where a Minister, after receipt of a complaint and examination of the complaint, decides that legislation for which he is responsible requires amendment, he must, then, submit his proposed change to current legislation to his ministerial colleagues.

Thus the federal Minister of Justice will, at certain times, decide that criminal legislation is required. In many instances, he reviews what may be termed a laundry list. An official of the Department of Justice, in charge of criminal legislation, will prepare a background document for the Minister to review, with a view to recommending legislative amendments. That list will detail a particular problem, give a background to the problem with alternative solutions, and a recommendation. A great number of problems may be outlined in that document. A meeting then will follow with the Minister, the Deputy Minister and various other officials to review the proposals. Oftentimes, of course, the document may contain various resolutions already passed by the Uniform Law Conference or at Attorneys-General meetings, or may reflect recommendations of the Law Reform Commission for legislating change.

When the Minister of Justice formally decides that legislative change is required, the commencement of the Cabinet process actually then begins. At this stage, Justice officials will be tasked with the requirement of preparing two documents termed, "A Discussion Paper" and a "Memorandum to Cabinet". The Discussion Paper is the larger of the two documents. It, in fact, will follow what appears to be the general government format outlining the particular program, a background to the problem, and listing various alternative approaches to the problem. However, that document makes no recommendations as to how that problem should be solved. Instead, it is a very neutral document made with the expectation that the document will eventually be made available to the general public. It tends therefore to be a scholarly analysis of theory as well as practice, showing a very detached approach to the problem.

By contrast, the Memorandum to Cabinet is a much shorter document and clearly outlines the particular recommendation of the Minister to his Cabinet colleagues. That document is considered confidential and protected by Crown privilege, and is not to be released to the public. It is a much shorter and tighter document outlining the problem, a brief background to the problem, and making a specific recommendation as to how the problem should be resolved.

Both the Discussion Paper and the Memorandum to Cabinet will be given to Cabinet numbers by Privy Council Office. In many cases, a communications plan is also required. The documents, after being extensively reviewed with the Department of Justice, will then be released on a confidential basis, before being submitted to the Cabinet, for review by various officials in the central agencies *i.e.*, Privy Council Office, the Prime Minister's Office and, in the case of criminal legislation, the Ministry for Social Development. As well, the documents may be sent to officials in the Department of the Solicitor-General, the Ministry of Health and Welfare or the Ministry of Consumer and Corporate Affairs, when those departments have an interest in proposed legislation.

As a result of a review by these officials, further changes may then be made to the documents. Finally, the documents will be translated, properly processed and sent to the Ministry of State for Social Development. A high level meeting of the Deputy Ministers for Social Development constitutes the first stage of official meetings to consider the policy of the proposed legislation. Those Deputy Ministers represent various departments within the federal government that are involved with social policy. Amongst those departments are the Department of Justice, Solicitor-General's Department, and National Health and Welfare. Status of Women is also represented by a designated Minister. Before the actual proposals are considered, the documents are formally tabled to be analyzed by officials from the Ministry of Social Policy as well as the various Deputy Ministers. Eventually the proposals will be formally discussed in detail, especially as to their financial implications. Finally, the Deputy Minister for Social Policy will make an assessment of the proposed legislation which he submits to the Minister in charge of Social Development for review by him and his colleagues at a later Cabinet meeting.

The next stage of official meetings to discuss the proposed legislation will occur at a standing committee called, "The Committee on Social Development". Again, the same departments are involved but, at this stage, the actual Ministers meet to discuss the implications of the proposed legislation. Of course, the meetings are secret and confidential, though the deliberations and decisions are, in fact, recorded. What occurs at the actual meetings cannot be discussed with outside officials. In fact, officials are permitted within the Cabinet room only when proposals from their department are being discussed.

Eventually, the chairman in charge of this committee will record the vote of his Cabinet colleagues on the proposed legislation. This vote and his recommendation will be forwarded to full Cabinet for further consideration. Justice officials are not permitted to attend the meeting of full Cabinet which tends to be a *"pro forma"* examination of proposed legislation. Only when the subject-matter is controversial or the vote at committee was very close will "full Cabinet" review the proposed legislation in great detail. In those cases, the matter may also be sent to "party caucus" for examination and recommendation by that group as to the political implications involved.

When Cabinet approves the proposed legislation, a record of decision (termed an "RD" in government circles) is sent by Privy Council officials to government draftsmen working for the Department of Justice. These draftsmen are charged with the duty of reflecting the policy decisions reached by Cabinet in legislative form, *i.e.*, with changing the policy decisions into legislative classes. That task is not an easy one.

Oftentimes various meetings will be held between the draftsmen and officials from the Department proposing the legislation to discuss the best means of reflecting the legislative policy in proper legislative language. That is an arduous task, whether conducted in English or French, and oftentimes five, six or seven drafts of the proposed legislation are reviewed before officials are satisfied with the proposed wordings of each clause of the proposed legislation. Often what is clear to the draftsmen is not clear to the departmental officials, and what is clear to the department officials is not clear to the draftsmen. Legislative drafting certainly is an art and not a science as is evidenced by the difficulty for the average person in comprehending modern-day legislation.

In any event, the agreed legislative form will eventually return to still another committee of Cabinet. That standing committee is called, "The Committee on Legislation and House Planning", chaired by the Deputy Prime Minister. Again, that is a partial committee of Cabinet, and various Cabinet members attend those meetings. At those meetings, the proposed Bill is reviewed on a clause-by-clause basis. The sponsoring Minister begins by outlining the general thrust and policy implications of the proposed legislation. The Minister will later respond to broad policy questions whereas Justice officials may explain the details of the proposed Bill, *i.e.*, the wording of the clauses and why the particular wording was chosen. Where Ministers, as they often do, choose to challenge the official as to the proper wording of the clause, a meticulous examination of the Bill results.

Oftentimes the clauses will be redrafted on direction of the chairman to reflect the problems encountered by Ministers with the wording. This is done with a view to simplifying language and to further the intelligibility of the Bill. If the committee then decides that the Bill is to be approved as worded, the chairman prepares a record of decision (RD) which is forwarded to full Cabinet for review.

Eventually the Bill, as yet unnumbered, will be sent to "Priorities and Planning" Committee of Cabinet, the most important sub-committee of Cabinet. That committee is comprised of the Prime Minister and his closest advisors, including the Deputy Prime Minister who advises the Prime Minister and his Cabinet colleagues as to, in the Deputy Prime Minister's view, the importance of the Bill and what priority it should receive in Parliament. After those decisions are made, and only then, will the Bill be tabled in Parliament. At the tabling in Parliament, the Bill ceases to be government property and only then comes within the official domain of Parliament.

## *Legislative Process*

A Bill receives either a Bill C- or Bill S- number, that is, a Commons or Senate number, on first reading, depending whether the Bill is tabled in the Commons or the Senate. Most criminal legislation originates in the Commons, as it must if financial considerations are involved. Contrary to the expression "first reading" there is in fact no reading. Instead, first reading entails only a formal tabling of a Bill. However, on first reading, a Minister in charge of a government Bill may decide to hold a press conference, where the Bill and a press release are distributed to the media. As well, this may involve a television appearance by the Minister or various officials. This, then, announces to the criminal justice community, as well as to the general public, that Parliament will be considering proposed criminal legislation in the near future.

The first formal statement in Parliament begins the second reading stage. At second reading, the Minister of Justice will make what has been termed a "second reading speech", outlining the general thrust and policy implications of the proposed legislation. In turn, the various Justice critics of the Official Opposition will reply with general statements either supporting or, as is more usual, attacking the Bill in principle. What then follows will be statements by various other members either of the Government or Opposition, and an eventual debate in principle of the Bill. If the Bill survives second reading, as it almost always does with a majority government, the Bill is forwarded to the "Standing Committee on Justice and Legal Affairs of the House of Commons" for consideration as to detail as well as principle.

At committee stage, the members of the committee are divided into approximately the same numbers as their respective parties are represented in the Commons. The Committee is chaired by a non-Cabinet member of the government, with the Justice critics represented at Committee.

The committee process generally begins with another speech by the Minister of Justice, again outlining in principle, but in more detail, the general policy implications of the Bill. This is followed by statements of the Justice critics. Eventually witnesses may be heard. These witnesses, in fact, represent various groups. Often the President of the Canadian Association of Chiefs of Police will attend, as will the President of Civil Liberties Association of Canada, as witnesses at committee stage, to proffer their opinion on the content of the Bill. As well, members of various public-interest groups may testify, as may various law professors, defence and Crown counsel.

It is considered good form for the Minister of Justice not to attend during the testimony of the witnesses so as not to give the impression of possibly intimidating the witnesses as to their testimony. Indeed the Minister of Justice or the sponsoring Minister, as the case may be, attends very few of the meetings other than his speech and the clause-by-clause stage of the Bill, which follows the testimony of witnesses.

The clause-by-clause process consists of a detailed examination of each clause of the Bill starting with clause one. Members of the committee may put questions to the Minister or his officials as to the wording of the particular clause, its implications and consequences, and make objections to the wording. A Minister may reconsider and amend the wording of the clause or in fact, at times, withdraw the actual clause. Eventually the clause will be voted on as worded, and the same process will follow in respect of each clause. Finally, the Bill as a whole will be voted upon and the committee will report back the Bill to the Commons as to the voting on the particular clauses and its general recommendations.

Assuming then that the Bill returns to the Commons for third reading, there is yet another speech by the sponsoring Minister and a further debate on principle, but one generally shorter in length. Then the Bill is voted upon and, if passed, goes to the Senate to begin the same process at the Senate level.

At the Senate level, the Minister of Justice is replaced by a particular Senator chosen by the Minister of Justice to represent his interests in the Senate, a so-called "Senatorial Minister of Justice ". That Senator will the represent the Minister at all levels, except for appearance before the Senate "Standing Committee on Legal and Constitutional Affairs", where the Minister of Justice may appear, make a statement and give testimony as will his officials. At that committee stage, a process usually somewhat shorter but essentially the same as that at the Commons Standing Committee, is repeated. At the Senate Standing Committee, more analysis is usually given to detail and the actual wording of the Bill and the making of grammatical and technical corrections, rather than to general policy. Often, however, matters of great weight and general policy importance are considered at the Senate level. Eventually, where the Bill is successfully passed at third reading, the Bill will then return to the Senate for formal enactment with the attendance of the Governor-General in the Senate to declare the law enacted.

The attendance of the Governor-General, or a Justice of the Supreme Court of Canada as his deputy, will usually occur on a Friday afternoon and usually in respect of a number of Bills. The Gentleman Usher of the Black Rod will summon to the Senate members of the Commons, "The Other Place", by banging on the doors of the Commons.

However, in most cases, government Bills now do not come into force on the day of enactment, but instead come into force on a day specified in the legislation, or on a day to be proclaimed in the future, by order of Council. This is required to give officials involved in the criminal justice process time to rearrange their affairs to meet the requirements of the proposed legislation, and to educate themselves and others as to the potential impact of the now-enacted legislation.

## CRIMINAL LAW REVIEW

The federal Minister of Justice steered through Parliament, in 1969, major criminal law amendments relating to abortion, gross indecency, and drinking and driving offences; in 1974, with respect to wiretap authorizations; in 1976, with respect to numerous procedural amendments: and in 1977, with respect to firearms, dangerous offenders and, again, wiretap amendments. As a result of this plethora of criminal legislation, a number of complaints had been made by various federal and provincial officials that his mass of legislation had literally inundated them. In particular, they complained that the legislation was very difficult to comprehend, digest and fully understand, especially given the complexity of the language used in drafting the legislation. Indeed, the usual complaint was that the legislation required simplification, especially in the language used. As well, with the numerous study and working papers, and reports produced by the Law Reform Committee of Canada, these officials felt that the time was ripe to totally revise the criminal laws of Canada.

Responding to those complaints, Senator Jacques Flynn, the federal Minister of Justice, in 1980, made a submission to Cabinet to authorize what has been called the criminal law review. Cabinet, receptive to that submission, in fact authorized the processing of a new Criminal Code to reflect modern language and values, such process to be completed within the course of the five years commencing April 1st, 1981. To that end, Parliament has authorized the expenditure of approximately eight million dollars.

The criminal law review process will reflect much of the present system but in a more developed and finely-tuned fashion, and will reflect in fact three stages of process. The first stage of the criminal law review commences with the examination and identification of problems in the major areas of the criminal justice system by the Law Reform Commission of Canada. The Commissioners, with the aid of their contract personnel, including a bevy of part-time law professors as advisors, conduct a theoretical review of the particular area, as well as a pragmatic review. In other words, the Law Reform Commission will examine the theoretical problems underlying the particular area as well as consult with various practitioners in the area to determine what are, in fact, the day-to-day problems.

In addition to its highly skilled staff, the Commissioners have a standing committee of judges to advise them on the working papers and reports. Furthermore, the Commission meets with a group of federal/provincial officials highly skilled in the area of the criminal justice system. The Commission also consults with the Canadian Bar Association and various other groups of lawyers and practitioners as well as other groups involved with the criminal law.

The Law Reform Commission process, after identification of the problems, will result in a study paper which is a document outlining the present law and problems with the operation of that present law. In turn, a working paper will follow outlining and describing in some detail the particular problems and a proposed manner to resolve those problems, giving emphasis to a general principles, rather than rules, approach to the solution of the problems. In other words, the solution to the problems must conform to a set of general principles enunciated at the start of the working paper. After more study and consideration, as well as more consultation, eventually a report endorsed by the Commissioners will be filed in Parliament. The report is then made public, delivered to the Minister of Justice and the "Standing Committee on Justice and Legal Affairs of the House of Commons", with a view to eventual enactment as criminal legislation by Parliament.

The second phase of the criminal law review entails what has previously been described as the Cabinet process. It involves of necessity the analysis and evaluation by Justice officials with their provincial counterparts as well as the Canadian Bar and other groups, of the Law Reform Commission reports and specific proposals contained in those reports. This may then result in various meetings between officials as well as meetings between Attorneys-General themselves. Again, many of the matters may be discussed at a Uniform Law Conference. Eventually, the Minister of Justice will decide whether legislation is required, and in what form, and will make his recommendations to Cabinet. After a legislative proposal has been drafted, the third stage of the criminal law review begins.

The third stage of the criminal law review, which has to date, not yet commenced with respect to any recommendations of the Law Reform Committee, is the parliamentary stage. The criminal law review project is guided by the principles that the legislation must reflect modern values, that the legislation must be clear and intelligible in language, and that restraint must be exercised in the use of the criminal law power. In other words, criminal offences should be enacted only when clearly required. Intervention by police must be utilized only when necessary and criminal procedure triggered by charges laid by police must be fair and expeditious in nature.

The resultant criminal legislation must reflect a wise blending of theory, practice and policy. The theory requires analysis of the applicable theory underlying the area considered, including its legislative history, its case law as well as comparative legislation in other countries. The practice requires discussion and consultation with practitioners involved in the system to ascertain their impressions and opinions as to work-a-day problems in the area, and an empirical evaluation of the area through statistical analysis. The latter has been made immensely more accessible through the recent establishment of the Canadian Centre for Justice Statistics. Finally the policy requires setting out of various alternatives as viable solutions to real problems in the areas under consideration. The solutions must satisfy present Canadian social needs, though change for change's sake must be avoided. In this fashion it is thus expected that the above process and methodology will guide eventual criminal law review recommendations through Parliament and result in a modern Criminal Code, reflecting present societal needs and values, and not those of previous centuries. It is in that fashion and with those expectations that modern criminal legislation will eventually be enacted.

# Ideology in the Work of the Law Reform Commission of Canada: The Case of the Working Paper on the General Part*
*Ross Hastings & R. P. Saunders*

* (1983), 25 Criminal Law Quarterly 206

## INTRODUCTION

The Law Reform Commission of Canada (hereinafter "LRC") has recently issued its latest contribution to the process of revising the Canadian Criminal Code. This contribution is in the form of a working-paper entitled *Criminal Law: The General Part — Liability and Defences* (hereinafter referred to as the "Working Paper") which attempts to present that portion of the General Part of a revised Code which expresses the "most central topic of that area of criminal law; criminal liability and general defences". Our paper will describe and evaluate some of the consequences of this attempt, and will focus specifically on the ideological implications of the proposed revision of the General Part.

The Working Paper states that the purposes of the General Part are to avoid repetition in the criminal law, to systematize the law and to provide it with a theoretical basis.

> Clearly the General Part has a threefold function to perform: to organize, rationalize and illuminate the criminal law. It organizes by providing general rules which obviate the need for endless repetition in the definitions of offences — the Special Part. It rationalizes by setting out these rules logically and systematically so as to bring order and coherence to the criminal law. It illuminates by articulating basic moral attitudes which underline the law and give it overall direction.

The need to engage in the task of rewriting the General Part of the present Criminal Code is based on the failure of the current version to meet these criteria. In the Working Paper, the LRC argues that the present General Part is incomplete, lacks the generality necessary to avoid repetitiveness in the Special Part, and is scattered and lacking in orderly arrangement. The task is thus necessary and timely.

We have no difficulty in agreeing with either the relevance or the priority of this task. However, law reformers should proceed cautiously; this is a complex and controversial task, and the manner in which it is executed will have profound implications for the nature and the quality of the final product. This is precisely why we are interested in the theoretical underpinnings and ideological implications of the revision process.

The process of legal reform is twofold. On the one hand, reform can concern itself with the systematization and rationalization of the law. The LRC's original mandate directed it, in part, to these kinds of technical considerations. The LRC was authorized to make recommendations, *inter alia*, on:

> 11. ...
> (a) the removal of anachronisms and anomalies in the law;
> (b) the reflection in and by the law of the distinctive concepts and institutions of the common law and civil law legal systems in Canada and the reconciliation of differences and discrepancies in the expression and application of the law arising out of differences in those concepts and institutions;
> (c) the elimination of obsolete laws ...

Technical reforms hold out the promise of facilitating the practice of law for professionals and of making the law more accessible and understandable to the public. Clearly, this is important work and the LRC's current effort in this area will hopefully generate an intense and productive debate among legal academics and practitioners over the appropriate direction and content of the General Part. However, this is a very limited type of legal reform, one which is perhaps best left to legal technicians.

A broader approach should incorporate the socio-political dimension of legal reform. The directive to engage in

> ... the development of new approaches to and new concepts of the law in keeping with and responsive to the changing needs of modern Canadian society and of individual members of that society.

was included in the original mandate of the LRC. The Working Paper focuses on this aspect through its attempt to illuminate the criminal law, and to articulate the link between law, morality and justice. A number of critical issues are involved in this process; unfortunately, there is a tendency for these to get lost in the more immediate, and usually more easily understandable concern with the technical contents and requirements of a new Criminal Code.

Our position is that the technical issues are important, but that a concentration on them may result in the debate over the theoretical underpinnings of the criminal law being downplayed. Law has a vital role to play in the over-all network of social institutions which constitutes our social system. At its best, it should both represent and foster the ideals of our society. In practice, however, the law is also one of the major areas where personal and social conflicts are manifested — as such, it has a corollary potential for bias.

For this reason, our immediate concern is less with the process of technical reform, and more with the socio-political dimensions of both the role of the Criminal Code and its General Part, and of the process of revising the criminal law. We will focus on three major questions:

1. the views of the commission on the aims of criminal law;
2. the views of the commission on the aims and content of the General Part of the Criminal Code; and
3. the nature and consequences of the way the revision process was undertaken and executed.

Our contention will be that the position of the LRC on these questions leaves it open to the charge of ideological bias, and that a great deal of work remains to be done in these areas.

## CRIMINAL LAW AND THE GENERAL PART

### *The Aims of Criminal Law*

Because we are concerned with the General Part of the Criminal Code and because the General Part should presumably reflect the general aims and purposes of the criminal law, we will begin with an examination of what the Working Paper has to say on this subject. As we shall try to show, one of the more disturbing aspects of this

Working Paper is the relative absence of a comprehensive and analytical discussion of what the criminal law should be trying to do.

The Working Paper states that "[t]he root of the problem concerns the aims of criminal law — the aims it ought to have". It then proceeds to specify one particular aim, the decreasing of "undesired activities", and to argue that the attainment of this goal is bounded by the need in a democratic society to "maximize freedom, justice and humanity". What is sought, therefore, is a criminal law which accommodates these values while achieving the desired end of the reduction of harmful activities. We are struck by the narrowness and vagueness of the aim stated and by the surprising absence of any attempt to address the premises and issues surrounding a normative term such as "undesired activities". There must surely be some set of standards or referents by which actions are classified as desired or undesired. The Working Paper does state that the "criminal law imposes objective standards ... [which] are not those of individual defendants but those of the whole community".

Such an approach begs the real questions involved in setting the relevant standards or in labelling certain activities as undesired. What are these standards, how are they set, and by whom? Unless these issues are addressed, the operationalization of the stated aim becomes a futile process. The Working Paper at several points implies that there is some general agreement on what these injurious activities might be; for example:

> In substance the rules are well understood, fundamentally accepted and based on general moral propositions.
>
> ... [O]ur criminal law's main contribution is to underline *our* values by forbidding conduct violating them. Guilt, blame and criminal liability rest after all on common-sense morality.

These contentions, however, do not illuminate the issues and dilemmas which underlie the criminal law, its goals, and its operation. Rather, they uncritically substitute unspecified values and common sense for theory. If the aim of the criminal law is fundamental to a revision of the General Part, then some real articulation of standards must be forthcoming. This is central to the process which was undertaken by the LRC, and yet is missing from the Working Paper. There should logically be some discussion of the "moral dilemmas" which must be recognized and hopefully reconciled. In spite of what the Working Paper seems to suggest, it is not enough to limit the illumination process to the contention that "moral causes" are, in fact, reflected in the criminal law.

The same criticism can be raised in regard to the short discussion in the Working Paper on the operationalization of the assumed aim of criminal law. If the pursuit of the aim is to be circumscribed by considerations of freedom, justice, and humanity, then some evaluative criteria must be specified. Normative constraints are relative and yet here they are used as absolutes. The Working Paper then argues for the paramount requirement of principle of responsibility — "no guilt without moral fault" — based on the belief that this principle maximizes freedom, justice, and humanity. This argument is a weak one because the Working Paper has selected only those meanings of freedom, justice, and humanity which best justify a commitment to the centrality of the principle of responsibility. It is this type of circular reasoning which characterizes much of the discussion of both the criminal law and the General Part.

In summary, if, as the Working Paper states, the aims and purposes of criminal law are fundamental to the Criminal Code (and in particular to its General Part), then these aims and purposes must be articulated theoretically and philosophically. We believe that this is an absolute minimum requirement in the attempt to lay a solid foundation for their use in the creation and operation of a new General Part. Without such illumination, the General Part will fail to fulfil its stated functions. It is to these functions which we now turn our attention.

## The Aims and Content of the General Part

The functions of the General Part are to avoid repetition in the criminal law, to facilitate its systematization, and to provide the criminal law with a theoretical basis. It is the third function which most concerns us here because it is crucial to a full understanding of a revised General Part. This theoretical basis is "concerned with the ultimate ideas which comprise the foundation of ... [any] social discipline", and in a criminal context, it "provides 'a set of ideas by reference to which every penal law can be significantly places, and thus explained'".

The problem, as was found in the previous discussion of the criminal law in general, is that these "ultimate ideas" are neither specified nor discussed. A written code of criminal law should express in its General Part the underlying concepts of wrongfulness and justice which society allegedly holds. What thus becomes imperative is an examination of the social and political contexts of these concepts. This examination is not attempted in any coherent fashion in the Working Paper, perhaps understandably so given the failure to adequately address at the outset the aims of criminal law in general. It is not sufficient to refer to such amorphous concepts as the "general moral attitudes" underlying the criminal law without noting the very real social, political, and moral dilemmas which are left unchallenged. It is an even graver failure to talk of such "given" values as if their content and substance were known and shared by all. As a consequence, the characterization of issues is distorted and the discussion which would profitably ensue is made impossible.

In order to fulfil the stated functions of the Criminal Code, the Working Paper argues that the contents of such should consist of three parts: (i) rules, which comprise the details of the specific offences and which are located principally in the Special Part; (ii) secondary principles, which are common to all rules and are for the most part in the General Part; and (iii) basic principles, which are found in the General Part and which "relate to the most broad and fundamental issues". It is the latter two elements which concern this paper.

According to the Working Paper, the General Part should articulate a set of basic principles or objects so as to provide a consistent and sustaining sense of direction for the secondary principles and the rules. These objects should be those of the General Part and not just those of the criminal law in general. In other words, although the General Part should embrace and promote the objects of the criminal law, it should also perform other functions, including those which

> ... express the basic values of our society in an accessible form, ... provide rules for the application of the criminal law and ... preserve the side-constraints that limit it.

If indeed the objects section is seen as fundamental to the General Part, it would have been interesting and enlightening to have read what "basic values" are or should be expressed in this section of the Code. Instead, we get yet another example of a tendency in the Working Paper to speak in empty generalities without reference to either the basis or content of such conclusions.

The same criticisms can be made of the secondary principles which are there to provide

> ... broad guidelines concerning considerations of fairness, justice and morality relating to the achievement of the objects of the *Code* and underlying the application of its operational rules.

The Working Paper makes the point that without such principles to guide the operation of the criminal law, the Code is merely a listing of rules "devoid of structure, rationale or moral underpinning". Of course, the argument might be made that this same charge can be levied against the Working Paper in its formulation of the General Part. If the principles on liability and defences are to articulate underlying values, then it is imperative to begin with these values, rather than to search them out in the formulas of the sections on liability and defences.

The one principle which is discussed at some length is that of responsibility which is a "guiding thrust throughout our criminal law". As the Working Paper puts it, "[h]ere is to be found the moral aspect of the criminal law reflected in the General Part provisions on liability and defences". The essence of the principle, as noted above, is clear: "no criminal liability without moral fault".

After a discussion of the centrality of the principle and its evolution, the conclusion is that the principle of responsibility is at the centre of criminal law. The notion that there should be no liability without fault is badly stated to be "a proposition enjoying general acceptance". The problem as stated in the Working Paper is that the proposition has at times been distorted in practice due in large part to "a move from the moral cogency of principles towards the legal authority of precedents and statutes". This has resulted in the development of more detailed, specific rules, with the principles underlying them tending to become obscured and sometimes lost. According to the Working Paper, the differences between rules and principles are threefold: (i) rules are more specific; (ii) rules are "more arbitrary than principles, which are largely self-evident and based on common sense"; and (iii) while rules merely state the law in a particular area, "principles articulate the reason for that law". The point it that as more and more reliance is placed on a rigid system of precedent and enacted criminal law, the common sense basis of the guiding principles is lost.

This difficulty has been compounded by the tendency of course to skew their method of reasoning towards an artificial and superficial "pure logic" and away from the type of legal reasoning which might have kept it acceptable and common sensical:

> Legal reasoning ... typically uses a kind of "yes, but" argument. We start with a general rule, follow with an objection and end up with a qualified rule. But this is only natural; for in law no general rules are complete in themselves but all are expressed against a background of competing principles and values, and besides while logic is concerned only with the validity of the inference, law and real life are concerned with the acceptability of the conclusion.

Criminal law in practice lost sight of the guiding principles of responsibility and substituted "pedigree for content, rigidity for flexibility and 'slot-machine' deduction for 'yes, but' arguments". The principal victim was a "common-sense morality" which had been the basis for "guilt, blame and criminal liability".

The focus of these arguments in regard to responsibility is that some undefined and atheoretical notion of a general common sense lies at the heart of criminal law and should be explicitly articulated in a new General Part. Two comments, however, can be made. In the first place, the concentration on the principle of responsibility is a rather narrow and distorting one. By focusing on responsibility, the Working Paper has reduced the debate on the issues surrounding criminality and criminal liability to the abstract application of an unspecified ideal of moral fault to individuals' actions. Important social, political, and moral dimensions of the larger debate are thereby ignored, dimensions which might have contributed to a better understanding of the "moral fault" concept.

Second, the reduction of the principle of responsibility to a concept of common sense is a limiting and ultimately shallow exercise. Such an argument substitutes an over-simplistic, unarticulated, sterile concept of common sense for a wider, more meaningful theoretical approach involving the full range of structural and relational positions in society. The use of a common-sense morality closes the debate without ever addressing and articulating the issues. A General Part based on a common-sense morality is not "justifiable" in analytic terms and lacks a theoretical base on which to proceed. It is unfortunate that the authors of the Working Paper have chosen so superficial a route when the need and the opportunity were there for the critical debate on the competing and at times conflicting values, policies, and rationales which lie beneath the surface of the criminal law.

## THE SOCIO-POLITICAL NATURE OF LEGAL REFORM

### *The Social Context of Legal Reform*

To this point, we have emphasized the content and limitations of the Working Paper on the General Part. However, our critique is intended to cut much deeper than that. We are also concerned with the process through which these recommendations were generated. Our contention is that this process cannot be fully understood without a discussion of the relationship of the LRC to the wider framework of institutions and events which has marked the last two decades. A failure to understand this relationship will result in a tendency to assume that the limitations of the current proposals are the "fault" of the authors of the Working Paper. We would argue that the scope of the problem is much larger than is suggested by so personal an approach to praise or blame.

The movement towards a creation of a Canadian law reform commission began in the late 1960s, and culminated with the creation of the Law Reform Commission of Canada in 1971. It was intended to be a response, and in part a solution, to the conflicts and social disjunctures which marked the 1960s. According to John Turner, who was the Minister of Justice at the time, this period was an "age of confrontation":

> We are witnessing today what has been called a "crisis of legitimacy" or as some would have it a "crisis of authority". All our institutions ... are being challenged.

In the face of this crisis, Turner nevertheless argued that "revolution" can be made possible through law, and that

> ... law is not just a "technical body" of rules; it is the organizing principle for the reconfiguration of society. Law is not just an agency of social control; it articulates the values by which men seek to live.

The LRC was thus designed to contribute to the challenge of coming to grips with social conflict and social change. There was a recognition that the old order was giving way to a new, more heterogeneous and more fragmented society, one in which the law would be called upon to provide "the means by which multiple sets of values can co-exist and develop". The goal was to codify, rationalize and rethink the law in order to adapt our legal instruments to the task of constructing a more harmonious world.

Such an approach, of course, assumes the validity of the pluralist conception of the state and the law as neutral institutions which are concerned only with the regulation of social conflicts, and which have no particular stake in their outcomes. There is, however, an alternate view, one which argues that the state and the law work in tandem with other institutions to assure the interests of the dominant groups in our society. One formulation of this position is the view that the LRC was never intended to be anything more than a political palliative or placebo. However, this only speaks to the motives which led to the establishment of the LRC, and tells us almost nothing about the goals or intentions of the people who are engaged in the actual work of legal reform.

The alternate view is nevertheless important, for it does direct our attention to the larger issue of the variable and dynamic relation of the LRC to the shifting nature of social conflicts. In this view, the LRC cannot avoid being a participant in these conflicts; this has obvious ramifications for how its recommendations were and are likely to be received by the state and by the competing groups within the community. More to the point, this view also directs us to the question of whether the consequences of the LRC's efforts are ideological in that they serve to rationalize, justify and/or defend a position favourable to the interests of one of the competitors in social conflicts. Specifically, for our immediate purposes, we feel that the work of the LRC in its attempt to rewrite the General Part of the Criminal Code is ideological not because it was intended to be — it is not a case of bad will — but because it has failed both to come to grips with the shifting nature of the conflicts, and to articulate its relationship to these conflicts.

This abstract point becomes clearer if we compare the Canada of the 1960s with the Canada of the 1980s. The conflicts of the 1960s centered for the most part on issues of morality and life-style; the perceived threat in this period was to the legitimacy of Parliament as a political decision-making body. For the most part, the battle-lines were drawn on the basis of age, race or sex and did not involve what a Marxist might call "class warfare". In this conjuncture, the concern of the state was to improve the capacity of the law to arbitrate these conflicts. However, moral and political debates of these types tend to be "luxuries" experienced during periods of relative economic prosperity.

The fiscal crises of the mid and late 1970s have fundamentally altered the nature and expression of social conflict. In plain terms, people have turned to "bread and butter" issues such as unemployment, mortgage interest rates and the rising cost of living. The attendant economic instability and uncertainty are usually assumed to be at the root of the conservative backlash of recent years. However, both these conflicts and the response of the state to them are much more complex than a simple-minded "pendulum" analogy might lead us to believe. The basis of these conflicts has shifted from life-styles and morality, and the corollary concern to politicize moral issues which characterized the 1960s; in its place, society is now experiencing social conflicts which are rooted in issues of class and power, and which represent a real attempt to alter the social and political cornerstones of our system. The urban riots in Great Britain during the summer of 1981 are perhaps the most obvious example of this danger. There has been no direct outbreak of such violence in Canada, most likely because the class divisions in Canadian society are less clear and less a part of everyday consciousness than in Great Britain. But extended political and constitutional debates over economic spheres of control have occurred, and there has been a significant level of union-type activity directed at redrawing the lines of economic and political policy. Clearly, though, we are neither in the throes of a Hobbesian nightmare, nor on the battle-lines of a full-blown revolution.

Nevertheless, the ground of conflict has shifted and, as a result, so has the fundamental response of the state. In simple terms, the strategy of the state has been to control the debate by redirecting it to another terrain. The enthusiasm of a Margaret Thatcher for a war over the Falklands is a good example of this strategy. The attraction of "law and order" politics has also been explained along these same lines. The so-called "new conservatism" is in part a mask for a shift in strategy from the attempt to arbitrate value debates to a concern to control fundamental social and class conflicts.

In practice, this means that different demands are made on the law. More specifically, the LRC as a mechanism for socio-political reform may no longer be a relevant part of the response of the Canadian state to the current social reality — time may have passed this strategy by. The LRC was an ideal liberal response to the desire to open the political arena, and to more effectively arbitrate issues of style. However, its very potential to transform the law makes it a risky proposition once the conflict escalates to the level of questioning the fundamental basis of our social organization. In plainer terms, the state is unlikely at this point to want or tolerate much more from the LRC than an exercise in technical reform. It is exactly to the extent that it restricts itself to the task of the technical revision of the law that the LRC runs the risk of becoming an ideological adjunct to current social conflicts and to the current distributions of social and political power.

### *Ideology and the Working Paper on the General Part*

As indicated in section 2, we have a number of criticisms to make of the LRC's view of the aims and functions of both the criminal law and of the General Part of the Criminal Code. These criticisms, however, do not directly address the issue of whether this Working Paper can be accused of ideological bias. Nor surprisingly, given our view of the current Working Paper, and our analysis of the place of the LRC within the wider political context, our contention is that the LRC is guilty of just such a bias. The implication of our earlier analysis is that a law reform agency cannot avoid having a relationship to the major conflicts of its time. This is neither good nor bad in and of itself. The important question is the extent to which this relationship reflects both a critical self-awareness of its own goals, and a consciousness of the impact of its own work on emerging or ongoing social conflicts and inequalities.

The LRC's Working Paper fails on exactly this level. By its own admission, the LRC seems to have settled for exactly the kind of technical reform or revision which many would have predicted would emerge from an analysis of our current social and political conjuncture. In its introduction and defence of the current proposals, the LRC argues that

> ... it remains faithful in substance to the tradition and thrust of our present law. In other words, the proposed Draft is more a codification than a reform of the present law.
> After all, the shortcomings of our present General Part relate less to substance than to form. In substance the rules are well understood, fundamentally accepted and based on general moral propositions. In form, however, they are articulated without sufficient clarity, scattered in a variety of sources and to a large extent left entirely to the common law.

In other words, the conclusion of the Working Paper is clearly that the traditional thrust of our law is good enough for the new challenges the law must face. This is surprising and disappointing, both in the face of the promise inherent in the original mandate of the LRC, and in light of its ongoing recognition that we live in a "society undergoing constant change".

In our view, in this Working Paper the LRC has abdicated its responsibility to articulate both its politics, and the politics of a new Criminal Code. The law is a part of the wider process of social control, and social control is, by definition, an attempt to preserve a given system, or at least to limit and shape the rate and direction of change. In spite of the social, political and economic inequalities which exist in this country, the Working Paper reverts to tradition. The law and common sense which failed in the 1960s are, ironically, good enough now.

This stand might be defensible, and even acceptable, if the LRC could:

1. prove the existence of homogeneous community standards across Canada;
2. articulate the relationship of those standards to the wider social and political context (that is, are they the products of an open democratic process, or do they reflect the workings of an ideology, and its constraints?);
3. theorize the role of the law in society (that is, whose law is it? who benefits from its control?); and
4. theorize its relationship to the reform of law and legal institutions (that is, whose reform is it? who benefits from this reform?).

The LRC fails to do any of these. Instead, it offers vague notions of common sense and community standards in lieu of a theory of law and of legal reform, and it foregoes the option of developing new approaches to the law which might be "responsive to the changing needs of modern Canadian society and of individual members of that society". The result is that it contributes to an ideology which seeks to manufacture public consent to and support of the current framework of social relations. Given the original mandate of the LRC, and its seeming recognition of changing social needs and conditions, this failure to address the basic issues of the debate is both disappointing and unsettling.

## Criminal Law in Canadian Society*

* Excerpts from *Criminal Law in Canadian Society* (Ottawa: Government of Canada, August, 1982), pp. 37-43, 52-54.

## SCOPE, PURPOSE AND PRINCIPLES

### *Introduction*

It was noted earlier that many thoughtful observers of the recent scene sense a state of crisis about the criminal law: a crisis of legitimacy, of effectiveness, of accountability. Furthermore, many of these same observers ascribe the crisis to a lack of "any clear or acceptable governing conception of what we as a society intend to accomplish under the rubric of criminality ... " (Parliamentary Subcommittee on Penitentiaries, 1977), to an "absence of any global concept or overall general policy which if woven into the various elements of the criminal justice system, would serve to guide the various services with a uniform philosophy" (Quebec Commission of Enquiry into the Administration of Justice, 1969). The Parliamentary Subcommittee on Penitentiaries, in fact, found a "corrosive ambivalence" concerning the very goals and purposes of criminal justice.

The current debate concerning the proper purpose and scope of criminal law is of comparatively recent vintage, although it entails renewed examination of issues of moral and political philosophy that have been argued since before the Golden Age of ancient Greece.

In addressing this basic issue of the nature of the criminal law — an issue critical to the approach that will be adopted to a host of more specific issues of criminal law and criminal justice policy — it seems useful to distinguish a set of interlinked subsidiary questions:

a) What is and what ought to be the basic purpose of criminal law sanctions: punishment or treatment? And why does criminal law impose sanctions: because it is right to do so or because it works to do so?

b) What conduct should be subject to criminal law sanctions: what is the proper scope of the criminal law?

c) On whom is it justifiable to impose sanctions: only on those who intend harm, or also on those who cause harm without intending it?

d) How far can we go in pursuit of our aims through use of criminal law powers and sanctions?

Answers to these questions will lead to the formulation of a general statement of the appropriate scope, purpose and principles of the criminal law.

### *The Nature of Criminal Law*

### **Purpose of the Criminal Law**

The basic problem confronting criminal law and the criminal justice system, it is often argued, is not the variety of specific concerns and complaints about particular phenomena — which are mere symptoms — but rather a debilitating confusion at the most basic possible level, concerning what the criminal law ought to be doing.

Part II of this paper traced the swing of the pendulum in the past century away from the so-called retributive orientation of criminal law and toward a utilitarian approach.

In this view, as has been seen, the retributive approach was identified with an anachronistic, backward-looking, punishment-oriented concern with the wrong that had been done. The utilitarian approach, on the other hand, was seen as a modern, forward-looking, non-punishment oriented concern with protecting society by preventing future wrongs — either through changing factors in the environment or the individual offender through rehabilitation, or through the deterrent or simple incapacitative effects of imposing penalties.

This trend in the philosophical justification of criminal law was very strongly felt over the past 100 to 150 years, and it is only in the past decade that the pendulum has reversed itself, in placing more emphasis on criminal law punishment for the sake of justice, to ensure appropriate denunciation for the wrong that has been committed.

In large part, this swing has come about because of growing doubts about and dissatisfaction with the efficacy of the utilitarian approach, as well as perceived loosening of moral bonds in society that has resulted in an allegedly undisciplined and unacceptable lax response to destructive anti-social behaviour.

The call to clarify goals and to resolve an ambiguity in objectives is an understandable one, given the confusion about aims and results, and the growing demand for demonstrated effectiveness in the use of taxpayers' money.

As discussed in the second Part of this paper, the combination of growing crime, growing public concern, and growing criminal justice resources has furthered the swing to control and protection. This trend was accompanied and reinforced by the optimistic belief that we had at hand the tools of individual treatment and social engineering that would permit realization of those goals, allowing us at the same time to lessen our reliance on primitive techniques that came increasingly to be identified with an old-fashioned retributive philosophy.

The recent recession of that optimism, and the recent renewed emphasis on both traditional "justice" and "equity" concerns in general, and on the legitimacy of a retributive justification for punishment, in particular, has defined the terms of the current debate over fundamental criminal law objectives.

Posing the debate in these terms can be a useful means of sharpening understanding of the issues at stake. Many have argued that the utilitarian interest of society in eliminating crime requires that "punishment" and retributive measures (seen as nothing more than vengeance), be replaced with a range of carefully-calibrated tools designed to deter and rehabilitate. Some recent observers argue the opposite case: that the utilitarian efforts of criminal justice have not only failed to protect society and rehabilitate offenders, they have also led us to lose sight of the legitimate interest of society in seeing justice done. On this basis, the justice objectives should not only be revived, they should be given paramount emphasis, with any utilitarian effects on safety or crime reduction being viewed as welcome side effects.

In the face of these apparently irreconcilable perspectives, it is important to clarify several points.

First, the criminal law, for all the efforts and rhetoric expended over the past century, is primarily a punitive institution at root. Certainly the sanctions it metes out — whether justified in the name of treatment, rehabilitation, denunciation, deterrence, incapacitation, or whatever — are and always have been perceived as punitive by almost all of those to whom they are applied. So, whether the question of the purpose of the criminal law is approached from a retributive or a utilitarian direction, it is important to understand that the fundamental nature of criminal law sanctions is punitive.

This should not be particularly surprising since, as Part II discussed, the criminal law and the criminal justice system constitute the end point on a continuum of informal and formal customs, beliefs and institutions of social-control — the end point in terms of the ultimately coercive intervention of the state in the lives of usually non-consenting citizens.

Although it may be agreed that the ultimate characteristic of criminal law sanctions is that they punish, this proposition does not mean that the sanctions awarded under the criminal law are to be harsh, cruel, inhumane, or uninterested in the ultimate effect they have on those subject to them. (Indeed, the concept of justice is seen as imposing limits on the extent to which punishment may be inflicted, in the sense that the traditional doctrine of "an eye for an eye" means that it is unjust to take more than an eye for an eye). Neither does the proposition imply that there is a necessary conflict in imposing punishment for retributive and for utilitarian reasons, although there may be such conflict in particular instances. In many cases, imposing punishment for retributive reasons may well have utilitarian effects in terms of deterrence, denunciation and reaffirmation of social values.

Second, on the basis of the long-term perspective adopted in this paper, it appears necessary to conclude that the debate, cast in "either/or" terms, is unresolvable because it is artificial and unrealistic.

This is so because the criminal law has, and should continue to have, two major purposes:

1. preservation of the peace, prevention of crime, protection of the public — security goals; and
2. equity, fairness, guarantees for the rights and liberties of the individual against the powers of the state, and the provision of a fitting response by society to wrongdoing — justice goals.

It must be admitted that there is continuing tension between these two clusters of objectives and that they sometimes come into conflict. Furthermore, while the criminal law is concerned with both sets of purposes, particular components of the criminal justice system place varying emphasis on those purposes.

By recognising the legitimacy of both the utilitarian and the retributive approaches, and by refusing to equate them with security and justice respectively, we may more productively debate the specific point of balance that is to be struck between the two major purposes of the law and the criminal justice system: justice and security. Thus, if the goal is to pursue "justice", utilitarian concerns about security, protection, prevention, treatment and rehabilitation need not be abandoned. Or, if the emphasis is to be on crime control and public protection, arguments appealing to a retributive justification for punishment in the name of "justice" or "just desserts" need not be dismissed as illegitimate. This is an important consideration to bear in mind, since most recent debates on the issue of the major purpose of criminal law are posed in such a way as to suggest there can be only one such legitimate purpose. Acceptance of this assumption of the necessity for a unique purpose may appear more logically or philosophically appealing, but it does not seem to be realistic in terms of the actual uses to which criminal law is put, and the actual effects it has in society.

In the case of the criminal law, most citizens would agree that criminals ought to be punished because they have done wrong, and therefore deserve punishment. But most would also like to see society protected either by the punishment of offenders in order to deter or simply incapacitate, or, perhaps preferably, by the rehabilitation of offenders.

The argument in this section is that no social institution as important or complex as the criminal law can afford the luxury of picking just one purpose — intellectually simple and satisfying though that selection might be. As Henry M. Hart wrote in 1958:

> A penal code that reflected only a single basic principle would be a very bad one. Social purposes can never be single or simple, or held unqualifiedly to the exclusion of all other social purposes; and an effort to make them so can result only in the sacrifice of other values which are also important. Thus, to take only one example, the purpose of preventing any particular crime, or crimes generally, is qualified always by the purposes of avoiding the conviction of the innocent and of enhancing that sense of security throughout society which is one of the prime functions of the manifold safeguards of ... criminal procedure. And the same thing would be true even if the dominant purpose of criminal law were thought to be the rehabilitation of offenders rather than the prevention of offences.

On the basis of this discussion, some important conclusions can be drawn. First, the criminal law and the criminal justice system must pursue two major clusters of objectives — "justice" and "security". Second, criminal sanctions, whether justified in terms of utilitarian or retributive aims, are primarily punitive in nature, and are understood as such by both society and by those on whom they are imposed. Third, acceptance of retributive justifications for punishment implies neither rejection or utilitarian justifications for such punishment, nor the acceptance of harsh, cruel or vindictive forms or levels of punishment. Indeed, the retributive approach that is often expressed in terms of the concept of "justice" acts as a brake in setting a maximum permissible limit on punishment that might otherwise be subject to no such limit in its pursuit of various utilitarian goals such as deterrence, incapacitation, or even rehabilitation. This distinguishes the concept of retribution from that of vengeance. Fourth, recognition of the legitimacy — and necessity — of pursuing two sometimes-conflicting purposes for criminal law directs attention to the need to devise an approach for defining the proper point of balance between these two purposes.

*Proper Scope of the Criminal Law*

Part II of the paper touched briefly on the trends in penal legislation over the past century, and Part III raised, as a major perceived problem, the question of the proper scope of the criminal law, as opposed to other forms of response to individual and collective behaviour within society.

Those Parts made the point that the criminal law and the criminal justice system should be conceived of as the ultimate recourse available to society along the continuum of informal and formal conventions, customs and institutions.

It is with this conception in mind that the Law Reform Commission, the Ouimet Committee, and many others have urged the doctrine of restraint in the use of the criminal law and the criminal justice system.

This notion — which has unfortunately and inaccurately been interpreted by some as a call for laxity and leniency — is properly understood as implying the need to examine carefully the appropriateness, the necessity, and the efficacy of employing the criminal law, rather than these other, less intrusive, less coercive means of dealing with particular social problems.

For some forms of conduct, this analysis can be quickly concluded. There is no question that the only adequate and fitting response to such "core" crimes as murder, assault, robbery, and so on is the criminal law. No one seriously suggests otherwise. For other new, sophisticated and potentially harmful forms of activities — especially those of large-scale organizations — use of the criminal law may also be appropriate in some circumstances, in light of the increased dependence of individuals on such organizations with respect to crucial aspects of everyday existence and, therefore, the increased vulnerability of individuals to harmful actions on the part of such organizations.

But, too often, the response to the emergence of a particular social problem has been almost routine or automatic invocation of the criminal law, or criminal-like sanctions. The discussion above concerning offences of a comparatively trivial or anachronistic nature contained in the Criminal Code, not to mention the huge array of "public welfare" legislation that has grown up in the past century and which relies heavily on criminal sanctions and criminal procedures for its enforcement, bears on this point.

Restraint should be used in employing the criminal law because the basic nature of criminal law sanctions is punitive and coercive, and, since freedom and humanity are valued so highly, the use of other, non-coercive, less formal, and more positive approaches is to be preferred whenever possible and appropriate. It is also necessary because, if the criminal law is used indiscriminately to deal with a vast range of social problems of widely varying seriousness in the eyes of the public, then the authority, credibility and legitimacy of the criminal law is eroded and depreciated. The lumping together off seriously harmful and wrongful conduct with a host of technical, minor, or controversial matters blunts the impact and undermines the effect the criminal law should have as society's institution of ultimate recourse.

The Law Reform Commission and others have argued persuasively for a "pruning" and clarification of the criminal law on the basis of arguments such as these. This process requires consideration of the boundaries that should be drawn to distinguish between criminal law and "public welfare" regulatory and administrative law, criminal law and private morality, and criminal law and civil law.

The Law Reform Commission strongly emphasized the need to distinguish more clearly between "regulatory" offences and "real" crimes. Regulatory processes designed to control certain socially and economically useful enterprises are sometimes viewed as being "too criminal" in nature, because of their inappropriate use of summary conviction criminal procedures to enforce compliance. For the Law Reform Commission, all "real" crimes should appear in the Criminal Code and not in regulatory law, though the Commission also recommends that such distinction be made between crimes and regulatory offences for a number of reasons. These include a need to be parsimonious with the criminal law, in order to preserve the impact of its symbolic and solemn condemnation of violations of "core values". Another reason is the need to observe the principle of equity by ensuring that the most serious transgressions are normally dealt with in a more serious manner and with a more elaborate procedure than other transgressions. In the boundary between criminal law and private morality, various concerns have been expressed about either decriminalizing or diverting from criminal prosecution many acts widely considered crimes of "going to Hell in one's own fashion", such as drug and gambling offences. Some of the offences are considered too minor to be treated with the heavy hand of the criminal law; others are thought to be more effectively dealt with through public education or regulation.

In the boundary between criminal and civil law, there has been considerable interest, in Canada and elsewhere, in diverting from the criminal process certain disputes which are more in the nature of civil wrongs between citizens, or staying criminal prosecutions for the purpose of allowing the offender to make financial or other redress to the victim. In this view, traditional criminal justice emphasis on allocating blame and punishing the blameworthy has not served the interests of the victim, righted the harm done, restored the "social harmony", nor had any positive impact on the offender. Opponents of this "diversion" approach argue that it may have a lesser deterrent effect on wrong-doing, may not serve social needs to denounce criminal behaviour, has not yet shown any success in diverting offenders who would in fact have been handled in criminal court caseloads, and may endanger the legal rights of the accused and the interests of the victim.

## STATEMENT OF PURPOSE AND PRINCIPLES

Recognizing that:

In the Charter of Rights and Freedoms, Canada has guaranteed certain rights and freedoms consonant with the rule of law and with principles of justice fundamental to a free and democratic society;

Canada has, in addition, undertaken international obligations to maintain certain standards with respect to its criminal justice system;

The criminal law is necessary for protection of the public and the establishment and maintenance of social order;

The criminal law potentially involves many of the most serious forms of interference by the state with individual rights and freedoms; and

Criminal law policy should be based on a clear appreciation of the fundamental purpose and principles of criminal law;

It is appropriate to set forth a statement of purpose and principles for the criminal law in Canada.

### *Purpose of the Criminal Law*

The purpose of the criminal law is to contribute to the maintenance of a just, peaceful and safe society through the establishment of a system of prohibitions, sanctions and procedures to deal fairly with culpable conduct that causes or threatens serious harm to individuals or society.

### *Principles to be Applied in Achieving this Purpose*

The purpose of the criminal law should be achieved through means consonant with the rights set forth in the Canadian Charter of Rights and Freedoms, and in accordance with the following principles:

(a) the criminal law should be employed to deal only with that conduct for which other means of social control are inadequate or inappropriate, and in a manner which interferes with individual rights and freedoms only to the extent necessary for the attainment of its purpose;
(b) the criminal law should clearly and accessibly set forth:
  (i) the nature of conduct declared criminal;
  (ii) the responsibility required to be proven for a finding of criminal liability;
(c) the criminal law should also clearly and accessibly set forth the rights of persons whose liberty is put directly at risk through the criminal law process;
(d) unless otherwise provided by Parliament, the burden of proving every material element of a crime should be on the prosecution, which burden should not be discharged by anything less than proof beyond a reasonable doubt;
(e) the criminal law should provide and clearly define powers necessary to facilitate the conduct of criminal investigations and the arrest and detention of offenders, without unreasonably or arbitrarily interfering with individual rights and freedoms;
(f) the criminal law should provide sanctions for criminal conduct that are related to the gravity of the offence and the degree of responsibility of the offender, and that reflect the need for protection of the public against further offences by the offender and for adequate deterrence against similar offences by others;
(g) wherever possible and appropriate, the criminal law and the criminal justice system should also provide for:
  (i) opportunities for the reconciliation of the victim, community, and offender;
  (ii) redress or recompense for the harm done to the victim of the offence;
  (iii) opportunities aimed at personal reformation of the offender and his reintegration into the community;
(h) persons found guilty of similar offences should receive similar sentences where relevant circumstances are similar;
(i) in awarding sentences, preference should be given to the least restrictive alternative adequate and appropriate in the circumstances;
(j) in order to ensure equality of treatment and accountability, discretion at critical points of the criminal justice process should be governed by appropriate controls;
(k) any person alleging illegal or improper treatment by an official of the criminal justice system should have ready access to a fair investigative and remedial procedure;
(l) wherever possible and appropriate, opportunities should be provided for lay participation in the criminal justice process and the determination of community interests.

## Questions/Discussion

1. What are the tests used by the courts to determine whether legislation falls within the criminal law power of the federal government? How useful and effective do you think they are? Are they perhaps the best we can hope for given the task which presents itself?
2. Do you think the provinces should be given an explicit, constitutionally empowered role in the formulation of criminal justice policy and legislation? Why or why not? What should be the proper role of the provinces in this area?
3. Describe the process of formulating criminal justice policy and note its weaknesses, strengths and potential? Where and how does it fail, and why? Are the problems in the process of a fundamental nature (i.e., the process itself is seriously flawed) or are they ones which can be corrected by better practices and better implementation?
4. Describe the development of the Criminal Code in Canada and state what has been wrong with that development. Are political pressures always going to be important in the creation of new criminal laws? Is this good or bad? Why? Do you think truly independent advisory bodies are possible or effective? Why or Why not? What would you do to change the process and do you think such changes would be politically feasible?
5. Do you think that the development of a set of guiding principles is necessary to the ordered evolution of criminal laws in Canada? Can any set of such principles ever be of much value and effect when it comes to actually deciding what will or will not enter the criminal arena? For example, to say that the criminal law should protect society from harm or that it should uphold, defend, and promote important or fundamental values in society does little to tell us what definition of "harm" one is using or what those values are and when the need bolstering in the criminal law.
6. Describe the role played by the now defunct Law Reform Commission of Canada. What criticisms are made of the LRCC in the Hastings and Saunders article? Do you agree or disagree with them? Why or why not? Do you think that the new "Law Commission of Canada" can perform a more useful or effective function?

## Further Reading
- Barnes, J., "The Law Reform Commission of Canada" (1975), 2 Dalhousie Law Journal 62.
- Goode, M.R. "The Law Reform Commission of Canada, Barnes and Marlin and the Value-Consensus Model" (1977), 4 Dalhousie Law Journal 793.
- Hartt, E.P., "The Limitations of Legislative Reform" (1974), 6 Manitoba Law Journal 1.
- Healy, P., "The Process of Reform in Canadian Criminal Law" (1984), 42 University of Toronto Faculty of Law Review 1.
- Kaiser, A., "New Directions for Canadian Criminal Law Reform: Ensuring an End to Complacency" (1993), 13 Windsor Yearbook of Access to Justice 264-86.
- Letourneau, G., and S. Zimmerman, "Recent Trends in Criminal Law Reform" (1992), 33 Cahiers de Droit 857-84.
- Samek, R., "A Case for Social Law Reform" (1977), 55 Canadian Bar Review 505.
- Wood, J., and R. Peck (eds.), 100 Years of the Criminal Code in Canada (Ottawa: Canadian Bar Association, 1993).

## 3.2 THE ROLE OF THE COURTS

**Introduction**

*R.P. Saunders*

The roles that the courts play in the development and production of the criminal law can be divided arbitrarily into four categories: i) an interpretive role; ii) a traditional common law role; iii) a Charter role; and iv) a process role. These roles are reflected in the readings which follow, though often not explicitly. First, the courts are responsible for the interpretation of the existing statute law and thus have a role to play in giving concrete meaning to the words in the statute through the various rules of interpretation that they employ. These rules do not concern us here as they are more useful in a practical sense and are often quite technical. However, the use of these rules may result at times in a distortion of the meaning and intent of the particular statute, or at least a re-interpretation of it.

The except from Kloepfer's article gives the reader an introduction to some of the problems inherent in the writing of criminal law and, therefore, in its interpretation. What is to be noted in this area are both the breadth of meanings that are possible even for seemingly simple phrases or terms and also how the courts, in giving meaning to the words of the statute, produce criminal law in a practical sense. This role is not to be undervalued, for not only is it necessary in the specific application of the law, but it is also important in setting out the limits of the law's coverage in the future. The *Paré* case provides an example of the court's fulfilling this role in interpreting the term "while committing" and the consequences of its interpretation on the accused in the case. The question to ask after the case is what guidelines are given for the future for the application of the interpretation of these words to other fact situations?

Another facet of the interpretation role is to give meaning to criminal law by filling out those requirements that are not explicitly set out in the legislation, specifically by addressing the issue of the mental requirement of an offence. This is a very important role and is examined in Chapter 6, for the provisions in the Code usually define only the physical elements of a crime and not the intention or knowledge which is needed for a conviction. As we shall see in Chapter 6, most crimes require some mental element; this is related to some notion of individual blameworthiness that arise *because* the accused did the wrongful acts intentionally or knowingly.

A final and important dimension of the interpretation role (though it could just as easily be classified as a constitutional function) is the court's role as to the constitutional division of powers which was addressed in the previous section. The tests that have been developed and examples of their use were given in that section. This "referee" function of the courts is a necessary one in a federal system such as Canada's and, as noted above, one should focus on the adequacy of the tests developed and their effective use by the courts.

Second, the courts have developed and continue to develop certain common law defences not yet found in statute. This power is explicitly set out in s. 8(3) of the Criminal Code where it is stated that:

> Every rule and principle of the common law that renders any circumstance a justification or excuse for an act or a defence to a charge continues in force and applies in respect of proceedings for an offence under this Act or any other Act of Parliament except in so far as they are altered by or are inconsistent with this Act or any other Act of Parliament.

By way of contrast, s. 9 of the Code expressly disallows common law offences except in the case of contempt of court. Examples of common law offences can be found in the defences of necessity, consent and entrapment, all of which are examined in Chapter 7. The courts will continue to have a free hand in the evolution of these defences until the federal government enacts the relevant provisions in the Code.

What can be said about these first two roles of the courts is that to date the courts have generally not done a particularly good job in the area of criminal law, notably at the highest level, the Supreme Court of Canada. The Supreme Court's interpretation and application of their own guiding principles, such as the need for actual subjective intention, have been at best inconsistent and confusing, and too often guided by what is practical and convenient in the circumstances of the case. In other words, the Supreme Court has not stepped in and filled the vacuum left by the failure of the legislators to articulate first principles.

The third function of the courts in relation to the production of criminal law arises from the constitutional entrenchment of the Charter of Rights and Freedoms in 1982. The Charter is similar to the well known American Bill of Rights, though major differences do exist. The courts derive from the entrenchment of the Charter the power to annul legislation or to intervene in the enforcement of legislation if that legislation or the enforcement procedures violate the rights and freedoms enunciated in the Charter, as interpreted by the courts. For example, in the criminal law sphere, if evidence was improperly obtained and the right to be secure against unreasonable search and seizure was thereby violated, the courts can rule that the evidence is inadmissible if by its admission the administration of justice would be brought into dispute.

Because the Charter is part of the Constitution Act, the "supreme law of Canada", it has given the judiciary much greater power than existed before 1982 in regard to the content and operation of the criminal law. The so-called rights and freedoms as set out in the Charter are not absolutes, but rather only take on the meaning and scope as given to them by the courts. In looking at the Charter's s. 9, the right not to be arbitrarily detained or imprisoned, what standard should we use for the term "arbitrarily" or, for that matter, when is a person "detained"? If the police stop you to ask you some questions, does this amount to being detained, or should something else be required before the right is available? You can look at virtually all the rights in the Charter in this manner. The Charter sections which most directly concern and impact on the criminal law are sections 7 to 14 ("legal rights") and section 24 (enforcement). Other sections, such as the "fundamental freedoms" in section 2, the qualifying guarantee given in section 1, and the equality provision in section 15 can also be used to intervene (or not to intervene) in the area of criminal law. Concrete examples of the courts' Charter use and interventions are presented in Chapter 7. The excerpts from the two cases of *Skapinker* and *Hunter*, which are reproduced below, highlight the Supreme Court's approach to the interpretation of the Charter and illustrate the freedom that the courts have in applying the vague principles in the document.

The final role of the courts is what has been referred to as a "process role", and is the focus of the excerpt from Cohen's article. This role has to do with the criminal law that is produced, because if we look at the process which the courts use to structure and control the disputes between the state and the offender in criminal law, we can see that it is up to the parties themselves to take an active role in the proceedings while the judge takes a more passive role. There is a basic assumption that the parties are equal before the court, not only as to the extant parties but also as to the types of defendants which come before the courts. In reality there is a substantial degree of variation in the resources and arguments which the parties can marshall for the courtroom and therefore different levels of access depending upon who you are and how much money you have. Legal aid may be of use in some situations but its availability is far from universal, not only as to the *type* of offence but also as to the income levels of the offender (see Chapter 4, section 2). Cutbacks in funding levels in 1996 in Ontario in particular will further reduce its availability. The point here is not to belabour the lack of equality between parties within the criminal justice system, but rather to illustrate the importance of the type of process that is used in court. In Canada, this process is an adversarial process that puts the burden on the parties to carry the case and that, consequently, gives an unfair advantage to some offenders as opposed to others. What type of lawyer one can hire and what resources one has for pretrial tests or investigations can be important determinants in cases and their results (witness the 1995 murder trial of O. J. Simpson in the United States and the resources he was able to employ in his defence). This is not only important as to the individual results of a case, but it can also be important in the larger sense of what issues get litigated (and therefore what law is produced). For example, who is using the Charter provisions and to what end: the *Hunter* case, excerpted below, gives an example of a corporation using the Charter to protect itself from state intervention in the anti-combines area of law, an area where the success rate by the state has traditionally been very poor. Who or what group has the resources and therefore the opportunity to use the courts to develop or manipulate the criminal law in a similar manner?

How the judge conducts the trial and reaches his or her decision can also have an important effect on the results of the trial and therefore the reality of criminal law for individuals or classes of individuals. If there are racist or sexist attitudes, or biases of any kind on the part of the judge that affect the ultimate decision or the legal rule that is expounded, then the results may be unfair. We know that the judiciary is not representative of the diversity of groups and classes found in the general population and that there are many examples of these biases being expressed by various judges, but what can be done? Presumably, there is a need for a better appointment process (see the articles by Baar and by Russell and Ziegel, for example, under Further Reading) to get better judges and a more representative judiciary, but the problem is greater than this. What is also required is a better and more representative "pool" of lawyers from which to select the judges, and this implies a much larger problem of ensuring more diversity on the basis of gender, ethnicity and class origin in our educational institutions, including high school, the university, and ultimately, law school. Of course, this problem of an unrepresentative judiciary is important in all the roles that the courts play in producing criminal law and affects the type of criminal law we have in Canada today. This problem is discussed in the context of feminist concerns in the Canadian Bar Association Task Force Report and in the article by Wilson listed under "Further Reading" and is addressed in the context of racism in Chapter 8, section 2.

In conclusion, it is important to note the overall expansion of judicial power and its exercise since 1982, and to realize what this has meant and will mean to the production of criminal law in this country, issues of expertise, democracy, accountability, accessibility and flexibility should be kept in mind as the reader proceeds through the readings below. What are the advantages and disadvantages of producing criminal law in this manner, and what are the ultimate effects of the criminal law that is produced and the crime that actually occurs?

## Ambiguity and Vagueness in the Criminal Law:
### An Analysis of Types*
*Stephen Kloepfer*

* Excerpt from (1984-85), 27 Criminal Law Quarterly 94.

### INTRODUCTION

A recurrent problem in legal analysis is to distinguish disputes about facts from disputes about *words*. That factual and verbal considerations impinge on one another renders this problem a formidable one. The distinction has, however, much to recommend it. Conceptual clarity can be gained by attempting to distil from a legal controversy the contribution linguistic considerations make to it. Traditional scholarship in the criminal law, for example, has tended to focus more on how the details of an accused's conduct should be differentiated and classified, than on the statutory verbal formulae by which the classification is ultimately effected. Problems of the latter sort have, for the most part, been relegated to the topic of statutory interpretation, and this has resulted in a particular imbalance in criminal law scholarship. The thoughtfulness expended on developing criteria for classifying criminal conduct has far exceeded that devoted to analyzing the technical problems of statutory drafting and interpretation which abound in Canadian criminal law.

The object of this article is to identify more precisely the sorts of semantic problems to which the criminal law recurrently gives rise, and to analyze how contemporary Canadian judges choose among possible statutory meanings and justify their choices. For however much Willis's adumbration of the "literal", "golden", and "mischief" rules was descriptive of judicial approaches to statutes at the time he wrote, it is today in no way descriptive of the complexity of interpretative problems which statutes give rise, of the sophistication with which the ablest of our judges resolve them, or of the various ways in which considerations of context influence the judicial attribution of meaning to statutory words. Indeed, some of the greatest insights into current judicial approaches to statutory interpretation are found in cases which, although presenting a problem of statutory meaning, are disposed of without any consideration of statutory interpretation at all. That received doctrine and current practice appear to have parted company recalls the anecdote about the eminent judge who confessed that "books on spiritualism and statutory interpretation were two types of literary ebullitions he had learned not to read".

The complexity of interpretative problems in the criminal law derives in part from the varieties of "meaning" in communication which insistence on a "literal" or "plain meaning" approach tends to obscure. Professor Dickerson has done much to clarify these distinctions, and he is surely correct in arguing that they constitute vital *matériel* in our continuing "battle against the bewitchment of our intelligence by means of language". Literal meaning is the "meaning carried by language when it is read in its dictionary sense unaffected by considerations of particular context". It must be distinguished from *actual* meaning, which is the meaning of a word or passage when read in a given context, and *true* meaning, which is the meaning disclosed when the word or passage is read in its "proper context".

The problem of what constitutes proper context is an elaborate one, but it may succinctly be described as "the context, shared by the communicant and his audience, that is presupposed by the communication". Although literal meaning may, in a given statutory provision, coincide with actual or true meaning, consideration of proper context typically yields a resultant meaning that differs significantly from literal meaning. Nor, on reflection, is this surprising. The literal meaning of a word or passage in a statute typically has a range of potential reference that is much wider when considered alone that when viewed through the reducing lens of proper context. Accordingly, only when "literal" or "plain meaning" corresponds to true meaning, that is, when it is arrived at by considering proper context, is the doctrine of literalism in statutory interpretation intelligible at all. "Legal meaning" is the meaning assigned to a statutory provision by a court adjudicating a particular legal controversy. The arguable disparity between "legal" meaning and "true" meaning provides the stuff of scholarly criticism and, one hopes, of appellate court emendations.

The necessity of adverting to proper context in order to approximate to true statutory meaning is highlighted by an appreciation of the deficiencies in the vehicle of language itself. Configurations of words have neither the clarity of crystals nor the austere precision of mathematical symbols nor the austere precision of mathematical symbols, and what they *should* be taken to mean in a given context is, in statutes as in other modes of communication, a semantic subset of what they *could* be taken to mean independently of context. Ambiguity and vagueness of language are the primary chronic "disease" which call for contextual therapy, and it is important to distinguish between the different forms of each disease and to identify the various symptoms by which each is recognized.

## AMBIGUITY

Ambiguity, "the condition of admitting of two or more meanings, or being understood in more than one way, or of referring to two or more things at the same time", is perhaps the most serious disease of language in that the intended meaning of an ambiguous word or passage, unlike that of homonymous words which also have multiple layers of reference, is not necessarily resolved by advertence to context. Indeed, legal terminology has exacerbated the problem, by designating additional meanings to words ambiguous in themselves. Examples are such words as "residence", "assignment", "user", "accounting", "process", "information", "tax", "bargain", "traffic", "service" and "fixture".

In a landlord and tenant statute, for example, in the stipulation that "the user of the premises shall be reasonable and all fixtures shall be kept in good repair", it is not clear whether the words "user" and "fixture" are employed in their legal or in their colloquial senses. Legal usage has rendered both terms essentially ambiguous, especially where they are used in a legal or *quasi*-legal context. Accordingly, special care must be taken by lawyers and legislative draftsmen to avoid using ambiguous words where the particular legal context will not render the intended meaning clear. The lawyer or draftsman "should avoid using the ambiguous word (*e.g.*, residence) whenever his intended meaning (*e.g.*, legal home) may be adequately expressed by an unambiguous word (*e.g.*, domicile)". In law, if not in politics, ambiguity is neither desirable nor defensible.

### *Semantic Ambiguity*

The most obvious form of ambiguity found in statutes is semantic ambiguity, where a word's inherent multiplicities of meaning derive from lexicographical usage and exist independently of context. Semantic ambiguity is not confined to single words however; often, whole phrases or passages are semantically ambiguous. For example, s. 237(5) of the Criminal Code provides:

> (5) No certificate shall be received in evidence pursuant to paragraph (2)(d), (e) or (f) unless the party intending to produce it has, before the trial, given to the accused reasonable notice of his intention *together with* a copy of the certificate.

The phrase "together with" in s. 237(5) is semantically ambiguous; it could mean either "at the same time as" or, alternatively, it could mean "in addition to". The admissibility of the certificate of analysis as Crown evidence in a case where a copy of such certificate was not given to the accused at the same time as the Crown notified the accused of its intention to produce the certificate would depend on which connotation of the phrase "together with" is judicially adopted as the legal meaning of that phrase. As it happens, the phrase "together with" in s. 237(5) has been judicially construed to mean "at the same time as", but it is surely better to avoid ambiguous terms at the drafting stage than to give judges yet another opportunity to deny that a term is ambiguous at all.

. . . .

## *Syntactic Ambiguity*

The examples cited above illustrate semantic ambiguity, where the uncertainty of meaning derives from lexicographical usage and does not always yield to suggestive features of context. Another conduit of muddled messages is syntactic ambiguity: a statement is syntactically ambiguous where its grammatical structure gives rise to uncertainties of reference. Syntactic ambiguity is the principal cause of the fallacy of "amphiboly", and expressions in which it occurs are often not without aspects of humour, intended or not. Advertising copy exhibits interesting variations on a theme of syntactic ambiguity, for example: "Safe Driving is No Accident"; "Save Soap and Waste Paper"; "We Dispense With Accuracy"; "Just received! A new stock of sports shirts for men with 15 to 19 necks"; "Siberian Husky, 2 yrs. old, eats anything and especially fond of children". Nor is this form of ambiguity entirely foreign to legal contexts, for example, in the rough-and-tumble of appellate advocacy: "May it please your Lordship to turn it over in what your Lordship is pleased to call your Lordship's mind?" or "Your Lordship is quite right, and I am quite wrong — as your Lordship usually is".

Although syntactic ambiguity often imparts an innocuous humour to poorly-formed sentences, where it finds its way into statutes, especially penal statutes, the consequences can be anything but humorous. An accused's procedural rights, legal culpability, or liability to punishment may depend on how a judge or appellate court construes a statutory provision that is syntactically ambiguous. Indeed, problems of syntactic ambiguity often necessitate the most delicate exercises of judicial judgment. For example, the question may arise, not whether a particular statutory provision applies to the details of an accused's actions, but whether the accused is a member of the class of persons the provision is intended to address.

. . . .

## *Contextual Ambiguity*

Apart from semantic and syntactic ambiguity, statutory provisions may be ambiguous because of competing contextual considerations arising either within the statute or between provisions of two or more statutes. Contextual ambiguities will occur notwithstanding that the meaning and syntax of the provisions in question may be unequivocal. A problem may arise concerning which of two inconsistent statutory directives should be considered controlling, or whether a particular implication should be inferred. For example, where general words in a statute follow a non-exhaustive enumeration of persons, things, or actions that appear to be instances of a single genus, there may arise a question whether the indeterminate "residue" should be restricted to persons, things, or actions of that genus. Although aspects of each of the sorts of contextual ambiguities will converge in a given case, problems of contextual ambiguity may useful be grouped into two broad classes: (i) *internal* contextual ambiguity, where the semantic problem is at least formally localized within the statute; and (ii) *external* contextual ambiguity, where the semantic problem results from the applicability of two or more statutes to the legal controversy. As will become clear below, the judicial resolution of contextual ambiguities typically involves the invocation of general legal principles which provide residual guidance where various forms of statutory uncertainty arise.

*Internal Contextual Ambiguity*

Problems of internal contextual ambiguity may take a number of forms, many of which have no counterpart in traditional doctrine on statutory interpretation. Even where the problem is a recurrent feature of statutory language, there is only seldom a rule or principle of interpretation that will reconcile in an acceptable way, and for the right reasons, the different thrusts of meaning occasioned by its occurrence. The uniqueness of proper context from one semantic problem to another usually renders inappropriate the reflexive invocation of alleged rules, canons, presumptions, and so forth. While the result reached in a given case may coincide with the dictates of an established precept of interpretation, such coincidence is often more, as it were, coincidental than casual.

. . . .

*External Contextual Ambiguity*

Contextual ambiguities are not confined to the interrelationships among provisions in the same statute, for it often happens that more than one statute is pertinent to the legal controversy. Where provisions from two or more enactments are relevant but seemingly irreconcilable, and where a choice has to be made about which provision has, in the circumstances, a greater claim to judicial attention, the problem is one of external contextual ambiguity. The most fertile source of external contextual ambiguity in Canadian criminal law is the often problematic relationship between the Criminal Code and various provisions in the Interpretation Act. For example, in *Re Purdy and The Queen*, the question arose whether s. 27(2) of the Interpretation Act, which makes certain provisions of the Code applicable to offences under all other federal enactments, coupled with the statutory power of a justice to issue search warrants where he is satisfied that there are reasonable grounds to believe that a Criminal Code offence has been committed, could be used to supply the absence of such a power regarding offences against the Broadcasting Act. Section 27(2) or the Interpretation Act and s. 443(1)(b) of the Code are extracted below:

> (2) All the provisions of the *Criminal Code* relating to indictable offences apply to indictable offences created by an enactment, and all the provisions of the *Criminal Code* relating to summary conviction offences apply to all other offences created by an enactment, except to the extent that the enactment otherwise provides.

> **443**(1) A justice who is satisfied by information upon oath in Form 1, that there is reasonable ground to believe that there is in a building, receptacle or place

. . . .

(b) anything that there is reasonable ground to believe will afford evidence with respect to the commission of an offence against this Act ...

. . . .

may at any time issue a warrant under his hand authorizing a person named therein or a peace officer to search the building, receptacle or place for any such thing, and to seize and carry it before the justice who issued the warrant or some other justice for the same territorial division to be dealt with by him according to law.

In a lucid and libertarian judgment, Mr. Justice Limerick for the New Brunswick Court of Appeal rejected any such implication. He asserted that "there is no right since the *Magna Carta* in any person to invade the home or enter privately occupied lands or buildings in the absence of contractual or statutory provisions", and that legislation derogating from common law rights must be expressed with irresistible clarity where it purports to override them. Since s. 443(1)(*b*) confers this authority only with respect to offences "against this Act", namely, against the Criminal Code, and since s. 27(2) of the Interpretation Act does not incorporate the expression *"mutatis mutandis"*, the inexorable conclusion was that the power to issue search warrants under s. 443(1)(*b*) was intended to be restricted to offences under the Criminal Code. Implicit in the court's conclusion was that the power to issue search warrants for offences against the Broadcasting Act must be grounded in a statutory sanction more emphatic than the one contended for by the Crown. On this and other of the issues raised by the appeal, Mr. Justice Limerick's opinion is exemplary of the principle of legality vigorously in play.

The effort required to disentangle the congeries of statutory interrelationships between, for example, the Criminal Code and the Interpretation Act, is highlighted by the Supreme Court of Canada decision in *Colet v. The Queen*. The Crown argued that the power to seize firearms pursuant to a warrant issued under the former s. 105 of the Code included the power to *search* for such firearms, even though s. 105 did not authorize search warrants for that purpose. To bolster this argument, the Crown sought to rely on s. 26(2) of the Interpretation Act, which provides that "where power is given to a person, officer or functionary, to do or enforce the doing of any act or thing, all such powers shall be deemed to be also given as are necessary to enable the person, officer or functionary to do or enforce the doing of the act or thing". It was contended that the power to search was a necessary incident of the power to seize, and therefore that s. 26(2) supplied the deficiency.

The Supreme Court of Canada rejected this contention. Mr. Justice Ritchie put the point forcibly:

It appears to me to follow that any provision authorizing police officers to search and enter private property must be phrased in express terms and the provisions of the *Interpretation Act* are not to be considered as clothing police officers by implication with authority to search when s. 105(1) and the warrant issued pursuant thereto are limited to seizure. The extensive number of sections of the *Criminal Code* to which reference was made by the trial Judge and which expressly include the dual authority "to search" and "to seize" are enough in themselves to indicate that the deeming provisions of s. 26(2) of the *Interpretation Act* are not applicable to the circumstances.

... It is my respectful opinion that if Parliament intended to include the power "to search" in the provisions of s. 105(1), the failure to do so was a clear case of legislative oversight, but that power which has not been expressly conferred cannot be supplied by invoking the provisions of the *Interpretation Act*.

. . . .

## VAGUENESS

The discussion thus far has concerned the various forms of ambiguity that occur in penal statutes, and has demonstrated how judges tend to resolve them by invoking principles which pertain, not to the ascertainment of meaning *per se*, but the socio-legal considerations which impel the adoption of one interpretation to the exclusion of another. Vagueness is a qualitatively different form of semantic uncertainty, and it is unfortunate that ambiguity and vagueness have occasionally been treated as though they implied the same contests of meaning.

The salient differences between ambiguity and vagueness have been well articulated by Dickerson:

> Where "ambiguity" in its classical sense refers to equivocation, "vagueness" refers to the degree to which, independently of equivocation, language is uncertain in its respective application to a number of particulars. Whereas the uncertainty of ambiguity is central, with an "either-or" challenge, the uncertainty of vagueness lies in marginal questions of degree. This uncertainty is said to result from the "open texture of concepts".

Statutory language may be ambiguous, vague, or both. For example, the phrase "by that person" in s. 214(5) of the Criminal Code is ambiguous; it is uncertain whether it refers only to the person who causes the death, or to any person who is a party to the murder, notwithstanding that the latter may have taken no part in the actual killing. On the other hand, the phrase "gross indecency" in s. 157 of the Criminal Code is vague: apart from the exceptions set forth in s. 158, whether or not a particular sexual behaviour is "grossly indecent" in law is a question more of putative social tolerance than of probable statutory meaning. That a term may simultaneously be ambiguous and vague is illustrated by the word "residence". For example, where a taxing statute provides a special deduction for taxpayers "having residence in Ontario", it may initially be unclear (a) whether the taxpayer is required to have a place of abode in Ontario, or to be domiciled in Ontario (in the legal sense of "domicile"), and (b) if the context suggest the former meaning, whether a particular place of abode is sufficiently "residential", for example, a yacht that is permanently moored in Toronto Harbour and in which the itinerant taxpayer from time to time resides.

Problems of vagueness in penal statutes may usefully be grouped into two broad categories: (1) internal contextual vagueness, in which vague statutory language is construed in light of its full statutory context and in light of general institutional assumptions such as *stare decisis*: and (2) external contextual vagueness, in which a statute or statutes other than the one directly in issue is relevant, at least formally, to the controversy, but is vague in its prescriptions.

## *Internal Contextual Vagueness*

The most cursory perusal of the Canadian Criminal Code betrays an abundance of vague statutory language. Whether the vagueness inheres in the definition of the offence itself, for example, "act of gross indecency"; "indecent act", and "undue exploitation of sex", "a purpose dangerous to the public peace"; "the course of justice"; "anything that is obscene, indecent, immoral, or scurrilous"; or in the definition of an institutional power, for example, "no substantial wrong or miscarriage of justice", it is obvious that Parliament, by couching its directives in such broad language, has delegated to officials charged with administering them, and ultimately to the courts, the discretionary power to determine whether a particular fact situation should be subsumed within the relevant statutory provision.

Vagueness and generality of statutory language are to some extent unavoidable. As H.L.A. Hart has pertinently observed:

> It is a feature of the human predicament (and so of the legislative one) that we labour under two connected handicaps whenever we seek to regulate, unambiguously and in advance, some sphere of conduct by means of general standards to be used without further official direction on particular occasions. The first handicap is our relative ignorance of fact: the second is our relative indeterminacy of aim.

## *External Contextual Vagueness*

A recurrent interpretive problem concerning the Criminal Code and other criminal statutes is that of external contextual ambiguity, in that it is grounded in the applicability of more than one statute to the proceedings in question, there are important distinctions between them. Where external contextual ambiguity arises, the "external" statutory provision has at least *some* relevance to the semantic issue presented; the question is not whether the external provision could, if applied, provide guidance, but whether its application is appropriate where the primary statute provides compelling contextual clues which support a different conclusion. Canadian courts have, for example, refused to allow various "all-purpose" sections in the Interpretation Act to be used to enlarge police powers, to lighten the evidentiary obligations of the Crown, or to erode vital distinctions between Criminal Code and juvenile delinquency proceedings.

Where the problem is one of external contextual *vagueness*, however, the external statutory provision offers no assistance on the semantic issue before the court. It is merely a vague exhortation to the judiciary, rather like a pre-game pep talk to a referee who is told that he should follow its dictates regardless of the rules of the game being played. That a conscientious referee will nonetheless adjudicate on the basis of the rules rather than the rhetoric is hardly surprising. Fortunately, this has been the Canadian experience concerning the criminal law and the "remedial" effect of s. 11 of the Interpretation Act thereon.

Section 11 of the Interpretation Act, which applies to all federal enactments, including the Criminal Code, is the primary source of problems of external contextual vagueness in Canadian criminal law. It provides:

> **11.** Every enactment shall be deemed remedial, and shall be given such fair, large and liberal construction and interpretation as best ensures the attainment of its objects.

The judicial controversy to which this section has given rise, especially within the last decade, has been the extent to which it prevails over common law principles of interpretation which lead to conclusions that, on some view at any rate, are not sufficiently "fair, large and liberal". In reference to the interpretation of the criminal law, the controversy has resolved itself into a contest between the arguable dictates of s. 11 and the principle that the accused should receive the benefit of any reasonable ambiguity in a penal statute. Although judicial exchanges on this issue have been lively of late, the principle of strict construction has emerged relatively unscathed.

. . . .

## CONCLUSION

The interpretation of modern day criminal legislation is plainly a more sophisticated enterprise than either judges, scholars, or legislative draftsmen have been apt to acknowledge. A better understanding of the different types of semantic problems in the criminal law, and of the range of considerations which judges canvass in attempting to resolve them, confers benefits over and above its intrinsic value to the scholar. The clarification of interpretative problems in the criminal law provides a basis for commentary and criticism where, under the guise of "merely interpreting the statute", important related issues of legality and fairness are not adequately addressed. It also can serve as an aid to legislative draftsmen, whose chosen words become the "fixed verbal form" of legislative policy. While the inherent deficiencies of language ensure that statutes will continue to be attended by an aura of imprecision, a heightened awareness of these deficiencies will, it is hoped, result in statutory texts that speak with greater clarity and structural consistency. This, in turn, would sharpen the criminal policy choices put forward for political assent. For, as Chief Justice Dickson has eloquently declared, "it is unnecessary to emphasize the importance of clarity and certainty where freedom is at stake".

## R. v. Paré
(1987), 60 C.R. (3d) 346 at 360 (S.C.C.).

Appeal by Crown from judgment of Quebec Court of Appeal setting aside accused's conviction of first degree murder and substituting conviction of second degree murder.

The judgment of the court was delivered by

WILSON, J.: — Section 214(5)(b) of the Criminal Code, R.S.C. 1970, c. C-34, as enacted by S.C. 1974-1975-1976, c. 105, which was in force at the time of the commission of the offence, provided that murder is first degree murder when the death is caused by a person while the person is committing indecent assault. The respondent, Marc-André Paré, indecently assaulted and murdered a 7-year-old boy, Steeve Duranleau. The central issue in this appeal is whether the respondent murdered the child "while committing" the indecent assault.

While ss. 213 and 214 were subsequently amended by "An Act to amend the Criminal Code in relation to sexual offences and other offences against the person and to amend certain other Acts in relation thereto or in consequence thereof". S.C. 1980-81-82-83, c. 125, the amendments are not germane to the issue on this appeal.

## THE FACTS

On 13th July 1982, at about 1:30 in the afternoon, the respondent, Marc-André Paré, then 17 years old, met Steeve Duranleau, a 7-year-old boy. At Paré's suggestion, the two went swimming. After about 15 minutes in the pool Paré offered to take Duranleau to look at some used cars. The offer was only a pretence. Paré's real motive was to get Duranleau alone in order to have sexual relations with him.

After changing, Paré and Duranleau went to a parking lot where they looked at some used cars. Near the parking lot was a bridge that crossed the St. Charles River. Paré lured Duranleau under the bridge. Duranleau wanted to leave, but Paré told him not to and held him by the arm. Paré sat there for the next ten minutes, holding Duranleau by the arm. Then Paré told Duranleau to lie on his back and keep quiet. Paré pulled Duranleau's shorts down and lowered his own pants and underwear. He then lay on top of Duranleau and indecently assaulted him. After ejaculating beside Duranleau's penis, Paré sat up and got dressed.

At this point Duranleau told Paré that he intended to tell his mother about the incident. Paré told him that he did not want him to tell his mother, and that if he did he would kill him. After this exchange of words Paré was certain that the boy would tell his mother as soon as he could. Paré made Duranleau lie on his back. He waited for two minutes with his hand on Duranleau's chest. He then killed Duranleau by strangling him with his hands, hitting him on the head several times with an oil filter, and strangling him with a shoelace.

The accused was charged as follows:

> [TRANSLATION] That in Quebec City, Quebec, on or around 13 July 1982, he illegally and intentionally killed Steeve Duranleau, thereby committing murder in the first degree contrary to ss. 212, 214(5) and 218 of the Criminal Code.

At trial the accused admitted all the facts outlined above. On 7th December 1982 the accused was found guilty of first degree murder. The accused's appeal to the Quebec Court of Appeal was dismissed on 2nd April 1985 (per L'Heureux-Dubé, Beauregard and LeBel JJ.A.), the court substituting a verdict of second degree murder for the jury's verdict of first degree murder: J.E. 85-556. Leave to appeal was granted to the Crown by this court (per Beetz, Lamer and Wilson JJ.) on 27th June 1985 [1985] 1 S.C.R. xii.

## THE COURTS BELOW

### The Superior Court

In his charge to the jury Bienvenue J. discussed the meaning of the words "while committing" in s. 214(5) of the Criminal Code. Since this appeal hinges upon the meaning of these words, it is necessary to reproduce the relevant comments of the trial judge:

> Alors l'art. 214(2)(5)(b) [sic-214(5)(b)] nous dit ce qui suit: "Est assimilé au meurtre au premier degré" — je ne pense pas que le mot "assimilé" fasse de difficulté entre vous et moi, c'est un mot qui veut dire tout simplement "*est* un meurtre au premier degré", ça va, c'est un meurtre au premier degré , ce qui va suivre — "le meurtre concommittant [sic]" — ou, si vous préférez, au lieu de "concommittant" je vais vous suggérer un éventail d'expressions qui veulent dire la même chose, c'est-à-dire "commis a l'occasion de", "commis au moment de", "qui accompagne", etc., ce qui va suivre, "qui c'est produit en même temps que", tous ces mots-là sont des synonymes de "concom-

mittant" — donc "le meurtre concommittant", ou, si vous préférez, "qui a été commis à l'occasion", du crime "prévu a l'art ... 156" du Code Criminel, "(attentat a la pudeur sur une personne de sexe masculin)" ...

Vous réalisez, je pense, que c'est même pas nécessaire de le dire, je fais droit à votre intelligence à tous, mais au cas ou on me reprocherait un jour de ne pas l'avoir dit que quant on dit "concommittant", c'est-à-dire "commis en même temps, à la même occasion, au même moment", vous réalisez que le Code ne vas pas jusqu'à exiger qu'au moment où je commets un attentat à la pudeur avec ma main droite je doive commettre mon meurtre avec la main gauche. N'est-ce pas? Le Code est logique dans cela, quant on dit "au même moment, commis dans, à la même occasion", ça veut dire: au cours des mêmes circonstances.

The jury found the accused guilty of first degree murder.

### *The Court of Appeal for Quebec*

Beauregard and LeBel J.A. gave separate reasons; L'Heureux-Dubé J.A. agreed with both. Beauregard J.A. examined the case law and decided that s. 214(5) of the Criminal Code should be restrictively interpreted. He concluded that "while committing" must be contrasted with "after having finished committing". A murder committed after the accused had committed the indecent assault was not a first degree murder. Accordingly, when the trial judge said to the jury that a murder committed "on the occasion of" an indecent assault was a first degree murder, he did not invite the jury to consider the really critical question, namely, whether the murder was committed during the commission of the indecent assault or after the indecent assault was over.

Beauregard J.A. was of the opinion that a properly-directed jury would not have been convinced beyond a reasonable doubt that the accused murdered his victim while committing the indecent assault. Consequently, he dismissed the appeal and substituted a verdict of second degree murder for the verdict of first degree murder.

LeBel J.A. did not agree with Beauregard J.A.'s conclusion that s. 214(5) required the murder and the indecent assault to be absolutely simultaneous. Even if the section were to be construed restrictively, he stated, it must not be deprived of all effect. By reading s. 214(5) in conjunction with s. 213 LeBel J.A. concluded that the words "while committing" demanded a close temporal connection between the indecent assault and the murder. Moreover, he concluded that the murder must be an immediate consequence of the first offence for s. 214(5) to apply. LeBel J.A. found it difficult to conclude that a jury more completely informed of the nuances of the sections in question would have necessarily returned the same verdict. The charge given to the jury, he stated, effectively prevented the jury from directing its attention to the proper meaning of s. 214(5). Therefore, despite his reservations about Beauregard J.A.'s conclusions of law, LeBel J.A. agreed with his disposition of the case.

## THE ISSUE

Counsel for the appellant submit that the Court of Appeal made two errors in law. First, it erred in concluding that s. 214(5) of the Criminal Code created a substantive offence of murder. Second, it erred in its interpretation of the words "while committing" in s. 214(5). I will address both issues, looking first at the general scheme of the murder provisions in the Criminal Code and then turning to the interpretation of the particular wording of s. 214(5).

## *The General Scheme*

Counsel for the appellant submit that the Court of Appeal viewed s. 214(5) of the Criminal Code as creating a substantive offence of murder. I find nothing in the judgments rendered by the Court of Appeal that suggests that this was the case. In any event, counsel for the respondent acknowledge that such an approach would be improper, and I agree. Section 214 has a completely different function.

The relevant provisions of the Criminal Code are as follows:

212. Culpable homicide is murder
(a) where the person who causes the death of a human being
   (i) means to cause his death, or
   (ii) means to cause him bodily harm that he knows is likely to cause his death, and is reckless whether death ensues or not;
(b) where a person, meaning to cause death to a human being or meaning to cause him bodily harm that he knows is likely to cause his death, and being reckless whether death ensues or not, by accident or mistake causes death to another human being, notwithstanding that he does not mean to cause death or bodily harm to that human being; or
(c) where a person, for an unlawful object, does anything that he knows or ought to know is likely to cause death, and thereby causes death to a human being, notwithstanding that he desires to effect his object without causing death or bodily harm to any human being.

213. Culpable homicide is murder where a persons causes the death of a human being while committing or attempting to commit high treason or treason or an offence mentioned in section 52 (sabotage), 76 (piratical acts), 76.1 (hijacking an aircraft), 132 or subsection 133(1) or sections 134 to 136 (escape or rescue from prison or lawful custody), 143 to 145 (rape or attempt to commit rape), 149 or 156 (indecent assault), subsection 246(2) (resisting lawful arrest), 247 (kidnapping and forcible confinement) 302 (robbery), 306 (breaking and entering) or 389 or 390 (arson), whether or not the person means to cause death to any human being and whether or not he knows that death is likely to be caused to any human being, if
(a) he means to cause bodily harm for the purpose of
   (i) facilitating the commission of the offence, or
   (ii) facilitating his flight after committing or attempting to commit the offence,
and the death ensues from the bodily harm;
(b) he administers a stupefying or overpowering thing for a purpose mentioned in paragraph (a), and the death ensues therefrom;
(c) he wilfully stops, by any means, the breath of a human being for a purpose mentioned in paragraph (a), and the death ensues therefrom; or
(d) he uses a weapon or has it upon his person
   (i) during or at the time he commits or attempts to commit the offence, or
   (ii) during or at the time of his flight after committing or attempting to commit the offence,
and the death ensues as a consequence.

214. — (a) Murder is first degree or second degree murder ...
(5) Irrespective of whether a murder is planned and deliberate on the part of any person, murder is first degree murder in respect of a person when the death is caused by that person
(a) while committing or attempting to commit an offence under section 76.1 (hijacking aircraft) or 247 (kidnapping and forcible confinement); or
(b) while committing an offence under section 144 (rape) or 145 (attempt to commit rape) or while committing or attempting to commit an offence under section 149 (indecent assault on female) or 156 (indecent assault on male).

It is clear from a reading of these provisions that s. 214 serves a different function from ss. 212 and 213. Section 212 and 213 create the substantive offence of murder. Section 214 is simply concerned with classifying for sentencing purposes the offences created by ss. 212 and 213. It tell us whether the murder is first degree or second degree. This view of s. 214 was expressly adopted by this court in *R. v. Farrant*, [1983] 1 S.C.R. 124, 32 C.R. (3d) 289, [1983] 3 W.W.R. 171, 4 C.C.C. (3d) 354, 147 D.L.R. (3d) 511, 21 Sask. R. 271, 46 N.R. 337 (per Dickson J. at p. 140), and in *Droste v. R.* [1984] 1 S.C.R. 208, 39 C.R. (3d) 26, 10 C.C.C. (3d) 404, 6 D.L.R. (4th) 607, 3 O.A.C.179, 52 N.R.176 (per Dickson J. at p. 218). In this case it is established that the respondent murdered Steeve Duranleau. The issue is whether s. 214(5)(b) makes the murder first degree.

## *Section 214(5): "while committing"*

### *The Literal Meaning*

Did the respondent murder Duranleau while committing an indecent assault? Counsel for the respondent submit that he did not. The argument here is simple. The murder occurred, it is submitted, after the indecent assault was complete. Thus, by a literal reading of s. 214(5) Paré did not murder Duranleau "while committing" an indecent assault.

This argument is a forceful one but by no means decisive. The literal meaning of words could equally be termed their acontextual meaning. As Professor Dworkin points out, the literal or acontextual meaning of words is "the meaning we would assign them if we had no special information about the context of their use or the intentions of their author": see R. Dworkin, Law's Empire (1986), Cambridge, Harvard University Press, at p. 17. Thus the words "while committing" could have one meaning when disembodied from the Criminal Code and another entirely when read in the context of the scheme and purpose of the legislation. It is the latter meaning that we must ascertain.

A preliminary problem in ascertaining the contextual meaning of the phrase "while committing" arises from an inconsistency between the French and English versions of s. 214(5). At the time of the offence the French version of the English words "while committing" was "concomitant". In 1983 the word "concomitant" was replaced by the phrase "en commettant". Is this change in wording in the French version significant to the interpretation of s. 214(5)? I think not. I would agree with Beauregard J.A. of the Quebec Court of Appeal, who said: "Il me semble que la modification n'a rien apporté de nouveau. Le mot 'concommittant' [sic] signifiait 'while committing' ou 'en commettant'."

## The Case Law

I now turn to cases which throw some light on the meaning of the words "while committing". Counsel for the appellant submit that these words in s. 214(5) should not be held to require the murder and the underlying offence to take place simultaneously. They seek to support this contention by reference to the judicial interpretation of the same words in s. 213.

Section 213 transforms culpable homicide into murder where a persons causes the death of a human being "while committing" any one of a number of serious offences, provided that the case falls within one of the four categories listed in ss. 213(a) to 213(d). The cases have consistently construed the words "while committing" in s. 213 to include cases where the homicide is committed during flight after commission of the underlying offence: see *R. v. Vaillancourt* (1974), 31 C.R.N.S. at 82, 16 C.C.C. (2d) 137, affirmed [1976] 1 S.C.R. 13, 31 C.R.N.S. 81, 21 C.C.C. (2d) 65, 54 D.L.R. (3d) 512, 4 N.R. 30 [Ont.]; *R. v. Stevens* (1984), 11 C.C.C (3d) 518, 2 O.A.C. 239 (C.A.). The appellant's argument is that because "while committing" is broadly construed in s. 213 it should also be broadly construed in s. 214(5).

This argument, in my view, is not sound. The particular construction placed on the words "while committing" in s. 213 was mandated by the reference to "flight" in subss. (a)(ii) and (d)(ii) of that section. As Martin J.A. noted in *Stevens* at p. 540: "Any other interpretation [of the words "while committing"] would deprive paras. (a)(ii) and (d)(ii) or s. 213 of any meaning and would render them inoperative ... ". Section 214(5), however, contains no such references to "flight". Thus no analogy may properly be drawn from judicial interpretation of the words "while committing" in s. 213. The same words appearing in s. 214(5) must be interpreted in the particular context of that section.

In *R. v. Gourgon* (1979), 9 C.R. (3d) 313, affirmed 19 C.R. (3d) 272 (B.C.C.A.), Anderson J. construed the words very narrowly. He stated at p. 319:

> (2) the words "while committing" in s. 214(5) ... relate to the time of the commission of the offence of "forcibly confining" and to no other time.
> I agree that the words "while committing" in s. 214(5) do not apply to "flight", and that unlike s. 213, the words "while committing" do not have to be given an extended meaning to make sense of s. 214(5).

It should be noted, however, that Anderson J.'s comments on the interpretation issue were obiter, since in that case the underlying offence of confinement was continuing at the very instant when the death took place.

. . . .

## Strict Construction

Counsel for the respondent argue that the doctrine of strict construction of criminal statutes requires that this court adopt the interpretation most favourable to the accused. According to this argument the words "while committing" must be narrowly construed so as to elevate murder to first degree only when the death and the underlying offence occur simultaneously. In order to assess the validity of this position we must examine the doctrine of strict construction.

The doctrine is one of ancient lineage. It reached its pinnacle of importance in a former age when the death penalty attached to a vast array of offences. As Stephen Kloepfer points out in his article "The Status of Strict Construction in Canadian Criminal Law" (1983) 15 Ottawa L. Rev. 553, at pp. 556-60, the doctrine was one of many tools employed by the judiciary to soften the impact of the Draconian penal provisions of the time. Over the past two centuries criminal law penalties have become far less severe. Criminal law remains, however the most dramatic and important incursion that the state makes into individual liberty. Thus, while the original justification for the doctrine has been substantially eroded, the seriousness of imposing criminal penalties of any sort demands that reasonable doubts be resolved in favour of the accused.

This point was underlined by Dickson J. in *Marcotte v. Can. (Dep. A.G.)*, [1976] 1 S.C.R. 108 at 115, 19 C.C.C. (2d) 257, 51 L.R. (3d) 259, 3 N.R. 613 [Ont.]:

> It is unnecessary to emphasize the importance of clarity and certainty when freedom is at stake. No authority is needed for the proposition that if real ambiguities are found, or doubts of substance arise, in the construction and application of a statute affecting the liberty of a subject, then that statute should be applied in such a manner as to favour the person against whom it is sought to be enforced. If one is to be incarcerated, one should at least know that some Act of Parliament requires it in express terms, and not, at most, by implication.

. . . .

*Applying the Doctrine*

As we have noted above, it is clearly grammatically possible to construe the words "while committing" in s. 214(5) as requiring murder to be classified as first degree only if it is exactly coincidental with the underlying offence. This, however, does not end the question. We still have to determine whether the narrow interpretation of "while committing" is a reasonable one, given the scheme and purpose of the legislation.

In my view, the construction that counsel for the respondent would have us place on these words is not one that could reasonably be attributed to Parliament. The first problem with the exactly simultaneous approach flows from the difficulty in defining the beginning and end of an indecent assault. In this case, for example, after ejaculation the respondent sat up and put his pants back on. But for the next two minutes he kept his hand on his victim's chest. Was this continued contact part of the assault? It does not seem to me that the important issues of criminal law should be allowed to hinge upon this kind of distinction. An approach that depends on this kind of distinction should be avoided if possible.

A second difficulty with the exactly simultaneous approach is that it leads to distinctions that are arbitrary and irrational. In the present case, had the respondent strangled his victim two minutes earlier than he did, his guilt of first degree murder would be beyond dispute. The exactly simultaneous approach would have us conclude that the two minutes he spent contemplating his next move had the effect of reducing his offence to one of second degree murder. This would be a strange result. The crime is no less serious in the latter case than in the former; indeed, if anything, the latter crime is more serious, since it involves some element of deliberation. An interpretation of s. 214(5) that runs contrary to common sense is not to be adopted if a reasonable alternative is available.

In my view, such an interpretation has been provided by Martin J.A. in *Stevens*, supra. As noted above, Martin J.A. suggested [at p. 541] that "where the act causing death and the acts constituting the rape, attempted rape, indecent assault or an attempt to commit indecent assault, as the case may be, all form part of one continuous sequence of events forming a single transaction" the death was caused "while committing" an offence for the purposes of s. 214(5). This interpretation eliminates the need to draw artificial lines to separate the commission and the aftermath of an indecent assault. Further, it eliminates the arbitrariness inherent in the exactly simultaneous approach. I would therefore respectfully adopt Martin J.A.'s single transaction analysis as the proper construction of s. 214(5).

This approach, it seems to me, best expresses the policy considerations that underlie the provision. Section 214, as we have seen, classifies murder as either first or second degree. All murders are serious crimes. Some murders, however, are so threatening to the public that Parliament has chosen to impose exceptional penalties on the perpetrators. One such class of murders is that found in s. 214(5), murders done while committing a hijacking, a kidnapping and forcible confinement, a rape, or an indecent assault. An understanding of why this class of murder is elevated to murder in the first degree is a helpful guide to the interpretation of the language.

The Law Reform Commission of Canada addressed this issue in its working paper 33, Homicide (1984). At p. 79 the paper states:

> ... there is a lack of rationale in the law. Subsection 214(5) provides that, whether planned and deliberate or not, murder is first degree murder when committed in the course of certain listed offences. It is curious that the list there given in considerably shorter than that given in section 213 which makes killing murder if done in the commission of certain specified offences. Inspection and comparison of the two lists, however, reveal no organizing principle in either of them and no rationale for the difference between them.

With respect, I disagree. The offences listed in s. 214(5) are all offences involving the unlawful domination of people by other people. Thus an organizing principle for s. 214(5) can be found. This principle is that, where a murder is committed by someone already abusing his power by illegally dominating another, the murder should be treated as an exceptionally serious crime. Parliament has chosen to treat these murders as murders in the first degree.

Refining, then, the concept of the "single transaction" referred to by Martin J.A. in *Stevens*, supra, it is the continuing illegal domination of the victim which gives continuity to the sequence of events culminating in the murder. The murder represents an exploitation of the position of power created by the underlying crime and makes the entire course of conduct a "single transaction". This approach, in my view, best gives effect to the philosophy underlying s. 214(5).

*The Charge to the Jury*

Given this interpretation of s. 214(5), was Bienvenue J.'s charge to the jury acceptable? The trial judge gave of number of definitions of "while committing". I do not think, however, that these definitions would have confused the jury or included events too remote from the underlying offence. The words "while committing" in s. 214(5) include conduct which is part of one continuous sequence of events forming a single transaction to the jury was in line with this interpretation, since it emphasized the need for connection between the two offences, but without demanding that they occur simultaneously.

## CONCLUSION

The respondent murdered Steeve Duranleau two minutes after indecently assaulting him. The killing was motivated by the fear that the boy would tell his mother about the indecent assault. The jury found the respondent guilty of first degree murder. They were entitled to do so. The murder was temporally and causally connected to the underlying offence. It formed part of one continuous sequence of events. It was part of the same transaction.

I would allow the appeal and restore the conviction of first degree murder.

*Appeal allowed; conviction restored.*

## S.C.C. Has Always Had Policy-making Role, Justice Says*
*Julia Gulej*

\* *The Lawyers Weekly*, February 23, 1990, p. 18.

Supreme Court of Canada Justice Clair L'Heureux-Dubé has shed light on the top court's "new importance as the watchdog of Parliament's legislative activities" since the inception of the *Canadian Charter of Rights and Freedoms*.

"These are truly great days for court watchers," Madam Justice L'Heureux-Dubé told lawyers at the Feb. 8 annual dinner meeting of the County of York Law Association in Toronto.

In her address "A View From the Top," she told the audience of lawyers and judges: "In less than five years, there have been attempts to stretch the Constitutional blanket as far as it has taken 200 years to extend south of the border ... .

"In our lifetime we will have answers to some of the most difficult human rights question. The protection you and I have from unfair governments will be determined. Laws will fall because the violate private rights. ...

"I have faith that in the end we are all, politicians, lawyers and judges alike, motivated by a real determination to improve the human condition," she said.

Not all "court watchers" share her excitement over the court's enhanced role, Madam Justice L'Heureux-Dubé acknowledged.

"How often do we hear journalists rave, in their infinite wisdom, about a 'government of judges' that would have taken over the country; an insidious power held by nine unknowns, half-gods or demons, for whom no-one voted and that are really hard to get rid of.

"Their argument goes something like this: The Charter makes it illegal for governments to infringe upon certain personal rights and freedoms. But the Supreme Court of Canada now has the final word in determining just what those rights and freedoms are.

"Therefore the Supreme Court is in fact making the law rather than Parliament or the provincial legislatures.

"What worries our critics," Madam Justice L'Heureux-Dubé noted, "is that justices are appointed and not elected and, in a democracy, law-making should be left to elected representatives."

It is important that this image of the courts' "evil powers" be dissipated, she said.

"Since the judicial system exists only for them and because of them, the citizens of this country have to know and understand that towards which they pay so much money."

The Supreme Court of Canada, as the country's last appellate court, has "always played a dual role," she said, as an adjudicator and policy-maker.

"Most of the public — and some lawyers too — still believe" the Supreme Court's main function to be its "traditional adjudicative role, as King Solomon deciding on the baby's fate ... .

"But there is another function that the court has performed for as long as it has existed: that of policy-maker.

"Laws are not ready-to-apply texts that require of the judge only a factual analysis. One has only to read the *Income Tax Act* to be sure of that," she said.

"Laws are not carved in stone but are rather malleable: They invariably are reshaped by their application. Were it not so and were statutes so inflexible, then the law would be even further from justice than some people think it already is."

The Charter merely added "another dimension to this aspect of the courts' function," she said, "that of direct control over legislative activities, not in regard of separation of powers, which implies only that the wrong level of government passes a law and that the appropriate legislative assembly could enact the same law, but in regard of the protection of individual rights."

Charter ss. 1, 24 and 52 seem to "give the courts a more interventionist role, somewhat different from the traditional principle of judicial restraint," she said, adding that this "new challenge facing the courts is only a step further than what the courts, and particularly the Supreme Court, were already doing."

The Supreme Court's decision *Roncarelli v. Duplessis*, [1959] S.C.R. 121, is an example, she said, of what the court was already doing.

When Parliament and the provinces enacted constitutional changes respecting individual rights back in 1982 and 1985, they "could have spelled out every detail of every right and freedom they intended to protect.

"Instead, they provided Canadians with guidelines and gave them access to the courts should they feel clarification is needed."

Since then "Charter arguments have often been used as shortcuts to change the system, a more direct way than legislative action ... ."

But the courts are "not always the best place to settle political issues," Madam Justice L'Heureux-Dubé warned, "and it sometimes ends up like trying to cure a headache with brain surgery."

In addition to affecting the courts' role, the Charter has "changed the Canadian public's perception of their judicial system and of the Supreme Court."

The Supreme Court of Canada found itself under a spotlight, its work attracting much closer scrutiny than it had in the past.

As a result, the "renewed importance of the independence of the judiciary, in substance and in appearance, is more crucial today than ever before," the justice said.

"The Charter, in recognizing certain rights, aims to regulate relations between the state and the individuals. Between the two, judges must act as mediators and arbitrators, balancing the individual's recognized rights and the right and obligation of a democratically elected government to manage the affairs of the state.

"This appears most clearly in the wording of s. 1 of the Charter," she said, "where the court must deal with notions such as 'reasonable limits' and 'demonstrably justified in a free and democratic society.'

"Faced with such vague social notions, where any expressed view will probably not be shared by at least part of the population, independence and impartiality are essential to maintain the legal system's integrity."

It took "centuries of hard work to insure the courts a systemic independence from the crowned and elected politicians, in order to allow the law to operate fairly and free from political pressure," Madam Justice L'Heureux-Dubé said.

"Now, a new player has appeared on the block and is making a lot of waves, demanding that its importance and legitimacy be recognized; the organized interest group."

They "may have a role to play, but the law cannot become their hostage."

This can be achieved by "drastically restructuring the court system itself," she said.

"If people were encouraged to utilize alternate dispute resolution methods and if politicians were slower to seek judicial solutions to policy problems, the public might well become less preoccupied by the heritage, background and gender of judges."

Are the courts "really suited" for their new role under the Charter? she asked.

The questions raised are far from being merely legal and judges have had to rely on lawyers to present them with a reliable picture of Canadian society.

"One may wonder if this is a task for which *they* are suited," the justice said, adding; "after all, it isn't something there were taught to do in law school."

Some believe "judges are all very conservative, some kind of dinosaurs, unaware of society's changing values or, at the other end of the spectrum since the advent of the Charter, too liberal, that will either slow down or accelerate too abruptly the development of a legal system reflective of society itself.

"Without going as far as saying that this criticism is totally unfounded," she said, "I feel it is generalizing far too much to think that all judges are alike.

"There are, even between judges of a same court, differences of opinion of a fundamental nature ... ."

Moreover, "judges are the product of their legal training and practice, two aspects of the legal world that usually evolve rapidly: consequently, applying a kind of Darwinian evolution theory to the judiciary, judges are bound to follow, although maybe at a different pace, the evolution of our society," Madam Justice L'Heureux-Dubé said.

"One thing seems certain: Courts will have to change with time one way or another.

"The Supreme Court has proven that it can change, though sometimes not without difficulties, and I am convinced that it can adjust to face any new challenge presented by the Charter."

Lawyers will have to assist the courts and play a strong supportive role, she said.

## Law Society of Upper Canada v. Skapinker
(1984), 9 D.L.R. (4th) 161 at 167 (S.C.C.).

[Only an excerpt from the judgment of Estey is reproduced below.]

We are here engaged in a new task, the interpretation and application of the *Canadian Charter of Rights and Freedoms* as adopted first as an appendage to the Resolution of Parliament on December 8, 1981, and then as an appendix to the *Canada Act, 1982*, 1982 (U.K.), c. 11. This is not a statute or even a statute of the extraordinary nature of the *Canadian Bill of Rights*, R.S.C. 1970, App. III, c. 44. It is part of the Constitution of a nation adopted by constitutional process which, in the case of Canada in 1982, took the form of a statute of the Parliament of the United Kingdom. The adoptive mechanisms may vary from nation to nation. They lose their relevancy or shrink to mere historical curiosity value on the ultimate adoption of the instrument as the Constitution. The *British North America Act, 1867* was such a law, albeit but a statute of the Parliament of the United Kingdom and albeit incomplete in the absence of an intra-national amending mechanism. In the interpretation and application of this document the Judicial Committee of the Privy Council of the United Kingdom, which until 1949 was the highest level of the judicial branch engaged in resolving constitutional issues, said: "The British North America Act planted in Canada a living tree capable of growth and expansion within its natural limits": *Edwards et al. v. A.-G. Can. et al.*, [1930] A.C. 124 at p. 136, per Viscount Sankey L.C., who reiterated this judicial attitude towards a "constituent or organic statute such as the [B.N.A.] Act" in *British Coal Corp. et al. v. The King* (1935), 64 C.C.C. 145 at p. 154, [1935] 3 D.L.R. 401 at p. 410, [1935] A.C. 500 at p. 518. This court recognized the distinction between simple "statutory interpretation" and "a constitutional role" when the court was called upon to determine the effect of the *Canadian Bill of Rights: Curr v. The Queen* (1972), 7 C.C.C. (2d) 181 at p. 191, 26 D.L.R. (3d) 603 at p. 613, [1972] S.C.R. 889 at p. 899, per Laskin J., as he then was. The *Canadian Bill of Rights* is, of course, in form, the same as any other statute of Parliament. It was designed and adopted to perform a more fundamental role than ordinary statutes in this country. It is, however, not a part of the Constitution of the country. It stands, perhaps, somewhere between a statute and a constitutional instrument. Nevertheless, it attracted the principles of interpretation developed by the courts in the constitutional process of interpreting and applying the Constitution itself.

There are some simple but important considerations which guide a court in construing the Charter, and which are more sharply focused and discernible than in the case of the federal *Bill of Rights*. The Charter comes from neither level of the legislative branches of government, but from the Constitution itself. It is part of the fabric of Canadian law. Indeed, it "is the supreme law of Canada": s. 52, *Constitution Act, 1982*. It cannot be readily amended. The fine and constant adjustment process of these constitutional provisions is left by a tradition of necessity to the judicial branch. Flexibility must be balanced with certainty. The future must, to the extent foreseeably possible, be accommodated in the present. The Charter is designed and adopted to guide and serve the Canadian community for a long time. Narrow and technical interpretation, if not modulated by a sense of the unknowns of the future, can stunt the growth of the law and hence the community it serves. All this has long been with us in the process of developing the institutions of government under the *B.N.A. Act, 1867* (now the *Constitution Act, 1867*). With the *Constitution Act, 1982* comes a new dimension, a new yardstick of reconciliation between the individual and the community and their respective rights, a dimension which like the balance of the Constitution, remains to be interpreted and applied by the court.

The courts in the United States have had almost 200 years' experience at this task and it is of more than passing interest to those concerned with these new developments in Canada to study the experience of the United States courts. When the United States Supreme Court was first concerned with the supervision of constitutional development through the application of the recently adopted Constitution of the United States, the Supreme Court of the United States, speaking through Chief Justice Marshall, stated (*Marbury v. Madison* (1803), 5 U.S. 137 at p. 176):

> The question, whether an act, repugnant to the constitution, can become the law of the land, is a question deeply interesting to the United States; but, happily, not of an intricacy proportioned to its interest. It seems only necessary to recognize certain principles, supposed to have been long and well established, to decide it.

There followed a lengthy discussion not dissimilar to that engaged in by the Privy Council and by this Court in considering the allocation of powers and institutional provisions in the Constitution as it existed, at least to 1981. As to the nature of a written Constitution in relation to the component governments, the Chief Justice continued (at p. 177):

> Certainly all those who have framed written constitutions contemplate them as forming the fundamental and paramount law of the nation, and, consequently, the theory of every such government must be, that an act of the legislature, repugnant to the constitution, is void.
> This theory is essentially attached to a written constitution, and is consequently to be considered, by this court, as one of the fundamental principles of our society. It is not therefore to be lost sight of in the further consideration of this subject.

The court then turned to the role of the court (at pp. 177-8):

> It is emphatically the province and duty of the judicial department to say what the law is. Those who apply the rule to particular cases, must of necessity expound and interpret that rule. If two laws conflict with each other, the courts must decide on the operation of each.
> So if a law be in opposition to the constitution; if both the law and the constitution apply to a particular case, so that the court must either decide that case conformably to the law, disregarding the constitution; or conformably to the constitution, disregarding the law; the court must determine which of these conflicting rules governs the case. This is of the very essence of judicial duty.

The court having staked out its constitutional ground then moved on in *M'Culloch v. State of Maryland et al.* (1819), 17 U.S. 316, to consider the techniques of interpretation to be applied in construing a Constitution. Again, speaking through Chief Justice Marshall (at p. 407):

> A constitution, to contain an accurate detail of all the subdivisions of which its great powers will admit, and of all the means by which they may be carried into execution, would partake of the prolixity of a legal code, and could scarcely be embraced by the human mind. It would probably never be understood by the public. Its nature, therefore, requires, that only its great outlines should be marked, its important objects designated, and the minor ingredients which compose those objects be deduced from the nature of the objects themselves ... In considering this question, then, we must never forget, that it is *a constitution* we are expounding.

In recognizing that both legislative and judicial power under the Constitution is limited, the Chief Justice observed that the court must allow the legislative branch to exercise that discretion authorized by the Constitution which will (at p. 412):

> ... enable that body to perform the high duties assigned to it, in the manner most beneficial to the people. Let the end be legitimate, let it be within the scope of the constitution and all means which are appropriate, which are plainly adapted to that end, which are not prohibited, but consist with the letter and spirit of the constitution, are constitutional.

. . . .

## Hunter v. Southam Inc.
(1984), 11 D.L.R. (4th) 641 (S.C.C.).

The judgment of the court was delivered by

DICKSON J.: — The Constitution of Canada, which includes the *Canadian Charter of Rights and Freedoms*, is the supreme law of Canada. Any law inconsistent with the provision of the Constitution is, to the extent of the inconsistency, of no force or effect. Section 52(1) of the *Constitution Act, 1982* so mandates. The constitutional question posed in this appeal is whether s. 10(3), and by implication s. 10(1), of the *Combines Investigation Act*, R.S.C. 1970, c. C-23 (the "Act"), are inconsistent with s. 8 of the Charter by reason of authorizing unreasonable searches and seizures and are therefore of no force and effect.

### "UNREASONABLE" SEARCH OR SEIZURE

At the outset it is important to note that the issue in this appeal concerns the constitutional validity of a statute authorizing a search and seizure. It does not concern the reasonableness or otherwise of the manner in which the appellants carried out their statutory authority. It is not the conduct of the appellants, but rather the legislation under which they acted, to which attention must be directed.

As is clear from the arguments of the parties as well as from the judgment of Prowse J.A., the crux of this case is the meaning to be given to the term "unreasonable" in the s. 8 guarantee of freedom from unreasonable search or seizure. The guarantee is vague and open. The American courts have had the advantage of a number of specific prerequisites articulated in the Fourth Amendment to the United States Constitution, as well as a history of colonial opposition to certain Crown investigatory practices from which to draw out the nature of the interests protected by that Amendment and the kinds of conduct it proscribes. There is none of this in s. 8. There is no specificity in the section beyond the bare guarantee of freedom from "unreasonable" search and seizure; nor is there any particular historical, political or philosophic context capable of providing an obvious gloss on the meaning of the guarantee.

It is clear that the meaning of "unreasonable" cannot be determined by resource to a dictionary, nor for that matter, by reference to the rules of statutory construction. The task of expounding a constitution is crucially different from that of construing a statute. A statute defines present rights and obligations. It is easily enacted and as easily repealed. A constitution, by contrast, is drafted with an eye to the future. Its function is to provide a continuing framework for the legitimate exercise of governmental power and, when joined by a Bill or a Charter of rights, for the unremitting protection of individual rights and liberties. Once enacted, its provisions cannot easily be repealed or amended. It must, therefore, be capable of growth and development over time to meet new social, political and historical realities often unimagined by its framers. The judiciary is the guardian of the Constitution and must, in interpreting its provisions, bear these considerations in mind. Professor Paul Freund expressed this idea aptly when he admonished the American courts "not to read the provisions of the Constitution like a last will and testament lest it become one".

The need for a broad perspective in approaching constitutional documents is a familiar theme in Canadian constitutional jurisprudence. It is contained in Viscount Sankey's classic formulation in *Re s. 24 of B.N.A. Act; Edwards v. A.-G. Can.*, [1930] 1 D.L.R. 98 at pp. 106-7, [1930] A.C. 124 at pp. 136-7, [1929] 3 W.W.R. 479, cited and applied in countless Canadian cases:

> The B.N.A. Act planted in Canada a living tree capable of growth and expansion within its natural limits. The object of the Act was to grant a Constitution to Canada.
> Their Lordships do not conceive it to be the duty of this Board — it is certainly not their desire — to cut down the provisions of the Act by a narrow and technical construction, but rather to give it a large and liberal interpretation ...

More recently, in *Minister of Home Affairs et al. v. Fisher et al.*, [1980] A.C. 319 at p. 329, dealing with the Bermudian Constitution, Lord Wilberforce reiterated that a constitution is a document "*sui generis*, calling for principles of interpretation of its own, suitable to its character", and that as such, a constitution incorporating a *Bill of Rights* calls for [at p. 328]: "a generous interpretation avoiding what has been called 'the austerity of tabulated legalism' suitable to give to individuals the full measure of the fundamental rights and freedoms referred to". Such a broad, purposive analysis, which interprets specific provisions of a constitutional document in the light of its larger objects, is also consonant with the classical principles of American constitutional construction enunciated by Chief Justice Marshall in *M'Culloch v. State of Maryland* (1819), 17 U.S. (4 Wheaton) 316. It is, as well, the approach I intend to take in the present case.

I begin with the obvious. The *Canadian Charter of Rights and Freedoms* is a purposive document. It purpose is to guarantee and to protect, within the limits of reason, the enjoyment of the rights and freedoms it enshrines. It is intended to constrain governmental action inconsistent with those rights and freedoms; it is not in itself an authorization for governmental action. In the present case this means, as Prowse J.A. pointed out, that in guaranteeing the right to be secure from unreasonable searches and seizures, s. 8 acts as a limitation on whatever powers of search and seizure the federal or provincial governments already and otherwise possess. It does not in itself confer any powers, even of "reasonable" search and seizure, on these governments. This leads, in my view, to the further conclusion than an assessment of the constitutionality of a search and seizure, or of a statute authorizing a search or seizure, must focus on its "reasonable" or "unreasonable" impact on the subject of the search or the seizure, and not simply on its rationality in furthering some valid government objective.

Since the proper approach to the interpretation of the *Canadian Charter of Rights and Freedoms* is a purposive one, before it is possible to assess the reasonableness or unreasonableness of the impact of a search or of a statute authorizing a search, it is first necessary to specify the purpose underlying s. 8: in other words, to delineate the nature of the interests it is meant to protect.

Historically, the common law protections with regard to governmental searches and seizures were based on the right to enjoy property and were linked to the law of trespass. It was on this basis that in the great case of *Entick v. Carrington* (1765), 19 State Tr. 1029, the court refused to countenance a search purportedly authorized by the Executive, to discover evidence that might link the plaintiff to certain seditious libels. Lord Camden prefaced his discussion of the rights in question by saying, at p. 1066:

> The great end, for which men entered into society, was to preserve their property. That right is preserved sacred and incommunicable in all instances where it has not been taken away or abridged by some public law for the good of the whole.

The defendants argued that their oaths as King's messengers required them to conduct the search in question and ought to prevail over the plaintiff's property rights. Lord Camden rejected this contention, at p. 1067:

> Our law holds the property of every man so sacred, that no man can set his foot upon his neighbour's close without his leave; if he does he is a trespasser though he does not damage at all; if he will tread upon his neighbour's ground, he must justify it by law.

Lord Camden could find no exception from this principle for the benefit of the King's messengers. He held that neither the intrusions nor the purported authorizations were supportable on the basis of the existing law. That law would only have countenanced such an entry if the search were for stolen goods and if authorized by a justice on the basis of evidence upon oath that there was "strong cause" to believe the goods were concealed in the place sought to be searched. In view of the lack of proper legal authorization for the governmental intrusion, the plaintiff was protected from the intended search and seizure by the ordinary law of trespass.

In my view, the interests protected by s. 8 are of a wider ambit than those enunciated in *Entick v. Carrington*. Section 8 is an entrenched constitutional provision. It is not therefore vulnerable to encroachment by legislative enactments in the same way as common law protections. There is, further, nothing in the language of the section to restrict it to the protection of property or to associate it with the law of trespass. It guarantees a broad and general right to be secure from unreasonable search and seizure.

The Fourth Amendment, of the United States Constitution, also guarantees a broad right. It provides:

#### AMENDMENT IV

The right of the people to be secure in their persons, houses, paper, and effects, against unreasonable searches and seizures, shall not be violated, and no warrants shall issue but upon probable cause, supported by oath or affirmation, and particularly describing the place to be searched, and the persons or things to be seized.

Construing this provision in *Katz v. United States* (1967), 389 U.S. 347, Stewart J., delivering the majority opinion of the United States Supreme Court, declared at p. 351 that "the Fourth Amendment protects people, not places". Justice Stewart rejected any necessary connection between that Amendment and the notion of trespass. With respect, I believe this approach is equally appropriate in construing the protection in s. 8 of the *Canadian Charter of Rights and Freedoms*.

In *Katz*, Stewart J. discussed the notion of a right to privacy, which he described at p. 350 as "the right to be let alone by other people". Although Stewart J. was careful not to identify the Fourth Amendment exclusively with the protection of this right, not to see the Amendment as the only provision in the *Bill of Rights* relevant to its interpretation, it is clear that this notion played a prominent role in his construction of the nature and the limits of the American constitutional protection against unreasonable search and seizure. In the Alberta Court of Appeal, Prowse J.A. took a similar approach to s. 8, which he described [at p. 503 C.C.C., p. 426 D.L.R., p. 150 C.P.R.] as dealing "with one aspect of what has been referred to as a right of privacy which is the right to be secure against encroachment upon the citizens' reasonable expectation of privacy in a free and democratic society".

Like the Supreme Court of the United States, I would be wary of foreclosing the possibility that the right to be secure against unreasonable search and seizure might protect interests beyond the right of privacy, but for purposes of the present appeal I am satisfied that its protection go at least that far. The guarantee of security from *unreasonable* search and seizure only protects a *reasonable* expectation. This limitation on the right guaranteed by s. 8, whether it is expressed negatively as freedom from "unreasonable" search and seizure, or positively as an entitlement to a "reasonable" expectation of privacy, indicates than an assessment must be made as to whether in a particular situation the public's interest in being left alone by government must give way to the government's interest in intruding on the individual's privacy in order to advance its goals, notably those of law enforcement.

The equation that remains, and the one upon which the present appeal hinges, is how this assessment is to be made. When is it to be made, by whom and on what basis? Here again, I think the proper approach is a purposive one.

### When is the Balance of Interests to be Assessed?

If the issue to be resolved in assessing the constitutionality of searches under s. 10 were whether *in fact* the governmental interest in carrying out a given search outweighed that of the individual in resisting the governmental intrusion upon his privacy, then it would be appropriate to determine the balance of the competing interests *after* the search had been conducted. Such a *post facto* analysis would, however, be seriously at odds with the purpose of s. 8. That purpose is, as I have said, to protect individuals from unjustified State intrusions upon their privacy. That purpose requires a means of *preventing* unjustified searches before they happen, not simply of determining, after the fact, whether they ought to have occurred in the first place. This, in my view, can only be accomplished by a system of *prior authorization*, not one of subsequent validation.

A requirement of prior authorization, usually in the form of a valid warrant, has been a consistent prerequisite for a valid search and seizure both at common law and under most statutes. Such a requirement puts the onus on the State to demonstrate the superiority of its interests to that of the individual. As such it accords with the apparent intention of the Charter to prefer, where feasible, the right of the individual to be free from State interference to the interests of the State in advancing its purposes through such interference.

I recognize that it may not be reasonable in every instance to insist on prior authorization in order to validate governmental intrusions upon individuals' expectations of privacy. Nevertheless, where it is feasible to obtain prior authorization, I would hold that such authorization is a pre-condition for a valid search and seizure.

Here also, the decision in *Katz, supra*, is relevant. In *United States v. Rabinowitz* (1950), 339 U.S. 56, the Supreme Court of the United States had held that a search without warrant was not *ipso facto* unreasonable. Seventeen years later, however, in *Katz*, Stewart J. concluded that a warrantless search was *prima facie* "unreasonable" under the Fourth Amendment. The terms of the Fourth Amendment are not identical to those of s. 8 and American decisions can be transplanted to the Canadian context only with the greatest caution. Nevertheless, I would in the present instance respectfully adopt Stewart J.'s formulation as equally applicable to the concept of "unreasonableness" under s. 8, and would require the party seeking to justify a warrantless search to rebut this presumption of unreasonableness.

In the present case the appellants make no argument that it is unfeasible or unnecessary to obtain prior authorization for the searches contemplated by the *Combines Investigation Act* and, in my view, no such argument could be made. I would therefore conclude that in the absence of a valid procedure for prior authorization searches conducted under the Act would be unreasonable. In the event, s. 10(3) *does* purport to establish a requirement for prior authorization, specifying, as it does, that searches and seizures conducted under s. 10(1) must be authorized by a member of the R.T.P.C. The question then becomes whether s. 10(3) provides for an acceptable prior authorization procedure.

. . . .

## Controlling the Trial Process: The Judge and The Conduct of Trial*
*Stanley A. Cohen*

* (1977), 36 C.R.N.S. 15.

### INTRODUCTION

The role of the judge in the conduct of a criminal trial is one calling for great sensitivity. If often requires the delicate balancing of important societal values. The actual manner in which a judge conducts a criminal trial will either enhance respect for the administration of justice or it will detract from it.

The purpose of this portion of this study is to place in high relief the nature and complexity of many of the vexing questions which must be confronted and adequately answered by our judiciary if the judicial system is to retain its credibility with the Canadian people.

The adversary system — the basic procedural structure of the criminal trial — merits and receives consideration in the pages which follow. The role and the response of the trial judge to counsel, and to the accused, is analyzed — both in terms of ideal types and of present shortcomings. In this regard, attention is focused upon the various forms of judicial intervention into the trial process which are presently manifest, and an attempt is made to discern the limitations upon such conduct.

Obviously the analysis offered infra cannot aspire to the final resolution of such highly complex and contentious issues. Nevertheless, the just resolution of them is absolutely crucial to the criminal justice system and to the administration of justice generally.

## PASSIVE AND ACTIVE MODELS OF JUDICIAL DEMEANOUR IN THE CONDUCT OF TRIAL

### *The Adversary Process and the Search for Truth*

"Truth, like all other good things, may be loved unwisely — may be pursued too keenly — may cost too much."

An eminent commentator and jurist reflecting on our legal system poses this question: "Is the quest for justice synonymous with the search for truth?" His answer is qualified: "In most cases, yes. Truth and justice will emerge in a happy coincidence. But not always. Nor should it be thought that the judicial process has necessarily failed if justice and truth do not end up in perfect harmony. Such a result may follow from the law's deliberate policy."

It cannot be denied that the criminal trial process is intimately concerned with the discovery of truth. But, over and above this, its concern is to do justice between man and man. Prejudice, innuendo, opinion and speculation are viewed as poor hand maidens in the cause of justice. Hence the criminal trial is not held "at large" and not "every piece of damning prejudice" will there be received into evidence. The truth is one thing. The law has regard for other values as well, as Freedman C.J.M. (the commentator above referred to) has advised us. A whole network of procedural and evidentiary rules exist to regulate and modulate Canadian trials and thus secure the end of fundamental justice.

The criminal trial process is therefore best regarded as a *qualified* search for truth.

This well-tempered inquiry is pursued in an unusual setting. The citizen and the state confront each other as opponents, or adversaries, and conduct a battle or "fight" according to age-hardened and time-tested rules and procedures.

The criminal trial is the paradigm of this adversary process. It has its detractors as well as its proponents. There are many who proclaim that it is well-suited to the task of discovering truth:

> Many lawyers maintain that the 'fight' theory and the 'truth' theory coincide. They think that the best way for a court to discover the facts in a suit is to have each side strive as hard as it can, in a keenly partisan spirit, to bring to the court's attention the evidence favorable to that side. Macaulay

said that we obtain the fairest decision 'when two men argue, as unfairly as possible, on opposite sides', for 'then it is certain that no important consideration will altogether escape notice'.

In the adversarial setting of the criminal trial this partisan battle involves a clash between the public interest in the suppression of crime and the protection of the public, and the countervailing public interest in the protection of individual rights and liberties.

Because the state is possessed of enormous manpower and economic resources to aid in the process of fact-finding and research, and because the individual does not have similar resources at his disposal, an attempt is made, through the formulation of evidentiary and procedural rules, to "right the balance". This is done in order that the battle of adversaries (which follows the laying of criminal charges) be perceived by the citizenry of the state as an essentially "fair" contest.

As mentioned, in purely objective terms this attempt to strike a balance between the competing claims of the individual and the state must on occasion work in such a way as to actually suppress some of the truth: A wife's evidence is not available in order to condemn her husband, the accused person is generally not obliged to criminate herself, and where the accused does not testify, evidence of his prior misdeeds is generally not available to the prosecution in its efforts to prove its case.

The adversary process as carried on in the criminal courts has (in complimentary terms) been described as an attempt to secure "justice between man and man". Truth is pursued, but not over-zealously and always with an eye toward relevancy and the avoidance of undue prejudice.

To continental lawyers the notion of fabled British justice is something of a puzzle:

> The continental courts claim to have only one aim — the discovery of the truth. The English adversary system claims to settle an issue between the prosecution and the defendant and it is a commonplace remark that this emphasises the sporting element in an English trial. This sporting element is a psychological factor of the greatest importance, for it is out of it that there arises the notion of 'fair play' for the accused. It has recently been argued that with the steady growth of professionalism in crime and the increase (as alleged) in the number of acquittals of those guilty of crime, this notion of a sporting element should be abandoned.

Abandoning the "sporting element" of Anglo-Canadian justice is an extreme suggestion. Freedman C.J.M. indicates that our law "makes its choice between competing values and declares that it is better to close the case without all the available evidence being put on the record. We place a ceiling price on truth".

Nevertheless, there are many who feel that we have fixed the price badly; that there has been "too much tenderness toward prisoners" and that in pursuing "justice" too avidly we have weakened the social fabric.

Jerome Frank is undoubtedly correct when he states that "frequently the partisanship of the opposing lawyers blocks the uncovering of vital evidence or leads to a presentation of vital testimony in a way that distorts it." At the same time, however, it must be remembered that "in the system of trial which we have evolved in this country the judge sits to hear and determine the issues raised by the parties, *not to conduct an investigation or examination on behalf of society at large*". Consequently the criminal trial, as we have noted, is not held "at large". Its terms of reference are circumscribed by many restraints. The requirement of "relevence" is as much an efficiency device designed to avoid needless tangential forays as it is a construct aimed at insuring fundamental fairness in the conduct of the inquiry.

But is there "too much tenderness towards prisoners in these matters"? Is "truth" being sacrificed at the mantle of "justice"? Jerome Frank, himself once a judge of the United States Court of Appeal for the Second Circuit, found many deficiencies to exist in the adversary trial — deficiencies which not only worked to deny truthful facts to the court, but which also worked to frustrate the cause of justice. Judge Frank felt that certain elements inherent in the nature of an adversarial contest operated so as to frustrate even the *qualified* search for truth which our courts presently conduct. He asserted that:

1. The whole atmosphere of the courtroom bewilders witnesses.
2. Lawyers, before trial, "coach" the witnesses who will appear for their clients, not only with regard to the story they will tell, but also the demeanour they should assume in testifying so as to give the most favourable personal impression.
3. Dishonest lawyers use this accepted practice to encourage perjury.
4. Lawyers attempt to discredit witnesses through exercise of the art of cross-examination, regardless of the truth of what these witnesses may be saying.
5. Lawyers refuse to concede facts harmful to their clients if they think the adversary cannot prove them, and they will not help to correct inaccurate statements of witnesses favourable to their clients.
6. Lawyers rely, wherever possible upon surprise as a tactic to keep the adversary from preparing to rebut particular testimony favourable to their clients.
7. The adversary process is deficient because a party may not have the funds to pay for an investigation, before trial, to assemble evidence on his behalf and to rebut evidence on which the other party may rely.

In fairness to Judge Frank much of the above commentary is directed at the adversary system in the context of a civil, rather than a criminal, trial. But the above remarks have much relevance to criminal trials as well.

Those criticisms of the adversary system are not insubstantial. Basically they imply that one of two serious options ought to be implemented:

1. The adversary system ought to be drastically altered in terms of its evidentiary and procedural structure. Irrationality ought to be weeded out and imbalances should be rectified.
2. The adversary system ought to be done away with altogether and should be replaced by an inquisitorial system.

Option (1) above is already in a protean state of existence. The drift of law reform in Canada is towards a whittling away of the historic rights and privileges which have been accorded to accused persons. The process has been slow, but it is inexorable. *Trial by jury* is not a commonplace of our criminal justice system; it is a rarity. Indications are that it will become rarer still. Our rules of evidence, their absurdities notwithstanding, are more honoured in the breach than in practice: see N. Brooks, book review on McWilliams, Canadian Criminal Evidence, and Sopinka and Lederman, "The Law of Evidence in Civil Cases" (1976), 54 Can Bar Rev. 179 at 182. Suggestions for criminal law reform emanating from the Law Reform Commission of Canada include the removal of the accused's right to silence. The present Canadian position with respect to the use of illegally obtained evidence (see *Regina v. Wray*, 11 C.R.N.S. 235, [1971] S.C.R. 272, [1970] 4 C.C.C. 1, 11 D.L.R. (3d) 673) renders much of our rhetoric about "fundamental fairness" a sham and an "embarrassment". Notwithstanding the protestations of some that "the Criminal is living in a Golden Age", the record does not support the charge.

Despite the benefit of reasonable doubt which is accorded to an accused; despite the burden of proof under which the prosecution must labour; and despite the prisoner's right to silence — despite all of these "heavily-weighted advantages" —"the scales of criminal justice are not balanced".

As mentioned, serious resource imbalances exist as between prosecution and accused. In many cases (and here the field is ever-expanding) the onus of proof has been shifted by legislation to the accused.

Against this backdrop our two adversaries are asked to join arms in regulated battle. While, indeed, we still have two adversaries left to fight this battle, the ground under foot is continually shifting. Many hands are "tinkering with the works". Coherency of vision, and unity of purpose, is absent from most of this process.

Its defects notwithstanding, it appears unlikely that there is substantial support in the Canadian legal community for the proposition that the adversary system ought to be *completely* dismantled. Proponents of such change favour the adoption of an inquisitorial system based upon the experience of continental Europe.

The adversary system possesses the "justifications" which (its proponents argue) cannot be compensated for by an inquisitorial process:

1. Truth is more likely to emerge if the parties themselves, motivated by their own self-interest, have control of investigating and presenting the facts to the tribunal; and
2. The tribunal's decision will be morally acceptable to the parties since it was made by one not involved in the presentation of evidence and therefore by one not committed to the particular cause of any single party.

Proponents of the inquisitorial system are more likely to take issue with the first of the propositions, than the second. In their view the continental-style inquiry is unparalleled as a truth-seeking device.

There is, of course, not simply one inquisitorial system utilized by all judicial systems not founded on the Anglo-Saxon. Great differences of approach are apparent from country to country. If a single distillation of the core elements of *the* inquisitorial system is possible, this admiring portrait offered by Edson Haines (Haines, J. of the Ontario Supreme Court) would represent its best qualities as well as any:

> ... the task of the judge in most foreign systems of law is akin to that of the scientist in the laboratory, to ascertain the real truth by all proper means. Essentially the enquiry into the circumstances devolves upon the court and the investigating judge or officer may take considerable time in developing the evidence both for and in favour of the accused. Frequently those injured in the incident giving rise to the charge are also represented, and it is not unusual for the verdict to deal

not only with guilt or innocence but also with civil responsibility, so that all matters may be concluded in the one proceeding. Complicated rules of evidence are unknown. The tendency is to admit all testimony on the theory that the court gives to all evidence the weight it deserves. The accused is questioned as the facts are developed during the investigation and his explanations are checked out by the court which also searches out and examines witnesses for the accused. Serious trials often commence with the examination of the accused which has the advantage at the outset of discovering those areas in dispute and those about which there is no controversy. They really try the man as well as the facts. Consequently the record of the accused, good or bad, is before the court. A feature emphasized in many jurisdictions is that the acquittal of the guilty is a threat to the security of society.

A discourse on the superiority of one system or another in this context is not a particularly useful or fruitful exercise. Our history, societal values and political institutions have quite naturally enclosed us in a cocoon of biases and predilections. However, certain features of the utopian paradigm sketched by Haines, J. do invite obvious responses from the common lawyer.

First among these is the grave risk of prejudice which is assumed in the portrait above mentioned. Innuendo, speculation, opinion and irrelevancies can present a damning trap for any accused person. To assert that judges will offset this danger by weighting evidence in relation to its perceived reliability is to saddle ordinary humans with a very unordinary burden.

"Judging the man as well as the facts" certainly carries with it the risk of convicting *the man* in absence of truly probative facts.

It may well be true that "the acquittal of the guilty is a threat to the security of society", but to the common law lawyer the graver risk to the *viability* of society is posed by the conviction of the innocent.

Not mentioned in the summary provided by Haines, J. is the standard to be utilized for the assessment of guilt. What contrast is there to the common law's presumption of innocence and the necessity for unanimity among our jurymen? In a French assize court, for example, there are three professional magistrates (a president and two assessors) and nine jurymen (selected from 25 drawn by lot for each assize). The whole tribunal deals with both law and fact. If the accused is unable to secure a majority in the vote as to his guilt he will be convicted — a far cry from our jury trials where one man's conscience may ultimately hold sway over jury's deliberations.

The inquisitorial system has been attacked on the basis that its paternalistic character "unavoidably raises suspicions of bias and tastes of despotism." The sufficiency of the inquiry conducted in terms of its fact-gathering mechanism, the ability of the party to bring his views and questions to the attention of the inquisition at the investigative phase, and the inability of the tribunal to contemplate all of the positions which a defendant might wish to advance are pointed to as serious, general defects of such a system.

### *The Role of the Trial Judge in the Adversary Process*

The greater part of this analysis will be devoted to exploring the specific limitations under which trial judges labour in handling various aspects of the trial process. How far a judge can or should proceed to enter into the trial arena is to a certain extent governed by the nature of the problem with which he is presented.

Obviously the role of the trial judge in dealing with an accused who is unrepresented by counsel will be far different from the considerations guiding his conduct when both parties are represented.

The proper response of the court to incompetency in counsel also may prompt the trial judge to deviate from otherwise normal standards of judicial conduct.

Other matters, such as the judicial examination or cross-examination of witnesses or judicial determinations to call witnesses to assist the court in its fact-finding enterprise or expressions of personal opinion by the trial judge, are not generally situation-inspired, but rather are usually expressions of a particular conception of the role of the trial judge in the entire trial process.

Is the trial judge to be an *active* force in the adversarial contest which he characteristically oversees and regulates? Or is his role more properly conceived as a *passive* one, with his interventions for the most part confined to clarifying obscurities and keeping the course of the trial within the orderly channels provided for by rules of evidence and procedure? Is the role of the trial judge essentially an active or a passive one? Does he play the role of pilot, participant or umpire?

In traditional terms, the role of the trial judge conducting a criminal trial has unquestionably been viewed as a passive one.

Denning L.J. in *Jones v. National Coal Bd.*, [1957] 2 Q.B. 55 at 64, [1957] 2 All E.R. 155, details the passive conception of the judicial role as well as it can be sketched:

> ... it is for the advocates, each in his turn, to examine the witnesses, and not for the judge to take it on himself lest by so doing he appear to favour one side or the other ... The judge's part in all this is to harken to the evidence, only himself asking questions when it is necessary to clear up any point that has been overlooked or left obscure; to see that the advocates behave themselves seemly and keep to the rules laid down by law; to exclude irrelevancies and discourage repetition; to make sure by wise intervention that he follows the points that the advocates are making and can assess their worth; and at the end to make up his mind where the truth lies. If he goes beyond this, he drops the mantle of a judge and assumes the role of an advocate; and the change does not become him well.

Sir Edmund Fry on the occasion of being named a Lord Justice of appeal in England summarized his view of the duty of a judge in *any* court:

> Give a benign and receptive listening to each side, so as to feel the full force of the argument on each side, and then judge between them.

It has been said that if a trial judge opts for a more active role — if he, so to speak, "descends into the arena" — he then is "liable to have his vision clouded by the dust of conflict": per Lord Greene M.R. in *Yuill v. Yuill*, [1945] P. 15, [1945] 1 All E.R. 183 at 189. To this it may be added that it then becomes difficult for him to avoid the appearance of bias or prejudice.

> Whatever the variations, a central core of agreed standards defines the trial judge as the neutral, impartial, calm, non-contentious umpire standing between the adversary parties seeing that they observe the rules of the adversary game. The bedrock premise is that the adversary contest is the ideal way to achieve truth and a just result rested upon the truth.

The author of the above-quoted statement acknowledges that even in the passive conception of the judicial role, the idea of the judge solely, or even primarily as "umpire", is not universally accepted. Denning L.J., to whom we have previously referred, also says as much [p. 63]:

> Even in England, however, a judge is not a mere umpire to answer the question 'How's that?' His object, above all, is to find out the truth, and to do justice according to law.

An American jurist commenting on the conception of the trial judge as purely playing an "umpireal" role claims that this view suffers from an inadequate appreciation of the true relationship between judges and lawyers in the trial process:

> Unfortunately, true understanding of the judicial process is not shared by all lawyers or judges. Instead of regarding themselves as occupying a reciprocal relationship in a common purpose, they are apt to think of themselves as representing opposite poles and exercising divergent functions. The lawyer is active, the judge passive. The lawyer partisan, the judge neutral. The lawyer imaginative, the judge reflective.

There is a grain of truth in this critique. The qualities of activism and imagination and, to a degree, even partisanship (where abuse and obstruction of the court's process is involved) are not foreign to the judicial demeanour, even within the parameters of the so-called "passive" conception of the judicial role. The fact is that our system does provide considerable latitude for effective or just intervention by the trial judge in the adversary fight about the facts. (These latitudes are explored more fully in the body of this work.)

However, a major limiting factor circumscribing both the role and aspirations of *any* trial judge is the fact that the trial judge is quintessentially (in criminal matters) unprepared in terms of both advance exposure to, and investigation of, the facts. (In civil cases he will at least have the benefit of the pleadings, affidavits and other supporting material including, on occasion, extensive factual admissions.) Unlike his counterpart in civil law countries he does not have the dossier of the investigating magistrate before him.

> Without an investigative file, the ... trial judge is a blind and blundering intruder, acting in spasms as sudden flashes of seeming light may lead or mislead him at odd times.

Its banality notwithstanding, what goes without saying in discussions centering on the nature of the judicial role is the sentiment that "the essence of the judicial role, active or passive, is impartiality and detachment, both felt and exhibited."

There is an activist conception of the judicial role, different in *kind* from the passive one. The activist ideal (if it can be so described) seeks to eschew the vision of a trial judge powerless to enter the fray in instances where he perceives an overt and patent thwarting of the pursuit of justice through the artful but unfair (not illegal) manipulation of rules and procedures. To such a trial judge the triumph of "justice" may appear as a different thing from the advocate's notion of victory.

The activist trial judge must basically, and most truthfully, be seen to be at odds with the adversary process. In order to be effective in his role he must constantly be straining and testing the very limits of the role which he has been asked to play. His efforts undoubtedly will on occasion meet with rebuke in the higher courts. But ultimately the disagreements between these two judicial levels must be perceived to be disagreements over basic philosophy.

The activist judge is a foe of the adversary system. He is most accurately described as an "adversary judge". Since his aim generally is to reform the system, in ideal terms he should do open battle with it. Characteristically such a judge is both "outspoken" and "creative", although his more traditional critics might employ less enthusiastic adjectives in describing his activity.

Jerome Frank and Marvin Frankel are two American jurists who admirably live up to this portrait. In Canada, Edson Haines (Haines J. of the Ontario Supreme Court) has played a similar role. By their learned commentary, their irascible and uncompromising courtroom demeanour, they vividly present without artifice or deceit — the alternative, full-blown. Basically, these and other "activist" judges do not favour the outright abolition of the adversary process but rather they operate under "the hypothesis that the tensions and contradictions in the trial judge's role may reflect remediable imperfections in the system he administers".

For the present, the activist model of judicial demeanour is out of the mainstream of normative judicial behaviour. However, as we have noted, many hands are at work tinkering with the mechanisms of the adversary process. As these mechanisms are altered the role of the trial judge will, in degree, be affected. If pre-trial discovery (even partial discovery) of the accused becomes a reality and this information becomes available to the court, the adequacy of the pre-trial preparation on the trial judge will be greatly enhanced. If pre-trial conferences between counsel for all parties and the trial judge become a common-place of the system this also will alter the role of the trial judge. If the right to silence of the accused is forfeited the adversary system will be immeasurably affected.

Not all, or indeed any, of these changes should be viewed as salutary. As suggestions for reform, however, they have been kicked about for a long time. And as we enter into yet another era of "law and order" (or, as we choose to call it in Canada, "peace and security") there is no predicting the mood of our legislators.

Yesterday's (or today's) judicial iconoclast may well become tomorrow's archetype. For the moment, however, this picture (which is really a description of the ideal-passive type) is the one which prevails:

> An overtly active judge may give the appearance of a meddler; but equally, a passive and quiescent trial judge may give the appearance of indifference. The public may have a legitimate complaint about the appearance and doing of justice — not just against counsel — but against a Bench which renders judgments based on technical evidentiary deficiencies or errors ... A trial judge who endeavours to assist counsel, parties, and witnesses in the proper, complete and logical development of all aspects of a case within the confines of the rules of evidence and the adversary system, neither favouring one side or the other, nor expressing any bias, but still remaining dispassionate and neutral (but not disinterested or indifferent) will gain the respect of all concerned with the administration of a viable system of justice.

## Questions/Discussion

1. Discuss the ways in which the courts produce criminal law in Canada, and assess the value and effectiveness of those roles. What do you see as the principal problems with the courts' roles in producing criminal law and why? Can these problems be corrected and, if so, how?
2. How can the problems of interpretation of the criminal law be overcome or perhaps minimized? Will problems of this type always be with us to some degree given the vagaries of the fact situations which can arise?

3. Do you agree that gender, class and racial biases on the part of judges are problems in the courts? Why or why not? Do you think that a different kind of criminal law might result, both in theory and in practice, if the judiciary were to become more representative of the Canadian mosaic? In what ways could such a change make itself felt in the criminal law?
4. Are there other types of review processes that might be useful in controlling the activities of the judiciary besides the internal controls exerted by the existing appeal process? Judicial councils do exist now and complaints can be laid with them against individual judges who explicitly state their biases or otherwise conduct themselves in unappropriate manner. Such councils, however, are for the most part secretive bodies and dominated by members of the judiciary.
5. The C.B.A. Task Force on Gender Equality recommended "that sensitivity courses for judges on gender and racial bias be made compulsory not only for newly appointed judges but for all judges" (p. 192). This recommendation was rejected by Chief Justice Lamer of the Supreme Court of Canada in a speech at the University of New Brunswick on March 14, 1996, as a threat to the independence of the judiciary. Do you agree or disagree with the recommendation? Why or why not?

**Further Reading**
- Baar, C., "Judicial Appointments and the Quality of Adjudication: The American Experience in a Canadian Perspective" (1986), 20 Thémis 1.
- Beatty, D., "Constitutional Conceits: The Coercive Authority of Courts" (1987), 37 University of Toronto Law Journal 183.
- Canadian Bar Association Task Force on Gender Equality. Touchstones for Change: Equality, Diversity and Accountability — The Report on Gender Equality in the Legal Profession (Ottawa: The Canadian Bar Association, 1993).
- Campbell, C., "The Canadian Left and the Charter of Rights" (1984), 2 Socialist Studies 30.
- Friedland, M., "Legal Rights Under the Charter" (1984), 24 Criminal Law Quarterly 430.
- Glasbeek, H. and M. Mandel, "The Legalisation of Politics" (1984), 2 Socialist Studies 84.
- Gold, M., "The Mask of Objectivity: Politics and Rhetoric in the SCC" (1985), 7 Supreme Court Law Review 455.
- Hovius, B. and R. Martin, "The CCRF and the Supreme Court of Canada" (1983), 61 Canadian Bar Review 354.
- Laforest, G., The CCRF — An Overview" (1983), 61 Canadian Bar Review 19.
- Martin, R., "The Judges and the Charter" (1984), 2 Socialist Studies 66.
- Olsen, D., *The State Elite* (Toronto: McClelland and Stewart Ltd., 1980).
- Ontario Law Reform Commission. Appointing Judges: Philosophy, Politics and Practice (Toronto: Ontario Law Reform Commission, 1991).
- Russell, P., The Judiciary in Canada: Third Branch of Government (Toronto: McGraw-Hill Ryerson, 1987).
- Russell, P., "The Political Purposes of the CCRF" (1983), 61 Canadian Bar Review 30.
- Russell, P., and J. S. Ziegel, "Federal Judicial Appointments: An Appraisal of the First Mulroney Government's Appointments and the New Judicial Advisory Committees" (199 ), 41 University of Toronto Law Journal 4-37.
- Weiler, K., "Of Courts and Constitutional Review" (1988-89), 31 Criminal Law Quarterly 121.
- Wilson, B., "Will Women Judges Really Make a Difference?" (1990), 24 Gazette 261.
- Ziegel, J.S. "Appointments to the Supreme Court of Canada" (1994), 5 Constitutional Forum 10-15.

# 4

# CRIMINAL LAW — PERSONNEL, PARTICIPANTS, AND POWERS

## 4.1 POLICE

### Historical Development
*C. Mitchell*

This section considers the law regarding police powers and limits on that power. Police history is largely a story of the eclipse of private prosecution and the rise of a professional law enforcement body capable of action against both individual tortfeasors (criminals) and rebellious groups (rioters, rebels, insurrectionists, and terrorists).

Law enforcement is a task requiring incentives. If enforcement is left in private hands, which is by far the cheapest method, the incentives can take four general forms. First, victims can be legally empowered to prosecute alleged wrongdoers in hope of receiving compensation. Second, citizens can be compelled by law to serve as volunteer police. Third, citizens may be rewarded on a bounty system for apprehending offenders and; finally, citizens can be hired by others to enforce the law as part of general private security services. In agricultural, non-commercial societies, such as England in 1285, the first two incentive schemes are employed because they require the least outlay or specialization. As Stenning (1981) comments "without some notable exceptions ... if the private victim or complainant in Medieval England did not initiate and conduct the prosecution of an alleged offender there would normally be no prosecution".

The private, self-policing of English towns and villages was based on custom and compulsion. All adult men served on the "watch" on a roster basis under the direction of a constable (Cooper, 1981). The constable was elected for each parish or shire from among the male citizens. Those who refused to serve as constables and those who failed to assist the watchmen in making an arrest were subject to penalties. But police service, while an imposition, was also a source of pride for small property holders elevated above the labouring poor by holding a minor parochial office such as constable. Evidently, this system is economical and effective in a stable, low population society because law enforcement in such a context is not a high-skilled, full-time, or specialized task. Government ranked military and tax matters a much higher priority than criminal law. Tort law was also economical because the aggrieved party acted as detective, prosecutor and witness without state subsidy or bounty. Historians generally agree that England from 1290-1485 experienced ineffective public policing. Part of the problem was official corruption. According to Bellamy (1973:12-14):

> Almost as productive of lawlessness as the king's absence on his military campaigns was the corruption of officials. In all but the most sophisticated societies the holding of office allows suitable

opportunity for illegal gain since the relative paucity of officials per head of population does not permit a comprehensive system of surveillance of one by another... [The] public order office which offered the greatest opportunity for dishonest behaviour and on which contemporaries cast the gravest aspersions was that of sheriff.

Complaints against sheriffs alluded to bribery, embezzlement and corrupting juries. Likewise of coroners it was said that every one practised some type of extortion. These minor law enforcement office holders were not alone, however, in their corruption, rather they were inspired by "the misapplication of the law and the misuse of office on the part of their social and feudal superiors" (Bellamy, 1973:13).

We noted earlier that the Crown weakened tort law incentives by creating "felonies" which individuals had to prosecute but for which they received no recompense. By the 1820s private prosecutors often wanted no part of a conviction for a new reason: because of the severe penalties inflicted on convicts. Police constables were also deterred by the expense of prosecution, which they incurred by having to jail the accused. Eventually, the *Criminal Justice Act* of 1826 in England made it possible for parish constables to recover the cost of detaining suspects in jail. The same Act also empowered courts to award payment to a private prosecutor of misdemeanours and by 1837 the death penalty was repealed for all property offences. Rude (1985) reports that while these reforms increased prosecutions somewhat, incentives remained inadequate. Tort incentives also decreased with greater social mobility, complexity and individuality since these changes meant that many wrongdoers could not or would not pay damages. When wrongdoers are "judgement-proof", one logical recourse is to substitute afflictive punishment for compensation. Another tactic is to enforce a period of personal service on the defendant in lieu of a money payment and this strategy was also employed in England. Writing about the 1700s in England, Douglas Hay (1975:40) explains:

Almost all prosecutions were initiated by private persons, at their discretion, and conducted in accordance with their views. Accustomed to organized state police and rigorous state prosecution, French visitors were inclined to marvel at this peculiar English institution... The victim of the crime could decide himself upon the severity of the prosecution, either enforcing the letter of the law, or reducing the charge. He could even pardon the offence completely by not going to court. The reformers' objections to this system are well known. Private prosecution was capricious and uncertain and too often rogues escaped due to the distaste, compassion or fear of the victims... In a rural parish with a relatively settled population there were many alternatives to a rigorous prosecution. The accused man could be made to post a bond not to offend again, or be given the choice of leaving the neighbourhood... He might also be allowed to escape the law by making compensation for his crime...

Perhaps more importantly, as social complexity increases private plaintiffs are less likely to know or be able to discover the tortfeasor's identity. Detective services, such as those provided for fictional Victorian clients by Sherlock Holmes, could be purchased, but for the bulk of petty torts, which included the wrongful appropriation of firewood, tools, food and livestock, the cost of finding and suing tortfeasors would be greater than the damages recoverable. One's resources were better spent on preventive security measures.

Under the same modern conditions, the volunteer police force also became problematic. Griffiths *et al.* (1980:44) explain that community policing began to collapse by the 1500s:

This was due in large measure to the movement of people from the rural areas into the cities. Many men declined to perform the duties of constable and it became commonplace for these individuals to pay someone to do the job for them. It soon developed that only the unemployed and uneducated were willing to assume the duties of constable . . . Because of . . . the failure of the watch and ward system, many cities including London were virtually unpoliced by the early nineteenth century. To protect their business and property, many people hired private merchant police.

An indication of the watchmen's quality by 1596 is conveyed in Shakespeare's *Much Ado About Nothing* where, in Act III, Scene III two constables, Dogberry and Verges, give the watchmen their instructions for the night which read, in part, as follows:

**Dogberry:** You shall also make no noise in the streets: for the watch to babble and talk is most tolerable and not to be endured.
**Watch:** We will rather sleep than talk: we know what belongs to a watch.
**Dogberry:** Why, you speak like an ancient and most quiet watchman for I cannot see how sleeping should offend; only have a care that your bills be not stolen. Well, you are to call at all the alehouses, and bid those that are drunk get then to bed.
**Watch:** How if they will not?
**Dogberry:** Why them, let them alone till they are sober: if they make you not then the better answer, you may say they are not the men you took them for . . .
**Watch:** If we know him to be a thief, shall we not lay hands on him?
**Dogberry:** Truly, by your office you may; but I think they that touch pitch will be defiled. The most peaceable way for you, if you do take a thief, is to let him show himself what he is and steal out of your company.
**Verges:** You have been always called a merciful man, partner.
**Dogberry:** Truly, I would not hang a dog by my will, much more a man who hath any honesty in him.

An unpaid citizen's police force requires compulsory service, otherwise "free riders" attempt to enjoy the benefits of policing without contributing their share. Since urban development is based on specialization and commercialization, both of which discourage citizen policing, the usual solution to free rider problems is to collect compulsory taxes and use the revenue to hire full time professional police. Commercial development increases taxable capacity while impeding the close, communal network necessary for volunteer forces.

The Royal Irish Constabulary, a model for the later Northwest Mounted Police in Canada, was established in 1786 and with the Metropolitan Police Act of 1829, the foundations of a professional police force were laid in London. Since the new police broke with a long tradition of citizen enforcement it was natural that they departed little from former procedures. Unlike soldiers, the new police were unarmed, under local civilian control and exercised no more powers of enforcement than ordinary citizens. Sir Robert Peel's principles of law enforcement of 1829 reflected the close legal connection between police and citizens. According to the 7th principle:

The police at all times should maintain a relationship with the public that gives reality to the historic tradition that the police are the public and that the public are the police; the police are the only members of the public who are paid to give full-time attention to duties which are incumbent on every citizen in the interests of community welfare.

Since their foundation, however, the police have rapidly diverged from this ideal of "professional" citizen by acquiring special legal authority, by effectively usurping the role of private prosecutor and by serving a government mandated social control function. Section 494 of the Code sets out arrest without a warrant. Subsequent sections, including 495 to 502, list additional powers given only to "peace officers". A brief description of the police powers of arrest can be found in the Solomon excerpt which follows in the next subsection. Even without special powers for the police there is a natural tendency for citizens to give up unremunerated police work once a professional body exists that is paid to perform the same function. Finally, unlike decentralized citizen enforcers, police forces routinely evolve into quasi-military outfits capable of assisting, then replacing the army in controlling riots and rebellions and in conducting surveillance operations over the "dangerous classes". According to Storch (1975:62) by the 1840s the upper and middle income classes believed that the urban lower classes were a threat to social survival and that only a strong police force securely and permanently lodged in the poorer neighbourhoods could preserve peace and property. This social control task was too delicate for the army, nor could it be left to local citizens because they themselves were members of the threatening 'dangerous class' that needed regulation:

> By 1830 the deficiencies of the army in order keeping were manifest. The inflexibility of the military, its inability to act with anything less than the maximum of force when compelled to intervene, and the consequent and frequent refusal of its commanders to act; but more important its inherent unsuitability to the task of providing the type of daily protection now demanded made its use increasingly inappropriate except in pressing emergencies. Similarly, the old parish constable system was now considered worse than useless. (Storch, 1975:64).

Local business owners and magistrates complained that constables from their districts were reluctant to act against their neighbours, refused to suppress "undesirable popular recreational activities" and had little interest in standing against employees in labour disputes (Storch:id). Rude (1985:99) considers Peel's new police were effective in their first thirty years in three areas: street patrols reduced mugging and pickpocketing, the "criminal class" came under greater surveillance and the police helped pacify civil unrest such as the Chartist agitation in the 1840s. The control of meetings, marches and public demonstrations remains an important police function in Canada (Grunis, 1978).

In Canada the NWMP illustrate the government's need for replacing local and/or private police with a quasimilitary police force under direct federal command. Founded in 1873 the NWMP ostensibly existed to police the western plains, shelter Indians from abusive American traders and keep the peace between settlers and Indians. Actually, there was scant evidence that local authorities, including Indian and Metis leaders, were unable to resolve their own problems. But what local interests would not do is loyally promote federal government policies favouring multinational railway, land development and trading corporations, nor would native leaders cooperate in programs designed to weaken, ignore or destroy their own land claims. Up to the present day the RCMP's deliberate policy includes minimizing the degree to which their officers identify with or become attached to their assigned community. The advantages of central command from Ottawa are lessened by local sympathies.

From a low cost, unprofessional police system still largely motivated by personal compensation, Western governments have moved towards a high cost, professional police system where little if any funds flow into victim compensation. In Canada, one police officer served on average over 700 people in 1962 while in 1994 this figure was reduced to 491; this is reflected in the rise in the per capita cost of policing from $137 in 1985 to $198 in 1994 (Statistics Canada, 1996). It is important to note as well that approximately two-thirds of the budget allocated for the criminal law system is devoted to police services (most of which comprised police salaries), while a very small amount goes to items such as legal aid and victim compensation.

In reviewing police development it is helpful to consider alternative models because we naturally grow accustomed to our own specific legal environment. Briefly, there are three basic legislative plans for police operations: police citizens, police bureaucrats and pure state police. These models may be explicitly designated but more often police officers' duties, powers and jurisdiction are not clearly specified in the enabling legislation (Stenning, 1981). As already noted, the early English and Canadian police, at least at the municipal level, exhibited many features of the police as citizen. Under a pure non-professional police model, there is free entry into police operations, the police enjoy no special powers and the great majority of their work is preventive, involving foot patrols, night watch, escort services and gathering information. This model is presently well represented in the form of private security services and, increasingly, businesses find it cheaper and more convenient to deal with theft and other crimes internally without involving the police or courts. Major advantages of private security personnel are their lack of special powers, their distance from political control, their profit incentive and their market discipline. Their major disadvantage is that certain people are either too poor or too disorganized to be able to hire their own security services. In many ways larger business organizations recreate the stability and structure of extended families or villages where almost all police work is private and internal. In contrast, heterogenous urban neighbourhoods are too diverse and fragmented to permit private policing so some form of public policing is called for.

One form public policing can take is the bureaucratic model represented in modern Japan and in 18th century Europe. In the police bureau model the police function as public servants performing a wide variety of government directed tasks. The city watchmen regulated garbage disposal, inspected food retailers, found shelter for the homeless and sought employment for the wayward. Concurrently in France, police acted as building and street inspectors, fire fighters, health inspectors, dog catchers, censors, trade regulators, rescue teams, builders and educators. Arresting suspected criminals was merely one task among many (Brannigan, 1984:46). Vogel (1979:215) describes the similar work of the Japanese *omawarisan*, "the one who makes his rounds".

> He usually travels by foot or by bicycle, scarcely distinguishable in attitude and type of dress from the local postman. The mini police station is also responsible for local household registration . . . policemen visit each home semi-annually to note any changes in a household. In addition, he gathers information about ownership and the ordinary location of cars and other valuable property . . . He aims to be helpful in giving first aid, assisting children across streets, finding lost items, and providing informal neighbourhood announcements on the bulletin board outside the mini police station . . . A crime prevention association is organized as part of every village or neighbourhood to ensure that certain local people have the responsibility of assisting the police.

In short, the local Japanese police act as census taker, foot patrol, traffic director, paramedic, watchman, probation officer and town crier. Furthermore, Japan's police system assumes that citizen assistance is a prerequisite to law enforcement.

A second feature of the bureaucratic model for Japanese police is a complex, multi-layered hierarchy of superior positions above the base level of the mini station officer who operates out of one of 5,800 urban stations each serving about 10,000 people. The large proportion of higher positions in the prefectural police structure and in the National Police Agency means police have more room for advancement and patrolmen are more closely supervised by higher officials. In direct crime work, the local officer makes immediate contact and begins questioning but even with minor misdemeanours specialists are sent out from the larger police stations above the mini stations.

The third police model is that of the state police pioneered in France and familiar from other European jurisdictions. State police are highly centralized, are relatively remote from the local community, and focus on political surveillance and national security rather than on social work and community service. State police typically depend on a network of paid informants to keep them advised of criminal activities, dissident groups and political opponents of the regime in power. Informants are even drawn from within families as when children are urged to inform on their parents, a practice carried on by the GESTAPO, the KGB and the Drug Enforcement Agency (DEA) in the U.S. One reason many English citizens feared Peel's proposed police force was that in the period 1790-1820 the French police operated a vast network of spies. Many Parisian housemaids took police bribes to inform on their employers and with some justification English critics were convinced that police were state agents who spied on citizens, searched their homes and dragged them off to jail (Wilson, 1984:469). By the mid-18th century Louis XV's Lieutenant General of Police could accurately boast that 'when three people chat in street, one of them is my man' (Cohen, 1982:631). Depending on the political climate, state police may be viewed with fear and suspicion by a significant portion of citizens. The FBI harassed Martin Luther King Jr. and spied on any group opposed to the Vietnam War. In the 1980's, the FBI under William Webster investigated more than 160 organizations supposedly opposed to the Reagan administration's Central American policy. Among those investigated were the United Auto Workers, the Maryknoll nuns in Chicago, the Knights of Columbus and the Southern Christian Leadership Conference. Because of their centralized command structure state police are normally the least responsive to public demands or sentiments. Conversely, state police are most likely to be elitist, sexist and racist. Hoover, for example, successfully preserved the FBI as a white male bastion; even today, women and blacks account for only a small percentage of all agents. Finally, as state agents such police forces enjoy enviable protection from local prosecutions. During the U.S. Volstead Act-Prohibition Era police agents killed 1,056 civilians (from 1920-1930). According to Lee (1963:168):

> It was the maddening practice of the federal authorities to intervene and protect a Dry agent who had killed, wantonly or otherwise. Late in 1928, the *Chicago Tribune* listed twenty-three cases in which local murder or manslaughter indictments had been returned against agents, all of whom escaped punishment through the over-riding federal power. As Democratic Senator Edwards of New Jersey pointed out, many killings resulted from shots fired 'as a warning' and many fatalities among

suspect culprits had been shot in the back, indicating they had been fleeing arrest, not resisting it
... By the nature of their jobs, Dry agents [federal Prohibition officers] were the most detested men
in the country, and through some perversity, they went out of their way to enhance their unpopularity.

In the 1970s 245 people died while in the custody of British police, 143 died from "unnatural causes". No criminal charges were laid in any case (Abraham et al., 1981). Between 1966-1976 6,000 people were shot and killed by American police. Most of these killed were fleeing from property offences and half were unarmed; still, only a very few cases tested the legality of police killings. During roughly the same period, Canadian police killed 88 persons with firearms and wounded another 200 or so.

Numerous state police systems flourish today. Butterfield (1982) reported that life in China under the surveillance of police informers at home and at work was, at the time of his report, equivalent to life in an army barracks. All public phones (only officials had private phones) were in shops, offices or apartments of people who worked for the police so all suspicious phone calls were reported. Members of the local street committee could search private homes without a warrant, decide which parents could have children and question neighbours about their guests or friends. Iraq's government operates three separate secret police organizations: the *mukhabarat*, the ordinary secret police, the ruling Baath party's security force and the so-called counterintelligence police. As usual, in Iraq security personnel are immune from prosecution. Consistent with the Chinese state police apparatus, Butterfield found a pervasive censorship and a mania for secrecy at all levels of government. Canadian governments are less secretive and the federal *Access to Information Act*, 1980-83, c. 111, Sch. I was proclaimed in 1983 but secrecy remains a major commitment in Canada as well as in Britain. If citizens seeking information about Canada's government under the act are not deterred by complex filing requirements and expensive "search charges" (as high as $10,000) they can be easily defeated by two key provisions. Section 21 of the Act allows government to refuse to release "advice or recommendations developed by or for a government institution or a minister" for twenty years. The Act also provides a total exemption for purported cabinet confidences with no time limit and no opportunity for review by a court to determine whether the document is actually a Cabinet confidence.

## Regulating Professional Police
### C. Mitchell

Professions, including lawyers, physicians and police can be regulated at two levels. Most regulatory activity occurs at the individual case level either when an aggrieved plaintiff launches a civil action against a member of the profession or when a disciplinary body, administered in whole or in part by the profession, considers cases of "unprofessional conduct". The other, less common form of regulation, occurs when government sets standards or applies limits to the entire profession. Cohen warns (1982:634) that the "police are arguably the agent to which we have granted the greatest power and widest discretion to interfere in our lives. The integrity of our processes is manifest only when such power is exercised according to law. The Rule of Law demands that this grant of power not be unstructured and unregulated".

The legal essence of monopolistic professions is the exclusion of competition and the severance of the profession from market discipline. Government limits police competition in a number of ways. First, as noted historically, self-policing by victims is minimized by raising impediments to private prosecutions, by limiting access to tort remedies and by granting special enforcement powers to police. Second, public police forces are protected from private competition by laws limiting the field of operations of enforcement companies like the Pinkerton agency. Allan Pinkerton founded a private detective agency in the U.S. and managed to make a profit preventing and solving crimes. So well-regarded was Pinkerton that Lincoln's administration during the Civil War (1860-65) commissioned him to run a spy agency called the Secret Service (Melanson, 1984). While many private companies and individuals sell services to government on a contract basis today, it is seldom if ever that police services are included in this semi-competitive process. Pinkerton's own tenure as head of the Secret Service was brief and he was replaced by General La Fayette Baker who ran the Secret Service like a vigilante organization and whole agents frequently made arrests and searches without regard to the law. Nor were they competent. The night Lincoln was assassinated, the officer guarding his box at Ford's theatre wandered away from his post (ld:2) In 1898, the Pinkerton Agency was again considered a leading candidate to receive a contract for spy services during the Spanish American War but ultimately lost out to the Secret Service bureau. Typically, while the Secret Service after 1865 was maintained to prevent counterfeiting — about 1600 American banks printed and circulated currency at that time — the agency expanded into other areas including the control of smuggling, piracy, mail and land fraud, and battling the Ku Klux Klan, and its budget now exceeds $200 million annually.

The performance of a profession is usually very difficult to judge because of citizens' limited access to information about the profession and because performance goals are not established. If police performance in general cannot be assessed then it cannot be effectively criticized. In an insightful article entitled "The Protection of the Inept" Goode (1967) explained that:

> All professions, while claiming to be the sole competent judge of their members' skill, and the guardians of their clients' welfare, refuse to divulge information about how competent any of them are, and under most circumstances their rules assert it is unethical to criticize the work of fellow members to laymen ... More generally, members of what Goffman calls 'teams' (army officers ... policemen ... ) protect each other from any exposure of their errors ... Perhaps the most difficult performances to measure are those of interpersonal skills or personal interaction.

Concerning the FBI, Wilson (1978:193) explains that until recently the Bureau did not pay "even fleeting consideration to investigative efforts. Since it had no bureaucratic rivals, it had no need to demonstrate any relative advantage ... " In contrast, the Drug Enforcement Agency (DEA) competed directly with Customs and with state police and so made repeated efforts to establish performance standards. From Britain the *Economist* (Feb. 13, 1988) reported that the most difficult problem assessing the value of public spending on police is to define output measures. While real spending increased 38% between 1979 and 1987 and 9% more police were employed, recorded crime increased and fewer offences were solved. They note that:

> There has been little scrutiny of police efficiency by outsiders. That is partly because the police are suspicious of them and remarkably good at keeping them at bay . . . Within police forces,

management has traditionally been haphazard. Until recently, hardly any forces tried to work out how much they were spending on their various tasks, or to set priorities between them . . . As yet, there are few rewards for forces that perform well.

Abandoning the standard municipal police monopoly in favour of competing police services may be one method of producing clear evaluative criteria for police work. Another possibility is private contracting where terms can be set out in some detail and the contract can be allowed to lapse if performance standards are not met. As an entrenched, bureaucratic profession the police successfully avoid this type of threat or scrutiny. Outside of deliberate withdrawal of service during a strike, it is not clear what would constitute overall police failure. More crime is interpreted as a signal to increase police funding yet less crime is also associated with increased spending on police services. As Brannigan (1984:48) noted, the Canadian increase in police manpower has "been independent of an increase in the number of serious crimes". An exception to this might be seen in the recent drops in the violent crime rates in the first half of this decade and a corresponding (slight) drop in the number of police officers. It can be argued, however, that this latter decrease may have more to do with concerns over fiscal restraint than with any response to official rates of crime falling. Also, we may be mistaken in using crime rates as a valid measure of police activity. Despite the media emphasis on crime fighting activities by police, the bulk of police work does not involve contact with people committing serious offences. Instead, police primarily engage in order maintenance (without making arrests) or provide social services. Ironically, police education consists of combat training, learning statute law such as the *Criminal Code*, the *Highway Traffic Act*, the *Liquor Control Act* and various city ordinances and discovering how to investigate minor crimes. Still, by a variety of measures we can see that the quality of police work can vary considerably. In the same year Japanese police, who report more of their crime than Americans, achieved an overall clearance rate through arrest of 69 percent whereas American police achieved an average rate of clearance of reported crimes through arrest of only 22 percent (Vogel, 1979:205). According to Bayley's calculations, American police obtain convictions in about 11 percent of all serious crimes reported and about 5 percent of total crimes (Bayley, 1980). The rate of on-duty police killed in the U.S. is about sixteen times higher than in Japan; the Japanese police respond to calls in an average time of three minutes, twenty-three seconds (far faster than American police). Japanese crime rates have been cut in half since 1946; furthermore, in all of Japan fewer police are dismissed for misbehaviour in one year than in six months in New York City and the rate of citizen complaints about police is far lower in Japan (ld.). Unfortunately, while North Americans can purchase Japanese VCRs, cameras, computers and automobiles in preference to domestic products they cannot purchase or import Japanese police services. Indeed, since few Canadians ever experience a different police system, they have no basis for judging their system as particularly good or bad. The police, like other professions, always profess to be doing their best but without the sort of competitive pressures which the Russians, for example, exerted on Canadian hockey, there is every reason to assume that the police are not operating close to an optimum level.

The discrepancy between formal police training and actual police practice and the failure of the police to provide cost-effective service to the public may also represent a conflict between public and government interests. If governments, who directly fund and supervise the police, want a quasi-military, crime-fighting police force capable of enforcing laws against a majority of citizens, then they will train the police in combat skills even though most police operations do not fit the state police model. From the government's perspective the police may be seen primarily as a reserve force, a "national guard" who in their "spare time" can respond to citizen requests but who exist mostly to enforce political order. This theory may explain why the government is indifferent to the rapid expansion of private security services because while such services compete with police crime prevention they do not compete with the state's monopoly of coercive, armed enforcement. Private security services do not engage in surveillance of suspect political groups, fight "drug wars", censor magazines or administer regulatory systems over drivers, drinkers, gamblers, smokers, prostitutes, students or juveniles. These political tasks are largely a police preserve and they lead naturally to police isolation (Barton, 1970). According to Brannigan (1984:54):

> [T]he police have traditionally been relatively isolated . . . They are also resistant to establishing contacts with non-police families or individuals; after all, what is a police officer going to do on a Saturday night when somebody pulls out a marihuana cigarette? . . . It appears that the isolation of police becomes more acute the longer they stay on the force.

Most people do not become "guarded" when they learn that someone is a Brinks guard precisely because the private security agent is not a threat to the average citizen whereas the police now are or can be such a threat should they choose (Wexler, 1974).

One of the more important issues facing the police in modern times has been the question of how to make them accountable to the needs and demands of the general public. The problem is that we do not want a police force that is under the direct control and direction of the government of the day, yet we also do not want a force which is not accountable and responsive to the general will of the citizens it serves. While various methods and schemes of accountability have been attempted over the years, the police today remain relatively free of outside interference. Several of the issues surrounding the demands for accountability and their implementation can be seen in the excerpt from the Hastings and Saunders paper reproduced below. Of course, it should be noted that this excerpt only covers one part of the accountability debates, specifically external review or oversight committees. Other ways in which the police are made accountable, for example through the filing of civil suits by individuals who feel aggrieved or through the intervention of the courts that supervise the police indirectly through the application of the Charter and its standards, are not discussed here.

## Bibliography
- Abraham, J., J. Field, R. Hardingt, S. Skurka, "Police Use of Lethal Force: A Toronto Perspective" (1981), 19 Osgoode Hall L.J. 199.
- Barton, P.G., "Civilian Review Boards and the Handling of Complaints Against the Police" (1970) University of Toronto L.R. 448.
- Bayley, D., "Ironies of American Law Enforcement" (1980), The Public Interest 45.
- Bellamy, J., *Crime and Public Order in England in the Later Middle Ages* (Toronto: University of Toronto Press, 1973).

- Blumberg, A., "The Practice of Law as a Confidence Game: Organization Cooperation of a Profession" (1967), 1 Law & Society Review 15.
- Boyd, N., J. Lowman, C. Mosher, "Case Law and Drug Convictions: Testing the Rhetoric of Equality Rights" (1987), 29 Criminal Law Quarterly 487.
- Brannigan, A., *Crimes, Courts and Corrections* (Toronto: Holt, Rinehart & Winston, 1984).
- Butterfield, F., "How the Chinese Police Themselves", New York Times Magazine, April 18, 1982, p. 31.
- Canadian Committee on Corrections, Report, "The Role of the Police in a Democratic Society", in Boydell, C., C. Grindstaff, P. Whitehead, eds., *The Administration of Criminal Justice in Canada* (Toronto: Holt, Rinehart & Winston, 1974).
- Casper, J., "Did You Have a Lawyer When You Went to Court? No I Had a Public Defender" (1971), 1 Yale Review of Law & Social Action. 4
- Chrétien, Jean, *The Criminal Law in Canadian Society, Report of the Criminal Law Review* (Ottawa: Ministry of Justice, 1982).
- Cohen, S.A., "Invasion of Privacy: Police and Electronic Surveillance in Canada" (1982), 27 McGill L.J. 619.
- Cooper, H.H., "Psychology: The Human Art of the Gentle Art of Espionage" (1981), 29 Chitty's Law Journal 251.
- Cousineau, D.F., J.E. Veevers, "Incarceration as a Response to Crime: The Utilization of Canadian Prisons" (1972), 14 Canadian J. Crim. & Corr. 19.
- Edwards, S.M., "Prostitutes: Victims of Law, Social Policy and Organized Crime", in Carlen, Pat & Anne Worral, eds., *Gender, Crime and Justice* (England: Open University Press, 1987).
- Foucault, Michel, *Discipline & Punish: The Birth of the Prison* (London: Allen Lane, 1977).
- Goode, W., "The Protection of the Inept" (1967), 32 American Sociological Review 1.
- Griffiths, C., et al., *Criminal Justice in Canada: An Introductory Text* (Toronto: Butterworths, 1980).
- Grunis, A., "Police Control of Demonstrations" (1978), 56 Canadian Bar Review 393.
- Hay;, Douglas, "Property, Authority and the Original Law", in Hay, F., P. Linebaugh, E.P. Thompson, eds., *Albion's Fatal Tree* (London: Allen Lane, 1975).
- Hogg, Peter, *Constitutional Law in Canada*, 2nd ed., (Toronto: Carswell, 1985).
- Lee, H., *How Dry We Were: Prohibition Revisited* (Englewood Cliffs: Prentice Hall, 1963).
- McGrath, W.T. & M.P. Mitchell, eds., *The Police Function in Canada* (Toronto: Methuen, 1981).
- Melanson, Philip H., *The Politics of Protection* (New York: Praeger, 1984).
- Milson, S.F.C., *Historical Foundations of the Common Law* (Toronto: Butterworths, 1981).
- Radcliff and Cross, *The English Legal System*, Hand, G. & D. Bentley, eds. (London: Butterworths, 1977).
- Rothman, David J., *The Discovery of the Asylum: Social Order in the New Republic* (Boston: Little, Brown & Co., 1971).
- Rude, G., *Criminal and Victim: Crime and Society in Early Nineteenth Century England* (Oxford: Clarendon Press, 1985).
- Samenow, S., *Inside the Criminal Mind* (New York: Times Books, 1984).
- Statistics Canada, "Police Personnel and Expenditures in Canada — 1994" (1996), 16(1) Juristat 1.
- Stenning, P., "The Legal Status of Police in Canada: A Study Paper Prepared for the Law Reform Commission of Canada" (1981).
- Storch, Robert, "The Plague of Blue Locusts: Police Reform and Popular Resistance in Northern England, 1840-57" (1975), 20 Int'l Review of Social History 61.

- Vogel, Ezra, *Japan as Number One — Lessons for America* (Cambridge: Harvard U. Press, 1979).
- Wexler, M., "Police Culture: A Response of Ambiguous Employment" in *The Administration of Criminal Justice in Canada* (Toronto: Holt, Rinehart & Winston, 1974).
- Wilson, J.Q., *The Investigators — Managing FBI and Narcotic Agents* (New York: Basic Books, 1978).
- Wilson, J.Q., and Herrnstein, Richard J., *Crime and Human Nature* (New York: Simon & Schuster, 1985).

**Introduction**
*R.P. Saunders*

The following excerpt briefly describes the statutory powers of arrest given to police officers in the Criminal Code (although the section numbers have changed). Note that there are also arrest and search powers given to the police in specific pieces of legislation, both criminal and non-criminal, as well as in provincial legislation which sets out the arrest powers pursuant to provincial legislation. For a full discussion of these and other aspects of arrest, see the Law Reform Commission's Working Paper 41, *Arrest*, under Further Reading. Note also that many of the investigation, arrest, detention and search and seizure practices of the police have been examined in light of the Charter, and have been modified to meet this standard. In this regard, see Chapter 7.3 dealing with policy defences and see also the Luther, Young and Moore references under Further Reading.

## Drug Enforcement Powers and The Canadian Charter of Rights and Freedoms*
### R. Solomon

* Excerpt from (1983), 21 University of Western Ontario Law Review 220.

### POLICE POWERS OF ARREST
*Sources of Police Powers to Arrest in Drug Cases*

It should be noted that a peace officer has the authority to enforce both federal and provincial law regardless of the police force that employs him, his assigned task, or any informal division of enforcement responsibilities that exists among police agencies. In appropriate circumstances, an officer may invoke his enforcement powers under the Code, other federal statutes, and provincial legislation. These independent sources of authority can be used indirectly to further a drug investigation. For example, a plain-clothed member of the Toronto RCMP drug squad may stop a suspected drug offender for violation of the provincial highway traffic act. If, in the course of that investigation, evidence of a drug offence is found, a drug charge may also be laid. Thus, the general arrest provisions of the Code represent only one of many discreet sources of police power in drug investigations.

## Arrest without Warrant

### Introduction

English common law protected individual freedom by strictly limiting police authority to arrest without a warrant. This power was not granted for misdemeanours, and even for felonies and treason it could only be invoked in a limited number of situations. In all other circumstances, an officer had to bring his information before a judge who would determine if there was sufficient evidence to justify issuing an arrest warrant. An officer who exceeded his authority was shown little sympathy, whether or not he had acted in good faith.

The English common law of crimes was largely supplanted in Canada by the enactment of the first Canadian Criminal Code in 1892. While many features of the common law have been maintained, the Code has greatly expanded both a police officer's powers to arrest without a warrant and his immunity from criminal and civil liability. Various sections of the Code authorize arrest without a warrant for specific offences, but section 450's general arrest powers are most relevant in drug cases.

### Section 450 of the Criminal Code

Section 450(1)(a) authorizes police to arrest without warrant in three situations involving indictable offences. The term "indictable offence" includes offences in which the prosecutor has the option of proceeding by indictment or summary conviction, commonly referred to as hybrid offences. Since all the common drug offences are either indictable or hybrid offences, they fall within the ambit of this subsection.

First, the police may arrest without a warrant a person who has committed an indictable offence. To rely on this provision, it is necessary to establish that the suspect actually committed an indictable offence. Second, the police may arrest without a warrant a person who, on reasonable and probable grounds, they believe has committed an indictable offence. The arresting officer need not prove that the suspect committed an indictable offence, only that there were reasonable and probable grounds for so believing. Third, an officer may arrest without a warrant a person who he believes, on reasonable and probable grounds, is about to commit an indictable offence. Although the purpose of this measure is to prevent the commission of indictable offences, its use necessarily entails the arrest, search, and detention of individuals who have not committed any criminal act.

Section 450(1)(b) provides that an officer may arrest without a warrant a person whom he finds committing a criminal offence, which includes both indictable and summary conviction offences. Rejecting an earlier Saskatchewan Court of Appeal decision, the Supreme Court of Canada in 1975 held that the terms "finds committing" should be read as "apparently finds committing". This interpretation dramatically increased both the scope of an officer's arrest powers and the number of situations in which an innocent suspect could be lawfully arrested. The courts have defined the term "criminal offence" to include only violations of federal statutes. Accordingly, this subsection cannot be used to arrest without a warrant suspects apparently found committing provincial offences.

Section 450(1)(c) authorizes an officer to arrest without a warrant a person who he has reasonable and probable grounds to believe is named in an arrest warrant in force within the territorial jurisdiction. The officer's conduct is lawful even if he arrests the wrong person, provided that he acts reasonably and in good faith. Prior to the enactment of the Code, an officer was held civilly liable in this situation.

*Reasonable and Probable Grounds*

The legality of an arrest frequently turns on whether the police had reasonable and probable grounds to suspect the accused. The courts apply an objective test in making this determination. The issue is often phrased in terms of whether the facts were sufficient to cause a reasonably careful and prudent man to have a strong and honest belief in the guilt of the accused. Suspicion alone is not enough. For example, a suspect's criminal record for similar offences, in itself, should not be relied upon as providing reasonable and probable grounds. An officer must approach the issue with an open mind, make reasonable inquiries, and listen to the explanations of the witnesses and suspect. The law requires that there be a fair and careful assessment of the facts at hand. The case against a suspect does not have to be conclusive, and reliance may be placed on evidence that would not be admissible in court. Having completed his initial investigation, an officer must make up his mind based on the facts, formulate a charge, and then arrest the suspect on that charge.

*Arrest with Warrant*

When executing an arrest warrant, a police officer acts as an agent of the court and not on his own initiative. Sections 455 and 456 of the Code set out the application procedure, content, and manner in which an arrest warrant is to be executed. Section 28 of the Code protects an officer from criminal liability if he arrests the wrong person under a warrant, provided he acts in good faith and on reasonable and probable grounds. At common law an officer was held civilly liable in this situation. The law protected the rights of the innocent suspect, regardless of how reasonable the officer's mistake had been. Canadian courts have rejected these common law principles and have extended an officer's immunity to civil liability. An individual confronted with an arrest warrant must submit to arrest, even in cases in which he knows that he is not the person named in the warrant. If the individual resists arrest, he may be held criminally and civilly liable.

# Strategies for Police Accountability and Community Empowerment*
*Ross Hastings and R.P. Saunders*

* Excerpts from: "Strategies for Police Accountability and Community Empowerment", a paper prepared for the CROP-IISL Seminar on *Law, Power and Poverty* held in Onati, Spain, in May, 1995.

. . .

## II. The Professional Model and Police Accountability: An Overview

It is the so-called professional or law-enforcement model which has dominated the conception of the police function and the approach to organizing police services and bureaucracies since the 1950's (See Leighton, 1991; Reiner, 1992; and Goldstein, 1990 for excellent detailed discussions of both the professional model and the later community models of policing). The professional model argues that the key roles of the public police are law enforcement (crime-fighting), order maintenance and emergency response. The police have two basic strategic approaches to accomplishing their mission. One is based on a commitment to prevention, usually through a reliance on some version of the tactic of random patrol. The idea in this case is that the awareness of the existence of patrols will raise the objective risks of arrest and sanction, and will thus deter individual offenders. The other is based on a faith in the deterrent effect of punishment. In this case, the police focus on their ability to clear cases, and to identify offenders and to deliver them for processing by the courts. Unfortunately, there is strong evidence in recent research findings that there are important limits to the ability of realistic changes in police tactics to have a significant impact on crime rates or on individual or community safety and security (see Reiner, 1992 for an overview of this research).

The key to the professional model, for the purposes of this paper, is that the police remain largely autonomous from outside control in the performance of their duties. They are obviously dependent on their political masters for issues related to resource allocation, but their basic responsibility is to the law. In this context, the police have argued for a model of "self-policing" which is characteristic of other professions (such as lawyers or doctors), and which thus leaves them with considerable automony in the control of their affairs. In practice, approaches to public accountability for their performance have tended to focus on the rule-breaking of individual officers, and have tended to exclude areas relating to police policies and practices.

In North America the history of the debates surrounding the accountability of the public police is a relatively short one. The debates have been most keen — and then only intermittently — since the 1960's. It is not that debates over the role, function and control of the police have not been a part of the research landscape since the creation of modern forces, but rather that questions over the responsiveness of the police to the wider citizenry have been a special focus of discussion only in the last 30 years. Interestingly, and certainly in Canada, the issue has not been one which has generated much public interest, particularly outside larger urban areas. Where debates about and around accountability have occurred, they have usually taken place within the broader framework of the control of crime, law and order, and the unique needs of the police to do their job, and have usually been overwhelmed by the broader context.

When such debates did focus specifically on the issue of accountability, they almost always arose (especially initially in the 1960's and 1970's) in the context of a crisis or confrontation between the police and minority groups in the community over their treatment at the hands of frontline police officers. Such explicit debates centring on accountability were usually framed around the civil rights of minorities and, importantly, around the individualized notions of officer misconduct; they were *not* structured in the context of larger organisational concerns or systemic misconduct. It is not that this larger context was not known or not spoken to, but simply that the principal thrust of the discourse around accountability quickly developed into one of the accountability of an officer for his or her misdeeds. The quest then became one of finding an appropriate method of ensuring that individual officers were brought to "justice", and that the mythic legalistic "balance" was restored in the community. In practical terms, the debate centred on attempting to wrest some of the traditional (legalistic) accountability mechanisms in the hands of the police administration (and chief) from the police department and vest them to some degree in the community or its representatives.

The debates, as they developed, were almost invariably framed in *negative* terms. The spotlight was on the alleged misconduct or wrongdoing of the officer(s). What this raised then was a criminal justice model of accusation and defence, giving rise to claims by aggrieved citizens for redress and counterclaims by the officers involved as to their legal rights and the unique requirements of the job. What happened in the case of civilian review where it was instituted was a juridification of the process of complaints by citizens. The civilial review-accountability models followed a route which was much more in harmony with the civil or criminal courts' focus on individual rights and wrongs rather than a less limiting path which might have allowed for more proactive and interventionist approaches. In fact, it was much the same route as had been followed by internal complaints systems within police departments though, arguably, with even less effect.

More importantly, the focus on this type of review served to divert attention from other meanings and practices of accountability. Given the "misconduct" orientation of the processes set up and their confining and legalistic nature which focused on the individual misdeed, a rights discourse tended to overwhelm the debates and practices around accountability, and transform the concept into an ineffective shell of what it could have been. The problem is how to transcend such a system, even one which is relatively "progressive" and citizen-oriented, and claim something more by way of accountability to the community served.

. . .

## IV. The Case of Civilian Review in Ontario

. . .

The province of Ontario has been in the forefront of attempts to breathe life into the concept of accountability and the notion of civilian review of the police in Canada. That experience, as in the rest of North America, has a relatively short history. In

Ontario, the movement for civilian review took root, not surprisingly, in Toronto where there has been a series of high-profile incidents (especially since the early 1970's) involving officers of the Metropolitan Toronto police force and members of visible minority communities, notably the Black community. Because of complaints from members of these communities and the impact of the surrounding publicity on the attributions of legitimacy in general, there had been a series of investigations and reports on the conduct of the Toronto police and on their handling of complaints against them (Lewis, 1991: 154-5). Each of the reports had come to the same conclusion: the existing internal complaints system of the police department was found wanting, and the creation of some form of external civilian oversight to restore confidence in the system, notably the confidence of the visibly minority communities in the city, was recommended (Lewis, 1991: 154-5).

In 1981, an initiative was launched in Toronto as a pilot venture under the authority of the Ontario legislature's Metropolitan Police Force Complainants Project Act (1981). It was, according to Lewis, the "first successful Canadian effort at 'civilianization' of police complaints procedures" (Lewis, 1991: 153). With a few modifications, it became a permanent feature of the Toronto system in 1984. In 1990, essentially the same system was instituted province-wide under the Police Services Act (1990). That same Act also introduced a new set of guiding principles for the police services in the province, focusing in particular on the need for community policing and partnerships. It should be noted that when the Toronto scheme was introduced, it met with vociferous opposition by the police officers themselves. This mirrors the experience of attempts to institute civilian review accountability procedures in most North American cities in recent years (see, for example, Terrill, 1991: 300-303, and Skolnick and Fyfe, 1993: 220-223). In the Toronto case, work action was taken against the legislation by members of the police service; as well, there were court challenges, union denunciations, concerted campaigns against it, and public calls to avoid compliance with the spirit, if not the letter of the Act (Lewis, 1991: 164-9). However, unlike many similar experiences in the United States, the Toronto scheme survived, in part due to the failure of the police to generate much public support for their cause. Currently there is, at best, an attitude of grudging acceptance of the system now in place Ontario-wide, a system which continues to reflect the basic principles and direction of the original pilot project legislation.

The Police Services Act essentially enshrines the Toronto scheme and applies it across the province. At its core is the review agency — the Office of the Police Complaints Commissioner — which is fundamentally an agency intended to *monitor* the complaints processing by individual police agencies in the province. The province's individual police agencies are mandated under the Act to establish complaint bureaus and it was these bureaus which were given the primary task of investigating complaints in the first instance. In regard to the review agency itself, Lewis, in referring to the original Act setting up the Toronto scheme, states:

The basic scheme of the Act provided that the Office would:

1. monitor the handling of complaints by the police;
2. perform initial investigation in unusual circumstances;

3. reinvestigate and review findings when the complainant was dissatisfied with action taken by the police;
4. when the public interest required a hearing, refer cases to a civilian adjudicative tribunal with direct disciplinary power; and
5. perform a preventive function, making recommendations to the chief of police, the board of commissioners of police, the Attorney-General, and the Solicitor-General, with respect to policing issues arising out of complaints. (Lewis, 1991: 157).

It should also be noted that the members of the "civilian" boards of inquiry are drawn from specific panels mandated by the Police Services Act: one-third of the members must be lawyers recommended by the Attorney-General of Ontario (the member from this group sits as the chair of the board) (ss.103(2)); one-third of the members are recommended for appointment by the Police Association of Ontario and cannot be serving police officers (ss.103(3)); and one-third of the members are recommended by the Association of Municipalities of Ontario (ss.103(4)). In other words, there is no direct public participation; the selection of board members is mediated by existing organizations, each of which has a specific orientation to (and interest in) law enforcement and the maintenance of community order. Organizations representing poor or disempowered groups must rely on the "good faith" of these organizations in selecting members who will represent their interests and concerns.

Like other agencies of its genre, it is not intended to replace the traditional method of discipline for officers who commit misdeeds or otherwise break department codes of policies. That power is meant to rest principally, though not exclusively, with the managerial sector of police bureaucracies (in spite of their very poor record in the area of disciplining officers who are accused of misconduct against citizens). Moreover, there are strong protections built into the Ontario system for ensuring due process and other constitutional guarantees for individual officers, as well as the right to appeal any discipline decisions to the courts (Lewis, 1991: 161-3).

In virtually all of these types of agencies, the "most pressing issue... remains the question of independence" (Terrill, 1991: 315). How "civilianized" and independent the agency is, and what powers of investigation and sanctioning it has are the issues which are most often at the heart of the debates over the relative merits of oversight agencies. By most accounts, the Ontario scheme provides for the functional independence of the oversight agency, and provides the agency with the tools necessary to enforce its decisions, at least in regard to the individual officer. In particular, the powers of independent investigation and direct discipline (including dismissal) are noted by supporters as evidence of the existence of an effective body against police misconduct and as an indication of its standing as a relatively potent agency for its type, especially when compared to many similar American agencies.

Furthermore, in regard to the practices and procedures of the police department as a whole, the Police Complaints Commissioner may, under section 101 of the Police Services Act, make recommendations and forward them to the Attorney-General, the Solicitor-General, the chief of police, the local police association and the police services board where such exist. This would appear to address, at least in a small way, the argument made by Goldsmith and other writers that review agencies can and should serve a broader policy function, using complaints as "sources of knowledge and opportunities for self-correction" (Goldsmith, 1991: 15). The chief, the association and the board can comment on these non-binding recommendations, but generally it is the chief who decides whether or not to implement any proposed changes.

In practice, the work of the Office of the Police Complaints Commissioner has not resulted in many changes in the disposition of complaints nor, many would argue, should it have been expected that many changes would result. As Skolnick and Fyfe state, "[n]o matter how effective civilian review, most of the time cops will be exonerated, and probably should be" (Skolnick and Fyfe, 1993: 229). Such sentiments are based on the fact that there are many spurious claims against the police due to unrealistic expectations and demands on the part of aggrieved citizens and the simple fact that many disputes cannot be resolved due to the lack of corroborating evidence (the Rodney King case in Los Angeles being a notable exception). Under the scheme, as was the case elsewhere under similar systems, the dismissal rate remained very high (Goldsmith, 1987: 621). As a result, some critics of the system have seen it as a farce, one serving more as a public relations vehicle than as an effective brake on police misconduct (see for example, early criticisms of the Toronto pilot project in McMahon and Ericson, 1987: 47). It can be argued that the state recognized that something had to be done to deal with the increasing public concerns about the police agency's ability to police itself, and the answer lay in the creation of an external, outwardly independent and civilian review process. However, the result might be called a triumph of form over substance along the lines of Sykes' criticism when discussing the reform of policing in more general terms: "Such reforms may provide an image of change without the substance . . . [T]he reform movements may have succeeded in creating the appearance without the substance of fundamental reform" (Sykes, 1989: 296-7).

The Ontario system has been praised in the civilian review literature as being among the more "progressive" systems of oversight, though it has received little attention in the popular press and therefore in the wider public mind in Ontario since its inception. The concerns expressed by representatives of various community and visible minority groups have not been picked up by the larger public. The public appears less concerned about police accountability, at least in regard to their alleged misdeeds, and more concerned with crime in the streets, personal and property safety, and fiscal responsibility. The larger public's sense of accountability lies less in the concern with the individual misconduct of the officer on the beat or with the larger issue of dealing with the structural anomalies which lie behind and even encourage such behaviour; instead, the focus appears to be more on the need for budgetary accountability, a traditional concern with politicians and the public writ large.

## V. Conclusion

The message which emerges from the experience of civilian review of police misconduct in Ontario is similar to findings from most other North American jurisdictions: there is little in either current legislation or practices which broadens the notion of police accountability beyond the assessment of the performance of individual officers and its fit with either the criminal law or other policy and procedural regulations.

There is little indication that the popular notion of police service and accountability to client communities has been translated into operational structures and processes which give these same communities a partnership role in decisions relating to the definition of problems and priorities within a community, nor in the design, implementation or evaluation of the programs or initiatives which constitute the service to these clients. This point is even more salient when one considers that many of the communities in which the police operate are characterized by high levels of disorder, tension and conflict. The performance of the police in such contexts can have a significant impact on the way a community evolves and develops.

At its heart, the problem begins at the conceptual level with the failure to distinguish adequately between the different potential operational meanings of the general notion of involving the community (as either a client or a partner) in policing, and of the more specific concern with the relation of police accountability mechanisms to this process. The concept of accountability should be conceived of as a continuum involving a number of different options and approaches. The continuum runs the gamut of possibilities between the two extremes of complete police autonomy and complete community control. Obviously, neither of these is desirable or realistic; they serve to provide end points for the debates over where exactly to locate a workable approach to accountability.

The first possibility is to involve the public as **complainants** in accountability processes. This has been the most popular position to date. It reflects the consensus that individual officers must work within the confines and constraints of the criminal law and other relevant regulations. In operational terms, the result is a tendency to involve the public as victims or witnesses of police abuse who may bring complaints to the attention of the relevant police authority (usually, at least initially, the police service in which the officer is employed). The key point here is that neither the complainant nor the general public exercise any control over the process beyond the point of the complaint, and many of these processes also fail the test of transparency. Even if it were possible to develop a perfect system for identifying and sanctioning individual officers, this approach does little or nothing to address problems at the corporate level of a police service. In addition, it neglects the broader structural factors responsible for current trends in crime and disorder, and in the maintenance of the legitimacy of the police among client groups and communities.

The second possibility is to include the public as either an **advisor** to the police or as a **participant** in the delivery of policing services. The benefit of this approach is that it goes part of the way towards opening up a police service to public input. Moreover, the participation of the public seems to have a beneficial impact on the quality of the contacts and relations between the police and the public. The problem is that it is still the relatively autonomous police professionals who retain control over what to do with the public's input, and over the nature of the activities in which the public is allowed to participate. At this level, we really have little more than a new approach to the *delivery* of traditional types of police services, with little or no real increase in community power or control.

The third possibility is to involve the community as a **partner** in the design and delivery of policing services. The focus of accountability here shifts from the individual officer to the police service. The concern is to develop structures and processes for addressing and redefining the problem of the redistribution of power and control in what are supposed to be partnerships between the police and the community in the co-production of social order. At this level, accountability involves giving mobilized community groups and their representatives a real and significant role within these partnerships. It also places a responsibility on either the police or other levels of government to assist in the mobilization of disadvantaged groups. Current accountability mechanisms fail this test: they not only are unable to address the larger notions of police accountability and responsiveness but, more importantly, in appropriating the discourses of accountability they mask the real challenge which remains to be faced in the next few years.

**References**

- Goldsmith, Andrew J. (1987) "Complaints Against the Police in Canada: A New Approach", *Criminal Law Reports* [1987]: 615
- Goldsmith, Andrew J. (1991) "External Review and Self-Regulation: Police Accountability and the Dialectic of Complaints Procedures", in Andrew J. Goldsmith, ed., *Complaints Against the Police: The Trend to External Review*. New York: Oxford University Press.
- Goldstein, Herman (1990) *Problem-Oriented Policing*. Toronto: McGraw-Hill.
- Goode, Matthew (1991) "Complaints Against the Police in Australia: Where we are Now, and What we Might Learn about the Process of Law Reform, with Some Comments about the Process of Legal Change", in Andrew J. Goldsmith, ed., *Complaints Against the Police: The Trend to External Review*. New York: Oxford University Press.
- Hastings, Ross (1993) "La Prévention du Crime: L'Illusion d'un Consensus", *Problèmes Actuels de Science Criminelle* VI:49-69.
- Kerstetter, Wayne A. (1985) "Who Disciplines the Police? Who Should?", in William A. Geller, ed., *Police Leadership in America: Crisis and Opportunity*. New York: Praeger Publishers.
- Leighton, Barry N. (1991) "Visions of Community Policing: Rhetoric and Reality", *Canadian Journal of Criminology* 33: 485-522.
- Lewis, Clare E. (1991) "Police Complaints in Metropolitan Toronto: Perspectives of the Public Complaints Commissioner", in Andrew J. Goldsmith, ed., *Complaints Against the Police: The Trend to External Review*. New York: Oxford University Press.
- McMahon, Maeve W. and Richard V. Ericson (1987) "Reforming the Police and Policing Reform", in R.S. Ratner and John L. McMullan, eds., *State Control: Criminal Justice Politics in Canada*. Vancouver: University of British Columbia Press.
- Petterson, Werner E. (1991) "Police Accountability and Civilian Oversight of Policing: An American Perspective", in Andrew J. Goldsmith, ed., *Complaints Against the Police: The Trend to External Review*. New York: Oxford University Press.
- Reiner, Robert (1992) *The Politics of the Police (2nd ed.)*. Toronto: University of Toronto Press.
- Skolnick, Jerome and James J. Fyfe (1993) *Above the Law: Police and the Excessive Use of Force*. New York: The Free Press.
- Sykes, Gary W. (1989) "The Functional Nature of Police Reform: The Myth of Controlling the Police", in R.G. Dunham and G.P. Alpert, eds., *Critical Issues in Policing. Comtemporary Readings*. Prospect Heights, Illinois: Waveland Press, Inc.
- Terrill, Richard J. (1991) "Civilian Oversight of the Police Complaints Process in the United States: Concerns, Developments, and More Concerns", in Andrew J. Goldsmith, ed., *Complaints Against the Police: The Trend to External Review*. New York: Oxford University Press.

## Questions
1. Why should anyone bother to enforce the law? Describe the different incentive schemes by which people are motivated to involve themselves in law enforcement. Which systems do you think would work best for the following crimes: shoplifting, assault, illegal gambling, environmental offences, murder.
2. Despite the lack of effective public policing in Britain in the period 1770-1830, many citizens were reluctant to support the formation of such a police force. Explain their reluctance.
3. Argue the case for and against the police having special authority to carry handguns.
4. Analyse and comment on the rapid rise of private security forces.
5. Investigate the complaints procedure in your local police force. What is the most effective way to make the police accountable to the public? What are the dangers of a police force which is not accountable?
6. How can you determine whether a given police force is performing adequately and behaving appropriately? What sort of information would you like to have to make this determination? Is such information available anywhere?

## Discussion
1. "The pursuit of a professionalized, politically neutral police force — narrowly focused on 'serious crime' and relying on new technologies — eventually weakened the bonds between private citizens and the police, and shifted the burdens of enforcement to a public agency that could not succeed by itself." Excerpt from M. Moore & G. Kelling, "'To Serve and Protect': Learning from Police History" (1982-3), 69-72 *The Public Interest* 49-65.
2. The deaths of Helene Betty Osborne in The Pas, J.J. Harper in Winnipeg, and the Nova Scotia case of Donald Marshall, Jr. suggest very strongly that Canadian police are often racist regarding native persons. Besides assigning blame in individual cases, what might be done to better protect Unit, Metis and other aboriginal peoples from police discrimination? For further discussion of these issues, see Chapter 8.2.

## Further Reading
- Archibald, B., "Police and Citizens' Powers to Arrest and Detain" in Pink, J. and D. Perrier (eds.), *From crime to punishment: an introduction to the criminal law system* (Toronto: Carswell, 1988), p. 55-66.
- Cohen, S., "Invasion of Privacy: Police and Electronic Surveillance in Canada" (1982), 27 McGill Law Journal 620.
- Cryderman, B. and A. Fleras, *Police, Race and Ethnicity. 2nd ed.* (Toronto: Butterworths, 1992).
- Delisle, R.J., "Judicial Creation of Police Powers" (1993), 20 C.R. (4th) 29-33.
- Ericson, Richard, *Making Crime: A Study of Detective Work* (Toronto: Butterworth, 1981).
- Ericson, Richard, *Reproducing Order: A Study of Police Patrol Work* (Toronto: University of Toronto Press, 1982).
- Goldsmith, A.J. (ed.), *Complaints Against the Police: The Trend to External Review* (New York: Oxford University Press, 1991).
- Hogan, M., D. Brown & R. Hogg, *Death in the Hands of the State* (Australia: Redfern Legal Centre, 1988).
- Law Reform Commission of Canada, *Arrest. Working Paper 41* (Ottawa: Law Reform Commission of Canada, 1985).
- Law Reform Commission of Canada, *Recodifying Criminal Procedure. Volume 1* (Ottawa: Law Reform Commission of Canada, 1991).

- Luther, G., "Police Power and the Charter of Rights and Freedoms: Creation or Control?" (1986/87), 51 Saskatchewan Law Review 217-227.
- Macleod, R.C. and D. Schneiderman, *Police Powers in Canada: The Evolution and Practice of Authority* (Toronto: University of Toronto Press, 1994).
- Moore, K., "Police Implementation of Supreme Court of Canada Charter Decisions: An Empirical Study" (1992), 30 Osgoode Hall Law Journal 547-577.
- Ontario Race Relations and Policing Task Force, *Report of the Race Relations and Policing Task Force* (Toronto: Race Relations and Policing Task Force, 1989).
- Weiler, Paul, "'Who Shall Watch the Watchmen?' Reflections on some Recent Literature about the Police" (1969), 11 Criminal Law Quarterly 420.
- Young, A., "All Along the Watchtower: Arbitrary Detention and the Police Function" (1991), 29 Osgoode Hall Law Journal 329-397.

## 4.2 DEFENCE/PROSECUTOR

### THE CRIMINAL PROSECUTION

After arrest comes prosecution. The prosecution function can be organized in a variety of ways. Some of the prime variables include private versus state prosecution, the political independence of prosecutors and the degree of discretion exercised by prosecutors. The prosecutor's function is vital because it is usually the prosecutor, not the victim or the police, who decides whether a case proceeds to trial. Where prosecution is carried on by officials or state agents, the most common concern is that powerful and politically influential people will not be prosecuted, while dissidents will be zealously pursued.

### Background and Issues
*Barry Wright and Chet Mitchell*

Historically, criminal prosecutions in English law derived their procedural form from tort practices. It was the victim or a relative who commenced and conducted the prosecution. A victim was able to go to the criminal courts and seek punishment of an accused offender (as opposed to seeking compensation in civil proceedings) if the wrong committed could be considered a breach of the "King's peace". Indeed, the private citizen was under a common law duty to prosecute offenders so as to preserve the King's peace. The victim was only limited by the grand jury's or magistrate's decision in preliminary proceedings as to whether there was sufficient evidence to proceed to trial. The state only undertook prosecutions where it had a particular interest, and these usually involved political offences such as treason or sedition. In 1472 all such state prosecutions were supervised by the Attorney General. Nonetheless, even in the 1700s, over 80% of indictable offences were privately prosecuted and less than 1% were prosecuted by the Attorney General's office (Hay, 1983:166). The situation only started to change in the 19th century when the newly established professional police forces started to prosecute criminal cases on behalf of victims. In 1879 the office of Director of Public Prosecutions (D.P.P.) was created to prosecute the most serious cases while police (unassisted by lawyers) prosecuted most cases in the lower courts. Although the rights of private prosecutors in England in this century have been reduced (in favour of the D.P.P. in 1908 legislation, and again in 1985, with the creation of a new Crown prosecution service under the Attorney General), a dual public-professional/private non-professional system persists. Most private prosecutions are conducted by police although ordinary citizens still initiate and conduct prosecutions in areas of shoplifting and common assault.

Elsewhere, in Scotland, the United States and Europe, private prosecutions are generally excluded. Under Scottish law the "procurators fiscal" are lawyers employed as Crown servants who prosecute crime on behalf of the Crown in each sheriff court district. Unlike in England, all prosecutions in Scotland until 1982 were undertaken by these public prosecutors. Scottish practice was altered in 1982 because of the famous Glasgow Rape Case. In that case a young woman alleged that she had been assaulted, disfigured and raped by several young men but the Lord Advocate refused to prosecute them. The victim's application for private prosecution was granted by the High Court and the accused were convicted (Harper & McWhinnie, 1984).

Generally, Canadian criminal law is much closer to the English model than the others because both the substantive law and procedure is based on the formal legislative "reception" of English criminal law during the colonial period and because of the extensive influence of James Fitzjames Stephen's Draft English Code on our own Criminal Code. Nonetheless, as explained below, a significant early Canadian departure from the English model was in the area of prosecutorial authority. The state, acting through crown lawyers under the authority of Attorneys General, has enjoyed a virtual monopoly over prosecutions.

Canadian criminal litigation is started by the laying of an "information" according to section 504 of the Code. That section states that "Any one who, on reasonable grounds, believes that a person has committed an indictable offence may lay an information in writing and under oath before a justice . . . " An information may be submitted by the victim or any one else with knowledge of the relevant events. In practice, "informants" are almost always police, but police do not have a legal monopoly in this area. A private prosecutor, however, faces a number of legal hurdles. For example, while the justice must receive the information, the justice can decide not to compel the accused to appear in court (L.R.C.C., 1986).

If the justice does issue a summons or warrant on the basis of the privately laid information, a distinction must be made between summary and indictable conviction offences. With summary offences, the "prosecutor" means the Attorney-General, or where the Attorney-General does not intervene, the informant (section 802). The prosecutor is entitled, under section 802 of the Code, "personally to conduct his case" with or without the help of counsel. The law regarding indictable offences is more complex because there the private prosecutor may require the permission of the Attorney-General or a judge. In either case, the private prosecutor is always subject to the Attorney-General's power to intervene by assuming control of the case or by staying proceedings, which amounts to stopping the prosecution (*ibid.*).

Should citizens, businesses and activists groups enjoy a broad right to private prosecution or should officials hold a prosecutory monopoly? Arguments in favour of private prosecution include the importance of citizens being able to prosecute police and other officials when the government itself refuses to act, the value in private groups prosecuting environmental and regulatory infractions overlooked by prosecutors focusing on standard crimes and the individual's interest in vindicating personal injuries. What can be said against private prosecutors? Some critics assert that private vengeance is not a proper goal but this objection is rarely backed up with extensive reasoning or any research. Along the same lines, some worry that private prosecution will lead to prosecutions for private gain, malice or blackmail. Little evidence accompanies such claims. Laws already prohibit malicious prosecutions and the ethical case against blackmail is not as obvious as many commentators assume. Also unsubstantiated is the concern that broad access to private prosecution will overburden the courts.

Canadian judges speaking against private prosecution have warned that it would result in "anarchy" or that it would "destroy the whole fabric of the recognized fairness of our criminal prosecutions" (Hay, 1983:166). As indicated below, these views show little awareness of English legal history. Until well into the 19th century, victims controlled the vast majority of prosecutions and the result was not anarchy. Parliament also had evidence by 1850, when most prosecutions came to be handled by police, that police were conducting many malicious prosecutions in search of costs and reward (Hay, 1983). Perhaps the central question here is: Why should individuals pursue private justice at public expense, particularly when they could start a civil action in tort law in many instances? (Tort law will usually not be helpful because of the accused's judgment-proof status). Further, it is mistaken to claim that private prosecution does not produce public benefit

Another claim is that professional prosecutors, as lawyers, possess the necessary expertise to understand complex laws as well as the disinterested objectivity to make decisions in the public interest. Studies of professional prosecutors in Scotland do not support this argument (Moody & Tombs, 1982). Research there revealed that lawyers use their specialized, technical knowledge about one hour per week. In examining why prosecutors decided not to prosecute, it is also apparent that legal training was not a major factor in the process. (This is not surprising given that state prosecutors must usually learn their trade almost entirely on the job.) Some cases were not prosecuted because of evidentiary concerns but others were rejected because prosecutors decided that the matter was "trivial", which is obviously a political judgment. Decisions also hinged on the accused's character. For example, old age pensioners arrested for shoplifting were not charged in 88% of the cases (ibid.,67). There was also a split between those who were enthusiastic about prosecuting husbands for wife assault and those who opposed such cases being brought to court. In short, public prosecutors make policy decisions about which offences will be fully prosecuted, which offences will not be prosecuted at all and which offenders will be prosecuted. In Katz's (1980:110) judgment: "Not only does the [American] prosecutor make the initial policies upon which decisions to charge are based, at every stage of a criminal case he has virtually unlimited power to dismiss or pursue a prosecution". Katz mentions one county in the state of Maryland, for example, where the State Attorney directed prosecutors not to file charges involving the possession of small amounts of marijuana.

Supporters of state prosecution also argue that crimes are such serious wrongs that they offend not just against the individual victim but also against the state, therefore the state should serve as the plaintiff or prosecutor. This reasoning does not accurately describe the nature of most modern crime. Offences between friends, families and neighbours, consumer fraud, shoplifting, and the many minor offences contained in the Code either do not constitute major blows to society or are very intimate. Certainly prosecutions against gaming houses, brothels, drug users, and other so-called vice offences must depend entirely on state officials but a strong case can be made against such activities being made crimes in the first place. Finally, even major public crimes like treason, sedition, armed robbery and rioting could be prosecuted privately given the right financial incentives. Perhaps then the major reason for the general domination of state prosecution is that a state bureaucracy will cooperate with the government in creatively modifying the law to achieve covertly desired results such as imprisoning native persons or excusing old age pensioners or selectively enforcing narcotic laws.

## Some Consequences of Public Prosecutorial Power: The Decision to Proceed with a Prosecution
### Barry Wright

As indicated in the previous section, public prosecutions are a recent development in our system of law. Although crimes have been considered breaches of the "king's peace" since medieval times, it was only in the eighteenth century that victims began to retain lawyers on a large scale to prosecute on their behalf, and not until the nineteenth century that the state began to manage the prosecution of most routine offences. Although public prosecutions have brought greater certainty and consistency to law enforcement, the role of the victim has receded to the background and bureaucratic priorities around the administration of justice have come to play a dominant role in the exercise of prosecutorial discretion. Concerns about the victim's rights have been fuelled in recent years by overburdened courts, more plea bargaining, trial delays and stayed charges. Section 11(*b*) of the Charter of Rights and the Supreme Court of Canada decision in *R. v. Askov* (1990), 59 C.C.C. (3d) 449, have only increased the tensions. Is there a modern role for private prosecutions which might address these concerns?

It is useful to revisit the main justifications for the state's domination of the prosecution process. The main support is that crimes involve wrongs of such magnitude that public interests are involved as well as those of the individual victim. Rule of law claims demand consistent and certain law enforcement and public prosecutorial power minimizes discretionary abuses, including malicious and frivolous private prosecutions that might arise out of private initiatives. It may also be argued that public prosecutions serve a redistributive measure to give all victims, regardless of economic means, legal representation and access to criminal justice. On these various bases, crown prosecutors in Canada are seen as representatives of the public interest as well as, in some vague way, agents of the victim.

Many questions are left unanswered by this modern model of Canadian prosecutorial authority, especially since the Attorneys General acting through crown prosecutors enjoy a virtual monopoly over prosecutions. This power extends from the basic decision on whether to proceed with a prosecution to a wide variety of important decisions during the course of the prosecution. How accountable is the public prosecutor? What if there is a conflict between the public interest (involving political or bureaucratic imperatives) and the victim's concerns? What are the rights of the victim in the prosecutorial process and what has become of the historical practice of private prosecutions?

These questions are especially pertinent and most dramatically posed in light of the most basic prosecutorial decision: the discretion exercised in whether or not to proceed with a prosecution in the first place. The Crown may be reluctant to proceed against criminal activity engaged in by powerful and established interests. Where does this place the victim of questionable activities by police or other public officials? What about environmental, workplace or consumer concerns involving the activities of corporations? Can the victim of sexual assault or domestic violence be confident that the Crown will pursue her case with determination and sensitivity?

The Crown's modern monopoly over prosecutions flies in the face of historical constitutional concerns. The right to launch a private prosecution was once regarded as guarantee of civil liberties and a means to check an oppressive state (Hay, 1983, 165). This was hardly surprising since up until the nineteenth century the rare public prosecutions taken on behalf of the Crown by the Attorney General usually had oppressive political overtones. State prosecutions were abused during the reign of the Tudors. The Crown's prerogative powers over prosecutions were associated with the Court of Star Chamber. These included the *ex officio* information, which provided the state the means to prosecute political offences such as treason and sedition, and the limitation of *nolle prosequi*, which formed the basis of the Attorney General's power to intervene and stay private prosecutions, a prerogative power usually exercised to terminate cases that threatened to be politically embarrassing for the authorities. These prerogative powers survived the demise of the Star Chamber and the constitutional advances of the Glorious Revolution and the Act of Settlement, but in Britain they were understood to be exercised in a circumspect manner.

Such civil libertarian concerns were in little evidence in early Canada. Prosecutions in British North America were almost exclusively exercised by the Crown. This monopoly was achieved through early practices, cemented in the 19th century through legislative provisions which expanded public prosecutorial power, and through judicial decisions which have deferred to the public prosecutor (Stenning, 1986).

Colonial government and the administration of justice were far more executively-dominated than Britain. Centralized control over prosecution served imperial strategic purposes. Colonial attorneys general were directly accountable to the lieutenant governors who in turn answered directly to the British Colonial Office. Public prosecutions facilitated close supervision over the important social control processes of colonial criminal law. Security concerns were particularly acute in Quebec and it is interesting to note that although there were private prosecutions for some years after the Conquest of 1759, they became very rare after the Quebec Act, 1774. There were other factors at play: the shortage of lawyers to serve as agents for private prosecutors (Stenning, 1986:41) and the lineal influences of the French and Scottish models of public prosecutions (the French system prevailed in Quebec before the Conquest, and many of the early lawyers were from Scotland (Hay, 1983:185). Others have suggested that the availability of fees and rewards available for conducting prosecutions were monopolized by the colonial Attorney General or his designate as a jealously-guarded privilege of holding office (Romney, 1986: 17, 37, 47).

Over time, early practices were put on more formal footing and re-enforced through legislation and judicial review. After confederation, the *Department of Justice Act* (S.C. 1867-8, c.39) was the first explicit legislative statement of the powers of the law officers of the crown which was replicated in provincial definitions of the role of their attorneys general. The adoption of the *Criminal Code* in 1892, further strengthened the role of the public prosecutor under by spelling out prosecutorial procedures for the crown prosecutors the authority of Attorneys General for the new classification of indictable and summary offences (Stenning, 1986: 75, 166). Judicial review of issues involving public prosecutorial powers suggests a lack of independence, or at least a strong judicial difference to Crown prerogatives and executive discretion.

Recognition of the potential for public prosecutorial abuse was not entirely absent in the early years. Romney has examined how constitutional crises were set off in Upper Canada in the 1820's over the Attorney General's partisanship, most notably the Crowns' refusal to prosecute the young Tories who destroyed radical William Lyon Mackenzie's press and the crown's power to stay contemplated private prosecutions. When radicals argued the colony's departure from contemporary English practice, the courts sided with the government, and the one judge who was sympathetic to the radicals' argument (John Walpole Willis who was recently arrived from England) was promptly removed from the bench (Romney, 1986: 130-39,146,150).

The courts have continued to defer to public prosecutorial decisions, justifying public monopoly on the basis of highly inaccurate historical arguments and modern justifications based on concerns about private prosecutors acting as "obsessed, vindictive, unscrupulous, self-styled saviours" and equality under the law (see Supreme Court of Canada, *R. v. Smyth* [1971] S.C.R. 680, (1971), 3 C.C.C. (2d) 366 (Ontario Court of Appeal)). The most recent authoritative decision on the powers of the public prosecutor and the relative rights of the victim is the 1983 *Dowson* (sub nom *Dowson v. the Queen*, [1983] 2 S.C.R. 159). While the Supreme Court of Canada *appeared* to be favourably inclined towards the private rights of the victim, in practical effect it merely continued the pattern of deference to the Crown's powers.

*Dowson* is a good illustration of political controversy involving the Crowns' refusal to proceed against powerful interests. The case of Dowson and another named Buchbinder involved some of the many victims of the R.C.M.P.'s "dirty tricks" campaign against political radicals during the early seventies. Despite evidence that the police had committed a number of criminal acts, the Crown refused to prosecute them, at first on the basis that criminal proceeding would jeopardize the findings of the MacDonald Commission Inquiry into the R.C.M.P.'s activities. However, proceedings were not forthcoming after the commission reported. Dowson and Buchbinder initiated private prosecutions on a number of charges against the R.C.M.P. including vandalism, forgery and uttering false documents. After a number of delays the Attorney General for Ontario directed a stay of the proceedings, in effect terminating the private prosecutions. The stay was upheld by the courts.

On appeal, the Ontario Court of Appeal declared: "The right of a private citizen to lay an information, and the right and duty of the Attorney General to supervise criminal prosecutions are both fundamental parts of our criminal justice system". (*Re Dowson and the Queen* (1982), 62 C.C.C. (2d) 286 at 288). The Court went on to declare that the Attorney General has the inherent power to intervene and withdraw any information laid by private prosecutors and therefore upheld the stay.

The matter was appealed again to the Supreme Court of Canada which unanimously upheld the Court of Appeal's position on the distribution of power between private and the public prosecutor. However, the Supreme Court emphatically added one limitation — a private information must be "heard and considered" in a preliminary proceeding before the Crown is entitled to intervene. Since this was not done, the appeal was allowed and both Dowson and Buchbinder were entitled to a hearing before the Crown exercised its right to a stay. (*Dowson v. the Queen*, [1983] 2 S.C.R. 144 at 152; (1983), 7 C.C.C. (d3) 527 at 536 — Buchbinder's case was decided at the same time and for the same reasons [1983] 2 S.C.R. 159).

The Supreme Court of Canada's decision in *Dowson* represents the most authoritative statement on the relative rights of public and private prosecutorial interests. While private citizens have the full right to lay a criminal information, the Attorney General has the full authority to control subsequent procedures, subject to the limitation that an information cannot be stayed before a justice has "heard and considered" and decided whether or not to issue process. Despite superficial appearances was the Supreme Court really balancing the conflicting interests involved? Did it really address concerns about the Attorney General's accountability? Does this current state of the law deal with concerns about the public prosecutor's failure to deal with other offences committed by powerful interests?

Certainly from a historical perspective the private prosecutors' rights in Canada are now fairly limited indeed. As Stenning observes in light of the Dowson case:

> It will be evident . . . that what was once historically regarded as a cherished right of private individuals to launch and *conduct* criminal prosecutions has now been substantially eroded, and perhaps entirely eliminated in Canada. (Stenning, 1986: 263)

On this basis Stenning has advocated an expansion, or perhaps more accurately a reaffirmation, of private prosecutorial rights as a check on the vast discretionary powers of the public prosecutor. Along similar lines, although stressing the need to maximize the role played by the victim in the criminal justice system, the Law Reform Commission of Canada also advocates expanded rights of private prosecution (L.R.C.C., 1986).

This is not to suggest a return to the old system of private prosecutions. The public interest justifications underlying the role of public prosecutor are indeed important. There are concerns in giving victims a free hand in invoking the considerable public powers involved in the modern criminal process. Yet it cannot be denied that victims might be fruitfully given a more active role in the prosecution process. The main rationale for facilitating private prosecutions is to provide an effective check on the exercise of public prosecutorial authority. Greater range should be given to the private prosecutor to subject powerful interests to criminal proceedings when the state is reluctant to do so. There should also be greater accountability, enabling an individual to challenge the public prosecutor who fails to provide reasonable grounds for not proceeding to trial. In short, there is a difference between privatization of prosecutions to replace parts of a faltering public system and freeing up private prosecutions as a means to contest executive abuses or failures.

Public prosecutorial failure also involves less dramatic, but no less significant situations than *Dowson*. The more routine instances of the Crown's decision whether or not to prosecute can detrimentally affect large categories of victims in cases such as sexual assault and domestic violence. As McGillivray's article suggests below, the Crowns' gathering, review and evaluation of evidence in these situations can involve questionable assumptions and understandings of the problem. The prosecutor may also have concerns about the victim appearing as a witness. These factors obviously influence the Crown's decision whether to prosecute or to conduct a prosecution in a determined manner. This suggests that more is required than expanding the rights of the private prosecutor to check the public prosecutor. Public policy may demand that explicit special procedures to be followed for particularly troublesome and neglected offences.

## Battered Women: Definition, Models and Prosecutorial Policy*
### A. McGillivray

\* (1987), 6 Canadian Journal of Family Law 15.

### INTRODUCTION

Perhaps, the last bastion of unregulated individualism and closed to public scrutiny, the family may shield acts of violence equal to any atrocity committed by stranger upon stranger, or by an act of war or terrorism. The family is not considered a legal entity by the state, nor has the issue of state responsibility for family order been widely addressed in light of broader goals of peace and social order. Ours is a violent society divided in its pursuit of peace. The family — autonomous, hierarchical in structure and separated into discrete arenas of authority — is a microcosm reflecting and influencing the structure and attitudes of the larger sphere. Despite the mutuality of social and family reform, there remains tremendous reluctance to involve the blunt processes of the state in the delicate and sacrosanct web of family relationships.

Wife battering appears to be an anomaly in a liberal democracy overtly committed to social order, but is in fact a deviance so widespread it is almost a social norm. Violence toward women by their husbands has at the least been tolerated and, in many societies, institutionalized. Throughout the world, both historically and presently, it is a phenomenon so large that its existence has become accepted as part of the social milieu. "Only rarely is the objective condition interpreted as worthy of attention." The legal right of the *pater familias* to punish his wife, children and slaves found support in church doctrine and in the common law, and this doctrine continues to influence legal judgments in this century.

Historically, the state's interest has been the control, rather than the denunciation, of wife battering, as evidenced by a regulation limiting the size of the stick used by a husband to discipline his wife to the size of a man's thumb — hence, the rule of thumb.

. . . .

In sheer numerical terms, wife battering is a major social problem. One in ten Canadian women in an intimate marital-type situation will be assaulted by her partner this year. The assault will be repeated for one in twenty and those who bring criminal charges will have been assaulted an average of thirty-five times. The rate is much higher for native women, who comprise fifty percent of battered women in Saskatchewan. The Law Reform Commission of Canada calls the wife battering problem "serious" and the Canadian Association of Social Work Administrators identifies it as the "current most pressing concern within the spectrum of domestic violence".

In 1983, in response to this major problem, Saskatchewan's Minister of Justice announced the implementation of a range of policies directed at reducing spousal violence including expanded shelter and counselling programs, batterer therapy, public education, statistical monitoring and reduction of discretion in the criminal prosecution of batterers. In the following discussion, Saskatchewan's new prosecutorial policy is examined within the context of the various definitions and the etiology of wife battering; the abuse models that have been formulated and the implications of criminal sanctions in wife battering cases; and also on the discretionary power exercised by the battered woman witness. Regrettably, the results of the Saskatchewan Department of Justice two-year study of this new policy were unavailable at the time of publication of this paper.

## THE CRIMINAL LAW

### *Prosecutorial Policy*

Efforts to ground policy in models are most difficult where the area is new, the data incomplete and the proposed policy heavily value-laden. In the final analysis, a policy choice is made in hopes that implementation will itself generate needed data and new models. Such a policy choice was the decision of Saskatchewan's Minister of Justice, announced in December 1983, to limit discretion in the prosecution of wife batterers.

Discretion — investigative, prosecutorial and judicial — is as much a hallmark of the Canadian legal system as is the right of the accused to make full answer and defence. Criminal acts are not equally prosecuted, nor are judges bound to dispose of cases in any rigidly controlled fashion to achieve absolutely uniform sentencing. The decision to control prosecutorial discretion in wife battering cases is properly a policy determination. It was made on the urging of feminist groups, who have historically been in the forefront of family law reform, in the belief that public attitudes toward family violence can be changed through enforcement of criminal sanctions.

### *The Saskatchewan No-Drop Policy*

The Director of Public Prosecutions for Saskatchewan, Kenneth McKay, described the policy and its rationale as follows:

> [T]he Minister of Justice instructed that the Crown press for more serious sentences in cases of spousal violence. In addition, the department instituted measures to ensure that the law was properly enforced in this area . . . .The efforts of the department were aimed at changing attitudes to family violence so that they were treated as any other offence — public, not private issues. Police were instructed not to put the onus on the complainant, but to lay charges as they would in any other case,

that is, where the evidence supported charges; prosecutors were instructed not to discontinue cases if the only reason for doing so was the reluctance of the complainant; and courts were pressed for firmer sentences.

A Saskatoon Crown prosecutor described the policy as "get the charges into Court" by doing everything possible at all costs to ensure that prosecutions of batterers go ahead, particularly where there has been a serious assault. Individual prosecutors now have no discretion to drop charges in wife-battering cases, but if circumstances warrant — the assault is minor, the victim vindictive— charges may be dropped upon approval by the Director of Public Prosecutions in Regina. This ensures province-wide consistency in policy application.

Prior to the institution of the policy, discretion was exercised primarily on the basis of the victim's choice. Implicit was an individual-level model of wife abuse, a model inappropriate to a situational-level judgment. The relationship between victim and offender and the repetitive nature of abuse led to an assumption by prosecutors that the victim in at least some cases had consented to the act. In any event, the domestic setting was a screen of privacy to be respected if the victim so desired. Police also took into account the factor of danger in interfering in domestic disputes: approximately seventy-five percent of all police injuries (including deaths) incurred on duty happened while responding to domestic calls. Also since women frequently wanted charges withdrawn, police and prosecutors tended to avoid the matter at the outset. The D.P.P. summed [up] the situation prior to the new policy:

> Because of the relationship of the persons involved in spousal violence cases, there was a tendency to consider them as personal matters — private disputes limited to parties involved. Thus, the police were reluctant to lay charges unless the complainant personally swore the information; where charges were laid, the prosecutor was reluctant to proceed if the victim was unwilling to continue; and where a conviction was registered the court appeared reluctant to sentence in any meaningful way.

The criminal law is less concerned with the interests of a particular victim than with deterrence of crime in general and the interest of society at large. Prosecuting the abuser not only requires the victim to testify against someone with whom she has had a close relationship; she must also undergo cross-examination ("isn't it true that you bruise easily?"), and she may be subjected to the offender's increased resentment and violence as a result. Criminal prosecution cannot prevent future violence by the batterer or assist his family in reorganizing their lives. It is not surprising, then, that a majority of theorists, therapists and family lawyers have ascribed only a minor role to criminal sanctions in wife abuse.

However, visible problems require visible solutions if the state is to be seen as responsive to social needs. Allocation of funding for research, education and therapy, as provided for in Saskatchewan, is an important step but lacks the firm disapproval expressed by criminal sanctions. The prosecution of abusers sends the clear message that society will not tolerate their acts. This didactic power of criminal justice is increasingly viewed by reformers as a vital component of programs aimed at the reformation of social attitudes. The no-drop prosecutorial policy is evidence of the consensus between reformers and the state that social interests are to take precedence over the immediate interests of the victim. Still, the policy is beneficial to a victim who wants the prosecution to proceed. As the D.P.P. noted:

Some of the results of the new efforts are obvious. By treating these cases as public issues, pressure was taken off the victim who is often locked in a cycle of violence. Since the matter is no longer her personal action, she is better able to resist pressure or intimidation from the offender, and in many cases psychological and emotional pressures she is subject to are lessened. It also appears to be better for the offender since it brings home the serious criminal nature of his activities.

On the other hand, based on preliminary data on the no-drop policy issued in 1985 by the Policy, Planning and Evaluation Branch of the Saskatchewan Department of Justice, a significant number of victims do not want the prosecution pursued. In thirty-five percent of the two hundred thirty-two reported cases during an eight-month period, the victim requested that charges be dropped. In twenty-five percent of cases the victim "actively hindered" prosecution.

The Branch is responsible for monitoring wife battering prosecutions over a two-year period and for compiling statistics from police and prosecution reports from across Saskatchewan. Preliminary statistics have been released for the eight-month period from January to August 1985. Police reports indicated that eight hundred fifty-four complaints of wife abuse were made; fifty percent resulted in charges being laid, thirty-five percent were diverted or otherwise cleared and fifteen percent were under investigation. Prosecutors reported two hundred thirty-three cases in sixty-one districts with a total of two hundred seventy-two charges. Of this total, seventeen percent were withdrawn or stayed. Physical violence was the basis of sixty-nine percent of charges, property offences comprised seven percent, weapons offences nine percent and peace bond applications ten percent. The accused pleaded guilty in seventy-one percent of instances and were found guilty in eleven percent. Probation was the single most common sentence imposed, followed by fines and incarceration. For third-time offenders, incarceration was imposed in every case.

Whether these initial figures approximate the final results is uncertain. The preliminary results of the two-year study, however, clearly disclose that the victim has retained control over prosecution despite the no drop policy.

*Social Workers and Police*

While statistics for the years preceding the introduction of the policy are unavailable, interviews with social workers, police, prosecutors and family court judges indicate the policy has resulted in perceptible changes. A social worker described the victim's situation prior to the introduction of the policy:

> It used to be a real problem. The wife would leave and return six to eight times before finally leaving. It's seldom a clean break. The police get angry: she would lay charges, get a peace bond or restraining order, then return to her husband and deny her previous statements. The police were frustrated, so they discouraged her. She would lay charges, go in the next day and find there was no record. This was especially true if she was native or had been in before. She would go to Legal Aid for a restraining order, but they discouraged her, telling her it's not effective, not very good. It's as though they have a quota. But in practice, if she had a restraining order and let the guy back in, then it was hard to get another order.

Workers recommend to their clients that they lay charges but contacting the police remains the victim's responsibility. The policy has changed the situation in that the laying of charges will now be followed up by police and prosecutors.

Attitudes, however, have yet to change. The attitude of the legal profession and the police [still] is, "Why go back? If she's stupid enough to go back the first time, why should we get involved again, especially the third or fourth time?" Because of those attitudes a crisis worker recently wondered whether the no-drop policy had been revoked.

> There was a brief flurry of police laying charges, but now they are backing off in the last couple of months. Police have recently been asking women who are bleeding in the emergency room if they want to lay charges, and saying to the husband "I'm here because your wife has decided to lay charges."

Pressure to establish wife battering crisis services has steadily increased over the past three years. One worker estimated that two to three requests per day for intervention or information are made to the Saskatoon Crisis Unit, and approximately twenty-five percent of calls come from the police. In an abusive situation the priority is to find a safe place for the victim so that counselling and legal services can begin. Crisis workers interact with the police during the "hot" times of the conflict, and from the workers' viewpoint this can be difficult.

> It is frustrating to go in after the police. They create a secondary situation which also has to be defused. If the police have taken the guy, it's easier — then the Unit just has to take care of the woman.

Representing police opinion are the comments of three high-ranking R.C.M.P. officers with long records of service in a number of Saskatchewan centres. They were in full agreement with the no-drop policy and commented on the situation prior to its adoption.

> The no-drop policy is designed so the victim is not coerced into doing what she doesn't want to do. Before, the victim would phone and withdraw charges the next day. There was suspicion of coercion but also battered women are notorious, consistently, for going back to their husbands. They may have no choice, or no alternatives, they may know they will be beaten, but they go back anyway.

However, police also experience a combination of pity and frustration and problems remain despite the policy.

> Police deal in facts and the beating is a fact. They have tunnel vision — they should take into account why she wants to withdraw the charges, but they don't. They see it as "do it or don't do it" — an irritation — how many times — not her again. Often they wish she would go ahead because she is so badly beaten.

When a victim changes her mind, police are irritated and if the violence has ended by the time police arrive, no charges can be laid if she is the sole witness. However, a conscientious officer can lay charges based on reasonable suspicion for breach of the peace, one of the most valuable tools for dealing with family violence.

The dual role police are expected to fulfil further complicates intervention. Trained to deal with violence through complex role-plays with actors using weapons, police respond to all calls fully prepared for violence. Instead, they may end up as unwilling arbitrators.

> The emotional flip-flop, from being tough, aggressive, to sympathy is really hard. There is very little satisfaction for police in dealing with domestic violence. How can the police undo in thirty minutes what it took the couple twenty-five years to do? If somebody has his watch stolen and the police get

it back for him, that's rewarding. Sometimes police are being used, just a tool, there to enforce personal wishes. Our training is for impartiality. We don't want to take sides.

The Director of Interval House, Saskatoon's shelter, preferred that police refrain from counselling. Offhand statements by police may lead a victim to think she is responsible for provoking the violence. Often the offender's apologetic charm can fool the police into thinking the situation has been resolved; but when they leave, the victim may be beaten for calling them. Police are not trained to counsel.

They don't understand and therefore they are frustrated by the wife's attacking them, because they are there for her safety. If they understood more of her fears they could deal with it without getting angry. They are there to deal with crime.

The director further observed that the criminal process is useful, though, because it shows the victim she is not to blame. Criminal charges also show the abuser that society views his acts as a crime. But in order for there to be any possibility of effective deterrence, the abuser must believe he will be caught. Secondly, sentencing must be appropriate. Neither circumstance is yet the case. The director stated that police take women to headquarters to lay the information and she is unaware of any case of refusal to comply. Although she has seen no change since the no-drop policy was introduced, she emphasized that she deals with only a small percentage of Saskatoon-area battered women at Interval House. While outlining legal options is part of the shelter's counselling service, usually the woman's priority is custody of her children and possession of the matrimonial home; criminal proceedings are not stressed.

## Prosecutors and the Court

According to one crown prosecutor, more people have been convicted subsequent to the policy than in the same time period preceding it. The estimate is one case per week for each of eleven Saskatoon prosecutors, twice the number before the policy. This prosecutor, like the police officers interviewed, would prefer to retain the discretion to drop cases involving very minor assaults or changed circumstances where proceeding is not the public interest. The policy does simplify dealing with victims, who can now be told, "Sorry, we have no choice but to go ahead with the charges." The frustration of dealing with reluctant witnesses, however, continues.

The police share this view. They may have put a lot of work into a case, and are often sympathetic to the woman and appalled by her injury. Without her full co-operation the best they can hope for in sentencing is probation instead of discharges. One officer took photographs of a terribly beaten woman and showed them to the judge when the victim was reluctant to testify, but it made no difference; the officer had not witnessed the beating itself and the man was acquitted. In most cases there is no witness except the victim herself. Photographs and circumstantial evidence are not sufficient for a conviction. The police are called only to corroborate. Any other witnesses, including children, will be subpoenaed but usually there are none.

Related to the problem of reluctant witnesses and another major source of frustration is sentencing. Despite the emphasis in the policy on pressing for stiffer sentences, sentencing continues to be lenient.

It depends on the nature of the offence. If it's an isolated incident and the couple has reconciled, then the court is disproportionately lenient. If he had broken his brother's tooth, he could get a fine, but if it's his wife, he gets an absolute discharge, so the leniency of sentencing is frustrating to prosecutors.

In the opinion of police officers, rules of evidence and procedure governing assault cases are at their discriminatory worst in spousal violence cases. Consent is an issue only where there is assault without physical injury; yet police corroboration may be required even where there is other evidence of injury. Evidence of injury is no substitute for the witness' own testimony as it is, for example, when the victim cannot testify in a murder trial. The co-operation of the victim is vital to conviction and meaningful sentencing and therefore to fulfilment of the overall policy goals.

There are two common scenarios. In the first, the victim testifies about the beating but claims that she and the accused have reconciled. The Saskatoon prosecutor used the following as an illustration:

> Monday morning, just before trial, the defence counsel came over and told me, "I think you should know they spent the weekend together". I asked the woman if this was true, and what about the restraining order. She said it was true and they had sexual relations. I asked her why, because she was still willing to testify about the beating. She said he would be going to jail for six months and she wouldn't have another chance to be with him. . . . I told the judge I had no recommendation for sentencing.

The woman testified, the accused was found guilty and put on probation. Because of the implications of reconciliation, the prosecutor decided it was pointless to recommend a jail term and, furthermore, the judge would not have awarded one under those circumstances. When reconciliation is claimed, or the incident is minor or minimized by the victim's testimony, the result is a discharge or, at most, probation. Madam Justice Mary Carter of the Unified Family Court summed it up this way:

> I don't like to send people to jail if they are earning money unless they are rich. Sometimes, the husband drinks but works steadily and the wife wants the courts to clean him up and send him back home. Counselling is not very effective. . . . I have gone over this with colleagues so often, and there are faults with it. A brutal attack is a different thing, but here we deal with anything from a shove to broken bones, and the problem may have been hidden for years.

Half of the forty cases on her Chambers list for the following day involved spousal cruelty.

The second scenario involves the witness who "can't remember". She may recognize her husband and remember her own name, but nothing else, even if she laid the charge. Nothing further can be done and the case is dismissed. The prosecutor may be told that there is no point in proceeding if the woman is not going to give evidence, particularly where the police have laid charges against the woman's wishes.

The Justice Department policy has removed discretion from the hands of the victim, the police and the prosecutor, but cannot remove it from the court. Whether it is fear of reprisal, mistaken belief in reconciliation, or the value for the victim in preserving the relationship, the court is reluctant to exacerbate her situation by removing the offender from the family against her wishes. The court, in dismissing the case for want of prosecution or in handing down lenient sentences, is in effect returning discretionary power to the victim. Women who want to withdraw from prosecution or are coerced into withdrawal have a number of options: they can avoid calling the police in the first place and thereby lose that source of protection; they can fail to appear in court; they can claim reconciliation, conveniently lose their memory or refuse to testify on the witness stand. In the final analysis, the victim controls every stage of the criminal process.

. . . .

## CONCLUSION

Wife battering has been and remains endemic to our society. Only recently has battering been brought out of the family unit into the open and been recognized as a serious social problem requiring attention and action. Deeply rooted in the patriarchal, male-dominated social and legal systems to which we belong, violence against women is a major problem requiring major system and social reform.

> [The ideology of violence against wives] remains imbricated in the legal system . . . . The ideology itself must be dismantled. The legal system has been committed to a patriarchal ideology. It is this that must be challenged if violence against women is to diminish and ultimately to cease.

Minor social reform measures do not directly address the need for major system and social reform. Advocacy and counselling programs, the unwritten policy against prosecuting victims who fail to testify and the no-drop policy all contradict, rather than further, gender equality ideals and it may argued that special treatment of battered women by a patriarchal male-dominated criminal justice system merely extends chauvinist protectionism into yet another arena. Short-term measures carry the message that the system is basically good and merely shore up a system which should be razed and rebuilt or left to crumble under the weight of its inadequacies.

Of the several models available, if the patriarchal one is chosen and social revolution along feminist lines is the selected remedy, then short-term measures will be rejected. Many supporters of this model bypass the criminal justice system and concentrate instead on service provision and public education to reduce society's glorification of violence and improve the social condition of women. But this extreme position denies both the immediate feminist interest in establishing wife-battering as a criminal concern and the interests of women caught up in the process. The position further pretends to a prescience of the means of revolution when, in reality, we lack both the tools and the shared vision required to engineer drastic social change. Moreover, reforms do not always appear to have the desired effects.

> Legal reforms have ambiguous and contradictory effects. Yet the only way to bring about major changes may be to begin with minor ones. We must make political decisions and act, even though our efforts may sometimes backfire. The more completely and accurately we analyze reforms, the greater the possibility we have to promote reforms that — sometime in the future — we will recognize to have been the beginnings of a revolution.

Any reform measure which promises a modicum of relief requires, along with careful analysis, acceptance of some degree of contradiction.

In the search for a new model of human relations it becomes practical to theorize about utopianism on a meta-societal level. World and social conditions have progressed well beyond the point where this can be dismissed as mere idealism. To solve the problem of wife battering, family violence must be viewed as a reflection of society which in turn reflects an outmoded ideology — which is detrimental to human civilization. While definition, model-building and police derivation for the curtailment of spousal violence are prerequisite to effective action, however refined and empirically accurate this process may become, policy-makers and court and agency personnel need to be reminded that the state of things as they are cannot dictate how things should be. A normative leap is required. The state's decision to intervene, and the formulation and implementation its intervention policy, remain in the realm of values and ethics.

. . .

## Other Discretionary Powers of the Prosecutor

As a case progresses beyond the initial decision to prosecute, the public prosecutor exercises a variety of further discretionary powers. Plea bargaining has received the most attention in this context. However, a whole variety of ongoing discretionary decisions can significantly affect the positions of both the victim and the accused.

### Prosecutorial Discretion on the Charges

According to Vanek (1988:219):

> Legal authorities appear to agree that the Attorney General is answerable to the legislature for the manner in which he exercises a discretion inherent in his office . . . but not to the courts; and hence, that the exercise of such discretionary authority is not subject to judicial control. Consequently, Crown prosecutors who derive their authority from the Attorney-General exercise their discretionary authority . . . on the same basis; namely, . . . that the exercise of their discretion is unfettered. In addition, the trend of recent legislation has been to increase rather than decrease the number of matters over which the Crown prosecutors are given discretionary authority.

Areas of concern mentioned by Vanek include Crown option offences in which Crown prosecutors have the power to decide before trial whether a "hybrid offence" will be dealt with summarily or by indictment. The choice is important because it affects the range of penalties applied and determines a number of procedural matters. Criminal law in the U.S. does not employ hybrid offences and Vanek suggests the same limit be observed in Canada. Where the accused has previous convictions, the Crown prosecutor by notice can require the court to impose the mandatory minimum sentence.

### Role of the Prosecutor and Discretionary Powers During the Proceedings

The Canada Constitution Act, 1867, establishes that the administration of criminal law is a provincial matter and so, it falls within the responsibility of provincial Attorneys-General and those delegated the powers of state prosecution. The powers of Crown Counsel include the power to detain in custody, to negotiate pleas, to utilize police forces, to disclose or not disclose evidence before trial, to proceed summarily or by indictment with hybrid offences, to stay proceedings, to intervene in private prosecutions and to appeal. The prosecutor's office is also of central importance because it is the one agency that works with every other element of the criminal law system. Prosecutors work closely with police concerning the gathering of evidence and the laying of charges. In addition, prosecutors coordinate with defence lawyers to transfer pre-trial information and to negotiate guilty pleas. Prosecutors also work with judges in a non-adversarial manner when they make sentencing recommendations or deal with accused who are possibly unfit to stand trial.

According to judicial and political pronouncements, Crown Prosecutors are quasi-judicial officers whose duty is not to seek conviction but to administer the criminal law fairly and free of political interference (Savage, 1959; Gourlie, 1982). In practice, this means that Crown Prosecutors should not use vindictive, inflammatory language, they should not express strong personal opinions about the guilt of the accused and they should willingly share information with defence counsel, even if that means weakening their own case (Bowen-Colthurst, 1969). Canadian courts have held that Crown Prosecutors must call all credible, relevant witnesses including those adverse to their case and they must cite all the cases on point known to them including those unknown to but of value to the defence (Savage, 1959). In short, the prosecutor is to put justice first and conviction second. To some extent, Crown Prosecutors are held to these standards by judges, particularly with respect to their conduct and language at trial, which is that part of their conduct most visible to judges. However, at a more fundamental level there are serious doubts about the neutrality of public prosecutors. The following case considers the acceptability of the Crown Prosecutor's language at trial.

## Regina v. Romeo
(1989), 47 C.C.C. (3d) 113 (N.B. C.A.)

Appeal by the accused from his conviction for first degree murder.

AYLES J.A. (dissenting): — I have read the reasons for judgment of my colleague Ryan J.A. I disagree with him as to what effect the inflammatory and prejudicial remarks of Crown counsel had on the decision of the jury. I am in accord with the remainder of his decision.

The question, as I see it, is what was the effect of the trial judge's failure to properly warn the jury to disregard the inflammatory and prejudicial remarks made by Crown counsel? In this case Crown counsel addressed the jury after defence counsel. The remarks in this case were made by Crown counsel in referring to the expert opinion of Dr. Suzanne Canning, a psychiatrist for the defence.

He referred to her as being good at telling stories and said in essence these stories were more exaggerated than fairy-tales. The prosecutor made other equally derogatory remarks:

> Now, I have no quarrel, really, with Suzanne Canning's qualifications, but like Dr. Akhtar, I submit that she is totally wrong, very wrong. I submit that, first of all, she's an excellent witness, very good witness, I think she — she can talk. I'm a lawyer, have been now 30 years, I don't come close to her. She is good, I'll say that, but I submit that *she is good in telling stories* and that's what she told you, *and somebody has made up a story in the whole case, a story of insanity*, and that's what was given to you, and this story can't be simple because it had to match so many other facts, so what was given to you was even much more than what you see in *fairy tales. Fairy tales* seem believable some but this is something I submit is far beyond fairy tales. You have to have a monster or a butcher, you have to have a phantom automobile, you have to have racketeering, some underworld going on, and because only when you have all these other delusions that you can answer every action of the accused, but on this monster, it's interesting, and every interesting, *a lot of things Suzanne Canning has tried to cover*. There is no description of the monster itself, and I bet — we didn't ask, but if we asked we probably would have had a painting of the monster from Dr. Suzanne Canning.

. . . .

> Just as I said, the monster is cast in front of us, and *it boggles my mind. I've heard many stories but this is the top.*

(Emphasis added.)

Several cases before the Supreme Court of Canada have dealt with the appropriate behaviour of Crown counsel during a criminal trial before a jury. In *Boucher v. The Queen* (1954), 110 C.C.C. 263, 20 C.R. 1, [1955] S.C.R. 16 (S.C.C.), Kerwin C.J.C. addressed the issue of Crown counsel's responsibility at p.265:

> In all this he has a duty to assist the jury, *but he exceeds that duty when he expresses by inflammatory or vindictive language his own personal opinion that the accused is guilty*, or when his remarks tend to leave with the jury an impression that the investigation made by the Crown is such that they should find the accused guilty.

(Emphasis added.) At p. 270 of *Boucher* Rand J. declared:

> It cannot be over-emphasized that the purpose of a criminal prosecution is not to obtain a conviction; it is to lay before a jury what the Crown considers to be credible evidence relevant to what is alleged to be a crime. Counsel has a duty to see that all available legal proof of facts is presented. It should be done firmly and pressed to its legitimate strength, but it must also be done fairly. The role of prosecutor excludes any notion of winning or losing; his function is a matter of public duty than which in civil life there can be none charged with greater personal responsibility. It is to be efficiently performed *with an ingrained sense of the dignity, the seriousness and the justness of judicial proceedings.*

(Emphasis added.)

The reasoning of the Supreme Court of Canada opinions in the Boucher case in relation to the role of Crown counsel was summarized in *Pisani v. The Queen* (1970), 1 C.C.C. (2d) 477, 15 D.L.R. (3d) 1, [1971] S.C.R. 738 (S.C.C.). In delivering the unanimous decision of the five-member panel, Laskin J., as he then was, started at p. 478 C.C.C., p. 740 S.C.R.:

> The reasons for judgment given separately in *Boucher* by Kerwin, C.J.C., Rand, Locke and Cartwright, JJ., amply point up the obligation of Crown counsel to be *accurate, fair and dispassionate* in conducting the prosecution and in addressing the jury. Over-enthusiasm for the strength of the case for the prosecution, manifested in addressing the jury, may be forgivable, especially when tempered by a proper caution by the trial Judge in his charge, where it is in relation to matters properly adduced in evidence. *A different situation exists where that enthusiasm is coupled with or consists of putting before the jury, as facts to be considered for conviction, matters of which there is no evidence and which come from Crown counsel's personal experience of observations.*

(Emphasis added.)

In my opinion, the impugned remarks of Crown counsel in this case do not meet the test set out in *Boucher* and *Pisani*. These remarks were calculated to inflame the jury by directing their attention to whether the hearsay statements of the appellant to Dr. Canning were a "fairy tale", instead of dealing with the proper question of which expert witness was to be believed.

As can be noted in the quotation from Crown counsel's remarks, there were both subtle and blunt attacks upon the credibility of the primary defence witness, Dr. Suzanne Canning. These remarks were unsupported by anything more than the personal observations of Crown counsel. Crown counsel described Dr. Canning's testimony regarding the details of the appellant's mental condition as being so incredible that it was "far beyond fairy tales". These remarks were focused upon the content of the appellant's alleged delusions, rather than the relevant issue of whether or not the appellant had experienced delusions that would affect his sanity at the time he killed Officer Aucoin. These comments attempted to undermine the credibility of

Dr. Canning without there being any evidence on which to base such an attack. The intemperate statements in my view were unfair and prejudicial and ought to have been commented upon by the trial judge so as to refocus the minds of the jurors on the real question in issue.

. . .

In the present case, the thrust of the defence was that the appellant had a history of psychotic behaviour and of paranoid delusional thoughts. Dr. Canning's psychiatric evidence in support of this contention was a central element in the appellant's case in order to support the plea of not guilty by reason of insanity. Crown counsel's improper and unsupported attack upon the credibility of Dr. Canning in his address to the jury bore directly upon the veracity of her testimony. The attack was prejudicial in respect of the central issue of the appellant's alleged insanity, which was the subject matter of Dr. Canning's testimony. In damaging the credibility of the witness, the content of the testimony given by that witness was also discredited. Because the improper remarks were not corrected by the trial judge, and these remarks directly affected the pivotal issues of Dr. Canning's credibility and the appellant's alleged insanity at the time the act of killing Officer Aucoin was committed, I cannot conclude that notwithstanding the remarks the verdict would necessarily have been the same.

In my opinion, the remarks of Crown counsel were prejudicial to a degree sufficient to impose a legal duty on the trial judge to comment and thus ensure that the position of the defence, in this case the appellant's alleged insanity at the time that Officer Aucoin was killed, was fairly put to the jury. The failure of the trial judge to comment on Crown counsel's improper remarks constituted an incorrect decision on a question of law.

In my view, no case has been made out for the application of s. 613(1)(b)(iii) of the *Criminal Code*. In the result I would allow the appeal, set aside the conviction and direct a new trial.

[Note: The majority in this case dismissed the appeal. On appeal to the Supreme Court of Canada, however, Ayles' dissent was supported and a new trial was ordered; see *R. v. Romeo* (1991), 62 C.C.C. (3d) 1 (S.C.C.).

Legal commentators often assert without any reference to evidence that prosecuting counsel do not aim to obtain convictions (Turner, 1962). But Grosman (1969) argues that the adversary system necessarily puts pressure on both the prosecution and defence to win. Furthermore, bureaucracies must measure job performance and the conviction rate obtained by prosecutors is likely to be used, perhaps covertly, as one criterion of competence. Since prosecutors enjoy the power to reject cases where conviction is unlikely, perhaps because of inconclusive evidence, it is natural when they do proceed they bring forward cases where they believe conviction is probable. In that context, prosecutors will naturally feel some commitment toward achieving conviction. In repeated courtroom struggles with often familiar defence lawyers, it may also be natural for prosecutors to take personal pride and pleasure in defeating their rivals. One can imagine contextual changes that would increase prosecutors impartiality. For instance, if prosecutors were required to prosecute every case or if some other agency made the initial decision to proceed, then they would have less at stake personally in conviction. Similarly, if criminal lawyers alternated daily between acting for the prosecution and for the defence, as they tend to in England, they are much less likely to develop biased orientation. This discussion, however, is somewhat academic for modern conditions where, increasingly, adversarial combat in court is used as a last resort. Most cases are settled by negotiations between prosecutor, defence counsel and judges. The adversarial process is being transformed into an administrative process where the trial court is no longer the central, controlling element. Still, parties seek to win at negotiation as well as at trial. Indeed, prosecutors may have more latitude to practise gamesmanship during plea bargaining because such bargaining is not closely scrutinized by judges.

The following case considers two issues central to the prosecutor's role: the legal status of offers to plea bargain, and the prosecutor's obligation to complete a trial in a "reasonable" time period.]

## Conway v. The Queen
(1989), 49 C.C.C. (3d) 289 at 300 (S.C.C.)

. . . .

L'HEUREUX-DUBÉ J.: — This appeal raises the question whether the appellant Conway should stand trial for a third time on a charge of murder. The facts are set out in ample detail by my colleague Mr. Justice Sopinka. While I agree with him and with the courts below that these facts do not disclose an abuse of process justifying a stay of proceedings, I cannot share his opinion that s. 11(b) of the *Canadian Charter of Rights and Freedoms* was infringed in the circumstances of the present case.

### ABUSE OF PROCESS

In considering the submission based on abuse of process at trial, Smith J. directed himself as follows:

[T]he residual discretion in a court to stay proceedings must not only be sparingly used, it must also be based on the prosecution being oppressive or vexatious, or follow upon the violation of the principles of fundamental justice and fair play or, again, there must be some other form of misconduct on the part of the authorities or some ulterior motive.

He found that there was no evidence to indicate that the prosecution had been "anything but fair and competent". He then went on to consider the main element in the appellant's claim, namely, that, in the circumstances, an abuse of process resulted from the Crown's objection to the appellant's re-election to be tried by a judge without a jury, and from the Crown's refusal to accept a plea of guilty of manslaughter in the absence of agreement on a joint submission for a sentence of 15 years. Smith J. did not find the Crown's position oppressive. He commented as follows on the insistence that there be a joint submission on sentencing:

The Crown ought not to be taken to task for doing that. The courts should encourage pre-trial discussions which have become much more frequent and numerous in recent years to the obvious benefit of the public. Such discussions are on their way to becoming completely institutionalized, at any rate. I feel compelled to say, though, that sentencing is for the courts and joint submissions, as is well understood by both Crown and defence, are never binding upon the court.

The Court of Appeal took a similar stand on this issue: 26 O.A.C. 389. In a unanimous decision, the court (Cory J.A., as he then was, and Grange and McKinlay

JJ.A.) rejected the appellant's submission that the Crown's requirement amounted to an abuse of process (at p.395):

> So far as the Crown was concerned, the aspect of sentence was inextricably bound up with the acceptance of the plea. There was no duty or obligation upon the Crown to accept the plea and the court should not impose such an obligation.

As well, the Court of Appeal rejected the contention based on the Crown's objection to the re-election before a judge without a jury, holding properly that "[t]he Crown could reasonably and properly determine that the issue should properly be determined by a jury as the representatives of the community" (p.394).

I am in agreement with these findings in the courts below and would only add the following remarks.

A trial judge has discretion to stay proceedings in order to remedy an abuse of the court's process. This court affirmed the discretion "where compelling an accused to stand trial would violate those fundamental principles of justice which underlie the community's sense of fair play and decency and to prevent the abuse of a court's process through oppressive or vexatious proceedings": *R. v. Jewitt* (1985), 21 C.C.C. (3d) 7 at p.14, 20 D.L.R. (4th) 651, [1985] 2 S.C.R. 128 (S.C.C.) borrowing from *R. v Young* (1984), 13 C.C.C. (3d) 1, 46 O.R. (2d) 520, 40 C.R. (3d) 289 (Ont. C.A.). The judge's power may be exercised only in the "clearest of cases": *Jewitt, supra,* at p.14.

Under the doctrine of abuse of process, the unfair or oppressive treatment of an appellant disentitles the Crown to carry on with the prosecution of the charge. The prosecution is set aside, not on the merits (see *Jewitt, supra,* at p.23), but because it is tainted to such a degree that to allow it to proceed would tarnish the integrity of the court. The doctrine is one of the safeguards designed to ensure "that the repression of crime through the conviction of the guilty is done in a way which reflects our fundamental values as a society": *Rothman v. The Queen* (1981), 59 C.C.C. (2d) 30 at p. 69, 121 D.L.R. (3d) 578, [1981] 1 S.C.R. 640 (S.C.C.), *per* Lamer J. It acknowledges that courts must have the respect and support of the community in order that the administration of criminal justice may properly fulfil its function. Consequently, where the affront to fair play and decency is disproportionate to the societal interest in the effective prosecution of criminal cases, then the administration of justice is best served by staying the proceedings.

Stays for abuse of process are not limited to cases where there is evidence of prosecutorial misconduct. In delivering the reasons of the court in *R. v. Keyowski* (1988), 40 C.C.C. (3d) 481 at pp. 482-3 [1988] 1 S.C.R. 657, 62 C.R. (3d) 349 (S.C.C.), Wilson J. made it clear that all relevant factors, including, but not restricted to, bad faith on the part of the Crown, are to be considered:

> To define "oppressive" as requiring misconduct or an improper motive would, in my view, unduly restrict the operation of the doctrine. In this case, for example, where there is no suggestion of misconduct, such a definition would prevent any limit being placed on the number of trials that could take place. Prosecutorial conduct and improper motivation are but two of many factors to be taken into account when a court is called upon to consider whether or not in a particular case the Crown's exercise of its discretion to re-lay the indictment amounts to an abuse of process.

While Wilson J. appears to contemplate that a sufficient number of trials may alone render the prosecution "oppressive", she suggests later in her reasons that the threshold is higher than two inconclusive trials (at p.483): "A third trial may, indeed, stretch the limits of the community's sense of fair play but does not of itself exceed them."

In the present appeal, the evidence supports no suggestion of prosecutorial misconduct or improper motive. As well, in light of the comments in *Keyowski* with respect to the number of trials, little weight can attach to the fact that the Crown is attempting to try the appellant a third time. Does the Crown's stand with respect to the re-election and the plea tip the scales in favour of prosecutorial oppression?

. . . .

[S].534(4) of the *Criminal Code* expressly recognizes the Crown's option to refuse a plea of guilty to an offence other than the offence charged:

> 534(4) Notwithstanding any other provision of this Act, where an accused . . . pleads not guilty of the offence charged but guilty of any other offence arising out of the same transaction, whether or not it is an included offence, the court may, *with the consent of the prosecutor*, accept such plea of guilty and, *if such plea is accepted*, the court shall find the accused . . . not guilty of the offence charged and find him guilty of the offence in respect of which the plea of guilty was accepted and enter those findings in the record of the court.

(Emphasis added.)

The requirement of prosecutorial consent is very strict and a plea of guilty which is not accepted by the prosecution is a "nullity" *R. v. Pentiluk and MacDonald* (1974), 21 C.C.C. (2d) 87 at pp. 90-1, 28 C.R.N.S. 324 (Ont. C.A.), reasons of the court delivered by Martin J.A.:

> Where the accused pleads not guilty to the offence charged, but guilty to the included offence and the plea of guilty to the included offence is not accepted, the only plea that has been made is one of not guilty. The plea of guilty to the included offence is not in accordance with the provisions of s. 534(6) [s. 534(4) in R.S.C. 1970, c. C-34] and is a nullity.

To allow pleas of guilty to lesser offences to be recorded without the consent of the Crown would be to negate the very premises of the administration of criminal justice. There can be no deterrence of crime nor any reinforcement of fundamental social values if a person charged with committing a particular offence is convicted and sentenced with respect to another offence of that person's choice. That is why the requirement of consent under s. 534(4) of the *Criminal Code* is so strict. Nevertheless, that provision furnishes some tools for tailoring the generally cumbersome system of criminal justice to the particular needs of individual cases. It makes room for a rational exercise by the Crown of its discretionary power, having regard to the interests of society and of the accused in each particular case.

. . . .

For these reasons, to hold a third trial in the circumstances would not in my view "violate those fundamental principles of justice which underlie the community's sense of fair play and decency" nor would it constitute an "abuse of a court's process through oppressive and vexatious proceedings". The present case is not one of the "clearest of cases" to which the Chief Justice referred in *Jewitt, supra*.

. . . .

SOPINKA J. (dissenting): — This appeal is from the Ontario Court of Appeal, 26 O.A.C. (3d) 389, which allowed the appeal from the decision of Smith J. of the High Court of Ontario. Pursuant to s. 11(b) of the *Canadian Charter of Rights and Freedoms*, Smith J. ordered a stay of proceedings by reason of the unreasonable delay in resolving a criminal charge of murder against the appellant.

In October, 1987, more than five years after the appellant was charged with murder, a third trial was scheduled to commence. At that time, the appellant brought a motion for a stay of proceedings based on an alleged violation of s. 11(b) of the Charter and abuse of process. The facts and procedural background are obviously central to the determination of this appeal and must therefore be considered in some detail.

## FACTS

On August 29, 1982, during the course of a bonfire party, a fight occurred between the appellant Conway and one Warren Leach. The appellant was then 21 years of age. There had been a history of animosity between the appellant and Leach. Leach was stabbed 16 times and died as a result of these injuries. Later that same day, the appellant was arrested on a charge of first degree murder in connection with Leach's death.

The appellant was detained in custody until September 13, 1982, at which time he was granted judicial interim release. The preliminary hearing was held in part on January 12 and 13, 1983, and was continued and concluded four months later on May 9 and 19, 1983, when the original two days scheduled in January proved insufficient to complete the inquiry. The appellant was committed to stand trial on the charge of first degree murder.

On June 24, 1983, the trial was adjourned on consent until December 5, 1983, to deal with the appellant's application to quash the committal for first degree murder. The application was dismissed, and on September 13, 1983, the trial date of December 6, 1983, was confirmed. Shortly thereafter, almost 16 months after the charge, on December 15, 1983, the jury returned a verdict of not guilty of first degree murder but guilty of the lesser included offence of second degree murder. The appellant was sentenced to life imprisonment without eligibility of parole for 10 years. The appellant was represented at this trial by Mr. Leonard Shore.

The appellant launched an appeal of his conviction which was heard in December, 1984. The appellant was represented by Mr. Brian Greenspan. On January 24, 1985, the Ontario Court of Appeal allowed the appeal partly on the grounds that the trial judge incorrectly instructed the jury relating to provocation. A new trial was ordered. The appellant was in custody for over 13 months between December 14, 1983, and February 1, 1985. On the later date he was released on bail.

. . . .

In this case, I am of the opinion that the Crown has failed to sufficiently justify the delay which it appropriately concedes is *prima facie* unreasonable. As well, the appellant has demonstrated prejudice to both his liberty and security interests at a minimum. I now turn to an examination of the reason for delay and the justification put forth by the Crown. I divide the five-year period into four segments:

(1) The date of the charge until the end of the first trial. August 29, 1982, to December 15, 1983. Almost 16 months.
(2) The end of the first trial until the Court of Appeal decision December 15, 1983, to January 24, 1985. More that 13 months.
(3) The Court of Appeal decision until the second trial. January 24, 1985, to May 1, 1986. More than 15 months.
(4) The end of the second trial until the scheduled start of the third trial. May 1, 1986, to October 26, 1987. Almost 18 months.

With respect to the first period, I am of the opinion that any delay can be justified on the basis of the inherent time requirements of the case with the possible exception of the period between January 12, 1983, and May 9, 1983. The preliminary hearing commenced on January 12th but was not completed on that date and was adjourned to May 9th and concluded on May 19, 1983. No explanation was offered for this delay of four months.

The second period is the 13 months from the end of the first trial until the decision of the Court of Appeal. This period alone is not abnormal or unreasonable. The decision itself was rendered in a very prompt fashion. Almost the entire deal was a result of the wait to be heard by the Court of Appeal. This delay has been explained adequately.

The third period is the 15-month delay leading up to the second trial. The Crown has argued that the accused's actions during this period comprised a waiver of his right to assert unreasonable delay. The Crown alleged that the accused's tardiness in retaining counsel was responsible for any delay. The appellant appeared in assignment court on March 4, 1985. For reasons that were not made clear to this court the matter was adjourned for over three and one-half months until June 25, 1985. The Crown failed to satisfactorily account for this delay. On June 25th, a trial date of January 7, 1986 was scheduled. This six-month period is part of the over-all systemic delay but in the circumstances would probably be well within the inherent time requirements. However, the actual trial did not commence until April 21, 1985.

On November 15, 1985, the counsel of record (and counsel at the first trial), Mr. Shore, brought an application to be removed from the record. The appellant apparently preferred to be represented by Mr. Greenspan who had conducted his successful appeal. The request was denied at that time due to a concern by the court that new counsel would not be available or would be unable to prepare by the January trial date. However, on a further motion on December 5, 1985, Mr. Shore was removed from the record. Predictably, on January 7, 1986, the appellant appeared without counsel and Osborne J. understandably declined to conduct the trial. The appellant provided the court with a list of 11 criminal lawyers who had stated they were unable to take the case.

This court must be very sensitive to an accused's right to choose counsel of choice. However, that right must be exercised with reasonable diligence: see *R. v. Ross* (1989), 46 C.C.C. (3d) 129, [1989] 1 S.C.R. 3, 67 C.R. (3d) 209 (S.C.C.). Normally, an attempt to secure the services of 11 different lawyers would demonstrate that the appellant had made a reasonable effort to secure representation. However, in this case, I am of the opinion that the appellant must answer for the delay caused by his lack of counsel.

I reach this conclusion because the first application to remove Mr. Shore from the record came only a month and a half prior to the trial date. This date had been known to the appellant since June. Section 11(b) must only protect those who demonstrate reasonable diligence in their selection of counsel when it affects the timing of the proceedings. Not all delays or adjournments sought by an accused will comprise a waiver as the underlying cause may be due to circumstances beyond the control of the accused. Here, however, the appellant must be held accountable for this delay. The trial was rescheduled for April 21, 1986. Because I attribute this delay to the appellant, this three and one-half month delay is satisfactorily explained by the Crown.

The fourth and longest period extends from the conclusion of the second trial until the scheduled start of the third, a period of close to 18 months. The Crown again argues that the appellant's actions were responsible for much of this delay such that he should be held to have waived his s. 11(b) rights. I am of the opinion, however, that most of this period has not been satisfactorily explained as being either within the inherent time requirements of the case or attributable to the accused. The Crown's conduct of the proceedings must now be scrutinized in light of the fact that through no fault of the appellant he had been tried twice and was still in jeopardy.

A month after the end of the second trial, the appellant appeared unrepresented in assignment court. The matter was adjourned two weeks until June 16th, to allow him to appear with counsel. Mr. Greenspan, counsel at the second trial, had informed the appellant that he could not conduct the third trial if it were again held in Ottawa. The appellant was also suffering financial difficulties and had been seeking legal aid for some time prior to the June 16th appearance. However, no legal aid was forthcoming by the time of that appearance at which the unrepresented appellant was given a trial date of September 22, 1986. Legal aid was only obtained upon appeal in July. This difficulty in obtaining legal aid was not the fault of the appellant and therefore be cannot be held responsible for any delay as a result. This is a different form of systemic delay which cannot be relied on here by the Crown as justification for any delay. I agree with counsel for the appellant that in view of what has occurred, the Crown had some responsibility to assist the accused in obtaining legal aid or indeed in funding the defence. The latter is, according to counsel, not an uncommon occurrence. While the Crown contends that its current practice concerning assistance extends only to appellate proceedings, there is no reason why in special circumstances it should not apply to trial proceedings which have been protracted due to appeals.

Mr. Greenspan on behalf of the appellant sought to obtain a change of venue to move the proceedings to Toronto. This application was opposed by the Crown and was dismissed on August 8, 1986, less than two months prior to the trial date. This application was a reasonably request by the appellant who would understandably desire representation by counsel very familiar with the case. Opposing this application in light of the appellant's known difficulties in obtaining counsel directly contributed to the plight in which he found himself on September 22, 1986. He had no counsel. Again, while the Crown has the right to oppose such motions, its actions here directly contributed to the mounting delay.

A new trial was set for November 10, 1986. Though the attempt to expedite the proceedings appears admirable in one sense, it also created the dilemma for the appellant of having to find counsel who was available on short notice. The appellant was reasonably diligent in his attempt to find a lawyer. Affidavits were filed from seven criminal lawyers who were approached between mid-September and the end of October. They were all unable to conduct the trial on November 10th. Mr. Donald Bayne on behalf of the appellant sought an adjournment on October 2nd so that he could represent the appellant. This application was denied as was a further application on November 4, 1986. After a several week postponement, the trial was finally moved to April 21, 1987. I am of the view that this delay was not the responsibility of the appellant that the Crown's insistence on an unrealistically short adjournment in light of the appellant's known predicament was the principal reason for not being able to retain counsel and hence caused the delay. It is an unfortunate illustration of the saying "haste makes waste".

On April 21, 1987, the appellant sought to be tried by judge alone. As the question whether this election was available to an accused was then before the Ontario Court of Appeal the trial was again postponed, this time until October 26, 1987. The Crown could have consented to this request pursuant to s. 473(1) of the *Criminal Code* but opposed it and argues that this delay is solely the responsibility of the appellant. Admittedly, the Crown had little control over the delay once it refused to allow a hearing before a judge alone. In view of the circumstances, however, and recognizing that refusal to consent if the prerogative of the Crown, I cannot accept the Crown's explanation of this delay. The antecedent delay was now chronic. The time for insisting on dubious procedural advantages had gone. This request by the appellant to be tried by judge alone was especially reasonable given his earlier experiences with jury trials. The appellant also demonstrated his sincerity in wanting to conclude the proceedings by offering to plead guilty to manslaughter.

Accordingly, I am of the opinion that substantial segments of the five-year period have not been justified or satisfactorily explained either on the basis of special circumstances of the case or that they have been waived by the appellant. As well, the appellant has demonstrated that the delay resulted in prejudice to his liberty and security interests. Furthermore, it is unlikely that a fair trial is now possible. Applying the principles in *Mills, supra*, and *Rahey, supra*, on any approach expressed therein, a breach of s. 11(b) is made out. I agree with the majority of this country in *Rahey* that the minimum remedy in the event of a violation of s. 11(b) is a stay of proceedings. In the result, I would have allowed the appeal, set aside the order of the Court of Appeal and restored the order of Smith J. at trial.

*Appeal dismissed.*

**Note**: In the case of *R. v Askov et al.* (1990), 59 C.C.C. (3d) 449, where the court held that the delay of a trial was unreasonable in the circumstances of the case, Cory summarized the relevant factors to be taken into account when considering whether the length of the delay has been unreasonable or not at pp. 483-4:

(i) The length of the delay

The longer the delay, the more difficult it should be for a court to excuse it. Very lengthy delays may be such that they cannot be justified for any reason.

(ii) Explanation for the delay

(a) Delays attributable to the Crown

Delays attributable to the action of the Crown or officers of the Crown will weigh in favour of the accused. The cases of *Rahey* and *Smith* provide examples of such delays.

Complex cases which require longer time for preparation, a greater expenditure of resources by Crown officers, and the longer use of institutional facilities will justify delays longer than those acceptable in simple cases.

### (b) Systemic or institutional delays

Delays occasioned by inadequate resources must weigh against the Crown. Institutional delays should be considered in light of the comparative test referred to earlier. The burden of justifying inadequate resources resulting in systemic delays will always fall upon the Crown. There may be a transitional period to allow for a temporary period of lenient treatment of systemic delay.

### (c) Delays attributable to the accused

Certain actions of the accused will justify delays. For example, a request for adjournment or delays to retain different counsel.

There may, as well, be instances where it can be demonstrated by the Crown that the actions of the accused were undertaken for the purposes of delaying the trial.

## (iii) Waiver

If the accused waives his rights by consenting to or concurring in a delay, this must be taken into account. However, for a waiver to be valid it must be informed, unequivocal and freely given. The burden of showing that a waiver should be inferred falls upon the Crown. An example of a waiver or concurrence that could be inferred is the consent by counsel for the accused to a fixed date for trial.

## (iv) Prejudice to the accused

There is a general, and in the case of very long delays an often virtually irrebuttable presumption of prejudice to the accused resulting from the passage of time.

Where the Crown can demonstrate that there was no prejudice to the accused flowing from a delay, then such proof may serve to excuse the delay. It is also open to the accused to call evidence to demonstrate actual prejudice to strengthen his position that he has been prejudiced as a result of the delay.

Unlike the Canadian civil servant model of public prosecutor, American prosecutors must often seek re-election to their office and typically they campaign on a platform of effective crime-fighting, proof of which lies in their conviction rate. In that context, it makes sense for prosecutors to lobby for systematic changes in administration that will either weaken the defence or strengthen the prosecution in order to increase their success rate in convicting racketeers, inside traders, drug traffickers and other popular targets. With the power to choose their cases, prosecutors enjoy the power to choose their defendants. As Jackson warned:

> With the law books filled with a great assortment of crimes, a public prosecutor stands a fair chance of finding at least a technical violation of some act on the part of almost any one ... it is in this realm — in which the prosecutor picks some person whom he dislikes or desires to embarrass, or selects some group of unpopular persons and then looks for an offence, that the greatest danger of abuse of prosecuting power lies. It is here that law enforcement becomes personal, and the real crime becomes that of being unpopular with the ... governing group, being attached to the wrong political views, or being personally obnoxious to or in the way of the prosecutor himself (Turner, 1962:447).

The political independence of Crown Prosecutors must also be doubted when their superior, the Attorney General, is an elected member of the provincial legislature and a member of the governing party's cabinet. Again, by its nature, partisan party politics favours decision making based on political advantage. If political independence is the goal, then private prosecution should arguably be encouraged and state prosecutors should be supervised not by politicians but by judges as tends to be the case in civil law countries such as France and Germany.

## THE ROLE OF DEFENCE COUNSEL

Until the 18th century, the accused did not have the right to be represented by legal counsel except in treason prosecutions mounted by the Crown. In the vast majority of cases, the accused defended himself or herself against a private prosecutor who was usually the victim. Often the accused did not even have an advance look at the prosecutor's evidence. The court was primarily concerned with the nature of the accused person's spontaneous responses to the prosecutor's case. The judge was thought to owe a limited responsibility to the accused in terms of explaining what had to be disproved in the prosecutor's case. All this started to change in the 1730s and 1740s and lawyers soon became the main "motor force" of the criminal trial. Much historical work on this transition remains to be done but it appears that the emergence of lawyers was due to two factors. One involved the increasing resort to lawyers acting on behalf of victims as agents in private prosecutions. The costs of legal counsel for the prosecutor were easier to bear with the rapidly increasing popularity of prosecution associations; property owners tended to subscribe to these to collectively deal with "crime problems". Another factor involved structural changes to the profession and the emergence of barristers who had the clear right to appear in all courts of law. With prosecutors increasingly resorting to skilled legal representation the accused's position in the trial was substantially disadvantaged and judges started to admit defence counsel on a discretionary basis when requested (Beattie, 1986:340-62). The clear legal right to defence counsel was only recognized in 1836 in Canada (at about the same time it was recognized in England). Of course the practical right to defence counsel has only emerged within the past fifty years with the emergence of legal aid.

Traditional descriptions of the role of defence counsel read very much like descriptions of the role of professional prosecutor. Both were said to have a duty to the court to see that justice was done. This meant that defence counsel was not to suppress or distort the truth on behalf of a client. Counsel owed a duty to their clients to represent their interests, of course, but this did not make counsel a mere agent of their clients (Savage, 1959). In formal terms, defence lawyers are "officers of the court". Historically, lawyers on either side of criminal trials in Canada were expected to owe their primary allegiance to the state and their profession (Maloney and Cassels, 1989). Criminal defendants themselves were not very important except in those rare cases when a famous, powerful figure was on trial. Unlike prosecutors, defence counsel were paid by their private clients but that has largely changed with the rise of legal aid in most jurisdictions. Now both sides are usually paid by the State.

Like most welfare schemes, legal aid is a complex, rule-laden program that was not designed with significant input from the people (criminal defendants) it is supposed to serve. While in the U.S. accused have a constitutional right to counsel, in Canada this right is qualified (except with young offenders) to cases where the judge determines that a fair trial demands counsel and where the accused lacks the means to employ a lawyer (see *R. v. Rowbotham* (1988), 41 C.C.C. (3d) 1 (Ont. C.A.). Provincial legal aid plans vary. Ontario's plan generally only covers criminal cases where there is a threat of imprisonment or loss of livelihood, and with drastic cuts in the funding of legal aid in 1996, it appears likely that only those facing imprisonment will receive legal assistance in the future. Applicants must pass a means test based on disposable income, assets and family composition. The focus of assistance is on the trial, but criminal defendants often need the most legal assistance at the time of arrest and questioning. Worse, the fee structures and incentives of legal aid may result in lawyers merely going through the motions of providing a defence, of making only "the noises of a defence" (Ericson & Baranek, 1982:201). The following case considers a number of issues central to the operation, adequacy and fairness of provincial legal aid plans:

## Regina v. Rockwood
### (1989), 49 C.C.C. (3d) 129 (N.S. C.A.).

Chipman J.A.: — This is an appeal from a decision of MacDonald J. denying the appellant's motion that the Attorney-General or the Nova Scotia Legal Aid Commission be compelled to fund competent counsel of his choice for the defence of charges against him, and until such funding and counsel were obtained, for a stay of proceedings.

The appellant describes himself in his affidavit as a self-employed real estate syndicator. On September 19, 1987, an information was sworn charging him with 20 counts of theft, breach of trust, and fraud. He appeared in court in answer to the charges on October 19, 1987. At that time he was represented by Lance Scaravelli who he was advised had expertise in criminal defence work. The preliminary hearing commenced on May 16, 1988. Saying that it was because of a shortage of funds, the appellant instructed Mr. Scaravelli to waive the preliminary hearing. Shortly thereafter the appellant was committed for trial on the charges and, as well, Mr. Scaravelli withdrew because the appellant was unable to pay for his services.

The date fixed for trial was April 3, 1989, and on being assigned to the case in the fall of 1988, MacDonald J. sought out the names of counsel and learned the appellant had none. He thereupon set a pre-trial conference for December 15, 1988, and arranged to have the R.C.M.P. notify the appellant thereof. As MacDonald J. said in his decision, the early pre-trial conference was chiefly to impress upon the appellant his need to obtain legal representation without further delay. At this pre-trial conference the appellant advised MacDonald J. that he had seen Nova Scotia Legal Aid regarding counsel the previous day. He was advised that there would be a further pre-trial conference at a later date and that it was "quite imperative" that he have counsel at that time to represent him.

In mid-February, 1989, a further pre-trial conference was called for March 1st. The appellant was unable to attend and it was rescheduled for March 7th. At this pre-trial conference the Crown prosecutor raised a summary of the facts which the Crown hoped to establish in support of the charges. At this time the appellant advised that his preliminary application for legal aid was turned down, but that he had appealed this decision and expected a ruling at the end of that week. The court then advised the appellant of his responsibilities in the matter and that the case would proceed to trial on April 3, 1989, with or without counsel.

On March 13, 1989, MacDonald J. was advised that the Nova Scotia Legal Aid Commission had issued a certificate to fund counsel on behalf of the name of counsel retained by Legal Aid on his behalf. A further pre-trial conference was held on March 23rd with the applicant's counsel and the Crown prosecutor present. Yet another pre-trial conference was held on March 28th at which time it appeared that the charges were ready for trial on April 3rd.

On Sunday afternoon, April 2nd, Victor Goldberg, a barrister, contacted MacDonald J. advising that the appellant had discharged his counsel and that he would be appearing on the appellant's behalf the following day to make a motion. On April 3rd, the schedule day of trial, the matter was adjourned to April 6th and the jury panel dismissed with instructions to return again on April 10th. After hearing both counsel,

MacDonald J. considered that it would be unfair both to the appellant and to the prosecution to hold the trial on April 10th.

On April 6, 1989, Mr. Goldberg presented his motion to MacDonald J.

. . . .

MacDonald J. . . . dismissed the motion and ordered the appellant to return on May 9, 1989, to answer to the charges and have a new trial date set. We are advised that this date has been set for November, 1989.

The appellant bases his claim to entitlement to "competent counsel of his choice" on both the common law and the Charter.

It has been said that legal aid, in its broadest sense, has existed as long as the law itself. There is a long-standing tradition in the Bar of service given either without charge or for less than it is worth to those unable to pay or pay adequately for a criminal defence. In particular, members of the Bar have responded, when called on by the court in the exercise of its inherent jurisdiction to do so, to defend indigents appearing without counsel. Such people have, over the years, been defended and defended well, often by inexperienced counsel. As the volume and complexity of criminal litigation increased, this system was inadequate to deal with the need. As was said by the Ontario Court of Appeal in *R. v. Rowbotham* (1988), 41 C.C.C. (3d) 1 at p 69, 63 C.R. (3d) 113, 35 C.R.R. 207 (Ont. C.A.):

> In former times, counsel (sometimes eminent counsel) were appointed by the trial judge to defend an indigent accused charged with a capital offence. Counsel appointed by the trial judge in those circumstances frequently acted without remuneration. Members of the defence Bar also defended many other kinds of criminal charges on a purely voluntary basis. Having regard to the increase in the length and complexity of modern trials and the increased overhead costs, the appointment of counsel to act without remuneration is no longer feasible and, indeed, in many cases, would be unfair to counsel.

In response to this inadequacy, legal aid programmes were established throughout Canada. In Nova Scotia, a formal legal aid system was constituted in 1972, and the service is now provided pursuant to the *Legal Aid Act*, S.N.S. 1977, c. 11. Such a programme has done much to respond to the ever increasing need, but no realist would argue that this system is perfect. As in other areas of service, provided by the government, budgetary constraints are a fact of life.

Under neither the legal aid system now in force nor under its predecessor of *ad hoc pro bono* service by individual members of the Bar does one think in terms of wide latitude of choice of counsel on the part of the recipients. Counsel for the appellant was unable to point to any authority showing that a choice outside of those counsel willing to serve within the system was a matter of entitlement.

. . . .

The position under the Charter is, I think, succinctly stated by the Ontario Court of Appeal in *R. v. Rowbotham, supra*, at pp. 65-6:

> The right to retain counsel, constitutionally secured by s. 10(b) of the Charter, and the right to have counsel provided at the expense of the state are not the same thing. The Charter does not *in terms* constitutionalize the right of an indigent accused to be provided with funded counsel. At the advent of the Charter, legal aid systems were in force in the provinces, possessing the administrative machinery and trained personnel for determining whether an applicant for legal assistance lacked the means to pay counsel. In our opinion, those who framed the Charter did not expressly

constitutionalize the right of an indigent accused to be provided with counsel, because they considered that, generally speaking, the provincial legal aid systems were adequate to provide counsel for persons charged with serious crimes who lacked the means to employ counsel. However, *in cases not falling within provincial legal aid plans*, ss. 7 and 11(d) of the Charter, which guarantee an accused a fair trial in accordance with the principles of fundamental justice, require funded counsel to be provided if the accused wishes counsel, but cannot pay a lawyer, and representation of the accused by counsel is essential to a fair trial.

It is submitted that this Charter guarantee contains three elements: (a) funded counsel; (b) competent counsel, and (c) counsel of choice. While it is not suggested that every indigent must be automatically provided with funded legal counsel, implicit in these guarantees is such funded counsel when the indigent faces a complex and serious charge. In *Panacui v. Legal Aid Society of Alberta* (1987), 40 C.C.C. (3d) 459, [1988] 1 W.W.R. 60, 54 Alta. L.R. (2d) 342 (Alta. Q.B.), McDonald J. said at p. 466:

> In my view, the foregoing statement of the purposes and interests which ss. 7, 10(b) and 11(d) are meant to protect when the issue is the scope and extent of the right to counsel, lead me irresistibly to the conclusion that a person charged with an offence that is serious and complex, when he cannot afford to retain counsel, is constitutionally entitled to have counsel provided to assist him at the expense of the state.

In making reference to funded counsel, nothing is said in these authorities about the degree of expertise of counsel an indigent accused is entitled to expect. In order to render the Charter rights meaningful, I believe counsel provided must be sufficiently qualified to deal with the matter at issue with a reasonable degree of skill.

Again, however, the case-law on the Charter aspect of this appeal does not go so far as to give the indigent a right of choice beyond those counsel willing to serve within the constraints of the Legal Aid programme. During the course of argument, counsel for the appellant conceded that the authorities did not establish that "choice" extended to any counsel, but only to those reasonably competent to handle the matter at hand. As MacDonald J. recognized in his decision, to extend the Charter right to the point contended for by the appellant could introduce chaos into the administration of justice.

*Appeal dismissed*

. . . .

Aside from the issue of fee-for-service, defence counsels' incentives must be examined to see where their primary interests lay. To begin with, criminal defendants are often from low income groups and unlike wealthier clients they do not tend to build a long term relationship with their lawyers. This may weaken the criminal lawyer's incentives to provide the level of service necessary to build repeat business. Second, defence counsel deal repeatedly with the same judges, prosecutors and court officers. In many ways, these people are all part of the same "team", a team that does not include the accused (Ericson & Baranek, 1982). Plea bargaining exaggerates this exclusionary effect, because bargaining does not take place in court where the accused can witness it and make some assessment of defence counsel's ability. Rather, bargaining occurs in secret between familiar "adversaries" away from the accused's view. Third, defence counsel are members of a monopoly profession and owe their livelihood to their profession's capacity to lobby government for laws that successfully exclude competitors, like former police officers or paraprofessionals, from courtroom advocacy. This protection is probably vital in the case of defence counsel because most of their work is routine and unsophisticated, and thus many could be readily replaced by low-cost competitors without law degrees, if such people were free to compete. Criminal lawyers, therefore, strive to maintain professional solidarity and to support a criminal law system that elevates them over their clients and over potential competitors. This reasoning does not suggest, however, that defence lawyers do not make spirited and sometimes personally risky efforts to protect their client's interests.

Issues of professional dominance and closed-shop union practices were not, however, matters traditionally discussed in connection with defence counsel (Larson, 1977). Legal "ethics" issues were instead relegated to peripheral questions such as whether lawyers should defend someone known to be guilty. According to Orkin (1958), the opinion of counsel as to a client's guilt or innocence is not just irrelevant but should not in any way be expressed in court by the lawyer. The usual argument in favour of this position is that, first, a lawyer should not usurp the function of the judge and jury who decide the question of guilt. This makes sense. Criminal guilt is a complex issue that often goes far beyond the simple question of whether the accused committed the specific acts charged. Numerous defences may be available. Some charges may be valid, others invalid. Difficult questions also arise about admissible evidence. The lawyer may not know all the evidence until trial is underway. The client may lie or the lawyer may mistakenly believe police testimony rather than accept the client's word. Determining guilt is also only one part of the process. Since judges have such wide discretion in sentencing, a lawyer's best defence work may consist of securing the best judge in the best district "(judge-shopping") and marshalling convincing evidence in support of a certain sentence. For example, on marijuana charges, a defendant is more likely to receive a lenient sentence in Ottawa-Carleton than in any of the surrounding districts (Maser, 1980). The difference between Ottawa and Hull on the same matter is also pronounced. Of 30 first-time offenders on marijuana possession charges who appeared in Ottawa courts in 1980, 25 received discharges, four were fined and one received a suspended sentence. By way of contrast, in Hull, of a similar group, 20 received fines and 10 got discharges (ibid.). Only a minority of accused are acquitted, so lawyers are accustomed to pursuing secondary goals, like reduced charges and lenient sentences.

## Bibliography

- Beattie, J.M., *Crime and the Courts in England, 1660-1800* (Princeton: Princeton University Press, 1986).
- Bowen-Colthurst, T.G., "Some Observations on the Duties of a Prosecutor" (1969), 11 Criminal Law Quarterly 377.
- Burns, Peter, "Private Prosecutions in Canada: The Law and a Proposal for Change" (1975), 21 McGill Law Journal 269.
- Davis, Kenneth, *Discretionary Justice* (Champaign: University of Illinois Press, 1971).
- Ericson, R. & Baranek, P., *The Ordering of Justice* (Toronto: University of Toronto Press, 1982).
- Gourlie, William, "Role of the Prosecutor: Fair Minister of Justice with Firm Convictions" (1982), 12 Manitoba Law Journal 31.
- Grosman, Brian, *The Prosecutor: An Inquiry into the Exercise of Discretion* (Toronto: University of Toronto Press, 1969).
- Grosman, Brian, "The Role of the Prosecutor: New Adaptations in the Adversarial Concept of Criminal Justice" (1969), 11 Canadian Bar Review 580.
- Harper, J. and McWhinnie, A., *The Glasgow Rape Case* (London: Hutchinson, 1984).
- Hay, Douglas, "Controlling the English Prosecutor" (1983), 21 Osgoode Hall Law Journal 165.
- Katz, Lewis R., *The Justice Imperative: An Introduction to Criminal Justice* (Cincinnati: Anderson Publishing, 1980).
- Larson, M.S., *The Rise of Professionalism: A Sociological Analysis* (Berkeley: University of California Press, 1977).

- Law Reform Commission of Canada, *Private Prosecutions*, Working Paper 52 (1986) (P. Burns, Principal Consultant).
- Maloney, M. and Cassels, J., "Critical Legal Education: Paralysis with a Purpose" (1989), 4 Canadian Journal of Law and Society 99.
- Maser, Peter, "Drug-Users Unequal Before the Courts", *The Ottawa Citizen*, June 2, 1980.
- Moody, S.R. and J. Toombs, *Prosecution in the Public Interest* (Edinburgh: Scottish Academic Press, 1982).
- Orkin, M.M., "Defence of One Known to be Guilty: An Extract from 'Legal Ethics'" (1958-59), 1 Criminal Law Quarterly 170.
- Romney, Paul, *Mr. Attorney: The Attorney General for Ontario in Court, Cabinet and Legislature, 1791-1899* (Toronto: The Osgoode Society, 1986).
- Savage, C.C., "The Duties and Conduct of Crown and Defence Counsel in a Criminal Trial" (1958-59) 1 Criminal Law Quarterly 164.
- Stenning, P.C., *Appearing for the Crown: A Legal and Historical Review of Prosecutorial Authority in Canada* (Brown Legal Publications, 1986).
- Turner, K., "The Role of Crown Counsel in Canadian Prosecutions" (1962), 40 Canadian Bar Review 439.
- Vanek, David, "Prosecutorial Discretion" (1988), 30 Criminal Law Quarterly 219.
- Wright, Barry, "Sedition in Upper Canada: Contested Legality" (1992), 29 Labour/Le Travail 7.

## Questions/Discussion

1. Compare and contrast the powers of private and public prosecutors in Canada.
2. In what way are Crown Prosecutors politically independent?
3. Why have both prosecutors and defence counsel largely abandoned the trial process? Does plea bargaining serve the interests of justice?
4. The Canadian Bar Association's Special Committee on Crown Disclosure examined disclosure rules in a number of countries and concluded that Canada has the weakest or "worst" disclosure rules because there is no legal compulsion for police or Crown Prosecutors to make disclosure of their evidence to the accused. According to the CBA Committee, the roots of injustice in the Donald Marshall case can be found in the disclosure issue. (This case is discussed in Chapter 8.2). The Crown failed, for example, to tell Marshall or his lawyers that witnesses who testified against him at trial had initially given statements to the police saying they had seen nothing of the killing. After his conviction, the Crown did not tell Marshall that a person had informed the police that he knew who the real killer was.
A survey done for the Marshall inquiry found that only 55 percent of defence lawyers were receiving complete disclosure from the Crown. But as the CBA points out, disclosure between accused and Crown is only part of the story. The first step is to have police make full disclosure to the Crown, something the CBA says occurs in only one case out of five. Unlike Matlock, Perry Mason and other criminal lawyers on television who spend most of their time investigating the facts, real defence lawyers are almost totally dependent on police and the Crown to provide information about their cases. Without compulsory disclosure rules, the defence will often be severely handicapped, and innocent people, like Donald Marshall, will continue to be wrongly convicted. Source: *National* "CBA Warning: Marshall Case Could Happen Again", February 1, 1990.
5. What are the legal and professional ethical bases for defending one known to be guilty?

## Further Reading

See the bibliography provided above at the conclusion of "The Role of Defence Counsel".

## 4.3 JUDGES

**Introduction**

Many of the issues which arise in the context of the personnel of the courts were addressed in Chapter 3. This section delineates the actual role which the judges play in directing the criminal trial process, but in looking at that role the problems which were witnessed previously should not be forgotten. As we saw in Chapter 3, it is evident that those who staff the courts can play a determining role in the formulation of criminal law, and these same agents can also have an important effect in the evolution of and on the consequences of particular trials. The technical role which judges play in the trial process and how they play it are discussed in the Silverman article below, while the important protections which are given judges by fellow judges are demonstrated in the *MacKeigan* case. The situation which gave rise to the *MacKeigan* case is discussed in more detail in Chapter 8.2, where the endemic racism in the criminal system is examined.

### The Trial Judge: Pilot, Participant, or Umpire?*
#### H. Silverman

- Excerpt from (1973), 11 Alberta Law Review 40 at 52-64.

Canadian courts dealing with the role of the trial judge emphasize that while there is an appropriate place and time for his intervention in the trial, and while he has the right to summarize and comment upon the evidence in a jury trial so long as he makes it clear that the jury are the sole judges of the facts, the prime prerequisite is that there must be a fair trial for the accused wherein the trial judge is not an umpire; nor should he assume the role of counsel for the defence or the prosecution (although when the accused is not represented his function is more all-embracing than that) or make remarks before the jury prejudicial to the accused such as indicating his conviction or the accused's guilt.

An eminent Canadian jurist, O'Halloran J.A. in *Regina v. Pavlukoff* lucidly explained the role and function of the trial judge in a statement worth quoting *in extenso*, and he concludes the following remarks by pointing out that judges are human and not objective-scientific recording machines, the "jury is not apt to reason in the abstract as if all men were alike, and attempt to force life into a plaster cast of law" and a judge does have a powerful influence upon the jury. He states:

> But the course of this case at trial and the argument on appeal demands the unpleasant appellate duty of adding two observations in a public interest that is concerned with whether the procreates of the common law shall decay or flower with a new vigour. The first is that a judge sitting with a jury is to a large degree an umpire and ought not to usurp the function of Crown counsel or appear to the spectators as a crusader for the conviction of a man on trial for his life. It may be that in some cases failure of counsel acting for the Crown to ask questions that ought to be asked may impel the judge for the assistance of the jury to interject himself into examination or cross-examination to a degree that he does not like to do and would not do if aided by experienced counsel. But that could not apply to this case, where counsel for the Crown as well as for the defence are well-known leaders of the bar, skilled in the practice of the criminal law. Experienced counsel for the Crown did not need judicial assistance in carrying on his cross-examinations.
>
> The second observation springs from the discussion of the extent to which a judge may express to the jury his own view of the credence to be attached to the testimony of a witness or directly or indirectly make clear his belief upon any factual phase of the case which would indicate his own

conviction that accused is guilty. There seem to be some generalized judicial *dicta* on the point, largely favouring a wide licence to the judge, and perhaps much more so traditionally in England than in Canada. There may be a view that the judge may express his own personal opinions to the jury as often as he wishes, provided that on a corresponding occasion he repeats to the jury the formula that 'the facts are for them alone'. With great defence and I hope with proper humility, in view of the eminence of some of the jurists who have given voice to *dicta* of apparently wide scope, I think it is appropriate to express a rationalized view that since the question of guilt is solely for the jury, a judge, under Canadian jurisprudence at least, who expresses his own opinions to a jury is doing nothing else than attempting to usurp the functions of the jury, the more so if strong and stubborn preconceptions are freely ventilated in the hearing of the jury prior to the conclusion of the defence case.

If the guilt is solely for the jury, and the judge in law so instructs them, what occasions can there be for the judge to express his own opinions as to factual matters of guilt?

It seems an absurdity for a judge, after telling the jury the facts are for them and not for him, then to volunteer his opinion of facts followed then or later by another caution to the jury that his own opinion cannot govern them and ought not to influence them. If his opinion ought not to govern or influence the jury, then why give his opinion to the jury? To a person who is not a lawyer, but has some training in the science of correct thinking and some knowledge of the workings of the human mind, a judge who expresses his own opinions to the jury is in effect unconsciously perhaps but nevertheless subtly and positively undermining the plain instruction he has given the jury that 'the facts are for them and not for him'; in reality he is in true effect attempting to persuade the jury not to exercise their own minds freely (as in law he has told them they must do) but instead to be guided by the factual conclusions he volunteers to them.

The judge in court officially and physically occupies a position of great power and prestige. His power and his control of the trial, which can be plainly seen in court, are matched by knowledge of the law and his experience in weighing and analyzing evidence. His lightest word or mannerism touching the reliability of a witness and the guilt of the accused cannot fail to bear heavily upon the members of the jury who naturally look up to him (and in more ways than one) as the embodiment of the great traditions of the law. To the jury the presiding judge appears as the great neutral. Anything that emanates from him carries for them at least all the ear-marks of balanced justice. In a widely publicized murder trial his every act and word are subjected to a merciless public scrutiny, which often wonders if he possesses natural penetrating shrewdness accompanied by a disciplined compassion.

There is every reason why the judge should confine himself strictly to his own responsibilities and leave the members of the jury alone to carry out their responsibility. There may be a tendency among some judges perhaps to feel constantly nervous whether a jury will bring in the verdict they may think the jury should bring in. But the law does not give the judge such a superior position. On the contrary the matter is beyond his jurisdiction and solely with the jurisdiction of the jury. The presiding judge is not an appellate court 'writ small'. It might easily be inferred that a judge who persists in giving his opinions to the jury is thoroughly convinced that a jury is not as competent as the judge himself to come to conclusion of the facts.

In a criminal case the trial judge can call witnesses. The position has been explained in this way in *Rex v. Skelly*:

As McDermott's name was endorsed on the indictment, the prisoner's counsel had the right to place him in the witness-box for examination. The prosecutor is not bound to call witnesses merely because their names are on the back of the indictment, but the prosecutor ought to have all such witnesses in court, so that they may be called by the defence if wanted. If, however, they are called by the defendant he makes them his own witnesses: per Alderson B., in *Regina v. Woodhead* (1847) 2 C.&K. 520.

The trial judge also, in the exercise of his discretion, might have called any witness whose name was on the indictment, as was done by Littledale J. in *Rex v. Beezley*

(1830) 4 C.&P. 220, and by Patteson J. in *Regina v. Holden* (1838) 8 C.&P. 606 at 610.

The trial judge cannot interfere with the Crown's right to determine which material witness to call, even where his name appears on the back of an indictment, especially where the Crown decides not to call such witness deeming him to be unreliable.

While the trial judge (and the Crown) need not provide witnesses for the accused, he should see to it that the Crown informs the accused so that the accused has "knowledge of the witnesses who are to be called against him and the general character of the evidence they are to give". A trial judge need not inform an indigent accused who requests assistance that the Crown will assist him in obtaining required witnesses. A trial judge can ask how an accused pleads, and "if the reply is not a clear admission of all the elements of the crime" he "must proceed to inquire into the charge without further questioning". Once the Crown closes its case, it is within the trial judge's discretion whether he will permit the Crown to re-open its case, as, for example, where the defence does not call evidence and the Crown motion to re-open is not based upon "any charge of position on the part of the defendant, nor of the discovery of fresh evidence by the Crown."

A trial judge should not be in a hurry to complete the proceedings. The limits of his intervention and his duties were delineated by Ferguson J.A. in *Rex. v. West*, where he said:

> We do not doubt that, objectionable as it may be, the trial judge has a right to ask leading questions, also to endeavour to speed the trial, and even to tell counsel that he is wasting time, and that he also has the right to suggest . . . that counsel waive their rights to address the jury. These . . . are matters of discretion and good judgement, not entitling us to interfere unless we are of opinion that they resulted in a manifest injustice being done to the accused.

. . . .

A compendium of a trial judge's functions would read as follows: he should not intervene inordinately during the trial; he should keep control of the proceedings, and should not, for example, permit the jury to examine and cross-examine witnesses; he should not usurp the function of counsel; within the bounds of proper advocacy he should allow counsel to proceed with the continuity of examination and cross-examination; and should give the fullest opportunity of cross-examination, so long as the right is not abused by prolix, irrelevant, insulting questions; and should not stop a trial without hearing all the available evidence, nor prejudge the outcome of the trial; nor should he indicate that he favours the prosecution or the accused or take the initiative by acting as counsel for the prosecution, which has been aptly stated by Rivard J. in *Regina v. Denis*:

> There is no doubt that a judge presiding over the criminal assizes has the right to intervene during the trial and to ask the witnesses questions. He has the right, and often the duty, to do this when it is necessary to clarify an answer, to render more precise a vague statement, or to remove the ambiguity from a comment. These interventions, however, must never leave the jury with the impression that the judge's opinion has been formed or that he does not believe a witness's statements, which statements could be favourable to the accused.
>
> During the examination of the witnesses, the judge must not intervene in such a way as to place the weight of his authority behind either the Crown or the defence. When he does intervene, moreover, he must not ask questions which might give the jury the impression that he is suggesting to them

that they should not believe the witness. Credibility of witnesses is a matter which falls to be decided entirely by the jury alone, without the judge's intervention.

It is irregular, unjust, and consequently unlawful for a judge in the trial of a case to lead the jury to believe that he is convinced of the guilt of the accused. Furthermore, the influence of a judge presiding over criminal assizes on the jury must not be underestimated. The jury is usually convinced, and with good reason, that the judge, who is accustomed to the proceedings taking place before them, and about which they know practically nothing, is the best guide for them to follow in the execution of their duty. In so far as questions of law are concerned, this is true, but it is not the case when the jury comes to analyze the facts presented to them. A question asked by the judge from the Bench, containing an analysis of evidence already given, or containing a statement of facts which have not been proved, certainly exerts a much greater influence on the jury than any cross-examination, however severe, which may be carried on by counsel.

The law prohibits the judge participating in the examination of witnesses where such participation is likely to indicate to the jury a predisposition in the judge's mind toward one side or the other. This would amount to the exercise of undue influence over the jury in the area of its own duties and jurisdiction.

The discretion of the trial judge to intervene, either to clarify an obscure answer, or to avoid the misinterpretation of an answer, is in many cases a matter of degree, and where the trial judge participates to excess, the line of demarcation between the lawful and unlawful conduct of the trial is drawn.

It is unlawful for the judge, during the conduct of a trial to usurp the function of counsel for the Crown. In many cases, the intervention of the judge wishing to make an answer clear and intelligible, or to move the trial further in the discretion of an area which he considers important, is desirable, but it must be remembered that all such interventions are subject to the over riding principle that none of the parties must have reason to believe that they have not had a fair and impartial trial.

During a trial (civil or criminal) the presiding judge need not be mute; but this does not give him a licence to make offensive and prejudicial remarks with respect to the accused or his case.

When he sums up for the jury he should not merely repeat or summarize the evidence, "nor should [he] place his own constriction upon the evidence or otherwise usurp the function of the jury . . . [but] the judge ought to make clear to the jury, in a way they cannot fail to understand, what are the determinative factual issues in dispute, upon which proof of guilt must stand or fall."

In this summing-up he must set out the accused's position and the evidence in support of it; he should present to the jury any defence that may arise from the evidence, whether or not it is raised by defence counsel, and tell the jury that they are the sole judges of the facts which does not preclude him from expressing his personal view as to the character of police witnesses, or from commenting upon the credibility of witnesses (but he must not do so during the testimony of the witness); and he need not spend the same amount of time, in his summing-up, for the defence and prosecution.

The trial judge is in a special position when the accused is not represented by counsel, and it has been said that the court "in effect acts as counsel for him and is vigilant to see that nothing is done that would prejudice him"; and "the court shall extend its helping hand to guide him throughout the trial in such a way that his defence, or any defence the proceedings may disclose, is brought out to the jury with its full force and effect".

## ASSESSORS AND EXPERTS

In *Phillips*, Evans J.A. says that an expert, under Rule 267, is appointed "solely to assist the judge in understanding the evidence" and the "drawing of inferences, the deciding of issues, the interpretation of the so-called phenomenon and the reaching of conclusion are all matters within the exclusive jurisdiction of the trial judge and cannot be delegated". He continues:

> I do not think that a court can say, in effect, 'I believe that this accident resulted from some unusual circumstance and I propose to call in an expert to assist me in discovering the cause.' Such a procedure is inquisitional rather than judicial.
> The expert is not a judicial officer charged with the responsibility of determining matters in issue, nor is he a Court-appointed investigator empowered to advance possible theories and state, as conclusions of fact, opinions based on matters not advanced in evidence.

The expert, he explains, should not examine, nor cross-examine; he is not a partisan advocate; a Court-appointed expert explains the evidence, as aduced in his special field, so that the trial judge may better comprehend complex factual matters, and he concludes that he doubts that a person appointed under Rule 267 is an assessor; more properly he should be called an expert.

. . . .

If Rule 267 is properly used, where there is extensive, complex evidence, the trial judge can profit from the assistance of an expert; however, even before the restrictions suggested in *Phillips* there was a reluctance by trial judges to avail themselves of the utility of this procedure, which has been attributed to the "mystique and sanctity of the adversary procedure."

## AN EVALUATION

The foregoing discussion has dealt with the civil and criminal trial process separately; and this is partly due to ease of organization of the material; and partly because this is an obvious division. It is trite to say that basically the rules of evidence in criminal and civil trials are the same. This is subject to obvious differences, *e.g.* the standards of proof required, and statutory requirements.

Having said this one could leave the subject of division of the material, but there are even more compelling reasons for this division. Chancellor Boyd explained the distinction between civil and criminal cases in this way:

> Though the rules of evidence may be the same in civil as in criminal cases, a wide and proper distinction exists in the application of the evidence, as to its effect, as to its extent, and as to its degree of certainty. Criminal prosecutions at the instance of the Crown, and for the vindication of public rights or public security are compulsory, and admit of no compromise . . . . A decision once pronounced against him is practically irrevocable, and the consequences of an error in branding as a criminal, one who is innocent cannot be effaced. Hence the safeguards which the law casts around an accused person, declaring in the language of the earlier judges that 'it is almost impossible to be too careful': *Thompson's Case* 1 Leach's C.C. 293. All these characteristic features of criminal prosecutions are wanting in civil litigation.

In civil cases the claims of competing private persons are set out in pre-trial proceedings (pleadings, discovery, interlocutory motions, particulars, and so on) which define the issues; in criminal trials it is the government (it would offend the Harold Laski concept of sovereignty to use the word "state" here) which claims that the citizen has transgressed against community rules; and in civil trials pecuniary damages result, whereas in the criminal trial the result is a fine and/or gaol.

By their nature, although each is a trial, the civil and criminal trials are different, and the role of the trial judge in each must necessarily differ. It could be said that in one sense the object of each is to determine facts objectively; but this feature of the trial process has been characterized as dubious.

Some of the *dicta* in both civil and criminal cases may well apply to both; however, it is suggested that a cleaner (for want of a better word) approach concerning the role of trial judges, would be for judges in civil actions to confine themselves as much as possible to the principles as set forth in civil cases, and for judges in criminal cases to look primarily to criminal case principles. In *Rex v. Harris* Lord Hewart C.J. distinguished between civil and criminal cases, and said that in a criminal case where the prosecution decides not to call a witness, the judge should not of his own motion use his discretion to call such a witness as the witness then testifies "with the imprimatur of the judge;" and he noted that in "civil cases the dispute is between the parties and the judge merely keeps the ring" which drew the ire or Wigmore who said: "This philosophy is not only low in its standard, but is false to the conduct and status of the English judge during the last three centuries".

. . . .

There are differences concerning the calling of witnesses in civil and criminal cases. In the former, of course, the stakes are different; but in any event it is a difference of proceeding — in the civil case counsel for the plaintiff develops the case as he wants, but in a criminal trial the prosecution has a duty to call all witnesses it considers fit for the prosecution, subject only to the limitations that

(a) it should make the defence aware of all of its witnesses, and
(b) that need not call witnesses it considers unreliable.

In civil cases the trial judge with the consent of counsel may call witnesses; but in criminal cases, in the situations discussed, we have seen that a trial judge may of his own motion call witnesses.

. . . .

In criminal cases too, where the defence fails to put to the jury a defence which could arise upon the evidence adduced, the trial judge, as pilot, should put that defence to the jury. Should he go so far as to suggest to defence counsel where there is an obvious gap or deficiency in the defence evidence that that should or could or may be developed?

So long as he does not usurp the function of counsel and refrains from entering into the dust of the arena, the trial judge should be able to act in all of the aforesaid matters as suggested. If there is some substantial area which a trial judge feels should be explored to fully expose the issues, then he should invite counsel to deal with the matters which appear critical to the Bench, and if counsel refuse, then the matter will probably end there. Moreover, as Wyzanski says, "a court . . . cannot rely on knowledge gained dehors the record, except in so far as it comes within the narrow ambit of the doctrine of judicial notice" but a judge, in certain cases, "has a duty to elicit facts in addition to those that are offered by the parties."

Wigmore wrote that the English judge "has never ceased to perform an active and virile part as a director of the proceedings and as an administrator of justice;" and he felt that the judge's right to interrogate should be left to his discretion. This viewpoint is obviously too broad a statement of the judge's role, in light of the jurisprudence we have surveyed; but, perhaps, it is the best overall test to apply in all actions, be they civil or criminal.

Those who would advocate a less active Bench should bear in mind the following:

(1) The adversary system is not perfect, and may tend to suppress or distort the truth. The inadequacies of counsel may detract from the effective operation of the adversary system; and unless we countenance judicial activity, as a supplement to counsels' role, the trial process may malfunction, *i.e.*, in the superior courts (County, District, Supreme), since at the lower trial level (small claim courts, summary conviction cases before magistrates and provincial court judges, and before justices of the peace who hear minor traffic violations), there may be no counsel and even if there is, strict adversary rules may be relaxed.

It is not too bold to admit to the fallibility of trial processes (*e.g.*, by allowing appeals, except for the statutory restrictions such as for lesser amounts of small claims), and to admit that counsel may even err (and if his error is substantial and grave enough, relief may be obtained, certainly in criminal matters); accordingly, there should be room within the adversary system for a trial judge to intervene in a neutral and dispassionate way to bring out facts, and define and refine the issues where the adversary system malfunctions.

(2) Lord Hewart's dictum concerning the doing, as well as the appearance of justice, should not be distorted beyond its ordinary meaning. Important as the appearance of justice may be, it is not more important than justice itself. Justice must first be done, and only then be seen to be done; and justice, obviously, should not be sacrificed for the appearance of justice. Justice should not only appear to be done, it must actually be done.

An overly active judge may give the appearance of a meddler; but equally, a passive and quiescent trial judge may give the appearance of indifference. The public may have a legitimate complaint about the appearance and doing of justice — not just against counsel — but against a Bench which renders judgements based on technical evidentiary deficiencies or errors (such as "had certain facts been proved" or "had a certain witness been called" the result might have been different). A trial judge who endeavours to assist counsel, parties, and witnesses in the proper, complete and logical development of all aspects of a case within the confines of the rules of evidence and the adversary system, neither favouring one side or the other, nor expressing any bias, but still remaining dispassionate and neutral (but not disinterested or indifferent) will gain the respect of all concerned with the administration of a viable system of justice.

(3) Law does not operate in a vacuum. Because of the interaction of the law and the public (and, hopefully, of democratically-based public opinion upon the law), it

is incumbent upon the judiciary to take appropriate steps in all trial proceedings to see to it they are conducted in a fair and equitable (in the broadest sense of the word) manner.

## CONCLUSION

A trial is a trial, whether civil or criminal; but the objectives, standards of proof, and applicable statutory materials vary greatly in these two arenas. The trial judge's functions in a civil and criminal trial are substantially similar. A trial judge is not a machine-formed computer and "often perceives the facts according to his idiosyncratic biases", nevertheless, in the absence of a clearer understanding of the actual functioning of the judicial mind in the decision-making process, and for the moment accepting the fact that the adversary-trial system, as we know it, operates reasonable well, we should be able to accept the following:

(1) A trial should not be a laboratory, but it should embark upon the ascertaining of all relevant and material facts concerning the issues of the case.
(2) When the evidence indicates that the issues have not been adequately defined in the pre-trial proceedings, counsel should be permitted to expand, re define and if necessary use other and wider and broader grounds of claim, subject to adjournment and full rights of amendment and examinations, and costs; and, of course, bearing in mind the need for finality to all proceedings.
(3) Where scientific or other experiments may shed light on the fact-finding process, subject to the rights of counsel to define the limits of same, the trial should embrace such possibilities.
(4) With the consent of counsel, the trial judge should be able to call and re-call witnesses; and in exceptional circumstances (*e.g.*, a custody and/or access application) he should be allowed leeway to call witnesses to clarify and expand upon areas he feels have not been adequately or properly developed.
(5) A trial judge should be able to make use of an expert where there is extensive and complex evidence so that he may better comprehend the same.
(6) A trial judge may intervene to assist the clarification of evidence, and to prevent prolix and lengthy proceedings; but his intervention should be infrequent, and should not interfere with the conduct of the trial by counsel as they want to present their cases.
(7) During the course of a trial a trial judge should never express any bias or favour for any side.
(8) In summing-up before a jury, the trial judge should deal adequately with the evidence, and while he can comment upon the credibility of witnesses, unless there are patent cases of gross manipulation of evidence by witnesses, he should leave the issue of credibility to the jury.
(9) In criminal cases, the trial judge should never of his own motion call any witness to which the defence objects; but he may call a witness in unusual circumstances (*Tregear*). In the summing-up he must deal fully with the defence theory and the evidence in support and indicate to the jury and defences which, although not presented, are available upon the adduced evidence; and he should never favour

the prosecution or the accused in his comments during the trial or in the summing-up.

The trial judge can be a pilot who guides the trial along sedate, orderly lines within the confines of the rules of evidence and the applicable law. He is certainly more than an umpire, watching the sporting-theory of litigation in action; and he is less than a participant in that he should not enter into the fray of combat nor take on the mantle of counsel. The interests of justice may best be served if the trial judge can call a witness, of his own motion, who would not become the witness of either side — if this had been done in the famous *Tichborne Case* it might have been helpful in resolving the case more quickly.

As Henry Cecil noted in the 1970 Hamlyn Lecture, *The English Judge*, the public puts great trust in judges and regards "a judge as a very special person". If for no other reasons than these, the trial judge is on display to the public as the epitome of our judicial system, and in his functioning it behooves him to remain fair, as objective as humanly possible, patient and willing to listen to all aspects of a case. In a sense he is a composite of the pilot, umpire and participant, with the tradition and legacy of common law. The respect which he engenders from those who appear before him is the touchstone of his success. His ability to act with equal impartiality to all who appear before him is the basic requirement of his office.

## Dispensing Justice in Courtroom 121*
### M. Valpy

* *The Globe and Mail*, June 29, 1988, p. A8.

The criminal division of the provincial courts in Metropolitan Toronto hears about one million charges annually. No other stratum of the court system has comparable contact with the public.

It is the same throughout the country. It is what happens in the provincial criminal courts — whether dignity and respect are extended to the accused, to witnesses, to the precepts of natural justice — that shapes Canadians' attitudes about the administration of justice.

Here is His Honor Lorenzeo DiCecco, sitting in Courtroom 121 of Toronto Old City Hall on June 1, 1988. The man before him is charged with communicating for the purpose of prostitution.

There is no dispute that, on March 15 between 8:25 and 8:33 pm., the man stopped his car to have a conversation with Constable Suzanne Beauchamp of the Metropolitan Toronto Police who was standing on a downtown corner, wearing pants and sweater, doing hooker detail.

There are, however, other elements to this case, beginning with the fact that the man's first language is not English. The transcript suggests he is having some difficulty understanding what is going on in court. There is no interpreter and he is not represented by counsel.

He first pleads guilty. But as he tries to explain the circumstances behind the charge — that he was trying to pick up Constable Beauchamp for free sex, not hire her —

Judge DiCecco abruptly cuts him off and says: "Forget it, we'll have a trial. Strike the plea. We'll have a trial".

He does not advise the man to get a lawyer. He merely tells him: "We'll test your intention under oath".

The trial begins.

It is Constable Beauchamp's evidence that within the space of a brief exchange — all the initiating being on the accused's part — she was offered $40 to engage in fellatio (at which point she signalled to her two backup officers to move in and join her in a bust).

Only the accused is available to cross-examine Constable Beauchamp. It is evident from the transcript that he is not familiar with how courtroom procedure works. No one assists him.

The accused's account of his conversation with Constable Beauchamp is a little confusing.

He stresses, however, that it lasted at least 10 minutes. He says he had stopped his car to talk to her because she "looked different than other girls I see in the streets".

The subject of sex did come up. He says Constable Beauchamp asked him variously: "How much you want to pay?" "How much can you afford?" and "You want free or you want for money?" He says he told her "more than 10 times that I'm not the type to do this (hire prostitutes)".

However, the man eventually says the figure of $40 was mentioned — he doesn't say how or by whom or under what circumstances and neither Judge DiCecco nor Crown counsel Catherine White seeks clarification.

But after the accused says he stopped to talk to Constable Beauchamp en route to a 9 p.m. appointment that was about three or four minutes' driving time from his house, Ms. White asks him how long he thinks an act of oral sex might take. The accused says he does not know.

**Ms. White:** "I have no further questions, Your Honour".
**Judge:** "Excuse me, you mean you never got a . . . job?"
**Accused:** "Your Honour . . . "
**Judge:** "No, just state your answer."
**Accused:** "Well, I don't have to bring my wife here, do I?"
**Judge:** "No, you don't have to. I'm not asking if your wife is a (a vulgar expression for someone who performs fellatio), I ask if you ever got . . . , because you said you do not know how long it takes."
**Accused:** "No, it takes longer than that."
**Judge:** "Oh, c'mon — you mean it takes more than 20 minutes?"
**Accused:** "Oh, I didn't say 20 minutes. I thought we're talking about three or four . . . "
**Judge:** "But your appointment was for nine o'clock. It was 8:30 — ample time to get . . . "

The accused is convicted. The judge discredits justice.

## MacKeigan v. Hickman
[1939] 2 S.C.R. 796 at 825

Only an excerpt from the judgment of McLachlin is reproduced below. For a full discussion of the issues and facts involved in the case, see the excerpt from the Marshall Inquiry in Chapter 8.2.

. . . .

### THE PRINCIPLE OF JUDICAL INDEPENDENCE

This Court has spoken of this cardinal principle, albeit in the context of s. 11(d) of the *Canadian Charter of Rights and Freedoms,* in two recent decisions, *Valente v. The Queen,* [1985] 2 S.C.R. 673, and *Beauregard v. Canada,* [1986] 2 S.C.R. 56. In *Valente v. The Queen, supra,* Le Dain J., speaking for the Court at p. 687, observes that the "constitutional" principle of judicial independence has two major elements, an individual element and an institutional element:

> It is generally agreed that judicial independence involves both individual and institutional relationships: the individual independence of a judge, as reflected in such matters as security of tenure, and the institutional independence of the court or tribunal over which he or she presides, as reflected in its institutional or administrative relationships to the executive and legislative branches of government.

In *Valente v. The Queen,* Le Dain J. trains his mind upon the function of the judiciary as the impartial adjudicator. The discussion turns on the relationship between judicial impartiality — a state of mind — and judicial independence — the relationship between judges and others, particularly others in the executive branch of government. Le Dain J., for the Court, enunciates three "essential conditions" for judicial independence: (1) security of tenure; (2) financial security; and (3) the institutional independence of judicial tribunals regarding matters affecting adjudication. Having enunciated these conditions, Le Dain J. makes it clear that he is not attempting an exhaustive codification of the elements necessary for judicial independence: identification of the essential conditions, he confesses, is a matter of some difficulty; moreover, the conditions themselves may vary and evolve with time and circumstances.

It should be noted that the independence of the judiciary must not be confused with impartiality of the judiciary. As Le Dain J. points out in *Valente v. The Queen,* impartiality relates to the mental state possessed by a judge; judicial independence, in contrast, denotes the underlying relationship between the judiciary and other branches of government which serves to ensure that the court will function and be perceived to function impartially. Thus the question in a case such as this is not whether the government action in question would in fact affect a judge's impartiality, but rather whether it threatens the independence which is the underlying condition of judicial impartiality in the particular case.

In *Beauregard v. Canada, supra,* the present Chief Justice (Estey and Lamer JJ. concurring; Beetz and McIntyre JJ. dissenting in part) quotes Le Dain J. in *Valente v. The Queen,* as above, and explains at p. 70 why the principle of judicial independence is so important in the liberal democratic society that is Canada:

The rationale for this two-pronged modern understanding of judicial independence is recognition that the courts are not charged solely with the adjudication of individual cases. That is, of course, one role. It is also the context of a second, different and equally important role, namely as protector of the Constitution and the fundamental values embodied in it — rule of law, fundamental justice, equality, preservation of the democratic process, to name perhaps the most important. In other words, judicial independence is essential for fair and just dispute-resolution in individual cases. It is also the life-blood of constitutionalism in democratic societies.

In *Beauregard v. Canada*, the discussion of the concept of judicial function is broadened to encompass not only the idea of impartial adjudication, but also the notion of the Court as protector of the Constitution. Both these functions must be borne in mind when determining the "reasonable ambit of judicial independence". The test, according to Dickson C.J., is stringent; the courts' function "as resolver of disputes, interpreter of the law and defender of the Constitution" requires that they be completely separate in "authority and function" from all other branches of government.

It is important to note that what is proposed in *Beauregard v. Canada* is not the absolute separation of the judiciary, in the sense of total absence of relations from the other branches of government, but separation of its *authority* and *function*. It is impossible to conceive of a judiciary devoid of any relationship to the legislative and executive branches of government. Statutes govern the appointment and retirement of judges; laws dictate the terms upon which they sit and are remunerated. Parliament retains the power to impeach federally-appointed judges for cause, and enactments such as the *Supreme Court Act,* R.S.C. 1970, c. S-19, stipulate on such matters as the number of judges required for a quorum. It is inevitable and necessary that relations of this sort exist between the judicial and legislative branches of government. The critical requirement for the maintenance of judicial independence is that the relations between the judiciary and other branches of government not impinge on the essential "authority and function", to borrow Dickson C.J.'s term, of the court. What is required, as I read *Beauregard v. Canada,* is avoidance of incidents and relationships which could affect the independence of the judiciary in relation to the two critical judicial functions — judicial impartiality in adjudication and the judiciary's role as arbiter and protector of the Constitution.

To summarize, judicial independence as a constitutional principle fundamental to the Canadian system of government possesses both individual and institutional elements. Actions by other branches of government which undermine the independence of the judiciary therefore attack the integrity of our Constitution. As protectors of our Constitution, the Courts will not consider such intrusions lightly.

**Questions/Discussion**
1. What is the proper role of the judge in controlling the trial process? Should the role be redefined in order to give the judge a more active part to play in the conduct of the proceedings? Why or why not?
2. Do you agree with the decision in *MacKeigan*? Why or why not? Does the case give too much power and/or protection to the judges, particularly in a case such as the Marshall inquiry (see Chapter 8.2)? What protections would you give to the judiciary and why?
3. The issue of the proper role for expert witnesses in the trial process is a difficult one and involves many facets: for example, what is an expert, how can we introduce technical matters and language into the courtroom, and what can we do about the problem of bias

and the hired expert. For full discussions of the relevant issues, see the articles by Cohen, Delisle and McDonald under Further Reading.

**Further Reading**
- Brooks, N., "The Judge and the Adversary System" in Allen Linden, ed., *The Canadian Judiciary* (Toronto: York University, 1976), p.89.
- ___ "Evidence" (1975), 7 Ottawa Law Review 600.
- Canadian Bar Association Task Force on Gender Equality. *Touchstones for Change: Equality, Diversity and Accountability - The Report on Gender Equality in the Legal Profession* (Ottawa: The Canadian Bar Association, 1993).
- Cohen, S., "The Role of the Forensic Expert in a Criminal Trial" (1978), 1 C.R. (3d) 289.
- Delisle, R.J., "The Admissibility of Expert Evidence: A New Caution Based on General Principles" (1994), 29 C.R. (4th) 267-273.
- Dickson, B., "The Rule of Law: Judicial Independence and the Separation of Powers" (1985), 9 Provincial Judges 4.
- Gibson, D., "Judges as Legislators: Not Whether but How: (1986), 25 Alberta Law Review 249.
- Laskin, B., "A Judge and His Constituencies" (1976), 7 Manitoba Law Journal 1.
- McDonald, D.C., "Opinion Evidence" (1978), 16 Osgoode Hall Law Journal 321.
- McLachlin, B., "The Role of The Court in the Post-Charter Era: Policy-Maker or Adjudicator?" (1990), 39 University of New Brunswick Law Journal 43-64.
- McLachlin, B., "The Role of Judges in Modern Commonwealth Society" (1995), 53 Advocate 681-687.
- Nemetz, N., "The Concept of an Independent Judiciary" (1986), 20 University of British Columbia Law Review 285.
- Ontario Law Reform Commission. *Appointing Judges: Philosophy, Politics and Practice* (Toronto: Ontario Law Reform Commission, 1991).
- Tollefson, E.A., "The Quality of Judicial Appointments: A Collateral Issue" (1971), 21 University of Toronto Law Journal 162.
- Volpe, P., "Psychiatric Testimony in The Criminal Prosecution Process" (1989), 10 Canadian Criminology Forum 26-39".
- Wilson, B., "Will Women Judges Really Make a Difference?" (1990), 24 Gazette 261.

## 4.4 VICTIMS

**Introduction**

*Ross Hastings*

The rise of interest during the last fifteen years in the plight of victims of crime and their proper role is an interesting one in the light of the developments which have actually occurred in the Canadian criminal justice system. The rhetoric on the part of the state in support of the victim of crime has not been matched by real initiatives and real funding and, moreover, it has not been translated into a more humane and more effective criminal justice system for any of the participants. However, the Canadian criminal justice system has come some way in its recognition of the problems experienced by victims of crime, and in its willingness to recognize that it bears some of the responsibility for responding to these problems in an effective and humane manner. The question to be asked is whether this new consciousness has been (or can be) translated into new policies and practices within the criminal justice system, and whether any of this can make a significant impact on the situation of victims of crime.

The so-called "costs" of criminal injuries, and the subsequent requirements of victims of crime, involve a broad range of physical, financial and emotional injuries which are discussed in more detail in the excerpt from the *Justice for Victims of Crime* report below. There is general agreement, however, that they can be summarized into three general types of concerns (Normandeau, 1983; Waller, 1981):

1. Access to the information and programmes necessary to prevent crime, or at last reduce the vulnerability to criminal injury;
2. Recovery of the physical, financial and emotional well-being which was experienced by the victim before the criminal act; and
3. Treatment by the criminal justice system which is just and humane, and which is responsive to the desire of victims to be fully informed and protected during their experience within the system.

There has been some optimism generated within both the criminal justice system and the victims' movement by the changes which have been made to date. There is also a degree of optimism that the rhetoric on the part of the state might actually be translated into policies and real support for victims of crime.

There are, however, a number of reasons to be guarded in assessing both the progress that the movement on behalf of victims has made, and its potential for further advances. The future may be less promising than it seems. The victim has acquired a presence in the public consciousness and within the policies and programmes of the criminal justice system; it can be said that victims are better treated than before, though perhaps not universally or uniformly, depending on the type of victim you are and the type of crime you have been subject to. It can also be argued that supporters and advocates within the victims' movement have been somewhat seduced by the appearance of a consensus around the definition of the problems experienced by victims of crime and the solutions to this situation, and as a result have neglected the ideological and political conflicts which are part of the attempt by the criminal justice system to respond to any new initiative. It is often assumed that the movement on behalf of victims has such a sound and legitimate moral base that progress is simply a question of raising people's consciousness about what needs to be done, and applying a little political pressure to the most responsive points of the state and its criminal justice system.

This is naive. It ignores the real debates over just exactly what victims need, who should provide for these needs, and who should pay the costs of this response. The fact of the matter is that there are very real options to choose on each of these questions. For the most part, the objectives of the victims' movement have been translated and operationalized on the basis of traditional or conservative approaches to social organization and the role of the criminal justice system. The practical result has been a tendency to favour programmes either based on the responsibility of the offender to repair the damage done to an innocent victim of crime, or which attempt to facilitate and encourage the participation of victims and witnesses of crimes in the criminal justice system in order to improve the efficiency and success of the system. At this point in time, there is little indication of any meaningful support for programmes which are based on the recognition of a collective responsibility for the kind of society we live in, and consequently for the types and rates of crime which we experience. In practice, this means the state is much more willing merely to "recognize" victims than it is to respond to their needs in an effective manner.

Compared to earlier times, victims have won recognition; it is difficult to imagine a criminal justice policy in today's society which would not at least acknowledge their existence and the responsibility of the criminal justice system or the state generally to do *something* for them. The real question remains as to who will be responsible for creating, financing, and delivering these new initiatives. It is here that the differences between the traditional and the critical perspectives are the most evident and the most important. The critical orientation will generally emphasize the collective responsibility for the consequences of the organization of the social system. The argument is that crime is in large part a function of our social and cultural arrangements, and thus the state (through the mechanism of the taxation system) should be responsible for taking care of the victims created by this situation. In this sense, victims of crime are just one category of people who suffer the consequences of our social arrangements. It is argued that they should be treated much the same way as unemployed people who receive state sponsored medical care.

On the other hand, the traditional orientation places the burden of responsibility to repair the damage done to an innocent victim of a criminal act on the offender who caused that damage. This reflects the tendency of these more conservative approaches to see the criminal act as an indicator of an unwillingness or a refusal on the part of the offender to accept the responsibilities which go along with citizenship. According to this point of view, the permissiveness and moral pluralism which characterize contemporary society require a concentration on strategies of deterrence (usually through more punishment) and control (usually through target hardening and increased surveillance). Within this perspective, social renewal has a moral rather than an economic meaning. This, in part, is how government cutbacks in social services and the expansion of the criminal justice system have been justified in recent years.

In an examination of the Canadian state's responses to date, it is evident that the policies and programmes on behalf of victims of crime have been much more characterized by the latter type of traditional or conservative approaches to criminal justice policy. An overview of initiatives in this field suggests that:

1. Relatively few new resources have been allocated to victims; public recognition and the expressed commitment of the criminal justice system have not been translated into a massive infusion of new programmes, services or resources.
2. A large part of the new resources which have been directed to victims have been invested in programmes designed to inform and support victims and witnesses of crime who participate in the criminal justice process. There is little doubt of the benefit of such programmes to these individuals, but it is also true that their basic justification lies in their potential to reduce the costs and increase the efficiency of the criminal justice system. In this sense, victims are a *means* to promote the organizational goals of the system — this does not represent a fundamental rethinking of the system.
3. There has been an indication of some increase in the use of reparative sanctions in sentencing. However, the primary motivation of this shift lies in the conviction that this represents a cheaper (but at least as effective) manner of denouncing and punishing criminal behaviour, and reintegrating the offender into society. The motivation, in other words, is not necessarily to help the victim; this is a worthwhile but secondary consequence of this development. There is also little indication that these measures constitute a significant means of repairing the damage done to victims of crime, given both the lack of funds on the part of the offender and the reluctance of judges to engage in this type of sentencing exercise. One should also not ignore that such measures are a means of reducing the number of new "clients" which the prisons must house, and thus can save the state some money on this level also. Finally, it can be asked whether these measures may not have the unanticipated consequence of increasing the number of people who come under the control of the criminal justice system, without really improving the lot of the victim. Because the system appears more humane, it is often the case that more people are brought within the ambit of the system who might otherwise not have been.
4. There is a tendency to look to the offender to find the new revenues which are necessary to fund victims' programmes, for example, through fine surcharges or other such measures.

This reflects the conservative tendency primarily to blame offenders and hold them responsible for the consequences of their behaviour. However, it is a limited approach, in light of the inability of the system to identify, arrest and convict a significant proportion of those who are guilty of offences.
5. The very notion of "victims of criminal acts" is restricted to the traditional categories of crimes against the person or property (the so-called predatory or street crimes). There has been almost no attention given to victims of corporate or white-collar crime, nor to victims of offences which fall under other types of regulatory legislation.
6. For the most part, only "innocent" victims of crime are likely to receive the state's sympathy or help. Those who have contributed to their own victimization, either through their "negligence" or "unworthiness", or by allegedly precipitating the act in question, are usually judged to be less worthy of consideration. In discussing the criminal injuries compensation schemes adopted in most of the provinces, Murphy (1982:544-55) states:

The applicant is also required to "co-operate fully with the Board" and will probably be expected to undergo a medical examination and testify under oath at the hearing.

The victim's behaviour at the time of the commission of the offence and subsequent to it, is a decisive factor in determining the amount, if any, to be awarded. The Board "shall consider and take into account any behaviour of the victim that directly or indirectly contributed to his injury or death." This broad wording gives the Boards considerable latitude in rendering a decision. The Ontario Reports supply an adequate number of examples as to what constitutes an unworthy victim. There are numerous instances where claimants have had their awards reduced or denied because of: failing to report to the police within a reasonable time, participation in criminal conduct, membership with the underworld, homosexuality, drunkenness, family disputes, immoral conduct, imprudent behaviour, as defined by the board members themselves.

The argument is, therefore, that the state, while quite vocal in its support of victims of crime, has been quite conservative in its approach to policies and programmes on behalf of these victims. For the most part these initiatives have reflected a humanitarian willingness to be charitable to worthy (blameless) victims. There is little indication of any large scale political movement towards funding the kinds of crime prevention and victim assistance programmes which would be necessary to insure victims against the damages caused by crime or the fear of crime. On the contrary, the creation and implementation of initiatives on behalf of victims have been dominated more by a concern to reduce the social and fiscal obligations of the state and to place the responsibility for the consequences of crime on individual offenders. And it seems unlikely that this political situation will change much in the near future. The result is that the victims' movement is likely to have to continue to content itself with fiscal crumbs, and to have to depend on the kindness and good will of volunteers who are willing to invest their own time and energy to come to the aid of victims of criminal acts.[1] What has been witnessed in the first half of the 1990's is a rise in the number and vigour of victims' groups that lobby for harsher criminal penalties for offenders as part of a broader package of victims' rights.

The final issue is the proper role of the victim in the criminal justice system. Once the state recognizes the needs of victims, then how should these needs be met? There is an argument that while the needs are real, the place to address them is *not* the criminal justice system. Better treatment of the victim in the system is required but the full-fledged participation of the victim in the criminal process would add little while at the same time creating an imbalance in a process which is already slanted against the offenders and the fulfilment of their rights in practice; the

---

[1] This is especially true for victims of sexual assault and domestic violence, where the victims of such crimes have always relied on the crisis centres and shelters which are set up, staffed and supported by women volunteers.

role of the victim in the prosecution process is discussed in the Clarke article below. What is required is an effective, well-advertised, and well-funded delivery system for the necessary counselling, compensation, and crime prevention services.

## Report of the Canadian Federal-Provincial Task Force on Justice for Victims of Crime*
*Ministry of Supply and Services*

* Excerpts from *Report of the Canadian Federal-Provincial Task Force on Justice for Victims of Crime* (Ottawa: Supply and Services, 1983).

### ISSUES — OVERVIEW

The victim and the victim's place in the criminal justice system have been the focus of increasing attention in several countries over the past twenty years. In some jurisdictions this interest has resulted in significant changes or additions being made to legislation. Starting with New Zealand in 1964, many countries have established various forms of state compensation to victims of crime. Some jurisdictions have delineated certain rights for victims of crime and encompassed these in legislation; some have enacted statutes which ensure that wherever possible restitution shall be made to the victim; others have passed legislation which legitimizes the victim's interest as an active participant in the criminal justice process.

Sometimes changes in administrative methods or in operational programmes have accompanied changes in legislation, or have occurred where the latter were seen to be unnecessary or untimely. Services have been developed to meet what are considered to be the legitimate needs of victims, particularly in the case of those perceived to be the most vulnerable such as women and young children.

France, South Australia and the U.S. A. are examples of jurisdictions which have passed legislation to establish services and procedures aimed at enhancing the role of the victim in the process. It is not surprising that Canadian citizens are more aware of the various thrusts made at the federal and state level in the U.S. A. than they are of developments elsewhere. In a sense this is unfortunate because the difference between the Canadian situation and that of the U.S. A. is more marked than the difference between Canada and the other examples chosen.

There is a vital and growing victims' movement in the U.S. A. whereas in Canada such a development is in an embryonic stage. It should be understood, however, that the victim in the United States faces problems of a different magnitude. The difference is not so much due to the difference in the two systems of justice, but rather to a different philosophy on state intervention. To take only three examples, albeit very important ones, in the U.S. A. there is only a limited degree of control of firearms and much more violent crime; there is no health service comparable to that in Canada and, therefore, the cost to the victim for crimes of violence can be much greater; finally, while most States have victim compensation funds, many have unstable funding or the legislation is not supported by an appropriation of funds to ensure its implementation.

. . . .

Increasing concern for the victim has arisen partly from humanitarian reasons such as having regard for the victim's loss or suffering, partly because it would seem to be only just or equitable that the state owes an obligation to the victim beyond that owed to citizens in general, and partly because the success of any criminal justice system is dependent upon the co-operation of victims and witnesses of crime. It should be a matter of grave concern that research and victimization surveys indicate that some victims are reluctant to report certain crimes and witnesses are often reluctant to cooperate with the agents of the system in their attempts to apprehend and prosecute the offender.

One of the reasons for this is that the victims themselves felt that the incident was too minor to report. In addition, however, research reveals an undercurrent of disillusionment. Indeed, many victims appear to feel that the system would only fail them or ignore them if they invoked it. These feelings may have resulted from a previous unsatisfactory experience with the system or from lack of information as to what it can and cannot be expected to accomplish.

The sense of disillusion takes many forms. If people no longer feel confident in the ability of society's institutions to protect them, then they look to their own protection. It is not by chance that private security forces have expanded remarkably in the past ten years, that the burglar alarm business is a growth industry or that self-defence classes flourish. Nor is it by chance that we have witnessed an emergence of groups who believe either that the law is not functioning or is not functioning as they want it to, and who attempt to provide their own response to what they perceive to be an absence of law and order; a growth in the number of commercial enterprises which deal privately with the fraudulent activities of their employees rather than report them; a number of witnesses who do not come forward because they know they will not be compensated adequately for the loss of wages incurred by adjournments and delays.

When society fails to protect its members from criminal activity, they may suffer physically, emotionally, or financially. These are the costs of victimization — but are not the only costs. Others are incurred by the manner in which our system of justice operates, and arise from the discomfort, the inconvenience, and sometimes — it must be said — the discourtesy and humiliation the victim faces as the process unfolds. Even though the very survival of the system rests upon the willing co-operation of victims to report crimes and of witnesses to testify, the manner in which they are dealt with often does little to inspire or encourage that co-operation. The victim is often given little assistance to overcome the effects of his victimization and provided with little, if any, information about the progress of the case; he may receive little or no compensation for his losses and it is unlikely that he will be consulted with regard to any decisions which are made. It is often the case that the victim is twice victimized: once by the offence and once more by the process.

It is understandable that victims contrast their neglect with the attention given to offenders. Their rights are made known to them, different agencies are prepared to assist them to obtain bail; the case against them must be disclosed to their legal representatives but the latter are under no similar obligation to make any disclosure to the prosecutor; probation officers, correctional workers and parole officers are prepared to give offenders all the assistance they can; alternatives to incarceration such as community resource centres, and measures such as temporary absence, day passes, etc., which are designed to reduce the negative effects of incarceration all work to the offenders' benefit.

While some generally view the sentences currently imposed by courts as being inadequate to properly protect society and the victims, others view any form of incarceration as being counter-productive. The Task Force believes that in appropriate cases there are many alternatives which are now available to the court to increase the offenders' chances of rehabilitation and decrease the damaging effects of prison life. In focussing more concern on the plight of the victim one must not lose sight of the need to safeguard the accused. The interests of the criminal justice system can only be served in securing criminal justice, not in seeking revenge. Consequently, it is with misgiving that we view legislation enacted or proposed in foreign jurisdictions which would appear to have that intention.

Focussing concern solely upon offenders can be a disservice to victims in many ways. For example, restitution as a sentence has been justified on the basis that it contributes to the rehabilitation of the offender. Rarely is it considered in light of its benefit to the victim. Bearing in mind that wherever possible victims should be restored to the position they enjoyed prior to the victimization, then restitution becomes a very important component of a sentence. The Report indicates that we believe restitution should be considered in all appropriate cases. Although this will present some difficulties, we believe that these will be outweighed by the benefits.

It is commonplace today to hear that the victim is the 'forgotten' actor in the criminal justice system. The Task Force does not believe that victims are forgotten — or even, as some would have it, ignored — but we do believe that victims have been neglected. We do not find it difficult to understand how easily this can occur within a system where it is the responsibility of the state, not the victim, to identify, prosecute and punish the offender; where the principal parties involved are the offender and the state — each being represented by others who speak for them — and where the victim's involvement is almost entirely limited to that of giving testimony. Ours is an adversarial system where the victim is not one of the adversaries.

This report does not take issue with the fact that the criminal justice system, which is designed to deal with public wrongs, must primarily focus on the public interest. It does express the view, however, that in doing so the criminal justice system has relegated the victim to a very minor role and left victims with the conviction that they are being used only as a means by which to punish the offender. It is not surprising that victims believe that their losses and needs or any change in their lifestyle resulting from the offence count for little, in light of the Crown's focus on the public interest and the focus of the offenders' representatives on the interests of their clients.

In their first experience with the process of criminal justice many victims are bewildered and confused. They find it difficult to understand why their stolen property cannot be returned to them promptly when it has been recovered; why they are not informed of the existence of a Criminal Injuries Compensation Board; why they are not informed well in advance of court hearings; why a case was delayed, then adjourned and again adjourned — and again; why a charge was reduced; why the true impact of the crime upon them and their family was not brought to light during the hearing; why the case was remanded for sentence and they were not informed of the date; why the offender was not ordered to make restitution. In many instances it is, unfortunately, the case that very few services are provided to victims and they receive little information about the process.

This somewhat depressing description of the bewilderment of the victim is far from uncommon. There are, however, encouraging signs provided by pilot projects. Some who work within the justice field recognize the extent to which the system itself can add to the victim's problems and are taking action to change it. Police, prosecutors, judges, and administrators in certain areas have encouraged the development of victim support services, often with the co-operation of voluntary agencies, and have vastly improved the flow of information from the system to the victim.

Examples are given in the Report of initiatives designed to provide support and information services which in our opinion will encourage the victims to believe that in fact the system can work for them, and can greatly minimize the effects of their double victimization. There are many other worthwhile projects in Canada which exemplify how much more can be done.

If adequate support services were provided and if every effort were made to keep the victim informed of the various steps taken or decisions made, one could take the view that the system had fulfilled its obligation to the victim; but services of this kind do not affect the extent to which the victim is involved in the process. If victims feel that they are ignored then their claims to participate more fully in the process should be examined.

Although it may appear to be sensible, appropriate and just to encourage the participation of the victim in the process, to achieve this in the context of our present system poses some problems. It has been argued that to do so would cause further delay in the courts, would increase the cost burden on the system, would result in more severe punishments for the offenders, would compromise the procedural safeguards which have been established to ensure civil rights of the offender, and so on.

It is the contention of this Report that the arguments advanced against any change in this regard are by no means convincing. Nor, can it be said, have other jurisdictions been persuaded by them. In France, in the U.S.A., and in Australia, we find examples of recent legislation which give the victim an expanded role in the criminal justice system. In our opinion the question to be addressed is no longer whether the victim should participate in the process or not. The question is rather the extent of this participation.

Few would quarrel with the decision, which has been reached in countries which have addressed the issue, that victims be provided the opportunity to inform the court of the impact of the crime upon them. Nor would many disagree that the Court should be required to give thought to the victim's concerns in the determination of a sentence since, in fact, attorneys and judges often take into consideration the effect upon the victim before arriving at a sentencing decision.

More disagreement is apparent, however, when the method of the victim's participation is considered at the time of sentencing and when victim participation is considered at other stages of the criminal process, e.g., at the determination of the charge, at bail hearings and at the time of parole decisions. We believe that the victim should most certainly be informed of these various decisions. We do not believe that the victim should be, or need be, involved at each of the critical points in the process. To take one example, it may seem appropriate that the victim should have some input into a decision regarding parole. However, if one takes the case of an offender who is sentenced to 10 years imprisonment and whose parole hearing occurs some four years after the offence was committed, certain questions must be addressed. Would the offender feel that he has paid his debt and that any input from the victim would be irrelevant? How long does one remain a victim?

Closely related to the issue of participation is the question of victims' rights. A number of foreign jurisdictions have delineated certain rights and enshrined them in legislation; however, some of these rights are very general in nature such as the right to be treated with dignity and sensitivity. Moreover, no effective remedies are available when the rights are abused. We believe that wherever possible specific rights which could properly be prescribed by the criminal law should be legislated. Guidelines should be issued for more general 'rights' by the Ministers responsible for law enforcement and court administration in order to establish policies and procedures ensuring that victims are treated with consideration.

. . . .

## THE NEEDS OF VICTIMS OF CRIME IN CANADA

As mentioned earlier the needs of victims of crime refer to those consequences of victimization which are not being dealt with through the practices of the justice or social services systems. The benefit of this approach is that it allows us to identify what remains to be done to satisfy the goals of the justice for victims of crime initiative. The purpose of this section is to attempt to present a more precise definition of the actual needs of victims of crime in Canada at this point in time.

Overall there would seem to be four broad types of needs. A discussion of these needs is summarized in the diagram below which attempts to specify the major responses to the consequences of victimization, and to identify the subsequent needs of victims. Obviously some of the responses can deal with more than one specific type of consequence or injury, but the diagram deals with each response terms of its *primary* impact.

*Report of the Canadian Federal-Provincial Task Force on Justice for Victims of Crime*

| Consequences of Victimization | Current Primary Responses | Gaps or Beneficiaries in Response (Needs) |
|---|---|---|
| 1. Physical Injury | state medical insurance | — limits or exclusions may discriminate against victims<br>— inconsistent service to rape victims |
| 2. Financial Injury or Property Damage | a) private insurance | coverage not universal |
| | b) civil justice system | little actual reparation is obtained |
| | c) criminal justice system | reparative sentencing does not result in a significant degree of reparation |
| | d) criminal injuries compensation | little impact due to low funding and public awareness |
| 3. Emotional Injury | services to victims of crime | lack of resources results in limited access to these services |
| 4. Secondary Injury | police and court services to victims and witnesses | such services are only beginning to emerge, and few are fully established |

## Needs Resulting from Physical Injury

The Canadian health care system adequately insures victims against most of the physical costs of victimization. Nevertheless, there are certain limits and exclusions built into every plan which may have the unintended consequence of discriminating against victims of crime. For example, some provinces are considering the adoption of user fees for hospital patients, or allowing doctors to engage in extra billing of patients for the services they provide. In either case, such practices can potentially affect many victims, and will obviously have their greatest impact on the most vulnerable economically.

Victims can attempt to recover these costs by civil suits, reparative criminal sentences, or criminal injuries compensation schemes. However, these options provide only limited remedies for the physical injury to the victim.

Certain medical practices can also be problematic. For instance, many victims of sexual assault find it difficult to receive the kinds of physical and legal treatment they require when they present themselves to hospital emergency wards. While there have been improvements in this area, there is reluctance on the part of some medical staff to become involved in the legal technicalities of the evidentiary requirements of sexual assault. Overall, then, it would seem that there are certain physical costs of crime which are not currently being remedied.

## Needs Resulting from Financial Loss or Property Damage

The Canadian justice system is much less able to deal successfully with the financial losses to victims of crime. Those victims who do obtain satisfaction generally do so through participation in private insurance schemes. However, not everyone can afford such coverage. Moreover, there are many forms of property which have an emotional or sentimental significance and which cannot be replaced for any amount of money. Victims of crime can also make use of the civil law process to obtain reparation for their losses. However, this is of limited value for most victims because it is difficult to identify and bring to justice the offender in question. Even assuming this can be done, there is still no guarantee that the accused will be found legally responsible, or will be willing and able to make reparation for the harm done.

Nor does the victim generally find satisfaction within the criminal law process. Little use is made of reparative sanctions; the focus of sentencing is on the needs of society, and the sanction chosen usually reflects the court's assessment of the fairest and most effective way to make the offender bend to those needs. The sentencing process is not designed to give priority to the wishes or desires of victims.

Finally, some financial reparation can be obtained through criminal injuries compensation schemes. However, these programmes are limited mostly to victims of violent crime. Moreover, they are underfunded by the jurisdictions which operate them, and almost unknown to the vast majority of the Canadian public. Overall, then, a number of changes are required in both the legal system and in government policy and practice before any significant improvements can be expected in this area.

### *Needs Arising from Emotional Injury*

One of the more promising trends in recent years is the emergence of a network of social services designed to meet the emotional needs of victims. The prototype of such service groups was the sexual assault centre which emerged over the last two decades. These centres provide information, guidance and support to victims of sexual assault. Similarly service groups are available for assaulted women and for a few other types of victims. The long-term benefits to victims of crime of immediate crisis counselling and support have been well documented and the value of such service cannot be overstated. It is, of course, important to recognize that when services of this kind are provided they must be delivered in such a way that the integrity of the victim's evidence will not be adversely affected.

The major problem faced by service groups of this kind is the difficulty of guaranteeing an adequate level of financial support. They are too often forced to go from one budgetary crisis to the next. This situation is demoralizing, and leaves these groups vulnerable to the vagaries of public opinion (as reflected in donations) and the cost-cutting realities of an era of fiscal restraint. Until there is some formal recognition of the value of such services, and a corollary decision to guarantee a higher level of priority to the support of these services, there is little reason to expect much improvement in this area. Obviously, the impact of this will be proportionately greater for the most vulnerable victims of crime.

### *Needs Resulting from Secondary Victimization*

The willingness of the criminal justice system to acknowledge the impact of their current practices is very promising. A great many police forces have already initiated programmes which are aimed at improving the quality of their service to victims and witnesses and others are planning to do so. The rate of development of services at the prosecutorial and court level has been slower, perhaps in part because of an expressed concern that services must be delivered in a manner which guards against interference with the evidence of potential witnesses.

Another problem is that there is so much to be done that the very enormity of the task can be intimidating. Moreover, the extra costs and labour required for such programmes, at least at the implementation stage, can be a disincentive, and it would appear that victims and witnesses are likely to be required to carry certain costs as a result of their participation in the criminal system.

## INFORMATION NEEDS

Almost every study made of victims of crime highlights the fact that victims place the need for information as their highest priority. What happens now? Who will tell me what to do? Will I have to go to court? What will happen at the court and what do I have to say? When will I get my property back? — these and many other questions are common to those working in the system. They should be dealt with patiently and thoroughly, given the emotional experience accompanying victimization, the complexities of the legal system and the desire to see that justice is done.

The system itself has information needs and these are dealt with later in the report but it would be logical to assume, in the light of what we have learned, that if the victims' needs are better satisfied, then the system will be perceived by them to be relevant and purposeful and its efficiency may thereby be improved. Victims will have a better understanding of what is expected of them and the reasons for those expectations. The more important information needs of victims fall into these categories:

- A need for information on matters specific to the case in which they are involved. Among other things this would include a need for information related to charges, hearings, adjournments, disposition of the case and the return of stolen property. Access to this information is important to reduce the victims' fears and to help them cope with some realities of the process. For example, a person charged with assault could well be back in the victim's neighbourhood shortly after a bail hearing. To help the victim to adjust to that reality it is important for the victim to know that bail has been granted.
- A need for basic introductory information on the relevant substantive law, the criminal justice process and the roles of such key players as the victim, witness, accused, police, prosecutor, judge, etc. This will serve to orient victims to the process and to their experience within it.
- A need to be aware of any services provided locally to assist victims, the focus of the service, its location, the hours during which assistance is provided and so on. Services in this context are not limited of course to those provided within the justice system but would include social services such as transition houses, sexual assault centres, etc., health services — particularly those offering counselling or emergency assistance — and businesses which provide lock and key repairs.
- A need for a central agency which can collect material on victims and disseminate it to all jurisdictions; it would be helpful, in addition, if such an agency would be

staffed with people experienced in the field who could act as consultants to those wishing to initiate programmes for victims.

## EXISTING SERVICES

What the Report has said so far on the consequences of victimization is not intended to imply that nothing is being done for the victims of crime. We have already established that the Canadian system of medical insurance provides protection against the direct physical consequences of a criminal injury. Moreover, victims have at least a limited potential for recovering their financial losses through civil suits, reparative criminal sentences or criminal injuries compensation schemes. The shortcomings of each of these options are significant. Nevertheless, these programmes and policies are in place and can be improved.

There has also been a recent trend towards providing services to victims of crime to assist them in overcoming the emotional and secondary consequences of victimization. The first such services were generally directed to dealing with the needs of special groups of victims, and focussed primarily on victims of sexual assault or child abuse. More recently, police forces, court systems and private agencies have become involved in this area, largely by attempting to provide information, assistance and support to victims or witnesses of crime.

The purpose of the section is to discuss the present services available to victims of crime in Canada. These services are not described in any great detail since there are already two excellent surveys in this area, and the interested reader can more profitably refer to these for further information (Norquay, Geoff and Weiler, Richard: *Services to Victims and Witnesses of Crime in Canada,* Solicitor General Canada, 1981; DeGagne, Jean-Guy; Weiler, Richard, and Poupart, Lise: *The Victim Services Survey,* Canadian Council on Social Development, 1983).

The focus of the section is on three major questions: what are the goals or objectives of providing services to victims of crime? who should provide these services? how should these services be delivered to victims?

### *The Objectives of Services to Victims*

Every needs-assessment study has illustrated the confusion and bewilderment of victims in the face of their involvement with the criminal justice system, and has detailed their lack of awareness of some of the programmes and services which are available to help them deal with the consequences of victimization. When available these different services to victims are a response to this expressed desire for information and support. There are differences in the specific goals or emphases of individual programmes. However, there seems to be a consensus that services to the victims or witnesses of crime have five major objectives.

- To provide victims and witnesses with information on the case in which they are involved, and on their rights and responsibilities within the criminal justice process.

. . . .

- To assist victims in dealing with the consequences of victimization, and in coping with the aftermath of crime.

- To provide crisis intervention services.

- To sensitize workers within the criminal justice system to the situation of victims, and to train those workers to recognize and respond to the needs of victims and witnesses.

- To co-ordinate victim-based efforts, and to assure that victims are aware of the services which are available to them.

Unfortunately, the consensus over objectives has not resulted in a widespread expansion of these services. The recent survey by the Canadian Council on Social Development (1983) suggests that the limited growth in this area is a result of a number of factors. Some jurisdictions have yet to clarify the extent of need for such services, or the appropriate auspices for delivering them. Hopefully, the rapid publication of the needs assessment studies undertaken by the Department of Justice which have now been completed, and which reveal a great deal of consistency in the needs which have been identified, will speed developments in this area. A more important consideration would seem to be the realities of fiscal restraint. It is interesting to note that services tend to be introduced or developed largely on the basis of redirecting resources: there is little political support for initiatives which require massive investments of new resources. The Report will deal with the further implications of financial or political constraints in its discussion of the responsibility for providing such services and of the models of service delivery.

### *The Responsibility for Providing Services*

The CCSD survey indicates that there is a great deal of controversy over which components of the justice system should provide services to victims, and over the range of services which should be provided. In large part, this reflects considerable differences of opinion as to the appropriate role of criminal justice agencies in relation to victims. While sensitive to the situation of victims, many practitioners are concerned that victim assistance may compromise the ability of the system to satisfy the needs of society and to guarantee the rights of the accused. The practical result of such concerns is a debate over the most appropriate manner for allocating the responsibility for such services. Some argue that the criminal justice system should fulfil this responsibility, while others insist that such work is better done by private social service agencies such as the Salvation Army, the John Howard Society, etc.

There is also a concern within both public and private agencies on the appropriateness of being involved with offenders while also dealing with victims. There is a sense that this may well represent a potential conflict of interest, especially to the extent that the services involve some form of victims' advocacy. This is compounded in the voluntary or private sector by the issue of the priority of services to victims, and the question of the specific role these agencies should play and the specific services they should provide. The problem is well illustrated by the difference of opinion regarding the extent of services which should be provided by sexual assault centres. For example, it is not clear whether sexually abused children can best be served by general child welfare agencies or by specialized sexual assault centres. Nor is it clear who can best provide crisis intervention, information or support to sexually abused adults. There is also considerable disagreement between sexual assault centres and provincial authorities over the political stances and advocacy actions of some such centres. There is little reason to believe that there will be an early or easy resolution of these questions. However, some encouragement can be taken from the interest most agencies have expressed in exploring possibilities for greater co-operation and co-ordination in the provision of services to victims.

## *The Organization and Delivery of Services*

The CSSD Survey found that there is a great deal of support for providing services to victims and witnesses within the framework of existing programmes and services, or by redeploying existing resources to deal with new responsibilities. This is accompanied by an increasing reluctance to adopt the 'special project' approach, largely because of a resistance to sharing the costs of these programmes or a reluctance to becoming involved in programmes which require major or sustained injections of new resources.

In practical terms, this has meant that services are either provided directly by agencies within the justice system, or indirectly by contracting the task out to the private social service network. In the former case, the services can be based in police departments, in the court system, in correctional agencies or in some combination of the three.

There are three approaches to a police-based system of providing services. The first is to create a specialized services unit within the police force to deal with the requirements of victims. This approach has been adopted by the police forces in Edmonton, Calgary and Kitchener-Waterloo. The second approach is to blend the victim services unit within an existing service or division of the police force. St. John and Regina are developing proposals based on this strategy. The third approach is to attempt to reorganize existing resources so that a police department can maximize the return on current resources. The city of Vancouver and the R.C.M.P. are perhaps the best examples of proposals for operationalizing such an initiative. As an illustration, the CCSD survey indicates a high level of recognition on the part of most R.C.M.P. detachments of the importance of victims' services as an inherent element of a police officer's responsibilities.

Moreover, the majority of detachments indicate that they provide services to victims and witnesses, especially in the area of linking the victim or witness to the legal system. Unfortunately, this commitment does not seem to be accompanied by a plan to develop services or by a participation in community-based planning or inter-agency co-ordination.

Court-based services are generally concerned primarily with the welfare and requirements of witnesses, and with the objective of improving the court process. This could involve an improved case management system such as the one being developed in British Columbia, or the provision of improved services to witnesses (e.g., transportation, babysitting). In either case, the product generally springs from the belief that such services will result in faster and more efficient justice by assuring the participation of more co-operative witnesses.

The final strategy is the combined victims/witnesses services approach, which directs the police to an emphasis on victims and the court-based unit to assisting witnesses. The only fully operational unit of this type is based in Winnipeg, where the victim and witness components were developed concurrently under a single advisory committee. It is too early to assess conclusively the potential advantages of this two-tiered approach, but it does seem to maximize the potential for rationalizing scarce resources in this area.

A number of programmes have also been developed within the volunteer social services network, by agencies such as the Salvation Army or the John Howard Society. Such programmes can best be distinguished on the basis of their targeted population. Some are designed for victims and witnesses in general and offer a broad range of services. The programmes offered by the Salvation Army in Ottawa, and by the John Howard Society in Lethbridge are examples of this. Others offer services to specific populations such as victims of family violence or sexual assault. The Restigouche Family Crisis Intervenors Program is an example of this type of service. Transition homes and rape crisis centres also generally use this approach.

In spite of this activity, we must conclude on a somewhat pessimistic note.

The CSSD survey discovered no substantial development of such services or projects over the last two years. A number of existing projects have either been terminated or given diminished levels of support, and some previously planned programmes have not been implemented. This appears to reflect a lack of resources more than anything else, although there is also some debate over the emphasis of proposed services or the appropriateness of the organizations requesting support. In sum, these various demonstration projects hold great promise for the future. However, it would appear that many jurisdictions are unwilling or unable to assume the financial burden of these projects once the federal government's demonstration grant funding is exhausted. Police and court-based programmes which can demonstrate their cost efficiency seem to be the best protected from such cutbacks. For the most part, however, it seems clear that fiscal restraint presents a significant hurdle for the victims' initiative to overcome. The contributions of existing programmes only serve to highlight the fact that most jurisdictions have done relatively little in this area. We can only hope that the lessons gained through existing programmes and demonstration projects will speed development.

## Is There a Place for the Victim in the Prosecution Process?*
*Patricia Clarke*

* (1986), 8 Canadian Criminology Forum 31.

Victims of crime once were the central actors in bringing offenders to justice. Today they are neglected outsiders in a system which could not function without them, yet is not accountable to them, provides no role for them and does not necessarily serve them, for ours is "an adversary system in which the victim is not one of the adversaries" (Federal-Provincial Task Force, 1983:5).

Victims are organizing, in one of the significant developments in the justice system, to complain of their expulsion and to demand more participation. Sometimes they bypass the system entirely, either by systems of private justice or in extreme cases by becoming their own prosecutor, judge and executioner.

A number of jurisdictions have tried a number of ways over the past twenty years to answer the demands of victims, and in Canada a Federal-Provincial Task Force on Justice for Victims has made recommendations some of which have been embodied in proposed legislation. The question is no longer, the Task Force says, "whether the victim should participate in the (criminal justice) process or not. The question is rather the extent of that participation" (1983:7).

This paper will look at the current status of the victim in the prosecution process, the reasons for that status in the historic development of the process, and some reasons for the growth of the victims' rights movement. It will review proposals to change the victim's status but will argue that, as far as genuine participation is concerned, the proposed changes will be more cosmetic than real. That is because of the nature of the process, the nature of bureaucratic systems to resist change, and the aims and purposes of the criminal justice system. The exclusion of victims is not an accident or oversight which can be remedied by minor tinkering with a process whose purpose is to provide justice for victims. It is a necessary and inevitable fact of a process with a totally different purpose. If victims dare to find remedies for their victimization, they must find them outside the prosecution process.

## EVOLUTION OF THE PROSECUTION PROCESS

Before there was a formal legal system, all wrongs were private wrongs. Victims and their families exacted the penalties. To temper and regulate such private justice, in Anglo-Saxon law there gradually grew a system of restitution with fixed payments for various wrongs. At the same time there grew the notion that while some incidents were private disputes, which in the development of law became torts to be dealt with in civil courts, other acts threatened the fabric of society and destroyed "the King's peace". For such acts the offender made payment not only to the victim but also to the lord or the king. Holdsworth (1909:38) claims this was "the germ of the idea that wrong is not simply the affair of the injured individual—an idea which is the condition precedent to the growth of a criminal law".

Gradually as this idea developed, the victim lost control of the conflict and it became the property of the state. The focus shifted from a dispute between the offender and the victim, in which the offender was bound to make reparation to the person he had injured, to the relationship between the offender and society, in which the offender had injured society and must be punished by society. Common law developed to prevent victims from receiving reparations until they did all they could to bring the offender to justice and forbid victims to agree not to prosecute in order to get back their property. Individuals could not condone a crime against the state (Hudson & Galway, 1975:24).

The key to a criminal proceeding thus became, in essence, the exclusion of the victim as one of the parties. Full participation by the victim, Christie says (1977:3), presupposes elements of civil law.

Just as the state came to replace the victim as the injured party, so it gradually replaced the victim as the prosecuting party. Until the late 18th century, trials normally were conducted by the victim-prosecutor and the defendant (Beattie, 1986:313). By the 19th century Blackstone was able to state categorically that the sovereign "is therefore the proper person to prosecute for all public offences and breaches of the peace, being the person injured in the eye of the law" (Hagan, 1983:268).

In the evolution of the prosecution process, then, two important things have happened, according to Christie (1977:3) one, that both parties are being represented; and second, that the one represented by the state, the victim, "is so thoroughly represented that for the most part he has been pushed completely out of the arena". The victim is a double loser: his property may have been stolen by the offender, but "his conflict has been stolen by the state" (Christie, 1982:93). When the private conflicts become state property, they are made to serve "the ideological interests of state-subject authority relations and the organizational interests of the individual citizens" (Ericson & Baranek, 1982:4).

## ROLE OF THE VICTIM IN THE PROSECUTION PROCESS

This transfer of the dispute between two persons into a dispute between one of them and the Crown means, according to Shearing and Stenning (1983:9), that victim neglect is not a "minor deficiency" in the justice system but arises from a "fundamental feature". The state owns the conflict and the roles left to victims are; (1) to supply the system with raw material; (2) to give the evidence the system requires; and (3) to serve as a "ceremonial" or "symbolic presence" (Hagan, 1983:7) which legitimizes the mobilization of the law against the accused.

The fundamental policy objectives of the criminal justice system are based on a classical concept of society as a contract between a neutral arbitrating state and rational individuals. The state provides society and its members with a reasonable degree of security, and ensures just treatment for the accused (Griffiths et al., 1980:6). Punishments must be established if the sovereign is to "defend the public liberty, entrusted to his care, from the usurpation of individuals" (Vold, 1979:24), and they must be fixed, known and in relation to the crime. These policy objectives ignore the victim as such, other than as a member of society. The second objective implies, far from participation by the victim, a moderation and rationality in the punishment the accused might otherwise receive from those who believe themselves wronged. The resulting court process may be seen as a sort of morality play where certain values are publicly affirmed, certain conduct publicly denounced, and certain persons identified, blamed and rejected as "criminals". "The process uses accused persons to help define the relationship between the individual and the state" (Ericson & Baranek, 1982:215). Victims and their needs simply are not part of the script.

As the process has evolved, the chief power left to victims is the power not to surrender their conflict to the state — not to report the victimization. More than half of victims appear to exercise this right (Task Force, 1983:14). Once the state takes over, they lose virtually all other power. They have no right to testify, although they may do so if they are called by the Crown and if theirs is the uncommon case which goes to trial. Approximately up to 70% of cases are settled by a guilty plea. They have no right to express their views on bail or sentencing, though a judge or prosecutor is free to ask for them. They have no right to receive restitution, although they may in certain circumstances have a right to apply for it.

In the prosecution, the Crown represents the interests of the community, which may or may not coincide with the interest of the victims. The Crown must consider, for example, priorities on police time and court time for investigating and prosecuting, availability of evidence, chances of a conviction, public attitudes toward the offence, desirability of plea negotiations, the protection of the community and the rehabilitation of the offender. The victim has no way to challenge these Crown decisions.

Not only does the Crown have to consider wider concerns than those of the victim, but it can be argued that to seem to represent the victim, or to press the victims' claim, might prejudice the Crown's function as an impartial presenter of all the evidence. Indeed, for the Crown to give any assistance or status to the alleged victim, which would not be given to any witness, might compromise the rights of the accused. Even to equate the complainant with a victim could prejudge facts to be proved, for instance in a sexual assault case where consent is an issue.

## THE VICTIM MOVEMENT

Having been detached over the centuries from the prosecution process, some victims have organized to attempt to get back in. In the last few years such groups have mushroomed across North America. In Canada 28 groups claim 150 chapters in every province and 250,000 to 400,000 members (Toronto Star, 1984:1). Their numbers comprise an effective lobby, but are only a fraction of those eligible. Individual victims in Canada number at least 1.6 million a year. Organizational victims may be even more numerous: in a study by Hagan (1983:35) they made up two-thirds of a random sample.

A number of factors appear to be involved in the birth and growth of victim groups. First, is "a widespread and apparently increasing fear of crime" of which Taylor (1983:93) says "countless research studies" have provided evidence. The fear, partly justified and partly promoted by the media, is expressed in purchases of burglar alarms and double-locks, in self-defence classes, in private security patrols and programmes such as Neighbourhood Watch, and in victim groups.

Second, is the law and order movement, which argues that the criminal justice system is "soft on criminals", thereby turning them loose to create more victims. It supports more "rights" for victims to balance what it claims are too many rights for "criminals".

Third, is the women's movement, which began with advocacy and assistance for rape victims and in some jurisdictions achieved changes in statues and rules of evidence which provided more rights for victim-witnesses.

Fourth, is the self-help movement, growing out of the protest movements of the 1960's, which leads people who don't trust big government or bureaucracy to form their own groups to represent themselves.

Fifth, is the general humanitarian impulse to help people in trouble (and earn political points) which in other fields has led to worker compensation programmes or the motorists' unsatisfied judgement fund.

Victim advocacy groups differ in their concerns and their goals. Some complain most about neglect, carelessness and insensitivity from police and the courts. They can't find out what is happening in their case, they can't understand what goes on in court and they are not notified when their case is coming up or when it is settled. These groups want more information, more support services, more "sensitivity".

Others complain that victims cannot get restitution for their losses, or even get back their stolen property promptly. According to a 1976 survey in Alameda County, California (Karmen, 1984:148), 30% of victims never got back the stolen property used as evidence, 42% never learned the outcome of their case, and 61% of those eligible for the state's crime compensation fund were not informed of its existence. These victims want more effective compensation schemes and help in applying to them.

Still others such as Mothers Against Drunk Driving want stiffer laws for specific offences. And some want an active role in the prosecution process. They want to be acknowledged as a party to the proceedings, to be given access to the crown case, to be supplied with reasons for every decision, even given a veto on plea negotiations and sentence submissions. Donald Sullivan, spokesman for a Canadian conference of victims groups, says they want laws to give victims "a place in the courtroom" and rights in court "equal to those of the offender" (Toronto Star, 1985:2).

## SOURCE OF RIGHTS FOR VICTIMS

A right has three key features (Task Force 1983:130). It is a legal recognition of interest, in this case the victim's interest in this court proceeding. A right for one party implies a responsibility or duty on another party. And it must be legally enforceable, so that one can secure either the right or damages.

At present the justice system is a balance (equal or not) of rights between prosecution and accused. If victims are to have more rights in the prosecution process, are they to come at the expense of the rights of police or the Crown or court officials? These have the greatest interest in encouraging the co-operation of victims, for as much as 87% of police workload — and consequently much of the court workload — comes from incidents reported by citizens (Griffiths et al., 1980:33). Clearly it is in the bureaucratic interests of the system to encourage a steady and increasing clientele. The more incidents that are reported, the higher the crime rate; and high crime rates are an effective argument for bigger budgets. Yet as we have seen, more than half of victimizations are not reported, and many victims "appear to feel that the system would only fail them or ignore them if they involved it" (Task Force, 1983:3).

Victims are essential not only to bringing in the cases but, as witnesses, to prosecuting them successfully. Treating victims in a "sensitive manner" will encourage their "constructive assistance", says a paper prepared for the federal department of justice (Weiler & Desgagne, 1984:27). Or as Weigend (1983:93) puts it, "Happy victims make better witnesses" — a claim he says is unsubstantiated by any evidence except the "feelings" of the staff of victim/witness assistance programmes.

Sensitivity however does not confer power. It is not a right enforceable by law (Task Force 1983:131). It does not conflict with any of the prerogatives of the prosecution. None of the proposals of the Task Force on Justice for Victims involves any mandatory transfer of power from police or court to victims. They contain phrases such as "to be considered" or "where appropriate". Indeed, the Task Force says the key words in its proposals for victims are "concern, consideration and communication" and that these words sum up how the system can respond to the concerns of victims "without compromising its basic aims") (1983:152).

But the "basic aims", as we have seen, have no necessary connection with justice for victims. There is no transfer of power to victims in proposals which allows them to participate in their cases only at the discretion of judge or Crown. There is no transfer of power, either in the guidelines for fair treatment of victims set out by the Victim Committee of the American Bar Association and quoted with approval by the Task Force (1983:152). They deal mainly with ways to improve communication between victims and decision-makers in the criminal justice system. Similarly, a case management programme in British Columbia "improved convenience" for victims with no change in the "aims and purposes" of the system (Task Force, 1983:96).

If rights for victims are not to come from the prosecution, then they must come from the accused. If the victim of sexual assault, for instance, wins the right not to have evidence of sexual reputation considered, the accused loses the right to present that evidence. The transfer of rights is particularly evident in the California Victims' Bill of Rights of 1982 (Karmen, 1984:232-3), which limits the accused's opportunities for bail, restricts plea bargaining, restricts insanity defences, broadens standards for admissibility of evidence, and permits victims to press for greater penalties in sentencing, to appeal sentences they view as lenient and to argue against parole.

That is further than Canadians appear willing to go. The rhetoric is that the rights of the accused are inviolate, and the Task Force cautions that in focussing on the plight of the victim "we must not lose sight of the need to safeguard the accused" (1983:5). Perhaps it would be more realistic to say, with Ericson and Baranek (1982:233), that both accused and victim are dependents in the prosecution process and that neither has more "rights" than is expedient to allow and not "upset the operation of criminal control in the interests of the state".

## PROPOSALS FOR CHANGE

It appears then that victims have almost no enforceable rights in the prosecution process. It also appears that they are excluded from any real rights in the process by its very nature as a conflict between the state and accused. Within those limits, several ways have been suggested to recognize and recompense the victim.

One is financial reparation. Three of the 79 recommendations of the Task Force deal with this. A second is a "victim impact" statement, to be requested before sentencing, the subject of another Task Force recommendation. A third is a "victims' advocate" who attempts to influence the prosecution process. Two such experiments have been tried in the United States (McDonald, 1976:153). In one a lawyer was employed as a "victim advocate" to attempt to influence the process through out-of-court negotiations. In the other, a volunteer group of victim advocates attended court hearings en masse for a time, until they tired of it, and claimed fewer charges were dismissed or remanded when they were present. The second programme raises questions about fairness to the accused. As Griffiths says (1980:32), "The prototype of community involvement . . . is the lynch mob". The first raises questions about who pays the advocate. If the victims pay, they may feel twice victimized. If the state pays, that may compromise its stance that the community, not the victim, is the injured party. In any case, such advocates have no standing in court since the victim is not one of the adversaries.

## RESTITUTION AND COMPENSATION

The Task Force proposals on reparation would; (1) amend s. 653 of the Criminal Code to require judges to consider restitution "in all appropriate cases" and to provide an opportunity for victims to make representation about their ascertainable losses; (2) empower the court to impose a jail term for wilful default on a restitution order; (3) amend s. 388 to raise its present limit on restitution for property damage from $50 to $500. Restitution as part of a probation order under s. 663 would continue unchanged.

"Whenever possible," the Task Force explains, "victims should be restored to the position they enjoyed prior to the victimization" (Task Force, 1983:35). The Law Reform Commission of Canada in its paper on Restitution and Compensation describes restitution as a "natural and just response" to the victim's plight which should be a "central consideration" in sentencing (Working Paper 5, 1974:6,8).

Yet such remedies for the victim already exist. Several sections of the Criminal Code make it possible for the court to order restitution. These remedies appear to be seldom used. While Canadian data are lacking (Burns, 1980:29), the Task Force thinks judges are "reluctant" to use them (Task Force, 1983:54). It does not explain why judges would be reluctant to use its new proposals.

Outside the criminal process, victims may apply to provincial crime injury compensation boards in all provinces except Prince Edward Island, or collect for property losses from private insurance, or file a civil suit both for property loss and for suffering and get judgement not only against the offender but, where negligence can be proved, against third parties.

Restitution provisions in other jurisdictions appear to be an ineffective remedy for victims. In Britain, after passage of new restitution legislation in 1972, of those sent to custody and also given restitution orders only 12% paid the whole sum (Burns, 1980:15). In practice, said the British Advisory Council on the Penal System, a victim's prospects for restitution through a criminal court order "are remote" (Burns, 1980:15). After a study of United States restitution schemes, Burns found them of relatively little use to victims and concluded that their popularity reflected a conception of them as "potentially useful tools for rehabilitating the offender rather than as devices for restoring the victim" (Burns, 1980:12).

The compensation schemes outside the criminal process are not well used either. They are usually limited to victims of violent crime but are available regardless of whether an offender has been identified or convicted. In Ontario, one in 55 eligible victims actually seeks compensation (Globe & Mail, 1984:2). A study of the New York and New Jersey schemes showed that fewer than 1% of all victims of violent crime even applied to the boards, and only 35% of those who applied were compensated (Elias, 1983:219).

As for the possibility of civil suit, Allen Linden reported that 1.5% of victims surveyed collected anything by suit, although 74.2% of those studied suffered some economic loss (Linden, 1968:29).

Whether or not restitution is a "natural response", there appear to be a number of reasons why judges are reluctant to use the existing provisions and legislators are reluctant to impose more effective ones — reasons involving the criminal process, the objectives of sentencing, constitutional division of powers, and sometimes no doubt a combination of ignorance and inertia. Judge Cartwright of York County, in *Regina v. Kalloo* (Unreported; quoted in Moskoff, 1983:11), commented:

> "those few Crown counsel who are even aware of the existence of this section (653) which allows the victim of an indictable offence to apply for an order to satisfy loss or damage to property caused in the commission of a crime are equally indifferent to its application."

He went on to suggest that if the Attorney General were paid by commission on completed restitution orders, "blood would be flowing from stones" all over Ontario (Moskoff, 1983:11).

The difficulty of getting blood from stones, however, is one reason restitution orders are seldom made, and civil suit is often useless as well. In making restitution a condition of probation under s. 663(2)(e), a judge is bound to consider an offender's ability to pay. (He is not so bound under 2.653.) Observation of the courts indicates that many offenders, particularly against property, have neither jobs nor assets.

A further reason for caution is the Supreme Court of Canada ruling in *R. v. Zelensky* (1978;2 C.R. (3d) 107 (S. C.C.)) that proceedings for restitution under s. 653 must not take on any character of a civil suit, and therefore the criminal court must not determine issues regarding the amount to be awarded. Restitution can be imposed, then, only when the amount is not in dispute, which Moskoff comments makes the section a "toothless tiger" (Moskoff, 1983:11). Burns comments that judges hesitate to order restitution under s. 663 as well, first because they fear using criminal law to enforce civil obligations, and second because they see it as suitable only for simple cases in which there is no dispute either over the amount involved or the offender's ability to pay (Burns, 1980:25).

In addition, a restitution order once made is hard to enforce. Those made under s. 653 must be enforced by the victim as a civil judgement, if the offender has assets and can be located. Those made under s. 663(2)(e) are intended to be monitored by probation officers. If the probation officers notice that payments have not been made, and if they decide to charge the offender with failure to comply with probation, and if the offender can be located, they must prove the offender "wilfully" defaulted. If they succeed, the maximum penalty is a $500 fine and/or six months in jail. Note that the victim is not the complainant in the enforcement procedure.

The most serious problem with restitution involves the nature of the criminal process. Civil wrongs have grown in law to be those for which injured persons seek their own monetary compensation. Criminal wrongs have become a public relationship between offenders and the state with a public response applied through penal sanctions. The historical tie between the two remains in the Criminal Code provisions for restitution (s. 653 and s. 663) which the Law Reform Commission describes as carry-overs "grudgingly grafted onto penal law to save the victim the expense of a civil suit" (Working Paper 5, 1974:9). They enable the victim to circumvent civil procedure by obtaining a criminal judgement, enforceable as if were civil, by a more expeditious and less expensive process. An example of the civil nature of s. 653 is that it comes into operation "on application" of the victim, not on the initiative of the court.

The British North America Act gives jurisdiction over criminal law and procedure to the federal parliament (1867:sect. 91(27) but authority over property and civil rights to the provinces. This division, says Burns, means "an almost insurmountable obstacle to the establishment of efficient restitution systems in Canada" (1980:29).

Further, criminal courts are constituted to determine a persons's criminal responsibility, not his/her civil liability. The two have different standards of proof and different rules of evidence. For example, examination for discovery is a civil procedure not available in the criminal court. An accused person would not have the same safeguards around challenging a victim's claim for damages in criminal court than would be available in civil court. For the criminal court to try and make such a determination raises the danger of infringing on the powers reserved to the civil court. Widespread use of restitution orders might encourage use of the criminal courts as a collection agency, and lead to threatening prosecution to collect a debt.

A further set of problems arises because the focus in sentencing is not on what is pleasing to the victim but on what is good for the offender and for society. Though the Law Reform Commission say restitution as a "rational sanction" and the Zelensky decision accepted its "valid character" as part of the sentencing process, restitution cannot be argued in the criminal court on the basis that it would return the victim to wholeness or compensate for suffering. The only constitutional way to make the civil liability to the victim a valid part of the criminal sentence is to actively locate it within criminal law. The purpose which has been alleged is that it will deprive the offender of the fruits of crime, deter those who might hope to profit illegally, and facilitate the rehabilitation of the accused.

The Law Reform Commission argues that restitution, "involves acceptance of the offender as a responsible person with the capacity to undertake constructive and socially approved acts . . . To the extent that restitution works toward self-correction and prevents or at least discourages the offender's commitment to a life of crime, the community enjoys a measure of protection . . . The offender too benefits . . . He is treated as a responsible human being" (1974:7-8).

These desirable effects, Burns comments, are "entirely speculative" (1980:8). The momentum toward restitution as a sentence seems to him to depend on little more than "an intuitive sense of its rationality" (1980:7).

The Task Force, although it supports expanded restitution proposals, admits "there is little of the kind of 'hard' evidence which might allow us to decide conclusively whether the benefits of restitution outweigh its costs" (1983:92). To be fair, there is little hard evidence on whether any other sentencing dispositions work any better (Griffiths et al., 1980:233-34). The "safest conclusion", says Klein, is that restitution "as a correctional measure simply will not make any difference" (1978:400).

And finally, there are difficulties in implementing effective and just restitution schemes.

Crown attorneys will have discretion whether to recommend restitution, and judges will have discretion whether to order it. Can justice then be equal for offenders, or victims? The victims cannot "shop" for a judge who is known to make restitution orders.

Would the law fall unevenly on the person who steals $10 million and cannot possibly make restitution, and the person who steals $100 and can? If restitution is a correctional measure, imposed for the good of the offender, should it not then be imposed regardless of whether the victim has been paid for the loss by insurance?

Defence counsel often tell the court, in a bid for a more lenient sentence, that full or partial restitution has been made. If this does in fact result in leniency, does that mean that if a rich man and a poor man both break a window, and the rich man can afford to replace it, then he receives a less severe sentence than the poor man for the same offence?

What happens if there are several offenders? If one has no ability to pay, or reneges on payment, do the others pay more to make up the victim's total loss? Suppose there are multiple victims, and as part of plea negotiations some charges are dropped. Which victims are then to receive restitution?

Finally, if victims of crime are entitled to be restored to their original status, why not every victim? Why limit the recompense to those cases of property loss in which an offender can not only be identified, charged, convicted, and sentenced to make restitution but can actually pay damages?

Yet with all their flaws, restitution programmes (inside the criminal process) and compensation schemes (outside of it) have been legislated in many jurisdictions in the last 20 years. Though often underfunded, unadvertised and underused, obviously they have merits for lawmakers. For one, they enable governments faced with rising crime rates and rising public concern over crime to say, "Look what we're doing for the victims." Roger Meiners points out that large numbers of compensation programmes were established at least in part as a palliative for increasing crime and relatively inefficient restitution (Meiners, 1978:9-44). Voters are told that something will be done for them when and if they are victimized and few will find out otherwise. Elias claims compensation has:

> "justified strengthened police forces, provided political advantages to its supporters, facilitated social control of the population and yet substantially failed in providing most victims with assistance" (1983:213).

A second purpose is to keep the victim from demanding a real role in the prosecution process. As Hagan says, such programmes open the possibility of bringing the victim back into the system without actually doing it, symbolically conveying a sense of concern while doing little to alter the actual origin of the concern (1983:160).

## VICTIM IMPACT STATEMENTS

The other proposal of the Task Force, aside from restitution, to bring the victim back into the prosecution process was to amend the Criminal Code to "permit" the introduction of a victim impact statement "to be considered" at the time of sentencing (Task Force, 1983:157). Such a statement would presumably enable victims to tell the judge of their suffering and of any monetary loss as a result of the crime. Presumably they would then feel that somebody was paying attention to what happened to them.

At present nothing, except pressure of time, prevents a judge from asking to hear from a victim, or when ordering a pre-sentence report from asking that the victim be consulted. The intent of the Task Force proposal is to require the judge to request such a statement.

That proposal raises serious questions. To the degree that the statement dealt with monetary loss, it could be considered in assessing restitution as part of a sentence, subject to concerns already discussed about the purposes of sentencing and conflict with civil courts, particularly if the amount of the loss were in dispute. Questions arise whether the determination of loss would have to be based on receipts of appraisals, which might be difficult for some victims to produce; whether the statement would have to be sworn; whether it would be subject to contest by the accused, and if contested, whether the whole question would not then have to be referred to a civil court for adjudication.

To the degree that the statement dealt with pain or suffering, its usefulness would be questionable as long as the focus in sentencing is on the protection of society and the rehabilitation of the accused. A shut-in widow whose television set is stolen may suffer more from its loss than the wealthy bachelor who is seldom home, but that should weigh less with the judge than the characteristics of the offence, the previous record of the offender and the perceived need to deter such behaviour in the community. If the purpose of the sentence is to rehabilitate the offender, then its nature should be determined by presumed experts. If its purpose is deterrence, then it should be certain and predictable, not subject to modification by the victim. If the purpose is retribution, then the punishment must fit the crime rather than the victim (Karmen, 1984:155).

Then there is the problem of how the statement will be submitted. Ninety-eight percent of cases are concluded in the provincial courts (Griffiths et al., 1980:146) and about 70% of these without a trial (Griffiths et al., 1980:147). Dockets are crowded, hearings are rushed and pre-sentence reports are rare. If the victim is not present when the accused pleads guilty, how often will judges be willing to delay sentence to hear from the victim?

Perhaps too, it is only an assumption that many victims really want this input, or any input, into their cases. A Philadelphia judge, Lois Porer, who routinely offers victims a chance to speak on sentence, says they seldom do (Karmen, 1984:230). Since victim impact statements were legislated in Connecticut in 1981, only 3% of victims appear at sentence hearings (Karmen, 1984:231). When as an experiment victims were invited to take part in plea-bargaining sessions on their cases in Dade County, Florida, only a third attended. Those who were present generally spoke only in answer to questions, approved what the professionals suggested and were "passive and docile" (Heinz & Kerstetter, 1980:172).

## RESISTANCE TO CHANGE

Having looked at the "rights" of the victim in the prosecution process and at proposals to give victims a larger role, it remains to ask: would these proposals, or any proposals, make any real difference in the conduct of the courts?

As we have seen, restitution is seldom ordered. Compensation schemes are seldom used. The majority of victims do not accept the limited opportunities to participate which are offered to them. It is not clear whether the last is because they don't care, or because they don't think it will make any difference, or because as the Dade County study suggests the system is not diligent in notifying them of opportunities (Heinz & Kerstetter, 1980:173).

One of the reasons advanced for helping victims is to encourage them to cooperate with the system in reporting more victimizations. In the United States, the percentage of incidents of violence which were reported to police went from 46% in 1973 to 47% in 1981, and of household burglaries from 47% in 1973 to 51% in 1981, despite the launching of numerous victim-assistance programmes during that period (Karmen, 1984:168).

After reviewing a decade of action and advocacy on behalf of victims in the United States, Weigend concluded it had generated "much rhetoric, more knowledge . . . but little change" (1983:91).

Criminal justice systems are like any bureaucracy. They operate in their own interests. They are subject to what Karmen calls "goal displacement" (1984:169), which means that they substitute for the official goals of doing justice and serving the public, the unofficial goals of getting through the workload expeditiously, covering up mistakes and making themselves look as essential as possible so funding won't be cut. As King points out:

> "Imagine for example the approach of the victim of a serious crime. He wishes to see the offender punished and deterred from further offences. Now compare that approach with that of a court administrator, whose major concern is the efficient running of the system, clearing the workload for the day and avoiding any unnecessary delays . . . The one looks to the magistrate to revenge his loss . . . and to compensate him, the victim, while the other looks at his watch and wonders how long the case is going to last and whether the morning list will be completed by one o'clock" (1981:13-14).

A place for victims in the prosecution process is limited to one that does not interfere with the smooth working of the system or the privileges and convenience of its principles.

Most reforms, as we have seen, seem to be intended to inform or assist or conciliate the victim, and these are worthy goals, but they involve no real rights or participation. Where the victim has been granted a role in the process, it appears to be subject to foot-dragging (the Dade County experiment), discretion (to be "considered" or to be applied "where appropriate") or co-opting.

The fate of reforms in the role of the victim is not surprising. Ericson and Baranek state:

> "It is a common feature of bureaucratic organizations that rules intended to influence the action of agents are routinely absorbed by the agents to conform with their existing practices" (1982:224).

Exciting reforms are "translated into mechanisms of convenience by control agents and relegated to their pragmatically appropriate place" (Ericson & Baranek, 1982:231).

## CONCLUSION

If the public criminal justice process is impervious to change which would allow the victim any real participation, what then?

Organizational victims already bypass the public prosecution and set up their own system to deal with incidents which are classified not as "crime" (which by definition involves the public interest) but as "loss" (Shearing & Stenning, 1983:7). In these victim-oriented systems, run by and for victims, the priority is on restitution or compensation for the loss and prevention of future losses.

Then there are proposals, for example Christie's (1977, 1982), for similar decriminalization of offences against individuals. Christie argues that we "create crime by creating systems that ask for the word" (1982:74). He proposes to remove conflicts from the professionals and return them to the accused and the victims, and to set up quasi-civil procedures to assess compensation and penalties. Pointing out that "several less-industrialized countries" apply civil law where Europe applies criminal law (1982:92), he asks, "Could we imagine social systems where the parties by and large relied on civil solutions?" (1982:96).

Ericson and Baranek, discussing such proposals, are skeptical. Decriminalization may simply imply some other form of social control. Diversion programmes may lead to more cumbersome procedures and increase the number of persons subject to control (1982:228). They add, "All reform alternatives include an added role for some group of professionals" (1982:233).

It is also important to note that there is the vigilante, who tries his own case and administers his own justice, celebrated in the movies *Death Wish* and *Deadly Force* ("When the cops won't and the courts can't . . . he will give you justice!" (Karmen, 1984:247)) and emulated by Bernhard Goetz of New York.

In Canada, at least, rates of reported crime are not escalating in a way that justifies the vigilante. But one of the arguments for compensating victims of crime rests on the assumption that they do not carry out their own justice. In Taylor's analysis (1983), a crucial function of the capitalist state is to maintain conditions under which production can flourish. One of these conditions is a "justice" system. There must be an overall sense in society of a free contract whereby the state protects the person and the property of its citizens, in exchange for those citizens subjugating themselves to the state. The loss of liberty thereby involved is offset and made legitimate by the overall protection of the freedom of the citizen which is provided by a police force and a legal and penal system (1983:135). In other words, citizens give up the right to protect themselves and to pursue their own vengeance, and the state contracts to protect them and collects taxes from them to do so. Therefore, it can be argued that if the state fails in its side of the contract, it should compensate the victims.

Similar arguments for compensating crime victims can be raised on the basis of sociologist Emile Durkheim's theories that crime is normal, even necessary to a healthy society (Vold, 1979:204-208). Durkheim argues that society makes certain demands on its members, and fulfilling these demands is an important source of social solidarity. But the demands are constructed so that inevitably a certain identifiable group will not be able to fulfil them. This enables the rest to feel a sense of moral superiority which he says is the primary source of the social solidarity.

Durkheim informed us that it is not only inevitable that some will oppose the collective conscience, it is also healthy. Progressive social change comes about because some people dare to differ. Thus crime is the price society pays for the possibility of progress — all the more reason why society should compensate those few who are martyrs to its health.

What would we do if we were really serious about helping victims of crime? We would fund adequately and advertise widely a government-supported compensation fund. It would not be funded, as is often suggested, by convicted offenders, for that would imply that offenders are a distinct group and would hold all in that group, who happened to be caught, liable for the damage inflicted by some. Rather it might be funded like medical insurance (one might contribute to OHIP and to VICE — Victims Insurance (against) Criminal Enterprises), recognizing first, that there are more offenders than ever that are caught; second, that the definition of which acts are crimes and therefore which persons are offenders is made by society and changes from time to time; and third, that society has an obligation to those who suffer from one of its inevitable features. We would allow compensation both for material loss and for pain and suffering, and whether or not an offender has been identified. Yes, there would be cheating, just as people cheat now on claims for private insurance. But if private insurers live with that risk, surely a public scheme can.

**References**
- Beattie, J., 1986 "Administering Justice Without Police; Criminal Trial Procedure in Eighteenth Century England", in R. Donelan (Ed.), The Maintenance of Order in Society: A Symposium. Ottawa: Canadian Police College (forthcoming).
- Burns, P., 1980 Criminal Injuries Compensation. Vancouver: Butterworths.
- Christie, N., 1977 "Conflicts as Property", British Journal of Criminology, Vol. 1.
- Christie, N., 1982 Limits to Pain. Oxford: Martin Robertson.
- Elias, R., 1983 "Symbolic Politics of Victim Compensation", Victimology, Vol 18.
- Ericson, R.V. & Baranek, P.M., 1982 The Ordering of Justice: A Study of Accused Persons as Dependents in the Criminal Process. Toronto: Butterworths.
- Federal-Provincial Task Force, 1983 Justice for Victims of Crime. Ottawa: Ministry of Supply and Services.
- Globe & Mail, 1985 "Subway Vigilante Describes Shooting in New York". Toronto, Jan 3.
- Globe & Mail, 1984 "Justice Secretary Proposes Fund Finances by Convicted Offenders". Toronto, April 10.
- Griffiths, C.T. et al., 1980 Criminal Justice in Canada. Toronto: Butterworths.
- Hagan, J., 1983 Victims Before the Law: The Organizational Domination of Criminal Law. Toronto: Butterworths.
- Heinz, A.M. & Kerstatter, W.A., 1980 "Victim Participation in Plea Bargaining: A Field Experiment", in W.F. McDonald and J.A. Cramer (Eds.) Plea Bargaining. Lexington, Mass. : D.C. Heath.
- Holdsworth, J., 1909 A History of English Law. Vol. II, Part II, Section II. London: Methuen.
- Hudson, J. & Galway, B., 1975 Considering the Victim: Readings in Restitution and Victim Compensation. Springfield Ill.: Charles Thomas.

- Karmen, A., 1984 Crime Victims: An Introduction to Victimology. Monterey: Brooks/Cole.
- King, M., 1981 The Framework of Criminal Justice. London: Croom Helm.
- Klein, J., 1978 "Revitalizing Restitution: Flogging a Horse that May Have Been Killed for a Just Cause:", Criminal Law Quarterly, Vol. 20.
- Law Reform Commission of Canada, 1974 Working Paper 5: Restitution and Compensation. Ottawa: Information Canada.
- Linden, A.M., 1968 Report of Osgoode Hall Study on Compensation for Victims of Crime. Toronto: Osgoode Hall Law School.
- McDonald, W.F., 1976 Criminal Justice and the Victim. Beverly Hills: Sage.
- Meiners, F., 1978 Victims Compensation: Economic, Legal, and Political Aspects. Toronto: D.C. Heath.
- Moskoff, F., 1983 "Compensation and Restitution as Part of the Criminal Process", Advocates Society Journal, Vol. 10.
- Shearing, C.D. & Stenning, P.C., 1983 Private Security and Public Justice: The Challenge of the 80's. Montreal: Institute for Research on Public Policy.
- Taylor, I., 1983 Crime, Capitalism, and Community. Toronto: Butterworths.
- Toronto Star, 1985 "Crime Victims — Conference Approves Organization of National Lobby Groups", Feb. 11.
- Toronto Star, 1984 "Victims of Violence: Too Many to Ignore", Nov 11.
- Vold, G.B., 1979 Theoretical Criminology New York; Oxford.
- Weigend, T., 1983 "Problems of Victim-Witness Assistance Programs", Victimology, Vol. 3.
- Weiler, D. & Desgagne, J.D., 1984 Victims and Witnesses of Crime in Canada: Ottawa: Ministry of Supply and Services.
- Zelensky, R.V. et al., 1978 2 C.R. (3rd) 197 (S. C.C.).

## Questions/Discussion

1. What are the needs of the victims of crime and how should they be met? Which of these needs have been met to date and how? What "gaps" remain in the provision of services?
2. What is the proper role of victims of crime in the criminal justice system? What roles do victims currently play in the system and how would you change those roles?
3. What is the role of the state in responding to the needs of the victims of crime? Should the state be fully responsible for preventing crime and repairing the damages caused by crime or should the state limit itself to the role of arresting and convicting offenders and extracting compensation from them for their crimes? What is the philosophical basis of your position?

## Further Reading

- Burns, P., Criminal Injuries Compensation *2nd Edition* (Toronto: Butterworths, 1992).
- Cooley, D., "Criminal Victimization in Male Federal Prisons" (1993), 35 Canadian Journal of Criminology 479-495.
- Langer, R., "Battered Women and the Criminal Injuries Compensation Board: Re A.L." (1991), 55 Saskatchewan Law Review 453-465.
- Murphy, R., "Compensation for Victims of Crime: Trends and Outlooks" (1982), 8 Dalhousie Law Journal 530.
- Normandeau, A., "Pour une Charte des Droits des Victimes d'Actes Criminels" (1983), 2 Revue de Science Criminel et de Droit Pénal Comparé 209.
- Skurka, S., "Two Scales of Justice: The Victim as Adversary" (1993), 35 Criminal Law Quarterly 334-354.
- Victims Symposium, "Perspectives on Proposals for a Constitutional Amendment Providing Victim Participation in the Criminal Justice System" (1987), 34 The Wayne Law Review 1.

- Waller, I., "Les Victimes d'Actes Criminels. Besoins et Services Canada/Etats-Unis" (1981), 5 Déviance et Société 263.
- Young, A., "Two Scales of Justice: A Reply" (1993), 35 Criminal Law Quarterly 355-375.

## 4.5 THE ACCUSED

### Selecting Accused: Characteristics of the Offender
### C. Mitchell

In this section we consider the legal process by which accused persons are selected to appear before the criminal court and we also consider the evolution of the accused's rights of due process. Accused are selected primarily by the nature of the criminal offence created and the social context in which offenders operate. We will compare in this regard three different types of offences: acquisitive crime, violent crime and vice crimes.

Rude's study (1985) of criminals and victims in early nineteenth century England provides some examples of the first type of offence: from 1805-1850 in England up to 80 percent of all crimes involved larceny. During a period when London police took 71,000 people into custody only six were tried for murder and less for rape or robbery. Crimes of violence were rare. Instead, common larcenists stole very common items — mostly food, clothing and household goods (Id.:10). In London, the typical larceny was an "inside job" by a servant or an employee. Not surprisingly in these conditions most offenders were classified by the court records as "labourers", with "gentlemen" comprising a mere 0-2% of convicted criminals. Gentlemen obviously did not need to take food or firewood from each other or steal their servants' meagre belongings. This does not imply that gentlemen refrained from criminal activities, merely that they did not commonly commit the sort of offences which resulted in police action. Assaults and other offences against servants may have been common but these would tend to be compensated, hushed up or left unreported for fear of reprisal and job loss.

Cesare Lombroso (1835-1909) made detailed anatomical measurements of Italian convicts searching for the physical and mental characteristics indicative of the "born criminal". Lombroso made two major errors: he failed to employ control groups which would have demonstrated that even paragons of official virtue had retreating foreheads and highly developed frontal sinuses or other criminal "traits", and he failed to account for those "criminals" not in prison because their social status or type of offence precluded criminal prosecution. Later, Goring in England and Hooton in the U.S. noted that "criminals" tended to be biologically inferior, shorter in stature and lighter in weight than average but again their work ignored the legal process by which offenders are "selected" by legislators, police, prosecutors, judges and juries. In modern acquisitive crimes such as tax evasion some studies indicate a greater or lesser propensity to offend depending on personal factors such as age and gender but it is generally recognized that opportunity is the major determinant. Self-employed persons such as farmers, waiters, plumbers, investors or artists evade tax far more often than employed persons whose tax is withheld at source by their employers (Mitchell, 1985). Since tax evasion is common and widespread and since the offenders' motives are so well-understood, forensic psychologists do not usually seek out personal flaws to explain the behaviour of tax evaders.

A different picture emerges when we turn to the violent and full-time offender who transgresses against norms common to every society, norms that prohibit theft, murder, assault, fraud and robbery. To begin with, serious crimes are perpetrated primarily by young men. Most apprehended property offenders are teenagers; the age peak for violent offences is the early twenties. Few serious crimes involve persons over forty years of age. Serious crimes are extreme examples of unethical or diseconomic behaviours and they are unethical, as noted, because they by-pass voluntary exchange mechanisms and thus take the shortest possible route to satisfaction. Logically, it should then follow that committed criminals in the conventional sense should exhibit an exaggerated degree of self-centredness. Wilson and Herrnstein (1985) found that the two personality traits most clearly associated with delinquency and crime are impulsiveness and contempt for others. These authors argue that foreshortened time horizons and relative lack of concern about approval render some people insensitive to social incentives (such as employment rewards and legal penalties) and unwilling to defer gratification. Samenow (1984) made a lengthy and detailed study of habitual and violent criminals for whom serious crime was a way of life, not an occasional aberration, and he concluded that such persons thought and behaved in similar ways. They demanded loyalty from family but were themselves completely disloyal; they felt contempt for their parents' advice and authority regardless of parental social status; they felt entitled to whatever they could grab or steal; they were profoundly anti-work and consistently irresponsible in almost every aspect of their lives. According to Samenow, if one counted every arrestable act committed by a typical forty year old career criminal "the toll would climb into the tens of thousands of crimes" (Id.,114).

Samenow's work is primarily descriptive and is noteworthy because of its accuracy and perception. It does not explain why one child in a family of four siblings happens to possess a "criminal personality" while the other children do not. Nor does it employ a control group in the sense of searching among people earning a legitimate living to find cases of the same extreme self-centredness unaccompanied by violence and crime. Wilson and Herrnstein (1985) do sketch out a tentative theory of crime causation noteworthy in part because it opposes conventional criminological wisdom which attributes crime to the social environment. In contrast, Wilson and Herrstein argue that once the influence of personality traits, family socialization and early school experiences are taken into account there is not much left to explain about serious offenders. Absent from their list are later influences such as employment rates, neighbourhoods, income level and peer influence.

Finally, theorizing a "criminal personality" does not foreclose a sociological analysis of crime. According to Beauchamp (1980) deviation from behavioral norms tends to follow a common pattern whether one examines alcohol intake, driving or serious crime. For example, with alcohol most people are abstainers or light users. Deviating from this norm are a smaller group who drink regularly and a much smaller group who consume very large quantities of the drug. As a result of this pattern, 10 percent of alcohol users consume more than 50 percent of all alcohol. Rule or law deviation appears to follow a similar distribution and again the small minority of extreme rule breakers commit the majority of all offences. Following Allports' work on conforming behaviour Beauchamp (Id.:109) argues that the distribution of conformity with a law or norm is unimodal and heavily weighted toward compliance:

> [T]he great majority of individuals conformed rather closely to the rule; a smaller group broke the rule noticeably and barely conformed; and, finally, a very small group flagrantly ignored the rule. Allport noted that when compliance was monitored (such as when a policeman is stationed at the intersection where the stop sign was located) the rate of conformity increased, with the rate of non-conformity and violation declining.

While alcohol users' physiology, age, sex and training play a part in their becoming heavy users a critical sociological factor is the per capita rate of intake of the entire population. If the total amount of alcohol consumption declines there is a concurrent decrease in the alcoholic intake of extreme users, a change that obviously occurs apart from any individualistic determinants. In other words, personal characteristics and circumstances affect who will be an extreme criminal or an alcohol abuser but general or sociological factors affect the quantity and the type of crime committed, as well as its style and severity. Wilson (1984:472) for example, traces the appearance of the grudge-against-society murderer back to Pierre Francois Lancenaire in 1834. Influenced by Rousseau, Lancenaire became a minor celebrity composing his *Memoirs* in prison and blaming "Society" for his murders and robberies. While the intelligent, articulate murderer is a familiar contemporary figure both in fact and in fiction (starting perhaps with Dostoevsky's *Crime and Punishment* in 1866) such crimes and criminals would probably have been impossible or incomprehensible to feudal societies.

Biased offender selection is most pronounced in the area of vice offences usually because the offence is designed legislatively or interpreted by police to regulate certain class, gender, or occupational subgroups. Two examples will illustrate the process from opposite sexual biases: prostitution and narcotics.

England's *Street Offences Act* of 1959 in subsection 1(1) prohibits a woman loitering or soliciting publicly for the purpose of sexual prostitution. In 1984 there were 8,836 prosecutions under this subsection (Edwards, 1987:43). Imprisonment for this offence was abolished in 1983 but a significant number of women offenders under this and other Acts, are still imprisoned for defaulting on fines. In England, as elsewhere, Parliament and police are preoccupied with the streetwalker whereas male customers and managers ("pimps") are either outside the law or rarely prosecuted. This bias is exaggerated in England because males are not liable to prosecution under subsection 1(1), only women are affected. The *Sexual Offences Act* provided, for the first time in 1985, a measure that criminalized "persistent soliciting" by customers (always men) seeking prostitutes. Canada follows Britain's lead in outlawing brothels, thereby forcing prostitutes into street soliciting in the first place and putting female-operated houses out of business. The stage was thus set for male managers and organized crime to exploit prostitutes and for the women to suffer from increased vulnerability from customers, managers and policemen. Comparing the police dynamics of chasing organized crime or street solicitors Edwards (Id.:56) notes that "evidence sufficient to convict a streetwalker is comparatively easy to obtain, being merely the word of two police officers "whereas convicting the manager of a club or massage parlour for procuring requires several days police observation" so higher, cheaper conviction rates are achieved by focussing on prostitutes.

In their study of Canadian cannabis convictions under the *Narcotic Control Act,* Boyd, Lowman and Mosher (1987) discovered inequalities between offenders by jurisdiction, sex and age. Between 1976 and 1981 when the average conviction rate per 100,000 population was 103, the rate in Quebec was 69 and in Alberta was 350. More striking was the discrimination correlated with gender. Between 1956-65 about 33 percent of persons convicted under the NCA were female, whereas by 1970 this proportion had fallen to seven percent. Now, the ratio of males to females convicted pursuant to the NCA is about twelve to one with a specific emphasis on young men: "it is male youth without access to private space who are disproportionately subject to the control of the criminal law ... It is the [cannabis] user and the context of that use that are controlled, not use or possession per se" (Id.:27).

## DEVELOPMENT OF THE ACCUSED'S RIGHTS

Since criminal law evolved to deal with political enemies, on one hand, and bandits, outlaws and highwaymen on the other, the king's agents and courts were not overly concerned with leniency or with protecting the accused from improper prosecution. Compared to private law, which tended to involve disputes between neighbours with continuing relations, criminal law was more akin to martial law. Wilson's comments (1984:403) are instructive:

> The miserable history of crime in England can be shortly told. Nothing worth-while was created. There are only administrative achievements to trace. So far as justice was done throughout the centuries, it was done by jurors and in spite of savage laws. The lawyers contributed humane but shabby expedients ... Until relatively modern times the lawyer was not even allowed to play any real part; and if he had been, few defendants could have paid him. The criminal law became segregated as one of the dirty jobs of society.

The first English statutes concerned with examining persons accused of crime were passed in 1554 and 1555. Accused could not be questioned at trial, indeed they were not permitted to give evidence until the *Criminal Evidence Act*, 1898. However, accused persons did testify at the preliminary inquiry. Prisoners, except in treason cases, received no copies of the indictment, were not allowed counsel, could give no evidence, could not call witnesses prior to the 17th century but could make a statement from the dock. According to one history (Radcliff and Cross, 1977:199) "the prisoner in those days laboured under great disadvantages ... many judges right down to the end of the seventeenth century were prepared, in political cases at least to take advantage of the defenceless condition of the prisoner to subject him to all sorts of abuse and ridicule". As to the specifics of trial procedure after the sixteenth century the following passage from Baker (1979:416) provides some guidance:

> When the justices were seated ... all the prisoners were brought to the bar of the court, chained together at the ankles ... Those who were to be tried were then arraigned individually by the clerk; their shackles were struck off, and they were asked to plead to the indictments against them. If a prisoner pleaded not guilty, he put himself on the country, and jurors were sworn in from the panel provided by the sheriff. The clerk then called for anyone to give evidence against the prisoner. The

witnesses who came forward were sworn to tell the truth, and in telling their story might have to dispute with the prisoner.

The blessing of trial by jury certainly benefited the accused in some ways. He was able to challenge up to thirty-five jurors without giving any reason, and more with cause. The twelve who were selected had to be unanimous before they could convict him. If the jury acquitted him, however perversely, the verdict was final and unimpeachable. Yet the accused was, to modern eyes, at a considerable disadvantage compared with the prosecution. His right to call witnesses was doubted, and when it was allowed the witnesses were not sworn . . . The defendant could not have the assistance of counsel in presenting his case, unless there was a point of law arising on the indictment; since the point of law had to be assigned before counsel was allowed, the unlearned defendant had little chance of professional help. This harsh rule was defended on the grounds that the evidence to convict the prisoner ought to be so clear that it could not be contradicted . . . Another reason, if not expressly articulated was the fear that trials would be lengthened if advocates took part. If counsel were allowed, it was pointed out with some alarm in 1602, every prisoner would want it. There was little of the care and deliberation of a modern trial before the last century. The same jurors might have to try several cases, and keep their conclusions in their heads, before giving in their verdicts; and it was commonplace for a number of capital cases to be disposed of in a single sitting. Hearsay evidence was often admitted; indeed, there were few if any rules of evidence before the eighteenth century. The judge's charge was usually short and uninformative, since there was no requirement that the judge should sum up the evidence as he now does. The unseemly hurry of Old Bailey trials in the early nineteenth century was disgraceful; the average length of a trial was a few minutes, and 'full two thirds of the prisoners, on their return from their trials, cannot tell of anything which has passed in court, nor even, very frequently, whether they have been tried". It is impossible to estimate how far these conditions led to wrong convictions, but the plight of the uneducated and unbefriended prisoner was a sad one.

Little is known about the conduct of criminal trials prior to 1500 and not much more is known until the 1700s but the contrast between then and now is clear. What explains the series of legal reforms, starting in the mid-1800s and continuing to the present day, which resulted in accused persons acquiring considerably more rights of due process? One possibility is heightened regard on the part of Parliament and judges for people accused of crimes but this was probably not a major factor given the preponderance of "labourers" before the criminal courts. A second possibility is the rise to power of an organized legal profession, a profession whose livelihood was dependent upon the creation and spread of legal rights and procedural rules. Accused were not allowed counsel at trial until 1696 for treason cases, until 1836 in felony cases and until 1848 in "petty sessions". These dates correspond in a rough way to the increase in cohesion, coherence and power of the English bar. Initially, the legal profession followed a number of lines and specialties as attorney, solicitor, barrister, apprentice, sergeant, proctor, advocate and notary. Judges were not first lawyers; that was a later development. By 1739, when the Society of Gentlemen Practicers in the Courts of Law and Equity was founded, legal experts dominated civil but not criminal cases. The establishment in 1831 of a new society of Gentlemen Practicers marked a much higher level of professionalization and this corresponded with greater procedural rights for accused in criminal trials. Many accused remained unrepresented, however, because they could not afford legal fees; thus well into the 20th century in England and Canada criminal trials remained brief and uncomplicated. Arguably, the recent revolution in procedural rights for the accused is due to legal aid and guaranteed legal counsel first in the U.S. following the Supreme Court's decision in *Gideon v. Wainwright*, 372 U.S. 335 (1963) and then in Canada. The concern expressed in the passage above that counsel for accused would lead to longer trials, has proved prophetic. The forty-five days required by an English court to try the accused persons charged in the Great Train Robbery set a duration record which is now almost routinely surpassed in American criminal trials (Tucker, 1985:245). The 1995 trial of O.J. Simpson is a good example of a case where the defendant has the resources to mount an effective and lengthy challenge to the state's case. Lawyers naturally seek procedural developments but such were slow arriving in criminal law primarily because criminal cases did not offer lawyers financial rewards. Another important point is that once all judges had to first practice as lawyers, criminal court judges became more sympathetic to rulings which created an increasingly sophisticated and lawyer-dependent crime law procedure.

The thesis ascribing accused's rights to the interests of lawyers is strengthened by an examination of the very subordinate role now occupied by defendants and the close, institutional ties between regular defence lawyers and the criminal law bureaucracy. Blumberg (1967:18-19) explains:

> Previous research has indicated that 'lawyer regulars' make no effort to conceal their dependence upon police, bondsmen, and jail personnel. Nor do they conceal the necessity for maintaining intimate relations with all levels of personnel in the court setting as a means of obtaining, maintaining, and building their practice... The client, then, is a secondary figure in the court system ... He becomes a means to other ends of the organization's incumbents. The accused's lawyer has far greater professional, economic, intellectual and other ties to the various elements of the court system than he does to his own client.

Blumberg warns that apparently libertarian, pro-defendant rulings by the U.S. Supreme Court such as *Miranda, Gideon and Escobedo* will eventually augment and enrich the lawyer-court organization rather than criminal defendants. Commenting on American public defenders in particular, Casper (1971:5) reports that among defendants represented by legal aid lawyers most "thought their major adversary in the bargaining process to be not the prosecutor or the judge, but rather their own attorney ... they saw him as the surrogate of the prosecutor ... rather than as their own representative".

Canadian researchers (Ericson & Baranek, 1982) draw similar conclusions about the relationship between legal rights for accused and professional and bureaucratic dominance:

> Accused people in the criminal process are dependent upon the actions of others in taking actions and procuring outcomes... criminal control agents... take over the accused's trouble or conflict and make it state property leaving the accused to await an outcome via a process that to him is complex, difficult to understand, mystical, and which makes him powerless. To be sure, the accused is asked to participate in this process at several points along the way. Of greatest importance are the many decisions he is asked to make, e.g. to give a police statement, to obtain legal counsel, to elect a court for the hearing, to plead, and to appeal the outcome. However... matters are foreclosed first by the police, and then by the lawyer, often to the point where only one course of action seems reasonable... The accused is also asked to participate by being physically present at *some* of the locations at which his case is decided... [but] the accused does not appear in the crown attorney's office, judge's chambers, or other sanctified locations where transactions are carried out among his lawyer and criminal control agents... At each stage of the process the accused not only fails to make what externally appear as his formal decisions, but he also does not take advantage of his formal rights because the costs of doing so are structured so that they usually exceed the benefits...

> Procedural rules are for the use of law enforcement agents in their efforts at criminal control. All procedural rules must be understood in the organizational context of their use . . . a flood of rights will result in excessive legalism. Excessive legalism might lead people to mistake due process for substantive relief from tyranny. It will also fill the pockets of lawyers, while still leaving most accused — especially poor ones who cannot afford much legalism — with a feeling of emptiness . . . A focus on rights can give legitimacy to neglect. It can also lead to greater professionalization and attendant control of the process by lawyers, a matter which must be examined in the context of contributions of other occupational groups. Furthermore, the greater the degree of adversarial conflict generated in the process, the greater the likelihood that the accused as the least powerful, by definition, will lose.

An additional reason for the relative overdevelopment of rights for the accused, as opposed to victims is the defense orientation of most criminal lawyers. In Canada, and more so in the U.S., public prosecutors earn less than defense lawyers so turn over is rapid amongst prosecutors who tend, as a result, to be inexperienced (Tucker, 1985:237). Prosecution is a state monopoly subject to the usual lack of performance incentives whereas defense work is a private enterprise concern with the usual rewards for innovation and skill. Proportionally, far more lawyers engage in defense rather than in prosecution.

In the end, an accused's rights in Canada have been affected to the greatest degree by the advent of the Charter of Rights and Freedoms in 1982. Defense lawyers and the courts have used the Charter to define and extend to the accused protections which previously did not exist. The accused's rights in the Charter, notably in sections 7-14, have been enforced not only through the use of section 24 and the exclusion of "tainted" evidence, but also by the overruling of legislation deemed unconstitutional as violating the Charter. In this way, an accused's rights have been enhanced and expanded since 1982. Several of these new rights and protections are looked at in the cases reported in section 3 of Chapter 7. For further reading generally in this area, see the bibliography in section one of this chapter.

**Bibliography**
- Baker, J.H., *An Introduction to Legal History* (Toronto: Butterworths, 1979).
- Beauchamp, D.E., *Beyond Alcoholism — Alcohol and Public Health Policy* (Philadelphia: Temple University Press, 1980).
- Beaudoin, G.-A. and E. Ratushny (eds.), *The Canadian Charter of Rights and Freedoms* (Toronto: Carswell, 1989).
- Bryden, P. (ed.), *Protecting Rights and Freedoms: Essays on the Charter's Place in Canada's Political, Legal, and Intellectual Life* (Toronto: University of Toronto Press, 1994).
- Blumberg, A. "The Practice of Law as a Confidence Game: Organizational Cooperation of a Profession" (1967), 1 Law Society Review 15.
- Boyd, N., *et al.*, "Case Law and Drug Convictions: Testing the Rhetoric of Equality Rights" (1987), Criminal Law Quarterly 487.
- Casper, J., "Did You Have a Lawyer When You Went to Court? No, I Had a Public Defender" (1971), 1 Yale Review of Law and Social Action 4.
- Delisle, R.J. and D. Stuart, *Learning Canadian Criminal Procedure. 3rd Edition* (Scarborough, Ontario: Carswell, 1994).

- Edwards, S. M., Prostitutes: Victims of Law, Social Policy and Organized Crime", in P. Carlen and A. Worral, eds., *Gender, Crime and Justice* (London: Open University Press, 1987).
- Ericson, R. and P. Baranek, *The Ordering of Justice: A Study of Accused Persons as Dependents in the Criminal Justice Process* (Toronto: University of Toronto Press, 1982).
- Gold, A. and M. Fuerst, "The Stuff That Dreams are Made Of!: Criminal Law and the Charter of Rights" (1992), 24 Ottawa Law Review 13-37.
- Mitchell, C.N., "Willingness to Pay: Taxation and Taxation Compliance" (1985), 15 Memphis State University Law Review 127.
- Peck, R., "Section 10(b) of The Charter of Rights and Freedoms: New Vistas" (1987), 45 Advocate 31-39.
- Radcliffe, Lord, and R. Cross, *The English Legal System* (London: Butterworths, 1977).
- Rosenberg M., "Controlling Intrusive Police Investigative Techniques Under Section 8" (1991), 1 Criminal Reports (4th) 32-44.
- Rude, G., *Criminal and Victim: Crime and Society in Early Nineteenth Century England* (Oxford: Clarendon Press, 1985).
- Samenow, S., *Inside the Criminal Mind* (New York: Times Books, 1984).
- Stuart, D., *Charter Justice in Canadian Criminal Law* (Scarborough, Ontario: Carswell, 1991).
- Tanovich, D., "Charting the Constitutional Right of Effective Assistance of Counsel in Canada" (1994), 36 Criminal Law Quarterly 404-422.
- Tucker, W., *Vigilante — The Backlash Against Crime in America* (New York: Stein & Day, 1985).
- Wilson, C., *A Criminal History of Mankind* (New York: G.P. Putnam's, 1984).
- Wilson, J.Q., and Herrnstein, R.J., *Crime and Human Nature* (New York: Simon and Schuster, 1985).

## Questions/Discussion
1. List the infractions of provincial and federal laws that you know you have committed in the last five years. Of the total, what portion resulted in: some police response, arrest, trial, and conviction.
2. As a group, attempt to estimate the laws or types of laws that are: least enforced, most frequently broken, and broken by the greatest proportion of Canadians. What elements, if any, do these laws have in common? Then determine, what laws are: most vigorously enforced, least frequently broken, and broken by the smallest proportion of the population?
3. Considering the relatively minor penalties for impaired driving infractions, speculate about why a disproportionate number of criminal trial and appeal court decisions involve "breathalyser" cases? Is it the nature of the penalties, the offence or perhaps the offenders?

## Further Reading
- Burchfiel, K., "The Economic Organizations of Crime: A Study of the Development of Criminal Enterprise" (1977-78), 20 Criminal Law Quarterly 478.
- Cornish, D., & R. Clarke, eds., *The Reasoning Criminal: Rational Choice Perspectives on Offending* (New York: Springer-Verlag, 1986).
- Irwin, J., *The Felon* (Englewood Cliffs: Prentice-Hall, 1970)
- Linden, Rick, *Criminology: A Canadian Perspective* (Toronto: Holt, Rinehart, & Winston, 1987).
- Mann, W.E., ed., *Social Deviance in Canada* (Toronto: Copp Clark, 1971).
- Reiman, J., *The Rich Get Richer and the Poor Get Prison: Ideology, Class and Criminal Justice* (New York: John Wiley, 1979).

- West, W.G., "The Short-Term Careers of Serious Thieves" (1978), 20 Canadian Journal of Criminology 169.

## 4.6 CRIMINAL PENALIZERS

### Introduction

Next to the police, the most numerous and expensive public servants engaged in the criminal legal system are those employed in penalizing convicted criminals. In 1979 there were approximately 8,000 staff to handle the 9,500 federal prison inmates incarcerated in Canada at a cost of well over a billion dollars (Chrétien, 1982:118). By 1985, 12,000 federal inmates cost $1.5 billion to imprison; there are also 20,000 provincial prisoners (Correctional Law Review, 1985). In 1994-95, there were approximately 11,000 staff to handle 14,000 federal inmates and over 16,000 staff to handle 20,000 provincial inmates in Canada at a cost of $1.9 billion. In addition, the National Parole Board supervised about 5,500 persons and an army of court clerks and sheriffs administered and collected fines from the majority of convicted persons. Attention usually concentrates on prison and post-prison supervision because these penalties are labour-intensive, extremely expensive compared to the levying of fines and severely intrusive. Canadian judges, more than most of their counterparts elsewhere, rely on incarceration so the administration of jails and prisons is of particular concern here (Cousineau & Veevers, 1972).

**Table 1**

*Detention Rate per 100,000 Inhabitants*

| | |
|---|---|
| Canada | 116 |
| Netherlands | 44 |
| Sweden | 55 |
| Spain | 92 |
| U.S.A. | 519 |
| France | 84 |
| England-Wales | 92 |

Generally, prison services are administered by both the provincial and federal governments. Convicts are allotted to one level or the other according to the length of their prison sentence: two years or longer (not including consecutive sentences) and the prisoner goes into a federal penitentiary. Half of the admissions to provincial jails served sentences under one month with only about 5 percent sentenced to more than a year. At the federal level, the Canadian Penitentiary Service and the National Parole Service merged in 1979 into the Correctional Service of Canada (CSC). The CSC operates about 60 institutions including maximum, medium and minimum security prisons, camps, farms, community centres and psychiatric facilities. The more secure prisons average less than 500 inmates and are considerably smaller than the largest American prisons. At the provincial level, a variety of institutions exist which differ from federal prisons in two important respects. First, as noted, all the convicted inmates at provincial facilities are serving short sentences, usually under a month, and many are locked up only on weekends. Second, in many cases the convicted share space with the non-convicted, usually persons on remand awaiting trial. At the provincial level, therefore, there is no stable, long term population of convict inmates and little emphasis on "correctional" programs.

The *Constitution Act, 1867* in subsection 91(2) provides that the 'establishment maintenance and management of Penitentiaries' is a matter of exclusive federal jurisdiction but also grants the provinces power over 'public and reformatory prisons' in subsection 92(6). Criminal Code section 731 sets out the 'two year rule' by which the two levels of government divide prisoners. The rationale for this division is not clear. The distinction may be historical: in pre-1867 a "penitentiary" meant a place of confinement for convicts sentenced to two or more years of incarceration. Another possibility is that the federal government's exclusive power to make criminal law is consistent with authority over prisons containing "real criminals" whereas the provincial prisons contain those convicted of regulatory offences to which little moral condemnation attaches. In this latter case perhaps the provincial 'reformatory prison' parallels a school or a hospital, both of which fall under exclusive provincial jurisdiction. Regardless of the reason for the jurisdictional split, the division of prisoners creates certain difficulties among which are the impediment to national standards and national record keeping. Another concern is that a lengthy prison term can mean a transfer to a distant federal prison out of the home province. On a minor note, jurisdiction over offenders depends on the type and length of sentence not on the jurisdiction which enacted the relevant statutory offence. Persons convicted under federal or provincial laws may be sent to ether provincial or federal jails. In practice, few provincial offences lead to penitentiary because such offences rarely authorize lengthy confinement and, if they do, judges will rarely impose such penalties under provincial law (Hogg, 1985).

Modern prisons generate numerous administrative problems because they interfere massively with normal legal rights and personal autonomy. Voting rights, privacy rights, freedom of association, right to counsel and numerous other indices of normal citizenship and denied by prison authorities and by prison conditions. These denials and social deprivations flow logically from the guiding principles espoused by the inventors of prisons. Though they are now being challenged in the courts under the Charter. The primary thesis behind prisons was that criminals required the rehabilitating influences only the carefully controlled prison environment could deliver. Writing about the Auburn and Pennsylvania prison systems of the early to mid 1800s, Rothman (1971:82) explains their common assumptions:

> Convinced that deviancy was primarily the result of the corruptions pervading the community . . . they believed that a setting which removed the offender from all temptations and substituted a steady and regular regimen would reform him . . . The penitentiary, free of corruptions and dedicated to the proper training of the inmate, would inculcate the discipline that negligent parents, evil companions, taverns, houses of prostitution, theatres, and gambling halls had destroyed. Just as the criminal's environment had led him into crime, the institutional environment would lead him out of it. The duty of the penitentiary was to separate the offender from all contact with corruption . . . There was obviously no sense to removing a criminal from the depravity of his surroundings only to have him mix freely with other convicts within the prison.

Supporters of the Pennsylvania system could boast that their inmates were 'perfectly secluded' from the world and 'hopelessly separated' from family and friends. The exclusion ideal led prison wardens to prohibit letters, visits and even news from outside the prison walls. Later, New York officials relented somewhat allowing prisoners to receive one visit in the course of their sentence and to send one letter (written by the chaplain and censored by the warden) every four months. Wardens of that period also considered the whip, the iron gag, the ball and chain and other corporal punishments indispensable for maintaining the strict order necessary to achieve their rehabilitative ends. The appropriateness of prison as either a retributive or rehabilitative instrument is one which is subject to much debate, and prisons are generally viewed as breeding grounds of criminal activity and violence.

In the following selections, the Correctional Law Review, working for the Solicitor General, attempts a more positive analysis of current prison practices. The particular problems and concerns of female inmates are addressed in the final reading by Moffatt.

## A Framework for the Correctional Law Review, Working Paper No. 2*
### Solicitor General of Canada

* Excerpts from *A Framework for the Correctional Law Review, Working Paper No. 2* (Ottawa: Solicitor General of Canada, 1986).

### Part I:
### PRESENT FRAMEWORK-RULES GOVERNING CORRECTIONS

The rules which currently govern the federal correctional system have several sources — the constitution, which includes the *Canadian Charter of Rights and Freedoms*; international law; legislation, consisting of statutes and regulations; and judicial decisions involving the application and interpretation of all these as well as the development of the common law. Other rules which shape our system are found in Commissioner's Directives, policy and procedures manuals, and manuals of standards. This part examines the form of our current rules, and some of the characteristics of each. It concludes with an assessment of our present legislative scheme.

. . . .

### *Judicial Attitudes and Decisions*

Case law relating to corrections has generally been dependent upon the attitude of the courts to the prospect of going behind prison walls to scrutinize correctional practices and to review the internal decision-making procedures of prison officials.

Until relatively recently, Canadian courts exhibited a marked reluctance to assume an active role in reviewing the activities and decisions of prison administrators. This judicial reticence, known as the "hands-off" approach, had the effect of immunizing prisons and the actions of prison officials from public scrutiny.

One justification for the courts' approach was the belief that, having regard to the difficulties inherent in running a prison and safe-guarding prison security, the job should be left to those best equipped to handle the situation—the prison administrators themselves. A second reason for the "hands-off" approach was the suggestion that confrontations between inmates and prison administrators would escalate, and would in fact be fuelled by the courts' open reception to suits brought to challenge conditions in Canadian prisons. Furthermore, the enormity of the task of rectifying conditions was regarded as a cogent factor militating against judicial interference. In this regard, the *Parliamentary Sub-Committee on the Penitentiary In Canada stated:*

> The gross irregularities, lack of standards and arbitrariness that exist in our penitentiaries, by their very quantity, make and always have made, the possibility of judicial intervention into prison matters a rather impracticable, time consuming and dismaying prospect . . . The sheer immensity of the task of straightening it out is enough to discourage even the most committed members of the judiciary.

One of the strongest reasons offered in explanation of the courts' "hands-off" attitude was the once-popular notion that, once convicted and sentenced to a term of incarceration, a prisoner became automatically stripped of all rights.

Although the concept of civil death, whereby a person lost all rights upon conviction, was abolished in Canada in 1892, the traditional view of courts, that review of prison administration was something beyond their jurisdiction, lingered.

Further factors involved two vitally important administrative law principles: first, that the only decisions which could be characterized as judicial or quasi-judicial were those which affected a person's rights; and second, that only decisions which could be characterized as judicial or quasi-judicial were subject to judicial review. Since prisoners were regarded as having few "rights", most of the decisions made by prison officials were regarded as being purely administrative in nature and were therefore immune from review by the courts. As a consequence, "inmates who had few rights, also had few remedies and were left essentially defenceless against the wide-ranging administrative decision-making power of the prison authorities".

Only as recently as the 1970's did changes begin to take place. A series of decisions which relied, essentially, on the argument that an individual in prison does not lose "the right to have rights" served to strengthen the position of those in favour of offender rights. In *R. v. Solosky* the Supreme Court of Canada expressly endorsed the proposition that a person confined to prison retains all civil rights, except for those necessarily limited by the nature of incarceration or expressly or impliedly taken away by law. Moreover, the Supreme Court endorsed the "least restrictive means" approach which recognized that the courts have a balancing role to play to ensure that any interference with inmates' rights by institutional authorities is for a valid correctional goal and must be the least restrictive means available.

In other cases, the Federal Court applied the cruel and unusual punishment clause of the *Canadian Bill of Rights* to administrative segregation, and the courts began to develop the common law duty to act fairly in decisions affecting both inmates and parolees.

It is not entirely clear why the courts gradually began to assume a more active role in reviewing prison officials' decision-making procedures and to intervene to recognize and protect offender rights. It has been suggested from a sociological perspective that the increased awareness of inmates' rights paralleled a growing movement, which was particularly strong in the United States, for the extension of legal rights to a broad spectrum of groups in society such as racial minorities, children, women and the handicapped. It came to be recognized that prisons operated as autonomous systems insulated from public scrutiny and external review and that this lack of public visibility made it impossible for prisoners to assert their claims on their own behalf. Strong and persistent activist groups were formed to challenge the status quo. Reminiscent of John Howard's model of outside inspection, public scrutiny and judicial intervention came to be regarded as effective ways of controlling abuses of power behind prison walls.

It has also been suggested that the gradual acceptance of the rehabilitative ideal within corrections as a primary goal of correctional institutions was one of the most important factors which set the stage for the growth of judicial scrutiny of penitentiary operations. Despite the drawbacks of the rehabilitative model, it was reasoned that since most inmates are expected to be eventually released into society, they should learn to respect authority and to participate in the democratic control of that authority by being able to challenge what may appear to be unfair or arbitrary exercises of power by prison officials.

Apart from these explanations, the shift in judicial attitudes may be looked upon as a practical consequence of the significant and radical developments which occurred in the sphere of administrative law generally. The recognition in England of a duty of procedural fairness in administrative matters opened the door to permit judicial review of decisions which could not be properly characterized as either judicial or quasi-judicial.

The notion was transported to Canada and first appeared in a dissenting judgment of Dickson J. in *Howarth v. National Parole Board.* In that case, Dickson J. stated, *inter alia,* that an administrative decision must be made "judicially" where the decision has a serious impact on the person involved.

> "It is not necessary that a body should be a court of law . . . before it falls under a duty to act judicially.
>
> . . . .
>
> Generally speaking if 'rights' are affected by the order or decision . . . the function will be classified as judicial or quasi-judicial and this is particularly so when the exercise of administrative power seriously encroaches on property rights or the enjoyment of personal liberty."
>
> . . . .

The role of the courts in requiring that certain restrictions be placed on the penitentiaries' ultimate carceral power was reflected in the simultaneous treatment of three cases by the Supreme Court of Canada in December, 1985: *Morin v. National Special Handling Unit Review Committee et al,; R. v. Miller*; and *Cardinal et al. v. Director of Kent Institution.* The court dealt with largely procedural questions relating to inmates' access to the *habeas corpus* remedy in a manner which reaffirms recognition of inmate rights, in this case of rights to "residual liberty" in regard to placing inmates in administrative segregation and special handling units. Characterizing such practices as creating "a prison within a prison", the Court held that even though inmates have a limited right to liberty, they must be treated fairly in regard to any limitations on the liberty they retain as members of the general prison population.

Emerging from this examination of the impact of the courts on corrections is the fact that the courts now seem willing to scrutinize the administration and practices of penitentiaries. Even prior to the Charter, the courts played an important role in recognizing and legitimizing the rights of inmates. At this stage, it appears that the power of the courts has been strengthened under the Charter and that their efforts to provide procedural protections and substantive content to the rights of offenders continue.

## *International Law*

Canada has entered into a variety of obligations under international law to maintain standards with respect to the criminal justice system.

Foremost amongst these are Canada's obligations under United Nations treaties. Not only is Canada subject to the provisions of the UN Charter and the *Universal Declaration of Human Rights,* it is also signatory to the *International Covenant on Civil and Political Rights* and its *Optional Protocol,* and the *International Covenant on Economic, Social and Cultural Rights.*

Specific provisions of the Civil and Political Rights Covenant relate to prisoners and penitentiaries. All persons deprived of their liberty are to be treated with humanity and with respect for the inherent dignity of the human person. The individual's right to be protected against torture, or cruel, inhuman or degrading treatment or punishment is upheld. It is also stipulated that the penitentiary system shall provide for treatment of prisoners, the essential aim of which shall be their reformation and social rehabilitation. Other provisions state that no one shall be subjected to arbitrary or unlawful interference with their privacy.

In addition to being party to these treaties, Canada has also endorsed in the United Nations *Standard Minimum Rules for the Treatment of Offenders*. The obligations that are imposed as a result of international law on Canada, where treaties are not self-executing, will be considered in the next chapter, which deals with "factors shaping the form and content of legislation".

## *Legislation*

Currently there are several federal statutes dealing with the field of corrections — the *Penitentiary Act*, the *Parole Act*, the *Prisons and Reformatories Act*, the *Transfer of Offenders Act* and the *Criminal Code*. The following is a brief description of these pieces of legislation.

The *Penitentiary Act* deals with a variety of matters, many of an organizational nature such as the establishment of the correctional service, the agency head, national and regional headquarters. Other matters in the *Penitentiary Act* include federal/provincial transfer agreements (s. 15), the right to earn remission (s. 24), and powers of correctional officers (s. 10). Subordinate legislation, in the form of regulations, is authorized under s. 29 of the Act.

. . . .

The Penitentiary Service Regulations enacted under section 29 deal with a number of organizational matters such as the duties of institutional heads (s. 5), and authority to delegate routine matters. The right of inmates to adequate food and clothing (s. 15) and the provision of essential medical and dental care (s. 16) are found in the regulations. The creation of Inmate offences and penalties, and the disciplinary process are in regulations. Section 3 of the regulations outlines the duty of every member of the Service to use his best endeavours to achieve the purpose and objectives of the Service, namely "the custody, control, correctional training and rehabilitation of persons who are sentenced or committed in penitentiary." This is the only statement of mandate of corrections and it is remarkable that, vague as it is, it appears in a regulation instead of a statute.

Similarly the *Parole Act* provides for the organizational structure of the National Parole Board (including number of members, provision for regional panels, agency head), powers of the Board (s. 6), and the duty to review every penitentiary inmate for parole (s. 8), authorizes the establishment of provincial parole boards, and provides for mandatory supervision (s. 15). Section 9 authorizes the making of regulations by Governor in Council. This section is very specific, and outlines the exact subject matter which Cabinet may prescribe (for example, prescribing the minimum number of members to vote on a case). The Parole Regulations contain very detailed rules on a wide range of topics. The Regulations, rather than the statute, contain rules concerning eligibility for parole, including the time an inmate must spend in custody before being eligible. As well, they provide for the right to assistance at hearings (s. 20.1), the right to information upon which the Board will base its decisions (s. 17), and the right to reasons for parole decision (s. 19). This detailed regulation-making power is in sharp contrast to the extremely broad power in s. 29 of the *Penitentiary Act.*

The *Prisons & Reformatories Act* governs certain aspects of incarceration in provincial institutions of persons serving sentences for offences against federal statutes. It covers such areas as the granting of remission, temporary absences, and authority for transfers of inmates between provinces.

The Act has undergone extensive revisions in recent years. The trend has been to remove unnecessary detail to permit provincial governments greater control over correctional operations. At the same time, consistency in certain key areas, such as the granting of remission, is maintained.

The *Transfer of Offenders Act* establishes the eligibility of Canadian offenders imprisoned in a foreign state with which Canada has a treaty to be transferred to Canada to serve the remainder of their sentence in a Canadian prison or penitentiary. There is also provision for the transfer to Canada of Canadian offenders on parole or probation in a foreign state.

Foreign nationals incarcerated in Canada may be transferred to their homeland if the conditions in the Act are met, and if they are from a country with which Canada has a treaty for the transfer of offenders. Regulations under this Act may be made by the Governor in Council to prescribe the form and manner of application for transfer, and for factors which the minister shall take into consideration in making a decision.

*Criminal Code* provisions which directly affect corrections include s. 659 (sentences of two years or more to be served according to rules governing the institution), s. 674 (prohibiting parole consideration for cases of life imprisonment until expiration of specified number of years of imprisonment), and s. 695.1 (review of dangerous offenders for parole). Section 2(b) of the Code specifies that a "peace officer" includes "a warden, deputy warden, instructor, keeper, gaoler, guard and any other officer or permanent employee of a prison" (prison is defined as including a penitentiary). Thus any consideration of the powers and responsibilities of correctional staff will involve an analysis of the many other provisions relating to peace officers found in the *Criminal Code.*

. . . .

## Correctional Philosophy, Working Paper No. 1*
*Solicitor General of Canada*

* Excerpts from *Correctional Philosophy, Working Paper No. 1* (Ottawa: Solicitor General of Canada, 1986).

### Part II:
### THE PURPOSE AND PRINCIPLES OF THE CRIMINAL LAW AND IMPLICATIONS FOR CORRECTIONS

*Rehabilitation*

Although rehabilitation has generally been discredited as a legitimate justification for *sentencing* an offender to imprisonment, no major report has ever recommended an end to rehabilitation as a goal of *corrections*. Even the 1977 Parliamentary Sub-committee, which rejected the use of imprisonment *in order* to rehabilitate offenders, said that "once a decision to imprison has been taken . . ., the correctional techniques employed should be aimed at encouraging and assisting personal reformation by wrongdoers". Thus, imprisonment (and corrections generally) contribute to the protection of society, in the Sub-committee's view, in two ways:

> "Protection of society" as a purpose of imprisonment includes not only protection during a term of imprisonment by the physical removal of a person who is dangerous or who has failed to respect values that are protected by the criminal law, but also the protection of society after his release by means of a prison system designed to assist him towards personal reformation.

Corrections is the only segment of the criminal justice system which is supposed to assist and encourage the offender to overcome the factors which contribute to his criminality. Other stages in the criminal justice system may occasionally or accidentally have this effect, but it is only after sentencing that any government agency is authorized to try to "treat" an offender. Even in an era of financial restraint, most corrections professionals, academics, and even members of the public still support the principle of rehabilitation, perhaps simply on the grounds that it would be irresponsible and cynical to give up so soon.

Despite the foregoing, it is nonetheless true that during the 1970's in Canada, rehabilitation fell into disfavour as a correctional ideal. The disfavour was on two fronts: first, that rehabilitation had been costly and ineffective, and second, that it had caused more cruelty and longer punishment than the intentionally "punitive" model which had preceded it.

In fact most of the allegations that treatment is "tyrannical" stem from the study of a few jurisdictions, primarily California and Maryland, and the concerns arose from the use of extremely lengthy or indeterminate prison sentences combined with a highly interventionist treatment philosophy. Nonetheless, there is probably some truth to the notion that offenders see an element of unfairness in almost any attempt to rehabilitate them. After all, virtually any type of personal change is in some respects painful. For offenders, "personal reformation" (as the 1977 Parliamentary Sub-committee on the Penitentiary System put it) can entail a painful and difficult struggle to give up alcohol or drugs, working at a low-paying and unsatisfying job instead of pursuing the risk and excitement of less legitimate earnings, or a protracted process of acquiring new methods of recognizing and dealing with anger and frustration.

Despite this painful element to rehabilitation, however, it is probably fair to say that most people would support rehabilitation if it were proven to be effective and if it did not create excessive additional punishment, costs and risks. How strong is the case, then, that rehabilitation is proven to be ineffective?

Some criminologists have in fact characterized this as one of the greatest over-generalizations in criminal justice. They argue that most evaluated programs in corrections could, in the word of one official, be characterized (as was one particularly well-documented one) as "a poorly conceptualized program that was inadequately delivered by unqualified personnel to individuals who might have been inappropriately assigned to it".

Has "rehabilitation", even in the form just described, been "proven" ineffective, however? Is the evaluative research on programs definitive? Here again, the bulk of expert opinion has it that the quality of evaluative research has, in the main, approached that of the programs themselves. Probably the most authoritative review of the literature, by the U.S. National Academy of Science Panel on Research and Rehabilitation Techniques, concludes that most of the research in the area has been inconclusive if not meaningless, because of poor methodology and a tendency to "evaluate" a multifaceted correctional experience (such as probation) as if it were a single phenomenon. Very little correctional research to date has been sophisticated enough to differentiate which offenders are helped — and which are made worse — by which techniques under which conditions. Most programs, with good and bad results, thus are felt to have, overall, "no effect".

We are of the view then, that it cannot be concluded that rehabilitation is ineffective. The evidence is too sparse, and the actual attempts to design, fund, and carry out a rehabilitative model for corrections have, to date, been inconsistent and incomplete. Should corrections therefore continue to try to correct offenders?

The best protection for society is widely acknowledged to be the re-integration of offenders into the community as law-abiding citizens. Actively pursuing the goal of encouraging and assisting the personal reformation of offenders, rather than relying on punishment and deterrence to achieve the same goal, is thought by the Working Group to be more appropriate for three reasons.

First, it treats individual offenders as responsible individuals capable of change and taking charge of their lives.

Second, it gives a role to correctional authorities which is positive, humane and which actively supports the long term criminal justice objectives. This role, rather than one which emphasizes the containment of inmates and maintenance of order, is far more rewarding for staff who assume responsibility for assisting and encouraging offenders to take advantage of rehabilitation opportunities.

Finally, the rehabilitative approach holds more potential than a simple punishment/deterrence approach, simply because it recognizes the inevitable reality that there are causal factors which contribute to criminality which no amount of punishment will remedy. By this we means such things as unemployment, poor impulse control, lack of job skills, low frustration tolerance, functional illiteracy, poor social and problem-solving skills, inability to cope with emotional stress. Many of these problems can be effectively dealt with through teaching offenders cognitive and behavioral skills. Offenders are extremely unlikely to learn the necessary skills themselves, and punishment through deterrence or simple incapacitation will not teach them. Experience also suggest that offenders are unlikely to take advantage of program opportunities unless they are actively encouraged to do so, and one of the most effective incentives to program participation is a high-quality program.

## Reconciliation

Reconciliation — of the offender with society, or the offender with the individual victim — has gained greater legitimacy in recent years. Long considered more appropriate to the civil courts which resolve disputes between individuals, restitution to victims as a sentence in criminal matters has grown with the increased recognition of victims' rights in the past decade. In addition, sentences which involve service to the community generally, such as community service orders, have become more common. All these reflect a greater recognition of the need to make reconciliation more prominent as a criminal justice goal.

## The Influence of Public Attitudes on the Delineation of a Correctional Philosophy

What the public has a right to reasonably expect from corrections should and will affect how corrections views its mandate. First and foremost, the public expects protection from crime, especially violent crime. For corrections, this means carrying out the requirements of the sentence, including the maintenance of a sufficient degree of security to prevent escapes from correctional institutions. It means always having regard for the potential risk to the public interest in all decisions about the treatment and handling of offenders. The public also has a right to expect that the punitive and deterrent aspects of the sentence will be respected by correctional authorities, and that any conditional release from imprisonment following the service of the punitive portion of a sentence will be made in accordance with the overall criminal justice goals of justice and security.

Once a decision has been made by the court to use imprisonment in an individual case, the public also has a right to expect that what goes on inside institutions will be optimally directed towards reducing the offender's chances of coming back. The 1977 Parliamentary Sub-committee on the Penitentiary System said that "society has spent millions of dollars over the years to create and maintain the proven failure of prisons. Incarceration has failed in its two essential purposes — correcting the offender and providing permanent protection to society". The Sub-committee went on to recommend both the availability of more community based alternatives to incarceration, and the wiser use of the time which imprisoned offenders spend incarcerated. In the Sub-committee's view, imprisonment too often becomes just a very expensive warehousing operation. "Personal reformation" instead was what the Sub-committee felt should be the goal of prisons. The public too has a right to expect more for its imprisonment dollars than a revolving-door warehouse.

The public also reasonably expects that its tax monies will be spent in the most effective possible way. Public attitude surveys suggest that it is violent crime which most concerns Canadians, and that the public is more willing to accept non-carceral handling of nonviolent offenders than many criminal justice professionals assume. This is a reasonable approach, especially in view of the high costs of imprisonment. As competition among social programs for increasingly scarce tax dollars increases, it makes sense to reserve the most costly correctional intervention for those who most deserve or require it.

# A Framework for the Correctional Law Review, Working Paper No. 2*
## *Solicitor General of Canada*

* Excerpts from *A Framework for the Correctional Law Review, Working Paper No. 2* (Ottawa: Solicitor General of Canada, 1986).

. . .

## Part III:
## MEETING THE GOALS OF THE CORRECTIONAL LAW REVIEW

### *Offenders*

In considering the rights and interests of offenders, who for purposes of our discussion are persons undergoing sentences of incarceration, the first questions are to what extent their rights differ from the rights of other citizens and, if they do differ in what respects.

The obvious distinction is in relation to liberty; incarceration necessarily results in loss or restrictions on the offender's right to liberty. However, in all other respects the offender has a right to live as full and normal a life as is compatible with incarceration. Indeed, the offender acquires rights through loss of liberty and dependence on the state, such as the right to be provided with the basic amenities of life, including adequate food, clothing, and accommodation.

This situation derives from the fundamental precept that inmates are sent to prison *as* punishment, not *for* punishment. This precept has been accepted in almost every Western democracy and is recognized as a fundamental starting point by the Correctional Law Review. It requires a justice system within the institution that ensures that an inmate's rights will be respected. Such a system would operate to protect the inmate if he is denied his rights, as well as deal with the transgressor. As well, it would provide a rational basis for ordering the prison community according to rules which take into account inmate interests and which are known to all in advance. This system would be manifested by fair and impartial procedures that must be strictly observed, would proceed from rules that cannot be avoided at will, and would treat all who are subject to it equally. In essence, such a system would ensure that the rule of law would prevail inside the institution.

This type of system was recommended by the *Parliamentary Sub-Committee in Canada* in 1977. As stated in its Report, "justice for inmates is a personal right and also an essential condition of an inmate's socialization and personal reformation. Justice implies both respect for the persons and property of others and fairness in treatment."

Such a system has advantages for everyone involved. Failure to provide a just system to protect inmates' rights increases the tensions of prison life. An inmate who is sent to prison for breaking the law can only resent finding himself in a closed society ruled not by law, but by discretionary power which may be wielded arbitrarily. The ensuring tension could create an atmosphere of mistrust, which could lead to violence, and which is contrary not only to the interests of inmates, but to staff, management and the larger community as well.

Related to this is the interest than an inmate has in seeing that he does not leave prison with fewer skills or in a worse psychological state than when he entered it. In addition, he may legitimately have an interest in improving his educational and vocational skills, getting appropriate medical and psychiatric care, maintaining and improving family relationships and so on. Opportunities must be available for an inmate to meet these goals in the general interest of the rehabilitation of the individual and the benefit it would bring the community.

## *Correctional Staff*

The rights and interests of correctional staff are key elements to be kept constantly in mind throughout the course of the Correctional Law Review. It is important to recognize two facts: that staff are as integral a part of penitentiary life as the inmates, and that no correctional system will be effective unless their rights, interests and concerns are taken into account.

The job of a correctional staff member is a difficult one, often exacerbated by a misunderstanding of their concerns on the part of inmates, management, and the public. It is important that persons with this job not be seen only as "guards" but as members of an important social service demanding ability, appropriate training, and good teamwork. This is especially important today, when many correctional staff, such as parole officers, have a duel role to play in relation to inmates. Staff are often expected to function as counsellors as well as police. Conflicts which arise as a result must be recognized and dealt with. It is important that conditions of service that will attract and retain the best qualified persons be implemented. As well, all staff should have access to continuous support and training programs.

Correctional staff perform a job which is characterized by constant fear of making a mistake which may result in an escape, or some form of violence. This situation leads to an inclination to solve inmate-staff problems through increased security measures rather than through more individualized problem-solving techniques.

"Security" has been described as the ultimate weapon to be used by the staff to demonstrate that they are the official masters, in physical terms. It has also been noted that correctional officers perceive the increased freedom and new programs for inmates as not only eroding their power but also causing a deterioration in security.

There is no doubt that security is a legitimate concern of staff and the institution, and that it must be a top priority in operating an effective system. Along the same line, it is also important to recognize that proper safeguards must exist to allow a correctional official to perform his functions safely. In addition, however, there is a need for re-orientation in the training of correctional staff. Staff should be trained to solve problems in constructive ways to enable them to deal humanely with staff-inmate and inmate-inmate problems. This could be aided by an increased emphasis during training on the objectives of the correctional system and of the role of staff in achieving these objectives. The view that "good programs are good security" should guide staff in their work.

Another issue of primary concern to correctional staff concerns their powers. The powers of correctional staff are by their nature defined in relation to the rights of inmates. For example, the powers available to a correctional official to conduct body searches of inmates must be balanced with the inmates' right to privacy and to be secure against unreasonable search or seizure.

It is essential that correctional officials be granted sufficient power and authority to enable them to perform their function, but it is also important to correctional officials that the limit and extent of their powers be clearly set out in law and easily accessible and understandable to them. Otherwise if they overstep their powers they may leave themselves open to civil suits or criminal charges.

Under current law, the primary source of powers, privileges and protections for correctional officials is the *Criminal Code* which contains over 75 provisions that bestow powers upon "peace officers". As a result of the definition of "peace officer" in s. 2 of the Code, the full range of police powers are bestowed on "a warden, deputy warden, instructor, keeper, gaoler, guard, and any other officer or permanent employee of a prison".

This automatic attachment of expansive law enforcement powers upon correctional officials should be reexamined, especially in light of the principle of restraint adopted in CLICS. Even more critical is the confusing state of the law in regard to how much power an official can use in a particular situation. As a result of the vague or general language used in the *Criminal Code*, this type of question can only be answered by an *ex-post facto* judicial determination.

For example, the degree of force which may be used is basically that which is "reasonable in the circumstances". What may be regarded as reasonable in one situation, may not be reasonable in another. Lawyers and the courts may take months to decide the legality of an action which the staff-member had only minutes, or even seconds, to decide upon. The extent of an official's powers is a matter which has serious consequences for both the official and the inmates, and the present uncertainty in the law is not conducive to a fair or effective correctional system. It is in the interests of both correctional officials and inmates that the law be clear and accessible in regard to powers.

. . . .

# Creating Choices or Repeating History: Canadian Female Offenders and Correctional Reform*
## K. Moffatt

\* Excerpts from: (1991), 18 Social Justice 184-203.

The treatment of women in the criminal-justice system has been scrutinized and vigorously debated over the last two decades. Authors have repeatedly argued that paternalistic and patriarchal attitudes have dominated criminological research and penal policy; one well-documented consequence of this dominance has been inferior and sexist programming afforded to female inmates (Sargent, 1985; Edwards, 1989; Feinman, 1980; Berzins and Cooper, 1982; Carlen, 1988; Adelberg and Currie, 1987; Morris, 1987). It has also been argued that criminology, like most academic disciplines, is primarily concerned with the activities and interests of men and thus focussed away from women and areas of concern to women (Morris, 1987:1). Female offenders have been systematically ignored by criminological researchers and correctional planners who have focussed their attention, money, and program efforts on male offenders. Correctional programs for women are largely unsatisfactory and inferior in quantity, quality, and variety to those for male offenders. However, the recent increase in women's involvement in correctional administration, criminology, and private organizations has resulted in greater acknowledgement and awareness of female offenders and their dilemmas.

. . . .

## Canadian Women in Conflict with the Law

Women comprise a small minority of those who come into conflict with the law.[1] However, those who do offend tend to be young, poor, under-educated, unskilled, and drug or alcohol dependent. A large number of women in prison have reported that they have been victims of physical and sexual abuse,[2] and many are emotionally or financially dependent on abusive male partners (Adelberg and Currie, 1987). In Canada, the *Badgley Report* found an association between child sexual abuse and future prostitution. Similarly, and unpublished study shows that 52% of the women in a sample of inmates reported being sexually abused as children and estimates put the proportion as high as 80% to 85% (Axon, 1989:25). In addition, an increasing number of women inmates tend to be single parents. Researchers suggest that 30% to 40% of convicted women are caring for children at the time of their incarceration, and that 50% to 70% of all incarcerated women have had at least one child.

A disproportionate number of these women tend to be Native. Native women make up about 20% of federally sentenced women although they represent only 3% of Canada's total female population. The types of offences committed by Native women are different from those committed by non-Native women. The report of a recent Task Force (1990) on the criminal justice system and its impact on the Indian and Metis People of Alberta indicates that violent offences and offences against persons accounted for a higher portion (67.4%) of Native female federal-offender admissions than of non-Native female federal-offender admissions (31.5%). Aboriginal offenders often experience racism, discrimination, and a devaluation of their culture that is intensified and complicated by their interaction with the law. It seems that the high rate of criminalization of Native women is clearly linked to their bleak socioeconomic profiles (Johnson, 1987:39).

According to *Statistics Canada 1989*, women accounted for 15% of all criminal charges laid. If convicted and sentenced to a period of less than two years, women offenders would serve their sentence in a provincial correctional facility. According to Ontario Ministry of Correctional Services, in 1988-1989 approximately 8.5% of the people admitted to provincial jails and detention centres were female. If sentenced to two years or more, convicted women are required to serve their time in a federal penitentiary. Women who are sentenced to two years or more are sent to the Prison for Women in Kingston, Ontario — the only federal institution for women in Canada. Correctional Services Canada reports that as of March 1989 there were 285 women serving federal sentences in institutions, compared with 13,066 men, indicating that only 2% of people serving federal time are women. It has been suggested that the lower rates of incarceration for women may be related to the comparatively minor nature of their offences, their shorter criminal histories, and the often ancillary role that women play to men in serious crimes (Ibid.: 33-34). Likewise, the lack of alternatives to the Prison for Women may influence the length of a women's sentences.

Federal/provincial exchange of service agreements allows some female inmates, while under federal jurisdiction, to serve their sentences in provincial institutions so that they may be closer to their families and community. Approximately 40% of all federally sentenced women use this option. Participation in exchange of service agreements is based on sentence length, severity of offence, and the personality of the offender. Some provinces refuse to take women serving more than five years (Saskatchewan, Manitoba) or more than 10 years (Alberta, British Columbia). Unfortunately, the program and facilities available in provincial institutions are designed for short-term inmates, and as a result they cannot satisfy the needs of federally sentenced women. There is a wide gap between the level of services at the Prison for Women versus that available at provincial facilities. Despite the inadequacies in programming, these agreements are the only alternative to the Prison for Women. The program location choices imposed by current exchange of service agreements is further complicated by the fact that most provincial jurisdictions have only one facility for women (*Creating Choices*, 1990:78). Initially, these agreements were designed to accommodate Canada's unique geographical features, which include the enormous size of the land mass, and a relatively sparse and scattered population with significant cultural and language differences.

Another difficulty with these agreements is that they are not equally available to all federally sentenced women. MacLeod (1986:54-55) notes that there is an uneven geographical distribution of these agreements, which puts women from certain parts of the country at a disadvantage. She further suggests that this imbalance in distribution has existed since the inception of exchange of service agreements. Between 1975 and 1984, 60% of the female federal inmates serving their sentences in provincial institutions were serving them in Quebec, another one-third were in Alberta or British Columbia, and only one percent were incarcerated in the Atlantic provinces (*Ibid.*). One explanation for this inequity is the existence of a formal agreement allowing

French-speaking federal female prisoners to reside at Maison Tanguary, in Montreal, Quebec, to ensure the provision of French-language staff and services (Hatch and Faith, 1990:453).

This research, like most on incarcerated women in Canada, focuses on the federal system. Historically, there has been a major concern about what to do with federally sentenced women. Debates have generally concentrated on centralization of prisons for women in one institution versus the decentralization of services. Despite various recommendations for dispersion, a decision was made in the early 1920's to build one central institution for women (Berzins and Cooper, 1982:402). Since the construction of the facility, several task forces and Royal Commissions have indicated a preference for decentralized services for federal women prisoners. Likewise, there seems to be continuing confusion and disagreement among correctional administrators, community organizations, and the government concerning the needs of the female offender. Not until the most recent Task Force *Creating Choices* (1990) has anyone seriously bothered to investigate women prisoners' perception of their needs. For the most part, reforms, methods, techniques, and ideologies of prison management in women's institutions have been predominantly associated with particular views as to women's "proper place" in society (Reid, 1985:129). Increasingly, it is being recognized that women, although underrepresented in the criminal-justice system, are overrepresented in the welfare and mental-health systems as well as in programs for victims of violence. As a result, penal regimes for women cannot function in isolation from other community and social services if they are to adequately evaluate and satisfy the needs of female offenders. The Task Force on federally sentenced women (*Creating Choices*, 1990) is one of the first formal government recognitions of these realities of women's lives. The members of this Task Force made a conscious effort to deal with the social circumstances that often contribute to women's criminal behaviour. Their report states:

> Women in Canada, and in other Western nations, live with inequalities flowing from traditions and values which emphasize their dependency on men and institutions. As well, the discrimination within discrimination experienced by Aboriginal women in this social reality is also ignored in the past understanding of the problem (*Ibid:*73).

The Task Force supported the belief that:

> Women in prison have more in common with other women than they do with male inmates, and that programs and services should be designed to meet local needs and circumstances, or planned individually, not on the basis of some centralized blueprint (Shaw, 1989:11, in *Creating Choices*, 1990:82).

. . .

## Prisoners' Struggles for Equality

Although the Prison for Women has been incessantly scrutinized and investigated, deplorable and inequitable conditions remain. Besides these inquiries, several legal challenges have graphically illustrated the injustices facing federally sentenced women. Most of these challenges, both past and present,[3] have occurred under the equality and other provisions of *The Canadian Charter of Rights and Freedoms*. These cases have revealed that:

in certain institutions the rights of federally sentenced women have been breached by the failure of the system to provide equal means for women to serve their sentences within a reasonable distance from their home, to provide equal opportunities, to provide equal programming, and to provide equal standards of facilities both in comparison to men and in comparison to federally sentenced women serving their sentences in another institution (*Creating Choices,* 1990:84).

When pursuing rights arguments, caution must be exercised. Federally sentenced women have discovered that although the state may concede a right, that does not mean that it will make the structural alterations that will allow for the exercise of that right. For example, in the case of the female offender, the courts have ruled that imprisoned women should be given the same rights as male prisoners; however, they do not require the funding and resource provisions necessary to implement and improve programs and treatment services.

Although the rhetoric of rights and equality has helped empower women prisoners in some cases, there is reason to be sceptical of any reform attempts that merely try to make women equal to men instead of addressing women inmates' unique experiences. Admittedly, litigation based on equality can improve conditions for women prisoners somewhat (e.g., educational and vocational opportunities). However, these legal arrangements are often poorly adapted to the specific realities of women, such as childcare and medical needs. In accord with this argument, Ross and Fabiano (1985:123) argue in their report to the Solicitor General of Canada, *Correctional Afterthoughts: Programs for Female Offenders,* that there has been increasing pressure on the government to provide equal services for women. However, they feel that this demand for equality, although warranted, may serve to "limit female offenders to the quantity, quality, and variety of services which are available to men; services which may not meet the needs of either group." They further indicate that by focussing only on providing women the same services as men, we may inadvertently succeed in marginalizing them by providing them with services that are not designed to meet their needs.

Public awareness of these problems has resulted in government pressure for change. This pressure for change stems from a variety of sources. There are many individual crusaders (such as Claire Culhane) and groups concerned with women's rights (such as Women for Justice and the Elizabeth Fry Society) who advocate on behalf of incarcerated women. These individuals and groups have brought considerable attention to the treatment of women in the criminal-justice system. Similarly, the revelations of senational cases and tragedies have exposed women's prisons to further public scrutiny. In Canada, the Marlene Moore case[4] and recent Native inmate suicides have been instrumental in revealing the deplorable conditions of women's prisons. For many, these cases symbolize the failure of our mental-health and penal institutions to respond to the problems and pain of women prisoners. Allegations that women have been mistreated and discriminated against in prisons have lead to demands (and sometimes court orders) for equal opportunity in correctional facilities, programs, and services (Ross and Fabiano, 1985:1). Considering these difficulties, there has been increased political pressure on the government and on correctional management to improve the availability of services and accommodations for female offenders.

## Task Force on Federally Sentenced Women

One consequence of this pressure was *Creating Choices* (1990), the report of a Task Force on federally sentenced women in Canada. The Task Force was designed to remedy the problem of inadequate research on women's prisons and alternatives to incarceration. This project was fully supported by Ole Instrup, Commission of Correctional Services Canada, who made a clear commitment to reviewing the needs of federally sentenced women. Interest in developing a Task Force to address women prisoners' issues was shared by the Elizabeth Fry Society and Native groups. Likewise, trends and events such as feminist criticism of the existing system, Aboriginal demands for more control over justice for their people. Charter challenges, repeated recommendations for the closure of the Prison for Women, rethinking of Corrections Canada Mission Statement, and tragedies at the Prison for Women reinforced a ground swell of consensus that fundamental reform is urgently required.

The recommendations of the Task Force were presented in a report to the government in April 1990, and a few months later the federal government announced that they would implement the Task Force's recommendations. On recommendation to be implemented immediately is the elimination of transfers from provincial correctional institutions to the Prison for Women. In the past, provincially sentenced women who posed a security threat could be transferred from a provincial facility to a federal facility.

Other proposals were to recruit more feminist and Aboriginal counsellors, and to establish a daily presence of an Aboriginal counsellor at the Prison for Women. Also, there is a recommendation to admit prisoners who have self-injured to the prison or community hospital and return them to the general population as soon as possible instead of treating these individuals punitively. It has also been recognized that geographic dislocation can cause many hardships, and, as a result, it has been recommended that prisoners should have access to funded visits with family members and enhanced telephone contacts.[5]

The most significant long-term recommendation of the Task Force is for the closure of the notorious Prison for Women, and the construction of four small regional facilities and one Aboriginal "healing lodge." Each regional facility would be developed and operated under a program philosophy that approximates community norms, focuses on the use of community services and expertise, and is geared to the safe and earliest possible release of federally sentenced women. Programs available at each of these facilities are expected to be culturally sensitive and responsive to the needs of women. Programming will concentrate on individual and group counselling that would be sensitive to sexual, emotional, and physical abuse, and teach everyday skills and coping techniques. The primary programming will also include health care, mental-health services, addiction programs, family visiting, mother and child programs, spirituality and religion, Aboriginal programs, education, and vocational training. These facilities will also rely extensively on volunteer services. Many local community groups will be encouraged to interact with the inmates to foster a community responsibility for the facility and to provide important community connections for women about to be released (*Ibid.*: 138-147).

The Aboriginal healing lodge would allow federally sentenced Aboriginal women to serve all or part of their sentences in a culturally sensitive environment. The intention is that the physical space and programs for the healing lodge should reflect Aboriginal culture. This facility would address the needs of federally sentenced Aboriginal women through Native teachings, ceremonies, contact with elders and children, and interaction with nature (*Ibid.:* 147-150). Presently, the breadth of problems facing Aboriginal women in the criminal-justice system has not been adequately researched and analyzed. We do not have a clear understanding of the realities of Native women's lives.

Although the closure of the Prison for Women can be viewed as progress, the construction of five more women's prisons across the country raises serious concerns about the future of women's imprisonment. One curious aspect of this recommendation is the endorsement of the construction of these new "facilities" (prisons) by the Elizabeth Fry Society, which has historically supported the abolition of prisons. Rather than a shift in ideology, the Elizabeth Fry Society's participation in the Task Force and support of these recommendations may reflect increased private-sector involvement in corrections. Griffiths and Verdun-Jones (1989:592) note that in recent years:

> there has been an increase in the number of contracts between the federal and provincial governments and the John Howard Society, Elizabeth Fry Society, the Salvation Army, and other private non-profit agencies for the delivery of programs and services, particularly in the supervision of adult offenders.

Another difficulty with the construction of these new prisons is that it would not necessarily solve the problems outlined in the Task Force report. Two of the most serious difficulties facing federally sentenced women are geographic dislocation and overclassification. If the recommendations for the construction of these new facilities are implemented, there will be some improvement in geographic isolation, but the problem of security still exists. Depending on the location of these centres, and provided that they accept all inmates from the surrounding area, women will be permitted to be closer to their families and communities. However, due to practical and monetary constraints, some dislocation will remain. Furthermore, if an Aboriginal inmate wants to serve her sentence in the Aboriginal healing lodge, depending on the location of her home province, she must choose between services and proximity to her community and family. This problem is quite similar to those associated with previously mentioned exchange of service agreements. To further improve and reduce imprisoned women's isolation and alienation from the family, these new institutions must have improved visiting and family contact programs.

Classification and security concerns were not adequately dealt with in the Task Force report. The lack of proposals that deal with these issues is problematic. The assumption here is that each facility will be able to adapt to different levels of security needs. This assumption is problematic, and a similar mistake was made when the Prison for Women was constructed in 1934. Furthermore, past task forces and Royal Commissions have been sceptical of the effectiveness of housing offenders with diverse security needs in the same institution. The proposals for these regional facilities concentrate on women prisoners with low-to medium-security classifications and not the offender who poses a security risk. The Task Force recommends the use of dynamic security and unit management, which is based on the idea of integrating concepts of control, support, and assistance. However, the Task Force recognizes that "the full expression of such integration, because it is dependent on establishing stable, productive, personal relationships rather than institutional ones, will be difficult to achieve in traditional correctional environments" *(Creating Choices,* 1990: 107). Although the Task Force was aware of these complications, it still advocated a non-authoritative security structure and the creation of an environment "where relationships are based on role modelling, support, trust, and democratic decision-making can thrive between staff and federally sentenced women" *(Ibid.*:108). Given that these facilities would still effectively be prisons, it will be interesting to see if this rhetoric is ever translated into correctional practice. Under the current system, and in any institution that limits inmate rights, the notion of truly democratic decision-making between inmates and guards is inconceivable.

Instead of traditional male-oriented and culturally specific classification systems, the Task Force favours development of a woman-centered and culturally relevant assessment system. The assessment system would be designed to look at the whole spectrum of a women's needs from a holistic perspective, including needs relating to programming, spirituality, health, family, culture, and release plans. Through this assessment it is hoped that staff will be better able to respond to the needs of federally sentenced women *(Ibid.:* 112). The Task Force feels that an emphasis on security classification is nonproductive when dealing with the female offender and that it is not conducive to rehabilitation. However, the fact remains that these women are in prison and there are bound to be some complications with this approach, especially with "high need" or "high risk" offenders, where the protection of society is a paramount concern.

A final concern with the proposals for the expansion of women's prisons is the effect this might have on judicial attitudes and sentencing patterns. Presently there is a lack of good empirical research on the sentencing of women. Judges have been reluctant to give dispositions of federal time to women since there was only one institution for federally sentenced women. In some cases, judges have publicly indicated that the conditions at the Prison for Women are deplorable and, as a result, they are reluctant to issue sentences of two years or more. With these proposed changes, there is some concern that there may be an increase in the number of women being sentenced to federal institutions who would have otherwise received a less severe sentence. There is a danger of a resurgence of paternalistic thinking and lengthy sentences for the "benefit of the offender". There is currently no attempt by the government to assess the likelihood of these problem. If this potential complication is not attended to, women's imprisonment may be affected by problems of overcrowding since the institutions being proposed would not be designed to hold large numbers of women.

The Task Force also recommended that the government develop a community-release strategy that would expand and strengthen residential and nonresidential programs and services for federally sentenced women on release. These facilities are to be developed by community groups and other interested agencies, including halfway houses, Aboriginal centres, satellite units, home placements, addiction-treatment centres, multi-use women's centres, mixed-group housing, and mother and childcare centres *(Ibid:* 152-153). In response to this proposal, the Ministry of the Solicitor

General recently opened a minimum-security institution for female offenders in Kingston to provide inmates with the opportunity to prepare for release into the community (Pale Green Paper on Correctional Reform, 1990:39). A community approach allows women prisoners the use of services and programs available in the community, since it does not attempt to duplicate these costly services in the institution. This proposal would be particularly beneficial to women prisoners who have historically had a difficult time acquiring funding and resources for programming and treatment services. The mobilization of community resources provides the distinct advantage "in providing community-based services to offender, including better access to community resources, a greater ability to involve the local community in program initiatives, and the capacity to provide services beyond those mandated by the government" (Ekstedt and Griffiths, 1988:276). Overall, proposals with respect to women's imprisonment in Canada seem to be following the broader trend toward "community-based corrections. "

The Ministry of the Solicitor General of Canada endorsed these proposals and announced that the Prison for Women shall be closed by 1994. According to the federal government and the Canadian Association of Elizabeth Fry Societies, these recommendations have received a tremendous amount of community support and enthusiasm.

A fundamental precondition for successful reform for women prisoners is the recognition that their life experiences are different from those of men. To effectively deal with the female offender, we must recognize and challenge our assumptions of punishment. Furthermore, we must be aware of the fact that the very

structure and fabric of Corrections Canada, the basic definitions, working tools, mechanisms, and philosophies, policies, methodologies, and procedures that form the backbone and flesh of our penological system have all without exception been born, raised, and sometimes died, male (Berzins and Cooper, 1982:405).

Not only is the structure of our penal system inherently male, it is also, to a great extent, culturally ignorant and intolerant. Penological reforms must acknowledge, without exploiting, the existence of gender and cultural differences that are defined by the social, political, and economic structures of our society. Only recently have attempts been made to address these crucial issues of women's imprisonment. In spite of the Task Force's recommendations, however, almost all of the problems facing Canadian women prisoners remain unresolved. If Correctional Services Canada again fails to convert the Task Force's proposals into a plan for action, the apathy and neglect that have characterized Canadian women's prisons for over a century will continue.

**Notes**

1. See Hatch and Faith (1990: 432-456) and Johnson (1987) for more detailed statistical analysis of female offenders.

2. At present, research on the physical and sexual abuse of women prisoners is inconclusive. Most Canadian research in this area has used self-report data as a measure of abuse. No attempts have been made to independently verify and substantiate this research. As a result, current figures may underrepresent the extent of this tragedy.

3. The most recent (1990) litigation involving federally sentenced women is the Saskatchewan Court of Appeal case between the Attorney General of Canada and Carol Maureen Daniels. This case was sponsored by LEAF (Women's Legal Education and Action Fund). Ms.

Daniels is a Native woman convicted of murder. In the ruling of this case, the Court of Appeal overruled a lower-court order that placed a ban on imprisoning Saskatchewan women in the Prison for Women at Kingston. The lower-court ruling argued that sending women to the Prison for Women in Kingston was discriminatory and cruel and unusual punishment. They further indicated that this prison constituted a threat to the lives of the women and that it deprived them of their cultural and family ties.

4. Marlene Moore committed suicide at age 31 while serving her sentence in the federal Prison for Women in Kingston, Ontario, after many previous self-mutilations and suicide attempts. Many women have killed themselves in this frequently condemned prison, but none of their deaths has struck the same degree of horror as that of Marlene Moore. The book entitled *Rock-a-Bye Baby* (1991) by Anne Kershaw and Mary Lasovich tells the story of Marlene Moore's life and death in Canadian prisons.

5. A more detailed and comprehensive discussion of the recommendations proposed by the Task Force on federally sentenced women can be located in *Creating Choices* (1990). For this article, I have only summarized what I believe are the most significant recommendations with respect to the problems outlined by the research for the Task Force.

## References

- Adelberg, Ellen and Claudia Currie, (1987), *Too Few to Count: Canadian Women in Conflict with the Law*, Vancouver: Press Gang Publishers.
- Archambault Report, (1938), *Report of the Royal Commission to Investigate the Penal System in Canada* (Archambault Report).
- Axon, Lee, (1989), "*Model and Exemplary Programs for Female Inmates: An International Review,*" Ottawa: Ministry of the Solicitor General.
- Berzins, Lorraine and Sheelagh Cooper, (1982), "The Political Economy of Correctional Planning for Women: The Case of Bankrupt Bureaucracy." Canadian Journal of Criminology (October).
- Brown Commission, (1849), "Report of the Royal Commission to Inquire and Then Report upon the Conduct, Economy, Discipline, and Management of the Provincial Penitentiary" (The Brown Commission Report).
- Canadian Bar Association, (1988), "Justice Behind the Walls: Legislate to Compel Closure of Prison for Women." The Canadian Bar Association.
- Carlen, Pat, (1988), "*Women's Imprisonment: Current Issues.*" Prison Service Journal (April): 7-12.
- Cooper, Sheelagh, (1987) "*The Evolution of the Federal Women's Prison.*" Adelberg and Currie (eds.), *Too Few To Count: Canadian Women in Conflict with the Law.* Vancouver: Press Gang Publishers.
- Daubney Committee, (1988) *Report of the Standing Committee on Justice and Solicitor General on Its Review of Sentencing, Conditional Release, and Related Aspects of Corrections: Taking Responsibility* (Daubney Committee). Ottawa: Supply and Service.
- DeCostanzo, Elaine and Janet Valente, (1985) "Designing a Corrections Continuum for Female Offenders: One State's Experience." Prison Journal 64,1: 120-135.
- Edwards, Anne, (1989), "Sex/Gender, Sexism, and Criminal Justice: Some Theoretical Considerations." International Journal of Sociology of Law.
- Ekstedt, John and Curt Griffiths, (1988), *Corrections in Canada: Policy and Practice.* Toronto: Butterworths.
- Evans, Maureen, (1989) "*A Survey of Institutional Programs Available to Federally Sentenced Women.*" Ottawa: Ministry of the Solicitor General.
- Feinman, Clairice, (1980), "An Historical Overview of the Treatment of Incarcerated Women: Myths, Realities, and Rehabilitation." In Women in the Criminal Justice System.

- Griffiths, Curt and Simon Verdun-Jones, (1989), *Canadian Criminal Justice.* Toronto: Butterworths.
- Hatch, Alison and Karlene Faith, (1990), "The Female Offender in Canada: A Statistical Profile." Canadian Journal of Women and the Law 3,2: 432-456.
- Johnson, Holly, (1987), "Getting the Facts Straight: A Statistical Overview," Adelberg and Currie (eds. ), Too Few to Count: *Canadian Women in Conflict with the Law.* Vancouver: Press Gang Publishers.
- LaPrairie, Carol, (1987), "Native Women and Crime in Canada." In Adelberg and Currie (eds. ), Vancouver: Press Gang Publishers.
- MacGuigan, M. (Chair), (1977), *Report to Parliament by the Sub-Committee on the Penitentiary System in Canada* (MacGuigan Report). Ottawa: Supply and Services.
- MacLeod, Linda, (1986), *Sentenced to Separation: An Exploration of the Needs and Problems of Mothers Who are Offenders with Children.* Ottawa: Ministry of the Solicitor General.
- Morris, Allison, (1987), *Women, Crime, and Criminal Justice.* Oxford: Basil Blackwell.
- Moyer, Imogene (1985), "Deceptions and Realities of Life in Women's Prisons." Prison Journal 64, 1:45-56).
- Ouimet, R. (Chair), (1969), *Report of the Canadian Committee on Corrections* (Ouiment Report). Ottawa: Queen's Printer
- Pale Green Paper, (1990), *Directions for Reform Corrections and Conditional Release.* Ottawa: Ministry of the Solicitor General.
- Reid, Susan, (1985), "The Reproduction of Women's Dependence as a Factor in Treating the Female Offender." Canadian Criminology Forum 7 (Spring): 129-143.
- Report by Cassey, (1991), *Report of the Task Force on the Criminal Justice System and Its Impact on the Indian and Metis People of Alberta* (Cassey Report). Ottawa: Supply and Services (March).
- Report by Chinnery, (1978), *Report of the National Planning Committee on the Female Offender* (Chinnery Report). Ottawa: Solicitor General Canada.
- Report of the Macdonald Commission, (1914), *Report of the Royal Commission on Penitentiaries* (The Macdonald Commission). Ottawa: Ministry of the Solicitor General.
- Report of the Task Force on Federally Sentenced Women, (1990), *Creating Choices,* Ottawa: Ministry of the Solicitor General (April).
- Ross, Robert and Elizabeth Fabiano, (1985), *Correctional Afterthoughts: Progress for Female Offenders.* Ottawa: Ministry of the Solicitor General.
- Sargent, John, (1985), "Evolution of a Stereotype: Paternalism and the Female Inmate." Prison Journal 64,1.
- Shaw, Margaret et al. (1989), "Survey of Federally Sentenced Women." Prepared under contract for the Ministry of the Solicitor General Canada. Ottawa: Ministry of the Solicitor General.
- Smandych, Russell, (1991), "Beware of the Evil American Monster: Upper Canada Views on the Need for a Penitentiary, 1830-1834." Canadian Journal of Criminology (April): 125-147.
- Strange, Carolyn, (1985), "The Criminal and Fallen of Their Sex: The Establishment of Canada's First Women's Prison." Canadian Journal of Women and the Law 1:79-92.
- Sugar, Fran and Lana Fox, (1990a), "Nistum Peyako Seht' wawin Iskwewak: Breaking Chains. " Canadian Journal of Women and the Law 3,2: 465-483.
- 1990b, "Survey of Federally Sentenced Aboriginal Women in the Community." Prepared for the Native Women's Association of Canada for submission to the Task Force on Federally Sentenced Women (January).

- *Task Force on Aboriginal Peoples in Federal Corrections,* (1990), Final Report. Ottawa: Ministry of the Solicitor General.
- Women for Justice, (1980), "Brief to the Canadian Human Rights Commission." Ottawa: Women for Justice.

## Bibliography
See Bibliography following Chapter 4.1

## Questions/Discussion
1. According to the Correctional Law Review the public has a right to expect that its taxes are being spent effectively to provide criminal justice and protection. What evidence does the Review consider in determining whether this goal is being met?
2. To what extent could some Canadian prisoners be said to be "political prisoners"?
3. Further to the Moffatt article, the current plan is to close the Prison for Women and transfer all the inmates to the new regional centres by the fall of 1996. Greater urgency was added to the situation with the April, 1996, release of the report by Louise Arbour on the 1994 use of a male riot squad which was called into the women's prison to put down a disturbance. The subsequent treatment of the inmates (which included strip-searches) was condemned in the report and it was recommended that such squads never again be used in women's prisons. Other recommendations included compensation for the inmates involved, making the correctional service more accountable and subject to greater public scrutiny, and better access by inmates to the courts.

## Further Reading
- Ekstedt J. & Griffiths C., *Corrections in Canada: Policy and Practice* (Toronto: Butterworths, 1988).
- Brannigan, A., *Crimes, Courts and Corrections* (Toronto: Holt, Rinehart and Winston, 1984).
- Cohen, S., *Visions of Social Control* (Cambridge: Polity Press, 1985).
- Lowman, John, "Images of Discipline in Prison" in Neil Boyd, ed., *The Social Dimensions of Law* (Toronto: Prentice-Hall, 1986).
- Lowman, J. and B. MacLean, "Prisons and Protest in Canada" (1991), 18 Social Justice 130.

# 5

# SENTENCING AND PAROLE

**Introduction**

There is little consensus on solutions to problems in the sentencing process; what is agreed upon is that there are a great many problems in the area and that few solutions have been successful to date. The principal problem is usually stated as being one of disparity, the fact that there may be a great deal of difference between the sentences which are given to two separate individuals who commit the same crime and in the same circumstances. It is not that all types of disparity are wrong. For example, when cases are not alike, there might be very good reasons to attach different sentences to the convictions. It is only when the cases are virtually the same that the question of unfairness arises. This is not to say that all factors determine the "sameness" of a case. The fact that the offender's eyes may be different colours would not be a relevant difference, while the previous criminal records of the individuals may be. The questions, therefore, are what are the causes of the unwarranted and unfair disparity which does occur in this country and how can it be reduced. These questions, among others, are addressed in the excerpts from the article by Jobson and Ferguson. The article by Roberts and Von Hirsch addresses the matter of statutory sentencing principles and Bill C-41 which was passed by Parliament in June, 1995 (though it has yet to be proclaimed). The three cases which follow deal with various aspects of sentencing in the courts: *Hollinsky* examines the application of sentencing principles to a particular fact situation; *Shropshire* looks at the relevant principles guiding a judge in extending parole ineligibility in the case of second degree murderers; and, finally, *Morin* sets out the criteria which should guide the courts in the use of "sentencing circles", a relatively new device being employed in the sentencing of aboriginal offenders.

Another problem in sentencing is the type and severity of punishment which is given out. Canada has one of the highest incarceration rates in the world, and yet it is a self-evident fact that prisons do little but brutalize and harden those who have been put into them. The rates of homicide, sexual assault, assault, and suicide within prisons are very high, but there is little concern or interest on the part of the general population. There is an attitude that those who are imprisoned deserve everything they get, in spite of the argument that most of those imprisoned are not convicted of violent offences. For example, the profile of those in federal prisons, that is, those institutions which presumably house those convicted of the most serious offences, indicates that only 35 percent of the inmates have been convicted for violent offences. In fact, the public overestimates the amount of violent crime generally, as documented in the Report of the Sentencing Commission (see Further Reading). The simple fact is that prisons do not work, and yet the courts and legislators continue to turn to them as a solution.

The issues surrounding parole in section 2 are closely linked to those of sentencing. Disparity relates not only to the sentences which are given by the judge, but also to the actual sentence which is ultimately served. This is because the parole authorities have a great deal of discretion as to the amount of time which an offender spends in custody. Release on full parole can be granted after only one-third of the sentence has been served, and day parole can come after one-sixth of the sentence has been served. The first reading in section two briefly describes the various kinds of conditional release which currently exist. As a result of this system of release, the fact is " . . . that most people given custodial sentences serve between one- and two-thirds of their sentence in custody" (Sentencing Commission, p. 66). How this discretion is exercised by the parole authorities can therefore have a very great effect on the actual time spent in custody. The factors which go into the exercise of this discretion are critically examined in Mandel's article. The case of *Gallichon* deals with the situation of a person sentenced to "preventive detention" and his challenge to this regime in the Criminal Code. The final case of *Cunningham* deals with a challenge to the 1986 amendments to the *Parole Act* which allowed the authorities to keep persons in prison after the time set for their statutory release (after serving two thirds of their sentences). These amendments were incorporated into the *Corrections and Conditional Release Act*, S.C. 1992, c. 20, which replaced various pieces of correctional legislation, including the *Parole Act*. The legislation sets "protection of society" as the paramount consideration in any conditional release decision.

## 5.1 SENTENCING

### Toward a Revised Sentencing Structure for Canada*
*Keith Jobson & Gerry Ferguson*

* Excerpts from (1987), 66 Canadian Bar Review 1.

### INTRODUCTION

On an average day, about one in every 670 Canadians is in prison. Who are these people, and why are they there? What have they done to deserve the most drastic sanction available? Is it necessary that more that 25,000 adults be imprisoned on any given day at an estimated annual cost of one-half billion dollars in order to make our society a better and safer place? What purposes do we seek to achieve through imprisonment, and at what risk and cost? Most people would agree that prison is the only realistic sentence for those who commit serious offences against the person, but is imprisonment necessary in less serious cases? If not, how are we to determine when imprisonment is necessary? What principles or factors of a legal, social or economic nature should influence the questions of who goes to prison and for how long?

Every society must eventually confront these difficult questions in a conscious, rational way. A point is reached where the available evidence begins to suggest that the old ways may not be the best or the only ways. Over the past ten years, the Law Reform Commission of Canada has produced various publications addressing the critical questions of the role of criminal law in our society and the place of imprisonment in our sentencing structure. This work and analysis have stimulated discussion and debate. The Department of Justice, for example, has released policy papers, and building on the work of the Commission, introduced proposed amendments to the Criminal Code relating to sentencing policy and practice. Meanwhile, the Canadian Sentencing Commission was set up with a broad mandate to examine Canadian sentencing policies and practices and to make recommendations.

This mandate is especially relevant considering the potential impact the Canadian Charter of Rights and Freedoms may have on sentencing. Section 7 of the Charter guarantees the right to life, liberty, and security of the person and the right not to be deprived thereof except in accordance with the principles of fundamental justice. Under section 1, limitations on this or other Charter rights are valid only if they are reasonable limits which are prescribed by law and can be justified in a free and democratic society. The guarantee under section 15 to equality before and under the law, and the recitation in the Preamble that our legal system is founded upon the rule of law, are also of obvious relevance to Canadian sentencing law.

Even prior to the Charter, the Supreme Court of Canada emphasized the importance of certain fundamental values in the administration of justice including a widely held revulsion against convicting or punishing the morally innocent. The court recently reaffirmed this principle, explaining that it is founded upon a belief in the dignity and worth of the human person and on the rule of law. In other recent Charter cases, the Supreme Court has referred to the principle of proportionality as a standard to be applied in assessing whether legislative provisions, in curtailing a protected liberty, have gone beyond what is necessary. The court noted that it is relevant to ask whether the state could achieve its legislative aim through less intrusive measures.

In light of these Charters considerations, it is our thesis that the relationship between proportionality, the restraint principle, and the retributive principle of "just deserts" is of critical importance and lends further urgency to the necessary task of reforming our sentencing laws. In this article we will briefly address the current problems with Canada's sentencing laws, focusing on the issue of imprisonment and its relationship to a fair and rational sentencing framework. We will then turn to a consideration of our proposals for reform, which include reclassification of offences, creation of "benchmark" sentences, abolition of parole and creation of a permanent Sentencing Commission.

Our approach proceeds on the assumption that Canadian sentencing policy should be rational and consistent with Canadian values. Victim and community relationships to sentencing cannot be ignored. Moreover, sentencing reform cannot proceed in a legal vacuum, ignoring research results or failing to relate those results to principles and practice. Account must be taken of the reality that sentencing is but one part of a legal process that starts with the apprehension of offenders and the laying of charges, and continues through plea bargaining and trials, convictions and sentencing, and the supervision and administration of those sentences, including parole and remission. Finally, Canada's sentencing policies and practices should be understandable, clear, fair and equitable.

. . . .

## OVERVIEW OF RECENT PROPOSALS

In its working paper, Principles of Sentencing and Disposition, the Law Reform Commission of Canada asserted that a primary value in sentencing is respect for the dignity of persons. Presumably this value implies that sentencing policy ought not to use individuals only as a means to some identifiable public "good" but rather must treat them as autonomous ends, as persons capable of choice and accountable for their actions.

Sentencing, suggested the Commission, should be based on the "just deserts" principle of righting the wrong. This principle, however, was not to be relied on absolutely; thus, where it could be shown that punishment did not serve any useful end, condemnation and punishment should not be imposed. In this sense the Commission suggested a "just deserts" theory of punishment conditioned upon a preliminary premise that punishment serves to prevent or reduce crime:

> Thus, there are two bases upon which to justify an initial invention by criminal law and sentencing: the common good and the sense of justice which demands that a specific wrong be righted. In other words, state intervention to deprive offenders of their property or freedom may be justified on a theory of justice according to which the wrong done ought to be righted. It would seem, however, that as a preliminary justification, it should be shown that state intervention would serve the common good; otherwise it could be said that men should be subject to sanctions, even though such sanctions appear useless ...
> Justice, on the other hand, in focusing on the wrong done and the need to restore the rights of the victims, provides an opportunity to individualize the sentence and to emphasize the need for reconciliation between the offender, society and the victim. Thus, within the context of a sentence which reflects the gravity of the harm done and is humane, there is room for restitution and rehabilitation.

For all practical purposes, then, the Commission suggested that in sentencing, "just deserts" be the operational principle with the gravity of the offence and the culpability of the offender determining the severity of punishment. It is a sentencing policy under which "just deserts" governs the quantum of punishment as well as its distribution. The imposition of imprisonment, then, was to be governed by some scale of punishment tied to the gravity of the offence and the culpability of the offender rather than to factors related to prevention or treatment. This "just deserts" philosophy is reflected in the Commission's Report on Dispositions and Sentences. Sentences serve to stigmatize and denounce, said the Commission, and must be proportionate to the harm done. At the same time, within these parameters the Commission urged restraint, reconciliation, and repairing the harm done. Proportionality, it should be noted, derives from a retributive principle of "just deserts"), but this principle is modified to some extent by the Commission's recommendation that in a limited number of cases sentencing power be used for protective purposes, and, specifically, to incapacitate the dangerous or to coerce obedience in cases of contempt of court. The principal purpose of imprisonment, said the Commission, was to denounce seriously grave conduct and, thus, to underline core values. Accordingly, it can be seen that the Commission recommended to Parliament a basically retributive position limited to some extent by a protective principle in a restricted class of cases.

The Commission's work was followed up by the Department of Justice as part of its criminal law review program. In its 1984 discussion paper, Sentencing, the Department stated that while the overall aim of sentencing is protection of the public, such protection could be achieved through a "just deserts" principle wherein the punishment fits the crime, or through incapacitation, deterrence, restitution or rehabilitation. In the end, the departmental paper did not choose between the competing retributivist (or "just desert's) philosophy and utilitarian counterparts. Some hint of preference for "just deserts" is indicated in the departmental paper, but in the end this principle is relegated to but one of a number of competing factors. This failure to set a priority among competing and disparate sentencing philosophies was reflected later in proposed sentencing amendments as set out in Bill C-19. Commendably, the Bill purported to include a statement of sentencing philosophy in the Criminal Code, presumably in the interests of fair notice to the public for the better guidance of courts. The Bill could be interpreted as espousing a limited "just deserts" philosophy. Thus, while the Bill proposed that the ultimate goal of sentencing be protection, it contemplated that such a goal could be achieved in a number of ways, namely through (1) imposing "just sentences", (2) incapacitation of offenders, (3) deterrence (both specific and general), (4) redress for victims, and (5) providing opportunities for offenders to become law abiding.

While such a statement, without more, might be regarded simply as an invitation to anarchy in sentencing purposes, this criticism was forestalled by the Bill imposing restrictions on discretion to pursue any or all of the above aims. In particular the Bill stated that any sentence had to be:

(1) proportionate to the gravity of the offence and the degree of responsibility of the offender for the offence and any other aggravating or mitigating circumstances;
(2) similar to other sentences imposed on other offenders under like circumstances; and
(3) the least onerous disposition appropriate under the circumstances.

By virtue of these limitations the operational sentencing policy was for all intents and purposes one of "just deserts". This effect was reinforced by other provisions of the Bill prohibiting imprisonment solely for purposes of rehabilitation. Lingering doubts about the overall philosophy were corroborated, however, by further statements in the Bill that imprisonment could be used either "to protect" society or to reflect the gravity of the offence. As it turned out Bill C-19 died on the order paper, but its very existence attested to the serious questioning of sentencing principles and practices in Canada.

Sentencing reforms in the United States in recent years also generated substantial debate over the re-emergence of "just deserts" as the primary goal of sentencing. At the core of legislative reforms in Minnesota, Washington, Illinois, New Jersey, and California is the priority to be given to "just deserts" as opposed to rehabilitation. At the same time, Illinois has enacted a sentencing framework that ostensibly aims at "determinate" imprisonment, without parole. In other sentencing reforms, Maine has abolished parole, and the United States federal criminal law reforms affirm the importance of "just punishment" and the need for the sentence to reflect the seriousness of the offence and promote respect for the law. The United States Supreme Court, too, has said in the context of capital punishment cases that punishment serves retributive purposes.

## CURRENT SENTENCING FRAMEWORK AND POLICY

### *Origins*

Our current sentencing scheme was not originally derived from the realities of modern life in Canadian society. It was adapted, with little alteration or discussion, from an English model during the colonial period: Stephen's English Draft Code of 1879. Following that model, every offence, no matter how minor, may be dealt with by imprisonment. The maximum terms of life, fourteen, ten, five, two years and six months in prison, in the Criminal Code, can be traced to nineteenth century legislation and penal practices in England. There, during the first half of the last century, the death penalty was prescribed for a wide range of offences including some which were relatively trivial, such as theft of a sheep. The harshness of this regime was mitigated to some extent through administrative action. For example, in England in 1717, and later, in the Canadian colonies, officials could arrange the commutation of death sentences, on condition that the person consent to be transported for fourteen years, or such other term as specified, to penal work in various English colonies. Over time the most common terms to which the offender could be transported to work in penal servitude were life, twenty-one, fourteen or seven years. This administrative practice was later reflected in legislation permitting judicial sentences of transportation. Still later, in England in the 1840s, after transportation was abolished, sentences of imprisonment (penal servitude) were introduced with terms of fourteen or seven years. Preference for penal terms of life, fourteen, ten and seven years was reflected in colonial legislation and in the current Code.

The Canadian colonies also retained the English distinction of imprisonment for less than two years in a local prison and sentences of more than two years in "penal servitude" in a penitentiary. The reason for the distinction was that conditions in local prisons, in England, as documented by John Howard, were thought to be so bad that it was considered inhumane to keep people in them for longer than two years. As a result, those serving longer sentences were sent to a "penitentiary", where it was believed that conditions were more humane. By the 1830s, English legislation authorizing penal servitude (imprisonment in excess of three years) was being copied into Canadian colonial statute books. With Confederation, in 1867, criminal law became a federal matter, along with penitentiaries, but terms of less than two years were to be served in provincially controlled prisons.

The first real break from English legislation, but not English values and ideas, came in 1892, when Sir John Thompson presented the Canadian Parliament with a Code of Criminal Law. This Code was based closely on the English Draft Code of 1879 which drew heavily on the existing statutory law of England at the time. Stephen's Draft Code, however, abolished the common law classification of offences as felonies and misdemeanours and replaced it with a classification of indictable and summary conviction offences. The terms of imprisonment in Sir John Thompson's Code of 1892 drew on English and pre-Confederation Canadian colonial statutes. The sentencing provisions of the Code were adopted by the Canadian Parliament with little discussion or debate. Over the years sentencing provisions have been amended to provide for probation and conditional discharges; parole was added on. Still, the 1892 Code remains basically unchanged today in its classification and sentencing structure.

### *Characteristic Features*

The current sentencing structure, including classification of offences, is scattered in legislation, case law, and administrative regulation and practice. The Criminal Code, as indicated, provides the basic framework by allocating the more severe punishments to the more serious offences according to a scale of proportionality. Appeals against sentence by both Crown and defence have been provided for since 1925. Such appeals are based on whether or not the sentence imposed is "fit", a retributivist principle. The Code sets out a maximum punishment for each offence based on the worst imaginable case; thus, robbery is punishable by life imprisonment. The very high maximum punishments provide no real guidance for judges in dealing with the average case. In a few selected offences the Code or other federal statutes set out mandatory minimum punishments. No guidelines or factors are included in the Code to indicate when imprisonment as opposed to a non-carceral sentence is appropriate, nor is there guidance as to an appropriate range of sentence in the "average" or "normal" case.

While the 1892 Code could be recognized for its unmistakably retributivist and deterrent features, legislative changes in 1921, authorizing probation as a sentence for first offenders, added a rehabilitative element and this was strengthened by enactment of the Parole Act in 1958. Under the Act, in the interest of rehabilitation and protection of society, all sentences of imprisonment were eligible for modification by possibility of early release on parole supervision. Thus, the original architecture of the sentencing framework was modified at the federal level by rehabilitative assumptions, just as it had been modified at the provincial level in earlier years by rehabilitative correctional programs facilitated by the provisions of the Prisons and Reformatories Act. It is characteristic that the Code does not contain an express statement of sentencing philosophy. Apart from an express reference to "rehabilitation" and "public protection" in the Parole Act and reformist principles in the Prison and Reformatories Act, sentencing policy under the Code is implicitly retributivist, but express policy has been left to the discretion of the judges and the enunciation of principles on a case by case basis.

Case law states that sentencing principles include protection of society through rehabilitation, deterrence, incapacitation, denunciation and retribution. This eclectic approach, endorsing a range of philosophies and principles, has gained the support of all ten courts of appeal in the various provinces, at different times and to different degrees. How helpful is such a broadly based approach in giving guidance to the sentencing judge? Various courts of appeal have said that no single principle is overriding and that the sentencing court must balance the principles and related factors in any given case. Notwithstanding the direction that the principles are to be "balanced" in any given case, it is also clear from the cases that rehabilitation and factors relevant to it are basically used only to mitigate punishment in appropriate cases; rehabilitation is not used as a principle to override proportionality. Support for rehabilitation as a sentencing principle has been strongest in Ontario, and was probably influenced by the growth of rehabilitative assumptions in prisons and "corrections" in the 1950s and 1960s in that province and elsewhere. As an illustration of the thinking of the times, the prestigious Ouimet Committee, reporting in 1969, rejected "just deserts" (or retribution as it was referred to then) as a sentencing principle in these words:

> The primary purpose of sentencing is the protection of society. Deterrence, both general and particular, through knowledge of penalties consequent upon prohibited acts; rehabilitation of the individual offender into a law abiding citizen; confinement of the dangerous offender as long as he is dangerous, are a major means of accomplishing this purpose. Use of these means should, however, be devoid of any connotation of vengeance or retribution.

In the years following the Ouimet report, however, the rehabilitative ideal and other utilitarian assumptions began to crumble in the light of social science research showing limited human capacity to reform, rehabilitate or deter, and the destructive and costly effects of prisons. In this context of changing perceptions and increased awareness of the immorality of punishing persons not because they deserved it, but because they served as convenient examples to others, the Law Reform Commission of Canada affirmed the role of the criminal court as an instrument of "doing justice" rather that "social engineering".

More recently, some courts of appeal have frankly and expressly announced that the governing principle in sentencing is now to be seen as retributive: let the punishment fit the crime. Thus, some courts at least have affirmed a priority for the principle that punishment cannot be excessive, and that it must be proportionate to the gravity of the offence and the culpability of the offender. There is, then, an observable cycle from retributivist principles to rehabilitative and incapacitative assumptions back to retribution.

The current framework, characterized by uneven offence descriptions, ranks offences according to a scale of seriousness, with very high statutory maxima. Thus punishment is left to the broad discretion of the judge, guided by such direction as offered through the case law. Sentencing practices are also affected by broad prosecutorial discretion to select charges and broad parole discretion to release on supervision. As can be expected, in the absence of a clearly articulated sentencing policy, the current framework has given rise to various criticisms. It is said that the high statutory maxima are productive of inequity and disparity in sentencing and are misleading.

A further feature of current sentencing policy is that, for all practical purposes, sentencing law is inaccessible and unknowable to the ordinary person except through the help of experienced lawyers. Should sentencing policy make it possible for the ordinary person to know what the average or "normal" sentences in given offences are, as opposed to the statutory maxima sentences? From the reported cases one would hope to be able to determine the "normal" range of punishments in the more common cases taken on appeal such as robbery, but, unfortunately, only a limited number of sentencing decisions are taken on appeal and few are reported. In some provinces a more extensive publication of sentencing decisions from the courts of appeal is available through a report series providing a short summary of the outcome. The most reliable information on what are the "normal" or "usual" sentences in any given offence is picked up by lawyers practising before the courts; such information is not accessible in any printed form to the general public. Indeed, the "usual" sentence will vary from one part of the province to another and from one part of the country to another. A new judge in a particular county or district will want to inquire beforehand how much a moose is worth and whether it is worth more than two pheasants; that is, what are the outer limits of punishment in typical cases and how do they relate to other offences, proportionately. As already indicated, the normal range of punishments is very much lower that the maximum punishments set out in the Code.

A further characteristic of the present sentencing framework is the degree to which prosecutorial discretion affects sentencing outcomes. For example, police and crown prosecutors in laying or reviewing the charge will sometimes have an option between laying a charge which carries a mandatory sentence of imprisonment upon conviction and one which does not. Should the offender be charged, for example, with importing a narcotic or simply with possession for the purpose of trafficking, the former carrying a minimum seven year term, the latter providing for discretionary imprisonment or even a suspended sentence? Similarly, an offence may be "hybrid", one which allows the charging official to choose between charging by way of a summary conviction (with a maximum of six months imprisonment), or proceeding upon indictment where the maximum term will be two, five, ten or fourteen years as provided in the particular offence. For example, everyone who commits mischief in relation to public property can be charged on summary conviction (maximum punishment being up to a $2,000 fine or six months imprisonment, or both) or charged with an indictable offence (maximum punishment being fourteen years). Thus the Crown prosecutors have a large discretion to affect sentencing through the power conferred upon them by these "hybrid" offences. Since such discretion is not reviewable any may not even be subject to internal administrative guidelines, any future sentencing and classification scheme should seriously consider whether these "hybrid" offences should be continued.

## CURRENT PROBLEMS

Given that there is no clear statement of policy and a want of accessible guidelines and precedents in Canadian sentencing law, that the judiciary and prosecution are obliged to exercise the broad discretion which that law confers on them in the absence of a coherent philosophical basis, and that we still rely for the most part on a system of crime classification that dates back to Colonial days, it is not surprising that a number of serious problems plague the present Canadian sentencing process. With the adoption of the Charter as part of the supreme law of the land, Canada has entered an era where charges of arbitrariness, disparity, inequity and vagueness will receive strict scrutiny. The various aspects of this nation's sentencing law which contribute to its present unsatisfactory state have been analyzed by us extensively elsewhere. Hence, these problems will here by given only such brief mention as is required to lay the foundations for the central focus of this paper: our discussion of reform proposals.

### Mandatory Punishment

A number of statutory provisions in Canadian law compel our courts to impose a prescribed minimum punishment in the event of conviction of certain offences. Whether they manifest themselves in absolute liability offences, where the accused is denied an opportunity to justify his or her breach of the law, or are of the nature such as section 5(2) of the Narcotic Control Act, where on conviction of the charge the court must impose seven years of imprisonment, such provisions raise serious issues on both a constitutional and a practical level.

. . . .

### Excessive Punishment

Several factors contribute to the problem of excessive punishment. First, many of the maximum penalties set by statute are historically high. In various offences, in practice, the actual punishments imposed are so far from these maximum penalties that the latter are rendered useless as guidelines. Second, the present system of ranking punishments in terms of such maxima contributes to the problem. The need for review is apparent in many provisions. For example, do we agree that forgery of passports (punishable by up to fourteen years) is a more serious crime than assault causing bodily harm (punishable by no more than 10 years)? Related to these issues is the matter of uneven offence descriptions. A number of offences are described in very broad terms. Take, for example, robbery. Is it realistic to leave open the possibility of a life sentence in all cases of robbery? A better approach would be to categorize that crime into, perhaps, three offences, simple robbery, armed robbery and aggravated armed robbery, with different terms for each.

Finally, excessive punishment results from the judicial tendency to impose prison terms in many cases where imprisonment is inappropriate. Until such time as statutory guidance is provided to assist the judiciary in determining what types of cases warrant imprisonment as opposed to probation, fines and other less intrusive penalties, the unnecessary over-crowding of Canadian jails will no doubt continue. Of course, some would argue that the imposition of guidelines would unduly fetter the courts' present ability to individualize punishment. But as it stands today, the Code does more than permit the individualization of treatment of offenders; it encourages sentencing anarchy. Since some appellate courts generally defer to the sentence prescribed by a court of first instance unless the sentence is illegal, the offender who has been subjected to individualized punishment that is apparently excessive may be without remedy. This is particularly the case given the underfunding of legal aid and the very conservative approach by legal aid societies to the funding of sentence appeals.

## *Disparity*

Quite apart from ethical concerns relating to the justice of individualized sentencing, sections 7 and 15 of the Charter call into question the constitutionality of excessive disparity. Although it may be argued that no two cases are alike, wide disparity in the sentences given to offenders who commit virtually the same offence cannot be supported solely on the basis of "individualized" justice. Indeed, the typical factors taken into account in "individualizing the sentence", namely, the personality of the offender, the likelihood of recidivism and the circumstances of the offence, may have little to do with the harshness of the sentence. Instead, the skill of the defence counsel in negotiating a plea bargain or in representing an accused in a sentencing hearing, or whether counsel are involved at all, are believed to be far more weighty factors in obtaining lenient sentences.

## *Lack of Fair Notice*

In *R. v. Robson* the British Columbia Court of Appeal proposed the following test of what constitutes fair notice: does the law serve to give a person of ordinary intelligence fair notice of what is forbidden? It is suggested here that fair notice extends even further; that it should include notice not only of the conduct that is forbidden, but also the consequences of conviction for such conduct. The wide discretion and high statutory maximum terms which prevail in present offence provisions do not fulfil this latter requirement. In light of the wide disparity of sanctions which are imposed for many crimes, can it be said that the law is accessible and capable of being understood by ordinary persons in the criminal courts; or are the law and the outcome too frequently inaccessible to them — another institutional mystery?

## Parole

It is our conclusion that parole and remission laws are complex, inaccessible and unknowable. In fact, since parole and remission laws do not set firm standards for release, revocation or suspension, it might even be said that parole is not governed by law at all in many cases. Briefly, the parole-remission system may be explained as follows.

In practice, while remission is to be "earned", offenders are credited by law with "good time" to a maximum of one-third of the term of imprisonment, subject to its being taken away for various reasons. Originally, at the two-thirds mark of the sentence, with full credit for good behaviour, the prisoner was discharged and the sentence legally ended. This is still the case for prisoners serving sentences of less than two years in those provinces which do not have a provincial parole board, and for all prisoners serving less that three months regardless of what province they are in. Inmates of federal institutions (sentences of two years or more) and those serving more than three months in Ontario, Quebec and British Columbia, however, are subject to a more complex agreement because of the parole system.

Generally, inmates are eligible for consideration for parole at the one-third mark of their sentences. Exceptions exist where minimum parole eligibility is prescribed by statute (for example, twenty-five years in first degree murder), or where parole regulations state otherwise (one half of sentence or seven years, whichever is the lesser, must be served for certain violent offences). The Parole Act provides that where parole is not granted before the expiry of two-thirds of the sentence the prisoner shall be released under mandatory supervision. The result is that what is legally prescribed as remitted time may be required to be spent under the watchful eyes of parole authorities. Further, these authorities are given the power to revoke or suspend parole or mandatory supervision for a wide number of reasons. If this is done, offenders frequently lose the benefit of what good time they have earned. The problem of calculating the correct release date in some cases is so complex that even the prison sentence administrator may be unsure and the courts are bewildered by the complexity. Such uncertainty and, arguably, arbitrary processes offend the principles of fundamental fairness.

## Dangerous Offenders

Sections 687 and following of the Criminal Code permit the Crown prosecutor to seek a special hearing following the conviction of a person of a "serious personal injury offence". At that hearing, a determination of whether the person is a dangerous offender may be made. If the court concludes that the person is dangerous as defined by the Code, it may impose an order of preventive detention for life. Recent challenges to these provisions as contrary to the Charter guarantee against arbitrary detention or imprisonment (section 9) have been unsuccessful. However, the Supreme Court of Canada has yet to rule on their constitutionality.

We are of the opinion that sentencing provisions must address the incarceration of particularly dangerous individuals. However, the present Code provisions and the application of those provisions raise serious concerns. It must be noted that the reliability of predictions of dangerousness is far from accurate, and further, that the provisions are presently applied in a very inconsistent fashion. Webster and Dickens point out that of the thirty-two dangerous offenders who had been sentenced to preventive detention at the date of their study, eighteen were in Ontario. The apparent reluctance of courts in some provinces to use the provisions, the excessive length of the indeterminate term, and the need for a periodic judicial review of such sentences require a re-examination of the Code provisions. A preferable approach, in our view, is to be found by turning to the Netherlands. There, a five year term, reviewable and renewable every five years, was used for several years, apparently with satisfactory results. A system similar to that appears far more desirable than the current system which imposes a life sentence subject only to uncertain parole release authorized under vague criteria.

### Role of the Victim

Another problematic aspect of the Canadian sentencing process is its failure to address the role of the victim. Historically, victims played a large part in the system. They brought a charge and reparation orders were a common sentencing feature. Today, however, criminal charges are generally a prosecutorial concern, and punishments are comprised primarily of imprisonment, fines and probation orders. Some movement has been made toward giving victims some recognition in pilot projects where victim impact statements are heard at the time of sentencing as well as in the conditions judges attach to probation orders. Still, the majority of victims remain a peripheral concern of the system. The extant sentencing structure does little to address the injury suffered by those against whose person and property crimes are committed. It is an inherent feature of our proposed "just deserts" model for punishment that attempts be made through sentencing to repair the harm done by offenders.

. . . .

## Statutory Sentencing Reform: The Purpose and Principles of Sentencing*
### Roberts, J. and A. von Hirsch

* Excerpts from (1995), 37 *Criminal Law Quarterly* 220.

### 1. INTRODUCTION

Sentencing reform has been advocated for many years now, by academics, criminal justice practitioners, advocacy groups, members of the public and the news media.[1] One of the reasons for this continued interest in sentencing has been the succession of commissions of inquiry and government reports that have examined the topic and recommended reform.[2] Sentencing reform now seems at hand: in June, 1994, the federal government introduced Bill C-41, "An Act to amend the Criminal Code (sentencing) and other Acts in consequence thereof", which is likely to pass into law in 1995. This bill is the successor to Bill C-90, which represented the federal government's rather belated response to two landmark reports, one by the Canadian Sentencing Commission[3] (released in 1987) and the other by the House of Commons Standing Committee on Justice and Solicitor General (the Daubney Committee) in

1988.[4] The process of parliamentary review of Bill C-90 was brought to a premature conclusion within a month and the mandate of the government expired shortly thereafter. The new Bill (Bill C-41) received 2nd Reading on October 18, 1994, and was referred to the Standing Committee on Justice and Legal Affairs. At the time of publication hearings are expected to be held in the near future. In light of the widespread interest in sentencing reform and the fact that the government is just beginning its mandate, Bill C-41 stands a very good chance of receiving passage in the spring of 1995. If a sentencing bill is passed it will constitute the first major statutory revisions to sentencing in many years.[5]

Bill C-41 would introduce several changes to the sentencing process. The bill provides the courts with more options to distinguish between serious violent offenders and less serious property offenders. As well, there are provisions to assist the victims of crime and proposals to ensure that offenders motivated by hate or who take advantage of a position of trust are dealt with more severely. The bill also creates a new disposition known as a conditional sentence. In this article we critically examine the most important component in Bill C-41: a statement regarding the purposes and principles of sentencing that would become part of the *Criminal Code*[6] of Canada. The reason for focusing upon the statement of purpose is that it could have far-reaching symbolic and practical effects upon the sentencing system. This is particularly true for this bill, since the government's sentencing reform initiative no longer contains a sentencing guideline scheme. Although federal government policy documents and ministerial statements have always included some form of guideline scheme (whether presumptive or merely advisory in nature), formal sentencing guidelines no longer appear to be part of the current sentencing reform initiative in Canada.

## 2. STATEMENT OF THE PURPOSE AND PRINCIPLES OF SENTENCING

The potential benefits of a statutory statement of the purpose(s) of sentencing are clear. At the present, in the absence of such a statement, judges are free to follow their own individual sentencing philosophies, which can vary greatly from case to case, and from judge to judge. And since sentencing means many things to different people, the result is a great deal of variation in both the choice and application of the various sentencing purposes. This alone must be responsible for a substantial amount of variation in sentencing practices across the country.[7] What is needed is a clear pronouncement from Parliament which would guide judges at the trial court level, and also the appellate courts across the country. It is a professed aim of Bill C-41 to provide such guidance.

. . .

The challenge to drafters of a statement of sentencing purpose and principle is to reconcile diverse and frequently conflicting sentencing aims. The task is not impossible, and nor does it necessarily mean promoting a single sentencing purpose at the expense of all others. Multi-purpose statements can still offer guidance and affect sentencing practices at the trial court level but they must specify the conditions under which certain aims are favoured over others. This section of the article will also necessitate some discussion of the utility of sentencing guidelines, for guidelines are the means by which a statement of purpose effects changes in sentencing practices.

The statement of purpose is the compass and guidelines the road map. Without the guidelines, judges know roughly where they are going but not necessarily how to get there. Without the statement, judges would be following instructions in the absence of a clear sense of over-all direction.

### (1) Bill C-41

The statement of purpose and principle contained in Bill C-41 is a hybrid containing elements of several previous proposals, notably those advanced by the Canadian Sentencing Commission and the Daubney Committee. This latest incarnation of a statement of the purposes of sentencing was the culmination of widespread consultation by the federal Department of Justice. It is unlikely then that a radically different statement of purpose will appear in the near future. In our view, while it is important to have a statutory statement, the proposal contained in Bill C-41 can be significantly improved.

. . . .

The statement of purpose proposed by Bill C-41[11] contains four elements: (i) A fundamental purpose of sentencing, which might be termed the *raison d'etre* of the whole process; (ii) a series of fully 10[12] objectives or goals, the fulfilment of which would promote the fundamental purpose of sentencing; (iii) a fundamental principle to limit, presumably, the influence of the objectives; and finally (iv) a series of five subordinate sentencing principles that interact with the fundamental principle. We shall discuss each element in turn (see Appendix A for the full text of the statement).

#### (a) The Fundamental Purpose of Sentencing

According to Bill C-41, the fundamental purpose of sentencing is to "contribute, along with crime prevention initiatives, to respect for the law and the maintenance of a just, peaceful and safe society by imposing just sanctions that have one or more of the following objectives".[13] We shall not dwell at length upon the fundamental purpose,[14] except to note that it draws upon, but is not the same as, the Canadian Sentencing Commission's proposed statement.[15] It is worth noting also that the language of the fundamental purpose reflects the dual nature of the whole statement, which incorporates elements of both the utilitarian and the retributivist traditions. By talking of "crime prevention initiatives" the statement raises the notion that a particular sentencing policy can have an important impact upon crime rates. At the same time, the phrase "just sanctions" clearly anticipates the principle of proportionality and sentencing according to a desert-based philosophy.

#### (b) The Objectives of Sentencing

According to the statement in Bill C-41, no matter what kind of sanction is selected by the judge, it must have at least one of the sentencing objectives specified in the bill. The statement enunciates 10 objectives that the "just sanctions" are designed to fulfil. These are the usual candidates that have been advanced over the years, namely: denunciation; individual deterrence; general deterrence; incapacitation; reparation to the individual; restitution to the community; the promotion of a sense of responsibility in offenders; acknowledgement of the harm done to victims; acknowledgement of the harm to communities, and the creation of opportunities to assist in the offender's rehabilitation. Since the judge may pick and choose from among this menu of sentencing purposes, the result is little more than a legislated statement of the status quo.

Whatever one's reaction to the fundamental purpose ascribed to the sentencing process by Bill C-41, there can be little disagreement that its role will be largely symbolic. It conveys a message that will have little *practical* impact in terms of sentencing practices. In contrast, the list of sentencing objectives is more instrumental than symbolic: it provides judges with a number of alternatives which may all lead to different dispositions. What it does not do, however is inform judges as to the conditions under which one objective should be privileged over the rest. No indication is provided to the sentencing judge as to when deterrence is appropriate, or when denunciation might take precedence of restitution or reparation.

An hypothetical example illustrates the difficulties. Consider a case of domestic violence in which a judge is about to impose sentence upon an offender convicted of assaulting his wife. The fundamental purpose of sentencing advocated by Bill C-41 prompts the judge to seek a just sentence, and then points him or her towards the specific objectives. Which of the 10 sentencing objectives is relevant in this particular case? Should the judge choose objective (a) ("to denounce unlawful conduct") and send the man to prison in order to convey a message that Canadian society will not tolerate spousal assault? Or should the offender be allowed to remain at liberty (and at home), provided he attends some form of counselling programme for husbands who assault their wives? If the latter objective is more appropriate, their objective (d) "to assist in rehabilitating offenders" is the relevant aim to be pursued. The choice provides judges with a dilemma that they are likely to resolve in their own individual way, as they have done in the past. The Bill C-41 formulation will not prove of much *practical* assistance to judges, for it fails to inform them of the conditions under which different sentencing purposes are appropriate. The likely consequence is that judges will continue to sentence as before and sentencing practices at the trial court level will not be affected.

### (c) The Fundamental Principle of Sentencing

The next section of the statement makes a sentencing judge's task still more complex. It contains a list of principles, in accordance with which the sentencing decision is to be taken. These principles include a fundamental principle — that of proportionality — and subordinate principles relating to the use of mitigating and aggravating factors, consistency in sentencing, totality, restraint and the use of incarceration. The fundamental principle states that: "A sentence must be proportionate to the gravity of the offence and the degree of responsibility of the offender."[16]

This straightforward expression of proportionality in sentencing is important and represents a clear departure from the current vacuum in the *Criminal Code*. By endorsing a fundamental principle of this nature, the drafters of Bill C-41 took a step towards making sentencing more consistent and philosophically coherent. In theory at least, this desert-based principle should limit the influence of the utilitarian sentencing objectives that precede it. Thus, a judge wishing to impose a severe, exemplary sentence to "send a message to others" will be restricted to the limits of a proportionate disposition. The imposition of disproportionately harsh or lenient sentences imposed in pursuit of some utilitarian goal (usually deterrence or rehabilitation) will be discouraged by this fundamental principle. In our view, the fundamental principle is the best part of the bill's proposed statement.

The weakness of this section of the proposed statement is that the fundamental principle is embedded within a lengthy statement and confined on two sides: first by the preceding 10 objectives, and second by the five subsequent principles. This gives rise to two problems. First, the influence of the principle of proportionality could be undermined by all these objectives. Second, there is no guidance provided for sentencing judges as to exactly how the objectives and principles affect the principle of proportionality, or how they relate to each other. Some articulation of the interrelationships between all these components is necessary; none is, in fact, provided.

### (d) Secondary Sentencing Principles

Three of the five principles are simply old bromides with which judges are already familiar. The first principle, for example, states that: "a sentence should[17] be increased or reduced to account for any relevant aggravating or mitigating circumstances relating to the offence or the offender...."[18] Since an important part of the process of determining the nature and quantum of punishment consists of evaluating relevant mitigating and aggravating factors, this principle is an enunciation of the obvious[19] and will come as little surprise to judges in Canada. The same can be said for principle (b) that "a sentence should be similar to sentences imposed on similar offenders for similar offences committed in similar circumstances".[20] This principle modestly strengthens the bill's statement on proportionality, by stating that there should be parity between the penalties assigned to offenders whose crimes are equally serious. Thus it has some degree of usefulness, in contrast to its predecessor, principle (a), which has little or no practical significance.[21]

The third principle (c) states that "where consecutive sentences are imposed, the combined sentence should not be unduly long or harsh".[22] This is a statutory enunciation of the totality principle, which the sentencing process has for some time articulated to prevent the imposition of excessively long sentences upon offenders convicted of multiple offences. Canadian Courts of Appeal have long provided guidance to trial court judges in this regard. Accordingly, few judges are unaware of the problem, or the solution that has evolved in Canada as well as England and Wales.[23] It is not clear why the principle needs to be enshrined in the *Criminal Code*.[24] The remaining two principles are more interesting, and in their final incarnation (as with other provisions of this bill) differ significantly from earlier formulations. They both relate to the issue of the over-use of incarceration in Canada.

### (i) Restricting the use of incarceration in Canada

The emphasis on incarceration as a sanction in Canada has been noted by many groups and individuals. Statistics have long demonstrated the high rates of imprisonment in this country. Comparison of international incarceration rates reveals that

Canada ranked third in the West (after the United States and Switzerland) with an incarceration rate of 92 per 100,000 population.[25] Accordingly, a fundamental policy goal supported by a wide constituency of experts has been effecting a reduction in Canada's reliance on incarceration as a sentencing option. Any sentencing bill should attempt to reduce, to the extent possible, the number and duration of sentences of imprisonment, particularly for non-violent offenders. In fact, this has been a stated aim of federal government policy for some time.[26] Bill C-41 attempts to restrict the use of imprisonment by means of principles (d) and (e).

*(ii) Principle of Restraint*

Principle (d) declares that "an offender should not be deprived of liberty, if less restrictive alternatives may be appropriate in the circumstances".[27] This is the principle of restraint, which has a long tradition in this country. As the Canadian Sentencing Commission noted in its report, restraint in the application of the criminal law is consistent with the position taken by every commission of inquiry in Canada from the Brown Commission[28] in the mid-19th century to the Nielsen Task Force that reported in 1986.[29] The notion of restraint is most closely associated with the work of the Law Reform Commission of Canada. However, earlier versions were far more general than the wording adopted in Bill C-41.

As formulated by the Law Reform Commission of Canada, the principle of restraint encompasses many aspects of the criminal law and is not restricted to the issue of sentencing. With relation to sentencing in particular, both the Law Reform Commission[30] and the Sentencing Commission argued that restraint should encompass *all* kinds of dispositions. Thus in the latter's proposed statement of sentencing purpose, the principle of restraint followed the paramount principle (that the sentence be proportionate to the gravity of the offence and the degree of responsibility of the offender) and was expressed in the following way: "a sentence should be the least onerous sanction appropriate in the circumstances".[31] Bill C-41 restricts the application of restraint to sentences of imprisonment. While it is important to affirm this principle in statutory form, in our view, the application used here is too narrow. Judges need to constantly question whether a less intrusive sanction would be appropriate if the law is to be truly faithful to the spirit of parsimony in sentencing. This means that if a discharge is appropriate, a fine should not be imposed, and so forth. The more restrictive wording contained in Bill C-41 is also a change from the Department of Justice policy document of 1990, which endorsed the exact wording of the Sentencing Commission's statement.[32]

*(iii) Alternatives to Incarceration*

Continuing the spirit of the preceding principle, the last principle (e) argues that "all available alternatives to imprisonment that are reasonable in the circumstances should be considered for all offenders, with particular attention to the circumstances of aboriginal offenders".[33]

### (iv) Imprisonment and Offenders from Visible Minorities

It has long been known that Canada's penal institutions contain a disproportionate number of aboriginal offenders. The most recent statistics from provincial correctional systems across the country show that almost one inmate in four is aboriginal. Over half of all admissions in some provinces such as Saskatchewan and Manitoba, are aboriginals.[34] It might seem churlish to criticize any attempt to redress this problem, but the issue of over-incarceration touches all kinds of offenders, not simply aboriginals.

Aboriginal Canadians are not the only visible minority that is over-represented in penal institutions. In fact, data from the province of Ontario show that the racial disproportion of blacks in the province's jails is far greater than that associated with aboriginals. Thus custodial admissions data for 1992-93 reveal that 16% of inmates admitted were black, compared to 6% for aboriginals.[35] Research is now accumulating that shows a sustained pattern of discrimination against blacks in the province's criminal justice system. It seems clear that Black inmates in the Province of Ontario are subject to negative treatment that is not accorded other categories of inmate.[36] Imprisonment also poses special problems for female offenders. The Daubney Committee reported a survey which found that over 80% of female inmates were mothers and over half of these were single parents. Incarceration clearly creates conditions of exceptional hardship for these categories of offenders, but Bill C-41 focuses exclusively on aboriginal offenders.

Will Bill C-41 accomplish its stated goal of curbing the use of incarceration as a sanction in Canada? Simply *suggesting* that judges consider other sentencing options is unlikely to have much impact upon sentencing practices across the country. In all probability, judges already consider alternatives to incarceration before they imprison offenders.[37] Bill C-41 should restrict judges from imposing imprisonment *unless specific conditions are met*. This would be the first step towards effective guidance. The second would consist of specific guidelines which would specify the kinds of cases and conditions that should give rise to different dispositions.[38]

The wording of Bill C-41's principle regarding incarceration represents a significant dilution of the original formulation. The discussion document published by the Department of Justice in 1990 followed a much stronger tack. It laid down specific conditions that *had* to be fulfilled *before* a sentence of imprisonment could be imposed.

The exclusionary nature of this 1988 document is modeled upon the Sentencing Commission's statement, but is to be found in formulations in other jurisdictions as well. For example, s. 1(2) of the English *Criminal Justice Act 1991* states:[39] the court shall not pass a custodial sentence on the offender unless it is of the opinion —

(a) that the offence, or the combination of the offence and one other offence associated with it, was so serious that only such a sentence can be justified for the offence; or

(b) where the offence is a violent or sexual offence, that only such a sentence would be adequate to protect the public from serious harm from him.

In contrast to both these formulations, Bill C-41 would permit judges considerably greater latitude in terms of imposing sentences of incarceration. In short, the diluting of the principle of restraint is a clear weakness of the statement. The imposition of sentences of imprisonment needs to be constrained to a substantially greater degree if any consequential impact upon incarceration rates to be achieved. This is particularly true since sentencing guidelines are no longer a part of the government's reform package. In the absence of guidelines, all hope of changing sentencing practices resides with the statement of purpose, which accordingly must be expressed in language that is both unequivocal and forceful.

*(v) Summary*

Would the statement of purpose proposed in Bill C-41 (in the words of the Minister's press release) provide "clear direction from Parliament on the purpose and principles of sentencing"? In our view, the answer is that with one exception, the proposed statement merely codifies themes that have evolved about the sentencing process and would not provide direction in the sense of giving judges a tool to promote consistency. The only practical advice for judges contained in the statement is to be found in the fundamental principle, which, it will be recalled, states that a sentence "must be proportionate to the gravity of the offence and the degree of responsibility of the offender". This may well constrain judicial behaviour. It will, in theory at least, discourage judges from imposing disproportionately harsh sentences to achieve deterrence, of disproportionately lenient sentences in order to promote the rehabilitation of the offender. The major hope of success for Bill C-41 lies with this fundamental principle.

The weakness of the over-all bill is that a rather confusing statement of purpose is all that is offered to effect changes in sentencing practices. This statement is the only means of giving life to the acknowledged policy goals of limiting unwarranted disparity and reducing the use of imprisonment as a sanction. It is unlikely to prove sufficient. If the statutory statement is the sole means of effecting change, then it should clearly specify the conditions under which certain sentencing options such as custody should be imposed. The statute contained in Bill C-41 closes off few options for the sentencing judge, and accordingly offers little *practical* guidance.

. . . .

[After formulating and discussing an alternate statute, the authors continued:]

## 3. CONCLUSIONS

The importance of a statutory statement of sentencing purpose and principle cannot be over-stated. Judges, criminal justice professionals and indeed all those with an interest in sentencing will look to such a document as a statement from Parliament about sentencing policy. The importance of the statement is enhanced in the Canadian context, because unlike other jurisdictions (such as the United States) sentencing reform in this country does not involve a formal guideline system. Thus the goals of reducing the use of incarceration, promoting proportionality in sentencing and reducing the amount of sentencing disparity must all be accomplished, in larger degree, by the statement of purpose. Finally, after so much time coming, a statement of sentencing purpose passed in 1995 is unlikely to be changed in the near future. Once legislation is passed, sentencing will disappear from the criminal justice radar screen for years to come. The attention of the criminal justice system will turn elsewhere and the opportunity for further reform will not arise again for some time. The statement of purpose that enters the *Criminal Code* as a result of this sentencing reform initiative is likely to remain with us for years. It is important that the best possible statement be drafted.

## APPENDIX A
## Bill C-41: Statement of Purpose and Principles of Sentencing

718. *The fundamental purpose of sentencing is to contribute, along with crime prevention initiatives, to respect for the law and the maintenance of a just, peaceful and safe society by imposing just sanctions that have one or more of the following objectives:*

*(a) to denounce unlawful conduct;*
*(b) to deter the offender and other persons from committing offences;*
*(c) to separate offenders from society, where necessary;*
*(d) to assist in rehabilitating offenders;*
*(e) to provide reparations for harm done to victims or to the community; and,*
*(f) to promote a sense of responsibility in offenders, and acknowledgement of the harm done to victims and to the community.*

718.1 *A sentence must be proportionate to the gravity of the offence and the degree of responsibility of the offender.*

718.2 *A court that imposes a sentence shall also take into consideration the following principles:*

*(a) a sentence should be increased or reduced to account for any relevant aggravating and mitigating circumstances relating to the offence or the offender, and without limiting the generality of the foregoing.*

  *(i) evidence that the offence was motivated by bias, prejudice or hate based on the race, nationality, colour, religion, sex, age, mental or physical disability or sexual orientation of the victim, or*
  *(ii) evidence that the offender, in committing the offence, abused a position of trust or authority in relation to the victim*

  *shall be deemed aggravating circumstances;*

*(b) a sentence should be similar to sentences imposed on similar offenders for similar offences committed in similar circumstances;*
*(c) where consecutive sentences are imposed, the combined sentence should not be unduly long or harsh;*

*(d) an offender should not be deprived of liberty, if less restrictive sanctions may be appropriate in the circumstances; and*

*(e) all available sanctions other than imprisonment that are reasonable in the circumstances should be considered by all offenders, with particular attention to the circumstances of aboriginal offenders.*

. . .

1   See, for example, editorial commentary on the previous sentencing reform bill (Bill C-90) in *The Globe and Mail*, Toronto, July 2, 1992, at p. A18.
2   For a summary of recent events in the area of sentencing, see J. Roberts and A. von Hirsch, "Sentencing Reform in Canada: Recent Developments" (1992), 23 Revue Générale de Droit 491.
3   *Report of The Canadian Sentencing Commission: Sentencing Reform: A Canadian Approach* (Ottawa: Ministry of Supply & Services Canada, 1987). Chair O. Archambault (hereafter the commission), pp. 1-592.
4   House of Commons Standing Committee on Justice and Solicitor General, *Report of the Standing Committee on its Review of Sentencing, Conditional Release and Related Aspects of Corrections* (Ottawa: Ministry of Supply & Services Canada, 1988), pp. 1-300.
5   The closest Canada has come to significant sentencing reform was the *Criminal Law Reform Act of 1984*, Bill C-19, which died on the order paper when Parliament was dissolved in 1984
6   R.S.C. 1985, c. C-46, as amended
7   for recent data on variation in sentencing practices, see Canadian Centre for Justice Statistics, *Sentencing in Adult Criminal Provincial Courts* (Ottawa: Statistics Canada, 1993). As well, a great deal of empirical research has demonstrated the importance of the sentencing objective in determining the nature and quantum of the sentence: see, for example R. McFatter, "Sentencing Strategies and Justice: Effects of Punishment Philosophy on Sentencing Decisions" (1978), 36 Journal of Personality and Social Psychology 1490.

. . .

11   Bill C-41, s. 718.
12   There are only six actual subsections in the bill but some contain more than one objective. For example, s. 718(*b*) includes both general and special deterrence. For the purposes of clarity, we discuss the objectives independently here.
13   Bill C-41, s 718. This statement of purpose is derived from the report of the Canadian Sentencing Commission. The commission attributed this purpose to the criminal law rather than sentencing *per se*. For further information on this issue, see J. Roberts and A. von Hirsch, "Sentencing Reform in Canada: Recent Developments' (1992), 23 Revue Générale de Droit 319.
14   See J. Roberts and A. von Hirsch, "Sentencing Reform in Canada", *supra*, footnote 2.
15   The commission proposal had two purposes, one for the criminal law and a related one for the sentencing process: see *Commission, supra*, footnote 3, at pp. 125-56.
16   Bill C-41, s. 718.1.
17   Bill C-41 contains a subtle shift in language from its predecessor, Bill C-90. The earlier bill simply suggested that a sentence "may" be changed to account for aggravating and mitigating circumstances.
18   Bill C-41, s. 718.2(*a*).
19   It is the conceptual equivalent of saying to professors that the grade assigned to a student's paper should reflect both the good and the bad points.
20   Bill C-41, s. 718.2(*b*).
21   In between principles (a) and (b), Bill C-41 introduces a statutory aggravating factor. It states that evidence that the offence was motivated by hate, or that the offender abused a position of trust, shall be deemed an aggravating circumstance. This clause — not present in the preceding Bill C-90 — raises its own set of problems. However, restrictions on space prevent us exploring the issue further in this article.
22   Bill C-41, s. 718.2(*c*).

23 See A. Ashworth, *Sentencing and Penal Policy* (London: Weidenfeld & Nicolson, 1983), pp. 259-68; D.A. Thomas, *Principles of Sentencing* (London: Heinemann, 1979), pp. 56-61.
24 A statement of purpose and principle need not, and in fact cannot, include all relevant sentencing principles. For example, a great deal has been written about the principle that has evolved whereby defendants who plead guilty are accorded a more lenient sentence than accused who are found guilty. Should this "discount" be enshrined in the guiding statute as well?
25 See S. Mihorean and S. Lipinski, "International Incarceration Patterns, 1980-1990" (1992), 12 Juristat Service Bulletin 12.
26 See for example, the report on sentencing published by the Government of Canada in 1982: "Sentencing" (Ottawa: Department of Justice Canada, 1982) at p. 34, and also the discussion documents released by the federal government in 1990.
27 Bill C-41. s/ 718.2(*d*).
28 Brown Commission, *Second Report of the Commissioners of the Penitentiary Inquiry* (Ottawa, 1849).
29 Nielsen Task Force Report on the Justice System, *The Justice System — A Study Team Report to the Task Force Program Review* (Ottawa, Minister of Supply & Services, 1986).
30 See Brief submitted to the Canadian Sentencing Commission by the Law Reform Commission of Canada (Ottawa: Law Reform Commission of Canada, March, 1985).
31 See *Commission, supra*, footnote 3, at p. 154.
32 See Government of Canada, *Directions for Reform: A Framework for Sentencing, Corrections and Conditional Release* (Ottawa: Ministry of Supply & Services Canada, 1990).
33 Bill C-41, s. 718.2(*e*).
34 Canadian Centre for Justice Statistics, *Adult Correctional Services in Canada, 1992-1990* (Ottawa, Statistics Canada, 1993).
35 Data supplied to the authors by the Ontario Ministry of the Solicitor General and Correctional Services, August 15, 1994.
36 See Commission on Systemic Racism in the Ontario Criminal Justice System, *Racism Behind Bars: Interim Report* (Toronto, Queen's Printer for Ontario, 1994).
37 See C. Laprairie "The role of sentencing in the over-representation of aboriginal people in correctional institutions" (1990), 32 Can. J. Crim. at pp. 429-40 for a thoughtful discussion of this issue.
38 For further discussion of this issue, see A. Doob, "Community Sanctions and Imprisonment" (1990), 32 Can. J. Crim. at pp. 415-28.
39 See *Criminal Justice Act* (U.K.), *supra*, footnote 9. The Act has subsequently been revised.

## R. v. Hollinsky
(1995), 103 C.C.C. (3d) 472 (Ont. C.A.)

Appeal by the Crown from a sentence imposed by Nosanchuk Prov. Div. J., *infra*, following the accused's conviction on two counts of dangerous driving causing death. The judgment appealed from is as follows:

*March 9, 1995.*

NOSANCHUK PROV. DIV. J. (orally): — On July 30, 1994, at 1:45 a.m. an automobile accident with very tragic consequences occurred. An 1985 Pontiac Sunbird, driven by Kevin Hollinsky, age 19, in an easterly direction on Wyandotte St. E. near St. Luke Rd. in Windsor, went out of control. It struck two hydro poles and ended up on a lawn next to a house. Two passengers, Joseph Camlis and Andrew Thompson died as a result of the injuries sustained in the accident. Todd Giles, another passenger, suffered injuries to his mouth and a punctured lung. These injuries had no lasting effect and were not life-threatening. The driver, Kevin Hollinsky, escaped uninjured.

The Sunbird was observed driving at a speed in excess of the speed limit about two blocks before the accident occurred. It overtook and cut in front of one auto; it then drove close behind a second auto, and, in the process of overtaking the second auto, the auto driven by Kevin Hollinsky skidded out of control and a single car accident with the tragic consequences indicated earlier occurred.

On February 2, 1995, Kevin Hollinsky pleaded guilty to a count in an information alleging that on July 30, 1994, he drove a motor vehicle in a manner that was dangerous to the public, thereby causing the death of Joseph Camlis, contrary to s. 249 of the *Criminal Code* [s. 249 [rep. & sub. R.S.C. 1985, c. 27 (1st Supp.), s. 36; am *idem*, c. 32 (4th Supp.), s. 57; 1994, c. 44, s. 11] and to a further count alleging an identical offence causing the death of Andrew Thompson.

The prosecution in this case has submitted that the court ought to impose a prison term of from eight to 12 months in an Ontario reformatory to deter other potential dangerous drivers from committing similar offences. The prosecutor concedes that in this case there is no real issue as to specific deterrence of Kevin Hollinsky. The victims were his very best friends and the enormity of the loss will unquestionably deter him from committing a similar offence in the future. The prosecutor argues, however, that a message must be sent out to any prospective offenders that the penalty of a prison term in at least the range indicated must follow for similar criminal conduct.

Defence counsel has urged the court to impose a non-custodial term on the accused. He has argued that a non-custodial sentence in cases of dangerous driving causing death are not entirely unprecedented. He has contended that this is a unique case, submitting that, "No punishment could possibly make up for the loss of the lives that occurred".

In the support of his submission in this case, defence counsel has the overwhelming and unqualified support of the families of both deceased victims, Andrew Thompson and Joseph Camlis. This court was exceedingly impressed and moved by the outpouring of compassion on the part of these families for Kevin Hollinsky, and their collective determination to respond to their own terrible losses in a constructive manner.

There was a recognition by them of the obvious guilt that would be suffered by Kevin Hollinsky for many years, if not for the rest of his life, as the result of the commission of the offence. There was a recognition of the torment that he has gone through and will continue to go through. There was an absence of bitterness and a desire to take positive and healing steps. There was a determination to participate in a program of public education to prevent such a tragedy from reoccurring as a tribute to the memories of Joseph Camlis and Andrew Thompson.

To accomplish that purpose, the families have already contacted the Windsor Police Services, and have volunteered their personal participation in attending schools throughout the area on a program of public education. They propose to have Kevin Hollinsky join them, which he is willing to do. They propose to use by way of demonstration the debris of the automobile in which their sons perished. They have committed themselves to going out and telling young students, in their own words, about the horrible and devastating tragedy of July 30, 1994, in the company of Kevin Hollinsky, in order to educate the young students about the need for responsible driving.

The conduct and attitude of the parents of the victims in this case is, indeed, a tribute to the capacity of the human spirit to respond affirmatively and with profound compassion to an awful tragedy.

The families of the victims have pleaded with the court, both in correspondence and in oral testimony, not to impose a custodial term on Kevin Hollinsky. "What useful purpose could be served", they have contended, "by sending Kevin Hollinsky to prison? Has he not suffered enough? Surely, the loss of his two very best friends is ample punishment".

Counsel for the accused has also reminded the court of the deep psychological wounds that could well be suffered by Kevin as a result of the offence. These pleas that were made on behalf of Kevin Hollinsky by the families of the victims were very powerful, very sincere, and have made the task of sentencing in this case incredibly difficult.

The sworn duty of this court is to uphold the law and to impose a just sentence according to the law. The court is obliged to balance the interests of the accused and the state. The fact that a criminal prosecution has been launched makes this case a matter of public concern. The commission of a criminal offence can never be simply a private matter between the accused and the family of the victim.

In determining the appropriate sentence in this case, the court must bear in mind that the overriding consideration in sentencing is the protection of the community and society. The sentencing court has the duty of imposing a fit and just sentence according to well-established sentencing principles of specific deterrence, general deterrence rehabilitation and denunciation. Any sentence that is imposed on an accused person ought to involve a wise blending of all of the above elements.

The court has been referred to numerous trial and appellate decisions delivered by courts across the country. As counsel for the accused has pointed out, sentences for the commission of the offence of dangerous driving causing death range from a suspended sentence to a penitentiary term . . . .

While alcohol may have been a factor in the case before the court, it must be observed that the prosecutor withdrew the charges of operating a motor vehicle while impaired by alcohol and causing death, stating that in his opinion, it could not be established that the death was related to operating a motor vehicle while impaired by alcohol. In addition, the prosecutor withdrew a charge alleging that the accused operated a motor vehicle with a concentration of alcohol in his blood that exceeded 80 mg of alcohol in 100 ml of blood. . . .

At the time of the commission of the offence, Kevin Hollinsky was a young man of 19 years of age. He has an unblemished past with no criminal record or record of traffic offences. He comes from a caring, devoted, and loving family. He was described as a kind, gentle, and loving young man by the families of both of the deceased victims, and by a former teacher.

His employer indicated that he has proven to be a trustworthy and loyal employee, that he has a good sense of values, and shows a great amount of loyalty to the company and to fellow workers. His employer describes him as always friendly and professional in dealing with customers and suppliers. He has always shown a willingness to learn new tasks and carries out work assigned to its full completion. His punctuality, neatness, and enthusiasm make him a person one can trust and respect.

The relationship of Kevin Hollinsky to his two deceased friends was unique. The devotion and loyalty of one to the other was remarkable. The impact of the deaths upon Kevin Hollinsky has been devastating. Joseph Camlis and Andrew Thompson were like brothers to him. The court has no doubt that Kevin Hollinsky would gladly serve any amount of time in prison in exchange for the return of his deceased friends.

Kevin Hollinsky has demonstrated great remorse and feels enormous guilt. He is currently receiving psychotherapy from a family physician who has indicated that he has, to quote the doctor, "undergone a great deal of anxiety and a depressive reaction that has changed his life tremendously". The doctor was impressed that Kevin Hollinsky was, to quote the doctor, "a decent young man who made a mistake and suffered a tremendous loss". The doctor is of the opinion that Kevin can learn from his mistake and be helpful to others.

Kevin Hollinsky has accepted responsibility for the offences and pleaded guilty before the commencement of the preliminary inquiry. The public has been saved the considerable expense of a preliminary inquiry and a trial. He is prepared to perform extensive community service to atone for the offence. As part of this service, he would attend on a regular basis to speak to students at local schools, and to openly explain the circumstances of the tragic event of July 30, 1994, with a view to impressing them with the immense risks involved in driving an automobile, particularly in driving it in a dangerous manner.

In this endeavour, the accused is fully supported by the parents of the victims and members of their families. The message delivered would undoubtedly leave an indelible and lasting impression on the students to whom it is delivered.

In addition, Kevin Hollinsky has been found suitable to perform community service work under the special work assignment program set up by Reaching Out in this community. This program involves a specified number of hours of labour-intensive work, doing litter pick-up and other heavy labour with non-profit organizations in a community, that need assistance with special projects. The program is designed for offenders who would otherwise serve a period of custody in prison were it not for the availability of the program. It can serve as a concrete alternative to imprisonment in this case.

Kevin Hollinsky has also been found suitable to do further community service that would be required of him over the balance of any probationary period to which he is sentenced. That service would involve working with youth groups in his community and doing other community service work that would benefit the community.

The court has no doubt that the accused is highly motivated and will perform all of the community service that has been outlined previously in an exemplary fashion. This court is convinced that there are, indeed, extraordinary circumstances in this case that lead the court to conclude that a term of imprisonment is not necessary in order to achieve the objective of general deterrence. The arrest of the accused, his public prosecution in court, the fact that he now has a record of conviction for two serious offences under the *Criminal Code* of Canada, the fact that he will lose his licence to drive a motor vehicle for an extended period of time, the fact that as an alternative to imprisonment he will be performing worthwhile and extensive community service, personally attending as required to repeatedly send a message of public education to other young persons, serves the need for general deterrence in this community in relation to the offences before this court.

The court has decided to seize the opportunity presented by this unique set of circumstances to make available the voices of the accused and the families of the victim through public education in this community. What more compelling message in the service of deterrence could be sent than the knowledge of the crushing devastation caused by the loss of the young person's two best friends as a result of the commission of the offences that are before the court? The elaborate community service program that has been arranged in the unique circumstances of this case as an alternative to imprisonment will serve the principle of general deterrence more effectively than simply the knowledge that a reformatory term of eight to 12 months was imposed. . . .

In conclusion, this court emphasizes that this is a unique and exceptional case. No member of the public ought to conclude that the fact that you have not gone to prison is a precedent for other cases of dangerous driving. The exceptional support and the affirmative action taken by the families of the victims, and your own family, have convinced this court that in this unique case as an alternative to imprisonment, the kind of community service that you will undertake will serve the ends of justice and will, in the long run, serve protection of the community far more effectively than would the imposition of any prison term. . . .

The following judgment was endorsed on the appeal record.

BY THE COURT: — Although an offence of this nature would usually require a custodial sentence, we have reviewed the carefully considered reasons of the trial judge and having regard to the exceptional circumstances of this case, we are in general agreement with these reasons. The Crown concedes that there is no concern on its part in this case with respect to the specific deterrence or rehabilitation of the appellant. It is only concerned with the matter of general deterrence. We have had the benefit of viewing the results of the performance by the respondent of the community service required from him as part of his sentence and in particular his participation in appearing before more than 8,300 students on 14 occasions emphasizing the terrible consequences of dangerous driving while drinking. This fresh evidence filed on behalf of the respondent is indicative of the powerful deterrent effect of this type of program as projected by the trial judge.

Moreover, the fresh evidence indicates that the respondent has successfully performed all but 75 hours of the 750 hours of community service required of him and it would be considerably more harsh to impose a custodial sentence at this time than it would have been in the first instance. For these reasons, although leave to appeal is granted, the appeal is dismissed.

*Appeal dismissed.*

## R. v. Shropshire
(1995), 102 C.C.C. (3d) 193 (S.C.C.)

Appeal by the Crown from a judgment of the British Columbia Court of Appeal, 90 C.C.C. (3d) 234, 45 B.C.A.C. 252, 72 W.A.C. 252, 24 W.C.B. (2d) 39, allowing the accused's appeal from sentence and reducing the period of parole ineligibility to 10 years following his plea of guilty to a charge of second degree murder.

The judgment of the court was delivered by

[1] IACOBUCCI J., — This appeal was allowed on June 15, 1995, with reasons to follow. These are those reasons.

[2] At issue in this appeal are the factors and principles that should guide a trial judge in determining whether to extend the period of parole ineligibility on a second degree murder conviction beyond the statutory minimum of 10 years. This appeal also touches on the appropriate standard of appellate review to be exercised when considering a trial judge's decision to postpone the period of parole eligibility. Both of these issues engage the broad theme of when the discretion of a sentencing judge ought to be altered.

I
BACKGROUND

[3] The respondent, Michael Thomas Shropshire, pleaded guilty to the second degree murder of Timothy Buffam. The offence was committed at the respondent's home in Abbotsford, British Columbia, on May 26, 1992, during a marijuana transaction between the respondent, the deceased, and Lorne Lang, a third person accompanying the deceased. Lang is otherwise known as "Animal". The respondent was acquainted with Buffam and Lang as the trio had had prior narcotics dealings. Without any warning, the respondent shot Buffam three times in the chest as they were about to enter the garage to complete the marijuana deal. The respondent then chased Lang in his vehicle shouting, "Hacksaw told me to do it!". Hacksaw is the nickname of another associate.

[4] Two days later, the respondent gave himself up to the police. After a preliminary hearing the respondent pleaded guilty to second degree murder. He professed remorse for his actions but was unwilling or unable to explain them. No motive for the killing was ever ascertained. The respondent has a prior criminal record including two convictions in youth court for robbery, a conviction for impaired driving, and two narcotic offences as an adult.

[5] On June 17, 1993, McKinnon J. of the Supreme Court of British Columbia sentenced the respondent to life imprisonment without eligibility for parole for 12 years. This period of non-eligibility is two years more than the minimum (and most common) period of parole ineligibility for second degree murder, namely, 10 years. Trial judges are permitted, by virtue of the discretionary power accorded to them by s. 744 of the *Criminal Code*, R.S.C. 1985, c. C-46, to extend the period of parole ineligibility beyond the statutory minimum. The respondent challenged the discretionary s. 744 decision of the trial judge.

[6] On May 4, 1994, a majority of the Court of Appeal for British Columbia allowed the respondent's appeal against sentence, and reduced the period of parole ineligibility to 10 years: 90 C.C.C. (3d) 234, 45 B.C.A.C. 252, 72 W.A.C. 252, 24 W.C.B. (2d) 39. Goldie J.A. dissented and would have dismissed the appeal.

## II
## RELEVANT STATUTORY PROVISIONS

*Criminal Code*, R.S.C. 1985, c. C-46

744. Subject to section 744.1, at the time of the sentencing under paragraph 742(*b*) of an offender who is convicted of second degree murder, the judge who presided at the trial of the offender or, if that judge is unable to do so, any judge of the same court may, having regard to the character of the offender, the nature of the offence and the circumstances surrounding its commission, and to the recommendation, if any, made pursuant to section 743, by order, substitute for ten years a number of years of imprisonment (being more than ten but not more than twenty-five) without eligibility for parole, as the judge deems fit in the circumstances.

[7] Section 744.1 applies to offenders under the age of 18. Section 742(*b*) specifies a sentence of life imprisonment with a period of parole ineligibility of at least 10 years and not more than 25 years for a person convicted of second degree murder. Section 743 relates to a recommendation by a jury as to minimum parole ineligibility.

. . .

## IV
## ISSUES ON APPEAL

[15] I would state the issues in the following manner:

1. What are the appropriate factors for a sentencing judge to consider in determining whether a period of parole ineligibility of longer than 10 years should be awarded for an individual convicted of second degree murder?
2. Given the discretionary nature of an extended period of parole ineligibility order under s. 744 of the *Criminal Code*, what is the appropriate standard of appellate review of such an order?

## V
## ANALYSIS

A. What are the appropriate factors for a sentencing judge to consider in determining whether a period of parole ineligibility of longer than 10 years should be awarded for an individual convicted of second degree murder?

[16] The majority of the British Columbia Court of Appeal held that there are *only two* factors to consider in justifying an enhanced period of parole ineligibility: (1) an assessment of future dangerousness, and (2) denunciation. With respect, I disagree. Although these factors are of relevance in justifying an extension of the period of parole ineligibility, they are by no means determinative or exclusive.

[17] Section 744 of the *Criminal Code* authorizes a trial judge to impose a period of parole ineligibility greater than the minimum 10-year period.

. . .

[18] The determination under s. 744 is thus a very fact-sensitive process. The factors to be considered in fixing an extended period of parole ineligibility are:

(1) the character of the offender;
(2) the nature of the offence; and
(3) the circumstances surrounding the commission of the offence;

all bearing in mind the discretionary power conferred on the trial judge.

[19] No reference is made to denunciation or assessments of future dangerousness in the statutory language. By elevating "denunciation" and "assessment of future dangerousness" as the only criteria by which extended periods of parole ineligibility can be determined, the majority of the British Columbia Court of Appeal has, in effect, judicially amended the clear statutory language. This is not to say, however, that these two criteria should not be part of the analysis. For example, "denunciation" can fall within the statutory criterion of the "nature of the offence". Similarly, "future dangerousness" can fall within the rubric of the "character of the offender" . . . .

[21] "Deterrence" is also a relevant criterion in justifying a s. 744 order. Parole eligibility informs the content of the "punishment" meted out to an offender: for example, there is a very significant difference between being behind bars and functioning within society while on conditional release. Consequently, I believe that lengthened periods of parole ineligibility could reasonably be expected to deter some persons from reoffending.

. . .

[23] The only difference in terms of punishment, between first and second degree murder is the duration of parole ineligibility. This clearly indicates that parole ineligibility is part of the "punishment" and thereby forms an important element of sentencing policy. As such, it must be concerned with deterrence, whether general or specific. The jurisprudence of this court is clear that deterrence is a well-established objective of sentencing policy.

. . .

[24] The exercise of a trial judge's discretion under s. 744 should not be more strictly circumscribed than the sentencing itself. The section does not embody any limiting statutory language; rather, it is quite the contrary.

. . .

[26] I also find it necessary to deal with Lambert J.A.'s conclusion that a period of parole ineligibility in excess of 10 years will not be justified unless there are "unusual circumstances" . . . . In my opinion, this is too high a standard and makes it overly difficult for trial judges to exercise the discretionary power to set extended periods of parole ineligibility. The language of s. 744 does not require "unusual circumstances". As a result, to so require by judicial pronouncement runs contrary to parliamentary intent.

[27] In my opinion, a more appropriate standard, which would better reflect the intentions of Parliament, can be stated in this manner: as a general rule, the period of parole ineligibility shall be for 10 years, but this can be ousted by a determination of the trial judge that, according to the criteria enumerated in s. 744, the offender should wait a longer period before having his suitability to be released into the general public assessed. To this end, an extension of the period of parole ineligibility would not be "unusual", although it may well be that, in the median number of cases, a period of 10 years might still be awarded.

. . .

[31] If the objective of s. 744 is to give the trial judge an element of discretion in sentencing to reflect the fact that within second degree murder there is both a range of seriousness and varying degrees of moral culpability, then it is incorrect to start from the proposition that the sentence must be the statutory minimum unless there are unusual circumstances. As discussed *supra*, a preferable approach would be to view the 10-year period as a minimum contingent on what the "judge deems fit in the circumstances", the content of this "fitness" being informed by the criteria listed in s. 744. As held in other Canadian jurisdictions, the power to extend the period of parole ineligibility need not be sparingly used.

. . .

[34] On another note, I do not find that permitting trial judges to extend the period of parole ineligibility usurps or impinges upon the function of the parole board. I am cognizant of the fact that, upon the expiry of the period of parole ineligibility, there is no guarantee of release into the public. At that point, it is incumbent upon the parole board to assess the suitability of such release, and in so doing it is guided by the legislative objectives of the parole system: see ss. 101 and 102 of the *Corrections and Conditional Release Act*, S.C. 1992, c. 20. However, it is clear that the parole board is not the only participant in the parole process. All it is designed to do is, within the parameters defined by the judiciary, decide whether an offender can be released. A key component of those parameters is the determination of when the period of parole eligibility (*i.e.*, when the parole board can commence its administrative review function) starts to run. This is the manner in which the system is geared to function — with complementary yet distinct input from both the judiciary and the parole administrators. It is the role of the sentencing judge to circumscribe, in certain statutorily defined circumstances, the operation of the parole board . . . .

[35] Applying these legal principles to the particular facts of this case, I do not see any error on the part of the trial judge. He adverted to the fact that the respondent had pleaded guilty and was only 23 years old. He recognized that the Crown was not seeking a period of parole ineligibility beyond the minimum. Nevertheless, in a legitimate exercise of his discretionary power, and after correctly reviewing the factors set out in s. 744, he imposed a 12-year period of parole ineligibility. He referred to the following factors as specifically justifying the 12-year period of parole ineligibility:

(a) the circumstances of the killing were strange in that they provided no real answer as to why it took place, and the respondent was unwilling or unable to explain his actions;
(b) the murder was committed during the course of committing another offence, namely, a drug transaction; and
(c) the respondent has a record for both narcotic offences and violence.

. . .

B. Given the discretionary nature of an extended period of parole ineligibility order under s. 744 of the *Criminal Code*, what is the appropriate standard of appellate review of such an order?

[43] In my view, the British Columbia Court of Appeal not only erred in law regarding the factors justifying the issuance of an extended period of parole ineligibility order, but also in the standard of appellate review it espoused.

[44] Lambert J.A. suggested that an appellate court should reduce the period of parole ineligibility imposed by the trial judge unless the trial judge has given specific reasons which, in the opinion of the appeal court, justify the increased period. This is a very broad standard of review, focusing in an exact manner on the appellate court's assessment of the correctness of the sentencing judge's decision. In my opinion, this standard of review is inappropriate.

[45] Orders made under s. 744 are defined by s. 673 of the *Criminal Code* as forming part of the "sentence". They are thus to be appealed pursuant to the statutory right of appeal provided by s. 687(1) of the *Criminal Code*. Section 687(1) reads as follows:

> 687(1) Where an appeal is taken against sentence, the court of appeal shall, unless the sentence is one fixed by law, consider the *fitness* of the sentence appealed against, and may on such evidence, if any, as it thinks fit to require or to receive
>
> (*a*) vary the sentence within the limits prescribed by law for the offence of which the accused was convicted; or
> (*b*) dismiss the appeal.

(Emphasis added).

[46] The question, then, is whether a consideration of the "fitness" of a sentence incorporates the very interventionist appellate review propounded by Lambert J.A. With respect, I find that it does not. An appellate court should not be given free reign to modify a sentencing order simply because it feels that a different order ought to have been made. The formulation of a sentencing order is a profoundly subjective process; the trial judge has the advantage of having seen and heard all of the witnesses whereas the appellate court can only base itself upon a written record. A variation in the sentence should only be made if the Court of Appeal is convinced it is not fit. That is to say, that it has found the sentence to be clearly unreasonable.

. . .

[50] Unreasonableness in the sentencing process involves the sentencing order falling outside the "acceptable range" of orders; this clearly does not arise in the present appeal .

. . .

## CONCLUSIONS AND DISPOSITION

[54] The trial judge considered the relevant factors in exercising the discretionary jurisdiction given to him under s. 744. The Court of Appeal erred in postulating an unduly restrictive and narrow approach to s. 744 and by adopting a standard of appellate review that was tantamount to substituting its opinion for that of the trial judge. Consequently, I would allow the appeal, set aside the decision of the British Columbia Court of Appeal, and restore the trial judge's s. 744 order of a period of parole ineligibility of 12 years.

*Appeal allowed; order of period of parole ineligibility restored.*

## R. v. Morin
### (1995), 101 C.C.C. (3d) 124 (Sask. C.A.)

Only excerpts from the judgement of Sherstobitoff are reproduced below:
**Note that an application for leave to appeal to the Supreme Court of Canada was filed in October, 1995.

The secondary ground of appeal is that the judge erred in law in holding a sentencing circle. The Crown, in its factum, said that the appeal was launched in an effort to have this court lay down some "guiding principles or limigations which should be placed on a court requested to hold a sentencing circle". This ground of appeal will be dealt with first.

## SENTENCING CIRCLES

There is no contest over the use of sentencing circles; their use in this province is now well established. This is the position of the Crown as stated in its factum:

. . .

> It must be emphasized that the Crown does not, as noted above, suggest that sentencing circles are illegal. The Crown is of the view that sentencing circles are legal, appropriate and helpful in the right circumstances. Upwards of 100 sentencing circles have been conducted in the Province of Saskatchewan. Out of those, two have been appealed by the Crown and are presently being heard before this Court at this time. Again, the Crown does have concerns about the use of sentencing circles in all cases where one is requested. While the Crown is quite prepared to commit the considerable resources necessary to support sentencing circles in appropriate cases, if there are no restrictions to the availability of this process it could cause significant court delays which could aversely affect other offender's rights.
>
> Sentencing circles can and do work most effectively in communities which are relatively small and close knit and are particularly effective where both the victim and the accused come from and live in the same community . . . .
>
> This type of community control is lacking in an urban setting or at least, very much more difficult to obtain. Additionally, in small, relatively homogeneous communities, the beneficial use of the circle can easily be seen by the community as a whole. It's a visble [sic] means to effect acknowledgement by the offender to the victim of the harm caused. It promotes reconciliation

between the victim and the offender and offender and the community. Finally, it encourages the mobilization of community resources to ensure the community supports both the offender and the victim with a view to maintaining harmony in the community.

The question is how to determine what guidelines should operate when those pre-conditions do not exist; that is, when the offences did not occur in a small community, the victim and the offender are from different racial, ethnic or geographic communities or the accused is not a resident of the geographic community where the offence occurred.

. . . .

The transportation of a social control process developed within the context of small, homogeneous, tribal community to a large, heterogeneous, urban community is not an easy process. Not surprisingly, there are differing views from the lower courts as to how this change is to be effected.

. . .

A recent judgment of the Provincial Court, *R. v. Joseyounen*, [1995] 6 W.W.R. 438, sets out the criteria developed by the judges of the Provincial Court sitting in the northern part of the province to determine whether use of a sentencing circle is appropriate in a given case. By way of preface, Fafard Prov. Ct. J. said this at pp. 439:

The first sentencing circle to be held in Saskatchewan took place in Sandy Bay in July of 1992. I was the presiding judge. Since then many sentencing circles have been held in Northern Saskatchewan (I estimate that I have dealt with over 60 cases in that manner myself), and out of this experience by me and my colleagues on the Provincial Court in the north, there have emerged seven criteria that we apply in deciding if a case for sentencing should go to a circle. These criteria are not carved in stone, but they provide guidelines sufficiently simple for the lay public to understand, and also capable of application so that our decisions are not being made arbitrarily.

It is imperative that the public, aboriginal and others, be able to know and understand what is happening in the development of sentencing circles: the credibility of the administration of justice depends on it.

The criteria are as follows [at pp. 442-5]:

(1) The accused must agree to be referred to the sentencing circle.

(2) The accused must have deep roots in the community in which the circle is held and from which the participants are drawn.

(3) That there are elders or respected non-political community leaders willing to participate.

(4) The victim is willing to participate and has been subjected to no coercion or pressure in so agreeing.

(5) The court should try to determine beforehand, as best it can, if the victim is subject to battered spouse syndrome. If she is, then she should have counselling made available to her and be accompanied by a support team in the circle.

(6) Disputed facts have been resolved in advance.

(7) The case is one in which a court would be willing to take a calculated risk and depart from the usual range of sentencing.

. . .

There is no provision in the *Criminal Code* for the use of sentencing circles. The foundations for their use consist, first, of the sentencing hearing, with its wide scope and measure of informality, as set down in *R. v. Gardiner* (1982), 68 C.C.C. (2d) 477, 140 D.L.R. (3d) 612, [1982] 2 S.C.R. 368; and, second, of the principles of sentencing as set forth in *R. v. Morrissette* (1970), 1 C.C.C. (2d) 307, 12 C.R.N.S. 392, 75 W.W.R. 644, including, in particular, the need to consider the rehabilitation of the offender in determining a fit sentence.

In *Gardiner*, the Supreme Court of Canada observed at pp. 513-14:

> One of the hardest tasks confronting a trial judge is sentencing. The stakes are high for society and for the individual. Sentencing is the critical stage of the criminal justice system, and it is manifest that the judge should not be denied an opportunity to obtain relevant information by the imposition of all the restrictive evidential rules common to a trial. Yet the obtaining and weighing of such evidence should be fair. A substantial liberty interest of the offender is involved and the information obtained should be accurate and reliable.
>
> It is a commonplace that the strict rules which govern at trial do not apply at a sentencing hearing and it would be undesirable to have the formalities and technicalities characteristic of the normal adversary proceeding prevail. The hearsay rule does not govern the sentencing hearing. Hearsay evidence may be accepted where found to be credible and trustworthy. The judge traditionally has had wide latitude as to the sources and types of evidence upon which to base his sentence. He must have the fullest possible information concerning the background of the accused if he is to fit the sentence to the offender rather than to the crime.

In *R. v. Morrissette*, Culliton C.J.S., commented upon the longstanding requirement that the courts, when sentencing, have regard for "the reformation and rehabilitation of the offender". It is this requirement in particular which may be best met in some cases by holding a sentencing circle, since the circle emphasizes "healing", or in other words reformation and rehabilitation.

In the light of these foundations, and given the wide latitude accorded judges as to the sources and types of evidence and information upon which to base their sentencing decisions, it is doubtful that this court should attempt to lay down guidelines in respect of a decision whether or not a sentencing circle should be used in a given case.

. . .

As a matter of principle, however, we should say that it would be futile, for the reasons given in both Joseyounen and Cheekinew, to use a sentencing circle in those cases where it is clear that the circumstances require, at a minimum, a penitentiary term. If a sentence exceeds two years' imprisonment, the court is without power to impose any conditions on the accused after he has served his term. There is, accordingly, no means of enforcing any obligations undertaken by an accused as a result of the recommendations of the community through a sentencing circle. That does not preclude voluntary action on the part of the community and the accused such as that contemplated by Fafard Prov. Ct. J. in Joseyounen when he indicated that he was prepared to use what he termed a "healing circle" which might make suggestions for parole conditions to the Parole Board if and when the accused made application for parole.

### FITNESS OF SENTENCE: PRINCIPLES AND STANDARD OF REVIEW

Since there is no provision in the *Criminal Code* for the use of sentencing circles, it is implicit in their use, and recognized by all of the judgments mentioned above, that when sentencing circles are used, the power and duty to impose a fit sentence remains vested exclusively in the trial judge. If a sentencing circle is used, and it recommends a sentence which is not a fit sentence, the judge is duty bound to ignore the recommendation to the extent that it varies from what is a fit sentence. And the duty of this court in reviewing the fitness of a sentence under s. 687 is the same.

The crux of this case is how, and the extent to which a meaningful use of sentencing circles may be integrated into this framework. This requires a brief examination of the principles which apply in determining a fit sentence in the first instance, and to the standard of review used by this court in determining whether those principles have been properly applied when it reviews a sentence.

This court still adheres to the statement of principles to be considered in the determination of proper sentences made by Culliton C.J.S. in *Morrissette* at p. 309:

> As has been stated many times, the factors to be considered are:
>
> (1) punishment;
> (2) deterrence;
> (3) protection of the public; and
> (4) the reformation and rehabilitation of the offender.
>
> The real problem arises in deciding the factor to be emphasized in a particular case. Of necessity, the circumstances surrounding the commission of an offence differ in each case so that even for the same offence sentences may justifiably show a wide variation.

...

It is to be noted that, according to *Morrissette*, one of the duties of the Court of Appeal is to prevent disparity in sentences. Disparity between the sentence imposed on Mr. Morin in this case and other sentences for like offences in like circumstances in other cases, and between Mr. Morin and his co-accused, is the Crown's main ground of appeal in this case.

...

The question, then, is to what extent can the sentencing judge make meaningful use of the recommendations of sentencing circles?

The very purpose of sentencing circles seems to be to fashion sentences that will differ in some mix or measure from those which the courts have up to now imposed in order to take into account aboriginal culture and traditions, and in order to permit and to take into account direct community participation in both imposition and administration of the sentence. It also seems implicit in all discussions of sentencing circles that they will in many cases, if not most of them, recommend sentences imposing lesser terms of incarceration than would have been imposed by a judge alone and to substitute alternative sanctions, usually involving the community in the administration of those sanctions.

The question posed above was answered by the seventh criterion developed by the judges of the Provincial Court, as outline in *Joseyounen*: the case must be one in which a court is justified in taking a calculated risk and departing from the usual range of sentencing.

...

This fits very well into and complies with the sentencing principles developed by the court. *Morrissette* says that the possibility of rehabilitation is a factor which must be taken into account in any sentence.

...

Before leaving the subject of fitness of sentence in relation to sentencing circles, reference should be made to Bill C-41, 42-43-44 Eliz. II, 1994-95, *An Act to amend the Criminal Code (sentencing) and other Acts in consequence thereof,* S.C. 1995, c.22. It was assented to on July 13, 1995, and will come into effect on a date or dates to be fixed by order of the Governor in Council. This legislation enacts a new Part XXIII of the *Criminal Code* which, for the first time, embodies in the *Code* itself some of the most important principles of sentencing. We can see no conflict between the sentencing principles developed by the courts, as outlined above, and those in the new legislation to the extent that they apply to this case.

Section 718.2(*b*) maintains the principle of parity as outlined above by requiring that a sentence should be similar sentences imposed on similar offenders for similar offences committed in similar circumstances.

Section 718.2(*d*) and (*e*) require that sanctions other than imprisonment, if appropriate or reasonable in the circumstances, should be considered for all offenders, with particular attention to the circumstances of aboriginal offenders. These provisions maintain the requirement, outlined above, that rehabilitation be considered in all cases, and that departure from the normal range of sentence is acceptable if circumstances warrant. The use of sentencing circles in appropriate cases fits with the requirement that there be particular attention to the circumstances of aboriginal offenders.

[After discussing the particular facts of this case in light of the above principles, Sherstobitoff allowed the appeal and varied the sentence.]

## 5.2 PAROLE

### Protecting Society Through Community Corrections*
*Correctional Service of Canada*

* Excerpt from Correctional Service of Canada, *Protecting Society Through Community Corrections* (Ottawa: Minister of Supply and Services Canada, 1995), pp. 2-4

### *Types of Release*

The different kinds of conditional release are:

**Escorted and unescorted temporary absence:** These are short absences granted for various reasons including contact with family and medical consultations. Offenders on such leave may be *escorted* by prison staff or volunteers. Offenders who are *unescorted* are monitored by community staff.

**Program release:** Offenders considered low risk are released for longer periods to take part in treatment or educational programs. These releases are granted by either wardens of prisons or a separate agency — the National Parole Board.

The National Parole Board has exclusive authority to grant two other forms of release — day parole and full parole — based on information and assessments prepared by CSC prison and community staff. Before granting such releases, Board members must be satisfied that the offender will not pose undue risk to the community and will fulfil specific conditions.

**Day parole:** Offenders participate in community-based activities and return nightly to a supervised residence. Day parole generally occurs during a six-month period prior to full parole. It allows offenders to prepare for the next stage in their return to community life.

**Full parole:** Offenders live by themselves or their families. Most offenders are eligible for full parole after serving one third of their sentences.

All the above forms of release are granted at the discretion of the National Parole Board or CSC. In addition, Canadian law decrees two forms of mandatory release.

**Statutory release:** By law, offenders not considered dangerous must be released after serving two thirds of their sentences. Only those who meet the criteria set to ensure public safety are let out. The National Parole Board may add conditions to those imposed on all offenders to protect society and assist the offender begin a new life. These offenders, like all others on conditional release, are supervised in the community by CSC staff.

**Release on expiry of sentence:** This is not a conditional release but the full release required when someone has served the entire sentence. It applies to offenders who were considered too dangerous to return to the community under statutory release. In addition, some offenders eligible for conditional release choose to stay in prison until the end of their sentences.

## *Conditions*

When released, all offenders must adhere to certain *standard conditions* set out in the release certificate. For example, they must travel directly to their homes and report regularly to their parole supervisor *Additional conditions* may also be imposed to control behaviour. These may include curfews, restrictions on movement, prohibitions on drinking, and prohibitions on associating with certain people (such as children, former victims, etc.) CSC staff can take action if they believe the offender is violating release conditions or may commit another crime. They can suspend the release and return the offender directly to prison until the risk is reassessed. Some offenders may remain in prison. Others may be released again but under more severe restrictions and after more supervision or community support services are in place.

## Democracy, Class and the National Parole Board*
### M. Mandel

* (1985), 27 Criminal Law Quarterly 159.

"Every individual is equal before and under the law and has the right to the equal protection and equal benefit of the law" proclaims the Canadian Charter of Rights and Freedoms (s. 15). Marxists have generally derided this sort of proclamation as completely incompatible with the enormous disparities in economic power and social class which exist in Canadian society. We have, indeed, argued that, far from standing apart from these class divisions, the law is "superstructural", that is its precise function is to maintain the class structure ("relations of production") by providing norms and institutions which allow this structure to flourish. This is subtly, though importantly, different from merely saying that the law and legal institutions are there to protect the "status quo", because it specifies the aspect of the status quo protected, not the legal or democratic status quo of equal citizens but the productive relations status quo of massive inequality, of dominance and subordination. Individual interests are protected, but only according to their placement in the relations of production, that is as *class* interests.

Marxism has often called in aid of its point of view the persistent and severe over-representation of subordinate classes in institutions of legal repression such as prisons. For example, in Susan Binnie's study of Ontario reformatory inmates, "managerial, professional and technical" occupations had less than one-quarter of their strength in the ordinary population (3.87% to 17.8%), while "labourers" were over-represented by a factor of 2.6 (16.02% to 6.24%). And in Irvin Waller's sample of Ontario penitentiary releases, it was found that on "all three indicators of job functioning (longest job, level of skill and wage) before admission the ex-prisoners held a lower-order job than the average male, a finding now well documented in criminology". Unemployment rates (at arrest) of male prisoners admitted to the provincial institutions of five provinces in 1978 ranged from 60% to 75% and were from two to over four times the age-adjusted unemployment rate for each province (see Appendix). Finally, though all ethnic groups are represented in the prison population, the native peoples of Canada, unquestionably the economically worst off ethnic group, are over-represented by a factor of about six in Canada's prison population.

Thus the prison population is heavily skewed in favour of the economically marginal groups in the social structure. Lest it be thought that the under-representation of women is a contradiction of this, it should be pointed out that *among women*, the economically most marginal are also over-represented.

These data, striking as they are, are nevertheless ambiguous because they do not rule out the possibility that people are being treated equally by the law. It might be that crime itself varies in amount and seriousness by class and that the social skew in prison is due merely to an impartial law being applied to the same social skew in criminal behaviour.

In fact, analysis of the actual practices of the law and even the specific ideologies which are used to legitimate these practices reveals that this is not the case. I have argued elsewhere that the Canadian sentencing system departs substantially from democratic principles of equality before (and "under") the law and is as much concerned with the enforcement of the social relations of production, that is the class relations, as it is with the prevention of harm to individuals through crime and that it is this that, at least partly, accounts for the social skew in the prison population. Sentencing judges consistently tailor their sentences to the degree to which an offender fulfils his or her role in the productive system, whatever the offence, and to the degree to which offences, whatever their legal severity and the harm they do to individuals, oppose or protect the productive relations status quo. This is made possible by an institutional structure reposing great discretionary authority in sentencing courts and by a legal theory which both guides and legitimates the exercise of this discretion on the basis of "denunciation" and "rehabilitation".

Though sentencing thus contains many undemocratic elements, it also contains some democratic ones. As can be seen from the empirical studies which establish sentencing's class bias and from the law in the statutes and the cases, the legal nature of the offence does exert *some* control on the outcome. However, whatever democratic elements remain in sentencing are completely undermined by what Foucault has called *"the principle of the modulation of penalties"*. This principle comprehends all those variations in penalty which penal authorities administer, including the location of the prisoner on the infinitely graded continuum between minimum and super-maximum security, temporary absences, various forms of "remission" and the largest single modulator, the parole system. According to Foucault, the establishment of the penitentiary system in the context of the massive economic and political transformations which took place at the end of the eighteenth century brought with it a fundamental transformation in the judicial function, albeit under the cover of a relative stability in the law with respect to offences: Judges have been led "to judge something other than crimes" — namely the criminal — "to do something other than judge" — namely to rehabilitate — "and the power of judging has been transferred, in part to other authorities than the judges of the offence". This latter aspect Foucault calls a "fragmentation of the legal power to punish" and in Canada's case it has reposed enormous powers in the hands of parole authorities, who supervise virtually the entire length of virtually every prison sentence. One recent example will be instructive. This is the case of *McNamara (No. 2)* otherwise known as the "Hamilton Dredging Scandal".

This case involved charges of conspiracy to defraud the government of over five million dollars through a "bid-rigging" scheme which went on for five years among nine corporations and eleven corporate executives. The trial lasted more than 14 months and took up 197 court days earning the title of "the longest criminal trial in Canadian history" and presumably the most expensive. The *Globe and Mail* reported that six of the accused were listed in the Canadian Who's Who and their lawyers were the best that money could buy. The *Globe* also reported this statement from one of the jurors:

> We realized they were very important businessmen and we wanted to be as fair as possible. It's just an awesome responsibility. It's an experience I won't forget.

In the result, only five persons and eight corporations were convicted. After further appeals, concluded another year and a half later, three human and one corporate convictions were quashed. The remaining seven corporations were fine six million dollars and the two humans, McNamara and Cooper, received prison terms of five years and three years respectively, taking into account their age (they were both 14 years older than when the conspiracies had started) and previous good character. About the latter, the trial judge said the following and the Court of Appeal agreed:

> "All of the accused are persons of previous good character. All may be considered as first offenders. This does not reduce the seriousness of the offences, but is a factor when considering sentence.
>
> ....
>
> The evidence indicates that not only has [Cooper] been a person of good reputation but that he has contributed a great deal in public service to his community and is capable of making a great contribution in the future. Counsel for Mr. Cooper submitted that this is a proper case for a fine plus an order for community service. There is no doubt Mr. Cooper would be of value to the community but I am afraid that the need for a deterrent sentence has a much higher priority."

Their appeals to the Supreme Court of Canada were dismissed a few months later and they finally went to prison.

The point of all this is that Cooper was out in six months in time for a winter holiday in Florida and the Caribbean and McNamara was out in ten months, both under the authority of the National Parole Board. When the facts become known, an NDP member stood up in the House of Commons and screamed that there was "one law for the rich, powerful friends of the Liberal Government and another law for the poor". Were the authorities embarrassed? Not at all. The National Parole Board chairman's response in a letter to the editor of the *Globe and Mail* is worth quoting in full:

> Your editorial Privileged Parole (April 28) implies that the National Parole Board decides when an inmate is eligible for parole. The board decides *if* an inmate is to be released *when* he becomes eligible; the law and, in certain cases, the courts, set the date of possible release, not the board. Sydney Cooper and Harold McNamara were by law eligible for parole and the board, taking into account that they were first-time, non-violent offenders and that their release plans were sustained by excellent community support, decided to release them.
>
> Ever since the 1899 Ticket of Leave Act, the question of political interference in parole decisions has been investigated, notably by the Archambault Commission (1938) and the Fauteux Committee (1956). To suggest that "powerful friends of the Liberal Government" receive special treatment and that there is a law for the poor and another for the rich, is completely contrary to fact.
>
> The opprobrium attached to Mr. Cooper and Mr. McNamara during their trial and incarceration is the greatest deterrent to this type of non-violent crime. Releases on any type of parole are restricted by specified conditions. As a consulting engineer and chairman of the building committee of the Baycrest Centre for Geriatric Care in Toronto since 1978, Mr. Cooper was in this rare instance, allowed to travel outside of his designated area for professional reasons.
>
> The National Parole Board, in releasing Mr. Cooper and Mr. McNamara, is not condoning their crimes. All we are saying is that deserving, not privileged, inmates should be given the opportunity to return to society to lead productive and law-abiding lives.
>
> W.R. Outerbridge
> National Parole Board
> Ottawa

There are a few interesting things to note about this affair:

(1) The chairman's attempt to disclaim responsibility for parole is dubious. Only about one-third of those eligible for *full parole* ever receive it and less than half of these receive it as soon as they are eligible. McNamara and Cooper were released on *day parole*, a privilege granted to only about half those again who receive parole. So the mechanism is highly selective.
(2) The National Parole Board's interpretation of the day parole provisions, which in the case of certain prisoners is apparently full parole by another name, extends "normal eligibility" for parole from one-third of the sentence to one-sixth of the sentence. Even this can be eclipsed by a similarly broad interpretation of the phoenix-like "parole by exception" provisions. This means that the Parole Board's jurisdiction over the sentence is virtually total.
(3) Though the courts in this case had justified the prison terms on the basis of the need for "general deterrence" of the offence, this is directly contradicted and almost completely wiped out by the Parole Board.
(4) The "individual" factors of no criminal record and "good character" which were taken into account in mitigation of the original sentences are further intensified by the Parole Board, and to them is added the feature of "release plans sustained by excellent community support" which in this case is entirely dependent on the offender's class status as wealthy business persons.
(5) The Parole Board seems as interested in the "productive" as in the "law-abiding" future of the offenders.

This is perhaps an extreme case, but extreme cases often shed light on the general workings of the system. I want to emphasize two factors about this case which are characteristic of the general workings of the system. They are the complete substitution of individual preventive for general preventive concerns on the one hand, and the class nature of the individual preventive concerns on the other. With respect to the substitution of individual preventive for general preventive concerns, it is fairly clear that this is the aim of the Parole Act itself which provides, in s. 10, that the board "may" grant parole if it considers that:

10(1) . . .
(i) in the case of a grant of parole other than day parole, the inmate has derived the maximum benefit from imprisonment;
(ii) the reform and rehabilitation of the inmate will be aided by the grant of parole; and
(iii) the release of the inmate on parole would not constitute an undue risk to society;

The Act evidently leaves to the Parole Board a great deal of freedom in making its determination. According to the board's chairman for the past 14 years, these statutory criteria "are wide enough to drive a truck through, and they are really not that much help...But essentially, when you come right down to it, what the alchemy is by which you come to the decision of yes or no is a subjective judgment, sure. It is a value judgment made by the Board members." Nevertheless, there seem to be a few regularities in this "value judgment" which can be inferred from the "General

Guidelines" from the National Parole Board's current *Policy and Procedures Manual* (s. 104-6):

> 1.1. In making its decision, the Board generally considers, but is not limited to, the following guidelines:
> (a) The nature and gravity of the inmate's offence;
> (b) the inmate's history of law-violation, his past and present behaviour;
> (c) the inmate's total personality as it reflects the presence or absence of potential for serious harm to society;
> (d) the possibility that on release the offender would return to a life of criminal conduct and the possible effect on society if he did so;
> (e) the efforts made by the inmate during his imprisonment to improve himself through educational and vocational training and how well they demonstrate his desire to become a law-abiding citizen;
> (f) the inmate's plans for release and whether they are realistic enough to aid in his ultimate rehabilitation;
> (g) the extent of support available from family, friends and other contacts in the community;
> (h) whether employment possibilities exit;
> (i) how well the inmate appears to understand the circumstances that contributed to his criminal behaviour;
> (j) how well he can identify his personal goals and his capacity to maintain his motivation;
> (k) community response to release.

At first sight this appears to be a bewildering set of criteria in which *everything* is considered relevant. However, on reflection and having regard to other sources, it is possible to discern a working model.

In the first place, the primary concern seems to be with individual prevention, that is with the extent to which the prospective parolee can be expected to offend against the law when released and, indeed, when the parole is finished. The references to the offences in items (a) and (k) seem perfunctory and are certainly outnumbered by other concerns. In order to assess this likelihood of future criminality the board deems literally everything relevant, but there is an emphasis on the prisoner's *attitude* which the board is to gauge from his or her behaviour in prison, plans for release and understanding of the crime. In addition to these attitudinal matters, the board also considers the concrete factors of the criminal record, and the social and economic environment into which the prisoner will be released.

The expressed goals and the concrete factors are easy to grasp, but the attitudinal factors require further investigation. Elsewhere in the manual, one is given some indication of what this means. Under "Police Reports", the board "wishes to know if the inmate was co-operative when apprehended" (s. 103-3: 2.2.2.). From judges, the board wants an "impression of the inmate and his attitude and demeanour at the time of sentencing" (s. 103-3: 2.3.2.(*b*)). Sentencing courts generally consider "demeanour" in the sense of whether it is respectful or not. A disrespectful demeanour is said to show "lack of remorse", remorse being a mitigating factor. The required court-room demeanour has recently been characterized as "deferential". Indeed, the attitudinal references in the guidelines of the Parole Board seem designed to elicit *humility* from the prospective parolee: he or she must have made an effort to "improve", and his or her plans must be "realistic". Another aspect of this attitude seems to be how the prospective parolee explains his or her offence. The board seems concerned that the prisoner "accepts responsibility" for the offence. Two written comments by board members in cases observed by Carriere and Silverstone bring this out quite nicely:

> 0-13 The inmate clearly had a tendency to rationalize and excuse his behaviour both in terms of the offence itself and his institutional offences. He showed little insight into his pattern of irresponsible behaviour which included his fathering three children by three different women.
>
> . . . .
>
> 0-43 This inmate had no prior record and was a highly intelligent university student who had been trying to accumulate sufficient funds to attend a university in England. Though the inmate was not prepared to state that marijuana was dangerous or destructive, the Board managed to have him admit that he had broken the law and that he would not engage in such activities again.

This concern with "responsibility" pervades the prison system. The first "basic principle" of the Correctional Service of Canada, at least as endorsed by the Federal Corrections Agency Task Force Report, endorsed in turn by the then Solicitor-General is: "The offender is ultimately responsible for his criminal behaviour". And the whole goal of prison programmes is said to be to allow the offender "to demonstrate responsible conduct". The *MacGuigan Report* based its approach on the notion of "personal reformation" which it said "emphasises the personal responsibility of the prisoners interested". This was also endorsed by the Solicitor-General.

So the proper attitude is one that exhibits an acceptance of one's responsibility for the crime, an acceptance that it was "wrong" and a deferential and co-operative attitude with authority. What does all this mean concretely in the actual parole decision? Canadian empirical research into this question is somewhat more extensive than in the case of sentencing. Several very revealing studies have been undertaken.

In MacNaughton-Smith's study of approximately 800 National Parole Board decisions to grant or deny parole taken during the period 1962 to 1964, the factors that emerged as most important were the recommendation of the prison authorities, the parolee's proposed occupation and the criminal record. The institutional recommendation by itself was more important that any of the individual elements of institutional behaviour combined, some of which were entirely unrelated to parole granting (for example, formal discipline reports) and some of which were rather strongly related. These latter factors included, in order of importance: whether the prisoner received complete trades training, whether there was a favourable custodial report on his "industry" and whether he had a record of steady work. This suggests that the mere absence of rule-breaking behaviour is not enough to influence the decision and that, though certain definite, positive activities have an impact, there is something extra that cannot be captured in these terms which results in a favourable institutional recommendation. With respect to employment prospects on release, the question seems not to have been the nature of the job but whether or not there was one. Strongly but apparently only indirectly related to the parole decision was whether the applicant was employed at the time of the offence or not. The more extensive the criminal record and the greater the history of imprisonment, the lower was the chance of receiving parole, though the nature of the offences in the record did not seem to make an independent contribution. The legal type of the current offence did not seem to figure at all in factors strongly associated with parole. There were some weak associations between certain types of offences and parole, namely those convicted of murder and robbery were more likely to receive parole than others and those convicted of breaking and entering were less likely to receive parole. But this seemed entirely due to the strong effect of the length of the sentence, those with longer sentences being more likely to receive parole.

While MacNaughton-Smith's study was concerned with a mixture of "hard" and "soft" data, Demers' study of 541 parole decisions made by the National Parole Board during 1972 dealt mostly with hard data, including age, sex, race, socio-economic status, education, employment record, employment status on arrest, current offence type, aggregate sentence, number of previous convictions and previous institutional experience. When comparing this study with that of MacNaughton-Smith it should be noted that no attempt was made by Demers to gauge the impact of institutional behaviour or of the opinions of institutional authorities on the parole decision.

Demers found that the strongest relationship of all was between the parole officer's recommendation and the decision, meaning that in most cases the recommendation and decision were the same. However, controlling for the officer's recommendation he found the remaining important factors to be: (1) whether there had been a previous parole violation (which reduced the chances of parole); (2) current offence a non-violent property offence (reduced); (3) drug offender (reduced); (4) age (younger offenders had a better chance of parole; and (5) education (the better educated had a better chance of parole). Demers also investigated the factors influencing the parole officer's recommendation, given its importance in determining the final result. Here three factors emerged as significant: employment history (the better it was, the greater the chance of parole); sex (women had a better chance of parole); and race (whites had a better chance of parole than natives).

Race seemed to play a completely independent role. It was not systematically related to such "legal" factors as current offence or criminal record or to any other variable. In short, it could not be explained away. It should be noted that the absence of race as a relevant factor in MacNaughton-Smith's study seems to have been due to the fact that information on this variable was lacking in over 75% of the cases. MacNaughton-Smith made no effort to study the effect of sex on parole decisions.

Socio-economic status seems to have made little difference to the parole decision in Demers' study, but as the author noted, the range was extremely small. The fact that employment history did have an impact is evidence that, with parole as with sentencing, it is the fact of a job and not the nature of the job that counts. It should also be noted that unlike MacNaughton-Smith, Demers did not study job prospects on *release*, which might explain the prominence of employment *history*, because the two appear to be very strongly related.

MacNaughton-Smith's and Demers' studies were largely corroborated by Nuffield's recently published study of 2,500 releases from federal penitentiaries during 1970-72. This was a study of the *proportion of sentence served before release* and thus would include questions of remission as well as of parole, but parole would still be the major factor involved. Another difference from the other studies is that the race variable was not included, nor were such matters as institution or parole officer recommendation. This may account for Nuffield's ability to explain so little of the variation in her sample. Perhaps her finding that the security rating of the prisoner's institution bore a strong direct relationship to the proportion of sentence served can be used as a proxy for institutional evaluation, thus providing indirect support for the importance of this factor.

Once again, prior penal record emerges as the most important factor in explaining the variation in the proportion of sentence served. This is followed by the demographic variables of age and employment status at arrest (the younger and employed serving smaller portions of their sentences). These are followed by length of aggregate sentence, which, as in the other studies, varied directly with chances of early release. Apart from this, the offence type was not related to early release.

An interesting aspect of Nuffield's study is her attempt to relate parole decision-making to the risk of recidivism, defined as re-arrest for an indictable offence within three years of release. The factors analyzed by Nuffield were able to account for only 7.7% of the variation, but they are at least very suggestive. Penal record is the most important factor in recidivism as in release, and aggregate sentence also figures prominently in the expected direction, indicating that if the Parole Board's goal is to select for early release those least likely to be re-arrested, it is on the right track with these variables. On the other hand, age, which was more important than aggregated sentence in predicting recidivism, went in the *opposite* direction from what the Parole Board would seem to expect, as the younger parolees were more likely to be re-arrested. Finally, employment status at arrest, to which the board seems to attach so much importance on the release decision, was only very weakly related to recidivism.

Waller's earlier study of parole covered similar ground to Nuffield's and also found that aggregate sentence, previous record, age and employment at arrest predicted recidivism, but "extremely inefficiently". The finding with respect to aggregate sentence was also reproduced with respect to type of offence, with those serving the longer sentences that accompany offences against the person (homicide, sex and wounding) being less likely to re-offend (and more likely to get parole) than those serving the shorter sentences for offences against property (breaking and entering, theft and fraud). Narcotics offences fell into the low recidivism group. Waller's study also examined post-release variables. A very important one was employment status and it had a special relevance for those on parole. Parolees were pressured into accepting low-paying jobs and keeping them. But the effect of this was only to *delay* re-arrest beyond six months. This delay factor was the only "rehabilitative effect" that Waller could attribute to parole. Otherwise, the observed differences in recidivism between those released on parole and those discharged were attributable to the Parole Board practice of selecting "good risks" (by virtue of penal record and employment on arrest) for parole.

Not everyone who gets parole keeps it, of course, though most (about two-thirds) do. Since the abolition in 1977 of automatic forfeiture upon conviction of an indictable offence, all terminations are within the discretion of the board. Furthermore, where federal prisoners are concerned, the board's power has been enormously increased with the introduction, in 1970, of mandatory supervision. Virtually every federal prisoner is therefore released to the custody of the National Parole Board, which retains the power of returning the person to prison. Though most revocations follow upon conviction for an indictable offence, about 40% do not (36% of revoked paroles and 44% of revoked mandatory supervisions). From the studies reviewed so far we know that in some cases revocations are associated with variables making release upon parole less likely, thereby exacerbating the effects of parole with respect to these variables. They include: previous convictions (MacNaughton-Smith, Demers), race (Demers) and employment status at arrest (MacNaughton-Smith). With respect to sentence length, those with longer sentences are more likely to be revoked, thus counteracting to some small extent the "smoothing" effect of the granting process.

We lack extensive information on the grounds of post-release variables, apart from offences, which account for revocation, although a study by Nicolas of parole suspensions in Quebec is of some help. It suggests that employment plays an important part in whether or not one keeps parole. This would be expected from the standard conditions of parole themselves, all of which essentially require the parolee to be under the authority of his or her supervisor except for the one that requires that he or she "endeavour to maintain steady employment" (*Policy and Procedures Manual*, s. 5.105-2).

The supervisors Nicolas interviewed all thought that the employment condition was the most important one of all. And while the proportion of suspended paroles ultimately revoked was only slightly higher for the unemployed, the suspensions in total included a much higher number of unemployed than employed parolees (though, understandably, there is no information as to the proportion of unemployed who did *not* have their parole suspended). Breach of *general* conditions (which includes but is not restricted to the employment condition) also accounted for a higher proportion of suspensions of unemployed parolees than of employed parolees and a much higher proportion if suspensions for offences are excluded. Both Nicolas' and Waller's studies indicate that contacts with the parolee's employer are an important part of the job of parole supervisor.

From this brief review of Canadian studies, a number of conclusions can be drawn about parole. First, in the decision as to what proportion of his or her sentence a prisoner will serve, the offence itself recedes entirely into the background and the important factors have almost all to do with the individual. Who the person is becomes the main factor. This is something about which the board has from time to time been quite frank: "the policy of the Board is, as far as possible to . . . treat the offender rather than the offence". In this connection, the primary factor remains the criminal record, but demographic factors (class, race, sex, age) are intensified from their position at sentence, both directly and indirectly through the criminal record. The result of this is to completely destroy the "gravity" ranking which has been done by the courts both within legal categories of offences and between them. The Solicitor-General has recently published figures showing that, on the average, for each category of offence, parolees have longer sentences than those released on mandatory supervision, but the relative amount of time actually served before release is reversed in most cases and drastically reduced in others. It also appears that the large category of non-violent property offences have relatively low parole rates, while crimes against the person have high parole rates, with robberies somewhere in the middle. It should be pointed out, finally, that the over-all effect of this is probably to raise the *absolute* as well as the relative level of punishment for those who do not benefit from parole, because courts appear to have increased in severity the general level of sentencing in response to parole in a manner that more than compensates for the small reduction in average time served which is actually effected by parole.

Now it seems that the board's emphasis of these personal factors has partly to do with selecting for parole those least likely to be re-arrested. But this cannot be the complete explanation because several factors associated with parole are unrelated to official recidivism or at least less related than their importance in parole decisions would require. These include the general evaluation of the prison authorities, job status at arrest, and age.

As we have seen, the studies suggest that the prison evaluation is entirely unconnected to rule-breaking, so its effect is not merely to enforce the prison's explicit rules through the threat of parole denied. It certainly has the *effect* of increasing the personal authority of prison officials and this must also be the effect of the parole board's practice of receiving reports and "evaluations" for all "staff in the institution who deal with the inmate" and "psychiatrists", "psychologists" and "medical reports" (*Policy and Procedures Manual*, s. 3.103-3:2). Naturally it would also increase the personal authority of parole supervisors and, indeed, employers. Furthermore, it seems that those who submit to this authority are to that extent those who, in general, succeed in obtaining and keeping parole. Naturally, submission to authority is not the only thing, as the case of McNamara illustrates, and, since the Parole Board also purports to take into account co-operation with police, courts and other social agencies, it would be stretching the imagination somewhat to think that the *point* of parole was to enhance the authority of all these agencies. In my opinion there is a more attractive alternative hypothesis which better accounts for all these phenomena and accounts as well for the Parole Board's practice of giving parole to younger prisoners even though they are most likely to re-offend. In the old but often-cited sentencing case of *Warner* leniency with respect to youth as assimilated to severity with respect to long criminal records in the following terms:

> Wilful persistence in the deliberately acquired habit of crime marks the offender as an enemy of society in proportion to the extent of such persistence. An individual's actions may indicate his permanent tendencies, or, on the other hand, they may merely be the result of transient moods or momentary impulses. Where we find an individual, over a period of time, pursuing a course of conduct, it is thereby possible reasonably to determine his character or mental attitude. That is why Judges consider the previous record of a delinquent in determining the penalty to be imposed upon him. The older and more mature the individual is, the easier it is to determine his character and attitude from his conduct. In a youth the testing time is short; in the mature man it has been longer.

So an alternative explanation is that the Parole Board seeks to *discover*, through a variety of tests stretching back before the offence and continuing through the prison sentence to the parole period, who among those in its charge will and who will not accept their assigned role in the general authority structure, which, over the vast realm of the "private sphere" is none other than the class structure. For those few who hold dominant positions, such as McNamara and Cooper, there is no difficulty in making this determination. Prison was not meant for them in the first place. But for most people, the role which the productive process assigns to them is subordination to the arbitrary personal authority of capital. Consequently, they must demonstrate their willingness to submit to arbitrary personal authority wherever it exists.

Parole thus intensifies those undemocratic features of the sentencing process which make punishment depend upon who one is and not what he has done. In doing so, it further sacrifices, to the point of complete abandonment, the goal of prevention of harm to victims of crime to the goal of strengthening class relations. The preference in parole of personal over property crimes is just the logical result of a "rehabilitation" orientation. Of course, parole does not "rehabilitate" anyone, even in the conventional sense of preventing recidivism. At its best it merely selects for parole those less likely, for reasons closely connected to their class, to be re-arrested. Even in this respect its success rate is little better than what could be achieved by random selection. Moreover, even preventing recidivism would not reduce the level of crime, because the causes of crime are not individual but structural. In the permanent structural unemployment of modern capitalism, giving one person a job merely means taking it away from someone else.

Naturally, parole is undemocratic in other ways as well. For one thing, it further removes the penalty in any case and in all cases from popular control. Indeed, its *point*, according to some of its supporters, is precisely to deceive the public about penalties. Waller considers one of the "valuable functions" of parole to be "to placate public opinion with the claim that justice is being done and protection being given, even though criminals are being set free" and Norval Morris considers it an important "latent purpose of the division of power between judge and parole board...to give the possibility of some clemency while appearing in the public eye to be imposing a more severe punishment". It should not be forgotten, of course, that this "clemency" is for the benefit of the few at the expense of the many and is not exactly randomly distributed. Finally, parole is undemocratic, like sentencing, in reposing extraordinary personal discretionary power in the hands of parole authorities and, more importantly, in thus being the foundation stone for the subjection to arbitrary personal power throughout the prison system which largely characterizes the status of prisoners.

## CONCLUSION

We owe to Foucault the insight that the penitentiary system "is not intended to eliminate offences but rather to distinguish them, to distribute them, to use them"; that the goal of the penitentiary invention was the "discipline" of offenders and not the prevention of crime; and that the task of the new penal technicians was "to produce bodies that were both docile and capable" through "perpetual assessment" and "permanent observation". However, Foucault is somewhat coy about the precise nature or object of that docility which remains for him and abstract "normalization". Melossi and Pavarine, on the other hand, in examining the same historical terrain from the point of view of material reality and not just expressed ideas, are more explicit. The penitentiary "is like a factory producing proletarians".

> The whole secret of the workhouse and the *Rasphuis* lay, right from the very start, in the way they applied bourgeois *ideals* of life and society to the preparation of people, particularly poor people, proletarians, so that they would accept an order and discipline which would render them docile instruments of exploitation.

Thus is solved the apparent paradox in Paterson's often quoted aphorism: "It is impossible to train men for freedom in a condition of captivity". It turns out that they are not being trained for "freedom" at all but for the captivity of subjection to arbitrary personal power which is the worker's concrete situation in capitalism. In this way the penal system is put at the service of the oppressive social relations of production, the relations of inequality, of dominance and subordination which characterize Canada as they do all capitalist societies. Pushed aside, no matter how often repeated in Bills and Charters of Rights, are all of the bourgeois ideals of democracy which, as usual, find it impossible to co-exist with bourgeois reality.

## APPENDIX

*Prisoner Unemployment Rate (Male) compared to Unemployment Rate in General Male Population 15 years and over for 1978*

| Province | Nfld. | P.E.I. | N.S. | N.B. | Man. |
|---|---|---|---|---|---|
| Participation Rate | 51.7% | 57.8% | 56.4% | 55.0% | 63.1% |
| Participation Rate adjusted for age and sex (male)* | 61.7 | 70.6 | 67.3 | 65.7 | 75.6 |
| % Students adjusted for age and sex** | 15.1 | 13.8 | 18.8 | 16.7 | 16.9 |
| "Unemployment Rate" | 16.4 | 9.9 | 10.6 | 12.6 | 6.5 |
| Unemployment Rate adjusted for age and sex*** | 20.6 | 10.6 | 13.3 | 15.7 | 7.9 |
| Real Unemployment Rate adjusted for age and sex (excluding Students) | 35.9 | 23.1 | 22.9 | 27.9 | 13.5 |
| Prisoner Unemployment Rate at arrest (excluding Students) (admissions 1978) | 74.6 | 70.1 | 62.0 | 59.7 | 59.6 |
| Factor by which Prisoner Unemployment Rate exceeds Real Unemployment Rate | 2.1 | 3.0 | 2.7 | 2.1 | 4.4 |

\* Males have a higher participation rate than the total population but the difference is greater for the over-25 age group than for the 15 to 24 group. The latter group is greatly over represented in prison. To reflect this, the provincial participation rates were adjusted to achieve a rate specific to males of the same age composition as that of the prison population for the province involved. The sex and age differences in participation rates had to be derived from figures for the whole of Canada, so they can only be approximate where each province is concerned.

\*\* For simplicity's sake, I have retained the cut-off at between 15 and 24 on the one hand and 25 and over on the other, though finer calculations are possible for students. It should be noted that occasional Bulletin 2.8 of the 1976 Census says that the 15-19 school attendance rate may be underestimated by as much as 25% which would mean that the provincial R.U.R. would be considerably over-estimated.

\*\*\* Fifteen to twenty-four year-old-males have a higher "unemployment rate" than the total population but those twenty-five and older have a lower one. Similar adjustments to those for participation rates were made to achieve an age and sex specific rate for each province.

## Cunningham v. Canada
(1993), 20 C.R. (4th) 57 (S.C.C.)

Appeal from judgment of Ontario Court of Appeal affirming judgment of Smith J. dismissing prisoner's application for habeas corpus.

April 22, 1993. The judgment of the court was delivered by

MCLACHLIN J.: — On February 14, 1981, the appellant was sentenced to 12 years' imprisonment for manslaughter following a brutal slaying in Chatham Head, New Brunswick. Under the *Parole Act* in force at the time of his sentencing, he was entitled to be released on mandatory supervision after serving approximately two-thirds of his sentence, on April 8, 1989, provided that he was of good behaviour.

In 1986 the *Parole Act* was amended to allow the Commissioner of Corrections, within six months of the "presumptive release date", to refer a case to the National Parole Board where he has reason to believe, on the basis of information obtained within those six months, that the inmate is likely, prior to the expiration of his sentence, to commit an offence causing death or serious harm: *Parole Act*, R.C.S. 1985, c. P-2, s. 21.3(3)(*a*)(ii) (en. c. 34 (2nd Supp.), s. 5.) The Parole Board may, if it sees fit, deny release of the inmate.

The appellant had maintained a good behaviour record in prison. In 1988, his parole officer recommended him for parole and requested a community assessment, since the appellant had indicated he would be returning to his home community, not far from the scene of the crime. The appellant expected to be released on April 8, 1989.

This, however, was not to be. Shortly before his release date, the appellant received a notice that the Commissioner had decided to seek the continued detention of the appellant under the 1986 amendments to the *Parole Act*. His community, alerted to his release by the community assessment, evinced concern at his early release given the violence of the crime. Further assessments made in the six months preceding the early release date suggested that he remained homicidal when drunk. There was said to be a 50 per cent chance of his returning to alcohol, and a 50 per cent chance that if drunk he would commit an act of violence. There was also evidence that he was somewhat unstable and had not accepted his responsibility for the crime. While this evidence was brought forward in the six months preceding the anticipated release date, similar observations may be found in the prison records for preceding years.

Following a detention hearing, the appellant was ordered to be detained until his sentence expired on February 13, 1993, subject to annual reviews. The appellant brought an action to the Supreme Court of Ontario for a writ of habeas corpus. The application was refused. The appellant appealed to the Court of Appeal for Ontario, but his appeal was dismissed. The appellant now appeals to this court.

Three issues arise before us:

1. Does the 1986 amendment to the *Parole Act* changing the conditions for release on mandatory supervision amount to a denial of the appellant's liberty contrary to the principles of fundamental justice under s. 7 of the *Canadian Charter of Rights and Freedoms*?
2. If the appellant's s. 7 rights were violated, is the violation justifiable under s. 1 of the *Charter*?

3. Did the Commissioner act lawfully in accordance with the legislation in referring the appellant to the National Parole Board for a hearing within six months of his release date?

## 1. *Were the Appellant's Rights under Section 7 of the Charter Violated?*

In order for the appellant to succeed in this argument, he must establish two things:

(1) that he was deprived of his liberty by the amendment to the *Parole Act* which resulted in denial of his release on mandatory supervision; and
(2) that the deprivation of his liberty was contrary to the fundamental interests of justice.

My conclusion is that while the appellant's liberty may be said to have been adversely affected by the changes to the *Parole Act*, the deprivation was not contrary to the principles of fundamental justice.

The first question is whether the appellant has suffered a deprivation of liberty which attracts the protection of s. 7 of the *Charter*. This raises two subsidiary questions: (1) has the appellant shown that he has been deprived of liberty? and; (2) if so, is the deprivation sufficiently serious to attract *Charter* protection?

In my view, the appellant has shown that he has been deprived of liberty. The argument that because the appellant was sentenced to twelve years' imprisonment there can be no further impeachment of his liberty interest within the twelve-year period runs counter to previous pronouncements, and oversimplifies the concept of liberty. This and other courts have recognized that there are different types of liberty interests in the context of correctional law. In *Dumas v. Centre de Detention Leclerc de Laval*, [1986] 2 S.C.R. 459, at p. 464, Lamer J. (as he then was) identified three different deprivations of liberty: (1) the initial deprivation of liberty; (2) a substantial change in conditions amounting to a further deprivation of liberty; and (3) a continuation of the deprivation of liberty. In *R. v. Gamble*, [1988] 2 S.C.R. 595, at p. 645, this court held by a majority, per Wilson J. (Lamer and L'Heureux-Dubé JJ. concurring), that the liberty interest involved in not continuing the period of parole ineligibility may be protected by s. 7 of the *Charter*:

> . . . the continuation of the 25-year period of parole ineligibility deprives the appellant of an important residual liberty interest which is cognizable under s. 7 and which may be appropriately remedied by way of *habeas corpus* if found to be unlawful.

. . . .

I do not find it useful to ask whether the liberty interest was "vested" or "not vested". The only questions which arise under the *Charter* are whether a protected liberty interest is limited, and if so, whether that limitation accords with the principles of fundamental justice. To qualify an interest as "vested" or "not vested" does not really advance the debate, except in the sense that a vested interest might be seen as being more important or worthy of protection than one which is not vested. In that event, I think it better to speak directly of the importance of the interest, rather than introducing the property law concept of vesting. At the same time, it is important to recognize that liberty interests may cover a spectrum from the less important to the fundamental. A restriction affecting the form in which a sentence is served, the issue here, may be less serious than would be an ex post facto increase in the sentence.

In the case at bar, the appellant was sentenced to twelve years and was required under his warrant of committal, both before and after the amendment of the *Parole Act*, to serve that sentence in its entirety. Thus the duration of the restriction of his liberty interest has not been affected. As Lamer J. held for the court in *Dumas*, supra, at p. 464, "In the context of parole, the continued detention of an inmate will only become unlawful if he has acquired the status of a parolee". The appellant had never acquired parolee status, and his sentence, contrary to his counsel's submissions, has not been increased.

However, the *manner* in which he may serve a part of that sentence, the second liberty interest identified by Lamer J. in *Dumas*, supra, has been affected. One has "more" liberty, or better quality of liberty, when one is serving time on mandatory supervision than when one is serving time in prison. The appellant had a high expectation, contingent on his good behaviour, that he would be released on mandatory supervision on April 8, 1989, had the *Parole Act* not been amended; indeed, he would automatically have been released on mandatory supervision given his good behaviour. The effect of the 1986 amendment of the *Parole Act* was to reduce that expectation of liberty, in the sense that it curtailed the probability of his release on mandatory supervision. This resulted from the new power of the Commissioner to refer exceptional cases to the Parole Board based on events and information in the six months immediately preceding the presumptive release date. As the British Columbia Court of Appeal put it in *Ross v. Kent Institution* (1987), 34 C.C.C. (3d) 452 [57 C.R. (3d) 79] (B.C. C.A.), at p. 454 [C.C.C., p. 81 C.R.]: "The effect of the 1986 amendments . . . is to alter the right of an inmate to serve a portion of his sentence on mandatory supervision by *qualifying that right*". [Emphasis added.]

I conclude that the appellant has suffered deprivation of liberty. The next question is whether the deprivation is sufficiently serious to warrant *Charter* protection. The *Charter* does not protect against insignificant or "trivial" limitations of rights. . . . It follows that qualification of a prisoner's expectation of liberty does not necessarily bring the matter within the purview of s. 7 of the *Charter*. The qualification must be significant enough to warrant constitutional protection. To require that all changes to the manner in which a sentence is served be in accordance with the principles of fundamental justice would trivialize the protections under the Charter. To quote Lamer J. in *Dumas*, supra, at p. 464, there must be a "substantial change in conditions amounting to a further deprivation of liberty".

The change in the manner in which the sentence was served in this case meets this test. There is a significant difference between life inside a prison versus the greater liberty enjoyed on the outside under mandatory supervision. Such a change was recognized as worthy of s. 7 protection in *Gamble*, supra.

Having concluded that the appellant has been deprived of a liberty interest protected by s. 7 of the *Charter*, we must determine whether this is contrary to the principles of fundamental justice under s. 7 of the *Charter*. In my view, while the amendment of the *Parole Act* to eliminate automatic release on mandatory supervision restricted the appellant's liberty interest, it did not violate the principles of fundamental justice. The principles of fundamental justice are concerned not only with the interest of the person who claims his liberty has been limited, but with the protection of society. Fundamental justice requires that a fair balance be struck between these interests, both substantively and procedurally . . . . In my view the balance struck in this case conforms to this requirement.

The first question is whether, from a substantive point of view, the change in the law strikes the right balance between the accused's interest and the interest of society. The interest of society in being protected against the violence that may be perpetrated as a consequence of the early release of inmates whose sentence has not been fully served needs no elaboration. On the other side of the balance lies the prisoner's interest in an early conditional release.

The balance is struck by qualifying the prisoner's expectation regarding the form in which the sentence would be served. The expectation of mandatory release is modified by the amendment permitting a discretion to prevent early release where society's interest are endangered. A change in the form in which a sentence is served, whether it be favourable or unfavourable to the prisoner, is not, in itself, contrary to any principle of fundamental justice. Indeed, our system of justice has always permitted correctional authorities to make appropriate changes in how a sentence is served, whether the changes relate to place, conditions, training facilities, or treatment. Many changes in the conditions under which sentences are served occur on an administrative basis in response to the prisoner's immediate needs or behaviour. Other changes are more general. From time to time, for example, new approaches in correctional law are introduced by legislation or regulation. These initiatives change the manner in which some of the prisoners in the system serve their sentences.

The next question is whether the nature of this particular change in the rules as to the form in which the sentence would be served violates the *Charter*. In my view, it does not. The change is directly related to the public interest in protecting society from persons who may commit serious harm if released on mandatory supervision. Only if the Commissioner is satisfied on the facts before him that this may be the case can he refer the matter to the Parole Board for a hearing. And only if the Board is satisfied that there is a significant danger of recidivism can it order the prisoner's continued incarceration. Thus the prisoner's liberty interest is limited only to the extent that this is shown to be necessary for the protection of the public. It is difficult to dispute that it is just to afford a limited discretion for the review of parole applicants who may commit an offence causing serious harm or death. Substantively, the balance is fairly struck.

Nor does the procedure established under the Act and regulations violate the principles of fundamental justice. The change was made by law. The new procedure provides for a hearing to consider whether the expectation of release on mandatory supervision was warranted. The prisoner is entitled to representation throughout . . . .

I conclude that the appellant has not established that the changes to the *Parole Act* deprived him of his liberty contrary to the principles of fundamental justice. No violation of s. 7 having been made out, it is unnecessary to consider the arguments under s. 1 of the *Charter*.

## 2. Did the Commissioner Act Lawfully?

I turn to the final issue: whether the Commissioner's referral of the appellant's case to the Parole Board was illegal and contrary to the law. Under s. 21.3(3), the Commissioner may refer an inmate's case to the Board no later than six months preceding his "presumptive release" on mandatory supervision. An exeption to this general rule is permitted where, due to the inmate's behaviour or information received within the six-month period, the Commissioner has reason to believe that the inmate is likely, prior to the expiration of his sentence, to commit an offence causing death or serious harm. The Commissioner must have formed the belief on the basis of "information obtained within those six months" (s. 21.3(3)(*a*)(ii)).

The Commissioner referred the appellant's case as a "Commissioner's Referral based upon new information", offering the opinion that "without treatment intervention there are reasonable grounds to believe that this inmate is likely to commit an offence causing death or serious harm prior to warrant expiry date". The Commissioner's memorandum included two psychiatric reports, a letter from the Crown prosecutor and an updated R.C.M.P. report. All this information was received within the six months before the presumptive release date. It is argued that the information relied on by the Commissioner, while nominally arising within the six-month period before the appellant's prospective date for release on mandatory supervision, in fact is no more than an update of information which was on the appellant's file before that period. It is true that references to the appellant's volatility, drinking problems, lack of acceptance of guilt and tendency to violence when drunk may be found in the files prior to the six-month period. But that should not, in my view, prevent the Commissioner from relying on new and revised reports to the same effect when they come to his attention within the six-month pre-release period did not find its echoes and antecedents in the previous prison record, given the long-standing nature of the problems typically involved in these cases.

I would agree with the motions judge that an objective test is appropriate. The issue put before this court was whether the information could be said to be "new" in the substantive sense, rather than merely the temporal sense. The motions judge, having considered all the material, concluded on an objective test that it had not been established that the Commissioner had acted illegally in the sense of not forming his opinion on the basis of information obtained within six months. My review of the record does not persuade me that he was wrong.

In my view, the Commissioner did not violate the Act by referring the appellant's case to the National Parole Board for reconsideration of his eligibility for release on mandatory supervision.

I would dismiss the appeal.

*Appeal dismissed.*

## Gallichon v. Canada (Commissioner of Corrections)
(1995), 101 C.C.C. (3d) 414 (Ont. C.A.)

APPEAL by applicant from the dismissal of his application for *habeas corpus*. The judgment of the court was delivered by

AUSTIN J.A.: — This is an appeal from the dismissal of the application of George Gallichon, then a prisoner in a federal institution, for an order for the issuance of a writ of *habeas corpus*. The object of the application was to secure a post-Charter review of the legality of Gallichon's continued incarceration pursuant to findings made in 1967 that he was an habitual criminal and that he be confined in preventive detention.

The application for *habeas corpus* was made July 24, 1992, and heard October 23, 1992. It was dismissed on that date and reasons for dismissal were delivered April 21, 1993. The judge of first instance held that she had jurisdiction to review the decision of the National Parole Board not to release the applicant on full parole, but found that there were no "highly unusual circumstances" in the case and so followed the recommendation of Cory J. in *Steele v. Mountain Institution (Warden)* (1990), 60 C.C.C. (3d) 1, [1990] 2 S.C.R. (3d) 1385, 80 C.R. 257, that such matters be left to the Federal Court.

On January 19, 1993, between the time of the decision of the trial judge and the release of her reasons six months later, Gallichon was released on day parole. On February 23, 2993, he was released on full parole.

On August 20, 1993, Gallichon moved for an extension of time within which to appeal. The motion was opposed by the respondent upon the ground that any appeal would be moot and by the Attorney General for Ontario upon the ground that the proper course was an application for judicial review in the Federal Court. An order extending the time for appealing was granted on October 8, 1993. The Attorney General of Ontario intervened on the application in the court below. She was served with notice of this appeal but elected not to participate.

*Facts*

Gallichon was born July 30, 1929. His criminal career appears to have begun in Thorold, Ontario, in 1948, at age 18 or 19 with a breach of the *Canada Shipping Act*, S.C. 1934, c. 44. A 1988 report suggests that this involved damage to a vessel during a strike of the Seafarers' International Union. He received a sentence of seven months. The same month, he was convicted in Welland, Ontario of mischief and assault occasioning actual bodily harm. He was released on parole on March 22, 1949.

. . .

Of the 37 offences committed before his sentence of preventive detention in 1967, four may be said to have involved violence, the most serious resulting in a sentence of 15 months. The specific offences which immediately preceded Gallichon's being found to be an habitual criminal were theft over $50, for which he received nine months, breaking and entering with intent to commit an indictable offence, for which he received 18 months concurrent, and mischief, for which he received a sentence of eight months consecutive. The last of these apparently involved damaging the contents of his cell in Oakalla Prison in British Columbia.

On the basis of his record he was found by the trial judge to be an habitual criminal.

. . .

*The period 1967 to 1992*

Gallichon was sentenced to preventive detention in February, 1967. In 1972, he went unlawfully at large for 10 days and was sentenced on August 29, 1972, to six months' imprisonment.

On July 24, 1973, he escaped from prison. He was recaptured three weeks later and sentenced on August 27, 1973, to two years for escaping lawful custody. On August 15, 1973, he was sentenced in Winnipeg to two years for theft over $200.

On January 30, 1975, the applicant was released from B.C. Penitentiary on full parole to the Anchorage Residence. On February 20, 1975, Gallichon left the residence in the morning and did not return for several days. His parole was to be suspended; however, arrangements were made to have him enter the Tri-Con Society, a half-way house in Richmond, B.C. On March 19, 1975, he failed to return to Tri-Con and his parole was suspended on March 27, 1975, and revoked by the Board on May 8, 1975.

On February 21, 1977, Gallichon went unlawfully at large while on an escorted temporary absence. He was returned to custody on March 15, 1977, having on that date engaged in robbery with violence against an individual from whom he stole approximately $80. He was sentenced for this offence on June 1, 1977, in Nanaimo, B.C. to one year.

The Board considered the appellant's case on October 4, 1977, and deferred parole. He was reviewed annually, with each review resulting in a denial of further conditional release.

In 1979, Gallichon was tried and acquitted on a charge of murder. Apparently his association with a particular group within the penitentiary led to his being charged along with them for the murder of another prisoner. The evidence against Gallichon was that he was seen talking with the group shortly before the victim was attacked by the others. He was acquitted of all charges. This matter was not mentioned by either counsel, either in the facts or in oral argument.

A progress summary on September 27, 1983, concluded with the recommendation by the case management team that unescorted temporary absences be granted. A month later, the Board granted the applicant unescorted temporary absences of 48 hours per month from Mountain Institution to Robson Centre in Vancouver where he was to spend the night. A special condition was that the applicant was required to abstain from all intoxicants. To March 13, 1984, however, no absences had been granted because Gallichon had been charged with possessing contraband in the institution.

On September 27, 1984, the Board granted the appellant day parole of 10 days per month to Howard House in Surrey, B.C. to run for six months. Gallichon, however, went unlawfully at large on December 12, 1984, and his parole was suspended two days later. He was arrested in Vancouver on December 19th and returned to the institution.

On March 27, 1985, the Board permitted Gallichon to return to his program at Robson Centre for 10 days per month. This day parole was ended as a result of his being unlawfully at large.

On June 6, 1985, the Board denied full parole but granted day parole to Robson Centre for six months. On September 20th, Gallichon left Robson Centre and failed to return. His day parole was suspended. A month later he was located in Toronto where he had been arrested by the police.

On December 12, 1985, the Board granted day parole to Gallichon, to be spent at Montgomery Centre in Toronto.

On June 5, 1986, the Board continued day parole for another four months, reserving full parole until accommodation suitable to Gallichon's needs could be located.

On June 16, 1986, a special report was prepared for the Board indicating that Gallichon's day parole had been suspended for misrepresenting to his parole officer his activities in the community, failing to advise her that he had quit his employment, and for suspected use of drugs and possible involvement in dealing. The Board held a hearing on August 21, 1986, and reserved its decision for up to six months to investigate further potential residences of Gallichon.

On November 28, 1986, the Board held a further day parole hearing and granted day parole to Gallichon to Keele Community Centre in Toronto, to commence when space was available, under specified conditions. Before being released, however, parole was cancelled on February 10, 1987.

. . .

On November 23, 1988, Gallichon's parole officer recommended unescorted temporary absences be granted for up to 72 hours per month plus travel time to Keele Community Correction Centre in Toronto from Frontenac Institution in Kingston.

On January 11, 1989, the Board granted the applicant escorted temporary absences of up to 24 hours per month for six months. On June 9, 1989, the Board granted unescorted temporary absences of up to 72 hours plus travel time to the Portsmouth Community Correctional Centre for up to six months under specified conditions involving abstention from alcohol and drugs and submitting to urinalysis. On September 6, 1989, the Board granted day parole to Portsmouth Centre for up to six months, subject to the availability of accommodation.

On May 30, 1990, a special report was prepared indicating that Gallichon had tested positive for marijuana use and warning that action would be taken in the event of a further positive test result on him. On July 10, 1990, the Board continued day parole for a further six months but denied full parole. On November 2, 1990, however, day parole was suspended because of a further positive test for marijuana.

The Board reconsidered the matter on December 6, 1990, and cancelled the suspension of parole on condition that Gallichon participate in a treatment program.

On January 7, 1991, the Board continued his day parole for a further seven months.

On May 21, 1991, Gallichon was arrested for attempting to steal a steak from a supermarket in Kingston, Ontario. No action was recommended in this regard. On June 18, 1991, he was fined $200 for theft under $1,000.

On June 17, 1991, the Board decided to take "no action" and stated that: "Continued day parole under increased Community Correctional Centre restrictions does not constitute an unmanageable risk to the community".

On November 19, 1991, the Board revoked Gallichon's parole because he had been arrested by police in Kingston on July 13, 1991, for shoplifting a pair of shorts from Sears and had in his possession a prescription drug from which the label had been removed. He was convicted and received 14 days for theft on October 3, 1991. The Board noted that it agreed:

> ... with your assistant that you require an in-house drug program prior to any expansion of release. The risk you present without that is not manageable. We are revoking your day parole but would consider your case again on receipt of a submission with acceptance into a CRF with an in-house substance abuse program. We would waive the six-month waiting period if necessary.

On April 9, 1992, the Board granted day parole for a five-day assessment at Serenity House in Belleville, Ontario, to be followed by day parole of up to six months upon successful completion of the assessment and acceptance by Serenity House. On July 17, 1992, the Board terminated day parole because Gallichon had tested positive for THC, and marijuana seeds were found in his pocket. The Board expressed the hope that "some appropriate release plan will be completed in the very near future".

This application was launched on July 24, 1992.

*The records of the National Parole Board*

In this context, regard must be had for the relevant provision of the *Parole Act*, R.S.C. 1985, c. P-2 (now the *Corrections and Conditional Release Act*, S.C. 1992, c. 20). Until 1968, s. 8(*a*) [S.C. 1958, c. 38] established the following criteria for the granting of parole:

> 8. The Board may
>
> (*a*) grant parole to an inmate if the Board considers that the inmate has derived the maximum benefit from imprisonment and that the reform and rehabilitation of the inmate will be aided by the grant of parole;

From 1970 on, the criteria were set out in s. 10 [R.S.C. 1970, c. P-2] as follows:

> 10(1) The Board may
>
> (*a*) grant parole to an inmate, subject to any terms or conditions it considers desirable, if the Board considers that
>   (i) in the case of a grant of parole other than day parole, the inmate has derived the maximum benefit from imprisonment,
>   (ii) the reform and rehabilitation of the inmate will be aided by the grant of parole, and
>   (iii) the release of the inmate on parole would not constitute an undue risk to society.

As an habitual offender, Gallichon was entitled to an annual review.

. . .

*Habitual offender legislation*

Gallichon was sentenced in 1967 under what was then known as the "habitual offender/preventive detention" section. Originally enacted in 1947, s. 660 of the *Criminal Code* provided as follows in 1967 [S.C. 1953-54, c. 51]:

> 660(1) Where an accused has been convicted of an indictable offence the court may, upon application, impose a sentence of preventive detention in lieu of any other sentence that might be imposed for the offence for which he was convicted or that was imposed for such offence, or in addition to any sentence that was imposed for such offence if the sentence has expired, if

(a) The accused is found to be an habitual criminal, and
(b) the court is of the opinion that because the accused is an habitual criminal, it is expedient for the protection of the public to sentence him to preventive detention.

(2) For the purposes of subsection (1), an accused is an habitual criminal if

(a) he has previously, since attaining the age of eighteen years, on at least three separate and independent occasions been convicted of an indictable offence for which he was liable to imprisonment for five years or more and is leading persistently a criminal life, or
(b) he has been previously sentenced to preventive detention.

This legislation provided for an indefinite life sentence in lieu of or in addition to any other sentence where an offender had, on at least three separate occasions since attaining the age of 18, been convicted of an indictable offence for which he was liable to imprisonment for five years or more and was "leading persistently a criminal life".

. . .

The habitual offender legislation was repealed by the *Criminal Law Amendment Act, 1977*, S.C. 1976-77, c. 53, s. 14. Also repealed were the sections dealing with dangerous sexual offenders. In their place was enacted a provision dealing with dangerous offenders. It read as follows:

688. Where, upon an application made under this Part following a conviction of a person for an offence but before the offender is sentenced therefor, it is established to the satisfaction of the court

(a) that the offence for which the offender has been convicted is a serious personal injury offence described in paragraph (a) of the definition of an expression in section 687 and the offender constitutes a threat to the life, safety or physical or mental wellbeing of other persons on the basis of evidence establishing
  (i) a pattern of repetitive behaviour by the offender, of which the offence for which he has been convicted forms a part, showing a failure to restrain his behaviour and a likelihood of his causing death or injury to other persons, or inflicting severe psychological damage upon other persons, through failure in the future to restrain his behaviour,
  (ii) a pattern of persistent aggressive behaviour by the offender, of which the offence for which he has been convicted forms a part, showing a substantial degree of indifference on the part of the offender as to the reasonably foreseeable consequences to other persons of his behaviour, or
  (iii) any behaviour by the offender, associated with the offence for which he has been convicted, that is of such a brutal nature as to compel the conclusion that his behaviour in the future is unlikely to be inhibited by normal standards of behavioural restraint, or
(b) that the offence for which the offender has been convicted is a serious personal injury offence described in paragraph (b) of the definition of that expression in section 687 and the offender, by his conduct in any sexual matter, including that involved in the commission of the offence for which he has been convicted has shown a failure to control his sexual impulses and a likelihood of his causing injury, pain or other evil to other persons through failure in the future to control his sexual impulses

the court may find the offender to be a dangerous offender and may thereupon impose a sentence of detention in a penitentiary for an indeterminate period, in lieu of any other sentence that might be imposed for the offence for which the offender has been convicted.

Clearly, for the non-sexual offender, the criteria for preventive detention were very much narrowed by these amendments, with the primary focus now resting on an individual's demonstrated capacity for violence against and injury to people.

Those amendments did not provide for the release of the habitual offenders then in custody . . . .

*Law*

This appeal raises a number of legal questions, including the following:

1. Gallichon having been released on full parole following the decision below, is the appeal moot?
2. What relief, if any, can this court grant?
3. What relief, if any, should the court grant?

Having regard to the manner in which the law has developed, it is probably most helpful to begin the inquiry with the second and third questions.

In *Hatchwell v. The Queen* (1974), 21 C.C.C. (2d) 201, 54 D.L.R. (3d) 419, [1976] 1 S.C.R. 39, the Supreme Court of Canada considered the ambit of s. 688 (formerly s. 660) with respect to preventive detention. At p. 206, Dickson J., speaking for the majority, said:

> Habitual criminal legislation and preventive detention are primarily designed for the persistent dangerous criminal and not for those with a prolonged record of minor offences against property. The dominant purpose is to protect the public when the past conduct of the criminal demonstrates a propensity for crimes of violence against the person, and there is a real and present danger to life or limb. In those cases the way is clear and the word "menace" seems particularly apt and significant. That is not to say that crimes against property can never be the cause for the invocation of preventive detention legislation, for the legislation contains no such exclusion and society is undoubtedly entitled to reasonable protection against crimes involving loss or damage of property. It would seem to me, however, that when one is dealing with crime of this type, seeking to distinguish between that which is menace and that which is nuisance, there is greater opportunity and indeed necessity to assess carefully the true nature and gravity of the potential threat. For it is manifest that some crimes affecting property are very serious and others are not.

Dickson J. added at pp. 206-7:

> The appellant is emotionally unstable and immature. The great majority of crimes committed by him appear to proceed from an uncontrolled aberration or fixation about cars. They are not motivated by gain nor by any destructive urge, for in every case, according to the evidence, the property taken was recovered undamaged. The appellant simply drives the stolen vehicles, until such time as he is apprehended. Of late he has shown a preference for large tractor-trailer units. This sort of irrational, senseless conduct is no doubt of annoyance to everyone, incommoding owners and vexing authorities, but it would seem to me that it partakes more of the quality of a nuisance than of a menace. Hatchwell is a bane rather than a danger to society.

In the result, the judgment at trial, which imposed a sentence of preventive detention, and the confirming judgment of the Court of Appeal for British Columbia were set aside.

It can be said without qualification that at no time did Gallichon meet the criteria of habitual criminal or preventive detention laid down by the Supreme Court of Canada in *Hatchwell*.

. . . .

In the present case, the Board has no jurisdiction to interfere with the original sentence of indefinite preventive detention. If, as in the present case, the attack is on the continued effect of that sentence, then any remedy must be found in the courts, not at the Board.

It was argued by counsel for the respondent on this appeal that there was no remedy available from either the Board or the court and that the only remedy available to Gallichon would be by way of application for a pardon: see Letters Patent Constituting the Office of Governor General of Canada, effective October 1, 1947, art. XII. . . . .

The argument in this case is not that the sentence was illegal when imposed but that it has become illegal, that is, contrary to the Charter, by virtue of the enactment of the Charter and the passage of time.

In *Steele v. Mountain Institution (Warden), supra*, the court was concerned with an application for *habeas corpus* to review Steele's continued detention in the penitentiary pursuant to a sentence of indeterminate detention imposed in 1953 following a declaration that he was a criminal sexual psychopath. Since the time of his sentencing, Steele had been released on several occasions on parole or temporary absence, but on each occasion his parole had been revoked either because of his consumption of alcohol or because he breached conditions, such as curfew. When first incarcerated, the trial judge recommended that the applicant receive treatment. None was available until the mid-70s and by that time, by reason of the years that he had spent in prison, he was not considered a suitable candidate for the program. In December, 1988, he filed a petition for *habeas corpus* with *certiorari* in aid and relief pursuant to s. 24(1) of the Charter alleging that his continued detention constituted cruel and unusual treatment or punishment. Following a hearing at which several psychiatrists testified, Paris J. concluded that Steele's rights under s. 12 had been violated, that he no longer remained a dangerous offender, and accordingly, that he should be released unconditionally [72 C.R. (3d) 58, 8 W.C.B. (2d) 7].

An appeal by the Crown was dismissed by the British Columbia Court of Appeal [54 C.C.C. (3d) 334, 76 C.R. (3d) 307, 45 B.C.L.R. (2d) 273]. That court, however, varied the release order to provide that the Crown could apply to the British Columbia Supreme Court for an order that the respondent be returned to custody should his conduct after release be such as to demonstrate that he did, in fact, represent so clear a danger of such serious harm as to render resumption of incarceration under the indeterminate sentence justifiable.

The appeal to the Supreme Court of Canada was dismissed. Cory J. gave the judgment of the court. At pp. 16-17, in reviewing the decision of the trial judge, he said:

> The majority reasons given by LaForest J. in *Milne* had expressly left undecided the validity of Linden J.'s ruling in *Mitchell*, Paris J. concluded that the decision in *Mitchell* could still be applied and that he was therefore entitled to review Steele's continuing detention to determine whether, even though it was lawfully imposed, it now violated s. 12 of the Charter.

. . .

I, of course, do not quarrel with the reasoning that judicial review in the Federal Court is appropriate in some cases. . . . But neither the Board nor the Federal Court would have had jurisdiction to give Gallichon a complete release, and that question would have remained to be dealt with by the Ontario Court (General Division) or, on appeal, by this court.

By granting Gallichon parole in early 1993, the Board has, in effect, rendered moot the question of the propriety of its decisions, or non-decisions, over the period 1967 to 1993.

Applying to Gallichon's record, criminal and otherwise, a comparative analysis similar to that performed by Linden J. in *Mitchell*, would yield a similar result: he is no more than a social nuisance; he is not a danger to the public; to continue to detain him in prison or restrain him by conditions of parole after 26 years in prison would surpass all rational bounds of treatment or punishment; it would be so excessive as to outrage standards of decency.

. . .

Many aspects of this case are troubling. These include the original sentence, the refusal of an extension of the time for appealing, the lack of any review in the light of *Hatchwell*, the failure to review the sentence when the basis for indeterminate detention was substantially altered, the failure to respond more positively to the Jackson report, the failure to follow the recommendations of the Leggatt report, and the failure to treat this matter with more urgency, a failure in which this court shares responsibility. In the light of those considerations, together with the appellant's age, health, lack of education, and lack of access to legal advice and legal aid, I cannot believe that justice would be served by requiring him to start over again by commencing an action for the relief which is his due.

The respondent argues that the appeal is moot because the Board has released Gallichon on full parole. The object of Gallichon's application, however, was not to secure parole but to achieve his unconditional release. While on parole, he remains subject to the restraints imposed by the *Corrections and Conditional Release Act* and other restraints which may be imposed by the Board as, for instance, the need to secure the Board's permission to travel beyond the Kingston area. Should he be charged with any offence, however minor, Gallichon is subject to reincarceration by order of the Board. The appeal is therefore not moot.

It is argued that as Gallichon is no longer in prison, but on parole, the remedy of *habeas corpus* is no longer available to him. In *Ex Parte Hinks* (1972), 7 C.C.C (2d) 316 at p. 318, 27 D.L.R. (3d) 593, [1972] 3 O.R. 182 (H.C.J.), Grant J. said of the applicant, a parolee: "Because he is not confined the applicant is not entitled to the remedy of *habeas corpus*".

. . .

In any event, it is questionable whether *Hinks* is applicable to the instant case. In this case, Gallichon was in prison when the application was launched and when it was heard. If the appeal is allowed, this court will simply be substituting its decision for that of the judge of first instance who clearly did have jurisdiction.

. . .

In the case now before the court, an unconditional release is sought. This is relief which is beyond the jurisdiction of the Board; it can be granted only by a court. Having regard to the length of Gallichon's incarceration, his record in recent years of non-violence, his age and health, and the lack of any indication that he presents a danger to anyone but himself, I would allow the appeal and set aside the order made below dismissing the application.

To satisfy any technical requirements of the *habeas corpus* process, I would order that the appellant, within 30 days of the release of these reasons, surrender himself to the authorities at the institution from which he was paroled: see *Masella v. Langlais, supra, per* Locke J. at p. 8. Upon such surrender, I would order that the order of preventive detention be set aside and that he be released unconditionally.

*Appeal allowed.*

## Questions/Discussion
1. Describe and explain the historical background of Canada's sentencing regime.
2. What are the causes of disparity in the Canadian criminal justice system? How can disparity be reduced in the system? What factors should be important in distinguishing similar cases and giving different sentences?
3. How would a judge determine the usual or normal sentence for a given crime? What guidance about maximum and minimum penalties is available in the *Criminal Code*? See, for example, section 236.
4. What are the primary arguments against the indeterminant sentence applied to "dangerous offenders" in ss. 752-761 of the Criminal Code?
5. Should it matter when sentencing a bank robber whether $5,000 or $50,000 was stolen, or whether bank robberies are increasing or decreasing in the jurisdiction?
6. What factors are important in the granting (or withholding) or parole? What factors should be important in this exercise of discretion? Do you agree with the "idea" of parole? Why or why not? If you agree, what functions should it serve and what goals should it have? If you disagree, what alternative do you see to parole and what would you gain by abolishing parole? In this regard, see Brodeur, J.-P., "The Attrition of Parole": (1990), 32 Canadian Journal of Criminology 503-510.
7. One of the more visible issues in 1996 is whether or not to repeal section 745 of the Criminal Code which allows first degree murderers sentenced to the mandatory 25 years with no parole the possibility after 15 years' imprisonment to apply to a jury to have the period of parole ineligibility reduced. This provision also applies to second degree murderers whose parole ineligibility has been set at more than 15 years. The government has undertaken to review the issue after pressure from victims' groups and Liberal MP John Nunziata. Would you agree with this? Why or why not? What purposes would be served by such a move?

## Further Reading
- Baum, D.J., *Discount Justice* (Toronto: Burns & MacEachern Ltd., 1979), ch. 5.
- Benzvy-Miller, S., "Integrating Sentence and Parole" (1990), 32 Canadian Journal of Criminology 493-502.
- Canada, *Sentencing Reform: A Canadian Approach: Report of the Canadian Sentencing Commission* (Ottawa: Supply & Services, 1987).
- Correctional Service of Canada, *Contributing to the Protection of Society Through Assistance and Control: An Overview of Canada's Correctional Service* (Ottawa: Correctional Service of Canada, 1993).
- "Criminal Sentencing Symposium" (1982), 4 Loyola University of Chicago Law Journal.
- Jull, K., "Sentencing, Corrections and Conditional Release: Principles or a Penitentiary by Any Other Name?" (1992), 34 Criminal Law Quarterly 443-468
- Landreville, P., "Prison Overpopulation and Strategies for Decarceration" (1995), 37 Canadian Journal of Criminology 39-60.

- LaPrairie, C., "The Role of Sentencing in the Over-representation of Aboriginal People in Correctional Institutions" (1990), 32 Canadian Journal of Criminology 429-440.
- Nadin-Davis, P., *Sentencing in Canada* (Toronto: Carswell, 1982).
- National Parole Board, *Balancing Public Safety and Personal Responsibility* (Ottawa: National Parole Board, 1994).
- Ouimet, M. and E. Coyle, "Fear of Crime and Sentencing Punitiveness: Comparing the General Public and Court Practitioners" (1991), 33 Canadian Journal of Criminology 149-162.
- Palys, T. and S. Divorski, "Explaining Sentence Disparity" (1986), 28 Canadian Journal of Criminology and Corrections 347.
- Pink, J. and D. Perrier (eds.), *From Crime to Punishment* (Toronto: Carswell, 1989)
- Roberts, J. and A. von Hirsch, "Sentencing Reform in Canada: Recent Developments" (1992), 23 Revue Générale de Droit 319-355.
- Ruby, C., *Sentencing* (Toronto, Butterworths, 1994).
- Schiffer, M., "The Sentencing of Mentally Disordered Offenders" (1976), 14 Osgoode Hall Law Journal 307.
- "Sentencing Symposium" (1989), 7 Behavioural Sciences and the Law.
- Statistics Canada (Canadian Centre for Justice Statistics), *Adult Correctional Services in Canada 1994-95* (Ottawa: Minister of Industry, 1996).
- Watson, J. et al., *Principles of Sentencing in Canada* (Scarborough Ontario: Carswell, 1993).

# 6

# CRIMINAL LAW LIABILITY

**Introduction**

This chapter examines the issues surrounding the definition and attachment of criminal law liability. The first section, 6.1 provides an introduction to the elements of criminal liability, looking at what are the definition and requirements of a crime in (general) legal terms and what are the problems in practice which are encountered when applying these elements to real fact situations? The two elements of a crime usually required are the actus reus (see subsection 6.1.1) and the mens rea (see subsection 6.1.2), the physical and the mental elements of a crime.[1] We will see that while the physical elements are delineated in the legislation, the mental elements are often left unspecified. In these situations it is up to the court to specify the requirements as to the intention, knowledge, or mental state needed. Furthermore, there are crimes and quasi-crimes which do not require any mental element; the crime is complete on the completion of the actus reus. Such offences are called strict and absolute liability offences, and are dealt with in subsection 6.1.3 of this chapter.

The second section of this chapter is entitled "Incomplete Offences" and at first sight this term might appear to be contradictory, in that if the offence is not complete, then there is no offence. However, the term refers to a class of offences where the intended purpose is, with the possible exception of conspiracy, not fully carried out, offences that present special problems in regard to their rationale, formulation and application. Subsection 6.2.1 addresses the subject of "attempts" in criminal law and deals with those situations where the offence which was planned has not been completed for some reason, yet the law still attaches criminal liability for the attempt which was made. At what stage the law intervenes and according to what rationale will concern us in this subsection.

Subsections 6.2.2 and 6.2.3 concern two crimes, neither of which requires the full completion of the planned offence. Counselling involves those situations where one party counsels another to commit a crime and the crime which has been counselled is never committed; but criminal liability will attach to the person who did the counselling in the first place, even though the person's goal was never achieved. The final part of the second section deals with "conspiracy", an offence where an agreement to carry out another crime results in criminal liability to those who enter the agreement, whether or not the agreement is put into action. How close this comes to punishing people for their bad thoughts or intentions — something the criminal law does not do if only one person is involved — is one question to keep in mind, particularly when examining the rationale behind the offence.

The last section in this chapter examines the attachment of criminal liability to individuals for their acts. For example, how and for what acts does the law attach blame to certain people who may not have physically done the required acts, but who did assist in or encourage the offence in some way? While this section on "parties to the offence" does not deal with crimes

---

[1] The terms have been criticized because they derive from the common law and are not used in criminal legislation. For the purposes of our analysis, however, the terms will suffice to provide a framework for the examination of some of the important issues which present themselves in the area of criminal law liability.

per se or the elements of a crime, it is important because it sets out the circumstances under which criminal liability will be attached to individuals for their actions.

A final question to keep in mind throughout the chapter is to what extent is there a convergence of theory and practice: what do the courts say are the theoretical requirements for finding criminal liability and what do they do in practice in the actual application of the legal rules to the fact situations? Serious discrepancies in this regard might tell us that the theoretical underpinnings of the courts' approaches might need to be rethought or, on the other hand, might suggest that the practice of the courts must be reoriented to put it in line with criminal law principles and ideals.

## 6.1 ELEMENTS OF AN OFFENCE

### 6.1.1. Actus Reus

**Introduction**

Traditionally, each criminal offence is made up of two distinct elements. The first element is referred to as the "actus reus", or guilty act. The second element is referred to as the "mens rea", or guilty mind, and will be discussed in detail in subsection 2 of this chapter. In order for Crown Prosecutors to secure a conviction, they have the legal or persuasive burden of proving both of these elements beyond a reasonable doubt.

The words "actus reus" and "mens rea" are derived from the legal maxim, *actus non facit reum nisi mens sit rea*, which when translated means there is no guilty act without a guilty mind. Interestingly, however, the Criminal Code and other criminal legislation does not make use of these terms expressly. Rather, these terms are merely the traditional language used by the courts when analyzing a particular criminal offence. Some legal scholars, have argued that the use of these expressions is confusing and should be abandoned.[1]

These issues surrounding actus reus are few and not complex, and for the most part are well highlighted in the cases which follow. In practice, what is at issue is the proof being adduced to prove that the accused actually committed the physical elements of the crime as outlined in the relevant legislation. As a rule, such questions of fact concerning actus reus do not concern us too much since they relate to evidentiary questions such as the cause of death of the victim in murder cases, the cause of fire in arson cases, or the source of pollution in environmental offences. What is of interest is the way in which the courts view the actus reus as a question of law; that is, how do they deal with the causal factors within the confines of the legislation and particularly, how do they deal with the situation where a person omits to do something (rather than does a criminal act) which results in harm being done?

Actus reus can refer to just the prohibited conduct or act of omission of the accused, or it can refer to the prohibited conduct and/or the consequences of the prohibited conduct or omission. An example of the former would be found in perjury in section 131 of the Criminal Code, where the wrongful conduct is the giving of a false statement under oath knowing that the statement is false (and with the intent to mislead the Court). An example of the latter would be one of the classes of murder (see sections 229-232 of the Criminal Code), where the death of a human being must have occurred as a consequence of the accused's actions; the question is "Did the accused cause the death of the victim?" In this regard, the issue of causation is an important one in connecting the acts of the accused to the death. Obviously there is a need for some causal relationship between the act done and the consequences which are required for the crime, as well as a common law voluntariness requirement. In the case of murder, death may have resulted from a number of different factors, and three of the cases (*Jordan, Smith and Beardsley*) which follow set out the test and guidelines that the courts use in making a determination as to whether or not the accused can be held liable for his or her actions. Essentially, such tests are applied to determine whether a valid legal causal connection has been made between the act and the consequences. In addition, the Code contains several provisions which relate to the issue of causation; for example, section 227 effectively limits the possible causal link between the acts of an accused and the death of the victim to a year and a day, a provision which has been criticized in light of today's medical technology.[2]

The final four cases deal with the issue of omissions in the criminal law, the principal point being that a legal duty generally must be found in the criminal law in order to hold the person liable for omitting to do something, i.e., for a failure to fulfil the duty. *Lavin* is an example where there was no legal duty to do anything and therefore no offence for omitting to do something. In regard to omissions, ask yourself what is the content of the duty and how well is it set out; is the nature and extent of the duty understandable to the ordinary citizen? What does it take to breach a particular duty? These duties are often set out in only the most general terms; see, for example section 215 of the Code where a duty to provide the "necessaries of life" is created in respect of certain relationships, including those of parent/child and husband/wife. Even when a duty is not explicitly set out in the legislation, courts can sometimes find that an omission to do something amounts to a criminal act. This was the situation in the *Thornton* case where the donation of blood which Mr. Thornton knew contained H.I.V. antibodies constituted a common nuisance and thereby endangered the life, safety and health of the public.

The *Fagan* case highlights not only a situation where there was no duty to act, but also illustrates a further requirement in regard to actus reus and mens rea. The usual requirement is that the two elements occur simultaneously. In *Fagan*, the court, faced with the fact that there was no duty to act on the part of the accused when he failed to act, effectively "stretched out" the actus reus so that in the majority's interpretation of the events there was a coincidence of the actus reus and mens rea. Such "continuing acts" may be valid in some circumstances,[3] but in this case the construction appears to be a rather artificial device which the courts can use to achieve the coincidence of actus reus and mens rea. Compare *Fagan* with the Supreme Court of Canada's decision in *Cooper*, where the court held that in the context of a death caused by manual strangulation it was sufficient that the intent and the act of strangulation coincided at some point. Which analysis do you prefer and why?

**Footnotes**
1. See, for example, Stuart, D. and R. Delisle, Learning Canadian Criminal Law. 5th ed. (Toronto: Carswell, 1995).
2. See also sections 223-226 and 228.
3. See *Meli v. The Queen*, (1954), 1 W.L.R. 228 (P.C.), where the accused struck the victim and, thinking him dead, threw the body over a cliff. But the victim was not dead and only died from the fall. The defence argument was that when the actus reus of killing was done there was no mens rea to kill, only to dispose of the body, and when there was the mens rea to kill, there was not the actus reus of murder because the victim had not died.

## Regina v. Jordan
(1965), 40 A.C. 152

Only the judgment of Hallet J. is reproduced below.

HALLET J.: — This is an exceedingly unusual case, and it might from one point of view be described as a difficult case, but we think that it can be dealt with with comparative brevity. We have considered the points that arise and have no doubt about any of them and it is the desire of the court that I should deliver judgement at once.

The facts of the case, so far as I need refer to them, are as follows. The appellant, together with three other men, all serving airmen of the United States Forces, were charged with the murder of a man named Beaumont as the result of a disturbance which arose in a cafe at Hull. Beaumont was stabbed with a knife. There was no evidence that any one of the other three used a knife on Beaumont or was acting in concert with the man who did use the knife, and accordingly Byrne J., who tried the case, directed the acquittal of those three men. With regard to the appellant it was ultimately conceded by Mr. Veale, who appeared for him in the court below and in this court, that he did use the knife and stab Beaumont. Beaumont was admitted to hospital very promptly and the wound was stitched up, but none the less he died not many days after. In those circumstances the appellant was tried for murder. Various defences were raised, accident, self-defence, provocation and stabbing in the course of a quarrel. On all of those defences the direction of the learned judge is not in any way challenged and the jury rejected them.

Mr. Veale told us, with his usual frankness, that the original intention of the defence was not to lodge an appeal, but certain information reached the United States authorities and the defence became in a position to put forward further evidence, and in particular the evidence of two doctors, Dr. Keith Simpson and Mr. Blackburn, whose standing is beyond question.

Application was made to the court for leave to call this additional evidence. It is only in the most exceptional circumstances, and subject to what may be described as exceptional conditions, that the court is ever willing to listen to additional evidence. There are most obvious reasons, which I need not restate, because they have been stated with authority on more than one occasion before, why such applications should be granted only with great restraint.

. . . .

[After referring to the summing-up and the medical evidence at the trial, his Lordship continued.] The further evidence is said to show that death was not, to use the words of Byrne J., "consequent upon the wound inflicted". On the contrary, both the doctors called are of opinion that, from the medical point of view, it cannot be described as caused by the wound at all. Whether from the legal point of view it could be described as caused by the wound is a more doubtful question. There are a number of cases in which the judges have discussed in what circumstances a death can be regarded as the result of a wound where something other than the inflicting of the wound has been the immediate cause of death. The circumstances vary very much. The judges in each case have ruled in the light of the circumstances with which they had to deal, and out of four cases the jury acquitted in two and convicted in two. First, as to the requirements allowing fresh evidence to be called; in the present case it seems clear to us that the fresh evidence was not in any true sense available at the trial. It did not occur to the prosecution, the defence, the judge, or the jury that there could be any doubt but that the stab caused death. The trial proceeded upon that basis. In those circumstances we thought it right to take the view that this was the case where the evidence sought to be given had not been in any true sense available at the trial.

. . . .

I have not yet referred to what is perhaps the most important case from the present point of view, HARDING (1936) 25 Cr. App. R. 190. The headnote is short: "Conviction of murder quashed after the court had heard fresh medical evidence as to the cause of death, the court emphasizing the fact that such reception of fresh evidence was to be regarded as wholly exceptional". I hope I have made it plain that this court has well in mind that such reception must be wholly exceptional.

As to the second requisite, namely, that the evidence proposed to be tendered is such that, if the jury had heard that evidence, they might very likely, and indeed probably would, have come to a different verdict, we feel that, if the jury had heard two doctors of the standing of Dr. Keith Simpson and Mr. Blackburn give evidence that in their judgement death was not due to the stab wound but to something else, the jury might certainly have hesitated very long before saying that they were satisfied that death was due to the stab wound. The jury, of course, would not be bound by medical opinion, but flying in the face of it, particularly in a capital case, is a thing any jury would hesitate to do. When Mr. Stanley-Price was trying to assist the court by cross-examining those doctors with a view to showing that they were mistaken in their opinions, and when he told us that he was prepared to tender the evidence of doctors who would, according to his instructions, probably express other opinions, we felt bound to say that the question is not whether we, if we were a jury, would have accepted and acted on the opinions those gentlemen expressed, but whether the jury in all probability would have allowed their verdict to be affected by them.

There is one further aspect that it is important I should emphasize lest this case is cited in some other case. There were two things other than the wound which were stated by these two medical witnesses to have brought about death. The stab wound had penetrated the intestine in two places, but it was mainly healed at the time of death. With a view to preventing infection it was thought right to administer an antibiotic, terramycin.

It was agreed by the two additional witnesses that that was the proper course to take, and a proper dose was administered. Some people, however, are intolerant to terramycin, and Beaumont was one of those people. After the initial doses he developed diarrhoea, which was only properly attributable, in the opinion of those doctors, to the fact that the patient was intolerant to terramycin. Thereupon the administration of terramycin was stopped, but unfortunately the very next day the resumption of such administration was ordered by another doctor and it was recommended for the following day. The two doctors both take the same view about it. Dr. Simpson said that to introduce a poisonous substance after the intolerance of a patient was shown was palpably wrong. Mr. Blackburn agreed.

Other steps were taken which were also regarded by the doctors as wrong — namely, the intravenous introduction of wholly abnormal quantities of liquid far exceeding the output. As a result the lungs became waterlogged and pulmonary oedema was discovered. Mr. Blackburn said that he was not surprised to see that condition after the introduction of so much liquid, and that pulmonary oedema leads to broncho-pneumonia as an inevitable sequel, and it was from broncho-pneumonia that Beaumont died.

We are disposed to accept it as the law that death resulting from any normal treatment employed to deal with a felonious injury may be regarded as caused by the felonious injury, but we do not think it necessary to examine the cases in detail or to formulate for the assistance of those who have to deal with such matters in the future the correct test which ought to be laid down with regard to what is necessary to be proved in order to establish causal connection between the death and the felonious injury. It is sufficient to point out here that this was not normal treatment. Not only one feature, but two separate and independent features, of treatment were, in the opinion of the doctors, palpably wrong and these produced the symptoms discovered at the post-mortem examination which were the direct and immediate cause of death, namely, the pneumonia resulting from the condition of oedema which was found.

The question then is whether it can be said that, if that evidence had been before the jury, it ought not to have, and in all probability would not have, affected their decision. We recognize that the learned judge, if this matter had been before him, would have had to direct the jury correctly on how far such supervening matters could be regarded as interrupting the chain of causation; but we feel that in the end it would have been a question of fact for the jury depending on what evidence they accepted as correct and the view they took on that evidence. We feel not uncertainty at all that, whatever direction had been given to the jury and however correct it had been, the jury would have felt precluded from saying that they were satisfied that death was caused by the stab wound.

For these reasons we come to the conclusion that the appeal must be allowed and the conviction set aside.

*Conviction quashed.*

## Regina v. Smith
(1959), 47 A.C. 121

[Only the judgment of The Lord Chief Justice is reproduced below.]

The appellant was convicted by a general court-martial at Verden, Germany, on July 2, 1958, of the murder of Pte. William Creed and was sentenced to imprisonment for life.

The appellant was a private soldier in the King's Regiment. On April 13, 1958, a company of that regiment was sharing a barracks with a company of the Gloucestershire Regiment. On that night a fight developed in which three men of the Gloucestershire Regiment were stabbed and one of them, Pte. Creed subsequently died. Immediately after the fight the regimental sergeant-major of D Company of the King's Regiment paraded a number of soldiers, including the appellant, and said: "I am going to get to the bottom of this fighting and whoever did it must step forward". No one then stepped forward and the regimental sergeant-major questioned each man about his movements at the material time. The appellant said that he was in bed. The regimental sergeant-major then said: "I am not leaving; I am staying here until you give me an answer about this fight". The appellant then stepped forward and said that he had done the stabbing with a bayonet. He was then taken into custody. About 7.30 on the following morning he was interviewed by a sergeant of the Special Investigations Branch who, after administering the usual caution, referred to what had happened the night before and the appellant's admission at that time. The appellant replied: "Yes,

I am not denying it. I stabbed three of them all right," and then made a written statement under caution to the same effect.

The deceased man had received two bayonet wounds, one in the arm and one in the back, the latter of which, unknown to anybody, had pierced the lung and caused haemorrhage. A fellow-member of his company, who was trying to carry him to the medical reception station, twice tripped and let the deceased man fall on the ground. When he ultimately was brought to the reception station, a transfusion of saline solution was attempted and failed. When his breathing seemed impaired he was given oxygen and artificial respiration was applied. He died after he had been in the station about an hour and about two hours after the original stabbing. There were no facilities whatsoever for blood transfusion. A medical witness who gave evidence for the defence said that had those facilities been available and blood transfusion been administered, the chances of the recovery of the deceased man would have been 75 per cent.

The Lord Chief Justice: In this court a number of points have been taken, and quite properly taken, by Mr. Bowen on his behalf, but there are, in the view of the court, only two which merit consideration. The first one is the question whether two alleged confessions given by the appellant were wrongly admitted in evidence . . . . [After finding the confessions were admissible, the Chief Justice continued:]

The second ground concerns a question of causation. The deceased man in fact received two bayonet wounds, one in the arm and one in the back. The one in the back, unknown to anybody, had pierced the lung and caused haemorrhage. There followed a series of unfortunate occurrences. A fellow member of his company tried to carry him to the medical reception station. On the way he tripped over a wire and dropped the deceased man. He picked him up again, went a little further, and fell apparently a second time causing the deceased man to be dropped on to the ground. Thereafter he did not try a third time, but went for help and ultimately the deceased man was brought into the reception station. There, the medical officer, Captain Millward, and his orderly were trying to cope with a number of other cases, two serious stabbings and some minor injuries, and it is clear that they did not appreciate the seriousness of the deceased man's condition or exactly what had happened. A transfusion of saline solution was attempted and failed. When his breathing seemed impaired, he was given oxygen and artificial respiration was applied, and in fact he died after he had been in the station about an hour, which was about two hours after the original stabbing. It is now known that, having regard to the injuries which the man had in fact suffered, his lung being pierced, the treatment that he was given was thoroughly bad and might well have affected his chances of recovery. There was evidence that there is a tendency for a wound of this sort to heal and for the haemorrhage to stop. No doubt his being dropped on the ground and having artificial respiration applied would halt or at any rate impede the chances of healing. Further, there were no facilities whatsoever for blood transfusion, which would have been the best possible treatment. There was evidence that, if he had received immediate and different treatment, he might not have died. Indeed, had the facilities for blood transfusion been available and been administered, Dr. Camps, who gave evidence for the defence, said that his chances of recovery were as high as 75 per cent.

In these circumstances Mr. Bowen urges that not only was a careful summing-up required, but that a correct direction to the court would have been that they must be satisfied that the death of Private Creed was a natural consequence and the sole consequence of the wound sustained by him and flowed directly from it. If there was, says Mr. Bowen, any other cause whether resulting from negligence or not, or if, as he contends here, something happened which impeded the chance of the deceased recovering, then the death did not result from the wound. The court is quite unable to accept that contention. It seems to the court that if at the time of death the original wound is still an operating cause and a substantial cause, then the death can properly be said to be the result of the wound, albeit that some other cause of death is also operating. Only if it can be said that the original wounding is merely the setting in which another cause operates can it be said that the death does not result from the wound. Putting it another way, only if the second cause is so over-whelming as to make the original wound merely part of the history can it be said that the death does not flow from the wound.

There are a number of cases in the law of contract and tort on these matters of causation, and it is always difficult to find a form of words when directing a jury or, as here, a court, which will convey in simple language the principle of causation. It seems to the court enough for this purpose to refer to one passage in the judgement of Lord Wright in The Oropesa, reported in [1943] p. 32, where he says (at p. 39): "To break the chain of causation it must be shown that there is something which I will call ultroneous, something unwarrantable, a new cause which disturbs the consequence of events, something which can be described as either unreasonable or exraneous or extrinsic." To much the same effect was a judgement on the question of causation given by Denning J., as he then was, in *Minister of Pensions v. Chennel* in [1947] K.B. 250.

Mr. Bowen placed great reliance on a case decided in this court, Jordan (1956) 40 Cr. App. R. 152, and in particular on a passage in the headnote which says "*Semble*, that death resulting from any normal treatment employed to deal with a felonious injury may be regarded as caused by that felonious injury, but that the same principle does not apply where the treatment employed is abnormal." Reading those words into the present case, Mr. Bowen says that the treatment that this unfortunate man received from the moment that he was struck to the time of his death was abnormal. The court is satisfied that Jordan (*supra*) was a very particular case depending upon its exact facts. It incidentally arose in this court on the grant of an application to call further evidence, and leave having been obtained, two well-known medical experts gave evidence that in their opinion death had not been caused by the stabbing, but by the introduction of terramycin after the deceased had shown that he was intolerant to it and by the intravenous introduction of abnormal quantities of liquid. It also appears that at the time when that was done the stab wound which had penetrated the intestine in two places had mainly healed. In those circumstances the court felt bound to quash the conviction, because they could not say that a reasonable jury, properly directed, would not have been able on that to say that there had been a break in the chain of causation; the court could only uphold the conviction in that case if they were satisfied that no reasonable jury could have come to that conclusion.

In the present case it is true that the Judge-Advocate did not, in his summing-up, go into the refinements of causation. Indeed, in the opinion of this court, he was probably wise to refrain from doing so. He did leave the broad question to the court whether they were satisfied that the wound had caused the death in the sense that the death flowed from the wound, albeit that the treatment he received was in the light of after-knowledge a bad thing. In the opinion of this court, that was on the facts of the case a perfectly adequate summing-up on causation: I say "on the facts of the case", because in the opinion of the court they can only lead to one conclusion. A man is stabbed in the back, his lung is pierced and haemorrhage results; two hours later he dies of haemorrhage from that wound; in the interval there is no time for a careful examination and the treatment given turns out in the light of subsequent knowledge to have been inappropriate and, indeed, harmful. In those circumstances no reasonable jury or court could, properly directed, in our view possibly come to any other conclusion that than the death resulted from the original wound. Accordingly, the court dismisses this appeal.

*Appeal dismissed.*

## People v. Beardsley
(1907), 113 N.W. 1128 (Michigan Sup. Ct.)

McALVAY, C.J. Respondent was convicted of manslaughter before the circuit court for Oakland county, and was sentenced to the state prison at Jackson for a minimum term of one year and a maximum term not to exceed five years.

He was a married man living at Pontiac, and at the time the facts herein narrated occurred he was working as a bartender and clerk at the Columbia Hotel. He lived with his wife in Pontiac, occupying two rooms on the ground floor of a house. Other rooms were rented to tenants, as was also one living room in the basement. His wife being temporarily absent from the city, respondent arranged with a woman named Blanche Burns, who at the time was working at another hotel, to go to his apartments with him. He had been acquainted with her for some time. They knew each other's habits and character. They had drunk liquor together, and had on two occasions been in Detroit and spent the night together in houses of assignation. On the evening of Saturday, March 18, 1905, he met her at the place where she worked, and they went together to his place of residence. They at once began to drink, and continued to drink steadily, and remained together, day and night from that time until the afternoon of the Monday following, except when the respondent went to his work on Sunday afternoon. There was liquor at these rooms, and when it was all used they were served with bottles of whisky and beer by a young man who worked at the Columbia Hotel, and who also attended respondent's fires at the house. He was the only person who saw them in the house during the time they were there together. Respondent gave orders for liquor by telephone. On Monday afternoon, about 1 o'clock, the young man went to the house to see if anything was wanted. At this time he heard respondent say they must fix up the rooms, and the woman must not be found there by his wife, who was likely to return at any time. During this visit to the house the woman sent the young man to a drug store to purchase, with money she gave him, camphor and morphine tablets. He procured both articles. There were six grains of morphine in quarter-grain tablets. She concealed the morphine from respondent's notice, and was discovered putting something into her mouth by him and the young man as they were returning from the other room after taking a drink of beer. She in fact was taking morphine. Respondent struck the box from her hand. Some of the tablets fell on the floor, and of these respondent crushed several with his foot. She picked up and swallowed two of them, and the young man put two of them in the spittoon. Altogether it is probable she took from three to four grains of morphine. The young man went away soon after this. Respondent called him by telephone about an hour later, and after he came to the house requested him to take the woman into the room in basement which was occupied by a Mr. Skoba. She was in a stupor, and did not rouse when spoken to. Respondent was too intoxicated to be of any assistance, and the young man proceeded to take her downstairs. While doing this, Skoba arrived, and together they put her in his room on the bed. Respondent requested Skoba to look after her, and let her out the back way when she waked up. Between 9 and 10 o'clock in the evening, Skoba became alarmed at her condition. He at once called the city marshal and a doctor. An examination by them disclosed that she was dead.

Many errors are assigned by respondent, who asks to have his conviction set aside. The principal assignments of error are based upon the charge of the court and refusal to give certain requests to charge, and are upon the theory that under the undisputed evidence in the case, as claimed by the people and detailed by the people's witnesses, the respondent should have been acquitted and discharged. In the brief of the prosecutor, his position is stated as follows: "It is the theory of the prosecution that the facts and circumstances attending the death of Blanche Burns in the house of respondent were such as to lay upon him a duty to care for her, and the duty to take steps for her protection, and failure to take which was sufficient to constitute such an omission as would render him legally responsible for her death. . . .

There is no claim on the part of the people that the respondent was in any way an active agent in bringing about the death of Blanche Burns, but simply that he owed her a duty which he failed to perform, and that in consequence of such failure on his part she came to her death." Upon this theory a conviction was asked and secured.

The law recognizes that under some circumstances the omission of a duty owed by one individual to another, where such omission results in the death of the one to whom the duty is owing, will make the other chargeable with manslaughter. . . . This rule of law is always based upon the proposition that the duty neglected must be a legal duty, and not a mere moral obligation. It must be a duty imposed by law or by contract, and the omission to perform the duty must be the immediate and direct cause of death. . . . Although the literature upon the subject is quite meager and the cases few, nevertheless the authorities are in harmony as to the relationship which must exist between the parties to create the duty, the omission of which establishes legal responsibility. One authority has briefly and correctly stated the rule, which the prosecution claims should be applied to the case at bar, as follows: "If a person who sustains to another the legal relation of protector, as husband to wife, parent to child, master to seaman, etc. knowing such person to be in peril, wilfully and negligently fails to make such reasonable and proper efforts to rescue him as he might have done, without jeapordizing his own life, or the lives of others, he is guilty of manslaughter at least, if by reason of his omission of duty the dependent person dies." "So one who from domestic relationship, public duty, voluntary choice, or otherwise, has the custody and care of a human being, helpless either from imprisonment, infancy, sickness, age, imbecility, or other incapacity of mind or body is bound to execute the charge with proper diligence, and will be held guilty of manslaughter, if by culpable negligence he lets the helpless creature die." 21 Am. & Eng. Enc. of Law (2d Ed.) p. 192, notes and cases cited.

The following brief digest of cases gives the result of our examination of American and English authorities, where the doctrine of criminal liability was involved when death resulted from an omission to perform a claimed duty. We discuss no cases where statutory provisions are involved. In Territory v. Manton, 8 Mont. 95, 19 Pac. 387, a husband was convicted of manslaughter for leaving his intoxicated wife one winter's night lying in the snow, from which exposure she died. The conviction was sustained on the ground that a legal duty rested upon him to care for and protect his wife, and that for his neglect to perform that duty, resulting in her death, he was properly convicted. State v. Smith, 65 Me. 257, is a similar case. A husband neglected to provide clothing and shelter for his insane wife. He left her in a bare room without fire during severe winter weather. Her death resulted. The charge in the indictment is predicated upon a known legal duty of the husband to furnish his wife with suitable protection. In State v. Behm, 72 Iowa, 533, 34 N.W. 319, the conviction of a mother of manslaughter for exposing her infant child without protection was affirmed upon the same ground. . . . In a federal case tried in California before Mr. Justice Field, of the United States Supreme Court, where the master of a vessel was charged with murder in omitting any effort to rescue a sailor who had fallen overboard, the learned justice, in charging the jury, said: "There may be in the omission to do a particular act under some circumstances, as well as in the commission of an act, such a degree of criminality as to render the offender liable to indictment for manslaughter. . . .

In the first place, the duty omitted must be a plain duty. . . . In the second place, it must be one which the party is bound to perform by law, or by contract, and not one the performance of which depends simply upon his humanity, or his sense of justice and propriety. United States v. Knowles, 4 Sawy. (U.S.) 517, Fed. Cas. No. 15,540. . . . The case of Reg. v. Nicholls, 13 Cox. Crim. Cases, 75, was a prosecution of a penniless old woman, a grandmother, for neglecting to supply an infant grandchild left in her charge with sufficient food and proper care. The case was tried at Assizes in Stafford, before Brett J., who said to the jury: "If a grown up person chooses to undertake the charge of a human creature, helpless either from infancy, simplicity, lunacy, or other infirmity, he is bound to execute that charge without, at all events, wicked negligence, and if a person who has chosen to take charge of a helpless creature lets it die by wicked negligence, that person is guilty of manslaughter." The vital question was whether there had been any such negligence in the case designated by the trial judge as wicked negligence. The trial resulted in an acquittal. The charge of this nisi prius judge recognizes the principle that a person may voluntarily assume the care of a helpless human being and, having assumed it, will be held to be under an implied legal duty to care for and protect such person; the duty assumed being that of caretaker and protector to the exclusion of all others. . . .

These adjudicated cases and all others examined in this investigation we find are in entire harmony with the proposition first stated in this opinion. Seeking for a proper determination of the case at bar by the application of the legal principles involved, we must eliminate from the case all consideration of mere moral obligation, and discover whether respondent was under a legal duty towards Blanche Burns at the time of her death, knowing her to be in peril of her life, which required him to make all reasonable and proper effort to save her, the omission to perform which duty would make him responsible for her death. This is the important and determining question in this case. If we hold that such legal duty rested upon respondent, it must arise by implication from the facts and circumstances already recited. The record of this case discloses that the deceased was a woman past 30 years of age. She had been twice married. She was accustomed to visiting saloons and to the use of intoxicants. She previously had made assignations with this man in Detroit at least twice. There is no evidence or claim from this record that any duress, fraud or deceit had been practiced upon her. On the contrary, it appears that she went upon this carouse with respondent voluntarily, and so continued to remain with him. Her entire conduct indicates that she had ample experience in such affairs.

It is urged by the prosecutor that the respondent "stood towards this woman for the time being in the place of her natural guardian and protector, and as such owed her a clear legal duty which he completely failed to perform." The cases cited and digested establish that no such legal duty is created based upon a mere moral obligation. The fact that this woman was in his house created no such legal duty as exists in law and is due from a husband towards his wife, as seems to be intimated by the prosecutor's brief. Such an inference would be very repugnant to our moral sense. Respondent had assumed either in fact or by implication no care or control over his companion. Had this been a case where two men under like circumstances had voluntarily gone on a debauch together and on had attempted suicide, no one would claim that this doctrine of legal duty could be invoked to hold the other criminally responsible for omitting to make effort to rescue his companion. How can the fact that in this case one of the parties was a woman change the principle of law applicable to it? Deriving and applying the law in this case from the principle of decided cases, we do not find that such legal duty as is contended for existed in fact or by implication on the part of respondent towards the deceased, the omission of which involved criminal liability. We find no more apt words to apply to this case than those used by Mr. Justice Field, in United States v. Knowles, supra: "In the absence of such obligations, it is undoubtedly the moral duty of every person to extend to others assistance when in danger . . . and, if such efforts should be omitted by any one when they could be made without imperilling his own life, he would by his conduct draw upon himself the just censure and reproach of good men; but this is the only punishment to which he would be subjected by society."

Other questions discussed in the briefs need not be considered.

The conviction is set aside, and respondent is ordered discharged.

## Regina v. Lavin
(1992), 76 C.C.C. (3d) 279 (Que. C.A.)

Appeal by the accused from a judgment of Boilard J., 23 M.V.R. (2d) 273, dismissing his appeal from conviction on a charge of obstructing a peace officer.

VALLERAND J.A. concurs with TYNDALE J.A.

TYNDALE J.A.: — The details of this case are summarized in the opinion of Madam Justice Tourigny; with respect, I come to a different conclusion.

As a preliminary, I wish to bring up a point of fact. My colleague writes, in the fourth paragraph [translation]: "For the second time, Lavin replied that he had no radar warning device . . ." That is from the version of Officer Lépine, but it is not the version accepted by the trial judge.

Appellant testified as follows [translation]:

Q. Now the, during the time you heard, you heard the second constable who testified, who was Mister Lépine . . .
R. Hum, hum.
Q. . . . say that when he asked you about the radar detector, that you denied having one, is that a fact?
R. No, I never denied having a radar detector.
Q. Was there any discussion between you and he about whether — and the fact you had one or not?
R. No, the discussion was whether or not he could search me and get it from me. He knew I had it, and I knew that he knew I had it, there was no discussion about that.

The trial judge said [translation]: ". . . I cast no doubt on Mr Lavin's testimony; he is an honest man — who in fact decided to do only what the law obliged him to do, in his opinion . . .". And so I take it as a fact that appellant did not deny possession of the detector.

Appellant was charged with wilfully obstructing a peace officer in the execution of his duty. He was found guilty, not of unlawful possession of a detector, not because he put the detector in his pocket, but because he refused to hand it over. I am not aware of any provision of law by which he was obliged to agree with the officer's request to give him the detector. If he was under no obligation, surely he had the right to refuse and did not thereby obstruct the officer.

On appellant's refusal, he was arrested; knowing that the arrest gave the officer the right to search him, he immediately handed over the offending apparatus.

The officer's knowledge, and not mere suspicion, of appellant's unlawful possession makes this case distinguishable from the precedents cited by Tourigny J.A.

. . .

*Moore v. The Queen* (1978), 43 C.C.C. (2d) 83, 90 D.L.R. (3d) 112, [1979] 1 S.C.R. 195 (not cited), was a case of refusal to identify himself; the majority held that, in the circumstances, there was a duty to answer; in our case, I see no duty to deliver. The minority, denying the duty to answer (and I suppose the majority would have agreed if there were no duty), held that a person is not guilty of obstruction merely by ding doing nothing, unless there is a legal duty to act; that *omission to act in a particular* way will entail criminal liability only where a *duty to act* arises at common law or by statute. The constable had the right to arrest if necessary to establish identity, but it did not follow that refusal amounted to obstruction; as in our case, the constable had the right to arrest if necessary to search, but refusal did not amount to obstruction.

It seems to me that wilful obstruction requires either some positive act, such as concealment of evidence, or an omission to do something which one is legally obliged to do, and that neither requirement is fulfilled in this case.

I would allow the appeal with costs.

TOURIGNY J.A. (dissenting) (translation): — The appellant (Lavin) appeals from a decision of the Superior Court [23 M.V.R. (2d) 273] affirming his conviction by a judge of the Quebec Court on a charge of obstructing a peace officer in the execution of his duty, pursuant to s. 129 of the *Criminal Code*.

The facts are of some importance in this case. Lavin was driving toward Montreal over a bridge when he saw a police car approaching from behind. He thought the vehicle was pursuing someone in front of him, but put in his pocket "just in case", the radar warning device attached to his car's sun visor. It turned out that it was Lavin whom the police officer wished to stop, because he had seen the wire of the device hanging from the sun visor and had subsequently seen Lavin concealing the object on his person.

After the vehicles were stopped, Lavin, informed of the situation by the officer, telephoned his lawyer and refused to hand over the warning device as the officer requested; the officer also telephoned for instructions and a second police officer arrived on the scene.

The officer who had followed Lavin in his car repeated to Lavin that he had seen the warning device and that he had also seen him performing the act of concealing it, and again requested that he hand it over. For the second time, Lavin replied that he had no radar warning device and suggested that the police officer search his car.

After the second refusal to hand over the device, the officer informed Lavin that he could be charged with obstructing a peace officer.

Later, after informing Lavin of his rights, the second officer who had arrived on the scene arrested him. Lavin then offered to hand over the device.

He was accused of obstructing an officer in the execution of his duty.

In this court, Lavin submitted that the refusal to hand over the device did not constitute an obstruction. "It is a non-action", he argues, in contrast to situations in which a person has performed the act of putting his hand in his pocket or of grabbing at his coat, for example.

Lavin argues that he did nothing to prevent the search, and that, in fact, the police officer did not attempt to search him. He submits as well that the factual evidence does not demonstrate any intention on his part to inhibit the work of the police officers.

The deputy prosecutor, for his part, argues that, once informed by the police officer that he had observed the presence of the warning device and the action to conceal it, his refusal to hand over the object was a voluntary act of obstruction that must be seen in the context of all the actions taken by Lavin. These actions, says the deputy prosecutor, demonstrate that Lavin knew he was committing an offence, that at a minimum he did not want the police officer to notice the device in passing, even if he initially thought the officer's attention was directed at someone else and that, in this context, the refusal to hand over the device cannot be anything but a voluntary act.

. . .

Even on the assumption that Lavin did not conceal the warning device *for the purpose* of concealing it from the police but only "just in case" they were to see it in passing, it is true none the less that, after being accosted by the police and informed by them of what they had seen, he continued to deny the facts and to conceal the offending object. In my opinion, this is sufficient intention to satisfy the requirements of the law — not to mention the invitation to search the vehicle when he knew the police would find nothing there. The need for the police in such circumstances to ensure that the evidence will be preserved justifies their attempt, in the performance of their duties, to get their hands on relevant objects, particularly when they have seen them and observed the action taken to conceal them.

It is, therefore, my opinion that we should reach the same conclusion as this court did in *Lajoie*, and dismiss the appeal.

*Appeal allowed.*

## Regina v. Thornton
(1991), 1 O.R. (3d) 480 (Ont. C.A.)

Appeal by the accused from his conviction on a charge of committing a common nuisance and from sentence

The judgment of the court was delivered by

GALLIGAN J.A.: — The presence in a person's blood of antibodies to Human Immunodeficiency Virus (HIV) indicates that the person is probably infected with Acquired Immune Deficiency Syndrome (AIDS). AIDS is a grave illness which is usually fatal. It is infectious and particularly contagious through the blood.

All of this is now well known. The appellant knew it in November 1987. In fact, he was well informed about AIDS and its means of transmission. He knew as well that he was a member of a group which was highly at risk of contracting AIDS. Moreover, he knew that he had twice tested positive for HIV antibodies and that he was therefore infectious. He knew that the Canadian Red Cross collected blood for transfusion to persons in need of it and that AIDS is transmitted by blood. He also knew that the Red Cross would not knowingly accept donations of blood from persons who had tested positive to HIV antibodies or who were members of his high risk group. Nevertheless, on November 16, 1987, he donated blood to the Red Cross at a clinic in Ottawa. Fortunately, the Red Cross's screening process detected the contaminated blood and it was put aside.

The appellant was charged with an offence contrary to s. 176(1)(*a*) of the *Criminal Code*, R.S.C. 1970, c. C-34. That provision is now s. 180 of the *Criminal Code*, R.S.C. 1985, c. C-46, and in these reasons for judgment reference will be made to the present provision. He was charged that he:

> ... on or about the 16th day of November, 1987, at the City of Ottawa in the said Judicial District did commit a common nuisance endangering the lives or health of the public by donating to the Canadian Red Cross Society a quantity of his blood knowing that his blood had previously been found to contain antibodies to Human Immunodeficiency Virus and intentionally withholding the information for the Canadian Red Cross Society, contrary to Section 176(a) [*sic*] of the Criminal Code of Canada.

He was convicted of the charge by Flanigan J., sitting without a jury, and sentenced to a term of 15 months' imprisonment. He appeals both his conviction and his sentence.

Counsel for the appellant attacked the conviction on three grounds:

1. that, reprehensible as the appellant's conduct may have been, it did not amount to an offence known to the law;
2. that it was not proved that his conduct endangered the lives or health of the public or any member of it;
3. that the appellant did not have the necessary *mens rea*.

The provisions of s. 180 of the *Code* are:

180.(1) Every one who commits a common nuisance and thereby

(*a*) endangers the lives, safety or health of the public, or

(*b*) causes physical injury to any person,

is guilty of an indictable offence and liable to imprisonment for a term not exceeding two years.

(2) For the purposes of this section, every one who commits a common nuisance who does an unlawful act or fails to discharge a legal duty and thereby

(*a*) endangers the lives, safety or health, property or comfort of the public; or

(*b*) obstructs the public in the exercise or enjoyment of any right that is common to all the subjects of Her Majesty in Canada.

I will deal first with the argument that the appellant's conduct did not amount to an offence known to law. If, in the circumstances, the appellant's act of donating blood which he knew was HIV-contaminated to the Red Cross was neither an unlawful act nor a failure to discharge a legal duty, then the indictment does not allege an offence known to law.

Section 180(2)(*a*) provides that a common nuisance is committed by either the doing of an unlawful act or the failure to discharge a legal duty which endangers the lives or health of the public. For the purposes of this appeal, I am prepared to assume the correctness of Mr. Greenspon's cogent argument that the words "unlawful act" must be taken to mean conduct which is specifically proscribed by legislation. The *Code* does not make it an offence to donate contaminated blood. Counsel were unable to refer the court to any other statutory provision, federal or provincial, which does so. On the assumption, therefore, that the appellant's conduct could not constitute an "unlawful act" I will examine whether it amounted to a failure to discharge a "legal duty".

I am unable to find any provision in the *Code* or any other statute which I can read as specifically imposing a legal duty upon a person to refrain from donating contaminated blood. The immediate issues therefore is twofold. Can a "legal duty" within the meaning of s. 180(2) be one which arises at common law or must it be one found in a statute? Is there a "legal duty" arising a common law the breach of which, assuming the other essential elements of the offence were proved, could be the basis of an offence under s. 180?

There are no cases deciding whether the "legal duty" in s. 180(2) must be a duty imposed by statute or whether it can be a duty according to common law. However, the "duty imposed by law" which forms part of the definition of criminal negligence set out in s. 219 of the *Code* has been held to be either a duty imposed by statute or a duty arising at common law. The provisions of s. 219 are as follows:

> 219. (1) Every one is criminally negligent who
>
> (a) in doing anything, or
>
> (b) in omitting to do anything that it is his duty to do, shows wanton or reckless disregard for the lives or safety of other persons.
>
> (2) For the purposes of this section, "duty" means a duty imposed by law.

In *R. v. Coyne* (1958), 124 C.C.C. 176, 31 C.R. 335, the New Brunswick Supreme Court Appeal Division considered the criminal negligence provision of the *Code* in relation to a hunting accident. Speaking for that court, Ritchie J.A. held at pp. 179-80 C.C.C.:

> The "duty imposed by law" may be a duty arising by virtue of either the common law or by statute. Use of a firearm, in the absence of proper caution, may readily endanger the lives or safety of others. Under the common law anyone carrying such a dangerous weapon as a rifle is under the duty to take such precaution in its use as, in the circumstances, would be observed by a reasonably careful man. If he fails in that duty and his behaviour is of such as character as to show or display a wanton or reckless disregard for the lives or safety of other persons, then, by virtue of s. 191, his conduct amounts to criminal negligence . . .

In *R. v. Popen* (1981), 60 C.C.C. (2d) 232, this court also had occasion to consider the nature of the "duty imposed by law" contained in the definition of criminal negligence. It was a child abuse case. In giving the judgment of the court, Martin J.A. said at p. 240 C.C.C.:

> . . . a parent is under a legal duty at common law to take reasonable steps to protect his or her child from illegal violence used by the other parent or by a third person towards the child which the parent foresees or ought to foresee.

The effect of that judgment is to hold that the common law duty, which was there described, was a "duty imposed by law" within the meaning of s. 219 because the court held that its breach could amount to criminal negligence.

These decisions lead me to the opinion that it is well settled that, for the purpose of defining criminal negligence, a "duty imposed by law" includes a duty which arises at common law.

While the words "legal duty" in s. 180(2) are not the same as a "duty imposed by law" used in s. 219, they have exactly the same meaning. It follows, therefore, that the meaning given to a "duty imposed by law" in s. 219 should also be given to the "legal duty" contained in s. 180(2). Thus, I am of the opinion that the legal duty referred to in s. 180(2) is a duty which is imposed by statute or which arises at common law. It becomes necessary, then, to decide whether at common law there is a duty which would prohibit the donating of blood known to be HIV-contaminated to the Red Cross.

While this is not a civil case and the principles of tort law are not directly applicable to it, the jurisprudence on that subject is replete with discussions about the legal duties of one person to another which arise at common law. The jurisprudence is constant that those duties are legal ones, that is, they are ones which are imposed by law. Throughout this century and indeed since much earlier times, the common law has recognized a very fundamental duty, which while it has many qualifications, can be summed up as being a duty to refrain from conduct which could cause injury to another person.

. . .

The editors [William James Byrne and Andrew Dewar Gibb] of the 4th edition of Thomas Bevin, *Negligence in Law* (London: Sweet & Maxwell, 1928), vol. 1 at p. 8, have described the fundamental common law duty of one person toward another and the rationale for it:

> Before the law every man is entitled to the enjoyment of unfettered freedom so long as his conduct does not interfere with the equal liberty of all others. Where one man's sphere of activity impinges on another man's, a conflict of interests arises. The debateable land where these collisions may occur is taken possession of by the law, which lays down the rules of mutual intercourse. A liberty of action which is allowed therein is called a right, the obligation of restraint a duty, and these terms are purely relative, each implying the other. Duty, then, as a legal term indicates the obligation to limit freedom of action and to conform to a prescribed course of conduct. *The widest generalisation of duty is that each citizen "must do no act to injure another".*

(Emphasis Added)

. . .

That brief reference to jurisprudence in civil matters shows that there is deeply embedded in the common law a broad fundamental duty which, although subject to many qualifications, requires everyone to refrain from conduct which could injure another. It is not necessary to decide in this case how far that duty extends. At the very least, however, it requires everyone to refrain from conduct which it is reasonably foreseeable could cause serious harm to other persons. Accepting, as I have said, that a "legal duty" within the meaning of that term in s. 180(2) includes a duty arising at common law, I think that the common law duty to refrain from conduct which it is reasonably foreseeable could cause serious harm to other persons is a "legal duty" within the meaning of that term in s. 180(2).

Donating blood which one knows to be HIV-contaminated to an organization whose purpose is to make the blood available for transfusion to other persons clearly constitutes a breach of the common law duty to refrain from conduct which one foresees could cause serious harm to another person. It is thus a failure to discharge a "legal duty" within the contemplation of s. 180(2). It is therefore my conclusion that the indictment which alleges the commission of a nuisance by the donation of blood which the appellant knew to be HIV-contaminated does allege an offence known to law. The first argument made by counsel for the appellant cannot be accepted.

Counsel for the Crown referred to a number of cases where, at common law, the courts held that the exposing of others to the risk of becoming infected by a contagious disease constituted a common nuisance. Those cases are: *R. v. Vantandillo* (1815), 4 M. & S. 73, 105 E.R. 762, *R. v. Burnett* (1815), 4 M. & S. 272, 105 E.R. 835, and *R. v. Henson* (1852), Dears. C.C. 24, 20 L.T.O.S. 63, 16 J.P. 711. I have not cited them as authority in this case because s. 9(*a*) [rep. & sub. R.S.C. 1985, c. 27 (1st Supp.), s.

6] of the *Code* abolishes common law offences. They are, however, very helpful for two reasons. The first is they seem to be based upon the fundamental duty recognized by the common law to refrain from conduct which one can foresee could cause injury to others. The second reason is perhaps a stronger one. It has been said by the editor of the 6th edition of *Tremeearr's Annotated Criminal Code* (Toronto: Carswell, 1964) at p. 241 that the statutory definition of a common nuisance contained in the *Code* "does not differ from a criminal common nuisance at common law". Those cases show that the conduct of donating blood known to be HIV-contaminated, if it exposed others to the risk of infection, is conduct very similar to that which the law has recognized to be a criminal common nuisance for almost 200 years. Finding that conduct to constitute a common nuisance under s. 180 is consistent with the common law position and does not extend it.

. . .

In the light of the findings of the trial judge on the issue of credibility and in the light of all of the other evidence, there can be no doubt that this appellant had personal knowledge that he should not donate his blood, that it was possible for it to get through the testing screen and that it could cause serious damage to the life and health of members of the public. It follows that he knew that, by giving his blood to the Red Cross, he was endangering the lives and health of other members of the public. It therefore becomes necessary to decide whether some lesser form of *mens rea* could satisfy the requirements of s. 180. This appellant knew personally the danger to which the public was subjected by his donation of blood. He clearly had *mens rea*. Mr. Greenspon's third argument fails.

It is my opinion that the appellant was properly convicted of the offence under s. 180. Accordingly, I would dismiss the appeal from conviction.

With respect to sentence, the trial judge did not impose the maximum sentence prescribed by law. The maximum sentence must be reserved for the worst offender committing the worst category of the offence. The sentence imposed took into account that, because of his prior good record, the appellant would not fall into the category of the worst offender. The offence, however, can certainly be categorized as among the worst offences. The appellant's conduct verges on the unspeakable. It cried out for a sentence which would act as a deterrent to others and which would express society's repudiation of what he did. One must have great compassion for this man. He faces a terrible future. Nevertheless, the sentence demonstrates no error in principle and is one that is eminently fit.

While I would allow the application for leave to appeal sentence, I would dismiss the appeal from sentence.

*Appeal dismissed.*

[Note: An appeal to the Supreme Court of Canada was dismissed in June, 1993.]

## Fagan v. Commissioner of Metropolitan Police
(1969), 1 Q.B. 439.

[Only the judgments of James J. and Bridge J. are reproduced below.]

On October 25, 1967, the appellant, Vincent Martel Fagan, appealed to Middlesex Quarter Sessions against his conviction at Willesden magistrates' court upon a charge preferred by David Morris, a constable of the Metropolitan Police Force, for and on behalf of the respondents. He had been convicted of assaulting David Morris when in the execution of his duty on August 31, 1967, contrary to section 51 of the Police Act, 1964. The appellant's appeal was dismissed.

. . . .

*Cur. adv. vult.*

. . . .

JAMES J.: — The appellant, Vincent Martel Fagan, was convicted by the Willesden magistrates of assaulting David Morris, a police constable, in the execution of his duty on August 31, 1967. He appealed to quarter sessions. On October 25, 1967, his appeal was heard by Middlesex Quarter Sessions and was dismissed. This matter now comes before the court on appeal by way of case stated from that decision of quarter sessions.

The sole question is whether the prosecution proved facts which in law amounted to an assault.

On August 31, 1967, the appellant was reversing a motor car in Fortunegate Road, London, N.W. 10, when Police Constable Morris directed him to drive the car forwards to the kerbside and standing in front of the car pointed out a suitable place in which to park. At first the appellant stopped the car too far from the kerb for the officer's liking. Morris asked him to park closer and indicated a precise spot. The appellant drove forward towards him and stopped it with the offside wheel on Morris's left foot. "Get off, you are on my foot," said the officer. "Fuck you, you can wait," said the appellant. The engine of the car stopped running. Morris repeated several times "Get off my foot." The appellant said reluctantly "Okay, man, okay." and then slowly turned on the ignition of the vehicle and reversed it off the officer's foot. The appellant had either turned the ignition off to stop the engine or turned it off after the engine had stopped running.

The justices at quarter sessions on those facts were left in doubt as to whether the mounting of the wheel on to the officer's foot was deliberate or accidental. They were satisfied, however, beyond all reasonable doubt that the appellant "knowingly, provocatively and unnecessarily allowed the wheel to remain on the foot after the officer said 'Get off, you are on my foot.'" They found that on those facts an assault was proved.

Mr. Abbas for the appellant relied upon the passage in Stone's Justices' Manual (1968), Vol. 1, p. 651, where assault is defined. He contends that on the finding of the justices the initial mounting of the wheel could not be an assault and that the act of the wheel mounting the foot came to an end without there being any mens rea. It is argued that thereafter there was no act on the part of the appellant which could constitute an actus reus but only the omission or failure to remove the wheel as soon as he was asked. That failure, it is said, could not in law be an assault, nor could it in law provide the necessary mens rea to convert the original act of mounting the foot into an assault.

Mr. Rant for the respondent argues that the first mounting of the foot was an actus reus which act continued until the moment of time at which the wheel was removed. During that continuing act, it is said, the appellant formed the necessary intention to constitute the element of mens rea and once that element was added to the continuing act, an assault took place. In the alternative, Mr. Rant argues that there can be situations in which there is a duty to act and that in such situations an omission to act in breach of duty would in law amount to an assault. It is unnecessary to formulate any concluded views on this alternative.

In our judgement the question arising, which has been argued on general principles, falls to be decided on the facts of the particular case. An assault is an act which intentionally — or possibly recklessly — causes another person to apprehend immediate and unlawful personal violence. Although "assault" is an independent crime and is to be treated as such, for practical purposes today "assault" is generally synonymous with the term "battery" and is a term used to mean the actual intended use of unlawful force to another person without his consent. On the facts of the present case the "assault" alleged involved a "battery". Where an assault involves a battery, it matters not, in our judgement, whether the battery is inflicted directly by the body of the offender or through the medium of some weapon or instrument controlled by the action of the offender. An assault may be committed by the laying of a hand upon another, and the action does not cease to be an assault if it is a stick held in the hand and not the hand itself which is laid on the person of the victim. So for our part we see no difference in principle between the action of stepping on to a person's toe and maintaining that position and the action of driving a car on to a person's foot and sitting in the car whilst its position on the foot is maintained.

To constitute the offence of assault some intentional act must have been performed: a mere omission to act cannot amount to an assault. Without going into the question whether words alone can constitute an assault, it is clear that the words spoken by the appellant could not alone amount to an assault: they can only shed a light on the appellant's action. For our part we think the crucial question is whether in this case the act of the appellant can be said to be complete and spent at the moment of time when the car wheel came to rest on the foot or whether his act is to be regarded as a continuing act operating until the wheel was removed. In our judgement a distinction is to be drawn between acts which are complete — though results may continue to flow — and those acts which are continuing. Once the act is complete it cannot thereafter be said to be a threat to inflict unlawful force upon the victim. If the act, as distinct from the results thereof, is a continuing act there is a continuing threat to inflict unlawful force upon the victim. If the act, as distinct from the results thereof, is a continuing act there is a continuing threat to inflict unlawful force. If the assault involves a battery and that battery continues there is a continuing act of assault.

For an assault to be committed both the elements of actus reus and mens rea must be present at the same time. The "actus reus" is the action causing the effect on the victim's mind (see the observations of Park B. in *Regina v. St. George*). The "mens rea" is the intention to cause that effect. It is not necessary that mens rea should be present at the inception of the actus reus; it can be superimposed upon an existing act.

On the other hand the subsequent inception of mens rea cannot convert an act which has been completed without mens rea into an assault.

In our judgement the Willesden magistrates and quarter sessions were right in law. On the facts found the action of the appellant may have been initially unintentional, but the time came when knowing that the wheel was on the officer's foot the appellant (1) remained seated in the car so that his body through the medium of the car was in contrast with the officer, (2) switched off the ignition of the car, (3) maintained the wheel of the car on the foot and (4) used words indicating the intention of keeping the wheel in that position. For our part we cannot regard such conduct as mere omission or inactivity.

There was an act constituting a battery which at its inception was not criminal because there was no element of intention but which became criminal from the moment the intention was formed to produce the apprehension which was flowing from the continuing act. The fallacy of the appellant's argument is that it seeks to equate the facts of this case with such a case as where a motorist has accidentally run over a person and, that action having been completed, fails to assist the victim with the intent that the victim should suffer.

We would dismiss this appeal.

BRIDGE J.: — I fully agree with my Lords as to the relevant principles to be applied. No mere omission to act can amount to an assault. Both the elements of actus reus and mens rea must be present at the same time, but the one may be superimposed on the other. It is in the application of these principles to the highly unusual facts of this case that I have, with regret, reached a different conclusion from the majority of the court. I have no sympathy at all for the appellant, who behaved disgracefully. But I have been unable to find any way of regarding the facts which satisfies me that they amounted to the crime of assault. This has not been for want of trying. But at every attempt I have encountered the inescapable question: after the wheel of the appellant's car had accidentally come to rest on the constable's foot, what was it that the appellant did which constituted the act of assault? However, the question is approached, the answer I feel obliged to give is: precisely nothing. The car rested on the foot by its own weight and remained stationary by its own inertia. The appellant's fault was that he omitted to manipulate the controls to set it in motion again.

Neither the fact that the appellant remained in the driver's seat nor that he switched off the ignition seem to me to be of any relevance. The constable's plight would have been no better, but might well have been worse, if the appellant had alighted from the car leaving the ignition switched on. Similarly I can get no help from the suggested analogies. If one man accidentally treads on another's toe or touches him with a stick, but deliberately maintains pressure with foot or stick after the victim protests, there is clearly an assault. But there is no true parallel between such cases and the present case. It is not, to my mind, a legitimate use of language to speak of the appellant "holding" or "maintaining" the car wheel on the constable's foot. The expression which corresponds to the reality is that used by the justices in the case stated. They say, quite rightly, that he "allowed" the wheel to remain.

With a reluctantly dissenting voice I would allow this appeal and quash the appellant's conviction.

*Appeal dismissed.*

## Regina v. Cooper
(1993), 78 C.C.C. (3d) 289 (S.C.C.)

Appeal by the Crown from a judgment of the Newfoundland Court of Appeal, 89 Nfld. & P.E.I.R. 1, 12 W.C.B. (2d) 424, allowing an appeal by the accused from his conviction for second degree murder.

LAMER C.J.C. (dissenting): — I have read the reasons of my colleague, Justice Cory, and adopt his exposition of the facts, the law and, save what is hereinafter said, his comments with respect to s. 212(*a*)(ii) of the *Criminal Code*, R.S.C. 1970, c. C-34 (now R.S.C. 1985, c. C-46, s 229 (*a*)(ii).

It is crucial to a correct charge under s. 212(*a*)(ii) that the jury understand that there must be intention to cause bodily harm which the accused knows is likely to cause death. Intention to cause bodily harm, without knowledge that such is likely to cause death, is not sufficient. Given the position of the defence in this case, a clear understanding of this aspect was essential to a fair trial.

Intentionally and consciously choking someone for only a few seconds might or might not constitute the infliction of "bodily harm" is not defined in that section, there is a statutory definition in s. 245.1 (now s. 267) which also applies to ss. 245.3 (now s. 269) and s. 246.2 (now s. 272):

> 245.1(2) "bodily harm" means any hurt or injury to the complainant that interferes with his or her health or comfort and that is more than merely transient or trifling in nature.

This definition provides some general guidance about the interpretation of the term "bodily harm" in s. 212(*a*)(ii) and makes the point that bodily harm includes a broad spectrum of hurts and injuries.

I do not raise this point to question whether the accused here intended to cause bodily harm. That was conceded in the argument before us. I raise it rather to emphasize that the intention to cause bodily harm by no means leads inexorably to the conclusion that the accused knew that the bodily harm was likely to cause death. It is, of course, this second aspect which is essential to a finding of guilt of murder under s. 212(*a*)(ii). Particularly with respect to an action such as grabbing by the neck, there may be a point at the outset when there is no intention to cause death and no knowledge that the action is likely to cause death. But there comes a point in time when the wrongful conduct becomes likely to cause death. It is, in my view, at that moment or thereafter, that the accused must have a conscious awareness of the likelihood of death. This awareness need not, however, continue until death ensues.

Cooper intended to choke the deceased and cause her bodily harm. Under s. 212(*a*)(i), it was open to the jury to infer from his conduct and on all of the evidence that in doing so he intended to kill her. To be found guilty under s. 212(*a*)(ii), however, he must have been aware of the fact that he persisted in choking her long enough for it to become likely that death would ensue.

This instruction, given the particular facts of this case and the nature of the defence presented by the accused, had to be given. Additionally, the jury should have been instructed to consider the evidence of drunkenness in relation to this awareness. In my respectful view, upon a reading of the whole charge, this was not done adequately.

I would dismiss the appeal.

L'HEUREUX-DUBÉ, SOPINKA AND GONTHIER JJ. concur with Cory J.

CORY J.: — At issue, on this appeal, is the nature of the intent required to found a conviction for murder pursuant to s. 212(a)(ii) of the *Criminal Code*, R.S.C. 1970, c. C-34 (now R.S.C. 1985, c. C-46, s. 229(a)(ii).

*Factual background*

The respondent Lyndon Cooper and the deceased Deborah Careen lived in Labrador City, Newfoundland. At one time, they had been friends and lovers. On January 30, 1988, they met at a gathering place known as the K-Bar in Labrador City. Although by this time the respondent was living with somebody else, they spent the evening together at the bar. There is no doubt that they consumed a considerable amount of alcohol. Eventually, Cooper, the deceased and a mutual friend left the bar in a taxi. After they dropped off the friend they continued in the cab to the residence of another of Cooper's friends where he borrowed a Jeep. Cooper then drove the deceased to the secluded parking-lot of a power station.

At the parking-lot the respondent testified that he and the deceased engaged in some form of consensual sexual activity. He said that they began to argue at one point and that the deceased struck him. At this he became angry. He hit the deceased and grabbed her by the throat with both hands and shook her. He stated that this occurred in the front seat of the Jeep. He then said that he could recall nothing else until he woke in the back seat and found the body of the deceased beside him. He had no recollection of causing her death. He pushed her body out of the Jeep and drove away. Later during the drive to his home he found one of her shoes in the vehicle and threw it out into the snow.

The expert evidence established that the deceased had in fact been struck twice. However, these blows could not have killed her. Rather death was caused by "a classic pattern of one-handed manual strangulation". That same evidence confirmed that death by strangulation can occur as quickly as 30 seconds after contact with the throat and that a drunken victim is likely to die from asphyxiation more quickly than a sober one. None the less, the presence of *petechial haemorrhages* on the neck of the deceased and the finding that the hyoid bone in her throat was not fractured suggested to the expert that death occurred rather more slowly, probably after two minutes of pressure. The position of the defence was that the respondent was so drunk that he blacked out shortly after he started shaking her with both hands. Thus, it was said that the respondent did not have, (i) the required intent to commit murder, or (ii) alternatively, did not foresee that holding someone by the neck was likely to cause death. . . .

*Analysis*

*The nature of the intent required to secure a conviction under s. 212(a)(ii).*

Section 212(a)(ii) provides:

212. Culpable homicide is murder

(a) where the person who causes the death of a human being

. . . . .

(ii) means to cause him bodily harm that he knows is likely to cause his death, and is reckless whether death ensues or not;

This section was considered in *R. v. Nygaard, supra*. On the issue of the requisite intent the court was unanimous. At p. 435, it was said: The essential element is that of intending to cause bodily harm of such a grave and serious nature that the accused knew that it was likely to result in the death of the victim. The aspect of recklessness is almost an afterthought. . . .

The aspect of recklessness can be considered an afterthought since to secure a conviction under this section it must be established that the accused had the intent to cause such grievous bodily harm that he knew it was likely to cause death. One who causes bodily harm that he knows is likely to cause death must, in those circumstances, have a deliberate disregard for the fatal consequences which are known to be likely to occur. That is to say he must, of necessity, be reckless whether death ensues or not.

The concept of recklessness was considered by this court in *R. v. Sansregret* (1985), 18 C.C.C. (3d) 223, 17 D.L.R. (4th) 577, [1985] 1 S.C.R. 570. At p. 233 it was said:

> [Recklessness] is found in the attitude of one who, aware that there is danger that his conduct could bring about the result prohibited by the criminal law, nevertheless persists, despite the risk. It is, in other words, the conduct of one who sees the risk and who takes the chance.

The same words can apply to s. 212(*a*)(ii) with this important addition: it is not sufficient that the accused foresee simply a *danger of death: the accused must foresee a likelihood* of death flowing from the bodily harm that he is occasioning the victim.

It is for this reason that it was said in *Nygaard* that there is only a "slight relaxation" in the *means rea* required for a conviction for murder under s. 212(*a*)(ii) as compared to s. 212(*a*)(i). The position was put in this way at p. 436:

> . . .[where] two accused form the intent to repeatedly and viciously strike a person in the head with a baseball bat realizing full well that the victim will probably die as a result. None the less they continue with the bone-splintering, skull-shattering assault. The accused . . . must have committed as grave a crime as the accused who specifically intends to kill . . . I would conclude that the crime defined in s. 212(*a*)(ii) [now s. 229(*a*)(ii)] can properly be described as murder and on a "culpability scale" it varies so little from s. 212(*a*)(i) as to be indistinguishable.

The intent that must be demonstrated in order to convict under s. 212(*a*)(ii) has two aspects. There must be (a) subjective intent to cause bodily harm; (b) subjective knowledge that the bodily harm is of such a nature that it is likely to result in death. It is only when those two elements of intent are established that a conviction can properly follow.

*What degree of concurrency is required between the wrongful act and the requisite mens rea?*

There can be no doubt that under the classical approach to criminal law it is the intent of the accused that makes the wrongful act illegal. It is that intent which brings the accused within the sphere of blameworthiness and justifies the penalty or punishment which is imposed upon him for the infraction of the criminal law. The essential aspect of *mens rea* and the absolute necessity that it be present in the case of murder was emphasized by Lamer J. (as he then was) in *R. v. Vaillancourt* (1987), 39 C.C.C. (3d) 118, 47 D.L.R. (4th) 399, [1987] 2 S.C.R. 636. At p. 133, he stated: " It may well be that, as a general rule, the principles of fundamental justice require proof of a subjective *mens rea* with respect to the prohibited act, in order to avoid punishing the 'morally innocent'."

. . .

However, not only must the guilty mind, intent or *mens rea* be present, it must also be concurrent with the impugned act. Professor D. Stuart has referred to this as "the simultaneous principle": see *Canadian Criminal Law*, 2nd ed. (1987), p. 305. The principle has been stressed in a number of cases. For example in *R. v. Droste* (1979), 49 C.C.C. (2d) 52, 18 C.R. (3d) 64 (Ont. C.A.), the accused had intended to murder his wife by pouring gasoline over the interior of the car and setting fire to it while she was within it. Before he could light the gasoline the car crashed into a bridge and ignited prematurely. As a result both his children were killed rather than his wife. He was charged with their murder and convicted. On appeal Arnup J.A., speaking for the Court of Appeal in directing a new trial, stated at pp. 53-4:

> . . . the trial Judge did not instruct the jury of the necessity of the Crown showing that at the time of the occurrence at the bridge, the appellant, intending to kill his wife, had done an act with that intention, and in the course of doing so his children were killed. *In short, he did not tell them that the mens rea and the actus reus must be concurrent* . . .

(Emphasis added).

Yet, it is not always necessary for the guilty act and the intent to be completely concurrent: see, for example, *Fagan v. Metropolitan Police Commissioner*, [1983] 3 All. E.R. 442 (Q.B.)

There is, then, the classic rule that at some point the *actus reus* and the *mens reas* or intent must coincide. Further, I would agree . . . that an act (*actus reus*) which may be innocent or no more than careless at the outset can become criminal at a later stage when the accused acquires knowledge of the nature of the act and still refuses to change his course of action.

The determination of whether the guilty mind or *mens rea* coincides with the wrongful act will depend to a large extent upon the nature of the act. For example, if the accused shot the victim in the head or stabbed the victim in the chest with death ensuing a few minutes after the shooting or stabbing, then it would be relatively easy to infer that the requisite intent or *mens rea* coincided with the wrongful act (*actus reus*) of shooting or stabbing. As well, a series of acts may form part of the same transaction. For example the repeated blows of the baseball bat continuing over several minutes are all part of the same transaction. In those circumstances if the requisite intent coincides at any time with the sequence of blows then that could be sufficient to found a conviction.

An example of a series of acts that might be termed a continuous transaction appears in *Meli v. The Queen*, [1954] 1 W.L.R. 228 (P.C.). There the accused intended to kill the deceased, and to this end struck a number of blows. The effect of the blows was such that the accused thought the victim was dead and threw the body over a cliff. However, it was not the blows but rather the exposure suffered by the victim while he lay at the base of the cliff that resulted in the death. It was argued on behalf of the accused that when there was the requisite *mens rea* (during the beating) death did not ensue and when death did ensue there was no longer any intention to kill. The judicial committee of the Privy Council concluded that the entire episode was one continuing transaction that could not be subdivided in any way. At some point, the requisite mens rea coincided with the continuing series of wrongful acts that constituted the transaction. As a result, the conviction for murder was sustained. I agree with that conclusion.

*Application of the "contemporaneous" principles to this case*

Gushue J.A. indicated that persisting or continuing knowledge by the accused that the act he was performing was likely to cause death was required in order to obtain a conviction. He wrote at p. 5:

> A simple reading of what the Supreme Court said in this regard in *Nygaard* makes it very clear that an extremely high degree of knowledge by an accused of what he is doing and *persisting* in must be demonstrated before the requisite intent may be found to exist.

(Emphasis added.)

Yet, with respect, I do not think that it is always necessary that the requisite *mens read* (the guilty mind, intent or awareness) should continue throughout the commission of the wrongful act. There is no question that in order to obtain a conviction the Crown must demonstrate that the accused intended to cause bodily harm that he knew was ultimately so dangerous and serious that it was likely to result in the death of the victim. But that intent need not persist throughout the entire act of strangulation. When Cooper testified that he seized the victim by the neck, it was open to the jury to infer that by those actions he intended to cause her bodily harm that he knew that was likely to cause her death. Since breathing is essential to life, it would be reasonable to infer the accused knew that strangulation was likely to result in death. I would stress that the jury was, of course, not required to make such an inference but, on the evidence presented, it was open to them to do so.

Did the accused possess such a mental state after he started strangling the victim? Here death occurred between 30 seconds and two minutes after he grabbed her by the neck. It could be reasonably inferred by the jury, that when the accused grabbed the victim by the neck and shook her that there was, at that moment, the necessary coincidence of the wrongful act of strangulation and the requisite intent to do bodily harm that the accused knew was likely to cause her death. Cooper was aware of these acts before he "blacked out". Thus although the jury was under no compulsion to do so, it was none the less open to them to infer that he knew that he was causing bodily harm and knew that it was so dangerous to the victim that it was likely to cause her death. It was sufficient that the intent and the act of strangulation coincided at some point. It was not necessary that the requisite intent continue throughout the entire two minutes required to cause the death of the victim.

Gushue J.A. in his reasons relied upon and stressed the following quotation from *R. v. Nygaard, supra*, at p. 435:

> Thus the section requires the accused to intend to cause the gravest of bodily harm that is so dangerous and serious that he knows it is likely to result in death and to *persist in that conduct* despite the knowledge of the risk.

(Emphasis added.)

The emphasized words refer to the *conduct* of an accused. Those words should not be taken as requiring a persistent or continued *awareness* of a likelihood of death right up to the moment of death or until the precise moment when it is established that death was likely to occur. Once it is demonstrated beyond a reasonable doubt that an accused has knowingly caused bodily harm that he knew was likely to cause the death of the victim and the victim dies as a result of the injuries inflicted, then he may be found guilty of murder under s. 212(*a*)(ii).

The Court of Appeal asked whether "continuing awareness on his part was what he was doing and its probable result [was] established". The accused argued that in using this expression the Court of Appeal was not going so far as to require the presence of a continuous intent up to the moment of death. Rather, he contended that the court was merely stating that in order for there to be a conviction under this section the *mens rea* must be present at or after the point at which it becomes likely the death will ensue. It was his position that if the intent to cause bodily harm that the accused knew was likely to cause death should disappear before the point was reached at which death became likely then the accused could not be found guilty. He stated that it was only at this point that the *mens rea* and *actus reus* could coalesce into the crime described in s. 212(*a*)(ii).

This argument should not be accepted. It would require the Crown to provide expert evidence as to the moment at which death physiologically became a likelihood. It would be impossible to fix the time of the "likelihood" of death and difficult to provide evidence as to the duration of the requisite intent of the accused. That cannot be the meaning of this section. Neither the plain wording of this section nor any concept of fairness require the Crown to demonstrate such a complex chronological sequence. In order to obtain a conviction under s. 212(*a*)(ii), the Crown must prove that the accused caused and intended to cause bodily harm that he knew was likely to cause the death of the victim. If death results from a series of wrongful acts that are part of a single transaction then it must be established that the requisite intent coincided at some point with the wrongful acts.

On this issue the trial judge correctly instructed the jury when he stated:

> When he grabbed her by the neck and shook her, did he intend to cause her bodily harm, which he knew was likely to cause her death and was reckless whether death ensued or not. In other words, he wouldn't have to be there until she died . . . He could formulate all of that intent at that point in time, even th[o]ugh he doesn't remember the final outcome.

It was on this ground that the Court of Appeal directed the new trial. Although it can never be determinative of the issue, it is significant that defence counsel at trial took no objection to this or any other aspect of the charge. In any event for the reasons set out earlier, I must disagree with the Court of Appeal's conclusion on this issue. A new trial should not have been granted on this ground.

## The knowledge of the likelihood of death

The appellant seeks to uphold the order directing a new trial on two other grounds. The first, and the more important of these, is the issue raised before the Court of Appeal that the trial judge did not adequately instruct the jury that the Crown must establish that Cooper *knew* that the bodily injury that he was inflicting was likely to cause the death of the victim. I cannot agree with that contention.

It is true that from one or two excerpts from the charge the jury could have inferred that an intent to cause bodily harm was all that was required in order to convict. Yet on numerous occasions the trial judge stated and repeated that the jurors had to be satisfied beyond a reasonable doubt that Cooper meant to cause bodily harm that he *knew* was likely to cause death and was reckless whether death ensued or not . . .

Upon a careful reading and review of the charge as a whole, I am satisfied that there were no errors committed by the trial judge that would justify a new trial.

In the result, I would set aside the order of the Court of Appeal directing a new trial and restore the conviction.

McLachlin and Iacobucci JJ. concur with Cory J.

*Appeal allowed; conviction restored.*

## Questions/Discussion

1. Do you think the results in the cases of *Jordan* and *Smith* can be reconciled? Why or why not?
2. What is your liability in the situation where you shoot A but just before A dies, B comes along and shoots A through the head, effectively killing A? What if after being shot by you, A in agony finishes himself off by cutting his own throat? If in both of these situations, the original wound is one of the causes of death, then attaching liability is no problem, for your actions need not be the only cause of death, just one of the causes. For example, in an American case, *People v. Lewis* (1899), 57 Pac. 470, the defendant mortally wounded the victim, but before dying of the wound, the victim slits his own throat. In the case, the court said that both wounds were operative at the time of death and both contributed to the death. In *Bradley v. The Queen*, [1956] S.C.R. 723, the victim was in a fight with the defendant which left the victim with a fractured skull; the defendant then removed the victim's coat and left him unconscious in the cold. The victim died partly as a result of exposure. The Supreme Court of Canada said that the exposure was caused by the abandoning of the victim in these circumstances and therefore the defendant was liable.
3. If A goes to kill B by shooting him, but misses and B escapes from the building only to be hit and killed by a bus a hundred metres down the street, should A be held liable for "causing" the death of B? What breaks the chain of causation in such situations? Would your answer be the same if B were killed two hours later by a bus or if B were killed by a bus the next day on the way to the police station to report the attempted killing?
4. Under the current law, if I watch a blind person walk into traffic or toward a cliff there is no duty on my part to do anything, assuming there is no special relationship between the two of us. Should there be such a duty created in the Criminal Code? Why or why not? The former Law Reform Commission of Canada proposed the following provision for a new code:

> Failure to Rescue.
> (a) General Rule. Everyone commits a crime who, perceiving another in immediate danger of death or serious harm, does not take reasonable steps to assist him [or her].
> (b) Exception Clause . . . (a) does not apply where the person cannot take reasonable steps to assist without risk of death to himself [or herself] or another person or where he [or she] has some other valid reason for not doing so.

Do you agree with such a provision? What problems do you see in actually applying such a rule? For example, how does one define the content of such a duty in any particular

circumstances. Should the law incorporate such a moral duty to assist or should we continue to rely on other social or moral pressures to accomplish the same ends?
5. If I drop poison in my soup by mistake and then say nothing when V comes along by chance and starts to eat it, should I be held liable for the death which is caused? I did nothing intentionally or knowingly, and when it could be argued I had formed an evil intent (when I knowingly watched V eat my poisoned soup), I merely omitted to do or say anything.
6. What are the nature and the significance of "continuing acts" in criminal law as expressed in *Fagan*? Does the concept pose any danger to traditional principles of criminal liability? Why (or why not)? What is your opinion of decision of the dissenting judge in the case?

**Further Reading**
- Mewett, A. and M. Manning, *Mewett and Manning on Criminal Law, 3rd ed.* (Toronto: Butterworths, 1994).
- Samek, R. "The Concepts of Act and Intention and Their Treatment in Jurisprudence" (1963), 41 Australasian Journal of Philosophy 198.
- Stuart, D., and R. Delisle, *Learning Canadian Criminal Law, 5th ed.* (Toronto: Carswell, 1995).
- Verdun-Jones., *Criminal Law in Canada: Cases, Questions and the Code* (Toronto: Harcourt Brace Jovanovich Canada, 1989), pp. 19-41, 57-82.

## 6.1.2 Mens Rea

### Introduction

Theoretically, the notion of individual intention and/or knowledge in the criminal law (and therefore individual "fault" or blameworthiness) is central to a finding of guilt or criminal liability. As stated by the Law Reform Commission of Canada,

> The basic thrust of the responsibility principle is clear and simple but its detailed analysis and application have become confusing. Its basic thrust is *no liability without fault* — a proposition enjoying general acceptance.[1]

In practice, it can be argued that the requirement of a guilty mind is at times ignored in the interests of protecting society. This tension between the requirement of individual moral fault and the desire to protect society is a very real one both in the literature and in the day-to-day work of the courts. A difficulty is that while lip service is often paid to this traditional subjectivist approach, it is not unusual for the courts in practice to either ignore the requirement or *assume* that it is present; this is particularly true, as we shall see, in cases of criminal negligence.

This section of the chapter examines the meanings of mens rea, the difficulties of applying those meanings to real life fact situations, and what the courts do in response to those problems. A general criticism in this area of criminal law is that there is too often an inconsistency between what the courts say they are doing in applying a so-called fundamental principle of criminal liability (i.e., the requirement of actual and subjective intent of knowledge) and what they actually do. Keep this criticism in mind as you read through the cases, and assess the validity and value of the principle.

One of the first difficulties we find in this area is in regard to the meaning of guilty intention and its operation within the criminal justice system. The problem of defining what is meant by intention or individual responsibility is a vexing one—how we explain notions of responsibility on the part of an individual is coloured by one's own particular perspective on or approach to the role of individual agency and free will in human conduct. Are individual actions to be interpreted in light of the social structures in which they operate? Should we see human actions strictly as the reflection of biological urges or needs? And what of the problems of the differing attributes and developmental environments of individuals — should these factors be reflected in our concept of individual blameworthiness and the determination of guilt?

The criminal justice system in theory assumes that all people are alike when determining guilt or innocence, yet in reality this assumption is far from the truth. People are vastly different in their backgrounds, abilities, opportunities, and resources: should these differences be pertinent to the issue of individual responsibility in the criminal law? As is obvious from the cases which follow, the courts adopt a relatively unproblematic view of mens rea in this regard. *Beaver* and *King* discuss the requirement for mens rea while *Ladue* deals (not satisfactorily) with the situation where the intent of the individual does "match" the physical acts of the accused.[2] *Droste* is a case where the intended victim and the actual victims differed, and involves a discussion of the type of liability which will attach in such situations.

Another problem with the meaning of mens rea is raised in the area of recklessness where less than a full intention or less that full knowledge is sometimes found sufficient to satisfy the requirement of mens rea. There is, as with full intention, the notion of individual blameworthiness to the extent that there is some degree of fault which can be attributed to the accused, for example in a situation where the accused has knowingly run a risk and harm has resulted. The accused does not have full intention or knowledge in regard to his or her actions and its consequences, but there is a sense of wrongfulness nonetheless. This mental state is still required to be subjective, however, and the question is what mental state is sufficient to satisfy the mens rea requirement and what are the problems which are involved. These issues are explored in Fruchtman's article below.

While in theory mens rea is a necessary element to be present in order to be convicted of a crime, there are many exceptions to this very general rule. For example, as we shall see in the final subsection (7.1.3.), there are criminal laws where no mens rea element need be proven at all. This is perhaps less of a problem than those situations where the courts, though seemingly requiring mens rea, in practice ignore the traditional call for actual, subjective intent. As noted above, this is particularly true in the area of criminal negligence where the courts seem to punish for actions or for conduct which on their face demonstrate a wanton disregard for the safety of others, even though the accused may not actually have addressed his or her mind to the dangerousness of the conduct (whether of stupidity, thoughtlessness, or just lack of intent). The courts, rightly or wrongly, are balancing the requirement of subjective intent and the protection needs of the public. When the choice is exercised in favour of the latter, the test becomes more of an objective one: that is, did the conduct of the accused breach standards of reasonableness in the conduct to be expected by the general public. The test then is *not* one of what was the intent or knowledge of the accused at the time of the act (for example, did she actually foresee the danger and run the risk anyway?) These issues are looked at in the last three cases in this section.

1. Law Reform Commission of Canada, *Working Paper 29: The General Part* — Liability and Defences (Ottawa: Ministry of Supply and Services, 1982), p. 172.
2. The issues raised in *Ladue* are more fully explored in Chapter 7, section 2.1, in regard to the *Kundeus* case.

## Beaver v. The Queen
## (1957), 118 C.C.C. 129 (S.C.C.)

Appeal by accused from a decision of the Ontario Court of Appeal, 116 Can. C.C. 231, affirming a conviction for possession and sale of a drug and from another decision of the same Court finding the accused an habitual criminal. Reversed in part.

[Only excerpts from the judgment of Cartwright is reproduced below.]

CARTWRIGHT J.: — The appellant was tried jointly with one Max Beaver before His Honour Judge Forsyth and a jury in the Court of General Sessions of the Peace for the County of York on an indictment reading as follows:

> "The jurors for our Lady the Queen present that
>
> "LOUIS BEAVER and MAX BEAVER, at the City of Toronto, in the County of York, on or about the 12th day of March, in the year 1954, unlawfully did sell a drug, to wit, diacetylmorphine, without the authority or a licence from the Minister of National Health and Welfare or other lawful authority, contrary to Section 4(1)(f) of the Opium and Narcotic Drug Act, Revised Statutes of Canada, 1952, Chapter 201 and amendments thereto.
>
> "The said jurors further present that the said Louis Beaver and Max Beaver, at the City of Toronto, in the County of York, on or about the 12th day of March, in the year 1954, unlawfully did have in their possession a drug, to wit, diacetylmorphine, without the authority of a licence from the Minister of National Health and Welfare or other lawful authority, contrary to Section 4(1)(d) of the Opium and Narcotic Drug Act, Revised Statutes of Canada 1952, Chapter 201, and amendments thereto;
>
> AND FURTHER that the said Louis Beaver is an habitual criminal;
>
> "AND FURTHER that the said Max Beaver is an habitual criminal."

On September 19, 1955, the accused were found guilty on both counts and on the same day the learned trial judge found them to be habitual criminals. On October 17, 1955, the learned Judge sentenced them to 7 years' imprisonment on each count, the sentences to run concurrently, and also imposed sentences of preventive detention.

Max Beaver has since died and we are concerned only with the case of the appellant.

The appellant appealed to the Court of Appeal for Ontario against both convictions and against the finding that he was an habitual criminal. These appeals were dismissed.

On February 19, 1957, the appellant was given leave to appeal to this Court [117 Can. C.C. 340, [1957] S.C.R. 119] from the convictions on the two counts on the following grounds:

1. The learned trial Judge erred in failing to instruct the jury that, if they accepted the evidence of Louis Beaver or were in doubt as a result of it, he was not guilty of the offence.
2. The learned trial Judge erred in holding that the accused Louis Beaver was guilty of the offence charged whether he knew the package handed by the accused Max Beaver to the Police were drugs or not.
3. The learned trial Judge erred in instructing the jury that the only point that they had to decide was whether in fact the package handed the police by the accused Max Beaver was diacetylmorphine.
4. The charge to the jury by the learned trial judge and the Court of Appeal is in error in holding that the accused Louis Beaver could be convicted of the offence

ELEMENTS OF AN OFFENCE 399

charged in the absence of knowledge on his part that the substance in question was a drug.

By the same order, leave to appeal from the finding that the appellant was an habitual criminal was granted, conditionally upon the appeals from the convictions being successful.

It is not necessary to set out the facts in detail. There was evidence on which it was open to the jury to find (i) that Max Beaver sold to a police officer, who was working under cover, a package which in fact contained diacetylmorphine, (ii) that the appellant was a party to the sale of the package, (iii) that while the appellant did not have the package on his person or in his physical possession he and Max Beaver were acting jointly in such circumstances that the possession which the latter had of the package was the possession of both of the accused, and (iv) that the appellant had no knowledge that the substance contained in the package was diacetylmorphine and believed it to be sugar or milk.

I do not mean to suggest that the jury would necessarily have made the fourth finding but there was evidence on which they might have done so, or which might have left them in a state of doubt as to whether or not the appellant knew that the package contained anything other than sugar or milk.

The learned trial Judge, against the protest of the appellant, charged the jury, in effect, that if they were satisfied that the appellant had in his possession a package and sold it, then, if in fact the substance contained in the package was diacetylmorphine, the appellant was guilty on both counts, and that the questions (i) whether he had any knowledge of what the substance was, or (ii) whether he entertained the honest but mistaken belief that it was a harmless substance were irrelevant and must not be considered. Laidlaw J.A. who delivered the unanimous judgment of the Court of Appeal, [116 Can. C.C. 231], was of opinion that this charge was right in law and that the learned trial Judge was bound by the decision in *R. v. Lawrence*, 102 Can. C.C. 121, [1952] O.R. 149, to direct the jury as he did. The main question on this appeal is whether this view of the law is correct.

The problem is one of construction of the *Opium and Narcotic Drug Act*, R.S.C. 1952, c. 201, and particularly the following sections, which at the date of the offences charged read as follows:

"**4**(1) Every person who . . .

"(d) has in his possession any drug save and except under the authority of a licence from the Minister first had and obtained, or other lawful authority; . . . .

(f) manufactures, sells, gives away, delivers or distributes or makes any offer in respect of any drug, or any substance represented or held out by such person to be a drug, to any person without first obtaining a licence from the Minister, or without other lawful authority; . . .

is guilty of an offence, and is liable

"(i) upon indictment, to imprisonment for any term not exceeding seven years and not less than six months, and to a fine not exceeding one thousand dollars and not less than two hundred dollars, and, in addition, at the discretion of the judge, to be whipped; or "(ii) upon summary conviction, to imprisonment with or without hard labour for any term not exceeding eighteen months and not less than six months, and to a fine not exceeding one thousand dollars and not less than two hundred dollars.

"(2) Notwithstanding the provision of the *Criminal Code*, or of any other statute or law, the court has no power to impose less than the minimum penalties herein prescribed, and shall, in all cases of conviction, impose both fine and imprisonment."

"**11**(1) No person shall, without lawful authority or without a permit signed by the Minister or some person authorized by him in that behalf, import or have in his possession any opium pipe, opium lamp, or other device or apparatus designed or generally used for the purpose of preparing opium for smoking, or smoking or inhaling opium, or any article capable of being used or as part of any such pipe, lamp or other device or apparatus.

"(2) Any person violating the provisions of this section is liable, upon summary conviction, to a fine not exceeding one hundred dollars, and not less than fifty dollars, or to imprisonment for a term not exceeding three months, or to both fine and imprisonment."

"**15**. Where any person is charged with an offence under paragraph (a), (d), (f), or (g) of subsection (1) of section 4, it is not necessary for the prosecuting authority to establish that the accused had not a licence from the Minister or was not otherwise authorized to commit the act complained of, and if the accused pleads or alleges that he had such licence or other authority the burden of proof thereof shall be upon the person so charged."

"**17**. Without limiting the generality of paragraph (d) of sub-section (1) of section 4, any person who occupies, controls, or is in possession of any building, room, vessel, vehicle, enclosure or place, in or upon which any drug or any article mentioned in section 11 is found, shall, if charged with having such drug or article in possession without lawful authority, be deemed to have been so in possession unless he prove that the drug or article was there without his authority, knowledge or consent, or that he was lawfully entitled to the possession thereof."

In the course of the argument counsel also referred to the following provisions of other statutes of Canada:

The *Interpretation Act*, R.S.C. 1952, c. 158, s. 28(1):

"**28**(1) Every act shall be read and construed as if any offence for which the offender may be

"(a) prosecuted by indictment, howsoever such offence may be therein described or referred to, were described or referred to as an indictable offence;

"(b) punishable on summary conviction, were described or referred to as an offence; and all provisions of the *Criminal Code* relating to indictable offences, or offences, as the case may be, shall apply to every such offence."

The *Criminal Code*, R.S.C. 1927, c. 36, s. 5:

"**5**(1) In this Act, unless the context otherwise requires, . . .

"(b) having in one's possession includes not only having in one's own personal possession, but also knowingly,

"(i) having in the actual possession or custody of any other person, and

"(ii) having in any place, whether belonging to or occupied by one's self or not, for the use or benefit of one's self or of any other person.

(2) If there are two or more persons, and any one or more of them, with the knowledge and consent of the rest, has or have anything in his or their custody or possession, it shall be deemed and taken to be in the custody and possession of each and all of them."

The judgment in appeal is supported by earlier decisions of Appellate Courts in Ontario, Quebec and Nova Scotia, but a directly contrary view has been expressed by the Court of Appeal for British Columbia. While this conflict has existed since 1948, this is the first occasion on which the question has been brought before this Court.

It may be of assistance in examining the problem to use a simple illustration. Suppose X goes to the shop of Y, a druggist, and asks Y to sell him some baking soda. Y hands him a sealed packet which he tells him contains baking soda and charges him a few cents. X honestly believes that the packet contains baking soda but in fact it contains heroin. X puts the package in his pocket, takes it home and later puts it in a cupboard in his bathroom. There would seem to be no doubt that X has had actual manual and physical possession of the package and that he continues to have possession of the package while it is in his cupboard. The main question raised on this appeal is whether, in the supposed circumstances, X would be guilty of the crime of having heroin in his possession?

It will be observed at once that we are not concerned with the incidence of the burden of proof or of the obligation of adducing evidence. The judgment of the Court of Appeal states the law to be that X must be convicted although he proves to the point of demonstration that he honestly believed the package to contain baking soda.

I have examined all the cases referred to by counsel in the course of their full and helpful arguments but do not propose to refer to them in detail as the differences of opinion which they disclose are not so much as to the principles by which the Court should be guided in construing a statute which creates a crime as to the result of applying those principles to the Act with which we are concerned.

The rule of construction has often been stated.

. . . .

In *R. v. Tolson* (1889), 23 Q.B.D. 168 at p. 188, Stephen J. says: "I think it may be laid down as a general rule than an alleged offender is deemed to have acted under that state of facts which he in good faith and on reasonable grounds believed to exist when he did the act alleged to be an offence. I am unable to suggest any real exception to this rule, nor has one ever been suggested to me." And adds at p. 189: "Of course, it would be competent to the legislature to define a crime in such a way as to make the existence of any state of mind immaterial. The question is solely whether it has actually done so in this case."

I adhere to the opinion which, with the concurrence of my brother Nolan, I expressed in *R. v. Rees*, 115 Can. C.C. 1 at p. 11, 4 D.L.R. (2d) 406 at p. 415, [1956] S.C.R. 640 at p. 651 that the first of the statements of Stephen J. quoted above should now be read in the light of the judgment of Lord Goddard C.J., concurred in by Lynskey and Devlin JJ. in *Wilson v. Inyang*, [1951] 2 All E.R. 237, which, in my opinion, rightly decides that the essential question is whether the belief entertained by the accused is an honest one and that the existence or non-existence of reasonable grounds for such belief is merely relevant evidence to be weighed by the tribunal of fact in determining that essential question.

. . . .

When the decisions as to the construction of the *Opium and Narcotic Drug Act* on which the respondent relies are examined it appears that two main reasons are assigned for holding that *mens rea* is not an essential ingredient of the offence created by s. 4(1)(d), these being (i) the assumption that the subject-matter with which the Act deals is of the kind dealt with in the cases of which *Hobbs v. Winchester Corp.*, [1910] 2 K.B. 471, is typical and which are sometimes referred to as "public welfare offence cases", and (ii) by implication from the wording of s. 17 of the Act.

As to the first of these reasons, I can discern little similarity between a statute designed, by forbidding the sale of unsound meat, to ensure that the supply available to the public shall be wholesome, and a statute making it a serious crime to possess or deal in narcotics; the one is to ensure that a lawful and necessary trade shall be carried on in a manner not to endanger the public health, the other to forbid altogether conduct regarded as harmful in itself. As a necessary feature of his trade, the butcher holds himself out as selling meat fit for consumption; he warrants that quality; and it is part of his duty as trader to see that the merchandise is wholesome. The statute simply converts that civil personal duty into a public duty.

. . . .

As to the second reason, the argument is put as follows. Using again the illustration I have taken above, it is said (i) that the words of s. 17 would require the conviction of X if the package was found in his bathroom cupboard "unless he prove that [it] was there without his authority, knowledge or consent", that is, he is *prima facie* presumed to be guilty but can exculpate himself by proving lack of knowledge, and (ii) that since no such words as "unless he prove that the drug was in his possession without his knowledge" are found in s. 4(1)(d) it must be held that Parliament intended that lack of knowledge should be no defence.

In my view all that s. 17 accomplishes, still using the same illustration, is, on proof that the package was in his cupboard, to shift to X the onus of proving that he did not have possession of the package. To this X would answer: "Of course I had possession of the package, I bought it, paid for it, carried it home and put it in my cupboard. My defence is that I thought it contained baking soda. I had no idea it contained heroin." If it be suggested that X could not usefully make this reply if what was found in his house was not a sealed package but an article of the sort described in s. 11 the answer would appear to be that any person might not recognize an opium lamp or an article capable of being used as part of such a lamp. The wording of s. 17 does not appear to me to compel the Court to construe s. 4 as the Court of Appeal has done. It still leaves unanswered the question: Has X possession of heroin when he has in his hand or in his pocket or in his cupboard a package which in fact contains heroin but which he honestly believes contains only baking soda? In my opinion that question must be answered in the negative. The essence of the crime is the possession of the forbidden substance and in a criminal case there is in law no possession without knowledge of the character of the forbidden substance.

. . . .

In my view the law is correctly stated in the following passage in the judgment of O'Halloran J.A., with whom Robertson J.A. concurred, in *R. v. Hess* (1948) 94 Can. C.C. 48 at pp. 50-1: "To constitute 'possession' within the meaning of the criminal law it is my judgment, that where as here there is manual handling of a thing, it must be co-existent with knowledge of what the thing is, and both these elements must be coexistent with some act of control (outside public duty). When those three elements exist together, I think it must be conceded that under s. 4(1)(d) it does not then matter if the thing is retained for an innocent purpose."

If the matter were otherwise doubtful I would be drawn to the conclusion that Parliament did not intend to enact that *mens rea* should not be an essential ingredient of the offence created by s. 4(1)(d) by the circumstance that on conviction a minimum sentence of 6 months' imprisonment plus a fine of $200 be imposed.

. . . .

The conclusion which I have reached on the main question as to the proper construction of the word possession makes it unnecessary for me to consider the other points raised by Mr. Dubin in his argument as to the construction of s. 4(1)(d). For the above reasons I would quash the conviction on the charge of having possession of a drug.

As to the charge of selling, as is pointed out by my brother Fauteux, the appellant's version of the facts brings his actions within the provisions of s. 4(1)(f) since he and his brother jointly sold a substance represented or held out by them to be heroin; and I agree with the conclusion of my brother Fauteux that the conviction on the charge of selling must be affirmed.

For the above reasons, I would dismiss the appeal as to the first count (that is, of selling) but would direct that the time during which the appellant has been confined pending the determination of the appeal shall count as part of the term of imprisonment imposed pursuant to that conviction. As to the second count (that is, of having possession) I would allow the appeal.

*Appeal from conviction for possession of drug allowed; appeals from conviction for sale of a drug and finding of being an habitual criminal dismissed.*

## Regina v. King
### (1962), 133 C.C.C. 1 (S.C.C.)

Appeal from a decision of the Ontario Court of Appeal, 129 Can. C.C. 391 [1961] O.W.N. 37, quashing a conviction for impaired driving. Affirmed.

Only the judgment of Ritchie is reproduced below.

Ritchie, J.: — This is an appeal by Crown at the instance of the Attorney-General for Ontario from a judgment rendered by the majority of the Court of Appeal of that Province (MacKay, J.A., dissenting) which allowed the respondent's appeal from a conviction entered against him after a trial *de novo* held before Judge Timmins of the County Court of the County of York for the offence of driving a motor vehicle while his ability to do so was impaired by a drug contrary to s. 223 of the *Cr. Code.*

The circumstances giving rise to this appeal are that on October 8, 1959 the respondent went to his dentist's office, by appointment, for the purpose of having two teeth extracted, and that he was there injected with a drug known as sodium pentothal, a quick-acting anaesthetic which produces unconsciousness, removes pain and gives a certain amount of relaxation during the period of an operation, and before using which the dentist stated that it was the practice of his office to have patients sign a printed form containing the following warning: "Patients are cautioned not to drive after anaesthetic until head clears." After he had regained consciousness, the respondent paid his bill by cheque to a nurse who was in attendance and who stated that at this time he appeared "perfectly normal" and that she warned him not to drive his car until his head was "perfectly clear" to which he replied that he intended to walk. The respondent says that he heard no such warning and remembers signing no form containing any warning, but he does remember getting into his car which he had parked about a block away and proceeding across an intersection, after which he became unconscious, and his car ran into the left rear portion of a parked vehicle, whereafter the police appeared to find that he was staggering and that his physical co-ordination was poor. This was later verified by a sergeant at the police station where the respondent was submitted to certain tests. Medical evidence was given to the effect that this mental and physical condition was consistent with the after-effects of being injected with sodium pentothal and that this drug may induce a state of amnesia accompanied by a period during which the subject may feel perfectly competent to get in a car and drive and in the next second or so be in a condition in which he would not know what was happening. The respondent stated that he did not know anything about the drug which was administered to him.

The learned County Court judge convicted the respondent on the ground that "he knew that he had a drug and he was given a warning with respect to driving a motor car" and also that "he took the responsibility of going to the car, he took the responsibility of driving his car knowing that he had had a drug".

The respondent's sole defence was that he had no knowledge of the effect of the drug which resulted in his being unaware of any warning and unaware of the fact that he was impaired when he took the responsibility to drive and did drive his car.

. . . .

The question of law so determined was made a ground of appeal and for leave to appeal to the Court of Appeal of Ontario, and Mr. Justice MacKay, in the course of his dissenting opinion, stated the issue before the Court in the clearest terms, saying [at p. 396 Can. C.C.]: "I think all of these grounds of appeal raise only one issue, that is, to what extent, if at all, does the doctrine of *mens rea* apply to this offence?"

. . . .

The provisions of s. 223 of the *Code* are as follows:

"**223.** Every one who, while his ability to drive a motor vehicle is impaired by alcohol or a drug, drives a motor vehicle or has the care or control of a motor vehicle, whether it is in motion or not, is guilty of an indictable offence or an offence punishable on summary conviction and is liable

(a) for a first offence, to a fine of not more than five hundred dollars and not less than fifty dollars or to imprisonment for three months or both,

(b) for a second offence, to imprisonment for not more than three months and not less than fourteen days, and

(c) for each subsequent offence, to imprisonment for not more than one year and not less than three months."

. . . .

As there is no express language in s. 223 of the *Cr. Code* disclosing the intention of Parliament to rule out *mens rea* as an essential ingredient of the crime therein described, it becomes necessary to determine whether it can be said that such an intention is disclosed by necessary implication.

In classifying the types of statute in which such an intention has been implied, the learned authors, writing under the title "Criminal Law and Procedure" in 10 Hals., 3rd ed., p. 275, adopt the three exceptions to the general rule which are suggested by Wright, J., in *Sherras v. DeRutzen, supra*, at p. 921 and state:

> "Most statutes creating a strict liability fall under three heads. First, where the acts are not criminal in any real sense, but are prohibited under a penalty in the public interest. Secondly, where the acts are public nuisances; thus, an employer has been held liable on indictment for a nuisance caused by workmen without his knowledge and contrary to his orders. Thirdly, where, although the proceeding is criminal in form, it is really only a summary mode of enforcing a civil right."

Mr. Justice MacKay concluded that s. 223 of the *Cr. Code* comes within the first exception to the general rule in that it is "an act perhaps not criminal in any real sense but which is in the public interest prohibited". He finds that [at p. 403 Can. C.C., p. 52 O.W.N.]:

> "A person whose ability to drive is impaired by alcohol or drugs, driving on the highway, is a danger to the general public and in my view the offence falls within the first classification referred to by Wright J. in the *Sherras* case. It is an act perhaps not criminal in any real sense but which is in the public interest prohibited."

. . . .

In my view the enactment of s. 223 of the *Cr. Code* added a new crime to the general criminal law, and neither the language in which it was enacted nor the evil which it was intended to prevent are such as to give rise to a necessary implication that Parliament intended to impose absolute liability unless the impaired condition which the section prohibits was brought about by some conscious act of the will or intention.

Consideration of this phase of the question should not be concluded without noting the decision in *Armstrong v. Clark*, [1957] 1 All E.R. 433, in which the Queen's Bench Division had to consider the question of "whether the taking of insulin by the respondent was, in the circumstances which occurred, to be regarded as taking a drug which would make him liable to be found guilty of an offence under s. 15(1)" of the *Road Traffic Act*, and in which Lord Goddard said [at pp. 435-6]:

> "This case must go back with a direction that the justices may take into account a great many things, but they must remember, and everyone must remember, that this section was designed for the protection of the public, and if people happen to be in a condition of health that renders them subject to going into a coma, or forces them to take remedies which may send them into a coma, the answer is that they must not drive because they are a danger to the rest of Her Majesty's subjects.

I do not think that anything that was said by Lord Goddard in that case can be taken as changing the Law with respect to *mens rea* in statutory offences as it was stated by the same learned Judge and adopted by this Court in the cases hereinbefore referred to. It is noteworthy, however, that in the course of this decision, Lord Goddard does make the observation [at p. 435] with respect to the statutory offence with which he was dealing: "The penalty, I need hardly say, is entirely at the discretion of the bench."

The existence of *mens rea* as an essential ingredient of an offence and the method of proving the existence of that ingredient are two different things, and I am of opinion that when it has been proved that a driver was driving a motor vehicle while his ability to do so was impaired by alcohol or a drug, then a rebuttable presumption arises that his condition was voluntarily induced and that he is guilty of the offence created by s. 223 and must be convicted unless other evidence is adduced which raises a reasonable doubt as to whether he was, through no fault of his own, disabled when he undertook to drive and drove, from being able to appreciate and know that he was or might become impaired.

If the driver's lack of appreciation when he undertook to drive was induced by voluntary consumption of alcohol or of a drug which he knew or had any reasonable ground for believing might cause him to be impaired, then he cannot, of course, avoid the consequences of the impairment which results by saying that he did not intend to get into such a condition, but if the impairment has been brought about without any act of his own will, then, in my view, the offence created by s. 223 cannot be said to have been committed.

The existence of a rebuttable presumption that a man intends the natural consequences of his own conduct is a part of our law, but its application to any particular situation involves a consideration of what consequences a man might be reasonably expected to foresee under the circumstances.

In the course of the lecture on "The Criminal Law" which is contained in the well-known work by O.W. Holmes, Jr. on *The Common Law* that learned author says [at p. 57]:

> "As the purpose is to compel men to abstain from dangerous conduct, and not merely to restrain them from evil inclinations, the law requires them at their peril to know the teachings of common experience, just as it requires them to know the law."

It seems to me that it can be taken as a matter of "common experience" that the consumption of alcohol may produce intoxication and, therefore, "impairment" in the sense in which that word is used in s. 223, and I think it is also to be similarly taken to be known that the use of narcotics may have the same effect, but if it appears that the impairment was produced as a result of using a drug in the form of medicine on a doctor's order or recommendation and that its effect was unknown to the patient, then the presumption is, in my view, rebutted.

For all the above reasons, I do not think that the Court of Appeal erred in holding that *mens rea* was an essential element of the offence of driving while impaired contrary to s. 223 of the *Cr. Code*, but I am of opinion that that element need not necessarily be present in relation both to the act of driving and to the state of being impaired in order to make the offence complete. That is to say, that a man who becomes impaired as the result of taking a drug on medical advice without knowing its effect cannot escape liability if he became aware of his impaired condition before he started to drive his car just as a man who did not appreciate his impaired condition when he started to drive cannot escape liability on the ground that his lack of appreciation was brought about by voluntary consumption of liquor or drug. The defence in the present case was that the respondent became impaired through no act of his own will and could not reasonably be expected to have known that his ability was impaired or might thereafter become impaired when he undertook to drive and drove his motor vehicle.

I would dismiss this appeal.

*Appeal dismissed.*

## Regina v. Ladue
[1965] 4 C.C.C. 264 (Y.T. C.A.)

Appeal by accused from a conviction for indecently interfering with a dead human body contrary to s. 167(b) of the *Cr. Code*.

The judgment of the Court was delivered by

DAVEY, J.A.: — Ladue either copulated or attempted to copulate with a dead woman and was convicted under s. 167(b) of the *Criminal Code* of indecency interfering with a dead human body. The material part of the section reads as follows:

"**167.** Every one who

(b) improperly or indecently interferes with or offers any indignity to a dead human body or human remains, whether buried or not,

is guilty of an indictable offence and is liable to imprisonment for five years."

The only point of substance in Ladue's appeal against his conviction is whether the learned trial Judge was right in holding that it was not open to the appellant to contend that he was not guilty because he did not know the woman was dead. There was considerable evidence upon which the learned Judge might have held, if he had not considered the defence untenable in law, that while Ladue knew what he was doing physically, he was so intoxicated that he did not realize the woman was dead. Subject to what I have to say later that would have been a good defence.

In his oral reasons the learned trial Judge, in dealing with the effect of intoxication upon the appellant's understanding, said this:

"What does the argument amount to? The only way you can make it, the only way in which you could make this argument—certainly I don't know. She was dead. He thought she was unconscious. Because she was dead? No. That is about it. At the time of the incident can a person be heard to say 'that it didn't occur to me she was dead, and I am therefore innocent.' I will tell you, I will not listen to such an argument. That would be an admission he was having intercourse with a person ..."

It is a fundamental principle of criminal law that, unless excluded by statute, *mens rea*, that is guilty intention, is necessary to constitute a crime, and that a person doing an act is not guilty of a crime if his mind be innocent: *R. v. Prince* (1875), L.R. 2 C.C.R. 154: *R. v. Tolson* (1889), 23 Q.B.D. 168, *per* Willis, J., at pp. 171-2. I see nothing in s. 167(b) to exclude that principle. Accordingly it was open to the appellant to attempt to rebut the inference of *mens rea* flowing from what he deliberately did to the body by proving that he did not know the woman was dead.

But in attempting to defend himself in that way the appellant runs into the insuperable difficulty alluded to by the learned trial Judge. The appellant could not have failed even in his drunken state, to perceive that the woman was unconscious, and incapable of giving her consent to copulation. Indeed the appellant does not suggest that he thought he had her consent to the act. So if the woman was alive he was raping her. Therefore it is impossible for him to argue that, not knowing her to be dead, he was acting innocently. An intention to commit a crime, although not the precise crime charged, will provide the necessary *mens rea* under a statute in the form of s. 167(b):

. . . .

It follows that in my respectful opinion the learned trial Judge was right in the particular circumstances of this case in saying that he would not entertain an argument that appellant was innocent because he did not know the woman was dead.

It becomes necessary at this point to notice our decision in *R. v. McLeod* (1954), 111 C.C.C. 106, 20 C.R. 281, 14 W.W.R. 97, in which we dismissed a Crown appeal against an accused's acquittal on a charge of assaulting a peace officer engaged in the execution of this duty on the ground that knowledge that the victim was a peace officer and was engaged in the execution of his duty was an essential ingredient of the crime, and that the accused did not know those essential facts. Of the three Judges who sat on that appeal I alone held that the accused had committed a common assault; consequently it became essential for me to consider the submission of Crown counsel that on the authority of *R. v. Prince*, the fact that the accused had in any event committed a common assault supplied the necessary *mens rea* and made him guilty of the aggravated offence even though he did not know the victim was a Peace Officer. In the course of my reasons I considered *R. v. Prince* and *R. v. Tolson*, I adhere to the views I expressed there, and it is unnecessary to repeat them. The neat distinction between *R. v. McLeod*, and the case at bar is that in the former we held as a matter of interpretation that knowledge that the victim was a peace officer and was engaged in the execution of his duty was a specific ingredient of the crime charged in that case, and that the charge had not been established in the absence of proof of that specific knowledge. But as a matter of interpretation I do not consider knowledge that the body is dead to be a specific ingredient of an offence against s. 167(b). All that is required is *mens rea* in the widest sense.

*Mens rea* is an uncertain term, and what it means varies with the different crimes and the statutes defining them . . . .

The nature of the offence under s. 167(b) and the language of that section would not seem to require knowledge that the body is dead as a specific ingredient of an offence under that section, because in most cases that fact would be clear, and proof of a deliberate act improperly or indecently interfering with a body that was in fact dead would be sufficient proof of a criminal intention or *mens rea*. It would be only in the most exceptional case where the offender might have any doubt whether a body was quick or dead, and in such a case he might defend himself by showing that he did not know the body was dead and that according to his understanding he was acting lawfully and innocently. That is what the appellant cannot show in this case, because if the woman was alive he was raping her.

I would dismiss the appeal.

*Appeal dismissed.*

## Regina v. Droste
(1982), 34 O.R. (2d) 588 (C.A.)

Appeal by accused against his conviction on two counts of first degree murder.
The judgement of the Court was delivered orally by
MARTIN J.A.: — The appellant was convicted on two counts of first degree murder and now appeals from those convictions. Count 1 charged the appellant with having on February 27, 1977, committed first degree murder on the person of Rolf Maurice Droste; count 2 charged the appellant with having on the same day committed first degree murder on the person of Monique Jean Droste. Rolf Maurice Droste and Monique Jean Droste are the children of the appellant.

The case for the Crown was that the appellant formed a plan to kill his wife. The plan involved saturating his car with gasoline, simulating an accident by running the car into the abutment of a bridge, rendering his wife unconscious by hitting her on the head with an instrument, setting fire to the car and escaping therefrom himself. The Crown alleges that in carrying out the plan, the appellant by accident or mistake caused the death of his two children.

A fellow employee of the appellant, one Holdsworth, testified that the appellant disclosed to him a number of plans to kill his wife. Holdsworth testified to the following effect. He said that the appellant's final plan to kill his wife, as disclosed to him, was that the appellant intended to crash his car into a bridge near St. Mary's, after soaking the interior of the car with gasoline, filling the gasoline tank and placing a five-gallon can of gasoline in the trunk of the car. The occupants would be wearing seat belts. The appellant had made a pipe at work inside of which he had poured molten zinc, and which the appellant said he would use to render his wife unconscious. Holdsworth said that the appellant told him he would ignite the fire by placing fuel-soaked rags under his seat, and told him on the Wednesday prior to Sunday, February 27th, that he was going to carry out the plan the following Sunday. Holdsworth said that he did not inform the police about what the appellant had told him because he did not take the appellant seriously. However, when he read the newspaper account of the accident on Monday, February 28th, he contacted the police.

Brenda Lee Lukings, also a co-worker at the plant where the appellant was employed, testified that the appellant told her that he was going to kill his wife by doing something to the automobile, such as fixing the brakes so that his wife would die in a car crash.

Linda May Sears, another co-worker testified that the appellant told her that he wished to kill his wife so he could live with his girl-friend down the street.

The appellant was sexually involved with a married woman at the time of the occurrence in question, although both the appellant and the woman denied that it was a serious relationship. The Crown, however, alleged that the relationship constituted a motive for the appellant's intention to kill his wife.

The appellant and his wife had been invited to attend a birthday party at the home of a friend on February 27, 1977. The friend lived a distance of 2.5 miles away by the most direct route or 4.8 miles by the route which the appellant, in fact, took. On the morning of February 27th the appellant went to a gas station where he had the tank of the car filled with gasoline. He also had a five-gallon container filled with gasoline which was placed in the trunk. There was also evidence that the appellant had used gasoline that day to clean the interior of the car. The appellant said that he had used, perhaps, a pint from the container which was used to soak rags which were applied to the car to remove grease from the interior. The appellant that morning also re-activated the seat belts of the car which had not been in use; he said that he re-activated the seat belts because there had been a number of accidents which had occurred in his own family and accidents involving close friends.

In the early afternoon of February 27, 1977, the appellant, his wife and the two children left in the car to attend the birthday party. The appellant's wife complained that the car smelled of gasoline fumes.

The appellant's wife testified that as they approached a bridge over the Otter Creek she noticed flames shooting up into the vehicle between the two seats by the gear shift. She testified that the appellant began to put out the flames with his right hand. She said that at this point the appellant reached down in the seat and took a screwdriver with an orange handle on it and proceeded to hit her on the left side of the back of the head with the handle part of the screwdriver. He continued to yell at her and told her to let go of the steering wheel. The car then crashed into the abutment. The appellant denied that he had hit wife on the head with a screwdriver or with any other instrument and said that the collision with the bridge was caused by the car pulling sharply and unexpectedly to the right. No screwdriver was found at the scene but a pipe to which adhered melted metal, composed principally of zinc, was found under the springs of the front seat.

Among the other injuries sustained by the wife was a laceration of the scalp. The medical evidence indicated that the injury was more consistent with having been caused by a blow on the head with an instrument than by striking her head on the front of the car.

The appellant's wife was able to extricate herself from the car through the driver's door and she then helped the appellant out of the vehicle. They then endeavoured to get the children from the back seat, but were unable to do so. At this point a Mr. Arnott arrived at the scene and he observed that the fire at this time was in the front of the vehicle. When Mr. Arnott opened the door to remove the children from the vehicle he said that he was met by flames which shot over his head and made a roaring sound. The appellant's wife sat in Mr. Arnott's car and the appellant ran up a laneway and began knocking on the door of a farmhouse seeking to get assistance. The children unfortunately were not able to be removed from the car and they both died of asphyxia as a result of the fire.

Samples taken from the interior of the car contained gasoline. There was also a plastic container found in the trunk of the car and evidence was given of the results of tests, from which an inference might be drawn, that some four gallons had been removed from the five-gallon can. Expert evidence was called by the Crown, the effect of which was, that the fire did not emanate in the engine, but was caused by an accelerant applied to the interior of the car. Professor Sandler was called by the defence and, he concluded, on the basis of the observations of persons at the scene and the quantity of gasoline found in the samples removed from the car, that the fire originated in the engine and travelled to the back of the car. He was also of the view that the fire burned naturally and was not due to an accelerant. He was of the opinion that the quantity of gasoline found in the interior of the car got there after the fire had started as a result of the burning and possibly by gasoline flowing from the container in the trunk into the interior of the car.

The appellant testified in his own defence, denied that he had planned to kill his wife and said that the collision with the bridge was an accident. He also denied that he had told Holdsworth that he planned to kill his wife.

On that evidence the jury found the appellant guilty of first degree murder on both counts. It was not, and in our view, it could not successfully be contended that the verdict of the jury was unreasonable or unsupported by the evidence.

The first ground of appeal is that the trial judge erred in instructing the jury that, if they found that the appellant's intention to kill his wife was the result of planning and deliberation, it was open to the jury to convict him of first degree murder in respect of the death of the children. Mr. Kluwak's submission was that a conviction for first degree murder cannot be supported on the basis that the accused planned and deliberated the killing of his wife and by accident or mistake caused the death of his children; that ss. 212(b) and 214(2) of the *Criminal Code*, R.C.S. 1970, c. C-34 cannot be combined to found a conviction for first degree murder and the trial judge erred in failing to so instruct the jury. He contended that the death of the victim must be planned and deliberate. Section 212(b) reads:

212. Culpable homicide is murder

. . . .

(b) where a person, meaning to cause death to a human being or meaning to cause him bodily harm that he knows is likely to cause his death, and being reckless whether death ensues or not, by accident or mistake causes death to another human being, notwithstanding that he does not mean to cause death or bodily harm to that human being . . .

Section 214(2) [rep. & sub. 1974-75, c. 105, s. 4] reads:

214(2) Murder is first degree when it is planned and deliberate.

The trial judge instructed the jury with respect to s. 212(b) and directed them that if the Crown had satisfied them beyond a reasonable doubt that the appellant caused the death of the children by asphyxia resulting from the fire, and at the time he caused their death he intended to kill Mrs. Droste, then the prosecution had proved second degree murder. The trial judge did not put to the jury that part of s. 212(b) which provides that it is murder if a person meaning to cause bodily harm that he knows is likely to cause death and being reckless whether death ensues to one human being by accident or mistake causes death to another human being. He further instructed the jury that it was only if they were satisfied beyond a reasonable doubt that the appellant had committed second degree murder that they could then consider whether the appellant was guilty of first degree murder. He then accurately instructed the jury with respect to the elements of planning and deliberation.

We think that the trial judge correctly instructed the jury that if they were satisfied beyond a reasonable doubt that the appellant's intention to kill his wife was planned and deliberate and that in the course of carrying out that intention he caused the death of the children by accident or mistake, that the resulting murder constituted first degree murder.

Section 214(2) provides that "murder" is first degree murder when "it" is planned and deliberate. Where murder as defined by s. 212(b) is committed and that murder is planned and deliberate the murder is first degree murder even though the planned and deliberate intention to kill took effect on a person other than the intended victim.

As we have indicated, we are satisfied that a conviction for first degree murder may be supported on the basis of a combination of ss. 212(b) and 214(2) and we are unable to accept the submission of Mr. Kluwak that in order to constitute first degree murder under s. 214(2) the planning and deliberation must be with respect to the person actually killed.

. . . .

We are also of the view that the transference of a planned and deliberate intention to kill one person to the actual victim is in accord with the general principles of the criminal law. Clearly, the moral culpability of one who intends to kill one person, preceded by planning and deliberation, but who by accident or mistake kills another person, is the same as if he had succeeded in killing his intended victim.

. . . .

It is well established that if an accused acting under such provocation as would reduce murder to manslaughter, shoots at one person with the intention of killing him, but accidently kills a third person the intention extenuated by provocation is transferred from the intended victim to the actual victim and the accused in those circumstances is guilty of manslaughter only. See *R. v. Gross* (1913), 23 Cox C.C. 455. By parity of reasoning the transferrence of an intention which is aggravated by the fact that it is planned and deliberate is transferred from the intended victim to the actual victim.

. . . .

*Appeal dismissed.*

## Recklessness and the Limits of Mens Rea: Beyond Orthodox Subjectivism
### Earl Fruchtman

* Excerpts from (1987), 29 Criminal Law Quarterly 315.

## PART I

*Introduction*

Our system of criminal justice can be said to rest ultimately on a single principle: *actus non facit reum, nisi mens sit rea* (the "principle of *mens rea*"). But this principle is not self-evident and therefore must be established on the basis of some more fundamental ground. The criminal law is in the business of punishing people; considerations of justice and fairness dictate that punishment requires fault. In so far as the principle of *mens rea* requires that criminal liability be based on fault, it is justified as the foundation of criminal responsibility.

This much is largely controversial. What is more difficult is to develop a theory of criminal responsibility which adequately defines the kinds of fault that satisfies the requirement of *mens rea* and thereby establishes the appropriate conditions for the ascription of the criminal sanction. The prevailing theory takes its inspiration from the literal translation of the *mens rea* principle, namely that an act is not a guilty one unless it is done with a guilty mind, and therefore equates fault with the existence of a positive "state of mind" or mental element. I shall call this theory "orthodox subjectivism".

Although it may indeed be the case that fault requires a subjective basis for liability, it does not follow that this requires the identification of a "state of mind", at least not in the way that this construct has been defined by orthodox subjectivism.

. . .

## *Orthodox Subjectivism*

Orthodox subjectivism posits that if criminal liability must depend upon fault, then liability must be subjective and therefore must be based on the presence of a mental state on the part of the accused. *Mens rea* is defined by orthodox subjectivism as follows:

> . . . [*mens rea*] denotes the mental state (subjective element) required for the particular crime in question.
>
> . . . Normally, the required mental element is either:
>
> — an *intention* to do the forbidden act, or otherwise to bring about the external elements of the offence . . . , or
>
> — (in most crimes) *recklessness* as to such elements. Intention includes knowledge.

Orthodox subjectivism represents the current state of the law in Canada. One can find judicial pronouncements of this theory in passages from three judgments of Dickson C.J.C.:

> The concept of *mens rea*, that the prohibited act must be accompanied by a certain *mental element*, has been authoritatively established by this Court . . . The notion that a Court should not find a person guilty of an offence against the criminal law unless he has a blameworthy *state of mind* is common to all civilized penal systems. . . . The *mental state* basic to criminal liability consists in most crimes in either (a) an intention to cause the *actus reus* of the crime, *i.e.,* an intention to do the act which constitutes the crime in question, or (b) foresight or realization on the part of the person that his conduct will probably cause or may cause the *actus reus*, together with assumption of or indifference to a risk, which in all of the circumstances is substantial or unjustifiable. This latter *mental element* is sometimes characterized as recklessness. [Emphasis added.]
>
> Where the offence is criminal, the Crown must establish a *mental element*, namely, that the accused who committed the prohibited act did so intentionally or recklessly, with knowledge of the facts constituting the offence, or with the wilful blindness toward them. Mere negligence is excluded form the concept of the mental element required for conviction. [Emphasis added.]
>
> . . . a man cannot be adjudged guilty and subjected to punishment, unless the commission of the crime was voluntary directed by a willing mind . . . Proof of the *mental element* is an essential and constituent step in establishing criminal responsibility. . . Subject to . . . [certain] exceptions, *mens rea*, consisting of some *positive state of mind*, such as evil intention, or knowledge of the wrongfulness of the act, or reckless disregard of consequences, must be proved by the prosecution. [Emphasis added.]

Although orthodox subjectivism acknowledges that each crime has its own mental element, all crimes are said to require one or two general states of mind, namely intention (or knowledge) and recklessness. Negligence does not qualify as *mens rea*. There are said to be two reasons for this: (i) negligence involves inadvertence and is not, therefore, a state of mind; and (ii) negligence does not involve a subjective evaluation and therefore imposes objective liability. Orthodox subjectivism finds historical support for the exclusion of negligence from *mens rea* because, at common law, negligence is not sufficient to establish criminal liability (except for homicide where "gross" negligence must be shown). In modern criminal law systems, liability for negligence is based on express statutory provision and is seen by orthodox subjectivism as either exceptional or inappropriate. Thus, for orthodox subjectivism, recklessness is the limit of *mens rea*.

## Recklessness, According to Orthodox Subjectivism

Recklessness, like intention, involves a *positive mental element* on the part of the accused with respect to the consequences or circumstances of his conduct. It is this defined positive element that renders "recklessness" a state of mind and thus part of *mens rea*.

A person is said to be "reckless" when he acts with what has been variously described as "knowledge", "foresight", "realization", or "conscious awareness" that an unreasonable risk of harm is created by his conduct, or that there is a risk that certain proscribed circumstances exists, and the conduct is pursued none the less.

Thus a person hastily packaging nitroglycerine for airplane transport who realizes that the package could explode in flight, but does nothing about it, is reckless and will be criminally responsible for any damage to property or death of passengers that may result. This is recklessness with respect to consequences. Recklessness also exists when a man intends to have sexual intercourse with a woman, realizes that she may not be consenting, but proceeds to have intercourse with her regardless. In this case, the recklessness is said to be with respect to the circumstances, *i.e.,* the woman's lack of consent.

Although orthodox subjectivism subscribes to the view that fault requires a subjective evaluation, the mental element required for recklessness is not entirely subjective. Recklessness requires the conscious creation of an unreasonable risk but the agent's own view of the reasonableness of the risk is irrelevant. So long as the risk is determined to be inconsistent with the risks taken by reasonable people, and the agent has adverted to the existence of this risk, he is reckless.

In fact, the issue of the reasonableness of the risk is determined in the same way as it is in cases of negligence: it requires a complex calculation of the social utility of the risk-attendant activity, the probability of risk eventuating, and the gravity of the harm created by the risk, all of which are ascertained objectively.

A surgeon performing a dangerous heart operation is aware that it creates a risk that the patient may die. But the surgeon is not described as reckless, because the risk he creates is not unreasonable. Conversely, a doctor carrying out an unorthodox form of treatment, denounced by medical experts as unquestionably dangerous and unnecessary, is not exculpated even if he honestly believes such treatment to be in the best interests of the patient.

Orthodox subjectivism concedes this objective element of fault. It justifies it on the basis that, almost invariably, the agent has a rationalization for his behaviour; if it is left to the individual to decide whether his conduct was reasonable or not, the law could become subject to the views of heretics and fanatics. Indeed, if this were the rule, any individual explanation of the reasonableness of the risk would necessarily have the effect of exculpating the agent. This would render the law inefficacious.

The orthodox subjectivist reconciles this apparent inconsistency by pointing out that, at common law, the nobility of an individual's motives is not relevant to the question of his *mens rea*. The very purpose of the criminal law is to set out the conditions of acceptable conduct and it would be repugnant to this purpose if the law permitted the individual to determine whether his proposed conduct is acceptable or not. Orthodox subjectivism maintains that:

> It is right to apply a subjective test to ascertain the defendant's knowledge of material facts and foresight of consequences but once these have been ascertained they should be judged by an objective standard applicable to all persons alike except of course in cases such as infancy and insanity.

However, awareness of or advertence to the risk is entirely subjective. If the heretical doctor is unaware that his treatment is dangerous and that is poses a risk to the patient's life or health, he is not reckless. It is said that the positive mental element is missing. He may be negligent (in not knowing that the treatment is dangerous), but that is insufficient *mens rea* under the offence explicitly provides otherwise. Thus, orthodox subjectivism distinguishes between the doctor who does something dangerous thinking it is right, and the doctor who does something dangerous without awareness of the danger.

To date, Canadian courts have had little occasion to analyze recklessness head-on but their *obiter dicta* suggest adherence to orthodox subjectivism.

. . .

## Conceptual Problems With Orthodox Subjectivism

Increasingly, orthodox subjectivism is criticized for a host of conceptual problems engendered by its reliance on the identification of a state of mind. Although we no longer speak of a "vicious will" as being necessary to establish criminal liability, the idea that an active human mind (whose contents are conscious thoughts) somehow controls the body's actions still seems to be the underlying model for orthodox subjectivism. This model has been colourfully criticized as requiring a metaphysical search for a "ghost in the machine".

A cogent historical case can be made which evinces the close relationship between the development of criminal law theory along subjectivist lines with the then prevailing philosophical views. At a time when the dominating concern of the criminal law was to punish evildoing, the central philosophical theory opined that the human being consisted of two separate elements: the mind (or soul) and the body. It was thought that the mind, through the faculty of the will, caused the physical body to carry out certain movements; human action was thought to be the result of volition. Thus, one finds in Blackstone: "To constitute a crime against human laws, there must be first, a vicious will; and secondly, an unlawful act consequent upon such vicious will." Although perfect sense can be made of the language of mental states without requiring a dualistic metaphysical conception of "mind", the will theory of human action has been generally discredited.

Moreover, the ontological issue should not be confused with a separate evidentiary one, namely, the difficulty the Crown has in proving the existence of a qualifying state of mind. This evidentiary difficulty, requiring proof in most cases by circumstantial evidence, is common to many criminal trials. Where an accused denies any involvement in a crime and there are no eyewitnesses, the evidence tendered to prove identity will be circumstantial and the Crown will ask the trier of fact to draw inferences from such evidence. This case is little different, in evidentiary terms, from one in which the accused concedes his involvement but disputes that he either intended the injury or foresaw that it was a probable consequence of his actions.

Nor is it a problem for orthodox subjectivism that the trier of fact may use an objective standard as a basis for drawing such inferences. There is a difference between using an objective standard to resolve an evidentiary issue and using an objective standard to determine what the issues are. Orthodox subjectivism requires that the trier of fact find that the accused had a particular state of mind, although in deciding, for example, whether the accused foresaw the probable harmful result, the trier of fact can consider what the accused *must* have foreseen on the basis of the evidence. This will inevitably involve a consideration of what a reasonable person in the accused's situation would have foreseen. But the accused can try at least to persuade the trier of fact otherwise.

The real problem with orthodox subjectivism is not so much its use of the language of mental states, but its view of the role of the mind in human action. Orthodox subjectivism, by focusing on a positive mental element, defined by intention and recklessness, commits itself to seeing human action as the causal result of thought-process." They are the crux of culpability. This view arises out of two related misconceptions. The first is the belief that if a person is able to articulate what he is doing without observing it, he must have already thought about it: "in saying what he is actually doing he is simply recalling the previous decision." This belief does not accord with the simple *fact* that many voluntary actions occur without any prior deliberations, and the agent is able to describe what he is doing even though he has not previously thought about it.

We do distinguish between intentional and non-intentional action, but this distinction does not depend upon the existence of positive mental elements. The agent himself is able to describe what he was trying to do without observing it, and a third person would be able to determine the agent's intention by considering the action within the context of its surrounding circumstances. Neither party need look for a mental act to make sense of this description. The problem arises when we try to go behind the intentional act to discover the "intent", *i.e.*, to find what it is that makes the action intentional. This inevitably leads to speculation about mental events which results in a general model of human action in terms of a causal relationship between mental acts and physical acts. This is not to deny the existence of such things as mental events (*e.g.* imagining, dreaming, deliberating), nor the contingent relationship which sometimes exits between such events and consequent action, but only to disassociate these with the general theory of human action.

The second misconception suffers from what Wittgenstein called the main cause of philosophical disease — "a one-sided diet: one nourishes one's thinking with only one kind of example". He gives this example:

> I deliberate whether to lift a certain heavyish weight, decide to do it, I then apply my force to it and lift it. Here, you might say, you have a full-fledged case of willing and intentional action. Compare with this such a case as reaching a man a lighted match after having lit with it one's own cigarette and seeing that he wishes to light his; or again the case of moving your hand while writing a letter, or moving your mouth, larynx, etc. while speaking. — Now when I called the first example a full-fledged case of willing, I deliberately used this misleading expression. For this expression indicates that one is inclined in thinking about volition to regard this sort of example as one exhibiting most clearly the typical characteristic of willing. One takes one's ideas, and one's language, about volition from this kind of example and thinks that they must apply — if not in such an obvious way — to all cases which one can properly call cases of willing.

Clearly, some intentional actions are the result of a deliberate decision. But there is no necessary causal relation between thought and action. Much intentional action occurs without any prior or contemporaneous thought. This is particularly exemplified by incidents which occupy a split second, or activities which are regularly performed. They are certainly voluntary actions, and in some cases intentional actions, but do not necessarily result from "acts of thought". Although there is a *theoretical* distinction between (a) acts which are preceded by some conscious thought process and (b) acts which are not so preceded, liability for intentional action does not in fact depend upon this distinction.

Criminal liability is not restricted to intentional action. For orthodox subjectivism, recklessness or culpable non-intentional action is restricted to those actions which are accompanied by the positive mental element of advertence. The same focus on a cognitive element as explaining intentional action is used to define the relevant class of culpable non-intentional actions. But since this model is an inaccurate description of intentional action, all of which is accepted as culpable, the extrapolation of this model to non-intentional action creates an underinclusive relevant class.

. . . .

## Normative Problems with Orthodox Subjectivism

### Inadvertence does not Involve Culpability

It is sometimes argued that inadvertence does not involve any moral culpability and for this reason should not attract the criminal sanction. This is, however, an overstatement. Although certain instances of inadvertence may be devoid of moral culpability, the very ascription of "negligence" suggest moral culpability: a failure to live up to the standards reasonably expected of ordinary persons. As H.L.A. Hart explained:

> One hundred times a day persons are blamed outside the law courts for not being more careful, for being inattentive, and not stopping to think.

Indeed, the basis of common law tort liability is fault. The question, therefore, is not whether inadvertence is ever more culpable but whether, and in what circumstances, it is sufficiently morally culpable to justify the criminal sanction. This question can only be answered upon consideration of other normative arguments for orthodox subjectivism.

*Criminal Liability Requires Choice*

A more persuasive argument for orthodox subjectivism is found in the "choice" theory. The following passage from the dissenting judgment of Dickson J. in *Leary v. The Queen* outlines this theory:

> [The criminal law] is founded upon respect for the person and for the freedom of human will. A person is accountable for what he wills. When, in the exercise of the power of free choice, a member of society chooses to engage in harmful or otherwise undesirable conduct proscribed by the criminal law, he must accept the sanctions which that law has provided for the purpose of discouraging such conduct. Justice demands no less. But to be criminal, the wrongdoing must have been consciously committed.

The choice theory certainly explains many of the substantive rules of criminal law relating to excuses. An individual may "intend" a proscribed result while insane or while acting under duress, provocation, or a means of self-defence. However, it cannot be said that such action is freely "chosen" by the agent and it is therefore unfair to subject that individual to punishment. Likewise, the choice theory applies perfectly to the paradigm of intentional conduct — where the agent's very purpose in acting is to bring about certain consequences. Even the reckless agent, although not choosing to bring about the proscribed result, certainly chooses to take the risk that the proscribed result may eventuate. It is argued that the culpability of the reckless person lies in this choice. And it is said that the negligent person, who does not avert to the risk of harm caused by his conduct, does not *choose* to take the risk and therefore ought not to be subject to the criminal sanction.

Implicit in the proposed correlation between choice and culpability is the theory which sees human action in terms of volition. Thus, Dickson C.J.C. explicitly refers to "free will" as the conceptual foundation for the ascription of responsibility; choice is seen as an "act of will", itself a mental event which precedes and causes a subsequent action. I have criticized this metaphysical model as creating significant conceptual problems, both philosophically and for the criminal law. Once again, the orthodox view makes one kind of choice paradigmatic, namely a decision to perform some action resulting from deliberations. Not all intentional actions result from choices of this nature, and not all choices themselves take this form. An action set within a context of alternatives can be viewed as indicating the agent's "choice" without requiring prior conscious decision by the agent.

In fact, depending upon one's characterization of the "act", all voluntary acts, including inadvertent ones, involve some choice: the intentional agent chooses to bring about some specific consequence; the reckless agent chooses to take a risk that harmful consequences may result (although he does not choose those consequences and may even hope that they will not occur); the negligent agent chooses to act in a certain way albeit unaware that any risk attends his conduct. It is not clear why the choice of the reckless agent qualifies for criminal liability and the choice of the negligent agent does not. The difference between them, that the reckless agent is aware of the possible consequences and the negligent agent is not, cannot be used to justify their different treatment, for that is what the choice theory itself is supposed to explain. The argument becomes circular.

. . . .

Moreover, whatever the connection between choice theory and the law relating to excuses, it is clear that choice theory does not apply "across the board" of most operative criminal justice systems. For example, there are a variety of instances in which liability is imposed as a result of omissions. It may be difficult to conclude that an agent has chosen *not* to act in the same way as when he chooses to act. In any event, liability of omissions is not dependent upon such choice: it simply requires a duty to act coupled with a failure to act (and an absence of an excuse for such failure).

Second, the existence of constructive and vicarious liability is inconsistent with choice theory. Of course this feature does not in principle refute orthodox subjectivism, which would oppose all forms of constructive liability, but it makes clear that a system of criminal law which permits constructive or vicarious crimes is not a system grounded entirely on choice.

Finally, it must be noted that our system of criminal law distinguishes between crimes requiring a "general intent" and those requiring a "specific intent". In the former case, self-induced intoxication, rendering the agent incapable of choice is no excuse.

## Criminal Liability Depends on Control

Closely related to the choice theory is the theory that criminal liability depends upon the agent's ability to "control" his actions so as to avoid harmful consequences. Only those agents who intend or foresee a consequence are able to take action to prevent that consequence from occurring, either by stopping themselves or by taking some precautions. It is assumed that an inadvertent agent cannot avoid the harm because he did not advert to it.

In fact, it cannot be said that an inadvertent agent necessarily lacks control over his conduct, or that he could not have helped acting in the way he did or that he could not have avoided causing the harm. By definition, the agent failed to act in the way in which an ordinary and prudent person would have in the circumstances. Since ought implies can, if the inadvertent agent ought to have acted differently, it is presumed that he could have.

Both the choice and control theories presuppose that it is the possession of knowledge by the agent which makes control or choice possible such that consequent action is wilful and therefore culpable. In contrast to the agent who acts intentionally or recklessly, orthodox subjectivism describes the negligent agent in almost "deterministic" terms:

> Many studies have been made of accident proneness; and it has been found that large categories of people are more accident prone than others... But some individuals are particularly accident prone. They are *born negligent*, so to speak, or become so through their experiences. A person has an innate temperament, which may in course of time be modified by many circumstances over which he has no control. The result may be that he is impulsive, unable to stop and consider the consequences of what he is doing, or too dull in mind to imagine them; that he is selfish, preferring his own convenience to the safety of others; that he is clumsy, unable to control his own movements (or

those of a machine he is using) with due precision, or with a slow reaction-time in case of emergency. [Emphasis added.]

Such a deterministic view, depending on one's philosophical allegiances, can be equally descriptive of the agent guilty of intentional or reckless conduct — the "born reckless": aggressive, thrill-seeking and lacking in moral conscience. Yet such a congenital make-up has never been seriously regarded as a satisfactory reason to reject criminal liability in these instances. Why is a distinction made between agents who could have acted differently and those who could not on the basis of some positive mental element like knowledge or advertence? Once again it is incorrectly assumed (rather than argued for) that the presence of this positive mental element is determinative of choice or control. Unless inadvertent conduct is seen in deterministic terms, this is certainly not necessarily the case.

. . . .

### Criminal Liability Must be Subjective if Based on Fault

I shall conclude this discussion of orthodox subjectivism by considering the fundamental claim that the principle of *mens rea* — a principle of fault — requires that criminal liability be subjective and that subjective liability requires an inquiry into the accused's state of mind at the time of the criminal activity.

The argument which links fault with subjectivity has cogency, since it would be clearly unjust to punish someone for bringing about a criminal event that he could not possibly have prevented or foreseen. A driver of a motor vehicle who unexpectedly suffers a heart attack, loses control of the vehicle and kills a pedestrian has committed a homicide, but fault could not fairly be ascribed to such person under these circumstances. This person truly could not have helped doing what he did. If criminal liability depends on fault, then an inquiry into the circumstances surrounding the commission of the offence is required; and in particular the accused's position must be considered. But to conclude from this that a positive mental element is required is *non sequitur*. The requirement of a positive mental element does not in itself preclude objective liability, "if, in considering whether a person acted intentionally, we were to attribute to him foresight of consequences which a reasonable man would have foreseen but which he did not.

Conversely, to impose liability for inadvertence is not to impose objective liability, so long as the inadvertence is culpable and the accused can be blamed for such inadvertence. According to orthodox subjectivism, the inquiry must be with respect to what the accused actually foresaw. His defence will be "I did not foresee". Expanding the inquiry to include consideration of what the accused ought to have foreseen, even if he did not do so, will not render liability objective if he can defend on the basis that "I could not have foreseen." The "reasonable man" is used as a test for what the accused *did* foresee in many instances. In this extended inquiry, the reasonable person would also be used as a test for what the accused "ought to have foreseen", as was the case in *Parker*, but the accused can show that he is not a reasonable person, as was the case in *Stephenson*.

# R. v. Tutton
[1989] 1 S.C.R. 1392.

Appeal from a judgment of the Ontario Court of Appeal (1985), 18 C.C.C. (3d) 328, setting aside convictions by Salhany Co. Ct. J. sitting with jury and ordering a new trial. Appeal dismissed.

The judgment of DICKSON C.J. and WILSON and LaFOREST JJ. was delivered by

WILSON J.: — I have had the benefit of the reasons of my colleagues Justices McIntyre and Lamer and I agree with them that the appeal should be dismissed and a new trial ordered because the trial judge's charge failed to make clear to the jury that the Crown had the burden to prove all the elements of the offence of manslaughter by criminal negligence. I do not, however, agree with my colleagues' conclusion that criminal negligence under s. 202 of the *Criminal Code*, R.S.C. 1970, c. C-34, consists only of conduct in breach of an objective standard and does not require the Crown to prove that the accused had any degree of guilty knowledge. I also have reservations concerning the approach my colleagues suggest is available in order to relieve against the harshness of the objective standard of liability which they find in s. 202 and to ensure that the morally innocent are not punished for the commission of serious criminal offences committed through criminal negligence.

The facts and the judgments below are fully set out in the judgment of my colleague McIntyre J. I wish only to emphasize two points. The respondent's defence in this case centred around their claim of honest but mistaken belief as to the nature of their son's condition. Although the respondents were aware that their son was a diabetic who needed regular insulin injections, they claimed that because of their religious convictions they sincerely believed that he had been cured by divine intervention and were unaware of the serious nature of his illness following the withdrawal of insulin. For example, in a statement provided to the police shortly after her son's death from the complications of diabetic hyperglycemia the respondent Carol Anne Tutton stated:

> Complete faith in Jesus and obedience to the word of God is the reason for our decision to cease giving Chris insulin. Since I have accepted Jesus as my personal Saviour and Lord, He has revealed himself to me in vision and spoke in words of his own that Christopher is healed and further that complete faith in Him not man's doctrine or shall I say the world's teachings will bring forth the manifestation of this healing. Standing on the promises of God and His holy Word 100%, Wednesday, October 14, 1981 I did not administer Christopher insulin. Thursday and Wednesday Christopher ate, played normally although Thursday evening he became sick to his stomach. Friday I kept him home from school and he kept liquids in his stomach. Saturday morning until approximately 1:00 PM he was resting comfortably. I left him to make myself a sandwich about five perhaps ten minutes, rechecked him and found he was not breathing. My husband administered mouth to mouth resuscitation until the police department arrived about five minutes later.

The second point which I wish to emphasize is that the Ontario Court of Appeal (1985), 18 C.C.C. (3d) 328) would not have applied an objective standard of liability in this case. Dubin J.A. stated at p. 345:

> I do not think, however, that a loving and caring parent who omits to seek medical assistance because of the honest but mistaken belief that his or her child was not in need of such assistance should be found to have shown a wanton or reckless disregard for its life or safety merely because it can be said that reasonable parents would have responded otherwise, or even that in omitting to seek

medical assistance, there was a marked and substantial departure from the standard of care of reasonable parents. In such a case, I think a distinction should be made between acts of commission and acts of omission and, in the latter case, a subjective test should be used.

The Court of Appeal concluded that the trial judge erred in instructing the jury that no *mens rea* was required for the crime of manslaughter by means of criminal negligence.

. . . .

For convenience, I reproduce here the relevant sections of the *Criminal Code*:

**197**(1) Every one is under a legal duty

(a) as a parent, foster parent, guardian or head of a family, to provide necessaries of life for a child under the age of sixteen years;

. . . .

(2) Every one commits an offence who, being under a legal duty within the meaning of subsection (1), fails without lawful excuse, the proof of which lies upon him, to perform that duty, if

(a) with respect to a duty imposed by paragraph (1)(a) or (b),

 (i) the person to whom the duty is owed is in destitute or necessitous circumstances, or
 (ii) the failure to perform the duty endangers the life of the person to whom the duty is owed, or causes or is likely to cause the health of that person to be endangered permanently; or

. . . .

**202**(1) Every one is criminally negligent who

(a) in doing anything, or

(b) in omitting to do anything that it is his duty to do,

shows wanton or reckless disregard for the lives or safety of other persons.

**205**(1) A person commits homicide when, directly or indirectly, by any means, he causes the death of a human being.

(2) Homicide is culpable or not culpable.

(3) Homicide that is not culpable is not an offence.

(4) Culpable homicide is murder or manslaughter or infanticide.

(5) A person commits culpable homicide when he causes the death of a human being,

(a) by means of an unlawful act,

(b) by criminal negligence,

(c) by causing that human being, by threats or fear of violence or by deception, to do anything that causes his death, or

(d) by wilfully frightening that human being, in the case of a child or sick person.

**219.** Every one who commits manslaughter is guilty of an indictable offence and is liable to imprisonment for life.

I wish to deal first with the implications of my colleagues' approach in this case. By concluding that s. 202 of the *Criminal Code* prohibits conduct and the consequences of mindless action absent any blameworthy state of mind, they have, in effect, held that the crime of criminal negligence is an absolute liability offence. Conviction follows upon proof of conduct which reveals a marked and substantial departure from the standard expected of a reasonably prudent person in the circumstances regardless of what was actually in the accused's mind at the time the act was committed.

. . . .

My colleague Mcintyre J. has concluded that upon the wording of s. 202 it is an inescapable conclusion that Parliament intended liability to follow upon proof of the act or conduct described in the section. In particular, he stresses the reference to conduct which *shows* wanton or reckless disregard for the lives and safety of others and the fact that what is prohibited is criminal *negligence*.

. . . .

Section 202 of the *Code* is, in my view, notorious in its ambiguity. Since its enactment in its present form in the 1955 Amendments to the *Criminal Code* it has bedevilled both courts and commentators who have sought out its meaning. The interpretation put upon it usually depends upon which words are emphasized. On the one hand, my colleague's judgment demonstrates that emphasizing the use of the words "shows" and "negligence" can lead to the conclusion that an objective standard of liability was intended and the proof of unreasonable conduct alone will suffice. On the other hand, if the words "wanton or reckless disregard for the lives or safety of other persons" are stressed along with the fact that what is prohibited is not negligence *simpliciter* but "criminal" negligence, one might conclude that Parliament intended some degree of advertence to the risk to the lives or safety of others to be an essential element of the offence. When faced with such fundamental ambiguity, it would be my view that the court should give the provision the interpretation most consonant, not only with the test and purpose of the provision, but also, where possible, with the broader concepts and principles of the law: see also *R. v. Paré*, [1987] 2 S.C.R. 618.

It is obviously important to give meaning and effect to each word employed in s. 202. Under that section every one is criminally negligent who in doing or in omitting to do anything that it is his duty to do shows wanton or reckless disregard for the lives or safety of other persons. As I have stated, the presumption when we are dealing with a serious criminal offence should be in favour of a requirement of some degree of mental blameworthiness if the text and purpose of the section are susceptible of such an interpretation. This Court, in its previous consideration of s. 202, concluded that it was intended to prohibit advertent negligence in the sense that the accused must be fixed with an awareness of the risk that is being prohibited.

. . . .

It is my view that the jurisprudence of this Court to date establishes that the criminal negligence prohibited under s. 202 is advertent negligence. I would not hesitate to depart from these precedents for solid reasons but I cannot, with due respect to those who think otherwise, agree that the case for the adoption of an objective standard of liability has been made out to the extent required to justify a departure from this Court's previous decisions.

. . . .

As I have suggested above, the words of the section can reasonably bear an interpretation which leaves room for the mental element of awareness of advertence to a risk to the lives or safety of others or wilful blindness to such risk. Conduct which shows a wanton or reckless disregard for the lives and safety of others will by its nature constitute *prima facie* evidence of the mental element, and in the absence of some evidence that casts doubt on the normal degree of mental awareness, proof of the act and reference to what a reasonable person in the circumstances must have realized will lead to a conclusion that the accused was aware of the risk or wilfully blind to the risk.

Professor Glanville Williams in his work *Criminal Law: the General Part* (2nd ed. 1961) explained the minimal nature of the mental element for advertent negligence and the important evidentiary use of objective standards in determining the subjective state of mind of what he terms advertent negligence. He defined the requirements of recklessness in advertent negligence as follows at pp. 53-55:

> If the actor foresaw the probability of the consequences he is regarded as reckless, even though he fervently desired and hoped for the exact opposite of the consequence, and even though he did his best (short of abandoning his main project) to avoid it . . . Recklessness is any determination to pursue conduct with knowledge of the risk involved though without a desire that they should eventuate.
>
> . . . .
>
> . . . recklessness may be a mere passing realization, instantly dismissed, which leaves no mark upon conduct.

. . . .

The minimal nature of the requirement of a blameworthy state of mind and the relevance of the objective standard as a rebuttable mode of proof suggests to me that a holding that s. 202 requires proof of the mental element of advertence to the risk or wilful blindness to the risk will not undermine the policy objectives of the provision. The loss in terms of deterrence and social protection would seem to be negligible when the retention of a subject standard would at most offer protection for those who due to some peculiarity or unexpected accident commit conduct which, although it shows a reckless or wanton disregard for the lives or safety of others, can be explained as inconsistent with any degree of awareness of or wilful blindness to such a risk. Should social protection require the adoption of an objective standard it is open to Parliament to enact a law which clearly adopts such a standard. In my respectful view this Court should not do it for them.

. . . .

To sum up, although I agree with my colleagues as to the proper disposition of this appeal, I am unable to agree with their conclusion that the offence of manslaughter by criminal negligence consists of conduct in breach of an objective standard.

The reasons of McINTYRE and L'HEUREUX-DUBÉ JJ. were delivered by

McINTYRE J.: — This appeal raises again the question of criminal negligence, as defined in s. 202 of the *Criminal Code*, R.S.C. 1970, c. C-34, and the test to be applied by a jury in its application to a given case.

The respondents, Carol Anne Tutton and Arthur Thomas Tutton, were the parents of a five-year-old child, Christopher Tutton, who died on October 17, 1981. After a trial before judge and jury, the Tuttons were convicted of manslaughter because of his death. They appealed the conviction. The Court of Appeal (Dubin, Goodman, Tarnopolsky JJ.A.) in a judgment written for the court by Dubin J.A. (as he then was) allowed the appeals, set aside the convictions, and directed new trials. This appeal is taken by the Crown, by leave granted May 23, 1985.

The Tuttons, according to the evidence, which was unquestioned on this point, had a good reputation in their community for honesty and integrity and, as well, they were loving and responsible parents. They were also deeply religious and they belonged to a religious sect which believes in faith healing. Their religious convictions did not prevent them from seeking and acting on medical advice nor from taking medicines, but they believed that Divine intervention could miraculously effect cures for illnesses and ailments beyond the power of modern medical science.

In April of 1979, their family physician, a general practitioner named Love, diagnosed the child, Christopher, as a diabetic and admitted him to hospital where he remained for some weeks. While the child was in hospital, his mother attended classes at a diabetic education centre where she received instruction regarding insulin injections and the impact of diet and exercise on diabetes and diabetics. She also attended in July of 1979 a full week of seminars at a juvenile diabetic clinic to gain an understanding of her son's condition and to learn how to deal with it. There was then evidence upon which the jury could conclude that Mrs. Tutton has made herself competent to deal with her child's illness under general supervision from the family physician.

Throughout the son's illness, the Tuttons main concern was to find a cure for the boy. They both believed that there would be a spiritual cure. They discussed the possibility with Dr. Love who considered that there was no possibility of a miraculous cure, and in November of 1979 a diabetic specialist from the Sick Children's Hospital in Toronto advised the respondents that their son would never be able to discontinue his insulin injections. He told the respondents not to discontinue the insulin treatments. However, on October 2, 1980, Mrs. Tutton stopped giving the child insulin in the belief that he was being healed by the power of the Holy Spirit. In two days, the child became quite ill and was taken to a hospital emergency unit. The physician who attended the child said that on admission to hospital the child was dangerously ill, suffering from diabetic acidosis, a potentially fatal disorder which was due to the absence of insulin. The doctor admonished the parents when he learned that they had consciously withheld the insulin. He told the parents that insulin would be required by their son for life, and after this incident Mr. Tutton assured the family physician that insulin would not be withheld in future without consulting a doctor. A year later, however, insulin was again stopped. Mrs. Tutton believed that she had a vision of God in which she was told that Christopher was cured, that no more insulin was needed, and that God would take care of her son. The insulin injections were stopped on October 14, 1981. Mr. Tutton did not know of the withdrawal of insulin until October 15 but on learning of it he approved. The child sickened quickly. On October 17, he was taken to the hospital where he was pronounced dead on arrival. The forensic pathologist who conducted a postmortem examination gave his opinion that death was caused by complications of diabetic hyperglycemia. The respondents were jointly charged with manslaughter in an indictment which provided:

ARTHUR TUTTON and CAROL TUTTON stand charged that between the period of the 14th day of October, 1981, and the 17th day of October, 1981, both dates inclusive, at the Township of Wilmot, in the Judicial District of Waterloo, being the parents of Christopher Tutton, they did cause the death of Christopher Tutton, age five years, by criminal negligence, to wit, they did, without lawful excuse, omit to provide necessaries of life to Christopher Tutton, which was their duty to provide, thereby showing wanton and reckless disregard for the life or safety of the said Christopher Tutton, and did thereby commit manslaughter contrary to the Criminal Code.

Particulars were given in these terms:

It is further particularized that the said Arthur Tutton and Carol Tutton failed, without lawful excuse, while their said son, Christopher, was in necessitous circumstances,
(1) to provide insulin to him
(2) to obtain timely medical assistance for him.

. . . .

At trial, the defence was that as far as the Crown's case rested on the failure to provide insulin the Tuttons honestly believed that Christopher had been cured by Divine intervention and, therefore, no further insulin was necessary. This would raise the defence of an honest though mistaken belief in the existence of a circumstance or circumstances which, if present, would render their conduct non-culpable. It was also argued that as far as the Crown's case depended upon a failure to provide timely medical assistance for their son, the parents were unaware of the fact that he was seriously ill as a result of the withdrawal of the insulin and, accordingly, their conduct in this regard could not be said to exhibit a wanton or reckless disregard for the life or safety of their son.

. . . .

In reaching a conclusion as to whether the conduct of an accused person has shown, within the meaning of s. 202 of the *Criminal Code*, wanton or reckless disregard for the lives or safety of other persons, the authorities dictate an objective test: see the review of the authorities on this subject by Cory J.A. for the Court of Appeal in *R. v. Waite* (1986), 28 C.C.C. (3d) 326, approved in this court, [1989] 1 S.C.R. 1436. Indeed, in the Court of Appeal, Dubin J.A. accepted the objective test as one of general application, but made an exception in cases where the conduct complained of consisted of an act or acts of omission, as opposed to those of commission. In such cases, it was his view that occasions would arise where a subjective test would be required where acts of omission were under consideration. He considered this was such a case. It is my view, however, that no such distinction as Dubin J.A. would adopt may be made. I am wholly unable to see any difference in principle between cases arising from an omission to act and those involving acts of commission. Indeed, the words of s. 202 of the *Code* make it clear that one is criminally negligent who, in <u>doing anything</u> or <u>in omitting to do anything</u> that it is duty to do, shows wanton or reckless disregard for the lives or safety of other persons. The objective test must, therefore, be employed where criminal negligence is considered for it is the conduct of the accused, as opposed to his intention or mental state, which is examined in this inquiry.

Our concept of criminal culpability relies primarily upon a consideration of the mental state which accompanies or initiates the wrongful act, and the attribution of criminal liability without proof of such a blameworthy mental state raises serious concerns. Nonetheless, negligence has become accepted as a factor which may lead to criminal liability and strong arguments can be raised in its favour. Section 202 of the *Criminal Code* affords an example of its adoption. In choosing the test to be applied in assessing conduct under s. 202 of the *Code*, it must be observed at once that what is made criminal is negligence. Negligence connotes the opposite of thought-directed action. In other words, its existence precludes the element of positive intent to achieve a given result. This leads to the conclusion that what is sought to be restrained by punishment under s. 202 of the *Code* is conduct, and its results. What is punished, in other words, is not the state of mind but the consequence of mindless action. This is apparent, I suggest, from the words of the section, which make criminal, conduct which *shows* wanton or reckless disregard. It may be observed as well that the words "wanton or reckless" support this construction, denying as they do the existence of a directing mental state. Nor can it be said that criminal negligence, as defined in s. 202, imports in its terms some element of malice or intention. This point was made in the Crown's factum in paragraph 41, which provided, in part:

> The plain and ordinary meaning of the terms "wanton" and "reckless" when used in connection with the concept of negligence would seem to include a state of being heedless of apparent danger. Section 202(1) does not use the term "reckless" as an extended definition of intention or malice, but rather employs the terms as part of a definition of conduct which amounts to "negligence" in a criminal context.

In my view, then, an objective standard must be applied in determining this question because of the difference between the ordinary criminal offence, which requires proof of a subjective state of mind, and that of criminal negligence. In criminal cases, generally, the act coupled with the mental state or intent is punished. In criminal negligence, the act which exhibits the requisite degree of negligence is punished. If this distinction is not kept clear, the dividing line between the traditional *mens rea* offence and the offence of criminal negligence becomes blurred. The difference, for example, between murder and manslaughter, both unlawful killings, is merely one of intent. If the question of an accused's intent had to be considered and separately proved in offences under s. 202 of the *Code*, the purpose of the section would be defeated because intentional conduct would perforce be considered under other sections of the *Code* and s. 202, aimed at mindless but socially dangerous conduct, would have no function. For these reasons, the objective test should be employed and, in my view, the Court of Appeal was in error in concluding in this case that a subjective test would be required. The test is that of reasonableness, and proof of conduct which reveals a marked and significant departure from the standard which could be expected of a reasonably prudent person in the circumstances will justify a conviction of criminal negligence.

. . . .

The application of an objective test under s. 202 of the *Code*, however, may not be made in a vacuum. Events occur within the framework of other events and actions and when deciding on the nature of the questioned conduct surrounding circumstances must be considered. The decision must be made on a consideration of the facts existing at the time and in relation to the accused's perception of those facts. Since the test is objective, the accused's perception of the facts is not to be considered for the purpose of assessing malice or intention on the accused's part but only form a basis for a conclusion as to whether or not the accused's conduct, in view of his perception of the facts, was reasonable. This is particularly true where, as here, the accused have raised the defence of mistake of fact. If an accused under s. 202 has an honest and reasonably held belief in the existence of certain facts, it may be a relevant consideration in assessing the reasonableness of his conduct. For example, a welder, who is engaged to work in a confined space believing on the assurance of the owner of the premises that not combustible or explosive material is stored nearby, should be entitled to have his perception, as to the presence or absence of dangerous material, before the jury on a charge of manslaughter when his welding torch causes an explosion and a consequent death.

As noted earlier, the Tuttons raised the defence of mistake of fact at trial. They argued that the failure to supply insulin was based on the belief that the child had been cured by Divine intervention and that the failure to provide medical care in timely fashion was based upon the belief that the child was not seriously ill, so medical assistance was not necessary. The trial judge, it was argued, was in error in telling the jury that for any such belief to be effective as a defence it must have been reasonably held. It was held in this Court in *Pappajohn v. The Queen*, [1980] 2 S.C.R. 120, that an honest, though mistaken, belief in the existence of circumstances which, if present, would make the questioned conduct non-culpable would entitle an accused to an acquittal. It was also held in *Pappajohn v. The Queen* that the honest belief need not be reasonable, because its effect would be to deny the existence of the requisite *mens rea*. The situation would be different, however, where the offence charged rests upon the concept of negligence, as opposed to that of the guilty mind or blameworthy mental state. In such case, an unreasonable though honest belief on the part of the accused would be negligently held. The holding of such a belief could not afford a defence when culpability is based on negligent conduct. I would therefore conclude that the trial judge made no error in charging the jury to the effect that any mistaken belief which could afford a defence in a charge of criminal negligence would have to be reasonable.

. . . .

I would dismiss the appeal and confirm the direction for a new trial.

*Appeal dismissed.*

## Regina v. Hundal
(1993), 79 C.C.C. (3d) 97 (S.C.C.)

Appeal by the accused from a judgment of the British Columbia Court of Appeal, 63 C.C.C. (3d) 214, 6 C.R. (4th) 215, 29 M.V.R. (2d) 108, 12 W.C.B. (2d) 475, dismissing his appeal from conviction on a charge of dangerous driving causing death.

[Only the judgement of Cory is excerpted below.]

CORY J.: — At issue on this appeal is whether there is a subjective element in the requisite *mens rea* which must be established by the Crown in order to prove the offence of dangerous driving described in s. 233 of the *Criminal Code*, R.S.C 1970, c. C-3, as amended by 1985, c. 19, s. 36 (now R.S.C. 1985, c. C-46, s. 249).

*Factual background*

The accident occurred at about 3:40 in the afternoon in downtown Vancouver. The streets were wet at the time, a situation not uncommon to that city. The downtown traffic was heavy. The appellant was driving his dump truck eastbound on Nelson Street, a four-lane road, approaching its intersection with Cambie Street. At the time, his truck was overloaded. It exceeded by 1160 kilograms the maximum gross weight permitted for the vehicle. He was travelling in the passing lane for eastbound traffic. The deceased was travelling southbound on Cambie Street. He had stopped for a red light at the intersection with Nelson Street. When the light turned green, the deceased proceeded into the intersection through a crosswalk, continued south across the two lanes for westbound traffic on Nelson Street and reached the passing lane for eastbound traffic. At that moment, his car was struck on the right side by the dump truck killing him instantly.

The appellant stated that when he approached the intersection of Nelson and Cambie Streets he observed that the light had turned amber. He though that he could not stop in time so he simply honked his horn and continued through the intersection when the impact occurred. Several witnesses observed the collision. They testified that the appellant's truck entered the intersection after the Nelson Street traffic light had turned red. It was estimated that at least one second had passed between the end of the amber light and the time when the dump truck first entered the intersection. A Vancouver police officer gave evidence that the red light for Nelson at this intersection is preceded by a three-second amber light and there is a further one-half-second delay before the Cambie light turned green. One witness observed that the deceased's vehicle had travelled almost the entire width of the intersection before it was struck by the truck. Another witness, Mr. Mumford, had been travelling close to the appellant's truck through some 12 intersections. He testified that on an earlier occasion, the appellant went through an intersection as the light turned red. He estimated the speed of the truck at the time of the collision was between 50 and 60 km/h. . . .

*Analysis*

The relevant portion of s. 233 read as follows:

233(1) Every one commits an offence who operates

(a) a motor vehicle on a street, road, highway or other public place in a manner that is dangerous to the public, having regard to all the circumstances, including the nature, condition and use of such place and the amount of traffic that at the time is or might reasonably be expected to be on such place;

. . . .

(4) Everyone who commits an offence under subsection (1) and thereby causes the death of any other person is guilty of an indictable offence and is liable to imprisonment for a term not exceeding fourteen years.

At the outset it must be admitted that the cases dealing with driving offences are not models of clarity. Professor Stuart in his book *Canadian Criminal Law*, 2nd ed. (1987), p. 202, states quite frankly that the law with regard to driving offences is a mess. He writes:

As a matter of theory the law of driving offences has long been in a mess. The offence of careless driving may require simple or gross negligence, the more serious offence of dangerous driving involves simple negligence although sometimes the courts talk about an "advertence" requirement; and the most serious offence of negligent driving required on one view, advertent recklessness and, on another gross inadvertent negligence. The law has been so confused that it has almost certainly been ignored. There is a fairyland quality to the esoteric analysis involved. Statistics indicate that most prosecutors have been content to rely on the provincial careless driving offence.

Professor Peter Burns aptly described the search for the appropriate *mens rea* for dangerous driving as being as "elusive as the legendary Minotaur": Burns, "An Aspect of Criminal Negligence or How the Minotaur Survived Theseus Who Became Lost in the Labyrinth", 48 Can. Bar Rev. 47 (1970), at p. 60.

*Earlier cases dealing with this section . . .*

These cases unfortunately support the contention of academic writers that decisions relating to dangerous driving are somewhat confusing if not contradictory and provide little in the way of guidance. For their part, lower courts have increasingly tended to fix an objective standard for the offence.

. . .

*The constitutional requirement of mens rea*

The appellant contends that the prison sentence which may be imposed for a breach of s. 233 (now s. 249) makes it evident that an accused cannot be convicted without proof beyond a reasonable doubt of a subjective mental element of an intention to drive dangerously. Certainly every crime requires proof of an act or failure to act, coupled with an element of fault which is termed the *mens rea*. This court has made it clear that s. 7 of the *Canadian Charter of Rights and Freedoms* prohibits the imposition of imprisonment in the absence of proof that the element of fault: see *Reference re: s. 94(2) of Motor Vehicle Act* (1985), 23 C.C.C. (3d) 289, 24 D.L.R. (4th) 536, [1985] 2 S.C.R. 486, and *R. v. Vaillancourt* (1987), 39 C.C.C. (3d) 118, 47 D.L.R. (4th) 399, [1987] 2 S.C.R. 636.

Depending on the provisions of the particular section and the context in which it appears, the constitutional rquirement of *mens rea* may be satisfied in different ways. The offence can require proof of a positive state of mind such as intent, recklessness or wilful blindness. Alternatively, the *mens rea* or element of fault can be satisfied by proof of negligence whereby the conduct of the accused is measured on the basis of an objective standard without establishing the subjective mental state of the particular accused. In the appropriate context, negligence can be an acceptable basis of liability which meets the fault requirement of s. 7 of the Charter: see *R. v. Wholesale Travel Group Inc.* (1991), 67 C.C.C. (3d) 193, 84 D.L.R. (4th) 161, [1991] 3 S.C.R. 154. Thus, the intent required for a particular offence may be either subjective or objective.

A truly subjective test seeks to determine what was actually in the mind of the particular accused at the moment the offence is alleged to have been committed. In his very useful text, Professor Stuart puts it this way in *Canadian Criminal Law, ibid.*, at pp. 123-4, and p. 125:

> What is vital is that *this accused* given his personality, situation and circumstances, actually intended, knew or foresaw the consequence and/or circumstance as the case may be. Whether he "could", "ought", or "should" have foreseen or whether a reasonable person would have foreseen is not the relevant criterion of liability.
>
> . . . .
>
> In trying to ascertain what was going on in the accused's mind, as the subjective approach demands, the trier of fact may draw reasonable inferences from the accused's actions or words at the time of his act or in the witness box. The accused may or may not be believed. To conclude that, considering all the evidence, the Crown has proved beyond a reasonable doubt that the accused "must" have thought in the penalized way is no departure from the subjective substantive standard. Resort to an objective substantive standard would only occur if the reasoning became that the accused "must have realized it if he had thought about it".

(Emphasis in original.)

On the other hand, the test for negligence is an objective one requiring a marked departure from the standard of care of a reasonable person. There is no need to establish the intention of the particular accused. The question to be answered under the objective test concerns what the accused "should" have known. The potential harshness of the objective standard may be lessened by the consideration of certain personal factors as well as the consideration of a defence of mistake of fact: see McIntyre J., and Lamer J, as he then was, in *R. v. Tutton* (1989), 48 C.C.C. (3d) 129, [1989] 1 S.C.R. 1392, 69 C.R. (3d) 289, and *R. v. Waite* (1989), 48 C.C.C. (3d) 1, [1989] 1 S.C.R. 1436, 69 C.R. (3d) 323. Nevertheless, there should be a clear distinction in the law between one who was aware (pure subjective intent) and one who should have taken care irrespective of awareness (pure objective intent).

*What is the mens rea required to prove the offence of dangerous driving?*

The nature of driving offences suggests than an objective test, or more specifically a modified objective test, is particularly appropriate to apply to dangerous driving. I say that for a number of reasons.

(a) *The licensing requirement*

First, driving can only be undertaken by those who have a licence. The effect of the licensing requirement is to demonstrate that those who drive are mentally capable of doing so. Moreover, it serves to confirm that those who drive are familiar with the standard of care which must be maintained by all drivers. There is a further aspect that must be taken into consideration in light of the licensing requirement for drivers. Licensed drivers choose to engage in the regulated activity of driving. They place themselves in a position of responsibility to other members of the public who use the roads.

As a result, it is unnecessary for a court to establish that the particular accused intended or was aware of the consequences of his or her driving. The minimum standard of physical and mental well-being coupled with the basic knowledge of the standard of care required of licensed drivers obviate that requirement. As a determining subjective intent, is simply not necessary in light of the fixed standards that must be met by licensed drivers.

## (b) *The automatic and reflexive nature of driving*

Secondly, the nature of driving itself is often so routine, so automatic that it is almost impossible to determine a particular state of mind of a driver at any given moment. Driving motor vehicles is something that is familiar to most adult Canadians. It cannot be denied that a great deal of driving is done with little conscious thought. It is an activity that is primarily reactive and not contemplative. It is every bit as routine and familiar as taking a shower or going to work. Often it is impossible for a driver to say what his or her specific intent was at any moment during a drive other than the desire to go from A to B.

It would be a denial of common sense for a driver, whose conduct was objectively dangerous, to be acquitted on the ground that he was not thinking of his manner of driving at the time of the accident.

## (c) *The wording of s. 233 (now s. 249)*

Thirdly, the wording of the section itself which refers to the operation of a motor vehicle "in a manner that is dangerous to the public, having regard to all the circumstances" suggests that an objective standard is required. The "manner of driving" can only be compared to a standard of reasonable conduct. That standard can be readily judged and assessed by all who would be members of juries.

Thus, it is clear that the basis of liability for dangerous driving is negligence. The question to be asked is not what the accused subjectively intended but rather whether, viewed objectively, the accused exercised the appropriate standard of care. It is not overly difficult to determine when a driver has fallen markedly below the acceptable standard of care. There can be not doubt that the concept of negligence is well understood and readily recognized by most Canadians. Negligent driving can be thought of as a continuum that progresses, or regresses, from momentary lack of attention giving rise to civil responsibility through careless driving under a provincial Highway Traffic Act to dangerous driving under the *Criminal Code*.

## (d) *Statistics*

Fourthly, the statistics which demonstrate that all too many tragic deaths and disabling injuries flow from the operation of motor vehicles indicate the need to control the conduct of drivers. The need is obvious and urgent. Section 233 (now s. 249) seeks to curb conduct which is exceedingly dangerous to the public. The statistics on car accidents in Canada indicate with chilling clarity the extent of the problem. The number of people killed and injured each year in traffic accidents is staggering. Data from Transport Canada shows that, in 1991, the number of deaths related to traffic accidents in Canada was 3,654. In 1990, there were 178,423 personal injury traffic accidents, 630,000 property-damage accidents and 3,442 fatal accidents. These figures highlight the tragic social cost which can and does arise from the operation of motor vehicles. There is therefore a compelling need for effective legislation which strives to regulate the manner of driving vehicles and thereby lessen the carnage on our highways. It is not only appropriate but essential in the control of dangerous driving that an objective standard be applied.

In my view, to insist on a subjective mental element in connection with driving offences would be to deny reality. It cannot be forgotten that the operation of a motor vehicle is, as I have said so very often, automatic and with little conscious thought. It is simply inappropriate to apply a subjective test in determining whether an accused is guilty of dangerous driving.

(e) *Modified objective test*

Although an objective test must be applied to the offence of dangerous driving, it will remain open to the accused to raise a reasonable doubt that a reasonable person would have been aware of the risks in the accused's conduct. The test must be applied with some measure of flexibility. That is to say the objective test should not be applied in a vacuum but rather in the context of the events surrounding the incident.

There will be occasions when the manner of driving viewed objectively will clearly be dangerous, yet the accused should not be convicted. Take, for example, a driver who, without prior warning, suffers a totally unexpected heart attack, epileptic seizure or detached retina. As a result of the sudden onset of a disease or physical disability the manner of driving would be dangerous, yet those circumstances could provide a complete defence despite the objective demonstration of dangerous driving. Similarly, a driver who, in the absence of any warning or knowledge of its possible effects, takes a prescribed medication which suddenly and unexpectedly affects the driver in such a way that the manner of driving was dangerous to the public, could still establish a good defence to the charge although it had been objectively established. These examples, and there may well be others, serve to illustrate the aim and purpose of the modified objective test. It is to enable a court to take into account the sudden and unexpected onset of disease and similar human frailties as well as the objective demonstration of dangerous driving.

A modified objective test was aptly described by McIntyre J. in *R. v. Tutton, supra*, at pp. 140-1. Although he was dealing with criminal negligence, his words, at p. 140, are apt in considering the dangerous driving section which is essentially concerned with negligent driving that constitutes a marked departure from the norm:

> The application of an objective test under s. 202 of the *Criminal Code*, however, may not be made in a vacuum. Events occur within the framework of other events and actions and when deciding on the nature of the questioned conduct, surrounding circumstances must be considered. The decision must be made on a consideration of the facts existing at the time and in relation to the accused's perception of those facts. Since the test is objective, the accused's perception of the facts is not to be considered for the purpose of assessing malice or intention on the accused's part but only to form a basis for a conclusion as to whether or not the accused's conduct, in view of his perception of the facts, was reasonable ... If an accused under s. 202 has an honest and reasonably held belief in the existence of certain facts, it may be a relevant consideration in assessing the reasonableness of his conduct. For example, a welder, who is engaged to work in a confined space believing on the assurance of the owner of the premises that no combustible or explosive material is stored nearby, should be entitled to have his perception, as to the presence or absence of dangerous materials, before the jury on a charge of manslaughter when his welding torch causes an explosion and a consequent death.

In summary, the *mens rea* for the offence of dangerous driving should be assessed objectively but in the context of all the events surrounding the incident. That approach will satisfy the dictates both of common sense and fairness. As a general rule, personal factors need not be taken into account. This flows from the licensing requirement for driving which assures that all who drive have a reasonable standard of physical health and capability, mental health and a knowledge of the reasonable standard required for all drivers.

In light of the licensing requirement and the nature of driving offences, a modified objective test satisfies the constitutional minimum fault requirement for s. 233 (now s. 249) of the *Criminal Code* and is eminently well suited to that offence.

It follows then that a trier of fact may convict if satisfied beyond a reasonable doubt that, viewed objectively, the accused was, in the words of the section, driving in a manner that was "dangerous to the public, having regard to all the circumstances, including the nature, condition and use of such place and the amount of traffic that at the time is or might reasonably be expected to be on such place." In making the assessment, the trier of fact should be satisfied that the conduct amounted to a marked departure from the standard of care that a reasonable person would observe in the accused's situation.

Next, if an explanation is offered by the accused, such as a sudden and unexpected onset of illness, then in order to convict, the trier of fact must be satisfied that a reasonable person in similar circumstances ought to have been aware of the risk and of the danger involved in the conduct manifested by the accused. If a jury is determining the facts, they may be instructed with regard to dangerous driving along the lines set out above. There is no necessity for a long or complex charge. Neither the section nor the offence requires it. Certainly the instructions should not be unnecessarily confused by any references to advertent or inadvertent negligence. The offence can be readily assessed by jurors who can arrive at a conclusion based on common sense and their own everyday experiences.

*Application of these principles to the facts*

Let us now consider whether the modified objective test was properly applied in this case. The trial judge carefully examined the circumstances of the accident. He took into account the busy downtown traffic, the weather conditions, and the mechanical conditions of the accused vehicle. He concluded, in my view very properly, that the appellant's manner of driving represented a gross departure from the standard of a reasonably prudent driver. No explanation was offered by the accused that could excuse his conduct. There is no reason for interfering with the trial judge's finding of fact and application of the law.

In the result the appeal must be dismissed.

*Appeal dismissed.*

## Regina v. Creighton
(1993), 83 C.C.C. (3d) 246 (S.C.C.)

[Only the judgement of McLachlin is excerpted below.]
McLACHLIN J.: — This appeal considers the constitutional status of s. 222(5)(*a*) of the *Criminal Code*, R.S.C. 1985, c. C-46. In particular, the constitutional question

stated by the Chief Justice asks: "Does the common law definition of unlawful act manslaughter violate s. 7 of the *Canadian Charter of Rights and Freedoms?*" The facts and judgments below have been set out by the Chief Justice. In brief, Mr. Creighton was convicted of manslaughter, arising from the death of Kimberly Ann Martin, who died as a result of an injection of cocaine given by Mr. Creighton. The trial judge found that the death constituted manslaughter either on the ground that it was caused by an unlawful act, or on the ground that it was caused by criminal negligence.

I respectfully disagree with the Chief Justice on two points. The first is his conclusion that the common law offence of manslaughter in unconstitutional because it does not require foreseeability of death. The Chief Justice concludes that the offence of manslaughter must be "read up" to include this requirement in order to bring it into line with the principles of fundamental justice enshrined in s. 7 of the *Canadian Charter of Rights and Freedoms*, and in particular with the principle that the moral fault required for conviction be commensurate with the gravity and the stigma of the offence. In my view, the offence of unlawful act manslaughter as defined by our courts and those in other jurisdictions for many centuries, is entirely consistent with the principles of fundamental justice. There is no need to read up its requirements; as it stands, it conforms to the Charter.

The second point on which I respectfully diverge is the Chief Justice's conclusion that the standard of care on the objective test in manslaughter and in crimes of negligence varies with the degree of experience, education, and other personal characteristics of the accused. This leads the Chief Justice to hold Mr. Creighton to a higher standard of care than that of the reasonable person in determining if he would have foreseen the risk in question, because of Creighton's long experience as a drug user (at p. 20, reasons of Chief Justice) [*ante*, p. 360]. For the reasons set out below I believe the appropriate standard to be that of the reasonable person in all the circumstances of the case. The criminal law is concerned with setting minimum standards of conduct; the standards are not to be altered because the accused possesses more or less experience than the hypothetical average reasonable person.

I will turn first to the common law test for manslaughter, and address the constitutional question as stated by the Chief Justice.

A. *Constitutionality of the requirement of foreseeability of bodily injury in manslaughter*

1. *The mens rea of manslaughter*

The *Criminal Code* defines three general types of culpable homicide. There is murder, the intentional killing of another human being. There is infanticide, the intentional killing of a child. All other culpable homicides fall into the residual category of manslaughter (s. 234).

Manslaughter is a crime of venerable lineage. It covers a wide variety of circumstances. Two requirements are constant: (1) conduct causing the death of another person, and (2) fault short of intention to kill. That fault may consist either in committing another unlawful act which causes the death, or in criminal negligence.

The common law classification of manslaughter is reflected in the definition of culpable homicide in s. 222(5) of the *Criminal Code*:

> 222(5) A person commits culpable homicide when he causes the death of a human being,
>
> (a) by means of an unlawful act;
> (b) by criminal negligence;

The structure of the offence of manslaughter depends on a predicate offence of an unlawful act or criminal negligence, coupled with a homicide. It is now settled that the fact that an offence depends upon a predicate offence does not render it unconstitutional provided that the predicate offence involves a dangerous act, is not an offence of absolute liability, and is not unconstitutional: *R. v. DeSousa* (1992), 76 C.C.C. (3d) 124, 95 D.L.R. (4th) 595, [1992] 2 S.C.R. 944. But a further objection is raised in this case. It is said that the offence of manslaughter is unconstitutional because it requires only foreseeability of the risk of bodily harm and not foreseeability of death, and that the trial judge erred in requiring only foreseeability of bodily harm.

The cases establish that in addition to the *actus reus* and *mens rea* associated with the underlying act, all that is required to support a manslaughter conviction is reasonable foreseeability of the risk of bodily harm. While s. 222(5)(*a*) does not expressly require foreseeable bodily harm, it has been so interpreted: see *R. v. DeSousa, supra*. The unlawful act must be objectively dangerous, that is, likely to injure another person. The law of unlawful act manslaughter has not, however, gone so far as to require foreseeability of death. The same is true for manslaughter predicated on criminal negligence; while criminal negligence, *infra*, requires a marked departure from the standards of a reasonable person in all the circumstances, it does not require foreseeability of death.

Certain early authorities suggest that foreseeability of the risk of bodily harm is not required for manslaughter. . .

In more recent times, the prevailing view has been that foreseeability of bodily harm is required for manslaughter. . .

This court in *R. v. DeSousa, supra*, confirmed that a conviction for manslaughter requires that the risk of bodily harm have been foreseeable. . .

So the test for the *mens rea* of unlawful act manslaughter in Canada, as in the United Kingdom, is (in addition to the *mens rea* of the underlying offence) objective foreseeability of the risk of bodily harm which is neither trivial nor transitory, in the context of a dangerous act. Foreseeability of the risk of death is not required. The question is whether this test violates the principle of fundamental justice under s. 7 of the Charter.

### 2. Constitutionality of the "foresight of bodily harm" test for manslaughter

Before venturing on analysis, I think it appropriate to introduce a note of caution. We are here concerned with a common law offence virtually as old as our system of criminal law. It has been applied in innumerable cases around the world. And it has been honed and refined over the centuries. Because of its residual nature, it may lack the logical symmetry of more modern statutory offences, but it has stood the practical test of time. Could all this be the case, one asks, if the law violates our fundamental notions of justice, themselves grounded in the history of the common law? Perhaps. Nevertheless, it must be with considerable caution that a twentieth century court approaches the invitation which has been put before us: to strike out, or alternatively, rewrite, the offence of manslaughter on the ground that this is necessary to bring the law into conformity with the principles of fundamental justice.

As I read the reasons of the Chief Justice, his conclusion that the offence of manslaughter as it stands is unconstitutional, rests on two main concerns. First, it is his view that the gravity or seriousness of the offence of manslaughter, and in particular the stigma that attaches to it, requires a minimum *mens rea* or foreseeability of death. Secondly, considerations of symmetry between the element of mental fault and the consequences of the offence mandate this conclusion. I will deal with each concern in turn.

(a) *Gravity of the offence*

A number of concepts fall under this head. Three of them figure among the four factors relevant to determining the constitutionality of a *mens rea* requirement, as set out by this court in *R. v. Martineau* (1990), 58 C.C.C. (3d) 353, [1990] 2 S.C.R. 633, 79 C.R. (3d) 129:

1. the stigma attached to the offence, and the available penalties requiring a *mens rea* reflecting the particular nature of the crime;
2. whether the punishment is proportionate to the moral blameworthiness of the offender, and
3. the idea that those causing harm intentionally must be punished more severely than those causing harm unintentionally.

The Chief Justice in his reasons places considerable emphasis on the first factor of stigma. He argues that "there may well be no difference between the *actus reus* of manslaughter and that of murder; arguably both give rise to the stigma of being labelled by the state and community as responsible for the wrongful death of another" (at p. 11) [*ante*, p. 355]. But later in his reasons he concedes that "the stigma which attaches to a conviction for unlawful act manslaughter", while "significant . . . does not approach the opprobrium reserved in our society for those who *knowingly* or *intentionally* take the life of another" (emphasis is original). The Chief Justice goes on to observe that "[I]t is for this reason that manslaughter developed as a separate offence from murder at common law." Nevertheless, in the end the Chief Justice concludes that the "constitutional imperative", taken with other factors, requires a minimum *mens rea* of foreseeability of the risk of death, suggesting that stigma may remain an important factor in his reasoning.

To the extent that stigma is relied on as requiring foreseeability of the risk of death in the offence of manslaughter, I find it unconvincing. The most important feature of the stigma of manslaughter is the stigma which is *not* attached to it. The *Criminal Code* confines manslaughter to non-intentional homicide. A persons convicted of manslaughter is *not* a murderer. He or she did *not* intend to kill someone. A person has been killed through the fault of another, and that is always serious. But by the very act of calling the killing *manslaughter* the law indicates that the killing is less blameworthy than murder. It may arise from negligence, or it may arise as the unintended result of a lesser unlawful act. The conduct is blameworthy and must be punished, but its stigma does not approach that of murder.

To put it another way, the stigma attached to manslaughter is an appropriate stigma. Manslaughter is not like constructive murder, where one could say that a person who did not in fact commit murder might be inappropriately branded with the stigma of murder. The stigma associated with manslaughter is arguably exactly what it should be for an unintentional killing in circumstances where the risk of bodily harm was foreseeable. There is much common sense in the following observation:

> The offender has killed, and it does not seem wrong in principle that, when he is far from blameless, he should be convicted of an offence of homicide. To some extent it must be an intuitive conclusion, but it does not seem too difficult to argue that those who kill, and who are going to be convicted of something, should be convicted of homicide. That, after all, is what they have done.

(Adrian Briggs, "In Defence of Manslaughter", [1983] Crim. L.R. 764 at p. 765.)

It would shock the public's conscience to think that a person could be convicted of manslaughter absent any moral fault based on foreseeability of harm. Conversely, it might well shock the public's conscience to convict a person who has killed another only of aggravated assault — the result of requiring foreseeability of death — on the sole basis that the risk of death was not reasonably foreseeable. The terrible consequence of death demands more. In short, the *mens rea* requirement which the common law has adopted — foreseeability of harm — is entirely appropriate to the stigma associated with the offence of manslaughter. To change the *mens rea* requirement would be to risk the very disparity between *mens rea* and stigma of which the appellant complains.

I come then to the second factor mentioned in *Martineau*, the relationship between the punishment for the offence and the *mens rea* requirement. Here again, the offence of manslaughter stands in sharp contrast to the offence of murder. Murder entails a mandatory life sentence; manslaughter carries with it no minimum sentence. This is appropriate. Because manslaughter can occur in a wide variety of circumstances, the penalties must be flexible. An unintentional killing while committing a minor offence, for example, properly attracts a much lighter sentence than an unintentional killing where the circumstances indicate an awareness of risk of death just short of what would be required to infer the intent required for murder. The point is, the sentence can be and is tailored to suit the degree of moral fault of the offender. This court acknowledged this in *Martineau*, at p. 362: "The more flexible sentencing scheme under a conviction for manslaughter is in accord with the principle that punishment be meted out with regard to the level of moral blameworthiness of the offender." It follows that the sentence attached to manslaughter does not require elevation of the degree of *mens rea* for the offence.

This brings me to the third factor relating to the gravity of the offence set out in *Martineau*, the principle that those causing harm intentionally must be punished more severely than those causing harm unintentionally. As noted, this principle is strictly observed in the case of manslaughter. It is by definition an unintentional crime. Accordingly, the penalties imposed are typically less than for its intentional counterpart, murder.

I conclude that the standard of *mens rea* required for manslaughter is appropriately tailored to the seriousness of the offence.

(b) *Symmetry between the element of fault and the consequences of the offence*

The Chief Justice correctly observes that the criminal law has traditionally aimed at symmetry between the *mens rea* and the prohibited consequences of the offence. The *actus reus* generally consists of an act bringing about a prohibited consequence, e.g., death. Criminal law theory suggests that the accompanying *mens rea* must go to the prohibited consequence. The moral fault of the accused lies in the act of bringing about that consequence. The Chief Justice reasons from this proposition that since manslaughter is an offence involving the prohibited act of killing another, a *mens rea* of foreseeability of harm is insufficient; what is required is foreseeability of death.

The conclusion that the offence of manslaughter is unconstitutional because it does not require appreciation of the consequential risk of death rests on two propositions: (1) that risk of bodily harm is appreciably different from risk of death in the context of manslaughter, and (2) that the principle of absolute symmetry between *mens rea* and each consequence of a criminal offence is not only a general rule of criminal law, but a principle of fundamental justice which sets a constitutional minimum. In my view, neither of these propositions is free from doubt.

I turn first to the distinction between appreciation of the risk of bodily harm and the risk of death in the context of manslaughter. In my view, when the risk of bodily harm is combined with the established rule that a wrongdoer must take his victim as he finds him and the fact that death did in fact occur, the distinction disappears. The accused who asserts that the risk of death was not foreseeable is in effect asserting that a normal person would not have died in these circumstances, and that he could not foresee the peculiar vulnerability of the victim. Therefore, he says, he should be convicted only of assault causing bodily harm or some lesser offence. This is to abrogate the thin-skull rule that requires that the wrongdoer take his victim as he finds him. Conversely, to combine the test of reasonable foreseeability of bodily harm with the thin-skull rule is to mandate that in some cases, foreseeability of the risk of bodily harm alone will properly result in a conviction for manslaughter.

What the appellant asks us to do, then, is to abandon the "thin-skull" rule. It is this rule which, on analysis, is alleged to be unjust. Such a conclusion I cannot accept. The law has consistently set its face against such a policy. It decrees that the aggressor must take his victim as he finds him. . . .

The principle that if one engages in criminal behaviour, one is responsible for any unforeseen actions stemming from the unlawful act, has been a well-established tenet for most of this century in Canada, the U.S. and U.K. . . .

The thin-skull rule is a good and useful principle. It requires aggressors, once embarked on their dangerous course of conduct which may foreseeably injure others, to take responsibility for all the consequences that ensue, even to death. That is not, in my view, contrary to fundamental justice. Yet the consequence of adopting the amendment proposed by the Chief Justice would be to abrogate this principle in cases of manslaughter.

In fact, when manslaughter is viewed in the context of the thin skull principle, the disparity diminishes between the *mens rea* of the offence and its consequence. The law does not posit the average victim. It says the aggressor must take the victim as he finds him. Wherever there is a risk of harm, there is also a practical risk that some victims may die as a result of the harm. At this point, the test of harm and death merge.

The second assumption inherent in the argument based on symmetry between *mens rea* and each consequence of the offence is that this is not only a general rule of criminal law, but a principle of fundamental justice — a basic constitutional requirement. I agree that as a general rule the *mens rea* of an offence relates to the consequences prohibited by the offence. As I stated in *R. v. Theroux* (1993), 79 C.C.C. (3d) 449 at p. 458, 100 D.L.R. (4th) 624, [1993] 2 S.C.R. 5: Typically, *mens rea* is concerned with the consequences of the prohibited *actus reus*." Yet our criminal law contains important exceptions to this ideal of perfect symmetry. The presence of these exceptions suggests that the rule of symmetry is just that — a rule — to which there are no exceptions. If this is so, then the rule cannot be elevated to the status of a principle of fundamental justice which must, by definition, have universal application.

It is important to distinguish between criminal law theory, which seeks the ideal of absolute symmetry between *actus reus* and *mens rea*, and the constitutional requirements of the Charter. As the Chief Justice has stated several times, "the Constitution does not always guarantee the 'ideal'": *R. v. Lippé* (1991), 64 C.C.C. (3d) 513 at p. 532. . . .

I know of no authority for the proposition that the *mens rea* of an offence must always attach to the precise consequence which is prohibited as a matter of constitutional necessity. The relevant constitutional principles have been cast more broadly. No person can be sent to prison without *mens rea*, or a guilty mind, and the seriousness of the offence must not be disproportionate to the degree of moral fault. provided an element of mental fault or moral culpability is present, and provided that it is proportionate to the seriousness and consequences of the offence charged, the principles of fundamental justice are satisfied.

The principles of fundamental justice, viewed thus, empower Parliament to recognize that, notwithstanding the same level of moral fault, some offences may be more or less serious, depending on the consequences of the culpable act. . . .

Thus it cannot be said that the law in all circumstances insists on absolute symmetry between the *mens rea* and the consequences of the offence. Sometimes it does not insist on the consequences at all, as in crimes of attempts. Sometimes, as in unlawful act manslaughter, it elevates the crime by reason of its serious consequences while leaving the mental element the same.

Just as it would offend fundamental justice to punish a person who did not intend to kill for murder, so it would equally offend common notions of justice to acquit a person who has killed another of manslaughter and find him guilty instead of aggravated assault on the ground that death, as opposed to harm was foreseeable. Consequences can be important. . . .

Thus when considering the constitutionality of the requirement of foreseeability of bodily harm, the question is not whether the general rule of symmetry between *mens rea* and the consequences prohibited by the offence is met, but rather whether the fundamental principle of justice is satisfied that the gravity and blameworthiness of an offence must be commensurate with the moral fault engaged by that offence. Fundamental justice does not require absolute symmetry between moral fault and the prohibited consequences. Consequences, or the absence of consequences, can properly affect the seriousness with which Parliament treats specified conduct.

### 3. *Policy considerations*

I have suggested that jurisprudential and historic considerations confirm a test for the *mens rea* of manslaughter based on foreseeability of the risk of bodily injury, rather than death. I have also argued that the considerations of the gravity of the offence and symmetry between the *mens rea* of the offence and its consequences do not entail the conclusion that the offence of manslaughter as it has been historically defined in terms of foreseeability of the risk of bodily harm is unconstitutional. It is my view that policy considerations support the same conclusion. In looking at whether a long-standing offence violates the principles of fundamental justice, it is not amiss, in my view, to look at such considerations.

First, the need to deter dangerous conduct which may injure others and in fact may kill the peculiarly vulnerable supports the view that death need not be objectively foreseeable, only bodily injury. To tell people that if they embark on dangerous conduct which foreseeably may cause bodily harm which is neither trivial nor transient, and which in fact results in death, that they will not be held responsible for the death but only for aggravated assault, is less likely to deter such conduct than a message that they will be held responsible for the death, albeit under manslaughter not murder. Given the finality of death and the absolute unacceptability of killing another human being, it is not amiss to preserve the test which promises the greatest measure of deterrence, provided the penal consequences of the offence are not disproportionate. This is achieved by retaining the test of foreseeability of bodily harm in the offence of manslaughter.

Secondly, retention of the test based on foreseeability of bodily harm accords best with our sense of justice. I have earlier alluded to the view, attested to by the history of the offence of manslaughter, that causing the death of another through negligence or a dangerous unlawful act should be met by a special sanction reflecting the fact that a death occurred, even though death was not objectively foreseeable. This is supported by the sentiment that a person who engages in dangerous conduct that breaches the bodily integrity of another and puts that person at risk may properly be held responsible for an unforeseen death attributable to that person's peculiar vulnerability; the aggressor takes the victim as he finds him. The criminal law must reflect not only the concerns of the accused, but the concerns of the victim, and where the victim is killed, the concerns of society for the victim's fate. Both go into the equation of justice.

Finally, the traditional test founded on foreseeability of the risk of bodily harm provides, in my belief, a workable test which avoids troubling judges and juries about the fine distinction between foreseeability of the risk of bodily injury and foreseeability of the risk of death — a distinction which, as argued earlier, reduces to a formalistic technicality when put in the context of the thin-skull rule and the fact that death has in fact been inflicted by the accused's dangerous act. The traditional common law test permits a principled approach to the offence which meets the concerns of society, provides fairness to the accused, and facilitates a just and workable trial process.

### 4. *Summary on the constitutionality of the test of foresight of bodily harm for manslaughter*

The foregoing considerations lead me to conclude that the fact that the *mens rea* of manslaughter requires foreseeable risk of harm rather than foreseeable risk of death does not violate the principles of fundamental justice. In the final analysis, the moral fault required for manslaughter is commensurate with the gravity of the offence and the penalties which it entails, and offends no principle of fundamental justice. The next issue is the nature of the objective test establishing foresight of bodily harm, to which I now turn.

### B. *The nature of the objective test*

I respectfully differ from the Chief Justice on the nature of the objective test used to determine the *mens rea* for crimes of negligence. In my view, the approach advocated by the Chief Justice personalizes the objective test to the point where it devolves into a subjective test, thus eroding the minimum standard of care which Parliament has laid down by the enactment of offences of manslaughter and penal negligence.

By way of background, it may be useful to restate what I understand the jurisprudence to date to have established regarding crimes of negligence and the objective test. The *mens rea* of a criminal offence may be either subjective or objective, subject to the principle of fundamental justice that the moral fault of the offence must be proportionate to its gravity and penalty. Subjective *mens rea* requires that the accused have intended the consequences of his or her acts, or that, knowing of the probable consequences of those acts, the accused have proceeded recklessly in the face of the risk. The requisite intent or knowledge may be inferred directly from what the accused said or says about his or her mental state, or indirectly from the act and its circumstances. Even in the latter case, however, it is concerned with " ' what was actually going on in the mind of this particular accused at the time in question'": L'Heureux-Dubé J. in *R. v. Martineau, supra*, at p. 367, quoting Stuart, *Canadian Criminal Law,* 2nd ed. (1987), p. 121.

Objective *mens rea*, on the other hand, is not concerned with what the accused intended or knew. Rather, the mental fault lies in failure to direct the mind to a risk which the reasonable person would have appreciated. Objective *mens rea* is not concerned with what was actually in the accused's mind, but with what should have been there, had the accused proceeded reasonably.

It is now established that a person may be held criminally responsible for negligent conduct on the objective test, and that this alone does not violate the principle of fundamental justice that the moral fault of the accused must be commensurate with the gravity of the offence and its penalty: *R. v. Hundal* (1993), 79 C.C.C. (3d) 97, [1993] 1 S.C.R. 867, 19 C.R. (4th) 169.

However, as stated in *Martineau*, it is appropriate that those who cause harm intentionally should be punished more severely than those who cause harm inadvertently. Moreover, the constitutionality of crimes of negligence is also subject to the caveat that acts of ordinary negligence may not suffice to justify imprisonment. . . . To put it in the terms used in *Hundal*: The negligence must constitute a "marked departure" from the standard of the reasonable person. . . .

It follows from this requirement, affirmed in Hundal, that in an offence based on unlawful conduct, a predicate offence involving carelessness or negligence must also be read as requiring a "marked departure" from the standard of the reasonable person.

. . .

To this point, the Chief Justice and I are not, as I perceive it, in disagreement. The difference between our approaches turns on the extent to which personal characteristics of the accused may affect liability under the objective test. Here we enter territory in large part uncharted. To date, debate has focused on whether an objective test for *mens rea* is ever available in the criminal law; little has been said about how, assuming it is applicable, it is to be applied. In *R. v. Hundal, supra*, it was said that the *mens rea* of dangerous driving should be assessed objectively in the context of all the events surrounding the incident. But the extent to which those circumstances include personal mental or psychological frailties of the accused was not explored in depth. In these circumstances, we must begin with the fundamental principles of criminal law.

*Underlying principles*

The debate about the degree to which personal characteristics should be reflected in the objective test for fault in offences of penal negligence engages two fundamental concepts of criminal law.

The first concept is the notion that the criminal law may properly hold people who engage in risky activities to a minimum standard of care, judged by what a reasonable person in all the circumstances would have done. This notion posits a uniform standard for all persons engaging in the activity, regardless of their background, education or psychological disposition.

The second concept is the principle that the morally innocent not be punished. . . . This principle is the foundation of the requirement of criminal law that the accused must have a guilty mind, or *mens rea*.

I agree with the Chief Justice that the rule that the morally innocent not be punished in the context of the objective test requires that the law refrain from holding a person criminally responsible if he or she is not capable of appreciating the risk. Where I differ from the Chief Justice is in his designation of the sort of educational, experiential and so-called "habitual" factors personal to the accused which can be taken into account. The Chief Justice, while in principle advocating a uniform standard of care for all, in the result seems to contemplate a standard of care which varies with the background and predisposition of each accused. Thus an inexperienced, uneducated, young person, like the accused in *R. v. Naglik*, S.C.C. Nos. 22490 and 22636, September 9, 1993, could be acquitted, even though she does not meet the standard of the reasonable person. . . . On the other hand, a person with special experience, like

Mr. Creighton in this case, or the appellant police officer in *R. v. Gosset, supra*, will be held to a higher standard than the ordinary reasonable person.

I must respectfully dissent from this extension of the objective test for criminal fault. In my view, considerations of principle and policy dictate the maintenance of a single, uniform legal standard of care for such offences, subject to one exception: incapacity to appreciate the nature of the risk which the activity in question entails.

This principle that the criminal law will not convict the morally innocent does not, in my view, require consideration of personal factors short of incapacity. The criminal law, while requiring mental fault as an element of a conviction, has steadfastly rejected the idea that a person's personal characteristics can (short of incapacity) excuse the person from meeting the standard of conduct imposed by the law....

In summary, I can find no support in criminal theory for the conclusion that protection of the morally innocent requires a general consideration of individual excusing conditions. The principle comes into play only at the point where the person is shown to lack the capacity to appreciate the nature and quality or the consequences of his or her acts. Apart from this, we are all, rich and poor, wise and naive, held to the minimum standards of conduct prescribed by the criminal law. This conclusion is dictated by a fundamental proposition of social organization. As Justice Oliver Wendell Holmes wrote in *The Common Law* (1881), p. 108: "... when men live in society, a certain average of conduct, a sacrifice of individual peculiarities going beyond a certain point, is necessary to the general welfare".

The ambit of the principle that the morally innocent shall not be convicted has developed in large part in the context of crimes of subjective fault — crimes where the accused must be shown to have actually intended or foreseen the consequences of his or her conduct. In crimes of this type, personal characteristics of the accused have been held to be relevant only to the extent that they tend to prove or disprove an element of such offences, personal factors can come into play. But beyond this, personal characteristics going to lack of capacity are considered under the introductory sections of the *Code* defining the conditions of criminal responsibility and have generally been regarded as irrelevant.

What then is the situation for crimes of inadvertence? Here actual intention or knowledge is not a factor; hence personal characteristics are not admissible on that ground. Nor, in my view, can a case be made for considering them on any other basis, except in so far as they may show that the accused lacked the capacity to appreciate the risk. This appears to be the settled policy of the law, applied for centuries to offences involving manslaughter or penal negligence based on objectively assessed fault. Here, as in crimes of subjective intent, the courts have rejected the contention that the standard prescribed by the law should take into account the individual peculiarities of the accused, short of incapacity....

To the principle of a uniform minimum standard for crimes having an objective test there is but one exception — incapacity to appreciate the risk....

Consistent with these principles, this court has rejected experiential, educational and psychological defences falling short of incapacity. Thus it has excluded personal characteristics short of incapacity in considering the characteristics of the "ordinary person" for the defence of provocation for the offence of murder....

To summarize, the fundamental premises upon which our criminal law rests mandate that personal characteristics not directly relevant to an element of the offence serve as excuses only at the point where they establish incapacity, whether the incapacity be the ability to appreciate the nature and quality of one's conduct in the context of intentional crimes, or the incapacity to appreciate the risk involved in one's conduct in the context of crimes of manslaughter or penal negligence. The principle that we eschew conviction of the morally innocent requires no more.

This test I believe to flow from the fundamental premises of our system of criminal justice. But drawing the line of criminal responsibility for negligent conduct at incapacity is also socially justifiable. In a society which licenses people, expressly or impliedly, to engage in a wide range of dangerous activities posing risk to the safety of others, it is reasonable to require that those choosing to undertake such activities and possessing the basic capacity to understand their danger take the trouble to exercise that capacity: see *R. v. Hundal, supra*. Not only does the absence of such care connote moral fault, but the sanction of the criminal law is justifiably invoked to deter others who choose to undertake such activities from proceeding without the requisite caution. Even those who lack the advantages of age, experience and education may properly be held to this standard as a condition of choosing to engage in activities which may maim or kill other innocent people.

The criminal law, as noted, is concerned with setting minimum standards of behaviour in defined circumstances. If this goal is to be achieved, the minimum cannot be lowered because of the frailties or inexperience of the accused, short of incapacity.

. . .

But the social justification for a uniform standard of care stops at the point of incapacity. Convicting and punishing a person who lacks the capacity to do what the law says he or she should have done serves no useful purpose. . . .

These considerations suggest that the practical as well as the theoretical concerns of the criminal law in the field of penal negligence are best served by insisting on a uniform standard of conduct for everyone, subject to cases where the accused was not capable of recognizing and avoiding the risk attendant on the activity in question. Beyond this, the standard should not be individualized by reason of the peculiar personal characteristics of the accused. . . .

As I see it, the recognition that those lacking the capacity to perceive the risk should be exempted from criminal conviction and punishment does not entail the conclusion that the standard of care must be adjusted to take into account the accused's experience and education. The only actor-oriented question apposite to *mens rea* in these cases is whether the accused was capable of appreciating the risk, had he or she put her mind to it. If the answer is yes . . . that is an end of the matter.

It may be that in some cases educational deficiencies, such as illiteracy on the part of a person handling a marked bottle of nitroglycerine in the Chief Justice's example, may preclude a person from being able to appreciate the risk entailed by his or conduct. Problems of perception may have the same effect; regardless of the care taken, the person would have been incapable of assessing the risk, and hence been acquitted. But, in practice, such cases will arise only exceptionally. The question of *mens rea* will arise only where it has been shown that the accused's conduct (the *actus reus* constitutes a dangerous and unlawful act (as in unlawful act manslaughter), or a marked departure from the standard care of a reasonably prudent person (as in manslaughter by criminal negligence, or penal negligence offences). This established, conflict with the prohibition against punishing the morally innocent will arise only rarely. . . .

Mental disabilities short of incapacity generally do not suffice to negative criminal liability for criminal negligence. The explanations for why a persons fails to advert to the risk inherent in the activity he or she is undertaking are legion. They range from simple absent-mindedness to attributes related to age, education and culture. . . .

This is not to say that the question of guilt is determined in a factual vacuum. While the legal duty of the accused is not particularized by his or her personal characteristics short of incapacity, it is particularized in application by the nature of the activity and the circumstances surrounding the accused's failure to take the requisite care. . . . The question is what the reasonably prudent person would have done in all the circumstances. Thus a welder who lights a torch causing an explosion may be excused if he has made an inquiry and been given advice upon which he was reasonably entitled to rely, that there was no explosive gas in the area. . . .

The matter may be looked at in this way. The legal standard of care is always the same — what a reasonable person would have done in all the circumstances. The *de facto* or applied standard of care, however, may vary with the activity in question and the circumstances in the particular case. . . .

A person may fail to meet an elevated *de facto* standard of care in either of two ways. First, the person may undertake an activity requiring special care when he or she is not qualified to give that care. Absent special excuses like necessity, this may constitute culpable negligence. An untrained person undertaking brain surgery might violate the standard in this way. Secondly, a person who is qualified may negligently fail to exercise the special care required by the activity. A brain surgeon performing surgery in a grossly negligent way might violate the standard in this second way. The standard is the same, although the means by which it is breached may differ.

Just as the adoption of a uniform standard of care which is blind to personal characteristics of the accused short of incapacity precludes lowering the standard for deficiencies of experience and temperament, so it precludes raising the standard for special experience or training. Since the criminal law is concerned with setting minimum standards for human conduct, it would be inappropriate to hold accused persons to a higher standard of care by reason of the fact that they may be better informed or better qualified that the person of reasonable prudence. Some activities may impose a higher *de facto* standard than others; brain surgery requires more care than applying an antiseptic. But as discussed earlier, this flows from the circumstances of the activity, not from the expertise of the actor.

The foregoing analysis suggests the following line of inquiry in cases of penal negligence. The first question is whether *actus reus* is established. This requires that the negligence constitute a marked departure from the standards of the reasonable person in all the circumstances of the case. This may consist in carrying out the activity in a dangerous fashion, or in embarking on the activity when in all the circumstances it is dangerous to do so.

ELEMENTS OF AN OFFENCE    447

The next question is whether the *mens rea* is established. As is the case with crimes of subjective *mens rea*, the *mens rea* for objective foresight and risking harm is normally inferred from the facts. The standard is that of the reasonable person in the circumstances of the accused. If a person has committed a manifestly dangerous act, it is reasonable, absent indications to the contrary, to infer that he or she failed to direct his or her mind to the risk and the need to take care. However, the normal inference may be negated by evidence raising a reasonable doubt as to lack of capacity to appreciate the risk. Thus, if a *prima facie* case for *actus reus* and *mens rea* is made out, it is necessary to ask a further question: did the accused possess the requisite capacity to appreciate the risk flowing from his conduct? If this further question is answered in the affirmative, the necessary moral fault is established and the accused is properly convicted. If not, the accused must be acquitted. . . .

I conclude that the legal standard of care for all crimes of negligence is that of the reasonable person. Personal factors are not relevant, except on the question of whether the accused possessed the necessary capacity to appreciate the risk.

C. *Application of the law to this appeal*

The trial judge properly found that Mr. Creighton committed the unlawful act of trafficking in cocaine. He also found that he was guilty of the criminal negligence, using the standard which I view as correct, the standard of the reasonable person. The only remaining question, on the view I take of the law, was whether the reasonable person in all the circumstances would have foreseen the risk of bodily harm. I am satisfied that the answer to this question must be affirmative. At the very least, a person administering a dangerous drug like cocaine to another has a duty to inform himself as to the precise risk the injection entails and to refrain from administering it unless reasonably satisfied that there is no risk of harm. That was not the case here, as the trial judge found.

The conviction was properly entered and should not be disturbed. Like the Chief Justice, I find it necessary to consider the alternative ground of manslaughter by criminal negligence.

I would answer the constitutional question in the negative and dismiss the appeal.

*Appeal dismissed.*

**Questions/Discussion**
1. Why does the law continue to use terms like actus reus and mens rea when such terms could be put into everyday language which would be better understood by all? The use of Latin terms is found throughout the law and it can be argued that the purpose best served is that of denying access to the law to the greatest number of citizens, as well as that of increasing the mystique of the law (whether deserved or not).
2. What is the meaning of mens rea for you? Should it continue to be regarded, at least in theory, from a subjectivist point of view, or would you favour an explicitly objectivist approach to the doctrine? Why or why not?
3. If A is given a package in Columbia to take into Canada and is arrested by customs on entering the country because it turns out the package contains cocaine, under what circumstances should A be held liable for importing cocaine? For example, if A did not address her mind as to what might be in the package because a good, trusted friend had given it to her and told her it was a gift for his mother? What if the package was given to

her by a stranger on the street but A never bothered to check the package or make any inquiries because she is an exceptionally trusting individual who thinks well of everyone? Should such naivety or blindness to the possible consequences relieve A of criminal liability on the grounds she did not have the intent to import the drugs? What role should the protection of the public play in these determinations (assuming for the moment that the public requires protection) as opposed to considerations of individual responsibility or blameworthiness?

4. What are the problems in theory and practice posed by laws involving criminal negligence and recklessness for traditional concepts of individual responsibility and blameworthiness?
5. Should Parliament attempt to specify a definition and test for the requisite mens rea for criminal negligence rather than leaving such to the courts? What type of mens rea do you think would be sufficient for criminal negligence? Should the test be subjective or objective? What is your rationale for the definition and test which you would adopt?

**Further Reading**
- Buxton, R., "Some Simple Thoughts on Intention", [1988] Criminal Law Review 484.
- Galloway, D., "Why the Criminal Law is Irrational" (1985), 35 University of Toronto Law Journal 25.
- Mewett, A. and M. Manning, *Mewett and Manning on Criminal Law*, 3rd ed. (Toronto: Butterworths, 1994.
- Salvatori, P., "Criminal Law — Criminal Negligence — Punishment" (1980), 58 Canadian Bar Review 660.
- Stuart, D., *Canadian Criminal Law: A Treatise*, 2nd ed. (Toronto: Carswell, 1987), pp. 117-156, 183-203.
- Stuart, D., "Progress on the Constitutional Requirement of Fault" (1988), 64 C.R. (3d) 352.
- Stuart, D., and R. Delisle, *Learning Canadian Criminal Law*, 5th ed. (Toronto: Carswell, 1995).
- Verdun-Jones, S., *Criminal Law in Canada: Cases, Questions and the Code* (Toronto: Harcourt Brace Jovanovich Canada, 1989), pp. 83-150.
- Verdun-Jones, S., and C. Griffiths, *Canadian Criminal Justice* 2nd ed. (Toronto: Butterworths, 1994).
- Weiller, P., "The Supreme Court of Canada and the Doctrine of Mens Rea" (1971), 49 Canadian Bar Review 280.

## 6.1.3 Strict and Absolute Liability

**Introduction**

This area of criminal law creates an exception to the general rule that crimes consist of an actus reus and mens rea. For a variety of reasons which are detailed in the *Sault Ste. Marie* case below, there a large number of crimes and quasi-crimes which do not require a mens rea to be present for criminal liability to attach. Before *Sault Ste. Marie*, these types of offences were referred to as either strict or absolute liability offences (or, generally public welfare offences), as opposed to so-called "true crimes" which required a mens rea. Subsequent to the case, public welfare offences were divided into two categories: strict liability offences, which allowed for a defence of due diligence or reasonable care, and absolute liability offences, for which no defences were available once the actus reus was proven. The old category of true crimes remained the same. The rationale for this new categorization of strict versus absolute liability offences is detailed quite clearly in the *Sault Ste. Marie* case. The situation as it existed before 1978 and the unfairness which such gave rise to are illustrated in the judgment of the first case,

*Rex. v. Ping Yuen.* Finally, the important effect of the Charter in this area is seen in the *Burt* and *Wholesale* cases. In addition to the legal questions and the rationales and problems presented by these types of offences, this area of the law is a very good example of the courts explicitly creating new criminal law rather than waiting for Parliament to act.

## Rex v. Ping Yuen
(1921), 36 C.C.C. 269 (Sask. C.A.)

Appeal by defendant from the judgment of Brown C.J.K.B, refusing defendant's application to quash the summary conviction made by the Magistrate under the Sask. Temperance Act, 1917, ch. 23, see 35 (*Cf.* Sask. Temperance Act R.S.S. 1920, ch. 194, sec. 522) The appeal was dismissed, Lamount, J.A. dissenting.

Only the judgment of Turgeon, J.A. is reproduced below.

TURGEON, J.A.: — The appellant is a vendor of soft drinks at Moosomin. On December 6th, 1920, a police officer, acting under a search warrant, found upon his premises three bottles of beer which were shown under analysis to contain more than 1.13% of alcohol per weight. This beer was, therefore, an "intoxicating liquor" within the definition of the Saskatchewan Temperance Act, and an information was laid against the appellant under sec. 35 of that Act (then c. 23 of the Statutes of 1917), which is, in part, as follows:

> 35.(1) In case any person engaged in the business of selling soft drinks or non-intoxicating liquors keeps or has with his stock of such drinks or liquors or on his business premises any liquor as defined by this Act, such person shall be guilty of an offence, etc.

The magistrate found the accused guilty and his memorandum of conviction reads as follows:

> The accused is found guilty. In my opinion the accused did not know that the contents of the bottles contained more than 1.13% absolute alcohol by weight and the fine and cost were paid under protest. Judgment, fine $50.00 and costs $4.50, and in default of payment of the said sums to imprisonment in the common gaol at Regina for a period of 15 days.

It was admitted by the Director of Prosecutions, on the hearing of this appeal, that the accused was innocent of any guilty intention. He bought the bottles from a firm of wholesale grocers and they purported to contain, and he believed that they contained, a beverage not prohibited by the act; that is, beer of less than the prohibited strength.

He could not have ascertained the fact that they contained liquor in excess of the alcoholic strength allowed by law without having each bottle opened and its contents analyzed, a proceeding which, of course, nobody suggests he should have followed. Under these circumstances the question to be decided is: Was the appellant really guilty of an infraction of the Act, in view of the total absence on his part of any wrongful knowledge or intention, of that usual but not invariable element of guilt known as *mens rea*?

A great number of authorities were cited to us by counsel on both sides. The older cases have been reviewed in recent years in decisions given in the various provinces of Canada, and the result is certainly very confusing. I think, however, that it can be said that the well-known rule of *mens rea* applies to infractions of all penal statutes (whether the subject matter of the Statute lies, in Canada, within the jurisdiction of the Dominion Parliament or of the Provincial Legislatures), unless the Statute itself expressly or by necessary implication excludes its application, and provides that the mere doing of the act shall call forth the penalty, regardless of the state of mind of the accused. If I am right in this, it remains to be determined whether the appellant in this case can be said to be guilty of the offence charged against him, when it is admitted that no knowledge, or intention, or neglect to take feasible precautions against mistakes, can be imputed to him.

. . . .

I am of the opinion that the case at Bar is governed by the authority of *Reg. v. Woodrow*. . . the same considerations apply, I think, as in that case, and for the same reasons I am forced to the conclusion that the real intent of the section of the Temperance Act, 1917 (Sask.), under which the charge was laid, is to penalise the mere "keeping" or "having" of intoxicating liquors in a stock of soft drinks which are offered for sale to the public. "Soft drinks" or "non-intoxicating liquors" as referred to in the statute are liquors of various sorts, some alcoholic and some non-alcoholic, but containing in the case of the former such a small proportion of alcohol as not to render them intoxicating. Among this variety is beer, which is the specific article dealt with in this case. When the proportion of alcohol in this beer is greater than that allowed by the Act the beer is deemed to be intoxicating, and the merchant who keeps it in stock is guilty of a breach of the Act. Therefore in the case of beer in this Province, it seems to me to be the true intent of the Act that persons who deal in the article are made responsible for its being of a certain quality, namely, not more than 1.13% of alcoholic content, and when they have a too strong alcoholic article in their possession they are liable to the penalty just as the tobacco dealer is liable under the English Tobacco Act when his tobacco is adulterated. It is true that the accused in *Reg. v. Woodrow* could have avoided trouble by having his tobacco analyzed, and that this precaution was not feasible in this case where the beer was purchased and left in bottles, but I do not think that this provided a sufficient distinction to affect the result.

. . . .

I think, therefore, that the order of the Chief Justice of the King's Bench should be affirmed, and the appeal dismissed with costs.

*Appeal dismissed.*

## R. v. Sault Ste. Marie
(1978), 3 C.R. (3d) 30 (S.C.C.)

The judgment of the court was delivered by

DICKSON J.: — In the present appeal the court is concerned with offences variously referred to as "statutory", "public welfare", "regulatory", "absolute liability", or "strict responsibility", which are not criminal in any real sense but are prohibited in the public interest: *Sherras v. De Rutzen*, [1985] 1 Q.B. 918 (D.C.) Although enforced as penal laws through the utilization of the machinery of the criminal law, the offences are in substance of a civil nature and might well be regarded as a branch of administrative law to which traditional principles of criminal law have but limited application. They relate to such everyday matters as traffic infractions, sales of impure food, violations of liquor laws, and the like. In this appeal we are concerned with pollution.

The doctrine of the guilty mind expressed in terms of intention or recklessness, but not of negligence, is at the foundation of the law of crimes. In the case of true crimes there is a presumption that a person should not be held liable for the wrongfulness of his act if that act is without mens rea: *R. v. Prince* (1875), L.R. 2 C.C.C. 154 (C.C.R.); *R. v. Tolson* (1989), 23 Q.B.D. 168 (C.C.R.); *R. v. Rees*, [1956] S.C.R. 640, 24 C.R. 1, 115 C.C.C. 1, 4 D.L.R. (2d) 406; *Beaver v. R.*, [1957] S.C.R. 531, 26 C.R. 193, 118 C.C.C. 129; *R. v. King*, [1962] S.C.R. 746, 38 C.R. 52, 133 C.C.C. 1, 35 D.L.R. (2d) 386. Blackstone made the point over 200 years ago in words still apt: "to constitute a crime against human law, there must be first a vicious will, and secondly, an unlawful act consequent upon such vicious will": Blackstone's Commentaries, vol 4, p. 21. I would emphasize at the outset that nothing in the discussion which follows is intended to dilute or erode that basic principle.

The appeal raises a preliminary issue as to whether the charge, as laid, is duplicitous and, if so, whether ss. 732(1) and 755(4) [re-en. 1974-75-76, c. 93, s. 94] of the Criminal Code, R.S.C. 1970, c. C-34, preclude the accused city of Sault Ste. Marie from raising the duplicity claim for the first time on appeal. It will be convenient to deal first with the preliminary point and then consider the concept of liability in relation to public welfare offences.

The city of Sault Ste. Marie was charged that it did discharge or cause to be discharged or permitted to be discharged or deposited, materials into Cannon Creek and Root River, or on the shore or bank thereof, or in such place along the side that might impair the quality of the water in Cannon Creek and Root River, between 13th March and 11th September 1972. The charge was laid under s. 32(1) of the Ontario Water Resources Act, R.S.O. 1970, c. 332 [title am. 1972, c. 1, s. 70(1)], which provides so far as relevant, that every municipality or person that discharges or deposits or causes or permits the discharge or deposit of any material of any kind into any water course or on any shore or bank thereof or in any place that may impair the quality of water, is guilty of an offence and, on summary conviction, is liable on first conviction to a fine of not more than $5,000 and on each subsequent conviction of a fine of not more than $10,000 or to imprisonment for a term of not more than one year or to both fine and imprisonment.

Although the facts do not rise above the routine, the proceedings have to date had the anxious consideration of five courts. The city was acquitted in Provincial Court (Criminal Division) but was convicted following a trial de novo on a Crown appeal. A further appeal by the City to the Divisional Court was allowed and the conviction was quashed [30 C.C.C. (2d) at 260]. The Court of Appeal for Ontario on yet another appeal directed a new trial [30 C.C.C. (2d) 257 at 283]. Because of the importance of the legal issues, this court granted leave to the Crown to appeal and leave to the city to cross appeal.

To relate briefly the facts, the city on 18th November 1970 entered into an agreement with Cherokee Disposal and Construction Co. Ltd. for the disposal of all refuse originating in the city. Under the terms of the agreement, Cherokee became obligated to furnish a site and adequate labour, material and equipment. The site selected bordered Cannon Creek which, it would appear, runs into the Root River. The method of disposal adopted is known as the "area" or "continuous slope" method of sanitary land fill, whereby garbage is compacted in layers which are covered each day by natural sand or gravel.

Prior to 1970, the site had been covered with a number of fresh-water springs that flowed into Cannon Creek. Cherokee dumped material to cover and submerge these springs and then placed garbage and wastes over such material. The garbage and wastes in due course formed a high mound sloping steeply toward, and within 20 feet of, the creek. Pollution resulted. Cherokee was convicted of a breach of s. 32(1) of the Ontario Water Resources Act, the section under which the city has been charged. The question now before the court is whether the city is also guilty of an offence under that section.

In dismissing the charge at first instance, the judge found that the city had had nothing to do with the actual disposal operations, that Cherokee was an independent contractor and that its employees were not employees of the city. On the appeal de novo Judge Vannini found the offence to be one of strict liability and he convicted. The Division Court in setting aside the judgment found that the charge was duplicitous. As a secondary point, the Divisional Court also held that the charge required mens rea with respect to causing or permitting a discharge. When the case reached the Court of Appeal that court held that the conviction could not be quashed on the ground of duplicity because there had been no challenge to the information at trial. The Court of Appeal, however, that the charge was one requiring proof of mens rea. A majority of the court (Brooke and Howland JJ.A.) held there was not sufficient evidence to establish mens rea and ordered a new trial. In the view of Lacourciere J.A., dissenting, the inescapable inference to be drawn from the findings of fact of Judge Vannini was the city had known of the potential impairment of waters of Cannon Creek and Root River and had failed to exercise its clear powers of control.

The divers, and diverse, judicial opinions to date on the points under consideration reflect the dubiety in these branches of the law.

. . . .

## THE MENS REA POINT

The distinction between the true criminal offence and the public welfare offence is one of prime importance. Where the offence is criminal, the Crown must establish a mental element, namely, that the accused who committed the prohibited act did so intentionally or recklessly, with knowledge of the facts constituting the offence, or with wilful blindness toward them. Mere negligence is excluded from the concept of the mental element required for conviction. Within the context of a criminal prosecution a person who fails to make such inquiries as a reasonable and prudent person would make, or who fails to know facts he should have known, is innocent in the eyes of the law.

In sharp contrast, "absolute liability" entails conviction on proof merely that the defendant committed the prohibited act constituting the actus reus of the offence. There is no relevant mental element. It is no defence that the accused was entirely without fault. He may be morally innocent in every sense yet be branded as a malefactor and punished as such.

Public welfare offences obviously lie in a field of conflicting values. It is essential for society to maintain, through effective enforcement, high standards of public health and safety. Potential victims of those who carry on latently pernicious activities have a strong claim to consideration. On the other hand, there is a generally held revulsion against punishment of the morally innocent.

Public welfare offences evolved in mid-19th century Britain (*R. v. Woodrow* (1846), 15 M. & W. 404, 153 E.R. 907, and *R. v. Stephens* (1986), L.R. 1 Q.B. 702) as a means of doing away with the requirement of mens rea for petty police offences. The concept was a judicial creation, founded on expediency. That concept is now firmly embedded in the concrete of Anglo-American and Canadian jurisprudence, its importance heightened by the ever-increasing complexities of modern society.

Various arguments are advanced in justification of absolute liability in public welfare offences. Two predominate. Firstly, it is argued that the protection of social interests requires a high standard of care and attention on the part of those who follow certain pursuits and such persons are more likely to be stimulated to maintain those standards if they know that ignorance or mistake will not excuse them. The removal of any possible loophole acts, it is said, as an incentive to take precautionary measures beyond what would otherwise be taken in order that mistakes and mishaps be avoided. The second main argument is one based on administrative efficiency. Having regard to both the difficulty of proving mental culpability and the number of petty cases which daily come before the courts, proof of fault is just too great a burden in time and money to place upon the prosecution. To require proof of each person's individual intent would allow almost every violator to escape. This, together with the glut of work entailed in proving mens rea in every case, would clutter the docket and impede adequate enforcement as virtually to nullify the regulatory statutes. In short, absolute liability, it is contended, is the most efficient and effective way of ensuring compliance with minor regulatory legislation and the social ends to be achieved are of such importance as to override the unfortunate by-product of punishing those who may be free of moral turpitude. In further justification, it is urged that slight penalties are usually imposed and that conviction for breach of a public welfare offence does not carry the stigma associated with conviction for a criminal offence.

Arguments of greater force are advanced against absolute liability. The most telling is that it violates fundamental principles of penal liability. It also rests upon assumptions which have not been, and cannot be, empirically established. There is no evidence that a higher standard of care results from absolute liability. If a person is already taking every reasonable precautionary measure, is he likely to take additional measures, knowing that however much care he takes it will not serve as a defence in the event of a breach? If he has exercised care and skill, will conviction have a deterrent effect upon him or others? Will the injustice of conviction lead to cynicism and disrespect for the law, on his part and on the part of others? These are among the questions asked. The argument that no stigma attaches does not withstand analysis, for the accused will have suffered loss of time, legal costs, exposure to the processes of the criminal law at trial and, however one may downplay it, the opprobrium of conviction. It is not sufficient to say that the public interest is engaged and, therefore, liability may be imposed without fault. In serious crimes, the public interest is involved and mens rea must be proven. The administrative argument has little force. In sentencing, evidence of due diligence is admissible and therefore the evidence might just as well be heard when considering guilt. Additionally, it may be noted that s. 198 of the Highway Traffic Act of Alberta, R.S.A. 1970, c. 169, provides that upon a person being charged with an offence under this Act, if the judge trying the case is of the opinion that the offence (a) was committed wholly by accident or misadventure and without negligence and (b) could not by the exercise of reasonable care or precaution have been avoided, the judge may dismiss the case. See also s. 230(2) [am. 1976, c. 62, s. 48] of the Manitoba Highway Traffic Act, R.S.M. 1970, c. H60, which has a similar effect. In these instances at least, the legislature has indicated that administrative efficiency does not foreclose inquiry as to fault. It is also worthy of note that historically the penalty for breach of statutes enacted for the regulation of individual conduct in the interests of health and safety was minor — $20 or $25; today, it may amount to thousands of dollars and entail the possibility of imprisonment for a second conviction. The present case is an example.

Public welfare offences involve a shift of emphasis from the protection of individual interests to the protection of public and social interests: see Sayre, "Public Welfare Offences" (1933), 33 Colum, L. Rev. 55; Hall, "Principles of Criminal Law", [1947] Ch. 13; Perkins, "The Civil Offence" 91952), 100 U. of Pa. L. Rev. 832; Jobson, "Far From Clear" (1975-76), 18 Cr. L.Q. 294. The unfortunate tendency in many past cases has been to see the choice as between two stark alternatives: (i) full mens rea; or (ii) absolute liability. In respect of public welfare offences (within which category pollution offences fall) where full mens rea is not required, absolute liability has often been imposed. English jurisprudence has consistently maintained this dichotomy: see 2 Hals. (4th), para. 18, Criminal Law, Evidence and Procedure. There has, however, been an attempt in Australia, in many Canadian courts, and indeed in England to seek a middle position, fulfilling the goals of public welfare offences while still not punishing the entirely blameless. There is an increasing and impressive stream of authority which holds that where an offence does not require full mens rea, it is nevertheless a good defence for the defendant to prove that he was not negligent.

Dr. Glanville Williams has written: "There is a half-way house between *mens rea* and strict responsibility which has not yet been properly utilized, and that is responsibility for negligence": Criminal Law, The General Part, 2nd ed., p. 262. Morris and Howard in Studies in Criminal Law (1964), p. 200, suggest that strick responsibility might with advantage be replaced by a doctrine of responsibility for negligence strengthened by a shift in the burden of proof. The defendant would be allowed to exculpate himself by proving affirmatively that he was not negligent.

. . . .

There have been several cases in Ontario which open the way to acceptance of a defence of due diligence. In *R. v. McIver*, [1965] 2 O.R. 475, 45 C.R. 401, [1965] 4 C.C.C. 182, the Court of Appeal held that the offence charged, namely, careless driving, was one of strict liability but that it was open to an accused to show that he had a reasonable belief in facts which, if true, would have rendered the act innocent. MacKay J.A., who wrote for the court, relied upon *Sherras v. De Rutzen*, supra, *Proudman v. Dayman*, supra, *Maher v. Musson* (1934) 52 C.L.R. 100, and *R. v. Patterson*, [1962] 2 Q.B. 429, 46 Cr. App. R. 106, [1962] 1 All E.R. 340 (C.C.A.), in availing an accused the opportunity of explanation in the case of statutory offences that do not by their terms require proof of intent.

. . . .

We have the situation therefore in which many courts of this country, at all levels, dealing with public welfare offences favour: (1) *not* requiring the Crown to prove mens rea; (2) rejecting the notion that liability inexorably follows upon mere proof of the actus reus, excluding any possible defence. The courts are following the lead set in Australia many years ago and tentatively broached by several English courts in recent years.

It may be suggested that the introduction of a defence based on due diligence and the shifting of the burden of proof might better be implemented by legislative act. In answer, it should be recalled that both the concept of absolute liability and the creation of a jural category of public welfare offences are the product of the judiciary and not of the legislature. The development to date of this defence, in the numerous decisions I have referred to of courts in this country as well as in Australia and New Zealand, has also been the work of judges. The present case offers the opportunity of consolidating and clarifying the doctrine.

The correct approach, in my opinion, is to relieve the Crown of the burden of proving mens rea, having regard to *Pierce Fisheries* and to the virtual impossibility in most regulatory cases of proving wrongful intention. In a normal case, the accused alone will have knowledge of what he has done to avoid the breach and it is not improper to expect him to come forward with the evidence of due diligence. This is particularly so when it is alleged, for example, that pollution was caused by the activities of a large and complex corporation. Equally, there is nothing wrong with rejecting absolute liability and admitting the defence of reasonable care.

In this doctrine it is not up to the prosecution to prove negligence. Instead, it is open to the defendant to prove that all due care has been taken. This burden falls upon the defendant as he is the only one who will generally have the means of proof. This would not seem unfair as the alternative is absolute liability which denies an accused any defence whatsoever. While the prosecution must prove beyond a reasonable doubt that the defendant committed the prohibited act, the defendant must only establish on the balance of probabilities that he has a defence of reasonable care.

I conclude, for the reasons which I have sought to express, that there are compelling grounds for the recognition of three categories of offences rather than the traditional two:

1. Offences in which mens rea, consisting of some positive state of mind such as intent, knowledge, or recklessness, must be proved by the prosecution either as an inference from the nature of the act committed or by additional evidence.
2. Offences in which there is no necessity for the prosecution to prove the existence of mens rea; the doing of the prohibited act prima facie imports the offence, leaving it open to the accused to avoid liability by proving that he took all reasonable care. This involves consideration of what a reasonable man would have done in the circumstances. The defence will be available if the accused reasonably believed in a mistaken set of facts which, if true, would render the act

or omission innocent, or if he took all reasonable steps to avoid the particular event. These offences may properly be called offences of strict liability. Estey C.J.H.C. so referred to them in *Hickey's* case.
3. Offences of absolute liability where it is not open to the accused to exculpate himself by showing that he was free of fault.

Offences which are criminal in the true sense fall in the first category. Public welfare offences would prima facie be in the second category. They are not subject to the presumption of full mens rea. An offence of this type would fall in the first category only if such words as "wilfully", "with intent", "knowingly" or "intentionally" are contained in the statutory provision creating the offence. On the other hand, the principle that punishment should in general not be inflicted on those without fault applies. Offences of absolute liability would be those in respect of which the legislature had made it clear that guilt would follow proof merely of the proscribed act. The overall regulatory pattern adopted by the legislature, the subject matter of the legislation, the importance of the penalty and the precision of the language used will be primary considerations in determining whether the offence falls into the third category.

## ONTARIO WATER RESOURCES ACT, s. 32(1)

Turning to the subject matter of s. 32(1) — the prevention of pollution of lakes, rivers and streams — it is patent that this is of great public concern. Pollution has always been unlawful and, in itself, a nuisance: *Groat v. Edmonton*, [1928] S.C.R. 522, [1928] 3 D.L.R. 725. A riparian owner has an inherent right to have a stream of water "come to him in its natural state, in flow, quantity and quality": *Chasemore v. Richards* (1859), 7 H.L. Cas. 349 at 382, 11 E.R. 140. Natural streams which formerly afforded "pure and healthy" water for drinking or swimming purposes become little more than cesspools when riparian factory owners and municipal corporations discharge into them filth of all descriptions. Pollution offences are undoubtedly public welfare offences enacted in the interests of public health. There is thus no presumption of a full mens rea.

There is another reason, however, why this offence is not subject to a presumption of mens rea. The presumption applies only to offences which are "criminal in the true sense", as Ritchie J. said in *R. v. Pierce Fisheries*, supra, at p. 278. The Ontario Water Resources Act is a provincial statute. If it is valid provincial legislation (and no suggestions was made to the contrary), then it cannot possibly create an offence which is criminal in the true sense.

. . . .

The Divisional Court of Ontario relied on these latter authorities in concluding that s. 32(1) created a mens rea offence.

. . . .

One comment on the defence of reasonable care in this context should be added. Since the issue is whether the defendant is guilty of an offence, the doctrine of respondeat superior has no application. The due diligence which must be established is that of the accused alone. Where an employer is charged in respect of an act committed by an employee acting in the course of employment, the question will be whether the act took place without the accused's direction or approval, thus negating wilful involvement of the accused, and whether the accused exercised all reasonable care by establishing a proper system to prevent commission of the offence and by taking reasonable steps to ensure the effective operation of the system. The availability of the defence to a corporation will depend on whether such due diligence was taken by those who are the directing mind and will of the corporation, whose acts are therefore in law the acts of the corporation itself. For a useful discussion of this matter in the context of a statutory defence of due diligence see *Tesco Supermarkets v. Nattrass*, [1972] A.C. 153, [1971] 2 All E.R. 127 (H.L.).

The majority of the Ontario Court of Appeal directed a new trial as, in the opinion of that court, the findings of the trial judge were not sufficient to establish actual knowledge on the part of the city. I share the view that there should be a new trial, but for a different reason. The city did not lead evidence directed to a defence of due diligence, nor did the trial judge address himself to the availability of such a defence. In these circumstances, it would not be fair for this court to determine upon findings of fact directed toward other ends, whether the city was without fault.

I would dismiss the appeal and direct a new trial. I would dismiss the cross-appeal. There should be no costs.

*Appeal and cross-appeal dismissed.*

## Regina v. Burt
(1988), 38 C.C.C. (3d) 299 (Sask. C.A.)

Appeal by the Crown from the dismissal of its appeal by Gerein J., 21 C.C.C. (3d) 138, 47 C.R. (3d) 49, [1985] 5 W.W.R. 545, 40 Sask. R. 214, 35 M.V.R. 244, from the accused's acquittal on a charge contrary to ss. 141 and 253 of the *Vehicles Act (Sask.)*.

Only the judgment of Wakeling is reproduced below.

WAKELING J.A.: — This appeal places in question whether s. 253 of the *Vehicles Act*, R.S.S. 1978, c. V-3 (the Act), offends s. 7 of the *Canadian Charter of Rights and Freedoms* when it seeks to hold an owner of a vehicle responsible for the actions of the driver of that vehicle.

The facts indicated the respondent is the owner of a vehicle which was being driven, with his permission, by another in such a manner as to create an excessive noise which prompted the laying of a charge under s. 141 of the Act. The identity of the driver was not known, so the charge was laid against the respondent as the owner of the vehicle by virtue of the application of s. 253 of the Act which makes an owner liable for the action of the driver when such actions are in violation of the Act. Section 253 reads:

> **253.** The owner of a motor vehicle, tractor or trailer, other than a public service vehicle, is liable for violation of any provision of this Act in connection with the operation of the motor vehicle, tractor or trailer, unless he proves to the satisfaction of the provincial magistrate or justice of the peace trying the case that at the time of the offence the vehicle, tractor or trailer was not being operated by him, nor by any other person with his consent, express or implied.

The trial judge dismissed the charge on the bass that s. 253 offends s. 7 of the Charter. On appeal, Gerein J. upheld the decision of the trial judge and dismissed the appeal [21 C.C.C. (3d) 138, 47 C.R. (3d) 49, [1985] 5 W.W.R. 545].

The sections of the Charter in question are

> 1. The *Canadian Charter of Rights and Freedoms* guarantees the rights and freedoms set out in it subject only to such reasonable limits prescribed by law as can be demonstrably justified in a free and democratic society.
>
> 7. Everyone has the right to life, liberty and security of the person and the right not to be deprived thereof, except in accordance with the principles of fundamental justice.

It is obvious that s. 253 has created a situation where a person can be convicted of a driving offence under the Act without having anything to do with the driving of the vehicle. The appellant's position is that the establishment of such an offence by mere ownership has the effect of eliminating the need for *mens rea* which is so fundamental a concept in law that its absence constitutes a breach of the principles of fundamental justice.

There have been several cases dealing with the interpretation and application of s. 7 of the Charter with somewhat varied views expressed and results obtained. However, since the argument presented on this appeal, the Supreme Court decision in Reference re s. 94(2) of Motor Vehicle Act (the *B.C. Motor Reference* Case) (1985), 23 C.C.C. (3d) 289, 24 D.L.R. (4th) 536, [1985] 2 S.C.R. 486, has become available, and it has gone far to provide guidance on the interpretation to be given s. 7 of the Charter.

The *B.C. Motor Reference* case dealt with a law which provided that a person who drove a motor vehicle while prohibited from driving or where his licence had been suspended, was guilty of an offence and required to go to prison even though he might not have known he had been prohibited from driving or that his licence had been suspended. It was an absolute liability offence involving a mandatory sentence of imprisonment.

The basic concepts which can be distilled from the Supreme Court judgment include:

1. That s. 7 enshrines substantive and not merely procedural rights.
2. That the "principles of fundamental justice" referred to in the section do not constitute a protected right, but a qualifier to the protected right not to be deprived of "life, liberty and security of the person"; their function is to set the parameters of that right.
3. That is not only permissible but appropriate to review the legislation which is being challenged in order to determine whether the legislation offends against the rights established by s. 7.
4. The phrase, "principles of fundamental justice", does not have the same meaning as natural justice. It has a broader meaning that includes an element of substantive right in addition to the concept of procedural fairness which is contemplated in the application of the words "natural justice".
5. That absolute liability in the penal law is contrary to principles of fundamental justice and an absolute liability offence violates s. 7 only if and to the extent it

has the potential of depriving one of life, liberty or security of the person (*i.e.*, the penalty of imprisonment is an option open to the trial judge).
6. Administrative expediency will seldom serve as reason for the application of s. 1 of the Charter to save a violation of s. 7.

The question raised by this appeal requires a determination of the application of the above concepts to the facts in this case.

The legislation under review clearly intends that a person may be convicted of an offence even though that person has done nothing wrong. There is no reason to distinguish the situation here where the owner does not know how his vehicle is being operated, yet is responsible for the violations of the driver, from one where an owner is unaware that he has been prohibited from driving or that his licence has been cancelled, yet is guilty of operating the vehicle against the law.

In the *B.C. Motor Reference* case, the point was clearly made that the concept of imprisonment for an absolute liability offence was unacceptable as being contrary to the long-held view against imprisonment of the morally innocent. It then goes further to say that not every absolute liability offence is objectionable but it is if it violates the right to liberty given by s. 7 and that right is violated if the trial judge has the option of imposing imprisonment as a penalty for the offence. Lamer J., dealing with the above, had the following to say at p. 311 C.C.C., p. 515 S.C.R.:

> In my view it is because absolute liability offends the principles of fundamental justice that this Court created presumptions against Legislatures having intended to enact offences of a regulatory nature falling within that category. This is not say, however, and to that extent I am in agreement with the Court of Appeal, that, as a result, absolute liability *per se* offends s. 7 of the Charter.
> A law enacting an absolute liability offence will violate s. 7 of the Charter only if and to the extent that it has the potential of depriving of life, liberty, or security of the person.
> Obviously imprisonment (including probation orders) deprives persons of their liberty. An offence has that potential as of the moment it is open to the judge to impose imprisonment. There is no need that imprisonment, as in s. 94(2), be made mandatory.

All of this tends to narrow down the issue in this case rather considerably. If the trial judge was required to impose a sentence of imprisonment or had the option for such a sentence, it seems clear this appeal cannot succeed. The question then remaining is whether in this case, where imprisonment could only occur as the result of the non-payment of a fine, the appeal must likewise fail.

With reference to the application of s. 7, is there a basis to distinguish a sentence which is restricted to payment of a fine, with imprisonment for non-payment, from one where the sentence is for imprisonment in the first instance? To the person in prison, it is of little consequence to have it said the original sentence only required payment of a fine and he is in jail because of his failure to do so. The prisoner will surely be convinced he is in jail because he was found guilty of the original offence and will be inclined to accuse judges and lawyers who say otherwise of exercising their legal skills to distinguish where no real difference exists.

If the penalty of imprisonment or the prospect of imprisonment for the commission of an absolute liability offence is offensive to the principles of fundamental justice referred to in s. 7, it seems logical to conclude that imprisonment for failure to pay a fine for the same offence is also offensive. To conclude otherwise is to draw rather narrow distinctions which the Supreme Court has so far been careful not to do, no doubt for the reason that it prefers to take a broader more purposive approach to the interpretation of the Charter than it has done to other instruments.

An interesting and useful article has recently been published entitled "Imprisonment in Default and Fundamental Justice", 28 crim. L.Q. p. 251 (1985-86), in which the question of fines and resultant imprisonment for non-payment is discussed. The author seems to generally agree with the views already expressed as the following extract would indicate [p. 264]:

> The courts have already ruled that it is contrary to fundamental justice for the legislature to impose mandatory imprisonment in connection with an offence of absolute liability with no opportunity to explain. It is no less offensive to settled notions of decency to tolerate an administrative practice of imprisonment, not upon proof of some positive act such as driving while licence suspended, but merely upon the happenstance of financial incapacity, a condition that goes to status, not to wilful act or omission.

Having reached the conclusion that this case involves an absolute liability offence and that the prospect for imprisonment for non-payment of a fine brings it within the ambit of the principles drawn from the recent *B.C. Motor Reference* case, it follows that s. 7 of the Charter has been violated.

It is the necessary to consider the possible application of s. 1 of the Charter to determine if the violation of the right might be acceptable by reason that the legislation constitutes "a reasonable limit(s) prescribed by law as can be demonstrably justified in a free and democratic society".

One can readily conclude that the Crown perceives a social benefit in being able to hold a registered owner responsible for the actions of the driver of his vehicle in certain instances such as where identity of the driver is otherwise unavailable. It makes it possible to assess liability for an offence where society's interests are perceived to require some sanction, and makes vehicle owners more aware of the need to be sure their vehicle is in the hands of a responsible driver. If this benefit is categorized as an administrative expediency, then it is useful to consider the following comment of Lamer J. from the *B.C. Motor Reference* case at p. 313 C.C.C., p. 518 S.C.R.:

> Administrative expediency, absolute liability's main supportive argument, will undoubtedly under s. 1 be invoked and occasionally succeed. Indeed, administrative expediency certainly has its place in administrative law. But when administrative law chooses to call in aid imprisonment through penal law, indeed sometimes criminal law and the added stigma attached to a conviction, exceptional, in my view, will be the case where the liberty or even the security of the person guaranteed under s. 7 should be sacrificed to administrative expediency, successfully come to the rescue of an otherwise violation of s. 7 but only in cases arising out of exceptional conditions, such as natural disasters, the outbreak of war, epidemics, and the like.

The recent decision of *R. v. Oakes* (1986), 24 C.C.C. (3d) 321, 26 D.L.R. (4th) 200, 65 N.R. 87, has given further guidance on the approach to be taken to the application of s. 1 of the Charter. It has indicated [at p. 348 C.C.C., paraphrase] that the party who alleges its application has the obligation to establish:

> (a) the measures responsible for a limit in a Charter right must be of "sufficient importance to warrant overriding a constitutionally protected right or freedom": *R. v. Big M Drug Mart Ltd., supra*, at p. 430 C.C.C., p 366 D.L.R., p. 352 S.C.R.;

(b) and where (a) above has been established, the means chosen are reasonably and demonstrably justified.

The Crown was prepared to stand on the justification for this legislation being self-evident given the object and purpose of the Act and the existence of legislation of a similar nature in other provinces. While there is perhaps more than administrative expediency here, the Crown falls short of meeting the burden which is upon it to justify the violation of the Charter right involved in this case as a result of the application of either of the above-mentioned tests.

For the reasons mentioned, the appeal is dismissed.

*Appeal dismissed.*

## Wholesale Travel Group Inc. v. The Queen
(1991), 67 C.C.C. (3d) 193 (S.C.C.)

[Excerpts from the judgement of Cory are reproduced below.]

CORY J.: — The fundamental issue raised on this appeal is whether regulatory statutes which impose a regime of strict liability for breach of their provisions infringe ss. 7 and 11(*d*) of the *Canadian Charter of Rights and Freedoms*.

*Factual background and pertinent legislation*

The Wholesale Travel Group Inc. ("Wholesale Travel") was charged with five counts of false or misleading advertising contrary to s. 36(1)(*a*) of the *Competition Act*, R.S.C. 1970, c. C-23. The charges were laid after Wholesale Travel advertised vacation packages at "wholesale prices" while at the same time charging consumers a price higher than the cost incurred by the company in supplying those vacation packages. The matter proceeded to trial in Provincial Court. Before any evidence was heard, Wholesale Travel brought a motion challenging the validity of ss. 36(1) and 37.3(2) of the *Competition Act* on the basis that those sections violate ss. 7 and 11(*d*) of the *Canadian Charter of Rights and Freedoms* and are, therefore, of no force and effect.

The offence of misleading advertising is described in s. 36(1)(*a*) of the *Competition Act*. Although the Act has since been amended, the applicable provisions remain unchanged. I shall, therefore, refer to the old section numbers under which the appellant was charged. Section 36(1)(*a*) (now s. 52(1)(*a*)) reads as follows:

36(1) No person shall, for the purpose of promoting, directly or indirectly, the supply or use of a product or for the purpose of promoting, directly or indirectly, any business interest, by any means whatever,

   (*a*) make a representation to the public that is false or misleading in a material respect;

Subsection (5) prescribes the penalties available upon conviction. It states:

36(5) Any person who violates subsection (1) is guilty of an offence and is liable

   (*a*) on conviction on indictment, to a fine in the discretion of the court and to imprisonment for five years to both; or
   (*b*) on summary conviction, to a fine of twenty-five thousand dollars or to imprisonment for one year or to both.

The Act sets forth a statutory defence to the charge. Section 37.3(2) (now s. 60(2)) provides:

> 37.3(2) No person shall be convicted of an offence under section 36 or 36.1, if he establishes that
>
> (a) the act or omission giving rise to the offence with which he is charged was the result of error;
> (b) he took reasonable precautions and exercised due diligence to prevent the occurrence of such error;
> (c) he, or another person, took reasonable measures to bring the error to the attention of the class of persons likely to have been reached by the representation or testimonial; and
> (d) the measures referred to in paragraph (c), except where the representation or testimonial related to a security, were taken forthwith after the representation was made or the testimonial published.

It is important to note that all four conditions must be met before the statutory defence can prevail.

Wholesale Travel contends that the statutory scheme and, in particular, the combined operation of the offence prescribed in s. 36(1)(a) and the statutory defence set forth in s. 37.3(2), infringes ss. 7 and 11(d) of the Charter. . . .

*Issues*

On July 26, 1990, the Chief Justice stated the following constitutional questions:

1. Does s. 37.3(2) of the *Competition Act*, R.S.C. 1970, c. C-23, as amended, in whole or in part violate ss. 7 or 11(d) of the *Canadian Charter of Rights and Freedoms*?
2. Does s. 36(1)(a) of the *Competition Act*, in and of itself or when read in combination with s. 37.3(2) of the *Competition Act*, violate ss. 7 or 11(d) of the *Charter*?
3. If either question 1 or 2 is answered in the affirmative, is (are) the impugned provision(s) saved by s. 1 of the *Charter*?

I. *Regulatory offences and strict liability*

A. *The distinction between crimes and regulatory offences*

The common law has long acknowledged a distinction between truly criminal conduct and conduct, otherwise lawful, which is prohibited in the public interest. Earlier, the designations *mala in se* and *mala prohibita* were utilized; today prohibited acts are generally classified as either crimes or regulatory offences.

While some regulatory legislation such as that pertaining to the content of food and drink dates back to the Middle Ages, the number and significance of regulatory offences increased greatly with the onset of the Industrial Revolution. Unfettered industrialization had led to abuses. Regulations were, therefore, enacted to protect the vulnerable — particularly the children, men and women who laboured long hours in dangerous and unhealthy surroundings. Without these regulations many would have died. It later became necessary to regulate the manufactured products themselves and, still later, the discharge of effluent resulting from the manufacturing process. There is no doubt that regulatory offences were originally and still are designed to protect those who are unable to protect themselves. . . .

The distinction between true crimes and regulatory offences was recognized in Canadian law prior to the adoption of the Charter. . . .

The *Sault Ste. Marie* case recognized strict liability as a middle ground between full *mens rea* and absolute liability. Where the offence is one of strict liability, the Crown is required to prove neither *mens rea* nor negligence; conviction may follow merely upon proof beyond a reasonable doubt of the proscribed act. However, it is open to the defendant to avoid liability by proving on a balance of probabilities that all due care was taken. This is the hallmark of the strict liability offence: the defence of due diligence.

Thus, *Sault Ste. Marie* not only affirmed the distinction between regulatory and criminal offences, but also subdivided regulatory offences into categories of strict and absolute liability. The new category of strict liability represented a compromise which acknowledged the importance and essential objectives of regulatory offences but at the same time sought to mitigate the harshness of absolute liability which was found, at p. 363 C.C.C., p. 171 D.L.R., to "violate" "fundamental principles of penal liability".

*The rationale for the distinction*

It has always been taught that there is a rational basis for distinguishing between crimes and regulatory offences. Acts or actions are criminal when they constitute conduct that is, in itself, so abhorrent to the basic values of human society that it ought to be prohibited completely. Murder, sexual assault, fraud, robbery and theft are all so repugnant to society that they are universally recognized as crimes. At the same time, some conduct is prohibited, not because it is inherently wrongful, but because unregulated activity would result in dangerous conditions being imposed upon members of society, especially those who are particularly vulnerable.

The objective of regulatory legislation is to protect the public or broad segments of the public (such as employees, consumers and motorists, to name but a few) from the potentially adverse effects of otherwise lawful activity. Regulatory legislation involves a shift of emphasis from the protection of individual interests and the deterrence and punishment of acts involving moral fault to the protection of public and societal interests. While criminal offences are usually designed to condemn and punish past, inherently wrongful conduct, regulatory measures are generally directed to the prevention of future harm through the enforcement of minimum standards of conduct and care.

It follows that regulatory offences and crimes embody different concepts of fault. Since regulatory offences are directed primarily not to conduct itself but to the consequences of conduct, conviction of a regulatory offence may be thought to import a significantly lesser degree of culpability than conviction of a true crime. The concept of fault in regulatory offences is based upon a reasonable care standard and, as such, does not imply moral blameworthiness in the same manner as criminal fault. Conviction for breach of a regulatory offence suggests nothing more than that the defendant has failed to meet a prescribed standard of care.

That is the theory but, like all theories, its application is difficult. For example, is the single mother who steals a loaf of bread to sustain her family more blameworthy than the employer who, through negligence, breaches regulations and thereby exposes his employees to dangerous working conditions, or the manufacturer who, as a result of negligence, sells dangerous products or pollutes the air and waters by its plant? At this stage it is sufficient to bear in mind that those who breach regulations may inflict serious harm on large segments of society. Therefore, the characterization of an offence as regulatory should not be thought to make light of either the potential harm to the vulnerable or the responsibility of those subject to regulation to ensure that the proscribed harm does not occur. It should also be remembered that, as social values change, the degree of moral blameworthiness attaching to certain conduct may change as well.

Nevertheless there remains, in my view, a sound basis for distinguishing between regulatory and criminal offences. The distinction has concrete theoretical and practical underpinnings and has proven to be a necessary and workable concept in our law....

### B. *The fundamental importance of regulatory offences in Canadian society*

Regulatory measures are the primary mechanisms employed by governments in Canada to implement public policy objectives. What is ultimately at stake in this appeal is the ability of federal and provincial governments to pursue social ends through the enactment and enforcement of public welfare legislation.

Some indication of the prevalence of regulatory offences in Canada is provided by a 1974 estimate by the Law Reform Commission of Canada. The commission estimated that there were, at that time, approximately 20,000 regulatory offences in an average province, plus an additional 20,000 regulatory offences at the federal level. By 1983, the commission's estimate of the federal total had reached 97,000. There is every reason to believe that the number of public welfare offences at both levels of government has continued to increase.

Statistics such as these make it obvious that the government policy in Canada is pursued principally through regulation. It is through regulatory legislation that the community seeks to implement its larger objectives and to govern itself and the conduct of its members. The ability of the government effectively to regulate potentially harmful conduct must be maintained.

It is difficult to think of an aspect of our lives that is not regulated for our benefit and for the protection of society as a whole. From cradle to grave, we are protected by regulations; they apply to the doctors attending our entry into this world and to the morticians present at our departure. Every day, from waking to sleeping, we profit from regulatory measures which we often take for granted. On rising, we use various forms of energy whose safe distribution and use are governed by regulation. The trains, buses and other vehicles that get us to work are regulated for our safety. The food we eat and the beverages we drink are subject to regulation for the protection of our health.

In short, regulation is absolutely essential for our protection and wellbeing as individuals, and for the effective functioning of society. It is properly present throughout our lives. The more complex the activity, the greater the need for and the greater our reliance upon regulation and its enforcement. For example, most people would have no idea what regulations are required for air transport or how they should be enforced. Of necessity, society relies on government regulation for its safety.

II. *The offence in the present case*

*Competition legislation generally*

The offence of misleading advertising with which Wholesale Travel is charged is found in the *Competition Act* (the "Act"). This Act, like its predecessor, the *Combines Investigation Act* is aimed at regulating unacceptable business activity. . . .

The nature and purpose of the Act was considered in greater detail in *Thomson Newspapers, supra*. LaForest J. pointed out that the Act is aimed at regulating the economy and business with a view to preserving competitive conditions which are crucial to the operation of a free market economy. . . .

*The offence of false or misleading advertising*

Is the offence of false or misleading advertising regulatory in nature? It seems to me that the fact that the provision is located within a comprehensive regulatory framework would ordinarily be sufficient to demonstrate its regulatory nature. Several other considerations point to the same conclusion.

The offence of misleading advertising has existed in Canada since 1914. It is not without significance that it was, in 1969, transferred from the *Criminal Code* to the *Combines Investigation Act*, a step which confirms the regulatory nature of the offence. The provision was amended in 1975 to provide for a defence of due diligence, converting the offence from absolute to strict liability.

It is true that the availability of imprisonment as a sanction for breach of a statute might be taken to indicate that the provision is criminal in nature. However, this fact is not itself dispositive of the character of an offence. Rather, one must consider the conduct addressed by the legislation and the purposes for which such conduct is regulated. . . .

The appellant has argued that conviction for the offence of false advertising carries a stigma of dishonesty, with the inference that the accused falsely advertised for the purposes of obtaining economic advantage. It is said that nothing could be more damaging to a business that the implication that it has made dishonest representations. In my view, however, the offence does not focus on dishonesty but rather on the harmful consequences of otherwise lawful conduct. Conviction suggests only that the defendant has made a representation to the public which was in fact misleading and that the defendant was unable to establish the exercise of due diligence in preventing the error. This connotes a fault element of negligence rather than one involving moral turpitude. Thus, any stigma that might flow from a conviction is very considerably diminished.

In summary, the offence of false advertising possesses the essential characteristics which distinguish regulatory offences from those which are truly criminal. Accordingly, it should be considered to be a regulatory offence rather than a crime in the ordinary sense.

## III. *A contextual approach to Charter interpretation*

### A. *The importance of considering Charter rights in context*

. . .

It is now clear that the Charter is to be interpreted in light of the context in which the claim arises. Context is relevant both with respect to the delineation of the meaning and scope of Charter rights, as well as to the determination of the balance to be struck between individual rights and the interests of society.

A contextual approach is particularly appropriate in the present case to take account of the regulatory nature of the offence and its place within a larger scheme of public welfare legislation. This approach requires that the rights asserted by the appellant be considered in light of the regulatory context in which the claim is situated, acknowledging that a Charter right may have different scope and implications in a regulatory context than in a truly criminal one.

Under the contextual approach, constitutional standards developed in the criminal context cannot be applied automatically to regulatory offences. Rather, the content of the Charter right must be determined only after an examination of all relevant factors and in light of the essential differences between the two classes of prohibited activity.
. . .

The contextual approach first requires that the appellant's claim be considered and weighed in light of the realities of a modern industrial society, where the regulation of innumerable activities is essential for the benefit of all. It is vital that the fundamentally important role of regulatory legislation in the protection of individuals and groups in Canadian society today be recognized and accepted. Canadians rely on and expect their governments to regulate and control activities which may be dangerous to others.
. . .

The scale and importance of public welfare legislation in Canada is such that a contextual approach must be taken to the issues raised in this appeal.

### B. *The basis for the differential treatment of regulatory offences*

In the present case, the contextual approach requires that regulatory and criminal offences be treated differently for the purposes of Charter review. Before proceeding to the substantive analysis, however, it is necessary to consider the justifications for differential treatment. They are two-fold: the first relates to the distinctive nature of regulatory activity, while the second acknowledges the fundamental need to protect the vulnerable through regulatory legislation.

#### 1. *The licensing justification*

Those who argue against differential treatment for regulatory offences assert that there is no valid reason to distinguish between the criminal and regulatory accused. Each, it is said, is entitled in law to the same procedural and substantive protections. This view assumes equality of position between criminal and regulatory defendants; that is to say, it assumes that each starts out from a position of equal knowledge, volition and "innocence". The argument against differential treatment further suggests that differentiating between the regulatory and criminal defendants implies the subordination and sacrifice of the regulatory accused to the interests of the community at large. Such a position, it is argued, contravenes our basic concern for individual dignity and our fundamental belief in the importance of the individual. It is these assumptions which the licensing justification challenges.

Criminal law is rooted in the concepts of individual autonomy and free will and the corallary that each individual is responsible for his or her conduct. It assumes that all persons are free actors, at liberty to choose how to regulate their own actions in relation to others. The criminal law fixes the outer limits of acceptable conduct, constraining individual freedom to a limited degree in order to preserve the freedom of others. Thus, the basis of criminal responsibility is that the accused person has made a deliberate and conscious choice to engage in activity prohibited by the *Criminal Code*. The accused person who is convicted of an offence will be held responsible for his or her actions, with the result that the opprobrium of society will attach to those acts and any punishment imposed will be considered to be deserved.

The licensing argument is directed to this question of choice. Thus, while in the criminal context, the essential question to be determined is whether the accused has made the choice to act in the manner alleged in the indictment, the regulated defendant is, by virtue of the licensing argument, assumed to have made the choice to engage in the regulated activity. The question then becomes not whether the defendant chose to enter the regulated sphere but whether, having done so, the defendant has fulfilled the responsibilities attending that decision. . . .

The licensing concept rests on the view that those who choose to participate in regulated activities have, in doing so, placed themselves in a responsible relationship to the public generally and must accept the consequences of that responsibility. Therefore, it is said, those who engage in regulated activity should, as part of the burden of responsible conduct attending participation in the regulated field, be deemed to have accepted certain terms and conditions applicable to those who act within the regulated sphere. Foremost among these implied terms is an undertaking that the conduct of the regulated actor will comply with and maintain a certain minimum standard of care.

The licensing justification is based not only on the idea of a conscious choice being made to enter a regulated field but also on the concept of control. The concept is that those persons who enter a regulated field are in the best position to control the harm which may result, and that they should, therefore, be held responsible for it. . . .

The licensing justification may not apply in all circumstances to all offenders. That is, there are some cases in which the licensing argument may not apply so as to permit the imputation to an accused of choice, knowledge and implied acceptance of regulatory terms and conditions. This may occur, for instance, where the nature of the regulated conduct is so innocuous that it would not trigger in the mind of a reasonable person the possibility that the conduct was regulated.

The nature of the regulated conduct will itself go far to determining whether the licensing argument applies. It is useful to distinguish between conduct which, by virtue of its inherent danger or the risk it engenders for others, would generally alert a reasonable person to the probability that the conduct would be regulated, from that conduct which is so mundane and apparently harmless that no thought would ordinarily be given to its potentially regulated nature. In the latter circumstances, the licensing argument would not apply. . . .

By virtue of the decision to enter the regulated field, the regulated person (here the appellant) can be taken to have accepted certain terms and conditions of entry. To paraphrase LaForest J., the procedural and substantive protections a person can reasonably expect may vary depending upon the activity that brings that person into contact with the state. Thus, the extent of Charter protection may differ depending upon whether the activity in question is regulatory or criminal in nature.

In this way, the licensing argument provides a link between the distinction between criminal and regulatory offences and the differential treatment of those two categories for the purposes of Charter review. There is, as well, a second justification for differential treatment.

## 2. *The vulnerability justification*

The realities and complexities of a modern industrial society couples with the very real need to protect all of society and particularly its vulnerable members, emphasize the critical importance of regulatory offences in Canada today. Our country simply could not function without extensive regulatory legislation. The protection provided by such measures constitutes a second justification for the differential treatment, for Charter purposes, of regulatory and criminal offences. . . .

Regulatory legislation is essential to the operation of our complex industrial society; it plays a legitimate and vital role in protecting those who are most vulnerable and least able to protect themselves. The extent and importance of that role has increased continuously since the onset of the Industrial Revolution. Before effective workplace legislation was enacted, labourers — including children — worked unconscionably long hours in dangerous and unhealthy surroundings that evoke visions of Dante's *Inferno*. It was regulatory legislation with its enforcement provisions which brought to an end the shameful situation that existed in mines, factories and workshops in the nineteenth century. The differential treatment of regulatory offences is justified by their common goal of protecting the vulnerable. . . .

It follows that a contextual approach is required in the present case in order that the distinctive nature of regulatory offences and their fundamental importance in Canadian society may be considered. Both licensing and the vulnerability considerations justify differential treatment, for the purposes of Charter interpretation, of crimes and regulatory offences. This, then, is the basis upon which the present case must be approached.

## IV. *The constitutionality of strict liability*

The appellant argues that strict liability violates the Charter on two bases. First, it is said that, at least where imprisonment is available as a sanction, s. 7 of the Charter requires a minimum fault element of guilty intent or wilful blindness to be proven; it is argued that, under s. 7, negligence is an insufficient degree of fault to justify a conviction. Secondly, the appellant alleges that the traditional requirement in strict liability offences that the defendant establish due diligence on a balance of probabilities violates the presumption of innocence guaranteed by s. 11(d) of the Charter. Let us consider these submissions.

A. *Section 7: the mens rea issue*

Wholesale Travel contends that wherever imprisonment is available as a penalty for breach of a regulatory statute, the failure to require the Crown to prove guilty intent as an essential element of the offence violates s. 7 of the Charter. It is constitutionally impermissible, it is argued, to impose liability on the basis of lack of reasonable care. Thus, it is the appellant's position that strict liability as defined in *Sault Ste. Marie* has been superseded and rendered invalid by the Charter. The appellant's argument, if accepted, would eliminate any distinction between criminal and regulatory offences.

The question to be determined at this stage is what level of *mens rea* is required by s. 7 of the Charter. . . .

What emerges from *Reference re: s. 94(2) of Motor Vehicle Act* and *Vaillancourt* is that the principles of fundamental justice referred to in s. 7 of the Charter prohibit the imposition of penal liability and punishment without proof of fault. Fault was, thus, elevated from a presumed element of an offence in *Sault Ste. Marie* to a constitutionally required element under the Charter. These cases did not, however, decide what level of fault is constitutionally required for every type of offence; rather, they make it clear that the degree of fault required will vary with the nature of the offence and the penalties available upon conviction. *Reference re: s. 94(2) of Motor Vehicle Act* does establish, however, that where imprisonment is available as a penalty, absolute liability cannot be imposed since it removes the fault element entirely and, in so doing, permits the punishment of the morally innocent.

The question which must now be determined is as follows: in situations where imprisonment is available as a penalty, does s. 7 require proof of a degree of fault greater than negligence? That is to say, must a positive mental state be established in order to justify a conviction? . . .

Does s. 7 require in all cases that the Crown prove *mens rea* as an essential element of the offence? The resolution of this question requires that a contextual approach be taken to the meaning and scope of the s. 7 right. Certainly, there can be no doubt that s. 7 requires proof of some degree of fault. That fault may be demonstrated by proof of intent, whether subjective or objective, or by proof of negligent conduct, depending on the nature of the offence. While it is not necessary in this case to determine the requisite degree of fault necessary to prove the commission of particular crimes, I am of the view that with respect to regulatory offences, proof of negligence satisfies the requirement of fault demanded by s. 7. Although the element of fault may not be removed completely, the demands of s. 7 will be met in the regulatory context where liability is imposed for conduct which breaches the standard of reasonable care required of those operating in the regulated field.

It should not be forgotten that *mens rea* and negligence are both fault elements which provide a basis for the imposition of liability. *Mens rea* focuses on the mental state of the accused and requires proof of a positive mental state of mind such as intent, recklessness or wilful blindness. Negligence, on the other hand, measures the conduct of the accused on the basis of an objective standard, irrespective of the accused's subjective mental state. Where negligence is the basis of liability, the question is not what the accused intended but rather whether the accused exercised reasonable care. The application of the contextual approach suggests that negligence is an acceptable basis of liability in the regulatory context which fully meets the fault requirement in s. 7 of the Charter.

It is argued, however, that to place regulatory offences in a separate category from criminal offences, with a lower fault standard, puts the accused charged with the breach of a regulatory provision in a fundamentally unfair position. It is a violation of the principles of fundamental justice under s. 7, it is said to allow the defendant to go to jail without having had the protection available in criminal prosecutions — that is, proof of *mens rea* by the Crown.

I cannot accept this contention. Regulatory offences provide for the protection of the public. The societal interests which they safeguard are of fundamental importance. It is absolutely essential that governments have the ability to enforce a standard of reasonable care in activities affecting public welfare. The laudable objectives served by regulatory legislation should not be thwarted by the application of principles developed in another context.

It must be remembered that regulatory offences were historically developed and recognized as a distinct category precisely for the purpose of relieving the Crown of the burden of proving *mens rea*. This is their hallmark. The tremendous importance of regulatory legislation in modern Canadian industrial society requires that courts be wary of interfering unduly with the regulatory role of government through the application of inflexible standards. Under the contextual approach, negligence is properly acceptable as the minimum fault standard required of the regulatory legislation by s. 7.

What some writers have referred to as "licensing" considerations lead to the same conclusion. The regulated actor is allowed to engage in activity which potentially may cause harm to the public. That permission is granted on the understanding that the actor accept, as a condition of entering the regulated field, the responsibility to exercise reasonable care to ensure that the proscribed harm does not come about. As a result of choosing to enter a field of activity known to be regulated, the regulated actor is taken to be aware of and to have accepted the imposition of a certain objective standard of conduct as a pre-condition of being allowed to engage in the regulated activity. In these circumstances, it misses the mark to speak in terms of the "unfairness" of an attenuated fault requirement because the standard of reasonable care has been accepted by the regulated actor upon entering the regulated sphere.

Further, from a practical point of view, it is simply impossible for the government to monitor adequately every industry so as to be able to prove actual intent or *mens rea* in each case. In order to do so, governments would have to employ armies of experts in every conceivable field. For example, it would be necessary to continuously monitor a myriad of complex activities that are potentially dangerous to members of society. Such activities include manufacturing and mining procedures, food and drug manufacturing, processing and packaging.

In our complex society, the government can, as a practical matter, do no more than to demonstrate that it has set reasonable standards to be met by persons in the regulated sphere and to prove beyond a reasonable doubt that there has been a breach of those standards by the regulated defendant. . . .

For these reasons, I conclude that the appellant's claim that strict liability offences violate s. 7 of the Charter cannot succeed. The requirements of s. 7 are met in the regulatory context by the imposition of liability based on a negligence standard. Therefore, no violation of s. 7 results from the imposition of strict liability.

### B. *Section 11(d): onus and the due diligence defence*

Wholesale Travel argues that the placing of a persuasive burden on the accused to establish due diligence on a balance of probability violates the presumption of innocence as guaranteed by s. 11(*d*) of the Charter. As the due diligence defence is the essential characteristic of strict liability offences as defined in *Sault Ste. Marie*, the appellant's s. 11(*d*) claim represents a fundamental challenge to the entire regime of regulatory offences in Canada. . . .

This court has recently considered the meaning of the presumption of innocence in the criminal context, particularly as applied to reverse onus provisions. It is now clear that it is the net effect of a reverse onus provision on the determination of the guilt or innocence of an accused rather than the precise nature of the provision that must be examined under s. 11(*d*). . . .

What must now be determined is whether the s. 11(*d*) standard which has been developed and applied in the criminal context should be applied to regulatory offences.

### *The content of the presumption in the regulatory context*

Much of what has been said in regard to the validity of strict liability under s. 7 of the Charter is applicable as well to the s. 11(*d*) question of onus. The importance of regulatory legislation and its enforcement strongly support the use of a contextual approach in the interpretation of the s. 11(*d*) right as applied to regulatory offences. . . .

The reasons for ascribing a different content to the presumption of innocence in the regulatory context are persuasive and compelling. As with the *mens rea* issue, if regulatory mechanisms are to operate effectively, the Crown cannot be required to disprove due diligence beyond a reasonable doubt. Such a requirement would make it virtually impossible for the Crown to prove regulatory offences and would effectively prevent governments from seeking to implement public policy through regulatory means.

It has been suggested that requiring the Crown to prove negligence beyond a reasonable doubt, either as part of its case or after the accused adduces some evidence raising a reasonable doubt as to due diligence, would represent an acceptable compromise: it would, it is said, lessen the burden on the accused while still allowing for the effective pursuit of the regulatory objective. I cannot accept this contention. While such an approach would undoubtedly be beneficial to the accused, it would effectively eviscerate the regulatory power of government by rendering the enforcement of regulatory offences impossible in practical terms. Under this approach, the Crown would be forced to prove lack of reasonable care where the accused raises a reasonable doubt as to the possibility of due diligence.

It is difficult to conceive of a situation in which a regulated accused would not be able to adduce *some* evidence giving rise to the possibility that due diligence was exercised. For instance, an environmental polluter would often be able to point to *some* measures it had adopted in order to prevent the type of harm which ultimately resulted. This might raise a reasonable doubt that it had acted with due diligence no matter how inadequate those measures were for the control of a dangerous situation. . . .

Thus, the question is not whether the accused has exercised *some* care, but whether the degree of care exercised was sufficient to meet the standard imposed. If the false advertiser, the corporate polluter and the manufacturer of noxious goods are to be effectively controlled, it is necessary to require them to show on a balance of probabilities that they took reasonable precautions to avoid the harm which actually resulted. In the regulatory context, there is nothing unfair about imposing that onus: indeed, it is essential for the protection of our vulnerable society. . . .

Nor can I accept the contention that there is little practical difference between requiring the accused to prove due diligence on a balance of probabilities and requiring only that the accused raise a reasonable doubt as to the exercise of due diligence. Professor Webb, in his article, *ibid.*, deals with this argument in the following terms, at p. 467:

> Some might argue that in practice there is no workable distinction between an offence which requires the accused to prove due diligence on the balance of probabilities to avoid conviction, and one that permits the accused to raise a reasonable doubt as to the existence of due diligence. Trial judges will find a way to convict those whom they feel are guilty of negligence, the argument would go, regardless of burdens of proof. This type of reasoning certainly contradicts the statement of the trial judge in *Whyte, [supra]*, who contended that in the absence of a balance of probability presumption, he would have found reasonable doubt as to whether the accused had "care and control" of a motor vehicle.

Webb then goes on, at p. 467, to identify the deleterious effects on prosecution of regulatory offences which would result from requiring the Crown to prove negligence:

> The "there is no difference in practice anyway" argument also fails to recognize the different quantity and quality of evidence which administrators would be forced to provide to prosecutors in preparation for a case. If an evidential rather than a persuasive burden is adopted, merely raising a reasonable doubt as to the existence of due diligence would then shift the burden of proof to the prosecutors to *prove negligence*. Prior to any case reaching the prosecution stage, administrators would be under an obligation to collect all the evidence necessary to prove negligence. In effect, prosecutors would be more likely to turn down a request from administrators for a prosecution unless proof of negligence could be established. Given the difficulty in accumulating such information, it is not unlikely that there would be a chilling effect on use of the prosecution mechanism. Once it became noticeable that less cases were reaching the courts, it is possible that regulatees would receive the signal that, in most circumstances, the offence of negligence was not enforceable.

(Emphasis in original.)

I agree with these conclusions of Professor Webb. To reduce the onus on the accused would, from a practical point of view, raise insurmountable barriers for the Crown seeking to enforce a regulatory scheme.

In these circumstances, it cannot be contended that requiring the prosecution to prove negligence beyond a reasonable doubt would still allow for the effective achievement of regulatory objectives. To the contrary, its effect would be, in practical terms, to render the regulatory power of governments ineffectual.

Nor can it be argued that other solutions would be satisfactory; there is simply no other practical solution. Both with respect to the consumption of government resources and the intrusiveness of regulatory measures, the consequences of a finding that the due diligence defence violates s. 11(*d*) of the Charter would be extremely severe. Governments would be forced to devote tremendous expenditure, in terms of monetary and human resources, to regulatory enforcement mechanisms. Armies of investigators and experts would be required in order to garner sufficient evidence to establish negligence or disprove due diligence beyond a reasonable doubt.

Further, a marked expansion in enforcement mechanisms by definition implies an escalation in the intrusiveness of regulatory measures. The greater the burden of proof on the Crown, the greater the likelihood that those charged with the enforcement of regulatory measures would have to resort to legislation authorizing search and surveillance in order to gather sufficient evidence to discharge that onus.

As with the s. 7 challenge, licensing considerations support the conclusion that strict liability does not violate s. 11(*d*) of the Charter. The licensing argument attributes to the regulated actor knowledge and acceptance, not only of the standard of reasonable care itself, but also of the responsibility to establish on a balance of probabilities the exercise of reasonable care. Acceptance of this burden is an implied term and a pre-condition of being allowed to engage in activity falling within the regulated sphere. Regulated actors are taken to understand that, should they be unable to discharge this burden, an inference of negligence will be drawn from the fact that the proscribed result has occurred.

I wish to emphasize, however, that the difference in the scope and meaning of s. 11(*d*) in the regulatory context does not imply that the presumption of innocence is meaningless for a regulated accused. The Crown must still prove the *actus reus* of regulatory offences beyond a reasonable doubt. Thus, the Crown must prove that the accused polluted the river, sold adulterated food, or published a false advertisement. However, once having established this beyond a reasonable doubt, the Crown is presumptively relieved of having to prove anything further. Fault is presumed from the bringing about of the proscribed result, and the onus shifts to the defendant to establish reasonable care on a balance of probabilities.

For these reasons, I conclude that the presumption of innocence as guaranteed in s. 11(*d*) of the Charter is not violated by strict liability offences as defined in *Sault Ste. Marie*. The imposition of a reverse persuasive onus on the accused to establish due diligence on a balance of probabilities does not run counter to the presumption of innocence, notwithstanding the fact that the same reversal of onus would violate s. 11(*d*) in the criminal context.

C. *The imprisonment concern*

Much has been made in this appeal of the potential use of imprisonment as a sanction for breach of strict liability offences. The Chief Justice considers the use of imprisonment to be determinative of the Charter analysis. With respect, I am unable to agree. The availability of imprisonment in no way alters my conclusion that strict liability does not violate either ss. 7 or 11(*d*) of the Charter.

The Charter does not guarantee an absolute right to liberty: rather, it guarantees the right not to be deprived of liberty except in accordance with the principles of fundamental justice. Thus, while the availability of imprisonment undoubtedly triggers Charter review, it does not resolve the ultimate question. What must be determined is whether, in a given case, the possibility of a sentence of imprisonment comports with the principles of fundamental justice. It is whether the principles of fundamental justice have been violated, not the availability of imprisonment, which is the determinative consideration. . . .

The ultimate question is whether the imposition of imprisonment on the basis of strict liability comports with the principles of fundamental justice. For the reasons set out earlier concerning the underlying rationale of regulatory offences, I am of the opinion that it does.

Regulatory schemes can only be effective if they provide for significant penalties in the event of their breach. Indeed, although it may be rare that imprisonment is sought, it must be available as a sanction if there is to be effective enforcement of the regulatory measure. Nor is the imposition of imprisonment unreasonable in light of the danger than can accrue to the public from breaches of regulatory statutes.

. . .

E. *Section 1*

In light of my conclusion regarding the appellant's ss. 7 and 11(*d*) claims, there is no need to proceed to s. 1. However, had it been necessary to consider the matter, the same reasons I have set forth in finding that neither ss. 7 nor 11(*d*) are necessarily infringed by strict liability offences would have led me to conclude that strict liability offences can be justified under s. 1 of the Charter.

V. *Application to s. 36(1)(a) and s. 37.3(2)*

Section 36(1)(*a*) of the *Competition Act* creates the offence of false or misleading advertising. Section 37.3(2) provides a statutory defence to that charge. The defence will only lie where all four conditions set out in paras. (*a*) through (*d*) are met. While paras. (*a*) and (*b*) in essence describe the common law defence of due diligence, paras, (*c*) and (*d*) create additional conditions which must be met before the defence will lie.

*The validity of paras. (c) and (d) of s. 37.3(2)*

Paragraph (*c*) of s. 37.3(2) requires an accused who has made a misleading representation to take positive steps to bring the error to the attention of those to be likely affected by it. Paragraph (*d*) requires this to be done promptly. The effect of these provisions is to impose an obligation on the accused to make a prompt retraction as a precondition to relying on the defence of due diligence.

The Court of Appeal unanimously held that paras. (*c*) and (*d*) of s. 37.3(2) may in some circumstances require conviction where there is no fault on the part of the accused. I agree with this conclusion. Even where an accused can establish the absence of negligence in the making of misleading representations, paras. (*c*) and (*d*) none the less require conviction if the accused has failed to make a prompt correction or retraction. In these circumstances, the accused would be deprived of the defence of due diligence and the offence would be tantamount to absolute liability, since liability could be imposed in the absence of fault on the part of the accused.

Such a result clearly violates s. 7 of the Charter. As Lamer J. stated in *Reference re" ss: 94(2) of Motor Vehicle Act, supra*, at p. 293 C.C.C., p. 541 D.L.R.:

> A law that has the potential to convict a person who has not really done anything wrong offends the principles of fundamental justice and, if imprisonment is available as a penalty, such a law then violates a person's right to liberty under s. 7 of the *Canadian Charter of Rights and Freedoms*.

Nor do I think that paras. (*c*) and (*d*) can be justified under s. 1 of the Charter. The Crown has filed little evidence to support its position that paras. (*c*) and (*d*) can be saved by s. 1. Perhaps this is itself a sufficient basis for finding that those paragraphs are not justifiable.

There are, however, additional grounds for reaching this conclusion. Assuming that there is a rational connection between the requirement of corrective advertising and the legislative objective of seeking to prevent the harm resulting from misleading representations, it cannot be said that the impugned provisions constitute a minimal impairment of the rights of the accused. Further, the availability of imprisonment as a sanction far outweighs the importance of the regulatory objective in correcting false advertising after the fact. In short, there is no proportionality between means and ends. Paragraphs (*c*) and (*d*) cannot then be justified under s. 1 of the Charter.

*The validity of paras. (a) and (b)*

These paragraphs in essence put forward the common law defence of due diligence. Where imprisonment is available as a penalty for breach of a statute, s. 7 of the Charter requires proof of fault before liability can be imposed. I have concluded, however, that the fault requirement is different for regulatory than for criminal offences. In the regulatory context, it is appropriate that fault should be imposed on the basis of negligence. There is, therefore, no violation of s. 7 resulting from the removal of the *mens rea* requirement in strict liability offences. It follows that paras. (*a*) and (*b*) of s. 37.3(2 do not violate s. 7 of the Charter.

It has been noted earlier that the s. 11(*d*) presumption of innocence has a different scope and meaning in relation to regulatory as opposed to criminal offences. In my view, the imposition in strict liability offences of a reverse persuasive onus on the accused to establish due diligence is proper and permissible and does not constitute a violation of the s. 11(*d*) and presumption of innocence. I, therefore, conclude that paras. (*a*) and (*b*) of s. 37.3(2) do not violate s. 11(*d*) of the Charter.

VI. *Conclusion*

Strict liability offences, as exemplified in this case by the combination of s. 36(1)(*a*) and s. 37.3(2)(*a*) and (*b*) of the *Competition Act*, do not violate either ss. 7 or 11(*d*) of the Charter. Neither the absence of a *mens rea* requirement nor the imposition of an onus on the accused to establish due diligence on a balance of probabilities offends the Charter of rights of those accused of regulatory offences.

Regulatory legislation is essential to the functioning of our society and to the protection of the public. It responds to the compelling need to protect the health and safety of the members of our society and to preserve our fragile environment. The imposition of strict liability is both reasonable and essential to the operation of regulatory schemes.

## VII. Disposition

Since paras. (*c*) and (*d*) of s. 37.3(2) of the *Competition Act* violate s. 7 of the Charter and cannot be justified under s. 1, they must be struck down and declared to be of no force or effect. What remains in s. 36(1)(*a*) and s. 37.3(2)(*a*) and (*b*) is a strict liability regulatory offence. These provisions are valid and enforceable. In the result I would dismiss the appeal and allow the Crown's Appeal to the extent required to reflect this disposition.

*Appeal by accused dismissed; appeal by Crown allowed in part.*

**Questions/Discussion**

1. What is the distinction between strict and absolute liability offences, and do you think the distinction is a valid one? What are the policy reasons given in *Sault Ste. Marie* to justify the categories? Do you agree with them? What problems remain after the case? For example, if public welfare offences are not "true crimes", then why do we continue to treat them as such and process offenders within the criminal justice system? Now that a defence is possible, might the courts be more likely to require less than a full mens rea?
2. Do you think that the possibility of a defence of due diligence will give companies an incentive to take preventive measures? Also, should the "reasonableness" of the steps taken be judged differently for corporations versus individuals, or for those who are engaged in profit-making versus others? Is there an argument that those who profit should have a higher standard of due diligence to meet that those who do not profit from the activity?
3. There has been a concern raised that the new categorization will make it more difficult to prosecute polluters successfully; see the Jeffery article listed below. The concern is that standards of care or due diligence will be set by the polluters themselves because they have knowledge of, and expertise in, the industry's practices — advantages which the courts and prosecutors lack.
4. What is the effect of the Charter in this area as seen in the *Burt* and *Wholesale* cases. Do you agree with the way the Charter is being used in this area of criminal law? Why or why not?

**Further Reading**
- Hutchinson, A., "*Sault Ste. Marie, Mens Rea* and The Halfway House: Public Welfare Offences Get a Home of Their Own" (1979), 17 Osgoode Hall Law Journal 415.
- Jeffrey, M., "Environmental Enforcement and Regulation in the 1980's: *Regina v. Sault Ste. Marie* Revisited" (1984), 10 Queen's Law Journal 43.
- Mewett, A. and M. Manning, Mewett and Manning on Criminal Law, 3rd ed. (Toronto: Butterworths, 1994).
- Reid, A., "*Sault Ste. Marie*: A Comment" (1979), 28 University of New Brunswick Law Journal 205.
- Richardson, G. "Strict Liability for Regulatory Crime: the Empirical Research", [1987] Criminal Law Review 295.
- Ruby, C. and K. Jull, "The Charter and Regulatory Offences: A Wholesale Revision" (1992) 14 Criminal Reports (4th) 226-44.

- Stuart, D., *Canadian Criminal Law: A Treatise*, 2nd ed. (Toronto: Carswell, 1987), pp 157-183.
- Stuart, D., and R. Delisle, *Learning Canadian Criminal Law*, 5th ed. (Toronto: Carswell, 1995).
- Verdun-Jones, S., *Criminal Law in Canada: Cases, Questions and the Code* (Toronto: Harcourt Brace Jovanovich Canada, 1989), pp. 159-185.
- Verdun-Jones, S., and C. Griffiths, Canadian Criminal Justice, 2nd ed. (Toronto: Butterworths, 1994).

## 6.2 INCOMPLETE OFFENCES

### 6.2.1. Attempts

**Introduction**

The issues surrounding attempts in the criminal law arise due to the fact that the intended object of the person's criminal intent was not completed, yet one tends to think in terms of a fully completed act. Conceptually, it is problematic because ordinarily in the criminal law the state is attaching liability for the action *and* the wrongful intent; in attempts, that action has been halted or thwarted at some stage before the completion of the act for a variety of possible reasons. For example, D may plan to rob a bank, may buy the gun she intends to use and map out her getaway route. However, on the chosen day, D may decide to abort the plan for any number of reasons. She may decide to give up a life of crime and pursue another career, or she may merely decide to try out her plan on another day. In the alternative, D may arrive at the scene of the planned crime and discover that the bank is closed due to a holiday, that police are present in the area of the bank, or perhaps that the target bank has closed permanently. In which of these situations should D be guilty of attempted robbery? In any one of them? In all of them? Or do we have enough information? For example, was D on her way into the bank when she changed her mind or was she merely getting up on the morning of the planned robbery when she had a change of heart or of plan? Was she headed into the bank when she saw the police in the vicinity and decided to abort her plan?

This type of information is often crucial because an attempt takes place before the completion of the intended crime. Therefore, the courts have to decide at what point in time the attempt is complete and liability will attach for an attempted crime; in other words, they decide what constitutes a valid actus reus in attempts. Obviously, the courts will not wait until the full crime has been completed before saying the police can intervene, for that approach would destroy the preventative ideal behind the concept of attempts. But at what point does liability occur? The courts in Canada, following the wording in section 24 of the Criminal Code, the principal "attempts" provision, say that an attempt is complete if the accused's acts have gone beyond "mere preparation". As for what is "mere preparation" and therefore attracting no penal consequences versus what is beyond preparation and consequently an attempt which is subject to sanction, the answer depends upon the facts of each case. The cases of *Sorrell* and *Bondett* and *Deutsch* provide examples of where (and why) the courts will find a valid attempt in differing fact situations.

Another issue in this area is that of "impossibility", the situation where the actus reus of the completed offence is impossible to complete under the circumstances. Examples here include the case of *Scott* below where the pickpocket attempted to steal from an empty pocket; they also include the situation where D tries to kill someone who is already dead but D does not know it, or the situation where D tries to kill someone by sticking pins in a model of that person. Should the law excuse impossible attempts and if so why? Section 24 states that a criminal attempt is made "whether or not it was possible under the circumstances to commit the offence", and this has been taken to mean that all types of impossible attempts are criminal regardless of the reason for the impossibility. Some jurisdictions have tried to distinguish between types of impossible attempts (legally versus physically impossible) and the *Smith* case below is an example of that sort of reasoning. Brown's article presents a full discussion of the issues in this area. Do you think such distinctions are valid or useful, particularly if one purpose of attempts is to discourage the individual from trying again and considering that the accused is being convicted for his or her wrongful intent to do the crime coupled with overt actions towards completing it? Should we reward the incompetent or the stupid when they attempt impossible criminal ends or when they use impossible means to accomplish their goals? Of course, if we look at the penalty provisions for attempts in section 463 it might be argued that those who fail in their criminal purpose are indeed being rewarded with lower maximum penalties in most cases. If liability attaches essentially for the evil purpose, then why are the maximum penalties not the same as if the accused was successful?

Another issue is raised in the situation where the accused has abandoned the criminal purpose for "good", altruistic reasons (for example, where the accused has realized the wrongfulness of his or her ways and decides to reject the criminal purpose). What is the argument for punishment in such cases? Under the current law, once an attempt has been made, it cannot be abandoned in the legal sense and liability will still attach, though the sentence will likely be more lenient. The rationale is that once a crime of any type has been committed, it cannot be "disowned" by the perpetrator, and that this is as true for attempts as for any other crime.

A final point about the actus reus of attempts is that in regard to certain offences, it is difficult to envisage attempts of them being made. We see this in criminal negligence (sections 219-221), for example, where it is difficult to comprehend situations where someone attempts to be negligent, or in offences involving being a found-in in a common gaming house (section 201) or a found-in in a common bawdy-house (section 210). Also, in strict and absolute liability offences it is difficult to see liability attaching for an attempt, if not because such fact situations are hard to conceive, then because the courts would be reluctant on policy grounds to extend liability for these types of offences too far. And attempts are just that, extensions of criminal liability to include acts which have yet to culminate in a full offence.

In general, the mens rea of an attempt is the intent to commit the full offence, but in certain crimes this may not be appropriate. The *Ancio* case is an example of this problem where the court attached a narrow mens rea to the crime of attempted murder, specifically an intent to kill. This intent is narrower than the intention which is sometimes sufficient in certain types of the full murder offences. Given the murder provisions in the Code, and the fact that attempts are one step removed from the full offence, the courts are perhaps justly concerned about extending liability too far. In a similar vein, there is a reluctance to put two incomplete crimes "together", for example in "attempted counselling" or "counselling conspiracy", due to a fear that this would result in extending criminal liability too far from the completed offence.[1]

## R. v. Deutsch
(1986), 52 C.R. (3d) 305 (S.C.C.)

Appeal by accused from judgment of Ontario Court of Appeal, 5 C.C.C. (3d) 41, reversing accused's acquittal of attempting to procure females for illicit intercourse with other persons, and ordering new trial.

---

[1] See, under "Further Reading", references to "Attempts" in Mewett and Manning or Stuart and Delisle

[Only the judgment of LeDain is reproduced below. Also, this is a case where the appellant represented himself before the Supreme Court, a situation which rarely happens.]

LEDAIN J. (BEETZ, McINTYRE and WILSON JJ. concurring): — This appeal [from 5 C.C.C (3d) 41], which involves a charge of attempting to procure a person to have illicit sexual intercourse with another person contrary to s. 195(1)(*a*) of the Criminal Code, raises two issues: the distinction between attempt and mere preparation, and the meaning of "illicit sexual intercourse".

The appeal is from the judgment of the Ontario Court of Appeal on 17th March 1983 setting aside the acquittal of the appellant by Graburn Co. Ct. J. on 13th August 1982 of the charge of attempting to procure a person to have illicit sexual intercourse with another person and ordering a new trial of the appellant on that charge.

During the period covered by the indictment, which is the three months ending on or about 3rd September 1981, the appellant was carrying on a business known as "Global Franchises Marketing", which was engaged in selling franchises of various kinds. During this period the appellant placed an advertisement in newspapers in Ottawa, Hamilton and Toronto inviting applications for the position of secretary/sales assistant and conducted interviews with three women who responded to the advertisement and with a police officer who posed as an applicant for the position and recorded the interview on a tape-recorder. The advertisement read as follows:

---

ENJOY TRAVEL
Secretary-Sales Assistant to Sales Executive, $600-$800 per month to start plus commission, bonuses, company benefits and expenses. Must be free to travel extensively. Call 746-2440 ask for Mel.

---

In the interviews the appellant indicated that a secretary/sales assistant would be expected to have sexual intercourse with clients or potential clients of the company where that appeared to be necessary to conclude a contract. The appellant also indicated that a successful secretary/sales assistant could earn as much as $100,000 per year through commission or bonus on the sale of franchises. The appellant did not make an offer of employment to the three applicants who testified at his trial. After hearing what the position required they said they were not interested and the interviews were terminated. Nor did he make an offer of employment to the police officer who posed as an applicant, but when she told him she was interested in the position despite its requirements he told her to think it over and let him know.

The appellant was tried upon an indictment containing two counts: attempting to procure female persons to become common prostitutes, and attempting to procure female persons to have illicit intercourse with another person. Graburn Co. Ct. J. acquitted the appellant on both counts. He found that the appellant intended that a person hired for the position should have sexual relations with clients or potential clients, but he held, as a matter of law, that the acts of statements of the appellant did not, in the absence of an offer of employment, constitute the actus reus of an attempt to procure. In his opinion they were mere preparation. He accordingly did not find it necessary to decide whether the sexual intercourse contemplated by the appellant would be illicit sexual intercourse within s. 195(1)(a) or make those who engaged in it common prostitutes within s. 195(1)(d), as it then read.

The Ontario Court of Appeal (Martin, Houlden and Robins JJ.A.) dismissed the appeal from the acquittal on the charge of attempting to procure female persons to become common prostitutes, but allowed the appeal from the acquittal on the charge of attempting to procure female persons to have illicit sexual intercourse with another person and directed a new trial of the appellant on that count of the indictment. The court held that the trial judge erred in concluding that the acts or statements of the appellant could not, in the absence of an offer of employment, constitute an attempt to procure rather than mere preparation. It held that there was evidence from which the trial judge could have concluded that there was both the mens rea and the actus reus required for an attempt to procure. The court also held that the sexual intercourse contemplated by the appellant would be illicit sexual intercourse within s. 195(1)(a). The appellant appeals from the judgment of the Court of Appeal with respect to the second count of the indictment.

The appellant, who appeared in person on the appeal, expressed his grounds of appeal in several different ways, but in my opinion there are only two issues that require consideration by the court:

(1) whether the Court of Appeal erred in holding that the acts or statements of the appellant could, as a matter of law, constitute an attempt to procure rather than mere preparation; and

(2) whether the Court of Appeal erred in holding that the sexual intercourse contemplated by the appellant would be illicit sexual intercourse within s. 195(1)(a) of the Code.

I propose to begin with the consideration of what is meant by "illicit sexual intercourse" in s. 195(1)(a) of the Criminal Code, which, at the relevant time, provided:

> **195.**(1) Every one who
>
> (a) procures, attempts to procure or solicits a female person to have illicit sexual intercourse with another person, whether in or out of Canada.
>
> . . . .
>
> is guilty of an indictable offence and is liable to imprisonment for ten years.

Martin J.A., delivering the unanimous judgment of the Court of Appeal, said with reference to the meaning of "illicit sexual intercourse" at p. 52:

> "Illicit sexual intercourse" in s. 195(1)(a) merely connotes sexual intercourse with another not authorized by law and it is not necessary for the sexual intercourse procured with another to be in itself criminal: see *R. v. Robinson* (1946), 92 C.C.C. 223, [1948] O.R. 857, [1949] 2 D.L.R. 531.

. . . .

I am of the respectful opinion that the Court of Appeal did not err in holding that the sexual intercourse contemplated by the appellant would be "illicit sexual intercourse" within s. 195(1)(a) of the Code.

I turn now to the question whether the acts or statements of the appellant could, as a matter of law, constitute the actus reus of an attempt to procure a person to have illicit sexual intercourse with another person, contrary to s. 195(1)(a) of the Code. The general provision of the Code defining the constituent elements of an attempt to commit an offence is s. 24, which provides:

> **24.**(1) Every one who, having an intent to commit an offence, does or omits to do anything for the purpose of carrying out his intention is guilty of an attempt to commit the offence whether or not it was possible under the circumstances to commit the offence.
> (2) The question whether an act or omission by a person who has an intent to commit an offence is or is not mere preparation to commit the offence, and too remote to constitute an attempt to commit the offence, is a question of law.

The issue is whether, if there was the necessary intent, the acts of the appellant were mere preparation to commit the offence of procuring a person to have illicit sexual intercourse with another person or whether any of them was a step in the commission of the offence, and the extent to which that distinction is to turn on the relative remoteness of the act in question from what would have been the completion of the offence. This issue, as s. 24 indicates, is a question of law. The appellant contends that the Court of Appeal erred in holding that one of the acts of the appellant could, if there was the necessary intent, constitute the actus reus of an attempt to procure.

. . . .

The Court of Appeal held that the trial judge had not made a finding as to whether the appellant had the requisite mens rea of intent to commit the offence of procuring, but that the holding out of large financial rewards in the course of the interviews could, as a matter of law, constitute the actus reus of an attempt to procure. Martin J.A. said at p. 50:

> The trial judge, as previously mentioned, found that the respondent intended that "the women in question" should have sexual intercourse with clients or potential clients if necessary to obtain a contract. I interpret that finding in its context as a finding that the respondent in the interviews with the three young women who answered the advertisement and with Constable Barkey did state and meant to state that the position required them to have sexual intercourse with clients or potential clients, and further that he contemplated that such sexual intercourse would take place as incidental to the employment. The trial judge made no finding that the respondent endeavoured to persuade the applicants to take the job and it is, I think, clear on the evidence that the respondent did not expressly attempt to persuade them to take such employment and indeed the trial judge found that the respondent had never offered the position to any of them. The holding out of large financial rewards in the context of the interviews was capable, however, of not only providing evidence of an intention to induce the applicants to become so employed, but was also capable of constituting the *actus reus* of an attempt to procure the applicants to have illicit sexual intercourse contrary to s. 195.

. . . .

Several different tests for determining whether there is the actus reus of attempt, as distinct from mere preparation to commit an offence, have been identified as reflected at one time or another in judicial decisions and legislation. All of them have been pronounced by academic commentators to be unsatisfactory in some degree. For a thorough analysis of the various tests, with suggestions for an improved test, see Meehan, The Law of Criminal Attempt: A Treatise (1984), c. 5, pp. 79-146, and Stuart, Canadian Criminal Law: A Treatise (1982), p. 529 et seq.

. . . .

In my opinion the distinction between preparation and attempt is essentially a qualitative one, involving the relationship between the nature and quality of the act in question and the nature of the complete offence, although consideration must necessarily be given, in making that qualitative distinction, to the relative proximity of the act in question to what would have been the completed offence, in terms of time, location and acts under the control of the accused remaining to be accomplished. I find that view to be compatible with what has been said about the actus reus of attempt in this court and in other Canadian decisions that should be treated as authoritative on this question.

. . . .

In my opinion, relative proximity may give an act which might otherwise appear to be mere preparation the quality of attempt. That is reflected, I think, in the conclusion of the majority in *Henderson* and in the conclusion of the Ontario Court of Appeal with respect to actus reus in *R. v. Sorrell* (1978), 41 C.C.C. (2d) 9. But an act which on its face is an act of commission does not lose its quality as the actus reus of attempt because further acts were required or because a significant period of time may have elapsed before the completion of the offence.

In the case at bar the Court of Appeal agreed with the trial judge on the applicable meaning of "procure". The meaning selected by the trial judge and approved by the Court of Appeal was "to cause, or to induce, or to have a persuasive effect upon the conduct that is alleged". Martin, J.A. expressed his argument at p. 49 with the following statement of the issue by the trial judge:

> The question for decision is did Mr. Deutsch attempt to cause or attempt to induce or attempt to have a persuasive effect upon the woman in question to have illicit sexual intercourse with another person . . .

I agree that the sources referred to by the trial judge and Martin J.A. support the meaning given by them to the word "procure".

The Court of Appeal differed with the trial judge as to what would have constituted the completed offence of procuring a person to have illicit sexual intercourse with another person. The trial judge held that the offence of procuring would have been completed, in the particular context of this case, by the acceptance of an offer of employment. The Court of Appeal held, citing *R. v. Johnson*, [1964] 2 Q.B. 404, [1963] 3 W.L.R. 1031, 48 Cr. App. R. 25, [1961] 3 All E.R. 969, and *R. v. Gruba*, 66 W.W.R 190, [1969] 2 C.C.C. 365 (B.C.C.A.), that the offence of procuring a person to have illicit sexual intercourse with another person is not committed unless sexual intercourse actually takes place. In the appeal to this court the respondent accepted this statement of the law as to what is required for the complete offence of procuring a person to have illicit sexual intercourse with another person. It was not challenged, and I accept it for the purposes of deciding whether the acts of the appellant could, as a matter of law, constitute the actus reus of an attempt to procure.

I agree with the Court of Appeal that if the appellant had the necessary intent to induce or persuade the woman to seek employment that would require them to have sexual intercourse with prospective clients then the holding out of the large financial rewards in the course of the interviews in which the necessity of having sexual intercourse with prospective clients was disclosed could constitute the actus reus of an attempt to procure. It would clearly be a step, and an important step, in the commission of the offence. Before an offer of employment could be made in such circumstances an applicant would have to seek the position despite its special requirement. Thus such inducement or persuasion would be the decisive act in the procuring. There would be little else that the appellant would be required to do towards the completion of the offence other than to make the formal offer of employment. I am further of the opinion that the holding out of the large financial rewards in the course of the interviews would not lose its quality as a step in the commission of the offence, and thus as an actus reus of attempt, because a considerable period of time might elapse before a person engaged for the position had sexual intercourse with prospective clients or because of the otherwise contingent nature of such sexual intercourse.

For these reasons I would dismiss the appeal. I agree with the Court of Appeal that because the trial judge did not make a finding as to whether or not there was the necessary intent to procure there must be a new trial.

*Appeal allowed; new trial ordered.*

## R. v. Sorell and Bondett
(1978), 41 C.C.C. (2d) 9 (Ont. C.A.)

Appeal by the Crown from the accused's acquittal on a charge of attempted robbery.

BY THE COURT: — The Attorney-General of Ontario appeals against the acquittal of the respondents on a charge of attempted robbery.

The respondents were tried at Kingston before His Honour Judge Campbell, sitting without a jury, on an indictment containing three counts.

Count 1 charged the respondents jointly with, on or about March 3, 1977, attempting to rob Peter Mason of Aunt Lucy's Fried Chicken store at 240 Montreal St. in Kingston. Count 2 charged the respondent Sorrell with carrying, at the time and place aforesaid, a concealed weapon, to wit: a Smith and Wesson revolver. Count 3 charged the respondent Sorrell with having in his possession, at the time and place aforesaid, a Smith and Wesson revolver, knowing the same was obtained by an offence committed in Canada punishable on indictment. The respondent Sorrell, on arraignment, pleaded guilty to the charge of carrying a concealed weapon contained in count 2; his plea of guilty was accepted by the trial Judge after the evidence was completed, and he was sentenced to imprisonment for 18 months. The trial Judge acquitted the respondent for 18 months. The trial Judge acquitted the respondent Sorrell on count 3, on the ground that the Crown had failed to prove the necessary element of guilty knowledge. The Crown does not appeal the acquittal of Sorrell on count 3, and we are not further concerned with it.

On the evening of Thursday, March 3, 1977, Miss Dawn Arbuckle was the cashier at Aunt Lucy's Fried Chicken store at 240 Montreal St. in Kingston. The store is located at the corner of Montreal and Markland Sts., the customer entrances being on Montreal St. Mr. Peter Mason was the manager of the store. The regular closing time for the store was 11:00 p.m., but, on the evening in question, since almost all the chicken had been sold, the manager decided to close the store earlier, and locked the customer entrances at approximately 10:45 p.m. Around 10 minutes to 11:00 Miss Arbuckle noticed two men, wearing balaclavas, on the Markland St. side of the store; they then came to one of the customer entrances on Montreal St. The area outside the store was illuminated, and the lights normally on in the store, when open, were still on.

One of the men was wearing a blue ski jacket and the other was wearing a brown coat. The balaclavas worn by the two men were pulled down completely over their heads, and one man was also wearing sunglasses. Miss Arbuckle said that the balaclava worn by one man was blue and white in colour, and that worn by the other man was brown and white.

One of the men rapped on the door and on the window. The manager, who had been mopping the floor, turned around and said, "Sorry we are closed", and returned to his mopping. The two men turned toward each other, and made a gesture of surprise. At this time Miss Arbuckle noticed that one of the men had a silver-coloured gun in his hand. The two men then walked away on Montreal Street in the direction of Princess St.; whereupon Mr. Mason, the manager, telephoned the police. Two officers in a cruiser responded to the call, drove to the area and saw the two men, whose clothing corresponded to the description that the officers had been given, walking on Montreal St. The officers drove past the two men, then made a U-turn and drove back towards them.

As the officers passed the two men, before making the U-turn, they saw one of the men throw "an article of material" towards a snow bank on the side of the street. The two men, who proved to be the respondents, were then arrested. The respondent Sorrell had a loaded .357 Magnum revolver concealed in his waistband. The gun was loaded with six Dominion .38 shells, and another five Dominion .38 shells were removed from the respondent Sorrell's pants' pocket.

An officer conducted a search of the immediate area where the respondents had been arrested, and found a brown balaclava on a snowbank on the side of Montreal St. The point on Montreal St. where the respondents were arrested was some 411 yards from the Aunt Lucy's store, where the attempted robbery is alleged to have occurred. The officer proceeded along Montreal St. in the direction of the Aunt Lucy's store, and found a blue balaclava in the middle of the sidewalk on Montreal St. at the intersection of Raglan St.

Neither of the respondents testified in his defence.

The Crown appeals against the acquittal of the respondents on the charge of attempted robbery on the ground that the trial Judge erred in law in holding that the acts of the respondents did not go beyond mere preparation, and hence did not constitute an attempt.

Section 24 of the *Code* defines an attempt as follows:

**24**(1) Every one who, having an intent to commit an offence, does or omits to do anything for the purpose of carrying out his intention is guilty of an attempt to commit the offence whether or not it was possible under the circumstances to commit the offence.

(2) The question whether an act or omission by a person *who has an intent to commit an offence* is or is not mere preparation to commit the offence, and too remote to constitute an attempt to commit the offence, is a question of law.

(Emphasis supplied.)

In order to establish the commission of the offence of attempted robbery charged, it was necessary for the Crown to prove that the respondents:

(i) Intended to do that which would in law amount to the robbery specified in the indictment (*mens rea*), and
(ii) took steps in carrying out that intent which amounted to more than mere preparation (*actus reus*).

By virtue of s. 24(2) of the *Code*, the existence of element (i) is a question of fact, but whether the steps taken are sufficient to satisfy element (ii) is a question of law.

. . . .

In the present case, there was no evidence of the intent to rob other than that furnished by the acts relied on as constituting the *actus reus*. There was no extrinsic evidence in the form of statements of intention, or admissions by the respondents showing what their intention was.

The prosecution in this case was forced to rely exclusively upon the acts of the accused, not only to constitute the *actus reus*, but to supply the evidence of the necessary *mens rea*. This Court in *R. v. Cline, supra*, rejected the so-called "unequivocal act" test for determining when the stage of attempt has been reached. That test excludes resort to evidence *aliunde*, such as admissions, and holds that the stage of attempt has been reached only when the acts of the accused show unequivocally on their face the criminal intent with which the acts were performed. We are of the view that where the accused's intention is otherwise proved, acts which on their face are equivocal, may none the less, be sufficiently proximate to constitute an attempt. Where, however, there is no extrinsic evidence of the intent with which accused's acts were done with the intent to commit the crime that the accused is alleged to have attempted to commit, and hence insufficient to establish the offence of attempt.

Counsel for the respondents while conceding that the trial Judge's reasons are not free of ambiguity, submitted that they are reasonably open to the interpretation that he was searching for evidence that satisfied him beyond a reasonable doubt that the accused intended to rob the store in question, and at the end of his quest was not satisfied beyond a reasonable doubt, that the acts done by the accused supplied the necessary proof of intent.

We think that this submission accurately states the basis upon which the trial Judge acquitted the respondents, and the Crown has not satisfied us that but for the self-misdirection with respect to which complaint is made, that the verdict of the trial Judge would not necessarily have been the same. It is not to the point that, on the evidence, we would have reached a different conclusion with respect to the respondent's intentions.

Because of the view which we have taken, it is unnecessary to consider the difficult question whether, in the circumstances, the conviction of the respondent Sorrell on the charge of carrying a concealed weapon "at the time and place aforesaid" would preclude his conviction of the charge of attempted robbery, by virtue of the principle enunciated in *Kienapple v. The Queen* (1974), 15 C.C.C (2d) 524, 44 DL.R. (3d) 351, [1975] 1 S.C.R. 729.

For the reasons given the appeal must be dismissed.

*Appeal dismissed.*

## "Th'attempt, and Not the Deed, Confounds Us": Section 24 and Impossible Attempts
### Barry Brown

* Excerpts from (1981), 19 University of Western Ontario Law Review 226.

### INTRODUCTION

In this paper I shall examine that area of criminal law which is concerned with attempts to do that which, under the circumstances, is impossible. Although this area comprises a peculiar kind of attempt and hence presents a unique set of difficulties and necessary policy decisions, in order to understand those difficulties one must first try to discover the basic principles of attempts in general: only in that way can one hope to arrive at a consistent and workable approach to the narrower, more problematic area. Hence, I shall begin this examination by considering the basic nature of criminal attempts and from there proceed to study the particular problems which describe the area of impossibility.

Section 24 of the Canadian Criminal Code makes it an offence for anyone who has an intent to commit an offence to do or to omit to do anything for the purpose of carrying out that intention. Section 24(2) provides that the issue of whether a particular act or omission is too remote to constitute an attempt is a question of law. Obviously, the section requires the same two basic requirements demanded in most criminal offences: an *actus reus* and a *mens rea*. But although the latter is the more important element of an offence under section 24, the determination of what the *actus reus* consists of in a particular case usually becomes the major difficulty simply because the offence defined by section 24 necessarily represents in some way a frustrated purpose. And, as we shall see, the uncertain relationship between the two elements of the offence accentuates this difficulty.

In order to clarify the issues involved before proceeding to an analysis of them, let us consider two situations which raise those issues. In example 1, A, intending to poison V, pours what he believes to be poison into V's coffee. V drinks the coffee but suffers no harm: the substance was really sugar. In example 2, D, intending to rape his neighbour Mary, waits in ambush for her to cross his lawn. When a woman whom he mistakes for Mary passes by, D attacks and rapes her. Only afterwards does D realize that he has, in fact, attacked his wife, P. The issues we must consider amount to the question of whether one or both of A and D can or ought to be convicted of an attempt to commit their respective intended crimes.

As soon as we ask ourselves what did A and D intend to do and what did they actually do, the problems begin to appear. The courts accept that the acts done need not themselves be a crime: the intention of the actor can make acts innocent in themselves criminal. This aspect of the law of attempts requires that the *actus reus* be considered together with the *mens rea*. One cannot discuss the former without reference to the latter. For example, in *Jones v. Brooks,* where the defendants had been seen testing the locks on several parked cars with the admitted purpose of stealing one, Parker L.C.J. rejected defence counsel's submission that the charge of attempted theft of a motor vehicle could not be supported because of the equivocality of the acts in question:

> I am quite unable to accept that contention. Of course, an expressed intention alone does not amount to an attempt; there must be an *actus reus* which is sufficiently proximate to the expressed intention. But that does not mean to say that the courts should disregard entirely as part of the surrounding circumstances and the evidence in the case the expressed intention of the respondents, both at the time and after the *actus reus*. It seems to me that the intention is relevant when the act concerned is equivocal in order to see towards what the act is directed.

This approach helps to solve the problems related to equivocality, but what of those acts which, as in our examples, when viewed from an objective perspective form no identifiable *actus reus* because they cannot, in the circumstances, lead to the commission of an offence? In other words, can the accused's intention to commit a crime, even when based upon a mistaken belief about certain material facts, be used to characterize his acts as sufficient to constitute an attempt?

The question, when applied concretely, becomes more straightforward. In our example 1, what did A intend to do? Did he intend to put poison into V's coffee, or did he intend, with the purpose of killing V, to put that substance which turned out to be sugar into V's coffee? The law does not punish intent alone. If we use the latter characterization, A's conduct cannot be described with enough certainty to support a conviction: his general malevolent intent is not sufficient to transform a harmless act into a criminal attempt. Similarly, in our second example, D has had non-consensual intercourse with his wife. Did he intend to rape Mary, or rather to force himself upon that particular woman who turned out to be his wife?

As Alan Gold has recently pointed out, our decision concerning whether or not to include the accused's mistaken belief when characterizing his intention and acts will usually determine, in cases involving impossible attempts, whether or not we convict him. The problem does not arise in most attempt cases because where the accused sets out to do something which constitutes an offence and proceeds upon an accurate perception of the relevant facts, but for some reason is prevented from realizing his goal, the court's only problem, once intent is established, will be to determine whether or not the acts represent an attempt or merely preparation. But where, as in our examples, the disparity between the actor's mistaken belief and reality renders his purpose impossible. One must determine whether or not such an impossible intention can render otherwise non-criminal acts criminal.

## DEFINITIONAL DIFFICULTIES

When dealing with cases in this area of the law, as in all areas, we must be wary of accepting a definition of attempts which reflects a particular approach to the problem. If we accept such a definition without being aware that our decision to accept one over another may determine the outcome of the case, we simply argue from conclusions rather than from reasons. Because of this inevitable effect of whichever definition we choose, our choice ought to be the last stage of our investigation — after we have asked those questions which must be asked in order to discover consistent, sound reasons for selecting a particular definition.

The obvious problem involved here is to describe attempts in a manner which does not arbitrarily circumscribe the scope of the offence. Most commentators in this area, although often in profound disagreement concerning the proper solution, do agree that the policy behind punishing failed criminal attempts consists of a desire to discourage subsequent attempts. However, courts in many jurisdictions have lost sight of this basic fact and have tried to deal with the various factual manifestations of impossibility by devising categories whose constituent situations can be definitively labelled as culpable or non-culpable, and then attempting to fit each particular case into the appropriate category. This approach does not help solve the basic problems involved; instead, it gives rise to a never-ending series of semantic distinctions and illogical exceptions.

. . . .

## IMPOSSIBILITY

Section 24(1) of the Criminal Code includes after the description of an attempt, the phrase "whether or not it was possible under the circumstances to commit the offence." The section was included, in a slightly different form, in the Code of 1892. That Code was influenced to a considerable extent by the English Draft Code of 1879. The latter included this principle in different language, but for the same purpose: to offset an 1864 case which had held that putting a hand into a empty pocket could not be an attempt at theft because it was not possible to steal anything. But the presence of this provision does not necessarily eliminate the problems already outlined. As a consideration of our two examples reveals, two different kinds of impossible attempts exist: those which are factually impossible and those which are legally impossible. The former, like example 1, refers to those cases in which the actor's objective is proscribed by law, but circumstances unknown to him prevent his bringing it about. The latter, like our example 2, consists of conduct which even when fully carried out does not constitute a crime because of the actor's mistaken belief about an important fact which renders that conduct lawful. And, since *Collins* dealt with what has become known as a case of factual impossibility, should the provision designed with that case in mind be extended to cover cases of legal impossibility as well? Or, in order to reduce the question's reliance on the historical genesis of section 24, do "the circumstances" referred to in that section include the legal status of the actor's conduct?

. . . .

## THE RATIONALE OF ATTEMPTS AND A CONCLUSION

If, as I have argued, the problem can only be understood if one has a clear conception of the issues and consequent questions to be answered, what are the basic principles or policies which provide the foundation of the law of attempts and which therefore must influence our answers to those questions? As noted earlier, the most common justification for punishing those who have attempted to commit a crime and have failed is the desire to deter subsequent attempts; he who has tried and failed will likely try again, regardless of the reason for his initial failure. This rationale makes considerable sense: since the accused has not necessarily done anything which of itself is unlawful, section 24 creates the offence of trying to do something unlawful. Clearly, that section at least partially reflects our concern that he will try again, and, in order to prevent that success, we punish the unsuccessful attempt.

Such an approach necessarily involves, at least to a much greater degree than in the case of a completed offence, emphasis upon the accused's intent: we punish not what he did but he tried to do. The only consistent way to define what the accused attempted to do in this context consists of construing his intent on the basis of the facts as he believed them to be. As we have seen, any attempt to discuss intention or, in the words of section 24, the intended offence in terms of the actual (though unknown to the accused) circumstances produces an approach which is full or arbitrary distinctions and is inconsistent with several basic principles of criminal law. On the other hand, the approach which defines intention on the basis of the accused's mistaken belief, which reflects a view of attempt as "essentially one of criminal purpose implemented by an overt act strongly corroborative of such purposes," most effectively provides the necessary protection to society while at the same time remaining consistent with those basic principles. The attack most frequently made against this position, that it allows for a conviction in the absence of an *actus reus*, proceeds from a misconstrual of the argument. To take an extreme example, the man who contemplates murdering his wife but does nothing to achieve that purpose, we would all agree, commits no crime: we do not punish intent alone. But if that man puts what he believes to be poison into her coffee, he has attempted to fulfil his criminal purpose. Regardless of section 24, logic demands that we convict that man irrespective of the actual nature of that substance: he has attempted to murder his wife.

To return to our original problem, however, what is the effect of this historical distinction between legal and factual impossibility on the application of section 24? The House of Lords considered the two kinds of attempts to be practically the same: the New Zealand and New York Courts of Appeal thought that the distinction ought to be maintained. But as we have seen, that distinction is founded upon irrelevant considerations and bases the determination of guilt upon circumstances out of the control and knowledge of the accused. If we aim to prevent further attempts, the question of culpability out to be determined by the acts and intent of the accused just as it is in the other areas of criminal law. The question of whether or not the accused's acts formed part of a series which would, in uninterrupted, have led to the commission of a crime is irrelevant to the simple question of whether the accused intended to do something which the law proscribes and went beyond preparation in his attempt to commit that offence. This approach does not arbitrarily use as a reason a conclusion disguised as a definition: it merely follows the direction provided by section 24 in a manner consistent with criminal law principles and with the policy which informs that section.

So, in our second example, we ought to convict D of attempted rape. He intended to rape his neighbour Mary and went far beyond mere preparation in an attempt to fulfil that plan. To argue that he intended to attack that woman who turned out to be his wife does violence to the language and to any rational conception of human thought. Because of the importance which the law of attempts attaches to the *mens rea*, in order to convict we must assume as a precondition that D acted after reflecting on the matter: otherwise no sufficient *mens rea* would exist. Hence, it makes no sense to say he intended to attack a woman who he believed to be elsewhere. Indeed, in our example, he planned his attack with Mary in mind. But even if he had chosen his victim more haphazardly, he would have intended, at the very least, to attack a woman who was not his wife. Recklessness or indifference as to the identity of his victim would be sufficient to establish the *mens rea* of the offence: only if D had intended to attack his wife specifically could he escape conviction. In the same way that the Crown would have to prove that a man in Donnelly's position believed the goods to be stolen, it would have to prove that D believed that his victim was not his wife or was reckless concerning her identity. Perhaps one ought to remember at this point that I am not suggesting that D's mistaken belief should override the wording of section 143: the fact that he mistook his wife for Mary does not mean that D can be convicted of rape, for the simple reason that he has not committed the offence. The point here is, and must be, that he has tried to do that which according to our law is criminal but which, in the circumstances, was impossible.

The British government has recently introduced legislation which will eliminate the confusion created by the *Smith* decision by refusing to recognize impossibility of completion as a defence. This, I submit, represents the only logical, consistent approach; hence, when a Canadian court is called upon to decide a case similar to those of *Smith, Donnelly,* and *Jaffe*, it ought to refuse to draw the artificial distinctions found in those cases. In cases such as the famous example of the man who steals his own umbrella, provided such a case ever gets to trial and the requisite intent can be proved, the court can use its wide discretionary powers in sentencing. To acquit would be to introduce an element of confusion into a straightforward section of the Canadian Criminal Code.

## Regina v. Scott
### [1964] 2 C.C.C. 257 (Alta. C.A.)

MacDONALD, J.A.: — This is an appeal from a conviction made by Magistrate Read whereby the appellant Kenneth Scott was convicted upon a charge that he,

> "on the 13th day of July A.D. 1963, at Calgary in the said province, did, unlawfully attempt to commit an indictable offence, to wit: did unlawfully attempt to steal cash valued at less than $50.00, the property of Leonard Dodd, contrary to Section 406(c) of the Criminal Code."

The case was tried under Part XVI of the *Criminal Code*. Section 467(b) states:

> "**467.** The jurisdiction of a magistrate to try an accused is absolute and does not depend upon the consent of the accused where the accused is charged in an information

"(b) with attempted theft."

During Stampede week in Calgary, the complainant Dodd, shortly after midnight on July 13, 1963, was attending a street dance. He felt something in his right-hand back pocket, and on reaching back he found a hand in his pocket. While the hand was still in his pocket, Dodd grabbed the wrist above the hand and managed to hold the person whose wrist he had grabbed until the police arrived. The accused was the person whose hand was in Dodd's pocket.

There was a wallet in Dodd's pocket containing a credit card, driver's licence, birth certificate, and other valuable papers, but there was no money in the wallet. There is no evidence that Dodd had any money in that pocket.

There can be no doubt about the appellant's attempt to steal from the pocket of Dodd. The difficulty arises from the fact that he was charged with attempting to steal money, while there is nothing in the evidence to show that Dodd had any money in his pocket.

. . . .

In the present case, the appellant pickpocket could not know what was in the pocket of Dodd. I think, however, it is a self-evident fact that a pickpocket is desirous of stealing money. A pickpocket could not be convicted of stealing money unless the money was there, but it does seem that an attempt to steal money stands on an entirely different footing.

It seems to be that the proper and reasonable inference to be made under the circumstance that existed was that the appellant had the intent to steal money from the pocket of Dodd. The evidence established that the appellant did an act towards the accomplishment of that objective.

. . . .

The fact that the Crown failed to prove that there was money in Dodd's pocket cannot, in my view, make the charge bad in law.

It follows that the conviction must be affirmed.

The appellant also appeals against the sentence of one year imposed by the Magistrate. The maximum sentence for stealing when the value of what is stolen is less than $50, is two years: see *Code*, s. 280(b). For an attempt to steal less that $50, the maximum sentence would be one year: see *Code*, s. 406(b).

In the case at bar, the learned Magistrate imposed the maximum sentence, undoubtedly taking into consideration the fact that the accused had two previous convictions for breaking and entry since March of 1960. I do not think this is a case where the maximum sentence should have been imposed. I would accordingly reduce the sentence to six months.

JOHNSON, J.A. (dissenting): — The complainant was attending a street dance in the early hours of the morning of July 13, 1963, at the City of Calgary. He was standing in a crowd watching the dancing when he felt a hand in his pocket. He grabbed the wrist of the appellant while the hand was still in the pocket, and, after grappling with him, was able to hold the appellant until the police arrived. The pocket contained a wallet; it contained no money but did contain a credit card, driver's licence, birth certificate, and "other valuable papers" not enumerated or otherwise described. The appellant was charged that he did,

> "unlawfully attempt to commit an indictable offence, to wit: did unlawfully attempt to steal cash valued at less than $50.00, the property of Leonard Dodd, contrary to Section 406(c) of the Criminal Code."

. . . .

The neat point for consideration in this appeal is whether a charge is good that attempts to particularize what the Crown believes the accused was attempting to steal when the Crown fails to prove the intent to steal that particular object, either by direct evidence or by a reasonable inference.

When a pickpocket puts his hand in a person's pocket, very likely he does not know what he will get. He is, of course, after some property of the victim. If it is a purse or a billfold that he is seeking, as appears to have been the case with this appellant, it was in the past possible to draw the inference that cash in some form was all that the thief was after. It is not so easy to draw such an inference at the present time when wallets and billfolds contain other items which may be at least as valuable, such as credit cards, letters of credit, cheques, and other documents which can be used to obtain money or for identification by which money can be obtained. The information in the present case has the additional objection that it mentions "cash valued at less than $50.00". No doubt this sum was inserted to give the Magistrate absolute jurisdiction, but the inference that the appellant's expectation was so limited when he put his hand in the complainant's pocket is difficult to draw.

. . . .

It would appear than an information or indictment simply charging the appellant with an attempt to commit theft from the person of the complainant would have been good in this case: *R. v. Ring, supra*. Certainly one which charged him with an attempt to steal a wallet would have been good. A charge of an attempt to steal "the property of the complainant" would also appear to be good, and the Court in such case would not require that such property" be particularized: *R. v. Johnson et al.* (1864), 34 L.J.M.C. 24.

Though I do so with some hesitation, I have concluded that a conviction based upon the information in this case, having regard to the evidence, is not justified. The appeal is allowed and the conviction quashed.

KANE, J.A., concurs with MacDONALD, J.A.

*Appeal from conviction dismissed; appeal from sentence allowed.*

## Regina v. Smith
(1973), 2 W.L.R 942

LORD WIDGERY C.J. gave the judgment of the court. On September 28, 1972, at the Liverpool Crown Court this defendant was convicted of attempted handling of stolen goods. It is perhaps as well to read the terms of the count in the indictment. The particulars of the offence were:

"On or about September 28, 1971, in the County of Hertford, dishonestly attempted to assist in the disposal by or for the benefit of Alan Christopher Dixon, George James Mooney, Paul John Maeder and other persons unknown of 890 cartons of corned beef, the property of Arbuckle Smith & Co. Ltd., knowing or believing the same to have been stolen."

The essence of it was dishonestly attempting to assist in the disposal of those goods. He was convicted on that count and sentenced to 12 months' imprisonment. There was another count in the indictment charging conspiracy, arising out of the same circumstances, but the jury were directed to return a verdict of not guilty on that count.

What had happened was this. On September 18, 1971, there was a burglary at a warehouse in Liverpool, and a very large quantity of corned beef in cartons was stolen. Ten days later on September 28 two police officers on duty at night saw a large van proceeding down a main road near Sutton Coldfield, and their attention was directed to it because it was obviously overloaded, or had a load which had shifted, in other words it was all down on one side. They stopped the vehicle, the driver was a man called Dixon; he had a man named Nicholson with him. The van was loaded with cartons of corned beef, and for the purposes of this judgment I shall state the facts as the jury must have found them to be, and the jury clearly accepted that the cartons of corned beef in this van were part of the proceeds of the theft in Liverpool 10 days before.

The van and the two men in it were taken by the police officers to Sutton Coldfield police station. There was a brief conference between the police officers and members of the regional crime squad. The upshot of it was that it was decided to let this van go on its way to London with the police keeping an eye on it with a view to catching some of the other people who were concerned in the theft and disposal of these goods. So after what was really quite a brief interval, the van set off for London; it had two police officers on board and was trailed by other police officers in a car. They got to the London end of the M1 motorway at about seven o'clock at the Scratchwood Service Area, as it is called, because this was the place where Dixon, the driver of the vehicle, told the police that he was to rendezvous with those who were to take the corned beef on. At the Scratchwood Service Area there were a number of people, including the defendant, who were obviously there to receive this vehicle, and who were responsible for the transfer of the goods to other vehicles and the ultimate distribution of the goods to the ultimate receivers. I take the matter quite briefly, and I do not consider further the fact that many of these facts were disputed in the trial. It suffices for present purposes to say that in view of the jury's verdict, one can regard the defendant as being one, if not, the leader, of a party waiting at the Scratchwood Service Area for this van with a view to disposing of the contents.

It is clear that not only were they there for that purpose, but that when the van arrived the defendant took a leading part in making arrangements for the future disposal of the goods. There were such troubles as a burst tyre and things of that kind, and he evidently was taking a leading part in seeing that the goods were made mobile again and went on to their ultimate destination. In the end the police officers made their identity known, and the defendant was eventually arrested.

The reason why he was not charged with handling stolen goods was a perfectly simple one, namely, that by the time the vehicle got to Scratchwood Service Area and the defendant began to take an active part in the affair, the corned beef was, as a matter of law, no longer stolen goods. The reason is that by section 24(3) of the Theft Act 1968, which deals with certain offences relating to stolen goods, there is this provision:

> "But no goods shall be regarded as having continued to be stolen goods after they have been restored to the person from whom they were stolen or to other lawful possessions or custody, or after that person and any other person claiming through him have otherwise ceased as regards those goods to have any right to restitution in respect of the theft."

So in brief, as a matter of law, although the goods were undoubtedly stolen goods when they left the Liverpool warehouse, they ceased to be stolen goods as soon as the police got hold of them at Sutton Coldfield, and they were then restored to lawful custody. Consequently when the defendant began to perform his functions at the Scratchwood Service Area, the goods with which he was dealing, totally unknown to him, were not stolen goods at all. Accordingly there could be no question of charging him with handling stolen goods. Instead he was charged with attempting to handle stolen goods. And this is another case in which the court has to consider whether a person can be said to commit the offence of attempting to commit a criminal offence, if the offence is not capable of being committed by reason of circumstances unknown to the accused. The fact that an attempt is charged means, of course, that the prosecution are not able or minded to try and prove the full offence. It goes without saying that a man is not to be charged with or convicted of an attempt except on the basis that he had not gone the whole distance and actually committed the full offence itself.

Attempts arising out of a failure on the part of the accused to complete the full offence usually fall into two main classes. The first class is the type of case where the accused has embarked on a course of conduct which, if completed, will result in an offence but for some reason breaks off that course of conduct and never completes the action required to amount to the offence. There are dozens of examples of which one can think of attempts which come into that class: the pickpocket who puts his hand in a man's pocket only to find it empty; the burglar who is disturbed by the police when he is in the process of trying to break open the window; the safebreaker who finds when he gets to the safe, it is too difficult for him and he cannot open it. these are all people who have set out on a course of conduct which if completed in accordance with their intention would have amounted to a criminal offence, but who have desisted for one reason or another before the full course of criminality has been pursued. In general, and I emphasise that this court is only concerned to deal with those cases in generality, a charge of attempt can properly be laid in that type of case. It matters not that the accused might never have completed the major offence in any event.

But the second class is the one into which the present facts fall. The second class of case where attempt is sought to be charged is where the accused has meticulously and in detail followed every step of his intended course believing throughout that he was committing a criminal offence and when in the end it is found he has not committed a criminal offence because in law that which he planned and carried out does not amount to a criminal offence at all. That is this case, and the question whether in such circumstances the accused can properly be charged with an attempt is on the authorities a very much more difficult one, and indeed the questions raised are question which have been canvassed in New Zealand and the United States of America as well as in the courts of this country.

I think one can conveniently start with the modern cases and not take too long going through the earlier authorities of which counsel's industry has reminded us this morning. I approach this question first of all by looking at *Rex. v. Percy Dalton (London) Ltd.* (1949) 33 Cr. App. R. 102. This is an immediate post-war case when there were still controlled prices or maximum permitted prices for the sale of various commodities. The accused in *Rex v. Percy Dalton (London) Ltd.* were charged with having sold pears at a price in excess of the current permitted price for pears. It seems fairly clear that the accused thought that they were breaking the law, in their words, that they knew the maximum price and thought that they were charging a price in excess; but when the case was heard out to its end and the details were examined, it was found that in fact they had not exceeded the maximum price and that therefore an offence of breach of the appropriate regulation had not been made out. The question then arose as to whether it was possible to charge then with attempting to commit the offence of selling in excess of the maximum price. The court held that it was not, and there is a passage which this court finds of particular value, and which indeed has been approved on other occasions in this court also. It appears in the judgment of the court given by Birkett J., at p. 110:

> "All the acts of the company" — the defendant in that case —"have been considered by the jury in coming to that conclusion; and we feel it impossible to say on the same facts that the company can be convicted of the attempt to sell above the maximum price when the completed transaction was no offence. Steps on the way to the commission of what would be a crime, if the acts were completed, may amount to attempts to commit that crime, to which, unless interrupted, they would have led; but steps on the way to the doing of something, which is thereafter done, and which is no crime, cannot be regarded as attempts to commit a crime."

That principle, as I say, has been adopted with approval in *Reg. v. McDonough* (1962) 47 Cr. App. R. 37; it is a principle which this court regards as being laid down by *Rex v. Percy Dalton London Ltd.*, 33 Cr. App. R. 102 and one which prima facie we ought to follow, and of course if we follow that principle it means that the defendant in this case must succeed, because in the end when he had carried out the full course of conduct which he had in mind, he had not committed the offence of having stolen goods because the goods were no longer stolen.

. . . .

One comes therefore finally to the most recent case on this topic, which is *Reg. v. Curbishley* (1970) 55 Cr. App. R. 310, decided in this court. This was a case in which the appellants as parties to a plan concerned with the movement of stolen goods had been assigned as their part in the plan to take a vehicle to a certain place, there to pick up the stolen goods now before us. They knew that the goods were going to be stolen goods; they knew that they were going to handle stolen goods in the technical sense. They went there in accordance with the plan, but when they got there the goods were not there and they therefore had to turn round and come home again. The convictions which had been recorded at the Buckinghamshire quarter session of dishonestly attempting to assist in the removal or disposal of stolen goods were upheld. We do not think that *Reg. v. Curbishley* is really in any way inconsistent with Birkett J.'s dictum in *Rex v. Percy Dalton (London) Ltd.*, 33 Cr. App. R. 102, nor do we think that it really carries weight against the defendant in the present appeal, because on the brief facts which I have outlined you have on the face of it a clear example of a man who sets out to commit a criminal offence, and who is unable to complete the full course of action which would amount to the commission of that offence by reason of some intervention on the part of others. The only reason why they did not commit the full offence was because the goods were not there when they went to pick them up. That seems to me to fall into the first of the two classes of attempt cases to which I earlier referred, and not to be in any way inconsistent with the argument put forward by Mr. Hytner today. Mr. Morgan picks up a sentence on p. 315 and seeks to put a somewhat different complexion on the case, because it is to be observed on p. 315 that the goods had not only been removed when the appellant arrived to collect them, but had been removed by the police. Of course if they had been removed by the police they might well have go back into lawful custody as a result of that, and *Reg. v. Curbishley* might then become on all fours with the case we are deciding.

We are not impressed by that argument because there is not a word in the report to suggest that anyone regarded removal by the police as significant or that the point we have to decide was argued at all. On its face it seems to be a straightforward example of class one attempts where the only reason why the full offence was not committed was that the accused broke off the course of events at some stage before the full details of the crime had been worked out. We do not therefore regard *Reg. v. Curbishley* as being any significant obstacle in the path of the appellant in this case.

In the end we have come to the conclusion that we ought to follow the principle in *Rex v. Dalton (London) Ltd.*, 33 Cr. App. R. 102 enunciated by Birkett J. supported by *Reg. v. Donnely* [1970] N.Z.L.R. 980 and against which, as far as English authority is concerned, we only have to set the authority of *Reg. v. Miller*, 49 Cr. App. R. 241 which, for the reasons I have already given, does not seem to us to be a compelling one. Accordingly, we think the conviction was wrong in this case, that the appeal should be allowed and the conviction should be quashed.

*Appeal allowed.*
*Conviction quashed.*
*Prosecution costs to be paid out of central funds.*

. . . .

## Regina v. Ancio
(1984), 10 C.C.C (3d) 385 (S.C.C.)

Appeal by the Crown from a judgment of the Ontario Court of Appeal, 63 C.C.C. (2d) 309, 34 O.R. (2d) 437, allowing an appeal by the accused from his conviction for attempted murder.

[Only the judgment of McIntyre J. is reproduced below.]

McINTYRE J.: — This appeal involves consideration of the mental element required for proof of the crime of attempted murder, the subject of this Court's earlier judgment in *Lajoie v. The Queen* (1973), 10 C.C.C (2d) 313, 22 D.L.R. (3d) 618, [1974] S.C.R. 399.

At the date of the events which give rise to this appeal the respondent had been married some 25 years. His wife had left the matrimonial home and was living with one Kurely. The respondent was depressed and had been drinking to excess on the date in question. He telephoned his wife at Kurely's residence and told her he was afraid that their 23-year-old son was about to commit suicide and asked her to meet him. She refused to co-operate. Later the same evening the respondent broke into a friend's home while its owners were absent and took away three shot-guns. He sawed off the barrel of one, loaded it, and taking some extra ammunition with him went to Kurely's apartment building and gained entry by breaking the glass in the front door. On hearing the noise caused by the breaking glass, Kurely came from his bedroom to investigate, carrying a chair with a jacket hanging on it. He saw the respondent, carrying the shot-gun, ascending the stairs to the second floor. He threw the chair and jacket, hitting the respondent. The gun went off. The blast missed Kurely by some three feet but put a hole in the jacket which had been on the chair. A struggle followed in which Kurely appears to have wrested the gun from the respondent. When the police arrived, having been called during the course of the fight between the two men, Kurley was on the floor with his head partly under a bed and with the respondent upon him striking him weakly.

Shortly after his arrest the respondent stated to the police:

> I just went over to see my wife. I had phoned her earlier. I broke the window and went in. Then I heard what sounded like a gun go off. You are lucky you got here when you did. I had him by the throat and I would have killed him.

According to the respondent's account of events, the gun was discharged accidentally, although under tests conducted by the police the weapon was not found to be prone to accidental discharge.

The respondent was charged with a number of offences arising out of this affair but only one, that of attempted murder, is involved in the appeal. It was contained in the first count of the information and was in these terms:

> ... did attempt to murder Michael Kurely by discharging a sawed off shotgun at him contrary to s. 222 of the *Criminal Code* of Canada.

He elected trial by judge alone and was convicted. The conviction was quashed in the Court of Appeal and a new trial directed [63 C.C.C. (2d) 309, 34 O.R. (2d) 437]. This appeal is taken by leave of this Court.

The trial judge disposed of the other charges against the respondent and made a finding that he had broken into Kurely's apartment building with intent to use the shot-gun to force his wife to leave. He said:

> I turn now to the very real point of the charge of attempted murder, and having made the finding I have of the break and enter at the house at 108 6th Street, with intent to commit an indictable offence, wither [sic] forceable confinement or worse. Forceable confinement if you accept the evidence of the accused, I feel probably worse than that.

He then referred to s. 213(d) of the *Criminal Code* which is in these terms:

> 213. Culpable homicide is murder where a person causes the death of a human being while committing or attempting to commit. . .(kidnapping an forcible confinement). . .(breaking and entering). . .whether or not the person means to cause death to any human being and whether he knows that death is likely to be caused to any human being, if
>
> . . .
>
> (d)  he uses a weapon or has it upon his person
>   (i)  during or at the time he commits or attempts to commit the offence, or

(ii) during or at the time of his fight after committing or attempting to commit the offence, and the death ensues as a consequence.

Noting that breaking and entering with intent to commit an indictable offence is one of the offences named in the section, he convicted the respondent of attempted murder on the basis that the respondent had carried and used a weapon int the course of a breaking an entry with intent to effect forceable confinement of his wife.

The judgment of the Court of Appeal (MacKinnon A.C.J.O., Dubin and Lacourciere JJ.A.) was written by MacKinnon A.C.J.O. He accepted the submission by counsel for Ancio that the finding of fact which formed the basis of the conviction were that the respondent committed the offence of breaking and entering Kurely['s residence and that he had in his possession a weapon during the commission of the offence. He then considered whether these findings of fact in the absence of any finding of an intent to kill or cause bodily harm were sufficient to support a conviction for attempted murder by the interaction of ss. 24(1) and 213(d) of the *Criminal Code*, and said [at p. 319]:

> There is no question in the instant appeal that the trial Judge was satisfied beyond a reasonable doubt that the appellant intended to break and enter the Kurrelli [sic] premises and intended to have in his possession the sawed-off shot-gun. The appellant was charged with the offence of attempted murder and the "offence" referred to in s. 24(1) is the offence of "attempted murder" and not the offence of break and enter while carrying a weapon on his person. If death had ensued in the instant case it would have been constructive murder, but from the standpoint of an attempt, can there be an intention to attempt an unintentional act without more?

and further [at p. 320]:

> In the law of attempts it is the *mens rea* which is fundamental and in the circumstances of this case there must be the intention either to mean to cause death or in the case of attempted murder, as now established by *R. v. Lajoie* (1973), 10 C.C.C. (2d) 313, 33 D.L.R. (3d) 168, [1974] S.C.R. 399, meaning to cause the victim bodily harm knowing it is likely to cause his death, and reckless whether death ensues or not. The trial Judge, accordingly in this case, had to be satisfied beyond a reasonable doubt (or a jury if one is present) that the Crown has established the required intent under s. 212(a)(i) or 212(a)(ii).

He then went on to hold that while there was evidence before the trial judge from which he could have drawn the necessary inferences regarding the intent to kill or cause bodily harm likely to cause death, he had not done so, and as a result had not made the finding necessary to support the conviction. Accordingly, the conviction was quashed and a new trial was ordered.

The Crown contended in this Court that the Court of Appeal was in error in holding that the *mens rea* in attempted murder was limited to an intention to cause death (s. 212(a)(i)), or an intention to cause bodily harm knowing it to be likely to cause death and being reckless whether death ensues (s. 212(a)(ii)). The Crown's position was stated in its factum in these words:

> ...the intention for attempted murder is not restricted to an actual intention to kill or an intention to cause grievous bodily harm that one knows is likely to cause death and is reckless whether death ensues or not, but *extends to an intention to do that which constitutes the commission of the offence of murder as defined in ss. 212 and 213 of the Criminal Code. It is the Crown's position that s. 24 and s. 213(d) in combination can for the basis for a conviction of attempted murder.*

(Emphasis added.)

. . . .

The common law recognition of the fundamental importance of intent in the crime of attempt is carried forward into the *Criminal Code*. A reading of s. 24 of the *Code* and all its predecessors since the enactment of the first *Code* in 1892 confirms that the intent to commit the desired offence is a basic element of the offence of attempt. Indeed, because the crime of attempt may be complete without the actual commission of any other offence and even without the performance of any act unlawful in itself, it is abundantly clear that the criminal element of the offence of attempt may lie solely in the intent. As noted by Glanville Williams, *Criminal Law: The General Part*, 2nd ed. (1961), -207, p. 642, in discussing attempts: "An *actus reus*. . .need not be a crime apart from the state of mind. It need not even be a tort, or a moral wrong, or a social mischief." The question now arises: What is the intent required for an attempt to commit murder? As has been indicated earlier, the Crown's position is that the intent required for a conviction on a charge of attempt to murder is the intent to do that which will, if death is caused, constitute the commission of murder as defined in ss. 212 and 213 of the *Code*, so that a combination of ss. 24 and 213(d) can form the basis for a conviction of attempted murder. The respondent, on the other hand, argues that although the authorities presently limit the intent to that which would constitute murder as defined in s. 212 of the *Code*, logic and principle dictate that the intent should be limited to the specific intent to kill described in s. 212(a)(i).

While it is clear from ss. 212 and 213 of the *Criminal Code* that an unintentional killing can be murder, it is equally clear that whatever mental elements may be involved and whatever means may be employed there cannot be a murder without a killing. Section 24 of the *Code* defines, in part, the offence of attempt as "having an intent to commit an offence". As Estey J. observed in *R. v. Quinton* (1947), 88 C.C.C. 231 at pp. 236-7, [1948] D.L.R. 625 at p. 630, [1947] S.C.R. 234 at pp. 235-6, in referring to the then s. 72(now s. 24):

> This section requires that one to be guilty of an attempt but intend to commit the completed offence and to have done some act toward the accomplishment of that objective.

The completed offence of murder involves a killing. The intention to commit the complete offence of murder but therefore include an intention to kill. I find it impossible to conclude that a person may intent to commit the unintentional killings described in ss 212 and 213 of the *Code*. I am then of the view that the *mens rea* for an attempted murder cannot be less than the specific intent to kill.

As I have said earlier, there is a division of opinion upon this point and strong arguments have been raised in favour of the Crown's position that a "lesser intent" such as that provided in s. 212(a)(ii) or even no intent at all relating to the causing of death as provided in s. 213(d), may suffice to found a conviction for attempted murder. This view is supported in *Lajoie*. In my view, with the utmost respect for those who differ, the sections of the *Criminal Code* relied on in that case to not support that position.

. . . .

It was argued, and it has been suggested in some of the cases and academic writings of the question, that it is illogical to insist upon a higher degree of *mens rea* for attempted murder, while accepting a lower degree amounting to recklessness for murder. I see no merit in this argument. The intent to kill is the highest intent in murder and there is no reason in logic why an attempt to murder, aimed at the completion of the full crime of murder, should have any lesser intent. If there is any illogic in this matter, it is in the statutory characterization of unintentional killing as murder. The *mens rea* for attempted murder is, in my view, the specific intent to kill. A mental state falling short of that level may well lead to conviction for other offences, for example, one or other of the various aggravated assaults, but not a conviction for an attempt at murder. For these reasons, it is my view that *Lajoie* should no longer be followed.

I would accordingly dismiss the Crown's appeal and confirm the Court of Appeal's order for a new trial.

*Appeal dismissed.*

**Questions/Discussion**
1. What is the rationale behind "attempts" in criminal law? What should we be punishing for in regard to attempts?
2. What is the test for deciding when the actus reus of a criminal attempt has occurred? Do you think this is a "real" test or is it so vague as to amount to "I know an attempt when I see one"? Are you in favour of a test which would give greater or less freedom of action to an individual who is thinking of committing a crime?
3. Should individuals who voluntarily abandon their criminal purpose for altruistic reasons be completely relieved of criminal liability? What is the purpose of punishing such people?
4. Explain the differences between "legal impossibility" and "physical impossibility" as they relate to attempts in criminal law. Are the differences of any relevance in Canadian criminal law today? Do you think that they should or should not be relevant in attaching criminal liability for attempts? Why or why not?
5. Do you agree with the decision in *Ancio*? Why or why not?

**Further Reading**
- Galloway, D., "Patterns of Trying: A Critique of Fletcher on Criminal Attempts" (1982), 7 Queen's Law Journal 232.
- MacKinnon, P., "Making Sense of Attempts" (1982), 7 Queen's Law Journal 254.
- Meehan, E., *The Law of Criminal Attempt: A Treatise* (Toronto: Carswell, 1984).
- Mewett, A. and M. Manning, *Mewett and Manning on Criminal Law, 3rd ed.* (Toronto: Butterworths, 1994).
- Stuart D., *Canadian Criminal Law: A Treatise*, 2nd ed. (Toronto: Carswell, 1987), pp. 535-562.
- Stuart, D., and R. Delisle, *Learning Canadian Criminal Law, 5th ed.* (Toronto: Carswell, 1995).
- Verdun-Jones, S., *Criminal Law in Canada: Cases, Questions and the Code* (Toronto, Harcourt Brace Jovanovich Canada, 1989), pp 354-367.
- Verdun-Jones, S., and C. Griffiths, *Canadian Criminal Justice, 2nd ed.* (Toronto: Butterworths, 1994).

## 6.2.2 Counselling

**Introduction**

Counselling is an offence under section 464 of the Criminal Code which states that it is a crime when someone counsels another person to commit an offence *and* that person does not commit the counselled offence. In situations where the person *does* commit the offence, the provisions relating to "parties to the offence" in section 21 or section 22 are then applicable; these provisions are looked at in section 6.3 below. As for the requirements of the offence in section 464, first, something must be done which amounts to counselling, and this may be words, actions, or gestures. There must also be, as is evident it *McLeod*, a recipient for the counselling though the recipient need not be influenced by the counselling. Finally, what is counselled must be either an indictable offence or an offence punishable on summary conviction.

Problems which are raised in regard to counselling relate to issues surrounding the actus reus and mens rea of the offence. As for the actus reus, there is no clear meaning of the term "counselling" and what amounts to such activity. There is thus a need to rely heavily on the cases for its meaning, rather than having it clearly set out in the Code. Second, it is unclear what the mens rea requirements are for the offence. Is a full wrongful intent needed or is recklessness sufficient? Both of these issues are important, particularly in the area of legitimate dissent and its boundaries. For example, is a writer breaking the law on counselling by advocating withholding of the payment of income taxes as one method of protesting the testing of Cruise missiles in Canada or by suggesting the blocking of roads to protest hazardous waste dumping in that area? What is the meaning of counselling and is the running of the risk than offence may be encouraged as a result of one's actions enough (that is, recklessness versus a full intention to have an offence carried out)? The code provision does not distinguish between these examples of dissent and the hiring of someone to kill your spouse. Obviously, differences in motive are important at the penalty stage, but perhaps we need clearer distinctions and boundaries set out in the legislation itself, rather than leaving it to the vagaries of prosecutors' policies or personalities. The case which follows is in fact a very good example of the dangers of an open-ended provision such as counselling in that the case against the counter culture newspaper was arguably borderline at best.

### Regina v. McLeod
### (1970), 1 C.C.C. (2d) (B.C. C.A.)

Appeal by the accused from their conviction on a charge of counselling another person to commit an indictable offence contrary to s. 407(a) of the *Criminal Code*.

The judgment of the Court was delivered by

MacLEAN, J.A.: — This is an appeal by Georgia Straight Publishing Ltd. and its Editor-in-Chief Dan McLeod, against convictions of the company and McLeod for that:

> between the 27th day of March, A.D. 1969 and the 4th day of April, A.D. 1969 unlawfully did counsel another person, to wit, Penelope Ann York, to commit an indictable offence, which was not committed, to wit, to cultivate marihuana, contrary to the provisions of Sec. 6 of the Narcotic Control Act, S.C. 1960-1961 Chapter 35.

Section 407(a) of the *Criminal Code* under which the charge is laid provides that:

(a) every one who counsels, procures or incites another person to commit an indictable offence is, if the offence is not committed, guilty of an indictable offence and is liable to the same punishment to which a person who attempts to commit that offence is liable;...

Then s. 6(1) and (2) of the *Narcotic Control Act*, 1960-61 (Can.), c. 35, provides that:

6(1) No person shall cultivate opium poppy or marihuana except under authority of and in accordance with a licence issued to him under the regulations.

(2) Every person who violates subsection (1) is guilty of an indictable offence and is liable to imprisonment for seven years.

The prosecution arose from an article which appeared in the issue of the weekly newspaper Georgia Straight of March 28th-April 3, 1969, in the centre two pages of the publication. The left-hand page is occupied by a picture of the plant *cannabis sativa*.

The article starts with a paragraph reading as follows:

THIS IS A CHAIN LETTER. WITHIN THE NEXT FIFTY-FIVE DAYS YOU WILL RECEIVE THIRTY-ELEVEN-HUNDRED POUNDS OF CHAINS.

In the meantime, plant your seeds.

Then follows in large capital letters the legend "PLANT YOUR SEEDS". This is followed again by a number of paragraphs reading as follows under the heading "Growing and Cultivating Pot":

This should help you grow better quality plants in less time.

The first thing in growing a better plant, naturally, would be to start with seeds of good quality. If you or some of your friends have had access to good grass, use those seeds. After all, not all the grass we smoke does the same thing for us.

Select the largest seeds and place them between two napkins, blotting paper, etc. and add enough water to cover the napkins. The cover the top or put them in a dark closet for two or three days, until the seeds have sprouted at least a half inch or longer.

These paragraphs are followed by detailed instructions for planting, fertilizing, cultivating and harvesting of the plant.

The article concludes with the exhortation "Plant Your Seeds".

The evidence discloses that a copy of the allegedly offending issue was purchased by the witness, Miss York, at the corner of Georgia and Granville Streets in Vancouver. On April 2, 1970, Miss York admitted that she was not influenced by the counselling contained in the newspaper. She said that she was amused by that part of the article which referred to the chain letter.

The learned Provincial Judge has held, and I think correctly, that:

... if the person bought the paper and the only fair inference is that it was on public sale at the corner of Georgia and Granville Street and if the person bought the paper and read it, they were in fact being counselled to grow marijuana.

Defence counsel has suggested that "counselling" is not complete unless the person to whom the communication is directed has been influenced by the communication. I cannot accept this submission as it is in my view there is no justification for such a limited meaning to the word "counselling".

In *Brousseau v. The King* (1917), 29 C.C.C. 207, 39 DL.R. 114, 56 S.C.R. 22, Sir Charles Fitzpatrick C.J. said at p. 208:

> I construe "counsel" used in collocation with "procure" to mean "advise" or "recommend" and the demand made in the admitted circumstances means at least that.

In *Rex v. Higgins*, 2 East 5 at 17, Lord Kenyon said: —

> "It is argued that a mere intent to commit evil is not indictable, without an act done; but is there not an act done when it is charged that the defendant solicited another to commit a felony? The solicitation is an act."

At p. 209 of the report Davies, J. said:

> I think s. 69 of the Criminal Code clearly makes a person who counsels or procures another to commit an offence, guilty of a specific offence, whether the person so counselled actually commits the offence he is counselled to commit or not.

In my view the purchaser of this newspaper was counselled to cultivate marijuana.

It is submitted that if this conviction were to be upheld that the "freedom of the press" (as that expression is used in s.1(f) of the *Canadian Bill of Rights*, 1960 (can.), c. 44) would be interfered with.

In the case of *Koss v. Konn* (1961), 40 D.L.R. (2d) 242, 36 W.W.R. 100, this Court dealt with an allegation that a section of the *Trade-Unions Act* infringed "freedom of speech", as that expression is used in s. 1(d) of the *Canadian Bill of Rights*. The majority judgment was given by Tysoe, J.A., and he quoted [p. 264 D.L.R.] the following words of Lord Wright in *James v. Commonwealth of Australia*, [1936] A.C. 578:

> "'Free' in itself is vague and indeterminate... Free speech does not mean free speech; it means speech hedged in by all the laws against defamation, blasphemy, sedition and so forth; it means freedom governed by law."

The same principle applicable to freedom of speech must in my opinion apply to "freedom of the press". In my view s. 407 of the *Criminal Code* as it applies to the appellant does not interfere with "freedom of the press". The freedom which the appellant enjoys is as Lord Wright expressed it a freedom "hedged in by all the laws against defamation, blasphemy, sedition and so forth".

The offence committed by the appellant has been part of the criminal law of Canada for many years and is also an offence in many of the common law countries.

Lastly the appellant submits that there was no evidence of criminal intent. Counsel does not suggest that the offence was other than deliberate but he suggests that the offending article was a "spoof", or was written in a humorous vein "with tongue in cheek".

I have read the article and in fact the whole paper and I can find nothing which even suggests that the appellant was doing anything other than deliberately counselling readers of the paper to cultivate marijuana. I would dismiss the appeal of the company.

However, I think that the evidence falls short of being sufficient to convict the appellant Dan McLeod, and according I would allow his appeal and set aside his conviction.

*Appeal as to Georgia Straight Publishing Ltd. dismissed;*
*appeal as to McLeod allowed.*

## Questions/Discussion

1. Do you agree with the decision in *McLeod*? Why or why not? Do you think the decision poses any danger to the free communication of dissemination of ideas in society? Can you think of similar situations where information is provided which might be interpreted as counselling an offence? For you, what amounts to or should amount to the actus reus and the mens rea of counselling?
2. As noted in the introduction above, the Code does not distinguish between activities many people consider legitimate dissent and protest and the hiring of someone to kill your spouse. Should it? Why or why not? If you did want to make such a distinction, how would you do it in the Code?

## Further Reading

- Fitzgerald, O., and L. Douglas, "Counselling and Conspiracy" (1984), 16 Ottawa Law Review 331.
- Mewett, A. and M. Manning, *Mewett and Manning on Criminal Law*, 3rd ed. (Toronto: Butterworths, 1984).
- Stuart, D., *Canadian Criminal Law: A Treatise*, 2nd ed. (Toronto: Carswell, 1987), pp. 590-592.
- Stuart, D., and R. Delisle, *Learning Canadian Criminal Law*, 5th ed. (Toronto: Carswell, 1995).
- Verdun-Jones, S., *Criminal Law in Canada: Cases, Questions and the Code* (Toronto: Harcourt Brace Jovanovich Canada, 1989), pp. 351-354.
- Verdun-Jones, S., and C. Griffiths, *Canadian Criminal Justice*, 2nd ed. (Toronto: Butterworths, 1994).

## 6.2.3 Conspiracy

### Introduction

Conspiracy is a separate offence as set out in section 465 of the Criminal Code whereby it is an offence to conspire to commit murder, to commit an indictable offence other than murder, and to commit an offence punishable on summary conviction, and also to conspire to falsely prosecute someone. What is missing from the section is a definition of conspiracy" and for this definition it is necessary to go to the common law requirements for a conspiracy. The *O'Brien* case which follows set out well the provisions of conspiracy as it has been interpreted by the courts. Central to the offence is the presence of an agreement to carry out an offence; the required nature of this agreement is set out in the case.

The rationale behind the offence is one of prevention, the idea that when several people have a shared criminal purpose, there is a greater risk to society, and the state has the right to step in before the attainment of the purpose. The criticism, as seen in Wilson's article below, is that the state is sometimes punishing people for the thoughts which they hold in common, when those who hold such thoughts individually would not be sanctioned unless or until they act upon them. Yet individuals may hold those goals more strongly than those who share them and present more of an actual risk or danger than a group. In this context, Wilson gives several examples where the crime has been used for political ends to punish those whose views differed from those in authority.

Another criticism of the provision has to do with the uncertainty that arises over what offences are to be included in the term "offences punishable of summary conviction".[1] Does it include provincial offences and if so, should it? The criticism is that provincial offences are not as serious as most of those in the Code, ad that criminal conspiracy should not encompass minor offences. There is also the argument that only Parliament should be responsible for the production of criminal sanctions and "for the sake of certainty and comprehensiveness, the Criminal Code should be self-contained".[1]

## The Queen v. O'Brien
## [1954] S.C.R. 666

[Only the judgments of Taschereau J. and Rand J. are reproduced below.]

TASCHEREAU, J.: — The Attorney General of British Columbia appeals from a judgment of the Court of Appeal which ordered a new trial. It held that there had been misdirection.

The charge for which the respondent was convicted was that, in the City of Vancouver, British Columbia, between the 30th day of November, 1952, and the 14th day of January, 1953, the respondent unlawfully conspired with one Walter John Tulley and others, to commit a certain indictable offence, namely, kidnapping.

Tulley, the alleged co-conspirator, was not charged, but the trial, being called as a Crown witness, he gave an account of various meetings he had with the respondent, and explained that both had agreed, at the request of the latter, to kidnap one Joan Margaret Pritchard. He said in his evidence that he never had any intention of going through with this plan, but was just fooling the respondent, or hoaxing him. He also explained that he denounced the whole scheme to the police authorities, and the respondent was arrested.

The learned trial Judge in his charge said: —

> Counsel for the accused has suggested that the offence is not complete, because Tulley, in his own evidence, said that he had had at no time any intention of carrying out that agreement. I tell you as a matter of law, gentlemen, *that the offence was complete*, if, in point of fact, the accused and Tulley did make the agreement which is charged against him, *even though Tulley never at any time had any intention of carrying the agreement into effect.*

The Court of Appeal, Mr. Justice Robertson dissenting, held that this constituted misdirection, and therefore, ordered a new trial.

The contention of the respondent which was accepted by the majority of the Court of Appeal, is that Tulley, not having any intention to carry through the common design, could not be a party to the conspiracy, and that therefore, O'Brien the respondent, could not alone be found guilty of the crime. It is common ground that no others were involved in the conspiracy. The mere agreement, without any intention to carry into effect the common design would, according to the submission of the appellant, be sufficient.

I think there has been some confusion as to the element of intention which is necessary to constitute the offence. It is, of course, essential that the conspirators have the *intention to agree*, and this agreement must be complete. There must also be a common design to do something unlawful, or something lawful by illegal means. Although it is not necessary that there should be an overt act in furtherance of the

---

[2] See generally, O. Fitzgerald and L. Douglas, "Counselling and Conspiracy" (1984), 16 Ottawa Law Review 331, at 337.

[1] *Ibid.* p. 340.

conspiracy, to complete the crime, I have no doubt that there must exist *an intention to put the common design into effect*. A common design necessarily involves an intention. Both are synonymous. The intention cannot be anything else but the will to attain the object of the agreement. I cannot imagine several conspirators agreeing to defraud, to restrain trade, or to commit any indictable offence, without having the intention to reach the common goal.

I fully agree with some of the statements that have been made by the Court of Appeal of Quebec in *Rex v. Kotyszyn*. The head note reads: —

> There was no common design between the accused and the policewoman, and there was no agreement between them *since the policewoman had no intention of undergoing the operation*. Consequently there *was neither a conspiracy* nor an *attempt to conspire*.

In the same case, at page 269, Mr. Justice MacKinnon said:

> There can be no conspiracy when one wants to do a thing and the other does not want to do it.

Stephen (Commentaries on the laws of England, 21st Ed., Vol. 4) says at page 166: —

> The object of the agreement may be the accomplishment of an unlawful act, or of a lawful act by unlawful means. In other words it must be unlawful either in *its aims or in its methods*.

The two elements of agreement and of *common design* are specifically stated to be essential ingredients of the crime of conspiracy. Willes, J. in *Mulcahy v. The Queen:*

> A conspiracy consists not merely in the intention of two or more, but in the agreement of two or more to do an unlawful act, or to do a lawful act by unlawful means. So long as such a design rests in intention only, it is not indictable. When two agree to carry it into effect, the very plot is an act in itself, and the act of each of the parties . . . punishable if for a criminal object. . .

Vide also *Rex v. McCutcheon*.

This is not the case of the conspirator, who after having completed the crime, withdraws from the conspiracy. If a person, with one or several others, agrees to commit an unlawful act, and later, after having had the intention to carry it through, refuses to put the plan into effect, that person is nevertheless guilty, because all the ingredient of conspiracy can be found in the accused's conduct. But, when the conspiracy has never existed, there can be no withdrawal.

The definition of conspiracy itself supposes an aim. People do not conspire unless they have an object in view. The law punishes conspiracy so that the unlawful object is not attained. It considers that several persons who agree together to commit an unlawful act, are a menace to society, and even if they do nothing in furtherance of their common design, the state intervenes to exercise a repressive action, so that the intention is not materialized, and does not become harmful to any one. The intention must necessarily be present because it is the unlawful act necessarily flowing from the intention, that the state wishes to prevent.

In the case at bar, there is evidence that although he made an agreement with the respondent, Tulley never intended to carry the plan through and kidnap Mrs. Pritchard. On the other hand, there is also evidence that may indicate that he intended to attain the object of the agreement. Did Tulley have this intention or not? This is a question for the jury, and I would invade a domain which is not mine, if I attempted to answer it.

It has been said that if the submission of the respondent were the law, it would be impossible to obtain a conviction on a charge of conspiracy, because the mental state of the accused very often remains in the sphere of uncertainty. All crimes where intention is an essential element would then become impossible to prove. Various factors have come into play, and with their help i is then possible to determine what the intention was. There is a presumption for instance, that a person who does an act intends to do it. As well, numerous circumstances will indicate if an alleged thief intended to rob, or if a killer intended to murder. Conspiracy is not in a different class. It is within the exclusive province of the jury, to weigh all the evidence and to determine all these questions of fact, and to say whether the intentional element is revealed by the evidence.

But I do think that the jury were not properly instructed when they were told that, even without the intention to commit the kidnapping, which was necessarily the common design, the conspiracy was complete by the agreement. The jury were not free to weigh the evidence because, being improperly instructed, they had to disregard what is in my view one of the most important elements of the crime for which the accused was charged.

I agree with the Court of Appeal that there was misdirection, and that consequently there must be a new trial. It has been suggested that the Court of Appeal should have dismissed the appeal, on the ground that although there was misdirection, a properly instructed jury would have necessarily come to the same conclusion. (Cr. Code 1014). With this proposition, I entirely disagree. There is evidence that would justify a properly instructed jury to acquit or to convict, and I do not think in either alternative, that the verdict wold be set aside as unreasonable.

I would dismiss the appeal.

RAND J.: — I agree that a conspiracy requires an actual intention in both parties at the moment of exchanging the words of agreement to participate in the act proposed; mere words purporting agreement without an assenting mind to the act proposed are not sufficient. The point of difference between the judgments below is the meaning to be given the word "agreement". In the opinion of Robertson J.A. there was an agreement when Tulley in effect said "I will" even though at that moment his mind was "I won't". The mens rea here appears to lie in the intent to utter the words "I will"; but this severance of the intention to speak the words from that of carrying out the action they signify is a refinement that seems to me to be out of place in a common law crime. Modern statutes have introduced offences in which the objective or physical acts themselves are struck at but they are irrelevant to the unwritten offences. Bishop's Criminal Law, 9th Ed. Vol. II, p. 131 puts it thus: —

> Obviously there must be, between the conspirators, a concert of will and endeavour, not a mere knowledge, acquiescence or approval or a mere several attempt to accomplish the particular wrong... Where there are only two, and one simply joins in appearance to draw the other on, neither is a conspirator.

and at p. 132: —

> As soon as this union of will is perfected, the offence of conspiracy is complete, — no act beyond is required... It is sufficient if the minds of the parties meet understandingly so as to bring about an intelligent and deliberate agreement to do the acts an commit the offence charged, although such agreement be not manifested by any formal words.

The question raised is, in my opinion, concluded by the judgment of the House of Lords in *Mulcahy v. The Queen*. In that case a prosecution had been brought under *The Crown and Government Security Act*, 11 Vict., c. 12. The indictment following the language of the statute alleged that the accused with five other persons "did feloniously and wickedly compass, imagine, invent, devise, and intend to deprive and depose Our Lady the Queen from the style, honour, and royal name of the Imperial Crown of the United Kingdom of Great Britain and Ireland" and proceeded to declare that the accused did "express, utter, and declare by divers overt acts and deeds hereinafter mentioned, that is to say". The overt acts were then alleged: —

> In order to fulfill, perfect and bring to effect his felonious compassing, imagination, invention, devise and intention aforesaid, they ... feloniously and wickedly did combine, conspire, confederate, and agree with (19 other persons all named) and with divers other evilly disposed persons, to the jurors aforesaid unknown to raise, make, and levy insurrection and rebellion against Our said Lady the Queen within this realm.

The statute required the expression of compassing and intending by overt acts and it was necessary, therefore, to allege them. The question raised was whether a conspiracy was such an act.

The House held that it was. This means that the act of conspiracy was sufficient to establish both the compassing and the intention to do the forbidden act, or to put it in another form, that in conspiracy there is not only agreement to do the act proposed signified by words or other means of communication, but also the coexistent intent in each to do it. If that were not so, conspiracy would not have evidenced the *intention* of those charged "to deprive and depose, etc." The language of Willes J. at p. 317 of the report bears out that view. In the course of considering the argument that conspiracy rests in intention only and that an overt act must consist in some external manifestation or deed, he says: —

> A conspiracy consists not merely in the intention of two or more, but in the agreement of two or more to do an unlawful act, or to do a lawful act by unlawful means. So long as such a design rests in intention only, it is not indictable. When two agree to carry it into effect, the very plot is an act in itself, and the act of each of the parties, promise against promise, actus contra actum, capable of being enforced, if lawful, punishable if for a criminal object or for use of criminal means.

In that language he distinguishes between the intention of each person severally and the communicated assent between them to carry out the intention. In stressing the necessity for agreement he assumes the existence of intent.

. . . .

On the contrary view, even if both parties had been without the intent to carry out the scheme, each seeking to incriminate the other, they would have drawn guilt upon themselves.

Assuming, then, the truth of the evidence of Tulley that at no time did he ever intend to go along with the proposal made to him, there was no conspiracy.

I would therefore dismiss the appeal.

*Appeal dismissed.*

## The Political Use of Criminal Conspiracy*
*Wes Wilson*

* Excerpts from (1984), 42 University of Toronto Faculty of Law Review 60.

The law of criminal conspiracy has occasioned much critical commentary from both academic and judicial sources. A great deal of the literature on the subject over the last century or more has focused on the various substantive and procedural problems in the area, and has often been prompted by cases of prosecutorial abuse or judicial expansion of the offence. The purpose of this essay is not to review this literature, not to provide a general description and critique of the law, but rather to draw attention to a very real danger arising from criminal conspiracy offences. The substantive and procedural features of the law in this area offer the State a singularly convenient weapon with which to suppress political dissent or augment the criminality of essentially political trials. This threat to civil liberties and political activism, inherent in the vagueness of conspiracy doctrine, should be of concern to anyone seeking to reform the criminal law.

This paper will touch on some of the may problematic aspects of conspiracy and will, where possible, provide specific illustrations of how this law can be, and is used, as a political instrument. Of course, many of these considerations are equally applicable to "purely criminal" conspiracy charges, if there is such a thing. In such cases, civil liberties issues are also raised regarding the unfairness of the law for any accused facing a conspiracy indictment. It is hoped, however, that by pointing out the overt political utility of criminal conspiracy, the law reform process will go beyond a narrow patch-up attempt to resolve isolated problems raised by conspiracy, and will instead undertake a fundamental re-evaluation of the rationale for having such a doctrine for part of the criminal law in Canada.

Criminal conspiracy gained notoriety during the 18th and 19th centuries in its use by the State to crush the nascent tide of trade unionism. The systematic use of the weapon during this period is only the most salient example of its political utility in reacting to fundamental challenges to the social and economic order of society. The trade union experience is now of interest primarily as an historical footnote, showing the potential for concerted use of the criminal law power as a coercive instrument to frustrate change in social relations. Yet this period should not be thought of as anomalous, nor should it be assumed that conspiracy can no longer be used against the union movement to prevent the consolidation of class interests or the expansion of tactics beyond those presently recognized as legitimate in the Canadian system of industrial relations.

The strike is now recognized in common law countries as an integral part of the collective bargaining regime. The legitimacy of the tactic is preserved in Canada by ss. 42(2) and 425 of the Criminal Code. Yet the aftermath of the 1919 Winnipeg General Strike illustrates the capacity of the State to find creative and effective uses for conspiracy to restrain movement toward worker solidarity and to purge perceived radicalizing influences on the union movement. Several leaders of the strike were charged and convicted of seditious conspiracy, that is,

> To bring into hatred and contempt and to excite disaffection against the government and constitution of the Dominion of Canada and the Government of the Province of Manitoba and the administration of justice, and also to raise discontent and disaffection against His Majesty's subjects and to promote feelings of ill-will and hostility between different classes of such subjects...

This was essentially a "sympathy strike" — a tactic outside what has been considered the "legitimate" limits of industrial confrontation in Canada — in support of the building and metal trades union which were already out. The purpose of the strike was to support their calls for wage increases and, on a more general level, to push for industrial union recognition. The events must be seen in the context of a class conscious society with a history of growing labour radicalism pushing for unionization and bargaining rights. The war had just ended and the availability of police and scab labour, expected increases in unemployment, rising costs of living, the recent success of the Russian revolution, and the rise of industrial unionism all were factors in seizing on the general strike as a method of political expression. The strike lasted for six weeks and, until the final confrontation with the R.N.W.P., was essentially non-violent.

Because *R. v. Russell* remains the most powerful instance of politically-motivated conspiracy charges in the Canadian experience, extensive comment on three of its most salient features is warranted. First, this case serves to illustrate the evidentiary rules which facilitate ease of conspiracy prosecution. Second, the statements of the Court of Appeal indicate the extent to which a seditious conspiracy charge will allow the politicization of a trial. Third, the case illustrates the advantages afforded the prosecution in its even being able to *charge* the conspiracy.

The essence of conspiracy is agreement — the *actus reus* of the offence. It is, however, seldom the case that the agreement itself can be proved by direct evidence, and so the agreement is usually proved by inference from acts or statements after (or, less often, before) the formation of the alleged agreement. If the conspiracy and the participation of the accused can be *prima facie* made out by independent evidence, then the co-conspirators' exception to the hearsay rule will allow the introduction of a wide range of evidence concerning declarations and conduct of others. *Russell* is an excellent example of the absurd lengths to which a court can apply the evidentiary laxity of conspiracy charges in political trials.

In addition to documents found in the possession of the accused and of those charged as the parties to the conspiracy, documents found in the possession of third parties were admitted insofar as they related "... to the actions and conduct of the persons charged with the conspiracy or to the spread of seditious propaganda as one of the purposes of the conspiracy". The purpose of this conspiracy was apparently to be effected by the spreading of seditious propaganda. Any printer matter found with third parties traceable to a party to the conspiracy would be evidence against all. Russell was the provincial secretary for the Socialist party of Canada, and was on the trades and labour council of Winnipeg. Any publications of either were held properly admitted against him.

The Court of Appeal cited speeches and literature attacking capitalism and the present Canadian form of government, as well as advocating "dictatorship of the proletariat," socialization of industry, and state appropriation of land. It picked up on rhetoric about "blood running" if workers did not get their rights, and stating the comparative superiority of the Russian form of government. "These statements were made to large audiences, many of whom were foreigners, and were received with much applause." Labour newspapers containing statements by co-conspirators calling for worker solidarity and delivering a critique of capitalism, speeches made at labour conventions across Canada, pamphlets by Lenin, and *The Communist Manifesto* all were admitted as "evidence of agreement to aid and abet the commission of seditious acts." One of the "expressions freely used of an inflammatory character" in Russell's speeches was " 'Long live the working classes.'" Indeed, Dennistoun J.A. observed,

> In proving charges of conspiracy it is generally necessary to throw a wide net and to examine the catch carefully. If it contains evidence which is clearly relevant and pertinent to the charge such evidence should not be excluded for the sole reason that there may have been included facts or statements or documents which would not otherwise properly come under review.

The jury had been instructed to disregard evidence if the person to whom it pertained were found by them not to be a party to the conspiracy. But as Jackson J. noted in *Krulewitch v. United States*, "The naive assumption that prejudicial effects can be overcome by instructions to the jury . . . all practising lawyers know to be unmitigated fiction."

The second striking feature of the *Russell* case is the explicit politicization of the trial. Many politically-motivated conspiracy trials try to downplay this aspect in an attempt to "criminalize" the proceedings. One explanation for the difference here may lie in the object of this particular conspiracy — sedition.

The characterization of the events in question and the terms used to describe the activities of the alleged parties to the conspiracy illustrate the motivation for the prosecution. The Court held that the strike did not fall under the trade union exception (then s. 590 of the Criminal Code), and went on to state that the strike went beyond the confines of a labour dispute.

> During the period of six weeks business, industry and the ordinary pursuits of civil life in Winnipeg were interrupted and the citizens subjected to apprehension and terror. The city was, in effect, in a state of seige.

Perdue, C.J.M. rejected claims that this was a legitimate strike, though not on the ground of its being a sympathy strike:

> [T]o aid a brother union in its strike for higher wages, or to obtain higher wages for all, was not the real object of the combination. What took place before the strike shows that the accused and his associate 'Reds' aimed at something much more drastic. Their ultimate purpose, as declared in their public speeches, was revolution, the overthrow of the existing form of government in Canada and the introduction of a form of socialistic or soviet rule in its place. . . The agitation prior to and during the strike showed no desire on the part of the leaders to bring about by constitutional means an improvement in the position of the wage earner or the securing for him of greater share in the fruits of his labour.

According to Cameron J.A. "A widespread system of espionage, intimidation and terrorism was organized and executed with relentless vigilance and activity."

The third point to be taken from *Russell* concerns the advantages to the prosecution in having conspiracy available — advantages which accrue from the procedural and substantive peculiarities of criminal conspiracy doctrine. Two arguments of the Court of Appeal indicate that there were many substantive offences which *could* have been charged. First, as mentioned above, the actions of the accused were not seen to fit within the trade union exception to conspiracy. The reason the exemption would not have applied is because the acts alleged under the conspiracy involved offences: for example, including postal workers to strike (*Post Office Act*), including firefighters to strike (endangering life and property under the Criminal Code), and causing workers to break contracts (*Masters and Servants Act*). Yet none of these offences were charged.

Second, the activities of the strike committee were described as being the irresponsible, malicious actions of an "autocratic junta" with no concern for the people of Winnipeg. "The general strike of last summer was in fact an insurrectionary attempt to subvert the authority of governments . . . and substitute for them an irresponsible 'strike committee', an attempt attended for a time with a measure of success. . ." In addition, the printed matter disseminated at the time was described by the Court of Appeal as "seditious" and "treasonable." Nevertheless, it was conspiracy that was charged, rather than a substantive offence.

Because of the vagueness of the offence and the attendant evidentiary rules, it may be to the advantage of the prosecution to charge conspiracy instead of any substantive offences alleged to have been committed in pursuit of the object of the conspiracy. This would be useful, for instance, if it were felt that the substantive offences could not be proved, as apparently was the case in *Russell*.

It should also be noted that the prosecution can also charge conspiracy in addition to any substantive offence which may form part of its object. If there is a weak case for the latter, then at least there is a chance of securing a conviction on the former. This "rolling up" of the charge allows the prosecution to bring others into the trial (co-conspirators will usually be tried together) who may not have been chargeable on the substantive offences, but whose declarations and conduct will be admissible against the primary targets once they are joined in the conspiracy charge. By charging both the conspiracy and the substantive offence, evidence would then be admissible which would not be if only the latter were charged. A defence may thereby be prejudiced even if the jury is later directed to disregard certain evidence concerning the substantive charge. Finally, the prosecution may get a conviction on both charges. This is so because the offence of conspiracy is completed upon agreement. Its object, if committed, is a separate and distinct offence, and does not preclude a conspiracy prosecution. However objectionable the concept, this does not constitute double jeopardy, nor does the rule in *Kienapple* apply.

The central point to be noted from the *Russell* case is that mentioned by the Law Commission of Great Britain in its assessment of conspiracy:

> Where there has been conduct which it has been thought merited punishment but there has been no substantive offence which could be charged, a conspiracy charge . . . has proved a useful weapon in the armour of the criminal law.

*Russell* indicates that this usefulness extends to situations where substantive offences could be charged, but whether from lack of evidence, expediency, or political/tactical considerations, are not.

In *R. v. Greenfield*, an indictment containing a total of eleven counts was brought against eight defendants, four of whom were acquitted of all charges. One count charged all accused with conspiracy to cause explosions between January 1968 and

August 1971. The prosecution led evidence of 25 explosions or attempts over the period having common features. It was alleged that all the defendants were associated with all the incidents. The other ten counts included attempting to cause explosions, possession of explosives, and possession of rounds of ammunition, a pistol, and automatic firearms. Apart from the conspiracy, the four appellants were also convicted of possession of explosives, ammunition, a pistol, and automatic firearms. Greenfield had been charged with two counts of attempting to cause explosions and was acquitted of both. The appellants got ten years on the conspiracy conviction — the other lesser sentences were to run concurrently.

In order to prove membership in the broad-ranging conspiracy, the prosecution led evidence that (1) there had been a long period of "association" of the accused, (2) Greenfield's fingerprints had been found on a newspaper used to wrap a bomb, (3) fingerprints of Greenfield and one other appellant were found on documents in a bag containing a bomb, and (4) the accused shared a flat, in which the police "found explosives having characteristics which were alleged to be shared with many of those used in the 25 incidents, "firearms, ammunition, documents," and "sundry articles which could have been used either in the making of bombs or in the preparation of publicity material about the Angry Brigade and its activities." (It was claimed by the defendants that these had been planted in the flat.)

Apart from the nature of the evidence used to prove the existence of and membership in the conspiracy, the issue of concern here is the inclusion of the conspiracy count with the other charges which, it was claimed by the appellants, resulted in an unfair trial. The appeal on this ground was dismissed. Yet there was an indication that the court was at least aware of the potential political import of conspiracy doctrine. According to Lawton L.J., "Conspiracy charges have long been regarded with suspicion by English lawyers... There have been times in our history...when prosecutions for conspiracy were used by the Crown to stifle criticism and prevent agitation for religious, social and economic changes."

The objection raised by the appellants in *Greenfield* is evident in a much more striking current example. The ongoing case of the Vancouver Five illustrates the unfairness to the accused in being able to join conspiracy with other counts. Not only does it allow in evidence which will prejudice a jury on related substantive charges, but just charging the offence (the vagueness of the offence makes it a fairly easy one to charge) adds to the appearance of criminality of the accused on other joined charges.

In the third trial scheduled in British Columbia, the indictment contains five counts: sabotage of the B.C. Hydro Dunsmuir substation, possession of explosives with intent to cause damage to property, conspiracy to damage B.C. Hydro substations, conspiracy to damage the Terry Fox Icebreaker (a Gulf Oil ship which is to be used in oil exploration in the North), and conspiracy to sabotage aircraft/equipment at the Canadian Forces Base, Cold Lake, Alberta (future site of the Cruise Missile tests). When the Five are sent to Toronto, the indictment will contain four counts: placing of explosives with intent to damage property (Litton Industries), causing an explosion (likely to cause serious bodily harm), possession of explosives with intent to damage property, and conspiracy to damage the property of Litton Systems.

The *Russell* and *Greenfield* cases raise many of the most objectionable aspects of conspiracy doctrine—considerations which open the offence to instrumental coercive use by the State, and procedural abuse by prosecutors.

With some variations, many of the attempts to set out the rationale for the conspiracy offence fall within two main categories. First, it is often seen as an adjunct to the law of attempts, designed to serve a pre-emptive or preventive role. Second, it is justified as a means of responding to a perceived danger to society arising from the fact of combination and the threat, presumably, of greater efficacy in the pursuit of any object by greater numbers of people than would be the case with one individual vis-a-vis that object. Goode argues that both of these concepts may be subsumed by a general rationale of "social danger." Noting the broad range of criticism that has been levelled at the rationale for conspiracy he concludes,

> ... the concept of social danger as a general rationale of conspiracy is merely a rationalization of judicial reaction to particular cases that have arisen... It is apparent that, if it is accepted that a concept of social danger lies behind the crime of conspiracy, and if the concept is open to serious criticism, then the role of the criminal law in attaching sanctions to criminal agreement must be seriously considered..."

The social danger rationale has been criticized extensively, particularly with respect to the factual basis of the concept, and the assumptions which underpin it. Essentially, the central problem is the assumed correlation between numbers and threat to society. This is both logically indefensible and empirically unfounded. Conspiracy doctrine is incongruous with the body of criminal law if it is true that the latter serves to publish the effects of certain acts, because the same effect may result from the actions of one as from those of many in combination. If the same effect may result from one as from ten persons' action, what is the basis for augmenting the criminality of the latter? And more important, on what basis can the fact of combination elevate what would be, if committed, a summary conviction offence, to an indictable offence? The *mens rea* component is effectively the same for co-conspirators as for the individual intending or planning to commit an offence, except that in the former there must also be intent to agree. As well, agreement does not necessarily make commission of an offence more likely or certain, making the attempt rationale dubious. In view of these considerations, it is difficult to accept the social danger rationale (as Goode defines it) as serving to justify criminal conspiracy.

If the general law of criminal conspiracy cannot be fully supported by a coherent and well-articulated rationale, then the many problems in the doctrine, compounded by the considerations set out in this paper, dictate that conspiracy has no place in the criminal law. In this paper, an attempt has been made to point to the danger criminal conspiracy poses for the existence and expression of political dissent. That it has proven itself not only capable of being utilized as a weapon against various forms of political activity, but also has been so used in a number of contexts, indicates that a fundamental re-evaluation of the underpinning rationale for the doctrine is called for. That rationale must not only be capable of justifying the existence of criminal conspiracy, it must also outweigh the dangers pointed to above.

It may be that certain very serious offences may legitimately constitute the unlawful object around which conspiracy offences can be shaped. If so, however, it is important that these situations be specifically identified by Parliament and be fully codified. The prerequisites for the charge must be concisely set out, and it must be demonstrated that no other means are available for dealing with the problem. The dangers of abuse and the experience of political application of the doctrine as an instrument of coercion demand no less.

### Questions/Discussion

1. What are the elements of criminal conspiracy in Canada today? What problems exist in the definition of and the rationale for the law on conspiracy?
2. Do you agree with the test for agreement in *O'Brien* that it should be essentially a subjective and not an objective one? Is the public less protected by the use of such a test? Why didn't the court focus on the subjective belief of O'Brien rather than the intention of Tulley?
3. Wilson's article highlights the dangers with this offence. What are those dangers? Do you agree with Wilson's analysis? Why or why not? Do you think that people who agree in common to commit a crime are necessarily more dangerous than a lone individual who holds a strong criminal intent? Is there a danger with this offence of punishing people for the ideas they hold rather than the criminal acts they do? How could the offence be more narrowly defined to protect against such dangers?

### Further Reading

- Goode, M., *Criminal Conspiracy in Canada* (toronto: Carswell, 1975).
- Groberman, H., "The Multiple Conspiracies Problem in Canada: (1982), 40 University of Toronto Faculty of Law Review 1.
- MacKinnon, P., "Developments in the Law of Criminal Conspiracy" (1981), 59 Canadian Bar Review 301.
- Mewett, A., and M. Manning, *Mewett and Manning on Criminal Law, 3rd ed.* (Toronto: Butterworths, 1994).
- Stuart, D., *Canadian Criminal Law: A Treatise*, 2nd ed. (Toronto: Carswell, 1987), pp. 562-590.
- Stuart, D., and R. Delisle, *Learning Canadian Criminal Law, 5th ed.* (Toronto: Carswell, 1995).
- Verdun-Jones, S., *Criminal Law in Canada: Cases, Questions and the Code* (Toronto: Harcourt Brace Jovanovich Canada, 1989), pp. 368-379.
- Verdun-Jones, S., and C. Griffiths, *Canadian Criminal Justice, 2nd ed.* (Toronto: Butterworths, 1994).

## 6.3 ATTACHING LIABILITY: THE LIMITS OF LIABILITY

### Introduction

This section focuses on "parties to the offence" and examines the ways in which and the degree to which the criminal law will attach liability for the actions of individuals. Specifically, it focuses on the operation of section 21 of the Code, a device by which criminal liability is attached. Section 21 is examined through the cases in regard to its two subsections.[1] Subsection

---

[1] S. 22 contains analogous provision to those in s. 21 in the matter of counselling where the offence has been committed, as opposed to s. 464 which was looked at in section 6.2.2, above.

(1) of section 21 states that a person becomes a party to an offence in one of three ways: by actually committing it, by doing or omitting to do anything for the purpose of aiding someone to commit it, or by abetting someone to commit it.

The first method is not problematic, for it concerns the person who actually shoots someone and is liable for murder or who actually robs the bank and is liable for armed robbery. Problems of proof may present themselves in individual cases as to who did or caused what, but these issues do not concern us. It is the latter two methods that raise more difficult issues, particularly if we keep in mind that the liability that attaches for an offence is equal in all three cases (though the extent of participation may be a factor at sentencing). A person is equally (legally) guilty for murder whether that person pulls the trigger or sells the gun knowing what it is to be used for.

If one is held liable for an offence by virtue of acts or omissions which assist in or encourage the doing of that offence by another person, that what acts or omissions do the courts find amount to aiding or abetting? Such questions can be answered in the particular only in the context of individual fact situations, but generally speaking, the courts have said that "mere presence" is not enough to constitute sufficient assistance or encouragement. But what types of activities or relationships make presence more than mere presence? We see in *Kulbacki* a situation where the car owner's presence and failure to do or say something was transformed into encouragement of the crime, even though he did nothing explicitly or overtly to encourage the offence. What other situations or relationships might be found sufficient to satisfy the attachment of criminal liability where one party *fails* to do something to *discourage* another party from committing a crime? Also, what would Kulbacki have to have done to satisfy the court: protest, protest strongly or threaten? We are left with a great deal of uncertainty after this case as to what is expected in such situations or, for that matter, when such situations occur and under what circumstances.

The *Salajko* case gives us an example of mere presence, where the accused was seen with his pants down during a gang rape but did nothing else. Can you envisage scenarios where for the very same actions the defendant would be found liable, for example if he had been the gang's leader? The final case on section 21(1), *Madigan*, deals with the common example of trafficking in drugs and the question of holding the purchaser liable for the trafficking offence in addition to the seller. It is evident that in some senses of the terms in section 21(1), a buyer of drugs does aid in or encourage the trafficking in drugs, yet should we hold such purchasers liable for trafficking as well as possession? How persuasive or realistic do you find the court's reasoning?

Subsection (2) of section 21 is a provision which enlarges the liability of an accused to include offences which the individual did not necessarily knowingly aid or encourage. The classic situation is where two or more persons agree to rob a bank and in the course of the robbery one of the gang members kills or injures an innocent third party. To what extent should other members of the gang be liable for the death or injuries? This provision sets out the requirements for attaching liability to the other gang members for such actions and consequences. The subsection states that when two or more persons have formed a common intention to carry out an unlawful purpose and to assist each other therein, each is liable for the actions of the other if in the carrying out of the common purpose the other gang member commits an offence which each knew or ought to have known would be a probable consequence of carrying out the plan.

It is important, then, to determine what that common design is, as the case of *Henderson* demonstrates. A criticism here is that the term "unlawful purpose" is too vague and all-encompassing, and that it should be restricted to truly criminal or serious purposes. For example, illegal parking is an unlawful purpose, yet it would not seem to be the type of planned criminal activity envisaged by the drafters of the Code. Finally, it is important to note the objective test which is used for attaching liability in this subsection, for even if the accused did not subjectively foresee the type of offence which a fellow gang member would commit in the course of the planned crime, that accused will still be guilty for the other member's crime if a reasonable person would have foreseen it as a probable consequence of carrying out the plan. How far the courts will go in attaching liability through this subsection is seen in *Trinneer*, although the results in the case may now be questioned if we refer to the reasoning in the case of *Ancio* which we looked at in section 6.2.1 and which was decided after *Trinneer*, Also, the decision in *Vaillancourt* (see section 7.3.2, below) might change the way the courts would approach this type of case in the future.

## Regina v. Kulbacki
[1966] 1 C.C.C. 1676 (Man. C.A.)

The judgment of the Court was delivered by
MILLER, C.J.M.: — This is an appeal by way of stated case from B.P. McDonald, P.M., under the provisions of s. 734 of the *Criminal Code*.

The accused was charged with driving a motor vehicle in a manner dangerous to the public contrary to s. 221(4) [enacted 1960-61, c. 43, s. 3] of the *Criminal Code*, and the learned Magistrate, after hearing the evidence, convicted the accused.

The accused, a young man 20 years of age, was not actually driving the motor vehicle himself but was the owner of it and had permitted a female infant, 16 years of age, although duly licensed to drive, to take the wheel of the car and drive the motor vehicle over an unimproved municipal highway in excess of 90 m.p.h. The accused, who was sitting in the front seat beside the driver, was charged with the substantive offence. According to the stated case, the accused did or said nothing to stop, prevent, or attempt to stop or prevent the driver of the car from driving in the manner in which she did.

The Crown contended that the conviction was proper in that the accused had aided and abetted the commission of the offence and, as such, under s. 21(1) of the *Code*, was liable to the same extent as if he had been driving the vehicle.

The defence was strictly one of law that the accused, although present, did nothing to encourage the commission of the offence and did not omit to do anything that [would have] contributed to its commission. The defence maintained that, although the accused was present, he did not participate in the commission of the crime but was merely a passive observer, and, at the most, guilty of mere passive acquiescence. Accused argued that he did not have nay duty and was not under any liability to do anything as long as he did not in some way encourage the commission of the offence...

Each of the above-cited cases was decided on its own special facts and the only principles of application to the instant case are that the accused, in order to have been convicted, must have done something to encourage the commission of the offence or omitted to do something which assisted in its commission. It appears to me that when the accused, the owner of car, sat in the front seat on the passenger's side and permitted this young lady to increase the speed to such a dangerous rate, he did, by his lack of action, encourage her to violate the law. Certainly it would not have been wise for him to have grabbed the wheel at this dangerous speed, not at any time when the car was being driven in excess of 60 m.p.h., as to do so would probably have been catastrophic. To turn off the ignition, as was suggested to us by the Crown, might not have been the best course either. In no uncertain terms he should have told this young lady, the minute she started to speed on this municipal road, to desist and slow down. In my opinion, the failure to even protest is equivalent to encouragement and is fatal to his defence.

The Crown cited to us two very pertinent cases with which I will deal briefly:

The first was *Du Cros v. Lambourne*, [1907] 1 K.B. 40, 21 Cox C.C. 311. The facts of that case are very similar to the facts in the instant case. There, the accused, who had permitted a young lady to drive his car, was charged with the substantive offence when she drove it in an improper manner, and was convicted on the ground that he was an aider and abettor. In 21 Cox C.C. at p. 315, Lord Alverstone, C.J., said:

> "'If Miss Godwin was then driving, she was doing so with consent and approval of the appellant, who was the owner and in control of the car, and was sitting by her side, and he could and ought to have prevented her driving at such excessive and dangerous speed, but instead thereof he allowed her to do so, and did not interfere in any way.'"

The Court of Appeal held that on that finding of fact it was justified in convicting the accused as if he were the driver, as he was an aider, abettor, etc.

The other case in *R. v. Halmo*, 76 C.C.C. 116, [1941] 3 D.L.R. 6, [1941] O.R. 99, a decision of the Ontario Court of Appeal. In that case the owner of the vehicle was found guilty o the offence of reckless driving committed by his chauffeur.

It is true that in the *Halmo* case, *supra*, the accused, owner of the car, had full knowledge that his chauffeur was intoxicated; in fact, they became intoxicated together. Perhaps in the *Halmo* case circumstances are stronger than in the instant case but, nevertheless, it is an authority in support of the Crown's position. The *Halmo* and the *Du Cros* cases were discussed with apparent approval by the Manitoba Court of Appeal in *R. v. Harder*, 88 C.C.C. 21, 3 C.R. 49, [1947] 2 D.L.R. 593. The *Halmo* case was referred to by the Supreme Court of Canada in another *R. v. Harder* case reported (1956), 114 C.C.C. 129, 23 C.R. 295, 4 D.L.R. (2d) 150, and apparently approved. The following quotation from the *Halmo* case has some application to the instant case (At p. 127 [C.C.C.]):

> "The facts combine to make the accused a person who had in his charge and under his control the motor vehicle in question: (a) He was the owner of the motor vehicle; (b) He was the master of Mayville, his hired servant, who was driving the car; (c) He was personally present at all material times both before and at the time when the motor vehicle was being driven in a manner dangerous to the public.

> "Being personally present and having in his charge and under his control the motor vehicle, he is a principal party to the offence of a breach of s. 285(60(a) of the *Code, Reg. v. Brown* (1878), 14 Cox C.C. 144. He was guilty of negligence in that being so in charge and control of a dangerous machine, he failed and omitted to control his drunken chauffeur and to prevent him from driving the car to the danger of the public."

Every passenger is an unlawfully driven motor vehicle is not necessarily subject to conviction as an aider and abettor, as it is conceivable that a passenger might not have any authority over the car or any right to control the driver, but that is not the situation in the instant case. As above stated, he failed to make any effort to stop or prevent the commission of the offence when he was in a position to do so and when he had the authority to do so.

Therefore, as intimated, I am of the opinion that the learned Magistrate was right in convicting the accused of the substantive offence on the ground that he was an aider and abettor and liable to conviction by virtue of s. 21(1) of the *Criminal Code*. The learned Magistrate's question ought to be answered in the affirmative. The appeal should be dismissed and the conviction affirmed.

*Appeal dismissed.*

## Regina v. Salajko
## [1970] 1 C.C.C. 352 (Ont. C.A.)

The judgment of the Court was delivered orally by

GALE, C.J.O.: — This particular appellant was present when some 15 young men, if one can dignify them by that term, raped a girl in a lonely field near New Dundee in this province. Because of the frightful circumstances the girl was able to identify only three of those who were present. They were charged with rape and all were found guilty. Two of the appellant's co-accused, Francis and White, were identified as having had intercourse with the girl. She admitted, however, that this appellant did not have intercourse with her. The Crown placed its case against him on the basis of s. 21(1)(b) and (c) of the *Criminal Code*.

At the conclusion of the Crown's case, counsel for Salajko moved for a directed verdict of acquittal but it was denied. Eventually, after a recharge by the learned Judge on aiding and abetting and after the jury had come back for further instructions in that regard, the jury found the appellant guilty.

In our view there was no evidence upon which a jury, properly charged, could reasonably come to the conclusion beyond any reasonable doubt that this man had aided or abetted the outrages performed by the others. When this proposition was put to Mr. Hachborn for the Crown he candidly admitted that the evidence was very weak and relied solely on the fact that at one stage the accused was seen to be near the girl with his pants down while she was being raped by others. The accused gave an explanation as to the incident but quite apart from it we do not think that the evidence can be translated into a conclusion that the accused was aiding or abetting the others when they were ravaging the girl. Passive acquiescence is not sufficient to induce such a finding and Mr. Hachborn can point to no other evidence to suggest anything in the way of aiding or counselling or encouragement on the part of the accused with respect to that which was being done by the others. Accordingly, there simply was no evidence upon which a jury could properly arrive at a verdict of guilty against this particular accused.

We are also of the view that the learned Judge's direction with respect to abetting was in error. In this respect, and in answer to a question put to him by the jury, he seemed to indicate that a person could abet another in the commission of an offence and so be guilty of the offence if knowingly he stands by while the offence is being committed. I have in mind the following which appears at p. 401 of the transcript:

> HIS LORDSHIP: To my mind in the context of the word "abet" it would involve the understanding of what was going on in a particular situation and without active encouragement, because the word "encourage" is used, to stand by and, I suppose, in the sense, adopt and approve . . . it is a rather negative word. . .what is taking place.
>
> "Encourage" and "uphold" to my mind import something that is an active thing. "Countenance" is the passive encouragement. That is the way I would understand it.

We do not think that passive encouragement, if there be such a thing, can render a person guilty of an offence and refer to the following taken from Jowitt, Dictionary of English Law, p. 9, where abet is defined "to encourage or set on" and an abettor is "an instigator or setter on, one who promotes or procures a crime to be committed".

The evidence indicates clearly that this accused did not either aid or instigate or promote or procure the commission of the crime of the others, and accordingly the appeal will be allowed, the conviction quashed and a verdict of acquittal entered with respect to this accused.

*Appeal allowed; accused acquitted.*

## Regina v. Madigan
[1970] 1 O.R. 80 (C.A.)

MACKAY J.A.: — This is an appeal by the Crown from the acquittal of the respondent on a charge that he did on or about January 23, 1963, unlawfully traffic in a controlled drug, to wit, derivatives of barbituric acid, namely, amobarbital (amytal) and secobarbital (seconal) contrary to s. 32(1) [rep. & sub. 1960-61, c. 37, s. 1] of the *Food and Drugs Act*, 1952-53 (Can.), c. 38. There was evidence that an undercover police officer had met and cultivated the acquaintance of the respondent over a period of time. He had on a number of occasions, without success, asked the respondent to obtain controlled drugs for him. What transpired on the date in respect of which the charge is laid, as stated in evidence by the undercover police officer, was as follows:

At about 1.20 a.m. the accused asked me if I still wanted some goofballs or bombers and I said...

Q. Well how did he know you at one time wanted them?
A. Well, when myself and the accused had left the New Service Tearoom, I had said to him that I wanted some bombers and at that time he said that he wished I — he wished he had known I wanted them then, but this was sort of a carry-over, he asked me if I still wanted some bombers at 1.20 a.m. in the Rhodes Restaurant.
Q. I see. And what did you say?
A. I said: "Seconals or Tuinals" and he replied "I don't know, but I know who's got some and approached a female known to me as Joan Fortnen(?) She was sitting alone at the south side of the fourth table on the east side of the restaurant and this is the fourth booth from the rear.
Q. How far would that be from your booth?
A. Oh approximately 20 feet.
Q. And did he then return to your table?
A. No, he didn't sit down, he just — he leaned over and whispered to the female and in a minute's time he did return. At this time he told me "She's only got grain and a half tuinals, she's just got two of them". He then asked me if I wanted them and I said "Yeah, okay" and in a matter of seconds Joan got up and came over to the table and sat beside the accused who had, like I say, rejoined me and sat in his original seat and she sat beside him and she said "I've only got two grain and a halfs left, do you want them" and I said "Okay". At this time the accused told me to give her the money. I took a $2.00 bill from my wallet and handed it to her. I told her like I only had a two dollar bill and she said she'd change it. She got up and left the table and went downstairs. In a couple of minutes she came back up and returned tot he table, she sat again beside the accused and she handed him a one dollar bill which he in turn handed to me, this was my change. Joan the said "Here, they're in the bottle" and she handed them to me under the table. I asked her what they were and she replied "Tuinals" and I took the bottle and I place it in my left coat pocket and about — this all took place in a matter of a few minutes. And then in another couple of minutes

the accused said to me "I'll try and get you some more". He then left the table again and got up and approached two other unknown males and about five minutes later he returned and I asked him if he had any more and he said no.

. . . .

The ground of appeal advanced by the Crown is that the learned trial Judge erred in law in failing to consider and apply s. 21(1)(b) of the *Criminal Code*. In fairness to the trial Judge I should say that counsel for the respondent, who was at the trial, informed the Court that neither counsel made any reference to or argued the effect or application to the facts of this case of s. 21 of the *Code*, This section is as follows:

21.(1) Every one is a party to an offence who

. . .

(b) does or omits to do anything for the purpose of aiding any person to commit it, or

(c) abets any person in committing it.

The argument of the respondent is that the accused was acting only as agent for the undercover officer in the purchase of the drug and that it is not an offence under the Act to purchase a controlled drug.

While I agree that he was acting as agent for the constable, I am of the opinion that in going over to the woman who sold the drug and bringing her to the undercover constable, he was aiding and abetting her in the sale of the drug within the meaning of s. 21 of the *Code* and I would, therefore, allow the appeal, set aside the verdict of acquittal and register a conviction against the respondent.

As to sentence, we were informed that the respondent is 28 years of age, has recently been honourably discharged from the Royal Canadian Air Force after some years of service and that his only prior record is for one unrelated offence. These facts, together with the circumstances of the offence with which he is charged, that is, that he had obviously on a number of occasions refused to obtain drugs for the undercover agent and that on this occasion the quantity and value of the drugs was very small, I would impose a sentence of three months' suspended sentence.

MCGILLIVRAY, J.A., concurs with JESSUP, J.A.

JESSUP, J.A.: — The circumstances of this appeal and the facts are fully set forth in the judgment of MacKay, J.A., which I have been privileged to read.

The appeal being made by the Crown must involve "a question of law alone". It is said such a question arises in the failure of the Provincial Court Judge either to charge himself with respect to s. 21 of the *Criminal Code* or in his failure to apply that section to the facts of the case.

It is true that in his brief reasons the judge does not mention s. 21. What he said is:

Now on the evidence in this case before me, Mr Madigan certainly did not manufacture the drug, he did not export from or import into Canada the drug, and I suppose it resolves itself tot he point of did he sell or did he transport or deliver the drug.

Now the evidence is that at the request of the undercover policeman he introduced the policeman to a person who ultimately did in fact sell some drugs to the policeman. I think the words have to be taken in their normal and ordinary connotation and meaning in the English language and on that basis I can't be satisfied, I am not satisfied beyond all reasonable doubt — as I must be — that the accused man did in fact traffic. Because what he did, his actions in my opinion do not come within the definition of trafficking and for that reason I must dismiss the charge against the accused.

However, I do not think that simply from the failure to expressly mention s. 21 it can be presumed that provisions of so fundamental a provision of the criminal law were not present to his mind. On the other hand, if he had the section present to his mind, the contention is that he failed to apply it. This amounts to a complaint that he drew the wrong inference from the facts. I think it is clear from the judgments of the Supreme Court of Canada in *Sunbeam Corp. (Canada) Ltd. v. The Queen,* [1969] S.C.R. 221, [1969] 2 C.C.C. 189, 56 C.P.R. 242, and *Lampard v. The Queen,* as yet unreported [later [1969] S.C.R. 373, [1969] 3 C.C.C 249, 4 D.L.R. (3d) 98], that the inference of guilt even from undisputed facts, including the intention of an accused, is an inference of fact. That a verdict of not guilty is unreasonable and cannot be supported by the evidence does not raise a question of law. Accordingly, I am of the opinion that in this case an appeal is not available to the Crown.

Even assuming otherwise I am not prepared to hold that the Judge of first instance was in error. It is not an offence under the statute to purchase controlled drugs. Accordingly, no criminal liability would attach to the acts of the accused if he had been the purchaser. It follows that similarly no criminal liability attaches to such acts if they were on behalf of the purchaser as his agent. In my opinion, on the peculiar facts of this case, it cannot be said they are consistent only with the accused acting as an agent either for the vendor or for both the vendor and the purchaser; they are equally consistent with him acting as agent for the purchaser alone. Accordingly, there must be a reasonable doubt that what the accused did was "for the purpose of aiding" the vendor in the words of s. 21(1)(b), *i.e.,* that his intention was to aid the vendor rather than simply to aid the purchaser. What the section says is "for the purpose of aiding", not "with the effect of aiding".

Accordingly I would dismiss the appeal.

*Appeal dismissed.*

## Henderson v. The King
[1948] S.C.R. 226

[Only the judgment of Taschereau, J. is reproduced below.]

TASCHEREAU, J.: — The appellant Henderson and one Harry Medos were jointly indicted at Vancouver B.C. for the murder of Charles Boyes, a police officer. The two accused were given separate trials, as a result of which Medos was found guilty and executed, and Henderson who was tried before Manson, J. was also convicted.

It appears from the evidence that the appellant, Medos, and one Cartier conspired together to commit a holdup at the premises of the Royal Bank of Canada, on the east side of Renfrew Street, directly opposite the Java Inn at Vancouver. The next day, the three men were seen in a maroon Mercury car, coming west, on 2nd Avenue. It was observed that the car turned into the first lane facing south, and backed out to 2nd Avenue again, and then went east, from whence it had come, and proceeded to the stop sign at Renfrew Street, and turned north on Renfrew Street in the direction of the bank, but proceeded only about two car lengths when it swerved to the right, making a U turn and proceeded at a fast rate of speed east on 2nd Avenue. The bandits who were on their way to the bank to commit the intended hold-up, had obviously detected a police car that was parked in front of the Java Inn facing south, and found that the occasion was not favourable to carry out their plot. After having made this U turn, the proceeded in their car for about a mile and a half, and then abandoned it on Kitchener Street, and walked west toward the Great Northern Railway yards.

They had admittedly been under close observation by the police, for when they arrived in the yards, Officers Boyes and Ledingham drove their car into the yards near the roundhouse, and accosted them on the railway track where all five crossed the line of tracks they were on, to another set of tracks. A few seconds later, Detective Sergeant Hoare arrived, and standing directly opposite the appellant, he said: "Who are you fellows anyway?" and coming nearer the appellant, Hoare said: "What is your name?" The two questions remained unanswered, and looking at the appellant, Hoare saw a gun tucked in the top of his overalls which he pulled out. He had just taken this gun, when the whole line of men broke up and the appellant, Medos and Carter sprang in different directions. Medos who was the first to move was pursued by Officer Boyes, Ledingham going after Carter. Medos had hardly ran six or seven steps when he turned and shot Boyes, and Carter fired at Ledingham. Medos then aimed at Hoare. Unfamiliar with the appellant's revolver, and therefore unable to use it, Hoare moved rapidly towards a pile of steel plates, trying to reach for his gun, but a bullet struck him in the left thigh and he fell to the ground. He however tried to get his gun out of the holster, but was at that moment struck by another bullet in the upper part of his right arm, and another shot passed by the left side of his face. He succeeded in sitting up, and he saw Boyes lying dead on the ground, and Medos still running. He then raised his gun to his right knee, and aimed at Medos, but seeing Carter running in an north-westerly direction, he transferred his aim to Carter and shot him to the ground. He then aimed at Medos who fell. He fired another shot which killed Carter, and a second shot at Medos.

As a result of the shooting, Officer Boyes and Ledingham and Carter were killed. Medos succeeded in escaping with the appellant, but both were discovered soon after in the basement of a house on 5th Avenue where they were arrested. In the interval, appellant had changed his outer clothing, and later Medos' gun was found in the basement containing one live shell. The gun taken from Henderson by Detective Sergeant Hoare was fully loaded with live shell, and in appellant's pocket were found also five other live shells which fitted his gun.

It is the contention of the Crown that Henderson, together with Medos and Carter, formed a common intention to commit a crime by violence, viz. to hold up and rob the Royal Bank of Canada on Renfrew Street, and to assist each other therein, and that it was a part of the common intention to overcome all resistance by force of arms, either in the bank or outside the bank, and to resist lawful apprehension by the police, and if pursued to shoot if necessary. The Crown further states that such common intention *was at no time abandoned* by appellant, that the common design was frustrated by the police and that it was only the presence of a Police car immediately across the street form the bank, which caused the bandits to change their mind, so that instead of continuing their unlawful purpose, they then directed their attention to resisting lawful apprehension.

The Crown further submits that in view of section 69(2) of the *Criminal Code*, which reads as follows: —

**2.** If several persons form a common intention to prosecute any unlawful purpose, and to assist each other therein, each of them is a party to every offence committed by anyone of them in the prosecution of such common purpose, the commission of which offence was, or ought to have been known to be a probable consequence of the prosecution of such common purpose.

the jury being properly instructed by the learned trial judge, could find that such a common intention was formed, and that in the *prosecution* of such common purpose one or more of the trio shot and killed Officer Boyes, and that the commission of that offence was or ought to have been known to be a probable consequence of the *prosecution* of such common purpose.

The Crown also submits that it was put to the jury by Crown counsel, that even if the jury could not find that the common purpose was as comprehensive as was put to them, there was another view which could be taken, namely, that when the trio abandoned the motor car on Kitchener Street, they had already committed a crime, that is to say, they had *attempted* to hold up and rob the bank, within the meaning of section 72 of the *Code* which is in the following words: —

**72.** Every one who, having an intent to commit an offence, does or omits an act for the purpose of accomplishing his object is guilty of an attempt to commit the offence intended whether under the circumstances it was possible to commit such offence or not.

. . .

**2.** The question whether an act done or omitted with intent to commit an offence is or is not only preparation for the commission of that offence and too remote to constitute an attempt to commit it, is a question of law.

It is said that these three men, when their attempt to hold up the bank was frustrated, formed a common intention to resist lawful apprehension, which is in itself an unlawful purpose within the meaning of section 69, and that during the *prosecution* of such common purpose, murder was committed by one of their number.

. . . .

I would first like to deal with the contention that the three conspirators while on their way to the bank, were guilty of *an attempt* to commit a hold-up and rob the Royal Bank of Canada. With deference with other views expressed, I cannot agree with this submission. Of course, the conspiracy to rob the bank was complete and this in itself was a crime, but I do not believe that the subsequent facts revealed by the evidence show the essential ingredients of an attempt, within the meaning of section 72 of the *Criminal Code*.

An intent, an act of preparation, and an attempt must not be confused. A mere intent is not punishable in criminal law, even if coupled with an act of preparation. As it was said in *Regina v. Eagleton* at p. 538: —

The mere intention to commit a misdemeanour is not criminal. Some act is required, and we do not think that all acts towards committing a misdemeanour are indictable. Acts remotely leading towards the commission of the offence are not to be considered as attempts to commit it, but acts immediately connected with it are . . .

. . . .

I entirely agree with what Mr. Justice O'Halloran says in his dissenting judgment:

For an act to be an attempt, it must take place between the attemptor and the attemptee and be proximate to the crime about to be committed.

Here, the trio were seen in an automobile in the direction of the bank; but the plot was frustrated by the presence of the police. There was nothing done by the trio, no overt act *immediately connected* with the offence of hold-up and robbing. Although it may be said that no one could doubt the express purpose of the bandits, I do not believe that it can be held that the mere fact of going to the place where the contemplated crime is to be committed, constitutes an attempt. There must be a closer relation between the victim and the author of the crime; there must be an act done which displays not only a preparation for an attempt, but a commencement of execution, a step in the commission of the actual crime itself.

. . . .

Section 72, para. 2 of the *Criminal Code* says that the question whether an act done or omitted with intent to commit an offence, is or is not only preparation for the commission of that offence, and too remote to constitute an attempt to commit it, is a question of law.

The jury were told by the learned trial judge that:

the (trio) could not be prosecuted for robbing a bank, but they could be prosecuted for attempting to rob a bank . . . the attempt is complete when they take any steps in connection with it.

This statement of law, is, I think, erroneous. The jury might have thought that it was while trying to escape, after having committed an act, which they were told was *a crime*, that the bandits started the shooting as a result of which the killing ensued. this obviously confused the issue and was prejudicial to the accused.

I further believe, however, that the question whether or not the bandits were guilty of an attempt, is entirely foreign to the case.

There is no possible doubt that the three accused in view of the evidence produced, were guilty of conspiracy. The common unlawful purpose was to hold up and rob the Royal Bank of Canada, and it is also common ground that they intended to assist each other in the prosecution of that purpose. But, their common purpose have been frustrated, was obviously not pursued, and it was not therefore in the *prosecution* of such common purpose that Officer Boyes was killed.

To my mind the real issues are the following: —

Was there at any moment a concerted plot formed by Medos, Carter and Henderson to resist legal apprehension with violence? It may well be that this plot if it did exist, was made originally when it was agreed to rob the bank, or it may be that it was formed after the bandits were frustrated in the prosecution of the hold-up. If such a plot did exist, the shooting being the result of a conspiracy, the two of course might be guilty of murder. The common intention would then be to resist legal apprehension; that would be the unlawful purpose. Each one of the trio wold be a party to any other offence, committed by any one of them, in the prosecution of the common purpose, if he had known, or ought to have known, that it was a probable consequence of the original common purpose. It may happen, however, and this was the for the jury to determine, that Henderson had ceased to be a party to the conspiracy, and that the shooting which started after he had been disarmed and under virtual arrest, was the spontaneous act of Medos. Then, the act of one, would not have been the act of all.

In order that section 69(2) may find its application, the co-conspirators must form not only a common intention to prosecute an unlawful purpose, but they must agree also "to assist each other therein", and therefore, if a man is disarmed and made incapable of furnishing the promised assistance, the situation is obviously changed. It is settled law that a person who has been a party to prosecute a common illegal purpose, amy disassociate himself with his original co-conspirators. As early as in 1828, in *Rex v. Edmeads*, Baron Vaughan said at the Berkshire Assizes (Carrington & Paynes Reports, Vol. 3): —

> If it could be shown that either of them separated himself from the rest, and showed distinctly that he would have no hand in what they were doing, the objection would have much weight in it.

. . . .

In *Rex v. Croft* it was held that the agreement may be expressly determined and that if it comes to an end before the crime is committed, the party who has put an end to the agreement is not guilty. The question whether the agreement has been put to an end, must be judged in view of all the circumstances revealed by the evidence, and I have no doubt that it is a question for the jury. It was for them to say, if in view of the evidence the appellant had been a party to the conspiracy, if such a conspiracy was ever formed, and it was also within their exclusive province to find, after have been properly instructed, that he had detached himself from any further association with the other conspirators.

Unfortunately, all these aspects of the case were not dealt with, and these omission were, I believe, highly prejudicial to the accused. The defence was not presented so as to give it all its force and effect. It is true that no witnesses were called on behalf of the appellant, but it is nevertheless the duty of the trial judge, in his charge to the jury, to explain the exculpatory effect of the evidence, whether it is given by the witnesses for the Crown or for the accused. *Wu v. The King*. It was the fundamental right of the appellant, who has been charged of murder, purely by construction of the law, which in this particular case creates a presumptive guilt, to have all the features of his defence adequately put to the jury.

I have come to the conclusion that this has not been done, and that the Crown has not established to my satisfaction that the verdict would have been the same, if the proper direction had been given.

The appeal should be allowed, the conviction quashed and a new trial directed.

*Appeal allowed and new trial directed.*

## The Queen v. Trinneer
[1970] S.C.R. 638

The judgment of the Court was delivered by

CARTWRIGHT C.J.C.: — This appeal is brought, pursuant to leave granted by this Court on December 15, 1969, from an unanimous judgment of the Court of Appeal for British Columbia pronounced on November 20, 1969, quashing the conviction of the respondent before Ruttan J. and a jury on February 26, 1969, on the charge that on December 19, 1967, he together with Isaac Darryl Frank did commit the non-capital murder of Rose Vollet.

A brief summary of the facts will be sufficient for an understanding of the points raised before us.

The respondent and another youth by the name of Isaac Darryl Frank were in the east part of Vancouver, B.C., early n the morning of December 19, 1967, having spent the night out together. Later that morning, a hunting knife, the blade of which was five or six inches long, was purchased by Frank in the presence of the respondent. Following this, Frank told the respondent "that he needed money to get back down to the States and that he was going to rob somebody."

At approximately 9:30 that morning, the respondent and Frank went over to a gas station a few block from the store where the knife had been purchased and they were seen by an attendant talking to a woman who had driven in for some gas. This woman was Rosie Vollet, a forty-year old married woman, who later died from knife wounds inflicted by Frank. The attendant noticed the hunting knife in the hand of one of the youths but was unable to say which one.

Both Frank and the respondent got into Mrs. Vollet's car with her and after it was filled with gas the three left in the car with Mrs Vollet driving. Mrs. Vollet had paid for the gas with a twenty-dollar bill and had other bills in her purse. After travelling a short distance, Frank "pulled a knife on her and told her that if she wouldn't say nothing, she wouldn't get hurt". Mrs. Vollet was then directed to pull over, following which the respondent took over the driving. He drove some distance out of Vancouver and eventually turned up a side road to a small clearing which was a lonely spot approximately thirty-six miles from the gas station. Frank and Mrs. Vollet got out of the car and the respondent turned the car around and topped it but left the engine running. Some distance from the car, Frank inflicted multiple stab wounds on Mrs. Vollet, from which she died at least twenty minutes and possibly two hours later. The respondent helped Frank move Mrs. Vollet from the road and the two then returned together to Vancouver in the Vollet car with the respondent driving. There, they picked up the respondent's "girl friend" and the three proceeded in the Vollet car to Corvallis in the State of Oregon where they were arrested.

Mrs. Vollet's body was later found by the police and nearby was her purse which contained no bills.

The respondent and Frank were charged with the non-capital murder of Mrs. Vollet and were granted separate trials. No witnesses testified directly at the respondent's trial as to the events which occurred from the time the car left the gas station until after it started back to Vancouver. The above facts were disclosed in statements made by the respondent and admitted in evidence at his trial.

The defence called no evidence.

Leave was granted to appeal to this Court on the following question of law:

> Did the Court of Appeal err in holding that the learned trial Judge was wrong in failing to direct the jury that before they could find the respondent guilty of non-capital murder they must find that the respondent knew or ought to have known that the death of Rosie Vollet would be a probable consequence of carrying out the robbery?

The submission of the Crown at the trial and before us was that the respondent was guilty of non-capital murder by virtue of the combined effects of s. 202 and s. 21 of the *Criminal Code* which so far as applicable to the facts of this case read as follows:

> **202.** Culpable homicide is murder where a person causes the death of a human being while committing or attempting to commit ... robbery ... whether or not the person means to cause death to any human being and whether or not he knows that death is likely to be caused to any human being, if
>
> (a) he means to cause bodily harm for the purpose of
>
>> (i) facilitating the commission of the offence, or
>> (ii) facilitating his flight after committing or attempting to commit the offence,
>
> and the death ensues from the bodily harm;
>
> . . . .
>
> (d) he uses a weapon or has it upon his person
>
>> (i) during or at the time he commits or attempts to commit the offence, or
>> (ii) during or at the time of his flight after committing or attempting to commit the offence,
>
> and the death ensues as a consequence.
>
> **21.**(1) Every one is a party to an offence who
>
> (a) actually commits it,
>
> (b) does or omits to do anything for the purpose of aiding any person to commit it, or
>
> (c) abets any person in committing it.
>
> (2) Where two or more persons form an intention in common to carry out an unlawful purpose and to assist each other therein and any one of them, in carrying out the common purpose, commits an offence, each of the who knew or ought to have known that the commission of the offence would be a probable consequence of carrying out the common purpose is a party to that offence.

In his charge to the jury, the learned trial Judge reviewed the sections of the *Criminal Code* dealing with homicide, culpable homicide, manslaughter and murder and then dealt with ss. 202 and 21(2). In effect he told the jury that before they could find the respondent guilty it was necessary that they should find that he knew or ought to have known that in carrying out the robbery Frank would cause bodily harm to the deceased for the purpose of facilitating the commission of the robbery or flight after its commission but that it was not necessary that they should find that the respondent knew or ought to have known that the death of the deceased was likely to be caused.

. . . .

The reasons given in the Court of Appeal make it clear that that Court was unanimously of opinion that the learned trial Judge should have told the jury that they could not find the respondent guilty unless they found that the respondent knew or ought to have known that the deceased's death would be a probable consequence of carrying out the robbery.

. . . .

Before referring to these cases I think it desirable to consider the words of s. 202 and s. 21(2) of the *Criminal Code*, which have been quoted above. In my opinion the learned trial Judge rightly interpreted and applied those sections and his charge to the jury was correct in law. He made it clear to the jury that before they could convict the respondent of murder they must find that he and Frank formed an intention in common to rob the deceased, that in carrying out that common purpose Frank committed the murder of the deceased *as defined in s. 202(a) and/or (d)* (my italics) and that the respondent knew or ought to have known that the commission of murder *as so defined* (my italics) would be a probable consequence of carrying out the common purpose. The offence of murder which Frank committed and the commission of which the respondent ought to have foreseen as probable was complete when, while committing the robbery. Frank intentionally caused bodily harm to the deceased and her death in fact resulted therefrom. With respect, the construction of the sections adopted by the Court of Appeal appears to me to fail to give effect to the words in s. 202 "whether or not the person means to cause death to any human being and whether or not he knows that death is like to be caused to any human being."

If the respondent ought to have known that it was probable that bodily harm would be inflicted on the deceased to facilitate the carrying out of the robbery, then it was unnecessary for the Crown to establish that he ought to have foreseen that her death was likely to result. The offence contemplated by s. 21(2) (that is murder as defined in s. 202(1) and/or (d)) was committed when Frank inflicted the bodily harm on the deceased for the purpose of facilitating the robbery or flight. Its character was determined when her death ensued.

I can find nothing in the words of s. 21(2) to support the view that foresight of the victim's death as a probable consequence of the robbery, an element expressly excluded in the definition of the offence of murder in s. 202, should have to be found to exist before the respondent could be convicted of such murder by the application of s. 21(2).

. . . .

At the risk of repetition, it is my opinion that on the true construction of s. 202 and s. 21(2) as applied to the circumstances of this case it was necessary to support a verdict of guilty against the respondent that the Crown should establish (i) that it was in fact a probable consequence of the prosecution of the common purpose of the respondent and Frank to rob Mrs. Vollet that Frank for the purpose of facilitating the commission of the robbery would intentionally cause bodily harm to Mrs. Vollet, (ii) that it was known or ought to have been known to the respondent that such consequence was probable and (iii) that in fact Mrs. Vollet's death ensued from the bodily harm. It was not necessary for the Crown to establish that the respondent knew or ought to have known that it was probable that Mrs. Vollet's death would ensue. In my opinion the jury were accurately instructed on this vital issue and there was ample evidence to support their verdict.

It appears from what I have said above that, if the only ground of appeal from the verdict of guilty have been that on which the Court of Appeal proceeded, I would allow the appeal but in the course of their reasons the Court of Appeal stated that they did not find it necessary to deal with the other grounds of appeal which were argued before them.

. . . .

I would allow the appeal, set aside the order of the Court of Appeal and restore the judgment of the learned trial judge.

*Appeal allowed.*

## Questions/Discussion
1. Describe and discuss the nature and operation of section 21(1) of the Criminal Code. Do you think that it has been fairly interpreted in the cases which you have read? For example, do you agree with the decisions in *Kulbacki* and *Salajko*? Why or why not? What types of relationships do you think might give rise to the results which are seen in *Kulbacki*? Is this case a dangerous precedent in that we are left with a great deal of uncertainty after the decision as to what relationship will transform mere presence into something more and also as to what was "required" of the accused?
2. Do you think that there should be a separate provision in the Code to distinguish the nature and degree of criminal liability of those who actually do the crime from the liability of those who aid or abet? In situations of offences with minimum penalties, leniency in sentencing is not possible in order to take account of the varying degrees of blameworthiness.
3. Describe and discuss the nature and operation of section 21(2) of the Criminal Code. Do you think that the subsection is fair in light of traditional principles of individual blameworthiness? Should an objective test be used to determine what might take place in the course of carrying out a planned offence? What are the problems with using a subjective test in such situations?
4. Do you agree with the court's decision in *Henderson* as to its interpretation of what was the planned offence? Note that unlike criminal attempts and conspiracy, there is the possibility of "withdrawal" from the plan and therefore being relieved of liability for other offences which may occur in its carrying out; depending on the circumstances, however, liability may still attach for an attempt of conspiracy in regard to the planned offence.
5. Do you agree with the decision in *Trenneer* or do you think that it stretches the web of liability too far from the concept of individual responsibility? As noted earlier, in light of the decision and reasoning in *Ancio* (see 6.2.1) as well as those in *Vaillancourt* (see 7.3.2)., the decision may not hold too much weight in the future.

## Further Reading
- Mewett, A., and M. Manning, *Mewett and Manning on Criminal Law 3rd ed.* (Toronto: Butterworths, 1994).
- Rose, V.G., *Parties to an Offence* (toronto: Carswell, 1982).
- Sornarajah, M., "Common Intention and Murder Under the Criminal Codes" (1981), 59 Canadian Bar Review 727.
- Stuart, D., and R. Delisle, *Learning Canadian Criminal Law, 5th ed.* (Toronto: Carswell, 1995).
- Verdun-Jones, S., *Criminal Law in Canada: Cases, Questions and the Code* (Toronto: Harcourt Brace Jovanovich, Canada, 1989). pp. 323-349.
- Verdun-Jones, S., and C. Griffiths, *Canadian Criminal Justice, 2nd ed.* (Toronto: Butterworths, 1994).

# 7

# DEFENCES AND DENIALS

**Introduction**

This chapter outlines defences to and denials of criminal liability, both complete and limited. Complete defences result in the acquittal of the accused whereas limited or partial defences can result in a conviction on a less serious charge, for example in the defences of provocation and intoxication. The four sections which follow are divided according to four arbitrary categories of defences: justifications, absence of intent or knowledge, policy defences, and mental or emotional impairment.

Justifications for our purposes are those types of defences which essentially admit that the offence was done, but offer an excuse for the defendant's actions. The defendant may argue that there were threats or force involved in the doing of the crime and for that reason he or she ought to be excused under section 17 of the Code. On the other hand, the argument of self defence may be raised by virtue of section 34 or the common law defence of consent may be used. These latter two defences raise particular concerns in the area of women and the criminal justice system. For example, there is the issue of the "battered women's defence" and its acceptance in and use by the courts. In the case of consent, we return to this defence in the final chapter in the section on sexual assault and the concerns raised by women's groups and others over the treatment of consent and the related issues in mistake of fact (see 7.2.1, below, and particularly the *Pappajohn* case).

Section 2 focuses on an absence of intent or knowledge, and is in essence an argument that the mens rea element of the offence has not been satisfied. At issue in this section is the type of mistaken belief or knowledge which is necessary to obviate guilt. Mistakes of fact are valid legal mistakes and the first subsection deals with the requirements of such mistakes. The second subsection examines mistakes (or ignorance) of law, mistakes which are not usually valid in relieving liability. The important question is how to determine what is a mistake of fact and what is a mistake of law because so many issues involve mixed questions of fact and law; for example, matters such as divorce and ownership involve legal relationships yet also encompass assertions as to fact in the everyday sense of the terms.

Section 3 highlights the increasing role played by the courts in the formulation of criminal justice policy, notably due to the advent of the Canadian Charter of Rights and Freedoms. The first subsection introduces us to the common law defence of entrapment where some of the problems associated with traditional judge-made law — uncertainty and lack of expertise — can be seen. The second topic on Charter protections reveals the developing role of the courts in the production of criminal law and illustrates many of the issues raised in Chapter 3 in a concrete manner. The selection of cases and defences is not exhaustive and is meant to provide only an introduction to this rapidly developing area of criminal law.

The fourth and final section deals with certain pleas which are all based on some type of mental or emotional impairment. The impairment may be caused by mental illness, drug use, disease, a blow to the head, or anger. The source of impairment determines whether the impaired accused falls within the scope of the defences of mental disorder, intoxication, provocation or automatism. Controversy surrounds all of these pleas. The main concern with provocation is the application of the "ordinary person" test in determining whether the accused's loss of control is acceptable. This question is addressed in *Hill*. Law reformers argue that the provocation section in the Code is inadequate and their reform suggestions are considered below. A final issue is whether provocation should continue to be restricted to murder.

A glance at the legal literature on the defence of mental disorder will confirm that this plea remains highly contentious. Dozens of articles call for the complete abolition of the plea and just as many argue for its retention. Some psychiatric experts argue that mental illness, the cornerstone of this defence, is a myth. Critics also suggest that while the mentally ill are sent away for treatment to be released when they are cured or at least not dangerous, the treatment given is not effective and mental health experts cannot predict accurately. Sorting the mad from the bad may be impossible, and even if theoretically possible, may be confounded by opposing institutional interests. Recent changes to the law in Canada are discussed in the excerpts from the O'Marra article.

The intoxication doctrine is controversial both legally and scientifically. Scientifically, the intoxication plea is questioned because there is considerable doubt that alcoholic or other drug impairments have the effects assumed by the courts. In particular, while the entire plea is premised on intoxicated offenders acting without intention, researchers report that drug impairment rarely, if ever, negates intent. With this background in mind, note the Supreme Court's most recent pronouncement in *Daviault* and Parliament's response in enacting section 33.1(1) of the Criminal Code. This new section effectively takes away the defence of extreme self-induced intoxication for general intent crimes of violence, and the question is now whether this section will withstand Charter scrutiny.

With automatism, a major difficulty is drawing the line between mental disorder and automatism, a problem illustrated by the *Rabey* case. Automatism cases often deal with physical or functional causes for the alleged involuntary behaviour. Such causes include epilepsy, brain tumour and blows to the head. Much more problematic are the cases involving so-called "psychological blows" which psychiatrists claim can be equivalent to physical blows. It is questionable whether any such "dissociative" states are valid excuses. Indeed, it is not clear how a psychological blow leading to violence differs in fact from provocation.

## 7.1 JUSTIFICATIONS

### 7.1.1 Duress

**Introduction**

One of the first questions that arises in regard to duress is why is it necessary to have a separate defence for duress or compulsion; if a person has been forced through threats to commit a crime, then it might be argued that the mens rea for the crime is not present. However, it must be kept in mind that "why" a person commits a crime is usually not important and many crimes merely require that an accused has knowingly or intentionally done the acts which make up the actus reus of the crime. People who do criminal acts under duress do so knowingly or intentionally, but there is an understandable excuse for their doing the acts. It is this excuse which the defence of compulsion in section 17 of the Code is permitting, though in a strictly limited way. Other types of excuses or reasons for doing the acts, such as "I needed the money to buy food so I robbed the bank" or "I killed him because I was mad at him" do not work, because they are either not viewed as socially valid excuses or might excuse too many people for their harmful acts.

We can see in section 17 that the law is allowing for people who have been subject to physical threats (though not necessarily *against* themselves) to be relieved of criminal liability for their actions. But this is not a blanket relief; it is one which is strictly circumscribed. First, it can be used only for threats of immediate death or grievous bodily harm, which has been interpreted in *Carker* below to mean that the threat must be one which is to be carried out immediately. The facts in the case show how unfair and unrealistic that interpretation can be, particularly in a prison environment like Carker's. Second, the person making the threat must be present when the offence is committed; again, the situation in *Carker* shows how narrow an interpretation the courts take of this. As for either of these requirements, the person threatened may realistically be motivated to commit the offence out of fear, even though the harm may be in the future or the person threatening may not be present when the offence is committed. Surely it would be more just and also more true to the rationale of the excuse to forgive those who subjectively believe that the threat will be carried out and who act as a direct result of that threat whether or not these first two requirements are met.[1]

Two major exceptions are given in section 17 as to who can make use of the defence. First, the defence is not available to a person who is "a party to a conspiracy or association whereby the person is subject to compulsion". In other words, the section is saying that such people have put themselves at risk in the first place and should not now be able to take advantage of the defence; they are not blameless in the circumstances. The second exception is that duress is not available as a defence in regard to certain crimes listed in section 17, crimes such as murder, sexual assault, robbery, and arson. The Code in effect is making a policy choice for the individual in such threatening situations, that if you go ahead and do one of the listed crimes, the excuse of duress can never be used.

It is this second exception which formed the basis of the *Paquette* case. The accused had been charged with murder and therefore, presumably, could not avail himself of the defence of duress. Yet he was successful in being able to use the common law defence of duress which is effective against murder charges. In such a situation the accused attempts to argue that the defence in section 17 does not apply to his or her case for the purpose of using the wider common law defence. The *Paquette* case outlines the situations under which the accused can escape the restrictions of the statutory defence. The last case, *Hibbert*, is the most recent and most exhaustive treatment of the defence by the Supreme Court.[2]

---

[1] See also the Supreme Court of Canada decision in this regard in *R. v. Hebert* (1989), 49 C.C.C. (3d) 59 (S.C.C.).
[2] See also an earlier case, *R. v. Langlois* (1993), 80 C.C.C. (3d) 28, in the Quebec Court of Appeal in which the court struck out section 17 as violating section 7 of the Charter.

## The Queen v. Carker (No. 2)
(1966), [1967] 2 C.C.C. 190 (S.C.C.).

Appeal by the Attorney-General of British Columbia from the judgment of the British Columbia Court of Appeal, [1966] 4 C.C.C. 212, 48 C.R. 313, 56 W.W.R. 65, quashing the accused's conviction on a charge of committing mischief and directing a new trial.

The judgment of the Court was delivered by

RITCHIE, J.: — This is an appeal by the Attorney-General of British Columbia from a judgment of the Court of Appeal of that Province, from which MacLean, J., dissented, and by which it was ordered that the respondent's conviction, for unlawfully and wilfully damaging public property and thereby committing mischief, should be set aside and that a new trial should be had.

At the trial the respondent admitted having damaged the plumbing fixtures in the cell where he was incarcerated at Oakalla Prison Farm in British Columbia but, through his counsel, he sought to introduce evidence to show that he had committed this offence under the compulsion of threats and was therefore entitled to be excused for committing it by virtue of the provisions of s. 17 of the *Criminal Code* and that he was also entitled to avail himself of the common law defence of "duress" having regard to the provisions of s. 7(2) of the *Criminal Code*.

Under the latter section it is provided that:

"7(2) Every rule and principle of the common law that render any circumstance a justification or excuse for an act or a defence to a charge continues in force and applies in respect of proceedings for an offence under this Act.. *except in so far as they are altered by or are inconsistent with this Act or any other Act of the Parliament of Canada"* (The italics are my own.)

I agree with the learned trial Judge and with MacLean, J.A., that in respect of proceedings for an offence under the *Criminal Code* the common law rules and principles respecting "duress" as an excuse or defence have been codified and exhaustively defined in s. 17 which reads as follows"

"17. A person who commits an offence under compulsion by threats of immediate death or grievous bodily harm from a person who is present when the offence is committed is excused for committing the offence if he believes that the threats will be carried out and if he is not a party to a conspiracy or association whereby he is subject to compulsion, but this section does not apply where the offence that is committed is treason, murder, piracy, attempted murder, assisting in rape, forcible abduction, robbery, causing bodily harm or arson."

At the outset of the proceedings at the trial in the present case and in the absence of the jury, Mr. Greenfield, who acted on behalf of the accused, informed the Court that he intended to call evidence of compulsion and duress and he elected to outline the nature of this evidence which was that the offence had been committed during a disturbance, apparently organized by way of protest, to damage property at the Prison Farm in the course of which a substantial body of prisoners, shouting in unison from their separate cells, threatened the respondent who was not joining in the disturbance that if he did not break the plumbing fixtures in his cell he would be kicked in the head, his arm would be broken and he would get a knife in the back at the first opportunity.

The question which the learned trial Judge was required to determine on Mr. Greenfield's application was whether the proposed evidence which had been outlined to him indicated a defence or excuse available at law; he decided that it did not and the majority of the Court of Appeal having taken a different view, the Attorney-General now appeals to this Court.

There can be little doubt that the evidence outlined by Mr. Greenfield, which was subsequently confirmed by the evidence given by the ringleaders of the disturbance in mitigation of sentence, disclosed that the respondent committed the offence under the compulsion of threats of death and grievous bodily harm, but although these threats were "immediate" in the sense that they were continuous until the time that the offence was committed, they were not threats of "immediate death" or "immediate grievous bodily harm" and none of the persons who delivered them was present in the cell with the respondent when the offence was committed. I am accordingly of opinion that the learned trial Judge was right in deciding that the proposed evidence did not afford an excuse within the meaning of s. 17 of the *Criminal Code*.

In the course of his most thoughtful judgment in the Court of Appeal, [[1966] 4 C.C.C. 212 at p. 224, 48 C.R. 313, 56 W.W.R. 65], Norris J., had occasion to say:

> "The question as to whether or not the person threatening was present goes to the question of the grounds for the fear which the appellant might have. In my opinion a person could be present making a threat although separated by the bars of the cell. These are all matters which should have gone to the jury, as was the question of whether or not the threat of death or grievous bodily harm was an immediate one — a question of degree. They might well consider that the threat was immediate as being continuous, as it was in this case, that it would be all the more frightening because of the uncertainty as to when it actually might happen, and therefore force him to act as he did."

With the greatest respect it appears to me that the question of whether immediate threats of future death or grievous bodily harm constitute an excuse for committing a crime within the meaning of s. 17 and the question of whether a person can be "present" within the meaning of that section when he is locked in a separate cell from the place where the offence is committed are both questions which depend upon the construction to be placed on the section and they are therefore questions of law and not questions of fact for the jury. (See *Vail v. The Queen, ex rel. Dickson*, 129 C.C.C. 145, at p. 150, 26 D.L.R. (2d) 419, [1960] S.C.R. 913, 33 W.W.R. 325; *Sikyea v. The Queen*, [1965] 2 C.C.C. 129 at p. 131, 44 C.R. 266, [1964] S.C.R. 642.

In support of the suggestion that the threat in the present case was "immediate and continuous" Norris J., relied on the case of *Subramaniam v. Public Prosecutor*, [1956] 1 W.L.R. 965, in which the Privy Council decided that the trial Judge was wrong in excluding evidence of threats to which the appellant was subjected by Chinese terrorists in Malaya. In that case it was found that the threats were a continuous menace up to the moment when the appellant was captured because the terrorists might have come back at any time and carried them into effect. Section 94 of the *Penal Code* of the Federated Malay States, which the appellant sought to invoke in that case provided [see p. 968]:

> "'94. Except murder and offences included in Chapter VI punishable by death, nothing is an offence which is done by a person who is compelled to do it by threats, which, at the time of doing it, reasonably cause the apprehension that instant death to that person will otherwise be the consequence: . . . '"

The distinctions between the *Subramaniam* Case and the present one lie in the fact that Subramaniam might well have had reasonable cause for apprehension that instant death would result from his disobeying the terrorists who might have come back at any moment, whereas it is virtually inconceivable that "immediate death" or "grievous bodily harm" could have come to Carker from those who were uttering the threat against him as they were locked up in separate cells, and it is also to be noted that the provisions of s. 17 of the *Criminal Code* are by no means the same as those of s. 94 of the *Penal Code* of the Federated Malay States; amongst other distinctions the latter section contains no provision that the person who utters threats must be present when the offence is committed in order to afford an excuse for committing it.

Both Norris, J., and Branca, J., in delivering their separate reasons for judgment in the Court of Appeal, expressed the view that the evidence which was tendered should have been admitted on the issue of whether the respondent acted wilfully in damaging the prison plumbing or whether he was so affected by the threats uttered against him as to be incapable of adopting any other course than the one which he did.

The relevant provisions of the *Criminal Code* read as follows:

"**372**(1) Every one commits mischief who wilfully
(a) destroys or damages property . . . .

"(3) Every one who commits mischief in relation to public property is guilty of an indictable offence and is liable to imprisonment for fourteen years."

On this phase of the matter, Norris, J., had this to say [pp. 225-6]:

"In making the ruling which he did, the learned trial Judge deprived the appellant of what could be a substantial defence to the charge or an excuse under s. 17. Without hearing the evidence, the jury could not decide whether the act was in fact wilful. This was not a matter on which the Judge might rule. The lengths to which the evidence might go to disprove the essentials of the charge or to prove the requirements of s. 17 could never, in the absence of the evidence of witnesses, be apparent either to the learned Judge or to the jury."

With the greatest respect, this portion of Mr. Justice Norris' reasons for judgment appears to overlook the fact that "the length to which the evidence might go . . . " was fully outlined to the learned Judge by counsel for the respondent when he was making the application.

In this regard it is important to bear in mind the fact that "wilful" as it is used in Part IX of the *Criminal Code* is defined in s. 371(1) which reads, in part, as follows:

"**371**(1) Every one who causes the occurrence of an event by doing an act or by omitting to do an act that it is his duty to do, knowing that the act or omission will probably cause the occurrence of the event and being reckless whether the event occurs or not, shall be deemed, for the purposes of this Part, wilfully to have caused the occurrence of the event."

The evidence outlined to the learned trial Judge discloses that the criminal act was committed to preserve the respondent from future harm coming to him, but there is no suggestion in the evidence tendered for the defence that the accused did not know that what he was doing would "probably cause" damage. Accepting the outline made by defence counsel as being an accurate account of the evidence which was available, there was in my view nothing in it to support the defence that the act was not done "wilfully" within the meaning of s. 371(1) and 372(1) of the *Criminal Code* and there was accordingly no ground to justify the learned trial Judge in permitting the proposed evidence to be called in support of such a defence.

In view of all the above, I would allow this appeal, set aside the judgement of the Court of Appeal and restore the conviction.

*Appeal allowed; conviction restored.*

## Paquette v. The Queen
[1977] 2 S.C.R. 189

The judgment of the Court was delivered by
MARTLAND, J.: — The facts which give rise to this appeal are as follows:
During the course of a robbery at the Pop Shoppe, in the City of Ottawa, on March 18, 1973, an innocent bystander was killed by a bullet from a rifle fired by one Simard. The robbery was committed by Simard and one Clermont, both of whom, together with the appellant, were jointly charged with non-capital murder. Simard and Clermont pleaded guilty to this charge.

The appellant was not present when the robbery was committed or when the shooting occurred. The charge against him was founded upon s. 21(2) of the *Criminal Code*. Section 21 provides as follows:

21.(1) Every one is a party to an offence who
(a) actually commits it,
(b) does or omits to do anything for the purpose of aiding any person to commit it, or
(c) abets any person in committing it.

(2) Where two or more persons form an intention in common to carry out an unlawful purpose and to assist each other therein and any one of them, in carrying out the common purpose, commits an offence, each of them who knew or ought to have known that the commission of the offence would be a probable consequence of carrying out the common purpose is a party to that offence.

The appellant made a statement to the police, which was admitted in evidence at the trial and which described his involvement in the matter as follows: On the day of the robbery Clermont telephoned the appellant for a ride as his own car was broken. Clermont asked the appellant where he used to work and was told at the Pop Shoppe. Clermont told him to drive to the Pop Shoppe because Clermont wanted to rob it, and when the appellant refused, Clermont pulled his gun and threatened to kill him. Simard was picked up later and also a rifle. The appellant drove them to the Pop Shoppe. The appellant had been threatened with revenge if he did not wait for Clermont and Simard. The appellant, in his statement, stated he was afraid and drove around the block. After the robbery and homicide Clermont and Simard attempted twice, unsuccessfully, to get into the appellant's car. Three of the Crown's witnesses supported this latter statement. The appellant did not testify at trial but relied on the above statement and two other statements also introduced at the trial by the Crown to support his argument that he had no intention in common with Simard and Clermont to carry out the robbery; i.e.:

(1) An oral statement to a police officer on his arrest that he had been threatened with death "if he squealed".
(2) The written statement to the police outlined above in which he stated that he had only participated in the robbery by driving because he was threatened with death;
(3) A statement to his girl friend the day after the robbery that he was forced to do it.

The trial judge charged the jury as follows:

Now, the defence are asserting that Paquette participated in this robbery because he was compelled to do so, and in that connection I charge you that if Paquette joined in the common plot to rob the Pop Shoppe under threats of death or grievous bodily harm, that would negative his having a common intention with Simard to rob the Pop Shoppe, and you must find Paquette not guilty.

The appellant was acquitted. The Crown appealed to the Court of Appeal for Ontario. The reasons delivered by that Court make it clear that the appeal would have been dismissed had it not been for the decision of this Court in *Dunbar v. The King*.

. . . .

Counsel for the Crown submits that the principles of law applicable to the excuse or defence of duress or compulsion are exhaustively codified in s. 17 of the *Criminal*

*Code*, and that the appellant is precluded from relying upon this provision because of the exception contained at the end of it. Section 17 provides:

> 17. A person who commits an offence under compulsion by threats of immediate death or grievous bodily harm from a person who is present when the offence is committed is excused for committing the offence if he believes that the threats will be carried out and if he is not a party to a conspiracy or association whereby he is subject to compulsion, but this section does not apply where the offence that is committed is treason, murder, piracy, attempted murder, assisting in rape, forcible abduction, robbery, causing bodily harm or arson.

In my opinion the application of s. 17 is limited to cases in which the person seeking to rely upon it has himself committed an offence. If a person who actually commits the offence does so in the presence of another party who has compelled him to do the act by threats of immediate death or grievous bodily harm, then, if he believes the threats would be carried out, and is not a party to a conspiracy whereby he is subject to such compulsion, he is excused for committing the offence. The protection afforded by this section is not given in respect of the offences listed at the end of the section, which include murder and robbery.

The section uses the specific words "a person who commits an offence". It does not use the words "a person who is a party to an offence." This is significant in the light of the wording of s. 21(1) which, in para. (a), makes a person a party to an offence who "actually commits it". Paragraphs (b) and (c) deal with a person who aids or abets a person committing the offence. In my opinion s. 17 codifies the law as to duress as an excuse for the actual commission of a crime, but it does not, by its terms, go beyond that. *R. v. Carker*, in which reference was made to s. 17 having codified the defence or excuse of duress, dealt with a situation in which the accused had actually committed the offence.

The appellant, in the present case, did not himself commit the offence of robbery or of murder. He was not present when the murder occurred, as was the case in *R. v. Farduto*, and *R. v. Warren*, to which counsel for the Crown referred. In the former case the accused provided the razor with which the murderer cut the throat of the victim in his presence. The Court was of the view that the trial judge could conclude that there was no case of such compulsion as would constitute an excuse. In the latter case the accused, the brother of the actual murderer was present with him over a period of time after the robbery occurred and before the deceased was killed in his presence. The report does not indicate the nature of the compulsion alleged. The emphasis appears to have been on the subnormal intelligence of the accused making him willing to go along with what was suggested to him.

The appellant could only be considered to be a party to the murder on the basis of the application of s. 21(2). Section 21(1) is not applicable because the offence to which he is alleged to be a party is murder, and it is clear that he did not commit murder, nor did he aid or abet in its commission.

Subsection (2) is only applicable if it is established that the appellant, in common with Simard and Clermont, formed an intention to commit robbery. The question in issue is as to whether the trial judge erred in law in telling the jury that if the appellant joined in the plot to rob under threats of death or of grievous bodily harm, this would negative such common intention.

I have already stated my reasons for considering s. 17 to be inapplicable. That being so, the appellant is entitled, by virtue of s. 7(3) of the *Code*, to rely upon any excuse or defence available to him at common law. The defence of duress to a charge of murder against a person who did not commit the murder, but who has alleged to have aided and abetted, was recently considered by the House of Lords in *Director of Public Prosecutions for Northern Ireland v. Lynch*, in which the decided cases were fully reviewed.

. . . .

I am in agreement with the conclusion reached by the majority that it was open to Lynch, in the circumstances of that case, to rely on the defence of duress, which had not been put to the jury. If the defence of duress can be available to a person who has aided and abetted in the commission of murder, then clearly it should be available to a person who is sought to be made a party to the offence by virtue of s. 21(2). A person whose actions have been dictated by fear of death or of grievous bodily injury cannot be said to have formed a genuine common intention to carry out an unlawful purpose with the person who has threatened him with those consequences if he fails to co-operate.

. . . .

I would allow the appeal, set aside the judgment of the Court of Appeal, and restore the verdict of acquittal.

*Appeal allowed.*

## Hibbert v. The Queen
(1995), 99 C.C.C (3d) 193 (S.C.C.)

Appeal by the accused from a judgment of the Ontario Court of Appeal dismissing his appeal from conviction for aggravated assault.

The judgment of the court was delivered by

[1] LAMER, C.J.C.: — This appeal presents a number of important questions, each having to do with the role of duress as a defence to criminal charges. In order to resolve these issues, we must first examine the theoretical basis underlying the rule that criminal liability does not attach to a person who commits the *actus reus* of an offence as a result of threats of death or bodily harm from a third party. In particular, this court must decide whether it is open to a person charged as a party to an offence to argue that, because his or her actions were coerced, he or she did not possess the *mens rea* necessary for party liability. This argument must be weighed against the alternative position — namely, that duress does not "negate" the *mens rea* for party liability, but that persons who commit certain criminal acts under duress may none the less be excused from criminal liability under the common law "defence of duress". It is also necessary for the court to address certain questions having to do with limitations on this defence's availability. Specifically, we are asked to determine whether accused persons are foreclosed from recourse to the defence if they failed to avail themselves of a "safe avenue of escape" from the situation of coercion when such a safe avenue was available. If this is indeed the case, we must go on to consider whether the

existence of such a "safe avenue" is to be determined on an objective basis, or from the subjective viewpoint of the accused.

# I
# FACTUAL BACKGROUND

[2] On November 25, 1991, shortly before 1:00 a.m. Fitzroy Cohen was shot four times with a semi-automatic handgun as he stood in the lobby of the apartment building he lived in. The shots were fired by Mark Bailey, an acquaintance of Cohen whom Cohen knew by his street names, "Quasi" or "Dogheart". At the time of the shooting, Bailey was accompanied by the appellant, Lawrence Hibbert, who was a close friend of Cohen. Cohen had descended from his apartment to the lobby at the appellant's request, unaware that Bailey was waiting below with gun in hand.

[3] Cohen survived the shooting. At the appellant's trial, Cohen testified that for some time prior to the shooting he had been aware that Bailey was seeking a confrontation with him. Bailey, Cohen believed, was seeking revenge for an incident that had taken place the previous year, in which Bailey had been robbed by a rival drug dealer named Andrew Reid while Cohen and several others stood by, watching and laughing. Cohen testified that he had been told that Bailey had subsequently attacked one of the men involved in the robbery on a busy street, firing several shots at him (but missing). He also knew that Andrew Reid had been murdered. Cohen said that he had told the appellant, whom he described as his "best friend", about the robbery of Bailey.

[4] The appellant, who testified at trial, stated that at the time of the shooting he owed Bailey $100 as payment for drugs he had purchased from him some months earlier. He testified that he had been attempting to avoid Bailey, but that on the evening of November 24, 1991, he had accidently run into him in the lobby of an apartment building in Etobicoke where he had gone to visit friends. Bailey had approached the appellant and indicated that he was armed with a handgun. The appellant testified that Bailey ordered him to take him to Cohen's apartment. When he refused, the appellant stated, Bailey had led him to the basement and punched him in the face several times. The appellant testified that he feared for his life, and that he believed that Bailey would shoot him if he continued to refuse to assist him. He stated that it was this fear that led him to agree to lead Bailey to Cohen's apartment.

[5] Bailey and the appellant went out to Bailey's car, where Bailey's girlfriend and another young woman were waiting. The appellant got into the back seat, while Bailey drove. The women testified that the appellant was quiet during the drive, but that his mood was neither noticeably happy or unhappy. At trial, one of the young women recalled that the appellant had made a remark to the effect that "this might be the last time I'm going to see you".

[6] Bailey dropped the two women off at their apartment, and told the appellant to get into the front seat. The appellant testified that they stopped at a telephone booth, and that Bailey ordered him to call Cohen and ask him to meet him downstairs in 20 minutes. The appellant did so, telling Cohen that he "had something for him". According to the appellant, Bailey stood by the phone booth during his conversation with Cohen, and could hear what the appellant said to Cohen. Cohen and his girlfriend,

Beverley St. Hillaire, confirmed that they had received a telephone call from the appellant, essentially as the appellant described. They testified that the appellant had sounded "normal", but that he had been more abrupt than he usually was.

[7] Bailey and Hibbert arrived at Cohen's apartment building approximately half an hour after making the phone call. The appellant testified that Bailey drew his gun and pointed it at him as they got out of the car. They went to the front door of the building where, following Bailey's orders, the appellant called Cohen's apartment on the building intercom, while Bailey kept his gun trained on him. The appellant's testimony, which was confirmed by Cohen, was that ordinarily when visiting Cohen he would not use the building's front door, but would instead enter the building through a side door that could be opened from the outside using a technique Cohen had taught him. Cohen also confirmed the appellant's testimony that he had asked Cohen to "come down" to the lobby, but that he had not asked Cohen to "buzz him in" (*i.e.*, press a button on the intercom that would unlock the building's outer door). The appellant testified that he had hoped that Cohen would not unlock the building's front door, so that when he came downstairs he would see Bailey through the locked glass outer door and have a chance to retreat to safety. However, Cohen buzzed the outer door open without being asked to do so, and Bailey and the appellant went into the lobby.

[8] According to the testimony of both Cohen and Hibbert, Cohen took the stairs from his second-floor apartment to the lobby. When he emerged into the lobby, he was met by Bailey, who grabbed him and pointed the gun at his chest, saying "You're dead now, pussy." Bailey led Cohen into the ground-floor hallway, where (according to both Cohen and the appellant's testimony) he turned to Hibbert and told him to "stay some place where I [can] see you." After a brief exchange of words with Cohen, Bailey pushed Cohen away and fired four shots at him, striking him in the groin, legs and buttocks. Saying "Come, Pigeon" (the appellant's nickname), Bailey and the appellant left the building by the side door. Cohen testified that during the incident the appellant said nothing, and made no effort to intervene. He described the appellant as "all sweating", and said that the appellant was unable to look at him. The appellant, however, testified that he had repeatedly pleaded with Bailey, "Quasi, don't kill him."

[9] The appellant testified that from the moment he first encountered Bailey that evening he had believed Bailey would shoot him if he refused to co-operate, and stated that he had been "terrified" throughout his time in Bailey's company. Under cross-examination, he declared that he believed that he had had no opportunity to run away or warn Cohen without being shot.

[10] After leaving the building, Bailey drove the appellant back to Etobicoke. The appellant testified that Bailey threatened to kill him if he went to the police. Upon his return to Etobicoke, the appellant spoke to Cohen's brother about what had happened, and called Cohen's mother and Cohen's apartment. He subsequently called his own mother, before going to sleep. The next morning, he turned himself in to the police. Bailey, however, was never apprehended.

[11] The appellant was charged with attempted murder. On March 19, 1992, following a trial by jury in the Ontario Court of Justice (General Division) presided over by Webber J., he was acquitted of this charge, but was convicted of the included offence of aggravated assault and sentenced to four years' imprisonment. On July 15,

1993, his appeal of his conviction to the Court of Appeal for Ontario was dismissed, although the court allowed his appeal from sentence, reducing his sentence from four years to time served (some 15 months).

## II
## RELEVANT STATUTORY PROVISIONS

*Criminal Code*, R.S.C. 1985, c. C-46

8(3) Every rule and principle of the common law that renders any circumstance a justification or excuse for an act or a defence to a charge continues in force and applies in respect of proceedings for an offence under this Act or any other Act of Parliament except in so far as they are altered by or are inconsistent with this Act or any other Act of Parliament.

. . . . .

17. A person who commits an offence under compulsion by threats of immediate death or bodily harm from a person who is present when the offence is committed is excused for committing the offence if the person believes that the threats will be carried out and if the person is not a party to a conspiracy or association whereby the person is subject to compulsion, but this section does not apply where the offence that is committed is high treason or treason, murder, piracy, attempted murder, sexual assault, sexual assault with a weapon, threats to a third party or causing bodily harm, aggravated sexual assault, forcible abduction, hostage taking, robbery, assault with a weapon or causing bodily harm, aggravated assault, unlawfully causing bodily harm, arson or an offence under sections 280 to 283 (abduction and detention of young persons).

. . . . .

21(1) Every one is a party to an offence who

(*a*) actually commits it,
(*b*) does or omits to do anything for the purpose of aiding any person to commit it; or
(*c*) abets any person in committing it.

(2) Where two or more persons form an intention in common to carry out an unlawful purpose and to assist each other therein and any one of them, in carrying out the common purpose, commits an offence, each of them who knew or ought to have known that the commission of the offence would be a probable consequence of carrying out the common purpose is a party to that offence.

. . .

## IV
## GROUNDS FOR APPEAL

[16] Lawrence Hibbert appeals his conviction to this court on the grounds that the trial judge's charge to the jury on the issue of duress contained several errors. First, he argues, the trial judge erred by instructing the jury that the defence of duress operated by "negativing common intention". The appellant objects further to the trial judge's statement that the defence of duress was unavailable to an accused who failed to avail himself or herself of a "safe avenue of escape". As an alternative to the latter argument, the appellant submits that even if the "safe avenue of escape" rule exists, the trial judge erred by not advising the jury that the existence or non-existence of such an avenue was to be determined by reference to the appellant's subjective belief.

# V
# ANALYSIS

## A. *Introduction*

[17] The issues raised in this appeal must be analyzed in several stages. First, it is necessary to consider the fundamental question of why it is that a person who performs an act that would otherwise constitute the *actus reus* of a criminal offence will not be held criminally liable at common law if he or she did so as a result of threats of death or bodily harm. That is, we must examine the theoretical nature of the common law defence of duress, and determine its relationship to basic *mens rea* principles. We must also consider the question of whether the availability of the defence of duress is limited by a "safe avenue of escape" rule. Once these questions have been addressed, it will then be possible to assess the learned trial judge's charge to the jury on duress, and to determine whether the jurors were correctly advised of the principles they were to apply to their deliberations.

## B. *The relationship between mens rea and the defence of duress*

### (1) *The common law defence of duress in Canada*

[18] The defence of "duress *per minas*" ("duress by threat") has a long history at common law. References to the defence can be found in the writings of such venerable commentators as Hale and Blackstone (see J. Ll. J. Edwards, "Compulsion, Coercion and Criminal Responsibility (1951), 14 Mod. L. Rev. 297 at pp. 298-9; and P. Rosenthal, "Duress in the Criminal Law" (1989-90), 32 C.L.Q. 199 at pp. 200*ff*). In spite of the defence's antiquity, however, many important aspects of its nature and its details have remained unresolved, or have been shrouded with uncertainty. As Professor Edwards, *supra*, observed in 1951 (at p. 297):

> Judged by the absence of any satisfactory modern authority, it must be very rare for the accused to set up as a defence that he committed the alleged crime under the compulsion of another person. Indeed, the whole field of learning on this defence to criminal liability is both meagre and unsatisfactory.

[19] In Canada, a defence of duress was included in the first *Criminal Code*, enacted in 1892 (S.C. 1892, c. 29). Section 12 of the original *Code* (the predecessor of the current *Code*'s s. 17) provided that "compulsion by threats of immediate death or grievous bodily harm from a person actually present at the commission of the offence shall be an excuse for [its] commission" (subject to certain specified conditions being met). For many years, it seems to have been generally assumed (although never conclusively established) that the existence of a codified version of the defence of duress left no room for further development of the common law defence in Canada. As Ritchie J. remarked, *obiter*, in *R. v. Carker*, [1967] 2 C.C.C. 190 at p. 191, [1967] S.C.R. 114, 2 C.R. (N.S.) 16: "[I]n respect of proceedings for an offence under the *Criminal Code* the common law rules and principles respecting "duress" as an excuse or defence have been codified and exhaustively defined in s. 17". In *R. v. Paquette* (1976), 30 C.C.C. (2d) 417, 70 D.L.R. (3d) 129, [1977] 2 S.C.R. 189, however, this

court determined that s. 17 of the *Code* does not constitute an exhaustive codification of the law of duress. Rather, the court held, s. 17 applies only to persons who commit offences as *principals*. Accordingly it remains open to persons who are liable as *parties* to offences to invoke the common law defence of duress, which remains in existence by virtue of s. 8(3) of the *Code* (which preserves those common law defences not expressly altered or eliminated by Parliament). The common law rules governing situations of duress thus remain an important aspect of Canadian criminal law.

[20] The holding in *Paquette* that the common law defence of duress is available to persons liable as parties is clear and unambiguous, and has stood as law in Canada for almost 20 years. The case has a second aspect, however, that is less firmly established, having given rise to differing interpretations, and having been the subject of considerable debate in the legal community. The controversy stems from certain comments made by Martland J. on the issue of the relationship between duress and the *mens rea* for party liability under s. 21(2) of the *Code*. The facts in *Paquette* were as follows. The accused had been charged as a party to non-capital murder. He had driven two acquaintances, Clermont and Simard, to a store. After Paquette had dropped them off, Clermont and Simard robbed the store, and during the course of the robbery an innocent bystander was shot and killed. Paquette was not present at the shooting, having driven away from the store once Clermont and Simard had entered. Although he circled the block and returned to the store, there was evidence that he had refused to let Clermont and Simard get back into the car. In a statement made to the police, Paquette indicated that he had driven Clermont and Simard to the scene of the crime only after Clermont had pointed a gun at him and threatened to kill him if he refused. At trial, the issue of duress had been left to the jury, which acquitted the accused. On appeal, the Ontario Court of Appeal ordered a new trial, on the grounds that the statutory defence of duress contained in s. 17 of the *Code* could not, by the express terms of the section, be invoked as a defence to a charge of murder or robbery.

[21] As noted above, the main holding of the court was that s. 17 applied only to principals and not to parties, from which it followed that Paquette could rely on the common law defence of duress, to which the restrictions set out in s. 17 did not apply. Martland J. went on, however, to make an observation regarding duress and the mental element of party liability under s. 21(2) of the *Code*, stating (at p. 423):

> A person whose actions have been dictated by fear of death or of grievous bodily injury cannot be said to have formed a *genuine* common intention to carry out an unlawful purpose with the person who has threatened him with those consequences if he fails to co-operate.

(Emphasis added). The significance of this comment in terms of the judgment as a whole is rather difficult to determine. Martland J. had earlier endorsed the decision of the House of Lords in *Director of Public Prosecutions for Northern Ireland v Lynch*, [1975] A.C. 653, in which a majority of the House of Lords had clearly taken the view that the common law defence of duress provided an *excuse*, rather than operating by negating *mens rea*. Thus, Martland J. evidently did not intent to suggest that duress provides a defence at common law *only* when the accused's culpable mental state can be said to have been "negated". Instead, he appears to have been holding out an alternative route by which a person charged as a party under s. 21(2) could escape criminal liability, distinct from the "defence of duress" *per se* — that is, a "defence" founded not on concepts of excuse or justification, but based instead on the absence of an essential element of the offence.

[22] Seen in this way, *Paquette* stands for the proposition that duress can provide a "defence" in either of two distinct ways — as an excuse, or by "negating' *mens rea*. In the present case, the appellant argues that this is a correct view of the law, and submits that the trial judge erred by not placing both alternatives before the jury. What falls to be considered, therefore, is the validity of the proposition that the *mens rea* for party liability under the *Criminal Code* can be "negated" by threats of death or bodily harm. That is, the court is called upon to reconsider whether the second aspect of our judgment in *Paquette* reflects a correct understanding of the law of duress in Canada.

*(2) Duress and mens rea*

[23] That threats of death or serious bodily harm can have an effect on a person's state of mind is indisputable. However, it is also readily apparent that a person who carries out the *actus reus* of a criminal offence in response to such threats will not necessarily lack the *mens rea* for that offence. Whether he or she does or not will depend both on what the mental element of the offence in question happens to be, and on the facts of the particular case. As a practical matter, though, situations where duress will operate to "negate" *mens rea* will be exceptional, for the simple reason that the types of mental states that are capable of being "negated" by duress are not often found in the definitions of criminal offences.

[24] In general, a person who performs an action in response to a threat will *know* what he or she is doing, and will be aware of the probable consequences of his or her actions. Whether or not he or she *desires* the occurrence of these consequences will depend on the particular circumstances. For example, a person who is forced at gunpoint to drive a group of armed ruffians to a bank will usually know that the likely result of his or her actions will be that an attempt will be made to rob the bank, but he or she may not desire this result — indeed, he or she may strongly wish that the robbers' plans are ultimately foiled, if this could occur without risk to his or her own safety. In contrast, a person who is told that his or her child is being held hostage at another location and will be killed unless the robbery is successful will almost certainly have an active subjective desire that the robbery succeed. While the existence of threats clearly has a bearing on the *motive* underlying each actor's respective decision to assist in the robbery, only the first actor can be said not to *desire* that the robbery take place, and neither actor can be said not to have knowledge of the consequences of their actions. To determine whether *mens rea* is "negated" in a particular case, therefore, the first question that must be asked is whether the mental element of the offence in question is defined in such a way that either an actor's motives or his or her immediate desires have any direct relevance. As A.W. Mewett and M. Manning explain:

> *Mens rea* ... has more than one meaning. It can entail a purpose, a desire to achieve an objective; it can entail merely knowledge that consequences will follow or that circumstances exist; it can entail only recklessness, that is, some advertent or perhaps inadvertent disregard of the consequences or circumstances. What suffices for liability depends upon the particular offence with which we are dealing. If a person is compelled to do an act which he does not wish to do, and therefore does it "against his will", why, it may be asked, does he have a defence not of compulsion but simply of lack of *mens rea* The answer is that this is quite true, but only if the *mens rea* required for the

particular offence in question is of the sort that is negatived by a person being compelled to do something against his will.

(*Mewett and Manning on Criminal Law*, 3rd ed. (Toronto: Butterworths, 1994), at p. 520.)

[25]As Dickson J. (as he then was) observed in *Lewis v. The Queen* (1979), 47 C.C.C. (2d) 24 at p. 33, 98 D.L.R. (3d) 111, [1979] 2 S.C.R. 82, "[t]he mental element of a crime ordinarily involves no reference to motive". Instead, he noted, "[i]n most criminal trials the mental element, the *mens rea* with which the Court is concerned, relates to 'intent'". Intention, however, is distinct from desire or subjective wish. As Lord Simon of Glaisdale stated in *Lynch, supra* (dissenting, but on another issue), at p. 690:

> [A]n *intention* to bring about a consequence of an act can co-exist with a *desire* that such consequences should not ensue ... [A] *wish* is a particular instance of *desire* .... [T]herefore, an *intention* to perform an act with foreseen consequences can co-exist with a *wish* not to perform the act or that its consequences should not ensue (this is crucial in considering the juridical effect of duress).

(Emphasis in original.) Parliament is, of course, entitled to define the mental element of criminal offences in whatever manner it sees fit (subject, of course, to the requirements of s. 7 of the *Canadian Charter of Rights and Freedoms*: see, for instance *Reference re: Section 94(2) of the Motor Vehicle Act* (1985), 23 C.C.C. (3d) 289, 24 D.L.R. (4th) 536, [1985] 2 S.C.R. 486; *R. v. Vaillancourt* (1987), 39 C.C.C. (3d) 118, 47 D.L.R. (4th) 399, [1987] 2 S.C.R. 636; *R. v. Martineau* (1990), 58 C.C.C. (3d) 353, [1990] 2 S.C.R. 633, 79 C.R. (3d) 129; and *R. v. Logan* (1990), 58 C.C.C. (3d) 391, 73 D.L.R. (4th) 40, [1990] 2 S.C.R. 731). Thus, Parliament could choose to make it an element of a given offence that the perpetrator have some particular *desire* at the time of the commission of the *actus reus*, or even make it a precondition for liability that an actor have a particular *motive* for performing a prohibited act. In the present appeal, of course, we are not called upon to conduct an exhaustive review of the *Criminal Code* for the purposes of identifying any or all offences with mental elements that might be capable of being negated by duress. Rather, the present case, like *Paquette*, involves the special situation of liability under s. 21 of the *Code*. Thus, our analysis can be restricted to the question of whether the *mens rea* requirements for party liability contained in s. 21 are of the sort that can, in some circumstances, be "negated" by coercion. Since the sole aspect of s. 21 left with the jury in the appellant's trial was s. 21(1)(*b*), the analysis could, strictly speaking, be restricted to that subsection. It is difficult, however, to embark upon an examination of the mental element of s. 21(1)(*b*) without being seen as inferentially commenting on s. 21(2), thereby calling into question the court's holding in *Paquette, supra*. In my view, in order to avoid creating undue confusion and uncertainty in the law, it is appropriate that we address the issue of the continued validity of *Paquette's* statements on the relation between duress and *mens rea* under s. 21(2), head on. I will thus extend my analysis beyond what is strictly necessary for the resolution of the present appeal by considering s. 21(2) in addition to s. 21(*b*).

### (3) *The mens rea requirements for party liability under s. 21*

(a) *Section 21(1)(b)*

[26] As noted earlier, s. 21(1)(*b*) imposes criminal liability as a party on anyone who "does or omits to do anything for the purpose of aiding any person to commit" an offence. Although a person who is a party to an offence is guilty of committing *that* offence, rather than a separate crime (as in the case for accessories after the fact), s. 21(1)(*b*) contains its own *mens rea* requirement, distinct from that applicable to the principal who actually commits the underlying offence. As the subsection states, party liability as an "aider" requires acts or omissions "for the purpose" of aiding the commission of the offence. In order to understand what effect, if any, duress might have on the *mens rea* of an aider, it is thus necessary to determine what "for the purpose" means in this context.

[27] It is impossible to ascribe a single fixed meaning to the term "purpose". In ordinary usage, the word is employed in two distinct senses. One can speak of an actor doing something "on purpose" (as opposed to by accident), thereby equating purpose with "immediate intention". The term is also used, however, to indicate the ultimate ends an actor seeks to achieve, which imports the idea of "desire" into the definition. This dual sense is apparent in the word's dictionary definition. For instance, the Oxford English Dictionary, 2nd ed. (1989), defines "purpose" alternatively as "[t]hat which one sets before oneself as a thing to be done or attained; the object which one has in view" and as "[t]he action or fact of intending or meaning to do something; intention, resolution, determination". The first of these definitions reflects the notion of one's "purpose" as relating to one's ultimate object or desire, while the latter conveys the notion of "purpose" as being synonymous with "intention".

. . .

My conclusions in the present case on the proper interpretation of the word "purpose" as it is employed in s. 21(1)(*b*) of the *Code* are thus restricted to this particular subsection. It may well be that in the context of some other statutory provision a different interpretation of the term will prove to be the most appropriate.

[31] As I said, when Parliament drafts a statute in language that, on its face, supports more than one meaning, it is appropriate for a court to consider which of the alternative interpretations that are available best accords with Parliament's intention (see my remarks in *R. v. McIntosh* (1995), 95 C.C.C. (3d) 481 at pp. 489*ff.*, [1995] 1 S.C.R. 686, 36 C.R. (4th) 171). As I will explain, I am of the view that in the context of s. 21(1)(*b*) of the *Code*, the second of the two meanings of "purpose" discussed above — that is, the interpretation that equates "purpose" with "intention" — best reflects the legislative intent underlying the subsection.

. . .

[38] Finally, I am satisfied that the interpretation of the *mens rea* for liability under s. 21(1)(*b*) that I am proposing will not result in unjust convictions in cases involving coercion by threats of death or bodily harm, since in these cases the common law

defence of duress will remain available to the accused. As I will explain shortly, this defence, properly understood, provides an excuse to persons who assist in the commission of offences as a result of threats of serious violence. On the other hand, interpreting "purpose" as equivalent to "desire" in s. 21(1)(*b*) would result in the introduction of unnecessary complication into the law. Under such an interpretation, juries in duress cases would have to be provided with extremely complex instruction that would, in the end, have very little, if any, impact on the final determination of guilt or innocence. As a matter of logic, the issue of whether an accused can invoke an excuse or justification arises only *after* the Crown has proven the existence of all the elements of the offence, including *mens rea*. Thus, if "purpose" were understood as incorporating "desire", and hence as being susceptible to "negation" by duress, trial judges would have to instruct juries accordingly. This would require judges, and juries, to delve into the arcane issue of whether a person who intentionally commits an offence in order to save his or her own skin commits the offence "on purpose" — a question of some philosophical significance, perhaps, but no easy matter for a judge to explain succinctly, or for a jury to comprehend readily. At the same time, trial judges would *also* have to provide juries with alternative instructions on the excuse-based common law defence of duress. While in many cases an aider who actively desires the commission of the offence he or she aids will not be able to legitimately claim that he or she acted under duress, this will not inevitably be so (consider, for instance, the hypothetical example, discussed earlier, of the parent whose child is held hostage by confederates of robbers, who is told that the child will be released unharmed only if he or she assists in the *successful* commission of a robbery). Consequently, in at least some cases juries would be forced to consider two alternate legal routes leading to an acquittal by reason of duress. This complication would, however, have little or no practical effect, since there will be few, if any, cases involving parties in which a "defence" of "negation of *mens rea* by duress" would succeed where recourse to the excuse-based common law defence of duress would not also lead to an acquittal. As Professor Stuart observes (D. Stuart: *Canadian Criminal Law: a Treatise*, 3rd ed. (Scarborough, Ont: Carswell, 1995)), introducing the notion of duress "negating" *mens rea* into the analysis serves only to muddy the conceptual waters. As he points out (at p. 420):

> The advantages [of viewing the operation of duress solely in terms of an excuse] are more than linguistic. If the defence of duress is viewed like any other justification or excuse as based squarely on policy considerations allowing one who has committed an *actus reus* with *mens rea* to escape in certain circumstances, the policy issues are focused without confusing the matter as one of *mens rea*.

[39] For these reasons, I conclude that the expression "for the purpose of aiding" in s. 21(1)(*b*), properly understood, does not require that the accused actively view the commission of the offence he or she is aiding as desirable in and of itself. As a result the *mens rea* for aiding under s. 21(1)(*b*) is not susceptible of being "negated" by duress. The trial judge's charge to the jury in the present case was thus incorrect in two respects. First, the reference to the relevant mental state in the present case as being a "common intention to carry out an unlawful purpose" was erroneous since, unlike *Paquette*, what was at issue in the present case was s. 21(1)(*b*), as opposed to s. 21(2). Second, in light of the mental element for commission of an offence under s.

21(1)(b), the suggestion that duress might "negate" the accused's *mens rea* was also incorrect.

(b) *Section 21(2) and the decision in Paquette*

[40] The preceding discussion suffices to resolve the question of the relation between duress and *mens rea* that directly arises in the present case. As I indicated earlier, however, I believe that in the interests of avoiding undue confusion in the law that applies to duress cases I should proceed further, and look expressly at the question of whether the interpretation of s. 21(2)'s mental element that was adopted by the court in *Paquette, supra*, remains correct in light of the interpretation of s. 21(1)(b) I am now adopting. To be sure, the respective *mens rea* requirements of the two subsections are defined differently — while s. 21(1)(b) imposes party liability on persons who "do or omit to do anything *for the purpose* of aiding any person to commit [an offence]", s. 21(2) establishes that "persons [who] form *an intention in common* to carry out an unlawful purpose and to assist each other therein" are liable for criminal offences committed by the principal that are foreseeable and probable consequences of carrying out the "common purpose." There is, however, a close connection between the two subsections, arising from the evident similarities that exist between certain aspects of s. 21(2)'s requirements and the terms of s. 21(1)(b). As I have explained in the previous section, a person who does something "for the purpose of aiding" another to commit a criminal offence (and who is thus liable under s. 21(1)(b)) invariably "intends" to assist the principal to carry out "an unlawful purpose" — an "intention" that its not susceptible of being "negated" by the fact that it arises as the result of threats of death or bodily harm. Furthermore, the terms "aid" and "assist" are virtually synonymous. Section 21(2), however, contains two further qualifications — the accused's intention must be "an intention in common" with the principal, and the intention to assist must be reciprocal (that is, two or more persons must have "an intention in common . . . to *assist each other* therein"). The question that must be addressed, therefore, is whether these additional qualifications on the requisite "intention" raise the prospect of an accused's *mens rea* being "negated" by duress. In particular, we must consider whether the requirement that the accused have an "intention *in common*" with another person has this effect.

. . .

[44] For these reasons, I am of the view that the comments of Martland J. in *Paquette, supra*, on the relation between duress and *mens rea* in the context of s. 21(2) can no longer be considered the law in Canada. I hasten to point out, however, that overturning this holding in *Paquette* does not affect the validity of that case's first aspect, namely, that the common law defence of duress continues to apply in cases involving party liability under s. 21 of the *Code*. Furthermore, it can be noted in passing that, on the facts of *Paquette*, the accused's acquittal could well have been supported on the basis of the excuse provided by the common law defence of duress rather than on the notion that his intention to assist in the commission of the robbery was "negated" by duress.

### (4) *Conclusions on duress and mens rea*

[45] The conclusions that can be extracted for the discussion in the previous sections may be summarized as follows:

1. The fact that a person who commits a criminal act does so as a result of threats of death or bodily harm can in some instances be relevant to the question of whether he or she possessed the *mens rea* necessary to commit an offence. Whether or not this is so will depend, among other things, on the structure of the particular offence in question — that is, on whether or not the mental state specified by Parliament in its definition of the offence is such that the presence of coercion can, as a matter of logic, have a bearing on the existence of *mens rea*. If the offence is one where the presence of duress is of potential relevance to the existence of *mens rea*, the accused is entitled to point to the presence of threats when arguing that the Crown has not proven beyond a reasonable doubt that he or she possessed the mental state required for liability.
2. A person who commits a criminal act under threats of death or bodily harm may also be able to invoke an excuse-based defence (either the statutory defence set out in s. 17 or the common law defence of duress, depending on whether the accused is charged as a principal or as a party). This is so regardless of whether or not the offence at issue is one where the presence of coercion also has a bearing on the existence of *mens rea*.
3. The mental states specified in s. 21(1)(*b*) and (2) of the *Criminal Code* are not susceptible to being "negated" by duress. Consequently, it is not open to persons charged under these sections to argue that because their acts were coerced by threats they lacked the requisite *mens rea*. Such persons may however, seek to have their conduct *excused* through the operation of the common law defence of duress.

It should be reiterated, however, that the holding in the present case is based on an interpretation of the particular terms of two specific offence-creating statutory provisions, s. 21(1)(*b*) and (2) of the *Criminal Code*. The question of whether other offences can be found either in the *Code* or in some other statute, that are defined in such a way that the presence of coercion *is* relevant to the existence of *mens rea*, remains open.

### C. *The "safe avenue of escape" requirement in the common law of duress*

[46] The second and third issues raised by the appellant have to do with the so-called "safe avenue of escape" rule. The court must decide whether such a rule in fact exists, and, if it does, whether the availability of a "safe avenue" is to be determined on an objective or subjective basis. In my opinion, it is best to start the analysis by examining the juristic nature of the defence of duress and its relationship to other common law defences, since I am of the view that by so doing the answers to the questions posed in the present appeal will become clear.

. . .

*Is the existence of a safe avenue of escape to be determined subjectively or objectively?*

[56] The remaining question on this appeal raises a potentially more difficult issue, namely, the question of whether the existence of a "safe avenue of escape" is to be determined objectively or on the basis of the accused's own subjective knowledge and awareness at the time. How this question is answered depends, in my view, on how one conceives of the notion of "normative involuntariness" upon which the defence of duress is based. That is, is an action "normatively involuntary" when the actor *believes* that he has no real choice, or is this the case only when there is *in fact* no reasonable alternative course of action available?

. . .

*Conclusions on duress and "safe avenue of escape" requirement*

[62] My conclusions on the second and third issues raised by the appellant can thus be summarized as follows. An accused person cannot rely on the common law defence of duress if he or she had an opportunity to safely extricate himself or herself from the situation of duress. The rationale for this rule is simply that in such circumstances the condition of "normative involuntariness" that provides the theoretical basis for both the defences of duress and necessity is absent — if the accused had the chance to take action that would have allowed him or her to avoid committing an offence, it cannot be said that he or she had no real choice when deciding whether or not to break the law. Furthermore, I believe that the internal logic of the excuse-based defence, which has theoretical underpinnings directly analogous to those that support the defence of necessity (as set out in *Perka, supra*), suggests that the question of whether or not a safe avenue of escape existed is to be determined according to an objective standard. When considering the perceptions of a "reasonable person", however, the personal circumstances of the accused are relevant and important, and should be taken into account.

. . .

[67] Although the errors identified above are in themselves sufficient, in my opinion, to entitle the appellant to a new trial, I will briefly address the other points raised by the appellant. As I have explained, I am of the view that the trial judge did not err in instructing the jury that the appellant could not rely on the defence of duress if the Crown established that he had failed to avail himself of a safe avenue of escape. Furthermore, while I believe the trial judge should have instructed the jury that the existence of such an avenue was to be determined objectively, taking into account the personal circumstances of the appellant, on the particular facts of this case, I am not persuaded that his failure to do so affected the jury's decision, since there was no indication, on the facts, that any of the appellant's personal attributes or frailties rendered him unable to identify any safe avenues of escape that would have been apparent to a reasonable person of ordinary capacities and abilities.

## VI
## CONCLUSION

[68] With respect, I am of the view that the trial judge erred in his instructions to the jury on the law of duress. Since I do not believe that it can be said that this error necessarily had no impact on the jury's verdict, I believe that there should be a new trial. According, the appeal is allowed, the appellant's conviction is set aside, and a new trial is ordered.

*Appeal allowed; new trial ordered.*

**Questions/Discussion**
1. Do you think the reasoning in the court in *Carker* was correct? Do you think the decision was fair? If not, then how would you interpret section 17? Do you think that the court had a real choice in light of the wording of the section? Should the section be as restrictively worded as it is now? If you had the opportunity, how would you rewrite the section? What goals or purposes in criminal justice are you trying to accomplish?
2. Why do we not allow the defences in certain types of offences? Do you agree with such exclusions? Why or why not? If a person is effectively forced to do a crime, then why shouldn't the defence be available in the interests of fairness?
3. Do you agree with the provision excepting those who have been involved in an association whereby they have been subject to the duress? If the defence is in effect withdrawn, can it be argued that they are being punished for the wrong reasons, i.e., that they were a member of a criminal group, and not for the crime which they were forced to commit?
4. Do you agree with the decision in *Paquette*? Why or why not? Are your reasons based on the legal reasoning in the decision or ultimately on the "fair" result which was achieved? Do you think that in fact it was the result which the court decided on first and then found a purely technical means to reach it? Would the court have been more "honest" to admit that in situations such as Paquette's, an exception should be made on policy grounds, that it was an obvious oversight on the part of the legislators when they passed the law?
5. Do you agree with the reasoning and the decision in *Hibbert*? Why or why not?
6. A recent case in the Quebec Court of Appeal struck down section 17 of the Code as unconstitutional under section 7 of the Charter. The case, *R. v. Langlois* (1993), 80 C.C.C. (3d) 28, was not appealed to the Supreme Court. For a discussion of the case and its effects, see Healy, P., "Innocence and Defences" (1993), 19 C.R. (4th) 121-131.

**Further Reading**
- Borins, Stephen, "The Defence of Duress" (1981-82), 24 Criminal Law Quarterly 191.
- Elliott, D.W., "Necessity, Duress and Self-Defence", [1989] Criminal Law Review 611.
- Mewett, A. and M. Manning, *Mewett and Manning on Criminal Law*, 3rd ed. (Toronto: Butterworths, 1994).
- Rosenthal, P., "Duress in the Criminal Law" (1990), 32 Criminal Law Quarterly 199-226.
- Stuart, D., *Canadian Criminal Law: A Treatise*, 2nd ed. (Toronto: Carswell, 1987), pp. 393-405.
- Stuart, D., and R. Delisle, *Learning Canadian Criminal Law*, 5th ed. (Toronto: Carswell, 1995).
- Verdun-Jones, S., *Criminal Law in Canada: Cases, Questions and the Code*, (Toronto: Harcourt Brace Jovanovich Canada, 1989), pp. 265-275.
- Verdun-Jones, S., and C. Griffiths, *Canadian Criminal Justice*, 2nd ed. (Toronto: Butterworths, 1994).

## 7.1.2 Necessity

**Introduction**

In using the common law defence of necessity, the accused is making the argument that "I had to commit the crime, I had no realistic choice in the matter". In the three cases which follow, the decisions outline the circumstances when this argument will be successful and excuse the accused from being held liable for the offence. In particular, *Perka* outlines the factors which a court will look for in assessing whether the defence is available. Furthermore, this case also presents an interesting debate on the proper rationale or foundation for the defence. The majority in *Perka* argues for the restricted basis of "excuse" (i.e., it is right to excuse people for acts which are "normatively involuntary", acts which ordinary people would feel compelled to do), while Wilson in her dissenting opinion states that the defence's basis rests in the broader and more inclusive conception of "justification" (i.e., the idea that it is wrong to punish those who do wrongful acts when those acts are "morally justified", though as the reader will see Wilson takes a rather narrow view of what is morally justified in linking such moral obligations to legal duties). The second case, *Roberts*, presents an application of the tests laid out in *Perka* to a much more common fact situation. In the final selection, *MacMillan Bloedel*, the court held that the defence is not available where the accused had lawful alternatives to the course of action followed.

One limitation which is suggested as to the use of the defence is that in situations where the accused has been negligent to some extent in creating the emergency in the first place, then perhaps the defence should not be available. In such cases defendants would be taking advantage of situations which they brought about. This is an argument which is raised in the *Breau* case in the "Self Defence" section below (see 7.1.3).

### Perka v. The Queen
(1984), 14 C.C.C. (3d) 385 (S.C.C.)

[Only the judgments of Dickson J. and Wilson J. are reproduced below.]

DICKSON J.: — In this case we consider (i) a recurring legal problem, the "necessity" defence; (ii) what is commonly known as the "botanical" or "*cannabis* species" defence.

#### FACTS

The appellants are drug smugglers. At trial, they led evidence that in early 1979 three of the appellants were employed, with 16 crew members, to deliver, by ship, (the "Samarkanda") a load of *cannabis* (marijuana) worth $6,000,000 or $7,000,000 from a point in international waters off the coast of Colombia, South America to a drop-point in international waters 200 miles off the coast of Alaska. The ship left Tumaco, Colombia, empty with a port-clearance document stating the destination to be Juneau, Alaska. For three weeks the ship remained in international waters off the coast of Colombia. While there, a DC-6 aircraft made four trips, dropping into the water shrimp-nets with a total of 634 bales of *cannabis* which were retrieved by the ship's long-boats.

A "communications" package was also dropped from a light aircraft, giving instructions for a rendezvous with another vessel, the "Julia B", which was to pick up the cargo of *cannabis* from the "Samarkanda" in international waters off the coast of

Alaska. *En route*, according to the defence evidence, the vessel began to encounter a series of problems; engine breakdowns, overheating generators and malfunctioning navigation devices, aggravated by deteriorating weather. In the meantime, the fourth appellant, Nelson, part-owner of the illicit cargo, and three other persons left Seattle in a small boat, the "Whitecap", intending to rendezvous with the "Samarkanda" at the drop-point in Alaska. The problems of the 'Samarkanda" intensified as fuel was consumed. The vessel became lighter, the intakes in the hull for sea-water, used as a coolant, lost suction and took in air instead, causing the generators to overheat. At this point the vessel was 180 miles from the Canadian coastline. The weather worsened. There were eight-to-ten-foot swells and a rising wind. It was finally decided for the safety of ship and crew to seek refuge on the Canadian shoreline for the purpose of making temporary repairs. The "Whitecap" found a sheltered cover on the west coast of Vancouver Island, "No Name Bay". The "Samarkanda" followed the "Whitecap" into the bay but later grounded amidships on a rock because the depth sounder was not working. The tide ran out. The vessel listed severely to starboard, to the extent that the captain, fearing the vessel was going to capsize, ordered the men to off-load the cargo. That is a brief summary of the defence evidence.

Early on the morning of May 22, 1979, police officers entered No Name Bay in a marked police boat with siren sounding. The "Samarkanda" and the "Whitecap" were arrested, as were all the appellants except Perka and Nelson, the same morning. The vessels and 33.49 tons of *cannabis* marijuana were seized by the police officers.

Charged with importing *cannabis* into Canada and with possession for the purpose of trafficking, the appellants claimed they did not plan to import to Canada or to leave their cargo of *cannabis* in Canada. They had planned to make repairs and leave. Expert witnesses on marine matters called by the defence testified that the decision to come ashore was, in the opinion of one witness, expedient and prudent and in the opinion of another, essential. At trial, counsel for the Crown alleged that the evidence of the ship's distress was a recent fabrication. Crown counsel relied on the circumstances under which the appellants were arrested to belie the "necessity" defence; when the police arrived on the scene most of the marijuana was already onshore, along with plastic ground sheets, battery-operated lights, liquor, food, clothing, camp stoves and sleeping-bags. Nevertheless, the jury believed the appellants and acquitted them.

The acquittal was reversed on appeal.

. . . .

## THE NECESSITY DEFENCE

### *History and Background*

From earliest times it has been maintained that in some situations the force of circumstances makes it unrealistic and unjust to attach criminal liability to actions which, on their face, violate the law. Aristotle, *Ethics* (Book III, 1110 a), discusses the jettisoning of cargo from a ship in distress and remarks that "any sensible man does so" to secure the safety of himself and his crew.

. . . .

To much the same purpose Kant, in *The Metaphysical Elements of Justice* (translator Ladd, 1965), discussing the actions of a person who, to save his own life sacrifices that of another, says at p. 41:

> A penal law applying to such a situation could never have the effect intended, for the threat of an evil that is still uncertain (being condemned to death by a judge) cannot outweigh the fear of an evil that is certain (being drowned). Hence, we must judge that, although an act of self-preservation through violence is not inculpable, it still is unpunishable.

In those jurisdictions in which such a general principle has been recognized or codified it is most often referred to by the term "necessity". Classic and harrowing instances which have been cited to illustrate the arguments both for and against the principle include the mother who steals for food for her starving child, the shipwrecked mariners who resort to cannibalism (*R. v. Dudley and Stephens* (1884), 14 Q.B.D. 273), or throw passengers overboard to lighten a sinking lifeboat (*United States v. Holmes* (1842), 26 Fed. Cas. 360), and the more mundane case of the motorist who exceeds the speed-limit taking an injured person to the hospital.

. . . .

In Canada the existence and the extent of a general defence of necessity was discussed by this Court in *Morgentaler v. The Queen* (1975), 20 C.C.C. (2d) 449, 53 D.L.R. (3d) 161, [1976] 1 S.C.R. 616. As to whether or not the defence exists at all I had occasion to say, at p. 497 C.C.C., p. 209 D.L.R., p. 678 S.C.R.:

> On the authorities it is manifestly difficult to be categorical and state that there is a law of necessity, paramount over other laws, relieving obedience from the letter of the law. If it does exist it can go no further than to justify non-compliance in urgent situations of clear and imminent peril when compliance with the law is demonstrably impossible.

Subsequent to *Morgentaler*, the courts appear to have assumed that a defence of necessity does exist in Canada. On the later trial of Dr. Morgentaler, the defence of necessity was again raised on a charge of procuring a miscarriage. Some admissible evidence was made in support of the plea and the case went to the jury, which rendered a verdict of not guilty.

. . . .

In the present appeal the Crown does not challenge the appellants' claim that necessity is a common law defence preserved by *Criminal Code* s. 7(3). Rather the Crown claims the trial judge erred in (1) instructing the jury on the defence in light of the facts, and (2) imposing the burden of disproof of the defence upon the Crown, rather than imposing the burden of proof on the appellants.

## The Conceptual Foundation of the Defence

In *Morgentaler, supra*, I characterized necessity as an "ill-defined and elusive concept". Despite the apparently growing consensus as to the defence of necessity that statement is equally true today.

. . . .

Working Paper 29 of the Law Reform Commission of Canada, *Criminal Law The General Part: Liability and defences* (1982), p. 93, makes this same point in somewhat more detail:

> The rationale of necessity, however, is clear. Essentially it involves two factors. One is the avoidance of greater harm or the pursuit of some greater good, the other is the difficulty of compliance with law in emergencies. From these two factors emerge two different but related principles. The first is a utilitarian principle to the effect that, within certain limits, it is justifiable in an emergency to break the letter of the law if breaking the law will avoid a greater harm than obeying it. The second is a humanitarian principle to the effect that, again within limits, it is excusable in an emergency to break the law if compliance would impose an intolerable burden on the accused.

Despite any superficial similarities, these two principles are in fact quite distinct and many of the confusions and the difficulties in the cases (and, with respect, in academic discussions) arise from a failure to distinguish between them.

Criminal theory recognizes a distinction between "justifications" and "excuses". A "justification" challenges the wrongfulness of an action which technically constitutes a crime. The police officer who shoots the hostage-taker, the innocent object of an assault who uses force to defend himself against his assailant, the good Samaritan who commandeers a car and breaks the speed laws to rush an accident victim to the hospital, these are all actors whose actions we consider *rightful*, not wrongful. For such actions people are often praised, as motivated by some great or noble object. The concept of punishment often seems incompatible with the social approval bestowed on the doer.

In contrast, and "excuse" concedes the wrongfulness of the action but asserts that the circumstances under which it was done are such that it ought not to be attributed to the actor. The perpetrator who is incapable, owing to a disease of the mind, of appreciating the nature and consequences of his acts, the person who labours under a mistake of fact, the drunkard, the sleepwalker: these are all actors of whose "criminal" actions we disapprove intensely, but whom, in appropriate circumstances, our law will not punish.

. . . .

As a "justification" this residual defence can be related to Blackstone's concept of a "choice of evils". It would exculpate actors whose conduct could reasonably have been viewed as "necessary" in order to prevent a greater evil than that resulting from the violation of the law. As articulated, especially in some of the American cases, it involves a utilitarian balancing of the benefits of obeying the law as opposed to disobeying it, and when the balance is clearly in favour of disobeying, exculpates an actor who contravenes a criminal statute. This is the "greater good" formulation of the necessity defence: in some circumstances, it is alleged, the values of society, indeed of the criminal law itself, are better promoted by disobeying a given statute than by observing it.

With regard to this conceptualization of a residual defence of necessity, I retain the scepticism I expressed in *Morgentaler, supra*, at p. 497 C.C.C., p. 209 D.L.R., p. 678 S.C.R. It is still my opinion that, "[n]o system of positive law can recognize any principle which would entitle a person to violate the law because in his view the law conflicted with some higher social value". The *Criminal Code* has specified a number of identifiable situations in which an actor is justified in committing what would otherwise be a criminal offence. To go beyond that and hold that ostensibly illegal acts can be validated on the basis of their expediency, would import an undue subjectivity into the criminal law. It would invite the courts to second-guess the Legislature and to assess the relative merits of social policies underlying criminal prohibitions. Neither is a role which fits well with the judicial function. Such a doctrine could well become the last resort of scoundrels and, in the words of Edmund Davies L.J. in *Southwark London Borough Council v. Williams et al.*, [1971] Ch. 734 [ at p. 746], it could "very easily become simply a mask for anarchy".

Conceptualized as an "excuse", however, the residual defence of necessity is, in my view, much less open to criticism. It rests on a realistic assessment of human weakness, recognizing that a liberal and humane criminal law cannot hold people to the strict obedience of laws in emergency situations where normal human instincts, whether self-preservation or of altruism, overwhelmingly impel disobedience. The objectivity of the criminal law is preserved; such acts are still wrongful, but in the circumstances they are excusable. Praise is indeed not bestowed, but pardon is, when one does a wrongful act under pressure which, in the words of Aristotle in *The Nicomachean Ethics* (translator Ress, p. 49), "overstrains human nature and which no one could withstand".

. . . .

At the heart of this defence is the perceived injustice of punishing violations of the law in circumstances in which the person had no other viable or reasonable choice available; the act was wrong but it is excused because it was realistically unavoidable.

Punishment of such acts, as Fletcher notes at p. 813, can be seen as purposeless as well as unjust:

> . . . involuntary conduct cannot be deterred and therefore it is pointless and wasteful to punish involuntary actors. This theory . . . of pointless punishment, carries considerable weight in current Anglo-American legal thought.

Relating necessity to the principle that the law ought not to punish involuntary acts leads to a conceptualization of the defence that integrates it into the normal rules for criminal liability rather than constituting it as a *sui generis* exception and threatening to engulf large portions of the criminal law. Such a conceptualization accords with our traditional legal, moral and philosophic views as accords with our traditional legal, moral and philosophic views as to what sorts of acts and what sorts of actors ought to be punished. In this formulation it is a defence which I do not hesitate to acknowledge and would not hesitate to apply to relevant facts capable of satisfying its necessary prerequisites.

. . .

## Preliminary Conclusions as to the Defence of Necessity

It is now possible to summarize a number of conclusions as to the defence of necessity in terms of its nature, basis and limitations:

(1) the defence of necessity could be conceptualized as either a justification or an excuse;

(2) it should be recognized in Canada as an excuse, operating by virtue of s. 7(3) of the *Criminal Code*
(3) necessity as an excuse implies no vindication of the deeds of the actor;
(4) the criterion is the moral involuntariness of the wrongful action;
(5) this involuntariness is measured on the basis of society's expectation of appropriate and normal resistance to pressure;
(6) negligence or involvement in criminal or immoral activity does not disentitle the actor to the excuse of necessity;
(7) actions or circumstances which indicate that the wrongful deed was not truly involuntary do disentitle;
(8) the existence of a reasonable legal alternative similarly disentitles; to be involuntary the act must be inevitable, unavoidable and afford no reasonable opportunity for an alternative course of action that does not involve a breach of the law;
(9) the defence only applies in circumstances of imminent risk where the action was taken to avoid a direct and immediate peril;
(10) where the accused places before the court sufficient evidence to raise the issue, the onus in on the Crown to meet it beyond a reasonable doubt.

### *The Judge's Charge*

The trial judge concluded that there was before him an adequate body of evidence to raise the issue of necessity and proceeded to direct the jury with respect to the defence. As I have earlier indicated, the Crown disputes whether the defence was open to the accused in the circumstances of the case and submits further that if it was in fact available, the trial judge erred in his direction.

In my view, the trial judge was correct in concluding that on the evidence before him he should instruct the jury with regard to necessity. There was evidence before him from which a jury might conclude that the accuseds' actions in coming ashore with their cargo of *cannabis* were aimed at self-preservation in response to an overwhelming emergency.

. . . .

In the course of his charge on the issue of necessity the trial judge instructed the jury, using the specific words that appear in *Morgentaler v. The Queen* (1975), 20 C.C.C. (2d) 449, 53 D.L.R. (3d) 161, [1976] 1 S.C.R. 616, to the effect that they must find facts which amount to "an urgent situation of clear and imminent peril when compliance with the law is demonstrably impossible" in order for the appellants' non-compliance with the law against importation and possession of *cannabis* to be excused. That is the correct test. It is, with respect, however, my view that in explaining the meaning and application of this test, the trial judge fell into error.

The trial judge was obliged, in my opinion, to direct the jury's attention to a number of issues pertinent to the test for necessity.

. . . .

In my view, this was a serious error and omission going to the heart of the defence of necessity. The error justifies a new trial.

I would dismiss the appeals.

. . . .

WILSON J.: — The factual background of this case, the history of the litigation in the courts below and the grounds on which the appeal was taken in this Court are very fully set out in the reasons for judgment of the Chief Justice (Dickson J. at the date of the hearing) and it is not necessary for me to repeat them. Indeed, inasmuch as the Chief Justice's conclusion as to the defence of necessity seems clearly correct on the facts of this case and his disposition of the appeal manifestly just in the circumstances, I am dealing in these reasons only with the proposition very forcefully advanced by the Chief Justice in his reasons that the appropriate jurisprudential basis on which to premise the defence of necessity is exclusively that of excuse. My concern is that the learned Chief Justice appears to be closing the door on justification as an appropriate jurisprudential basis in some cases and I am firmly of the view that this is a door which should be left open by the court.

As the Chief Justice points out, criminal law theory recognizes a distinction between justification and excuse. In the case of justification the wrongfulness of the alleged offensive act is challenged; in the case of excuse the wrongfulness is acknowledged but a ground for the exercise of judicial compassion for the actor is asserted. By way of illustration, an act may be said to be justified when an essential element of the offence is absent, so that the defence effectively converts the accused's act from wrongful to rightful. Accordingly those defences which serve to establish a lack of culpable intent on the part of the accused, or which demonstrate that, although the accused intended to commit the act, the act was one which the accused was within his rights to commit may be labelled justification in so far as they elucidate the innocent nature of the act giving rise to the charge. Such doctrines as mistake of fact, automatism, etc., which, in the words of Lord Hailsham of St. Marylebone in *Director of Public Prosecutions v. Morgan*, [1975] 2 All E.R. 347 (H.L.), are raised in order to "negative" *mens rea*, may be appropriately placed in this category as they are invoked in order to undermine the very ingredient of culpability. Similarly, the accused who claims to have acted out of self-defence or provocation is utilizing aggressive force against another individual raises a justificatory defence in that he asserts the essential rightfulness of his aggressive act.

On the other hand, an excuse requires the court to evaluate the presence or absence of the accused's will. In contemporary jurisprudence the most forceful champion of excuse in criminal law has been Professor George Fletcher who has advocated a trend toward individualizing the conceptual basis for culpability so that all circumstances subjectively relevant to the accused be considered by the court. As such, the jury is requested to exercise compassion for the accused's predicament in its evaluation of his claim: "I couldn't help myself": Fletcher, "The Individualization of Excusing Conditions", 47 So. Cal. L.R. 1264 at p. 1269 (1974).

. . . .

Thus, the nature of an excuse is to personalize the plea so that, while justification looks to the rightness of the act, excuse speaks to the compassion of the court for the actor.

As Chief Justice Dickson points out, although the necessity defence has engendered a significant amount of judicial and scholarly debate, it remains a somewhat elusive concept. It is, however, clear that justification and excuse are conceptually quite distinct and that any elucidation of a principled basis for the defence of necessity must be grounded in one or the other.

Turning first to the category of excuse, the concept of "normative involuntariness" stressed in the reasons of the Chief Justice may, on one reading, be said to fit squarely within the framework of an individualized plea which Professor Fletcher indicates characterizes all claims of excusability. The notional involuntariness of the action is assessed in the context of the accused's particular situation. The court must ask not only whether the offensive act accompanied by the requisite culpable mental state (i.e., intention, recklessness, etc.) has been established by the prosecution, but whether or not the accused acted so as to attract society's moral outrage.

. . . .

On the other hand, the necessity of an act may be said to exempt an actor from *punishment*, since the person who acts in a state of what the Chief Justice calls "normative involuntariness" may be viewed as having been moved to act by the instinct for self-preservation. If so, the defence does not invoke the court's compassion but rather embodies an implicit statement that the sanction threatened by the law (i.e., future punishment in one form or another) could never overcome the fear of immediate death which the accused faced. Accordingly, in such a case the law is incapable of controlling the accused's conduct and responding to it with any punishment at all. Although such an act dictated by the necessity of self-preservation is a voluntary one (in the normal sense of the word), its "normative involuntariness" (in the sense that the actor faced no realistic choice) may form the basis of a defence if this is conceived as based on the pointlessness of punishment rather than on a view of the act itself as one of the accused was entitled to commit.

. . . .

Returning to the defence of necessity as a justification, it may generally be said than an act is justified on grounds of necessity if the court can say that not only was the act a necessary one but it was rightful rather than wrongful. When grounded on the fundamental principle that a successful defence must characterize an act as one which the accused was within his rights to commit, it becomes immediately apparent that the defence does not depend on the immediacy or "normative involuntariness" of the accused's act unless, of course, the involuntariness is such as to be pertinent to the ordinary analysis of *mens rea*. The fact that one act is done out of a sense of immediacy or urgency and another after some contemplation cannot, in my view, serve to distinguish the quality of the act in terms of right or wrong. Rather, the justification must be premised on the need to fulfil a duty conflicting with the one which the accused is charged with having breached.

. . . .

Similarly, the Chief Justice in his reasons for judgment in the present case correctly underlines the fact that a utilitarian balancing of the benefits of obeying the law as opposed to disobeying it cannot possibly represent a legitimate principle against which to measure the legality of an action since any violation of right permitted to be justified on such a utilitarian calculus does not, in the Chief Justice's words "fit[s] well with the judicial function". The maximization of social utility may well be a goal of legislative policy but it is not part of the judicial task of delineating right and wrong.

. . . .

Accordingly, not only can the system of positive law not tolerate an individual opting to act in accordance with the dictates of his conscience in the event of conflict with legal duties, but in cannot permit acts in violation of legal obligations to be justified on the grounds that the social utility is thereby increased. In both situations the conflicting "duty" to which the defence arguments point is one which the court cannot take into account as it invokes considerations external to a judicial analysis of the rightness or wrongness of the impugned act. As Lord Coleridge C.J. succinctly put it in *Dudley and Stephens, supra*, at p. 287: "Who is to be the judge of this sort of necessity?"

On the other hand, in some circumstances defence counsel may be able to point to a conflicting duty which courts can and do recognize. For example, one may break the law in circumstances where it is necessary to rescue someone to whom one owes a positive duty of rescue (see *R. v. Walker* (1979), 48 C.C.C. (2d) 126, 5 M.V.R. 114 (Ont. Co Ct.)), since failure to act in such a situation may itself constitute a culpable act or omission: see *R. v. Instan*, [1893] 1 Q.B. 450. Similarly, if one subscribes to the viewpoint articulated by Laskin C.J.C. in *Morgentaler, supra* and perceives a doctor's defence to an abortion charge as his legal obligation to treat the mother rather than his alleged ethical duty to perform an unauthorized abortion, then the defence may be invoked without violating the prohibition enunciated by Dickson J. in *Morgentaler* against choosing a non-legal duty over a legal one.

It must be acknowledged, however, that on the existing state of the law the defence of necessity as justification would not be available to the person who rescues a stranger since the absence of a legal duty to rescue strangers reduces such a case to a conflict of a legal with a purely ethical duty. Such an act of rescue may be deserving of no punishment and, indeed, deserving of praise, but it is nevertheless a culpable act if the law is violated in the process of the rescue.

. . . .

In similar fashion the ethical considerations of the "charitable and the good" must be kept analytically distinct from duties imposed by law. Accordingly, where necessity is invoked as a justification for violation of the law, the justification must, in my view, be restricted to situations where the accused's act constitutes the discharge of a duty recognized by law. The justification is not, however, established simply by showing a conflict of legal duties. The rule of proportionality is central to the evaluation of a justification premised on two conflicting duties since the defence rests on the rightfulness of the accused's choice of one over the other.

As the facts before the court in the present case do not involve a conflict of legal duties it is unnecessary to discuss in detail how a court should go about assessing the relative extent of two evils. Suffice it to say that any such assessment must respect the notion of right upon which justification is based. The assessment cannot entail a mere utilitarian calculation of, for example, lives saved and deaths avoided in the aggregate but must somehow attempt to come to grips with the nature of the rights and duties being assessed. This would seem to be consistent with Lord Coleridge's conclusion that necessity can provide no justification for the taking of a life, such an act representing the most extreme form of rights violation. As discussed above, if any defence for such a homicidal act is to succeed, it would have to be framed as an excuse grounded on self-preservation. It could not possibly be declared by the court to be rightful. By contrast, the justification analysis would seem to support those cases in which fulfilment of the legal duty to save persons entrusted to one's care is preferred over the lesser offences of trespass or petty theft: see *Mouse's Case* (1608), 12 Co. Rep. 63, 77 E.R. 1341; *Amiens, Ch. corr. April 22, 1898*, S. 1899.2.1 (*Menard's Case*). The crucial question for the justification defence is whether the accused's act can be said to represent a furtherance of or a detraction from the principle of the universality of rights.

In summary, it seem to me that the category of "normative involuntariness" into which an act done in the interests of self-preservation falls is characterized not by the literal voluntariness of the act but by its unpunishable nature. As such, the act may be exempted from culpability if it arose in a life-threatening situation of necessity. Where, however, a defence by way of excuse is premised on compassion for the accused or on a perceived failure to achieve a desired instrumental end of punishment, the judicial response must be to fashion an appropriate sentence but to reject the defence as such. The only conceptual premise on which necessity as an excuse could rest is the inherent impossibility of a court's responding in any way to an act which, although wrongful, was the one act which any rational person would commit.

Where the defence of necessity is invoked as a justification the issue is simply whether the accused was right in pursuing the course of behaviour giving rise to the charge. Thus, where the act otherwise constitutes a criminal offence (i.e., it embodies both *mens rea* and the *actus reus*) the accused must show that he operated under a conflicting legal duty which made his seemingly wrongful act right. But such justification must be premised on a right or duty recognized by law. This excludes conduct attempted to be justified on the ground of an ethical duty internal to the conscience of the accused as well as conduct sought to be justified on the basis of a perceived maximization of social utility resulting from it. Rather, the conduct must stem from the accused's duty to satisfy his legal obligations and to respect the principles of the universality of rights.

I would dismiss the appeals.

*Appeals dismissed.*

## R. v. Roberts
### (1987), 65 Nfld. & P.E.I.R. 343 (P.E.I. C.A.)

[Only the judgment of Carruthers, C.J. is reproduced below.]

[1] CARRUTHERS, C.J.: — This is an appeal from a conviction of an offence of impaired driving contrary to s. 237(a) of the Criminal Code.

[2] The notice of appeal sets forth two grounds of appeal, namely:

"1. That the learned trial judge erred in finding that the appellant was in fact impaired.

"2. That the learned trial judge erred in law by misinterpreting the defence of necessity and by not leaving the defence of necessity open to the appellant."

[3] The facts giving rise to the charge occurred sometime around 1 a.m. on March 24, 1986, at Charlottetown. The appellant's mother, who had not been well for two or three weeks previous to this incident, developed "an awful pain below the heart" and asked the appellant to drive her to the hospital. The appellant testified:

> "Well, Mum had come downstairs, she wasn't fully dressed and I had to get her dressed. She wanted to go to the hospital because she had an awful pain below the heart. So we got her dressed and I said 'do you want to take the ambulance?' and she said 'no, I am not going in the ambulance, you will drive me.' So I knew I had a bottle of beer in me or two bottles and I said 'well, probably get a taxi' and 'no' she said, 'you drive me right now.' So on the way out . . . "

[4] The appellant left with her mother for the hospital and on the way to the hospital she was stopped by Cpl. Walker who testified that he had observed the vehicle driven by the appellant swerve onto the sidewalk area, strike a snowbank, and return to the center of the street. As a result he stopped the vehicle and later charged the appellant with impaired driving.

. . . .

[12] It is clear from the transcript that the trial judge was satisfied beyond a reasonable doubt as to the guilt of the appellant.

. . . .

[14] I dismiss the appellant's first ground of appeal as I cannot say that the conclusions reached by the trial judge are either unreasonable or that they are unsupported by the evidence.

[15] The second ground of appeal raises the defence of necessity. The appellant submits that the trial judge did not give proper consideration to the defence of necessity and erred by not applying the defence.

[16] It is clear from the transcript that the trial judge did deal with the defence of necessity. He states:

> "Defence of necessity, again the law is quite clear and I don't think there is any argument on the law, it's on the facts. Was there a necessity for the accused to drive her mother? I hold there was not. Indeed (she) herself could have called the taxi, could have called the ambulance. The only reason she wanted to drive her mother was because her mother was insisting to save $3. She was not 50 kilometers away as that case was. She didn't call a taxi and get no answer. Anybody could have driven her mother that night. There was no urgency so as that she had to drive her herself."

[17] The leading decision in Canada on the defence of necessity is *Perka et al. v. The Queen*, [1984], 2 S.C.R. 232; 55 N.R. 1; 13 D.L.R. (4th) 1; 42 C.R. (3d) 113; [1984] 6 W.W.R. 289; 14 C.C.C. (3d) 385 (S.C.C.) in which Dickson, C.J.C., made a very thorough analysis of the matter.

. . . .

[18] Counsel for the appellant submits that the trial judge erred as he did not consider all of the conclusions enumerated by Dickson, C.J.C. It may well be that he did not consider each and every one of these conclusions. In my opinion it was not necessary

for him to do so in this case. He has dealt with what Dickson, C.J.C., said would almost certainly be the most important consideration in most cases when the defence is raised; was there any reasonable legal alternative to the legal response open to the accused?

[19] He held that there was a reasonable legal alternative open to the accused. I am satisfied that he did not make any error of law in dealing with the defence of necessity. I dismiss the appellant's second ground of appeal.

[20] I cannot say that the conclusions reached by the trial judge are either unreasonable or that they are unsupported by the evidence.

[21] The appeal is dismissed.

*Appeal dismissed.*

## MacMillan Bloedel Ltd. v. Simpson
(1994), 89 C.C.C. (3d) 217 (B.C.C.A.)

Appeal by the accused from their conviction by Bouck J., 12 C.E.L.R. (N.S.) 81, 43 A.C.W.S. (3d) 914, for contempt of court.

*The facts*

In the summer of 1991, and subsequently, the Supreme Court of British Columbia issued successive injunctions, on the application of MacMillan Bloedel Limited ("M. & B.") to prevent obstruction of its logging crews in the Clayoquot Sound area of Vancouver Island.

On July 5, 1993, protestors began to blockade road access to M M. & B. logging areas in the Clayoquot area. Starting July 6, 1993, and on many subsequent working days, over 600 such protestors were arrested for contempt of court. A small number of those arrested persons pleaded guilty. The trial court was faced with the daunting task of trying the others.

The first contested trial, of a group of 44 defendants who were arrested between July 6 and 20, 1993, began on September 2, 1993, before Bouck J. Some of the background facts are described in the reasons for judgment of this court delivered February 11, 1994, on sentence appeals by some of the defendants on that trial. Those appeals are styled *MacMillan Bloedel Ltd. v. Brown et al.*, February 11, 1994, Victoria V02013; V02001; V02024; V01990; Vancouver CA017849; CA018076 (B.C.C.A.) [indexed as: *MacMillan Bloedel Ltd. v. Simpson*, reported 88 C.C.C. (3d) 148, 22 W.C.B. (2d) 457]. I shall quote some of those reasons in a moment. The appellants on those appeals did not appeal their conviction. These are reasons for judgment on the appeals against conviction brought by 31 of those defendants.

In pre-trial proceedings in Victoria on July 26, 1993, Cowan J. directed that a special assize would be established commencing August 30, 1993, with cases being set for trial in groups selected by date of arrest, and trials commencing immediately upon the completion of an earlier trial until all were dealt with. Later, it became necessary to establish more than one assize because of the number of cases to be heard.

The Crown initially estimated that the trial of the first set of 44 defendants would require about two weeks trial time. The trial before Bouck J. actually required about six weeks. Bouck J. found 42 of the alleged contemnors guilty of criminal contempt [12 C.E.L.R. (N.S.) 81, 43 A.C.W.S. (3d) 914]. The other two pleaded guilty during the trial. He imposed custodial sentences ranging from 45 to 60 days in jail and he also imposed fines. On the six sentence appeals, the custodial sentences were affirmed, Lambert J.A. dissenting, and the fines were set aside.

The names of the 31 defendant-appellants on these appeals are set out in Schedule "A" to these reasons. Some of them, we were told, have sentence appeals pending. With commendable professionalism, counsel for these appellants joined forces and presented useful joint submissions, which permitted the court to complete the hearing of these conviction appeals in just three days.

Some of the facts set out in this court's reasons for judgment on the earlier sentence appeals, delivered February 11, 1994, include the following [at pp. 155-9]:

> The forested areas in the Clayoquot Sound area of Vancouver Island are amongst the loveliest land and seascapes to be found anywhere on earth. As these areas are environmentally rich, so also are they rich in economic potential for forestry exploitation. Since the early part of this century, there has been some logging in these areas and MacMillan Bloedel Limited has extensive logging rights under Tree Farm License No. 44, which covers much of the Clayoquot area. This logging must be carried out, if at all, in accordance with the provisions of the *Forestry Act*, R.S.C. 1985, c. F-30, and other relevant legislation and regulations.
>
> As might be expected, some members of the public sincerely believe there should be no logging, or very limited logging, in the Clayoquot area. When MacMillan Bloedel Limited began to make preparations to log some Clayoquot areas in 1991, various individuals sought to prevent such work by various forms of protest, including the obstruction of highways leading to the logging areas.
>
> . . . .
>
> On Wednesday, September 18, 1991, Spencer J. made an order on the application of the plaintiff, MacMillan Bloedel Limited, enjoining three named defendants together with John and Jane Doe and "Persons Unknown" and "all persons having notice of [his] Order," from obstructing or impeding the plaintiff's logging operations. This order, and successive orders, have been disobeyed by a number of persons whom, for descriptive purposes, I shall call "protestors".
>
> On September 20, 1991, Spencer J. made a further order authorizing peace officers to arrest any persons whom they believed on reasonable and probable grounds were or had contravened his order, and directing the police to release such persons upon their giving an undertaking to appear in court as required for the purpose of being proceeded against for contempt of court, and otherwise to be detained in custody.
>
> On September 25, 1991, Bouck J. made a fresh order which, in effect, continued the orders previously made by Spencer J. until trial. Subsequently, as sporadic disobedience continued, further orders were made by Hamilton J. on June 30, 1992, Holmes J. on July 13, 1992; Tysoe J. on July 17 and July 20, 1992, Esson C.J.S.C. on July 16, 1993, and Hall J. on August 26, 1993. These subsequent orders added further named defendants as they became known and expanded the geographic scope of the earlier orders.
>
> On December 9, 1991, Sheppard J. found six persons guilty of contempt.
>
> . . . . .
>
> On July 24, 1992, numerous further breaches of the court's order being alleged, Drost J. ordered that "these contempt proceedings be continued as criminal contempt proceedings" and that:

"THE COURT REQUESTS that the Attorney General of British Columbia intervene and take conduct of these proceedings."

This followed the practice established in the contempt proceedings taken with respect to the Everywoman's Health Clinic a year or so earlier where there was also massive disobedience of an order of the court. The Attorney-General responded affirmatively to the court's request and has properly assumed responsibility for the prosecution of alleged contempts against the orders of the court.

There were several "Clayoquot" contempt trials in 1992 and early 1993, where multiple convictions were entered for contempts committed by disobeying one or more of the above orders of the court enjoining interference with logging activities in the Clayoquot area of the province.

. . . . .

In April, 1993, the Government of British Columbia, acting through its executive council (the cabinet), pursuant to powers given to it by the legislature, made a well-publicized decision to permit logging in designated areas in the region of Clayoquot Sound, including some areas within Tree Farm License No. 44.

After considerable pre-arranged publicity, a large group of protesters gathered before 7:00 a.m. on July 5th at the Kennedy River Bridge for the purpose of preventing MacMillan Bloedel crews from proceeding to their work areas. Television crews were present in abundance. On the hearing of these appeals, we were shown two one-half hour videos, which clearly disclosed what happened on July 5th.

As the work crew approached, about 10 or 12 protesters including Mr. Svend Robinson M.P. donned distinctive T-shirts and, by locking arms, they formed a human chain across the bridge. Many others milled around in front of them.

When a work truck arrived, a process server read the order of Tysoe J. aloud over the chanting of the protesters but none of the human chain gave way. The process server then personally served the said order upon each member of the human chain by stuffing a copy between their arms and body and he asked each in turn if he or she would let the workers pass. None responded affirmatively, or moved away.

At this point the work crew retired to the cheers of the protesters. It is to the credit of the protesters that good humour prevailed. It is to the greater credit of the work crew that violence was avoided. There were no police at the scene that day.

More or less the same thing occurred on the early morning of subsequent days when another human chain or other configurations of protesters prevented work crews from proceeding to work. Mr. Robinson was not present after July 5th. Starting on July 6, 1993, police officers arrested those who refused to step aside upon being asked to do so, and upon being served with an injunction requiring them to do so. Some of those arrested on July 6th had also been present on July 5th, but no one was arrested only by reason of conduct on July 5th. Appellants' counsel argued that the absence of Mr. Robinson should in some way diminish their responsibility. I have already mentioned why Mr. Robinson was not charged with respect to his conduct on July 5, 1993, when no arrests were made. With respect, the question of whether or not Mr. Robinson should have been charged has no relevance to the fitness or unfitness of the sentences imposed upon these appellants.

There can be no doubt that these protests were carefully planned and deliberately carried out for the purpose of preventing logging in the Clayoquot area and to obtain local, national and international publicity for the views of the protesters. The protesters had earlier established a camp where instruction on passive resistance was given. Encouraging speeches were given and organizers maintained radio contact with look-outs on the road approaches to work sites.

By July 20, 1993, over 50 protesters had been arrested. Some determined protesters chose not to give undertaking and they were kept in custody. Most were released on undertakings to appear. There were many further arrests prior to and subsequent to the commencement of this trial. In pre-trial proceedings it was directed that a group later defined by date of arrest, including these appellants, should be tried together, commencing August 30, 1993.

It should be noted that except for one day in July when there was a huge gathering of protesters, and the work crews did not even try to go to work, the work stoppages were of short duration, but the trial judge noted in his reasons for conviction that the stoppages ". . . were only short lived because [the accused] were arrested. It is apparent that they would have blocked the road for a long time had they not been arrested."

## *The injunction orders*

The relevant orders on these appeals are those made by Tysoe J. on July 20, 1992, and by Esson C.J.S.C., which replaced the former; on July 16, 1993, during the period when these appellants were being arrested. These were interlocutory orders. . . .

The operative part of his order is in the following terms:

THIS COURT ORDERS that the Defendants and all persons having notice of this Order be restrained and enjoined until the 17th day of July, 1993 or until further order of this Court, from:

> (a) physically obstructing or otherwise physically impeding the logging operations of the Plaintiff or its employees, or contractors or other agents of the Plaintiff, and their employees, in the Cold Creek Watershed, Tofino Creek Watershed or Tranquil Creek Watershed;
> (b) physically creating a nuisance by obstructing the road near the Clayoquot Arm Bridge or such bridge or other access leading to the Plaintiff's operating areas in the Cold Creek Watershed, Tofino Creek Watershed or Tranquil Creek Watershed; and
> (c) physically preventing, impeding, restricting or in any way interfering with the Plaintiff or its employees, or with contractors or other agents of the Plaintiff, or their employees, from conducting logging operations in the Cold Creek Watershed, Tofino Creek Watershed or Tranquil Creek Watershed . . .

AND THIS COURT FURTHER ORDERS that the order of this Court pronounced the 30th day of June, 1992 in respect of the Bulson Creek Bridge, the Kennedy River Bridge and the Bulson Creek Watershed shall continue to apply to such bridges and watershed.

. . .

Lastly, Mr. Millar called in aid the defences of necessity and *Criminal Code*, s. 27. Generally speaking, Mr. Millar asserted that continued clear cut logging so damaged the environment that the defendants were entitled to disobey the law.

The leading decision on the defence of necessity is *R. v. Perka* (1984), 14 C.C.C. (3d) 385, 13 D.L.R. (4th) 1, [1984] 2 S.C.R. 232 (S.C.C.), where Dickson J. (as he then was), writing for the court, at p. 398 C.C.C., p. 14 D.L.R., said:

> [A] liberal and humane criminal law cannot hold people to the strict obedience of laws in emergency situations where normal human instincts, whether of self-preservation or of altruism, overwhelmingly impel disobedience.

In his judgment, however, Dickson J., made it clear that this unusual defence may be applied only in truly emergent circumstances, and only when the person at risk has no alternative but to break the law. This question was considered by my colleague Wood J. (as he then was) in *R. v. Bridges* (1989), 48 C.C.C (3d) 535, 61 D.L.R. (4th) 126, 7 W.C.B. (2d) 11 (B.C.S.C.), which was one of the abortion cases. At p. 541 C.C.C., p. 133 D.L.R., Wood J. said:

Thus it can be seen that the defence of necessity which the defendants seek to raise rests on the footing that disobedience of the order of this court was necessary in order to avoid the imminent peril or harm resulting from the conduct of the plaintiff's clinic which conduct was, and is in fact, lawful. This novel approach to necessity defies any description of the defence which I have been able to find in any recognized authority on the subject. On that basis alone, I must reject the notion that the defence of necessity can have any role to play in these proceedings.

In my judgment, this defence cannot be applied in this case for at least two reasons. First, the defendants had alternatives to breaking the law, namely, they could have applied to the court to have the injunction set aside. None of them did that prior to being arrested. I do not believe this defence operates to excuse conduct which has been specifically enjoined. By granting the order, the court prohibited the very conduct which is alleged against the defendants. An application to the court, which could be heard on fairly short notice, would have determined whether the circumstances were sufficient to engage the defence of necessity.

Secondly, I do not believe the defence of necessity can ever operate to avoid a peril that is lawfully authorized by the law: M. & B. had the legal right to log in the areas in question, and the defence cannot operate in such circumstances.

*Code*, s. 27 only justifies the use of force to prevent anything being done that, on reasonable grounds, is believed likely to cause immediate and serious injury to person or property. In my judgment, s. 27 does not contemplate the justification of force (if passively obstructing a road is the use of force) or other conduct which the court has already specifically enjoined. As with the defence of necessity; the remedy of persons such as the defendants is to apply to have the order modified or rescinded, not to disobey it. Further, the immediacy of serious injury by the logging operations in question was not of a quality that would engage s. 27: see *R. v. Walker*, January 27, 1994, Vancouver CA017058 (B.C.C.A.) [reported 64 W.A.C. 302, 22 W.C..B. (2d) 370]. I am unable to give effect to either of these defences.

*Conclusion*

It follows that I would dismiss these appeals against conviction.

*Appeals dismissed*

**Questions/Discussion**
1. Which rationale for the defence of necessity do you agree with in *Perka*? Why? Would you allow for an even wider defence in this area based upon a wider meaning of "justification" than Wilson in her judgment is willing to give?
2. Should people who steal to eat be free of liability, especially in an era of social service cutbacks and lack of real choice for the destitute in such situations?
3. Is the defence of necessity too restrictive as to the situations in which the court will accept it? Should the courts be the ones who make the law in this area or do we need legislation for greater clarity and certainty? In this regard, the Law Reform Commission of Canada (Report 31) has recommended the following:
    (a) General Rule. No one is liable if: (i) he [or she] acted to avoid immediate harm to the person or immediate serious damage to property; (ii) such harm or damage substantially outweighed the harm or damage resulting from that crime; and (iii) such harm or damage could not effectively have been avoided by any lesser means.

(b) Exception. This clause does not apply to anyone who himself [or herself] purposely causes the death of, or seriously harms, another person.

What changes would result from the addition of such a clause to the Code? How helpful do you think this provision would be?

4. Do you think the decision in *Roberts* is fair given the circumstances the accused found herself in? To what extent should the courts try to "second-guess" the choices made by individuals in extreme situations?

5. Do you think that the decision in *MacMillan Bloedel* was just given the circumstances the accused found themselves in? Were their actions justifiable in light of the possible environmental damage to the area?

**Further Reading**
- Elliott, D.W., "Necessity, Duress and Self-Defence" [1989] Criminal Law Review 611.
- Galloway, D., "Necessity as a Justification: A Critique of *Perka*" (1986), 10 Dalhousie Law Journal 158.
- Mewett, A. and M. Manning, *Mewett and Manning on Criminal Law*, 3rd ed. (Toronto: Butterworths, 1994).
- Morgan, E., "The Defence of Necessity: Justification or Excuse?" (1984), 42 University of Toronto Faculty of Law Review 165.
- Stuart, D., *Canadian Criminal Law: A Treatise*, 2nd ed. (Toronto: Carswell, 1987), pp. 432-448.
- Stuart, D., and R. Delisle, *Learning Canadian Criminal Law*, 5th ed. (Toronto: Carswell, 1995).
- Verdun-Jones, S., *Criminal Law in Canada: Cases, Questions and the Code*, (Toronto: Harcourt Brace Jovanovich Canada, 1989), pp. 255-265.
- Verdun-Jones, S., and C. Griffiths, *Canadian Criminal Justice*, 2nd ed. (Toronto: Butterworths, 1994).

## 7.1.3 Self Defence

**Introduction**

Self defence is a codified defence found in sections 34-37 of the Code (with the exception of a situation as in *Breau* and is, for the most part, well explained in the case of *Cadwallader* which follows. The defence applies principally to charges of murder, manslaughter and assault. The principal section which concerns us is section 34 which deals with unprovoked attacks on the accused and which is itself divided into two areas of applicability.[1] The first subsection of section 34 deals with those situations where the force used by the accused was not intended to cause death or grievous bodily harm. The test for the amount of force that is allowed in such circumstances in an objective one of no more force than is necessary. If the accused does not come within subsection (1), the subsection (2) might be applicable where the accused causes death or grievous bodily harm. The tests for the permissable use and amount of force in this case are found in paragraphs (a) and (b) of the subsection.

First, there must be a "reasonable apprehension of death or grievous bodily harm from the violence with which the assault was originally made or with which the assailant pursues his [or her] purposes". Second, as to the degree of force, the test is essentially a subjective one, that is, that the accused believes on reasonable grounds that she or he could not otherwise be preserved from death or grievous bodily harm. It is important, therefore, at the outset to determine which

---

[1] See section 36 for the meaning of "provocation" in this area.

subsection of section 34 applies as the tests are very different. Note as well that as to the amount of force which is permitted the test is not an exact one and the courts are willing to give some leeway in the degree of force applied, whichever test is employed.[2] Finally, note that when the accused passes the preliminary test yet misjudges and uses too much force, there is no reduction in the liability found. There is an argument that has been accepted in some jurisdictions that in a case of murder where the accused has used too much force but otherwise satisfies the tests for self defence, then the accused should be found guilty of manslaughter only. This type of qualified defence of self defence is discussed in *Brisson* below and rejected.[3]

The section of the Code dealing with situations where the accused has provoked the assault, section 35, is not dealt with here because its availability and usefulness are so restricted. Read the section and note its rather onerous and some might say unrealistic requirements. The other section which is dealt with in the cases, section 37, involves the prevention of an attack and was the focus of inquiry in the *Whynot (Stafford)* case. This case and the *Lavallée* case which follows it highlight a particular problem in the area of self defence relating to domestic violence. The various restrictions in the self defence provisions, coupled with regressive, mistaken and stereotypical attitudes towards the victims of domestic violence, have often made it difficult to effectively mount a defence in situations where the battered woman strikes back. Self defence is more readily available in situations where the death occurs in the course of a fight precipitated by the deceased and thus fits within the traditional mould. Many cases involving battered women, however, arise after a prolonged period of battering but not in the course of a contemporaneous attack; rather, the assault by the woman often occurs when the man is asleep or unconscious. It is ironic that the criminal law has been so slow to intervene in cases of domestic violence, yet has usually been unable or unwilling to deal effectively with cases where the woman ultimately protects herself or her children. The recognition in *Lavallée* of the complex issues surrounding the problems of battered women in Canada is a hopeful sign that the legal framework may be changing to meet their needs and circumstances.

A final section to note is section 43 which deals, not with self defence, but with statutory protection for parents and teachers who use force to correct a child's behaviour. In such cases there is not criminal liability if the person in authority uses no more force than is reasonable under the circumstances. Analogous protections are provided to masters of ships in section 44 and to surgeons in section 45.

## Regina v. Cadwallader
(1965), [1966] 1 C.C.C. 380 (Sask. Q.B.)

SIROIS, J.: — John Kenneth Marcella Cadwallader of Kyle, Saskatchewan, a 14-year-old boy, was charged that he was on or about October 24, 1964, at the White Bear District, in the Province of Saskatchewan, a juvenile, and that he did unlawfully kill and slay one John Cadwallader, thereby committing manslaughter and thus violating the *Criminal Code* of Canada, and did thereby commit a delinquency contrary to the provisions of the *Juvenile Delinquents Act*, R.S.C. 1952, c. 160.

The trial was held at Swift Current, Saskatchewan, before His Honour Judge J.H. Sunstrum, Judge of the Juvenile Court for Saskatchewan, commencing on January

---

[2] See *R. v. Ogal* (1928), 50 C.C.C. 71 (Alta C.A.) where the court said the accused need not "measure with nicety" the amount of force used.

[3] For a full discussion of this case and of "excessive self defence", see Noel O'Brien, "Excessive Self-Defence: A Need for Legislation" (1982-83), 25 Criminal Law Quarterly 441.

27th, and ending on February 1, 1965. At the close of the hearing the learned Juvenile Court Judge gave an oral judgment as follows:

> "Now you can just stand up, Mr. Cadwallader. You are charged on the 24th day of October, 1964, at the White Bear district, a juvenile, did unlawfully kill and slay one, John Cadwallader, thereby committing manslaughter, and thus violating a provision of the Criminal Code of Canada, and thereby commit a delinquency, contrary to the provisions of the Juvenile Delinquents Act.
>
> "Now we have heard evidence over the last few days as to the circumstances under which the body of your father was found, and the explanation you gave this morning. The explanation is that your father was coming up the stairs with a loaded 30-30 and apparently with the intention of carrying out a threat to kill you. Now your evidence is that you took your .22 and put a loaded magazine in it and then swung around and, without aiming, shot at your father, who then apparently fell down the stairs, and a total of five wounds were found in the body of your father. Now I feel that the last shot, particularly the one that was fired from a very close distance to the body of your father, and possibly any that were fired after the first one or two. You stated that the third one you were on the stairs at the time you fired the third shot, the fourth shot that you were possibly three-quarters of the way up the stairs, and then the fifth shot fired when the gun was only a few inches away. Now I feel that the extent of force used here was far more than was reasonable under the circumstances. I don't feel that you had any concern at that time that your father was in any condition to — able to carry out any threat to kill you, and therefore I find you guilty of the charge, and you will be found guilty of committing a delinquency contrary to the provisions of the Juvenile Delinquents Act."

The delinquent was committed to the Director of Child Welfare for the Province of Saskatchewan and a condition was imposed that he not be allowed to have or use firearms until he reaches the age of 21 years.

The special grounds for appeal against the judgment set out above as stated in the notice of appeal as amended are as follows:

> "(a) The learned Juvenile Court Judge erred in law in that he completely misconstrued the law and the evidence relating to self-evidence;
> (b) The learned Juvenile Court Judge erred in law in that he misconstrued the law and evidence relating to the amount of force used;
> (c) The learned Juvenile Court Judge should have dismissed the charge before him, in that the evidence clearly showed self-defence on the part of the applicant;
> (d) The learned Juvenile Court Judge erred in that there was no evidence whatsoever to support the finding that the applicant was guilty of committing a juvenile delinquency."

It may be of assistance to review the salient facts of the incident as well as some of the antecedent so as to better understand what took place and why it took place.

The appellant, an only child reached his 14th birthday a few months before the tragedy. His mother had passed away on July 19, 1956, before the boy was six years of age. The child was cared for by an uncle and aunt for approximately one school year after his mother died. Thereafter the father hired a housekeeper who reared the child in a fashion until the end of 1963, and from that time on the appellant and his father lived alone together. From the evidence it would seem that the father was reserved and quiet; his social contacts were very limited; he had a strange sense of humour and was inclined to be moody. While the father and son relationship seemed normal and healthy to outsiders, it in fact according to the boy's evidence left much to be desired. They lived in the father's house in Kyle during the week so the boy could attend school. But on weekends and during the summer holidays they would go to the farm and indulge in their favorite pastime — firing guns of various descriptions. The appellant in his evidence related over twenty incidents prior to the tragedy —

these occurring with increasing frequency in the years 1962 to 1964 — wherein the father seemed to want to do away with him or to kill him. The appellant, who is possessed of above average intelligence and who had always done well in school previously, began to slip badly academically in June and again in September and October of 1964. Something obviously was worrying and troubling him but he refused to tell anyone about his personal problems. During the week of October 18, 1964, remains of a mammoth were located in the Kyle district and specialists from the University came down to unearth the discovery. The appellant and his father drove down from Kyle, as did many others, to see the men at work on Wednesday, October 21st. The appellant found out that they would be busy on the project until the coming Saturday or Monday of the following week. The appellant and his father talked about the discovery on their return to Kyle, at which time the father told the boy, "You will be in the ground before the mammoth is out of the ground." The father was serious when he spoke these words and the boy's apprehension increased.

On Friday, October 23rd, the boy and his father went to the mammoth site again and continued on to the farm for the week-end as was the custom. On Saturday morning, the 25th, the father and son had breakfast together but the boy did not go out to work as he had just recovered from a cold and was not feeling his normal self. About 1:30 p.m. the father and son had a light dinner together, after which the father went outside to repair the fence. The boy went upstairs to lay down on his bed again as he was not feeling well. About 3:30 p.m. the boy heard his father make a lot of noise on the doorstep, he mumbled as he entered the house, slammed the door, and he was heard to say: "I'm going to kill that God Damned little bastard." The father walked noisily to his room (situated roughly beneath the boy's room), started loading a 30-30, pumped a shell into the barrel, and walked noisily again across the kitchen towards the stairway. The boy arose from his bed and peeked over the edge of the stairway; he saw his angry and determined father start up the stairs with the 30-30 rifle in his hand. The boy figured this was it — that his father was coming up to get him. The boy returned to his bed, quickly grabbed the magazine on the nail keg as well as his semi-automatic Cooey rifle leaning against the east wall, and slipped the magazine into the gun. The boy swung around and saw his father up the steps aiming at him with his 30-30 rifle. The boy took a quick shot without aiming; three followed four other shots, according to the evidence, but the accused at the time did not remember. He was "a little scared and excited" and "it all happened so quickly." The evidence of the pathologist as well as the photographs and the boy's recollection of the rapid series of events at the crucial moment seem to indicate that two shots followed quickly after the first one before or as the father and his gun started to fall back down the stairs. The fourth shot was fired with the boy standing near the top or about three quarters up the stairs, the father was still partly on the stairs and the bullet struck him in the back. The father was still moving around and the boy says he was still scared of his ability to shoot. The accused followed down the stairs and fired the fifth and last shot in the neck of the deceased from a distance of about three inches. Either the fourth or fifth shot could have been fatal whereas the first three shots were not.

The boy, under rigorous cross-examination, staunchly maintained that he did not want to kill his father but that up until the final or fifth shot he figured his father was still able to shoot him. The boy's feelings and reactions at the tragic moment were, I believe, adequately summarized in his answers to the following questions:

> "Q.4616. Well why did you hold the gun up to his head and hoot three inches away? Why did you do that?
> A. Well there is so much strain and everything . . . "

And again later on:

> "Q.4813. Why did you move the 30-30 rifle at all?
> A. I apparently didn't — I hadn't had sleep for a long time — and I didn't think at the time."

. . . .

The teachers who taught the boy all agreed he was a good boy, that he caused no problem in school and that he was of above intelligence. But they all agreed that from June, 1964, onward, when his marks mysteriously plummeted down, that the boy had a problem although he refused to communicate with them on the subject.

. . . .

The appellant's defence was self-defence. The Crown agrees with this but submits that the force used by the appellant was excessive and that the conviction for manslaughter should be upheld.

The evidence establishes that the events immediately prior to the actual shooting constituted an unprovoked assault by the deceased upon the appellant.

. . . .

While a person is not justified in killing another because of fear, there are many cases where killing in self-defence has been condoned on the ground of the necessity to preserve life.

. . . .

Self-defence proceeds from necessity and each case must therefore be determined upon its own facts. The force used can only be justified when it is necessary for the avoidance or prevention of an offered injury, and again it must be no more than is necessary under the circumstances. To use an extreme example, you could not use a tank against a chariot. But if one believes he is in danger of life or limb he is entitled to use such force as would effectually put his assailant out of action. Where the means of defence used is not disproportionate to the severity of the assault, the plea is valid although the defender fails to measure with nicety the degree of force necessary to ward off the attack and inflicts serious injury. The test as to the extent of justification is whether the accused used more force *than he on reasonable grounds believed necessary*. It is not an objective test; the determination must be made according to the accused's state of mind at the time. The question is: Did he use more force than he on reasonable grounds believed to be necessary?

To establish the defence there should be evidence — (a) that the facts amount to self-defence, and (b) that the mode of defence used was justifiable under the circumstances.

When the defence of self-defence is raised it does not affect the burden upon the Crown of establishing its case — that is of proving all accused guilty of the offence beyond a reasonable doubt. All that the accused has to do to establish this defence is introduce evidence raising at least a reasonable doubt as to his guilt; the burden rests on the prosecution of negativing that defence. If, on consideration of the whole of the evidence, the jury are either convinced of the innocence of the prisoner or are left, in doubt whether he was acting in necessary self-defence they should acquit.

The appellant in this instance is a 14-year-old boy, who barely remembers his mother — he was five years old when she died. For most of the time thereafter he lived a closed life with a father who was a strange man in many ways. Incidents punctured this boy's life with his father, especially in the two years prior to the tragedy and particularly in the summer and fall of 1964 which worried and frightened this boy. Such an incident, previously referred to, occurred in the course of a conversation with his father a few days only before the tragedy. On the afternoon of the fateful day the boy was lying on his bed, he was not well and was worried. His angry father was coming up the stairs with a 30-30 to kill him. The boy was trapped and he reacted in the only way it seems to me that an ordinary person would under the circumstances. Can one adequately visualize the fear, terror and confusion which would grip any man, let alone a 14-year-old boy in a situation such as this.

It is clear that he acted in self-defence. On his uncontradicted evidence he used only sufficient force as he reasonably thought necessary under the circumstances to put his assailant out of action. You cannot put a higher test on a 14-year-old boy than that known to our law.

In my respectful opinion the case against the appellant was not proved with that certainty, in the light of all the evidence, which is necessary in order to justify a verdict of guilty. Therefore upon that ground the appeal is allowed and it is directed that this conviction be quashed.

*Appeal allowed; conviction quashed.*

## Regina v. Breau
(1959), 125 C.C.C. 84 (N.B. S.C)

WEST J.: — The accused was convicted by Magistrate Morrissey of Northumberland County for that he "did kill a bull moose contrary to section 22(a) of the Game Act of New Brunswick". The case is before me on review under s. 46 of the *Summary Convictions Act*, R.S.N.B. 1952, c. 220. Under s. 115 of the *Game Act*, R.S.N.B. 1952, c. 95 it is my duty to hear and determine the review upon the merits of the case only.

The accused admits he killed the moose at the time and place charged, but contends he did so in self defence. He says he was hunting with two companions near Renous, Northumberland County on October 25, 1958. He separated from his companions and when alone met a bull moose on a woods road. The moose charged him and in self defence he shot it. Shortly after, his companions rejoined him and helped dress it. The moose had been shot in the breast. The three men then went out to the main highway where they met a truck driver who happened to be passing and told him they had shot a moose and asked where they might find a game warden. They were informed if they waited around one would probably be along. Shortly afterwards a game warden arrived and the accused told him he had shot a moose in self defence and went with the warden to show him the carcass. The story of the accused was corroborated in many important details by the evidence of the game warden and the truck driver.

The relevant sections of the *Game Act* are 22(a) and 106(1) which read as follows:

"**22.** Any one is guilty of an offence who hunts, takes, hurts, injures, shoots, wounds, kills or destroys,
"(a) a cow moose, calf moose, bull moose, cow caribou or calf caribou, at any time or season."

"**106**(1) Where on the prosecution of an offence under this Act it is proven that the person charged with such offence had in his possession the game or fur bearing animal or any part thereof in respect to which he is charged, the onus shall be on the person charged to prove that he did not commit the offence charged."

The submission of the accused is that the finding of the Magistrate is contrary to the evidence, and that he was justified in shooting the moose in self defence.

. . . .

I have come to the conclusion that the account given by the accused as to the shooting must be accepted as true. The only question remaining is whether under the *Game Act* self defence is available as a justification or excuse for shooting a moose. In the recent case of *R. v. Vickers* [unreported] which was before the Chief Justice of the Queen's Bench Division on review the learned Judge states "self defence is not open as an excuse or as a defence" to anyone who violates the provisions of s. 22(a) of the Act. Such was the view of an able Judge whose opinions are entitled to great respect. However, it must be considered as *obiter* as the case was decided on other grounds.

Apart from the *Vickers* case I have been unable to find any authority directly in point. It becomes necessary therefore to rely on certain fundamental legal doctrines. It has long been a principle of the common law that a person may with impunity kill another in self defence. It is recognized that in certain circumstances an individual may through necessity employ self help for his protection and preservation rather than wait for the protection of the law, which may come too late.

. . . .

These principles of the common law are given express statutory recognition in ss. 34 and 35 of the *Criminal Code*. See Crankshaw's Criminal Code, 7th ed., s. 17 and pp. 83 *et seq*. Such is in keeping with the statement of Blackstone, *supra*: "Self-defence, therefore, as it is justly called the primary law of nature, so it is not, neither can it be in fact, taken away by the law of society."

The same rule applies when a person is attacked by an animal.

. . . .

The Crown argues the accused voluntarily went into the woods and placed himself in a position where he might be attacked by a moose and therefore must accept the consequences. I cannot accept such a submission. The accused was lawfully in the woods and engaged on a lawful mission. Through no fault of his own he found himself in a situation of dire peril from which he could only extricate himself by taking the action he did. In my view his acts were warranted under the principles of the common law above noted.

To alter a clearly established principle of the common law a distinct and positive legislative enactment is necessary. Statutes are not presumed to make any alteration in the common law further or otherwise than the Act expressly declares. See Craies on Statute Law, 5th ed., p. 114. There is no specific language in the *Game Act* taking away the right of self defence nor is there any language which by necessary implication does so. Hence the defence remains open to the accused.

The finding of the Magistrate will be set aside and the conviction quashed. There will be no order for costs.

*Appeal allowed.*

## Brisson v. The Queen
(1982), 69 C.C.C. (2d) 97 (S.C.C.)

Appeal by the accused from a judgment of the Quebec Court of Appeal dismissing his appeal from conviction for first degree murder.

. . . .

[Only the judgment of Dickson J. is reproduced below.]

DICKSON, J.: — This is an appeal from the Court of Appeal of Quebec following conviction of the appellant Brisson, by a jury at Montreal, on a charge of first degree murder. The question of substance is whether the trial judge erred in failing to direct the jury that if they found that the accused had used excessive force in defending himself from his victim, they should find him guilty only of manslaughter, and not murder.

After study of the transcript and the authorities the views which I hold with respect to the self-defence issue are as follows. In the first place I question whether there was any evidentiary base for the defence. Secondly, in my view, the verdict is murder and not manslaughter if the Crown establishes the requisite deadly intent (means to cause death or means to cause bodily harm that he knows is likely to cause death and is reckless whether death ensues or not, s. 212 of the *Criminal Code*) and the defence of self-defence fails.

On the evidentiary point, the evidence gleaned from a statement of the accused to the police, was to the following effect. Brisson had met "un clochard" (a rubby-dub) with whom he had supper. He took the clochard by taxi to the parking-lot of the Hotel Loews and put him in his car. He gave the clochard a 40-oz. bottle of rye that was already in the trunk of the car. They drove about in the car for two and one-half hours, the clochard drinking throughout this time. At one point a dispute broke out and the clochard hit Brisson on the forehead with the half-empty bottle of rye. The statement by Brisson continues [translation]:

> I then brought the vehicle to a sudden stop. I asked him to calm down, which he had no intention of doing, pushed him into the corner, reached over to the back seat and took a bottle of beer from the case of 12 and hit him on the head to quieten him down, the bottle shattered and he stopped all movement, he was inert, crumpled over the front seat, his head resting against the door on the panel in front of the window.

On these facts it seems to me highly questionable whether there was evidence to warrant placing the defence of self-defence before the jury. Assuming, however, *arguendo* that the trial judge was correct in charging the jury on self-defence I pass to the substantial legal point which arises.

## Canadian Authorities

The defence of self-defence is codified in our *Criminal Code*, The *Code* preserves the common law with slight variation. Although it is to the *Code* and not the cases that we should primarily direct attention, the Canadian authorities which have considered the issue of excessive force in self-defence had paid scant heed to the *Code*. They have concentrated, in the main, on the jurisprudence as it has developed in Australia, in England and in Canada. For that reason I will turn to the cases before addressing s. 34 of the *Criminal Code*.

A number of Canadian cases have suggested that it is open to a jury to bring in a verdict of manslaughter if they find that the force used by an accused in self-defence is excessive. The first of these is *R. v. Barilla* (1944), 82 C.C.C. 228, [1944] D.L.R. 344, [1944] W.W.R. 305 (B.C.C.A.). O'Halloran J.A. found error on the part of the trial judge in failing to instruct the jury that if they found that firing the revolver as Barilla did was an unnecessary violent act of self-defence in the circumstances of the attack then launched, that it was open to them to find a verdict of manslaughter. There was no discussion in *Barilla* of the principles involved and no mention of the *Criminal Code*.

. . . .

Many of the Canadian cases simply follow *Barilla*: see for example, *R. v. Ouellette* (1950), 98 C.C.C. 153, 10 C.R. 397, [1950] 2 W.W.R. 875 (B.C.C.A.), and *R v. Basarabas and Spek* (1981), 62 C.C.C. (2d) 13 (B.C.C.A.).

. . . .

A review of the Canadian authorities shows a singular lack of uniformity in result and in reasoning. It is difficult to say that the cases follow any pattern, or the law of any country, or that, to date, any clear statement of principle has emerged.

. . . .

[After discussion of Australian and British authorities, he continued:]

## The Criminal Code

A consideration of the elements of murder, self-defence, and the consequences of that "defence" must begin with s. 212(a) and s. 34 of the *Criminal Code*. Culpable homicide is murder when the person who causes the death means to cause the death or means to cause bodily harm that he knows is likely to cause death and is reckless whether death ensues or not. An accused who is charged with murder or manslaughter may invoke the defence of self-defence.

On the construction of s. 34 it is difficult to see how the amount of force used will determine that a murder should be reduced to manslaughter. In such a case one must of necessity be dealing with s. 34(2), *i.e.*, there exists an intention to cause death. Otherwise we fall under s. 34(1) where there is no intention to cause death and thus no question of reducing murder to manslaughter. In s. 34(2) we are concerned primarily with the person who has caused death and intended to cause death. All of these elements of murder are present.

On a reasonable statutory interpretation of s. 34 it is apparent that a qualified defence of excessive force does not exist.

To summarize, I would reject the notion that excessive force in self-defence, unless related to intent under s. 212 of the *Code* or to provocation, reduces what would otherwise be murder or manslaughter.

I would dismiss the appeal.

. . . .

*Appeal dismissed.*

## R. v. Whynot (Stafford)
(1983), 61 N.S.R. (2d) 33

HART, J.A., delivered the following judgment for the Court of Appeal.

[1] HART, J.A.: — This is a Crown appeal from the acquittal of the respondent for the offence that she at or near Bangs Falls, in the County of Queens, Nova Scotia, on or about the 11th day of March, 1982 did unlawfully commit first degree murder upon the person of Lamont William Stafford, contrary to s. 218(1) of the *Criminal Code* of Canada. The trial took place at Liverpool before Mr. Justice C.D. Burchell with a jury.

[2] The point of law raised by the Crown is that the trial judge misdirected the jury as to the defence of justification, pursuant to s. 37 of the *Criminal Code*, which states:

> 37.(1) Every one is justified in using force to defend himself or any one under his protection from assault, if he uses no more force than is necessary to prevent the assault or the repetition of it.
>
> (2) Nothing in this section shall be deemed to justify the wilful infliction of any hurt or mischief that is excessive, having regard to the nature of the assault that the force used was intended to prevent.

[6] The facts of the matter are not complicated and may be stated simply as follows.

[7] In March of 1982, Jane Marie Stafford and her common law husband, Lamont William Stafford, resided in a house in the small community of Bangs Falls, Queens County. Their son, Darren, four years of age; and Jane's son, Allan Whynot, sixteen years of age; and a boarder, Ronald Wamboldt, lived with them. Near the Stafford house there was a trailer occupied by Margaret Joudrey and a boarder, Roger Manthorne. The Mersey River flowed through Bangs Falls close to the Stafford house and the Joudrey trailer.

[8] The evidence revealed that Billy Stafford was a very large and powerful man prone to violence, especially when drinking or under the influence of drugs. He dominated the household and exerted his authority by striking and slapping the various members and from time to time administering beatings to Jane Stafford and the others. He displayed very little respect for the law or the police, and had on occasion avoided responsibility for deer jacking by getting others to lie on his behalf. He was a great outdoorsman and had friends who shared this type of activity with him.

. . . .

[11] On March 11, 1982, Billy Stafford and Ronald Wamboldt had been drinking during the day at different places and when they returned home Billy demanded that

Jane drive them down to Leona Anthony's home. On the way going down, she said that Billy was "very angry, hollering, saying, referring to Margaret saying the old bag sat up all night last night, he said she was worried last night, he said her light was on all night. He said won't have to worry about seeing the light shine down there no more, he said after tonight. He said he was going to burn her out. And he kept this up pretty well the whole way."

[12] When they arrived at Anthony's they spent an hour during which Billie and Ronnie drank several beers, and Jane had one. A joint of marijuana was passed among the group. According to Jane there was no fuss while they were there, and after an hour or so Billy announced that they were going home. At that time Ronnie was in his usual state of being drunk.

[13] Jane Stafford drove home with Billy sitting in the middle and Ronnie on the outside of the seat of the truck. Her testimony then continued:

> A. We was driving up, I was driving, the stereo was still playing loudly. Bill's mouth was still running on about the same thing he said all the way down, he started right in again on the way back. He told me about the Mounties being out to talk to Allan. He said when he got done with him too, might as well clean everything up in one night. This went on pretty well the whole way up the road. A little bit before we got home he passed out or went to sleep, I don't know, one or the other, he was asleep anyway. We got in the driveway, Ronny got out and went in. I had to stay in the truck, I couldn't leave as long as Bill was out. Whenever we went anywhere and we came home and he did pass out or go to sleep like that I would have to stay there until he woke up. So I just sat there and the words, everything that he had been saying just started sinking in, Margaret, Allan, what he was going to do. I just said to hell with everything, I'm just not living like this anymore. I blew the horn on the truck and Allan came to the door, and I told him to get me the gun and load it, and I got out of the truck. When he came with the gun I just held it in the window and pulled the trigger. I don't know if I put the gun down there or what I did with it. I was telling him to do this and do that and do things.

. . . .

[16] On the day following the killing after the R.C.M.P. had found the body of Billy Stafford in the abandoned truck, Jane Stafford was arrested and charged with the first degree murder of her common law husband, Billy Stafford. On March 25 she gave a statement to the R.C.M.P. setting forth most of the facts that are given in her evidence, but alleging that the fatal shot was fired by her son, Allan Whynot. On March 27, however, she gave another statement to the police admitting that she was the person who had in fact killed Billy Stafford.

[17] At the trial, in addition to the facts already related, there was a great deal of evidence presented to the jury to indicate the terrible circumstances under which Jane Stafford had been living with Billy Stafford over the previous five years since the birth of their only child, Darren Stafford. This evidence was obviously admitted in an attempt to establish a certain state of mind as it related to the defence of provocation at the time Jane Stafford pulled the trigger. Whether any or all of this evidence should have been admitted will be discussed when I consider the defences raised on behalf of the respondent at her trial.

[18] The Crown adduced certain additional evidence to show that Jane Stafford had attempted to hire a person to kill Billy Stafford a few months earlier. This evidence was, of course, properly admitted since it tended to establish premeditation on the part of the accused person.

[19] There was also some psychiatric evidence adduced on behalf of the defence which tended to show that Jane Stafford was at her wit's end when she committed the killing. She had testified that she could not leave Billy because he had threatened to kill all of the members of her family, one at a time, should she do so, and there was no escape from her terrible plight. This evidence did not, however, establish any basis for a defence of not guilty by reason of insanity, nor was such defence raised.

. . . .

[37] In my opinion there are only two possible ways the jury could have reached the verdict of not guilty in light of the evidence before them. They may have had reasonable doubt as to whether Jane Stafford did, in fact, kill the victim, or whether the gun had been fired by her son, Allan Whynot, as had been originally alleged. This conclusion would require them to disbelieve the evidence of Jane Stafford and her son given at the trial, and such a defence was not pressed by her counsel or even referred to by the trial judge in his charge. The other route by which the jury could have arrived at its conclusion was if they understood from the judge's instructions that s. 37 of the *Criminal Code* permitted Jane Stafford to anticipate a possible assault against her son from threats made earlier in the evening, and that she used reasonable force to prevent such an assault. They had been given a copy of s. 37, isolated from the other provisions dealing with self-defence, and, in my view, after considering the overall instructions in the charge, this conclusion was left open to them. Furthermore, the legal definition of assault was not placed before them and the jury might well have understood that threats alone could amount to assault.

[38] The instructions given to the jury regarding s. 37 were broad enough to say that a person is justified in killing anyone who has threatened them and is likely to carry out such a threat. I do not believe that Parliament intended such an interpretation of the section.

[39] Section 37 is grouped together with provisions relating to the defence of the person. By s. 34 a person unlawfully assaulted is entitled to repel the assault if no more force is used than is necessary to defend himself and may kill his attacker if he is under a reasonable apprehension of death or grievous bodily harm and he believes on reasonable and probable grounds that he cannot otherwise preserve himself from death. By s. 37 he is justified in defending himself or anyone under his protection from an assault from happening, and by s-s. (2) "Nothing in this section shall be deemed to justify the wilful infliction of any hurt or mischief that is excessive, having regard to the nature of the assault that the force used was intended to prevent."

. . . .

A person who seeks justification for preventing an assault against himself or someone under his protection must be faced with an actual assault, something that he must defend against, before the provisions of s. 37 can be invoked, and that assault must be life threatening before he can be justified in killing in defence of his person or that of someone under his protection.

[40] At the time that Jane Stafford said she shot and killed Billy Stafford he was passed out or sleeping in the truck. There was no assault against her and only a general statement made sometime during the evening that he would deal with Allan. Allan was the only person who could be said to have been under her protection, and there was no evidence that Billy Stafford was about to assault him at the time he was killed. The remark of Jane Stafford, after having fired the lethal shot, to the effect that "It's all over, I ain't going to have to put up with it no more", was not in reference to any need to protect her son, but that she had brought to an end the problems which she had continually faced from her association with Billy Stafford.

[41] I do not believe that the trial judge was justified in placing s. 37 of the Code before the jury any more than he would have been justified in giving them s. 34. Under s. 34 the assault must have been underway and unprovoked, and under s. 37 the assault must be such that it is necessary to defend the person assaulted by the use of force. No more force may be used than necessary to prevent the assault or the repetition of it. In my opinion no person has the right in anticipation of an assault that may or may not happen, to apply force to prevent the imaginary assault.

. . . .

[43] I appreciate that it can be difficult for a trial judge to determine before all the evidence has been heard whether a particular defence should be placed before the jury. After the evidence has been completed, however, it becomes his responsibility to decide whether a sufficient foundation has been laid. In my opinion the trial judge in this case should have ruled that in law there was no legal foundation in the evidence to merit a justification of the act of killing the deceased as a means of defending Jane Stafford's son from any assault by Billy Stafford. As he did with s. 34 of the Code he should have refused to place before the jury any justification of her actions under s. 37. Nobody was being assaulted at the time Billy Stafford was killed. There was no need to protect anybody from any assault. The jury should not have been permitted to consider a possible assault as a justification of her deed, and s. 37 of the Code should not have been left with them.

[44] Since the jury was improperly instructed on the law relating to the offence alleged against the respondent, and since that improper instruction may well have permitted them to reach a conclusion that would not otherwise be open to them, I would allow the appeal, set aside the verdict of the jury and order a new trial upon the original indictment.

*Appeal allowed.*

## R. v. Lavallée
### (1990), 55 C.C.C (3d) 97 (S.C.C.)

[Excerpts from the judgment of Wilson J. are reproduced below.]

WILSON J.: — The narrow issue raised on this appeal is the adequacy of a trial judge's instructions to the jury regarding expert evidence. The broader issue concerns the utility of expert evidence in assisting a jury confronted by a plea of self-defence to a murder charge by a common law wife who had been battered by the deceased.

### THE FACTS

The appellant, who was 22 years old at the time, had been living with Kevin Rust for some three to four years. Their residence was the scene of a boisterous party on August 30, 1986. In the early hours of August 31 after most of the guests had departed the appellant and Rust had an argument in the upstairs bedroom which was used by the appellant. Rust was killed by a single shot in the back of the head from a .303 calibre rifle fired by the appellant as he was leaving the room.

The appellant did not testify but her statement made to police on the night of the shooting was put in evidence. Portions of it read as follows:

> Me and Wendy argued as usual and I ran in the house after Kevin pushed me. I was scared, I was really scared. I locked the door. Herb was downstairs with Joanne and I called for Herb but I was crying when I called him. I said, "Herb come up here please." Herb came up to the top of the stairs and I told him that Kevin was going to hit me actually beat on me again. Herb said he knew and that if I was his old lady things would be different, he gave me a hug. OK, we're friends, there's nothing between us. He said "Yeah, I know" and he went outside to talk to Kevin leaving the door unlocked. I went upstairs and hid in my closet from Kevin. I was so scared . . . My window was open and I could hear Kevin asking questions about what I was doing and what I was saying. Next thing I know he was coming up the stairs for me. He came into my bedroom and said "Wench, where are you?" And he turned on my light and he said "Your purse is on the floor" and he kicked it. OK then he turned and he saw me in the closet. He wanted me to come out but I didn't want to come out because I was scared. I was so scared. [The officer who took the statement then testified that the appellant started to cry at this point and stopped after a minute or two.] He grabbed me by the arm right there. There's a bruise on my face also where he slapped me. He didn't slap me right then, first he yelled at me then he pushed me and I pushed him back and he hit me twice on the right hand side of my head. I was scared. All I though about was all the other times he used to beat me, I was scared, I was shaking as usual. The rest is a blank, all I remember is he gave me the gun and a shot was fired through my screen. This is all so fast. And then the guns were in another room and he loaded it the second shot and gave it to me. And I was going to shoot myself. I pointed it to myself, I was so upset. OK and then he went and I was sitting on the bed and he started going like this with his finger [the appellant made a shaking motion with an index finger] and said something like "You're my old lady and you do as you're told" or something like that. He said "wait till everybody leaves, you'll get it then" and he said something to the effect of "either you kill me or I'll get you" and that was what it was. He kind of smiled and then turned around. I shot him but I aimed out. I though I aimed above him and a piece of his head went that way.

The relationship between the appellant and Rust was volatile and punctuated by frequent arguments and violence. They would apparently fight for two or three days at a time or several times a week. Considerable evidence was led at trial indicating that the appellant was frequently a victim of physical abuse at the hands of Rust. Between 1983 and 1986 the appellant made several trips to hospital for injuries including severe bruises, a fractured nose, multiple contusions and a black eye . . .

A friend of the deceased, Robert Ezako, testified that he had witnessed several fights between the appellant and the deceased and that he had seen the appellant point a gun at the deceased twice and threaten to kill him if he ever touched her again. Under cross-examination Ezako admitted to seeing or hearing the deceased beat up the appellant on several occasions and, during the preliminary inquiry, described her screaming during one such incident like "a pig being butchered" . . .

At one point on the night of his death Rust chased the appellant outside the house and a mutual friend, Norman Kolish, testified that the appellant pleaded with Rust to "leave me alone" and sought Kolish's protection by trying to hide behind him. A neighbour overheard Rust and the appellant arguing and described the tone of the former as "argumentative" and the latter as "scared" . . .

Three witnesses who attended the party testified to hearing sounds of yelling, pushing, shoving and thumping coming from upstairs prior to the gunshots. It is not disputed that two shots were fired by the appellant. The first one went through a window screen. It is not clear where Rust was at the time. The appellant in her statement says that he was upstairs, while another witness places him in the basement. The second shot was the fatal one . . .

The police officer who took the appellant's statement testified to seeing a red mark on her arm where she said the deceased had grabbed her. When the coroner who performed an autopsy on the deceased was shown pictures of the appellant (who had various bruises), he testified that it was "entirely possible" that bruises on the deceased's left hand were occasioned by an assault on the appellant. Another doctor noted an injury to the appellant's pinkie finger consistent with those sustained by the adoption of a defensive stance.

The expert evidence which forms the subject matter of the appeal came from Dr. Fred Shane, a psychiatrist with extensive professional experience in the treatment of battered wives. At the request of defence counsel Dr. Shane prepared a psychiatric assessment of the appellant. The substance of Dr. Shane's opinion was that the appellant had been terrorized by Rust to the point of feeling trapped, vulnerable, worthless and unable to escape the relationship despite the violence. At the same time, the continuing pattern of abuse put her life in danger. In Dr. Shane's opinion the appellant's shooting of the deceased was a final desperate act by a woman who sincerely believed that she would be killed that night:

> . . . I think she felt, she felt in the final tragic moment that her life was on the line, that unless she defended herself, unless she reacted in a violent way that she would die. I mean he made it very explicit to her, from what she told me and from the information I have from the material that you forwarded to me, that she had, I think to defend herself against his violence.

Dr. Shane stated that his opinion was based on four hours of formal interviews with the appellant, a police report of the incident (including the appellant's statement), hospital reports documenting eight of her visits to emergency departments between 1983 and 1985, and an interview with the appellant's mother. In the course of his testimony Dr. Shane related many things told to him by the appellant for which there was no admissible evidence. They were not in the appellant's statement to the police and she did not testify at trial. For example, Dr. Shane mentioned several episodes of abuse described by the appellant for which there were no hospital reports. He also related the appellant's disclosure to him that she had lied to doctors about the cause of her injuries. Dr. Shane testified that such fabrication was typical of battered women. The appellant also recounted to Dr. Shane occasions on which Rust would allegedly beat her, then beg her forgiveness and ply her with flowers and temporary displays of kindness. Dr. Shane was aware of the incidents described by Ezako about the appellant's pointing a gun at Rust on two occasions and explained it as "an issue for trying to defend herself. She was afraid that she would be assaulted". The appellant denied to Dr. Shane that she had homicidal fantasies about Rust and mentioned that she had smoked some marijuana on the night in question. These facts were related by Dr. Shane in the course of his testimony.

The appellant was acquitted by a jury but the verdict was overturned by a majority of the Manitoba Court of Appeal and the case sent back for retrial.

....

## ISSUES ON APPEAL

It should be noted that two bases for ordering a new trial are implicit in the reasons of the majority of the Court of Appeal. In finding that "absent the evidence of Dr. Shane, it is unlikely that the jury, properly instructed, would have accepted the accused's plea of self-defence" the Court of Appeal suggests that the evidence of Dr. Shane ought to have been excluded entirely. The alternative ground for allowing the Crown's appeal was that Dr. Shane's testimony was properly admitted but the trial judge's instructions with respect to it were deficient. Thus, the issues before this Court are as follows:

1. Did the majority of the Manitoba Court of Appeal err in concluding that the jury should have considered the plea of self-defence absent the expert evidence of Dr. Shane?
2. Did the majority of the Manitoba Court of Appeal err in holding that the trial judge's charge to the jury with respect to Dr. Shane's expert evidence did not meet the requirements set out by this Court in *Abbey*, thus warranting a new trial?

## ANALYSIS

### *Admissibility of Expert Evidence*

In *Kellier (Village of) v. Smith*, [1931] S.C.R. 672, at p. 684, this Court adopted the principle that in order for expert evidence to be admissible " the subject-matter of the inquiry must be such that ordinary people are unlikely to form a correct judgment about it, if unassisted by persons with special knowledge". More recently, this Court addressed the admissibility of expert psychiatric evidence in criminal cases in *R. v. Abbey, supra*. At p. 42 of the unanimous judgment Dickson J. (as he then was) stated the rule as follows:

> With respect to matters calling for special knowledge, an expert in the field may draw inferences and state his opinion. An expert's function is precisely this: to provide the judge and jury with a ready-made inference which the judge and jury, due to the technical nature of the facts, are unable to formulate. "An expert's opinion is admissible to furnish the Court with scientific information which is likely to be outside the experience and knowledge of judge or jury. If on the proven facts a judge or jury can form their own conclusions without help, then the opinion of the expert is unnecessary" (*turner* (1974), 60 Crim. App. R. 80, at p. 83, *per* Lawton L.J.).

. . . .

The need for expert evidence in these areas can, however, be obfuscated by the belief that judges and juries are thoroughly knowledgeable about "human nature" and that no more is needed. They are, so to speak, their own experts on human behaviour. This, in effect, was the primary submission of the Crown to this Court.

The bare facts of this case, which I think are amply supported by the evidence, are that the appellant was repeatedly abused by the deceased but did not leave him (although she twice pointed a gun at him), and ultimately shot him in the back of the head as he was leaving her room. The Crown submits that these facts disclose all the information a jury needs in order to decide whether or not the appellant acted in self-defence. I have no hesitation in rejecting the Crown's submission.

Expert evidence on the psychological effect of battering on wives and common law partners must, it seems to me, be both relevant and necessary in the context of the present case. How can the mental state of the appellant be appreciated without it? The average member of the public (or of the jury) can be forgiven for asking: Why would a woman put up with this kind of treatment? Why should she continue to live with such a man? How could she love a partner who beat her to the point of requiring hospitalization? We would expect the woman to pack her bags and go. Where is her self-respect? Why does she not cut loose and make a new life for herself? Such is the reaction of the average person confronted with the so-called "battered wife syndrome". We need help to understand it and help is available from trained professionals.

The gravity, indeed, the tragedy of domestic violence can hardly be overstated. Greater media attention to this phenomenon in recent years has revealed both its prevalence and its horrific impact on women from all walks of life. Far from protecting women from it the law historically sanctioned the abuse of women within marriage as an aspect of the husband's ownership of his wife and his "right" to chastise her. One need only recall the centuries old law that a man is entitled to beat his wife with a stick "no thicker than his thumb".

Laws do not spring out of a social vacuum. The notion that a man has a right to "discipline" his wife is deeply rooted in the history of our society. The woman's duty was to serve her husband and to stay in the marriage at all costs "till death do us part" and to accept as her due any "punishment" that was meted out for failing to please her husband. One consequence of this attitude was that "wife battering" was rarely spoken of, rarely reported, rarely prosecutive, and even more rarely punished. Long after society abandoned its formal approval of spousal abuse tolerance of it continued and continues in some circles to this day.

Fortunately, there has been a growing awareness in recent years that no man has a right to abuse any woman under any circumstances. Legislative initiatives designed to educate police, judicial officers and the public, as well as more aggressive investigation and charging policies all signal a concerted effort by the criminal justice system to take spousal abuse seriously. However, a woman who comes before a judge or jury with the claim that she has been battered and suggests that this may be a relevant factor in evaluating her subsequent actions still faces the prospect of being condemned by popular mythology about domestic violence. Either she was not as badly beaten as she claims or she would have left the man long ago. Or, if she was battered that severely, she must have stayed out of some masochistic enjoyment of it.

. . . .

## THE RELEVANCE OF EXPERT TESTIMONY TO THE ELEMENTS OF SELF-DEFENCE

In my view, there are two elements of the defence under s. 34(2) of the *Code* which merit scrutiny for present purposes. The first is the temporal connection in s. 34(2)(a) between the apprehension of death or grievous bodily harm and the act allegedly taken in self-defence. Was the appellant "under reasonable apprehension of death or grievous bodily harm" from Rust as he was walking out of the room? The second is the assessment in s. 34(2)(b) of the magnitude of the force used by the accused. Was the accused's belief that she could not "otherwise preserve herself from death or grievous bodily harm" except by shooting the deceased based "on reasonable grounds"?

The feature common to both 34(2)(a) and 34(2)(b) is the imposition of an objective standard of reasonableness on the apprehension of death and the need to repel the assault with deadly force.

. . . .

If it strains credulity to imagine what the "ordinary man" would do in the position of a battered spouse, it is probably because men do not typically find themselves in that situation. Some women do, however. The definition of what is reasonable must be adapted to circumstances which are, by and large, foreign to the world inhabited by the hypothetical "reasonable man".

I find the case of *State v. Wanrow*, 559 P.2d 548 (1977), helpful in illustrating how the factor of gender can be germane to the assessment of what is reasonable. In *Wanrow* the Washington Supreme Court addressed the standard by which a jury ought to assess the reasonableness of the female appellant's use of a gun against an unarmed intruder. The Court pointed out that the appellant had reason to believe that the intruder had molested her daughter in the past and was coming back for her son. The appellant was a 5'4" woman with a broken leg. The assailant was 6'2" and intoxicated. The Court first observed, at p. 558, that "in our society women suffer from a conspicuous lack of access to training in and the means of developing those skills necessary to effectively repel a male assailant without resorting to the use of deadly weapons." Later it found that the trial judge erred in his instructions to the jury by creating the impression that the objective standard of reasonableness to be applied to the accused was that of an altercation between two men. At p. 559, the Court makes the following remarks which I find apposite to the case before us:

> The respondent was entitled to have the jury consider her actions in the light of her own perceptions of the situation, including those perceptions which were the product of our nation's "long and unfortunate history of sex discrimination." Until such time as the effects of that history are eradicated, care must be taken to assure that our self-defence instructions afford women the right to have their conduct judged in the light of the individual physical handicaps which are the product of sex discrimination. To fail to do so is to deny the right of the individual woman involved to trial by the same rules which are applicable to male defendants.

I turn now to a consideration of the specific components of self-defence under s. 34(3) of the *Criminal Code*.

*Reasonable Apprehension of Death*

Section 34(2)(a) requires than an accused who intentionally causes death or grievous bodily harm in repelling an assault is justified if he or she does so "under reasonable apprehension of death or grievous bodily harm". In the present case, the assault precipitating the appellant's alleged defensive act was Rust's threat to kill her when everyone else had gone.

It will be observed that subsection 34(2)(a) does not actually stipulate that the accused apprehend *imminent* danger when he or she acts. Case law has, however, read that requirement into the defence: see *Reilly v. The Queen, supra; R. v. Baxter* (1975), 33 C.R.N.S. 22 (Ont. C.A. ): *R. v. Bogue* (1976), 30 C.C.C. (2d) 403 (Ont. C.A.). The sense in which "imminent" is used conjures up the image of "an uplifted knife" or a pointed gun. The rationale for the imminence rules seems obvious. The law of self-defence is designed to ensure that the use of defensive force is really necessary. It justifies the act because the defender reasonably believed that he or she had no alternative but to take the attacker's life. If there is a significant time interval between the original unlawful assault and the accused's response, one tends to suspect that the accused was motivated by revenge rather than self-defence. In the paradigmatic case of a one-time bar room brawl between two men of equal size and strength, this inference makes sense. How can one feel endangered to the point of firing a gun at an unarmed man who utters a death threat, then turns his back and walks out of the room? One cannot be certain of the gravity of the threat or his capacity to carry it out. Besides, one can always take the opportunity to flee or to call the police. If he comes back and raises his fist, one can respond in kind if need be. These are the tacit assumptions that underlie the imminence rule.

All of these assumptions were brought to bear on the respondent in *R. v. Whynot*, (1983) 9 C.C.C. 449 (N.S.C.A.) . . . .

The Court stated at p. 464:

> I do not believe that the trial judge was justified in placing s. 37 of the *Code* before the jury anymore than he would have been justified in giving them s. 34. Under s. 34 the assault must have been underway and unprovoked, and under s. 37 the assault must be such that it is necessary to defend the person assaulted by the use of force. No more force may be used than necessary to prevent the assault or the repetition of it. In my opinion, no person has the right in anticipation of an assault that may or may not happen, to apply force to prevent the imaginary assault.

The implications of the Court's reasoning is that it is inherently unreasonable to apprehend death or grievous bodily harm unless and until the physical assault is actually in progress, at which point the victim can presumably gauge the requisite amount of force needed to repel the attack and act accordingly. In my view, expert testimony can cast doubt on these assumptions as they are applied in the context of a battered wife's efforts to repel an assault.

The situation of the appellant was not unlike that of Jane Stafford in the sense that she too was routinely beaten over the course of her relationship with the man she ultimately killed. According to the testimony of Dr. Shane these assaults were not entirely random in their occurrence. The following exchange during direct examination elicited a discernible pattern to the abuse:

> Q. How did they react during the tension that preceded the beatings? How would her . . .
> A. Well, typically before a beating there's usually some verbal interchange and there are threats and typically she would feel, you know, very threatened by him and for various reasons.
>
> He didn't like the way she dressed or if she — didn't like the way she handled money or she wasn't paying him enough attention or she was looking at other men, all sorts of reasons, and she would be defending herself, trying to placate him, which was typical, saying, you know, trying to calm him down, trying to soothe him, you know, so nothing violent would happen and sometimes it would work. You know, as people's experiences indicated or as people who write about this process, if you will, have indicated. But often, as reflected by what she has told me, and the information I have from other people, such as her mother, often it would fail and she would end up being beaten and assaulted.
>
> Q. And that would be followed by this forgiveness state?
> A. It typically would be followed by, you know, this make-up period.

Earlier in his testimony Dr. Shane explained how this "make-up" period would be characterized by contrite and affectionate behaviour by Rust:

> In this particular case she documented many times, after he would beat her, he would send her flowers and he would beg her for forgiveness and he would love her and then the relationship would come back to a sense of equilibrium, if you will . . . But then, because of the nature of the personalities, it would occur again.

The cycle described by Dr. Shane conforms to the Walker Cycle Theory of Violence named for clinical psychologist Dr. Lenore Walker, the pioneer research in the field of the battered wife syndrome.

. . . .

Dr. Walker defines a battered woman as a woman who has gone through the battering cycle at least twice. As she explains in her introduction to *The Battered Woman* at p.. xv, "Any woman may find herself in an abusive relationship with a man once. If it occurs a second time, and she remains in the situation, she is defined as a battered woman".

Given the relational context in which the violence occurs, the mental state of an accused at the critical moment she pulls the trigger cannot be understood except in terms of the cumulative effect of months or years of brutality. As Dr. Shane explained in his testimony, the deterioration of the relationship between the appellant and Rust in the period immediately preceding the killing led to feelings of escalating terror on the part of the appellant:

> But their relationship some weeks to months before was definitely escalating in terms of tension and in terms of the discordant quality about it. They were sleeping in separate bedrooms. Their intimate relationship was lacking and things were building and building to a point where she couldn't — she felt so threatened and so overwhelmed that she had to — that she reacted in a violent way because of her fear of survival and also because, I think because of her, I guess, final sense that she was — that she had to defend herself and her own sense of violence toward this man who had really desecrated her and damaged her for so long.

Another aspect of the cyclical nature of the abuse is that it begets a degree of predictability to the violence that is absent in an isolated violent encounter between two strangers. This also means that it may in fact be possible for a battered spouse to accurately predict the onset of violence before the first blow is struck even if an outsider to the relationship cannot. Indeed, it has been suggested that a battered woman's knowledge of her partner's violence is so heightened that she is able to anticipate the nature and extent (though not the onset) of the violence by his conduct beforehand.

. . . .

Where evidence exists than an accused is in a battered relationship, expert testimony can assist the jury in determining whether the accused had a "reasonable" apprehension of death when she acted by explaining the heightened sensitivity of a battered woman to her partner's acts. Without such testimony I am skeptical that the average fact-finder would be capable of appreciating why her subjective fear may have been reasonable in the context of the relationship. After all, the hypothetical "reasonable man" observing only the final incident may have been unlikely to recognize the batterer's threat as potentially lethal. Using the case at bar as an example the "reasonable man" might have thought, as the majority of the Court of Appeal seemed to, that it was unlikely that Rust would make good on his threat to kill the appellant that night because they had guests staying overnight.

The issue is not, however, what an outsider would have reasonably perceived but what the accused reasonably perceived, given her situation and her experience.

Even accepting that a battered woman may be uniquely sensitized to danger from her batterer, it may yet be contended that the law ought to require her to wait until the knife is uplifted, the gun pointed or the fist clenched before her apprehension is deemed reasonable. This would allegedly reduce the risk that the woman is mistaken in her fear, although the law does not require her fear to be correct, only reasonable. In response to this contention, I need only point to the observation made by Huband J.A. that the evidence showed that when the appellant and Rust physically fought the appellant "invariably got the worst of it". I do not think it is an unwarranted generalization to say that due to their size, strength, socialization and lack of training, women are typically no match for men in hand-to-hand combat. The requirement imposed in *Whynot* that a battered woman wait until the physical assault is "underway" before her apprehensions can be validated in law would, in the words of an American court, be tantamount to sentencing her to 'murder by installment'; *State v. Gellegos*, 719 P.2d 1268 (N.M. 1986), at p. 1271) . . .

### Lack of Alternatives to Self-Help

Subsection 34(2) requires an accused who pleads self-defence to believe "on reasonable grounds" that it is not possible to otherwise preserve him or herself from death or grievous bodily harm. The obvious question is if the violence was so intolerable, why did the appellant not leave her abuser long ago? This question does not really go to whether she had an alternative to killing the deceased at the critical moment. Rather, it plays on the popular myth already referred to that a woman who says she was battered yet stayed with her batterer was either not so badly beaten as she claimed or else she liked it. Nevertheless, to the extent that her failure to leave the abusive relationship earlier may be used in support of the proposition that she was free to leave at the final moment, expert testimony can provide useful insights. Dr. Shane attempted to explain in his testimony how and why, in the case at bar, the appellant remained with Rust.

. . . .

> One is that the spouse gets beaten so badly — so badly —that he or she loses the motivation to react and becomes helpless and becomes powerless. And it's also been shown sometimes, you known, in — not that you can compare animals to human beings, but in laboratories, what you do if you shock an animal, after a while it can't respond to a threat on its life. It becomes just helpless and lies there in an amotivational state, if you will, where it feels there's no power and there's no energy to do anything.
> So in a sense it happens in human beings as well. It's almost like a concentration camp, if you will. You get paralyzed with fear.
> The other thing that happens often in these types of relationships with human beings is that the person who beats or assaults, who batters, often tries — he makes up and begs for forgiveness. And this individual, who basically has a very disturbed or damaged self-esteem, all of a sudden feels that he or she — we'll use women in this case because it's so much more common — the spouse feels that she again can do the spouse a favour and it can make her feel needed and boost her self-esteem for a while and make her feel worthwhile and the spouse says he'll forgive her and whatnot.

Apparently, another manifestation of this victimization is a reluctance to disclose to others the fact or extent of the beatings. For example, the hospital records indicate that on each occasion the appellant attended the emergency department to be treated for various injuries she explained the cause of those injuries as accidental. Both in its address to the jury and in its written submissions before this Court the Crown insisted that the appellant's injuries were as consistent with her explanations as with being battered and, therefore, in the words of Crown counsel at trial, "the myth is, in this particular case, that Miss Lavallee was a battered spouse". In his testimony Dr. Shane testified that the appellant admitted to him that she lied to hospital staff and others about the cause of her injuries. In Dr. Shane's opinion this was consistent with her overall feeling of being trapped and helpless:

> . . . she would never say that she'd been abused by the man with whom she was living and that usually happened because of this whole process. He would beg her. I mean she would tell me that on occasions he would beat her and then the police would be called by, I think, on one occasion a neighbour and he got down on his knees and he begged forgiveness and he loved her and he felt so terrible about it. And so this would be a typical scenario. Whenever she would go to the hospital, that he would attempt to, I think, attempt to have her forgive him and he would love her so much more.

. . . .

The account given by Dr. Shane comports with that documented in the literature. Reference is often made to it as a condition of "learned helplessness", a phrase coined by Dr. Charles Seligman, the psychologist who first developed the theory by experimenting on animals in the manner described by Dr. Shane in his testimony. A related theory used to explain the failure of women to leave battering relationships is described by psychologist and lawyer Charles Patrick Ewing in his book *Battered Women Who Kill* (1987). Ewing describes a phenomenon labelled "traumatic bonding" that has been observed between hostages and captors, battered children and their parents, concentration camp prisoners and guards, and batterers and their spouses. According to the research cited by Ewing there are two features common to the social structure in each of these apparently diverse relationships. At pp. 19-20, he states:

> The first of these common features is an imbalance of power "wherein the maltreated person perceives himself or herself to be subjugated or dominated by the other". The less powerful person in the relationship — whether battered women, hostage, abused child, cult follower, or prisoner — becomes extremely dependent upon, and may even come to identify with, the more powerful person. In many cases, the result of such dependency and identification is that the less powerful, subjugated persons become "more negative in their self-appraisal, more incapable of fending for themselves, and thus more in need of the high power person." As this "cycle of dependency and lowered self-esteem" is repeated over time, the less powerful person develops a "strong affective bond" to the more powerful person in the abusive relationship.
> The second feature common to the relationships between battered woman and batterer, hostage and captor, battered child and abusive parent, cult follower and leader, and prisoner and guard is the periodic nature of the abuse. In each relationship, the less powerful person is subjected to intermittent periods of abuse, which alternate with periods during which the more powerful, abusive person treats the less powerful person in a "more normal and acceptable fashion."

. . . .

This strong "affective bond" may be helpful in explaining not only why some battered women remain with their abusers but why they even profess to love them. Of course, as Dr. Ewing adds, environmental factors may also impair the woman's ability to leave — lack of job skills, the presence of children to care for, fear of retaliation by the man, etc. may each have a role to play in some cases.

This is not to say that in the course of a battering relationship a woman may never attempt to leave her partner or try to defend herself from assault. In *The Battered Woman Syndrome* Dr. Walker notes at p. 30 that women sometimes "react to men's violence against them by striking back, but their actions are generally ineffective at hurting or stopping the men. They may be effective in controlling the level of the man's violence against them."

. . . .

The same psychological factors that account for a woman's inability to leave a battering relationship may also help to explain why she did not attempt to escape at the moment she perceived her life to be in danger.

. . . .

I emphasize at this juncture that it is not for the jury to pass judgment on the fact than an accused battered woman stayed in the relationship. Still less is it entitled to conclude that she forfeited the right to self-defence for having done so. I would also point out that traditional self-defence doctrine does not require a person to retreat from her home instead of defending herself. *R. v. Antley* (1963), 42 C.R. 384 (Ont. C.A.). A man's home may be his castle but it is also the woman's home even if it seems to her more like a prison in the circumstances.

If, after hearing the evidence (including the expert testimony), the jury is satisfied that the accused had a reasonable apprehension of death or grievous bodily harm and felt incapable of escape, it must ask itself what the "reasonable person" would do in such a situation. The situation of the battered woman as described by Dr. Shane strikes me as somewhat analogous to that of a hostage. If the captor tells her that he will her in three days time, is it potentially reasonable for her to seize an opportunity presented on the first day to kill the captor or must she wait until he makes the attempt on the third day? I think the question the jury must ask itself is whether, given the history, circumstances and perception of the appellant, her belief that she could not preserve herself from being killed by Rust that night except by killing him first was reasonable. To the extent that expert evidence can assist the jury in making that determination, I would find such testimony to be both relevant and necessary.

In light of the foregoing discussion I would summarize as follows the principles upon which expert testimony is properly admitted in cases such as this:

1. Expert testimony is admissible to assist the fact-finder in drawing inferences in areas where the expert has relevant knowledge or experience beyond that of the lay person.
2. It is difficult for the lay person to comprehend the battered wife syndrome. It is commonly thought that battered women are not really beaten as badly as they claim, otherwise they would have left the relationship. Alternatively, some believe that women enjoy being beaten, that they have a masochist strain in them. Each of these stereotypes may adversely affect consideration of a battered woman's claim to have acted in self-defence in killing her mate.
3. Expert evidence can assist the jury in dispelling these myths.
4. Expert testimony relating to the ability of an accused to perceive danger from her mate may go to the issue of whether she "reasonably apprehended" death or grievous bodily harm on a particular occasion.
5. Expert testimony pertaining to why an accused remained in the battering relationship may be relevant in assessing the nature and extent of the alleged abuse.
6. By providing an explanation as to why an accused did not flee when she perceived her life to be in danger, expert testimony may also assist the jury in assessing the reasonableness of her belief that killing her batterer was the only way to save her own life.

Quite apart from Dr. Shane's testimony there was ample evidence on which the trial judge could conclude that the appellant was battered repeatedly and brutally by Kevin Rust over the course of their relationship. The fact that she may have exhibited aggressive behaviour on occasion or tried (unsuccessfully) to leave does not detract from a finding of systematic and relentless abuse. In my view, the trial judge did not err in admitting Dr. Shane's expert testimony in order to assist the jury in determining whether the appellant had a reasonable apprehension of death or grievous bodily harm and believed on reasonable grounds that she had no alternative but to shoot Kevin Rust on the night in question.

Obviously the fact that the appellant was a battered woman does not entitle her to an acquittal. Battered women may well kill their partners other than in self-defence. The focus is not on who the woman is, but on what she did.

. . . .

Ultimately, it is up to the jury to decide whether, *in fact*, the accused's perceptions and actions were reasonable. Expert evidence does not and cannot usurp that function of the jury. The jury is not compelled to accept the opinions proffered by the expert about the effects of battering on the mental state of victims generally or on the mental state of the accused in particular. But fairness and the integrity of the trial process demand that the jury have the opportunity to hear them.

. . . .

I would accordingly allow the appeal, set aside the order of the Court of Appeal, and restore the acquittal.

*Appeal allowed; acquittal restored.*

**Note:** In October, 1995, the government announced a federal review of murder cases involving women convicted of killing their abusive partners, spouses or guardians in self defence. Judge Lynn Ratushny has been appointed to undertake the review. The "Terms of Reference" of the task force are as follows (Excerpt from Department of Justice News Release, October 4, 1995):

> In recent years, there have been developments in our understanding of the law of self-defence as it relates to battered women who have been involved in abusive relationships. There are concerns that women convicted of homicide in these circumstances may not have received the benefit of the defence of self defence when it may have been available to them.
>
> We also now have an increased understanding of abusive relationships and their impact upon those who have been battered, and how this might support the use of the defence. Questions have also been raised about the circumstances under which these types of offences occurred and about whether our criminal law sentencing processes and sentencing tools are adequate to deal with these circumstances.
>
> Accordingly, the Honorable Lynn Ratushny, a judge of the Ontario Court of Justice (Provincial Division) is appointed:
>
> i) to review the cases of women under sentence in federal and provincial institutions who apply for a remedy and who are serving a sentence for homicide in circumstances in which the killing allegedly took place to prevent the deceased from inflicting serious bodily harm or death;
> ii) to make recommendations in appropriate cases to the Government of Canada for individual women whose circumstances merit consideration for the granting of the royal prerogative of mercy;
> iii) to clarify the availability and the scope of the defences available to women accused of homicide in the circumstances set out above; and
> iv) to make recommendations as considered appropriate with respect to possible law reform initiatives stemming from the review.

As a result of any forthcoming recommendations, the government could decide to release certain women, shorten their sentences or order new trials. Recommendations may also be made as to the reform of the law on self defence.

**Questions/Discussion**

1. Do you agree with the differing test in section 34? Why or why not? What do you think is the rationale for an objective test versus a subjective test in regard to the amount of force in subsections (1) and (2)?
2. Do you agree with the decision in *Brisson* or do you think that if an accused satisfies all the tests but the last as to the amount of force then some consideration should be given to this in attaching liability?
3. Should there be a special defence for women in the situation of the accused in *Whynot (Stafford)*? Why or why not? Was the court too restrictive in its interpretation of section

37 in this case? How and on what grounds would you have decided the case? Could you interpret section 34 or section 37 in such a way as to have allowed its successful application in such a fact situation?
4. Do you agree with the approach taken in the *Lavallée* decision? Why or why not? What problems do you foresee in the application of this decision in other cases? See also the recent case of *R. v. Pétal* (1994), 87 C.C.C. (3d) 97 (S.C.C). For a feminist critique of the use of the "Battered Women Syndrome", see Comack under Further Reading.
5. The then Law Reform Commission of Canada proposed in its Report 31, *Recodifying Criminal Law*, that there be one general rule relative to defence of the person: no one would be liable " ... if he [or she] acted as he [or she] did to protect himself [or herself] or another person against unlawful force by using such force as was reasonably necessary to avoid the harm or hurt apprehended". Do you agree with such a formulation? Do you think that such a section would change what the courts do in practice? Should it include a special provision for battered women who strike back to protect themselves or their children?

**Further Reading**
- Bailey, M., "The Fall of the Half-Way House: The Supreme Court of Canada in *Gee, Brisson and Faid*" (1984), 22 Alberta Law Review 473.
- Brodsky, D., "Educating Juries: the Battered Women Defence in Canada" (1987), 25 Alberta Law Review 461.
- Burt, L., "The Battered Woman Syndrome and the Plea of Self-Defence: Can the Victim and the Accused be Strangers" (1993), 27 University of British Columbia Law Review 93-98.
- Comack, E., "Justice for Battered Women?" (1988), vol. 22, no. 3, of Canadian Dimension 8.
- Martinson, D., et al., " A Forum on Lavallée v. R.: Women and Self-Defence" (1991), 25 University of British Columbia Law Review 23-68.
- McEachern, A., "On Self-Defence" (1985), 43 The Advocate 305.
- Mewett, A., and M. Manning, *Mewett and Manning on Criminal Law*, 3rd ed. (Toronto: Butterworths, 1994).
- O'Brien, N.C., "Excessive Self-Defence: A Need for Legislation" (1982-83), 25 Criminal Law Quarterly 441.
- Stalker, A., "Self Defence and Consent: The Use of Common Law Developments in Canadian Criminal Code Analysis" (1994), 32 Alberta Law Review 484-510.
- Stuart, D., *Canadian Criminal Law: A Treatise*, 2nd ed. (Toronto: Carswell, 1987), pp. 405-414.
- Stuart, D., and R. Delisle, *Learning Canadian Criminal Law*, 5th ed. (Toronto: Carswell, 1995).
- Verdun-Jones, S., and C. Griffiths, *Canadian Criminal Justice*, 2nd ed. (Toronto: Butterworths, 1994).

## 7.1.4 Defence of Property

**Introduction**

There is little to say about the defence of defence of property outside the two cases below. The main distinctions made in this area relate to the type of property being protected; is it real or movable (personal) property? If it is personal property (section 38) then you have the right to prevent someone from taking it or to take it back, if you do not strike or cause bodily harm to the trespasser. If the trespasser persists in trying to keep it or in trying to take it, then the trespasser is deemed to commit an unprovoked assault and your actions are then protected by the self defence provisions in section 34. If someone is trying to break into your home, then you have the right to use as much force as necessary to prevent that person from entering, or to remove the trespasser (sections 40-41). If the trespasser resists attempts at blocking or removing her or him, then it is deemed that an unprovoked assault has been committed by the trespasser and your actions are protected again by the provisions of section 34.[1]

## Regina v. Stanley
### (1977), 36 C.C.C. (2d) 216 (B.C. C.A.)

[Only the judgment of Branca J.A. is reproduced below.]

BRANCA, J.A.: — The appellant Stanley was charged with unlawfully committing murder punishable by life imprisonment. Stanley was charged with killing one Donald Blosky at Williams Lake in this Province on January 29, 1975.

He pleaded not guilty and was found guilty by the jury on September 15, 1975, and was then sentenced to imprisonment for life with a minimum period of 10 years to be served.

Blosky was admittedly stabbed by Stanley, on the day charged, at 1702 Renner Rd. in Williams Lake. That address was the dwelling-house of Stanley and his common law wife Debbie Chemko. I shall hereafter refer to her as "the wife". The stab wound caused Blosky's death. Stanley and Debbie voluntarily went to the police who arrived at his home immediately afterwards and they were arrested. As a result of a conversation with the appellant, the police took possession of a knife rack containing six knives, one of which was the weapon used to stab Blosky. The totality of the narratives of the events given is rather bizarre, and in a manner drug oriented.

The appellant and Chemko were in their home, asleep, and the dwelling was in darkness. A party of men made up of Jim Stole, Wayne Janz, Rick Croft and Rick Gunn and the deceased arrived at Stanley's residence at about 2:00 or 2:30 o'clock in the morning. The evidence established that four of the five, excluding Gunn, were drinking in the early morning at the home of Blosky's parents. The evidence proved that Blosky was intoxicated, he having consumed a large quantity of drugs and whisky. The four left Blosky's place and went in search of a party and during the search Rick Gunn was picked up on the street.

The party arrived at Stanley's residence and knocked on the door in an effort to awaken Stanley and his wife.

Finally, according to the Crown witnesses, Stanley came to the door, dressed only in his pants. All five immediately entered and Stanley retreated to the bedroom. One witness, Janz, stated that Debbie "got freaked out" and screamed to them to get out. They backed out of the bedroom into the kitchen. Janz said that Rick and the deceased, told the other three to leave the room and Rick Gunn said he was going to stay to make sure things did not get out of hand. The other three went out and Janz and Stole went

---

[1] For examples of cases where these deemed assault provisions have been used in the context of offences rather than in the creation of defences, see *R. v. Kellington* (1972), 7 C.C.C. (2d) 564 (B.C. S.C.) and *R. v. Spencer* {1977}, 38 C.C.C. (2d) 303 (B.C. S.C.).

to the car and sat down. Croft remained and stood near the window looking in. He said he was then called by Stole to the car and he went there and then he saw Blosky come flying out backwards and he fell. He then got up and ran some 20 ft. and fell again. The three picked him up and Janz drove Blosky to the hospital. There was blood all over Blosky about the stomach region and Blosky was unconscious. Before leaving he, Janz, had seen no weapons in the hands of anyone. He admitted that in January he saw Stanley and he had planned to rip off any drugs that Stanley may have had. By "rip-off" he meant "steal". On the occasion in question Stanley was working. Stole was with him, as was Blosky, together with a girl named Gay Newenhousen. They met the wife and took Debbie to Stole's home and Blosky stole the dope, and then told Debbie that if Stanley sold any more dope, he wasn't going to be in Williams Lake. After the dope was stolen, each took part of the seven caps that were stolen. The drug was heroin. He later corrected that to say that it was Tussionex. He said that Blosky had heard Stanley say the he, Stanley, could do Blosky in if he wanted to. Janz had heard of the threat. It was because of that that on the occasion in question they decided to go and see Stanley. He said that Blosky was "going to have a discussion and if they fight, they fight". Blosky did not discuss a threat allegedly made by Stanley, after the rip-off, to shoot him in the knee. He knew of that threat. He fixed the time of arrival at Stanley's home at 2:30 in the morning. He said that the door was locked and when they were inside he could not remember the conversation between Blosky and Stanley. Gunn did the talking.

Croft was called and confirmed the earlier events of the evening and said that finally the party arrived at Stanley's. All went inside. None had a weapon. When inside "they" were talking about having a fight. He thought that Blosky had said "*I want to take you outside*" or something like that. He said Stanley replied "*Okay, if we are going to have it out then the rest of you guys get outside*". He said he left with Janz and Stole when Blosky told them to leave. Croft stayed by the window to watch and looked in the window. He marked the position of Blosky and Stanley on a plan and placed them three or four feet apart. Gunn stood by the side of Blosky; Stanley was facing him. Something was being said that he, Croft, could not make out. There was no physical pushing, no clenched fists, and Blosky had no weapon. Stanley had no weapon at that time. It was then that Stole called and he went to join them at the car and had no further knowledge of what happened inside. He confirmed Blosky falling out through the door. He stated that earlier in the evening Blosky had had some Valium and the four polished off a 26-oz bottle of Scotch. He stated *it was Blosky who first suggested that they go and see Stanley after leaving Blosky's home*; the whole five "*were going to have a little talk with Stanley*". He said Blosky had heard about the threats and wanted to go and confirm the threats. Blosky said "*there might be a fight*". *He thought there would be. Croft went there looking for a fight.* He said Stanley said "If we are going to have it out, you guys have to leave". He heard Debbie screaming "You guys get out of here". He left and did not care whether she screamed or not.

. . . .

Stanley testified he said he was 20 years of age at the time. He lived with Debbie in a common law relationship. He knew Gunn who was a friend of one month's standing. He knew Stole. He did not know Blosky but had seen him about the town.

He had heard of the rip-off of his common law wife. He had found out who had done the job and he named Stole, Stole's girlfriend, Janz and Blosky. He described the incident at the home on the day charged and he first recalled them all in the home. He said he was high on Valium. Gunn and Blosky entered the bedroom. Debbie was with him in that room. *She got very upset and started screaming to them "to get out of the house".* He put on a shirt, took a knife off the rack and put it in his pants. He identified the knife.

. . . .

He described the incident as follows. He stabbed and Blosky opened the door and stumbled out. He was questioned about and admitted he made a statement in the beer parlour about a week before that he would blow off Blosky's knee-caps. He said he made the statement out of spite and it was the only time he mentioned that. *He was scared.* He did *not own a gun and had no weapon other than a knife. The phone was not working.*

. . . .

The issues to be left to the jury were discussed in the absence of the jury by the Court with counsel. Provocation, self-defence and defence of dwelling were dealt with as issues to be left to the jury for assessment. There was no evidence to support directions for a defence of provocation. There was, however, ample and abundant evidence to support a strong theory of self defence and of a defence of one's home or real property.

The fundamental picture established by the evidence was that of a bunch of five drunken goons going to a private dwelling of Stanley and Debbie, seeking a fight with Stanley and acting as a bunch of degenerate characters, virtually breaking into the premises and refusing to leave when asked to and forcing a fight upon Stanley in the most disgraceful circumstances.

Ever since *Semaynes Case* (1605), 5 Co. Rep. 91a, at p. 91b, 77 E.R. 194, it was said: "That the house of every one is to him as his (a) castle and fortress, as well for his defence against injury and violence as for his repose. . . ."

That is something that people who live in our country have been told to understand is the law of our land. The precept that a man's home is his castle is as true today as it was then.

Stanley and Debbie on the date charged were in lawful possession of their home when the bunch of five either knocked at the door or forcibly entered or were in the home as Stanley recalled and refused to leave when screamed at by Debbie, quite contemptuous of her rights and refusing to leave until Blosky told them to do so.

What is the state of the law dealing with self defence and the defence of property in such circumstances?

A number of sections in the *Criminal Code* come into play depending upon the view of the jury upon assessment of the evidence and proper judicial instruction. There is in this case not much contradiction in the evidence.

Section 34 deals with the rights of a person to repel force by force by way of self-defence and the extent of his justification to do so.

. . . .

Section 37 is relevant and states:

> 37(1) Every one is justified in using force to defend himself or any one under his protection from assault if he uses no more force than is necessary to prevent the assault or the repetition of it.
>
> (2) Nothing in this section shall be deemed to justify the wilful infliction of any hurt or mischief that is excessive, having regard to the nature of the assault that the force used was intended to prevent.

The foregoing sections are relevant to and have application upon the facts of this case viewed in the totality of the evidence and required careful directions: see *Wu v. The King* (1934), 62 C.C.C.90, [1934] 4 D.L.R. 459, [1934] S.C.R. 609.

Another two sections of the *Code* dealing with defence of a dwelling were applicable. Section 40 reads as follows:

> **40.** Every one who is in peaceable possession of a dwelling-house, and everyone lawfully assisting him or acting under his authority, is justified in using as much force as is necessary to prevent any person from forcibly breaking into or forcibly entering the dwelling-house without lawful authority.

Section 41 states:

> **41**(1) Every one who is in peaceable possession of a dwelling-house or real property and every one lawfully assisting him or acting under his authority is justified in using force to prevent any person from trespassing on the dwelling-house or real property, or to remove a trespasser therefrom, if he uses no more force than is necessary.
>
> (2) A trespasser who resists an attempt by a person who is in peaceable possession of a dwelling-house or real property or a person lawfully assisting him or acting under his authority to prevent his entry or to remove him, shall be deemed to commit an assault without justification or provocation.

. . . .

Section 34 applied, as here Blosky was committing a deemed unprovoked assault under the provisions of s. 41(2). So it was then justifiable for Stanley both for his self-defence and in the defence of his home to repel force by force, if the force used was not intended to cause death or grievous bodily harm and was no more than was necessary for Stanley's defence of himself and of Debbie, a person under his protection, or to remove Blosky, a trespasser, from his home.

Under s-s. (2) of s. 34 Stanley was justified in causing the death of or grievous bodily harm to Blosky by repelling Blosky's assault if the evidence disclosed that Stanley reasonably apprehended that his death might be caused or that he might suffer grievous bodily harm from the violence with which Blosky and the others originated the assault and the method that Blosky and the others pursued their purpose and if Stanley believed on reasonable and probable grounds, even though he was mistaken in that belief, that he could not otherwise preserve himself or Debbie from death and/or grievous bodily harm. The knife in Stanley's hands caused the death of Blosky. The question then presenting itself for solution by the jury was: did Stanley cause Blosky's death reasonably fearing death or grievous bodily harm to himself and/or Debbie from the violence which originally characterized Blosky's assault and with which he, Blosky, pursued that assault and did Stanley reasonably believe on reasonable grounds that he could not otherwise preserve himself and/or Debbie from death or grievous bodily harm.

What then were the pertinent facts proven in evidence which might satisfy the justification mentioned in s.s. (2) of s. 34. I list the following facts:

(a) Stanley and Debbie knew that their home or fortress was invaded by five drunken goons in a manner which could only be intended to terrorize both as to their safety. Neither one upon the evidence had any knowledge as to whether or not Blosky or anyone of the remaining four men were armed or how far they go in pursuing their assault. One thing appears to be certain. They must have known that the situation was dangerous in the extreme, and
(b) both knew that none of the five invaders had left the house when Debbie ordered them to do so and all were contemptuous of her rights and the right of Stanley in their home and according to Croft they did not care if Debbie screamed or yelled. They knew too that it was only after Blosky said "Everything is cool man, you can split" that three of the invaders left the room.
(c) they knew they were captives not masters of their castle or fortress; Stanley, when he picked up the knife knew he was facing five men who had invaded his home with the express purpose of doing him battle. He knew too that the odds were overwhelming, and
(d) there were no guns or weapons available in the house and the phone did not work. Stanley and Debbie knew or must have known that when Debbie was ripped off, Janz, the one who ripped her off in the company of Blosky and others, was one of the trespassers who were there. It will be remembered that it was Janz who pulled the knife on that occasion and said "If you come back here or if your old man ever comes back he will get this" pointing to a knife. Blosky also was there on that occasion, and
(e) both knew that the only avenue of escape was effectively blocked.

This was the picture painted by the uncontradicted evidence led at trial.

The law of necessity gave Stanley the right to protect himself or Debbie from death or grievous bodily harm even if Blosky had to be killed.

The law provides favourably for a person such as Stanley who is assaulted if he, in the agony of the occasion, reasonably but mistakenly believes that he must kill in order to save himself from death or grievous bodily harm.

The law does not expect one in such circumstances to weigh with too much nicety the force that might be necessary to repel the attack and too, the law does not expect one to wait until he is struck before he strikes back. If he does so it may well be that it will be too late for him to retaliate in order to preserve himself.

. . . .

The law of self-defence is founded upon the right of one to survive if attacked and is a paramount law subject only to the limitation set forth in the sections of the *Criminal Code* that I have mentioned and considered.

It is pertinent in my judgment to consider the intent which the evidence may show directly and inferentially accompanied Stanley's act in dealing the fatal blow.

Gunn said that after the stabbing he took off his sweater and challenged Stanley to fight. *He said that Stanley did not want to fight.* Stanley did not know that Blosky was fatally wounded.

Shortly thereafter, Gunn suggested that they all leave and go to his home because Blosky would come back with guns. He, too, had no idea that Blosky had suffered a fatal wound. He rather believed that Blosky would be on his way back with guns in order to finish them off. They went to Gunn's home where Gunn immediately took out his rifle and ran from window to window in his dwelling to see if Blosky or the others were coming back for revenge. Debbie, before she and Stanley left Gunn's home to go and see the police, suggested to Stanley that she would take the "rap" because "in no way did we think he was dead or anything like this".

Stanley said he did not want to fight. He said that immediately before he stabbed Blosky the latter took a step towards him and it was then that he stabbed him. Debbie confirmed this.

. . . .

If a jury in such circumstances would come to the conclusion that Stanley intended out of revenge to kill Blosky in circumstances amounting to murder, that in my judgment would amount to a verdict that would be set aside on the grounds that the evidence was of too dubious a nature to support such a conviction and would be considered as unreasonable or unsupported by the evidence.

The appeal was not taken under s. 613(1)(a) but that section becomes a powerful consideration on the facts of this case in deciding whether or not the indictment to follow on the new trial should be one of manslaughter rather than murder if justice requires.

. . . .

The appeal must be allowed as I have said and the conviction must be quashed and a new trial directed. I would further direct that under the provisions of s. 613(8) that the new trial should be on an indictment for manslaughter only and not murder and that the indictment be amended accordingly.

[MacLEAN and McINTYRE agreed with BRANCA.]

*Appeal allowed;*
*New trial ordered on a charge of manslaughter.*

## R. v. Born With a Tooth
(1992), 76 C.C.C. (3d) 169 (Alta. C.A.)

Appeal by the accused from his conviction on charges of possession of a weapon for purpose dangerous to the public peace, pointing a firearm, obstruction of police, assault police and use of a firearm while committing an offence.

BY THE COURT: — This is an appeal from conviction by a jury on seven of eight counts relating to an incident on September 7, 1990. The accused was found guilty of possession of a rifle for a purpose dangerous to the public peace, pointing a rifle at Constable Raymond Gaultier, obstruction of Constable Gaultier in the execution of his duty, obstruction of Constable Brian McKenna in the execution of his duty, assault of Constable Gaultier, use of a rifle while committing an assault, and use of a rifle while obstructing a peace officer.

The grounds of appeal alleged include the failure of the trial judge to put the defence theory fairly to the jury; refusal by the trial judge to admit evidence relevant to the defence theory; abuse or intimidation of defence counsel and defence witnesses, and failure to order a stay on at least some counts on invocation of the rule in *R. v. Kienapple* (1974), 15 C.C.C (2d) 524, 44 D.L.R. (3d) 351, [1975] 1 S.C.R. 729.

We shall, for the reasons now offered, order a new trial for failure to admit relevant evidence. In the result, it is not necessary to comment on all the grounds, although, as counsel observed during argument, there is considerable overlap among them.

Because of our decision, we shall avoid unnecessary discussion of the evidence of the case. Some factual background, however, is needed to explain the relevancy issues. What follows is, as far as it goes, not in dispute.

The incident occurred on the banks of the Oldman river where it flows through the Peigan Indian reserve, which the band members call the Peigan nation. The Peigan long ago surrendered a narrow strip of land alongside the river, and Alberta now has title to it under the *Land Titles Act*, R.S.A. 1980, c. L-5. This parcel, with other parcels, has been referred to as the "right of way". Many years ago, the river-bank included in the right of way was built up to form a dyke, or berm, and a weir and diversion canal were built, all as part of the irrigation system in that area. The Peigan later challenged the validity of the original surrender in a suit, which apparently the parties settled on June 11, 1981. The true meaning of the settlement agreement has, more recently, become a new matter of dispute between the Peigan (or perhaps more accurately some Peigan) and Alberta.

One term of the settlement agreement commits the Peigan to do what is needed to gain for Alberta a ministerial permit under the *Indian Act*, R.S.C. 1985, c. I-5, to enter the right of way to make dykes and other works, and to maintain and repair these works. On April 20, 1981, and again on June 2, 1981, the band council had resolved to request such a permit, and, also on June 11, the Minister of Indian Affairs issued a permit that authorized Alberta to ". . . enter upon and use . . ." the right of way (A.B., p. 708).

Sometime in 1990, at least by August 2nd, the accused and other Peigan, together with some well-wishers, made camp on Peigan lands about 200 feet from the dyke and not on the right of way. Save for the camp and the irrigation works, the area was not otherwise habited or developed. On August 7th, officers from Alberta Environment noted a hole in the dyke. The effect of that was to divert the water into an old river channel instead of a diversion canal. On August 29th, Alberta sought and received an injunction in Queen's Bench against interference, among other things, with

> . . . access to the . . . Right-of-Way by Her Majesty, her servants, employees . . . for the purpose of restoring . . . damage . . . and . . . operating and maintaining the Headworks System . . .

On August 29th, an officer of the R.C.M.P. attended at the Peigan camp to serve the injunction. The accused was not present, but others were served. The Assistant Deputy Minister for the Environment testified that he overflew the site regularly and that, between August 30th and September 7th, he saw the hole in the dyke grow larger. That witness then resolved to take workers to the site to make repairs, and requested the assistance of the R.C.M.P.

On September 7th, at 9:00 a.m., some of these workers, accompanied by police officers, moved across the reserve toward the right of way. About 10 people, including the accused, awaited them on the dyke. They called the new arrivals trespassers, and threw rocks. When they closed to a short distance, the accused raised his rifle and shot it into the air at least twice. (Some witnesses also said that the accused pointed the rifle at officers. This was challenged. The jury convicted on the charge of pointing it at one officer, and acquitted on the charge of pointing it at the other).

Just before her opening statement, counsel for the accused told the presiding judge (A.B., p. 372) that she relied upon the defence offered by s. 41(1) of the *Criminal Code*, which provides

> 41(1) Every one who is in peaceable possession of a dwelling-house or real property ... is justified in using force to prevent any person from trespassing on the dwelling-house or real property, or to remove a trespasser therefrom, if he uses no more force than is necessary.

The theory of the defence, as finally explained to us at the oral hearing of this appeal, was the following:

— The Peigan, including the accused, had been in actual possession of the right of way for some time prior to September 7th. Moreover, this occupation was peaceable because it had in fact not been challenged by Alberta.
— Alberta's failure to give reasonable notice made it a trespasser. It had *no* right of exclusive possession. Under the settlement agreement, it held only a licence to work the right of way. Even that right must be exercised reasonably, and in the circumstances of this case that meant, notwithstanding the injunction, on notice to the occupants.
— In any event, the R.C.M.P. did not enter the right of way merely to keep the peace or enforce the injunction; their real purpose was to attack and eject the occupants. This illegal purpose they demonstrated before entry by a huge show of force. They were thus trespassers.
— In all these circumstances, the action of the accused was reasonable force to prevent a trespass or eject a trespasser. The accused did not obstruct Alberta in a lawful entry to effect repairs, and did not act in breach of the injunction.

In our view, this defence should have been put to the jury if any support for it existed in the evidence, and if it is sound in law. It is probably correct to say that, at the close of the trial, the essential evidentiary base was absent. But we are bound to say that this may have been because of some exclusionary rulings.

The learned trial judge excluded evidence from the defence about what the Peigan were doing at the right of way prior to September 7th. Evidence of their activity could be relevant because it would be evidence of use and occupation, and might also be evidence of peaceable possession. It seems that at least some of this activity was religious and ceremonial in nature, and Ms. Gainer began by attempting to lead evidence about Peigan tradition generally. She explained to us, if not the learned trial judge, that she had sought to introduce this evidence so that the jury could better understand the significance of the activity of the campers, including the accused. For this reason, it was admissible as relevant to the defence theory.

The learned trial judge gained the impression that the sole purpose of the evidence was to lay a foundation for a claim to a right, based upon Peigan laws and traditions not Canadian law, to repel Alberta if it came on the right of way. This would be tantamount to a claim of right, based on higher law, to defy the injunction. That is not a defence known to Canadian law, and a jury must be so instructed. But that does not warrant keeping the evidence out if it is admissible for other reasons.

The evidence about activity and evidence explaining the cultural significance of activity, might also have been relevant to show the state of mind of the accused. The learned trial judge also rejected this ground. Assuming that the state of mind of the accused is relevant, the defence can show evidence of surrounding circumstances from which the jury might draw an inference about the state of mind of the accused, even if the accused shall not testify: see *Lampard v. The Queen*, [1969] 3 C.C.C. 249 at pp. 255-6, 4 D.L.R. (3d) 98, [1969] S.C.R. 373. See also *R.v. Nealy* (1986), 30 C.C.C. (3d) 460 at pp. 468-9, 54 C.R. (3d) 158, 17 O.A.C. 164 (Ont. C.A.)., and the cases discussed there.

The learned trial judge also curtailed cross-examination designed to raise a doubt with the jury about the true intentions of the police. Moreover, in his charge he instructed the jury that the police had behaved reasonably. He may express his views to the jury, but he must leave relevant issues of fact for them to decide.

In general terms, the learned trial judge forbad any evidence tending to show peaceable possession by the Peigan on the ground that the title to the lands held by Alberta conclusively decided all questions of that sort. His views were later repeated to the jury....

In short, he had concluded that, as a matter of law, the accused was himself a trespasser and could not possibly invoke the defence.

With respect, and even assuming these statements of law are correct, they would curtail but not eliminate the defence theory. One question posed for the jury by the defence theory was whether Alberta by its conduct had in fact granted or suffered peaceable possession of the right of way to the Peigan. That question is not foreclosed by production of title. Nor does the title necessarily answer a second question raised by the defence theory: whether the R.C.M.P. had come on the lands for an unlawful reason, one, for example, not sanctioned by Alberta. The Crown theory was that Alberta had a right to enter to work the dyke, and to invite the police to enter to keep the peace, and both did only that. The defence theory was that at least the police entered with another and illegal intent, that their conduct as they arrived evidenced that contrary intent, and that they were trespassers. That is a question of fact that survives resolution of the title dispute.

Moreover, it is not beyond argument that the settlement agreement did not "abrogate in any way" the title of Alberta. We make no definitive ruling because not enough material is before us and because it is neither necessary nor appropriate to do so. But, assuming the agreement applies to the titled lands, it contains terms that seem to derogate title, as, for example, this term in clause 4 (A.B., p. 718):

> Both parties recognize that the Band retains control and ownership of all mines, minerals and natural resources, including wildlife under their protection upon the subject lands.

In any event, the title and title disputes do not necessarily resolve a s. 41 defence. Here, the accused admitted, at least before us, that Alberta had a right to go on the right of way to repair and maintain the dyke. It is not clear to us that the Crown position was that the Peigan, and the accused, had *no* right to be on the right of way. The Crown position, as we understand it, was that they had no peaceable possession if their claim to possession extended to any control of the access by Alberta to the irrigation works. And that limit on a claim to possession was conceded before us by the accused, as indeed he must concede in the light of the injunction order and in the light of the terms of the settlement agreement and the permit, even if they receive the interpretation most generous to him. And the jury must be so instructed. But other aspects of the title dispute can await another day.

We agree, however, with the learned trial judge that the jury must be told, as a matter of law, that no notice need have been given by Alberta to the accused about its proposed exercise of its right of entry other than the notice required by the injunction, which is, simply, actual knowledge of it. To say otherwise would be to suggest that the injunction was itself illegal, a position not available to the accused as a matter of law. If he thought the injunction was illegal, he, like other Canadians, was none the less bound to obey it until he succeeded in having it vacated. Again, however, this circumscribes but does not eliminate the defence. Indeed the defence might be available if the entry by Alberta was lawful and by the R.C.M.P. was unlawful.

It would be extremely unfair to the trial judge to speak of these or any other errors at the trial without some explanatory comment. Simply put, the defence theory we heard and here expressed was never put to him, at least not in comprehensible terms. It became quite clear early in the trial that the learned trial judge found it difficult to comprehend how the defence could be available in this case. That difficulty, and the failure of the defence counsel to articulate compelling answers to his questions, largely account for almost all grounds of appeal. Counsel was at once argumentative and vague. She asserted positions but said almost nothing to explain them. This led to repeated clashes during the remainder of the trial, to the impugned admissibility rulings, to the sharp comments by the judge, and to the complaint about disparagement of the defence in the charge. Worse, counsel defied the rulings by repeatedly leading evidence like that already excluded. By the end of the trial, the trial judge was limiting himself to the occasional protesting interjection. . . .

To avoid a repeat of the confusion at the next trial, we conclude with some general comments about the rule in s. 41. while they express our understanding of the law, we caution that not all points were fully argued before us.

The defence contains four elements. This means that, before an accused can benefit from it, the jury must have at least a doubt about all four. If a jury is convinced beyond any reasonable doubt that any one element is missing, the defence must fail. The four elements are these: the accused must be in possession of land; his possession must be *peaceable*; the victim of the assault must be a trespasser, and the force used to eject the trespasser must be reasonable in the circumstances.

As to the first, the word "possession" has here its usual meaning in criminal law: see *Beaver v. The Queen* (1957), 118 C.C.C. 129, [1957] S.C.R. 531, 26 C.R. 193. The defence will fail if the accused, in fact, has no control over the land in question: see *R. v. Spencer* (1977), 38 C.C.C. (2d) 303, 3 R.P.R. 61, [1978] 1 W.W.R. 250 (B.C.S.C.). But for possession, control need not be exclusive: see *R. v. Dillabough* (1975), 28 C.C.C. (2d) 482 (Ont. C.A.), and *Re British American Oil Co. Ltd. and Halpert* (1959), 21 D.L.R. (2d) 110, [1960] O.R. 71 (Ont. C.A). Because control is largely a matter of fact, this element includes a question of fact to be decided by the jury.

The demand that the possession be "peaceable" greatly limits the defence. That word is *not* synonymous with peaceful. It is not enough for the accused to show he kept the peace while on the land. Historically, it meant a possession that did not provoke a breach of the peace: see Stephen, *A History of the Criminal Law of England*, vol. III, pp. 13-4 (London: MacMillan and Co., 1883).

. . .

For the purpose of the *Code*, the term must mean a possession not seriously challenged by others. If it were otherwise, then every property dispute could be resolved legitimately by force. The evident object of the law is the exact opposite: the defence should be available only to those whose possession has not been seriously questioned by somebody before the incident in question. It is not necessary for us to make a definitive statement how serious and immediate must the challenge be before the defence is lost. That is a question to be decided on the precise facts of each case. We but aside, as not necessary for decision, the question whether one can invoke the defence against a trespasser totally unaware that one's possession is under challenge from some third party.

Whether a previous serious challenge existed is a question of fact for decision by the jury. But the judge often will be required to inform the jury about questions of law to assist them in that determination. The strength in law of a claim to a *right* of possession, for example, will often be determinative. But the seriousness of the challenge will turn more on the likelihood of a breach of the peace than on the strength of a legal title. This is because, as the Law Reform Commission has suggested, the key to peaceable possession is whether the possession is such, and the challenge to it is such, the situation is "unlikely to lead to violence": see Law Reform Commission of Canada, report No. 30 (1987), p. 38. . . .

The third element is that the victim of the ejectment must be a trespasser. If that person has a right to be on the land, even if the accused also has a right to be on the land, the defence is not available. This element often will require a judge to direct the jury about matters of law, because the right to be on the land is a legal consequence. But that consequence always arises as a result also of matters of fact, and they must be left to the jury.

A nice question arises if the victim has the right to go on the land for one purpose, but goes on in fact for another, unlawful, purpose. A water meter inspector has a right of entry for one limited purpose. If she in fact enters to steal the refrigerator, and an irate home owner who knows her true purpose ejects her, can the accused owner invoke s. 41 and say that the inspector was a trespasser? Some authorities seem to suggest an affirmative answer: see *R. v. Collins*, [1973] 1 Q.B. 100 (C.A.), and *R. v. Jones*, [1976] 3 All E.R. 54 [1976] 1 W.L.R. 673 (C.A.) and *R. v. Walkington*, [1979] 2 All E.R. 716. . . . But see the criticism by Glanville Williams, *Textbook of Criminal Law*, 2nd ed, pp. 847-50 (London: Stevens & Son, 1983), albeit in the context of what amounts to proof of an element of the offence of breaking and entering. This court, in *R. v. Farbridge* (1984), 15 C.C.C. (3d) 521, 42 C.R. (3d) 385, [1985] 2 W.W.R. 56, 34 Alta. L.R. (2d) 394, accepted the criticism, and took a narrower view. We held that a person who enters lawfully does not become a trespasser unless and until he does something in furtherance of his unlawful purpose. Thus, in the example given, the homeowner might not be able to eject the meter inspector until she reaches for the refrigerator, or turns away from the path to the meter. But that contradictory activity might well arise before actual entry, as when the inspector is seen coming up the front walk pushing a large refrigerator dolly.

The last requirement is that only necessary force be used. Of course, all the other facts will also bear on that. But the issue can be quite separate.

In sum, the defence is available to an accused when the jury has at least a doubt whether the accused has a measure of control over the land, whether that assertion of control has been seriously challenged, whether the challenger has a right to come on the land, and whether, objectively speaking, the force used was reasonable in the circumstances.

As regards the first two elements, and the factual content of the third element, the defence of mistake is also available. . . . An accused might, honestly but mistakenly, believe that he has a measure of control over the lands, or that his supposed control is unchallenged, or he might believe in a set of facts which, if true, makes the victim a trespasser. But honest mistake of fact appears not to be enough for the last element, because that requires that the reasonableness of the force meet an objective, not just a subjective, test: see *R. v. Scopelliti* (1981), 63 C.C.C. (2d) 481, 34 O.R. (2d) 524 (C.A.).

Nor does honest but mistaken belief about entitlement trigger a defence. The general criminal rule, stated in s. 19 of the *Criminal Code*, R.S.C. 1985, c. C-34, is that all citizens of Canada have a duty to inform themselves correctly about the law, and failure to do so is no defence to a charge. A defence based on an error of law is not available on any of the charges before the court because none require, as a necessary element of the *mens rea*, that the accused be aware that he is interfering with the legal rights of others. In the result, the opinion of the accused about the merit of his title claim, or that of his victim, is not directly relevant to the defence.

Nor of course, does an honest opinion about the rightness of one's cause offer any justification, under Canadian criminal law, for violent acts. No doubt many criminals persuade themselves that their crime is somehow justified. But the principles of civil disobedience dissociate civil protest from other crime, and from revolution, by ready acceptance of the legal consequences of action forbidden by the state.

We allow the appeal and order a new trial. The accused shall appear at the next Queen's Bench arraignment at Fort Macleod for determination of the time and place of trial.

*Appeal allowed; new trial ordered.*

**Questions/Discussion**
1. Should there be a separate defence of property defence which is not related to a defence of person provision? The then Law Reform Commission of Canada in its Report 31, *Recodifying Criminal Law*, proposed the following:

    **3(11)** Protection of Movable Property. No one in peaceable possession of movable property is liable for using such force, not amounting to purposely causing the death of, or seriously harming, as is reasonably necessary to prevent another person from unlawfully taking it or to recover it from another person who has just unlawfully taken it.

**3(12)** Protection of Immovable Property. . . . General Rule. No one in peaceable possession of immovable property is liable for using such force, not amounting to purposely causing the death of, or seriously harming, as is reasonably necessary to prevent trespass, to remove a trespasser or to defend the property against another person taking possession of it.

Do you think that such clauses are better than the existing law. Why or why not?

**Further Reading**

- Kathol, T., "Defence of Property in the Criminal Code" (1993), 35 Criminal Law Quarterly, 453-479.
- Mewett, A., and M. Manning, *Mewett and Manning on Criminal Law*, 3rd ed. (Toronto: Butterworths, 1994).
- Stuart, D., *Canadian Criminal Law: A Treatise*, 2nd ed. (Toronto: Carswell, 1987), pp. 414-419.
- Stuart, d., and R. Delisle, *Learning Canadian Criminal Law*, 5th ed. (Toronto: Carswell, 1995).
- Verdun-Jones, S., and C. Griffiths, *Canadian Criminal Justice*, 2nd ed. (Toronto: Butterworths, 1994).

## 7.1.5 Consent

**Introduction**

Certain offences, such as assault, sexual assault, or theft, incorporate lack of consent into their very definition. Given stereotypical attitudes toward victims of sexual assault, the issue of consent or the lack of consent has been particularly important in such cases; these issues are examined in the next chapter. Generally, though, the argument as to the lack of consent in such cases is quite simply a defence that the actus reus of the crime has not been fulfilled. What becomes important in this defence, then, is what exactly has been consented to. We see this in the *Maki* case, in which one hockey player was charged for assaulting another. Technically, many sports allow for contact between players (and thus assaults) to occur; but legally the question is what is the limit of that consent? Normally, we agree to the usual types of assaults which may take place in the course of a game. When someone steps outside the usual rules, then it can be deemed that consent to such conduct is not present. A case in the Alberta Court of Appeal highlights this idea. In the course of a fist fight, one party bit off the left ear of the other party; the court said:

> We are all of the view that whatever consent was given did not extend to the infliction of injuries with the teeth.
>
> The two parties may have agreed to engage in a fist fight but the consent of neither of them went to the point where either of them consented to have the other apply his teeth in the manner which the appellant did in this contest.
>
> In our view, at the point where the complainant was attacked by the appellant using his teeth to bite the various appendages of the complainant's body, the consent ceased to be operative.[1]

The *Jobidon* decision below would further limit the notion of consenting to the normal rules within the context of so-called consensual fist fights. It quotes with approval the following passage from *Attorney-General's Reference (No. 6 of 1980)*, [1981] 2 All E.R. 1057 (C.A.):

---

[1] *R. v. Loonskin*, quoted in *the Lawyers Weekly*, February 9, 1990.

Where two persons fight (otherwise than in the course of sport) in a public place can it be a defence for one of those persons to a charge of assault arising out of the fight that the other consented to fight? . . .

The answer to this question, in our judgment, is that it is not in the public interest that people should try to cause or should cause each other actual bodily harm for no good reason. Minor struggles are another matter. So, in our judgment, it is immaterial whether the act occurs in private or in public; it is an assault if actual bodily harm is intended and/or caused. This means that most fights will be unlawful regardless of consent.

## Regina v. Maki
### (1970), 1 C.C.C. (2d) 333 (Ont. Prov. Ct.)

CARTER, PROV. CT. J.: — Mr. Maki is charged under s. 231(2) of the *Criminal Code*: assault causing bodily harm. The case is basically a simple one factually but complicated to some extent in that the alleged assault occurred during the playing of a National Hockey League exhibition game and that there has not been such a prosecution in the past. The game was between the St. Louis Blues and the Boston Bruins, played at the Ottawa Civic Centre in the City of Ottawa on September 21, 1969.

I have considered the facts carefully and, although, as would be expected in such a fast moving situation, there are some inconsistencies in the evidence, the occurrence appears to have taken place in the following manner.

I might say in reviewing the facts I have [given] a great deal of weight to the evidence of the referee Mr. Bodenistel and of course to the evidence of Mr. Maki himself. I found both to be credible witnesses, as in fact were all the witnesses in the case.

At about the 11-minute mark of the first period St. Louis had shot the puck into the Boston zone and behind and to the left of the Boston net. Mr. Maki and Mr. Green followed the puck into the area and collided at this point. Mr. Green pushed or punched Mr. Maki in the face with his glove and, it would appear, caused some injury to his mouth. At this point the referee signalled a delayed penalty for an infraction by raising his arm and play continued. The two players, it would appear, broke apart at this juncture with Mr. Maki skating to the area in front of the Boston net and the puck was moved into the centre ice area. There is some evidence of spearing by Maki against Green, but this fact is in some considerable doubt. There is evidence that Mr. Maki was somewhat dazed as a result of the incident behind the net. This is borne out by evidence given by Mr. Maki and by Mr. Larkin.

At this point the two players came together again at some point in front of the Boston net, sticks swinging, and as a result Mr. Green's unfortunate injury occurred at this time. There is no doubt that Mr. Green swung at Mr. Maki first and struck him on the neck or shoulders. Mr. Maki states that Mr. Green then made another move or motion towards him with his stick and that Mr. Green's stick was above his shoulders and held by both hands. Mr. Maki then swung at Mr. Green and his stick hit Mr. Green's stick and glanced from there to the side of Mr. Green's head causing the injuries in question. It seems clear from the photographs filed that this was the case and that if Mr. Green's stick had not been raised as it was, the blow would probably have landed on Green's shoulder. Most witnesses testified that the blow struck was not, as one witness testified, a baseball-type swing. These are the main facts as I find them. There were other motions or movements by the players during this period, but these are the main point that the fact that Mr. Green indicated that he wanted no prosecution of Mr. Maki is of little or no interest in this case. The fact that he did not testify either for the Crown or defence is somewhat unusual, but I place no weight on that fact as well.

I will deal first with the law upon which I have based my decision — that is, self-defence, as put forward by defence counsel.

This whole affair took place in a matter of two to five seconds in a game noted for its speed and bodily contact. We have evidence to indicate that Mr. Green is a very aggressive, hard-hitting player, and Maki of course is fully aware of this.

Section 34 of the *Criminal Code* reads as follows:

**34**(1) Every one who is unlawfully assaulted without having provoked the assault is justified in repelling force by force if the force he uses is no more than is necessary to enable him to defend himself.
(2) Every one who is unlawfully assaulted and who causes death or grievous bodily harm in repelling the assault is justified if
(a) he causes it under reasonable apprehension of death or grievous bodily harm from the violence with which the assault was originally made or with which the assailant pursues his purposes, and
(b) he believes, on reasonable and probable grounds, that he cannot otherwise preserve himself from death or grievous bodily harm.

The law in this regard briefly stated therefor is that on a charge of this sort there must be an acquittal if the Court is left in any doubt as to whether the accused was acting in self-defence, that is where self-defence is raised as a defence. The Court must also consider the reasonableness of the force used under the circumstances and the state of mind of the accused at the time in question.

Mr. Maki in his evidence states, and I am paraphrasing to some extent: "I was trying to protect myself"; "I didn't aim at any particular part of his body"; "I swung in desperation to protect myself". And in cross-examination he stated again that he was protecting himself: "trying to ward off Green"; "I was not angry at Green I was just protecting myself"; "I expected he would still come after me if I turned away"; "swung in desperation"; "I didn't know I would cause him serious injury", and so on. A number of witnesses including the referee could not assess clearly the severity of the blow. The referee also indicated in his evidence that Maki did not seem angry or to have lost his temper. He was the man who was watching the whole affair much more closely than anybody else. Mr. Finn, one of the linesmen, stated that he had no problem separating Maki from the fight area and that Maki did not appear to want to get back at Mr. Green.

It is to be emphasized that the paramount obligation is upon the Crown to have proved the guilt of the accused beyond all reasonable doubt. It is also important to note as in *R. v. Ogal*, 50 C.C.C. 71, [1928] 3 D.L.R. 676, 23 Alta. L.R. 511, cited by defence counsel, that where the means of defence used is not disproportionate to the severity of the assault a plea of self-defence is valid, although the defender, in this case Maki, fails to measure with nicety the degree of force necessary to ward off the attack and inflicts serious injury thereby. Green was the aggressor up to the point of Maki's blow to Green.

Can I, considering the fact situation as I have found it to be, find beyond any reasonable doubt that Maki intended to injure Green; that Maki should not have been under any reasonable apprehension of bodily harm, and that Maki used excessive force under the circumstances? I think not — I must have a doubt in my mind on all three points and the charge is dismissed.

I feel, however, that although it does not form part of my reasons for acquittal, I must comment on the merit of some of the Crown Attorney's submissions as to the defence of consent put forward by defence counsel. If the fact situation in this case had been such that no doubt was raised in my mind regarding self-defence, I would not have hesitated to convict the accused. The defence of consent would in my opinion have failed. Although no criminal charges have been laid in the past pertaining to athletic events in this country, I can see no reason why they could not be in the future where the circumstances warrant and the relevant authorities deem it advisable to do so. No sports league, no matter how well organized or self-policed it may be, should thereby render the players int hat league immune from criminal prosecution. I agree with Mr. Cassells when he states that consent to bodily injury as a defence to criminal prosecution has its limitations. I refer to the words of Stephen J., in *R. v. Coney et al.* (1882), 8 Q.B.D. 534 at p. 549, when he states:

> In cases where life and limb are exposed to no serious danger in the common course of things, I think that consent is a defence to a charge of assault, even when considerable force is used, as, for instance, in cases of wrestling, single-stick, sparring with gloves, football, and the like; but in all cases the question whether consent does or does not take from the application or force to another, its illegal character, is a question of degree depending upon circumstances.

Thus all players, when they step onto a playing field or ice surface, assume certain risk and hazards of the sport, and in most cases the defence of consent as set out in s. 230 of the *Criminal Code* would be applicable. But as stated above there is a question of degree involved, and no athlete should be presumed to accept malicious, unprovoked or overly violent attack. Bastin, J., states it this way in *Agar v. Canning* (1965), 54 W.W.R. 302 at p. 304; affirmed 55 W.W.R. 384:

> But a little reflection will establish that some limit must be placed on a player's immunity from liability. Each case must be decided on its own facts so it is difficult, if not impossible, to decide how the line is to be drawn in every circumstance. But injuries inflicted in circumstances which show a definite resolve to cause serious injury to another, even when there is provocation and in the heat of the game, should not fall within the scope of the implied consent.

The adoption of such principals in the future world, I feel certain, be a benefit to the players, of course, to the general public peace and, in particular, to young aspiring athletes who look to the professionals for guidance and example.

I would like at this point to thank counsel for the excellent manner in which the case was presented. Their arguments were extremely helpful to me and may form guide-lines in the future.

*Charge dismissed.*

## Regina v. Jobidon
(1988), 45 C.C.C. (3d) 177 (Ont. C.A.).

Appeal by the Crown from a judgment of Campbell J., 36 C.C.C. (3d) 340, 59 C.R. (3d) 203, acquitting the accused on a charge of manslaughter.

The judgment of the court was delivered by

ZUBER J.A.: — Jules Jobidon was tried by Mr. Justice Campbell sitting without a jury on a charge that he "did unlawfully kill Rodney Haggard and thereby did commit manslaughter, contrary to the Criminal Code of Canada". The learned trial judge found the respondent not guilty. The Crown now appeals on a question of law alone and asks that this court set aside the acquittal and convict the respondent. Alternatively, the Crown seeks a new trial.

### FACTS

On September 18, 1986, Rodney Haggart, who was then 25 years old, went with a group of friends to the Woodland Hotel near Sudbury, Ontario. At some point there was a conversation between Rodney Haggart, his brother Clinton Haggart and a friend named Glen Krolick concerning the fact that about a week earlier Krolick had been "sucker-punched" in the face. Rodney Haggart suspected that one or more of the Jobidon brothers had been involved in this previous incident relating to Krolick. The Haggart party, which had been drinking in a downstairs room at the Woodland Hotel, then moved upstairs to a bar where Jules Jobidon and his brother Raymond were sitting at separate tables.

Some time between 12:15 and 12:30 a.m. Rodney Haggart approached Jules Jobidon and asked him if his name was Jobidon. Shortly thereafter Haggart punched Jobidon in the face and a fight commenced. Each punched the other a few times but Haggart appears to have emerged the winner. The owner of the hotel separated them and told Jules Jobidon and his brother to leave the hotel. Jobidon thought it was unfair that he should be obliged to leave. He and Haggart exchanged angry words stating that "it was not over". It appeared to be understood that they would continue the fight later.

The respondent and his brother went outside where they waited. The respondent testified that he was waiting for a ride; the learned trial judge found that he was also waiting to renew the fight if the opportunity arose.

Meanwhile, the Haggart party finished their drinks, collected their jackets and about 15 minutes after the end of the first fight walked out of the front door of the hotel. At this time the Jobidon brothers were still standing about 10 to 20 feet away from the front door. Jules Jobidon and Rodney Haggart exchanged angry words and a crowd gathered. The learned trial judge found as a fact that the two of them exchanged mutual invitations to fight and that then Jobidon rushed at Haggart, struck him on the head with his fist with great force knocking Haggart unconscious onto the hood of a car. Jobidon in the next few seconds struck the unconscious Haggart a further four to six times on the head. A melee erupted around Jobidon and Haggart and Jobidon then retreated. Haggart slid off the car to the ground. He was taken to the hospital but did not regain consciousness and died the next day. The cause of death was one or more of the severe blows to the head.

With respect to the events surrounding the second fight the trial judge found as a fact that Haggart and Jobidon consented to a fair fist fight, that it was a fight in anger, and that physical injury was intended. The trial judge further found that Jobidon did not intentionally exceed that consent and that he struck the last blows under a reasonable but mistaken apprehension that Haggart was still capable of returning the fight and was trying to do so.

## THE JUDGMENT

It was the Crown's case that Jobidon assaulted Haggart causing his death and thereby committed manslaughter. The defence position was that the fight was consensual and therefore the blows struck in the course of the fight could not be an assault and therefore the acts of Jobidon were not unlawful. In this context consent is not an affirmative defence. It is said on behalf of Jobidon that the Crown failed to prove a necessary element of its case, *i.e.*, the absence of consent.

Mr. Justice Campbell engaged in an extensive review of the law referring to both English and Canadian authorities. He concluded that he was bound by a decision of this court in *R. v. Dix* (1972), 10 C.C.C. (2d) 324 (Ont. C.A.), and acquitted the respondent. It is clear from his reasons that the learned trial judge experienced a degree of discomfort in arriving at this result. The issue before this court is the correctness of the result in this case and in wider terms the correctness of the decision in *R. v. Dix*.

## THE LAW

As mentioned earlier it is an essential part of the Crown's case that the respondent was guilty of assault. Section 24(1) and (2) of the *Criminal Code* provide as follows:

**244**(1) A person commits an assault when
(a) without the consent of another person, he applies force intentionally to that other person, directly or indirectly;
(b) he attempts or threatens, by an act or gesture, to apply force to another person, if he has, or causes that other person toe believe upon reasonable grounds that he has, present ability to effect his purpose; or
(c) while openly wearing or carrying a weapon or an imitation thereof, he accosts or impedes another person or begs.

(2) This section applies to all forms of assault, including sexual assault, sexual assault with a weapon, threats to a third party or causing bodily harm and aggravated sexual assault.

Read literally and divorced from the rest of the *Criminal Code*, this section would appear to make the absence of consent a necessary element in establishing the guilt of a person charged with any form of assault.

The *Criminal Code* itself however, contains limitations on the ability of victims to consent to the use of force upon themselves. No person can consent to have death inflicted upon him (s. 14): se also s. 224 (counselling or aiding suicide), and s. 81 which prohibits prize fighting. Thus it will be seen that even within the *Criminal Code* there are certain limits placed on the concept of consent in s. 244.

There is, however, another basis upon which it may be said that the concept of consent in s. 244 is limited. The predecessor of s. 244 appeared in the *Criminal Code*, 1892, c. 29, in the following terms:

**258.** An assault is the act of intentionally applying force to the person of another directly or indirectly, or attempting or threatening, by any act or gesture, to apply force to the person of another, if the person making the threat has, or causes the other to believe, upon reasonable grounds, that he has present ability to effect his purpose, and it either case, without the consent of the other or with such consent if it is obtained by fraud.

Section 258 was, of course, not a statutory invention but represented a codification of what had been the common law for centuries. It would therefore be instructive to determine the breadth of the concept of consent within the common law crime of assault.

. . . .

## Canadian Cases

Early Canadian cases found little difficulty with the notion that the concept of consent with respect to assault should be limited even though the definition of assault was now embedded in the *Criminal Code*.

. . . .

However, in the 1970's a series of cases were decided which departed from the long-standing view of the limited extent to which a victim could consent to the application of force. In June, 1972, the New Brunswick Court of Appeal dealt with the case of *R. v. MacTavish* (1972), 8 C.C.C. (2d) 206, 20 C.R.N.S. 235, 4 N.B.R. (2d) 876 (N.B.C.A.). In that case MacTavish was charged with assault causing bodily harm to Douglas Mitchell. The defence was that the force complained of was applied in a fair fight. The trial judge held that consent was irrelevant and convicted MacTavish of common assault. The New Brunswick Court of Appeal dismissed the appeal on the ground that the force applied exceeded the fair fight agreed upon. On the appeal, the Crown took the position that consent could not justify the conduct of MacTavish, but in view of the fact that the conduct exceeded the ambit of the consent this last issue was directly addressed.

In November, 1972, the so-called fair fight doctrine came before the Ontario Court of Appeal in *R. v. Dix, supra*. Dix had been convicted of assault causing bodily harm. His defence at trial was that he caused the bodily harm in the course of a fair fight. Gale C.J.O., speaking for the court in an oral judgment, said at pp. 325-6:

> In essence, then, the Crown failed to prove the necessary element of lack of consent to that which was done. The two parties consented to a fight and the fight was had in a normal manner, if I might use that phrase. That is not the same situation as in *R. v. MacTavish* (1972), 8 C.C.C. (2d) 206, 20 C.R.N.S. 235, 4 N.B.R. (2d) 876, where the combatants expressly, or impliedly agreed to a fair fight and the accused did not fight fairly.

If it could be said that the decision in *MacTavish* had set the stage, the *Dix* case accepted the proposition that the Crown must prove the absence of consent even in cases where bodily harm was caused. The doctrine thus enunciated in *Dix* was approved by the Quebec Court of Appeal in *R. v. Abraham* (1974), 30 C.C.C. (2d) 332, 26 C.R.N.S. 390 (Que. C.A.)., and reached a high-water mark in *R. v. Setrum* (1976), 32 C.C.C. (2d) 109 (Sask. C.A.). In *Setrum*, the Saskatchewan Court of Appeal held that the absence of consent was a necessary element of the Crown's case even where the force administered resulted in death.

Thus, in a space of four years the law with respect to assault and the consensual fight had undergone a remarkable change. However, it appears that the change was neither complete nor lasting. Even before the decision in *Setrum*, doubt was cast upon the law as expounded in *Dix*. In *R. v. Squire* (1975), 26 C.C.C. (2d) 219, 10 O.R. (2d) 40, 31 C.R.N.S. 314 (Ont. C.A.), Martin J.A., speaking for this court, said at p. 230:

> The mere fact that the deceased and the appellant fought by mutual consent (if such be the case) did not, of itself, make subsequent blows struck by either of them lawful.
> In *R. v. Donovan* (1934), 25 Cr. App. R. 1, Swift, J., speaking for the Court of Criminal Appeal, said at p. 10:
>> "as a general rule, although it is a rule to which there are well-established exceptions, it is an unlawful act to beat another person with such a degree of violence that the infliction of bodily harm is a probable consequence, and when such an act is proved, consent is immaterial."
>
> Where two persons engage in a fight in anger by mutual consent the blows struck by each constitute an assault on the other, unless justifiable self-defence in accordance with the provisions of the *Code*: see *Russell on Crime*, 12th ed. (1964), vol. 1, p. 679; *R. v. Coney et al.* (1882), 15 Cox C.C. 46, *per* Cave, J., at pp. 49-50, *per* Hawkins, J., at pp. 60-1: *R. v. Knock* (1877), 14 Cox C.C. 1.

In *R. v. Kusyj* (1983), 51 A.R. 243, [1984] N.W.T.R. 152 (N.W.T.S.C.). Marshall J. of the Northwest Territories Supreme Court refused to follow *Dix* and *Setrum*.

The retreat from the rule in *Dix* continued when the Ontario Court of Appeal in *R. v. Charlebois*, released December 11, 1986, held that Charlebois was guilty of aggravated assault despite the fact that the victim had consented to being shot with a .22 calibre rifle.

. . . .

It now falls to this court to either revive (at least in this province) the somewhat dubious authority of the *Dix* case or conclude that it was wrongly decided.

In my respectful view, the concept of consent as it appears in s. 244 of the *Criminal Code* should be construed subject to the same limitations as are imposed by the common law. There are good reasons for so doing. First, this interpretation conforms with the traditional understanding of the law which existed for a very long time prior to 1972. Secondly, this interpretation is in accord with the over-all purpose of the *Criminal Code*, *i.e.*, the protection of the public and keeping the peace. Lastly, this interpretation accords with sound policy. The so-called consents to fight are often more apparent than real and are obtained in an atmosphere where reason, good sense and even sobriety are absent. In a case such as the one at hand it seems scarcely necessary to mention that often the results are very serious. To interpret the *Criminal Code* otherwise would continue to legitimize the uncivilized brawling which, because of *Dix*, is not the subject of the criminal sanction.

I conclude therefore that *R. v. Dix, supra*, was wrongly decided and that consent as used in s. 244 of the *Criminal Code* should be interpreted subject to the same limitations as are expressed in *Attorney-General's Reference (No. 6 of 1980), supra*.

In this case, Jobidon intended to cause bodily harm and in fact caused death. In view of my conclusions with respect to the law the Crown in this case was not obliged to prove the absence of consent. As a result, and in the light of the findings of fact by the trial judge, there is left no defence to the charge in this case. Leave to appeal is granted, the appeal is allowed, and the verdict of acquittal is set aside. A verdict of guilty of manslaughter will be entered in its place. The matter is remitted to Mr. Justice Campbell for sentence. A warrant will issue at the discretion of the Crown.

*Appeal allowed; conviction entered.*

**Note**: This decision of the Court of Appeal was upheld by the Supreme Court of Canada; see *Jobidon v. The Queen* (1991), 66 C.C.C. (3d) 454 (S.C.C.).

**Questions/Discussion**
1. Do you agree with the results in *Jobidon*? Why shouldn't people be able to agree to fight each other? What is special about hockey or other types of contact sports where assaults within the rules of the game are permitted? Is the court in *Jobidon* trying to accomplish another purpose (of stopping street fights) by subverting the defence of consent; in other words if we agree that lack of consent is an element of assault, then why *should* the courts ignore the existence of consent in many non-sports fights while deeming it available in sports?
2. If we allow the defence in fist fights, then what are the limits to "normal" fist fights? Does it depend upon who you are and your experience in such situations? Does it depend upon the location of the fight (for example, the sidewalk versus a private dwelling, or perhaps even "good" versus "bad" parts of town?
3. In the situation of domestic violence, stereotypical attitudes give rise to questions such as "why didn't the woman leave" and thus implicitly support the notion that she consented to some extent. Such attitudes ignore, of course, the lack of real choices in the woman's life. Obviously, such a defence could not be used explicitly by the violent husband or boyfriend in court, but such an attitude can contribute to the reluctance on the part of police agents, prosecutors, and the courts to get involved and to treat such assaults as real crimes.

**Further Reading**
- Bryant, A., "Consent and Constructive Manslaughter" (1989), 67 C.R. (3d) 193.
- Doherty, D. and D. Stuart, "Jobidon: Consensual Combat and the Crime of Manslaughter — Two Views:" (1987), 59 C.R. (3d) 216.
- Stuart, D., *Canadian Criminal Law: A Treatise,* 2nd ed. (Toronto: Carswell, 1987), pp. 469-480.
- Stuart D., and R. Delisle, *Learning Canadian Criminal Law*, 5th ed (Toronto: Carswell, 1995).

## 7.2 ABSENCE OF INTENT OR KNOWLEDGE

### 7.2.1 Mistake of Fact

**Introduction**
The common law defence of mistake of fact is available in those cases where the requisite mens rea of the crime has not been fulfilled. For example, if you take an umbrella believing it to be yours, then you lack the requisite intent to steal. In cases such as this, criminal liability will not attach given that you believed in a set of circumstances which, if true, would have made your acts innocent. The problem is what type of mistake of fact will relieve you of criminal responsibility? While the first case, *Williams*, gives an example of the successful use of the defence, the problem presented in *Kundeus* is that although the belief or knowledge of the

accused was not entirely innocent, his intent was *not* the intent to do the offence with which he was charged. In the case, the court seems to say that any wrongful intent will suffice, but this "transfer of intent", particularly involving the transfer of intent to do a less serious crime to the actus reus of a more serious crime, seems problematic and is given no limitations. Ordinarily, offences are legally defined as the actus reus plus the mens rea, and our common sense understanding is that both relate to the *same* crime. *Kundeus* challenges this conception and allows for the combining of the actus reus for crime "x" and the mens rea for crime "y" to find liability for crime "x". Ask yourself what limits should be placed on such transfers or if they should be allowed at all.

The last two cases, *Pappajohn* and *Laybourn, Bulmer and Illingworth*, deal with both the quality of the mistaken belief, a belief which we can see need not be reasonable but only "honest", and the conditions of its availability. This correlates well with the ideal of the mens rea as actual and subjective, yet presents certain problems in the area of sexual assault (or rape as the offence was known before 1983). In a society which promotes sexist stereotypes of women, which encourages attitudes suggesting that women do not really know what they want, and which teaches men to see women as essentially sexual objects, is it safe to rely solely on the accused's belief as to the existence of consent on the part of the woman? Parliament was of the view that it was not and responded by enacting section 273.2 of the *Criminal Code* which restricts the availability of apprehended consent as a defence to charges of sexual assault. The issues surrounding this matter are more fully explored in the next chapter.

Finally, note that certain types of mistakes of fact are obviously irrelevant to attaching liability. For example, it is no defence to say as a thief you only meant to steal $100 but by mistake you took $150, or that you mistakenly stole a car from A rather than your intended victim B. In addition, certain statutory provisions makes some types of mistakes irrelevant in criminal law. A good example can be found in section 150.1(4) of the Criminal Code where it is no defence in regard to some sexual offences against minors under 14 years of age that the accused believed that the minor was older (unless the accused took all reasonable steps to ascertain the complainant's age).

## R. v. Williams
(1987), 80 N.S.R. (2d) 220 (Prov. Ct.)

[1] CURRAN, P.C.J.: — I want to thank counsel for the way this matter was dealt with. I am satisfied that the facts were fully put before me at the time of the hearing in May and that the issues and arguments have been thoroughly canvassed in the extensive briefs that were filed.

[2] These three matters were heard separately, in accordance with proper criminal procedure. However, there were agreed statements of fact in all three cases that were in large part identical. Besides that, some of the Crown evidence heard in one trial was adopted as part of the other trials. Consequently, most of the issues in the three cases are the same. I will render one decision on the common issues and deal separately with any issue that is peculiar to any one case.

[3] For several years Mr. Williams has been Clerk of the Provincial Court in Yarmouth and Justice of the Peace for the Province of Nova Scotia. In the early 1980's he was asked by the local detachment of the R.C.M.P. to take pleas from persons, usually American tourists, charged with narcotics and drug offences upon their arrival aboard the ferries from Maine.

[4] Most of the charges were laid when court was not in session in Yarmouth. No Provincial Court judge resided in Yarmouth at that time. Apparently both the R.C.M.P. and Mr. Williams wanted to cause as little inconvenience as possible to the persons charged.

[5] From 1981 to 1984 Mr. Williams attempted to obtain some instructions from the Attorney-General's Department about whether he ought to handle such charges. Mr. Williams was aware of a statement on page 4 of the *Handbook for Justices of the Peace* issued by the Department of Attorney-General that:

"A justice shall not accept a plea of guilty except for charges arising from provincial legislation."

Nevertheless, he felt obliged to do what he could to assist with the problem brought to his attention by the R.C.M.P. Consequently, he took pleas on those charges.

[6] In 1984 Mrs. Crosby and Mrs. MacConnell were hired to work in the Provincial Court office in Yarmouth. Mrs. MacConnell was appointed a Justice of the Peace. Mrs. Crosby, who had been made a J.P. in 1978 during a previous stint with the Provincial Court, was declared to be "designated" as were the others.

[7] None of the accused ever received any instructions about their powers and duties as Justices. They were merely given the Handbook for Justices of the Peace and sent off on their own. Their knowledge about the position was very limited.

[8] By 1985 Mr. Williams had become annoyed with the R.C.M.P. because of the large number of drug charges laid against tourists. He thought that most of the matters should have been left in the hands of Customs authorities to seize the substances and levy administrative penalties. Consequently, Mr. Williams and the other accused began to grant absolute discharges in all but the more serious drug cases. The number of charges did not decrease.

[9] By the end of 1985, the R.C.M.P. had complained about the amount of paper work they had to do in relation to the charges. They convinced Mr. Williams that discharges were not always appropriate. Mr. Williams and the other accused then met and decided to grant discharges only when Customs had collected an administrative penalty. In cases where there was no Customs penalty they would impose fines. They agreed on fines of $50.00 for most circumstances. That was notwithstanding the fact that the typical Yarmouth Provincial Court fine against landlubbers was $300.00. It seems that the accused were attempting to do their bit for Nova Scotia tourism.

[10] Each of the accused dealt with several drug charges in 1986, particularly during the time covered by the information. More often than not they imposed absolute discharges. On just a few occasions they remanded persons for later appearance in Provincial Court. In all other cases they imposed fines, usually of $50.00. Almost all the charges were laid against American citizens.

[11] On one occasion when imposing sentence, Mrs. MacConnell said that the fine was $50.00 American or $65.00 Canadian. It is alleged that on three occasions Mr. Williams imposed such a two-tier fine. On all other occasions the three accused merely said there would be a fine of a certain number of dollars, usually $50.00, and would not state the currency. I am satisfied that they intended the fines in those cases to be in Canadian funds of the stated amount.

[12] On the two occasions when the face amount of the fine was paid in Canadian funds, Mrs. MacConnell turned those funds in full over to the Provincial Court in

Yarmouth. The nominal amounts of all other fines imposed by the three accused were paid in American funds. None of the persons who paid such a fine testified. There is no way of knowing whether or not they had any interest in what happened to the exchange on their American funds.

[13] As mentioned previously, there was one occasion on which Mrs. MacConnell assessed a fine of $50.00 American or $65.00 Canadian. She testified that as soon as she said those words, she knew something was wrong because, in her words, "the fine was fifty dollars." Whether or not she said so was not clear. In any event, I am satisfied that she did not explain to the person involved, Norman C. Schneider, that $50.00 Canadian would be sufficient. It seems clear to me that Mr. Schneider would have been left with the impression that the fine was $50.00 U.S.

. . . .

[17] Few, if any, of the transactions involving any of the accused took place during regular working hours or at the courthouse. Most, if not all, took place during odd hours at the R.C.M.P. detachment. There was no one available to collect fine payment other than the justices themselves. Each of them merely accepted payment of the nominal amount in the funds offered, usually American. Exchange was neither requested nor given. On the next work day, the justice took the U.S. funds to the bank, exchanged them for Canadian, paid the nominal amount of the fine in Canadian funds to the Provincial Court office and kept the difference.

[18] The entire amount so kept by the three accused amounted only to a few hundred dollars. None of the accused ever made any attempt to disguise what he or she was doing. In fact, the practice was obviously well known, at least by the R.C.M.P. Until the charges were laid, no one ever suggested to any of the accused that what they were doing was improper.

[19] It was not until March 2, 1987 that the Attorney-General's Department formulated a policy for Provincial Court offices in relation to the receipt of U.S. funds. The instructions direct that the first $5.00 of any exchange above the nominal amount outstanding be kept by the court office as a processing fee. The balance was to be returned to the person who made the payment.

. . . .

[36] I am satisfied that if there were any thefts they were from the persons who paid the American funds and not the federal Crown. On that basis, the prosecution has not made out its case, . . .

[37] In the alternative, I would say the following. Ownership or interest in the property, including U.S. currency, is clearly a matter of law. However, there have been countless disputes over property where more than one party incorrectly believed that it had a property interest or a right to the property without even having a property interest. It is clear that mistakes about the right to property are no mistakes of law, but mistakes of fact. Persons who make such mistakes because of honest beliefs may be civilly liable, but they are not guilty of crimes.

. . . .

[39] In order for there to be a theft, the taking must be done fraudulently, that is, with a dishonest intention: *R. v. Dalzell* (1983), 57 N.S.R. (2d) 148; 120 A.P.R. 148; 6

C.C.C. (3d) 112 (C.A.). Proof only that something was taken without lawful right does not establish a crime. Moral wrongdoing must be shown.

[40] I attach considerable significance to the fact that the accused did nothing whatever to disguise their actions. I recognize that just because something is done openly does not necessarily mean it is done honestly. Some particularly brazen thieves use openness as a way of, in effect, disguising their thievery. However, I am convinced that these three accused persons did everything in the open because the thought never even crossed their minds that they were doing something wrong.

[41] There is another significant point. If the accused had concocted a scheme to fleece unsuspecting tourists, one would have expected them to impose fines on every occasion possible and to make those fines as large as possible. Instead, they ordered more discharges than fines, and the fines they did impose were very small.

[42] If the accused were wrong about their right to the exchange, they were honestly wrong.

. . . .

[46] I am troubled as well by the way in which this investigation was carried out. Apparently by June of 1986 someone was aware of a problem in the handling of American funds used to pay drug fines. The authorities must have known the accused were basically honest people. For the life of me, I do not understand why they did not confront the accused about what was taking place. Instead, things were allowed to proceed with the full knowledge of at least some members of the R.C.M.P. Those members of the R.C.M.P. who were present when the fines were imposed and paid were put in the position of almost being accomplices. I doubt that any of the American tourists who overpaid their fines would be grateful to the R.C.M.P. for saying nothing and letting this happen. Application of a little common sense might have prevented any of these charges from arising.

[47] I find the three accused not guilty.

*Accused acquitted.*

## The Queen v. Kundeus
[1976] 2 S.C.R. 272

[Only the judgments of Laskin C.J.C. and De Grandpre J. are reproduced below.]

LASKIN C.J.C. (dissenting): — The issue in this appeal, brought by the Crown with leave of this Court, is whether the British Columbia Court of Appeal was right in concluding that the prosecution had failed to establish the necessary *mens rea* on a charge of trafficking in a restricted drug, namely lysergic acid dythalamide (LSD), contrary to the *Food and Drugs Act*, R.S.C. 1970, c. F-27. I take the factual considerations to be those narrated and found by the trial judge (who had convicted the accused) and which were accepted by the British Columbia Court of Appeal.

Briefly, they are as follows, based on the evidence of the undercover policeman who was involved in the transaction with the accused. The latter was at a table in a beer parlour calling out "speed, acid, MDA or hash" to passers-by. The policeman asked for hash or acid, to which the accused replied that he was all sold out. He then offered to sell mescaline at two dollars. The policeman accepted the offer and paid the accused four dollars for two "hits". The accused left, returned in five minutes, and handed the policeman two capsules. In fact, these capsules contained LSD. The British Columbia Court of Appeal took the reasons of the trial judge as involving a finding that although the accused in fact sold LSD he intended to sell and thought he was selling mescaline and the policeman thought he was buying mescaline. The record in this Court does not admit of any other view.

It was not contended by the Crown, and, indeed, could not be under the applicable legislation, that proof of the *actus reus* involved in the charge was alone enough to support the conviction; proof of *mens rea* also rested upon the Crown: see *Beaver v. The Queen*. The conviction can, of course, be easily supported if it be enough to establish that the accused intended to traffic in drugs and that is immaterial, save as a matter of description in the charge, what particular drug or class of drug was the subject of the trafficking. Such a view overlooks the legislative scheme governing various drugs and the applicable penal provisions. On that view, the accused would have to risk the range of penalties applicable to the trafficking in the drug which was in fact sold, albeit he thought that he was selling one with respect to which a much lighter scale of penalties was prescribed.

The scheme of the *Food and Drugs Act* is of considerable relevance in this case. Sections 40 and 42, on which the prosecution was based, are in Part IV of the Act dealing with "restricted drugs", which are those included in Schedule H, and LSD is one of those mentioned. Part III of the Act deals with "controlled drugs" which are those included in Schedule G, and among them are amphetamine and methamphetamine. Sections 33 and 34 are provisions in Part III (relating to controlled drugs) which are to the same effect as ss. 40 and 42 relating to restricted drugs under Part IV. Sections 40 and 42 read as follows:

**40.** In this Part,
"possession" means possession as defined in the *Criminal Code*;
"regulations" mean regulations made as provided for by or under section 45;
"restricted drug" means any drug or other substance included in Schedule H;
"traffic" means to manufacture, sell, export from or import to Canada, transport or deliver, otherwise than under the authority of this Part or the regulations.

**42.**(1) No person shall traffic in a restricted drug or any substance represented or held out by him to be a restricted drug.

(2) No person shall have in his possession any restricted drug for the purpose of trafficking.

(3) Every person who violates subsection (1) or (2) is guilty of an offence and is liable
(a) upon summary conviction, to imprisonment for eighteen months; or
(b) upon conviction on indictment, to imprisonment for ten years.

Mescaline is neither a controlled drug nor a restricted drug, but is a drug within Schedule F, included thereunder by virtue of s. 15 of the Act ("no person shall sell any drug described in Schedule F") and governed by regulations made pursuant to s. 25 of the Act. Section 15 of the Act is in Part I which deals with adulterated food, drugs and cosmetics, with deceptive advertising and labelling, with control of standards of manufacturing and with the sanitary condition of premises. Part II of the Act deals with administration and enforcement of the Act by inspectors and includes very wide regulation-making powers set out in s. 25. Penalties for violation of the Act or of the regulations are prescribed by s. 26 which reads as follows:

> **26.** Every person who violates any of the provisions of this Act or the regulations is guilty of an offence and is liable
> (a) on summary conviction for a first offence to a fine not exceeding five hundred dollars or to imprisonment for a term not exceeding three months, or to both, and for a subsequent offence to a fine not exceeding one thousand dollars or to imprisonment for a term not exceeding six months, or to both; and
> (b) on conviction upon indictment to a fine not exceeding five thousand dollars or to imprisonment for a term not exceeding three years, or to both.

It is common ground that any offence under the Act or regulations relating to the sale of mescaline would be punishable under s. 26. On the other hand, this provision would have no application to controlled or restricted drugs in the face of the penalty provisions of ss. 34 and 42 which alone govern illegal dealing in them. A comparison of the respective penalty provisions governing mescaline and LSD shows how much heavier the penalty is in respect of illegal dealing in the latter than in the former, both where the prosecution is on summary conviction and on indictment.

The regulation respecting mescaline is Regulation C.01.041 which prohibits the sale of any substance containing a drug listed or described in Schedule F unless on written or verbal prescription, and the regulation goes on to elaborate on these types of prescriptions. I may observe here that it is not an offence to possess mescaline but it is an offence to possess a controlled or a restricted drug for the purpose of "trafficking", defined (as already noted) to include, *inter alia*, selling transporting and delivering.

. . . .

It was the contention of the appellant Crown that the required proof of *mens rea* was furnished by evidence showing what Crown counsel called a general intention to traffic in drugs; and, this being shown, it was immaterial that the accused did not intend to traffic in the specific drug which was named in the charge but thought (as did his purchaser) that he was trafficking in another drug. Crown counsel thus takes the position to which I referred earlier in these reasons, and he stated in this connection that the accused could meet the case against him only by relying on mistake of fact which must be an honest mistake on reasonable grounds that the facts believed by him to be true would not attract culpability of any drug offence. That, according to Crown counsel, was not this case.

. . . .

The third issue, which is tied in with the first, is whether mistake of fact is shown on proof that, on the facts as the accused honestly believed them to be, he was innocent of the offence charged, albeit guilty of another offence, or whether he must show that he was innocent of any offence.

. . . .

Even if it be proper to describe trafficking in controlled drugs, whatever be the drug, or trafficking in restricted drugs, whatever be the drug as being, in each case, a description of the same crime. I think it is impossible to bring mescaline within either category when it stands entirely outside the group of controlled or restricted drugs and is governed by other statutory provisions than those governing controlled or restricted drugs. I am unable to agree that where *mens rea* is an element of an offence, as it is here, it can be satisfied by proof of its existence in relation to another offence unless, of course, the situation involves an included offence of which the accused may be found guilty on his trial of the offence charged.

Is any general principle deductible . . . ? Certainly, it cannot be said that, in general, where *mens rea* is an ingredient of an offence and the *actus reus* is proved it is enough if an intent is shown that would support a conviction of another crime, whether more or less serious than the offence actually committed. Coming to the particular, to the case before this Court, where proof is made of an *actus reus* that, in a general sense, is common to a range or variety of offences which require *mens rea* but those offences differ as to gravity by reason of different classifications and different penalties, is a charge of a more serious offence established by proof only that the accused intended to commit and could have been found guilty of a less serious, a lesser offence? The matter, in terms of principle, depends on how strict an observance there should be of the requirement of *mens rea*. If there is to be a relaxation of the requirement, should it not come from Parliament, which could provide for the substitution of a conviction of the lesser offence, in the same way as provision now exists in our criminal law for entering a conviction on an included offence?

This position is the one taken by the Model Penal Code of the American Law Institute (1962) which provides as follows in s. 2.04(2):

> Although ignorance or mistake would otherwise afford a defense to the offence charged, the defence is not available if the defendant would be guilty of another offense had the situation been as he supposed. In such case, however, the ignorance or mistake of the defendant shall reduce the grade and degree of the offense of which he may be convicted to those of the offense of which he would be guilty had the situation been as he supposed.

In the present case, and under present Canadian law, this sensible solution to a difficult problem is not open to this Court.

There may be some regret on the part of a court to free a person who appears to be guilty of an offence with which he has not been charged. That regret, if any there be, cannot be a vehicle for making a particular charge which cannot be proved serve as a foundation for imposing culpability of another, which is not an included offence. If there is to be a modification of principle in a situation like the present one, it must come from Parliament.

. . . .

There is another consideration which should be brought into account in this case. The Crown's case was built on evidence of an undercover policeman which must have been as well known to the prosecuting authorities before the trial. I can appreciate that there could have been some difficulty in determining what charge should be laid on the facts disclosed by the chief Crown witness. Although the Crown may have felt that it could support the charge actually laid, it could also, as a matter of precaution, have laid a charge of attempting to traffic in mescaline. Such a charge is supportable under s. 24 of the *Criminal Code* which makes it immaterial whether it was possible or not to commit the intended offence: see 10 Halsbury, 3rd ed., p. 306; *R. v. Scott*. I have already indicated the view of the facts that the record compels. If there should be any doubt on the evidence whether the accused offered and intended to sell mescaline, that doubt cannot be translated into an affirmative finding, certainly not in this Court, that he offered and intended to see LSD. At the worst, it would require a new trial.

I see no such doubt and, on the considerations I have canvassed, I would dismiss the appeal.

The judgment of MARTLAND, JUDSON, RITCHIE, PIGEON, DICKSON, BEETZ and De GRANDPRE JJ. was delivered by

De GRANDPRE J.: — With leave of this Court, the Crown appeals the unanimous judgment of the British Columbia Court of Appeal setting aside the conviction of respondent.

. . . .

The Court of Appeal disagreed with the conclusion reached by the trial judge and specifically refused to follow *R. v. Custeau.* The conviction was consequently set aside.

> *Mens rea* cannot, of course, be examined without reference to *Beaver v. The Queen.* In that case, there was evidence on which the jury might have found that Beaver had no knowledge that the substance was a drug but believed it to be sugar of milk. It is in that context that the following excerpt from the reasons of Cartwright J., as he then was, must be read (p. 538):
>
>> ... the essential question is whether the belief entertained by the accused is an honest one and that the existence or not-existence of reasonable grounds for such belief is merely relevant evidence to be weighed by the tribunal of fact in determining that essential question.
>
> The question to which Cartwright, J. was directing his attention is made very clear in the illustration he uses at p. 536:
>
>> It may be of assistance in examining the problem to use a simple illustration. Suppose X goes to the shop of Y, a druggist, and asks Y to sell him some baking soda. Y hands him a sealed packet which he tells him contains baking-soda and charges him a few cents. X honestly believes that the packet contains baking-soda but in fact it contains heroin. X puts the package in his pocket, takes it home and later put it in a cupboard in his bathroom. There would seem to be no doubt that X has had actual manual and physical possession of the package and that he continues to have possession of the package while it is in his cupboard. The main question raised on this appeal is whether, in the supposed circumstances, X would be guilty of the crime of having heroin in his possession.
>>
>> It will be observed at once that we are not concerned with the incidence of the burden of proof or of the obligation of adducing evidence. The judgment of the Court of Appeal states the law to be that X must be convicted although he proves to the point of demonstration that he honestly believed the package to contain baking-soda.
>
> Our facts are different. They are very simple and not contradicted. One reading of them is that Kundeus was offering LSD for sale, actually sold LSD and received payment therefor. On that reading, it is obvious that the conviction should have been affirmed.
>
> Another reading is that adopted by the Court of Appeal and expressed by McFarlane J.A., speaking for the Court (p. 345):

The evidence disclosed, and the trial Judge found, that the appellant offered to sell mescaline at two dollars to a police constable acting undercover. The constable accepted the offer and paid the appellant four dollars for two "hits". The appellant left, returned in about five minutes and handed the constable two capsules which were found, on analyses, to contain LSD.

I think I must interpret the reasons for judgment of the trial Judge as a finding that although the appellant did in fact sell LSD he thought he was selling, and intended to sell, mescaline and that the constable also thought he was purchasing Mescaline.

Assuming that this reading of the trial judgment is the proper one, was the Court of Appeal right in holding that the necessary *mens rea* had not been proved? I do not believe so.

. . . .

No evidence having been tendered by the accused, it is not possible to find that he had an honest belief amounting to a non-existence of *mens rea* and the Court of Appeal was in error in its conclusion.

The quality of respondent's conduct is not to be determined by the existence or non-existence of a binding civil agreement as to the purchase of LSD between him and the constable.

. . . .

I would allow the appeal, set aside the Order of the Court of Appeal of British Columbia and restore the judgment at trial together with the sentence imposed thereat.

*Appeal allowed.*

## Pappajohn v. The Queen
(1980), 52 C.C.C. (2d) 481 (S.C.C.)

[Only the judgment of McIntyre J. is reproduced below.]

MCINTYRE, J.: — The appellant appeals his rape conviction, which was affirmed in the Court of Appeal for British Columbia with one dissent [45 C.C.C. (2d) 67, 5 C.R. (3d) 1983, [1979] 1 W.W.R. 562], upon the ground that the trial Judge failed to put to the jury the defence of mistake of fact. That ground is expressed in the appellant's factum in these words:

> Did the learned trial judge err in failing to instruct the jury on the question of honest belief by the accused that the Complainant consented to intercourse and thus on the facts of this case, failed to put properly before the jury a defence, such failure being a non-direction amounting to mis-direction?

A consideration of the facts of the case is vital to a resolution of the problem it poses. The complainant was a real estate sales-woman employed by a well-known and well-established real estate firm in Vancouver. She was successful in her work. The appellant is a businessman who was anxious to sell his home in Vancouver and he had listed it for sale with the real estate firm with which the complainant was associated. She was to be responsible for the matter on her firm's behalf. On August 4, 1976, at about 1:00 p.m., she met the appellant by appointment at a downtown restaurant for lunch. The purpose of the meeting was to discuss the house sale. The lunch lasted until about 4:00 or 4:30 p.m. During this time, a good deal of liquor was consumed by both parties. The occasion became convivial, the proprietor of the restaurant and his wife joined the party, and estimates of the amount of alcohol consumed varied in retrospect, as one would expect. It does seem clear, however, that while each of the parties concerned had a substantial amount to drink, each seemed capable of functioning normally.

At about 4:00 p.m. or shortly thereafter, they left the restaurant. The appellant drove the complainant's car while she sat in the front passenger seat. They went to the appellant's house, the one which was listed for sale, to further consider questions arising in that connection. Up to the time of arrival at the home, at about 4:30 or 5:00 p.m., there is no significant variation in their accounts of events. From the moment of arrival, however, there is a complete divergence. She related a story of rape completely against her will and her protests and struggles. He spoke of an amorous interlude involving not more than a bit of coy objection on her part and several acts of intercourse with her consent. Whatever occurred in the house, there is no doubt that at about 7:30 p.m. the complainant ran out of the house naked with a man's bow tie around her neck and her hands tied behind her back with a bathrobe sash. She arrived at the door of a house nearby and demanded entry and protection. The occupant of the house, a priest, admitted her. She was in an upset state and exhibited great fear and emotional stress. The police were called and these proceedings followed. More detailed reference to the facts will be made later.

When the defence closed its case and before the trial Judge commenced his charge, the jury was excluded while counsel for the appellant argued that on the facts of the case as it appeared from the evidence, the trial Judge should put the defence of mistake of fact to the jury. He contended that the appellant was entitled to have the Judge tell the jury that if the appellant entertained an honest but mistaken belief that the complainant was consenting to the acts of intercourse as they occurred, the necessary *mens rea* would not be present, and the appellant would be entitled to an acquittal. Reliance for this proposition was placed upon *Director or Public Prosecutions v. Morgan*, [1975] All E. R. 347 (H.L.), and *R. v Plummer and Brown* (1975), 24 C.C.C. (2d) 497, 31 C.R.N.S. 220 (Ont. C.A.). The trial Judge refused to accede to the defence counsel's request.

. . . .

In the Court of Appeal, this ruling found support in the majority judgment of Farris, C.J.B.C., with whom Craig, J.A., agreed. The majority adopted the view that the issue emerging from the evidence was a simple one of consent or no consent. In a dissenting judgment, Lambert, J.A., was of the opinion that there was sufficient evidence to put the defence to the jury. He would have directed the jury that the accused was entitled to an acquittal if the jury found that he entertained an honest and *reasonably held* mistaken belief in the existence of consent. This is a view which I cannot share in view of the pronouncement in this Court in *Beaver v. The Queen* (1957), 118 C.C.C. 129 at pp. 136-7, [1057] S.C.R. 531 at p. 538, 26 C.R. 193.

. . . .

In relating the law to the facts of any case, we must keep in mind what it is that the trial Judge must look for in the evidence in deciding whether there is, in the words of Fauteux, J., "some evidence or matter apt to convey a sense of reality in the argument, and in the grievance". In this case, to convey such a sense of reality, there must be some evidence which if believed would support the existence of a mistaken but honest belief that the complainant was in fact consenting to the acts of intercourse which admittedly occurred. This requires a more detailed recital of the evidence than would ordinarily be necessary.

The complainant, after describing the events of the early afternoon in the restaurant, said that upon entering into the house where discussions were to take place regarding its sale, the appellant seized her and pushed her down the hallway to the bedroom. She resisted his pushing and tried to reason with him. He said that he was going to break her and began, as soon as the bedroom was reached, to remove her blouse. She said she protested and screamed and grew hysterical and tried to reason with him but was not fighting him in a physical way. When he continued to remove her blouse, she realized he was going to rape her. She tried to escape but he threw her onto the bed and she became totally hysterical. She just lay on the bed and screamed. She then said she tried to rise from the bed but he held out his arm and told her to remove his cuff-links, she refused and then she tried to escape. He pushed her back onto the bed, removed her skirt, nylons and panties, but not her brassiere or slip. She remained on the bed screaming, then she observed that he was undressed, although did not actually recall him undressing. She described various conversations in which she told him she was not able to take birth control pills and was without any contraceptive protection. She said that she and the man she lived with were attempting to have a baby and she was at that time ovulating. This information came, she said, from her lover who was a gynaecologist and he later gave evidence confirming these matters. She tried to persuade the appellant to desist but he would not be put off and finally had intercourse with her against her will. She said that the appellant had told her he would not ejaculate in her and she described three short acts of intercourse all against her will in which no ejaculation occurred. After some time the appellant left the bed and got a bow tie from a drawer and a sashcord from a dressing gown. Again, against her will, he tied the bow tie over her mouth as a gag and tied her hands behind her back. She struggled against this and threw herself from the bed onto the floor. He put her back on the bed and while her hands remained tied had intercourse again from the rear. During all this time she said she was at times pleading and reasoning with him, at times hysterical and screaming, and at times endeavouring to avoid and escape him. She said at one stage when she saw him get the tie and cord that she decided that he was going to kill her. Shortly after the incident of falling off the bed, and by this time some three hours had elapsed, she said he left the room. She seized the opportunity to escape and fled from the house naked with her hands still tied behind her back. She ran down an alley and pounded at the door of a nearby house. She was admitted and the police were called. During all this period, she insisted that she did not consent to any of the acts of intercourse. She insisted that she was hysterical, fearful and helpless in his hands and she escaped as soon as she could.

The appellant, in giving evidence on his own behalf, said that upon arrival at the house, he entered and went immediately to the bathroom. On this return to the front of the house, he led the complainant into the living room. They sat on the couch and began to kiss. During this episode, she removed her necklace and left her car keys on a table in the living room. They then moved into the bedroom where she consented to the removal of her clothes. He hung her blouse in the closet and put her other garments, after folding them, at the foot of the bed. He agreed that she refused to undo his cufflinks but he undressed and they then had intercourse with her consent. He admitted to three occasions and admitted that he had had no ejaculations. The whole performance, while with her consent, was not very successful. He admitting getting the tie to gag her and the cord to bind her, saying that it was done as an act of bondage to stimulate sexual activity. He said that when bound she suddenly threw herself from the bed and was hysterical and screaming. He said that he put her back on the bed. He left to find a cigarette and on his return she had gone. He did not know where. He waited for some time then put some clothes on and had a look around the house and the yard but could not find her. He insisted that everything was done with her consent. She made no serious resistance to his advances beyond making such coy inquiries as "George, what are you doing?" He says he would not have forced her if she had resisted, that she made no objection to his advances, and, that when she threw herself from the bed he desisted from any further efforts at intercourse and did not have intercourse after that event.

It will be seen at once that there is a fundamental conflict between the two stories. Her version excludes consent and any possible mistaken belief in consent. His version speaks of actual consent and no suggestion of any mistaken belief could arise. To find support for the defence asserted by the appellant, the other evidence must be considered.

When the complainant gained admission to the house where she sought help, she was observed to be in a distraught and emotional condition. She complained that she had been assaulted or raped or that someone was attempting to rape her. She was evidently fearful.

She wanted to have her gentleman friend called and the call was made. The police were called as well. The priest, who had admitted her to the house, removed the cords from her wrists and found that they had been tightly tied. He gave evidence that he had some difficulty in untying her.

After the complainant had spoken to the police, they went to the appellant's house. Some 40 minutes had elapsed since she had left it. The appellant asked if they came about the girl. He denied he had raped her. He said she was willing, that he didn't resist much and that she had suddenly become hysterical and had run away. He did not follow her because he did not know what to do and when he first discovered her absence he was naked himself. In the house, the police found the necklace in the living-room with the car keys. They found the complainant's blouse hanging in the closet in the bedroom, the complainant herself had seen it there before her escape. They found her underclothes folded at the foot of the bed with the exception of her slip which was in the bed sheets. Further examination revealed that the clothing of the complainant was undamaged, that is, untorn, though the complainant said that she did observe a torn shoulder strap in her slip the next day. Medical evidence found the following physical marking or injuries upon the body of the complainant. There were three scratches, two on her chest and one on her back, a red mark on the inside of her upper right arm, reddened areas on the front of both wrists. There was no bruising or redness on her mouth, throat, neck, the inside of her thighs or legs, and no injury or any kind of redness was observed about the vagina area.

In summary then, this was the state of evidence when the trial Judge was called upon to make his ruling. It became his task to apply the rule enunciated above. in assessing his resolution of the matter, we must consider the situation as it presented itself to him at the time. Speculation as to what the jury did, or would have done after being charged, is not relevant here.

With that thought in mind and, bearing in mind that the object of the judicial search must be evidence of a mistaken but honest belief in the consent of the complainant, one must first ask the question "Where is this evidence to be found?" It cannot be found in the evidence of the complainant. She denies actual consent and her evidence cannot provide any support for a mistaken belief in consent. Her conduct, according to her description, is that of a terrified, hysterical, non-consenting woman who resisted the appellant's advances, albeit unsuccessfully, and when able fled from his house in search of assistance. Turning then to the evidence of the appellant, it immediately becomes apparent that his evidence speaks of actual consent, even co-operation, and leaves little if any room for the suggestion that she may not have been consenting but he thought she was. The two stories are, as has been noted before, diametrically opposed on this vital issue. It is not for the trial Judge to weigh them and prefer one to the other. It is for him in this situation, however, to recognize the issue which arises on the evidence for the purpose of deciding what defences are open. In this situation the only realistic issue which can arise is the simple issue of consent or no consent. In my opinion, the trial Judge was correct in concluding that there simply was not sufficient evidence to justify the putting of the defence of mistake of fact to the jury. He left the issue of consent and that was the only one arising on the evidence.

In reaching this conclusion, I am not unmindful of the evidence of surrounding circumstance which were said to support the appellant's contention. I refer to the absence of serious injury suffered by the complainant and the absence of damage to clothing, as well as to the long period of time during which the parties remained in the bedroom. These matters may indeed be cogent on the issue of actual consent but, in my view, they cannot by themselves advance a suggestion of mistaken belief. The finding of the clothes at the foot of the bed, the necklace and the keys in the living-room, are equally relevant on the issue of actual consent and, in my view, cannot affect the issue which was clearly framed by the opposing assertions of consent and non-consent.

It would seem to me that if it is considered necessary in this case to charge the jury on the defence of mistake of fact, it would be necessary to do so in all cases where the complainant denies consent and an accused asserts it. To require the putting of the alternative defence of mistaken belief in consent, there must be, in my opinion, some evidence beyond the mere assertion of belief in consent by counsel for the appellant. This evidence must appear from or be supported by sources other than the appellant in order to give it any air of reality. In *R. v. Plummer and Brown, supra*, Evans, J.A. (as he then was), speaking for the Ontario Court of Appeal, considered that there was such evidence as far as Brown was concerned and directed a new trial because the defence had not been put. In that case, the complainant had gone to Plummer's "pad" where she had been raped by Plummer. Brown entered the room where the rape occurred after Plummer had gone. Apparently, he had arrived at the house separately from Plummer. It was open on the evidence to find that he was unaware then that

Plummer had threatened the complainant and terrorized her into submission. He had intercourse with her and she said that because of continuing fear from Plummer's threats, she submitted without protest. In these special circumstances, the defence was required. The facts clearly established at least an air of reality to Brown's defence. In *Morgan*, there was evidence of an invitation by the complainant's husband to have intercourse with his wife and his assurance that her show of resistance would be a sham. In other words, there was evidence explaining, however preposterous the explanation might be, a basis for the mistaken belief. In the case at bar, there is no such evidence.

Where the complainant says rape and the accused says consent, and where on the whole of the evidence, including that of the complainant, the accused, and the surrounding circumstances, there is a clear issue on this point, and where as here the accused makes no assertion of a belief in consent as opposed to an actual consent, it is unrealistic in the absence of some other circumstance or circumstances, such as are found in the *Plummer and Brown* and *Morgan* cases, to consider the Judge bound to put the mistake of fact defence. In my opinion, the trial Judge was correct in refusing to put the defence on the evidence before him.

I might add that I have had the advantage of reading the reasons of my brother Dickson, J., and while it is apparent that I am unable to accept his view on the evidentiary question, I am in agreement with that part of his judgment dealing with the availability as a defence to a charge of rape in Canada of what is generally termed the defence of mistake of fact.

I would dismiss the appeal.

*Appeal dismissed.*

## Laybourn, Bulmer and Illingworth v. R.
(1987), 58 C.R. (3d) 48 (S.C.C.)

Appeal by accused from judgment of British Columbia Court of Appeal, 10 C.C.C. (3d) 256, dismissing accused's appeals from two convictions for rape and one for indecent assault.

[Only the judgment of McIntyre J. is reproduced below.]

June 4, 1987, MCINTYRE J. (DICKSON C.J.C., WILSON, LeDAIN and LaFOREST JJ. concurring): —

This case involves an appeal from two convictions of rape and one of indecent assault. There are two issues involved. The first, whether on the facts of this case the defence of mistake of fact should have been left with the jury, and the second, whether the charge to the jury on the question was correct.

The complainant was a prostitute. Late on the evening of 13th July 1980 the three appellants were together in the appellant Bulmer's hotel room. Laybourn left and picked up the complainant on the street. According to the complainant, they discussed sexual acts and prices and struck a bargain. She agreed to provide her services for $80. They returned to Bulmer's room and on entering she discovered the other two. The complainant objected to their presence and they left. Before leaving, Illingworth sought to engage the favours of the complainant. She quoted her price and told him to come back in 20 minutes. When they left, Laybourn gave her $80. The other two returned to the room in a few minutes and Bulmer, learning that Laybourn had paid $80, said that the complainant was not worth that sum. He told her to return the money, which she did. She was frightened and Illingworth told her she would have to perform without payment. She then performed various sexual acts with the three appellants, asserting that she did so only out of fear. She denied giving consent. The police arrived at the room after some time and she left with them complaining of rape. She said there was not physical violence other that the various sexual acts and she received no payment.

Laybourn and Illingworth gave evidence. Bulmer did not. Laybourn confirmed the complainant's story of the departure and quick return of Illingworth and Bulmer. Then, according to his evidence, a discussion occurred. The complainant wanted $60 from each man. They said they would pay her $20 each. Laybourn told her she could take $20 or leave. She seemed "jumpy" but did not leave. She then asked if she could go when she had finished with them and he replied that she could go at once if she wished. She agreed to a price of $20 from each man and various sexual acts, including intercourse, followed. No threats were made. Generally, Illingworth's evidence supported Laybourn's.

Evidence of what went on in the hotel room was also given by one Jones, who occupied an adjoining room. From conversation overheard, he concluded that the woman was a prostitute. He heard Bulmer and Illingworth leave, go down the hall and return. He heard the woman complain at the presence of the two men in the room and her heard conversation, including a male voice saying, "You are in a tough business, baby, and you have got to learn to take it." At first, her voice seemed normal, but as time passed it took on a whining, wheedling tone. There was discussion about price, the woman saying she wanted $60 from each and a male voice saying they would pay her $20.

At trial, the appellants took the position that the complainant had consented to the acts. Counsel made the alternative submission that Laybourn had held an honest but mistaken belief in consent. The trial judge left the defence to the jury and told the jury that all three could rely upon the defence. They jury returned verdicts of guilty of rape against both Laybourn and Illingworth. Bulmer was acquitted of rape, but convicted of indecent assault. An appeal to the British Columbia Court of Appeal was dismissed, with Lambert J.A. dissenting [10 C.C.C. (2d) 256]. This appeal is taken, under s. 618(1)(a) of the Criminal Code, on the basis of dissent.

In the Court of Appeal (Taggart, Craig and Lambert JJ.A.), Taggart, J.A. was of the view that the trial judge was right in leaving the defence of mistake of fact to the jury. He considered that the jury would not be misled by the charge; that the trial judge's instructions would not leave the jury with the impression that the appellants were obliged to show that their mistaken belief in consent was a reasonable one. Craig J.A. considered that the defence of mistake of fact should not have been put to the jury. In this case, he said, the issue was consent or no consent and there was no basis in the evidence for defence of honest but mistaken belief in consent. He agreed with Taggart J.A., however, that taken as a whole, the trial judge's charge to the jury was adequate.

Lambert J.A. in his dissent was of the view that in the circumstances of this case the judge was required to put the defence of mistake of fact to the jury. He considered, however, that the defence was incorrectly put.

The dissent is recorded in the formal order of the Court of Appeal in these terms:

1. That the learned trial judge erred in instructing the jury that the defence of honest but mistaken belief in consent required something more than a genuine belief in consent in the mind of the accused and in instructing the jury that there must be some objective evidence from which an inference could be drawn that the complainant might be consenting.
2. That the learned trial judge erred in leaving with the jury, the impression that there must be reasonable grounds to support the defence of honest but mistaken belief in consent.

The appellants raised three grounds of appeal in a revised factum which was filed on behalf of all three. The first issue raised alleges error on the part of the trial judge, upon the same basis as that mentioned in ground 1 of the dissent of Lambert J.A. The other two grounds raised points not dealt with below, which required the leave of this court. There were expressed in the factum thus:

2. The learned trial judge was without jurisdiction to conduct a joint trial against the applicants as the Crown had proceeded against each of the applicants severally.
3. The learned trial judge erred in law having embarked on a trial of the applicants, in directing the jury that they acted jointly and further in not directing the jury that the actions and words in fact evidence of each one could not be used against each of the others.

An application for leave to appeal in respect of both grounds was refused. The court did not feel it necessary to call upon counsel for the Crown on that application. The appeal then turned on the "mistake of fact" issue. The appellants argued that the trial judge was in error in instructing the jury that the defence required objective evidence, apart from the complainant may have been consenting. The Crown contended that if the defence was open on the evidence, then the judge's charge was adequate and did not confuse the jury.

## *The Law Generally*

. . . .

The defence has been variously described and may be conveniently stated in these terms. If an accused entertains an honest belief in the existence of a set of circumstances which, if they existed at the time of the commission of an otherwise criminal act, would have justified his act and rendered it non-criminal, he is entitled to an acquittal. The law on this question as far as Canada is concerned has been stated authoritatively in *Pappajohn v. R.*, [1980] 2 S.C.R. 120, [1980] 4 W.W.R. 387, 14 C.R. (3d) 243, 19 C.R. (3d) 97, 52 C.C.C. (2d) 481, 111 D.L.R. (3d) 1, 32 N.R. 104 [B.C.].

. . . .

It is well settled law that in his charge the trial judge must put to the jury all defences that may arise upon the evidence, whether they have been raised by counsel for the defence or not. In doing so, he is obliged to explain the law respecting the defence and to refer the jury to the evidence which may be relevant on that issue. Before putting the defence, however, the trial judge is not bound to put every defence suggested by counsel in the absence of some evidentiary base. Indeed, he should not do so, for to put a wholly unsupported defence would only cause confusion.

This question was dealt with in some detail in *Pappajohn*. The majority of the court were of the view that a defence should be put when there was evidence before the court which would give an air of reality to the defence . . . .

In discussing the application of the "air of reality" test in the *Pappajohn* case, I said, at p. 133:

> To require the putting of the alternative defence of mistaken belief in consent, there must be , in my opinion, some evidence beyond the mere assertion of belief in consent by counsel for the appellant. This evidence must appear from or be supported by sources other than the appellant in order to give it any air of reality.

. . . .

When the defence of mistake of fact, or for that matter any other defence, is raised, two distinct steps are involved. The first step for the trial judge is to decide if the defence should be put to the jury. It is on this question, as I have said, that the "air of reality" test is applied. It has nothing to do with the jury and is not a factor for its consideration. If it is decided to put the defence, the second step requires the trial judge to explain the law to the jury, review the relevant evidence and leave the jury with the issue of guilt or innocence. The jury must consider all the evidence, and they must be satisfied beyond a reasonable doubt in the case of a rape charge that there was no consent before they may convict. Where they find there was consent or honest belief in consent, or if they have a doubt on either issue, they must acquit. They should be told as well that the belief, if honestly held, need not be based on reasonable grounds. Before going further, it should be observed that, since the decision of this court in *Pappajohn*, the Criminal Code has been amended by the addition of s. 244(4), which provides:

> (4) Where an accused alleges that he believed that the complainant consented to the conduct that is the subject-matter of the charge, a judge, if satisfied that there is sufficient evidence and that, if believed by the jury, the evidence would constitute a defence, shall instruct the jury, when reviewing all the evidence relating to the determination of the honesty of the accused's belief, to consider the presence or absence of reasonable grounds for that belief.

This section, in my view, does not change the law as applied in *Pappajohn*. It does not require that the mistaken belief be reasonable or reasonably held. It simply makes clear that in determining the issue of the honesty of the asserted belief, the presence or absence of reasonable grounds for the belief are relevant factors for the jury's consideration.

. . . .

The jury should then be instructed, in accordance with s. 244(4) of the Criminal Code, that, when considering all the evidence relating to the question of the honesty of the accused's asserted belief in consent, they must consider the presence or absence of reasonable grounds for that belief.

## Application to this Case

In the Court of Appeal, Taggart and Lambert JJ.A., while differing in the result, were both of the opinion that the evidence was sufficient to warrant the putting of the defence to the jury. I am in agreement with that view. From the evidence it is clear that, when the complainant was picked up on the street by Laybourn, after some discussion she did consent to sexual intercourse with Laybourn. This consent would, of course, not extend to the others, and it may well be that she withdrew her consent on learning that the others wished to participate in the evening's activities. But there was other evidence, that of the witness Jones in the adjoining room, which told of bargaining regarding price and conversation that could be considered equivocal at times, but which could raise questions on the issue of whether and to what extent the appellants may have understood her to be consenting. I would agree, as I have said, with Taggart and Lambert JJ.A. that there was then sufficient evidence to lend an air of reality to the defence of mistake of fact and the trial judge was not in error in deciding to put the defence to the jury.

The two points on which Lambert J.A. dissented in the Court of Appeal have been set out above. In summary, he was of the view that the trial judge was in error in telling the jury that more than a genuine belief in consent in the mind of the accused was required to support the defence and that there must be some objective evidence supporting the belief that the part of the trial judge in leaving the jury with the impression that there must be reasonable grounds for the honest but mistaken belief before the defence could prevail. Lambert J.A. based his dissent not upon the main charge but upon a supplementary charge requested by the jury after they had commenced their deliberations. On their return to the courtroom, after some evidence had been read back at the jury's request, the following occurred [at pp. 275-76]:

THE COURT: Thank you. Now that's the evidence of Mr. Jones that you asked for.
MR. FOREMAN, you've given me another question which is not quite as simple as the last one and you've asked for further address to the jury on the matter of reasonable belief. I'm hard pressed to do that. Is there anything specific that you're concerned about?
MR. FOREMAN" My lord, I believe when you were addressing us this morning on the definition of reasonable belief that you were going quite quickly.
THE COURT: Okay, I'll go over it again. You realize, of course, when I instructed you on honest belief, this is the third position as opposed to—opposed to the consent being asserted by the accused, denied by the complainant, this is something over and above that scenario, and that's where it is. If you find there is some evidence that might assist you in concluding that, even though the girl wasn't consenting, *you accepted that, if there is some basis upon which the accused thought she was consenting, that would be a defence, but that has to be based on something more than something in his mind, it has to be based on something else, some evidence from which an inference can be drawn that she might be consenting.*
I will read again — I dealt with the ingredients of the crime of rape as being complete upon (a) an act of sexual intercourse, (b) without consent. An affirmative finding as to each of these elements in this case does not end the matter, as a defence is not evidence that the accused believed Laybourn —believed Ms. [S.] to be consenting to the sexual intercourse.
The commission of a crime voluntarily directed by a willing mind, this we call mens rea. This consists of some positive state of mind such as an intention or the knowledge of the wrongfulness of the act or reckless disregard of the consequences which must be proved by the prosecution. The mental element may be established by inference on the nature of the act committed or by additional evidence. You will be concerned to consider the reasonableness of any grounds found or asserted to be available to support the accused's belief. Reasonable ground is not a pre-condition to the

### 634  AN INTRODUCTION TO CRIMINAL LAW IN CONTEXT

> availability of honest belief and consent, those grounds determine the weight to be given to the evidence. The reasonableness or otherwise of the accused's belief is only evidence for or against the view that the belief was actually held and the intent was therefore lacking. So if you conclude that the Accused of any of them honestly believed Miss [S] was consenting to the acts of intercourse and that then that necessary mental element would be lacking and you would acquit.
>
> *Now, this is* — that is only, of course, when there is some reasonable grounds to support the belief because it can hardly be an honest belief if it isn't based on anything to support the belief and it's not sufficient to say I believe she was opposing the rape, it has to be something else, something you can glean from the evidence to support that position.

The words of the foreman of the jury, quoted above, revealed that the jury was concerned on the question of reasonable belief. It was therefore important that the trial judge direct the jury fully on the question so that any misapprehension on their part could be dispelled. Lambert J.A. noted this point and, referring to the two emphasized passages in the part of the charge quoted above, he said, at pp. 276-77:

> The first passage is wrong. The defence of honest belief does not have to be based on something more than something in his mind. The trial judge should not put the "air of reality" question to the jury. That is for him. Once he has decided to put the defence to the jury, the "air of reality" question is over. All that is then required is for the jury to decide on the evidence whether the accused honestly believed in consent, in his own mind. There does not have to be "evidence from which an inference could be drawn that she might be consenting." That diverts the jury from the question that is truly before them, namely: did the accused believe that the complainant consented?
>
> The second passage is also wrong. There do not have to be reasonable grounds to support the belief. It can be an honest belief even if there are no reasonable grounds. I do not think that the previous paragraph can modify the impression that this last paragraph must have had on the jury. I doubt if what the trial judge actually said was ". . . it's not sufficient to say I believe she was opposing the rape . . ."

As I have indicated, I agree with Lambert J.A. that the "air of reality" test is for the judge and does not concern the jury. The issue facing the jury with respect to the defence which had been put to them related to the honesty of the appellant's asserted belief in consent. It was said to be error on the part of the trial judge to say that the belief entertained by the appellants had to be based on something from which the inference could be drawn that there might be a consent. In this, the trial judge may well have been confusing the "air of reality" test, which is for him alone, with the "reasonable doubt" test, which is for the jury, and his words may well have diverted the jury from their true task, which was to answer the question: Did the accused believe that the complainant consented? Regardless of its effect on them, however, the second passage attacked by Lambert J.A. is clearly wrong and, as he said, amounts to serious misdirection. I am unable to say that this specific direction that there must be some reasonable ground to support the asserted belief, being the last words the jury heard on the subject, would not override the earlier correct direction. I would, accordingly, allow the appeal and direct a new trial.

*Appeal allowed; new trial ordered.*

### Questions/Discussion

1. Do you agree with the results and the reasoning of the majority in *Kundeus*? Do you think the decision is theoretically correct as to what we are punishing or should be punishing for in criminal law? Should intent be "transferred" at all, even to an actus reus which turns out to be less serious than the intended criminal conduct? Is the intent or mens rea to be

considered that of the specific intent involved in the doing of an actus reus or is it a more general notion of some wrongful or blameworthy intent? Which should it be? For a full discussion of competing conceptions of mens rea, see Weiler's article in "Further Reading", below.

2. Is the requirement that the mistake need only be honest and not reasonable satisfactory? Should we include a reasonableness test to protect society from stupid or unreasonable people or should the focus be on individual moral culpability continue? If reasonableness is not generally included in the test, then should the law make special requirements in the case of sexual assault and claims of mistaken belief as to consent in light of the attitudes and stereotypes which surround women victims and the issues of consent (see section 273.2 of the Code)? What types of justifications can be advanced to require special criteria in one particular area of the criminal law to alter a general defence of mistake of fact?

## Further Reading

- Mewett, A., and M. Manning, *Mewett and Manning on Criminal Law*, 3rd ed. (Toronto: Butterworths, 1994).
- Pickard, T., "Culpable Mistakes and Rape: Relating Mens Rea to the Crime" (1980), 30 University of Toronto Law Journal 75.
- Stuart, D., *Canadian Criminal Law: A Treatise*, 2nd ed. (Toronto: Carswell, 1987), pp. 241-272.
- Stuart, D., and R. Delisle, *Learning Canadian Criminal Law*, 5th ed. (Toronto: Carswell, 1995).
- Verdun-Jones, S., and C. Griffiths, Canadian Criminal Justice, 2nd ed. (Toronto: Butterworths, 1994).
- Weiler, J., "*R. v. Kundeus*: the Saga of Two Ships Passing in the Night" (1976), 14 Osgoode Hall Law Journal 457.
- Williams, J., "Mistake of Fact: The Legacy of *Pappajohn v. The Queen* (1985), 63 Canadian Bar Review 597.

## 7.2.2 Ignorance of the Law

### Introduction

"Ignorance of the law is no excuse" is a well known phrase and one which is essentially true. The inability to use mistake of law as a defence is codified in section 19 of the Criminal Code. The difficulty in this area of law comes in trying to label mistakes as either those of fact or of law. As noted in the introduction to this chapter, many mistakes relate to combined matters of law and fact, yet how the mistake is categorized is vitally important as to its potential as a defence. The following cases give examples of how the courts treat various types of mistakes. We can see as well that in situations where the mistake of law has been genuine and has been relied upon, then it can be used as a mitigating factor at the time of sentencing.

There is an argument that certain types of mistake of law known as "officially induced errors" should be accepted as valid defences. The situation where such would arise is where a person has been directly misled by a government official; for example, you are told by a government official you do not need a licence to hunt and then you are arrested for hunting without a licence. The argument is that you have relied upon the advice of an official who should have known the applicable law, and that you should not be held liable for reasonably relying on the official's incorrect advice. The defence has been used successfully in some lower courts and an example is given in *Cancoil Thermal Corporation* and *Parkinson* below. The more established view, however, is that such a factor should only be important as a ground for an absolute discharge or in the mitigation of sentence.[1]

## Regina v. Shymkowich
(1954), 110 C.C.C. 97 (S.C.C.)

Only the judgment of Rand J. is reproduced below.

RAND J.: — The external facts in this appeal are few and simple. The accused removed from a booming ground, within which a lumber company, the prosecutor, had exclusive privileges for the putting down of mooring dolphins, the ancorage of booms, a line of piles and a log haul-up, two logs belonging to the company which at the time of removal had become lodged against the easterly end of a line of booms. He did that by entering the water area over a boundary line of single logs a distance of approximately 40 ft. and towing the two logs out and down the Fraser River where on the following day he sold them, along with 23 others, for $80 or so.

He was believed in saying that he did not intend to do anything wrong and that he thought he had the right to do what he did. This both the County Court Judge who tried him and the Court of Appeal [108 Can. C.C. 194] have found to be an answer to the charge laid.

. . . .

What, then, he believed was that by a general law he had a right to collect them as he did, to dispose of them, and in effect to require the owners to pay him or the person to whom he transferred them remuneration for his salvage work. Is that admissible as a defence? I have no doubt that it is not. As Kenny in his Outlines of Criminal Law, 1952 ed. at pp. 48-9 says: "The final condition is, that the mistake, however reasonable, must not relate to matters of law but to matters of 'fact'. For a mistake of law, even though inevitable, is not allowed in England to afford any excuse for crime. *Ignorantia juris neminem excusat.* The utmost effect it can ever have is that it may occasionally, like drunkenness, rebut the existence of the peculiar form of *mens rea* which some particular kind of crime may require."

This principle is embodied in s. 22 of the *Cr. Code*: "The fact that an offender is ignorant of the law is not an excuse for any offence committed by him."

A claim to ownership of a chattel, although it may depend on matter of law, is, in most cases, a question of fact, or its legal basis may, in the ordinary sense of the word, be subsumed in "fact". This enhances the difficulty of separating legal from factual elements in any relation to property and in any case it may resolve itself into a refined conceptual distinction. But a distinction between justifying an act as authorized by law and as a *bona fide* belief in a property interest does seem to correspond with an instinctive discrimination between the two concepts.

This idea is given its best expression by Lord Westbury in *Cooper v. Phibbs* (1867), L.R. 2 H.L. 149 at p. 170 in the following language: "It is said, '*ignorantia juris haud excusat;*' but in that maxim the word '*jus*' is used in the sense of denoting general law, the ordinary law of the country. But when the word '*jus*' is used in the sense of denoting

---

[1] For a full discussion of the issues involved, see N.S. Kastner, "Mistake of Law and the Defence of Officially Induced Error" (1985-86), 28 Criminal Law Quarterly 308.

a private right, the maxim has no application. Private right of ownership is a matter of fact; it may be the result also of matter of law; but if parties contract under a mutual mistake and misapprehension as to their relative and respective rights, the result is, that that agreement is liable to be set aside as having proceeded upon a common mistake."

This language was used in a civil proceeding but it furnishes a most helpful distinction for the application of the maxim in criminal law of which it has always been taken to be a basic principle.

The taking into possession and the conversion of the logs obviously was intended to deprive the owner temporarily at least of its property and this comes within the express language of the definition of theft given by the Criminal Code.

I would therefore allow the appeal and direct a judgment of conviction upon the second count, with a fine of $25 imposed on the accused.

[ESTEY J., with whom FAUTEUX J. concurred, held that the "respondent, in taking these logs out of the possession of the company, could not be said to have an honest and reasonable belief in the existence of facts which, if true, would have constituted a defence and, therefore . . . he possessed mens rea."]

[LOCKE J. dissented on the basis that "to constitute the offence, the act must be done fraudulently and without colour of right. In Stephen's History of the Criminal Law, vol. 3, p. 124, the learned author says " . . . A man who takes possession of property which he really believes to be his own does not take it fraudulently, however unfounded his claim may be. This, if not the only, is nearly the only case in which ignorance of the law affects the legal character of acts done under its influence."]

*Appeal allowed.*

## Regina v. Howson
[1966] 3 C.C.C. 348 (Ont. C.A.)

[Only the judgment of Porter C.J.O. is reproduced below.]

PORTER, C.J.O.: — This is an appeal from the conviction of the accused dated June 24, 1965, by J.L. Addison, Magistrate, on a charge that he did on January 28, 1965, at the Municipality of Metropolitan Toronto, steal one automobile of a value exceeding $50, the property of one Bruce Haines. On the evening on January 28th, Haines parked his 1956 automobile at the rear of 86 Bloor St. W., on private property. There were parking signs on the property, stating that there should be no parking day or night on the private property, or the unauthorized cars would be towed away at the owner's expense. When Haines returned to the place where he had parked his car it was not there. As a result of inquiries he found the car in a yard on Merton St. surrounded by a high fence and guarded by an attendant and a police dog. He was informed by the attendant that he could not have his car unless he paid a $10 towing charge and a $2 storage charge. The evidence discloses that some two hours earlier, the appellant had taken Haines' car from lot at 86 Bloor St. W., had towed it to Merton St. and had impounded it in the yard. The appellant said that it was taken on the authority of the owner of the building. There was no consent given by Haines to the removal or towing or storage of his car. Haines was deprived of his car until the following evening when it was released to him on payment of $14.

Haines, in his evidence stated that the appellant produced a letter signed by the superintendent of the parking lot, which reads as follows:

> "This letter gives the Ace Towing Service the sole authority to tow away cars parked on private parking lot at rear of building that is parked there without proper consent."

The Ace Towing Service was operated by the appellant and his brother, Walter Howson. The appellant appeared to be an employee of his brother.

The relevant sections of the *Criminal Code* read as follows:

> **269**(1) Every one commits theft who fraudulently and without colour of right takes, or fraudulently and without colour of right converts to his use or the use of another person, anything whether animate or inanimate, with intent,
> (a) to deprive, temporarily or absolutely, the owner of it or a person who has a special property or interest in it, of the thing or of his property or interest in it . . .
>
> "(3) A taking or conversion of anything may be fraudulent notwithstanding that it is effected without secrecy or attempt at concealment.
>
> "(4) For the purposes of this Act the question whether anything that is converted is taken for the purpose of conversion, or whether it is, at the time it is converted, in the lawful possession of the person who converts it is not material."

The *Criminal Code* and the *Larceny Act*, 1916 (U.K.), c. 50, are similar in so far as they apply to facts corresponding to those in issue here. If upon all the facts, the only inference which may reasonably be drawn points to an intent to steal, a conviction must follow. If the evidence shows, as in this case, that there was no legal right to withhold the vehicle, and unlike this case, that there was no other evidence, there would I should think, be an irresistible inference of theft. If, however, upon consideration of all the evidence before them, a jury, properly instructed, were satisfied that the accused honestly but mistakenly believe that he had a right in law or in fact, they should acquit. The question is whether upon all the evidence the proper inference to be drawn would be that the accused did have an honest belief. This is the question for the tribunal of first instance. The weight of authority would indicate, I think, that the test for the determination of the presence of an honest belief is a subjective rather than an objective one.

. . . .

Thus there is considerable authority in the English cases culminating in the decision of the Court of Criminal Appeal in *R. v. Bernhard, supra,* to establish that colour of right applies equally to fact and law. I think that in England, honest mistake of either fact or law would be a defence to a charge of theft. The Canadian authorities are less clear. In *R. v. Lyon, supra,* a Divisional Court dealt with a situation where the defendant had a right to demand payment. In *R. v. Laroche, supra,* it is doubtful whether the Supreme Court intended to overrule the judgment of McLennan, J.A., which was consistent with *R. v. Bernhard*. In *R. v. Shymkowich*, Rand J., adopted a statement from Kenny to the effect that mistake of law is not an excuse, and in this Taschereau, J, concurred. Estey, J., Fauteux, J., concurring, considered a mistake of law as well as of fact to be a defence.

Rand, J., did not deal with the question of colour of right. He relied upon s. 19 of the *Criminal Code* which states:

"**19.** Ignorance of the law by a person who commits an offence is not an excuse for committing that offence."

In my view the word "right" should be construed broadly. The use of the word cannot be said to exclude a legal right. The word is in its ordinary sense charged with legal implications. I do not think that s. 19 affects s. 269. Section 19 only applies when there is an offence. There is no offence if there is colour of right. If upon all the evidence it may fairly be inferred that the accused acted under genuine misconception of fact or law, there would be no offence of theft committed. The trial tribunal must satisfy itself that the accused has acted upon an honest, but mistaken belief that the right is based upon either fact or law, or mixed fact and law.

. . . .

The learned trial Judge held that the removal of the vehicle to Merton St. was not an unreasonable thing to do. Under the circumstances, I would agree with this finding. The real question here is whether the accused had, under the circumstances, a colour of right sufficient to justify his refusal to release the vehicle. If not, upon the facts of this case, he would be guilty of theft.

The accused was an employee of his brother, Walter Howson, who was the owner of the towing company. The evidence indicates that the accused acted upon instructions from his brother. He stated that he believed he had a right to retain the car until the towing charges were paid. He produced a letter from the building superintendent which ostensibly gave him the right to retain the car. Because the accused was asked to give up the car and refused to do so without payment, the Magistrate said that he was wrongfully withholding the car, the company having no lien upon it. He thereupon convicted the accused. However, the Magistrate then proceeded to make certain comments. He said that the accused was not trying to steal a car or intending to steal one. He then said that the type of business was not one that he would encourage.

I think that it is clear from this evidence that the Magistrate misdirected himself by failing to consider the question of colour of right. From what he said after the conviction, it was obvious that he did not believe that the accused was trying or intending to steal the car. Under these circumstances he should, I think, have acquitted the accused. There were other points raised in the argument, but since, upon the grounds stated, I would acquit, I do not think it necessary to deal with them.

I would, therefore, allow the appeal, quash the conviction and direct that a verdict of acquittal be entered.

*Appeal allowed; accused acquitted.*

## Regina v. Campbell and Mlynarchuk
(1972), 10 C.C.C. (2d) 26 (Alta. Dist. Ct.)

KERANS, D.C.J. (orally): — This is an appeal by Darlene Agatha Campbell from conviction and sentence.

. . . .

On a charge before the summary conviction Court that she did, between February 9, 1972, and February 21, 1972, at the City of Edmonton, in the Province of Alberta, unlawfully take part as a performer in an immoral performance at Chez Pierre's situated at 10615- Jasper Ave., Edmonton, contrary to s. 163(2) of the *Criminal Code*.

This matter, therefore, comes before me by way of a trial *de novo*. That section provides, in s-s. (2):

> (2) Everyone commits an offence who takes part or appears as an actor, performer, or assistant in any capacity, in an immoral, indecent or obscene performance, entertainment or representation in a theatre.

The facts before me are relatively straightforward. On the dates in question, at the place in question, the appellant danced on stage, before an audience. At the start of her performance, she was wearing some clothes. By the end of her performance, she was not wearing any clothes. The dance was described to me as a "go-go dance" which, I understand, is a violent movement of almost all part of the body, more or less in time to strongly rhythmic music.

I have no doubt in coming to the conclusion that this is a performance within the meaning of the section, and that, in doing what she did, the appellant took part as a performer in that performance. On the question of whether or not the performance was immoral, both counsel have agreed that I am bound to follow the recent decision of the Appellate Division of the Supreme Court of Alberta in *R. v. Johnson (No. 1)* (1972), 8 C.C.C. (2d) 1, [1972] 5 W.W.R. 638. This was a stated case before the learned Riley, J. [6 C.C.C. (2d) 462, [1972] 3 W.W.R. 226], and appealed from him to the Appellate Division.

In that case, McDermid, J.A., speaking for the Court, said, after drawing attention to the fact that s. 170 of the *Criminal Code* makes it a crime for anyone to appear nude in a public place, that he understood the enactment of that offence, by the Parliament of Canada, and, I quote, "declared that it is a breach of a moral standard in Canada". And he goes on,

"We know of no better way of establishing a moral standard than a declaration by the Parliament of Canada, so the Provincial Judge was justified in accepting this as his standard in finding that the dance by the respondent in the nude was an immoral performance." I understand, therefore, that since, to be nude in a public place is itself an offence; to perform in the nude, therefore, is an immoral performance within the meaning of the charging section. Therefore, I must conclude that the performance here was immoral within the meaning of that section.

I have been told that the decision of the Appellate Division has been appealed to the Supreme Court of Canada [8 C.C.C. (2d) 279n]. In some cases it is considered appropriate to adjourn or reserve, pending the outcome of an appeal. In my view, this rule should not be followed in the case of appeals from the Appellate Division to the Supreme Court of Canada, for various reasons. One is the delay of time involved. Therefore, on this point, the position of the parties would have to be that, should the Appellate Division decision not be upheld, my decision must also be appealed.

. . . .

The next argument raised on behalf of the appellant is that the appellant lacked the necessary *mens rea* for this offence. The facts in this respect were these: she engaged to do this performance, where, earlier, she had refused to engage to do this performance, because she relied upon the statement made to her, by Pierre Couchard, that he, in turn, had been informed that a Supreme Court Judge had, to use his words because he also gave evidence, "Ruled that we could go ahead with bottomless dancing." That decision arose out of a charge in the City of Calgary, of a business acquaintance of Couchard, who was the manager of the place where this performance took place. Ironically, the decision to which Couchard and the appellant referred is the decision at the Trial Division level in *R. v. Johnson (No. 1)*, to which I earlier referred, and which, the witnesses tell me, obtained some newspaper publicity. It was a decision then, that subsequently was reversed on appeal.

Mistake of fact is a defence to a criminal charge, where it can be said that the facts believed by the accused, if true, would have afforded him a defence. It is also said that a mistake of mixed fact and law is a defence. I understand that proposition to be correct, simply because, if there is a mistake of mixed fact and law, then there is a mistake of fact. In my view, there was no mistake of fact by the appellant here. What she was told had happened, in fact, did happen.

. . . .

This is not a situation like others, where a mistake of law can be a defence, not because a mistake of law is a defence, but because a mistake of law can negative a malicious intent required for that crime. Thus, for example, where the law requires that a person wilfully, or maliciously, or knowingly, does something wrong, it could conceivably be a defence as negativing intention, to show that, because of the mistake in the understanding of the law, there was no wilful intent or malice. This is not one of those situations as no such special intention is required for this offence. The only *mens rea* required here is that the appellant intended to do that which she did. And there is no suggestion, for a moment, that she lacked that *mens rea*.

This statement, that mistake of law is no defence, is contained in the *Criminal Code*, in s. 19, under the old numbering, which says:

> 19. Ignorance of the law by a person who commits an offence is not an excuse for committing that offence.

Excuse, or legal justification, is a defence at law, and I understand that defence to mean that it is a defence to a criminal charge to show that the act complained of was authorized by some other law. Section 19 says that defence is not available, in effect, when a person has made a mistake as to whether or not this act is excused by another law or authorized by another law.

Properly understood, in my view, the section removing ignorance of the law as a defence, in criminal matters, is not a matter of justice, but a matter of policy. There will always be cases, not so complicated as this, where honest and reasonable mistakes as to the state of the law will be the explanation of the conduct of an accused. In such a circumstance, one cannot help but have sympathy for the accused. But that situation, traditionally, is not a defence. It is not a defence, I think, because the first requirement of any system of justice, is that it work efficiently and effectively. If the state of understanding of the law of an accused person is ever to be relevant in criminal proceedings, we would have an absurd proceeding. The issue in a criminal trial would then not be what the accused did, but whether or not the accused had a sufficiently sophisticated understanding of the law to appreciate that what he did offended against the law. There would be a premium, therefore, placed upon ignorance of the law.

. . . .

I have given some consideration as to whether or not this position varies at all, because of the unique circumstances here, where the appellant relied upon a specific judgment of a Court very immediate in terms of time and place, as opposed to a solicitor's opinion or some understanding as to the law. There is not question that there is something of an anomaly here. Reliance on a specific order, of a specific Judge, granted at a specific time and place, seems, at first sight, not to be ignorance of the law, but knowledge of the law. If it turns out that that Judge is mistaken, then, of course, the reliance on that Judge's judgment is mistaken. The irony of this: people in society are expected to have a more profound knowledge of the law than are the Judges. I am not the first person to have made that comment about the law, and while it is all very amusing, it is really to no point.

The principle that ignorance of the law should not be a defence in criminal matters is not justified because it is fair, it is justified because it is necessary, even though it will sometimes produce an anomalous result.

When this appellant relied on the decision of the learned trial Judge, she relied on his authority for the law. As it turns out, that reliance was misplaced, as misplaced as reliance on any statement as to the law I might make. Less so, I am sure.

. . . .

I, therefore, conclude that the mistake of law of the appellant affords no defence to her on this charge. There being no other defences, and the facts necessary having been made out, the conviction of the Court below, in my opinion, was correct. The appeal as to conviction is dismissed.

. . . .

I should have been more careful in my language a moment ago, when I said the appeal as to conviction was dismissed. Under the new law, I should have more properly said that I find the appellant guilty of the charge, and will hear argument as to whether or not to allow or dismiss the appeal as to conviction.

. . . .

Well, I have already indicated, in a quotation from Kenny, that, in this awkward situation, the matter does not afford a defence, but should certainly be considered in mitigation of sentence. Indeed, there are several cases, not as awkward as this, in the law reports, involving a person who had an honest and reasonable mistake in belief as to the law, and for whom the Courts expressed sympathy, and, in respect of whom, sentence was mitigated.

It is at this stage where the scales of justice are balanced. Clothed with very recent power to refuse to enter a conviction I can now balance the scales of justice even more delicately.

. . . .

I have no power to give a pardon, but I do have power to give an absolute discharge. In my view, this is the proper case.

. . . .

I am not aware, perhaps I am naive, but I am not aware that these tawdry nude night-club acts, of this sort, have become a prevalent problem in our community. Therefore, I think, out of the sense of justice, and certainly not out of any sense of approval for what this lady did, it would be appropriate for me to grant her an absolute discharge, and that is what I do.

*Accused discharged absolutely.*

## Regina v. Cancoil Thermal Corporation and Parkinson
(1986), 27 C.C.C. (3d) 295 (Ont. C.A.)

Appeal by the Crown from the accused's acquittal on charges contrary to ss. 14 and 16 of the *Occupational Health and Safety Act* (Ont.).

The judgment of the court was delivered by

LACOURCIELE J.A.: — The Crown appeals by leave, on a pure question of law, against the order of the Honourable Judge Alan R. Campbell in the District Court of Ontario at Kingston dismissing two appeals from the judgment of His Honour Judge Baker acquitting the respondents. On January 10, 1985, the respondents had pleaded not guilty to the following charges:

> . . . Cancoil Thermal Corporation . . . as Employer on or about the 20th day of March, 1984 at the Township of Pittsburg in the County of Frontenac and Province of Ontario, did commit the offence of failing to ensure that the measures and procedures prescribed by section 28 of Revised Regulations of Ontario, 1980, Regulation 692 were carried out in the work place in an industrial establishment, to wit, a factory located at Kingston Mills Road East, Contrary to section 14(1)(c), the Occupational Health and Safety Act, R.S.O. 1980, c. 321.
> 
> *Particulars:* A machine having an exposed moving part that endangered the safety of a worker was not equipped with and garded by a guard or other device which prevented access to the moving part. Stewart Pare was injured as a result.
> 
> (2) and further that Cancoil Thermal Corporation, Part Lot 41, Conc. 4, Pittsburg Township, as Employer, on or about the 20th day of March, 1984, at the Township of Pittsburg in the County of Frontenac and the Province of Ontario, did commit the offence of failing to ensure that the equipment, materials and protective devices prescribed by Section 28 of Revised Regulations of Ontario, 1980, Regulation 692 were provided in an industrial establishment, to wit, a factory located at Kingston Mills Road East Contrary to section 14(1)(a), the Occupational Health and Safety Act, R.S.O. 1980, c. 321.
> 
> *Particulars:* [same as above]
> 
> . . . Terence Parkinson — on or about the 20th day of March, 1984 at the Township of Pittsburg in the County of Frontenac and Province of Ontario, did commit the offence of failing to ensure that a worker worked in the manner and with the protective devices, measures and procedures required

by section 28 of Revised Regulations of Ontario, 1980, Regulation 692 in an industrial establishment, to wit, a factory located at Kingston Mills Road East. Contrary to section 16(1)(a), the Occupational Health and Safety Act, R.S.O. 1980, c. 321.

*Particulars*: [same as above]

## The Facts

The respondent corporation is in the business of manufacturing heat transfer coils at a factory located outside of Kingston. In December, 1983, the company took delivery of a large metal shearing machine, known as a "Newton Shear", which was needed to cut the metal used in the production of the casings for the coils. The blade of this "Newton Shear" was operated by means of a "foot pedal" located seven and one-half inches from the floor. When this foot pedal was depressed, the clutch would engage, the "hold down" mechanism would clamp the inserted piece of metal in place, and the blade would come down and cut the metal. When the foot pedal was not depressed, the blade was in the up position and was not in motion. Needless to say, when the shearing mechanism was engaged by the depression of the foot pedal, the blade of the machine became dangerous to its operator.

When the respondent corporation took delivery of the Newton Shear, the machine was equipped with a "guard" which had been installed by its manufacturer to prevent access to the blade area of the machine by the operator during its operation. However, the respondent Parkinson, who was the supervisor and foreman of the factory, and Mr. Datta, its general manager, felt that the guard created a hazard in that its presence made it more difficult for the operator to clear away pieces of scrap metal. Accordingly, they decided to remove the guard from the machine. No other guard or similar safety device was installed on the machine as a replacement. It was felt that the hold down device provided sufficient safety to the operator of the machine. However, there were openings in the hold down mechanism which permitted physical access to the blade area of the machine. With the guard removed, there was nothing on the machine to prevent physical access to the blade.

On March 20, 1984, a 26-year-old employee, Stuart Bradford Pare, while engaged in the operation of the metal shearing machine, accidently cut off the tips of six of his fingers (three fingers on each had) down to approximately the first joint. After cutting large pieces of metal into smaller pieces of a specified size, Mr. Pare, following what he described as the accepted procedure, had used his fingers to push a small piece of scrap metal through the machine and onto the floor. In the process of doing this he accidently depressed the foot pedal on the machine, activating the blade mechanism.

There can be no doubt that the guard which came installed on the machine would have prevented this accident, acting as a barrier to prevent the operator's hands or fingers from going into the area of the cutting blade. Mr. Pare had been employed by the respondent as a machine operator for seven or eight months. Before March 20, 1986, he had operated the machine on one occasion and only for a short period; there was a conflict of evidence at trial as to the specific instructios given to him on safety precaution in the operation of the machine. Mr. Pare had helped Mr. Parkinson to modify the machine by removing the guard.

It will be more convenient to detail later the inspection of this machine made by an inspector of the Ministry of Labour before the accident in January, 1984, and on the day after the accident when he made an order that the machine could not be used until the guard was replaced.

## *The Statutory Provisions*

Generally, the *Occupational Health and Safety Act,* R.S.O. 1980, c. 321, is designed to protect the health and safety of workers in Ontario and is administered and enforced by the Ministry of Labour. Part VIII of the Act deals with enforcement. Inspectors are given broad powers to inspect the work place and to make orders, without the requirement of a hearing, where they find that a contravention of the Act or regulation creates a danger or hazard to the health or safety of a worker. Part IX deals with offences and penalties. The general penalty section is s. 37(1) which provides as follows:

> 37(1) Every person who contravenes or fails to comply with,
> (a) a provision of this Act or the regulations;
> (b) an order or requirement of an inspector or a Director; or
> (c) an order of the Minister,
> is guilty of an offence and on conviction is liable to a fine of not more that $25,000 or to imprisonment for a term of not more than twelve months, or to both.

The information alleged that the respondent corporation had breached s. 14(1)(a) and (c) which provide:

> 14(1) An employer shall ensure that,
> (a) the equipment, materials, and protective devices as prescribed are provided;
>
> . . . .
>
> (c) the measures and procedures prescribed are carried out in the workplace;

It was alleged that the respondent was in breach of s. 28 of the regulations, R.R.O. 1980, Reg. 692, which provides:

> 28. Where a machine or prime mover or transmission equipment has an exposed moving part that may endanger the safety of any worker, the machine or prime mover or transmission equipment shall be equipped with and guarded by a guard or other device that prevents access to the moving part.

The information against the respondent Parkinson was based on s. 16(1)(a) which states:

> 16(1) A supervisor shall ensure that a worker,
> (a) works in the manner and with the protective devices, measures and procedures required by this Act and the regulations;

I should note at this time that the Act provides a statutory equivalent of the defence of due diligence. This provision does not apply to the offence charged against the respondent corporation under s. 14(1)(a). Section 37(2) of the Act provides as follows:

> 37(2) On a prosecution for a failure to comply with,
> (a) subsection 13(1);
> (b) clause 14(1)(b), (c) or (d); or
> (c) subsection 16(1),
> it shall be a defence for the accused to prove that every precaution reasonable in the circumstances was taken.

The specific exclusion of this statutory defence in the case of offences under s. 14(1)(a) would suggest that the Legislature, as a matter of policy, had determined that the subsection creates an offence of absolute liability as defined in *R. v. City of Sault Ste. Marie*(1978), 40 C.C.C. (2d) 353, 85 D.L.R. (3d) 161, [1978] 2 S.C.R. 1299. However, it s. 14(1)(a) were treated as creating an absolute liability offence, it would offend s. 7 of the *Canadian Charter of Rights and Freedoms,* the right to life, liberty and security of the person and the right not to be deprived thereof except in accordance with the principles of fundamental justice. Under s. 37(1), a violation of s. 14(1)(a) may attract a term of imprisonment. In *Reference re. s. 94(2) of Motor Vehicle Act* (1985), 23 C.C.C. (3d) 289, 24 D.L.R. (4th) 536, [1985] 2 S.C.R. 486, the Supreme Court of Canada held that the combination of absolute liability and the potential penalty of imprisonment was a violation of s. 7 of the Charter. In the words of Lamer J. at p. 311 C.C.C., p. 515 S.C.R.:

> A law enacting an absolute liability offence will violate s. 7 of the Charter only if and to the extent that it has the potential of depriving of life, liberty or security of the person.
> Obviously, imprisonment (including probation orders) deprives persons of their liberty. An offence has that potential as of the moment it is open to the judge to impose imprisonment. There is no need that imprisonment, as in s. 94(2), be made mandatory.
> I am therefore of the view that the combination of imprisonment and of absolute liability violates s. 7 of the Charter. . .

To avoid a violation of s. 7 of the Charter, s. 14(1)(a) must be treated as creating a strict liability offence. The defence of due diligence was available to the respondents.

. . . .

### The Defence of Estoppel or Officially Induced Error

The difficult question is whether there exists on this record any room for the defence of estoppel or of "officially induced error" of law.

The inspector from the Ministry of Labour (Occupational Health and Safety Division), Mr. J.J. Ogoniek, had inspected the factory on January 16, 1984, more than two months before the accident. At the time of the inspection, the guard installed by the manufacturers had been removed. Although the machine had not been put into production, it was run while the inspector was present so that he could observe the cycle of operation. The absence of the manufacturer's guard was pointed out by the respondent Parkinson. According to the evidence of the respondent Parkinson, the inspector commented that it was "safe to remove the particular piece of metal in question and that with the machine being operated according to instructions that it was safe to do so." Mr. Pare who had not then operated the machine, stated that he had "no unresolved health and safety concerns". In any event, the inspector was satisfied apparently that no provision of the Act or regulations was being contravened and he made no order pursuant to his powers under s. 29 of the Act. However, on March 21st, the day after the accident, the inspector issued an order that the metal shear was not to be used until access to the blade area had been blocked. This order was complied with on the following day "by welding 1/4 inch x 1 inch steel bars across the openings in the hold down".

On the record, it is clear that the inspector was an official of the Occupational Health and Safety Division of the Ministry of Labour, appointed for the purpose of inspection and examination of the work place and that he was clothed with wide powers to enforce compliance with the Act and its regulations.

The defence of "officially induced error", exists where the accused, having adverted to the possibility of illegality, is led to believe, by the erroneous advice of an official, that he is not acting illegally. In *R. v. Walker and Somma* (1980), 51 C.C.C. (2d) 423, Martin J.A., in an *obiter dictum*, left open the possibility of this defence, and stated at p. 429:

> I would not wish to be taken to assent to the proposition that if a public official charged with responsibility in the matter led a defendant to believe that the act intended to be done was lawful, the defendant would not have a defence if he were subsequently charged under a regulatory statute with unlawfully doing that act: see "Excusable Mistake of Law", [1974] Crim. L.R. 652 at p. 660, by A.J. Ashworth. I leave aside that difficult question until it is necessary to decide it. Suffice it to say that no suggestion arises in this case that the respondents were misled by Customs officials.

An article by Professor P.G. Barton, "Officially Induced Error as a Criminal Defence: A Preliminary Look", 22 C.L.Q. 314 (1979-80), contains a helpful consideration of this defence.

In *R. v. MacDougall* (1981), 60 C.C.C. (2d) 137 at p. 160, 46 N.S.R. (2d) 47, 10 M.V.R. 236, the Nova Scotia Court of Appeal, *per* Macdonald J.A., recognized the defence in the following words:

> The defence of officially induced error has not been sanctioned, to my knowledge, by any appellate Court in this country. The law, however, is ever-changing and ideally adapts to meet the changing mores and needs of society. In this day of intense involvement in a complex society by all levels of Government with a corresponding reliance by people on officials of such Government, there is, in my opinion, a place and need for the defence of officially induced error, at least so long as a mistake of law, regardless how reasonable, cannot be raised as a defence to a criminal charge.

On a further appeal to the Supreme Court of Canada, Ritchie J. appeared to give approval to the defence [1 C.C.C. (3d) 65 at p. 71, 142 D.L.R. (3d) 216, [1982] 2 S.C.R. 605]:

> It is not difficult to envisage a situation in which an offence could be committed under mistake of law arising because of, and therefore induced by, "officially induced error" and if there was evidence in the present case to support such a situation existing it might well be an appropriate vehicle for applying the reasoning adopted by Mr. Justice Macdonald. In the present case, however, there is no evidence that the accused was misled by an error on the part of the registrar.

The defence of "officially induced error" is available as a defence to an alleged violation of a regulatory statute where an accused has reasonably relied upon the erroneous legal opinion or advice of an official who is responsible for the administration or enforcement of the particular law. In order for the accused to successfully raise this defence, he must show that he relied on the erroneous legal opinion of the official and that his reliance was reasonable. The reasonableness will depend upon several factors including the efforts he made to ascertain the proper law, the complexity or obscurity of the law, the position of the official who gave the advice, and the clarity, definitiveness and reasonableness of the advice given.

I agree with the following statement made by Professor Barton in the article referred to *op. cit.* at p. 331:

Where the advice is given by an official who has the job of administering the particular statute, and where the actor relies on this advice and commits what is in fact an offence, even if the agency cannot be estopped does it follow that the actor should be excused? To do so is not to condone an illegality or say that the agency is estopped into a position of illegality, but to recognize that the advice was illegal but excuse the actor because he acted reasonably and does not deserve punishment.

It may well be that the individual respondent and the respondent corporation in the s. 14(1)(c) count (either count against the corporation would probably fall under the *Kienapple* principle [see *Kienapple v. The Queen* (1974), 15 C.C.C. (2d) 524, 44 D.L.R. (3d) 351, [1975] 1 S.C.R. 729], if a conviction were entered against it under the other count) need not rely on this novel defence if they can satisfy the trier of fact that they acted with due diligence. But, although it may at times overlap with the defence of due diligence, the defence of "officially induced error of law" is separate and distinct and can be asserted, in the same way as other defences.

In the present case, it will be for the trier of fact to decide whether the accused has proved, by a preponderance of evidence, that he was misled by the inspector into thinking that the removal of the manufacturer's guard would not be in contravention of the law. The record makes it clear that the inspector was an official involved in the administration of the relevant law, presumably familiar with the Act and regulations and having the expertise to determine whether a machine was equipped with the prescribed safety devices. Ordinarily, mistake of law cannot be successfully raised as a defence to a criminal or *quasi*-criminal charge or regulatory offence, but an officially induced error of law may, in some circumstances, constitute a valid defence. This will, of course, depend on whether the opinion of the official was reasonable in the circumstances and whether it was reasonable for the accused to follow it.

The evidence in the present case is too sparse and inconsistent to allow an appellate court to determine the availability of the defence. Officially induced error was not relied on at trial and was only raised by the court, *proprio motu* during the argument of the appeal. However, I should, in fairness, point out that the respondent relied on the defence of estoppel which would encompass the other defence. If a new trial is directed, the prosecution as well as the defence may adduce further evidence. I note that the inspector of the Ministry, J.J. Ogoniek, was present at the trial but was not called by either party although his reports were filed.

### *Conclusion*

For these reasons, I would allow the appeal, set aside the acquittals of both respondents and direct a new trial.

*Appeal allowed; new trial ordered.*

## Forster v. The Queen
(1992), 70 C.C.C. (3d) 59 (S.C.C.)

APPEAL by the accused from a dismissal of her appeal by the Court Martial Appeal Court following her conviction by General Court Martial on a charge of being absent without leave.

LAMER C.J.C.: —

## The facts

The appellant, Ms. Forster, has been a commissioned officer in the Canadian Armed Forces since 1975. In June, 1987, she and her husband were transferred to the C.A.F. Base in Edmonton, where the appellant assumed the position of base comptroller. Prior to her difficulties with a particular superior officer at Edmonton, she had an excellent service record. Her difficulties evidently began during this new posting.

On January 29, 1988, Colonel Buckham (the Edmonton base commander) relieved the appellant of her duties as base comptroller, apparently due to his concerns regarding her management methods. Colonel Buckham testified that the appellant was advised to remain at home until called to a specific duty. On February 9th, Colonel Buckham sent a message to National Defence Headquarters, with a copy to Air Command, indicating the appellant was relieved of her duties as base comptroller. This same day, he also denied a redress of grievance that the appellant had submitted.

On February 15, 1988, the appellant was informed she had received an "attached posting" to the Directorate of Pay Services, Ottawa, her duties commencing February 19th. This was subsequently changed to 8:00 a.m., March 15th. The appellant did not report to her new posting on March 15th, but remained at her home in Edmonton where she was arrested by military police on March 16th. At the General Court Martial that followed, she gave the following explanation.

In early February, 1988, the appellant had engaged civilian legal counsel, because after researching the *Canadian Forces Administrative Orders,* the *Queen's Regulations and Orders for the Canadian Forces* ("Q.R. & O.") and the *National Defence Act,* R.S.C. 1985, c. N-5 (formerly R.S.C. 1970, c. N-4), she could not find any regulation or authority for Colonel Buckham to do what he had done. On February 18th, her counsel wrote a letter to Colonel Buckham, which stated: "Major Forster has no alternative but to treat these circumstances as a constructive dismissal of her employment from the Armed Forces."

On February 23, 1988, the appellant attended a meeting with Colonel Buckham, at which they discussed this letter. The appellant's request that her lawyer be present at this meeting was denied.

According to the appellant, she was told that she could not simply resign from the armed forces and that if she did not report for duty in Ottawa she could face charges under the *National Defence Act.* She was also advised to bring certain sections of the Act to the attention of her lawyer. However, the appellant further testified that at this meeting "[t]he invitation was extended to me by the Base Commander [Colonel Buckham] that I could, if I so wished, tender my release voluntarily at that point . . . Eventually I did tender my resignation, my lawyer sent a letter". With respect to this meeting, Colonel Buckham testified:

> In order to prevent what appeared to be a collision course with the *Code of Service Discipline,* I convened the meeting on the 23rd of February to lay out very clearly and explicitly, with a witness present so that there was no misunderstanding, just how serious a situation she was putting herself in. Indeed, with Major Gouin's assistance, we even brought to her attention the particular sections of the *National Defence Act* that applied to her and that would apply . . .

On March 10, 1988, the appellant's lawyer sent a second letter, this time to the commander of Air Command, indicating that the appellant "hereby resigns her position from the Armed Forces effective Monday, March 14, 1988".

The appellant testified that she did not attend at her posting in Ottawa because she had resigned. She felt this was her right, particularly because Colonel Buckham had told her at the meeting on February 23, 1988, that she could tender her release voluntarily. She testified that she did not intend to commit any offence, and that she believed that her resignation absolved her of the requirement of attending the posting in Ottawa.

On May 2, 1988, the appellant was convicted by a General Court Martial at Canadian Forces Base, Edmonton, on a charge of being absent without leave (s. 90 of the *National Defence Act* (formerly s. 80)). The judge advocate rejected her objections to the constitution and structure of the General Court Martial based on s. 11(*d*) of the *Canadian Charter of Rights and Freedoms*. The appellant's appeal to the Court Martial Appeal Court of Canada was unanimously dismissed.

[After discussing the constitutional issues involved in the case and deciding that the appeal would be allowed and a new trial ordered, Lamer continued:]

It is not therefore necessary to deal with the *mens rea* issue raised by the appellant. However, since this matter will be sent back for a new trial I consider it appropriate to deal with this question as well. The appellant did not contend before us that her purported resignation from the Canadian Forces was legally effective. What she claims is that she honestly believed that she had resigned from the forces, and that because of this she did not possess the requisite *mens rea* for the offence under s. 90 of the *National Defence Act* of being absent without leave. In my opinion, this submission can be dealt with very briefly. Even if we take the appellant's assertions about her beliefs at face value, she did not labour under any mistake about what she in fact did: she deliberately refrained from reporting to her new posting in Ottawa. Instead, she was mistaken about the legal consequences of her actions, because of her failure to understand that she was under a continuing legal obligation to report for duty notwithstanding her purported resignation by letter from the forces. Thus, while she may not have intended to commit any offence under military law, this lack of intention flowed from her mistake as to the continuing legal obligation to report for duty which that regime imposed upon her until properly released from service in accordance with the Q.R. & O.

It is a principle of our criminal law that an honest but mistaken belief in respect of the legal consequences of one's deliberate actions does not furnish a defence to a criminal charge, even when the mistake cannot be attributed to the negligence of the accused: *R. v. Molis* (1980), 55 C.C.C. (2d) 558, 116 D.L.R. (3d) 291, [1980] 2 S.C.R. 356. This court recently reaffirmed in *R. v. Docherty* (1989), 51 C.C.C. (3d) 1, at p. 15, [1989] 2 S.C.R. 941, 72 C.R. (3d) 1, the principle that knowledge that one's actions are contrary to the law is not a component of the *mens rea* for an offence, and consequently does not operate as a defence.

I do not rule out the possibility that, in an appropriate case, an officially induced error as to the state of the law might constitute a defence. However, I do not consider that it would be appropriate to rule on this question in the context of this appeal. At trial, defence counsel did raise the possibility of a defence based on an officially induced error of law. However, the precise theory advanced by the defence was somewhat unclear, and, in any case, the judge advocate concluded that there was no evidence to support such a defence, even if it existed. Defence counsel expressed complete satisfaction with the judge advocate's recharge, in which he repeated that there was no evidence to support a defence based on officially induced error. Consequently, the triers of fact received no instructions with respect to a possible defence of officially induced error of law, and made no finding as to whether it was supported by the evidence.

Before this court, the appellant in her statement of facts says that she relied upon certain remarks made to her by Colonel Buckham at the meeting of February, 1988, which led her to believe she could resign from the forces as she did. However, in argument the theory of officially induced error was not pressed and it is unclear whether, or to what extent, it was relied upon. Rather than attempt to unravel the somewhat confusing record, the availability of a defence of officially induced error of law, and whether such a defence arises on the facts of this case, should be left to be ruled upon, if raised, at a new trial.

In view of the above, it is not necessary to decide whether the offence of absence without leave is a *mens rea* offence or an offence of strict liability, for which the required mental state could simply be negligence. At trial, the appellant took the position, with which the judge advocate agreed, that absence without leave is a *mens rea* offence, not an offence of strict liability. Before this court, she argues that the judge advocate's charge may not have made this sufficiently clear. I am not convinced that the appellant is entitled to raise this issue at all, considering that her counsel at trial stated that he was "totally satisfied" with the recharge given by the judge advocate in response to defence counsel's objections to the part of the charge dealing with *mens rea*. Moreover, it is arguable that the offence of absence without leave is not a *mens rea* offence.

However, it is not necessary for me to decide this issue, because even assuming that absence without leave is a *mens rea* offence, the appellant was shown to have the requisite mental state. She was mistaken not about the factual context or the quality of her actions, but rather about their legal consequences. Without considering the possibility of a defence based on officially induced error of law, this is not a circumstance amounting to a defence.

. . . .

*Appeal allowed; new trial ordered.*

## Questions/Discussion
1. Do you agree that ignorance of the law should be no excuse or can you think of situations where it should affect criminal liability? Do you think that the result in *Campbell* and *Mylnarchuk* is fair or that an exception should have been made in the circumstances of the case?
2. Should the defence of officially induced error be accepted in Canada? If yes, then what rationale would you use to support its acceptance and what limitations would you place on it? If no, then why not?

3. Do you think that mistakes of law versus fact can be neatly categorized as one or the other? What tests can be used to delineate the two types of mistakes? Do we in the end have to rely solely on arbitrary distinctions made by the courts in previous cases?

**Further Reading**
- Kastner, N., "Mistake of Law and the Defence of Officially Induced Error" (1985-86) 28 Criminal Law Quarterly 308.
- Mewett, A., and M. Manning, *Mewett and Manning on Criminal Law*, 3rd ed. (Toronto: Butterworths, 1994).
- Stuart, D., *Canadian Criminal Law: A Treatise,* 2nd ed. (Toronto: Carswell, 1987), pp. 272-304.
- Stuart, D., and R. Delisle, *Learning Canadian Criminal Law*, 5th ed. (Toronto: Carswell, 1995).
- Ward, R., "Officially Induced Error of Law" (1988/89), 52 Saskatchewan Law Review 88-114.

## 7.3 POLICY DEFENCES
### 7.3.1 Entrapment
**Introduction**

Entrapment generally occurs when police go beyond the use of decoys, spies and informers, and instead encourage or even pressure a person into committing an offence for the purpose of securing an arrest. English courts reject a defence of entrapment, while U.S. courts have long accepted entrapment as a substantive defence. In Canada, there has been a great deal of uncertainty about the nature of the common law defence of entrapment in the past. Should it result in an acquittal, like self-defence, or should it merely allow the court to exclude certain evidence? Alternatively, should judges leave the issue to consideration at sentencing or should a successful plea of entrapment result in a stay of proceedings? Judicial views on the nature of entrapment depend in large part on whether they see it as a matter of abusive police practice, or as an issue affecting the blameworthiness of the accused.

In the landmark decision of *Mack* in 1988, the Supreme Court of Canada finally decided many of the issues surrounding the rationale and the availability of the defence. As you will see in the case, the focus of inquiry of the courts is now on the "objective assessment of the conduct of the police rather than on the effect of that conduct on the accused's state of mind" (Stuart, 1989:70). Such an approach illustrates the policy basis of the defence, that the courts do not want to be a party to abusive or coercive behaviour by the police. Because of this "abuse of process" approach, the remedy adopted is not an outright acquittal but rather a "stay of proceedings" by the judge which effectively ends the proceedings against the accused. The decision put an end to a great deal of uncertainty which had surrounded the defence for a long while. *Showman* and *Barnes* are examples of cases decided soon after *Mack* but in which the defence of entrapment fails on the facts.

### Mack v. R.
### (1989), 67 C.R. (3d) 1 (S.C.C.)

APPEAL by accused from judgment of British Columbia Court of Appeal, 49 C.R. (3d) 169, 23 C.C.C. (3d) 421, affirming accused's conviction of possession of narcotic for the purpose of trafficking, 34 C.R. (3d) 228, and refusing stay of proceedings.

December 15, 1988. The judgment of the court was delivered by
LAMER J.: —

## INTRODUCTION

The central issue in this appeal concerns the doctrine of entrapment. The parties, in essence, ask this court to outline its position on the conceptual basis for the application of the doctrine and the manner in which an entrapment claim should be dealt with by the courts. Given the length of these reasons due to the complexity of the subject, I have summarized my findings on pp. 68-71 [pp. 449-450] of these reasons.

## THE FACTS

The appellant was charged with unlawful possession of a narcotic for the purpose of trafficking. He testified at trial and, at the close of the case for the defence, brought an application for a stay of proceedings on the basis of entrapment. The application was refused and a conviction entered by Wetmore Co. Ct. J., sitting without a jury, in written reasons reported 34 C.R. (3d) 228. A notice of appeal from that decision was filed with the British Columbia Court of Appeal but the appeal books were not filed within the time prescribed. Counsel for the appellant sought and obtained, with the consent of Crown counsel, an order dispensing with the requirement that transcripts of evidence be filed and permitting counsel to base their arguments solely on the reasons for judgment of Wetmore Co. Ct. J. The Chief Justice of British Columbia directed that a panel of five judges hear the appeal. For the reasons given by Craig J.A., on behalf of the court, the appeal was dismissed. This decision is now reported at 49 C.R. (3d) 169, 23 C.C.C. (3d) 421. Leave to appeal was granted by this court.

It is necessary to describe in some detail the relevant facts. In view of the particular procedural history of this appeal, I think it is appropriate to reproduce in its entirety the summary of the evidence provided in the reasons for judgment of Wetmore Co. Ct. J. (at pp. 234-37).

> Through information obtained from an officer of the Ontario Provincial Police, one Momotiuk was brought to British Columbia. This man had apparently been dealing in narcotics in Kenora, Ontario. He was placed under police "handlers" in Vancouver, he visited the accused on a number of occasions, and eventually a transaction was set up whereby the accused would deliver cocaine to Momotiuk.
> The accused testified. He first met Momotiuk in 1979 in Montreal where the accused was visiting one Franks. The accused understood Franks and Momotiuk to be associated in some clothing franchise.
> The accused at this time was attempting to develop some property for sale near De Roche, British Columbia, and told Franks and Momotiuk of this and both expressed some interest in buying. Both arrived in British Columbia in October 1979. In the course of this visit the accused says that Momotiuk told him he was a drug trafficker in Kenora and wanted some "Thai pot". The accused says he had no interest.
> Momotiuk, according to the accused, called later still wanting to make drug deals, and the accused told him he was interested only in real estate deals.
> The accused again went to a yoga retreat near Montreal in December 1979. Franks and Momotiuk visited him there. Momotiuk produced some cocaine, which he and Franks used, and again asked the accused to become a supplier. A few days later they met again. At this time conversation was directed to show Momotiuk as an importer of drugs on a large scale, and again the accused was invited to join in and refused.

In January and February there were approximately seven telephone calls from Momotiuk to the accused soliciting his involvement. The accused says he refused.

In mid-February 1980 Momotiuk visited the accused again, asking him to supply drugs. The accused says he told Momotiuk he was not interested and asked to be left alone. Momotiuk continued to visit two or three times and telephoned.

In March the accused says Momotiuk arrived again. They went for a walk in the woods. Momotiuk produced a pistol and was going to show the accused his markmanship. He was dissuaded because of the probability of startling the horses nearby. The accused says that at this remote area Momotiuk said, "A person could get lost." This the accused says was a threat. He says the matter of drugs was again raised and the accused says he was adamant that he had no knowledge of drug sources.

The accused was asked to phone him twice and did not. One Matheson attended at the accused's residence on 13th March with a message that Momotiuk was very excited and wanted to see him at the Biltmore Hotel. The accused says he wanted nothing to do with Momotiuk but was terrified of him and agreed to go into town to the Biltmore. He also says that Matheson told him Momotiuk had some friends with him. This the accused took to be other members of this illegal syndicate.

While en route to the city he twice noted a car which seemed to be following him. This was probably so, because undercover police officers were doing a surveillance at the time.

On arrival at the hotel he met Momotiuk. Again he was informed of the syndicate. He was asked then if he wished to see the buying power. The accused agreed. He was directed to a car outside the hotel. In this car was an open briefcase with $50,000 exposed. The custodian, unknown to the accused, was an undercover policeman.

The accused returned to the hotel, Momotiuk asked him to get a sample and gave him $50 for this purpose.

The accused left and went to a supplier he had known of from years back. This supplier, one Goldsmith, now dead, heard the accused's story and agreed to supply "in order to get Doug (Momotiuk) off me". He obtained the sample and delivered it to Momotiuk, who tested it and said to get a much as he could. He returned to the supplier and offered $35,000 to $40,000 for a pound. At the meeting the following day the accused had still not acquired the drugs and he says that at this point he was told to get his act together, in a threatening way.

I need not detail the accused's evidence of the following two days. He obtained 12 ounces of cocaine, and was to pay $27,000 for it. This credit, he says, was extended to him by Goldsmith on the basis of payment when delivered to Momotiuk. It was in the course of this delivery that he was arrested. It is on the basis of this testimony that the accused says he was entrapped. Momotiuk, Matheson and Franks did not testify. Neither did "Bonnie", the accused's former wife, who was apparently present at one of the Montreal meetings, where cocaine was produced and some discussion took place.

The accused has drug convictions in 1972 and 1976, two in 1978 and one in 1979. Those in 1976, one in 1978 and one in 1979 involved cocaine. He says his former use of drugs arose to relieve back pain, but in 1978 he discovered relief from yoga and gave up the use of narcotics. The offence in 1979 was a fall from grace when he met up with old friends.

. . . .

## POSITION OF THE PARTIES

. . . .

### *Appellant*

The appellant asserts that there are two types of entrapment. The first is objective and involves an evaluation of police conduct in order to determine whether prosecution of the accused would amount to an abuse of the court's process. It is submitted that this analysis is a question of law to be addressed by the trial judge. If objective entrapment is found, the proper remedy is a stay of proceedings. This is purely a question of police misconduct and as such is determined wholly independently of the accused's state of mind.

The second type of entrapment is subjective and the focus is on the accused's state of mind. The test is whether the accused possesses the necessary predisposition to commit the crime; if he or she does not, then the element of mens rea is missing. This can exist, in the appellant's submission, even when the police are "blameless" in terms of the character of their conduct toward the accused.

The appellant draws an analogy to other excusing defences, such as necessity, which focus on the accused's response to a given set of facts. The appellant asserts that in subjective entrapment where the inquiry is on the accused's state of mind, like other mens rea issues, the question is one of fact to be decided by the jury. The onus would lie on the Crown to prove beyond a reasonable doubt that the accused was predisposed to commit the offence. In the result, the appellant submits, his conviction should be quashed as the trial judge stated he had a reasonable doubt as to whether the appellant was entrapped.

## *Respondent*

The respondent asserts that there is only one conception of entrapment and it is rooted in the doctrine of abuse of process. Entrapment is not a defence since the necessary mens rea will be present and the conduct of the accused will be neither excused nor justified. The respondent submits, however, that the test for determining whether or not there has been unlawful entrapment is an amalgam of subjective and objective tests: the defence is limited to situations where the conduct of the police has gone beyond permissible limits *and* the crime would not have been committed but for such activity. The police conduct must be, to use the respondent's phrase, the causa sine qua non of the offence.

With respect to procedural issues, the respondent asserts, the question of entrapment is one of law to be decided by the trial judge. The onus would be on the accused to establish on a balance of probabilities that the proceedings amounted to an abuse of the court's processes.

## ANALYSIS

### *The Context*

One need not be referred to evidence to acknowledge the ubiquitous nature of criminal activity in our society. If the struggle against crime is to be won, the ingenuity of criminals must be matched by that of the police; as crimes become more sophisticated so too must be the methods employed to detect their commission. In addition, some crimes are more difficult to detect.

....

I would note that in addition to so-called "victimless" or "consensual" crimes, active law enforcement techniques may be used to combat crimes where there are victims, but those victims are reluctant to go to the police because of intimidation or blackmail, as may be the case with the offence of extortion. Further, some criminal conduct may go unobserved for a long time if the victims are not immediately aware of the fact that they have been the subject of criminal activity, in the case, for example, of commercial fraud and also bribery of public officials. In general it may be said that many crimes are committed in secret and it is difficult to obtain evidence of their commission after the fact.

Obviously the police must be given considerable latitude in the effort to enforce the standards of behaviour established in the criminal law.

. . . .

*There is a crucial distinction, one which is not easy to draw, however, between the police or their agents — acting on reasonable suspicion or in the course of a bona fide inquiry — providing an opportunity to a person to commit a crime, and the state actually creating a crime for the purpose of prosecution.* The former is completely acceptable, as is police conduct that is directed only at obtaining evidence of an offence when committed: see *Amato*, per Estey J. at p. 446. *The concern is rather with law enforcement techniques that involve conduct that the citizenry cannot tolerate.* In many cases the particular facts may constitute a classic example of what may be referred to as "entrapment", which has been described by an American judge as *"the conception and planning of an offense by an officer, and his procurement of its commission by one who would not have perpetrated it except for the trickery, persuasion, or fraud of the officer"*: Sorrells v. U.S., 287 U.S. 435 at 454, 77 L. Ed. 413, 53 S. Ct. 210 (1932) per Roberts J., cited by Dickson C.J.C. in *Jewitt*, at p. 145.

. . . .

[After a discussion of Canadian and American cases, he continues:]

**The Rationale**

*The Regulation of the Administration of Justice*

It is critical in an analysis of the doctrine of entrapment to be very clear on the rationale for its recognition in Canadian criminal law. Much of what is contained in the opinion of Justice Estey in *Amato* provides this rationale. As was explained by Estey J., central to our judicial system is the belief that the integrity of the court must be attained. This is a basic principle upon which many other principles and rules depend. If the court is unable to preserve its own dignity by upholding values that our society views as essential, we will not long have a legal system which can pride itself on its commitment to justice and truth and which commands the respect of the community it serves. It is a deeply ingrained value in our democratic system that the ends do not justify the means. In particular, evidence or convictions may, at times, be obtained at too high a price. This proposition explains why as a society we insist on respect for individual rights and procedural guarantees in the criminal justice system. All of these values are reflected in specific provisions of the Charter, such as the right to counsel, the right to remain silent, the presumption of innocence and in the global concept of fundamental justice. Obviously, many of the rights in ss. 7 to 14 of the Charter relate to norms for the proper conduct of criminal investigations and trials, and the courts are called on to ensure that these standards are observed.

The principles expressed in the Charter obviously do not emerge in a legal, social or philosophical vacuum. With respect to criminal law in particular, the courts have, throughout the development of the common law and in the interpretation of statutes, consistently sought to ensure that the balance of power between the individual accused and the state was such that the interests and legitimate expectations of both would be recognized and protected. Lord Devlin, in *Connelly v. D.D.P.*, [1964] A.C. 1254, [1964] 2 W.L.R. 1145, 48 Cr. App. R. 183, [1964] 2 All E.R. 401 at 438 (H.L.), made the following apposite observation in this regard:

> ... nearly the whole of the English criminal law of procedure and evidence has been made by the exercise of the judges of their power to see that what was fair and just was done between prosecutors and accused. The doctrine of autrefois was itself doubtless evolved in that way.

It is my view that in criminal law the doctrine of abuse of process draws on the notion that the state is limited in the way it may deal with its citizens. The same may be said of the Charter, which set out particular limitations on state action and, as noted, in the criminal law context ss. 7 to 14 are especially significant.

. . . .

It is the belief that the administration of justice must be kept free from disrepute that compels recognition of the doctrine of entrapment. In the context of the Charter, this court has stated that disrepute may arise from "judicial condonation of unacceptable conduct by the investigatory and prosecutional agencies": *R. v. Collins*, [1987] 1 S.C.R. 265 at 281, [1987] 3 W.W.R. 699, 13 B.C.L.R. (2d) 1, 56 C.R. (3d) 193, 33 C.C.C. (3d) 1, 38 D.L.R. (4th) 508, 28 C.R.R. 122, 74 N.R. 276. The same principle applies with respect to the common law doctrine of abuse of process. Conduct which is unacceptable is, in essence, that which violates our notions of "fair play" and "decency" and which shows blatant disregard for the qualities of humanness which all of us share.

The power of a court to enter a stay of proceedings to prevent an abuse of its process was, as noted earlier, confirmed by this court in *Jewitt, supra*. The appropriateness of the court's exercise of the power, as well as the circumstances in which it may be used, is discussed in the following passage (at pp. 136-37, per Dickson C.J.C.):

> I would adopt the conclusion of the Ontario Court of Appeal in *R. v. Young, supra* [(1984), 40 C.R. (3d) 289], and affirm that "there is a residual discretion in a trial court judge to stay proceedings where compelling an accused to stand trial would violate those fundamental principles of justice which underlie the community's sense of fair play and decency and to prevent the abuse of a court's process through oppressive or vexatious proceedings". I would also adopt the caveat added by the Court in *Young* that this is a power which can be exercised only in the "clearest of cases".

It is essential to identify why we do not accept police strategy that amounts to entrapment. There could be any number of reasons underlying what is perhaps an intuitive reaction against such law enforcement techniques but the following are, in my view, predominant. One reason is that the state does not have unlimited power to intrude into our personal lives or to randomly test the virtue of individuals. Another is the concern that entrapment techniques may result in the commission of crimes by people who would not otherwise have become involved in criminal conduct. There is perhaps a sense that the police should not themselves commit crimes or engage in unlawful activity solely for the purpose of entrapping others, as this seems to militate against the principle of the rule of law. We may feel that the manufacture of crime is not an appropriate use of the police power. It can be argued as well that people are already subjected to sufficient pressure to turn away from temptation and conduct themselves in a manner that conforms to ideals of morality; little is to be gained by adding to these existing burdens. Ultimately, we may be saying that there are inherent limits on the power of the state to manipulate people and events for the purpose of attaining the specific objective of obtaining convictions. These reasons and others support the view that there is a societal interest in limiting the use of entrapment techniques by the state.

The competing social interest is in the repression of criminal activity. Further, our dependence on the police to actively protect us from the immense social and personal cost of crime must be acknowledged. There will be differing views as to the appropriate balance between the concepts of fairness and justice and the need for protection from crime, but it is my opinion that it is universally recognized that some balance is absolutely essential to our conception of civilized society. In deciding where the balance lies in any given case it is necessary to recall the key elements of our model of fairness and justice, as this is the only manner in which we can judge the legitimacy of a particular law enforcement technique.

It must be stressed, however, that the central issue is not the power of a court to *discipline* police or prosecutorial conduct but, as stated by Estey J. in *Amato* (at p. 461), "the avoidance of the improper invocation by the state of the judicial process and its powers". In the entrapment context, the court's sense of justice is offended by the spectacle of an accused being convicted of an offence which is the work of the state (*Amato*, at p. 447). The court is, in effect, saying it cannot condone or be seen to lend a stamp of approval to behaviour which transcends what our society perceives to be acceptable on the part of the state. The stay of the prosecution of the accused is the manifestation of the court's disapproval of the state's conduct. The issuance of the stay obviously benefits the accused but the court is primarily concerned with a larger issue: the maintenance of public confidence in the legal and judicial process. In this way, the benefit to the accused is really a derivative one. We should affirm the decision of Estey J. in *Amato*, that *the basis upon which entrapment is recognized lies in the need to preserve the purity of administration of justice.*

### The Guilt of the Accused.

Both the appellant and respondent agree that the rationale for recognition of the entrapment doctrine lies in the inherent jurisdiction of the court to prevent an abuse of it own processes. The respondent asserts that this is the exclusive rationale; the appellant submits that it is open to the court to view entrapment as also bearing on the accused's culpability and as such it would operated as a substantive defence.

It is not fruitful, in my view, to deal with impermissible police conduct through the vehicle of substantive criminal law doctrine. There are three problems with the appellant's proposition. Firstly, the conduct of the police or their agents in most cases will not have the effect of negativing mens rea or, for that matter, actus reus. (There may be exceptional cases, however: see, for example, the decision of this court in *Lemieux v. R.*, [1967] S.C.R. 492, 2 C.R.N.S. 1, [1968] 1 C.C.C. 187, 63 D.L.R. (2d) 75 [Ont.].) The physical act of the accused is a voluntary one and the accused will have an aware state of mind. The prohibited act will have been committed intentionally and with knowledge of the facts which constitute the offence and the consequences which flow from them.

However they may be defined, the essential elements of the offence in issue will have been met in most cases, and it is from this general position that the doctrine of entrapment should develop.

. . . .

Secondly, while the argument that the accused is not culpable because his or her conduct may be excused is more plausible, it is ultimately not compelling. For entrapment to be recognized as an excusing defence, it is clear that the focus must be directed at the effect of the external or internal circumstances on the accused.

. . . .

There is a third and perhaps more fundamental problem with the notion that entrapment relates to the blameworthiness or culpability of the accused: if this is the proper theoretical foundation for allowing the claim of entrapment, then on what principled basis can we justify limiting the defence to situations where it is the state, and not a private citizen, who is the entrapping party? Professor Colvin makes this point in the following passage (at p. 232):

> Considering entrapment from the standpoint of the theory of criminal culpability, the better arguments are for recognizing the defence in a procedural rather than an exculpatory form. This is not to deny that circumstances of entrapment can sometimes provide an excuse which might merit recognition by way of a special defence. But, if the argument for an excusing defence is accepted, it demands much more than the entrapment defence as it has been hitherto conceived. The arguments for an entrapment defence have been made with respect to entrapment by the police or their agents. Yet in almost all cases, the accused would not have known who was entrapping him. It is therefore immaterial to his culpability whether it happened to be the police or someone else. The argument for an excusing defence can only be sustained as an argument for a defence of wider application, available wherever someone has been pressured into committing an offence by another person. The defence of duress represents a limited concession to the view that exculpation can be appropriate in this kind of situation. There has, however, been little support for extending its rationale to cases of persistent solicitation. In addition, the arguments for making entrapment an excusing defence have generally been confined to entrapment by the police or their agents. If the defence is to be subject to this limitation, it is best conceived as an aspect of abuse of process. [citations omitted]

. . . .

I remain firmly of the view that the true basis for allowing an accused the defence of entrapment is *not* culpability. I will summarize the main reasons. Firstly, in most cases the essential elements of the offence will have been met. Secondly, the circumstances in which an accused is placed in an entrapment situation are not agonizing in the sense acknowledged by the defences of duress or necessity. Where the police conduct does amount to duress, that defence can be pleaded in conjunction with an abuse of process allegation. I would not, however, that any "threats" by the police, even if insufficient to support the defence of duress, will be highly relevant in the assessment of police conduct for the purpose of an abuse of process claim. The third reason why I am unwilling to view entrapment as relating to culpability is that if it did, there would not be a valid basis on which to limit the defence to entrapment by the state. The lack of support for an extension of the defence to provide against entrapment by private citizens demonstrates that the real problem is with the propriety

## The Proper Approach

. . . .

To summarize then, the police must not, and it is entrapment to do so, offer people opportunities to commit crime unless they have a reasonable suspicion that such people are already engaged in criminal activity or unless such an offer is made in the course of a bona fide investigation. In addition, the mere existence of a prior record is not usually sufficient to ground a "reasonable suspicion". These situations will be rare, in my opinion. If the accused is not alleging this form of entrapment, the central question in a particular case will be: Have the police gone further than providing an opportunity and instead employed tactics designed to induce someone into the commission of an offence?

There is, therefore, entrapment when (a) the authorities provide an opportunity to persons to commit an offence without reasonable suspicion or acting mala fides, as explained earlier, or (b) having a reasoning suspicion or acting in the course of a bona fide inquiry, they go beyond providing an opportunity and induce the commission of an offence. As I have already mentioned, the first form of entrapment is not likely to occur. The police of this country are generally resorting to the type of investigatory technique of providing opportunities only in relation to targeted people or locations clearly, and therefore reasonably, suspected of being involved in or associated with criminal activity, or again are already engaged in a bona fide investigation justifying the provision of such opportunities.

As regards the latter form of entrapment, to determine whether police conduct gives rise to this concern, it is useful to consider whether the conduct of the police would have induced the average person in the position of the accused, i.e., a person with both strengths and weaknesses, into committing the crime. I believe such a test is useful not only as an analytical mechanism that is consistent with objective analysis, but also because it corresponds to one of the reasons why the defence is thought desirable. In other words, it may be inevitable that when apprised of the factual context of an entrapment case, members of the community will put themselves in the position of the accused; if a common response would be that anyone could have been induced by such conduct, this is a valuable sign that the police have exceeded the bounds of propriety. The reasoning does not go so far as to imply that the accused is therefore less blameworthy; rather, it suggests that the state is involved in the *manufacture* as opposed to the detection of crime.

An objective approach which uses the hypothetical person test only is subject to some criticism. For example, Professor Park argues (at pp. 270-71):

> The defence creates a risk that dangerous chronic offenders will be acquitted because they were offered inducements that might have tempted a hypothetical law abiding person. More subtly, it creates a danger that persons will be convicted who do not deserve punishment. This danger stems from its attempts to evaluate the quality of government conduct without considering the defendant's culpability. The notion that sauce for the wolf is sauce for the lamb leads to unhappy consequences,

since the sauce will be brewed with wolves in mind. Because many targets are professional criminals, judges will be reluctant to rule that entrapment has occurred simply because an agent found it necessary to appeal to friendship, make multiple requests, or offer a substantial profit. Yet approval of such conduct would lead to unfair results in cases where the target was law-abiding but ductile. For example, conviction of someone who has been solicited by a friend may be fair enough in the general run of cases, but unfair if the target was a nonpredisposed person who would not have committed the type of crime charged but for a request from that particular friend.

The response to this is twofold. Firstly, I agree that there is a danger of convicting "lambs" or people who have a particular vulnerability such as a mental handicap or who are suffering from an addiction. In those situations, it is desirable for the purposes of analysis to consider whether the conduct was likely to induce criminal conduct in those people who share the characteristic which appears to have been exploited by the police. I am not, however, in agreement with the assertion that it is fair for the police in the general run of cases to abuse a close relationship between friends or family members, as compared to that between acquaintances, contacts or associates, for the purpose of inducing someone into the commission of an offence, and thus I do not consider this a valid criticism of the hypothetical person test. The nature of the relationship at issue is relevant and in certain cases it may be that the police have exploited confidence and trust between people in such a manner as to offend the value society places on maintaining the dignity and privacy of interpersonal relationships.

Secondly, I do not find the danger of acquitting wolves particularly troublesome. It assumes that it cannot be said that chance exists that a predisposed person would not have committed the particular offence were it not for the use of inducement that would have caused a nonpredisposed person to commit the offence. More fundamentally, this perspective is part of a larger view-point that in certain cases it would be better for society to send someone to jail for committing a crime, even if fundamental rights and procedural guarantees normally provided to an accused have been disregarded. The familiar refrain is that the end justifies the means. This view is, however, entirely inconsistent with the model of fairness which exists both within and alongside substantive criminal law doctrine. Could not the same comment of "acquitting wolves" be made where an accused's right to counsel or to remain silent have been flagrantly violated and the evidence of his or her confession to the crime is excluded? In the short term, it may well be "better" for society to convict such persons, but it has always been held that in the long term it would undermine the system itself. If the rule of law is to have any meaning and provide the security which all in society desire, it is axiomatic that it be extended to every individual.

I am not of the view that the hypothetical or average person model is the *only* relevant method of analysis. There may be situations where it cannot be concluded that a hypothetical person would likely have committed the offence under the same circumstances, and yet the presence of other factors supports the conclusion that the police involvement in the instigation of crime has exceeded the bounds of propriety.

. . . .

## SUMMARY

In conclusion, and to summarize, the proper approach to the doctrine of entrapment is that which was articulated by Estey J. in *Amato,* and elaborated upon in these reasons. As mentioned and explained earlier, there is entrapment when:

(a) the authorities provide a person with a opportunity to commit an offence without acting on a reasonable suspicion that this person is already engaged in criminal activity or pursuant to a bona fide inquiry; or
(b) although having such a reasonable suspicion or acting in the course of a bona fide inquiry, they go beyond providing an opportunity and induce the commission of an offence.

It is neither useful nor wise to state in the abstract what elements are necessary to prove an entrapment allegation. It is, however, essential that the factors relied on by a court relate to the underlying reasons for the recognition of the doctrine in the first place.

Since I am of the view that the doctrine of entrapment is not dependent upon culpability, the focus should not be on the effect of the police conduct on the accused's state of mind. Instead, it is my opinion that as far as possible an objective assessment of the conduct of the police and their agents is required. The predisposition, or the past, present or suspective criminal activity, of the accused is relevant only as a part of the determination of whether the provision of an opportunity by the authorities to the accused to commit the offence was justifiable. Further, there must be sufficient connection between the past conduct of the accused and the provision of an opportunity, since otherwise the police suspicion will not be reasonable. While disposition of the accused is, though not conclusive, of some relevance in assessing the initial approach by the police of a person with the offer of an opportunity to commit an offence, *it is never relevant* as regards whether they went beyond an offer, since that is to be assessed with regard to what the average non-predisposed person would have done.

The absence of a reasonable suspicion or a bona fide inquiry is significant in assessing the police conduct because of the risk that the police will attract people who would not otherwise have any involvement in a crime and because it is not a proper use of the police powers to simply go out and test the virtue of people on a random basis. The presence of reasonable suspicion or the mere existence of a bona fide inquiry will, however, never justify entrapment techniques: the police may not go beyond providing an opportunity, regardless of their perception of the accused's character and regardless of the existence of an hones inquiry. To determine whether the police have employed means which go further than providing an opportunity it is useful to consider any or all of the following factors:

— the type of crime being investigated and the availability of other techniques for the police detection of its commission;

— whether an average person, with both strengths and weaknesses, in the position of the accused would be induced into the commission of a crime;
— the persistence and number of attempts made by the police before the accused agreed to committing the offence;
— the type of inducement used by the police, including deceit, fraud, trickery or reward;
— the timing of the police conduct, in particular whether the police have instigated the offence or became involved in ongoing criminal activity;
— whether the police conduct involves an exploitation of human characteristics such as emotions of compassion, sympathy and friendship;
— whether the police appear to have exploited a particular vulnerability of a person such as a mental handicap or a substance addiction;
— the proportionality between the police involvement, as compared to the accused, including an assessment of the degree of harm caused or risked by the police, as compared to the accused, and the commission of any illegal acts by the police themselves;
— the existence of any threats, implied or express, made to the accused by the police or their agents; and
— whether the police conduct is directed at undermining other constitutional values.

This list is not exhaustive, but I hope it contributes to the elaboration of a structure for the application of the entrapment doctrine. Thus far, I have not referred to the requirement in *Amato*, per Estey J., that the conduct must, in all the circumstances, be shocking or outrageous. I am of the view that this is a factor which is best considered under procedural issues to which I will now turn.

## PROCEDURAL ISSUES

The resolution of the issues surrounding the manner in which an entrapment claim should be considered at trial is, in my view, entirely dependent upon the conceptual basis for the defence, outlined earlier. If I were of the opinion that there was a substantive or culpability-based defence of entrapment, I would readily come to the conclusion that the defence raised a question of fact, which should be decided by a jury when there is a sufficient evidentiary basis on which to raise the defence, and I would hold that the onus would rest on the crown to disprove the existence of entrapment beyond a reasonable doubt. Having come to the opposite view-point on the rationale for recognizing the doctrine of entrapment. I am not persuaded that the adoption of rules which historically, and by virtue of the Charter, conform to most substantive defences is either necessary or correct. It seems to me, however, that this court must be clear on how an entrapment claim is to be handled, as a brief review of some lower court decisions suggests that there is, at present, and understandably so, a great deal of confusion on the matter.

### *Who Decides: Judge or Jury?*

Both the appellant and the respondent agree that objective entrapment, involving police misconduct and not the accused's state of mind, is a question to be decided by the trial judge and that the proper remedy is a stay of proceedings. I too am of this view. The question of unlawful involvement by the state in the instigation of criminal conduct is one of law, or mixed law and fact. In *Jewitt*, in a passage cited previously, Dickson C.J.C. expressed this opinion (at p. 145): "Staying proceedings on the basis of abuse of process, and in particular, on the basis of the defence of entrapment, in my view, amounts to a decision on a complex question of law and fact."

. . . .

### *Who Bears the Burden of Proof and on What Standard?*

In my opinion the best way to achieve a balance between the interests of the court as guardian of the administration of justice and the interests of society in the prevention and detection of crime is to require an accused to demonstrate by a preponderance of evidence that the prosecution is an abuse of process because of entrapment. I would also note that this is consistent with the rules governing s. 24(2) applications (*Collins*, supra, at p. 277), where the general issue is similar to that raised in entrapment cases: Would the administration of justice be brought into disrepute?

. . . .

In conclusion, the onus lies on the accused to demonstrate that the police conduct has gone beyond permissible limits to the extent that allowing the prosecution or the entry of a conviction would amount to an abuse of the judicial process by the state. The question is one of mixed law and fact and should be resolved by the trial judge. A stay should be entered in the "clearest of cases" only.

## DISPOSITION

In determining whether the doctrine of entrapment applies to the present appeal, this court is restricted to the summary of evidence provided by Westmore Co. Ct J. in his reasons. I am of the view that a stay of proceedings should be entered in this case. While the trial judge had the advantage of hearing the testimony of the appellant, and normally findings on entrapment cases should not be disturbed because of this, I am concerned that in this case too much emphasis was placed on the appellant's state of mind. Earlier in my summary of the decisions below I cited a passage from the trial judge's reasons wherein he stated that the fundamental issue was the appellant's state of mind and his predisposition to crime. This, perhaps, explains why in his conclusion the trial judge stated the appellant was not entrapped because he acted out of a desire to profit from the transaction. If the trial judge had been permitted only to evaluate the conduct of the police objectively, I think he might well have and, in any event, ought to have come to the conclusion that the police conduct amounted to entrapment.

From the facts it appears that the police had reasonable suspicion that the appellant was involved in criminal conduct. The issue is whether the police went too far in their efforts to attract the appellant into the commission of the offence.

Returning to the list of factors I outlined earlier, this crime is obviously one for which the state must be given substantial leeway. The drug trafficking business is not one which lends itself to the traditional devices of police investigation. It is absolutely essential, therefore, for police or their agents to get involved and gain the trust and confidence of the people who did the trafficking or who supply the drugs. It is also a crime of enormous social consequence which causes a great deal of harm in society generally. This factor alone is very critical and makes this case somewhat difficult.

The police do not appear, however, to have been interrupting an ongoing criminal enterprise, and the offence was clearly brought about by their conduct and would not have occurred absent their involvement. The police do not appear to have exploited a narcotics addiction of the appellant, since he testified that he had already given up his use of narcotics. Therefore he was not, at the time, trying to recover from an addiction. Nonetheless, he also testified that he was no longer involved in drugs and, if this is true, it suggests that the police were indeed trying to make the appellant take up his former lifestyle. The persistence of the police requests, as a result of the equally persistent refusals by the appellant, supports the appellant's version of events on this point. The length of time, approximately six months, and the repetition of requests it took before the appellant agreed to commit the offence also demonstrate that the police had to go further than merely providing the appellant with the opportunity once it became evident that he was unwilling to join the alleged drug syndicate.

Perhaps the most important and determinative factor in my opinion is the appellant's testimony that the informer acted in a threatening manner when they went for a walk in the woods, and the further testimony that he was told to get his act together after he did not provide the supply of drugs he was asked for. I believe this conduct was unacceptable. If the police must go this far, they have gone beyond providing the appellant with an opportunity. I do not, therefore, place much significance on the fact that the appellant eventually committed the offence when shown the money. Obviously the appellant knew much earlier that he could make a profit by getting involved in the drug enterprise and he still refused. I have come to the conclusion that the average person in the position of the appellant might also have committed the offence, if only to finally satisfy this threatening informer and end all further contact. As a result I would, on the evidence, have to find that the police conduct in this case was unacceptable. Thus, the doctrine of entrapment applies to preclude the prosecution of the appellant. In my opinion the appellant has met the buren of proof and the trial judge should have entered a stay of proceedings for abuse of process.

I would accordingly allow the appeal, set aside the conviction of the appellant, order a new trial and enter a stay of proceedings.

*Appeal allowed.*

## Showman v. R.
## (1989), 67 C.R. (3d) 61 (S.C.C.)

Appeal by accused from judgment of British Columbia Court of Appeal, [1986] B.C.W.L.D. 1562, affirming accused's conviction of trafficking in marijuana.

December 15, 1988. The judgment of the court was delivered by

LAMER J.: —

### INTRODUCTION

The appellant was charged with unlawfully trafficking in a narcotic contrary to the provisions of the Narcotic Control Act, R.S.C. 1970, c. N-1. The charge arose as a result of a sale of marijuana made to an undercover police officer on 18th March 1982. He was convicted of this offence by Judge Catliff of the County Court of Vancouver, sitting with a jury. On a voir dire the appellant testified that he had been entrapped into committing the crime because of the pressure exerted on him by a friend, Ward Kirkus. The trial judge rejected the appellant's claim and the jury returned a verdict of guilty. The appellant appealed to the British Columbia Court of Appeal and in reasons for judgment given by Mr. Justice Macfarlane, concurred in by Carrothers and Aikins JJ.A., the appeal was dismissed [[1986] B.C.W.L.D. 1562]. Leave to appeal was granted by this court and the appeal was heard at the same time as the appeal in *R. v Mack*, the judgment in which is also being delivered today [reported ante, p. 1, also [1989] 1 W.W.R. 577]. I am of the view that this appeal must be dismissed.

## THE FACTS

The Crown called two witnesses on the voir dire, Constable Hickman and Constable Adam, and the appellant testified on his own behalf. Constable Hickman testified that Ward Kirkus, the alleged entrapper, was facing a potential narcotics charge and it was agreed that the police would give him some consideration with respect to his charge in exchange for Kirkus assisting the police. Constable Hickman had information, received from Kirkus and others, that the appellant was a supplier of narcotics. Constable Hickman instructed Kirkus to phone the appellant for the purpose of arranging a sale of narcotics. Following a discussion with Kirkus, Constable Hickman directed an undercover officer, Constable Adam, to go to a mall parking lot on 15th March, 1982, approach a person sitting in a specific vehicle and ask if he could purchase some drugs. Adam was provided with approximately $200 to that end. The person in the car was in fact Kirkus. Constable Hickman had told Kirkus that a man would approach him in his car. Neither Constable Adam nor Kirkus were informed of the fact that they were both working for the police, in accordance with standard police procedure. It is clear, however, that Constable Adam suspected Kirkus was acting on behalf of the police upon meeting him at the mall. At all material times Constable Hickman was assisting in the surveillance of this undercover investigation of the appellant.

There were three narcotics transactions arising from the association set up by Kirkus between the appellant and the undercover Constable Adam, with only the second of which the appellant was charged.

On 15th March 1982 Constable Adam met Kirkus and Kirkus drove him to the appellant's house. Kirkus introduced Constable Adam to the appellant. Constable Adam testified that Kirkus asked the appellant if he had any narcotics and the appellant, who had been told by Kirkus that a half-pound of marijuana would be purchased, stated that he was "doing pounds for $1,900". Constable Adam picked up a plastic bag containing approximately half an ounce of marijuana. Constable Adam inquired as to the amount and price and the appellant sold this package to Constable Adam at that time. The appellant was not charged with any offence as a result of this transaction.

As arranged, the appellant met with Constable Adam on 18th March and while driving in his car the appellant pulled out a bag containing three individually packaged half-pounds of marijuana. The two men discussed prices and Adam had the appellant stop so that Adam could obtain an additional $100 needed to buy one of the half-pounds. At this time the appellant, upon being asked by Constable Adam, indicated that he could supply cocaine and "red hair" (marijuana) and he stated that he had been dealing for years and was lucky to find some really good sources. The agreed-to transaction was then completed.

Constable Adam testified that he phoned the appellant on 13th April and the appellant phoned him the next day, and the two met on the 15th. Constable Adam gave evidence that a further drug transaction was set up and the appellant took him to the residence of a Scott Muirhead. The appellant introduced them and then left. A transaction involving five pounds of marijuana was concluded between Muirhead and the undercover officer. The appellant was not charged with respect to this sale, although Muirhead was.

The appellant testified that he and Wade Kirkus were friends and they had known each other for approximately seven years. He had not heard from him for about six months when he received a phone call on 6th March 1982. Kirkus told him he had a friend who was interested in buying marijuana and who was willing to pay "a lot of money". The appellant says he told Kirkus he was not really interested and while he may know someone, he was not willing to get involved.

The next day Kirkus called and repeated his request. The appellant again said he was not interested and he asked Kirkus how much money was involved. Kirkus told him that his friend was willing to buy 10 to 15 pounds. The appellant says he told Kirkus "you are talking to the wrong guy". Kirkus then asked about a half-pound. The appellant agreed to ask around for him and told Kirkus to phone him back.

The appellant asked a friend but that person did not want to deal with Kirkus. When Kirkus phoned back, he said he was unable to assist him. Then Kirkus asked if the appellant could please help him out, "just this once". The appellant then asked about Kirkus' friend and Kirkus again stressed the profit they would both make and the appellant said he would have to think about it. Similar conversations initiated by Kirkus occurred the next two nights and Kirkus emphasized that his friend might be getting impatient. The appellant suggested that he meet Kirkus' friend and if he thought he was "okay" he would try and arrange a meeting between his friend and the undercover officer.

The next day Kirkus phoned twice to see whether the appellant had made the arrangements and the appellant said he was too busy and unable to reach his friend and he agreed to check the next day. That following day Kirkus phoned and the appellant said he still had not reached his friend. Kirkus asked how long it would take and the appellant told him to call back in an hour. When Kirkus called, the appellant told him he could bring the officer to the appellant's home on Monday, 15th March. Kirkus said his friend, Constable Adam, had approximately $1,000 to spend.

The appellant gave evidence that he had never sold marijuana to anyone before and he made the following statement when asked what was going on in his mind as the phone calls from Kirkus continued:

> A. He was calling me every day. He would talk to me, and I told him I didn't think so, and I didn't know, and I would check it, and I started telling him I would call him back, and I never did. I never checked it, and finally it just got to be a bit of a problem, him calling me every day.
> Q. Why weren't you checking it?

> A. Because I wasn't interested in doing it.
> Q. And what did you think would happen?
> A. I thought he would maybe find someone else to deal with and he might stop calling me. I was hoping that he would work it out himself.

Then the appellant contacted Scott Muirhead, who supplied him with three separately wrapped half-pounds of marijuana. The appellant did not pay for them but arranged to share the proceeds with Muirhead with the appellant earning $250 on the sale of one half-pound. The appellant explained why he had two extra half-pounds in the following manner:

> Well, Scott gave me more than one-half pound, and I asked him why he was giving me more, and he told me, well, maybe the guy will like it and take more. It would just be more money for you, you are doing it now, so, you know, a few dollars for you would be even better. I just — I didn't say — I couldn't say no. He just asked if there was a problem and I told him, no, I guess not.

The appellant was asked why he sold the half-pound on the 18th following the first meeting with Constable Adam. He stated:

> Well, there is a various number of reasons. It was a combination of reasons, I guess. Ward [Kirkus] was a very good friend of mine at the time. He was persistently calling me, and the money was a factor. I just couldn't say no to a friend, who really wanted me to help him out. He sounded, not desperate, but almost desperate to the point where, you know, you've got to help me out just this once. So, his persistence, or his constant calling didn't stop, so I really didn't have the will to say no to a friend. So, I did it just the once.

The appellant insisted that the reason why he acted as if he knew about drugs and sources in his interactions with Constable Adam was because Muirhead told him to "talk big" and to appear like a drug dealer so as to impress the constable and that he just did what Muirhead told him to do. In cross-examination, the following exchange took place, which provides a useful summary of the appellant's position:

> Q. So, to sum up, you really got talked into this, is that what you are saying, by Kirkus and Muirhead?
> A. Well, I was beginning — it was beginning to be a problem with them calling me all the time, you know. He was a friend. He sounded like he needed help, and it was a one-shot deal, so I did it for a friend, a good friend.
> Q. But you got $250 out of it?
> A. I did get some money for it, yes. That wasn't the main reason, though.

. . .

## ANALYSIS

In *Mack* I outlined the proper approach to the doctrine of entrapment. I agree with the Court of Appeal in the present case that had the trial judge correctly applied the onus and standard of proof, the result would be the same. The appellant has not demonstrated that the conduct of the police, viewed objectively, constitutes entrapment.

Firstly, it is clear that the police acted on reasonable suspicion and they were fully entitled to provide the appellant with an opportunity to commit the offence. The issue, is, therefore: "Have the police gone further than providing an opportunity and instead employed tactics designed to induce someone into the commission of an offence?" (*Mack*, pp. 44-45).

The offence of drug trafficking is, as was noted in *Mack*, one which is especially difficult to detect and the use of undercover agents and informers, like Kirkus in the present case, is common and necessary. There has been no exploitation of a close personal relationship between Kirkus and the appellant. If the police were unable to rely on the existing connections and associations between people in the narcotics business they would be unduly hampered in their efforts at detecting crime and preventing further criminal activity. Certainly there was an appeal to the appellant because of his friendship with Kirkus but it was not unduly exploitive nor was the dignity of their relationship violated. This alone is not sufficient to establish the defence in the absence of any other factors.

The number of phone calls made by Kirkus occurred over a very short time span and, as described by the appellant himself, consisted generally of appeals to the profit they could each make by getting involved. Obviously the average narcotic supplier is not going to respond at the very first phone call and it would not be unusual for there to be a number of contacts made before a deal is arranged. I do not, therefore, find the fact that Kirkus had to phone the appellant a number of times to be significant, especially given the content of these calls and the short number of days involved. I have no doubt that the average person would not be induced into the commission of an offence as a result of this conduct.

In short, there are none of the circumstances which existed in *Mack* or which have been identified in that judgment as factors which may lead to a conclusion that the police conduct has gone beyond the limits that our society deems proper. I would, therefore, dismiss this appeal.

*Appeal dismissed.*

## Barnes v. R.
## (1991), 3 C.R. (4th) 1 (S.C.C.)

February 28, 1991. LAMER C.J.C. (WILSON, LA FOREST, SOPINKA, GONTHIER, CORY and STEVENSON JJ. concurring): —

This case involved a consideration of the defence of entrapment as set out by this Court in *R. v. Mack*, [1988] 2 S.C.R. 903, 67 C.R. (3d) 1, [1989] 1 W.W.R. 577, 90 N.R. 173, 44 C.C.C. (3d) 513, 37 C.R.R. 277. In particular, this Court is asked whether the accused was subjected to random virtue-testing by an undercover police officer in the city of Vancouver. This case also raises the question of whether this Court, at the request of the Crown, has jurisdiction to modify the decision of a court of appeal which has allowed an appeal by the Crown from a judicial stay of proceedings entered at trial.

### Facts

On January 12, 1989, the appellant sold one gram of hashish to an undercover police officer near the Granville Mall area of Vancouver. The parties do not dispute the facts surrounding the sale which are as follow:

The undercover officer was involved in a "buy-and-bust" operation conducted by the Vancouver Police Department. In a buy-and-bust operation, undercover police officers attempt to buy illicit drugs from individuals who appear, in the opinion of the officers, to be inclined to sell such drugs. If an officer is successful, the individual is immediately arrested for trafficking.

This particular operation was undertaken by the Department with respect to the Granville Mall area in the city of Vancouver, which covers a six-block section of Granville Street. On the day of the arrest, the undercover officer approached the accused, Philip Barnes, and his friend, as they were walking towards Granville Street. The officer testified at trial that she approached the accused and his friend because she had "a hunch, a feeling that they'd — possibly might be in possession." She believed that he and his friend fit the description of persons who possibly had drugs in their possession, and who would be willing to sell to her. "I had a feeling. They fit my general criteria. I look for males hanging around, dressed scruffy and in jeans, wearing a jean jacket or leather jacket, runners or black boots, that tend to look at people a lot." The officer indicated that there was nothing else that aroused her suspicions.

The officer approached the accused and asked him if he had any "weed". He said "no", but his friend repeated to him: "She wants some weed." The accused again responded negatively. The officer persisted and the accused then agreed to sell a small amount of cannabis resin to the officer for $15.00. Shortly afterwards, the accused was arrested by another officer and small amounts of cannabis resin and marijuana were seized from his person.

The accused was tried in the Country Court of Vancouver before Leggatt Co. Ct. J., and was found guilty of trafficking in cannabis resin, of the included offence of possession of cannabis resin for the purpose of trafficking, and of possession of marijuana. The accused conceded that he sold illicit drugs to the officer, but argued that a judicial stay for entrapment should be directed. He claimed that he had no intention of selling drugs on the day in question, but felt sorry for the undercover officer; he agreed to sell only because he believed that his friend wanted to meet a woman and that this was a way of gaining an introduction. The trial Judge held that the police officer had engaged in "random virtue testing", which was unacceptable according to the judgment of this Court in *Mack*, supra, and therefore ordered a judicial stay of the proceedings.

The British Columbia Court of Appeal allowed the Crown's appeal and ordered a new trial. . . .

## *Analysis*

### *Did the Police Officer Engage in Random Virtue-Testing?*

To resolve this appeal, this Court must consider whether the conduct of the undercover police officer was acceptable in light of the guidelines set out in *Mack*. In *Mack*, I attempted to define the circumstances in which police conduct in the course of investigating and uncovering criminal activity ceases to be acceptable and, instead, amounts to the unacceptable entrapment of individuals. The defence of entrapment is based on the notion that limits should be imposed on the ability of the police to participate in the commission of an offence. As a general rule, it is expected in our society that the police will direct their attention towards uncovering criminal activity that occurs without their involvement. . . .

It is apparent that the police officer involved in this case did not have a "reasonable suspicion" that the accused was already engaged in unlawful drug-related activity. The factors that drew the officer's attention to this particular accused — his manner of dress, the length of his hair — were not sufficient to give rise to a reasonable suspicion that criminal acts were being committed. Furthermore, the subjectiveness of the officer's decision to approach the accused, based on a "hunch" or "feeling" rather than extrinsic evidence, also indicates that the accused did not, as an individual, arouse a reasonable suspicion.

Consequently, the police conduct in this case will amount to entrapment *unless* the office presented the accused with the opportunity to sell drugs *in the course of a bona fide inquiry*. In my opinion, the police officer involved in this case was engaged in such a *bona fide* investigation. First, there is no question that the officer's conduct was motivated by the genuine purpose of investigating and repressing criminal activity. The police department had reasonable grounds for believing that drug-related crimes were occurring throughout the Granville Mall area. The accused was not, therefore, approached for questionable motives unrelated to the investigation and repression of crime.

Secondly, the police department directed its investigation at a suitable area within the city of Vancouver. As I noted in *Mack*, the police may present the opportunity to commit a particular crime to persons who are associated with a location where it is reasonably suspected that criminal activity is taking place. . . .

The police department in this case focused its investigation on an area of Vancouver, a section of Granville Street covering approximately 6 city blocks, where it was reasonably suspected that drug-related crimes were occurring. In my opinion, they would not have been able to deal with the problem effectively had they restricted the investigation to a smaller area. Although there were particular areas within the Granville Mall where drug trafficking was especially serious, it is true that trafficking occurred at locations scattered generally throughout the Mall. It is also true that traffickers did not operate in a single place. It would be unrealistic for the police to focus their investigation on one specific part of the Mall given the tendency of traffickers to modify their techniques in response to police investigations. The trial Judge admitted that the Mall was "known as an area of considerable drug activity." Similarly, the Court of Appeal found support in the evidence given at trial by Staff Sergeant Davies of the Vancouver City Police. . . .

It is, therefore, my opinion that the police department was engaged, in these circumstances, in a bona fide inquiry.

I note that in many cases, the size of the area itself may indicate that the investigation is not bona fide. This will be so particularly when there are grounds for believing that the criminal activity being investigated is concentrated in part of a larger area targeted by the police. In this case, however, for the reasons discussed above, it was reasonable for the Vancouver Police Department to focus its investigation on the Granville Mall.

The accused argues that although the undercover officer was involved in a bona fide inquiry, she nevertheless engaged in random virtue-testing since she approached the accused without a reasonable suspicion that he was likely to commit a drug-related offence. She approached the accused simply because he was walking near Granville Street.

In my respectful opinion, this argument is based on a misinterpretation of *Mack*. I recognize that some of my language in *Mack* might be responsible for this misinterpretation. In particular, as noted above, I stated, at p. 956 [S.C.R., pp. 42-43 C.R.]:

> "In those cases [where there is a particular location where it is reasonably suspected that certain crimes are taking place] it is clearly permissible to provide opportunities to people associated with the location under suspicion, even if these people are not themselves under suspicion. This latter situation, however, is only justified if the police acted in the course of a *bona fide* investigation and are not engaged in random virtue-testing."

This statement should not be taken to mean that the police may not approach people on a random basis, in order to present the opportunity to commit an offence, in the course of a bona fide investigation. The basic rule articulated in *Mack* is that the police may only present the opportunity to commit a particular crime to an individual who arouses a suspicion that he or she is already engaged in the particular criminal activity. An exception to this rule arises when the police undertake a bona fide investigation directed at an area where it is reasonably suspected that criminal activity is occurring. When such a location is defined with sufficient precision, the police may present *any* person associated with the area with the opportunity to commit the particular offence. Such randomness is permissible within the scope of a bona fide inquiry.

Random virtue-testing, conversely, only arises when a police officer presents a person with the opportunity to commit an offence *without* a reasonable suspicion that:

(a) the person is already engaged in the particular criminal activity, or

(b) the physical location with which the person is associated is a place where the particular criminal activity is likely occurring.

In this case, the accused was approached by the officer when he was walking near the Granville Mall. The notion of being "associated" with a particular area for these purposes does not require more than being *present* in the area. As a result, the accused was associated with a location where it was reasonably believed that drug-related crimes were occurring. The officer's conduct was therefore justified under the first branch of the test for entrapment set out in *Mack*.

For these reasons, it is my opinion that the officer did not engage in random virtue-testing in this case. I would, therefore, dismiss the appeal and uphold the decision of the Court of Appeal ordering a new trial. . . .

[Lamer then addressed the question of whether the court had jurisdiction to enter convictions with respect to the charges.]

*Appeal dismissed.*

## Questions/Discussion

1. What is the nature and availability of the defence of entrapment in Canada today? Do you agree with the defence as it is currently set out? Why or why not?

2. In practice, entrapment arises mostly in connection with vice offences, primarily narcotics. This occurs because police routinely pursue narcotics offenders with zealous aggression (Alexander, 1990). For example, while crossing a Vancouver street, and undercover R.C.M.P. officer was mistaken for a heroin user by two Vancouver police, who punched and kicked him to the ground and struck him with a flashlight. The police were convicted but probably only because their victim was also a police officer (*ibid.*). Because most Canadians, and most judges, mistakenly believe that the use and sale of narcotics is a major social threat, the courts in the past have been remarkably accepting of abusive police practices in the drug field. Take, for example, *R. v. Coupal* (1987). Mrs Bloome was in trouble. Police had charged her with possession of cocaine and possession of stolen goods worth about $61,000, which the police confiscated. She approached the police to make a deal: she would deliver to them a drug trafficker if they would drop charges against her. Mrs.Bloome then approached Gary Coupal, her daughter's former boyfriend. She told Coupal that she had cancer and needed cocaine. He refused to help her. She phoned and pestered him for some months, pleading that she was dying and needed money to pay her physicians. Eventually, he agreed to help to "get her off his back". Police then arrested Coupal for trafficking and dropped all charges against Mrs. Bloome. Coupal, who had no record and was not even a user of cocaine, was sentenced to six months' imprisonment. Apparently, police routinely employ known drug sellers to entrap people uninvolved with drugs (Alexander, 1990). Do you think that the decision in *Mack* will represent a real change either in the way the police go about their business or in the leeway the courts have given to police in the past?

3. Entrapment cases represent the problems that arise when narrow, legalistic solutions are sought for more fundamental failures. For example, in regard to the control of narcotics in Canada, the laws set police an impossible task: the legal system lacks the resources to arrest all drug offenders, let alone send them to trial and prison. Despite increased policing over the last decade, drug potency and availability have increased and prices have fallen. Worse, police are forced to risk their own safety when their sacrifice is not only useless, but destructive to society. Police leaders, however, find the drug war useful because it allows them to expand their budget and workforce, and to push police in the schools as "drug educators". The solution to abusive police practices in the narcotics field is to abolish all drug prohibitions, but this solution is political, not legal. Judges are limited in what they can do to remedy the problem of overly aggressive police work. But before *Mack*, judges had not come close to exploiting the limited powers they did possess. Given existing attitudes toward drug use in this country, do you think that there is much hope this situation will change after the decision in *Mack*?

## Further Reading

- Alexander, B., *Peaceful Measures: Canada's Alternatives to the War on Drugs* (Toronto: University of Toronto Press, 1990).
- France, S., "Problems in the Defence of Entrapment" (1988), 22 University of British Columbia Law Review 1.
- Frankel, S. D., "An Overview of the Law of Entrapment" (1991), 49 Advocate 591-594
- Stober, M., "Persistent Importuning for a Defence of Entrapment" (1988), 33 McGill Law Journal 400.
- Stober, M., "The Limits of Police Provocation in Canada" (1992), 34 Criminal Law Quarterly 290-348.
- Stuart, D., "*Mack*, Resolving Many But Not All Questions of Entrapment" (1989), 67 C.R. (3d) 68.

## 7.3.2 Charter Protections

**Introduction**

This section presents a number of examples where the courts have interpreted the Charter of Rights and Freedoms to date; it is not meant to be exhaustive but rather is meant to give a representative selection of such decisions by the Supreme Court of Canada. The cases themselves deal with a variety of issues arising in the Charter, including the presumption of innocence, the definition of murder, cruel and unusual punishment, and the right to counsel. The growth of Charter law has been great in the last few years and the prospect is that it will continue to grow as new arguments are introduced and work their way through the court system. There remain many areas of criminal law and procedure yet to be handled by the courts, so the ultimate effect on the criminal justice system is yet to be seen.

What can be seen to date is a plethora of legal arguments by defence counsel related to the Charter, coupled with a willingness on the part of the courts to intervene more forthrightly than many would have imagined given the conservative, non-interventionist record of the courts before 1982 (see Hovius and Martin, 1983). The decision striking down the abortion provisions in the Criminal Code is perhaps the most visible and well known intervention to date, and the case brought home forcefully to the general public the new role which the Charter and therefore the courts are playing in the formation of criminal justice policy (see Chapter 3). In this regard, the inherent dangers of the lack of accountability and expertise, of the use of narrow, legalistic approaches to social problems, and of the lack of access to the courts should be kept in mind as you examine the specific interventions by the courts in this area.

The sections of the Charter affecting criminal law and procedure are primarily the "legal rights" in sections 7-14, though certainly this is not exclusively so. For example, the so-called "fundamental freedoms" listed in section 2, listing such freedoms as freedom of thought, belief, opinion and expression, and freedom of association, could have a real effect on many aspects of the criminal law, notably as to the limits of state interference regarding obscenity. The equality provisions in section 15 could also play a role in the future, for example in regard to gender-biased sections of the criminal law such as infanticide.

Finally, note that the effects of the Charter can be felt in different ways. The courts may declare certain criminal provisions as contrary to the Charter and therefore of no validity and effect. On the other hand, certain procedures or tactics of the police may be found to be offensive to the principles expressed in the Charter and thus any evidence obtained as a result of such could be excluded from the case under section 24 of the Charter. In the latter situation, the police would presumably change their practices so as not to offend the Charter and to prevent the exclusion of evidence in the future (see the issue raised under "Discussion" number 2, below).

### Regina v. Oakes
### (1986), 24 C.C.C. (3d) 321 (S.C.C.)

APPEAL by the Crown from a judgment of the Ontario Court of Appeal, 2 C.C.C. (3d) 339, 145 D.L.R. (3d) 123, 40 O.R. (2d) 660, 32 C.R. (3d) 193, 3 C.R.R. 289, dismissing its appeal from a judgment of Walker Prov. Ct. J., 38 O.R. (2d) 598, convicting the accused of simple possession on a charge of possession of narcotics for the purpose of trafficking contrary to s. 4(2) of the *Narcotic Control Act* (Can.).

DICKSON C.J.C.: — This appeal concerns the constitutionality of s. 8 of the *Narcotic Control Act*, R.S.C. 1970, c. N-1. The section provides, in brief, that if the court finds the accused in possession of a narcotic, he is presumed to be in possession for the purpose of trafficking. Unless the accused can establish the contrary, he must be convicted of trafficking. The Ontario Court of appeal held that this provision constitutes a "reverse onus" clause and is unconstitutional because it violates one of the core values of our criminal justice system the presumption of innocence, now entrenched in s. 11(d) of the *Canadian Charter of Rights and Freedoms*. The Crown as appealed.

## *Statutory and Constitutional Provisions*

Before reviewing the factual context, I will set out the relevant legislative and constitutional provisions:

*Narcotic Control Act*

3(1) Except as authorized by this Act or the regulations, *no person shall have a narcotic in his possession.*

(2) *every person who violates subsection (1) is guilty of an indictable offence and is liable*
(a) upon summary conviction for a first offence, to a fine of one thousand dollars or to imprisonment for six months or to both fine and imprisonment, and for a subsequent offence, to a fine of two thousand dollars or to imprisonment for one year or to both fine and imprisonment; or
(b) *upon conviction on indictment, to imprisonment for seven years.*

. . . .

4(1) No person shall traffic in a narcotic or any substance represented or held out by him to be a narcotic.

(2) *No person shall have in his possession any narcotic for the purpose of trafficking.*

(3) *Every person who violates subsection (1) or (2) is guilty of an indictable offence and is liable to imprisonment for life.*

. . . .

**8.** *In any prosecution for a violation of subsection 4(2)*, if the accused does not plead guilty, *the trial shall proceed as if it were a prosecution for an offence under section 3,* and after the close of the case for the prosecution and after the accused has had an opportunity to make full answer and defence, *the court shall make a finding as to whether or not the accused was in possession of the narcotic contrary to section 3*; if the court finds that the accused was not in possession of the narcotic contrary to section 3, he shall be acquitted but *if the court finds that the accused was in possession of the narcotic contrary to section 3, he shall be given an opportunity of establishing that he was not in possession of the narcotic for the purpose of trafficking,* and thereafter the prosecutor shall be given an opportunity of adducing evidence to establish that the accused was in possession of the narcotic for the purpose of trafficking; *if the accused establishes that he was not in possession of the narcotic for the purpose of trafficking, he shall be acquitted of the offence* as charged but he shall be convicted of an offence under section 3 and sentenced accordingly; and *if the accused fails to establish that he was not in possession of the narcotic for the purpose of trafficking, he shall be convicted of the offence as charged and sentenced accordingly.*

(Emphasis added.)

*Canadian Charter of Rights and Freedoms*

11. Any person charged with an offence has the right

. . . .

(d) to be presumed innocent until proven guilty according to law in a fair and public hearing by an independent and impartial tribunal;

1. The *Canadian Charter of Rights and Freedoms* guarantees the rights and freedoms set out in it subject only to such reasonable limits prescribed by law as can be demonstrably justified in a free and democratic society.

## *Facts*

The respondent, David Edwin Oakes, was charged with unlawful possession of a narcotic for the purpose of trafficking, contrary to s. 4(2) of the *Narcotic Control Act*. He elected trial by magistrate without a jury. At trial, the Crown adduced evidence to establish that Mr. Oakes was found in possession of eight one-gram vials of *cannabis* resin in the form of hashish oil. Upon a further search conducted at the police station, $619.45 was located. Mr. Oakes told the police that he had bought 10 vials of hashish oil for $150 for his own use, and that the $619.45 was from a worker's compensation cheque. He elected not to call evidence as to possession of the narcotic. Pursuant to the procedural provisions of s. 8 of the *Narcotic Control Act*, the trial judge proceeded to make a finding that it was beyond reasonable doubt that Mr. Oakes was in possession of the narcotic.

Following this find, Mr. Oakes brought a motion to challenge the constitutional validity of s. 8 of the *Narcotic Control Act*, which he maintained imposes a burden on an accused to prove that he or she was not in possession for the purpose of trafficking. He argued that s. 8 violates the presumption of innocence contained in s. 11(d) of the Charter.

. . . .

## *The Issues*

The constitutional question in this appeal is stated as follows:

Is s. 8 of the *Narcotic Control Act* inconsistent with s. 11(d) of the *Canadian Charter of Rights and Freedoms* and thus of no force and effect?

Two specific questions are raised by this general question" (1) does s. 8 of the *Narcotic Control Act* violate s. 11(d) of the Charter, and (2) if it does, is s. 8 a reasonable limit prescribed by law as can be demonstrably justified in a free and democratic society for the purpose of s. 1 of the Charter? If the answer to (1) is affirmative and the answer to (2) negative, then the constitutional question must be answered in the affirmative.

## **Does s. 8 of the Narcotic Control Act violate s. 11(d) of the Charter?**

### *The Meaning of s. 8*

Before examining the presumption of innocence contained in s. 11(d) of the Charter, it is necessary to clarify the meaning of s. 8 of the *Narcotic Control Act*.

. . . .

8. . . . if the court finds that the accused was in possession of the narcotic . . . he shall be given an opportunity of establishing that he was not in possession of the narcotic for the purpose of trafficking . . . if the accused fails to establish that he was not in possession of the narcotic for the purpose of trafficking, he shall be convicted of the offence as charged.

In determining the meaning of these words, it is helpful to consider in a general sense the nature of presumptions. Presumptions can be classified into two general categories: presumptions *without* basic facts and presumption *with* basic facts. A presumption without a basic fact is simply a conclusion which is to be draw until the contrary is proved. A presumption with a basic fact entails a conclusion to be drawn upon proof of the basic fact (see *Cross On Evidence*, 5th ed. (1979), pp. 122-3).

Basic fact presumptions can be further categorized into permissive and mandatory presumptions. A permissive presumption leaves it optional as to whether the inference of the presumed fact is drawn following proof of the basic fact. A mandatory presumption requires that the inference be made.

Presumptions may also be either rebuttable or irrebuttable. If a presumption is rebuttable, there are three potential ways the presumed fact can be rebutted. First, the accused may be required merely to raise a reasonable doubt as to its existence. Secondly, the accused may have an evidentiary burden to adduce sufficient evidence to bring into question the truth of the presumed fact. Thirdly, the accused may have a legal or persuasive burden to prove on a balance of probabilities the non-existence of the presumed fact.

Finally, presumptions are often referred to as either presumptions of law or presumptions of fact. The latter entail "frequently recurring examples of circumstantial evidence" (*Cross on Evidence*, at p. 124) while the former involve actual legal rules.

To return to s. 8 of the *Narcotic Control Act*, it is my view that, upon a finding beyond a reasonable doubt of possession of a narcotic, the accused has the legal burden of proving on a balance of probabilities that he or she was not in possession of the possession is proven, a mandatory presumption of law arises against the accused that he or she had the intention to traffic. Moreover, the accused will be found guilty of the offence of trafficking unless he or she can rebut this presumption on a balance of probabilities.

. . . .

In some decisions it has been held that s. 8 of the *Narcotic Control Act* is constitutional because it placed only an evidentiary burden rather than a legal burden on the accused. The ultimate legal burden to prove guilt beyond a reasonable doubt remains with the Crown and the presumption of innocence is not offended: *R. v. Therrien* (1982), 67 C.C.C. (2d) 31, 37 O.R. (2d) 641, 1 C.R.R. 354 (Ont. Co. Ct.); *R. v. Fraser* (1982), 68 C.C.C. (2d) 433, 138 D.L.R. (3d) 488, 21 Sask. R. 227 (Sask. Q.B.); *R. v. Kupezyniski* (June 23, 1982, unreported, Ont. Co. Ct.) [summarized 8 W.C.B. 157].

. . . .

Those decisions which have held that only the secondary or evidentiary burden shifts are not persuasive with respect to the *Narcotic Control Act*. As Ritchie J. found in *R. v. Appleby, supra* (though addressing a different statutory provision), the phrase "to establish" is the equivalent of "to prove". The Legislature, by using the word "establish" in s. 8 of the *Narcotic Control Act*, intended to impose a legal burden on the accused. This is most apparent in the words "if the accused fails to establish that he was not in possession of the narcotic for the purpose of trafficking, he shall be convicted of the offence as charged".

. . . .

I conclude that s. 8 of the *Narcotic Control Act* contains a reverse onus provision imposing a legal burden on an accused to prove on a balance of probabilities that he or she was not in possession of a narcotic for the purpose of trafficking. It is therefore necessary to determine whether s. 8 of the *Narcotic Control Act* offends the right to be "presumed innocent until proven guilty" as guaranteed by s. 11(d) of the Charter.

### The Presumption of Innocence and s. 11(d) of the Charter

Section 11(d) of the Charter constitutionally entrenches the presumption of innocence as part of the supreme law of Canada. For ease of reference, I set out this provision again:

**11.** Any person charged with an offence has the right

. . . .

(d) to be presume innocent until proven guilty according to law in a fair and public hearing by an independent and impartial tribunal;

To interpret the meaning of s. 11(d), it is important to adopt a purposive approach. As this Court stated in *R. v. Big M Drug Mart Ltd.* (1985), 18 C.C.C. (3d) 385 at pp. 423-4, 18 D.L.R. (4th) 321 at pp. 359-60, [1985] 1 S.C.R. 295 at p. 344:

The meaning of a right or freedom guaranteed by the Charter was to be ascertained by an analysis of the *purpose* of such a guarantee; it was to be understood, in other words, in the light of the interests it was meant to protect.

In my view, this analysis is to be undertaken, and the purpose of the right or freedom in question is to be sough by reference to the character and the larger objects of the Charter itself, to the language chosen to articulate the specific right or freedom, to the historical origins of the concepts enshrined, and where applicable, to the meaning and purpose of the other specific rights and freedoms.

To identify the underlying purpose of the Charter right in question, therefore, it is important to begin by understanding the cardinal values it embodies.

The presumption of innocence is a hallowed principle lying at the very heart of criminal law. Although protected expressly in s. 11(d) of the Charter, the presumption of innocence is referable and integral to the general protection of life, liberty and security of the person contained in s. 7 of the Charter: see *Reference re s. 94(2) of Motor Vehicle Act*, December 17, 1985, unreported, *per* Lamer J. [since reported 23 C.C.C. (3d) 289, 48 C.R. (3d) 289, [1986] 1 W.W.R. 481]. The presumption of innocence protects the fundamental liberty and human dignity of any and every person accused by the State of criminal conduct. An individual charged with a criminal offence faces grave social and personal consequences, including potential loss of physical liberty, subjection to social stigma and ostracism from the community, as well as other social, psychological and economic harms. In light of the gravity of these consequences, the presumption of innocence is crucial. It ensures that until the State proves an accused's guilt beyond all reasonable doubt, he or she is innocent. This is essential in a society committed to fairness and social justice. The presumption of innocence confirms our faith in humankind; it reflects our beliefs that individuals are decent and law-abiding members of the community until proven otherwise.

The presumption of innocence has enjoyed longstanding recognition at common law. In the leading case, *Woolmington v. Direct of Public Prosecutions*, [1935] A.C. 462 (H.L.), Viscount Sankey L.C. wrote at pp. 481-2:

> Throughout the web of the English Criminal Law one golden thread is always to be seen, that it is the duty of the prosecution to prove the prisoner's guilt subject to what I have already said as to the defence of insanity and subject also to any statutory exception. If, at the end of and on the whole of the case, there is a reasonable doubt, created by the evidence given by either the prosecution or the prisoner, as to whether the prisoner killed the deceased with a malicious intention, the prosecution has not made out the case and the prisoner is entitled to an acquittal. No matter what the charge or where the trial, the principle that the prosecution must prove the guilt of the prisoner is part of the common law of England and no attempt to whittle it down can be entertained.

Subsequent Canadian cases have cited the *Woolmington* principle with approval: see, for example, *Manchuk v. The King* (1938), 70 C.C.C. 161 at p. 167, [1938]S.C.R. 341 at p. 349; *R. v. City of Sault Ste. Marie* (1978), 40 C.C.C. (2d) 353 at pp. 366-7, 85 D.L.R. (3d) 161 at p. 174, [1978] 2 S.C.R. 1299 at p. 1316.

Further evidence of the widespread acceptance of the principle of the presumption of innocence is its inclusion in the major international human rights documents. Article 11(1) of the Universal Declaration of Human Rights, adopted December 10, 1948, by the General Assembly of the United Nations, provides:

> **11**(1) Everyone charged with a penal offence has the right to be presumed innocent until proved guilty according to law in a public trial at which he has had all the guarantees necessary for his defence.

In the International Covenant on Civil and Political Rights, 1966, art. 14(2) states:

> **14**(2) Everyone charged with a criminal offence shall have the right to be presumed innocent until proved guilty according to law.

Canada acceded to this covenant, and the optional protocol which sets up machinery for implementing the covenant, on May 19, 1976. Both came into effect on August 19, 1976.

In light of the above, the right to be presumed innocent until proven guilty requires that s. 11(d) have, at the minimum, the following content. First, an individual must be proven guilty beyond a reasonable doubt. Secondly, it is the State which must bear the burden of proof. As Mr. Justice Lamer stated in *Dubois v. The Queen* (November 21, 1985, unreported), at p. 6 [since reported 22 C.C.C. (3d) 513 at p. 531, 23 D.L.R. (4th) 503 at pp. 521-2, [1985] 2 S.C.R. 350]:

> Section 11(d) imposes upon the Crown the burden of proving the accused's guilt beyond a reasonable doubt as well as that of making out the case against the accused before he or she need respond, either by testifying or by calling other evidence.

Thirdly, criminal prosecutions must be carried out in accordance with lawful procedures and fairness. The latter part of s. 11(d), which requires the proof of guilt "according to law in a fair and public hearing by an independent and impartial tribunal", underlines the importance of this procedural requirement.

. . . .

[After reviewing a number of these authorities, Dickson continues:]

*Conclusions Regarding s. 11(d) of the Charter and s. 8 of the Narcotic Control Act*

This review of the authorities lays the groundwork for formulating some general conclusions regarding reverse onus provisions and the presumption of innocence in s. 11(d). We can then proceed to apply these principles to the particulars of s. 8 of the *Narcotic Control Act*.

In general one must, I think, conclude that a provision which requires an accused to disprove on a balance of probabilities the existence of a presumed fact, which is an important element of the offence in question, violates the presumption of innocence in s. 11(d). If an accused bears the burden of disproving on a balance of probabilities an essential element of an offence, it would be possible for a conviction to occur despite the existence of a reasonable doubt. This would arise if the accused adduced sufficient evidence to raise a reasonable doubt as to his or her innocence but did not convince the jury on a balance of probabilities that the presumed fact was untrue.

The fact that the standard is only the civil one does not render a reverse onus clause constitutional.

. . . .

As we have seen, the potential for a rational connection between the basic fact and the presumed fact to justify a reverse onus provision has been elaborated in some of the cases discussed above and is now known as the "rational connection test". In the context of s. 11(d), however, the following question arises: if we apply the rational connection test to the consideration of whether s. 11(d) has been violated, are we adequately protecting the constitutional principle of the presumption of innocence? As Professors MacKay and Cromwell point out in their article "Oakes: A Bold Initiative Impeded by Old Ghosts", 32 C.R. (3d) 221 (1983), p. 233:

> The rational connection test approves a provision that *forces* the trier to infer a fact that may be simply rationally connected to the proved fact. Why does it follow that such a provision does not offend the constitutional right to be proved guilty beyond a reasonable doubt?

A basic fact may rationally tend to prove a presumed fact, but not prove its existence beyond a reasonable doubt. An accused person could thereby be convicted despite the presence of a reasonable doubt. This would violate the presumption of innocence.

. . . .

To return to s. 8 of the *Narcotic Control Act*, I am in no doubt whatsoever that it violates s. 11(d) of the Charter by requiring the accused to prove on a balance of probabilities that he was not in possession of the narcotic for the purpose of trafficking. Mr. Oakes is compelled by s. 8 to prove he is *not guilty* of the offence of trafficking. He is thus denied his right to be presumed innocent and subjected to the potential penalty of life imprisonment, unless he can rebut the presumption. This is radically and fundamentally inconsistent with the societal values of human dignity and liberty which we espouse, and is directly contrary to the presumption of innocence enshrined in s. 11(d). Let us turn now to s. 1 of the Charter.

## Is s. 8 of the Narcotic Control Act a Reasonable and Demonstrably Justified Limit Pursuant to s. 1 of the Charter?

The Crown submits that even if s. 8 of the *Narcotic Control Act* violates s. 11(d) of the Charter, it can still be upheld as a reasonable limit under s. 1 which, as has been mentioned, provides:

> 1. The *Canadian Charter of Rights and Freedoms* guarantees the rights and freedoms set out in it subject only to such reasonable limits prescribed by law as can be demonstrably justified in a free and democratic society.

The question whether the limit is "prescribed by law" is not contentious in the present case since s. 8 of the *Narcotic Control Act* is a duly enacted legislative provision. It is, however, necessary to determine if the limit on Mr. Oakes' right, as guaranteed by s. 11(d) of the Charter, is "reasonable" and "demonstrably justified in a free and democratic society" for the purpose of s. 1 of the Charter, and thereby saved from inconsistency with the Constitution.

It is important to observe at the outset that s. 1 has two functions: first, it constitutionally guarantees the rights and freedoms set out in the provisions which follow; and, secondly, it states explicitly the exclusive justification criteria (outside of s. 33 of the Charter) against which limitations on those rights and freedoms must be measured. Accordingly, any s. 1 inquiry must be premised on an understanding that the impugned limit violates constitutional rights and freedoms — rights and freedoms which are part of the supreme law of Canada. As Madam Justice Wilson stated in *Re Singh and Minister of Employment & Immigration and 6 other appeals* (1985), 17 D.L.R. (4th) 422 at p. 468, [1985] 1 S.C.R. 177 at p. 218, 58 N.R. 1: "... it is important to remember that the courts are conducting this inquiry in light of a commitment to uphold the rights and freedoms set out in the other sections of the Charter".

A second contextual element of interpretation of s. 1 is provided by the words "free and democratic society". Inclusion of these words as the final standard of justification for limits on rights and freedoms refers the court to the very purpose for which the Charter was originally entrenched in the Constitution: Canadian society is to be free and democratic. The court must be guided by the values and principles essential to a free and democratic society which I believe embody, to name but a few, respect for the inherent dignity of the human person, commitment to social justice and equality, accommodation of a wide variety of beliefs, respect for cultural and group identity, and faith in social and political institutions which enhance the participation of individuals and groups in society. The underlying values and principles of a free and democratic society are the genesis of the rights and freedoms guaranteed by the Charter and the ultimate standard against which a limit on a right or freedom must be shown, despite its effect, to be reasonable and demonstrably justified.

The rights and freedoms guaranteed by the Charter are not, however, absolute. It may become necessary to limit rights and freedoms in circumstances where their exercise would be inimical to the realization of collective goals of fundamental importance. For this reason, s. 1 provides criteria of justification for limits on the rights and freedoms guaranteed by the Charter. These criteria impose a stringent standard of justification, especially when understood in terms of the two contextual considerations discussed above, namely, the violation of a constitutionally guaranteed right or freedom and the fundamental principles of a free and democratic society.

The onus of proving that a limit on a right or freedom guaranteed by the Charter is reasonable and demonstrably justified in a free and democratic society rests upon the party seeking to uphold the limitation. It is clear from the test of s. 1 that limits on the rights and freedoms enumerated in the Charter are exceptions to their general guarantee. The presumption is that the rights and freedoms are guaranteed unless the party invoking s. 1 can bring itself within the exceptional criteria which justify their being limited. This is further substantiated by the use of the word "demonstrably" which clearly indicates that the onus of justification is on the party seeking to limit: *Hunter v. Southam Inc., supra*.

. . . .

To establish that a limit is reasonable and demonstrably justified in a free and democratic society, two central criteria must be satisfied. First, the objective, which the measures responsible for a limit on a Charter right or freedom are designed to serve, must be "of sufficient importance to warrant overriding a constitutionally protected right or freedom": *R. v. Big M. Drug Mart Ltd., supra*, at p. 430 C.C.C., p. 366 D.L.R., p. 352 S.C.R. The standard must be high in order to ensure that objectives which are trivial or discordant with the principles integral to a free and democratic society do not gain s. 1 protection. It is necessary, at a minimum, that an objective relate to concerns which are pressing and substantial in a free and democratic society before it can be characterized as sufficiently important.

Secondly, once a sufficiently significant objective is recognized, then the party invoking s. 1 must show that the means chosen are reasonable and demonstrably justified. This involves "a form of proportionality test": *R. v. Big M Drug Mart Ltd., supra*. Although the nature of the proportionality test will vary depending on the circumstances in each case courts will be required to balance the interests of society with those of individuals and groups. There are, in my view, three important components of a proportionality test. First, the measures adopted must be carefully designed to achieve the objective in question. They must not be arbitrary, unfair or based on irrational considerations. In short, they must be rationally connected to the objective. Secondly, the means, even if rationally connected to the objective in the first sense, should impair "as little as possible" the right or freedom in question: *R. v. Big M Drug Mart Ltd., supra*. Thirdly, there must be a proportionality between the *effects* of the measures which are responsible for limiting the Charter right or freedom, and the objective which has been identified as of "sufficient importance".

With respect to the third component, it is clear that the general effect of any measure impugned under s. 1 will be the infringement of a right or freedom guaranteed by the Charter; this is the reason why resort to s. 1 is necessary. The inquiry into effects must, however, go further. A wide range of rights and freedoms are guaranteed by the Charter, and an almost infinite number of factual situations may arise in respect of these. Some limits on rights and freedoms protected by the Charter will be more serious than others in terms of the nature of the right or freedom violated, the extent of the violation and the degree to which the measures which impose the limit trench upon the integral principles of a free and democratic society. Even if an objective is of sufficient importance, and the first two elements of the proportionality test are satisfied, it is still possible that, because of the severity of the deleterious effects of a measure on individuals or groups, the measure will not be justified by the purposes it is intended to serve. The more severe the deleterious effects of a measure, the more important the objective must be if the measure is to be reasonable and demonstrably justified in a free and democratic society.

Having outlined the general principles of s. 1 inquiry, we must apply them to s. 8 of the *Narcotic Control Act*. Is the reverse onus provision in s. 8 a reasonable limit on the right to be presumed innocent until proven guilty beyond a reasonable doubt as can be demonstrably justified in a free and democratic society?

The starting point for formulating a response to this question is, as stated above, the nature of Parliament's interest or objective which accounts for the passage of s. 8 of the *Narcotic Control Act*. According to the Crown, s. 8 of the *Narcotic Control Act* is aimed at curbing drug trafficking by facilitating the conviction of drug traffickers. In my opinion, Parliament's concern that drug trafficking be decreased can be characterized as substantial and pressing. The problem of drug trafficking has been increasing since the 1950's at which time there was already considerable concern: see Report of the Special Committee on Traffic in Narcotic Drugs, Appendix to Debates of the Senate, Canada, Session 1955, pp. 690-700; see also Final Report, Commission of Inquiry into the Non-Medical Use of Drugs (Ottawa, 1973). Throughout this period, numerous measures were adopted by free and democratic societies, at both the international and national levels.

At the international level, on June 23, 1953, the Protocol for Limiting and Regulating the Cultivation of the Poppy Plant, the Production of, International and Wholesale Trade in, and Use of Opium, to which Canada is a signatory, was adopted by the United Nations Opium Conference held in New York. The Single Convention on Narcotic Drugs, 1961, was acceded to in New York on March 30, 1961. This treaty was signed by Canada on March 30, 1961. It entered into force on December 13, 1964. As stated in the preamble, "addiction to narcotic drugs constitutes a serious evil for the individual and is fraught with social and economic danger to mankind . . . "

At the national level, statutory provisions have been enacted by numerous countries which, *inter alia*, attempt to deter drug trafficking by imposing criminal sanctions: see, for example, *Misuse of Drugs Act*, 1975 (N.Z.), No. 116; *Misuse of Drugs Act*, 1971 (U.K.), c. 38.

The objective of protecting our society from the grave ills associated with drug trafficking, is, in my view, one of sufficient importance to warrant overriding a constitutionally protected right or freedom in certain cases. Moreover, the degree of seriousness of drug trafficking makes its acknowledgement as a sufficiently important objective for the purposes of s. 1, to a large extent, self-evident. The first criterion of a s. 1 inquiry, therefore, has been satisfied by the Crown.

The next stage of inquiry is a consideration of the means chosen by Parliament to achieve its objective. The means must be reasonable and demonstrably justified in a free and democratic society. As outlined above, this proportionality test should begin with a consideration of the rationality of the provision; is the reverse onus clause in s. 8 rationally related to the objective of curbing drug trafficking? At a minimum, this requires that s. 8 be internally rational; there must be a rational connection between the basic fact of possession and the presumed fact of possession for the purpose of trafficking. Otherwise, the reverse onus clause could give rise to unjustified and erroneous convictions for drug trafficking of persons guilty only of possession of narcotics.

In my view s. 8 does not survive this rational connection test. As Martin J.A. of the Ontario Court of Appeal concluded, possession of a small or negligibly quantity of narcotics does not support the inference of trafficking. In other words, it would be irrational to infer that a person had an intent to traffic on the basis of his or her possession of a very small quantity of narcotics. The presumption required under s. 8 of the *Narcotic Control Act* is overinclusive and could lead to results in certain cases which would defy both rationality and fairness. In light of the seriousness of the offence in question, which carries with it the possibility of imprisonment for life, I am further convinced that the first component of the proportionality test has not been satisfied by the Crown.

Having concluded that s. 8 does not satisfy this first component of proportionality, it is unnecessary to consider the other two components.

**Conclusion**

The Ontario Court of Appeal was correct in holding that s. 8 of the *Narcotic Control Act* violates the *Canadian Charter of Rights and Freedoms* and is therefore of no force or effect. Section 8 imposes a limit on the right guaranteed by s. 11(d) of the Charter which is not reasonable and is not demonstrably justified in a free and democratic society for the purpose of s. 1. Accordingly, the constitutional question is answered as follows:

> *Question:* Is s. 8 of the *Narcotic Control Act* inconsistent with s. 11(d) of the *Canadian Charter of Rights and Freedoms* and thus of no force and effect?
>
> *Answer:* Yes.

I would, therefore, dismiss the appeal.

ESTEY J.: — I would dismiss this appeal. I agree with the conclusions of the Chief Justice with reference to the relationship between ss. 11(d) and 1 of the *Canadian Charter of Rights and Freedoms*. For the disposition of all other issues arising in this appeal, I would adopt the reasons given by Martin J.A. in the court below [2 C.C.C. (3d) 339, 145 D.L.R. (3d) 123, 40 O.R. (2d) 660].

MCINTYRE J. concurs with ESTEY J.

CHOUINARD, LAMER, WILSON and Le DAIN JJ. concur with DICKSON C.J.C.

*Appeal dismissed.*

## Smith v. The Queen
(1987), 34 C.C.C. (3d) 97 (S.C.C.)

[Only the judgment of Lamer J. is reproduced below.]
LAMER J.: —

### Introduction

Those who import and market hard drugs for lucre are responsible for the gradual but inexorable degeneration of many of their fellow human beings as a result of their becoming drug addicts. The direct cause of the hardship cast upon their victims and their families, these importers must also be made to bear their fair share of the guilt for the innumerable serious crimes of all sorts committed by addicts in order to feed their demand for drugs. Such persons, with few exceptions (as an example, the guilt of addicts who import not only to meet but also to finance their needs is not necessarily the same in degree as that of cold-blooded non-users), should, upon conviction, in my respectful view, be sentenced to and actually serve long periods of penal servitude. However, a judge who would sentence to seven years in a penitentiary a young person who, while driving back into Canada from a winter break in the U.S.A., is caught with only one, indeed, let's postulate, his or her first "joint of grass", would certainly be considered by most Canadians to be a cruel and, all would hope, a very unusual judge.

Yet, there is a law in Canada, s. 5(2) of the *Narcotic Control Act,* R.S.C. 1970, c. N-1, that gives no judge in the land any other choice.

Section 5 of the *Narcotic Control Act* reads as follows:

> **5.** (1) Except as authorized by this Act or the regulations, no person shall import into Canada or export from Canada any narcotic.
>
> (2) Every person who violates subsection (1) is guilty of an indictable offence and is liable to imprisonment for life but not less than seven years.

While no such case has actually occurred to my knowledge, that is merely because the Crown has chosen to exercise favorably its prosecutorial discretion to charge such a person not with the offence that person has really committed, but rather with a lesser offence. However, the potential that such a person be charged with importing is there lurking. Added to that potential is the *certainty* that upon conviction a minimum of seven year's imprisonment will have to be imposed. It is because of that certainty that I find that the minimum mandatory imprisonment found in s. 5(2) is in violation of s. 12 of the *Canadian Charter of Rights and Freedoms*, which guarantees to each and every one of us that we shall not be subjected to any cruel and unusual treatment or punishment.

The appellant returned to Canada from Bolivia with 7-1/2 oz of 85 to 90% pure cocaine on his person. He pleaded guilty in the County Court of Vancouver, British Columbia, to importing a narcotic contrary to s. 5(1) of the *Narcotic Control Act* and was sentenced to eight years in the penitentiary.

## The Issue

The following constitutional question which was stated by the Chief Justice is, as a result of appellant's having abandoned all others at the hearing, the only issue in this court:

> Whether the mandatory minimum sentence of seven years prescribed by s. 5(2) of the *Narcotic Control Act*, R.S.C. 1970, c. N-1 is contrary to, infringes, or denies the rights and guarantees contained in the *Canadian Charter of Rights and Freedoms*, and in particular the rights contained in ss. 7, 9 and 12 thereof?

For reasons I will give later I will address only s. 12 of the Charter. Since the appellant does not dispute the constitutionality of the maximum penalty of life imprisonment but only the minimum seven years' imprisonment, the question in issue is therefore limited to whether the concluding six words of s. 5(2) of the *Narcotic Control Act* will, under certain circumstances, leave the judge no other alternative but that of subjecting those convicted under the section to cruel and unusual punishment.

## The Meaning of s. 12

It is generally accepted in a society such as ours that the State has the power to impose a "treatment or punishment" on an individual where it is necessary to do so to attain some legitimate end and where the requisite procedure has been followed. The Charter limits this power: s. 7 provides that everyone has the right not to be deprived of life, liberty and security of the person except in accordance with the principles of fundamental justice, s. 9 provides that everyone has the right not to be arbitrarily detained or imprisoned, and s. 12 guarantees the right not to be subjected to any cruel and unusual treatment or punishment.

The limitation at issue here is s. 12 of the Charter. In my view, the protection afforded by s. 12 governs the quality of the punishment and is concerned with the effect that the punishment may have on the person on whom it is imposed. I would agree with Laskin C.J.C. in *Miller and Cockriell, supra*, where he defined the phrase "cruel and unusual" as a "compendious expression of a norm". The criterion which must be applied in order to determine whether a punishment is cruel and unusual within the meaning of s. 12 of the Charter is, to use the words of Laskin C.J.C. in *Miller and Cockriell, supra*, at p. 183 C.C.C., p. 330 D.L.R., p. 688 S.C.R., "whether the punishment prescribed is so excessive as to outrage standards of decency". In other words, though the State may impose punishment, the effect of that punishment must not be grossly disproportionate to what would have been appropriate.

In imposing a sentence of imprisonment the judgement will assess the circumstances of the case in order to arrive at an appropriate sentence. The test for review under s. 12 of the Charter is one of gross disproportionality, because it is aimed at punishments that are more than merely excessive. We should be careful not to stigmatize every disproportionate or excessive sentence as being a constitutional violation, and should leave to the usual sentencing appeal process the task of reviewing the fitness of a sentence. Section 12 will only be infringed where the sentence is so unfit having regard to the offence and the offender as to be grossly disproportionate.

In assessing whether a sentence is grossly disproportionate, the court must first consider the gravity of the offence, the personal characteristics of the offender and the particular circumstances of the case in order to determine what range of sentences would have been appropriate to punish, rehabilitate or deter this particular offender or to protect the public from this particular offender. The other purposes which may be pursued by the imposition of punishment, in particular the deterrence of other potential offenders, are thus not relevant at this stage of the inquiry. This does not mean that the judge or the legislator can no longer consider general deterrence or other phenological purposes that go beyond the particular offender in determining a sentence, but only that the resulting sentence must not be grossly disproportionate to what the offender deserves. If a grossly disproportionate sentence is "prescribed by law", then the purpose which it seeks to attain will fall to be assessed under s. 1. Section 12 ensures that individual offenders receive punishments that are appropriate, or at least not grossly disproportionate, to their particular circumstances, while s. 1 permits this right to be overridden to achieve some important societal objective.

One must also measure the effect of the sentence actually imposed. If it is grossly disproportionate to what would have been appropriate, then it infringes s. 12. The effect of the sentence is often a composite of many factors and is not limited to the quantum or duration of the sentence but includes its nature and the conditions under which it is applied. Sometimes by its length alone or by its very nature will the sentence be grossly disproportionate to the purpose sought. Sometimes it will be the result of the combination of factors which, when considered in isolation, would not in and of themselves amount to gross disproportionality. For example, 20 years for a first offence against property would be grossly disproportionate, but so would three months of imprisonment if the prison authorities decide it should be served in solitary confinement. Finally, I should add that some punishments or treatments will always be grossly disproportionate and will always outrage our standards of decency: for example; the infliction of corporal punishment, such as the lash, irrespective of the number of lashes imposed, or, to give examples of treatment, the lobotomisation of certain dangerous offenders or the castration of sexual offenders.

. . . .

There is a further aspect of proportionality which has been considered on occasion by the American courts: a comparison with punishments imposed for other crimes in the same jurisdiction: see *Solem v. Helm* (1983), 463 U.S. 277 at p. 291. Of course, the simple fact that penalties for similar offences are divergent does not necessarily mean that the greater penalty is grossly disproportionate and thus cruel and unusual. At most, the divergence in penalties is an indication that the greater penalty may be excessive, but it will remain necessary to assess the penalty in accordance with the factors discussed above. The notion that there must be a gradation of punishments according to the malignity of offences may be considered to be a principle of fundamental justice under s. 7, but, given my decision under s. 12, I do not find it necessary to deal with that issue here.

On more than one occasion the courts in Canada have alluded to a further factor, namely, whether the punishment was arbitrarily imposed. As regards this factor, some comments should be made because arbitrariness of detention and imprisonment is addressed by s. 9, and, to the extent that the arbitrariness, given the proper context, could be in breach of a principle of fundamental justice, it could trigger a *prima facie* violation under s. 7. As indicated above, s. 12 is concerned with the *effect* of a punishment, and, as such, the process by which the punishment is imposed is not, in my respectful view, of any great relevance to a determination under s. 12.

. . . .

Of course because we live in a free, democratic and progressive society, cruelty and gross discrepancy of treatment of those we punish has generally, under the rule of law, been kept in check through legislation imposing limitation on what we can do to others under the law and through the development of elaborate sentencing guidelines and review through appeals. Therefore when a cruel and unusual punishment is inflicted it will often be the result of a disregard for those laws and guidelines and as such will be the result of arbitrariness in the choice of punishment. However, as I said, a sentence is or is not grossly proportionate to the purpose sought or a punishment is or is not cruel and unusual irrespective of why the violation has taken place.

## Section 5(2) of the Narcotic Control Act

At issue in this appeal is the minimum term of imprisonment provided for by s. 5(2) of the *Narcotic Control Act*. It thus is not necessary to delimit the scope of the terms "treatment" and "punishment", since they clearly include the imposition by a judge of a term of imprisonment. The minimum seven-year imprisonment fails the proportionality test enunciated above and therefore *prima facie* infringes the guarantees established by s. 12 of the Charter. The simple fact that s. 5(2) provides for a mandatory term of imprisonment does not by itself lead to this conclusion. A minimum mandatory term of imprisonment is obviously not in and of itself cruel and unusual. The Legislature may, in my view, provide for a compulsory term of imprisonment upon conviction for certain offences without infringing the rights protected by s. 12 of the Charter. For example, a long term of penal servitude for he or she who has imported large amounts of heroin for the purpose of trafficking would certainly not contravene s. 12 of the Charter, quite the contrary. However, the seven year-minimum prison term of s. 5(2) is grossly disproportionate when examined in light of the wide net cast by s. 5(1).

As indicated above, the offence of importing enacted by s. 5(1) of the *Narcotic Control Act* covers numerous substances of varying degrees of dangerousness and totally disregards the quantity of the drug imported. The purpose of a given importation, such as whether it is for personal consumption or for trafficking, and the existence or non-existence of previous convictions for offences of a similar nature or gravity are disregarded as irrelevant. Thus, the law is such that it is inevitable that, in some cases, a verdict of guilt will lead to the imposition of a term of imprisonment which will be grossly disproportionate.

This is what offends s. 12, the certainty, not just the potential. Absent the minimum, the section still has the potential of operating so as to impose cruel and unusual punishment. But that would only occur if and when a judge chose to impose, let us say, seven years or more on the "small offender". Remedy will then flow from s. 24. It is the judge's sentence, but not the section, that is in violation of the Charter. However, the effect of the minimum is to insert the certainty that, in some cases, as of conviction the violation will occur. It is this aspect of certainty that makes the section itself a *prima facie* violation of s. 12, and the minimum must, subject to s. 1, be declared of no force or effect.

In its factum, the Crown alleged that such eventual violations could be, and are in fact, avoided through the proper use of prosecutorial discretion to charge for a lesser offence.

In my view, the section cannot be salvaged by relying on the discretion of the prosecution not to apply the law in those cases where, in the opinion of the prosecution, its application would be a violation of the Charter. To do so would be to disregard totally s. 52 of the *Constitution Act, 1982* which provides that any law which is inconsistent with the Constitution is of no force or effect to the extent of the inconsistency and the courts are duty-bound to make that pronouncement, not to delegate the avoidance of a violation to the prosecution or to anyone else for that matter. Therefore, to conclude, I find that the minimum term of imprisonment provided for by s. 5(2) of the *Narcotic Control Act* infringes the rights guaranteed by s. 12 and, as such, is a *prima facie* violation of the Charter. Subject to the section's being salvaged under s. 1, the minimum must be declared of no force or effect.

[After addressing issues arising in regard to s. 1 of the Charter, he continued:]

## Conclusion

In my view, the constitutional question should be answered in the affirmative as regards s. 12 of the Charter, and the minimum sentence provided for by s. 5(2) of the *Narcotic Control Act* should therefore be declared to be of no force or effect. It is not necessary, for reasons discussed above, to answer the question as regards ss. 7 and 9.

Now to deal with the appellant. The majority of the Court of Appeal upheld the eight-year sentence imposed by the trial judge. Because this is not a sentence appeal and because there was no suggestion that the sentence of eight years imposed on the appellant was cruel and unusual, I would normally dismiss the appeal. However, the Court of Appeal considered the fitness of the sentence in the context of a seven-year minimum, and we cannot ascertain whether or not they were influenced by that minimum, though I am inclined to think that they were not as they held that an eight-year sentence was not inappropriate. Counsel for the Crown, however, stated at the hearing that, were we to declare the minimum of no force or effect, the disposition preferable in his view of the appeal would be to allow the appeal and remit the matter to the Court of Appeal for a reconsideration of the sentence appeal in that court. Given this concession and my conclusion that the minimum is of no force or effect, I would so order.

I should add that I do not wish this manner of disposition to be taken as any indication whatsoever of what I may think the appropriate sentence in this particular case might be.

*Appeal allowed.*

## Vaillancourt v. R. and Attorney General of Ontario
(1988), 60 C.R. (3d) 289 (S.C.C.)

[Only the decision of Lamer J. is reproduced below.]
LAMER J. (DICKSON C.J.C. AND WILSON J. concurring): —

### INTRODUCTION

Vaillancourt was convicted of second degree murder following a trial before a sessions court judge and jury in Montreal. He appealed to the Quebec Court of Appeal, arguing that the judge's charge to the jury on the combined operation of ss. 213(d) and 21(2) of the Criminal Code, R.S.C. 1970, c. C-34, was incorrect. His appeal was dismissed and the conviction was affirmed [31 C.C.C. (3d) 75]. Before this court, he has challenged the constitutional validity of s. 213(d), alone and in combination with s. 21(2), under the Canadian Charter of Rights and Freedoms.

### THE FACTS

For the purposes of this appeal, the Crown does not contest the following statement of the facts.

The appellant and his accomplice committed an armed robbery in a pool hall. The appellant was armed with a knife and his accomplice with a gun. During the robbery, the appellant remained near the front of the hall while the accomplice went to the back. There was a struggle between the accomplice and a client. A shot was fired and the client was killed. The accomplice managed to escape and has never been found. The appellant was arrested at the scene.

In the course of his testimony, the appellant said that he and his accomplice had agreed to commit this robbery armed only with knives. On the night of the robbery, however, the accomplice arrived at their meeting place with a gun. The appellant said that he objected because on a previous armed robbery his gun had discharged accidentally, and he did not want that to happen again. He insisted that the gun be unloaded. The accomplice removed three bullets from the gun and gave them to the appellant. The appellant then went to the bathroom and placed the bullets in his glove. The glove was recovered by the police at the scene of the crime and was found at trial to contain three bullets. The appellant testified that at the time of the robbery he was certain that the gun was unloaded.

### CONSTITUTIONAL QUESTION

Before this court, the following constitution questions were formulated:

1. Is s. 213(d) of the *Criminal Code* inconsistent with the provisions of either s. 7 or s. 11(d) of the *Canadian Charter of Rights and Freedoms* and therefore, of no force or effect?
2. If not, is the combination of s. 21 and s. 213(d) of the *Criminal Code* inconsistent with the provisions of either s. 7 or s. 11(d) of the *Canadian Charter of Rights and Freedoms* and is s. 21 of the Criminal Code therefore of no force or effect in the case of a charge under s. 213(d) of the *Criminal Code*?

## THE LAW

### Narrowing the Issue

The appellant has framed his attack on s. 213(d) of the Code in very wide terms. He has argued that the principles of fundamental justice require that, before Parliament can impose any criminal liability for causing a particular result, there must be some degree of subjective mens rea in respect of that result. This is a fundamental question with far-reaching consequences. If this case were decided on that basis, doubt would be cast on the constitutional validity of many provisions throughout the Criminal Code, in particular s. 205(5)(a), whereby causing death by means of an unlawful act is culpable homicide, and s. 212(c), whereby objective foreseeability of the likelihood of death is sufficient for a murder conviction in certain circumstances.

However, the appellant was convicted under s. 213(d) and the constitutional question is limited to this provision. In my opinion, the validity of s. 213(d) can be decided on somewhat narrower grounds. In addition, the Attorney General of Canada has seen fit not to intervene to support the constitutionality of s. 213(d), which is clearly in jeopardy in this case, though he might have intervened to support ss. 205(5)(a) and 212(c) and other similar provisions. I will thus endeavour not to make pronouncements the effect of which will be to predispose in obiter of other issues more properly dealt with if and when the constitutionality of the other provisions is in issue. I do, however, find it virtually impossible to make comments as regards s. 213(d) that will not have some effect on the validity of the rest of 213 or that will not reveal to some extent my views as regards s. 212(c). However, the validity of those sections and of subss. (a) to (c) of s. 213 is not in issue here and I will attempt to limit my comments to s. 213(d).

The appellant has also challenged the combined operation of ss. 21(2) and 213(d). Given my decision on the validity of s. 213(d), and in view of the importance of s. 21(2) and the absence of the Attorney General of Canada, I do not find it necessary or advisable to deal with s. 21(2) in this appeal.

### Analysis of 213(d)

*Section 213(d) in the Context of the Murder Provisions*

It is first necessary to analyze s. 213(d) in the context of the other murder provision in the Code in order to determine its true nature and scope. Murder is defined as a culpable homicide committed in the circumstances set out at ss. 212 and 213 of the Code. There is a very interesting progression through s. 212 to s. 213 with respect to the mental state that must be proven.

The starting point is s. 212(a)(i), which provides:

**212.** Culpable homicide is murder
(a) where the person who causes the death of a human being

(i) means to cause his death . . .

This clearly requires that the accused have actually subjective foresight of the likelihood of causing the death, coupled with the intention to cause that death. This is the most morally blameworthy state of mind in our system.

There is a slight relaxation of this requirement in s. 212(a)(ii), which provides:

**212.** Culpable homicide is murder
(a) where the person who causes the death of a human being . . .

> (ii) means to cause him bodily harm that he knows is likely to cause his death, and is reckless whether death ensues or not . . .

Here again the accused must have actual subjective foresight of the likelihood of death. However, the Crown need no longer prove that he intended to cause the death, but only that he was reckless whether death ensued or not. It should also be noted that s. 212(a)(ii) is limited to cases where the accused intended to cause bodily harm to the victim.

Section 212(c) provides:

> **212.** Culpable homicide is murder . . .
> (c) where a person, for an unlawful object, does anything that he knows or ought to know is likely to cause death, and thereby causes death to a human being, notwithstanding that he desires to effect his object without causing death or bodily harm to any human being.

In part, this is simply a more general form of recklessness, and thus the logical extension is s. 212(a)(ii), in that it applies when the accused "does *anything* . . . he knows . . . is likely to cause death" (emphasis added). However, there is also a further relaxation of the mental element required for murder, in that it is also murder where the accused "does *anything that he . . . ought to know* is likely to cause death" (emphasis added). This eliminates the requirement of actual subjective foresight and replaces it with objective foreseeability or negligence.

The final relaxation in the definition of murder occurs at s. 213:

> **213.** Culpable homicide is murder where a person causes the death of a human being while committing or attempting to commit high treason or treason or an offence mentioned in section 52 (sabotage), 76 (piratical acts), 76.1 (hijacking an aircraft), 132 or subsection 133(1) or section 134 to 136 (escape or rescue from prison or lawful custody), 143 or 145 (rape or attempt to commit rape), 149 or 156 (indecent assault), subsection 246(2) (resisting lawful arrest), 247 (kidnapping and forcible confinement) 302 (robbery), 306 (breaking and entering) or 389 or 390 (arson), whether or not the person means to cause death to any human being and whether or not he knows that death is likely to be caused to any human being, if
> (a) he means to cause bodily harm for the purpose of
> > (i) facilitating the commission of the offence or
> > (ii) facilitating his flight after committing or attempting to commit the offence,
> 
> and the death ensues from the bodily harm;
> (b) he administers a stupefying or overpowering thing for a purpose mentioned in paragraph (a), and the death ensues therefrom;
> (c) he wilfully stops, by any means, the breath of a human being for a purpose mentioned in paragraph (a), and the death ensues therefrom: or
> (d) he uses a weapon or has it upon his person
> > (i) during or at the time he commits or attempts to commit the offence, or
> > (ii) during or at the time of his flight after committing or attempting to commit the offence, and the death ensues as a consequence.

Under this provision, it is murder if the accused causes the victim's death while committing or attempting to commit one of the enumerated offences if he performs one of the acts in subss. (a) to (d). Proof that the accused performed one of the acts in subss. (a) to (d) is substituted for proof of any subjective foresight, or even objective foreseeability, of the likelihood of death.

I should add that there appears to be a further relaxation of the mental state when the accused is a party to the murder through s. 212(2) of the Code, as in this case. However, as I have said, it is sufficient to deal with s. 213(d) in order to dispose of this appeal.

*The Historical Development of s. 213*

Although the concept of felony murder has a long history at common law, a brief review of the historical development of s. 213 indicates that its legitimacy is questionable.

In the early history of English criminal law, "murdrum", or murder, referred to a secret killing, or the killing of a Dane, or later a Norman, by an Englishman, and to the fine levied on the township where the killing occurred. By the early 14th century, the fines had been abandoned and murder had come to be the name used to describe the worst kind of homicide. The expression "malice aforethought" was subsequently adopted to distinguish murder from manslaughter, which denoted all culpable homicides other than murder. Malice aforethought was not limited to its natural and obvious sense of premeditation, but would be implied whenever the killing was intentional or reckless. In these instances, the malice was present and it is the premeditation which was implied by law.

Coke took this one step further and implied both the malice and the premeditation in cases where the death occurred in the commission of an unlawful act. He wrote in the Third Part of the Institutes of the Laws of England (1817), London, W. Clarke and Sons, at p. 56:

> *Unlawfull.* Of the act be unlawful it is murder. As if A. meaning to steale a deere in the park of B., shooteth at the deer, and by the glance of the arrow killeth a boy that is hidden in a bush: this is murder, for that the act was unlawful, although A. had no intent to hurt the boy, nor knew of him. But if D. the owner of the park had shot at his own deer, and without any ill intent had killed the boy by the glance of his arrow, this had been homicide by misadventure and no felony.
>
> So if one shoot at any wilde fowle upon a tree, and the arrow killeth any reasonable creature afar off, without any evil intent in him, this is *per infortunium*: for it was not unlawful to shoot at the wilde fowle: but if he had shot at a cock or a hen, or any tame fowle of another mans, and the arrow by mischance had killed a man, this had been murder, for the act was unlawful.

Coke's statement of the unlawful act murder rule has been much criticized. Stephen demonstrated that Coke's statement was not supported by the authorities cited: History of the Criminal Law of England (1883), vol. 3, pp. 57-58. Further, a recent author has suggested that Coke's statement was just "a slip of the quill" and that Coke intended to say that accidental killing by an unlawful act was manslaughter: see D. Lanham, "Felony Murder — Ancient and Modern" (1983), 7 Crim. L.J. 90, at pp. 92-94.

. . . .

In the 19th century, the felony murder rule was accepted as part of the common law; see Stephen's Digest of the Criminal Law, 9th ed. (1950), art. 264(c). However, the rule was strongly criticized by Stephen, who labelled it "cruel" and "monstrous": History of the Criminal Law, vol. 3, p. 75.

Despite the rule's questionable origins and the subsequent criticisms, s. 175 of the English Draft Code of 1879 included a restricted form of felony murder, which was subsequently adopted in the first Canadian Criminal Code, in 1892. Through subsequent amendments this provision has been widened, and it is now s. 213. It is more restricted than the common law rule, in that it is limited to deaths occurring in the commission of certain enumerated offences and it requires that the accused have committed one of the acts set out in subss. (a) to (d).

. . . .

### Section 213(d) and the Charter

This appeal calls into play two principles of fundamental justice.

**The First Principle:** The essential elements of certain crimes and s. 7 of the Charter

Prior to the enactment of the Charter, Parliament had full legislative power with respect to "The Criminal Law" (Constitution Act, 1867, s. 91(27)), including the determination of the essential elements of any given crime. It could prohibit any act and impose any penal consequences for infringing the prohibition, provided only that the prohibition served "a public purpose which can support it as being in relation to criminal law": *Ref. re s. 5(a) of the Dairy Indust. Act*, [1949] S.C.R. 1 at 50, [1949] 1 D.L.R. 433, affirmed (sub. nom. *Cdn. Fed. of Agriculture v. Can. (A.G.)*) [1951] A.C. 179, [1950] 4 S.L.R. 689 (P.C.). Once the legislation was found to have met this test, the courts had very little power to review the substance of the legislation. For example, in *R. v. Sault Ste. Marie (City)*, [1978] 2 S.C.R. 1299, 3 C.R. (3d) 30, 40 C.C.C.(2d) 353, 85 D.L.R. (3d) 161, 7 C.E.L.R. 53, 21 N.R. 295 [Ont.], Dickson J. (as he then was) held that, when an offence was criminal in the true sense, there was a presumption that the prosecution must prove the mens rea. However, it was always open to Parliament expressly to relieve the prosecution of its obligation to prove any part of the mens rea, as it is said to have done in s. 213 of the Criminal Code with respect to the foreseeability of the death of the victim. It is thus clear that, prior to the enactment of the Charter, the validity of s. 213 could not have been successfully challenged.

However, federal and provincial legislatures have chosen to restrict through the Charter this power with respect to criminal law. Under s. 7, if a conviction, given either the stigma attached to the offence or the available penalties, will result in a deprivation of the life, liberty or security of the person of the accused, then Parliament must respect the principles of fundamental justice. It has been argued that the principles of fundamental justice in s. 7 are only procedural guarantees. However, in *Ref. re s. 92(2) of Motor Vehicle Act*, [1985] 2 S.C.R. 486, 48 C.R. (3d) 289, [1986] 1 W.W.R. 481, 69 B.C.L.R. 145, 36 M.V.R. 240, 23 C.C.C. (3d) 289, 24 D.L.R. (4th) 536, 18 C.R.R. 30, 63 N.R. 266, this court rejected that argument and used s. 7 to review the substance of the legislation. As a result, while Parliament retains the power to define the elements of a crime, the courts now have the jurisdiction and, more important, the duty, when called upon to do so, to review that definition to ensure that it is in accordance with the principles of fundamental justice.

This court's decision in *Re Motor Vehicle Act* stands for the proposition that absolute liability infringes the principles of fundamental justice, such that the combination of absolute liability and a deprivation of life, liberty or security of the person is a restriction on one's rights under s. 7 and is prima facie a violation thereof. In effect,

*Re Motor Vehicle Act* acknowledges that, whenever the state resorts to the restriction of liberty, such as imprisonment, to assist in the enforcement of a law, even, as in *Re Motor Vehicle Act*, a mere provincial regulatory offence, there is, as a principle of fundamental justice, a minimum mental state which is an essential element of the offence. It thus elevated mens rea from a presumed element in *Sault ste. Marie*, supra, to a constitutionally-required element. *Re Motor Vehicle Act* did not decide what level of mens rea was constitutionally required for each type of offence, but inferentially decided that even for a mere provincial regulatory offence *at least* negligence was required, in that *at least* a defence of due diligence must *always* be open to an accused who risks imprisonment upon conviction. In *Sault Ste. Marie*, Dickson J. stated at pp. 1309-10:

> Where the offence is criminal, the Crown must establish a mental element, namely, that the accused who committed the prohibited act did so intentionally or recklessly, with knowledge of the facts constituting the offence, or with wilful blindness toward them. Mere negligence is excluded from the concept of the mental element required for conviction. Within the context of a criminal prosecution a person who fails to make such enquiries as a reasonable and prudent person would make, or who fails to know facts he should have known, is innocent in the eyes of the law.

It may well be that, as a general rule, the principles of fundamental justice require proof of a subjective mens rea with respect to the prohibited act, in order to avoid punishing the "morally innocent". It must be remembered, however, that Dickson J. was dealing with the mens rea to be presumed in the absence of an express legislative disposition, and not the mens rea to be required in all legislation providing for a restriction on the accused's life, liberty or security of the person. In any event, this case involves criminal liability for the result of an intentional criminal act, and it is arguable that different considerations should apply to the mental element required with respect to that result. There are many provisions in the Code requiring only objective foreseeability of the result or even only a casual link between the act and the result. As I would prefer not to cast doubt on the validity of such provisions *in this case*, I will assume, but only for the purposes of this appeal, that something less than subjective foresight of the result may sometimes suffice for the imposition of criminal liability for causing that result through intentional criminal conduct.

But, whatever the minimum mens rea for the act or the result may be, there are, though very few in number, certain crimes where, because of the special nature of the stigma attached to a conviction therefor or the available penalties, the principles of fundamental justice require a mens rea reflecting the particular nature of that crime. Such is theft, where, in my view, a conviction requires proof of some dishonesty. Murder is another such offence. The punishment for murder is the most severe in our society, and the stigma that attaches to a conviction for murder is similarly extreme. In addition, murder is distinguished from manslaughter only by the mental element with respect to the death. It is thus clear that there must be some special mental element with respect to the death before a culpable homicide can be treated as murder. That special element gives rise to the moral blameworthiness which justifies the stigma and sentence attached to a murder conviction. I am presently of the view that it is a principle of fundamental justice that a conviction for murder cannot rest on anything less than proof beyond a reasonable doubt of subjective foresight. Given the effect of this view on part of s. 212(c), for the reasons I have already given for deciding this case more narrowly, I need not and will not rest my finding that s. 213(d) does not, for reasons I will set out hereinafter, even meet the lower threshold test of objective foreseeability. I will therefore, for the sole purpose of this appeal, go no further than to say it is a principle of fundamental justice that, absent proof beyond a reasonable doubt of a least objective foreseeability, there surely cannot be a murder conviction.

**The Second Principle**: Section 11(d) and the burden of persuasion

The presumption of innocence in s. 11(d) of the Charter requires at least that an accused be presumed innocent until his guilt has been proven beyond a reasonable doubt: *Dubois v. R.,* [1985] 2 S.C.R. 350 at 357, 48 C.R. (3d) 193, [1986] 1 W.W.R. 193, 41 Alta., L.R. (2d) 97, 22 C.C.C. (3d) 513, 23 D.L.R. (4th) 503, 18 C.R.R. 1, 66 A.R. 202, 62 N.R. 50; *R. v. Oakes,* [1986] 1 S.C.R. 103 at 120-21, 50 C.R. (3d) 1, 24 C.C.C. (3d) 321, 26 D.L.R. (4th) 200, 19 C.R.R. 308, 14 O.A.C. 335, 65 N.R. 87. This means that, before an accused can be convicted of an offence, the trier of fact must be satisfied beyond reasonable doubt of the existence of all the essential elements of the offence. These essential elements include not only those set out by the legislature in the provisions creating the offence but also those required by s. 7 of the Charter. Any provision creating an offence which allows for the conviction of an accused notwithstanding the existence of a reasonable doubt on any essential element infringes ss. 7 and 11(d).

Clearly, this will occur where the provision requires the accused to disprove on a balance of probabilities an essential element of the offence by requiring that he raise more than just a reasonable doubt. It is for this reason that this court struck down the reverse onus provision in s. 8 of the Narcotic Control Act, R.S.C. 1970, c. N-1 in *R. v. Oakes.*

Sections 7 and 11(d) will also be infringed where the statutory definition of the offence does not include an element which is required under s. 7. As Dickson C.J.C. wrote for the majority of the court in *Oakes* at pp. 132-33:

> In general one must, I think, conclude that a provision which requires an accused to disprove on a balance of probabilities the existence of a presumed fact, which is an important element of the offence in question, violates the presumption of innocence in s. 11(d). If an accused bears the burden of disproving on a balance of probabilities an essential element of an offence, *it would be possible for a conviction to occur despite the existence of a reasonable doubt.* This would arise if the accused adduced sufficient evidence to raise a reasonable doubt as to his or her innocence but did not convince the jury on a balance of probabilities that the presumed fact was untrue. [Emphasis added.]

It is clear from this passage that what offends the presumption of innocence is the fact that an accused may be convicted despite the existence of a reasonable doubt on an essential element of the offence, and I do not think that it matters whether this results from the existence of a reverse onus provision or from the elimination of the need to prove an essential element. With respect, the Nova Scotia Supreme Court, Appeal Division, was thus clearly incorrect when it stated in *R. v. Bezanson* (1983), 8 C.C.C. (3d) 493 at 508, 61 N.S.R. (2d) 181, 144 A.P.R. 181:

> In my view, there was no attempt by Parliament to reverse the onus of proof under s. 213, and s. 11(d) of the Charter has no application. Parliament has not reversed the burden of proof, it has simply

omitted what the appellant argues is an essential element from the definition of the offence so that no evidence is required at all on that issue.

The omission of an essential element does bring s. 11(d) into play.

Finally, the legislature, rather than simply eliminating any need to prove the essential element, may substitute proof of a different element. In my view, this will be constitutionally valid only if upon proof beyond a reasonable doubt of the substituted element it would be unreasonable for the trier of fact not to be satisfied beyond reasonable doubt of the existence of the essential element. If the trier of fact may have a reasonable doubt as to the essential element notwithstanding proof beyond a reasonable doubt of the substituted element, the substitution infringes ss. 7 and 11(d).

Given the first principle I have enunciated earlier and my assumption for the sole purpose of disposing of this appeal with respect to objective foreseeability, an accused cannot be found guilty of murder absent proof beyond reasonable doubt of at least that essential element infringes ss. 7 and 11(d).

*Application of the Principles to s. 213*

The mens rea required for s. 213 consists of the mens rea for the underlying offence and the intent to commit one of the acts set forth in subss. (a) to (d): *Swietlinski v. R.*, [1980] 2 S.C.R. 956, 18 C.R. (3d) 231, 55 C.C.C. (2d) 481, 117 D.L.R. (3d) 285, 34 N.R. 569 [Ont.]. Section 213 does not impose on the accused the burden of disproving objective foreseeability. Further, it does not completely exclude the need to prove any objective foreseeability. Rather, s. 213 has substituted for proof beyond a reasonable doubt of objective foreseeability, if that is the essential element, proof beyond a reasonable doubt of certain forms of intentional dangerous conduct causing death.

The question is therefore: Can Parliament make this substitution without violating ss. 7 and 11(d)? As I have discussed earlier, if Parliament frames the section so that, upon proof of the conduct, it would be unreasonable for a jury not to conclude beyond a reasonable doubt that the accused ought to have known that death was likely to ensue, then I think Parliament has enacted a crime which is tantamount to one which has objective foreseeability as an essential element, and, if objective foreseeability is sufficient, then it would not be in violation of s. 7 or 11(d) in doing so in that way. The acid test of the constitutionality of s. 213 is this ultimate question: *Would it be possible for a conviction for murder to occur under s. 213 despite the jury having a reasonable doubt as to whether the accused ought to have known that death was likely to ensue?* If the answer is "Yes", then the section is prima facie in violation of ss. 7 and 11(d). I should add in passing that if the answer is "No" then it would be necessary to decide whether objective foreseeability is sufficient for a murder conviction. However, because in my view the answer is "Yes" and because I do not want to pass upon the constitutionality of s. 212(c) in this case, I will not address that issue.

To varying degrees it can be said that in almost any case a jury satisfied beyond a reasonable doubt that an accused has done one of the prohibited acts described in subss. (a) to (d) will be satisfied beyond a reasonable doubt that the accused ought to have known that death was likely to be caused. But not always. Indeed, as a first example, drunkenness would under certain circumstances leave the jury in doubt in that regard. The rule as regards the effect of drunkenness on objective foreseeability was unanimously laid down by this court in *R. v. Vasil*, [1981] 1 S.C.R. 469, 20 C.R. (3d) 193, 58 C.C.C. (2d) 97, 121 D.L.R. (3d) 41, 35 N.R. 451 [Ont.], a murder prosecution under s. 212(c). This court addressed the issue at some length and then summarized its conclusion as follows, per Lamer J. at pp. 500-501:

> (5) Whilst the test under [s.] 212(c) is objective and the behaviour of the accused is to be measured by that of the reasonable man, such a test must nevertheless be applied having regard, not to the knowledge a reasonable man would have had of the surrounding circumstances that allegedly made the accused's conduct dangerous to life, but to the knowledge the accused had of those circumstances;
>
> (6) As a result, drunkenness, though not relevant in the determination of what a reasonable man, with the knowledge the accused had of those circumstances, would have anticipated, is relevant in the determination of the knowledge which the accused had of those circumstances.

It is clear to me, under s. 213 as drafted, there will be cases where the effect of drunkenness on an accused's knowledge of the circumstances would leave a jury with a reasonable doubt as to whether the accused ought to have known of the likelihood of death ensuing even though it has been proven beyond a reasonable doubt that the accused actually did one of the acts described under subs. (a) to (d).

A second example, and this case amply illustrates the point, is the accused who is brought into s. 213 not as a principal but through the operation of s. 21(2) of the Criminal Code. In *R. v. Trinneer*, [1970] S.C.R. 638, 11 C.R.N.S. 110, 72 W.W.R. 677, [1970] 3 C.C.C. 289, 10 D.L.R. (3d) 568 [B.C.], this court had the opportunity to consider the combined operation of ss. 21(2) and 213 (s. 220 [of the 1953-54 Criminal Code] at the time). Cartwright C.J.C., delivering the judgment of the court, stated at pp. 645-46:

> At the risk of repetition, it is my opinion that on the true construction of s. 202 and s. 21(2) as applied to the circumstances of this case it was necessary to support a verdict of guilty against the respondent that the Crown should establish (i) that it was in fact a probable consequence of the prosecution of the common purpose of the respondent and Frank to rob Mrs. Vollet that Frank for the purpose of facilitating the commission of the robbery would intentionally cause bodily harm to Mrs. Vollet, (ii) that it was known or ought to have been known to the respondent that such consequence was probable and (iii) that in fact Mrs. Vollet's death ensued from the bodily harm. *It was not necessary for the Crown to establish that the respondent knew or ought to have known that it was probable that Mrs. Vollet's death would ensue.* [Emphasis added.]

It is clear that an accused can be convicted of murder under the combined operation of ss. 21(2) and 213 in circumstances where the death was not objectively foreseeable. As s. 21(2) requires proof of objective foreseeability, the culprit, in my view, must be s. 213.

These two examples suffice, in my view, for one to conclude that, notwithstanding proof beyond a reasonable doubt of the matters set forth in subss. (a) to (d), a jury could reasonably be left in doubt as regards objective foreseeability of the likelihood that death be caused. In other words, s. 213 will catch an accused who performs one of the acts in subss. (a) to (d) and thereby causes a death but who otherwise would have been acquitted of murder because he did not foresee and could not reasonably have foreseen that death would be likely to result. For that reason, s. 213 prima facie violates ss. 7 and 11(d). It is thus not necessary to decide whether objective foreseeability is sufficient for murder, as s. 213 does not even meet that standard. This takes us to s. 1 for the second phase of the constitutional inquiry.

[After addressing issues arising in regard to s. 1 of the Charter, he continued:]

## CONCLUSION

As a result of the foregoing, I would answer the first constitutional question in the affirmative, as s. 213(d) violates both s. 7 and 11(d) of the Charter, and I would declare s. 213(d) of the Criminal Code to be of no force or effect. I would, for the reasons which I have given, decline to answer the second constitutional question. It follows that the appeal must be allowed, the appellant's conviction for murder set aside, and a new trial ordered.

. . . .

*Appeal allowed; conviction quashed; new trial ordered.*

## Regina v. Mellenthin
(1992), 76 C.C.C. (3d) 481 (S.C.C.)

Appeal by the accused from a judgment of the Alberta Court of Appeal, 2 W.A.C. 165, [1991] 5 W.W.R. 519, 80 Alta. L.R. (2d) 193, 117 A.R. 165, 13 W.C.B. (2d) 139, allowing an appeal by the Crown from the accused's acquittal on a charge of possession of narcotics.

The judgment of the court was delivered by

CORY J.: — Can the police, conducting a random roadside check stop, in the absence of any reasonable grounds for doing so, interrogate a driver about matters other than those related to the vehicle and its operation and search the driver and the vehicle? That is the question to be resolved in this appeal.

I. *Factual background*

On September 4, 1988, Constable Watkins and two other members of the R.C.M.P. were operating an "Alberta Check Stop" as part of a program to check vehicles. At about 12:30 a.m. the appellant's vehicle was directed into the check stop. At this time, there was nothing unusual observed either with regard to the manner in which the appellant was driving the vehicle or the appellant himself. Constable Watkins observed that the appellant was not wearing his seatbelt and asked him for his driver's licence, vehicle registration and insurance papers. The appellant complied with the request without any difficulty. At this point, the officer shone his flashlight around the interior of the vehicle. He did this to check whether drugs were present in the vehicle and "for the safety of the officers conducting the check point". He saw neither liquor nor drugs but did see an open gym bag on the front seat beside the appellant. Inside the gym bag was a small brown bag with a plastic sandwich bag inside it.

Constable Watkins asked what was inside the bag and in response the appellant pulled the bag open and said there was food inside. The officer saw a reflection of what he thought was glass from inside the plastic bag. For the first time he became suspicious and "felt that there could have been narcotics inside". The officer asked the appellant what was in the brown bag and the appellant pulled the baggie out. It contained empty glass vials. The constable testified that because these types of vials were commonly used to store *cannabis* resin he considered that he had reasonable and probable grounds to believe that narcotics were present.

Constable Watkins asked the appellant to get out of the car. He searched the brown bag and found it contained some *cannabis* resin. He arrested the appellant for possession of a narcotic and properly instructed him as to his rights. The officer searched the car and found it contained vials of hash oil and some *cannabis* resin cigarettes. The appellant gave an incriminating statement a little later at the R.C.M.P. detachment....

III. *Issues*

There are in my view three questions that must be resolved in order to determine the result of this appeal.

(1) Was the appellant detained in the check stop?
(2) Was there an unreasonable search conducted by the police?
(3) If the search conducted was unreasonable, would the admission of the evidence bring the administration of justice into disrepute?

IV. *Analysis*

A. *Was the appellant detained in the check stop?*

It was decided in *R. v. Dedman* (1985), 20 C.C.C. (3d) 97, 20 D.L.R. (4th) 321, [1985] 2 S.C.R. 2, that stopping a vehicle as a part of a R.I.D.E. program constituted detention. The case arose prior to the passage of the Charter; however, the reasoning was relied upon in cases that did take into account Charter rights. . . .

There can be no question that the appellant was detained and, as a result, could reasonably be expected to feel compelled to respond to questions from the police.

It is true that a person who is detained can still consent to answer police questions. However, that consent must be one that is informed and given at a time when the individual is fully aware of his or her rights. This was certainly not the situation which was present in this case. Here it cannot be said that the appellant consented to either the questions pertaining to the gym bag or to the physical search. These are factors that will be of significance in the subsequent analysis.

B. *Was there a search and was it unreasonable?*

The Crown (the respondent) contends that what occurred in this case did not constitute a search. First, it was said that a visual inspection of the interior of the vehicle would not in itself constitute a search. Further it was submitted that the questions posed by the police officers pertaining to the gym bag were authorized by the provisions of s. 119 of Alberta's *Highway Traffic Act*, R.S.A. 1980, c. H-7. That section provides:

119. A driver shall, immediately upon being signalled or requested to stop by a peace officer in uniform, bring his vehicle to a stop and furnish any information respecting the driver or the vehicle that the peace officer requires and shall not start his vehicle until he is permitted to do so by the peace officer.

It was argued that the questions came within the ambit of the words "any information respecting the driver or the vehicle that the peace officer requires". These words, it was said, indicate that the objectives of the check-stop program in Alberta are wider than those referred to in Ontario's *Highway Traffic Act*, R.S.O. 1980, c. 198, considered in *Ladouceur, supra*. I cannot agree with this submission.

There can be no quarrel with the visual inspection of the car by police officers. At night the inspection can only be carried out with the aid of a flashlight and it is necessarily incidental to a check-stop program carried out after dark. The inspection is essential for the protection of those on duty in the check stops. There have been more than enough incidents of violence to police officers when vehicles have been stopped. Nor can I place any particular significance upon the fact stressed by the appellant that the police only made use of a flashlight after the request had been made of the appellant to produce the necessary papers and not when the constable first approached the car. Although the safety of the police might make it preferable to use the flashlight at the earliest opportunity, it certainly can be utilized at any time as a necessary incident to the check-stop routine.

However, the subsequent questions pertaining to the gym bag were improper. At the moment the questions were asked, the officer had not even the slightest suspicion that drugs or alcohol were in the vehicle or in the possession of the appellant. The appellant's words, actions and manner of driving did not demonstrate any symptoms of impairment. Check-stop programs result in the arbitrary detention of motorists. The programs are justified as a means aimed at reducing the terrible toll of death and injury so often occasioned by impaired drivers or by dangerous vehicles. The primary aim of the program is thus to check for sobriety, licences, ownership, insurance and the mechanical fitness of cars. The police use of check stops should not be extended beyond these aims. Random stop programs must not be turned into a means of conducting either an unfounded general inquisition or an unreasonable search.

The respondent next argued that the production of the gym bag and its contents came about as a result of the consent of the appellant. Once again, I cannot accept this submission.

It has been seen that as a result of the check stop the appellant was detained. The arbitrary detention was imposed as soon as he was pulled over. As a result of that detention, it can reasonably be inferred that the appellant felt compelled to respond to questions put to him by the police officer. In those circumstances it is incumbent upon the Crown to adduce evidence that the person detained had indeed made an informed consent to the search based upon an awareness of his rights to refuse to respond to the questions or to consent to the search. There is no such evidence in this case. In my view the trial judge was correct in her conclusion that the appellant felt compelled to respond to the police questions. In the circumstances it cannot be said that the search was consensual.

The police questions pertaining to the appellant's gym bag, the search of the bag and of the appellant's vehicle were all elements of a search. Furthermore, that search was made without the requisite foundation of reasonable and probable grounds. It was therefore an unreasonable search in contravention of s. 8 of the Charter.

C. *Should the evidence obtained as a result of the unreasonable search be admitted?*

A decision to exclude evidence on the grounds that it would bring the administration of justice into disrepute pursuant to s. 24(2) of the Charter raises a question of law: see *R. v. Collins* (1987), 33 C.C.C. (3d) 1 at p. 12, 38 D.L.R. (4th) 508, [1987] 1 S.C.R. 265. It has also been held that generally a deferential approach will be adopted when reviewing a decision of a provincial appellate court dealing with the exclusion of evidence pursuant to s. 24(2) of the Charter. . . .

However, it is significant that in *R. v. Collins, supra*, Lamer, J., also cautioned the provincial courts of appeal that they should not too readily interfere with the decision of trial judges on s. 24(2) issues. . . .

Here it does not appear that the trial judge made either an unreasonable find in of fact or an error in law. Nevertheless, the majority of the Court of Appeal overruled her decision. With respect I am of the view that the majority erred in this regard and too readily interfered with the findings of the trial judge.

*R. v. Collins, supra*, indicates that three sets of factors must be taken into account in determining whether evidence should be admitted pursuant to s. 24(2). First there are those factors which go to determining whether the admission of the evidence will affect the fairness of the trial. This is undoubtedly the most important issue and should be given the greatest weight. Second are those factors which demonstrate either the seriousness or the insignificance of the violation. Third are those factors which are concerned with the effect of the exclusion of the evidence on the reputation of the administration of justice. It is appropriate to now consider some of those factors.

(1) *Factors affecting the fairness of the trial*

*Collins, supra*, made it apparent that the admission of real evidence which was obtained in a manner that violated the Charter will rarely operate unfairly in the conduct of the trial. There can be no doubt that in this case the *cannabis* which was discovered constituted real evidence. However, it must also be remembered that in *R. v. Ross* (1989), 46 C.C.C. (3d) 129 at p. 139, [1989] 1 S.C.R. 3, 67 C.R. (3d) 209, it was said that: ". . . the use of any evidence that could not have been obtained but for the participation of the accused in the construction of the evidence for the purposes of the trial would tend to render the trial process unfair".

The trial judge recognized these competing principles. She found that the evidence, although real could never have been discovered but for the illegal search. The majority of the Court of Appeal disagreed with this finding. It was their view that since the appellant transported the drugs in an open gym bag on the front seat of his car, he could not have been concerned about his own privacy nor was he anxious to avoid detection. They concluded that so long as a person remains in possession of a prohibited substance it is not unlikely that the substance will be discovered. Be that as it may, it cannot be denied that the conclusion of the trial judge was a reasonable one. Had it not been for the illegal search, the drugs could not have been found. . . .

In the case at bar, the trial judge could certainly not be said to have acted unreasonably in concluding that the evidence (the marijuana) would not have been discovered without the compelled testimony (the search) of the appellant. To search a person who is stopped at a check stop, without any reasonable or probable cause, goes far beyond the purpose and aim of those stops and constitutes a very serious Charter breach. . . .

Unless there are reasonable and probable grounds for conducting the search, or drugs, alcohol or weapons are in plain view in the interior of the vehicle, the evidence flowing from such a search should not be admitted.

It would surely affect the fairness of the trial should check stops be accepted as a basis for warrantless searches and the evidence derived from them was to be automatically admitted. To admit evidence obtained in an unreasonable and unjustified search carried out while a motorist was detained in a check stop would adversely and unfairly affect the trial process and most surely bring the administration of justice into disrepute.

It follows that the conclusions of the trial judge in this regard are neither unreasonable nor an error in law. . . .

Yet in light of the extent of the argument that was submitted with regard to the seriousness of the Charter violation some brief comments on that subject might be appropriate.

(2) *Seriousness of the violation*

The trial judge was not unreasonable in her conclusion that the breach was a serious one. It is true that there was not, in this case, any bad faith on the part of the police. They conducted the search, before the reasons of this court in *Ladouceur* had been released. None the less, the violation must be considered a serious one. It was conducted as an adjunct to the check stop and was not grounded on any suspicion, let alone a reasonable and probable cause. It is the attempt to extend the random stop programs to include a right to search without warrant or without reasonable grounds that constitutes the serious Charter violation.

V. *Conclusion*

The appellant was detained at a check stop. While he was so detained, he was subjected to an unreasonable search. To admit the evidence obtained as a result of an unreasonable search of a motorist in a check stop would render the trial of the appellant unfair. Admitting such evidence would thus bring the administration of justice into disrepute. The evidence derived from the unreasonable search cannot be admitted.

VI. *Disposition*

In the result, the appeal will be allowed, the order of the Court of Appeal directing a new trial set aside, and the acquittal of the appellant restored.

*Appeal allowed; acquittal restored.*

## Bartle v. The Queen
(1994), 92 C.C.C. (3d) 289 (S.C.C.)

[Only excerpts from the judgement of Lamer are reproduced below.]

APPEAL by the accused from a judgment of the Ontario Court of Appeal, 81 C.C.C. (3d) 353, 22 C.R. (4th) 1, 15 C.R.R. 212, 45 M.V.R. (2d) 107, 63 O.A.C. 109, 20 W.C.B. (2d) 9, allowing an appeal by the Crown from a judgment of Cavarzan J., 41 M.V.R. (2d) 266, 17 W.C.B. (2d) 219, allowing an appeal by the accused from his conviction for "over 80".

LAMER, C.J.C.: — This case was heard in conjunction with four other cases also raising s. 10(*b*) of the *Canadian Charter of Rights and Freedoms*. These other cases, which are handed down concurrently with this one, consist of *R. v. Pozniak* (23642); *R. v. Harper (23160); R. v. Matheson* (23312), and *R. v. Prosper* (23178) [these cases are as yet unreported]. While all of the s. 10(*b*) cases concern the scope of the state's obligations with respect to duty counsel, in this case as well as in that of *Pozniak* and *Harper*, the issue under s. 10(*b*) is a relatively narrow one to do with disclosure upon arrest or detention of *existing and available duty counsel services*. Specifically, do persons who are detained and arrested have the right, under the information component of s. 10(*b*), to be advised as a matter of routine of the existence of a service which provides free, 24-hour preliminary legal advice and can be reached by dialling a 1-800 (toll-free) telephone number?

I. *Facts*

On June 22, 1991, at approximately 1:00 a.m., Constable Pray arrested the appellant for impaired driving after he failed the roadside A.L.E.R.T. test. The constable read the appellant his rights under the Charter from a pre-printed caution card. Specifically, the constable advised the appellant that:

You have the right to retain and instruct counsel without delay.

You have the right to telephone any lawyer you wish.

You also have the right to free advice from a Legal Aid lawyer.

If you are charged with an offence, you may apply to the Ontario Legal Aid Plan for legal assistance.

Constable Pray then asked the appellant if he understood, and the appellant responded affirmatively. Constable Pray did not make any reference to the specific availability of immediate, preliminary legal advice by duty counsel, or to the existence of the 24-hour, toll-free Legal Aid number which was printed on his caution card. Further, Constable Pray did not ask the appellant if he wanted to call a lawyer "now", a question printed on his caution card, because there was no telephone at the roadside. Constable Pray then gave the appellant the standard secondary caution regarding admissions and read him the breath sample demand. At this point, the appellant stated that he had five or six beers after baseball that evening.

Upon arrival at the police station, Constable Pray again asked the appellant if he wished to call a lawyer, making it clear that he could do so "now". The appellant said no, and was turned over to breathalyzer technician., Constable Hildebrandt. Constable Hildebrant also asked the appellant if he wanted to call a lawyer (again, no mention was made of the 1-800 number or the availability of immediate, preliminary legal advice by duty counsel). The appellant declined to call a lawyer, and then agreed to take the two breathalyzer tests, both of which he failed by a significant margin. The appellant was charged with having care or control of a motor vehicle while his blood-alcohol level was in excess of 80 mg. of alcohol in 100 ml of blood, contrary to s. 253(b) of the *Criminal Code*, R.S.C. 1985, c. C-46.

The appellant testified that he thought that the caution he received from Constable Pray meant that he could contact a lawyer "when one would be available like maybe Monday morning call one" (the arrest was on Friday night). He explained that he had refused to call counsel because he did not know whom to call, and was at a loss as to whom he could get a hold of. The appellant further testified that he indicated to Constable Hildebrandt that he wanted to call a lawyer, but that he did not know whom he could call. In response to Constable Hildebrandt's question "Why?", the appellant indicated that he had said "well I can't think of anybody to call, it's too late". He said that Constable Hildebrandt had no response to that comment, and that there was no indication that Constable Hildebrandt had heard him. Constable Hildebrandt, on the other hand, testified that the appellant had simply said "no" when asked whether he wanted to call a lawyer. The appellant testified that he had played baseball on the night in question and afterward had had some beers. He admitted at trial that he probably should not have been on the road that evening.

On December 6, 1991, the appellant was convicted by Perozak Prov. Div. J. of the Ontario Court (Provincial Division). On September 14, 1992, Cavarzan J. of the Ontario Court (General Division), allowed the appellant's appeal and quashed the conviction, concluding that the appellant's rights under s. 10(b) of the Charter had been infringed and that the evidence of the breathalyzer technician ought to be excluded. On May 28, 1993, the Court of Appeal for Ontario allowed the respondent's appeal and restored the appellant's conviction, *infra*. . . .

### III. *Points in issue*

The issues in this case are twofold:

1. Does the information component of s. 10(b) of the Charter require that police routinely refer to the existence and availability of a 24-hour duty counsel service which provides free, preliminary legal advice and can be reached by dialling a 1-800 (toll-free) telephone number?
2. If the answer is yes and if the appellant's rights under s. 10(b) of the Charter have, in the circumstances of this case, been violated, should the evidence obtained in the course of this infringement be excluded under s. 24(2) of the Charter?

### IV. *Analysis*

Section 10(b) of the Charter provides that:

10. Everyone has the right on arrest or detention

. . . . .

(b) to retain and instruct counsel without delay and to be informed of that right . . .

It is now well accepted that under s. 10(*b*) a person who is arrested or detained (the "detainee") must be promptly informed of his or her right to retain counsel without delay. Because s. 10(*b*) has already been extensively considered by this court, I propose to simply summarize some of the basic principles which have been developed with respect to the right to counsel under the Charter. This will provide the necessary framework in which to approach the disclosure-related issue raised by this case, *Pozniak* and *Harper*.

(a) *The purpose of s. 10(b)*

The purpose of the right to counsel guaranteed by s. 10(*b*) of the Charter is to provide detainees with an opportunity to be informed of their rights and obligations under the law and, most importantly, to obtain advice on how to exercise those rights and fulfil those obligations: *R. v. Manninen* (1987), 34 C.C.C. (3d) 385 at pp. 391-3, 41 D.L.R. (4th) 301, [1987] 1 S.C.R. 1233. This opportunity is made available because, when an individual is detained by state authorities, he or she is put in a position of disadvantage relative to the state. Not only has this person suffered a deprivation of liberty, but also this person may be at risk of incriminating him or herself. Accordingly, a person who is "detained" within the meaning of s. 10 of the Charter is in *immediate* need of legal advice in order to protect his or her right against self-incrimination and to assist him or her in regaining his or her liberty: *Bridges*, at p. 343; *R. v. Hebert* (1990), 57 C.C.C. (3d) 1 at pp. 35-6, [1990] 2 S.C.R. 151, 77 C.R. (3d) 145, and *Prosper*. Under s. 10(*b*, a detainee is entitled as of right to seek such legal advice "without delay" and upon request. As this court suggested in *R. v. Clarkson* (1986), 25 C.C.C. (3d) 207 at p. 217, 26 D.L.R. (4th) 493, [1986] 1 S.C.R. 383, the right to counsel protected by s. 10(*b*) is designed to ensure that persons who are arrested or detained are treated fairly in the criminal process.

(b) *The duties under s. 10(b)*

This court has said on numerous previous occasions that s. 10(*b*) of the Charter imposes the following duties on state authorities who arrest or detain a person:

(1) to inform the detainee of his or her right to retain and instruct counsel without delay and of the existence and availability of Legal Aid and duty counsel;
(2) if a detainee has indicated a desire to exercise this right, to provide the detainee with a reasonable opportunity to exercise the right (except in urgent and dangerous circumstances), and
(3) to refrain from eliciting evidence from the detainee until he or she has had that reasonable opportunity (again, except in cases of urgency or danger). . . .

The first duty is an *informational* one which is directly in issue here. The second and third duties are more in the nature of *implementation* duties and are not triggered unless and until a detainee indicates a desire to exercise his or her right to counsel.

Importantly, the right to counsel under s. 10(*b*) is not absolute. Unless a detainee invokes the right and is reasonably diligent in exercising it, the correlative duty on the police to provide a reasonable opportunity and to refrain from eliciting evidence will either not arise in the first place or will be suspended: *R. v. Tremblay* (1987), 37 C.C.C. (3d) 565 at p. 568, 45 D.L.R. (4th) 445, [1987] 2 S.C.R. 435; *R. v. Black* (1989), 50 C.C.C. (3d) 1 at pp. 13-4, [1989] 2 S.C.R. 138, 70 C.R. (3d) 97. Furthermore, the rights guaranteed by s. 10(*b*) may be waived by the detainee, although the standard for waiver will be high, especially in circumstances where the alleged waiver has been implicit: *Clarkson*, at pp. 217-9; *Manninen*, at p. 393; *Black*, at p. 14-5; *Brydges*, at p. 341, and *Evans*, at pp. 307-8.

Under these circumstances, it is critical that the information component of the right to counsel be comprehensive in scope and that it be presented by police authorities in a "timely and comprehensible" manner: *R. v. Dubois* (1990), 54 C.C.C. (3d) 166 at p. 190, 74 C.R. (3d) 216, [1990] R.J.Q. 681 (C.A.). Unless they are clearly and fully informed of their rights *at the outset*, detainees cannot be expected to make informed choices and decisions about whether or not to contact counsel and, in turn, whether to exercise other rights, such as their right to silence: *Hebert*. Moreover, in light of the rule that, absent special circumstances indicating that a detainee may not understand the s. 10(*b*) caution, such as language difficulties or a known or obvious mental disability, police are not required to assure themselves that a detainee fully understands the s. 10(*b*) caution, it is important that the standard caution given to detainees be as instructive and clear as possible: *R. v. Baig* (1987), 37 C.C.C. (3d) 181 at p. 183, 45 D.L.R. (4th) 106, [1987] 2 S.C.R. 537, and *Evans*, at p. 305.

Indeed, the pivotal function of the initial information component under s. 10(*b*) has already been recognized by this court, For instance, in *Evans*, McLachlin J., for the majority, stated, at p. 305 that a "person who does not understand his or her right cannot be expected to assert it". In that case, it was held that, in circumstances which suggest that a particular detainee may not understand the information being communicated to him or her by state authorities, a mere recitation of the right to counsel will not suffice. Authorities will have to take additional steps to ensure that the detainee comprehends his or her s. 10(*b*) rights. Likewise, this court has stressed on previous occasions that, before an accused can be said to have waived his or her right to counsel, he or she must be possessed of sufficient information to allow him or her to make an informed choice as regards exercising the right: *R. v. Smith* (1991), 63 C.C.C. (3d) 313 at pp. 320-4, [1991] 1 S.C.R. 714, 4 C.R. (4th) 125, and *Brydges*, at p. 342.

To conclude, because the purpose of the right to counsel under s. 10*(*b) is about providing detainees with meaningful choices, it follows that a detainee should be fully advised of available services *before* being expected to assert that right, particularly given that subsequent duties on the state or not triggered unless and until a detainee expresses a desire to contact counsel. In my opinion, the purpose of the right to counsel would be defeated if police were only required to advise detainees of the existence and availability of Legal Aid and duty counsel *after* some triggering assertion of the right by the detainee. Accordingly, I am unable to agree with the trial judge and the Court of Appeal below that information about duty counsel and how to access it need only be provided to detainees when they express some concern about affordability or availability of counsel. Indeed, in putting forward such a position, I can only conclude with respect that both the trial judge and the Court of Appeal erred in their interpretation and application of *Brydges*. It is, therefore, to a consideration of *Brydges* that I must now turn.

### (c) Brydges

In *Brydges*, the accused requested information about Legal Aid and expressed concern about his inability to afford a lawyer after being informed by police authorities of his right to counsel under s. 10(*b*) of the Charter. This court unanimously held that the failure by the police to inform the accused of the existence and availability of Legal Aid and duty counsel was a violation of his s. 10(*b*) rights and that the evidence obtained as a result of this violation — inculpatory statements — should have been excluded. This court was satisfied that by failing to inform the accused fully of his right to counsel in circumstances where he had raised concerns about being able to afford a lawyer and where free, preliminary legal advice was indeed available upon request, the police had improperly left the accused with an erroneous impression of the nature and extent of his s. 10(*b*) rights.

However, a majority of this court went further, holding that, besides telling detainees of their general right to retain and instruct counsel without delay, *in all cases* police must advise detainees of the existence and availability of Legal Aid and duty counsel. For the majority, I stated, at p. 349, that,

> ... the right to retain and instruct counsel, in modern Canadian society, has come to mean more than the right to retain a lawyer privately. It now also means the right to have access to counsel free of charge where the accused meets certain financial criteria set up by the provincial Legal Aid plan, and the right to have access to immediate, although temporary, advice from duty counsel irrespective of financial status. These considerations, therefore, lead me to the conclusion that *as part of the information component of s. 10(b) of the Charter, a detainee should be informed of the existence and availability of the applicable systems of duty counsel and Legal Aid in the jurisdiction, in order to give the detainee a full understanding of the right to retain and instruct counsel.*

(Emphasis added.) Accordingly, *Brydges* had the effect of adding two new elements to the information component of s. 10(*b*):

(1) information about access to counsel free of charge where an accused meets the prescribed financial criteria set by provincial Legal Aid plans ("Legal Aid"), and
(2) information about access to immediate, although temporary legal advice irrespective of financial status ("duty counsel").

At the same time, *Brydges* made it clear that the specific nature of the information provided to detainees would necessarily be contingent on the existence and availability of Legal Aid and duty counsel in the jurisdiction: *Prosper*. . . .

To conclude, *Brydges* stands for the proposition that police authorities are required to inform detainees about Legal Aid and duty counsel services which are in existence and available in the jurisdiction at the time of detention. In case there is any doubt, I would add here that basic information about how to access available services which provide free, preliminary legal advice should be included in the standard s. 10(*b*) caution. This need consist of no more than telling a detainee in plain language that he or she will be provided with a phone number should he or she wish to contact a lawyer right away. Failure to provide such information is, in the absence of a valid waiver (which, as I explain *infra*, will be a rarity), a breach of s. 10(*b*) of the Charter. It follows, therefore, that where the informational obligations under s. 10(*b*) have not been properly complied with by police, questions about whether a particular detainee exercised his or her right to counsel with reasonable diligence and/or whether he or she waived his or her facilitation rights do not properly arise for consideration. Such questions are simply not relevant under s. 10(*b*) (although they may be when it comes to considering whether the evidence obtained in the course of the Charter violation should be excluded under s. 24(2) of the Charter). The breach of s. 10(*b*) is complete, except in cases of waiver or urgency, upon a failure by state authorities to properly inform a detainee of his or her right to counsel and until such time as that failure is corrected. . . .

(e) *Summary of s. 10(b) principles*

A detainee is entitled under the information component of s. 10(*b*) of the Charter to be advised of whatever system for free, preliminary legal advice exists in the jurisdiction and of how such advice can be accessed (*e.g.*, by calling a 1-800 number, or being provided with a list of telephone numbers for lawyers acting as duty counsel). What remains to be decided, then, is whether the caution given to the appellant by the police in this case complied with the informational requirements under s. 10(*b*), or whether the appellant waived his informational s. 10(*b*) rights. It is to this question that I now turn.

. . .

[After applying the law to the facts of the case, Lamer continues:]

Under the circumstances of this case where no urgency was involved and where there was no valid waiver of s. 10(*b*)'s informational component, the breach of the appellant's s. 10(*b*) rights was complete upon his not being advised of the existence and availability of Ontario's duty counsel service and of the toll-free number by which it could be accessed. I find, therefore, that the appellant's rights under s. 10(*b*) of the Charter were infringed by the police. Accordingly, it is necessary to decide whether the evidence obtained as a result of this violation should be excluded under s. 24(2) of the Charter.

(g) *Exclusion of evidence*

The evidence at issue here are the results of two failed breathalyzer tests and the appellant's incriminating statement to the police at the roadside that he had had five to six beers that night.

Section 24(2) of the Charter provides as follows:

**24(2)** Where . . . a court concludes that evidence was obtained in a manner that infringed or denied any rights or freedoms guaranteed by this Charter, the evidence shall be excluded if it is established that, having regard to all the circumstances, the admission of it in the proceedings would bring the administration of justice into disrepute.

There are two requirements for exclusion of evidence under s. 24(2): *Strachan*, per Dickson C.J.C., at pp. 494-5, and *R. v. Therens* (1985), 128 C.C.C. (3d) 481 at p. 508, 18 D.L.R. (4th) 655, [1985] 1 S.C.R. 613, *per* Le Dain J. First, there has to have been a Charter violation in the course of obtaining the evidence. Secondly, it must be found that having regard to all the circumstances, admission of the evidence would bring the administration of justice into disrepute.

Under the first threshold requirement, there must be some connection or relationship between the infringement of the right or freedom in question and the obtaining of the evidence which is sought to be excluded. However, a strict causal link between the Charter infringement and the discovery of the evidence is not required: *Therens*, per Le Dain J., at p. 509; *Strachan*, per Dickson C.J.C., at pp. 494-9, and Lamer J. (as he then was), at p. 501, and *Brydges*, at pp. 345-6. Generally speaking, so long as it is not too remotely connected with the violation, all the evidence obtained as part of the "chain of events" involving the Charter breach will fall with the scope of s. 24(2): *Strachan*, per Dickson C.J.C., at p. 499, and Lamer J. at p. 501. This means that in the initial inquiry under s. 24(2) as to whether evidence has been "obtained in a manner that infringed or denied" Charter rights, courts should take a generous approach. However, it should be borne in mind that the presence and strength of the causal connection between the evidence and the Charter breach may be a factor for consideration under the second, more important, branch of s. 24(2): *Strachan*, per Dickson C.J.C., at p. 499; *R. v. I. (L.R.)* (1993), 86 C.C.C. (3d) 289 at p. 307, 109 D.L.R. (4th) 140, [1993] 4 S.C.R. 504, per Sopinka J.

In the case at bar, I am satisfied that the breathalyzer evidence as well as the self-incriminating statement were obtained in the context of the infringement of the appellant's right to counsel under s. 10(*b*) and, therefore, that they pass the first hurdle under s. 24(2).

The analysis must then proceed to the second stage of inquiry under s. 24(2), where it must be determined whether, in all of the circumstances, admission of the evidence would tend to bring the administration of justice into disrepute. In order to make this determination, a court must balance factors relating to the effect of admission on the fairness of the trial, the seriousness of the breach, and the effect of exclusion on the repute of the administration of justice: *R. v. Collins* (1987), 33 C.C.C. (3d) 1 at pp. 19-21, 38 D.L.R. (4th) 508, [1987] 1 S.C.R. 265. The overall burden of persuasion under s. 24(2) rests on the party seeking exclusion of the evidence: *Collins*, at p. 16; *R. v. Simmons* (1988), 45 C.C.C. (3d) 296 at p. 323, 55 D.L.R. (4th) 673, [1988] 2 S.C.R. 495, per Dickson C.J.C., and *R. v. Duarte* (1990), 53 C.C.C. (3d) 1 at pp. 22-3, 65 D.L.R. (4th) 240, [1990] 1 S.C.R. 30. That is, it is the applicant for exclusion under s. 24(2) who must ultimately satisfy the court on a balance of probabilities that admission of the evidence could bring the administration of justice into disrepute. . . .

In my view, the Crown should bear the legal burden (the burden of persuasion) of establishing, on the evidence, that the s. 24(2) applicant would not have acted any differently had his s. 10(*b*) rights been fully respected, and that, as a consequence, the evidence would have been obtained irrespective of the s. 10(*b*) breach. There are at least two reasons why the Crown should bear this burden.

First, breaches of s. 10(*b*) tend to impact directly on adjudicative fairness. Indeed, this court has consistently said that where self-incriminatory (as opposed to real) evidence has been obtained as a result of a s. 10(*b*) violation, its admission will generally have a negative affect on the fairness of the trial. . . .

Secondly, in light of the many warnings by this court about the dangers of speculating about what advice might have been given to a detainee by a lawyer had the right to counsel not been infringed (*infra*, pp 38-9) [*post*, p. 319] it is only consistent that uncertainty about what an accused would have done had his or her s. 10(*b*) rights not been violated be resolved in the accused's favour and that, for the purposes of considering the effect of admission of evidence on trial fairness, courts assume that the incriminating evidence would not have been obtained but for the violation. The state bears the responsibility for the breach of the accused's constitutional rights. If the state subsequently claims that there was no causal link between this breach and the obtaining of the evidence at issue, it is the state that should bear the burden of proving this assertion.

Section 24(2) applicants thus do not bear the burden of proving that they would have consulted counsel had their s. 10(*b*) rights not been infringed. Of course, once there is positive evidence supporting the inference that an accused person would *not* have acted any differently had his or her s. 10(*b*) rights been fully respected, a s. 24(2) applicant who fails to provide evidence that he or she *would* have acted differently (a matter clearly within his or her particular knowledge) runs the risk that the evidence on the record will be sufficient for the Crown to satisfy its legal burden (the burden of persuasion)....

A review of past decisions by this court clearly demonstrates that exclusion of evidence, even self-incriminatory evidence, will not necessarily follow each and every breach of the right to counsel under s. 10(*b*).... If the party resisting admission of the evidence is unable to establish in an overall sense that its admission would bring the administration of justice into disrepute, the evidence should be admitted.

(i) *Breathalyzer evidence and the issue of statutory compellability*

In the case at bar, not only is the appellant's statement about having five to six beers clearly self-incriminatory, but so too are the results of the breathalyzer tests. The breath samples provided by the appellant emanated from his body and, unlike real evidence, could not have been obtained but for the appellant's participation in their construction: *Ross* at p. 139. The conscriptive character of breathalyzer evidence in the impaired driving context warrants further discussion in light of a line argument which seeks to downplay or even deny the self-incriminatory nature of breath samples. This line of argument not only appears to be gaining acceptance amongst courts of appeal (*e.g.*, see the Nova Scotia Court of Appeals reasons in *Prosper*) [reported 75 C.C.C. (3d) 1, 38 M.V.R. (2d) 268, 113 N.S.R. (2d) 156], but is also urged upon us by the respondent Crown in this and the related case of *Pozniak*. The argument can be summarized as follows: because the breathalizer evidence was statutorily compellable whether or not the appellant spoke to counsel, it could not have affected the fairness of the trial, and, therefore, should be admitted under s. 24(2) of the Charter....

I am satisfied that there is sufficient scope for legal advice to a detainee who has received a breathalyzer demand pursuant to s. 254(3)(*a*) of the Code to say that the courts must not speculate about the nature of that advice and whether it would have made any difference to the outcome of the case. In addition, I must respectfully disagree with the Ontario Court of Appeal which adopts an *ex post facto* approach to determining whether or not the defence of "no reasonable and probable grounds" was actually available to the accused on the facts. One of the purposes of s. 10(*b*) is to provide detainees with an opportunity to make *informed* choices about their legal rights and obligations. This opportunity is no less significant when breathalyzer charges are involved. I am, therefore, not prepared to hold, *ipso facto*, either that breathalyzer evidence in the impaired driving context does not qualify as self-incriminating evidence or, if it does, that its admission does not affect the fairness of a trial.

(ii) *The impugned evidence*

Turning to the case at bar, I am satisfied that admission of the failed breathalyzer results and the appellant's self-incriminatory statement about having had five to six beers would adversely affect the fairness of the trial, which is the first factor which must be considered under the *Collins* test. Constable Hildebrandt, the breathalyzer technician, testified that the appellant simply answered "no" when asked if he wanted to contact a lawyer. The appellant, on the other hand, testified that he told the constable that he wanted to call a lawyer, but did not know who to call because it was so late. Notwithstanding that the trial judge *appears* to have preferred the evidence of the constable (and I would note that, contrary to what is suggested by the Court of Appeal below, no adverse finding of credibility against the appellant was expressly made), I find that it is speculative on the facts of this case to try and draw conclusions one way or the other as to what the appellant would have done had he been properly cautioned. In light of what I said above about the Crown's legal burden (the burden of persuasion), the uncertainty in this case must be resolved against the respondent Crown. As a result, I must conclude that the breathalyzer evidence might not have been obtained had the appellant's s. 10(*b*) rights not been infringed and, therefore, that admission would adversely impact on the fairness of the trial.

As for the second set of factors to do with the seriousness of the Charter breach, I would note that information about duty counsel and particularly the 1-800 number, which was actually printed on the caution card, were readily at hand. However, I am not prepared to interfere with Cavarzan J.'s conclusion that the police acted in good faith and in accordance with what they believed at the time to be proper procedure. Although this second set of factors favours the admission of the evidence in this case, this cannot cure the fact that admission would render the trial unfair. As this court held in *Elshaw*, at pp. 127-8, the first two factors in the *Collins* test are alternative grounds for the exclusion, not the admission, of evidence. Where the impugned evidence falls afoul of the "trial fairness" factor, admissibility cannot be saved by resorting to the "seriousness of the violation" factor.

With respect to the third element — namely, whether exclusion of the evidence would bring the administration of justice into disrepute — I would note that the appellant admitted at trial that he probably should not have been on the road on the evening in question, which is tantamount to an admission of guilt. However, notwithstanding this and the fact that drinking and driving poses a significant risk to public safety, I am of the view that exclusion of the evidence in this case is in the long-term interests of the administration of justice. Section 24(2) must work together with s. 10(*b*) to ensure that the privilege against self-incrimination and the principle of adjudicative fairness are respected and protected in our criminal justice system.

For the foregoing reasons, I find on balance and having regard to all the circumstances that the repute of the administration of justice favours the exclusion, not the admission, of both the breathalyzer evidence and the incriminatory statement.

(h) *Conclusion*

I am satisfied that the appellant's right to counsel under s. 10(*b*) of the Charter was infringed and that, having regard to all the circumstances of this case, the impugned evidence should be excluded under s. 24(2) of the Charter.

Accordingly, the appeal should be allowed and the conviction quashed. As this is not an appropriate case in which to order a new trial, a verdict of acquittal should be entered.

*Appeal allowed: acquittal entered.*

**Questions/Discussion**
1. Should the courts be intervening in the ways which you have seen in the above cases? Do you agree with the way in which the Charter is being interpreted in these cases? Why or why not? Do you feel it is the proper role of the courts to be deciding substantive criminal justice policy issues and altering criminal law passed by allegedly democratically elected officials? For example, is it the proper role of the Supreme Court to be deciding what the abortion law should or should not be in Canada; see *R. v. Morgentaler*, [1988] 1 S.C.R. 30.
2. It is important to question the true effects of these decisions on the everyday reality of law enforcement. Who will take advantage of their rights on the streets or who *can* take advantage of them? How will or can the decisions affect the bias of enforcement agents as to who is interfered with in the first place? What practical limits are placed on the "processing of the poor" in the current criminal justice system? Do you think that the Charter will make a real difference in how you interact with the police if and when you are stopped or detained?
3. Does the right to counsel mean different things to different people, or more specifically, to different classes of people? For example, if you have your own lawyer or the money to hire one, does this make a difference as opposed to someone who merely receives duty counsel at the last minute before the first appearance? What is the "content" of this right?
4. There have been a number of cases surrounding the "right to be tried within a reasonable time" under section 11(b) of the Charter. For the latest Supreme Court discussion of the issues, see *R. v. Morin* (1992), 71 C.C.C. (3d) 1 (S.C.C.).
5. Finally, note that the above cases only touch the surface of Charter activity and for a full discussion of the issues raised by the Charter, please refer to the readings below.

**Further Reading**
- Archibald, B., "The Constitutionalization of the General Part of Criminal Law" (1988), 67 Canadian Bar Review 403.
- Beaudoin, G.-A., and E. Ratushny (eds.), *The Canadian Charter of Rights and Freedoms* (Toronto: Carswell, 1989).
- Bryden, P. (ed.), *Protecting Rights and Freedoms: Essays on the Charter's Place in Canada's Political, Legal, and Intellectual Life* (Toronto: University of Toronto Press, 1994).
- Dawe, J., "Standing to Challenge Searches and Seizures Under the Charter: The Lessons of the American Experience and their Application to Canadian Law" (1993), 52 University of Toronto Faculty of Law Review 39-72.

- Epstein, M., "The Guiding Hand of Counsel: The Charter and the Right to Counsel on Appeal" (1987-88), 30 Criminal Law Quarterly 35.
- France, S., "Gains and Lost Opportunities in Canadian Constitutional Mens Rea" (1995), 20 Queen's Law Journal 533-555.
- Friedland, M., "Controlling the Administrators of Criminal Justice" (1988-89), 31 Criminal Law Quarterly 280.
- Gold, A. and M. Fuerst, "The Stuff that Dreams are Made of: Criminal Law and the Charter of Rights" (1992), 24 Ottawa Law Review 13-37.
- Hovius, B. and R. Martin, "The Canadian Charter of Rights and Freedoms in the Supreme Court of Canada" (1983), 61 Canadian Bar Review 354.
- Jull, K., "Exclusion of Evidence and the Beast of Burden" (1987-88), Criminal Law Quarterly 178.
- Knopff, R., *Charter Politics* (Scarborough, Ontario: Nelson Canada, 1992).
- MacLean, S., "Video Surveillance and The Charter of Rights" (1987-88), 30 Criminal Law Quarterly 88.
- Mahoney, R., "The Presumption of Innocence: A New Era" (1988), 67 Canadian Bar Review 1.
- Mandel, M., *The Charter of Rights and the Legalization of Politics in Canada (Updated and expanded edition)* (Toronto: Thompson Educational, 1994).
- Mitchell, G., "The Supreme Court of Canada on the Exclusion of Evidence in Criminal Cases Under Section 24 of the Charter" (1988), 30 Criminal Law Quarterly 165.
- Stuart, D., "Progress on the Constitutional Requirement of Fault" (1988), 64 C.R. (3d) 352.
- Stuart, D., *Charter Justice in Canadian Criminal Law* (Scarborough, Ontario: Carswell, 1991).
- Tanovich, D., "Charting the Constitutional Right of Effective Assistance of Counsel in Canada: (1994), 36 Criminal Law Quarterly 404-422.
- Way., R.C., "The Charter, the Supreme Court and the Invisible Politics of Fault" (1992), 12 Windsor Yearbook of Access to Justice 128-178.

## 7.4 INCAPACITY

### General Introduction

This section deals with special pleas that all involve some type of argument that the accused did not have the capacity due to mental or emotional impairment to form the necessary mental element or mens rea for the offence. Note, however, that capacity is also extremely relevant to the issue of whether the accused is in fact fit to stand trial. The accused's incapacity due to age may also become a relevant factor, particularly when dealing with young persons. Section 13 of the Criminal Code says that no person under the age of twelve may be convicted of an offence. The Young Offenders' Act, R.S.C. 1995, c. Y-1, defines "young persons" to be between the ages of twelve and eighteen; of this group, if the accused is at least 14 years of age, then there is the possibility of having the case tried in adult court. It issues and criteria involved in this area are discussed further in Chapter 8.

Four defences are considered in this section. The first is the defence of provocation which involves the ordinary person "losing control" because of some wrong committed by the victim. It only applies as a defence to charges of murder, reducing the conviction to one for manslaughter if successful. Provocation entails a claim of justification. It is not enough that a person lose control or act in the "heat of passion"; that passion must be directed at a justified target, namely the person who wronged the accused.

The defence of mental disorder was introduced in 1992 following the case of *Swain* which overturned sections of the former defence of insanity. While the defence of insanity was rarely used in criminal trials previously (due to the fact that the offender could be held indefinitely on a Lieutenant Governor's Warrant), it is argued by some that with the recent changes, the defence will arise more frequently. In any event, the question of the accused's mental capacity is of fundamental importance because it concerns the central issue of criminal responsibility. Also, many criticisms have been raised about the use and abuse of mental health experts in the courtroom. Such experts often testify from a deterministic perspective that seeks to blame criminal behaviour on forces outside the offender's control. For example, psychiatrists diagnose the majority of prison inmates as suffering from some sort of mental illness and some have argued that prisons should be replaced with therapeutic institutions where the inmates are converted into patients and released when "cured". This therapeutic agenda is a powerful competitor to the criminal law's traditional attribution of blame. While the defence of mental disorder remains relatively rare, it should be noted that mental illness is frequently raised as a mitigating factor at sentencing. It is also central to the issues surrounding fitness to stand trial and dangerous offenders. The important question you should consider while reading the materials is why does the law treat the mentally ill in an exceptional manner? What assumptions are made about the mentally ill concerning their dangerousness and their self-control? What evidence is considered by the courts?

Intoxication and automatism are the other defences considered in this section. The latter is a relatively recent common law defence, created by judges to cover seemingly random, motiveless acts. The classic example where the defence is used is that of an epileptic charged with assault after striking a bystander during a seizure. The defence negates the actus reus (according to most cases) and results in complete acquittal. It is therefore a far more appealing defence than that of mental disorder where the consequences can be very severe.

While automatism is rarely at issue, intoxication is commonly considered at trial. About half of all offenders, in crimes of both property and personal violence, consumed drugs (usually alcohol) prior to the commission of their offence. The common law defence of intoxication is rather complex and confused as the extract from *Daviault*, below demonstrates. As a result of this case and the government's response in section 33.1 of the Code, consider what assumptions the courts make about intoxicated offenders? Why should the law make any special rules about intoxication?

## 7.4.1 Provocation or Heat of Passion

### Introduction

The heat of passion or provocation doctrine involves both a justification and an excuse whereby murder is partially excused when the accused's impairing passion is triggered by the victim's wrongful act or insult. In Canada, provocation is the only statutory partial defence, and it is restricted to murder charges; attempted murder is not covered by section 232. The passionate, unpremeditated killing of an adultering spouse, caught in the wrongful act, traditionally fit within the defence whereas the killing of a philandering lover did not (Dressler, 1982). Passion must be present, as the offender must "act on the sudden and before there was time for his passion to cook", but passion by itself is no excuse. Instead, the passion must be inflicted upon the accused through no fault of their own by a wrongful act which would, in the words of section 232: "deprive an ordinary person of the power of self-control". The accused is thus to be judged by an objective standard — the "ordinary person" — but this leaves considerable doubt as to what characteristics should be attributed to the ordinary person. The modern position, analyzed in the case of *Hill* (1986), below, ascribes the accused's age, sex and race to the "ordinary" person but not specific peculiarities such as an excitable temperament.

The language of "self-control" and its loss is rather difficult in some ways to understand. Does provocation's passion cause another "self" to emerge the (Avenger)? This recalls the ancient bicameral perception featured in the Homeric epics (Jaynes, 1976) which did attribute provoked responses to vengeful gods. Do provocation and passion short-circuit inhibitions that hold back the savage within? This neo-Freudian thesis parallels the process by which the mild mannered Dr. Bruce Banner who, when provoked, is transformed into the raging, elemental Hulk. If this view is correct, the law on provocation is wrong because it only applies when the provoker is attacked; assaulting by-standers, even in passion, is not excused. Does passion focus our attention or does it blot out consciousness? Or is passion even relevant? Is the severely provoked person who calmly retaliates to be punished for their self-discipline?

Or is the main element the "wrongful act"? Is the provoked crime less severely punished because the victim deserved some degree of retaliation? (Some other jurisdictions do not require any wrongful act on the part of the victim.) If this logic is followed, one would think that the wrongful, provoking act would normally have to be quite serious but the courts have counted mere verbal insults as sufficient provocation.

The Law Reform Commission of Canada's *Recodifying Criminal Law*, Volume 1, (1986) excludes provocation as even a partial defence. Instead, the Commission would abolish the mandatory life sentence for second degree murder, find provoked killers guilty of murder, not manslaughter, and then permit provocation to be weighed as a mitigating factor at sentencing. Other reform agencies suggest retaining provocation but simplifying it by adopting a more subjective test of whether the accused killed under extreme mental or emotional disturbance, and by dropping all the complications about wrongful acts and acting on the sudden (Stuart, 1987:458). These changes would move provocation toward a diminished responsibility test (see section 7.4.2.).

## Bibliography
- Dressler, J., "Rethinking Heat of Passion: A Defence in Search of a Rationale" (1982), 73 Journal of Criminal Law and Criminology 421.
- Klimchuk, D., "Outrage, Self-Control, and Culpability" (1994), 44 University of Toronto Law Journal 441-468.
- Macklem, T., "Provocation and the Ordinary Person" (1987/88), 11 Dalhousie Law Journal 126-156.
- Quigley, T., "Battered Women and the Defence of Provocation" (1991) 55 Saskatchewan Law Review 223-261.
- Stuart, D., *Canadian Criminal Law: A Treatise,* 2nd ed. (Toronto: Carswell, 1987).

## R. v. Hill
(1986), 25 C.C.C. (3d) 322 (S.C.C.).

[Only excerpts from the judgment of Dickson C.J.C. are reproduced below.]

Appeal by the Crown from a judgment of the Ontario Court of Appeal, 2 C.C.C. (3d) 394, 32 C.R. (3d) 88, allowing an appeal by the accused from his conviction for second degree murder.

DICKSON C.J.C.: — Gordon James Elmer Hill was charged with committing first degree murder at the City of Belleville, County of Hastings, on the person of Verne Pegg, contrary to s. 218(1) of the *Criminal Code*, R.S.C. 1970, c. C-34. He was found by the jury not guilty of first degree murder but guilty of second degree murder. He was sentenced to imprisonment for life without eligibility for parole until 10 years of his sentence had been served.

Hill appealed his conviction to the Court of Appeal of Ontario. He raised many grounds of appeal, but the Court of Appeal called upon the Crown with respect to one ground only, relating to the charge on the issue of provocation. The ground of appeal was that the trial judge failed to instruct the jury properly as to the "ordinary person" in s. 215(2) of the *Criminal Code*. Section 215 of the *Code* reads in part:

> 215(1) Culpable homicide that otherwise would be murder may be reduced to manslaughter if the person who committed it did so in the heat of passion caused by sudden provocation.
>
> (2) A wrongful act or insult that is of such a nature as to be sufficient to deprive an ordinary person of the power of self-control is provocation for the purposes of this section if the accused acted upon it on the sudden and before there was time for his passion to cool.

These two subsections, given their plain meaning, produce three sequential questions for answer by the tribunal:

1. Would an ordinary person be deprived of self-control by the act or insult?
2. Did the accused in fact act in response to those "provocative" acts; in short, was he or she provoked by them whether or not an ordinary person would have been?
3. Was the accused's response sudden and before there was time for his or her passion to cool?

At this stage it is important to recall the presence of s-s. (3) of s. 215 which provides:

> 215(3) For the purposes of this section the questions
> (a) whether a particular wrongful act or insult amounted to provocation, and
> (b) whether the accused was deprived of the power of self-control by the provocation that he alleges he received,
> are questions of fact ...

In the answering of these successive questions, the first or "ordinary person" test is clearly determined by objective standards. The second *de facto* test as to the loss of self-control by the accused is determined, like any other question of fact as revealed by the evidence, from the surrounding facts. The third test as to whether the response was sudden and before passions cooled is again a question of fact.

At the time of the killing, Hill was male, 16 years of age. The narrow question in this appeal is whether the trial judge erred in law in failing to instruct the jury that if they found a wrongful act or insult they should consider whether it was sufficient to deprive an ordinary person "of the age and sex of the appellant" of his power of self-control. Was it incumbent in law on the trial judge to add that gloss to the section? That is the issue.

## The Facts

At trial both parties agreed that it was the acts of Hill which caused the death of Pegg but disagreed otherwise. The position of the Crown at trial was that Hill and Pegg were homosexual lovers and that Hill had decided to murder Pegg after a falling-out between them. The Crown argued that Hill deliberately struck Pegg in the head while Pegg lay in bed. This did not kill Pegg who immediately ran from the bedroom into the bathroom to try to stop the flow of blood from his head. Realizing he had been unsuccessful, Hill took two knives from the kitchen and stabbed Pegg to death.

Hill's version of the events was very different. He admitted to causing the death of Pegg but put forward two defences: self-defence and provocation. Hill testified that he had known Pegg for about a year through the latter's involvement with the "Big Brother" organization. Hill stated that on the night in question he had been the subject of unexpected and unwelcome homosexual advances by Pegg while asleep on the couch in Pegg's apartment. Pegg pursued Hill to the bathroom and grabbed him, at which time Hill picked up a nearby hatchet and swung it at Pegg in an attempt to scare him. The hatchet struck Pegg in the head. Hill then ran from the apartment but returned shortly afterward. Upon re-entering the apartment, he was confronted by Pegg who threatened to kill him. At this point, Hill obtained two knives from the kitchen and stabbed Pegg to death.

Hill was arrested, after a car chase with the police, at the wheel of a Pontiac automobile owned by Pegg. At the scene of the arrest Hill denied knowing Pegg, but later he made a statement to the police which was substantially similar to his oral testimony at trial.

## The Charge

. . . .

At trial, counsel for Hill objected to the instruction of the trial judge as to the objective requirement of the defence of provocation, submitting that the "ordinary person" referred to in s. 215(2) ought to have been defined as an ordinary person of the age and sex of the accused. Counsel submitted that the objective requirement would be satisfied if the judge were to recharge the jury by defining the "ordinary person" as an "ordinary person in the circumstances of the accused". The judge refused to recharge the jury in those terms.

## The Court of Appeal

In oral reasons Brooke J.A. (Martin and Morden JJ.A. concurring) noted that counsel for the defence, relying on *Director of Public Prosecutions v. Camplin*, [1978] A.C. 705 (H.L.). submitted that the judge should have instructed the jury to consider whether the wrongful act or insult was sufficient to deprive an "ordinary person" of the age and sex of the accused of his power of self-control. The court of Appeal held that because the trial judge declined to do so he erred. In reaching this conclusion, Brooke J.A. stated [2 C.C.C. (3d) 394 at p. 395, 32 C.R. (3d) 88]:

> The age and sex of the appellant are not "peculiar characteristics" excluded from consideration of the "ordinary person" in the objective test in s. 215(2) (see Fauteux J. (as he then was) in *Wright v. The Queen*, [1969] 3 C.C.C. 258 at pp 261-2 . . . discussing *Bedder v. D.P.P.*, [1954] 2 All E.R. 801).

He also added [at pp. 395-6]:

> In our respectful opinion, there is nothing in that judgment which precludes charging the jury as the defence requested. As the matter was left to the jury, the age of the appellant was only a consideration

if and when the jury turned to the question of whether the wrongful act or insult deprived him of his power of self-control. The effect of the charge was that an ordinary person did not include a 16-year-old or youth and may well have established as the standard an ordinary person more experience and mature than the ordinary 16-year-old or youth. If this is so, the jury may have rejected the defence judging the objective test on that basis.

In the result, the Court of Appeal held that the judge was in error and there may well have been misdirection which seriously prejudiced Hill and so the conviction could not stand. The appeal was allowed, the conviction set aside and a new trial on the charge of second degree murder ordered.

## *The Issue*

The issue in this appeal is whether the Ontario Court of Appeal erred in law in holding that the trial judge erred in law with respect to the elements of the objectives test relevant to the defence of provocation in failing to direct the jury that the "ordinary person" within the meaning of that term in s. 215(2) of the *Criminal Code* was an "ordinary person of the same age and sex as the accused".

## *The Defence of Provocation*

The defence of provocation appears to have first developed in the early 1800s. Tindal C.J. in *R. v. Hayward* (1833), 6 Car. & P. 157 at p. 159, 172 E.R. 1188, told the jury that the defence of provocation was derived from the law's "compassion to human infirmity". It acknowledged that all human beings are subject to uncontrollable outbursts of passion and anger which may lead them to do violent acts. In such instances, the law would lessen the severity of criminal liability.

Nevertheless, not all acts done in the heat of passion were to be subject to the doctrine of provocation. By the middle of the 19th century, it became clear that the provoking act had to be sufficient to excite an ordinary or reasonable person under the circumstances. As Keating J. stated in *R. v. Welsh* (1869), 11 Cox C.C. 336 at p. 338:

> The law is, that there must exist such an amount of provocation as would be excited by the circumstances in the mind of a reasonable man, and so as to lead the jury to ascribe the set to the influence of that passion.

The *Criminal Code* codified this approach to provocation by including under s. 215 three general requirements for the defence of provocation. First, the provoking wrongful act or insult must be of such a nature that it would deprive an ordinary person of the power of self-control. That is the initial threshold which must be surmounted. Secondly, the accused must actually have been provoked. As I have earlier indicated, these two elements are often referred to as the objective and subjective tests of provocation respectively. Thirdly, the accused must have acted on the provocation on the sudden and before there was time for his or her passion to cool.

## *The Objective Test of Provocation and the Ordinary Person Standard*

In considering the precise meaning and application of the ordinary person standard or objective test, it is important to identify its underlying *rationale*. Lord Simon of

Glaisdale has perhaps stated it most succinctly when he suggested in *Camplin*, at p. 726, that

> the reason for importing into this branch of the law the concept of the reasonable man [was] . . . to avoid the injustice of a man being entitled to rely on his exceptional excitability or pugnacity or ill-temper or on his drunkenness.

If there were no objective test to the defence of provocation, anomalous results would occur. A well-tempered, reasonable person would not be entitled to benefit from the provocation defence and wold be guilty of culpable homicide amounting to murder, while an ill-tempered or exceptionally excitable person would find his or her culpability mitigated by provocation and would be guilty only of manslaughter. It is society's concern that reasonable and non-violent behaviour be encouraged that prompts the law to enforce the objective standard. The criminal law is concerned among other things with fixing standards for human behaviour. We seek to encourage conduct that complies with certain societal standards of reasonableness and responsibility. In doing this, the law quite logically employs the objective standard of the reasonable person.

With this general purpose in mind, we must ascertain the meaning of the ordinary person standard. What are the characteristics of the "ordinary person"? To what extent should the attributes and circumstances of the accused be ascribed to the ordinary person?

. . . .

*Canadian case-law*

The Supreme Court of Canada has also had occasion to provide guidance on the ordinary person standard for provocation. In *Taylor v. The King* (1947), 89 C.C.C. 209 at pp. 217-8, [1948] 1 D.L.R. 545, at pp. 552-3, [1947] S.C.R. 462 at p. 471, a case in which the accused was drunk at the time of his alleged provocation., Kerwin J. made clear that for the purposes of the objective test of provocation, the "criterion is the effect on an ordinary person . . . the jury is not entitled to take into consideration any alleged drunkenness on the part of the accused".

This Court again rejected a consideration of the drunkenness of the accused in connection with the objective test in *Salamon v. The Queen* (1959), 123 C.C.C. 1, 17 D.L.R. (2d) 685, [1959] S.C.R. 404. Mr. Justice Fauteux endorsed the trial judge's instruction to the jury not to consider "the character, background, temperament, or condition of the accused" in relation to the objective test of provocation. Similarly, Cartwright J. (dissenting on another issue) wrote, at p. 5 C.C.C., p. 689 D.L.R., p. 415 S.C.R., that the trial judge correctly "made it plain that on this [objective] branch of the inquiry no account should be taken of the idiosyncrasies of the appellant and that the standard to be applied was that of an ordinary person".

Finally, in *Wright v. The Queen*, [1969] 3 C.C.C. 258, 2 D.L.R. (3d) 529, [1969] S.C.R. 335, a son was charged with the shooting death of his father. The evidence suggested that there had been some difficulties in their relationship. The father was said to have been a bad-tempered and violent man who had mistreated his son on a number of occasions. The accused had not seen his father for a period of about five years until a few days prior to the fatal incident. On the evening of the shooting, the accused had spent most of the day drinking with his friends. In considering the objective test of provocation, the court rejected the relevance of the quality of the accused's relationship with his father, the mentality of the accused or his possible drunkenness. Fauteux J. quoted, at p. 261 C.C.C., p. 532 D.L.R., p 340 S.C.R., the words of Lord Simonds L.C. in *Bedder*, that the purpose of the objective test is ". . . to invite the jury to consider the act of the accused by reference to a certain standard or norm of conduct and with this object the "reasonable" or the "average" or the "normal" man is invoked". The court went on to state, at p. 262 C.C.C., p. 532 D.L.R., p. 340 S.C.R.:

> While the character, background, temperament, idiosyncrasies, or the drunkenness of the accused are matters to be considered in the second branch of the enquiry, they are excluded from the consideration in the first branch. A contrary view would denude of any sense the objective test.

Appellate courts at the provincial level have also considered the nature of the ordinary person standard of provocation. In *R. v. Clark* (1974), 22 C.C.C. (2d) 1, [1975] 2 W.W..R. 385, 5 N.R. 601 (Alta. S.C.A.D.)., the "morbid jealousy and slight mental degeneration" suffered by the accused was held not to be relevant to the objective test. According to Clement J.A. at p. 16:

> In the first branch of the inquiry, the objective test, what in essence has to be determined as a standard of comparison is the reaction that might be expected from ordinary human nature to the wrongful act, or to the alleged insult in the present case.

In *R. v. Parnerkar* (1971), 5 C.C.C. (2d) 11, 16 C.R.N.S. 347, [1972] 1 W.W.R. 161, the Saskatchewan Court of Appeal held that the cultural and religious background of the accused was not relevant to the determination of the objective test. The accused, born in India, was alleged to have been provoked by, *inter alia*, the deceased's statement "I am not going to marry you because you are a black man". The court's ruling seems to narrow unduly the conception of the ordinary person and rigidly prohibit a consideration of the physical characteristics of the accused along the lines of the *Bedder* case. I should not that *Parnerkar* was affirmed by this Court on appeal (see 10 C.C.C. (2d) 253, 33 D.L.R. (3d) 638, [1974] S.C.R 449), however, this particular question was not addressed.

. . . .

*The appropriate content of the ordinary person standard*

What lessons are to be drawn from this review of the case-law? I think it is clear that there is a widespread agreement that the ordinary or reasonable person has a normal temperament and level of self-control. It follows that the ordinary person is not exceptionally excitable, pugnacious or in a state of drunkenness.

In terms of other characteristics of the ordinary person, it seems to me that the "collective good sense" of the jury will naturally lead it to ascribe to the ordinary person any general characteristics relevant to the provocation in question. For example, if the provocation is a racial slur, the jury will think of an ordinary person with the racial background that forms the substance of the insult. To this extent, particular characteristics will be ascribed to the ordinary person. Indeed, it would be impossible to conceptualize a sexless or ageless ordinary person. Features such as sex, age or race do not detract from a person;s characterization as ordinary. Thus particular characteristics that are not peculiar or idiosyncratic can be ascribed to an ordinary person without subverting the logic of the objective test of provocation. As Lord Diplock wrote in *Director of Public Prosecutions v. Camplin*, [1978] A.C. 705 at pp. 716-7:

> ... the "reasonable man" has never been confided to the adult male. It means an ordinary person of either sex, not exceptionally excitable or pugnacious, but possessed of such powers of self-control as everyone is entitled to expect that his fellow citizens will exercise in society as it is today.

It is important to note that, in some instances, certain characteristics will be irrelevant. For example,the race of a person will be irrelevant if the provocation involves an insult regarding a physical disability. Similarly, the sex of an accused will be irrelevant if the provocation relates to a racial insult. Thus the central criterion is the relevance of the particular feature to the provocation in question. With this in mind, I think it is fair to conclude that age will be a relevant consideration when we are dealing with a young accused person. For a jury to assess what an ordinary person would have done if subjected to the same circumstances as the accused, the young age of an accused will be an important contextual consideration.

I should also add that my conclusion that certain attributes can be ascribed to the ordinary person is not meant to suggest that a trial judge must in each case tell the jury what specific attributes it is to ascribe to the ordinary person. The point I wish to emphasize is simply that in applying their common sense to the factual determination of the objective test, jury members will quite naturally and properly ascribe certain characteristics to the "ordinary person".

. . . .

It has been suggested that the instruction of the trial judge on the subjective prong of the provocation defence had the effect of misleading the jury on the appropriate content of the ordinary person standard. The charge stated:

> ... you will then secondly consider whether the accused acted on the provocation on the sudden before there was time for his passion to cool. In deciding this question you are not restricted to the standard of the ordinary person. You will take into account the mental, emotional, the physical characteristics and the age of this accused.

. . . .

> You will also ask yourselves was the provocation such that it would have led a person with the mental and physical conditions and the age of the accused to respond in this way.

In my opinion, these words would not have misled the average juror with respect to the objective test, particularly when viewed in the context of the charge as a whole.

I have the greatest confidence in the level of intelligence and plain common sense of the average Canadian jury sitting on a criminal case. Juries are perfectly capable of sizing the matter up. In my experience as a trial judge I cannot recall a single instance in which a jury returned to the court-room to ask for further instructions on the provocation portion of a murder charge. A jury frequently seeks further guidance on the distinction between first degree murder, second degree murder and manslaughter, but rarely, if ever, on provocation. It seems to be common ground that the trial judge would not have been in error if he had simply read s. 215 of the *Code* and left it at that, without embellishment. I am loath to complicate the task of the trial judge, in cases such as the case at bar, by requiring him or her as a matter of law to point out to the members of the jury that in applying the objective test they must conceptualize an "ordinary person" who is male and young. The accused is before them. He is male and young. I cannot conceive of a Canadian jury conjuring up the concept of an "ordinary person" who would be either female or elderly, or banishing from their minds the possibility that an "ordinary person" might be both young and male. I do not think anything said by the judge in the case at bar would have led the jury to such an absurdity.

*Conclusion*

I find that the trial judge's charge to the jury on the ordinary persons standard in the defence of provocation was consistent with the requirements of the *Criminal Code* and correct in law. It was not necessary to direct the jury that the ordinary person means an ordinary person of the same age and sex as the accused. I would, therefore, allow the appeal and restore the conviction.

*Appeal allowed; conviction restored.*

## 7.4.2 Defence of Mental Disorder and Diminished Responsibility

**Introduction**
*C. Mitchell*

**INSANITY**
Prior to 1800, insanity was usually regarded as a general, seriously disabling condition that, like infancy, was presumed to prevent the formation of criminal intent. Under England's *Criminal Lunatics Act*, 1800 (U.K.), 39 & 40 Geo. 3, c. 94, a successful insanity defence resulted in acquittal and confinement in an asylum. Obviously mad offenders were probably not even brought before the courts.

The modern form of the insanity plea arose in 1843 when the House of Lords devised the McNaghten Rules. These Rules formed the basis for section 16 of the Code. They stated that to establish insanity, the accused must clearly prove that at the time of the offence he had a disease of the mind and thus did not know the nature and quality of the act he was doing, or, if he did know it, that he did not know that it was wrong. The Rules were a response to the insanity acquittal of Daniel McNaghten, tried for the murder of Edward Drummond, secretary of Prime Minister Robert Peel. Under the Rules named after him, McNaghten might well have been convicted.

Since 1843, judges and lawyers have repeated that McNaghten was insane because he suffered from delusions that he was being spied upon and persecuted by Peel's government. But in a fascinating piece of historical detective work, Richard Moran (1981) recently argued that McNaghten likely was being spied upon, that only a natural mistake of identity led him to shoot Drummond in place of Peel, and that he may have been paid to assassinate Peel. Perhaps Lord Chief Justice Tindal was anxious to find McNaghten insane so as to foreclose an embarrassing inquiry into government surveillance of political radicals. For similar reasons, many commentators now immediately characterize all American political assassins as insane; after all, only a crazy person would want to kill an American leader. McNaghten, of course, would go along with any deception to avoid execution — he died 23 years later in the Broadmoore Criminal Lunatic Asylum. Indeed, it was the death penalty that once made insanity such a critical issue. Insanity matters much less now in Canada because the plea's outcome most just affects the place and style of incarceration, though it can still avoid the minimum 25-year term for murder.

A number of controversial issues are raised by insanity (or "mental disorder" as it is now called in the Criminal Code). These include the role of volitional impairment, the meaning of "disease of mind" and "wrong", the ability of the courts to meaningfully distinguish between the mad and the bad, the acceptance of psychiatrists as "experts" and whether or not section 16 should be abolished outright.

Dissatisfaction with the McNaghten Rules was immediate. Juries dislike the all-or-nothing outcome and medical experts complained about the focus on cognitive incapacity to the neglect of volitional impairment. The concept of irresistible impulse was certainly known in 1843. Thomas Erskine, counsel in the famous case of *Hadfield* (1800), argued that Hadfield, an injured veteran with a messianic complex who tried to kill King George III, was impelled by "impossible phantoms of the mind" and "by motives irresistible".

Despite the strictures of McNaghten, Erskine's reliance on volitional impairment foreshadowed a leading interpretation of insanity. Mental illness is commonly alleged to act as an internal source of coercion whereby a person's "real self" is overpowered and compelled by his or her unconscious to act strangely and even criminally (Ehrenzweig, 1971). Blame is placed on the uncontrollable urge, not on the innocent person who caught the urge (Goldstein and Katz, 1963). Hospers (1961) offered an extreme version of this thesis claiming that a person's "conscious will is only an instrument, a slave, in the hands of a deep, unconscious motivation which determines his action . . . [like] a puppet whose motions are manipulated from behind by invisible wires . . . [thus] criminal actions in general are not actions for which their agents are responsible; the agents are passive, not active — they are victims . . . " Japanese robots killed ten people between 1978 and 1987 because of mechanical failure or rogue electromagnetic waves. Should these robots be punished? According to Hospers, humans who kill as unconscious puppets, should also be repaired not punished. Psychiatrists of this school believe that the unconscious processes allegedly behind mental illness are comparable to external forces that cause involuntary actions, i.e., "automatism", which even sounds robotic, or are comparable to duress. The insane are thus considered blameless but dangerous and somewhat inhuman, so they are locked away for protection and treatment, not punishment.

The Australian case of *Knatchbull* (1844) was probably the first to base a defence solely on irresistible impulse, an argument that was then supported by phrenology, the study of bumps on the skull. Indeed, Robert Lowe's defence address in the case was reproduced in *The Zoist*, a leading phrenological journal. Lowe claimed, using the language of duress, that if "the disease existed in that portion of the brain wherein the will held its seat, while the other portion of the brain in which the intellect of the patient was contained was free from any such disease, it naturally followed that the person so circumstanced might, with a full knowledge of what he was doing feel compelled — irresistibly compelled — to crimes which if a perfectly free agent he would be the last to commit." (White, 1984:175). Accepting this theory logically leads to the surgical removal or disconnection (lobotomy) of the brain's "diseased portion" in the interest of public safety. Lobotomy was popular in the 1950s.

Many American insanity provisions, such as *Durham* (1954) and the American Law Institute standard, expressly allow for volitional incapacity, that is, an inability "to conform one's conduct to the law". But unconscious compulsion need not be explicitly contained in a statutory definition of insanity to be employed in court. Judges can indirectly rule that someone suffering from such a compulsion resulting from a "disease of the mind" may not have knowledge of or appreciate the nature and quality of her act. The Canadian Supreme Court reasoned thusly in *Borg* (1969).

Some authorities report that historically, insanity was taken as a general condition, like infancy, which prevented formation of criminal intent (Smith, 1981). This comparison to infancy, however, suggests that the real issue was not lack of intent. Children under 12 can intentionally attack and seek to harm others, often they misbehave with passionate intent; nonetheless, they are not criminally liable. Youngster escape liability in crime, though not in tort, for policy reasons because they are not a threat to the state and because their parents, not the state, are primarily responsible for their control and punishment. Similarly, the seriously insane would have been of little criminal interest historically because they would normally be incarcerated already for their mental disorder.

Some 19th century opinion on insanity continued with comparisons to infancy. Isaac Ray argued that homicidal monomania and pyromania were diseases that paralyzed the reflective powers and caused blind, automatic impulses with which reason has as little to do as with the movements of a newborn infant (Geller, Erien, Pinkus, 1986:203). Other experts dismissed "pyromania" as a contrived disease and while that opinion dominates today, some Ray-type diagnoses are still offered in arson trials. But legal insanity over time expanded to include conditions that were not totally or even obviously debilitating; thus, comparisons to infancy, for example, are now seldom made.

Evidently, those found insane in modern trials do act with intent. According to Fingarette and Hasse (1979:52) criminally insane conduct is typically "purposeful, intentional and effectively executed; it is often premeditated, planned and prepared; and it is not infrequently tenaciously and ingeniously pursued in spite of external objects". Consistent with this observation is the finding that the pattern of homicide by the mentally disordered is identical to ordinary homicides where the victim is usually a family member or a familiar acquaintance. Insane killings are generally not random, so-called "motiveless attacks". As Dix explains in a recent survey, the insanity defence permits the introduction into criminal litigation of issues that are otherwise irrelevant. Absent insanity, there is no need "to address the defendant's ability to control his conduct, that is, to act upon his conscious perceptions, or to evaluate the moral or ethical implications of his conduct. If — but only if — the insanity defence is raised do these matters become the subject of dispute" (Dix, 1984:11-12). The courts have also expanded the number of conditions that constitute "disease of the mind", the criterion needed to fall within the insanity provision.

The special legal status of the insane, therefore, is not based on their lack of intent or lack of knowledge but rather on the theory that their unconsciously caused impairment somehow results in or contributes to their wrongful act. The Durham Rule (1954) spoke of the act being a "product of" mental abnormality. Both assumptions — that mental illness is unconsciously caused and that it contributes to dangerous behaviour — are open to qualification and debate (Mitchell, 1986b)

The supposed link between mental illness and anti-social behaviour is vulnerable to two criticisms. First, blaming irresistible impulses for crime is comparable to demonology with its notions of unconscious, evil spirits taking control of the possessed (Szasz, 1970). Both theories are circular, hence irrefutable. Proof that a mentally ill person was compelled to misbehave is the fact of the misbehaviour itself. And, since in the criminal trial context mental disorder is rarely raised except in connection with some serious misdeed, it is natural for judges, lawyers and forensic specialists to causally link crime and mental illness. Scientifically, however, the anecdotal evidence usually led in court about the relationship between an accused's health status and his or her criminality often has little predictive or explanatory power. What must be demonstrated is some general, stable causal relationship between mental illness and crime and it is on this issue that the second criticism focuses. Historically, the relationship between mental disorder and crime was presumed rather than demonstrated. Now many authorities advise that mental illness has not special connection with violent crime and that the mentally ill statistically are not over-represented in the category of dangerous persons (Kittrie, 1978; Morse, 1982a; Bartol, 1980). Some suggest mental illness should be "totally ignored or written off as a factor in understanding . . . dangerous" (Steadman and Bruff, 1975). Others report that the mentally ill may be less dangerous than average because of their predominantly female and mature composition (Monahan, 1981).

Recognizing these problems Bonnie wishes to grant exculpatory relevance to insanity merely because the "impairment of mental or emotional functioning" may affect the defendant's "perceptions, beliefs and motivations at the time of the offence" (Bonnie & Morris, 1987:135). This extremely open-ended view agrees with Meyer's perception that modern trials are complex clemency hearings that focus on the "inner mind" of the accused and that basically recycle, expand and "psychologically sanitize" the old "heat of passion" defence (Meyer, 1982:295-301). The trial of John Hinckley, Jr., attempted assassin of former President Reagan, illustrates the incredible lengths to which a court may go when all that is at issue is the character and personality of the accused. Testimony was given by Hinckley's sister, mother, father and brother. Hinckley's poems were read aloud, recordings of his songs were played and his short stories were entered into evidence (Caplan, 1984). The jury listened to tape recordings of his telephone calls to Jodi Foster and Foster herself appeared at trial on videotape. "Taxi Driver", Hinckley's favourite film, was screened for the jury. This introductory course in Hinckleyology was compounded by psychiatric evidence. Psychiatrists interviewed Hinckley for hundreds of hours and consumed weeks of court time expounding on their observations. Psychiatric services cost the prosecution about $300,000, the defence about $150,000. Excluding personnel already on the government payroll, the entire Hinckley trial cost $3 million. Afterward, 83 percent of respondents in a post-trial poll felt justice was not done (*ibid.*, 116).

The link between provocation and Bonnie's representation of the insanity plea is obvious since Bonnie contends that mental illness can trigger an inadvertent impairment in the ordinary person which, to some extent, deprives them of their self-control. This thesis is not new. Sir James Stephen's discussion of the McNaghten Rules in 1878 emphasized the incapacity of the mentally disordered to reason calmly because they are burdened by "wild and astonishing" delusions (Verdun-Jones, 1979:21). Once in an impaired state of chronic "heat of passion", the mentally ill can supposedly be provoked through no fault of their own into wrongful behaviour. Provocation doctrine requires that a person act "on the sudden and before there was time for the passions to cool" but the mentally ill need not act spontaneously because they are assumed to be chronically impaired. In the words of a New York Appeal Court in 1976, "it may be that a significant trauma has affected the defendant's mind for a substantial period of time, simmering in the unknowing unconscious and then inexplicably coming to the fore" (Meyer, 1982:301). Additionally, the mentally ill are allowed to be provoked by events that would not radically weaken an "ordinary" person's self-control.

Moore, like Bonnie, dismisses most of the usual reasons for absolving the insane of criminal responsibility and argues instead that the mentally ill as a class are excused because of their "irrationality". Moore claims that "persons who are seriously irrational or nonrational . . . have always been excused because they lack an essential attribute of personhood . . . Beings who lack this feature to some serious degree, such as plants, dogs, very young infants, and the mentally ill, cannot fairly be held responsible for some particular harm because they are not responsible (accountable) at all." (Moore, 1980:1662). In short, the mentally ill are like dogs, not full "persons", a characterization that paves the way for systematic maltreatment of the mentally ill. Moore defines "irrationality" as acting on the basis of "defective or conflicting beliefs", thus a person falsely believing themselves to be God or Elvis Presley would be irrational. But for non-believers, are not the beliefs of millions of Christians, Moslems and Jews similarly "irrational"? Has not modern science revealed many "defective beliefs" held by our ancestors and will not further revelation expose our own errors? Does this mean insanity is the norm?

Typically, the case examples discussed by Moore and Bonnie of "insane" accused acquitted as not guilty by reason of insanity amount to clemency hearings. Psychiatrists in *Pollard* (1960) testified that while the Detroit police officer said he robbed banks to obtain money he really acted out an unconscious desire to punish himself for failing to be at home two years previously to prevent the brutal death of his wife and child at the hands of a neighbour. His "unconscious" intent to be apprehended and punished supposedly accounted for his incompetent efforts at bank robbery; he "really" wanted to fail. Pollard was also said to be in a dissociative state, so his actions "may not have been consciously activated". A more realistic explanation of these bare facts starts with the common knowledge that bereavement is impairing, especially the loss of a spouse and child. The major loss experienced by Pollard often results in depression, poor health, carelessness, lack of attention, and so on. Extreme bereavement may help explain why Pollard embarked on such a risky business as bank robbery and why he did it badly. In addition, courts traditionally treat errant police officers with great leniency. Combining Pollard's mourning, his occupation and his incompetency produces the ingredients for a sympathetic response at sentencing. Legally, however, he should have been found guilty.

Bonnie's case involves Joy Baker, acquitted in Virginia for the shooting death of her aunt. Baker is a sympathetic figure, having been threatened with death by her husband who accused her of adultery. Furthermore, in the midst of Baker's paranoid panic that her children and neighbours were also a threat, Baker's aunt arrived and refused to leave, ignoring Baker's "frantic pleas to go away". When the aunt, against all orders, tried to unlock the back door and enter, Baker shot her. Subsequently, Baker became if anything even more distraught, and killed the wounded aunt. According to Bonnie, everyone agreed Baker was crazy because "she was clearly out of touch with reality and unable to understand the wrongfulness of her conduct" (Bonnie, 1987:125). Bonnie regards the insanity defence as an irreplaceable tool for acquitting Baker but the same result could be achieved by other means. First, Baker had a legal right to resist the trespassing aunt. Trespassers who refuse to leave when warned and who try to break through doors can probably be shot and killed in most U.S. states without the shooter even being charged with a criminal offence. The intruder need not be a stranger; indeed, family members are usually most dangerous to one another. Second, Baker allegedly made a mistake in viewing her aunt as someone determined to harm her. Without great doctrinal stress, the defence of mistake of fact in Virginia could require only honest mistakes, not reasonable ones, and could explicitly include honest mistakes based on delusions, illusions or hallucinations. Arguably, Bonnie could achieve his goal without any psychiatric input by seeking change in the law of mistake of fact that would end discrimination against the mentally ill. Why would judges and juries be unlikely to accept mental delusions as excusing mistakes of fact?

The current law on the defence of mental disorder is explained and discussed in the excerpts from the O'Marra article which follows a brief section on diminished responsibility. The final reading, the *Worth* case, is an example of a recent application of the law in this area in regard to the meaning of "wrong" in section 16(1) of the Code.

## DIMINISHED RESPONSIBILITY

Modelling the defence of insanity on "heat of passion" had much to recommend it because it allowed for a gradation of culpability and it honestly recognized that the mentally ill carried out their offences intentionally. This new defence, which is not formally recognized in Canada, was entitled "diminished responsibility" after 1909, and was first applied in the Scottish case of *Dingwall* (1867) and resulted not in an acquittal, like insanity, but in a verdict of culpable homicide (the Scottish equivalent of manslaughter) instead of murder. The legal distinction is important because while murder usually calls for a minimum sentence such as life imprisonment or execution, manslaughter typically grants judges nearly unfettered discretion in sentencing. Diminished offenders can therefore receive sentences ranging from life imprisonment to conditional discharges. Judges appreciate this defence because it leaves the disposition of mentally ill offenders entirely in their hands, unlike insanity where medical or political authorities determine the length and nature of the involuntary committal. For example, in Canada the insane are released only with the permission of the provincial government, i.e. the cabinet, but in many American jurisdictions the decision to release is made by the attending psychiatrists. Many defendants also prefer a known, fixed prison term to an indefinite stay in psychiatric detention. Being found guilty of manslaughter is probably also less stigmatizing than being found not guilty of murder by reason of insanity. Whatever the reason, the plea of insanity in England virtually disappeared after the passage of subsection 2(1) of the *Homicide Act,* 1957 (U.K.), 5 & 6 Eliz. 2, c. 11, which stated that a person shall not be convicted of murder "if he was suffering from such abnormality of mind . . . as substantially impaired his mental responsibility for his acts . . . " While not accepted in Canada, diminished responsibility is part of the law of Scotland, England and certain American and Australian states.

Diminished responsibility cases, in practice, allow the submission of almost every kind of evidence concerning intoxication, mental illness, personality disorder, dietary disorder or brain malfunction to indicate that the defendant was not fully "mentally responsible". Typically, *Dingwall* (1867), the first case on point, involved a husband who attacked his wife after a prolonged bout of Hogmanay (Scottish New Year)-inspired alcoholic excess. More broadly, the court in *Savage* (1909) spoke of the requirement for some "weakness of the mind", some form of "mental unsoundness" "bordering on insanity". Following *Byrne* (1960) in England, diminished responsibility included the concept of irresistible impulse, that is the incapacity of the accused to "exercise will-power to control his physical acts" (Gregory, Oxford Companion, 1987:194).

Both the concepts of "mental responsibility" and "irresistible impulse" are, according to critics, empty explain-alls used to disguise policy decisions. Persons who kill blackmailers or who mercifully dispatch elderly relatives suffering from terminal illnesses are conveniently discovered by English judges to be suffering from an abnormality of the mind. (Dell, 1982). Or more commonly, diminished responsibility allows judges to pass a greater range of sentences than would otherwise be possible. In a recent case similar to *Beard* (1920), an intoxicated alcohol-abuser broke into a house, attempted to rape a frail, elderly woman and managed somehow to asphyxiate her. On closely similar facts Beard was convicted of murder and executed, whereas in the modern case the killer was convicted of manslaughter and sentenced to five years' imprisonment of which only about half will probably be served (Dell, 1984:35-38).

California also adopted a diminished capacity test until amendments in 1981 severely restricted the defence (Dix. 1985:15). That the legal response to murder incites political discord can hardly be denied given the continual battle between death penalty advocates and abolitionists or given the 1986 voter recall of California Supreme Court Chief Justice Bird largely because of her efforts to block every execution order that came before her court (83% of Californians favor the death penalty for murder). Diminished capacity was arguably enacted and utilized by some judges as an ostensibly medical, apolitical device for avoiding first-degree murder convictions. In a series of decisions starting with *Wolff* (1964), the California Supreme Court used diminished capacity to raise the legal standard for premeditated murder so as to exclude more and more defendants. In *Wolff*, the Court held that if because of psychological impairments the defendant failed to "maturely and meaningfully reflect upon the gravity" of the killing, there was no premeditation and thus no death penalty. Subsequently in *Conley* (1966) and *Poddar* (1974) the same court set out equally vague tests for reducing murder to manslaughter including the inability to act in accordance with one's perceived legal duties because of psychological impairment. In *Conley*, the defendant threatened murder, purchased a gun, practiced shooting and then shot his ex-lover. Premeditation could hardly be plainer.

## Hadfield to Swain: The Criminal Code Amendments Dealing with the Mentally Disordered Accused*
### A.J. O'Marra

. . .

The case of *R. v.Swain* (1991), 63 C.C.C. (3d) 193, 5 C.R. (4th) 253, [1991] 1 S.C.R. 933, created a significant turning point in how we deal with mentally disordered accused. While there had been great debate throughout the years over the issues of when and how an accused should be declared not guilty by reason of insanity, largely starting with the famous M'Naghten rules and the resultant jurisprudence, there has been a relative paucity of legislative development or judicial comment on how mentally disordered accused should be dealt with at the post-verdict stage. . . .

It is probably fair to say that very few jurists who have been required to make a s. 614(2) strict-custody order knew what became of or happened to the accused once he became subject to the pleasure of the Lieutenant-Governor.

It has been well recognized that the provisions in the *Criminal Code* as they existed prior to the amendments were procedurally vague. In fact, when the case came before the Ontario Court of Appeal, *R. v. Swain* (1986), 24 C.C.C. (3d) 385, 50 C.R. (3d) 97, 53 O.R. (2d) 609, Mr. Justice Thorson observed that the provisions were "unnecessarily imprecise and sketchy and too often lacking in any clear expression of Parliament's purpose and intent". Indeed, other than remand provisions to obtain evidence as to an accused's psychiatric state and the inclusion of the provision which created advisory review boards with the annual task of determining whether the accused had recovered from his insanity, there has been little legislative change to the progenitor of these sections. The comprehensive legislative package known as Bill C-30, which was proclaimed in force on February 4, 1992, was designed to replace the remnants of the *Criminal Lunatics Act* found in ss. 614 and 617 of the *Criminal Code* with a new system, replete with specific procedures to strengthen due process and the other fundamental Charter rights of the mentally disordered accused, while at the same time protecting society from dangerous, mentally disordered accused.

The Supreme Court of Canada in *Swain* held that s. 614(2) which provides entry to the Lieutenant-Governor's Warrant System in the same manner as the *Criminal Lunatics Act* by way of "strict custody", was unconstitutional for failing to provide due process. Basically, due to the imperative nature of the provision, it did not permit the court to conduct a hearing to inquire into the accused's present state of mind and degree of dangerousness, and whether in fact the accused required confinement. Accordingly, the order for confinement had to be considered arbitrary, Section 614(2) directs that where an accused has been found not guilty by reason of insanity, the court "shall order that he be kept in strict custody . . . until the pleasure of the Lieutenant Governor of the Province is known". The focus of the trial is by necessity on the state of mind of the accused at the time of the offence. However, at the time the court is

---

* Excerpts from (1993), 36 Criminal Law Quarterly 49

directed to make a disposition of strict-custody, following a verdict of not guilty by reason of insanity, the only evidence it may have as to the accused's state of mind is in most instances dated. Moreover, the imperative nature of the legislation required a strict custody disposition even if the court had up-to-date evidence of the accused's present state of mind which indicated that such a disposition was not warranted. Accordingly, the court's order made pursuant to s. 614(2) was without due process and arbitrary. While the Supreme Court focused on s. 614(2), Chief Justice Lamer took the opportunity to observe that the other sections of the *Criminal Code* upon which the Lieutenant-Governor's Warrant System was based, were suspicious due to "a lack of procedural safeguards". In the result, there was a clear incentive on the part of Parliament to institute a comprehensive overhaul of the way in which courts and review boards dealt with mentally disordered accused. . . .

### 1. Summary of the Former Criminal Code Provisions Dealing with the Mentally Disordered Accused

As the law existed prior to February 4, 1992, an accused who was found not guilty by reason of insanity would be ordered into strict custody by the court, until the "pleasure of the lieutenant governor of the province is known": s. 614(2).

Section 615(2) provided for the psychiatric assessment of an accused who might be mentally ill and as a result of mental illness, unfit to stand trial. Upon trial of the issue of fitness (s. 615(1), if the court found that the accused was unfit, then the court was directed to order that the accused be kept in custody until, once again " the pleasure of the Lieutenant Governor of the Province is known": s. 615(7). As a practical matter, there was no distinction between "strict custody" under s. 614(2) and "custody" under s. 615(7). The custody which resulted from either order was the same.

Generally, once the court made the order that the accused was to be held in "strict custody" or "custody", the accused remained in a detention centre or jail, pending the issuance of the initial warrant of the Lieutenant-Governor directing the accused to a place of safe custody, namely, a psychiatric facility. Should the accused already have been in a psychiatric facility at the time of the verdict, or finding that the accused was unfit to stand trial, the accused would remain in the custody of the hospital pending the issuance of the initial warrant. The jurisdiction of the Lieutenant-Governor to issue the warrant was found in s. 617(1).

A review board was created under s. 619 of the Code. It was observed by Mr. Justice Arnup in *Abel v. Advisory Review Board, supra*, at p. 165 C.C.C., that the legislation created advisory review boards with a considerable and varied expertise which would ensure that no one languished indefinitely and half-forgotten in mental institutions. The purpose of the review board and the frequency of the reviews was set out in s. 619(5). The review board assumed the obligation to review the case of every person in custody as a result of a s. 617 order. Although there is nothing in the Code which directed the review board to assist the Lieutenant-Governor in the issuance of his initial order, the practice in Ontario had been that the review board would conduct placement hearings. The chairman of the review board would make a recommendation to the Lieutenant-Governor as to initial placement of the accused following the court ordered remand under either s. 614(2) for the not guilty by reason of insanity accused, or s. 615(7) for an accused who is found unfit to stand trial on account of insanity.

The review board inquired as to the progress of the accused at each of its periodic hearings as directed by s. 619(5) which required it to report to the Lieutenant-Governor as to whether an unfit accused had recovered sufficiently to stand trial, or whether an accused who is found not guilty by reason of insanity had recovered and, if not, to make recommendations that it considered to be in the interests of the accused's recovery and not contrary to the public interest. A report and recommendation would then be provided to the Lieutenant-Governor as to the appropriate disposition of the accused. Depending on the degree of dangerousness presented by the accused, an order would be issued directing that the accused be detained in the custody of a psychiatric hospital, however, with certain discretions afforded to the administrator to allow the accused degrees of community access if appropriate. The system was designed and continues to be one of a monitored conditional release. . . .

### (1) The Warrant System as Conducted in Ontario

In Ontario, the Lieutenant-Governor's Warrant System (hereafter the "L.G.W. system") utilized a monitored conditional release approach in the management of dangerous mentally disordered accused. The system can be described as a cascade system effected by the use of "loosened warrants". . . .

In order for the system to function there had to be a delegation of authority to hospital administrators. While there was no authority in the previous legislation to do so, such a delegation of authority allowed for the day-to-day management of the mentally disordered accused. The process of gradual reintegration continues under the new legislative regime virtually unchanged.

### 2. Highlights of the Mental Disorder Provisions

In summary form, some of the highlights of the new legislation are as follows:
(a) Section 16 has been altered to the extent that the notion of "insanity" has been removed and relegated to the historical waste bin which such terms as "lunatics" and "asylums" and has been replaced with that of "mental disorder". It has been done in an attempt to replace antiquated terminology, yet without changing the legal requirements of the defence. "Mental disorder" is still defined as a "disease of the mind" thereby retaining within s. 16 the notion that mental disorder, as a disease of the mind includes: any illness, disorder, or abnormal condition which impairs the human mind and its functioning, excluding, however self-induced states of alcohol or drugs; as well as transitory mental states such as hysteria or concussion": *R. v. Cooper* (1980), 51 C.C.C. (2d) 129, 13 C.R. (3d) 97, [1980] 1 S.C.R. 1149.
(b) On a verdict of not criminally responsible on account of a mental disorder (N.C.R.), the accused must first have been found to have committed the act. This particular provision will be seen to be important when the concept of capping is proclaimed in force. Certain offences will have a time-limit attached to them beyond which the review board will cease to have jurisdiction. In the instance of murder, there will be no cap, however, in the instance of manslaughter, the cap

will be 10 years. Accordingly, it will make a significant difference as to which case the Crown is able to make out prior to the accused being found not criminally responsible.

(c) The court is now authorized to order psychiatric assessments of the accused by medical practitioners to determine not only whether an accused is fit to stand trial, or not criminally responsible on account of mental disorder, but also to determine what the most appropriate disposition should be following such a finding or verdict.

It is important to note that the periods of assessment are generally restricted to five days to determine the issue of fitness and 30 days for any other purpose with a possible maximum increase to 60 days. The shortened assessment period to determine fitness has markedly increased the number of unfit accused who have been directed from the trial process into the review board system.

(d) Any statements made by an accused during the assessment process are protected from use against him, except to prove the issue for which the assessment was ordered, or to challenge the credibility of the accused if he elects to testify and gives testimony inconsistent with statements given during the assessment, or to establish perjury in a subsequent proceeding.

(e) In keeping with the concerns expressed in *R. v. Swain, supra,* after conducting a hearing, the court may render an initial disposition following a verdict of not criminally responsible or finding that the accused is unfit to stand trial by reason of a mental disorder. In addition, the court has the authority to make a time-limited treatment order for an unfit accused which would allow for the administration of a specific course of treatment, without the accused's consent, for a maximum period of 60 days on the testimony of a medical practitioner that it will likely result in a return to fitness.

(f) Review boards have been created in each province by Lieutenant-Governor's Order-in-Council with a composition largely as they have in the past. They have become independent tribunals with direct jurisdiction over the accused rather than merely advisory boards to their respective Lieutenant-Governors.

(g) In rendering a disposition, the court or review board may order the mentally disordered accused to be:
  (i) discharged absolutely, if he is not a significant threat to the safety of the public;
  (ii) discharged subject to conditions, or
  (iii) detained in the custody of a hospital.

The overriding principle that must be taken into account by both the court or review board, is that any disposition must reflect the principle that the disposition is to be the *"least onerous and least restrictive to the accused"*. In reaching a determination, the court and review board must take into consideration the same factors:
  (i) the need to protect the public from dangerous persons;
  (ii) the mental condition of the accused at the time;
  (iii) the reintegration of the accused into society;
  (iv) any other needs of the accused.

It should be noted that if an accused requires confinement at the time of the disposition, whether the disposition is rendered by the court or the review board, *he may only be detained in the custody of a hospital.*

(h) A court-ordered disposition following a verdict of not criminally responsible or finding of unfitness, will only last up to 90 days, other than an order for an absolute discharge for someone found not criminally responsible. The court cannot discharge absolutely a person who has been found unfit to stand trial on account of a mental disorder. Any disposition rendered by the court, other than an absolute discharge, must be reviewed by the review board within that 90-day period, or in the event that the court does not render an initial disposition, the review board must conduct a hearing and render its initial disposition within 45 days of the verdict or finding. Dispositions rendered by the review board are subject to a mandatory review within 12 months or they may be reviewed more often on the request of the accused or the person in charge of the hospital where the accused is detained, or as circumstances require.

(i) Disposition hearings conducted by the court or the review board may be as informal as circumstances permit, however, all parties are specifically entitled to representation by counsel as well as to examine and cross-examine all witnesses. The proceedings are to be recorded and the hearing process is open to the public, within a caveat that the court or review board may exclude the public or make publication bans under certain circumstances.

(j) There is a right of appeal against any disposition by an accused or any other party to the proceeding, which may include the Attorney-General of the province, a hospital in whose care the accused has been placed, and any person designated as a party to the proceedings having established a substantial interest in protecting the interests of the accused to the satisfaction of the court or the review board.

(k) The legislation now covers both indictable and summary conviction matters, whereas under the previous legislative scheme the Lieutenant-Governor had authority to issue warrants for persons found unfit or not guilty by reason of insanity on indictable offences only.

(l) There is a provision referred to as "capping" which will permit a maximum period during which a mentally disordered accused may be subject to a disposition of the review board. If the verdict of not criminally responsible or finding of unfitness is as a result of an act found to be first or second degree murder or high treason, the maximum period during which the review board may exercise jurisdiction over the accused is life. However, for those offences classified as "designated offences", which largely comprise all other crimes of violence, the maximum period for which the accused could be subject to a disposition, would be 10 years or the maximum period for which the accused would be liable to imprisonment for the offence, whichever is less. As to any other offence which does not fall within the "designated offences" category, the maximum period for which the accused could be subject to a disposition would be two years or the maximum confinement allowable, whichever is shorter. In the instance of young offenders, the maximum period for which the accused would be subject to a disposition would be the maximum period to which he could be confined under the *Young Offenders Act.*

At the end of the capping period, if, as a result of his continuing dangerousness, the accused has not been discharged or successfully reintegrated into the community the review board would no longer have jurisdiction to detain him. If the accused is to be detained, at that point, it would have to be accomplished by way of the civil commitment procedures for involuntary patients under the provincial mental health legislation.

(m) The cap period for designated offences may be extended for certain accused on an application by the prosecution at the time of the verdict to have the accused declared a *"dangerous mentally disordered accused"*. The same criteria and procedures which are used under the dangerous offender provisions of the *Criminal Code* will apply. On a finding by the court that an accused is a dangerous mentally disordered accused, it may increase the cap in respect of the offence to a maximum of life.

Similarly there is a transitional provision which allows for the appointment of a commissioner, who will be selected from the superior court judiciary, to whom applications will be made by the Crown to have accused who have been Lieutenant-Governor's warrant patients on designated offences, declared dangerous mentally disordered accused. On a successful application, an order may be obtained to extend the capping period for that individual accused to a maximum of life.

The proclamation of capping was intended to take place approximately one year after the other provisions had been proclaimed; however, that process has been delayed to allow the provinces to review and amend their mental-health legislation to accommodate the committal of dangerous accused. The transitional process to deal with Lieutenant-Governor's warrant patients who would be subject to release on the proclamation of capping, has not commenced as yet.

### 3. Pre-Verdict Provisions

### (1) Section 16 — Not Criminally Responsible (NCR)

Section 16 of the *Criminal Code* dealing with the defence of insanity has been repealed (see S.C. 1991, c. 43, s. 2) and the following has been substituted for it:

16(1) No person is criminally responsible for an act committed or an omission made while suffering from a mental disorder that rendered the person incapable of appreciating the nature and quality of the act or omission or of knowing that it was wrong.

(2) Every person is presumed not to suffer from a mental disorder so as to be exempt from criminal responsibility by virtue of subsection (1), until the contrary is proved on the balance of probabilities.

(3) The burden of proof that an accused was suffering from a mental disorder so as to be exempt from criminal liability is on the party that raises the issue.

There has been little change to s. 16 other than to replace the notion of insanity with that of mental disorder. Section 2 of the Code now sets out a definition of "mental disorder", which is defined to be "a disease of the mind". Previously, "insanity" had been equated with the concept of "disease of the mind", and as one can see from the definition of mental disorder, the concept of disease of the mind is still an essential element of s. 16. The difference between "insanity" and "mental disorder" is a distinction without a difference because all of the jurisprudence that has evolved from the phrase "disease of the mind" has been incorporated through the definition of "mental disorder". In any event, the Supreme Court in *R. v. Cooper* (1980), 51 C.C.C. (2d) 129, 13 C.R. (3d) 97, [1980] 1 S.C.R. 1149, indicated that a disease of the mind embraces any illness, disorder, or abnormal condition which impairs the human mind and its functioning, excluding, however, self-induced states caused by alcohol or drugs; as well as transitory mental states such as hysteria or concussion.

Aside from updating the terminology in s. 16, the two branches which may lead to the defence of "not guilty by reason of insanity" (NGRI), now "not criminally responsible on account of mental disorder" (NCR), remain the same. In order to meet the test of the first branch, the person must have a mental disorder, the result of which renders him incapable of appreciating the nature or quality of the act. The second branch or route to the defence is that the accused, who suffers from the mental disorder, must establish on a balance of probabilities, as with the first branch, that he is incapable of knowing that the act or omission was wrong. The second branch has presented the most recent and interesting development through a series of cases from the Supreme Court of Canada, *R. v. Chaulk and Morrissette* (1990), 62 C.C.C. (3d) 193, 2 C.R. (4th) 1, [1990] 3 S.C.R. 1303; *R. v. Ratti* (1991), 62 C.C.C. (3d) 105, 2 C.R. (4th) 293, [1991] 1 S.C.R. 68; *R. v. Landry* (1991), 62 C.C.C. (3d) 117, 2 C.R. (4th) 268, [1991] 1 S.C.R. 99; and *R. v. Rromeo* (1991), 62 C.C.C. (3d) 1, 2 C.R. (4th) 307, [1991] 1 S.C.R. 86. . . .

Now the issue is whether the accused is incapable of knowing either that the act is "morally wrong" by the standards of society or that it was legally wrong. Having extended the second branch to include a moral wrong, there was some consternation that it would open the door again to the amoral offenders, specifically psychopaths, who had been denied access to the insanity defence when the test was simply whether they knew that what they did was legally wrong. However, in *R. v. Chaulk and Morrissette, supra*, at pp 232-3 C.C.C., Lamer C.J.C., for the majority, stated that this change to the definition would not result in an opening of the floodgates to the insanity defence:

> An interpretation of s. 16(2) that makes the defence available to an accused who knew that he or she was committing a crime but was unable to comprehend that the act was a moral wrong will not open the floodgates to amoral offenders or to offenders who relieve themselves of all moral considerations. First, the incapacity to make moral judgements must be causally linked to a disease of the mind; if the presence of a serious mental disorder is not established, criminal responsibility cannot be avoided. Secondly, as was pointed out by Dixon J. in Schwartz, *supra*, ' "moral wrong' is not to be judged by the personal standards of the offender but by his awareness that society regards the act as wrong" (p. 13). The accused will not benefit from substituting his own moral code for that of society. Instead, he will be protected by s. 16(2) if he is incapable of understanding that the act is wrong according to the ordinary moral standards of reasonable members of society.

While a personality disorder or psychopathic personality is capable of constituting a disease of the mind according to *Cooper, supra* and *R. v. Simpson* (1977), 35 C.C.C. (2d) 337, 77 D.L.R. (3d) 507, 16 O.R. (2d) 129 (C.A., and *R. v. Kjeldsen* (1981), 64 C.C.C. (2d) 161, 28 C.R. (3d) 81, [1981] 2 S.C.R. 617, the defence of insanity is not made out where the accused understands the nature, character and consequences of his act, but merely lacks appropriate feelings for the victim, remorse or guilt, even though the lack of feeling stems from the disease of the mind.

Due to the confusion arising from the phrase "not guilty" contained in the former s. 16 in reference to someone found not guilty by reason of insanity, s. 672.34 of the new provisions indicates that if a person qualifies for the defence of being not criminally responsible on account of a mental disorder, the court shall render a verdict that the accused committed the act which constitutes the offence. This section is significant because there has to be formal finding of the *actus reus* of the offence, whereas in the past if the accused qualified for the defence of not guilty by reason of insanity, there was little attention paid to the offence charged and the offence proven because the consequences were the same regardless. In the instance of homicide, it made little difference whether the verdict was not guilty by reason of insanity for murder or manslaughter; however, when and if capping is proclaimed, it will make a marked difference as to how long the mentally disordered accused may be subject to dispositions by a review board.

## (2) Assessments

Section 672.12 permits the accused, the prosecution or the judge to initiate applications for assessment orders. The purposes for which the orders may be made are stated in s. 672.11.

> 672.11. A court having jurisdiction over an accused in respect of an offence may order an assessment of the mental condition of the accused, if it has reasonable grounds to believe that such evidence is necessary to determine:
>
> (a) whether the accused is unfit to stand trial;
> (b) whether the accused was, at the time of the commission of the alleged offence, suffering from a mental disorder so as to be exempt from criminal responsibility by virtue of subsection 16(1);
> (c) whether the balance of the mind of the accused was disturbed at the time of the commission of the alleged offence, where the accused is a female person charged with an offence rising out of the death of her newly born child;
> (d) The appropriate disposition to be made, where a verdict of not criminally responsible on account of mental disorder or unfit to stand trial has been rendered in respect of the accused; or
> (e) whether an order should be made under subsection 736.11(1) to detain the accused in a treatment facility, where the accused has been convicted of an offence. . . .

In terms of assessments which are ordered to determine if an accused comes within s. 16 of the *Criminal Code*, the Crown's application will not be granted unless the accused has first put his mental capacity for criminal intent into issue, or the court is satisfied that there are reasonable grounds to doubt that the accused was criminally responsible at the time of the offence. Section 672.12(3) should be read with the direction in mind of the Supreme Court of Canada in *R. v. Swain, supra*, to the effect that the Crown cannot lead evidence of an accused's insanity on its own motion, but only where the accused puts his mental capacity for criminal intent in issue, or at the end of the case after the accused has put forth his defence, other than in s. 16, and he would otherwise be found guilty. . . .

### (c) Protected statements

In recognition of an accused's right to remain silent, s. 672.21 directs that statements made during the course of these assessments are to be admissible only for the purpose for which they were ordered:

(a) at a hearing to determine fitness
(b) to determine what disposition to impose following a verdict of unfitness or not criminally responsible;
(c) whether the accused is a dangerous mentally disordered accused;
(d) to determine whether infanticide applies:
(e) at trial, to determine if the accused is criminally responsible, or if the accused raises mental disorder, automatism, or he puts his mental capacity for intent into issue, or if the prosecution raises a post-verdict s. 16.

The general rule as stated in s. 672.21(2) is that statements made by the accused during assessments are not admissible in evidence, without the consent of that accused unless it is for one of the above-noted purposes. . . .

### (3) Fitness: Determining the Issue

The definition of the phrase "unfit to stand trial" is now set out in s. 2 of the Code:

"Unfit to stand trial" means unable on account of mental disorder to conduct a defence at any stage of the proceedings before a verdict is rendered or to instruct counsel to do so, and, in particular, unable on account of mental disorder to:

  (*a*)  understand the nature or object of the proceedings,
  (*b*)  understand the possible consequences of the proceedings, or
  (*c*)  communicate with counsel.

Pursuant to s. 672.22 an accused is presumed fit to stand trial unless the court is satisfied on the "balance of probabilities" that the accused is unfit to stand trial. The onus, or burden of proof, is on the party, either accused or prosecutor, who makes the application to establish that the accused is unfit to stand trial. According to s. 672.24 when the court has reasonable grounds to believe that an accused is unfit to stand trial, and the accused is not represented by counsel, the court shall order that the accused be represented by counsel. . . .

In *Taylor*, the Ontario Court of Appeal indicated that the underlying rationale for the fitness rules is that an accused must have sufficient mental fitness to participate in the proceedings in a meaningful way "in order to ensure that the process of determining guilt is as accurate as possible, that he accused can participate in the proceedings or assist counsel in his or her defence, that the dignity of the trial process is maintained, and that, if necessary, the determination of a fit sentence is made possible". The appropriate test to determine whether an accused is fit, by the enumerated statutory criteria, is whether he has the *cognitive capacity*, rather than an *analytic capacity* to comprehend. The analytic capacity test establishes too high a threshold for fitness by requiring that the accused be capable of making rational decisions beneficial to himself: whereas the cognitive capacity test only requires that the accused understand the nature and object of the proceedings and the consequences. It is not necessary that he be able to act in his own best interests because to require him to do so, would derogate from the fundamental principle that an accused is entitled to choose and present his own defence. . . .

## 4. Post-Verdict Provisions

Under the new legislative regime the duty of the court does not necessarily stop with the rendering of a verdict of not criminally responsible on account of mental disorder or that the accused is unfit to stand trial, but rather the court as well as the review board have been empowered to participate in the "disposition" of the accused. "Court" by definition includes a summary conviction court as defined in s. 785, a judge, a justice and a judge of the Court of Appeal.

### (1) The Initial Disposition

Section 672.45 under the new legislative scheme grants an option to the courts to conduct the initial disposition, that is the disposition immediately following the court having found the accused either unfit to stand trial on account of mental disorder or not criminally responsible on account of a mental disorder.

> 672.45(1) Where a verdict of not criminally responsible on account of mental disorder or unfit to stand trial is rendered in respect of an accused, the court *may* of its own motion, and *shall* on application of the accused or the prosecutor, hold a disposition hearing.
>
> (2) At a disposition hearing, the court *shall* make a disposition in respect of the accused, *if* it is satisfied that it can readily do so and that a disposition should be made without delay. [Emphasis added.] . . .

The new regime further provides that if the court decides not to make an initial disposition, the review board must do so by virtue of s. 672.47 within 45 days following the finding of unfitness or that the accused is not criminally responsible. If the court does not render an initial disposition, any release process or detention order made by the court will continue in force pursuant to s. 672.46(1) unless cause is shown to the court why the release or detention order should be vacated. By virtue of s. 672.46(2), the court may also vary a detention order to direct that the accused be kept in the custody of a hospital, pending the initial review by the review board. Practice and experience thus far has shown that very few courts conduct initial disposition hearings but rather have taken to remanding the accused to an appropriate psychiatric hospital pending the initial disposition by the review board.

One of the significant deficiencies of the legislation is an omission to provide the review board with authority to order assessments. Whether or not the court renders the initial disposition, it should order an assessment pending the review board hearing, with a direction that the report is to be made available to the review board. In that way, the review board will have the best available evidence at its disposal as to the present state of mind of the accused at the time of the hearing and disposition.

## (2) Dispositions

In order to render a disposition, the court (and it should be noted the task of the review board is identical), shall take into account the following factors:

> 672.54 Where a court or Review Board makes a disposition pursuant to subsection 672.45(2) or section 672.47, it shall, taking into consideration the need to protect the public from dangerous persons, the mental condition of the accused, the reintegration of the accused into society and the other needs of the accused, make one of the following dispositions that is the *least onerous and least restrictive to the accused*:
>
> > (a) where a verdict of not criminally responsible on account of mental disorder has been rendered in respect of the accused, and in the opinion of the court or Review Board, the accused is not a significant threat to the safety of the public, by order, direct the accused be discharged absolutely;
> >
> > (b) by order, direct that the accused be discharged subject to such conditions as the court or Review Board considers appropriate; or
> >
> > (c) by order, direct that the accused be detained in custody in a hospital, subject to such conditions as the court or Review Board considers appropriate.

The overriding consideration as expressed in the preamble to s. 672.54 is that the disposition to be made must be "the least onerous and the least restrictive to the accused". To render a disposition, the court or review board must consider the following factors:

(1) the need to protect the public from dangerous persons;
(2) the mental condition of the accused;
(3) the reintegration of the accused into society, and
(4) the other needs of the accused.

After consideration of those factors, the court or review board may:

(1) grant an absolute discharge to a not criminally responsible accused who is not a "significant threat to the safety of the public";
(2) discharge the not criminally responsible or unfit accused subject to conditions; or
(3) detain the accused in the custody of a hospital.

The ultimate purpose of the statutory scheme is to protect the public from dangerous persons. The focus of the inquiry under this provision is by necessity as to the dangerousness of the accused and the risk that he presents to the public consequent to his mental condition. The process requires that a predictive and subjective appraisal be applied at each hearing in order to determine the level of security required, if any, leading to a disposition which is in the result the least onerous and least restrictive to the accused. The factors instanced in s. 672.54 are components of the objective to rehabilitate the accused in furtherance of the ultimate purpose which is to protect the safety of the public. . . .

### (3) Disposition Hearings

Disposition hearings conducted by the court or review board may be held in as an informal manner as is appropriate in the circumstances (s. 672.5(2)).

Section 672(5) envisions an open hearing process. The media, victims, and any others will have a right of access to the hearings. However, an exclusion of the public may be made under s. 672.5(6) when it is in the best interest of the accused and not contrary to the public interest. There shall be a publication ban pursuant to s. 672.51(11) *only* if disposition information has been withheld from the accused or any other person not a party because disclosure would seriously prejudice the accused, or there has been an order under s. 672.5(10)(*b*) removing the accused from the hearing because failure to do so would likely endanger the life or safety of another person or impair the treatment and recovery of the accused. . . .

### (5) Dealing With the Unfit

Once the issue has been tried and there has been a finding by the court that an accused is unfit, then the court may, pursuant to s. 672,45, render the initial disposition or, in turn, it may be left to the review board to render a disposition within 45 days of the finding pursuant to s. 672.47(1). As noted above, the court must hold a disposition hearing on an application of the accused or the prosecutor, however, the court shall make a disposition only if it is satisfied that: (1) it can readily do so; and (2) that a disposition should be made *without delay*. . . .

### (6) Reviews

In addition to the power of the review board to make an initial disposition which has already been dealt with above, s. 672.81(1) provides that the review board shall hold a hearing no later than 12 months after making a disposition and every 12 months thereafter for as long as the disposition remains in force in order to review any disposition that it has made in respect of an accused other than an absolute discharge. There is a further mandatory review pursuant to subsec. (2), where the person in charge of a hospital has increased the restrictions on the liberty of the accused significantly for a period exceeding seven days. Such an increase may arise where an accused, who is permitted to reside in the community, is removed therefrom, or placed in a circumstance of greater security, due to a deterioration of his mental condition and increase in the dangerousness that he presents.

Discretionary reviews may be held by the review board *at any time* pursuant to s. 672.82(1) at the request of the accused or any other party. . . .

## R. v. Worth
### (1995), 98 C.C.C. (3d) 133 (Ont. C.A)

Appeal by the accused from his conviction for second degree murder and from the period of parole ineligibility.

BY THE COURT: — After a trial in February and March, 1990, before Osborne J. and a jury, the appellant was found guilty of second degree murder and sentenced to life imprisonment without eligibility for parole for 23 years. The victim was a 12-year-old girl. The defence virtually conceded that the appellant killed the young girl. Indeed, when the appellant was arrested he had the child's dismembered head in a bag in his car. The principal issue for the jury was whether the appellant had established the defence of mental disorder within s. 16 of the *Criminal Code*. The Crown and the defence led expert psychiatric evidence on this issue. The appellant did not testify.

The appellant appealed against both his conviction and the period of parole ineligibility.

A. *The conviction appeal*

The appellant made six submissions on his conviction appeal.

. . .

(ii) The trial judge misdirected the jury by telling them that "wrong" in s. 16(1) of the *Code* meant only "legally wrong". In support of this ground of appeal, the appellant applied to introduce fresh evidence on the question whether the appellant knew that his act was "morally wrong".

(iii) The trial judge erred in instructing the jury that they could infer from the appellant's refusal to see a Crown psychiatrist that the appellant's s. 16 defence would not withstand scrutiny. . . .

(2) *Instruction on mental disorder*

The trial judge instructed the jury that on the second branch of the mental disorder test in s. 16 "wrong" meant "legally wrong". That was the law in February, 1990, when this case was tried: see *Schwartz v. The Queen* (1976), 29 C.C.C. (2d) 1, 67 D.L.R. (3d) 716, [1977] 1 S.C.R. 673. In December, 1990, however, in *R. v. Chaulk* (1990), 62 C.C.C. (3d) 193, [1990] 3 S.C.R. 1303, 2 C.R. (4th) 1, the Supreme Court of Canada held that the defence of mental disorder is available if an accused proves on the balance of probabilities that he is suffering from a disease of the mind that renders him incapable of knowing that his act was legally or morally wrong.

There was no evidence at trial to support a finding that the appellant did not know his actions were morally wrong. The appellant therefore concedes that on the trial record the trial judge's "misdirection" on the meaning of the word "wrong" did not amount to reversible error. He submits, however, that when the evidence at trial is considered with the fresh evidence, then he is entitled to a new trial. The appellant's fresh evidence consisted of an affidavit of Dr. Graham Glancy, a psychiatrist. In response, the Crown filed an affidavit of Dr. Andrew Malcolm, one of the psychiatrists who testified for the Crown at trial. Both psychiatrists were cross-examined on their affidavits. We reviewed this material in considering the appellant's fresh evidence application.

Both counsel accepted that the principles in *Palmer v. The Queen* (1979), 50 C.C.C. (2d) 193, [1980] 1 S.C.R. 759, 14 C.R. (3d) 22, governed the appellant's application to admit fresh evidence under s. 683(1) of the *Code*. The issue on this appeal is whether the fresh evidence meets the last of the four tests in *Palmer*: "the evidence must be such that, if it is believed, it could reasonably, when taken with the other evidence adduced at trial, be expected to have affected the result".

Dr. Glancy did not interview the appellant; instead, he relied on the diagnosis of those who had. He accepted that the appellant suffers from an antisocial personality disorder (in other words he is a "psychopath"). In *R. v. Oommen* (1994), 81 C.C.C.(3d) 8, [1994] 2 S.C.R. 507, 30 C.R. (4th) 195, McLachlin J. wrote at p. 19:

> Finally, it should be noted that we are not here concerned with the psychopath or the person who follows a personal and deviant code of right and wrong. . . . This is different from the psychopath or person following a deviant moral code. Such a person is capable of knowing that his or her acts are wrong in the eyes of society, and despite such knowledge, chooses to commit them.

Dr. Glancy, however, indicated that recent research in psychopathy suggests that psychopaths may suffer from a mental deficit that goes beyond not caring whether their acts are viewed as wrong by society, and that includes not knowing what is morally wrong. But his opinion of the appellant was guarded. He had not doubt that when the appellant killed the deceased, he knew his actions were legally wrong. On the crucial question whether the appellant knew his actions were morally wrong, Dr. Glancy stated in his affidavit that it is possible that at the time of the killing the appellant knew that his actions would be condemned by the majority of society as morally wrong; and that it is also possible the appellant was so lacking in moral sense due to psychopathy that when he killed the deceased he may not have known, "in the fullest sense", that his actions were morally wrong. He confirmed this opinion on cross-examination as the following exchange demonstrates:

> Q. So in terms of the bottom line of your opinion, it is possible that he knew it was morally wrong and it is possible that he did not and it is not clear one way or the other?
> A. That's correct. This is also a difficult issue. It is reasonable that the Court of Appeal decide that. I can only from a psychiatrist point of view, from the evidence I have read, try and put this into some sort of coherent argument from a psychiatrist point of view
>
> . . . . .
>
> Q. I take it that when you — before I ask you that, let me go back to where I started. So I take it, your opinion remains the same that it is possible that he knew that killing was morally wrong and also possible that he didn't?
> A. Yes.

At its highest, therefore, Dr. Glancy's opinion suggests only that it is possible, not probable, that when the appellant killed the deceased he may not have known that his actions were morally wrong. Since the appellant must prove the defence of mental disorder on the balance of probabilities, Dr. Glancy's opinion, even if accepted in the face of the substantial contrary evidence, could not reasonably have affected the result. In our view, it provides no additional weight to the evidence the jury heard. The fresh evidence therefore does not meet the fourth requirement for admissibility in *Palmer*. This motion to introduce fresh evidence is dismissed and accordingly this ground of appeal fails.

## (3) *The appellant's refusal to see a Crown psychiatrist*

In his charge to the jury, the trial judge commented on the defence's refusal to permit the Crown psychiatrist to interview and assess the appellant as follows:

> All doctors seem to me to agree that it is an advantage to have spoken to the accused about this general issue of the state of his mind, and that the Crown psychiatrists were denied that opportunity.
>
> .....
>
> Finally, on the insanity issue, you heard that the accused, through counsel, did not agree to be examined by the Crown psychiatrists or psychiatrist. That is the accused's right. Let there be no doubt about that. As a matter of law, however, this refusal is a fact from which you may, — not "must" but "may", infer that the accused's defence of insanity, that is his section 16 defence, would not withstand scrutiny. This is one among a number of facts which can be considered when you are discussing and considering the insanity issue.
>
> .....
>
> In dealing with the Crown not being given access to a psychiatric medical examination of the accused, Mr. Frost [defence counsel] asked you to consider that the accused was, through counsel, simply exercising his rights.

The trial judges's comments were consistent with this court's judgment in *R. v. Sweeney* (1977), 35 C.C.C. (2d) 245, 76 D.L.R. (3d) 211, 40 C.R.N.S. 37. The appellant submits, however, that by instructing the jury that they may draw an adverse inference from his refusal to be examined by the Crown psychiatrist, the trial judge infringed the appellant's right to remain silent guaranteed by s. 7 of the *Canadian Charter of Rights and Freedoms*.

We do not agree with this submission. In *R. v. Chaulk, supra*, in discussing the application of s. 1 of the Charter to s. 16 of the *Code*, Lamer C.J.C. referred to the difficulties the Crown faces in obtaining a conclusive psychiatric opinion of an accused's sanity at the time of the offence in cases in which the accused raises the defence of mental disorder. Having put his sanity in issue, we do not think the appellant could preclude the jury from drawing an adverse inference from his refusal to speak to the Crown psychiatrist. An accused's right to silence is not absolute. It is protected in the terms of s. 7, that is, an accused cannot be deprived of his right to silence except in accordance with the principles of fundamental justice. Since the appellant put his sanity in issue and had the burden of proving his mental disorder, we do not think that the trial judges's comments contravened the principles of fundamental justice. . . .

*Appeal dismissed.*

## 7.4.3 Intoxication

### Introduction

Issues of unconscious compulsion and irrationality are also played out within the context of the intoxication defence. While similar to the defence of mental disorder and to heat of passion, the issues are different enough in intoxication to warrant a separate analysis. Compared to mental disorder, intoxication is also of more practical importance to criminal and public law because typically half of all personal violence and property offenders are drug-impaired (usually with alcohol) and because the theories underlying intoxication's legal treatment are manifest publicly in narcotics legislation that has spawned a near-war on illicit drug users and dealers.

Legal commentators accept that drug impairment can negate intent, cause involuntary action, turn off consciousness, induce frenzy and produce temporary insanity (Goode, 1984; Orchard, 1977; Lynch, 1982; Stannard, 1982; Mackay, 1982. Stuart (1987:363) claims that the "mind of a severely intoxicated person may well be physiologically indistinguishable from a mind impaired as a result of severe mental disorder." Higher English courts have determined that intoxication can negate intent *Beard* (1920), and cause the intoxicant to act puppet-like "under the complete mastery of drink or drugs" (*Majewski* (1976)). Also in *Majewski*, Lord Simon assumed that criminal violence could result from drugs having "obliterated the capacity of the perpetrator to know what he was doing or what were its consequences" (p. 152). Both the doctrinal analysis and the cases themselves concerning intoxication are populated by odd, mythical creatures: "blind drunks" who can aim pistols, "dead drunks" who move openly among the living, intoxicated "automatons" who perform complex tasks and "mad drunks" who somehow always have a method to their madness.

A leading school of thought on drug impairment and crime can be fairly represented by a short and implausible fantasy tale in the tradition of phenomenologist Colin Wilson's *The Mind Parasites* (1968) or Robert Heinlein's *The Puppet Masters* (1955) in which slug-like aliens rob decent Americans of their "free will". Richard Condon's *The Manchurian Candidate* (1957) also provides an excellent model because its surrealistic tale of brain washing and unconscious killing combined two of the era's potent fantasies. Our story begins when one day some innocent people in South America come upon an alien substance that has fallen to earth in a meteor shower. The substance, which can assume plant form, contains a persona. Like some genie-in-a-pill, this ethereal substance entices people to take it by making them temporarily happy but meanwhile it gradually substitutes its will, personality and knowledge for that of its consumer. When people take enough of it, they truly become different characters under the control of another personality. Unfortunately for the alien persona, the effect is short-lived and the human will is reasserted after the dark night of the soul has passed. Now if the substituted persona were enlightened and altruistic and by replacing all humans saved Earth from ecological disaster, there would not be much of a story. So, of course, the alien persona is bad and commits murder and sabotage. When such crimes occur who is responsible? If the users are innocent, the evil substance is responsible. Recognizing the threat, a benevolent alliance of American and Soviet military forces eventually launches an attack against the substance and drives it from the planet, although not before much of the Colombian and Peruvian Andes lie in ruin

If people, however, know about the evil, alien substance and its role in driving humans to act criminally then different legal outcomes are possible. A person who slips the substance into an innocent victim's orange juice would be fully liable as an aider, abettor or procurer. The apparent perpetrator would be entirely innocent; her position being equivalent to a person knocked unconscious or tied in a chair and physically forced to grip the gun and pull the trigger. Next, we must consider the case of the foolish person who likes the euphoric effect of the evil substance so much that he knowingly takes enough to let the alien persona temporarily gain control. When the alien thing completes its usual nasty business and retreats from conscious control should we hold the user responsible? Legally, the answer should be yes since the user, though not intending the crime, knew of its almost certain likelihood and recklessly took the substance anyway. Finally, there is the person who wants to commit a murder but is too anxious: fear of discovery, of counter attack or of legal penalties saps his criminal initiative. If he takes the substance in order for the evil alien to commit the act, he is fully liable since his position parallels the husband who hires someone to kill his wife.

Though this fairy tale of humans taken over by an evil bio-chemical persona is fantastic, like Stevenson's *Dr. Jekyll and Mr. Hyde*, it actually corresponds with current legal thinking about drugs and it neatly reproduces the basic variations on the intoxication doctrine. First, it is well established legally that innocent or unknowing drug takers are not responsible for the ensuing offence allegedly "caused" by the drug. However, some legal authorities state flatly that cases of involuntary drug use causing crimes are completely non-existent (Hall, 1960:539). An exception may be the Ontario case of *King* (1962) where the accused was acquitted of impaired driving after receiving sodium pentothal at the dentist's. King, however, was warned beforehand and told not to drive (he denied this) and when he left the dentist he said that he was not driving so the case was probably wrongly decided on the facts. (See Chapter 6.1.2.)

On the second point, concerning recklessness, Lord Elywn-Jones held in *Majewski* that in allowing himself "to get drunk, and thereby putting himself in such a condition as to be no longer amenable to the law's commands, a man shows such regardlessness as amounts to mens rea for purpose of all ordinary crimes" (p. 475). The English Court of Appeal held in *Bailey* (1983) that as a matter of "common knowledge", excessive use of "alcohol and drugs" is so likely to cause dangerous behaviour, that such excessive use constitutes recklessness, a form of legal intent. Further in *Hardie*, (1985), the same court determined that the use of "dangerous drugs" raises a conclusive presumption of recklessness. In fact, the probability of a given person committing a violent act following intoxication is remote. Finally, courts have long held that people who imbibe with the aim of aiding the commission of an offence are fully liable.

The fairy tale of alien or demonic drug possession also reproduces accurately the anti-drug propaganda that for more than a century has warned that certain substances including alcohol, cocaine, heroin, PCP and the like, could transform ordinary people into maniacs bent on rape, murder and mayhem. Though laughable in some respects, the mentality that produced the anti-drug propaganda film "Reefer Madness" has been singularly successful in influencing mass opinion. In the mid-1800s, establishment figures begin to discover that the sorry state of industrial employees was due not to unjust laws or exploitive employers but to alcohol abuse. Medical investigations followed and many European psychiatrists, along with social Darwinists, adopted the model of alcohol-induced degeneration and applied it to antisocial and insane behaviour (Vogt, 1984). Authorities claimed that since industrial wage earners could not limit their drinking, they had to be controlled and "detoxified". More specifically, leading figures like W.B. Carpenter, a physiologist and avid teetotaller, argued that alcohol turned drinkers into uninhibited automatons (Smith, 1981). Alcohol-induced degeneration fit in nicely with the prevailing physiological determinism that attributed insanity to disordered nerves. Physiological nerve disorders, according to Maudsley, deadened the "moral sense" and led to sudden, overwhelming impulses whereby "homicidal mania", like a twitch, resulted from dysfunctional reflex actions (*ibid.*, 50-52; Bynum, 1984). Politically, this medical theory translated into pronouncements by American governors in 1900 that "three-fourths of the crime in the personal violence class are the result of a mind made mad by intoxication" (Ladouceur & Temple, 1985:270). Later the U.S. Narcotics Bureau made equally specious charges about hashish, opium and marijuana turning ordinary people into degenerate zombies bent on crime. H.J. Anslinger, commissioner of the Bureau for 33 years was still arguing in 1970 that marijuana use degraded moral capacity, signified incipient insanity and caused such abnormal violence that it took five police officers to subdue a "pot head". This last assertion is an imaginative embellishment on the evil, alien substance myth — one can distinguish genuine people from those taken over by the alien persona because the possessed, like vampires and werewolves, have superhuman strength. Recently PCP was without justification linked to violence and the latest target appears to be cocaine (Zetner, 1984). Illicit drug dangers are systematically exaggerated by government agencies and repeated by compliant judges. Most people now believe that heroin is incredibly harmful and enticing despite scientific reports that the drug is neither very dangerous nor especially euphoric (Grinspoon & Hedblom, 1975; Rosenberg, 1974; Goode, 1984).

Drugs are also seen as a threat because their addictiveness supposedly locks people into compulsive, unconscious behaviour. Alcoholism is popularly regarded as a disease because alcoholics are somehow infected with an irresistible desire to drink; they can never learn to use the drug moderately. The invention of alcoholism, however, was a political rather than a medical accomplishment (Wiseman, 1985; Levine, 1978; Poikolainen, 1982). The U.S. Supreme Court has tentatively rejected the theory of compelled alcohol use in *Powell* (1968). Slavery metaphors are frequently employed to describe drug addicts who, despite conscious resolutions to quit their habits, are supposedly powerless in the face of deep-seated drives (Kaplan, 1983). Especially in the case of illicit drugs like heroin or cocaine, the habituation process is regarded as pathological and incredibly compelling. One popular report recently stated that, "By definition, people addicted to cocaine are out of control. They are probably on or over the edge of ruin" (*Time*, April 11, 1983). The parallels to mental illness are striking. Both behavioural groups (drug takers and mentally ill) are stigmatized as dangerous and out of control; both are subject to a host of restrictive and discriminatory laws affecting employment, housing, immigration and civil rights; both are given compulsory treatment and both are granted a superficial leniency in terms of criminal liability. Removing persons from full criminal liability, as women traditionally were, is always part of a broader scheme that denies them autonomy and civil rights. It is not merciful or positive as many participants in the criminal law system assume.

Despite its reputation as a "devil drug" luring users into its evil clutches, most users of heroin are not strongly habituated. Many opiate users are dabblers, and even committed users often abstain voluntarily, consciously regulate their quantity and frequency of use and quit entirely, on average, after about ten years (Peele, 1985; Hughes & Brewin, 1979: Zetner, 1979: Lauderdale & Inverarity, 1984). Heroin withdrawal's much proclaimed agonies apparently result for the most part from cultural expectations and, objectively, are comparable to the discomforts of a bad flu (Grinspoon & Bakalar, 1984). Users of heroin and nicotine claim that nicotine is more difficult to quit, yet 30 million Americans have quit using tobacco and 95% of them quit without medical or professional assistance (Peele, 1985).

Both mental illness and drug use are frequently linked with violence. A central prohibitionist assertion is that cocaine, cannabis, morphine, alcohol and other nonmedically sanctioned drugs cause increased aggression by short-circuiting the self-conscious mind and releasing the pentup emotions of the unconscious (Wisotsky, 1986). If intoxication does amplify aggression, logically the law should increase criminal penalties against drug-impaired offenders on grounds that their drug use renders them more dangerous, just as carrying a firearm renders an offender more dangerous. But a review of the drug-violence literature finds that simple cause and effect theories about drugs and aggression have been abandoned (Myers, 1982; Wilson & Herrnstein, 1985). Drug effects on aggression are ambiguous: some people use alcohol to dampen hostility and persons already aggressive may become more or less aggressive on alcohol (Siann, 1985; Zillman, 1979). Most drugs, including those currently outlawed, have little apparent effect on aggression (Goldstein, 1985; Virkkunen, 1974). Drugs may facilitate crime, however, by tranquillizing would-be offenders whose fears and anxieties are impeding their resolve (Dengerink, 1976). Researchers now frequently note the importance of users' expectations where alcohol-related misbehaviour occurs to a large extent because drinkers entertain an illusion of irresponsibility or correctly calculate the exculpatory power of alcohol (Lange, *et al.*, 1975; Brian, 1986; Pihl, *et al.*, 1984). One research group provides a representative comment to the effect that our culture "established and maintains beliefs that alcohol increases the probability of aggressive behaviour. Independent of any pharmacological effect of alcohol, these experiences may underlie the observed increase in aggressive responses" (Cherak, *et al.*, 1985). Survey investigations reveal that people generally expect alcohol use to amplify their social assertiveness (Brown, *et al.*, 1980). Overall, the available evidence supports the expectancy thesis whereby people learn that normally inappropriate behaviour will often be tolerated when it occurs along with alcoholic intoxication.

The attribution of serious violence to alcohol use offers a convenient case study of questionable research method. Most crime-alcohol studies confuse correlation with causation and thus feel their task is complete when it is shown that a large portion of offenders took alcohol before committing their crime. A recent study of fights and marital assault avoided this mistake. A pattern of excessive alcohol use related strongly to fighting and marital conflict but the same strong connection did not exist for the amount of alcohol consumed. The researches explain this result by noting that chronic alcohol abusers are the type of person more likely to be violent and that the violence would continue without the alcohol (Leonard, et al,, 1985). Similarly, a study of impaired drivers found five personality groups which, holding alcohol intake constant, accounted for the differences in behaviour. The group having the most violations and accidents ranked highest on measures of hostility, resentment and sensation seeking. The second worst group ranked high on measures of depression, resentment and and being controlled by others. In both groups of aggressive personality drinkers, individuals tended to blame external elements, like alcohol, for their behaviour (Wilson & Herrnstein, 1985:360). This conscious strategy of shifting blame outside oneself is likely to be exacerbated by legal doctrines and psychological theories that permit intoxication to operated as an excuse.

Apart from the aggression issue, medical witnesses also testify that intoxication causes accused to act without knowledge or awareness of what they are doing so that they lack the necessary mens rea. *Reninger v. Feogossa* (1552), the earliest English intoxication case, spoke of a defendant being so drunk that "he had no understanding nor memory", and there is a long line of authority for the proposition that intoxication could take away a person's "wits" or render them non compos mentis (Singh, 1933). But the "blind drunk" thesis is not supported by the evidence. In controlled studies, impaired subjects demonstrated no significant deprivations concerning knowledge of identity, recognition or orientation in place or time (Hutchinson; *et al.*, 1964). Legal commentators agree that it is almost always a fiction to say intoxicated defendants did not know what they were doing (Morse, 1984; Gerber, 1975). In what was for many years the leading article on intoxication, Hall (1944:1062) recognized that the "harms committed by inebriates reveal not wild, disorganized, aimless motor activity but conduct well adapted to attain specific goals."

What alcohol and other sedatives can impair is memory. Alcohol-induced memory defects are common, they can occur at the dosage level of "social drinking" and they take a specific form where past history and immediate events can be recalled but short-term call back is impaired (Loftus & Loftus, 1976; Hutchinson, 1964). The type of anterograde amnesia induced by drugs involves incapacity to retain recent experiences but there is no loss in general intelligence or sense of identity. Chronic alcohol abuse may result in more serious defects as in Korsakoff's syndrome where memory storage vaults are permanent. Korsakoff sufferers understand causal relations and are capable of intelligent judgment but besides their memory problems their conduct is noteworthy for its lack of initiative (Talland, 1970:76). It is interesting to speculate on the possible relationship between memory and initiative. Perhaps loss of short-term memory makes self-conscious planning an impossibility since both continuity and feed-back are lost. If true, the passive Korsakoff cases may in some manner represent what humans would be like without conscious direction. On a similar note, Bywater (1982:616) observes that the consequence of drug-induced mental aberration is typically one of no activity rather than aberrant activity".

Since memory defects can occur at moderate dosage levels, memory loss does not by itself indicate extreme intoxication as courts sometimes assume. An Ontario Court of Appeal accepted medical opinion in *Bray* (1975) that the defendant was too drug-impaired to be aware he was driving a motor vehicle although the evidence only indicted that Bray had no memory of driving. (Bray was a police officer). Confusing memory defect with lack of intent and knowledge at the time of the offence is responsible for the ancient notion that intoxication can negate mens rea.

The correct legal approach to memory loss was taken in *Broadhurst* (1964), where Lord Devlin held that "subsequent loss of memory does not mean that the accused may not have had clear intent at the time of the act" (p 116).

Intoxication is also alleged to be a cause of automatic, involuntary acts: in *Szymusiak* (1972), a psychiatrist testified that after an evening of heavy drinking, the defendant acted involuntarily and irrationally in challenging, then shooting an apparent stranger. The shooting was described by the psychiatrist as purposeless and random, like a twitch. Earlier on similar facts in *Martin* (1947), the trial judge reasoned that the accused was in "a state of intoxication out of which the act arose without the consciousness of the accused . . . the complainant was an entire stranger to the accused. so that there can be no reason in the world for his wishing to injure him" (p. 318). Here, the judge established lack of motive by mere assertion and on that flimsy platform found the intoxicated accused to be without consciousness. As a final example, in *Bouchard* (1973) a police officer was acquitted of impaired driving after a physician testified that Bouchard's subconscious "took over control from the conscious mind" and caused him to lie about his occupation, refuse the breathalyzer and fight with police. Perhaps such behaviour by a police officer automatically establishes that he must have been so far out of character as to have lost all self-conscious control.

Finally, as with insanity, the more insightful analysts of intoxication have moved the emphasis from intent to "appreciation". Hall felt that the intoxicated were only partially responsible because they acted without "ethical sensitivity" and did not full understand the consequences of their conduct (Hall, 1944:1078). Hall admitted this test "closely resembles insanity" which was the result he desired since Hall was an uncritical booster of Freudian psychiatry, accepted alcoholism as a disease and further believed that excessive drinking was "symptomatic of serious mental disease" (p. 1073). Early American insanity cases usually involved serious intoxication or "dipsomania", and in an 1819 case it was held that intoxication made it more likely that a killing was done in "sudden heat" rather than being premeditated, so that the three pleas tend to fade into one another (Hovenkamp, 1981). In other words, a typical offender will be intoxicated, will kill in the heat of passion, and will be found to have some mental disorder (at least sociopathy) affecting his "appreciation" of the crime.

Chief Justice Dickson's dissent in *Leary* (1978), which was expanded upon in *Bernard* (1989), explained that the rule holding intoxication capable of negating specific intent "was conceived in response to humanitarian urgings which sought to distinguish between the homicide committed in coldblood by a sober person and one committed by a drunken person" (pp. 39-40). While much admired for rejecting the general-specific intent distinction and the other illogical oddities of the *Beard* rules, Dickson's approach matches Hall's in being psychologically unreasonable. The "cold-blooded" killer metaphor with its reptilian connotations is both physiologically and psychologically wrong since all humans are warm blooded and since reptiles are not particularly "evil". The distinction also requires a coherent argument as to why sober, well-reasoned acts deserve greater punishment than intoxicated, more impulsive acts. Is an impulsive killer not more of a danger than a person who kills once for a calculated reason? Perhaps the impulsive offender is much easier to apprehend since he has failed to take precautions or plan the "perfect crime" and is therefore less of a threat than the careful offender who strives, like Professor Moriarty, to avoid detection. These distinctions, however, are not moral ones since they merely relate to the issue of deterrence. Furthermore, judges seem to take an opposite position when they leniently sentence careful, sober and fraudulent stock brokers as compared to careless, intoxicated convenience store robbers. Judges perhaps assume that careful thieves are less likely than impulsive thieves to cause more damage than necessary.

Finally, both Dickson and Hall want to tie intoxication's mitigating effect to a universal result of drug use, namely some type of diminished capacity. Surveys of convicted criminals indicate that a large portion took alcohol prior to their crime for the express purpose of diminishing their capacity to be afraid of the consequences of their act. If fear of other people, fear of shame, fear of law and fear of being hurt are important factors in producing civilized behaviour, and if tranquillizing drugs like alcohol help relieve these fears, it seem rather odd to allow a criminogenic factor to serve as an excuse.

The case which is reproduced below, the Supreme Court decision in *Daviault*, gives a history and explanation of the defence of intoxication, and proceeds to expand the defence in the area of "extreme intoxication". As a result of this decision, the law in the area was fundamentally changed — at least until Parliament passed new legislation — when the court held for the first time that in the "rarest of cases" the defence of intoxication or extreme drunkenness could be advanced by persons charged with general intent offences. The person's state of drunkenness must be so extreme that the accused resembles an automaton or someone with a disease of the mind as defined by section 16 of the Code. Several acquittals based on a defence of "extreme intoxication" followed this decision and several interest groups, including women's and victims' groups, along with members of the public pressured the government to change the law. Parliament acted with unusual speed and passed section 33.1 of the Code in June, 1995; the new section purports to remove this defence for general intent offences. The issue now is whether the section will withstand Charter scrutiny.

## R. v. Daviault
(1994), 93 C.C.C. (3d) 21 (S.C.C.)

Appeal by the accused from a judgment of the Quebec Court of Appeal, 80 C.C.C. (3d) 175, 19 C.R. (4th) 291, [1993] R.J.Q. 692, 54 Q.A.C. 27, 20 W.C.B. (2d) 345, allowing an appeal by the Crown from the accused's acquittal by Grenier Q.C.J., [1991] R.J.Q. 1794, on a charge of sexual assault.

SOPINKA (dissenting):

*Facts*

The facts which give rise to this appeal are not in dispute. The complainant is a 65-year-old woman who is partially paralysed and, thus, confined to a wheelchair. She knew the appellant through his wife, who was the complainant's dressmaker and ran errands for her. The complainant testified that at approximately 6:00 p.m. on May 30, 1989, at her request, the appellant arrived at her home carrying a 40-oz. bottle of brandy. The complainant drank part of a glass of brandy and then fell asleep in her wheelchair. When she woke during the night to go to the bathroom, the appellant appeared, grabbed her chair, wheeled her into the bedroom, threw her on the bed and sexually assaulted her. The appellant left the apartment at about 4:00 a.m. The complainant subsequently discovered that the bottle of brandy was empty. The trial judge found as a fact that the appellant had drunk the rest of the bottle between 6:00 p.m. and 3:00 a.m.

The appellant was chronic alcoholic. He testified that he had spent the day at a bar where he had consumed seven or eight bottles of beer. He recalled having a glass of brandy upon his arrival at the complainant's residence but had no recollection of what occurred between then and when he awoke nude in the complainant's bed. He denied sexually assaulting her.

The defence called a pharmacologist, Louis Léonard to testify as an expert witness. Mr. Léonard testified that the appellant's alcoholic history made him less susceptible to the effects of alcohol. He hypothesized that, if the appellant had consumed seven or eight beers during the day and then 35 oz. of brandy on the evening in question, his blood-alcohol content would have been between 400 mg. and 600 mg. per 100 ml. of blood. That blood-alcohol ratio would cause death or coma in an ordinary person. Mr. Léonard testified that an individual with this level of alcohol in his blood might suffer an episode of "l"amnésie-automatisme", also known as a "blackout". In such a state the individual loses contact with reality and the brain is temporarily dissociated from normal functioning. The individual has no awareness of his actions when he is in such a state and will likely have no memory of them the next day.

Mr. Léonard further testified that it is difficult to distinguish between a person in a blackout and someone who is simply acting under the influence of alcohol. He stated that if a person acting under the influence of alcohol behaves in a manner which requires cognitive functions or reflection, it is unlikely that the person is in a blackout. On the other hand, if the person departs from his normal behaviour to act in a gratuitous or violent manner, it is more likely that he is in a blackout.

The appellant was charged with one count of sexual assault. The trial judge found as a fact that the appellant had committed the offence as described by the complainant. However, he acquitted the appellant because he had a reasonable doubt about whether the appellant, by virtue of his extreme intoxication, had possessed the minimal intent necessary to commit the offence of sexual assault: [1991] R.J.Q. 1794. The Quebec Court of Appeal overturned this ruling: 80 C.C.C. (3d) 175, 19 C.R. (4th)291, [1993] R.J.Q. 692, 54 Q.A.C. 27. The appellant now appeals to this court as of right, pursuant to s. 691(2)(*a*) of the *Criminal Code*, R.S.C. 1985, c. C-46. . . .

CORY J.: —

*Issue*

Can a state of drunkenness which is so extreme that an accused is in a condition that closely resembles automatism or a disease of the mind as defined in s. 16 of the *Criminal Code*, R.S.C. 1985, c. C-46, constitute a basis for defending a crime which requires not a specific but only a general intent? That is the troubling question that is raised on this appeal.

The facts of this case and the judgments below are set out in the reasons of Justice Sopinka. Although I agree with my colleague on a number of issues, I cannot agree with his conclusion that it is consistent with the principles of fundamental justice and the presumption of innocence for the courts to eliminate the mental element in crimes of general intent. Nor do I agree that self-induced intoxication is a sufficiently blameworthy state of mind to justify culpability, and to substitute it for the mental element that is an essential requirement of those crimes. In my opinion, the principles embodied in our *Canadian Charter of Rights and Freedoms*, and more specifically in ss. 7 and 11(*d*), mandate a limited exception to, or some flexibility in, the application of the *Leary* rule. This would permit evidence of extreme intoxication akin to automatism or insanity to be considered in determining whether the accused possessed the minimal mental element required for crimes of general intent.

*Analysis*

As this case involves the reconsideration of a common law principle in light of more recent developments in the principles of criminal law and particularly the enactment of the Charter, it may be useful to begin with a brief review of the historical developments of the relevant criminal law concepts. As well, it will be helpful to outline the various options adopted and suggested with respect to intoxication as a factor in determining whether an accused possessed the mental element required by the crime.

*The physical and mental aspects of criminal acts*

Originally a crime was considered to be the commission of a physical act which was specifically prohibited by law. It was the act itself which was the sole element of the crime. If it was established that the act was committed by the accused then a finding of guilt would ensue. However, as early as the 12th century, in large part through the influence of the canon law it was established that there must also be a mental element combined with the prohibited act to constitute a crime. That is to say that the accused must have *meant* or intended to commit the prohibited act. The physical act and the mental element which together constitute a crime came to be known as the *actus reus* denoting the act, and the *mens rea* for the mental element. Like so many maxims they are imprecise and in many instances misleading.

For my purposes, it is sufficient to say that for a great many years it has been understood that, unless the legislator provides otherwise, a crime must consist of the following elements. First a physical element which consists of committing a prohibited act, creating a prohibited state of affairs, or omitting to do that which is required by the law. Secondly, the conduct in question must be willed, this is usually referred to as voluntariness. Some writers classify this element as part of the *actus reus*, others prefer to associate it with the *mens rea*: however, all seem to agree that it is required: see, generally J.C. Smith and B. Hogan, *Criminal Law*, 7th ed. (1992), at pp. 37ff. . . .

With this concept of a crime established it soon came to be accepted that in certain situations a person who committed a prohibited physical act still could not be found guilty. A number of examples come to mind. For instance, if a person in a state of automatism as a result of a blow on the head committed a prohibited act that he was not consciously aware of committing, he could not be found guilty since the mental element involved in committing a willed voluntary act and the mental element of intending to commit the act were absent. Thus, neither the requisite *actus reus* or *mens rea* for the offence was present. . . .

A review of the history of the defence of intoxication shows that, originally, intoxication was never a defence to any crime. However, with the evolution of criminal law, this rule came to be progressively relaxed and the defence of intoxication was admitted for crimes of specific intent. Although one of the justifications for this was the courts' preoccupation with the harshness of criminal liability and criminal sanctions, clearly this development was also influenced by the development of the requirements for mental elements in crimes. The defence of intoxication was based on the recognition and belief that alcohol affected mental processes and the formulation of intention: see, for example D. McCord, "The English and American History of Voluntary Intoxication to Negate *Mens Rea*", 11 J. Legal Hist. 372 at p. 378 (1990). I would agree with the authors who feel that the progressive expansion of the intoxication defence has paralleled the progressive expansion of theories of the mental elements of crimes: see, for example, T. Quigley, "A Shorn Beard", 10:3 Dalhousie L.J. 167 (1987). In my view, the need for this historical expansion is justified and emphasized by the increased concern for the protection of fundamental rights enshrined in the Charter.

It can thus be seen that with the development of principles recognizing constituent elements of crimes, particularly the need for a mental element, there came the realization that persons who lack the requisite mental element for a crime should not be found guilty of committing that crime. For centuries it has been recognized that both the physical and the mental elements are an integral part of a criminal act. It has long been a fundamental concept of our criminal law.

This appeal is concerned with situations of intoxication that are so extreme that they are akin to automatism. Such a state would render an accused incapable of either performing a willed act or of forming the minimal intent required for a general intent offence. I will approach the issue primarily on the basis that the extreme intoxication renders an accused incapable of forming the requisite minimum intent.

. . .

*Categorization of crimes as requiring either a specific intent or a general intent . . .*

The distinction between crimes of specific and general intent has been acknowledged and approved by this court on numerous occasions. . . .

The categorization of crimes as being either specific or general intent offences and the consequences that flow from that categorization are now well established in this court. . . .

It may have been convenient to review the approach that courts have taken with regard to drunkenness as a factor in considering the mental element in crimes of general intent.

*Drunkenness as a factor in the consideration of criminal liability.*

The issue has been the subject of many judicial decisions in commonwealth countries. It is useful here to contrast the two opposite positions which have emerged in the absence of Charter considerations. The first position is illustrated by the decision of this court in *Leary, supra*, and also corresponds to the English position. The second position is that which prevails in Australia and New Zealand. It is best illustrated by *R. v. O'Connor* (1980), 4 A. Crim. R. 348.

*Leary v. The Queen*

Leary was charged with rape. In the course of his instructions, the trial judge advised the jury that "drunkenness is no defence to a charge of this sort". This position was taken on the grounds that rape was a crime of general intent and that in such a crime, the mental element could not be negated by drunkenness. The majority in this court confirmed that rape was, indeed, a crime of general intent and that the *mens rea* could not be affected by drunkenness. They relied upon *Director of Public Prosecutions v Majewski*, [1977] A.C. 443. There, the House of Lords held that, unless the offence was one which required proof of a specific intent, it was no defence to a criminal charge that, by reason of self-induced intoxication, the accused did not intend to do the act which constituted the offence. A charge to the jury to that effect was approved.

The minority (Dickson J., with Laskin C.J.C. and Spence J. concurring) would have required that the jury be satisfied that the accused knew the victim was not consenting or was reckless as to whether she was or not. On that issue it was said that drunkenness was an element that the jury could properly take into account in resolving the question. It was their position that drunkenness should be left to the jury, along with all the other relevant evidence, in deciding whether the accused knew the victim was not consenting.

The supporters of the *Leary* decision are of the view that self-induced intoxication should not be used as a means of avoiding criminal liability for offences requiring only a general intent. They contend that society simply cannot afford to take a different position since intoxication would always be the basis for a defence despite the fact that the accused had consumed alcohol with the knowledge of its possible aggravating effects. Supporters of the *Leary* decision argue that to permit such a defence would "open the floodgates" for the presentation of frivolous and unmeritorious defences.

Those who oppose the decision contend that it punishes an accused for being drunk by illogically imputing to him liability for a crime committed when he was drunk. Further, it is said that the effect of that decision is to deny an accused person the ability to negate his very awareness of committing the prohibited physical acts. That is to say the accused might, as a result of his drinking, be in a state similar to automatism and, thus, completely unaware of his actions, yet he would be unable to put this forward as a factor for the jury to consider because his condition arose from his drinking. In such cases, the accused's intention to drink is substituted for the intention to commit the prohibited act. This result is said to be fundamentally unfair. Further, it is argued that the floodgates argument should not have been accepted because juries would not acquit unless there was clear evidence that the drunkenness was of such a severity that they had a reasonable doubt as to whether the accused was even aware that he had committed the prohibited act: see, for example, Mewett and Manning, *Criminal Law*, 2nd ed. (1985), at pp. 214-5.

*The O'Connor case — A position taken contrary to Leary*

*O'Connor, supra*, is a decision of the High Court of Australia. O'Connor was seen removing a map holder and a knife from a car. A police officer saw him, identified himself and asked O'Connor why he had taken the articles. O'Connor ran away with the officer in pursuit. When he was arrested, O'Connor stabbed the officer with the knife. He was charged with theft of the map holder and knife and wounding with intent to inflict grievous bodily harm. O'Connor testified that he had consumed alcohol and car sickness tablets before these events and stated that he had no memory either of taking anything from the car or of his subsequent arrest. Medical evidence was given that the combined effect of the tablets and alcohol could have produced such a state of intoxication that O'Connor would have been incapable of reasoning or forming an intent to steal or wound. The trial judge directed the jury, in accordance with *Majewski, supra*, that evidence of self-induced intoxication, although relevant in determining whether the accused had acted with the intent to steal or to inflict grievous bodily harm, was not relevant with respect to the included alternative offence of unlawful and malicious wounding. O'Connor was acquitted on the charges of theft and wounding with intent and convicted of the included offence of unlawful wounding.

O'Connor appealed the conviction to a court of criminal appeal which declined to follow *Majewski, supra*, and quashed the conviction. The Attorney-General for Victoria then appealed to the High Court.

There, the majority upheld the decision of the Court of Appeal. They concluded that for all offences requiring proof of a mental element, evidence of intoxication, whether self-induced or not, was relevant and admissible in determining whether the requisite mental element was present. The majority went on to observe that evidence of intoxication which merely tends to establish loss of inhibition or weakening of the capacity for self-control would not provide a basis for denying that the mental element of an offence was present. However, where there was evidence that the accused was unconscious or that his mind was a blank through drunkenness at the time of the offence, this should be left to the jury in resolving the question as to whether there had been a voluntary act on the part of the accused. . . .

Following the decision of this court in *Leary*, important changes have occurred in the evolution of criminal law principles. Many of these changes were prompted by the enactment of the Canadian Charter of Human Rights and Freedoms. It must now be seen whether, as a result of the passage of the Charter or the reasoning in subsequent cases of this court, some modification of the rule established by *Leary* is required.

*Passage of the Charter and subsequent cases of this court*

The passage of the Charter makes it necessary to consider whether the decision in *Leary* contravenes ss. 7 or 11(*d*) of the Charter. Those sections provide:

> 7. Everyone has the right to life, liberty and security of the person and the right not to be deprived thereof except in accordance with the principles of fundamental justice.
>
> . . . . .
>
> 11. Any person charged with an offence has the right
>
> . . . . .
>
> (*d*) to be presumed innocent until proven guilty according to law in a fair and public hearing by an independent and impartial tribunal;

There have been some statements by this court which indicate that one aspect of the decision in *Leary* does infringe these provisions of the Charter. The first occurred in *R. v. Bernard, supra*. Bernard was charged with sexual assault causing bodily harm. He was tried by judge and jury and found guilty. Bernard admitted forcing the complainant to have sexual intercourse with him but stated that his drunkenness caused him to attack her. The issue was whether self-induced intoxication should be considered by the jury along with all the other relevant evidence in determining whether the prosecution had proved beyond a reasonable doubt the *men rea* required by the offence. Bernard's appeal was dismissed by a majority of the court. They all agreed that, as the defence of intoxication had not been made out on the evidence, s. 613(1)(*b*)(iii) (now s. 686(1)(*b*)(iii)) of the *Criminal Code* could be applied. Four sets of reasons were given. . . .

Wilson, J. (L'Heureux-Dubé J. concurring), agreed with the conclusion reached by McIntyre and Beetz JJ. However, she advocated a modification of the rule set out in *Leary*. Her reasoning proceeds in this way. Sexual assault causing bodily harm is an offence of general intent which requires only a minimal intent to apply force. Ordinarily the Crown can establish the requisite mental state by means of the inferences to be drawn from the actions of the accused. Wilson J. found that the *Leary* rule was perfectly consistent with an onus resting upon the Crown to prove the minimal intent which should accompany the doing of the prohibited act in general intent offences, but she would have applied it in a more flexible form. In her view, evidence of intoxication could properly go before a jury in general intent offences if it demonstrated such extreme intoxication that there was an absence of awareness which was akin to a state of insanity or automatism. Only in such cases would she find that the evidence was capable of raising a reasonable doubt as to the existence of the minimal intent required for a general intent offence. Wilson J. put forward her position in this way at pp. 41-2:

> I believe that the *Leary* rule is perfectly consistent with an onus resting on the Crown to prove the minimal intent which should accompany the doing of the prohibited act in general intent offences. *I view it as preferable to preserve the Leary rule in its more flexible form as Pigeon J. applied it, i.e., so as to allow evidence of intoxication to go to the trier of fact in general intent offences only if it is evidence of extreme intoxication involving an absence of awareness akin to a state of insanity or automatism. Only in such a case is the evidence capable of raising a reasonable doubt as to the existence of the minimal intent required for the offence.* I would not overrule *Leary*, as the Chief Justice would, and allow the evidence of intoxication to go to the trier of fact in every case regardless of its possible relevance to the issue of the existence of the minimal intent required for the offence.

(Emphasis added.)

She also noted that she had some real concerns about the validity of the use of self-induced intoxication as a substituted form of *mens rea* under the Charter. More specifically, she thought it would be unlikely that proof of the substituted element would lead inexorably to a conclusion that the minimum intent existed at the time of the commission of the criminal act. . . .

## The alternative options

What options are available with regard to the admissibility and significance or evidence of drunkenness as it may pertain to the mental element in general intent offences? One choice would be to continue to apply the *Leary* rule. Yet, as I will attempt to demonstrate in the next section, the rule violates the Charter and cannot be justified. Thus, this choice is unacceptable.

Another route would be to follow the *O'Connor* decision. Evidence relating to drunkenness would then go to the jury along with all other relevant evidence in determining whether the mental element requirement had been met. It is this path that is enthusiastically recommended by the majority of writers in the field. Yet it cannot be followed. It is now well established by this court that there are two categories of offences. Those requiring a specific intent and others which will call for nothing more than a general intent. To follow *O'Connor* would mean that all evidence of intoxication of any degree would always go to the jury in general intent offences. This, in my view, is unnecessary. Further, in *Bernard, supra*, the majority of this court rejected this approach.

A third alternative, which I find compelling, is that proposed by Wilson J. in *Bernard*. I will examine the justifications for adopting this position in more detail shortly, but before doing that it may be helpful to review the nature of the Charter violations occasioned by a rigid application of the *Leary* rule.

### How the Leary rule violates ss. 7 and 11(d) of the Charter

What then is the rule of law established by the decision in *Leary*? The conclusion of the majority in that case establishes that, even in a situation where the level of intoxication reached by the accused is sufficient to raise a reasonable doubt as to his capacity to form the minimal mental element required for a general intent offence for which he is being tried, he still cannot be acquitted. In such a situation, self-induced intoxication is substituted for the mental element of the crime. The result of the decision in *Leary* applied to this case, is that the intentional act of the accused to voluntarily become intoxicated is substituted for the intention to commit the sexual assault or for the recklessness of the accused with regard to the assault. This is a true substitution of *mens rea*. First, it would be rare that the events transpiring from the consumption of alcohol through to the commission of the crime could be seen as one continuous series of events or as a single transaction. Secondly, the requisite mental element or *mens rea* cannot necessarily be inferred from the physical act or *actus reus* when the very voluntariness or consciousness of that act may be put in question by the extreme intoxication of the accused.

It has not been established that there is such a connection between the consumption of alcohol and the crime of assault that it can be said that drinking leads inevitably to the assault. Experience may suggest that alcohol makes it easier for violence to occur by diminishing the sense of what is acceptable behaviour. However, studies indicate that it is not in itself a cause of violence: see "Interim Report of the Commission of Inquiry into the Non-Medical Use of Drugs", c. 3; "The LeDain Interim Report", referred to by S.H. Berner, in "Intoxication and Criminal Responsibility", Law Reform Commission (1975); Law Commission, Great Britain, "Intoxication and Criminal Liability", Consultation Paper No. 127 at pp. 4, 67 (1993); see also the references and additional information given in notes 14, 15, 16 and 18 at p. 4; C.N. Mitchell, "The Intoxicated Offender — Refuting the Legal and Medical Myths", Int. J.L. & Psychiatry 77 at p. 89 (1988); S.S. Covington, "Alcohol and Family Violence", Paper presented at the 34th International Congress on Alcoholism and Drug Dependence, August 4-10, 1985, Calgary, Alta, Canada, at p. 24; L. Wolff and B. Reingold, "Drug Use and Crime", 14:6 Juristat 1 at pp. 5-8 and 13 (1994), and Saskatchewan Alcohol and Drug Abuse Commission, "Legal Offences in Saskatchewan: The Alcohol and Drug Connection", Research Report (February, 1989). . . .

In my view, the strict application of the *Leary* rule offends both ss. 7 and 11(*d*) of the Charter for a number of reasons. The mental aspect of an offence, or *mens rea*, has long been recognized as an integral part of crime. The concept is fundamental to our criminal law. That element may be minimal in general intent offences; none the less, it exists. In this case, the requisite mental element is simply an intention to commit the sexual assault or recklessness as to whether the actions will constitute an assault. The necessary mental element can ordinarily be inferred from the proof that the assault was committed by the accused. However, the substituted *mens rea* of an intention to become drunk cannot establish the *mens rea* to commit the assault. . . .

The consumption of alcohol simply cannot lead inexorably to the conclusion that the accused possessed the requisite mental element to commit a sexual assault, or any other crime. Rather the substituted *mens rea* rule has the effect of eliminating the minimal mental element required for sexual assault. Furthermore, *mens rea* for a crime is so well-recognized that to eliminate that mental element, an integral part of the crime, would be to deprive an accused of fundamental justice. . . .

It was argued by the respondent that the "blameworthy" nature of voluntary intoxication is such that it should be determined that there can be no violation of the Charter if the *Leary* approach is adopted. I cannot accept that contention. Voluntary intoxication is not yet a crime. Further, it is difficult to conclude that such behaviour should always constitute a fault to which criminal sanctions should apply. However, assuming that voluntary intoxication is reprehensible, it does not follow that its consequences in any given situation are either voluntary or predictable. Studies demonstrate that the consumption of alcohol is not the cause of the crime. A person intending to drink cannot be said to be intending to commit a sexual assault.

Further, self-induced intoxication cannot supply the necessary link between the minimal mental element or *mens rea* required for the offence and the *actus reus*. This must follow from reasoning in *R. v. DeSousa* (1992), 76 C.C.C. (3d) 124, 95 D.L.R. (4th) 595, [1992] 2 S.C.R. 944 (S.C.C.), and *R. v. Théroux, supra*. Here, the question is not whether there is some symmetry between the physical act and the mental element but whether the necessary link exists between the minimal mental element and the prohibited act; that is to say that the mental element is one of intention with respect to the *actus reus* of the crime charged. . . .

In summary, I am of the view that to deny that even a very minimal mental element is required for sexual assault offends the Charter in a manner that is so drastic and so contrary to the principles of fundamental justice that it cannot be justified under s. 1 of the Charter. The experience of other jurisdictions which have completely abandoned the *Leary* rule, coupled with the fact that under the proposed approach, the defence would be available only in the rarest of cases, demonstrate that there is no urgent policy or pressing objective which need to be addressed. Studies on the relationship between intoxication and crime do not establish any rational link. Finally, as the *Leary* rule applies to all crimes of general intent, it cannot be said to be well tailored to address a particular objective and it would not meet either the proportionality or the minimum impairment requirements.

What then should be the fate of the *Leary* rule?

*Approach that should be taken when a common law principle is found to infringe the provisions of the Charter.*

In *R. v. Swain* (1991), 63 C.C.C. (3d) 481, [1991] 1 S.C.R. 933, 5 C.R. (4th) 253 (S.C.C.), Lamer C.J.C. (concurred in by Sopinka J. and myself), wrote on this issue. At p. 510, he stated:

> Before turning to s. 1, however, I wish to point out that because this appeal involves a Charter challenge to a common law, judge-made rule, the Charter analysis involves somewhat different considerations than would apply to a challenge to a legislative provision. For example, having found that the existing common law rule limits an accused's rights under s. 7 of the Charter, it may not be strictly necessary to go on to consider the application of s. 1. Having come to the conclusion that the common law rule enunciated by the Ontario Court of Appeal limits an accused's right to liberty in a manner which does not accord with the principles of fundamental justice, it could, in my view, be appropriate to consider at this stage whether an alternative common law rule could be fashioned which would not be contrary to the principles of fundamental justice.

> If a new common law rule could be enunciated which would not interfere with an accused person's right to have control over the conduct of his or her defence, I can see no conceptual problem with the court's simply enunciating such a rule to take the place of the old rule, without considering whether the old rule could none the less be upheld under s. 1 of the Charter. Given that the common law rule was fashioned by judges and not by Parliament or a legislature, judicial deference to elected bodies is not an issue. If it is possible to reformulate a common law rule so that it will not conflict with the principles of fundamental justice, such a reformation should be undertaken.

This then is the approach that should be adopted when a common law principle is found to infringe the Charter. This, again, militates in favour of the adoption of a flexible application of the *Leary* rule, as was suggested by Wilson J.

*Justifications for the adoption of the flexible approach suggested by Wilson J.*

As I have said, the position adopted by Wilson J. in *Bernard* has much to commend it and should be adopted. Indeed, the original case which is the basis for much of our jurisprudence pertaining to intoxication seems to confirm this position. In *Director of Public Prosecutions v. Beard*, [1920], A.C. 479, Lord Birkenhead set out the three propositions which have been so frequently referred to in cases involving intoxication and criminal behaviour, at pp. 500-2:

> 1. That insanity, whether produced by drunkenness or otherwise, is a defence to the crime charged. The distinction between the defence of insanity in the true sense caused by excessive drinking, and the defence of drunkenness which produces a condition such that the drunken man's mind becomes incapable of forming a specific intention, has been preserved throughout the cases. The insane person cannot be convicted of a crime . . . but, upon a verdict of insanity, is ordered to be detained during His Majesty's pleasure. The law takes no note of the cause of the insanity. If actual insanity in fact supervenes, as the result of alcoholic excess, it furnishes as complete an answer to a criminal charge as insanity induced by any other cause.

> . . . . .

> 2. That evidence of drunkenness which renders the accused incapable of forming the specific intent essential to constitute the crime should be taken into consideration with the other facts proved in order to determine whether or not he had this intent.

> 3. *That evidence of drunkenness falling short of a proved incapacity in the accused to form the intent necessary to constitute the crime, and merely establishing that his mind was affected by drink*

*so that he more readily gave way to some violent passion, does not rebut the presumption that a man intends the natural consequences of his acts.*

(Emphasis added.)

It does not appear to me that the decision was meant to create a complete bar to the defence of intoxication in the context of crimes of general intent. . . .

Further support for the modification of the *Leary* rule in favour of the more flexible rule suggested by Wilson J. comes from the fact that the decision in *Majewski, supra*, which was relied upon by the majority in *Leary*, has been the subject of severe criticism in the United Kingdom. The following extract from the Law Commission's "Intoxication and Criminal Liability", *supra*, at p. 34 is an example:

> The present law is therefore objectionable on three levels, It is very complicated and difficult to explain, to the extent that it is difficult to think that it operates in practice other than by its detailed rules being substantially ignored; it purports to apply a clear social policy, of ensuring that intoxicated people who commit criminal acts do not escape criminal sanctions, but only does so in an erratic and unprincipled way; and if taken seriously it creates many difficulties of practical application. It is therefore understandable that in other jurisdictions, and under the rational scrutiny of law reformers, other solutions have been sought to the problem of protecting society from those who commit criminal acts when in a state of intoxication.

Perhaps the result in these cases arose from the understandable desire to ensure that the accused persons should not escape criminal responsibility by the consumption of alcohol. . . .

Far more writers have supported the approach advocated by Dickson J. in *Leary*, and adopted in *O'Connor*. In my view, the most vehement and cogent criticism of both *Majewski* and *Leary* is that they substitute proof of drunkenness for proof of the requisite mental element. The authors deplore the division of crimes into those requiring a specific intent and those which mandate no more than a general intent. They are also critical of the resulting presumption of recklessness, and of the loss of a requirement of a true *mens rea* for the offence. They would prefer an approach that would permit evidence of drunkenness to go to the jury together with all the other relevant evidence in determining whether the requisite *mens rea* had been established. . . .

I find further support for adopting the approach suggested by Wilson J. in studies pertaining to the effect of the *O'Connor* and *Kamipeli* decisions which have been undertaken in Australia and New Zealand: reference to these studies can be found in the English Law Commission's "Intoxication and Criminal Liability", *supra*, at pp. 60-3. One of these studies was conducted in New South Wales, by means of a survey of approximately 510 trials: see Judge G. Smith, "Footnote to O'Connor's Case", *supra*. The author, Judge George Smith, concluded, at p. 277, that:

> Those figures disclose that a "defence" of intoxication which could not have been relied upon pre-*O'Connor* was raised in eleven cases or 2.16 per cent of the total. Acquittals followed in three cases or 0.59 per cent of the total, but only in one case or 0.2 per cent of the total could it be said with any certainty that the issue of intoxication was the factor which brought about the acquittal.

. . . . .

> It seems to me that no one with any experience of the criminal courts should be greatly surprised at this result for the simple practical reason that any "defence" of drunkenness poses enormous difficulties in the conduct of a case. To name but one, if the accused has sufficient recollection to

describe relevant events, juries will be reluctant to believe that he acted involuntarily or without intent whereas, if he claims to have no recollection, he will be unable to make any effective denial of facts alleged by the Crown.

. . . . .

Certainly my inquiries would indicate that the decision in *O'Connor's* case, far from opening any floodgates has at most permitted an occasional drip to escape from the tap.

That study clearly indicates that the *O'Connor* decision has not had an effect of any significance on trials or on the number of acquittals arising from evidence of severe intoxication. . . .

It is obvious that it will only be on rare occasions that evidence of such an extreme state of intoxication can be advanced and perhaps only on still rarer occasions is it likely to be successful. None the less, the adoption of this alternative would avoid infringement of the Charter.

I would add that it is always open to Parliament to fashion a remedy which would make it a crime to commit a prohibited act while drunk.

The appellant in this case is an elderly alcoholic. It is difficult if not impossible to present him in a sympathetic light. Yet any rule on intoxication must apply to all accused, including the young and inexperience drinker. The strict rule in *Leary* is not a minor or technical infringement but a substantial breach of the Charter eliminating the mental elements of crimes of general intent in situations where the accused is in an extreme state of intoxication. I would think that this judge-made rule should be applied flexibly, as suggested by Wilson J., so as to comply with the Charter. Such an approach would mean that except in those rare situations where the degree of intoxication is so severe it is akin to automatism that drunkenness will not be a defence to crimes of general intent.

It should not be forgotten that if the flexible "Wilson" approach is taken, the defence will only be put forward in those rare circumstances of extreme intoxication. Since that state must be shown to be akin to automatism or insanity, I would suggest that the accused should be called upon to establish it on the balance of probabilities. This court has recognized, in *R. v. Chaulk* (1990), 62 C.C.C. (3d) 193, [1990] 3 S.C.R. 1303, 2 C.R. (4th) 1 (S.C.C.), that although it constituted a violation of the accused's rights under s. 11(*d*) of the Charter, such a burden could be justified under s. 1. In this case, I feel that the burden can be justified. Drunkenness of the extreme degree required in order for it to become relevant will only occur on rare occasions. It is only the accused who can give evidence as to the amount of alcohol consumed and its effect upon him. Expert evidence would be required to confirm that the accused was probably in a state akin to automatism or insanity as a result of his drinking. . . .

Thus, it is appropriate to place an evidentiary and legal burden on the accused to establish, on a balance of probabilities, that he was in a state of extreme intoxication that was akin to automatism or insanity at the time he committed the offence.

*Result if the mental element relates solely to the actus reus which requires that the prohibited act be performed voluntarily*

Should it be thought that the mental element involved relates to the *actus reus* rather than the *mens rea* then the result must be the same. The *actus reus* requires that the prohibited criminal act be performed voluntarily as a willed act. A person in a state of automatism cannot perform a voluntary willed act since the automatism has deprived the person of the ability to carry out such an act. It follows that someone in an extreme state of intoxication akin to automatism must also be deprived of that ability. Thus, a fundamental aspect of the *actus reus* of the criminal act is absent. It would equally infringe s. 7 of the Charter if an accused who was not acting voluntarily could be convicted of a criminal offence. Here again the voluntary act of becoming intoxicated cannot be substituted for the voluntary action involved in sexual assault. To do so would violate the principle set out in *Vaillancourt, supra*. Once again to convict in the face of such a fundamental denial of natural justice could not be justified under s. 1 of the Charter.

*Summary of proposed remedy*

In my view, the Charter could be complied with, in crimes requiring only a general intent, if the accused were permitted to establish that, at the time of the offence, he was in a state of extreme intoxication akin to automatism or insanity. Just as in a situation where it is sought to establish a state of insanity, the accused must bear the burden of establishing, on the balance of probabilities, that he was in that extreme state of intoxication. This will undoubtedly require the testimony of an expert. Obviously, it will be a rare situation where an accused is able to establish such an extreme degree of intoxication. Yet, permitting such a procedure would mean that a defence would remain open that, due to the extreme degree of intoxication, the minimal mental element required by a general intent offence had not been established. To permit this rare and limited defence in general intent offences is required so that the common law principles of intoxication can comply with the Charter.

In light of the experience in Australia or New Zealand, it cannot be said that to permit such a defence would open the floodgates to allow every accused who had a drink before committing the prohibited act to raise the defence of drunkenness. As observed earlier, studies made in Australia and New Zealand indicate that there has not been any significant increase in the number of acquittals following the *O'Connor* and *Kemipeli* decisions.

*Disposition*

In the result, I would allow the appeal, set aside the order of the Court of Appeal [80 C.C.C. (3d) 175, 19 C.R. (4th) 291, [1993] R.J.Q. 692] and direct a new trial.

*Appeal allowed; new trial ordered.*

**[Note:**
The Criminal Code was amended in June, 1995, to negate the effect of the *Daviault* case as follows:

**Section 33**
The *Criminal Code* is amended by adding the following after section 33 (1995, c. 32, s.1):

## SELF-INDUCED INTOXICATION

33.1(1) It is not a defence to an offence referred to in subsection (3) that the accused, by reason of self-induced intoxication, lacked the general intent or the voluntariness required to commit the offence, where the accused departed markedly from the standard of care as described in subsection (2).

(2) For the purposes of this section, a person departs markedly from the standard of reasonable care generally recognized in Canadian society and is thereby criminally at fault where the person, while in a state of self-induced intoxication that renders the person unaware of, or incapable of consciously controlling, their behaviour, voluntarily or involuntarily interferes or threatens to interfere with the bodily integrity of another person.

(3) This section applies in respect of an offence under this Act or any other Act of Parliament that includes as an element an assault or any other interference or threat of interference by a person with the bodily integrity of another person.]

## 7.4.4 Automatism

**Introduction**

Since criminal acts or omissions must be voluntary, any involuntary act such as an epileptic spasm during a seizure cannot satisfy the first requirement and thus a full acquittal results. The automatism defence is uncontroversial where the actor is unconscious in the sense of being unaware at the time of movement, context and consequences. There is also little debate about laws which hold people responsible for their automatic behaviour when it is plainly foreseeable and dangerous. In *Shaw* (1938), an epileptic was charged and convicted for driving a vehicle on a public highway knowing his high risk of becoming unconscious. The difficulties arise with automatism where "unconsciousness" is confused with memory loss or with lack of self-consciousness and where psychiatric witnesses claim that dissociative disorders are equivalent in legal effect to unconscious reflex actions.

Sleepwalking is a classic instance where defective memory is elevated into full-blown unconsciousness. Standard criminal texts accept that a somnambulist is "unconscious" (Mewett & Manning, 1994:493). In *Fain* (1879), sleepwalking was accepted as a "species of mental unsoundness", a state in which people are "unconscious, though they seem to be awake" (p. 183). Fain fell asleep in the lobby of a Kentucky hotel and when wakened mistook the bell hop for an enemy and shot the unfortunate messenger boy. On its face, the case turns on a mistake of fact. If Fain honestly believed his life was in danger, the gunplay was legally justified and no reason exists for raising issues of unconsciousness. Arguably, a liberal mistake of fact defence is all that is required to handle such cases. (Fain would still be liable in tort for wrongful killing.) Courts, unfortunately, go much further and by equating sleepwalking with unconscious or involuntary behaviour, judges excuse acts, like killing a spouse, that look very much like ordinary crimes of familial murder. Some believe that the court's ready acceptance of sleepwalking as proof of involuntariness follows from the notion that personified entitles exist in the subconscious and are released from bondage at night in dreams (Morris, 1951). This idea has a long history — Plato believed that even in the most respectable persons there exists "a terrible, fierce and lawless brood of desires which it seems are revealed in our sleep" (Simon, 1978:169). By 1900, psycho-analytical schools had further developed Plato's idea as Fenwick (1987:343) relates: "The belief was that unfulfilled wishes were held at bay in the unconscious by the ego censor, and only allowed to come into consciousness in the dream. Even then they were disguised so that dangerous wishes would not wake the sleeper. It was the duty of the same censor to keep motor impulses away from the dreamer's psyche, for if they broke through and passed the censor, then sleepwalking . . . would occur. Even today, papers are published in which sleepwalking is seen as an ('ego defect') or an ('early fixation of the ego subsystem')."

During the same period William James took a different view. James was a foe of the Freudian unconscious, seeing it as a metaphysical device destined to impede the development of a psychological science. James suggested that somnambulists were not unconscious, but were comparable to the intoxicated who act with awareness but experience defects in memory (Klein, 1977:40). Sleepwalkers, in fact, do not wander about aimlessly or at random, rather they have their eyes open, avoid obstacles and know generally what they are doing, though they do make factual errors (Arkin, 1981).

All advanced mammals exhibit the indications of dreaming, namely rapid eye movements (REM), increased blood flow to the brain and genitals, irregular breathing and pulse and a sort of temporary sedation or paralysis. Sleep cycles also seem to involve oscillating levels of chemicals like acetylcholine and noradrenaline which have a role in memory processes. When these systems are artificially disrupted, the normal inhibitory effect during dreaming can be eliminated. Jouvet found that cats started to act out their complex behaviours during dreams after their brains suffered surgical disconnection (*Economist*, December 26, 1987, p. 93). Winson (1985) recently concluded, rather boldly, that the mechanisms involving REM sleep are the "Freudian unconscious" but the appearance in dreams of traumatic memories and instinctual wishes contradicts Freud's dream theory. But Winson's portrayal of dreaming as unconscious information processing, memory storage and strategy rehearsal posits an indispensably useful unconscious quite different that the murky, symbolic, repressed unconscious associated with Freud. Looking at sleepwalking from a chemical/drug perspective is probably more profitable that the Freudian ego defect hypothesis. The former perspective does not require personified unconscious forces, so in law it should not give rise to the current tendency to equate sleepwalking with involuntariness. Careful observation, however, may confirm that sleepwalkers frequently make honest, uncontrived mistakes of fact which, if relevant to a criminal act, should result in a full acquittal. The most recent example of the successful use of the "sleepwalking defence" is found in *Parks*, reproduced below.

The other dissociative states linked to automatism are hysteria, fugue, amnesia and split-personality. Multiple-personality cases naturally receive popular attention because they are bizarre and because they conflict with the orthodox view that every person has one basic identity with a diverse but single store of memories (Lasky, 1982). Speculation exists as to whether any such cases are genuine and that sometimes is the issue in court. Sands (1981) describes such a courtroom battle with the assumption that a genuine split-personality will excuse a defendant from criminal liability. Sometimes the accused's "core" personality is alleged to be unconscious, submerged under the fringe personalities. Legally that argument makes little sense. To exaggerate the case in Sand's favour, imagine an incredibly advanced process whereby the memories, personality and brain of a dying person could be transferred into someone else's central nervous system. The result would be a double-identity person with two distinct biographies. Yet even in this case the law should not allow special treatment. The criminal laws deal with human organisms identified singularly by their fingerprints, voice prints or DNA patterns. The law is concerned with the actions of that organism and any punishment inflicted will physically restrain, limit or hurt that organism. To exempt personality A because personality B committed the crime is, in effect, to exempt both.

The other dissociative states, particularly amnesia, are not infrequently associated with crime. Still, the legal relevance of these impairments is far from obvious despite the readiness of psychiatrists to equate memory loss with automatism (Parkin, 1987:66; Schacter, 1986). Certainly, memory loss will commonly raise evidentiary problems since an accused may be unable to remember her intent. If she killed, for example, was it provoked, in self-defence or done out of spite? A possible alibi may also be forgotten. Despite these concerns the courts properly determined in *Podola* (1959) that amnesia did not render an accused unfit to stand trial (Cocklin, 1981). Fitness to stand trial should involve only temporary incapacity or, where the impairment is chronic, only a temporary delay in trial (Savage, 1981).

Dissociative states have become legally relevant, however, through the confusion of memory loss with lack of intent and involuntariness. The Ontario Court of Appeal in *Kasperek* (1951) rejected a defence based on linking a memory "black out" with lack of intent but conceded that a different result was possible should a person be "walking in his sleep or otherwise acting with his mind a total blank" (p. 790). This "total blank" thesis was approved in *Minor* (1955) where medical evidence for the defence asserted that because of a blow to the head the accused was made "unconscious" for an unknown interval. In fact, the evidence only indicated memory loss. Judges define automatism in ways that make this mistake easy to make. In *Callum* (1973), the judge defined automatism to mean "unconscious involuntary action, that is, doing something without knowledge of it and without memory afterward of having done it" (p. 304). Since lack of knowledge at the time of the offense cannot be tested, all that is usually in evidence is lack of memory afterward. Lack of memory is obviously consistent with true unconscious behaviour but it is not sufficient evidence on which to conclude involuntariness. Memory loss with alcohol is common and alcohol-impaired offenders are common. Moreover, the possibly very unpleasant fact of having committed a serious wrong may trigger in amateur criminals an unconscious dissociation. Judges hold that "the state of automatism is a demonstration of a malfunction of the mind technically described as dissociation" (Sproule, 1975:98). Dissociation itself is an unconscious process but it does not mean that a dissociated person carried out complex, purposeful actions unconsciously. If the person themselves did not direct the activity who did? At this extreme, one is merely rephrasing the split-personality, split-brain theory or accepting the "small man" view of a personified unconscious capable of seizing control of "the body" once a drug, physical blow or trauma has knocked out Captain Consciousness.

Automatism leads to odd results. In *Gottschalk* (1974) the defendant was acquitted of theft because chronic anxiety and "depersonalization" made his shoplifting an unintentional "reflex". In *Rabey* (1980), set out below, under the psychological blow of being insulted, the defendant's conscious mind supposedly "shut off" and thereafter he struck the victim on the head and attempted to injure her by strangulation. The psychiatric expert claimed that when in a severe dissociative state people can perform complex actions like talking and strangling "without consciousness". As noted, this claim must be carefully filled out with an explanation of who or what is directing the action once the "mind" is shut off.

In *Rabey* much was made of his condition after the event. He was perspiring, was very nervous, pale, bewildered, clammy, depressed and perhaps dazed. All of this is consistent with the jealous rage/remorse cycle typical of men who kill or attack women they love-hate. Rabey also fits the mold in being essentially a medicalized heat of passion case extended beyond the legal limits traditionally allowed — even if Rabey was wrongly insulted, he did not act on the sudden (he brooded for a day) and it was not a provocation that would cause an "ordinary" person to "lose control" (Archibald, 1985:470). While Rabey and perhaps all the automatism defendants are in "altered states of consciousness", these do not indicate involuntariness. The psychiatrist for the prosecution in Rabey made a two-pronged argument — Rabey was simply in a rage but, if he was dissociated, that amounts to a "disease of the mind" (which opens up the abyss of insanity). Thus neither psychiatrist made what is probably the correct argument, namely that Rabey acted intentionally and voluntarily, but then from shame and remorse unconsciously repressed memory of his wretched behaviour. Such repression, however, does not mitigate or amplify his criminal or tortious liability.

The dubious nature of the medical evidence in *Rabey* raises a question central to all psychiatric testimony: should it be allowed in the criminal court? Many scholars contend that psychiatrists should be banished from criminal trials and from any procedure affecting a legal decision (Sutherland, 1956; Weisstub, 1978). Psychiatric testimony is said to "obscure our vast ignorance [and] . . . obfuscate familiar facts" (Fingarette & Hasse, 1979:172). Medical experts argue that disturbed accused did not intend, know about or recklessly risk their criminal acts when many lawyers, jurors and observers know otherwise (Gerber, 1975). Critics charge that courts are "bombarded with irrelevant, confusing and prejudicial testimony from mental health professionals" (Morse, 1984:37). Winslade and Ross (1983) advocate elimating all psychiatric testimony on the accused's state of mind at the time of the offence and Alan Stone (1984), a past President of the American Psychiatric Association, advises psychiatrists to stay out of the courtroom until they can achieve normal scientific standards of truth.

## Rabey v. The Queen
(1980), 54 C.C.C. (2d) 1 (S.C.C.)

[Only the judgments of Dickson J. and Ritchie J. are reproduced below.]

DICKSON, J. (dissenting): — The automatism "defence" has come into considerable prominence in recent years. Although the word "automatism" made its way but lately to the legal state, it is basic principle that absence of volition in respect of the act involved is always a defence to a crime. A defence that the act is involuntary entitles the accused to a complete and unqualified acquittal. That the defence of automatism exists as a middle ground between criminal responsibility and legal insanity is beyond question. Although spoken as a defence, in the sense that it is raised by the accused, the Crown always bears the burden of proving a voluntary act.

The issue in this appeal is whether automatism resulting from a "psychological blow" is available to an accused in answer to a charge of causing bodily harm with intent to wound. The appellant, Wayne Kenneth Rabey, suddenly and without warning assaulted a fellow student and friend, causing her injury. The theory of the defence was that his behaviour was caused by a "psychological blow, an intense emotional shock which induced a "dissociative state", during which for a time, the appellant was neither conscious of, nor able to control his conduct, so that it was involuntary. This is sometimes spoken of as non-insane automatism, to distinguish it from cases in which the state of automatism is attributable to disease of the mind.

At common law a person who engaged in what would otherwise have been criminal conduct was not guilty of a crime if he did so in a state of unconsciousness or semi-consciousness. Nor was he responsible if he was, by reason of disease of the mind or defect of reason, unable to appreciate the nature and quality of an act or that its commission was wrong. The fundamental precept of our criminal law is that a man is responsible only for his conscious, intentional acts. Devlin, J., summed up the position in *R. v. Kemp*, [1956] 3 All E.R. 294 at p. 251:

> In the eyes of the common law if a man is not responsible for his actions he is entitled to be acquitted by the ordinary form of acquittal, and it matters not whether his lack of responsibility was due to insanity or to any other cause.

In order to protect the public from dangerous criminally insane the common law was changed by statute, long ago. By the *Criminal Lunatics Act, 1800*, and the *Trial of Lunatics Act, 1883*, and in Canada by the *Criminal Code*, a verdict of not guilty by reason of insanity results in committal to an institution. The purpose of the qualified verdict of acquittal is, of course, to ensure custody and treatment for those who might pose a continuing threat to society by reason of mental illness. In Canada, an accused who is acquitted on the ground of insanity is kept in strict custody in the place and manner that the Court directs, until the pleasure of the Lieutenant-Governor of the Province is known (s. 542(2) of the *Code*).

The term "automatism" first appeared in the cases and in the periodical literature about 30 years ago. It is seen with increasing frequency. The defence of automatism is successfully invoked in circumstances of a criminal act committed unconsciously; and, in the past, has generally covered acts done while sleepwalking or under concussional states following head injuries.

The defence of automatism is, in some respects, akin to that of insanity. In both instances, the issue is whether an accused had sufficient control over, or the knowledge of, his criminal act, to be held culpable. The two defences are, however, separate and distinct. As Professor Edwards observed in 21 Mod. L. Rev. 375 at 384 (1958):

> ... Both circumstances are concerned to prove mental irresponsibility, the essential difference ... being that in the case of insanity the defect of the understanding must originate in a disease of the mind, whereas in the defence of automatism *simpliciter* the criminal law is not concerned with any question of the disease of the mind.

Although separate, the relationship between the two defences cannot be discounted. Automatism may be subsumed in the defence of insanity in cases in which the unconscious action of an accused can be traced to, or rooted in, a disease of the mind. Where that is so, the defence of insanity prevails.

. . . .

### The Facts

At the time of the alleged offence, March 1, 1974, the appellant, 20 years of age, was a third-year geology student in an honours science course at the University of Toronto. During the fall of 1973, he had spent some time with the complainant, also a third-year science student with whom he shared a number of classes. Along with two male classmates, the two studied and lunched together. Their social activities extended to walks together, dinner at one another's homes and forays to a local bar. The appellant was somewhat shy and though he began to develop strong feelings for the attractive, out-going complainant, the sentiment was not reciprocated.

Plans for a ski trip to Quebec were made in November and the two planned to share a room. The complainant then invited another student to accompany them, creating a more platonic overtone. The three did in fact go to Quebec. The appellant testified that his relationship with the complainant deteriorated in early 1974. They no longer went on walks or visited for dinner. He still saw much of her at school.

On February 28, 1974, the complainant asked the appellant to assist her with an assignment. While she was absent a few moments, he flipped through her books to locate an equation and found a letter she had written to a female friend. He took the letter without her knowledge and read it at home that evening. The letter contains a number of references to sexual activity, both actual and wished for. Toward the end of the letter, this paragraph appears:

And for some reason all the guys I know want to go out with me and not just be friends any more so I can't talk to them. I don't want to go out with them and they know it so there is static in the air which is why I want to leave. Hell I can insult Wayne [the appellant] and Rick and they still hug me in class. I want to be alone or with just one good guy, not with a bunch of nothings.

The appellant was hurt and angry as he read the letter. He marked the passages referred to above with a pen.

The following morning, he removed a rock sample of galena from the geology lab. This was not unusual, for he was permitted to take samples home for purposes of study. At about noon, as he left to watch a squash match, he met the complainant. He testified that, "just for about a second, not even that, I felt sort of strange, I can't describe how I felt". He referred to it as a flash. He suggested she watch the match with him. The two proceeded to the squash court. The game was not in progress, so they left by the far stairwell. The appellant remembered asking her what she though of Gord, a friend of theirs, hearing the reply that he was "just a friend", and "really the next thing I remember was choking her and I remember the face was a funny colour and I remember seeing a lot of blood and I stopped". He realized his hands were around her throat.

The complainant testified that following the question about Gord, the appellant then asked, "What do you think of me?" She replied, "You're just a friend too." As she opened a set of fire doors, she heard a crash and a "crumbling sound". The appellant grabbed her around the arms and struck her on the head. She lost consciousness momentarily. When she recovered consciousness, he was choking her.

A student happened along, to whom the appellant said, "there's been a terrible accident". He was pale, sweating, glassy-eyed and had a frightened expression. When the witness looked over the railing and saw the complainant's head, her body being under the stairs, the appellant said, "I've killed her and I am going to kill you too". The appellant had only a partial recollection of his encounter with this witness.

A professor who was summoned testified that the appellant was very pale and bewildered. His description of the appellant was that he was perspiring; very, very nervous; distraught; upset; absolutely pale, no colour in his face; had moisture about the mouth; was shaky, jerky in his speech; absolutely bewildered, "out of it". In reply, he said that although the appellant was halting in his speech, he was coherent. According to the nurse who next saw the appellant, he looked very upset. His pulse was very fast and not strong; he had a limp "clammy" appearance. She was unable to convince him he had not killed the complainant. To the Dean, the appellant said, "I don't know why I started or why I stopped" and that, "he liked her better than anyone he had ever known". The Dean testified that the appellant spoke slowly in a confused sort of way, was very depressed and perhaps dazed.

To Constable Pollitt, the appellant said, "I did it, I know I did it, I just couldn't stop hitting her". The appellant gave a statement to the police, which reads in part:

> I was asking her about the ballet, then I asked her if she liked this guy Gord. She said something about just a friend, then I guess I hit her right then on the head, she was bleeding from the head and the next thing I remember it all happened so fast she was on the floor and I was sitting on top of her choking her. I thought she was dead there was blood everywhere, I just don't know what happened.

The statement concluded:

I don't know why I did it because I wasn't even mad when this happened, and I don't remember parts of what happened and when I realized what I had done I went to the nurse's office and then to phone the police. I actually thought I'd killed somebody.

A number of character witnesses spoke highly of the appellant. Evidence was led that he had been a well-behaved young man until this incident. He had never lost his temper or displayed signs of anger.

The complainant made a complete recovery within a short time.

## *The Medical Evidence*

The appellant was remanded for psychiatric assessment and committed on March 5, 1974, to the Lakeshore Hospital. He was discharged on April 1, 1974. Detailed medical examinations disclosed no evidence of neurological disease. A psychological survey showed no indication of psychotic process. Dr. Slyfield conducted a number of interviews in the preparation of his report which concludes:

> Psychological testing done by Mr. Wejtko indicates superior intellectual ability, a personality profile within the range of normality, and a tendency to use the psychological defences of avoidance, repression and blocking. There was no evidence of psychotic disintegration.
>
> If Wayne is telling the truth about his amnesia for most of the incident, then it is probable that his consciousness was dissociated at the time. His somnambulistic episode lends some support to his explanation. However, such a psychological mechanism need not indicate mental illness.

In the opinion of Dr. Orchard, assistant professor of psychiatry at the University of Toronto and witness for the defence, the appellant entered into a complete dissociative state, a disorder of consciousness which occurs as a result of part of the nervous system "shutting off". A person in a severe dissociative state may be capable of performing physical actions without consciousness of such actions. When the appellant entered the dissociative state near the foot of the stairs his mind "shut off", and the return of consciousness was gradual. In Dr. Orchard's opinion the dissociative state which occurred was comparable to that produced by a "physical blow", though caused by a "psychological blow", certain physical effects were produced as observed by the student, the professor, the nurse and the Dean.

According to Dr. Orchard the appellant was a young man of average health, or better than average health, with no predisposition to dissociate. The severe dissociative state, such as the appellant suffered, usually occurs in persons within the category of normal people. According to Dr. Orchard it is rare for the severe dissociative state not caused by some underlying pathology to recur. In his opinion there was only a very slight possibility that the appellant would suffer a recurrence of this disorder of consciousness. Dr. Orchard could find no indication of any pathological condition, which he defined as a "diseased condition or abnormally sick condition". In his view the dissociative state itself is an "occurrence", not a mental illness and not a disease of the mind.

Dr. Rowsell who, like Dr. Orchard, is a psychiatrist of eminence, examined the appellant and testified on behalf of the Crown. In his opinion the appellant was not in a dissociative state, but rather was a controlled young man who went into an extreme state of rage at that moment and, while in that state, struck the complainant on the head and choked her. Dr. Rowsell felt that if, contrary to his opinion, the appellant was in a dissociative state, he suffered from disease of the mind. According to Dr. Rowsell, consciousness is the distinguishing factor of mental life; the dissociative state is, by definition, a subdivision of hysterical neurosis, which is a definite mental illness. It is by definition a disorder of the mind. Dr. Rowsell did not suggest there was an underlying pathology which induced the alleged dissociative state. His report reads in part:

> He shows no evidence of psychosis. (A psychosis is a disorder of thinking, feeling and behaviour, accompanied by a break with reality. This means that the individual is no longer able to interpret events, both internal and external, as would a person in good mental health.) . . .
> There is no evidence of any organic brain disorder which would impair his consciousness. Therefore, the issue could be raised as to whether he was in an automatic state at the time of the event. In my opinion he was not. The psychiatric term for such a state would be Dissociative Reaction.

The evidence of Dr. Rowsell was that Rabey was conscious at the time of the act but suffered hysterical amnesia *after the event*, which Dr. Rowsell categorized as neurosis, a disease of the mind.

Dr. Rowsell, unlike Dr. Orchard, was of the opinion that the appellant still had a psychiatric problem for which he required treatment to help him face up to what occurred. The treatment would take six months to a year, and could be undertaken on an out-patient basis. The prognosis was excellent.

Dr. Orchard, on the other hand, was of the view that inasmuch as the appellant had been a relatively normal person prior to the occurrence, the likelihood of any recurrence was negligible. In Dr. Orchard's words:

> I think he has a pretty healthy personality and he will find a healthy way through all this, So I don't see it in need of any treatment. I don't see him as sick. I do agree with Dr. Rowsell he is not in any way a criminal type of person.

Dr. Rowsell considered that the appellant was not "in any way a criminal type of person". Dr. Orchard shared that view.

## At Trial and on Appeal

The trial Judge, Dymond, Co. Ct. J., rejected the Crown theory of planned revenge and the medical opinion advanced by Dr. Rowsell of tremendous rage and loss of memory from protective hysterical amnesia. Referring to *R. v. K* (1970), 3 C.C.C. (2d) 84, [1971] 2 O.R. 401, and *Pernerkar v. The Queen* (1973), 10 C.C.C. (2d) 253 . . . (Sask. C.A.), the Judge concluded that a dissociative state brought on by psychological trauma can support a defence of automatism. The ruling in *Parnerkar* flowed from the medical evidence there, distinctly different from the evidence in this case.

. . . .

In acquitting the appellant the Judge made two findings of particular significance: first that the appellant was not insane within the meaning of s. 16 of the *Criminal Code* when the acts were committed and, secondly, that the appellant had acted in a state of automatism brought about by an external cause.

It is important to note that the Crown did not challenge the finding of automatism in this Court or in the Ontario Court of Appeal. We must therefore accept for the purposes of this appeal, that the acts to which I have referred occurred without will, purpose or reasoned intention on the part of the appellant. The only question for decision is whether, having found automatism, the trial Judge was bound in law to find that the appellant was a proper subject for indefinite detention as an insane person.

On appeal to the Ontario Court of Appeal, the acquittal on the charge of causing bodily harm was reversed and a new trial directed on that count. The Court held that the psychological blow suffered was not an externally originating cause of the dissociative state. The acquittal at trial on a companion charge of possession of a rock for the purpose of wounding was upheld.

. . . .

I turn now to the authorities, with the threshold observation that none of them is binding upon this Court or particularly helpful in the resolution of this case.

. . . .

The first Canadian decision is *R. v. Kasperek* (1951), 101 C.C.C. 375, [1951] O.R. 776, 13 C.R. 206, a case in which the defence raised was "temporary blackout" and "amnesia". It was held the denial of insanity, with an assertion of amnesia, was untenable. This decision predates the English authorities which recognized a defence of automatism.

In *R. v. Minor* (1955), 112 C.C.C. 29, 21 C.R. 377, 15 W.W.R. (N.S. 433 (Sask. C.A.), a death resulted from the accused's dangerous and erratic handling of his car. The facts indicated that just prior to driving, the accused, in attendance at a wedding reception, had been struck and knocked down. According to the medical evidence, he had suffered from an injury which rendered him unconscious for an unknown interval. The salient passage is at pp. 34-5:

> There is ample authority to the effect that when a person is unconscious from any cause and is in a condition when he cannot form an intent . . . he has a good defence . . . In my opinion the provisions with respect to insanity . . . do not apply to the defence set up in this case, namely, that the accused did not know what he was doing at the time of the accident.

. . . .

The jury charge in *R. v. K* (1970), 3 C.C.C. (2d) 84, [1971] 2 O.R. 401, as far as I am aware, contains the first plea of psychological blow automatism in this country. Both insanity and automatism were before the jury. In view of the uncontradicted evidence of an underlying pathological condition and a course of psychiatric treatment prior to the killing, one may seriously query whether the trial Judge correctly left the alternative defence of automatism with the jury. In the event, the defence gained the accused an acquittal.

A plea of automatism raised at trial was sustained before this Court in *Bleta v. The Queen*, [1965] 1 C.C.C. 1, 48 D.L.R. (2d) 139, [1964] S.C.R. 561, a case in which the Court was concerned, however, with an evidentiary matter. In the course of an affray between the appellant and the deceased, the former was knocked onto the pavement, whereupon he forcibly struck his head. Moments later, he got up and delivered a fatal blow. Witnesses testified that after the fall, the appellant was dazed. On medical evidence that the physical blow deprived him of voluntary control of his actions, the appellant was acquitted at trial. With no discussion as to the availability of the defence of automatism, which appears not to have been in issue in this Court, the acquittal was restored.

*Parnerkar v. The Queen* (1973), 10 C.C.C. (2d) 253, 33 D.L.R. (3d) 688, [1974] S.C.R. 449; affirming 5 C.C.C. (2d) 11, 16 C.R.N.S. 347, [1972] 1 W.W.R. 161, is perhaps the case most directly in point in the resolution of the present appeal. The trial Judge and appellate Court in the case at bar disagreed in their respective interpretations of the judgment rendered by Culliton, C.J.S. The case reached this Court, but the plea of non-insane automatism was not directly considered. Only Ritchie, J. (in whose judgment Spence, J., concurred), expressed a view on the issue of automatism. He agreed that the defence of automatism should not have been left with the jury.

The passage in the judgment of Culliton, C.J.S., which has given rise to uncertainty reads (p. 24):

> In my opinion, if the evidence of Dr. Benjamin is accepted, that Parnerkar was in a dissociated state at the time he killed Anna, he was, at the time, suffering from a disease of the mind within the M'Naghten rules as defined by this Court. If the acts committed by Parnerkar were unconscious acts, they depended upon a defect of reason from disease of the mind, and consequently the defence, if any, was one of insanity, and not of automatism. Therefore, in my respectful view, the learned trial Judge erred in law putting the defence of automatism to the jury. I would also point out that Dr. Benjamin stated, if Parnerkar was in a dissociated state, then during that time he was temporarily insane.

It is unclear whether Culliton, C.J.S., unsupported by earlier authority, made a finding that, as a matter of law, a dissociated state is a disease of the mind, or whether he merely accepted the medical opinion that, on these facts, there was a disease of the mind. In the present case Mr. Justice Martin took the former view of the meaning to be attributed to the words of Culliton, C.J.S.; the trial Judge took the latter view. There is little in the way of elaboration, beyond that contained in the quoted passage, on the issue of disease of the mind.

There are three or four decisions since *Parnerkar*, in which automatism induced by a psychological blow has been pleaded. In *R. v. James* (1974), 30 C.R.N.S. 65 (Ont. H.C.J.), dissociation caused by emotional stress was categorized as insanity rather than as a non-insane automatism but in that case the medical evidence disclosed an underlying pathological condition of psychotic proportion. In *R. v. Cullum* (1973), 14 C.C.C. (2d) 294 (Ont. Co. Ct.), Zalev. Co. Ct. J., acquitted an accused who was in a dissociated state due to situational emotional stress. In *Cullum*, there was evidence that the factors inducing the dissociative state were "alcohol and the girls"; there was also evidence of a predisposition to dissociate; recurrence could not be ruled out.

. . . .

Another case to which one might refer is *R. v. Sproule* (1975), 26 C.C.C. (2d) 92, 30 C.R.N.S. 56, decided by the Ontario Court of Appeal differently constituted than in the case at bar. In that case, the accused had an argument with a girl who had earlier informed him her interest was on the wane. A discussion between the two rapidly escalated into an argument, during which the girl was shot. The judgment of the Court was delivered by Kelly, J.A., who stated that the defence sought to tender evidence to prove that Sproule, at the time of the shooting, had been acting in a state of automatism.

. . . .

In *Cooper* and in the case at bar there was evidence of interruption of the thought processes in the course of committing certain acts and criminal responsibility was in issue. In *Cooper* the question was whether the trial Judge was required to charge on insanity. The inquiry in the present case goes somewhat deeper. The question here is whether the accused, having acted in a state of unconsciousness, while in a transitory mental state, must be committed to an institution.

This case raises interesting issues, and the judicial conclusion, in my view, should be guided by general principles of criminal responsibility. Before alluding to those principles, it is useful to recall s. 16(4) of the *Criminal Code* which reads:

> **16(4)** Every one shall, until the contrary is proved, be presumed to be and to have been sane.

In the usual case in which an accused pleaded insanity, he has the burden of overcoming the presumption of sanity. In the present case the appellant is not seeking to establish that he was insane on March 1, 1974. The Crown is asserting the insanity in answer to the defence of automatism raised by the appellant. The presumption of sanity runs in the appellant's favour.

We turn to s. 16(2): a person is insane when he is in a state of natural imbecility or has a disease of the mind to an extent that renders him incapable of appreciating the nature and quality of an act or omission or of knowing that an act or omission is wrong. The important words, for present purposes, are "disease of the mind".

The first principle, fundamental to our criminal law, which governs this appeal is that no act can be a criminal offence unless it is done voluntarily. Consciousness is a *sine qua non* to criminal liability.

The prosecution must prove every element of the crime charged. One such element is the state of mind of the accused, in the sense that the act was voluntary. The circumstances are normally such as to permit a presumption of volition and mental capacity. That is not so when the accused, as here, has placed before the Court, by cross-examination of Crown witnesses or by evidence called on his own behalf, or both, evidence sufficient to raise an issue that he was unconscious of his actions at the time of the alleged offence. No burden of proof is imposed upon an accused raising such a defence beyond pointing to facts which indicate the existence of such condition: *R. v. Berger* (1975), 27 C.C.C. (2d) 357 at p. 379. Whether lack of consciousness relates to *mens rea* or to *actus reus* or both may be important in a case in which the offence charged is one of absolute liability, but the conceptual distinction does not concern us in the case at bar.

The second principle is that no person should be committed to a hospital for the criminally insane unless he suffers from disease of the mind in need of treatment or likely to recur.

The Ontario Court of Appeal held that the excusing factor was insanity. This finding was reached though the appellant exhibited no pathological symptoms indicative of a previously existing, or ongoing, psychiatric disorder. On medical evidence accepted by the trial Judge, the prospect of a recurrence of dissociation is extremely remote. There was no finding that the appellant suffered from psychosis, neurosis or personality disorder. He does not have an organic disease of the brain. This was an isolated event. The appellant has already spent several weeks in a mental institution undergoing psychiatric, neurological and psychological assessment, the result of which did not indicate need for treatment.

There are undoubtedly policy considerations to be considered. Automatism as a defence is easily feigned. It is said the credibility of our criminal justice system will be severely strained if a person who has committed a violent act is allowed an absolute acquittal on a plea of automatism arising from a psychological blow. The argument is made that the success of the defence depends upon the semantic ability of psychiatrists, tracing a narrow path between the twin shoals of criminal responsibility and an insanity verdict. Added to these concerns is the *in terrorem* argument that the floodgates will be raised if psychological blow automatism is recognized in law.

There are competing policy interests. Where the condition is transient rather than persistent, unlikely to recur, not in need of treatment and not the result of self-induced intoxication, the policy objectives in finding such a person insane are not served. Such a person is not a danger to himself or to society generally.

The Ontario Court of Appear in the present case focused upon "external cause". The "ordinary stresses and disappointments of life" were held not to constitute an external cause. The Court considered that the "emotional stress" suffered by the appellant could not be said to be an external factor producing the automatism; the dissociative state had its source primarily in the psychological or emotional make-up of the appellant.

There is no evidence to support Mr. Justice Martin's statement attributing the dissociated state to psychological or emotional make-up of the appellant. To exclude the defence of automatism it lay upon the Crown to establish that the appellant suffered from a disease of the mind at the time of the attack. The existence of the mental disease must be demonstrated in evidence. Here there is no such evidence from any of the expert or other witnesses with references to the crucial period of the assault. Moreover as earlier noted, s. 16(4) presumes sanity. The Court of Appeal's conclusion was directly contrary to the testimony of Dr. Orchard, accepted by the trial Judge, and finds no support in the testimony of Dr. Rowsell.

Martin, J.A., left open the question whether it is possible to dissociate as a result of emotional shock rather than physical injury. The effect of the appellate Court judgment was to differ with the trial Judge's finding that the dissociation was brought about by an externally operating cause. In the circumstances, I do not think it is open to this Court to disturb the findings of fact at trial.

If the effect of the appellate Court judgment is that, as a matter of law, emotional stress can never constitute an external factor then, with respect, I disagree. Indeed, in the passage quoted below the Court seems to concede as much. If the controlling factor is one of degree of emotional stress, and the application of some form of quantitative test, then the question becomes one of fact for the trier of fact and not one of law for an appellate Court.

It is not clear to me why, as a matter of law, an emotional blow, which can be devastating, should be regarded as an external cause of automatism in some circumstances and an internal cause in others, as the Court of Appeal would seem to propose in this passage [at pp. 482-3 C.C.C., p. 435 D.L.R.]:

> I leave aside until it becomes necessary to decide them, cases where a dissociative state has resulted from emotional shock without physical injury, resulting from such causes, for example, as being

involved in a serious accident although no physical injury has resulted; being the victim of a murderous attack with an uplifted knife, notwithstanding the victim has managed to escape physical injury; seeing a loved one murdered or seriously assaulted, and the like situations. Such extraordinary external events might reasonably be presumed to affect the average normal person without reference to the subjective make-up of the person exposed to such experience.

I cannot accept the notion that an extraordinary external event, *i.e.*, an intense emotional shock, can cause a state of dissociation or automatism, if and only if all normal persons subjected to that sort of shock would react in that way. If I understand the quoted passage correctly, an objective standard is contemplated for one of the possible causes of automatism, namely, psychological blow, leaving intact the subjective standard for other causes of automatism, such a physical blow, or reaction to drugs.

As in all other aspects of the criminal law, except negligence offences, the inquiry is directed to the accused's actual state of mind. It is his subjective mental condition with which the law is concerned. If he has a brittle skull and sustains a concussion which causes him to run amok, he has a valid defence of automatism. If he has an irregular metabolism which induced an unanticipated and violent reaction to a drug, he will not be responsible for his acts. If he is driven into shock and unconsciousness by an emotional blow, and was susceptible to that reaction but has no disease, there is no reason in principle why a plea of automatism should not be available. The fact that other people would not have reacted as he did should not obscure the reality that the external psychological blow did cause a loss of consciousness. A person's subjective reaction, in the absence of any other medical or factual evidence supportive of insanity, should not put him into the category of persons legally insane. Nor am I prepared to accept the proposition, which seems implicit in the passage quoted, that whether an automatic state is an insane reaction or a sane reaction may depend upon the intensity of the shock.

M.E. Schiffer states in his text, *Mental Disorder and The Criminal Trial Process* (1976), that psychological blow automatism is described as a reaction to a shock (p. 101):

> However, in cases where the psychological stress has taken the form of a sudden jolt, or blow to the accused, the court may be more willing to treat a short-lived bout of automatism as sane. Because the automatism, in order to be a defence in itself, must be an "on the sudden" reaction to psychological stress, the defence of "psychological blow automatism" may be seen as somewhat analogous to the defence of provocation.

I agree with the requirement that there be a shock precipitating the state of automatism. Dissociation caused by a low stress threshold and surrender to anxiety cannot fairly be said to result from a psychological blow. In a recent decision of the British Columbia Court of Appeal, *R. v. MacLeod*, as yet unreported [since reported 52 C.C.C. (2d) 193], Craig, J.A., adopted the judgment of Martin, J.A., in *Rabey*. The facts of *MacLeod* cannot be compared with those in the instant appeal. There, the accused absorbed four double drinks of liquor prior to entering the alleged state of dissociation. His loss of consciousness cannot be traced to an immediate emotional shock. He had been subject to ongoing stress for some time, which was heightened by his wife's recent departure. Though unwilling to classify it a disease of the mind, the accused's medical witness described it as a "neurotic disorder" which could be induced by an "anxiety reaction". The Court of Appeal held non-instance automatism was not available.

Dr. Glanville Williams' new book *Textbook of Criminal Law* (1978), is helpful in this discussion, in particular chapter 27. The author cites as the main instances of automatism: "sleepwalking, concussion, some cases of epilepsy, hypoglycaemia and dissociative states". Williams says (pp. 608-9) that "automatism" has come to express "any abnormal state of consciousness (whether confusion, delusion or dissociation) that is regarded as incompatible with the existence of *mens rea*, while not amounting to insanity", adding: "It would better be called 'impaired consciousness', but the orthodox expression can be used if we bear in mind that it does not mean what it says" and in a footnote (p. 609):

> Because automatism is a legal concept, a psychiatrist should be asked to testify to the mental condition as psychiatrically recognized, not to "automatism". It is for the judge to make the translation. In most of the conditions referred to legally as automatism the psychiatrist would speak of an altered state of consciousness.

The *Parnerkar* case is discussed at some length and the following observations made with respect thereto (p. 613):

> The decision illustrates the difficulty that can be caused to the courts by over-enthusiastic psychiatrists. If such evidence were regularly given and accepted a considerable breach would be made in the law of homicide. A medical witness who proclaims that the defendant, though awake, did not know that he was stabbing a person because of his dissociated state invites incredulity, particularly where it is shown that the defendant immediately afterwards telephoned for an ambulance and the police. Further, to assert that this medical condition amounts to insanity ignores the distinction that has been developed between sane and non-sane automatism. *If Parnerkar was in a state of automatism at all it was on the non-insane variety, since there was no evidence of psychosis or brain damage or continuing danger.*

(Emphasis added.) At the conclusion of the discussion of *Parnerkar*, Williams makes the following comment, particulary apt in the present case:

> It may also be remarked that commitment to hospital is inappropriate in a case of hysterical dissociation, since once the episode is over the patient does not need to be detained.

Under the heading "Insanity versus Automatism" Williams states that before the decision in *Quick*, Lord Dnening's view in *Bratty* was generally accepted. The test of insanity was the likelihood of recurrence of danger. In *Quick* the Court of Appeal adopted what might seem at first sight to be a different test for insane *versus* non-insane automatism. But the real question is whether the violence is likely to be repeated. Williams concludes that "On the whole, it would be much better if the courts kept to Lord Denning's plain rule; the rule of *Quick* adds nothing to it" (p. 615).

This view, which the Ontario Court of Appeal appears to have rejected, finds ample support in the legal literature. See S.M. Beck, "Voluntary Conduct: Automatism, Insanity and Drunkenness" (1966-67), 9 Crim. L.Q. 315 at p. 321: "The cause of the automatic conduct, and the threat of recurrence, are plainly factors that determine the line between sane and insane automatism"; F.A. Whitlock, *Criminal Responsibility and Mental Illness* (1963), p. 120: "The test of whether or not an episode of automatism is to be judged as sane or insane action seems to rest on the likelihood of its repetition"; Professor J.Ll.J. Edwards, "Automatism and Criminal Responsibility", 21 Mod. L.

Rev. 375 at p. 385: "Where evidence is available of recurrent attacks of automatism during which the accused resorts to violence . . . inevitably leads to consideration of the imposition of some restraint"; S. Prevenzer, "Automatism and Involuntary Conduct", [1958] Crim. L.R. 440 at p. 441: "If . . . it can safely be predicted that his conduct is not likely to recur, having regard to the cause of the automatism, there can be no point in finding him insane and detaining him in Broadmoor"; G.A. Martin, "Insanity as a Defence", (1965-66) 8 Crim. L.Q. 240 at p. 253: "Perhaps the distinction lies in the likelihood of recurrence and whether the person suffering from it is prone to acts of violence when in that state."

In principle, the defence of automatism should be available whenever there is evidence of unconsciousness throughout the commission of the crime, that cannot be attributed to fault or negligence of his part, such evidence should be supported by expert medical opinion that the accused did not feign memory loss and that there is no underlying pathological condition which points to a disease requiring detention and treatment.

I would only add that s. 16 determines the consequences of the finding of "no consciousness", on the basis of a legal conclusion guided by the medical evidence of the day. What is disease of the mind in the medical science of today may not be so tomorrow. The Court will establish the meaning of disease of the mind on the basis of scientific evidence as it unfolds from day to day. The Court will find as a matter of fact in each case whether a disease of the mind, so defined, is present.

The circumstances in this case are highly unusual, uncomplicated by alcohol or psychiatric history. The real question in the case is whether the appellant should be confined in an institution for the criminally insane. The trial Judge negated an act of passion, lack of self-control or impulsiveness. The medical evidence negated a state of disease or disorder or mental disturbance arising from infirmity. Save for what was said by Dr. Rowsell, whose evidence as to *ex post facto* hysterical amnesia was rejected by the trial Judge, the medical experts gave the appellant a clean mental bill of health. I can see no possible justification for sending the case back for a new trial.

I would allow the appeal, set aside the judgment of the Ontario Court of Appeal, and restore the verdict of acquittal.

RITCHIE, J.:—This is an appeal from a judgment of the Court of Appeal for Ontario whereby that Court set aside the appellant's acquittal at trial for "causing bodily harm with intent to wound". The appellant had, at the same time, been charged with having a rock in his possession "for the purpose of committing the offence of wounding" but no appeal was taken from his acquittal on this charge.

. . . .

It should be observed also that the appellant was subject to a number of interviews with psychiatrists with the result that the Courts have found themselves involved in the shadowy area of mental disorders concerning which it is not surprising to find that there are wide differences in opinion amongst the "experts". The meaning of the word "automatism", in any event so far as it is employed in the defence of non-insane automatism, has in my opinion been satisfactorily defined by Mr. Justice Lacourciere of the Court of Appeal of Ontario in the case of *R. v. K* (1970), 3 C.C.C. (2d) 84, [1971] 2 O.R. 401:

> Automatism is a term used to describe unconscious, involuntary behaviour, the state of a person who, though capable of action, is not conscious of what he is doing. It means an unconscious, involuntary act, where the mind does not go with what is being done.

The defence of automatism as used in the present case of course involves a consideration of the provisions of s. 16 of the *Criminal Code* . . .

. . . .

What is said here is that although at the relevant time the appellant was in a state where, though capable of action he was not conscious of what he was doing, and more particularly that he was not suffering from a disease of the mind and was therefore not insane. The central question in deciding any case involving the defence of automatism is whether or not the accused was suffering from a disease of the mind. The opinions of psychiatrists go no further than characterizing the condition in which the appellant was found as being "a dissociative state" but it is clear at least since the case of *Bratty v. A.-G. Northern Ireland*, [1963] A.C. 386, that the question of whether or not such a state amounts to "a disease of the mind" is a question of law for the Judge to determine. The general rule is that it is for the Judge as a question of law to decide what constitutes a "disease of the mind", but that the question of whether or not the facts in a given case disclose the existence of such a disease is a question to be determined by the trier of fact. I think it would be superfluous for me to retrace the line of authorities in this area as they have been so exhaustively discussed by my brother Dickson and also by Mr. Justice Martin of the Court of Appeal and by the learned trial Judge. I am satisfied in this regard to adopt the following passages from the reasons for judgement of Mr. Justice Martin which are now conveniently reported in (1978), 37 C.C.C. (2d) 461, 79 D.L.R. (3d) 414, 40 C.R.N.S. 46. He said at pp. 477-8 C.C.C., pp. 430-1 D.L.R., pp. 62-3 C.R.N.S.:

> In general, the distinction to be drawn is between a malfunctioning of the mind arising from some cause that is primarily internal to the accused, having its source in his psychological or emotional make-up, or in some organic pathology, as opposed to a malfunctioning of the mind which is the transient effect produced by some specific external factor such as, for example, concussion. Any malfunctioning of the mind, or mental disorder having its source primarily in some subjective condition or weakness internal to the accused (whether fully understood or not), may be a "disease of the mind" if it prevents the accused from knowing what he is doing, but transient disturbances of consciousness due to certain specific external factors do not fall within the concept of disease of the mind. (For an interesting and helpful discussion see "The Concept of Mental Disease in Criminal Law Insanity Tests" by Herbert Fingarette in 33 University of Chicago Law Review 229.) Particular transient mental disturbances may not, however, be capable of being properly categorized in relation to whether they constitute "disease of the mind", on the basis of a generalized statement, and must be decided on a case by case basis.

The same learned Judge later stated in the same judgment at pp. 482-3 C.CC., p. 435 D.L.R., p. 68 C.R.N.S.:

> In my view, the ordinary stresses and disappointments of life which are the common lot of mankind do not constitute an external cause constituting an explanation for a malfunctioning of the mind which takes it out of the category of a "disease of the mind". To hold otherwise would deprive the concept of an external factor of any real meaning. In my view, the emotional stress suffered by the respondent as a result of his disappointment with respect to Miss X cannot be said to be an external

factor producing the automatism within the authorities, and the dissociative state must be considered as having its source primarily in the respondent's psychological or emotional make-up. I conclude, therefore, that, in the circumstances of this case, the dissociative state in which the respondent was said to be, constituted a "disease of the mind". I leave aside until it becomes necessary to decide them, cases where a dissociative state has resulted from emotional shock without physical injury, resulting from such causes, for example, as being involved in a serious accident although no physical injury has resulted; being the victim of a murderous attack with an uplifted knife, notwithstanding the victim has managed to escape physical injury; seeing a loved one murdered or seriously assaulted, and the like situations. Such extraordinary external events might reasonable be presumed to affect the average make-up of the person exposed to such experience.

For the above reasons, I am of the opinion, with deference, that the learned trial Judge erred in holding that the so-called "psychological blow", which was said to have caused the dissociative state, was, in the circumstances of this case, an externally originating cause, and should have held that if the respondent was in a dissociative state at the time he struck Miss X he suffered from "disease of the mind". A new trial must, accordingly, be had on count 2.

. . . .

It seems to me that his infatuation with this young woman had created an abnormal condition in his mind under the influence of which he acted unnaturally and violently to an imaged slight to which a normal person would not have reacted in the same manner.

It was contended on behalf of the appellant that a finding of disease of the mind and consequently of insanity in the present case would involve gross unfairness to the appellant who could be subject to the provisions of s. 545 of the *Criminal Code* and thus detained at the pleasure of the Lieutenant-Governor of the Province. That such a result does not carry with it the hardship contended for is illustrated by the following passage from the reasons for judgment of Mr. Justice Martin at p. 483 C.C.C., p. 436 D.L.R., p. 69 C.R.N.S.:

> It would, of course, be unthinkable that a person found not guilty on account of insanity because of a transient mental disorder constituting a disease of the mind, who was not dangerous and who required no further treatment should continue to be confined. The present provisions of s. 545(1)(b) [rep. & sub. 1972, c. 13, s. 45], however, authorize the Lieutenant-Governor to make an order, if in his opinion it would be in the best interest of the accused and not contrary to the interest of the public, for the discharge of a person found not guilty on account of insanity, either absolutely or subject to such conditions as he prescribes. In addition to the periodic reviews required to be made by a board of review appointed pursuant to s. 547(1) of the *Code* the Lieutenant-Governor under s. 547(6) of the *Code* may request the board of review to review the case of any person found not guilty on account of insanity, in which case the board of review is required to report forthwith whether such person has recovered and, if so, whether in its opinion it is in the interest of the public and of that person for the Lieutenant-Governor to order that he be discharged absolutely or subject to such conditions as the Lieutenant-Governor may prescribe.

For all these reasons, as well as for those expressed by Mr. Justice Martin in the Court of Appeal for Ontario, I would dismiss the appeal and dispose of the matter in the manner proposed by him.

*Appeal dismissed.*

# R. v. Parks
## (1992), 75 C.C.C. (3d) 287 (S.C.C.)

[Only excerpts from the judgement of Lamer are reproduced below.]

APPEAL by the Crown from a judgment of the Ontario Court of Appeal, 56 C.C.C. (3d) 449, 78 C.R. (3d) 2, 39 O.A.C. 27, 73 O.R. (2d) 129, 10 W.C.B. (2d) 236, dismissing an appeal by the Crown from the acquittal of the accused by Watt J., 6 W.C.B. (2d) 232, on charges of murder and attempted murder.

LAMER C.J.C. (dissenting in part): — In the small hours of the morning of May 24, 1987, the respondent, aged 23, attacked his parents-in-law, Barbara Ann and Denis Woods, killing his mother-in-law with a kitchen knife and seriously injuring his father-in-law. The incident occurred at the home of his parents-in-law while they were both asleep in bed. Their residence was 23 km. from that of the respondent, who went there by car. Immediately after the incident, the respondent went to the nearby police station, again driving his own car. He told the police:

> I just killed someone with my bare hands; Oh my God, I just killed someone; I've just killed two people; My God, I've just killed two people with my hands; My God, I've just killed two people. My hands; I just killed two people. I killed them; I just killed two people; I've just killed my mother- and father-in-law. I stabbed and beat them to death. It's all my fault.

At the trial the respondent presented a defence of automatism, stating that at the time the incidents took place he was sleepwalking. The respondent has always slept very deeply and has always had a lot of trouble waking up. The year prior to the events was particularly stressful for the respondent. His job as a project co-ordinator for Revere Electric required him to work 10 hours a day. In addition, during the preceding summer the respondent had placed bets on horse races which caused him financial problems. To obtain money he also stole some $30,000 from his employer. The following March his boss discovered the theft and dismissed him. Court proceedings were brought against him in this regard. His personal life suffered from all of this. However, his parents-in-law, who were aware of the situation, always supported him. He had excellent relations with them: he got on particularly well with his mother-in-law, who referred to him as the "gentle giant". His relations with his father-in-law were more distant, but still very good. In fact, a supper at their home was planned for May 24th to discuss the respondent's problems and the solutions he intended to suggest. Additionally, several members of his family suffer or have suffered from sleep problems such as sleep-walking, adult enuresis, nightmares and sleep-talking.

The respondent was charged with the first degree murder of Barbara Ann Woods and the attempted murder of Denis Woods.

The trial judge chose to put only the defence of automatism to the jury, which first acquitted the respondent of first degree murder and then of second degree murder. The judge also acquitted the respondent of the charge of attempted murder for the same reasons. The Court of Appeal unanimously upheld the acquittal. . . .

## Issue

Did the Ontario Court of Appeal err in law in holding that the condition of sleep-walking should be classified as non-insane automatism resulting in an acquittal instead of being classified as a "disease of the mind" (insane automatism), giving rise to the special verdict of not guilty by reason of insanity?

*Analysis*

This court has only ruled on sleep-walking in an *obiter dictum* in *R. v. Rabey* (1980), 54 C.C.C. (2d) 1, 114 D.L.R. (3d) 193, [1980] 2 S.C.R. 513. The court found that sleepwalking was not a "disease of the mind" in the legal sense of the term and gave rise to a defence of automatism. Should the court maintain this position? . . .

A large part of the defence evidence in this case was medical evidence. Five physicians were heard: Dr. Roger James Broughton, a neurophysiologist and specialist in sleep and sleep disorders; Dr. John Gordon Edmeads, a neurologist; Dr. Ronald Frederick Billings, a psychiatrist; Dr. Robert Wood Hill, a forensic psychiatrist, and finally, Dr. Frank Raymond Ervin, a neurologist and psychiatrist.

The medical evidence in the case at bar showed that the respondent was in fact sleep-walking when he committed the acts with which he is charged. All the expert witnesses called by the defence said that in their opinion Parks was sleep-walking when the events occurred. This is what Dr. Broughton said:

> Q. . . . assuming for a moment that Mr. Parks caused the death of Barbara Woods, did you, sir, reach an opinion as to his condition at the time he caused that death?
>
> A. Yes. My opinion is that he did it during a sleepwalking episode.

Though sceptical at the outset, the expert witnesses unanimously stated that at the time of the incidents the respondent was not suffering from any mental illness and that, medically speaking, sleep-walking is not regarded as an illness, whether physical, mental or neurological. . . .

The evidence also disclosed that sleep-walking was very common, almost universal, among children, and that 2% to 2.5% of "normal" adults had sleep-walked at least once. Dr. Hill further noted that he found it significant that there were several sleepwalkers in the respondent's family.

> Thirdly, I think, as I indicated, it turns out, as enquiries are made more and more, that there is a significant history in the background family of Mr. Parks of difficulties, of bedwetting difficulties, of sleeptalking and sleepwalking, that is in keeping with what we know about the phenomena of sleepwalking. We know that there are often family members so affected and that was present.

Dr. Broughton, for his part, indicated that he had never known of sleep-walkers who had acted violently who had repeated this kind of behaviour:

> Q. Yes. Now, with respect to Mr. Parks, do you have any opinion, sir, as to the probability of a recurrence of an event of sleepwalking with serious aggression involving physical harm to others?
>
> A. I think the risk of that is infinitesimal, I don't think it would exceed the risk of the general population almost. He has the family predisposition to sleepwalk, but it would only be in the likelihood of all precipitating and extenuating and so forth factors that built up to this crisis that would theoretically have to almost reappear.
>
> Q. And even if they were to reappear, would there be any probability of another homicidal event?
>
> A. It would still — As I say, there are no reported cases in the literature, so there is essentially — The probability of it occurring is not statistically significant. It is just absolutely improbable.

In cross-examination he also added that sleep-walking episodes in which violent acts are committed are not common. . . . Further, on being questioned about a cure or treatment, Dr. Broughton answered that the solution was sleep hygiene, which involved eliminating factors that precipitated sleep-walking such as stress, lack of sleep and violent physical exercise. . . .

Dr. Ervin in his turn stated that during the slow wave sleep stage the cortex, which is the part of the brain that controls thinking and voluntary movement, is essentially in coma. When a person is sleep-walking, the movements he makes are controlled by other parts of the brain and are more or less reflexive. . . .

Three very important points emerge from this testimony: (1) the respondent was sleep-walking at the time of the incident; (2) sleep-walking is not a neurological, psychiatric or other illness: it is a sleep disorder very common in children and also found in adults; (3) there is no medical treatment as such, apart from good health practices, especially as regards sleep. It is important to note that this expert evidence was not in any way contradicted by the prosecution, which as the trial judge observed did have the advice of experts who were present during the testimony given by the defence experts and whom it chose not to call. . . .

I am of the view that in the instant case, based on the evidence and the testimony of the expert witnesses heard, the trial judge did not err in leaving the defence of automatism rather than that of insanity with the jury, and that the instant appeal should be dismissed. For a defence of insanity to have been put to the jury, together with or instead of a defence of automatism, as the case may be, there would have had to have been in the record evidence tending to show that sleep-walking was the cause of the respondent's state of mind. As we have just seen, that is not the case here. This is not to say that sleep-walking could never be a disease of the mind, in another case on different evidence.

As I see it, however, that does not end the matter. Although the expert witnesses were unanimous in saying that sleep-walkers are very rarely violent, I am still concerned by the fact that as the result of an acquittal in a situation like this (and I am relieved that such cases are quite rare), the accused is simply set free without any consideration of measures to protect the public, or indeed the accused himself, from the possibility of a repetition of such unfortunate occurrences. In the case of an outright acquittal, should there not be some control? And if so, how should this be done? I am of the view that such control could be exercised by means of the common law power to make an order to keep the peace vested in any judge or magistrate. . . .

If conditions should be imposed on Mr. Parks they will restrict his liberty. It follows that the decision to impose such conditions and the terms of those conditions should not violate the rights guaranteed under s. 7 of the Canadian *Canadian Charter of Rights and Freedoms*. However, such a hearing is justified, as the sleepwalker has, although innocently, committed an act of violence which resulted in the death of his mother-in-law. Members of the community may quite reasonably be apprehensive for their safety. In those circumstances it cannot be said that the court has unduly intruded upon the liberty of the accused by exploring, on notice to the accused, the possibility of imposing some minimally intrusive conditions which seek to assure the safety of the community. If conditions are imposed, then they obviously must be rationally connected to the apprehended danger posed by the person and go no further than necessary to protect the public from this danger.

I would, therefore, refer this matter back to the trial judge so that he can hear the parties on this point and decide, upon the evidence before him, whether such an order is appropriate. If this proves to be the case, it will be up to the trial judge to determine the content of the order.

I would, accordingly, dismiss this appeal and uphold the acquittal of the respondent but refer the matter back to the trial judge for him to decide on the making of an order to keep the peace on certain conditions, pursuant to the "preventive justice" power which he possesses.

[Note: In the final result, the majority was not in agreement as to sending the case back to the trial judge for consideration of further measures against Mr. Parks.]

*Appeal dismissed.*

## Bibliography

- Abramson, J.B., *Liberation and Its Limits* — The Moral and Political Thought of Freud (New York: The Free Press, 1984).
- Abrahamsen, D., *The Psychology of Crime* (Columbia University Press, 1960).
- Allen, H., "At the Mercy of Her Hormones: PMS and the Law" (1984), 19 m/f 9 19.
- Allen, F., "Criminal Law and the Modern Consciousness: Some Observations on Blameworthiness" (1977), 44 Tennessee Law Review 413.
- Archibald, T., "The Interrelationship Between Provocation and Mens Rea: A Defence of Loss of Self-Control" (1985), 28 Criminal Law Quarterly 454.
- Arkin, A.M., *Sleep-Talking: Psychology and Psychophysiology* (Hillsdale: L. Erlbaum Ass., 1981).
- Bartol, Curt, *Criminal Behaviour* — A Psychosocial Approach (Englewood Cliffs: Prentice Hall, 1980).
- Beauchamp, D., *Beyond Alcoholism — Alcohol and Public Health Policy* (Philadelphia: Temple University Press, 1980).
- Becker, G., *The Economic Approach to Human Behaviour* (Chicago: University of Chicago, 1976).
- Blackstone, W., *Commentaries on the Laws of England* (1769), Book IV.
- Bonnie, R. & Morris, N.V., "Debate: Should the Insanity Defence Be Abolished?" (1987), 2 Journal of Law & Health 113.
- *Broadhurst v. The Queen*, [1964] 1 All E.R. 111 (P.C.).
- Brian, P., ed., *Alcohol and Aggression* (Dover, N.H.: Croom Helm, 1986).
- Brown, et al., "Expectations of Reinforcement From Alcohol" (1980), 48 Consult. Clinical Psychology 419.
- Bynum, W., "Alcoholism and Degeneration in 19th Century European Medicine and Psychiatry" (1984), 78 British Journal of Addictions 317.
- Bywater, C., "Drink, Drugs and Criminal Intent", [1982] New Law Journal 615.
- Caplan, L., *The Insanity Defence: The Trial of John W. Hinckley, Jr.* (Boston: David R. Godine, 1984).
- Chamblis, W., "Types of Deviance and the Effectiveness of Legal Sanctions", [1967] Wisconsin Law Review 703.
- Cherek, D., *et al.*, "Effects of Alcohol on Human Aggressive Behaviour" (1985), 46 Journal Studies in Alcohol 321.

- Churchland, P.S., *Neurobiology — Towards a Unified Science of the Mind-Brain* (Cambridge: MIT Press, 1986).
- Clanon, T., Shawver, L., Kurdys, D., "Less Insanity in the Courts" (1982), 68 American Bar Ass. Journal 829.
- Clune, P., *Guilty but Insane — Anglo-American Attitudes to Insanity and Criminal Guilt* (London: Nelson, 1973).
- Cocklin, K., "Amnesia: The Forgotten Justification for Finding an Accused Incompetent to Stand Trial" (1981), 20 Washburn Law Journal 289.
- Dell, S., "Diminished Responsibility Reconsidered", [1982] Criminal Law Review 809.
- Dell, S., *Murder into Manslaughter* (Oxford: Oxford University Press, 1984).
- Dengerink, H., "Personality Variables as Mediators of Attack-Instigated Aggression", in Green, Russell and O'Neal, *Perspectives on Aggression* (New York: Academic Press, 1976).
- Dix, G., "Mental Health Professionals in the Legal Process: Some Problems of Psychiatric Dominance" (1981), 6 Law & Psychology Review 1.
- Dix, G., "Criminal Responsibility and Mental Impairment in American Criminal Law: Response to the Hinckley Acquittal in Historical Perspective" in D. Weisstub, ed., *Law and Mental Health* (New York: Pergammon Press, 1984), vol. 1.
- *D.P.P. v. Beard*, [1920] A.C. 479 (H.L.).
- *D.P.P. v. Majewski*, [1976] 2 All E.R. 142 (H.L.).
- *Durham v. United States* (1954), 214 F.2d 862 (D. Cir.).
- Ehrenzweig, A., *Psychoanalytic Jurisprudence: On Ethics, Esthetics and Law.* (New York: Oceana Publications, 1971).
- Ennis, B., *Prisoners of Psychiatry* — Mental Patients, Psychiatrists and the Law (New York: Harcourt Brace Jovanovich, 1972).
- Ericson, R., "Penal Psychiatry in Canada: The Method of Our Madness" (1976), 26 University of Toronto Law Journal 17.
- Ericson, R., "Psychiatrists in Prison" (1974), 22 Chitty's Law Journal 29.
- Eysenck, H.J., *The Effects of Psychotherapy* (New York: Science House, 1969).
- *Fain v. Commonwealth* (1879), 78 Ky. 183.
- Fenwick, P., "Somnambulism and the Law: A Review" (1987), 5 Behavioural Science & The Law 343.
- Fingarette, H. & Hasse, A., *Mental Disabilities and Criminal Responsibility* (Berkeley: University of California Press, 1979).
- Fingarette, H., *Heavy Drinking — The Myth of Alcoholism as a Disease* (Berkeley: University of California Press, 1988).
- Gaylin, W., *The Killing of Bonnie Garland — A Question of Justice* (New York: Simon & Schuster, 1982).
- Geller, J., Erlen J., Pinkus, R., "A Historical Appraisal of America's Experience with 'Dyromania' — A Diagnosis in Search of a Disorder" (1986), 9 International Journal of Law & Psychiatry 201.
- Gerber, J., "Is the Insanity Test Insane" (1975), 20 American J. Juris 111.
- Glasbeek, H. & Mandel, M., "The Legalization of Politics in Advanced Capitalism: The Canadian Charter of Rights and Freedoms" (1984), 2 Socialist Studies 84.
- Goff, C., "Criminological Appraisals of Psychiatric Explanations of Crime: 1936-1950" (1986), 9 International Journal of Law & Psychiatry 245.
- Goldstein, J. & Katz, "Abolish the Insanity Defence — Why Not?" (1963), 72 Yale Law Journal 853.
- Goldstein, P.J., "The Drugs/Violence Nexus: A Tripartite Conceptual Framework" (1985), 15 Journal of Drug Issues 493.
- Goode, E., *Drugs in American Society* (New York: Randon, 1984).

- Gregory, R.L., ed., *The Oxford Companion to the Mind* (Oxford: Oxford University Press, 1987).
- Grinspoon, L. & Bakalar, J., *Drug Control in a Free Society* (Cambridge: Harvard U. Press, 1984).
- Grinspoon, L. & Hedblom, R., *The Speed Culture: Amphetamine Use and Abuse in America* (Cambridge: Harvard U. Press, 1975).
- Gross, M., *The Psychological Society* (New York: Random House, 1978).
- Hall, J., *General Principles of Criminal Law* (Indianapolis: Bobbs-Merrill, 1960).
- Hall, J., "Intoxication and Criminal Responsibility" (1944), 57 Harvard Law Review 1045.
- Halleck, S., *Psychiatry and the Dilemmas of Crime* (New York: Harper & Row, 1967).
- Haney, J., "Psychology and Legal Change: On the Limits of a Factual Jurisprudence" (1980), 4 Law & Human Behaviour 147.
- *H.M.A. v. Dingweall* (1867), 5 Irv. 466.
- *H.M.A. v. Savage* (1923), J.C. 49.
- Hospers, J., "Meaning and Free Will" in H. Morris, ed., *Freedom and Responsibility* (Palo Alto: Stanford U. Press, 1961).
- Hovenkamp, H., "Insanity and Criminal Responsibility in Progressive America" (1981), 57 North Dakota Law Review 541.
- Hughes, R., and R. Brewin, *The Tranquilizing of America* (New York: Harcourt Brace Jovanovich, 1979).
- Hutchinson, H., *et al.*, "A Study of the Effects of Alcohol on Mental Functions" (1964), 9 Canadian Psychology Ass. J. 33.
- Illich, I., *Medical Nemisis* (New York: Pantheon, 1976).
- Jacobs, F., *Criminal Responsibility* (London: London School of Economics and Political Science, 1971).
- Jaynes, J., *The Origins of Consciousness in the Breakdown of the Bicameral Mind* (Boston: Houghton Mifflin, 1976).
- Jeffery, "Criminology as an Interdisciplinary Behavioural Science" (1978), 16 Criminology 149.
- Kaplan, J., *The Hardest Drug: Heroin and Public Policy* (Chicago: University of Chicago Press, 1983).
- Kelly, D., "Stalking the Criminal Mind — Psychopaths, Moral Imbeciles, and Free Will" Harper's, August, 1985, vol. 53.
- Kenny, A., *Freewill and Responsibility* (Toronto: Methuen, 1978).
- Kittrie, N., "The Prediction of Dangerousness" in *Mentally Ill Offenders and the Criminal Justice System* (New York: Praeger, 1978).
- Klein, D.B., *The Unconscious: Invention or Discovery?* (Santa Monica: Goodyear Pub., 1977).
- Klein, D.B., *The Concept of Consciousness* (Lincoln: University of Nebraska Press, 1983).
- Korchin, S., *Modern Clinical Psychology* (New York: Basic Books, 1967).
- Ladouceur, P. & Temple, M., "Substance Use Among Rapists: A Comparison with Other Serious Felons" (1985), 31 Crime & Delinquency 269.
- Lange, *et al.*, "Effects of Alcohol on Aggression in Male Social Drinkers" (1975), 84 Journal of Abnormal Psychology 233.
- Lasky, R., *Evaluation of Criminal Responsibility in Multiple Personality and the Related Dissociative Disorders: A Psychoanalytic Consideration* (Springfield: Charles C. Thomas, 1982).
- Lauderdale, P. & Inverarity, J., "Regulation of Opiates" (1984), 14 Journal Drug Issues 567.
- Lazare, "Hidden Conceptual Models in Clinical Psychiatry" (1973), 288 New England Journal of Medicine 345.

- *Leary v. The Queen* [1978] 1 S.C.R. 29.
- Leonard, et al., "Patterns of Alcohol Use and Physically Aggressive Behaviour in Men" (1985), 46 Journal Studies in Alcohol 279.
- Levine, H., "The Discovery of Addiction: Changing Conceptions of Habitual Drunkenness in America" (1978) 39 Journal Studies in Alcohol 143.
- Lewis, H.D., *The Elusive Mind* (London: Allen & Unwin, 1969).
- Loftus, G. & Loftus, E., *Human Memory* — The Processing of Information (London: Halsted, 1976).
- Lyon, D., *Ethics and the Rule of Law* (Cambridge: Cambridge University Press, 1984).
- Lynch, A., "The Scope of Intoxication", [1982] Criminal Law Rev. 139.
- Mackay, R., "Intoxication as a Factor in Automatism", [1982] Criminal Law Review 146.
- Mackay, R., "Pleading Provocation and Diminished Responsibility Together", [1988] Criminal Law Review 411.
- Marcus & Conway, "Dangerous Sexual Offender Project" (1969), 11:3 Canadian Journal Corrections 198.
- Martinson, R., "What Works? Questions and Answers about Prison Reform" (1974), 33-36 Public Interest 35.
- Menninger, K., *The Crime of Punishment* (New York: The Viking Press, 1966).
- Mewett, A., and M. Manning, *Mewett and Manning on Criminal Law* 3rd ed. (Toronto: Butterworths, 1994).
- Meyer, P., *The Yale Murder* (New York: Empire Books, 1982).
- Milner, N., "Models of Rationality and Mental Health" (1981), 4 Int'l J. of Law & Psychiatry 35.
- Mitchell, C., "The Mispursuit of Happiness: Divorcing Normative Legal Theory from Utilitarianism" (1986a), 16 Manitoba Law Journal 123.
- Mitchell, C., "Culpable Mental Disorder and Criminal Liability" (1986b), 8 International Journal of Law and Psychiatry 273.
- Mitchell, C., "The Judging and Policing of Science: The Law's Need for Science Consumer Protection" (1989), 9 Windsor Yearbook of Access to Justice 3.
- *M'Naghten's Case* (1843), 8 E.R. 718, 10 Cl. & F.200.
- Monahan, J., "The Prediction of Violence" in *Violence and Criminal Justice* (Toronto: D.C. Heath & Co., 1981).
- Montagu, A. & Darling, E., *The Prevalence of Nonsense* (New York: Harper & Row, 1967).
- Moore, M., "Responsibility and the Unconscious" (1980), 53 Southern California Law Review 1563.
- Morris, N., "Somnambulistic Homicide: Ghosts, Spiders and North Koreans" (1951), 29 Res. Judicata 29.
- Morris, N., "Psychiatry and the Dangerous Criminal" (1968), 41 Southern California Law Rev. 514.
- Morse, S., "Failed Explanations and Criminal Responsibility: Experts and the Unconscious" (1982a), 68 Virginia Law Review 971.
- Morse, S., "A Preference for Liberty: The Case Against Involuntary Commitment of the Mentally Disordered" (1982b), 70 California Law Review 54.
- Morse, S., "Undiminished Confusion in Diminished Capacity" (1984), 75 Journal of Criminal Law & Criminology 1.
- Murphy, J., *Retribution, Justice and Therapy* (Norwell: MA: Kluwer Academic, 1979).
- Myers, T., "Alcohol and Violent Crimes Re-examined: Self: Reports from Two Sub-Groups of Scottish Male Prisoners" (1982), 77 British Journal of Addictions 399.
- Orchard, G., "Drunkenness as a 'Defence' to Crime" (1977), 1 Criminal Law Journal 59.
- Parkin, A.J., *Memory and Amnesia: An Introduction* (Oxford: Basil Blackwell, 1987).

- Peele, S., "The Pleasure Principle in Addiction" (1985), 15 Journal of Drug Issues 193.
- *People v. Conley* (1966), 64 Cal.2d 310, 411 P.2d 911, 49 Cal. Rptr. 815.
- *People v. Poddar* (1974), 10 Cal.3d 750, 518 P.2d 342, 111 Cal. Rptr. 910.
- *People v. Wolff* (1964), 61 Cal.2d 795, 394 P.2d 959, 40 Cal. Rptr. 271.
- Pepinsky, H. & Jesilow, P., *Myths that Cause Crime* (Washington: Seven Locks Press, 1984).
- Pihl, R., *et al.*, "Alcohol and Aggression in Men" (1984), 45 Journal Studies in Alcohol 278.
- Poikolainen, K., "Alcoholism: A Social Construct" (1982), 12 Journal of Drug Issues 361.
- Polier, W., *The Rule of Law and the Role of Psychiatry* (Baltimore: Johns Hopkins Press, 1968).
- *Pollard v. United States* (1960), 282 F.2d 450 (6th Cir.).
- Posner, R., *The Economics of Justice* (Cambridge: Harvard U. Press, 1981).
- *Powell v. Texas* (1968), 392 U.S. 514.
- *Rabey v. The Queen* (1980), 54 C.C.C. (2d) 1 (S.C.C.).
- Rachman, S. & Wilson, G., *The Effects of Psychological Therapy* (London: Pergamon Press, 1980).
- *R. v. Bailey*, [1983] 1 W.L.R. 760 (C.A.).
- *R. v. Borg*, [1969] 4 C.C.C. 262 (S.C.C.).
- *R. v. Bouchard* (1973), 12 C.C.C. (2d) 554 (N.S. Co. Ct.).
- *R. v. Bray* (1975), 24 C.C.C. (2d) 366 (Ont. Co. Ct.).
- *R. v. Byrne*, [1960] 2 Q.B. 396 (C.A.).
- *R. v. Cullum* (1973), 14 C.C.C. (2d) 294 (Ont. Co. Ct.).
- *R. v. Gottschalk* (1974), 22 C.C.C. (2d) 415 (Ont. Prov. Ct.).
- *R. v. Hadfield* (1800), 27 St. Tr. 1281 (K.B.).
- *R. v. Hardie*, [1985] 1 W.L.R. 64 (C.A.).
- *R. v. Kasperek*, [1951] O.R. 776 (C.A.).
- *R. v. King* (1962), 133 C.C.C. 1 (S.C.C.).
- *R. v. Martin* (1947), 4 C.R. 54 (Alta. S.C.).
- *R. v. Minor* (1955), 112 C.C.C. 29 (Sask. C.A.).
- *R. v. Podola* (1959), 3 All E.R. 418 (C.C.A.).
- *R. v. Shaw* (1938), 70 C.C.C. 159 (Ont. C.A.).
- *R. v. Smith*, [1982] Crim. L.R. 531 (C.A.).
- *R. v. Sproule* (1975), 26 C.C.C. (2d) 92 (Ont. C.A.).
- *R. v. Szymusiak*, [1972] 3 O.R. 602 (C.A.).
- Reiser, M,, *Mind, Brain, Body* — Towards a Convergence of Psychoanalysis and Neurobiology (New York: Basic Books, 1985).
- Reisner, R. & Semmel, H., "Abolishing the Insanity Defence" (1974), 62 California Law Rev. 753.
- *Reninger v. Feogossa* (1552), 15 E.R. 1.
- Robitscher, J. & Haynes, A., "In Defence of the Insanity Defence" (1982), 31 Emory Law Journal 9.
- Rosenberg, "The Abusers of Stimulants and Depressants", in Cull, J. & Hardy, R., eds., *Types of Drug Abusers and Their Abuses* (Springfield, Ill.: Charles C. Thomas, Publisher, 1974).
- Ryle, G., *The Concept of Mind* (London: Hutchinson, 1949).
- Sahlins, M., *Culture and Practical Reason* (Chicago: University of Chicago Press, 1976).
- Samenow, S., *Inside the Criminal Mind* (New York: Times Books, 1984).
- Sands, "The Mad Murderer in the Courtroom" (New Orleans: Paper presented to the Am. Psych. Assoc., 1981).
- Savage, H., "The Relevance of the Fitness to Stand Trial Provisions to Persons with Mental Handicap" (1981), 59 Canadian Bar Review 319.

- Schachter, D., "Amnesia and Crime — How Much Do We Really Know (1986), 41 American Psychologist 286.
- Schiffer, M.E., *Mental Disorders and the Criminal Trial Process* (Toronto: Butterworths, 1978).
- Schoenfeld, C.G., *Psychoanalysis Applied to the Law* (New York: Assoc. Faculty Press, 1973).
- Scitovsky, T., *The Joyless Economy* (Oxford: Oxford University Press, 1976).
- Sheleff, L., "The Illusions of Law — Psychoanalysis and Jurisprudence in Historical Perspective" (1986), 9 Int'l J. Law & Psychiatry 143.
- Siann, G., *Accounting for Aggression* — Perspectives on Aggression and Violence (Boston: Allen & Unwin, 1985).
- Sidgwick, H., *The Methods of Ethics* (New York: Macmillan Co., 1893).
- Simon, B., *Mind and Madness in Ancient Greece* — A Classical Roots of Modern Psychiatry (Ithaca: Cornell University Press, 1978).
- Singh, R., "History of the Defence of Drunkeness on English Criminal Law" (1933), 49 Law Quarterly Review 528.
- Smith, J.C. & Weisstub, D.N., *The Western Idea of Law* (Toronto: Butterworths, 1983).
- Smith, R., *Trial by Medicine — Insanity and Responsibility in Victorian Trials* (Edinburgh: Edinburgh University Press, 1981).
- Stannard, J., "The Demise of Drunkeness" (1982), 2 Legal Studies 291.
- Starke, J.G., *The Validity of Psycho-Analysis* (New York: Angus & Robertson, 1973).
- Steadman & Bruff, "Crimes of Violence and Incompetency Diversion" (1975), 66 J. Criminal Law & Corrections 73.
- Stone, A., *Law, Psychiatry and Morality* (New York: Am. Psychiatric, 1984).
- Stuart, D., *Canadian Criminal Law: A Treatise*, 2nd ed. (Toronto: Carswell, 1987).
- Sutherland, E.H., "The Sexual Psychopath Laws" in Cohen, *et al.*, eds., *The Sutherland Papers* (Bloomington: Indiana University Publications, 1956).
- Szasz, T., *Law, Liberty and Psychiatry* (London: Routledge & Kegan Paul, 1963).
- Szasz, T., *Ideology and Insanity* (London: Routledge, 1970).
- Szasz, T., *Insanity* — The Idea and Its Consequences (New York: John Wiley & Sons, 1987).
- Talland, G., "The Korsakoff Syndrome" in E. Strauss & R. Griffith, eds., *Phenomenology of Memory* (Pittsburgh: Duquesne University Press, 1970).
- Toch, H., *Legal and Criminal Psychology* (New York: Holt, Rinehart and Winston, 1964).
- Trebach, A., *The Great Drug War* (New York: Macmillan, 1987).
- Valenstein, E., "Causes and Treatments of Mental Disorders" in *The Psychosurgery Debate* (New York: W.H. Freeman, 1982).
- Van den Haag, E., *Punishing Criminals* (New York: Basic Books, 1976).
- Veblen, T., *Theory of the Leisure Class* (New York: Viking Press, 1899).
- Verdun-Jones, S., "The Evolution of the Defences of Insanity and Automatism in Canada from 1843 to 1979" (1979), 14 University of British Columbia Law Rev. 7.
- Virkkunen, M., "Alcohol as a Factor Precipitating Aggression and Conflict Behaviour Leading to Homicide" (1974), 69 British J. Addictions 149.
- Vogt, I., "Defining Alcohol Problems as a Repressive Mechanism: Its Formative Phase in Imperial Germany and its Strengths Today" (1984), 19 International Journal of Addiction 551.
- Warren, "The Economic Approach to Crime" (1978), 20 Canadian Journal Criminology 437.
- Weinberg & Vatz, "The Mental Illness Dispute: The Critical Faith Assumptions" (1981), 9 Journal Psychology & Law 9.
- Weiss, P., *Man's Freedom* (Carbondale: Southern Illinois University Press, 1950).
- Weisskopf, "The Image of Man in Economics" (1973), 40 Social Research 547.
- Weisstub, D., "Review of Psychiatry on Trial" (1978), 56 Canadian Bar Review 740.

- Weisstub, D., "The Theoretical Relationship Between Law and Psychiatry" (1978), 1 Inter'l J. Law & Psych 19.
- White, S., "Phrenology and the McNaughten Rules" (1984), 8 Criminal Law Journal 166.
- Whyte, L.L., *The Unconsciousness Before Freud* (New York: St. Martin's Press, 1978).
- Wilson, C., *Order of Assassins: The Psychology of Murder* (London: Rupert-Hart-Davis, 1972).
- Wilson, C., *A Criminal History of Mankind* (New York: G.P. Putnam's, 1984).
- Wilson, J. & Herrnstein, R., *Crime and Human Nature* (Cambridge: Harvard University Press, 1985).
- Wilson, J., *Thinking About Crime* (New York: Basic Books, 1983).
- Winsdlade, W. & Ross, J., *The Insanity Plea: The Uses and Abuses of the Insanity Defense* (New York: Charles Scribner's Sons, 1983).
- Winson, J., *Brain and Psyche — The Biology of the Unconscious* (New York: Anchor Press/Doubleday, 1985).
- Wiseman, S., "Communist Ideology and the Substance Abuser: A Peripatetic Look at the Use of the Medical Paradigm to Oppress Political Deviants" (1985), 15 J. Drug Issues 247.
- Wisotsky, S., *Breaking the Impasse on the War Against Drugs* (New York: Greenwood Press, 1986).
- Zeichner, A. & Pihl, R., "Effects of Alcohol and Instigator Intent on Human Aggression" (1980), 41 J. Studies Alcohol 265.
- Zetner, J., "Heroin: Devil Drug or Useful Medicine?" (1979), 9 J. Drug Issues 333.
- Zetner, J., "Review Essay" (1984), 14 J. Drug Issues 175.
- Zilbergeld, B., *The Shrinking of America — Myths of Psychological Change* (Boston: Little, Brown, 1983).
- Zillman, D., *Hostility and Aggression* (Hillsdale: Lawrence Erlbaum Assoc., 1979).

## Questions

1. How do the defences of mental disorder and automatism differ? How may they overlap?
2. You are defending an accused charged with armed robbery and assault. The accused has a history of psychiatric treatment, including hospitalization. Should you argue that your client is unfit to stand trial? Would it be advantageous to raise the issue of insanity? Or should the accused's possible mental problems be argued merely as a mitigating factor at sentencing? See, McIntyre, J., "Amendments to the Criminal Code (Mental Disorder): Bill C-30 and Review Boards" (1992), 50 Advocate (Vancouver) 574-592, and Bloom, H. and B. Butler, *Defending Mentally Disordered Persons 1995* (Scarborough, Ont.: Carswell, 1995).
3. What is the connection between the intoxication doctrine and the prohibition of psychoactive drugs?
4. Do you agree with the result in *Daviault*? Why or why not? Do you think that section 33.1 of the Code will withstand a Charter challenge? Why or why not?
5. In what way does the criminal law discriminate against the mentally ill? What is the theoretical basis for this policy?
6. Explain the legal outcome of replacing the insanity section with a pure mens rea test for all accused persons.
7. Three basic alternatives exist for dealing with intoxicated offenders: the *O'Connor* rule, the rule in *Leary*, and a special offence of being "drunk and dangerous". Describe these alternatives and explain the differences in legal outcome their use would cause. In this regard, see the four articles contained in "Criminal Reports Forum on *Daviault*: Extreme Intoxication Akin to Automatism Defense to Sexual Assault" in (1994), 33 C.R. (4th) 269-294 and Drassinower, M. and D. Stuart, "Nine Months of Judicial Application of the *Daviault* Defence" (1995), 39 C.R. (4th) 280-286.

# 8

# CURRENT ISSUES IN CRIMINAL JUSTICE

## 8.1 SEXUAL ASSAULT

### Issues in Sexual Assault
*R.P. Saunders*

The topic of sexual assault can be looked at from several different analytical perspectives including, for example, psychological, sociological, and legal. In this section we conduct an examination of the various legal issues involved and also try, more importantly and more generally, to illustrate the somewhat limited effectiveness of legal solutions to such problems facing women. To accomplish these two goals, we need, at the very least, a basic understanding of not only the legal response to the problem, but also the basic social dimensions to sexual assault.

Three points should be made at the outset by way of explanation. First, the terms "sexual assault" and the term "rape" are used throughout, though, as you will see, rape is an outdated and more narrowly defined term. It is, however, for good or for bad, one of the most widely used and recognizable term for sexual attacks against women. Second, there are many and varying views and theories on the issues related to sexual assault, and it should be recognised that what follows is not an attempt to present all of them, but rather is a selective and introductory presentation of several of these perspectives. To examine many of these views in more depth, please refer to the "Further Reading" section which follows. A final point to note is that the topics of prison rapes and child sexual assault are not considered here, though such assaults do present serious problems for those in detention and for children; the focus here is on the problem of sexual assaults which occur in everyday life.

In light of these qualifiers, then, we can begin with a very brief reference to earlier times. It is interesting to note that historically the goal of rape sanctions was often to protect a man's property, not to protect the integrity of women *per se*; for example, in certain societies, rape was seen as something which damaged a man's goods. The crime was seen in the context of the theft of property or the theft of a saleable item, that is, virginity or the woman's exclusive sexual services. It is this notion of the theft of property and not the desire to protect individual women which is sometimes seen as the historical basis of the rape and sexual assault laws which were or are in place in Western society today.

In a Canadian context, this attitude can be seen particularly in the old definition of rape which was in effect until January 4, 1983. This law, which dated from earlier this century, contained the four principal elements of rape. The first element was vaginal penetration by the penis; the consequence of this was a concentration on the sexual nature of the act itself, not on the assaultive or aggressive nature of the act. It is interesting that other types of violation of the person, for example, forcible oral and anal intercourse were not seen as rape. The prohibited act was seen in the context of the "normal" sexual act. Second, the victim had to be a woman — a man could not be legally raped. Somehow, it was only a woman's body and integrity which could be taken and not a man's. Again, this relates to very early notions of women as men's property, of women as "available victims" in society, and of women as objects capable of being appropriated. Third, a man could not rape his wife. It was assumed that if a woman said "I do", then the possibility of saying no to sexual relations in the future was forever gone. We can see in this element the idea that a woman became the husband's property on marriage and he could do with her as he wished sexually. The fourth and final factor was that of lack of consent. It is important to note, however, that the lack of consent was not necessarily the actual refusal of consent on the part of the victim; rather, it was the rapist's perception of the existence or non-existence of the consent which was the important issue. If the rapist was "honestly" mistaken as to the existence of consent, then he would not be guilty. It was the subjective belief of the rapist as to the existence of consent which was the important legal issue.

In sum, the old law presented rape in the context of normal sexual intercourse between a man and a woman who was not his wife where consent was lacking. The focus was on the sexual aspects of the crime, not on the assaultive nature of the crime. This was particularly true in the actual operation of the law where it was often the woman's actions and character which were put on trial, not the accused's. The law was a reflection of many of the "myths" which people held about the crime of rape (see generally, Rioux and Kinnon). It is important now to understand what these myths are so that we can see how the old laws failed us, and perhaps to better understand what the legislative reforms were attempting to rectify and their potential for success.

The first of these myths has to do with frequency. It is the belief that rape is not a "big" problem but rather that it is a relatively rare occurrence, and as a rule does not happen to so-called "good girls". This is coupled with the idea that the woman could have avoided the attack. Many people believe that if a woman really wants to avoid sexual assault, then she can, either by fighting back or by not putting herself in a dangerous situation. We see this view in the attitudes expressed in phrases such as "What was she doing in the park at that time of night? Why was she hitchhiking? Why did she go out with the person?" and so on. The difficulty is that participation in social interaction is regarded as a sexual invitation.

The second myth has to do with the "situation" of rape. Rape is often seen as a separate, deviant, or individualized type of behaviour. We have a definite image of the rapist as a "lurker" in alleys who pounces on his victim. What this means is we are taught to see rape as a *separate problem*. The rapist becomes a rapist because of bad genes or an extra hormone, or perhaps because of poor early social development. In this context, the rapist is also often seen as a sick predator, a stranger who preys upon more or less innocent victims. What this view does is teach us to avoid the need to put rape in the context of other behaviour and other attitudes in society which might be seen as contributing to the problem of rape. Under the individual-oriented view, if we "cured" the individual, then we could eventually "cure" the problem of rape. As we shall see later, it is more helpful to see rape as only one aspect of a larger set of problems in society.

The third myth has to do with the victim herself. As noted above, the victim is seen as "more or less" innocent: more innocent if the victim is white, middle or upper class, married, or is a virgin. Less innocent, and therefore more culpable, if she is a member of a minority group, single, independent, or career-oriented. If she falls within this latter group, she is viewed somewhat as a "loose" woman and has "asked for it", or at the very least has brought about the attack through some fault of her own.

This myth also encompasses several other ideas. First, we have the notion that the victim wanted sexual contact, and then to cover up that desire decided to call it rape. She might do this out of guilt, or because she was fearful of being caught by a husband or boyfriend, but essentially it is the belief that the victim initiated the contact and then alleged lack of consent. Second, we also have the fact that some rapists *believe* that they are releasing the victims from their innate sexual inhibition. Such attackers see themselves in a very perverse sense as sexual therapists. And finally, we have the idea that the victim, while not direct in asking for sexual contact, in fact precipitated the assault. There was allegedly implied consent by virtue of, for example, the clothing the woman was wearing, the area she was in, or the activity (for example, hitchhiking) in which she was engaged. It is the notion that these are signals to the attacker that the woman is available and even eager to some extent for sexual contact, even though she has not explicitly expressed her consent.

A fourth myth has to do with the nature of the act of rape itself as it is conceived in many people's minds. It is often perceived as an act of sexual passion in which the rapist could not control himself. We find this view well illustrated, for example, in the popular media when we look at the focus on the lurid sexual aspects of the crime found in the coverage of rape trials. The depictions are sensationalized and thereby trivialized; it is as if the sexual aspect somehow transformed the nature of the crime into something other than a real crime. An act which degrades and violates women is too often portrayed as an erotic act. This can be seen also in many pornographic magazines and films which depict the forcible violation of women as erotic.

A final myth is that "she enjoyed it". Again, this relates to the mistaken idea that rape is a type of sexual activity; the lack of consent and the assaultive nature of the crime are consequently downplayed. Rapists will sometimes tell the victim to "relax and enjoy it" even though the mutual agreement of consensual sexual intercourse is not present. Furthermore, the attacker will sometimes ask the victim if he was the best lover she ever had, or did she have an orgasm? Such sentiments obviously have nothing to do with the true nature of rape or sexual assault, and yet the attackers somehow believe (even if only as a self-justification) that rape is a sexual experience. Of course, one would find it ludicrous to think of a robber asking the victim "Did you enjoy it?" or "Was I the best person who ever robbed you?" Yet this is the type of justification used by the rapist and indeed, many would argue, by society as a whole.

In summary, in all these myths we have the underlying belief that women are primarily sexual beings; though they might use devious means to achieve sexual contact, the belief is that that is what they are often seeking. It is thought that the signals which women put out through their dress or their status, their activity or the area in which they might find themselves, are signals which can justifiably be interpreted by men as wanting that contact. Therefore, the act of rape or any type of forcible sexual contact is justified by the rapist, by the enforcement agencies and courts to some extent (as we shall see below), and by society itself.

The questions which now arise are what do we know about rape? what are the facts about rape? We can relate that knowledge to many of the issues which were raised above connected with the various myths. In regard to the issue of frequency, the first point is that rape is a major problem. But the difficulty is that it is a hidden crime. In 1992, the national rate for reported sexual assaults was 126 per 100,000 residents. However, only a small proportion of women report such assaults to the police. The point is that all women are vulnerable and live in danger of being sexually assaulted. The difficulty with the statistics is that it is very hard to determine the real number of assaults because the estimates vary widely for the report-occurrence ratio. Some argue that approximately only 1 in 3 survivors of sexual assault report the attack while others maintain that the figure is closer to 1 in 20. Whatever the figure, it is obvious that the problem is a serious one. An even more disturbing aspect of the problem is that only a very small percentage of actual assaults ever results in a conviction. What this means is that sexual assault remains a hidden crime and a hidden problem.

In regard to the myth of "situation", it is argued that it is misleading to see rape in the context of lovemaking; it is better understood as an act of aggression, as the violent appropriation of control over another person's body. As to the notion that rape is done by the lone lurker in alleys, it has been shown that most rapes are planned acts. The rapist knows what he is doing and the act is rationally constructed. In fact, 80 percent of single rapes are planned and more than 90 percent of group rapes are planned. The rapist follows a typical pattern, and within that pattern, more than 85 percent of rapes involve violence to the victim. In regard to the victim, two-thirds of the victims know the assailant and 30 to 40 percent know the assailant well. The assault most often occurs in a trust situation; that is, the victim is attacked by a boyfriend, a friend, a friend of the husband or the boyfriend, or a relative.

In light of these facts, how, then, can sexual assault be explained? Rather than as an individual act done by a lone predator who is individually disturbed, rape must be seen as an aspect of larger social relations. Sexual assault is an act which is integrated into the way society is organized; that is, ordinary men rape ordinary women. In this regard, we can look for an explanation of rape at two levels: first, at the societal level, and second, at the individual level.

On the societal level, we have to look at the social arrangements which many argue endorse rape in society. What is that social relation? Basically, it is that we have sexism as a relation in society. If we look at this relation on a cultural level, we see sexism existing as a normative system. Simply put, it is a relation which helps men to manage their world. It promotes the idea that there are winners and losers in society and that women are losers. Women are portrayed as emotional, as fragile, as silly, as subject to flights of fancy (particularly during menstruation), as gossipy and useful primarily as sexual beings or objects. We see this in the way that they are portrayed in ads on television, in the way business tries to sell products in newspapers and magazines, and generally, through their presentation in the entertainment media. One inference of this, of course, is that if a woman says no, does she really mean no? Perhaps one should search for other cues to determine the "real" answer. For example, if she is hitchhiking, or is drinking alone, or is wearing a low-cut dress, the belief is that perhaps it is legitimate to infer that the woman is available for sexual relations.

This is true as well if we look at the relation on an economic level. Women, again, are designated losers within the economic system. This is true not only in the continuing disparity in average wage levels between men and women, but also in society's willingness to tolerate sexual harassment on the job and the lack of opportunities for advancement by women in many career fields. The consequence of sexism as a relation or social arrangement in society is that women are designated as available victims in society. Society provides the justification for, even endorsement of, the act of rape or sexual assault in society.

Within this overall context of a sexist and patriarchal society, we can also look at the individual level of rape. At the individual level, one goal of rape is an attempt to deal with the anger and frustration felt by men in society; it is not an attempt to achieve sexual gratification. Sexual assault becomes a solution to problems because it is an easy solution. It is an easy solution because we have a weak and authorized victim, the crime is easy to justify through justification such as "she wanted it" or "she enjoyed it", and, finally there is little chance of punishment. Therefore, the individual man, in an attempt to deal with his frustration at "losing" in society, can turn to sexual assault as a means for solving or coping with his problems. It should be noted, however, that there are different explanations of rape at this individual level and this is only one. What is important here as to the issue of the response of criminal law is that in looking at this individual level we must not forget the origin of the problem in the sexist relations within society.

What, then, are the proposed solutions to the problem of sexual assault? In general, we have two solutions. One, we can change the system; we can rid society of the basic causes of sexual assault, that is rid society of sexism. The problem is, obviously, how one does that, particularly in the short term. Second, we have limited pragmatic solutions which involve two things: first, we want to raise the cost of rape to the aggressor. We can do this through more convictions, by making it more likely that an individual will be convicted and punished if he sexually assaults a woman. Also, we can raise the capacity of women to resist, not only through self defense classes, better and safer living environments, and the such, but also by lowering the cost to the victim, by ensuring that the victim is more willing to report, and by making the system more amenable to her needs in coming forth and reporting the offence.

By way of a pragmatic solution, Parliament passed legislation which came into effect in 1983 and which was modified in 1992. These amendments to the Criminal Code and the relevant case law are detailed in the Stuart article which follows. As can be seen, flaws remain in the law's treatment of this type of crime, but it can be said that the attempts to date represent major steps forward when compared to the old rape law. But very real difficulties do remain with such a pragmatic solution, notably in regard to the enforcement of the law. It is in the operation of the legislation that major hurdles remain. These hurdles, seen in the context of a sexist society, can be seen in several steps of the enforcement process.

On the front line are police enforcement agencies. The problem we find here is that according to a study published in late 1982 (when the old law was still in force), one-third of all rape complaints were disbelieved by the police. This meant that one-third of all complaints reported to the police were not investigated further. This figure had improved by 1985 to about 14 percent, a hopeful sign but still high given dismissal rates for other crimes. Unfortunately, the figure of 14% has remained virtually the same since then, though it should be noted that the actual rate varies considerably across the country (see, generally, Roberts, 1994). Police argue that many of the complainants are mistaken or lying and that a rape never occurred. By way of contrast, police believe that only 1 out of every 33 individuals who say they have been robbed are either mistaken or lying, and when it comes to police officers who say they have been assaulted in the course of their duty, only 1 in 250 will not be believed. As to the reasons why women are disbelieved, one often finds in the arguments of the police stereotypical beliefs and attitudes as to the nature of the crime itself. These attitudes have been criticized by rape crisis centre counsellors who argue that the police are clinging to outmoded and prejudicial attitudes towards women; they do not believe that when a woman says no she really means no. It is this type of police attitude toward the problem which obviously discourages women from coming forward to report the crime and prevents the prosecution of assailants. Some improvements have been made recently in the creation of specific units within police departments formed to deal with sexual assault victims and to aid them in the prosecution of this type of crime. However, the availability of this type of unit is not widespread, particularly in rural areas. Moreover, the complaint has been raised that these units often consist principally of male members of the force.

Another problem in the enforcement in this area has to do with the treatment of the victim at the hands of the medical profession. According to the former Attorney General of Ontario, Roy McMurtry, "there is a tradition of reluctance of doctors in emergency wards to get involved in cases that could end up at a criminal trial because of the time involved" (*Globe and Mail*, October 1, 1982). There have been several cases across the country where hospitals and doctors have refused to treat sexual assault victims and of situations where the victim had to "shop around" for a hospital which was willing to examine and treat her. While some hospitals now provide special units and personnel to deal with sexual assault victims, such units remain relatively rare. It is this reluctance and callousness on the part of the medical profession which have undoubtedly caused many women to hesitate before reporting the crime and seeking treatment.

The final problem has to do with the judiciary. Judges play a particularly important role under the legislation due to the lack of a definition for sexual assault, the Charter concerns over balancing the rights of the victims versus those of the accused, and the issues surrounding the defence of mistaken belief in consent (see excerpts from the *Livermore* case, reproduced below). There have been many instances in the past when, it can be argued, judges have been less than sympathetic or less than progressive in regard to the plight of the rape or sexual assault survivor. One can find numerous examples in statements by members of the judiciary reflecting outmoded and sexist attitudes towards women, not only in sexual assault cases but also in many other types of cases involving women (for example, where domestic violence has occurred). It is important to note that one of the first major cases to come forward in regard to the new sexual assault legislation evolved around the issue of whether women's breasts are indeed sexual. In this case, the Court of Appeal in New Brunswick ruled that female breasts are like men's beards, a secondary sexual characteristic. In contrast, the prosecutor had contended that it is the circumstances of an assault which determine whether it is sexual, not the parts of the body which are touched. In the case, however, the court reduced the sentence to six months from the eight months which had been imposed originally because it argued that the assault was not sexual as it involved only secondary sexual characteristics, that is, a woman's breasts. This is the type of inane argument which critics argued might result under the new legislation. The Court of Appeal decision was overturned by the Supreme Court in *R. v. Chase* (1987), 59 C.R. (3d) 193, but many of the attitudes surrounding the Court of Appeal decision and the ignorance reflected in it continue today. The *McCraw* case, below, though not a sexual assault case *per se*, is another good example of some existing judicial attitudes and their consequences. There are numerous other examples which one can point to which reveal attitudes on the part of many in the judiciary (both at the trial and appellate levels) which reflect the myths referred to above, but we can end here by noting the reasoning used by a judge in sentencing three convicted gang rapists in 1981 and the incredible double standard which was applied:

> In sentencing the men, Smith [the judge] said that because of all the exceptional circumstances of the case, a penitentiary term of two years or more . . . would be a gross error. . . .
> The rape took place in a ditch beside a country road after several hours of driving about and smoking marijuana.
> Smith said that the young men were of good character and came from remarkable family backgrounds, but because of excessive drinking and pot smoking that night, had stepped out of character for a brief period.
> The woman, on the other hand, "had behaved very foolishly".
> "She was rebellious, drank too much and started out on that *frolic* with no regard for the consequences."
> [Emphasis added]. (*The Ottawa Citizen*, October 31, 1981).

While the drinking and smoking served to excuse the men's behaviour, it was used on the other hand to blame the woman (at least partially) for the crimes which took place.

The attitudes we find towards sexual assault victims on the part of the police, the medical profession, and the legal profession are, of course, not surprising in light of the fact that we are dealing with male-dominated, conservative bodies. A real attack on the problem of sexual assault in society cannot be fully or effectively undertaken until women begin to have a real influence within these enforcement agencies and more importantly within the political power structures in this country. There will be little progress until sexism itself is eliminated.

In sum, what we have is a pragmatic solution which, though flawed, is certainly a positive step towards a real, comprehensive solution. The greatest problem in the short term remains in its enforcement within the context of a patriarchal enforcement process. Moreover, in the long term, in spite of the fact that we may eventually have more effective enforcement, the fundamental problem remains that sexual assault is too much an accepted and even acceptable activity within the context of current sexist relations in society. What progress has been made to date has been the result of women organizing amongst themselves to create lobby groups, crisis centres, and self-defence classes. Changes in the criminal legislation go only a very small way towards providing a solution and do not ensure either that the cause of the social problem will be eradicated or that the reforms will be given real effect in their enforcement. Unless and until these two issues are effectively addressed, any legislative reforms can have only a marginal effect.

## R. v. McCraw
### (1989), 72 C.R. (3d) 373 (Ont. C.A.).

Appeal by Crown from accused's acquittal of threatening serious bodily harm. October 16, 1989. BROOKE J.A. (TARNOPOLSKY J.A. concurring): — The Crown appeals from the acquittal of the respondent on three counts in an indictment, each of which counts charged him with an offence contrary to s. 243.4 (now s. 264.1) of the Criminal Code. The counts were as follows:

1. That he the said Stephen Joseph McCraw, between the 1st day of November, 1987 and the 26th day of November, 1987 at the City of Ottawa in the said Judicial District, did knowingly cause to be received a threat to Sandy Kobluk, by letter, to cause serious bodily harm to Sandy Kobluk, contrary to Section 243.4(2) of the Criminal Code of Canada.
2. And further that he the said Stephen Joseph McCraw, between the 1st day of November, 1987 and the 26th day of November, 1987 at the City of Ottawa in the said Judicial District, did knowingly cause to be received a threat to Johanne Robillard, by letter, to cause serious bodily harm to Johanne Robillard, contrary to Section 243.4(2) of the Criminal Code of Canada.
3. And further that he the said Stephen Joseph McCraw, between the 1st day of October, 1987 and the 30th day of October, 1987 at the City of Ottawa in the said Judicial District, did knowingly cause to be received a threat to Deborah Burgoyn, by letter, to cause serious bodily harm to Deborah Burgoyn, contrary to Section 234.4(2) of the Criminal Code of Canada.

The trial judge held that, although the respondent had written the letters and each contained a threat to rape the complainant, none of the threats necessarily involved the infliction of serious bodily harm. The finding that each letter contained a threat to rape is not attacked in this court.

The facts were that the complainants were cheerleaders of a football club. The respondent, who was not known to any of them, wrote to each a similar letter. The letter to the complainant Johanne Robillard stated:

Johanne
Let me tell you, your a beautiful woman, I am disappointed you weren't in the calendar, you are the most beautiful cheerleader on the squad. I think you should pose nude for playboy.

[After detailing in graphic and vulgar terms what he would like to do to the complainant, the defendant wrote:]

I am going to fuck you even if I have to *rape* you. Even if it takes me till the day I die. There should be more beautiful women around like you.
*See you later and have a nice day!*

In the case of Johanne Robillard only, that letter was followed by a letter which said:

Johanne
Meet me on Thursday, November 19, at 6:00 p.m., behind the N.A.C. (National Arts Centre) in Ottawa, be along the water of the Rideau Canal. If you dont show up I will go to Rockland and *get*

*you*. Dont forget I know where you live.
See you soon!

In dismissing the charges, the trial judge said:

> In this case, the threat to "rape", to have non-consensual sexual intercourse, may or may not involve serious bodily harm. It does not involve it necessarily. The court found that the words in *Gingras* might equally mean "I'm going to strike you," but not necessarily cause bodily harm, a separate concept. The words in our case may equally mean: "I'm going to have intercourse with you with or without your consent, but not necessarily by causing any serious bodily harm." The court concluded that the threat contemplated by s. 243.4(1)(a) has to contain with it clear words that would expressly or by necessary implication refer to serious bodily harm. Just as the words in *Gingras* are ambiguous and do not expressly or by necessary implication refer to causing serious bodily harm, so too the word "rape" in the case at bar is ambiguous and does not expressly or by necessary implication refer to the causing of serious bodily harm.

Later he said:

> ... s. 243.4(1)(a) specifically proscribes threats to cause serious bodily harm, and not a threat to have non-consensual intercourse.

In concluding he said:

> In this case, we are dealing with "serious bodily harm", which we equated in the section to "death". What we have here is a threat to have sexual intercourse with each of the complainants, with or without their consent. This is quite separate and distinct, in the court's view, from threatening serious bodily harm. Again, the threat to commit a sexual assault does not necessarily cause serious bodily harm.

In my respectful view, the trial judge erred in holding that the threat was simply to have sexual intercourse without the complainant's consent. The threat was not confined to the lawyer's meaning of "rape", but would be understood, in the circumstances, as meaning that the threatener intended to do all of the acts specified in his letter. His statement that he would rape her was a statement that he would resort to such physical force as was necessary to do what he wanted and to make her do what he wanted her to do.

The second letter to the complainant Johanne Robillard emphasizes the threat. It is a warning to the complainant that, if she does not meet him as he has told her to, he will come and take her against her will by force and carry out the threatened acts. Why these letters should be regarded as other than a threat to use physical force to take the complainant, hold her against her will and violate her body I do not know. But does all this amount to a threat to cause serious bodily harm? "Bodily harm" is defined in s. 267(2) [of the 1985 Criminal Code] as "any hurt of injury to the complainant that interferes with the health or comfort of the complainant and that is more than merely transient or trifling in nature". Where the bodily harm amounts to wounding, maiming, disfiguring or endangering life, the sexual assault which causes it is aggravated sexual assault. But "serious bodily harm" is not defined in the Code. Perhaps some assistance may be had from s. 752, defining "serious personal injury offences".

The learned trial judge interpreted serious bodily harm in s. 264.1 as equated to death. I do not agree. The section should not be read in that way. It is for the finder of fact to determine if a threat is a threat to cause bodily harm and whether or not such bodily harm is serious bodily harm. The word "serious" is not ambiguous, and should be given its ordinary meaning. The Crown submits that the ambit of bodily harm is not restricted to physical injury or harm but includes emotional or psychological injury, harm or damage. Putting aside any question of whether bodily harm includes emotional or psychological harm, does the threat in this case amount to a threat to cause serious bodily harm? In my opinion, it does. The object of this threat is to create fear of such a degree of bodily harm from the application of physical force that the complainant will submit to or not resist the sexual assault. The nature of bodily harm which would cause her to submit to such violations of her dignity and her body is not simply a hurt or injury that would interfere with her comfort, but rather something serious. In short, resistance means force, perhaps violence, and serious injury. That is this case.

While there is no evidence that the complainants other than Johanne Robillard received a letter similar to the second letter referred to above, each of the complainants received a letter similar to the first letter, in which the trial judge held that there was a threat to rape her. In the circumstances, that was enough.

In the result, I think the trial judge was wrong in his interpretation of s. 264.1 as to the meaning of "serious bodily harm" and he erred in holding that a threat to commit rape was no more than a threat to have sexual intercourse without the complainant's consent. Accordingly, the acquittal cannot stand, and must be set aside. In the circumstances, as the only issue was whether or not the threat was a threat to cause serious bodily harm, the respondent will be convicted on each of the three counts in the indictment. The case is remitted to the trial judge for sentencing.

FINLAYSON J.A. (dissenting): — The validity of this prosecution is very much one of first impressions. Its outcome depends upon the reaction of the reader to the letters which constitute the criminal acts alleged. To me, they do not constitute threats to commit a specific criminal act. It is thus not necessary for me to embark on an inquiry as to whether a threat to rape is a threat to cause serious bodily harm. Accordingly, I respectfully disagree with the assessment of the trial judge's findings made by Brooke J.A. and with his disposition of the appeal.

The letters to the three cheerleaders for the Ottawa Rough Riders Football Club that were alleged to be threats to cause serious bodily harm are virtually identical. Brooke J.A. has selected the letter to Johanne Robillard as representative, and it is set out in full in his reasons. The charge is that the sending of the letter is contrary to what is now s. 264.1(1)(a) of the Criminal Code. That section reads as follows:

> **264.1(1)** Every one commits an offence who, in any manner, knowingly utters, conveys or causes any person to receive a threat
> (a) to cause death or serious bodily harm to any person. . . .
>
> . . . . .

In my opinion, offensive as the letters are, they do not amount to a threat to cause serious bodily harm as contemplated by the Code. They are expressions of sexual fantasizing, and are clearly obscene. It is difficult to conceive of any defence that the respondent would have if he had been charged under s. 168 of the Code. It reads as follows:

> **168.** Every one commits an offence who makes use of the mails for the purpose of transmitting or delivering anything that is obscene, indecent, immoral or scurrilous, but this section does not apply

to a person who makes use of the mails for the purpose of transmitting or delivering anything mentioned in subsection 166(4).

Obscenity need not be restricted to matters sexual. The Code defines an obscene publication as follows:

**163.** ...

(8) For the purposes of this Act, any publication a dominant characteristic of which is the undue exploitation of sex, or of sex and any one or more of the following subjects, namely, crime, horror, cruelty and violence, shall be deemed to be obscene.

In her submissions, counsel for the appellant isolated the phrase "even if I have to rape you" from its context in the letter. The hearing before our court was taken up almost entirely with a discussion as to whether a threat to rape was a threat to cause serious bodily harm. This misses both the affront and the effect of the letter. It is not intended that its contents be taken literally. There is no purpose in close analysis of the conduct described to determine if it portrays deviance, fetishism or criminal acts. The letter is nothing more than a series of obscenities.

The case, as represented by the Crown, is complicated by the fact that the offence of rape as such no longer exists and has been replaced in the Code by various degrees of sexual assault, not all of which involve serious bodily harm. We are asked to accept a layman's definition of "rape" as a non-consensual, even forced, act of sexual intercourse and to assume that the "threat" in the letter was a threat to cause serious bodily harm, as opposed to sexual gratification regardless of consent. This begs the question, in that it assumes that the letters contain a series of explicit threats, including a threat to rape. I agree with the trial judge's finding, which I accept as a finding of fact, that: "The tenor of the letters, while immature and disgusting, reveals more of an adoring fantasy than a threat to cause serious bodily harm."

. . . . .

Even if I am wrong in concluding that the trial judge found as a matter of fact that the letters were not intended to be taken seriously, I certainly accept that the language of the letters, while clearly criminal, in that it is obscene, is ambiguous as a threat to cause serious bodily harm. The respondent was entitled to the benefit of any ambiguity in this language. To quote the trial judge against, "the court ought never to begin to speculate upon what the accused might have meant".

Accordingly, for the reasons given, I would allow leave to appeal but dismiss the appeal.

*Appeal allowed; conviction substituted.*

## Sexual Assault: Substantive Issues Before and After Bill C-49*
*Don Stuart*

*Excerpts from: (1992-93), 35 Criminal Law Quarterly 241

### 1. CONTEXT

#### (1) The 1983 Reform of Rape Laws

In 1983 the crime of rape was replaced by a three-tier structure of sexual assault offences: sexual assault (s. 271, maximum sentence of 10 years); sexual assault with a weapon, threats or causing bodily harm (s. 272, maximum sentence 14 years), and aggravated sexual assault (s. 273, maximum sentence life imprisonment). The aim, clearly expressed by the Honourable Flora MacDonald in the House of Commons, was to reflect the violence rather than the sexual nature of the offence and to increase both reporting and conviction rates:

> ... the current laws relating to rape and indecent assault are being changed to emphasize the violence as opposed to the sexual aspects of these crimes. In other words, we will no longer have the term "rape" in law.
>
> This legislation has a long history. Individual women and groups of women all across the country have been pushing for years to change the rape laws. It was apparent that this section of the Criminal Code cried out for reform. The number of reported rape cases was far below the actual number of offences. It has been estimated that only one in ten cases of rape was reported. That was due largely to the stigma which surrounded the rape victim — the idea that nice girls do not get raped and the belief that she must have asked for it ... The conviction rate for rape has traditionally been much lower than the conviction rate for other serious crimes — only 52 per cent conviction rate for rape, compared with an 82 per cent conviction rate in the case of other indictable offences.

Parliament also took the opportunity to abolish clearly discriminatory evidentiary rules based on notions of women as property or that women, particularly those "unchaste", are likely to make false rape claims. Parliament abolished the spousal immunity, restricted cross-examination of the primary witness as to her previous sexual history, abrogated the doctrine of recent complaint, repealed corroboration requirements and warnings and restricted evidence of prior sexual history of the complainant. It is clear that these legislative changes attempted to answer some of the complaints of legal bias against victims of sexual assault. Whether attitudes have changed is another matter.

The extent to which Parliament's 1983 objectives have been met is, unfortunately, uncertain. A comprehensive Department of Justice review of national statistics has confirmed that there is a much larger proportion of victims of sexual assault now reporting to police but that there has been no change in the percentage of reports designated by police as unfounded. The same report indicates that some half of all sexual assault reports result in charges and that this rate is no lower than that for other crimes against the person. There are no national statistics on conviction rates for sexual assault. A 1988 site study indicated comparable conviction rates of about 73% for those charged with either sexual or non-sexual assault. A number of instances where judges have not sufficiently emphasized the violence of a sexual assault in sentencing have been clearly documented. On the other hand, the conclusion of a Department of

Justice study of various sentencing data bases has concluded that the popular view that most sexual assaults are not punished severely relative to other offences is "in part at least a misperception, founded upon media coverage of cases that resulted in atypically lenient sentences being imposed."

As best one can tell from this empirical data, rape cases are now being routinely reported and charged as sexual assault *simpliciter*, the lowest level of seriousness. In all these sexual assault statistics, there is no longer a differentiation between sexual touching and rape. In this sense, the impact of the 1983 legislation on rape cannot be determined.

### (2) Changing Attitudes: No Means No

There would appear to be an emerging public awareness, particularly on university campuses and in the media that rape is by no means confined to a stranger emerging from the dark. Public concern seems to be increasingly focused on the fact that over 70% of all sexual assaults are committed by someone the victim knows. The need for a new attitude by men to sexual relations is captured by the often-repeated slogan "No Means No". It is quite clear that women are justifiably asserting the right to say no at any time, even if the woman has been drinking, has said yes earlier and is now changing her mind, or has had sex before with the particular man.

The importance of this movement was recently well expressed to me and my class by a female law student as follows:

> Men don't seem to understand why this right is so important to us. We feel we are in a bind. If we say no we are teasers; if we say yes we are sluts. All we want to do is to assert our autonomous right without anybody making a judgment.

This message has not got through to all quarters. Recently, a defence counsel was quoted as having said this about the right to revoke consent recognized in Bill C-49:

> It's ridiculous . . . this isn't contract law. She says "Let's have sex." They are having full sexual intercourse. She suddenly says: "That's it. I'm revoking my agreement." Now how long does the male have to withdraw before it's sexual assault? . . . It just denies the biological nature of human beings.

Given that the criminal law is meant to reflect fundamental human values and to punish and deter those who do not share those values and have harmed others, it seems only appropriate that the "no means no" philosophy be adequately reflected in our *Criminal Code* of 1992.

### (3) Right to a Fair Trial

It has been a fundamental value of our criminal justice system before and after the Charter that any accused is presumed innocent until proven guilty and that proof must be beyond reasonable doubt. It is obvious that the interests of victims of violence must be adequately addressed by the criminal law. It is also the reality that it is the accused who risks being sent to prison. However heinous the crime, the criminal justice system must be scrupulous in its attempt to punish the morally blameworthy and to ascertain the truth lest we convict the innocent. It may be that sexual assault will always be a type of crime where acquittal rates will be relatively high. The reality is that most sexual conduct takes place in private and communication is sometimes unclear. Where there is a conflict in testimony it will always be difficult for the trier of fact to determine the truth well after the event. It is a pernicious myth that women and children likely lie in such cases. There is also the reality that there are some false claims and some cases where what happened is unclear.

### (4) Realities of Prison

The criminal law is a blunt instrument and should be used with restraint. Prison sentences for violent offences are easy to justify on the grounds of the need for retribution and punishment proportionate to the crime committed. On the other hand, those glibly urging ever longer prison sentences for sexual offenders need to confront the reality that in the Canadian penitentiaries of today, there are some 1,500 sex offenders and only 150 of them are receiving treatment. There has not been sufficient political will since 1983 to provide the resources for treatment of offenders and real alternatives for victims of abuse. Such resources might be the best chance of protecting women and children in the future.

### (5) Impetus Behind Bill C-49

On August 22, 1991, a 7 to 2 majority of the Supreme Court of Canada in *R. v. Seaboyer; R. v. Gayme* held that the blanket exclusion by s. 276 of the *Criminal Code* of evidence of prior sexual history of a complainant subject to three specified exceptions violated the accused's right to make full answer and defence under ss. 7 and 11(*d*) of the Charter. The provision was held to exclude evidence without permitting a judge to engage in a determination of whether the possible prejudicial effect of the evidence would outweigh its value to the truth-finding process.

*Seaboyer* immediately produced an outcry in the media. Headlines blared that the Supreme Court had struck down the rape-shield provision and that women and children would be even less likely to pursue charges of sexual assault given that there would be unrestricted cross-examination of their prior sexual history. Such comments were an overreaction and unfair to the majority of the Supreme Court. For the majority, Madam Justice McLachlin had indeed struck down s. 276. However, expressing grave concern at leaving the matter to unfettered judicial discretion, she set out what she considered to be careful guidelines as to the admissibility of evidence of the complainant's prior sexual history. Her Ladyship also extended the protection to such conduct *with the accused*.

It is fair to say, however, that the majority of the Supreme Court took but a line to hold that although victims might have equality rights, these had to give way to the accused's right to make full answer and defence. It may well have been this weighing of rights that led usually moderate feminist writers to strong statement:

> It may not be the case that the majority betrayed women, or even necessarily made a wrong decision by neglecting the constitutional value of sex equality. They may have illustrated, in the clearest, most "rational" terms, the fact that law will inevitably value the interests of men and require women to pay the price.

The response from the Minister of Justice, the Honourable Kim Campbell was swift. She announced that Parliament would respond to protect women and children better. She called a meeting of national and regional women's groups. The record seems clear that the Minister thereafter worked very closely in drafting and revising the bill with the coalition of some 60 groups that emerged. The coalition reached unanimity at each point and agreed to oppose any attempt to water down the bill. In this sense, the process was partisan with voices of men, no doubt for the first time in the history of the development of Canadian criminal law, of little weight. By the time Bill C-49 reached the Senate, Professor Sheila McIntyre, the spokesperson for L.E.A.F. (Women's Legal Education and Action Fund), the sponsor of the bill, stated that the aim had been to reflect women's constitutional rights under s. 7 and women's equality rights under s. 15 and also to achieve formal education:

> We also wanted comprehensive judicial education not through weekend seminars but in the body of the law, and we got it. We are very happy with the codified guidelines to judges that framed Seaboyer's broad principles and very specific factors to keep in mind, many of which are mindful of equality. No prejudicial, discriminatory stereotype language made its way in there and we are very pleased with that.

Bill C-49 was enthusiastically welcomed by politicians of every stripe for having replaced *Seaboyer* with a new rape shield that would protect women and children. This is ironic given that the new rape-shield laws, which are not the subject of this article, so closely mirror the guidelines suggested by the majority in *Seaboyer*. It is certainly true, however, that the new statutory scheme does at one point, in declaring the factors for trial judges to consider, include concerns for interests of the victim on the same level as the accused's right to make full answer and defence. It remains to be seen whether the Supreme Court will change its earlier assessment of the proper balance.

Bill C-49 accomplished much more than a statutory rape-shield law. The Minister of Justice and the women's groups seized the opportunity to legislate on the question of what constitutes genuine consent and also on the long-controversial mistake-of-fact defence. These changes will here be examined in the course of a review of substantive issues surrounding sexual assault before and after Bill C-49.

## 2. Actus Reus

### (1) Sexual Nature of Assault

What makes an assault "sexual"? In *R. v. Chase* the Supreme Court adopted an objective test:

> Sexual assault is an assault, within any one of the definitions of that concept in [s. 265(1)] of the Criminal Code, which is committed in circumstances of a sexual nature, such that the sexual integrity of the victim is violated. The test to be applied in determining whether the impugned conduct has the requisite sexual nature is an objective one: "Viewed in the light of all the circumstances, is the sexual or carnal context of the assault visible to a reasonable observer?": *Taylor*, supra, per Laycraft C.J.A., at p. 269. The part of the body touched, the nature of the contact, the situation in which it occurred, the words and gestures accompanying the act, and all other circumstances surrounding the conduct, including threats, which may or may not be accompanied by force, will be relevant.

The court added that the intent and motive of the accused were factors to be considered. The Supreme Court rejected the much-criticized view of the court below that sexual referred to genital parts of the body and did not include female breasts.

### (2) No Consent

Under ss. 265(1) and (2) there can be no assault or sexual assault where the complainant consents to the application of force. In 1983, s. 265(3) was added:

> 265(3) For the purposes of this section, no consent is obtained where the complainant submits or does not resist by reason of
>
> (a) the application of force to the complainant or to a person other than the complainant;
> (b) threats or fear of the application of force to the complainant or to a person other than the complainant;
> (c) fraud; or
> (d) the exercise of authority.

The notion that submission as a result of fear cannot be consent is important in the sexual assault context. The provision is clearly designed to protect vulnerable victims who choose to "co-operate" as a defence strategy.

In *R. v. Jobidon* the Supreme Court held by a 5 to 2 majority that s. 265(3)'s list of four vitiating factors was not exhaustive and did not remove further common law limits on the legal effectiveness of consent. Notwithstanding s. 9 of the *Criminal Code* which outlaws common law offences, the majority held that it was open for the court to adopt policy-based limits on the role and scope of consent in s. 265. Their conclusion in the manslaughter case before them was that s. 265 "*vitiates consent between adults intentionally to apply force causing serious hurt or non-trivial bodily harm to each other in the course of a fist fight or brawl*".

Whether the *Jobidon* principle can be extended to vitiate apparent consent in cases of sexual practices that cause physical harm remains to be seen.

### (3) Consent Under New s. 273.1

The new s. 273.1 seeks to define consent in the case of sexual assault but, consistent with *R. v. Jobidon*, is expressly not exhaustive:

*Meaning of "consent"*

> 273.1(1) Subject to subsection (2) and subsection 265(3), "consent" means, for the purposes of sections 271, 272 and 273, the voluntary agreement of the complainant to engage in the sexual activity in question.

*Where no consent obtained*

> (2) No consent is obtained, for the purposes of sections 271, 272 and 273, where
>
> (a) the agreement is expressed by the words or conduct of a person other than the complainant;
> (b) the complainant is incapable of consenting to the activity;
> (c) the accused induces the complainant to engage in the activity by abusing a position of trust, power or authority;
> (d) the complainant expresses, by words or conduct, a lack of agreement to engage in the activity; or

(e) the complainant having consented to engage in sexual activity, expresses, by words or conduct, a lack of agreement to continue to engage in the activity.

*Subsection (2) not limiting*

(3) Nothing in subsection (2) shall be construed as limiting the circumstances in which no consent is obtained.

These provisions clearly set out to give courts better guidance as to situations in which consent can be held to have been not genuine and therefore not consent in law. Subsections (*b*), (*c*) and (*e*) were amended as the bill passed through Committee. The amendments were largely inconsequential, merely clarifying rather than changing the original intent. Subsection (*b*) had read that the complainant was incapable of consenting to the activity "by reason of intoxication or other condition". The provision was criticized as being vague, especially in its reference to "other condition". Parliament clearly decided to leave the matter to the discretion of trial judges while preserving the common law principle that one who, on the evidence was incapable of giving consent, cannot be considered to have consented.

These new consent provisions seem adequately drafted and a welcome assertion of the "No Means No" philosophy. With the exception of subsec. (*c*), which will require judicial interpretation, the provisions appear to merely restate existing legal principles.

Subsection (*d*) clearly preserves the existing common law that consent can be express or implied. A suggestion by the women's coalition, that consent should be limited to unequivocal communications, was rejected and would have produced unfairness to the accused.

Critics of Bill C-49 have suggested that in future written consent will be needed in advance for any sexual conduct, that there is an onus of proof on the accused or that Bill C-49 criminalizes seduction. Given the wording of the new provisions these criticisms have no validity.

### 3. Fault

#### (1) Former Mistaken Belief in Consent Defence

In debates surrounding Bill C-49 proponents often left the impression that the mistake defence had a lot to do with the low reporting of rape and high acquittal rates. It is, however, clear that the mistake-of-fact defence had had virtually no impact on the conviction rate.

In its controversial ruling in *R. v. Pappajohn* a majority of the Supreme Court determined that the normal moral blameworthiness requirement they had been applying for other serious offences also applied to rape. This was the notion of subjective *mens rea* where the accused must be proved to have been at least reckless in the sense that he was aware of the risk — in the case of sexual assault, that the woman had not consented. The court confirmed that, on general principles, the belief need merely be honest and whether it was reasonable went only to the question of whether the accused was to be believed. The court recognized that there were policy considerations advanced in support of the view that the mistake should be one a reasonable man would have made but suggested that such mistake offences would be few in number and that juries could be trusted to distinguish between the genuine and bogus defences. However, the most important *Pappajohn* ruling was by a differently composed majority of the court. This majority imposed the requirement that before the defence of mistaken belief could be put to the jury, it had to be supported by sources other than the accused in order to give it "any air of reality".

The evidentiary ruling in *Pappajohn* seems pragmatically designed to restrict the ambit of the mistaken-belief defence. It places a corroboration requirement on the accused which is required in no other type of case. Although this has led to criticism the Supreme Court of Canada has thus far refused to alter it. The court has also confirmed that the law on mistaken belief has not changed since Parliament added s. 265(4) to the *Criminal Code* in 1983. Section 265(4) enacts an express mistake-of-belief defence to apply to all types of assault and sexual assault.

It seems clear that the evidentiary ruling in *Pappajohn* has accounted for the reality that the mistaken-belief defence is rarely even put to the jury. Since *Pappajohn* was decided, there have been few decisions with written reasons basing an acquittal on a mistaken-belief defence and only one such acquittal confirmed by a Court of Appeal.

Two other Supreme Court decisions may well have contributed to the low success rate of mistake-of-fact defences in rape cases. In *R. v. Sansregret*, there had been an acquittal at trial on the basis of a mistake-of-fact defence. The air of reality had come from the testimony of the complainant. When the matter reached the Supreme Court, the court decided that, given the finding that the accused had an honest belief in consent, he could not have been reckless. However, the court convicted on the basis that, as there had been a previous incident involving the same victim, the accused must have been wilfully blind. *Sansregret* has been soundly criticized on the basis that the court could not have validly found wilful blindness in the face of the trial judge's finding of fact that the accused honestly believed in consent and that it wrongly imported knowledge where there was no awareness of risk.

Another holding which may account for mistake of fact defences being unlikely to succeed in sexual assault cases is the Court's deeply divided ruling in *R. v. Bernard*. The 4 to 3 majority hold that the common law rule that voluntary intoxication is no defence to a crime of general intent is not contrary to the Charter. The majority ruled that sexual assault was such a crime. However two of the majority (Wilson and L'Heureux-Dubé JJ.) recognize a "flexible" approach under which *extreme* intoxication may be a defence to general intent crimes. A minority of three justices hold that denying the intoxication defence imposes absolute liability inconsistent with fundamental principles of voluntariness and fault. The minority point to the Australian reality where voluntary intoxication is now a defence to any crime but rarely succeeds. Given the complex splits in the judgments *Bernard* can be read as a 5 to 2 holding that *extreme* intoxication is a defence to any crime, including sexual assault.

## (2) Effect of New s. 273.2

Where belief in consent not a defence

273.2 It is not a defence to a charge under section 271, 272 or 273 that the accused believed that the complainant consented to the activity that forms the subject-matter of the charge, where

- (a) the accused's belief arose from the accused's
    - (i) self-induced intoxication, or
    - (ii) recklessness or wilful blindness; or
- (b) the accused did not take reasonable steps, in the circumstances known to the accused at the time, to ascertain that the complainant was consenting.

The section creates special limits on the mistake-of-fact defence which apply to all sexual assault cases but not to assault offences. In the case of sexual assault Parliament has reversed the substantive but not the evidentiary ruling in *Pappajohn*. The accused still has to pass the air-of-reality test for a mistake defence. That defence will not now be open where his mistaken belief arose from self-induced intoxication, recklessness or wilful blindness or, most importantly, where he did not take reasonable steps in the circumstances known to him to ascertain that the complainant was consenting. At the First Reading stage the accused was to be required to take "all" reasonable steps. "All" was dropped at Third Reading, presumably accepting arguments that the standard was too severe and risked a Charter challenge that it restricted the minimum Charter standard of due diligence.

The irrelevance of self-induced intoxication is a change from the narrow majority ruling in *Bernard* because it excludes the possibility of the extreme intoxication defence. The exclusion of situations where the accused was reckless or wilfully blind is difficult to fathom. *R. v. Sansregret* itself points out that if the accused had an honest belief in consent, he could not have been reckless since he would not have been aware of the risk of consent. The same would be true of someone who was wilfully blind which requires a deliberate suppression of the possibility that the accused was not consenting. The proposed exclusion of reckless and wilful blindness is unnecessarily harsh and diverts attention from the inquiry into whether the accused was aware of the risk. This criticism seems academic given the further requirement that the accused have taken reasonable steps. This liability is clearly new and would impose a standard of not measuring up to a reasonableness test. Under the offence as so defined, the Crown could rest content with proof beyond reasonable doubt of unreasonable conduct in a sexual context.

In my judgment s. 273.2 is unjust in not fairly recognizing different forms of culpability of an accused and may be unconstitutional as a result.

## (3) Unfairness in Not Distinguishing Subjective and Objective Fault Standards

Few judges or writers would now dogmatically insist that criminal responsibility should always be based on a determination of subjective fault. There *is* a case to be made for the punishment of one who "ought", "should", "could", or "as a reasonable person would" have foreseen. But the key point is that whenever resort is had to this external objective negligence standard, there is a considerable extension of the reach of the criminal law. Such extension should be made cautiously. The advantage of the subjective awareness of risk approach which courts have usually insisted on for *Criminal Code* offences is that it is the fault test fairest to the accused since it takes into account all the capacities and incapacities of the individual. It has proved a valuable vehicle for restraint in the exercise of state power behind the criminal law.

The time had arrived for Parliament to declare some criminal responsibility for objectively unreasonable sexual behaviour. Some commentators have long advocated such a reform, either on the basis of an analysis of the nature of the act of sexual assault, or on the need to be consistent with the acceptance of the objective standard in the case of other crimes.

It is, however, vital for the criminal law to recognize that there is a distinction in culpability between a deliberate risk-taker and one who was unreasonable in that he did not anticipate the risk but ought to have. There is surely a qualitative distinction between a man who deliberately rapes a woman knowing that she is not consenting and one who engages in sexual intercourse where it was in the circumstances unreasonable for him to have assumed that the woman was consenting. These different forms of culpability should be reflected in different forms of conviction and different penalties. This would appear to be the basis upon which the Supreme Court of Canada has, in its Charter rulings striking down constructive murder rules, decided to distinguish between murder and manslaughter. Murder has to be based on subjective foresight of the likelihood of death to justify the life imprisonment sentence. On the other hand, it is likely that the Supreme Court will squarely hold that manslaughter can be based on an objective standard since the penalty is the reduced one of a maximum of life imprisonment, which allows for considerably more lenient sentences.

Parliament too had previously moved cautiously in its efforts to create some criminality based on the objective standard. When it created an offence of arson by negligence in 1990 it specifically declared that the offence required proof of a marked departure from the standard of care that a reasonably prudent person would use and reduced the penalty from a maximum of 14 years in the normal arson case to one of five years imprisonment. Similarly, the definition of the offence of careless use of a firearm was to be changed to require a gross departure from the objective norm.

Section 273.2 is also too inflexible on the issue of self-induced intoxication. Given the nature of any sexual act a man would have to be very drunk indeed before the trier of fact would accept that because of his intoxication he could not have been able to determine whether the alleged victim was consenting. A drunken rapist is usually also a deliberate rapist. But if the man is very drunk indeed there may be rare cases where he could not be said to have known what he was doing. In such cases the trier of fact may prefer to base culpability on a failure to measure up to the reasonable standard. Section 273.2 however precludes any such determination. Under s. 273.2(*a*)(i) the accused's intoxication, however severe, is irrelevant to any belief in consent defence. On the other hand, if the alleged victim is very intoxicated she will, under s. 273.1(2)(*b*), not have been capable of consent.

### (4) Four Possible Charter Challenges

Challenges based on the Supreme Court of Canada's assertion of a constitutional requirement of fault to safeguard the guarantee of principles of fundamental justice under s. 7 now seem far less likely to succeed. *R. v. DeSousa*, a unanimous judgment of five justices, holds that, while s. 7 still guards against absolute liability, absent very high stigma any federal or provincial offence will be constitutional if it has a subjective or objective fault requirement. The court further holds, in *obiter*, that the fault need not relate to all the essential ingredients of the crime.

There would nevertheless appear to be at least four possible Charter challenges to Bill C-49's substantive regime. Whether they would succeed will clearly depend on whether the Supreme Court acts consistently with its prior decisions and on the extent to which new members of the court may bring new attitudes.

#### (a) The air-of-reality test violates the accused's right to make full answer and defence

The requirement from *Pappajohn* and s. 265(4) as interpreted that the defence be grounded on evidence other than the accused's testimony sets up an unfair corroboration rule not found in the case of any other defence. It is far more onerous than the normal requirement of pointing to an evidentiary base. The rule's constitutionality was left open by the British Columbia Court of Appeal. Under Bill C-49 the rule could operate especially unfairly. Under s. 276.2(2)*a* the complainant is not compellable at an admissibility hearing respecting evidence of prior sexual history. She may well not testify. Without the complainant's testimony it may be impossible for the accused to point to independent evidence. Rather than striking down s. 276.2(2) the solution may be to modify the special air-of-reality test.

#### (b) Section 273.2's exclusion of any intoxication defence imposes absolute liability which threatens the liberty interest

It is quite clear that any penal law that imposes absolute liability will violate s. 7 of the Charter and be declared of no force and effect where there is a potential deprivation of the liberty interest. Absolute liability occurs where a conviction can be based on mere proof of the act without any necessity to prove any form of fault on the part of the accused. Absolute liability seems to occur where the extreme drunkenness of the accused is irrelevant but that of the victim determinative.

This would also necessitate the Supreme Court revisiting its complex, split decision in *R. v. Bernard* that denying a defence of voluntary intoxication to a general intent crime does not violate the Charter. Three new members of the court have already expressly indicated that issue is open.

In *R. v. Nguyen; R. v. Hess* the Supreme Court determined by a majority that the denial of a mistake of fact defence to the former statutory rape offence constituted an absolute liability which could not be demonstrably justified under s. 1. As part of its determination under s. 1, the majority of the court noted that the offence had been replaced by a series of measures that allowed a due diligence defence, showing that

Parliament had concluded that its objective could be effected in a less restrictive manner.

### (c) Sexual assault is one of those few offences requiring a minimum degree of mens rea in the form of subjective foresight

The Supreme Court has thus far identified a few offences for this constitutional requirement of subjective foresight and has placed considerable emphasis on the special nature of the stigma attached and the penalties. Thus far the list of offences is murder, attempted murder, and theft. The criterion of stigma has been often criticized as an inadequate and unreliable test but if it remains the discriminating factor, surely sexual assault is an offence calling for such special treatment?

### (d) Section 273.2 is unconstitutional because it violates the constitutional principle that those causing harm intentionally must be punished more severely than those causing harm unintentionally

In *R. v. Martineau* Mr. Justice Lamer rested the Supreme Court's ruling that there is a constitutional requirement of subjective foresight of death for murder, in part on the principle that punishment must be proportionate to the moral blameworthiness of the offender, and also on the principle that those causing harm intentionally must be punished more severely than those causing harm unintentionally.

These principles, which were not referred to in *DeSousa*, are sound and should be boldly asserted by all judges. Since the penalty for sexual assault remains the same, Parliament has now clearly criminalized, in the same prohibition, carrying the same penalty, one who is deliberately aware of a risk and one who was acting unreasonably. If the *Martineau* principles have any remaining vitality, the new sexual assault scheme should be struck down or at least read down to ensure that these fundamental principles are respected.

This writer presented a brief to both the House of Commons and the Senate Committees, suggesting that Bill C-49 be amended to create a separate new crime of negligent sexual assault with a lesser penalty of a maximum of five years' imprisonment. This would have achieved a pattern of criminal responsibility along the lines recently adopted for the crime of arson. It would have been much fairer to the negligent accused who would not face the same stigma as one convicted of deliberately committing sexual assault. The scheme would also have had the advantage that the determination of culpability would be made by the trier of fact. Accused may well have been more likely to plead guilty to the lesser offence, thus sparing victims from having to testify. Given current sentencing patterns, a five-year maximum seemed to offer adequate scope for punishment of a negligent offender for reasons of individual and general deterrence and retribution.

The response of the Minister, provided only at the last moment in the brief Senate Committee hearing, was that this was a matter that could be left to sentencing discretion:

> Clearly, each [sexual assault] case that comes before the Court is unique, and in the circumstances surrounding that case, the moral opprobrium attached to it may vary, depending on the particular

circumstances. I would argue that sentencing is the appropriate forum in which to reflect those judgments. Given the nature of sexual assault and how damaging it is, to create an offence of negligent sexual assault would communicate the opposite message of what we are trying to communicate.

In my view, it is fundamental that the key determination of whether the actor was deliberate or negligent should be made at trial and not left to the uncertain exercise of sentencing. A person charged with sexual assault is entitled to know whether he or she is convicted on the basis of having been deliberate or merely negligent. At least the British Columbia Court of Appeal is on record as holding that culpability is important to sentence. In *R. v. Tracy*, involving a charge of smuggling a vehicle into Canada, it mattered to the court whether the smuggling was committed knowingly and willingly rather than as a result of naive misunderstanding.

If the matter is left to sentence, one can only hope that judges will be careful to provide adequate reasons so that a clear jurisprudence as to the importance of culpability can be developed. In the case of jury trials there is also a practical problem. The prevailing Canadian view is that a judge cannot ask the jury for the basis for its verdict. In *R. v. Tuckey* the Ontario Court of Appeal rejected an exception in England for cases of manslaughter. According to the Ontario Court of Appeal, this practice would raise more difficulties than it would solve since the jury might not be unanimous on the evidential basis of the verdict. In *R. v. Brown* the Supreme Court acknowledged that a sentencing judge will be bound by the express or implied factual implications of a jury's verdict. In that case, the court held that where a jury had acquitted on charges of causing death or bodily harm by dangerous driving but had convicted of the included offence of dangerous driving, the sentencing judge could not take into account the deaths and injuries when imposing sentence. *Brown* would appear to be of no assistance in the new sexual assault era unless the Crown particularizes the charge contrary to the broad approach envisaged by Parliament. When jury trials reach the stage of sentence the trial judge will have to make an independent factual determination as to the culpability. There is authority for this approach in the decision of Mr. Justice Campbell in *R. v. Lawrence*. His Lordship decided to reach his own conclusion as to whether the Crown had proved beyond a reasonable doubt that the accused had shaken the young infant to death or that his common law spouse had shaken the child to death and he was criminally negligent for failing to prevent it.

### 4. Is Rape Always Sexual Assault Causing Bodily Harm?

Experience since 1983 suggests that rape prosecutions are now routinely prosecuted at the lowest level of sexual assault, as sexual assault *simpliciter*. In this way Parliament unwittingly trivialized rape in putting it into the same category as sexual touching. The problem is that the second category under s. 272 requires proof of bodily harm, a threat or the use of a weapon. This may be difficult to prove in many acquaintance-rape situations where there may be no physical injury such as bruises.

This reality may well have led to Judge Cole's recent decision in *B*. His Honour decided on his own motion to commit an accused charged with sexual assault *simpliciter* to trial on the more serious offence of sexual assault causing bodily harm. He utilized the recent ruling of the Supreme Court of Canada in *R. v. McCraw* where the Supreme Court interpreted bodily harm to include psychological injury. Judge

Cole recognizes that *McCraw* was reached in the different context of s. 264.1(1)(*a*) involving the crime of threatening serious bodily harm but holds that the Supreme Court clearly intended to make a general pronouncement.

There would appear to be dangers in the approach of Judge Cole. He holds that judges at preliminary inquiries and at trial must be satisfied that there is evidence of psychological harm and that it is non-trivial. This may well have the indirect effect of compelling victims to testify as to the consequences of the assault and to be submitted to cross-examination as to the extent of the injury. In this sense, the victim will be once again back on trial. Another problem is that it is difficult to see how any form of sexual assault will not involve at least some psychological harm. If this is true, sexual assault *simpliciter* will have ceased to exist by judicial fiat.

When testifying before the Committees of the House of Commons and the Senate on Bill C-49, this commentator unsuccessfully sought the addition of an amendment that sexual assault involving any form of attempted penetration would be automatically placed in the second level of sexual assault, where the maximum penalty is raised from 10 to 14 years. This would have emphasized the seriousness of all rapes and would have made it unnecessary and indeed irrelevant to hear evidence as to the consequences for the victim. The victim would have been less on trial. Furthermore, if rapists were again to be singled out for special legal treatment, it would have been much easier to track and assess responses to rape. At the moment, no separate statistics are kept for rape as opposed to sexual assault.

## R. v. Livermore
(1996), 43 C.R. (4th) 1 (S.C.C.)

Appeal from judgment reported at (1994), 31 C.R. (4th) 374, 18 O.R. (3d) 221, 89 C.C.C. (3d) 425, 71 O.A.C. 340 (C.A.) dismissing appeal from acquittal on charge of sexual assault.

[Excerpts from the judgment of MacLachlin.]

November 16, 1995. McLACHLIN J. (LAMER C.J.C., CORY and IACOBUCCI JJ. concurring): — Mr. Livermore is charged with sexual assault of a 15-year-old girl, V. At the time of the alleged assault, Livermore was 28 years old. It is common ground that V. and her 14-year-old friend T. had willingly gone with Livermore and another young man, the co-accused, who picked them up in Livermore's car at an Oshawa pizza store at 1:30 a.m. Livermore drove to a parking lot behind an apartment building where the four consumed some beer and talked. Both T. and V. testified that T. asked to go home after approximately 30 minutes; the accused stated that the four mutually agreed to drive to another location. Livermore drove past T.'s building to a second parking lot, where the two girls exchanged seats. Livermore then drove to a third parking lot where he had sexual intercourse with V. After this he drove the two girls to T.'s home.

V. testified that she resisted Mr. Livermore's advances throughout. She stated that although she told the accused to stop kissing her and pushed him away, he climbed over the gear shift, pulled her pants down and had sexual intercourse with her. She stated that she told him "no" during intercourse and tried to push him away. She testified that although the accused was not violent and the windows were open and the doors unlocked, she was afraid to scream or try to escape because in the movies "people that don't say nothing, don't do nothing, just get away". V. stated that when they arrived at T.'s apartment, Livermore hugged her. V. said that it was possible that she had hugged him back, before saying "bye". When asked by counsel for the accused why, on returning to T.'s apartment building, she didn't run into the apartment with T. to escape, she stated that she didn't because she didn't want the men "to know that anything was wrong".

The girls testified that on their return to T.'s home they locked themselves in the bathroom and concocted a story to explain their absence to T.'s mother. They told T.'s mother a story that involved the presence of a third girl at the pizza store, whose threatening manner had prompted them to go with Livermore and the co-accused for safety. They also told her that V. had been raped. V. related the same story in her first statement to the police later that morning. She testified that the only part of the story that was untrue was the explanation of how the girls came to get into the car with Livermore and the co-accused. V. says she told her own mother the truth "from the start", at the hospital later in the morning, and subsequently told the police the truth in a second statement. A medical examination of V. revealed extensive genital bruising consistent with "traumatic" or "very forceful" sexual intercourse.

Livermore's testimony contradicted V.'s on the issue of consent. He testified that V. had been a willing partner while they mutually kissed and touched each other and that he climbed over the gear shift onto her side of the car after she touched his leg and penis. He stated that V. lowered her own pants and underpants prior to intercourse. Livermore testified that on the way back to T.'s apartment, T. and V. discussed how they would explain their absence to T.'s mother. He stated that V. hugged him before she left the car. Livermore also testified that he gave a slip of paper to T. on which he had written his name and telephone number before she and V. switched places in the car.

In his defence, Livermore maintained that V. had consented to the sexual intercourse. He also argued that, in light of V.'s denial that she had consented, circumstances were such that he had entertained an honest but mistaken belief in consent. The trial judge put this defence to the jury, which acquitted him and his co-accused. The Ontario Court of Appeal dismissed the appeal: (1994), 18 O.R. (3d) 221. Abella J.A., dissenting, would have ordered a new trial.

Both in the Court of Appeal and in this court, the Crown alleged that the trial judge made the following four errors:

> 1) The trial judge erred in his review of V.'s lack of consent and in his treatment of the jury's question on this issue; . . .
> 4) The defence of honest but mistaken belief should not have been left with the jury.

In my view, the cumulative effect of the errors made at trial requires that the appeal be allowed and a new trial ordered, despite the heavy onus on the Crown when it seeks to have an acquittal set aside.

With respect to the first alleged error, V.'s evidence was clear that she had repeatedly said "no" to Livermore and had resisted the assault. There is nothing in the record to indicate that her statements to the police or her testimony at the preliminary hearing were contradictory on this point. The contradiction with respect to her saying "no" to the co-accused when he tried to kiss her does not negate the consistency of her testimony with respect to Livermore. The trial judge in his charge to the jury did not mention V.'s resistance and incorrectly stated that she had not said "no" to Livermore. Since the sole issue was consent, this constituted a serious error.

The jury was understandably confused by the trial judge's erroneous direction, as indicated by the question it put to the judge after an hour of deliberation:

> The jury would like to hear evidence repeated with respect to the witness [V.] ... answering to both the Crown and the defence questioning *about when [V.] said, no, to Carson Livermore. Further, can also we also hear [V.]'s comments of, no, during the preliminary hearing?* [Emphasis added.]

The judge's response to this question was accurately described by the dissenting judge in the Court of Appeal as, in essence, telling them they ought to try harder to remember the evidence. This was an inadequate response to the jury's question, which indicated difficulty on the main issue in the case — consent. Combined with the other errors, its effect is serious. . . .

It remains to consider the allegation that the trial judge should not have left the defence of honest but mistaken belief with the jury. The Court of Appeal was unanimous in concluding that it should not have, since the defence was unsupported by the evidence. I agree with that assessment.

Livermore testified that he believed V. was consenting to intercourse. The only question is whether there was sufficient foundation in the facts to lend an air of reality to the defence of mistaken but honest belief in consent. There was evidence that V. had said no; there was no evidence that she had said yes. The trial judge in putting this defence to the jury relied on the fact that the girls were out after midnight, that they willingly entered the car of the accused, that they changed seats without trying to escape, that the windows of the car were down and the doors unlocked, that the girls did not scream and the erroneous conclusion, discussed earlier in these reasons, that there was no evidence of verbal complaint. Abella J.A. was of the view that these circumstances did not provide the required air of reality to the defence of honest but mistaken belief in consent (at p. 226):

> Not screaming, drinking beer while under age, being out at 1:00 a.m., parking, cavalierly trusting a stranger, switching places in a car after a casual physical encounter, and staying too long in a car someone else has control over, are neither individually nor collectively any basis at all, let alone realistic ones, for assuming that someone is agreeing to sexual intercourse. In my view, there were no reasonable grounds for the accused's beliefs found in the package of factors listed by the trial judge.

Galligan J.A., for the majority, suggested that "this case was one of consent or no consent and there was no air of reality to a defence of honest but mistaken belief in consent" (p. 232).

The common law has long recognized that defences for which there is no factual basis or evidentiary foundation should not be put to the jury. In *R. v. Pappajohn*, [1980] 2 S.C.R. 120, this court articulated the minimum threshold for mistake of fact defences, including an accused person's honest but mistaken belief in consent, as requiring an air of reality to be raised on the evidence and circumstances to support the defence.

In *R. v. Osolin*, [1993] 4 S.C.R. 595, Cory J. noted that the air of reality test as it relates to honest but mistaken belief in consent in all assault offences has been codified by the requirement in s. 265(4) of the *Criminal Code*, R.S.C. 1985, c. C-46, that there be "sufficient evidence" in order for the judge to put the defence of mistake to the jury.

. . .

The defence of mistake of fact in the context of sexual assault involves two elements: 1) that the accused *honestly believed* the complainant consented; and 2) that the accused have been *mistaken* in this belief. In order for the defence to be put to the jury, there must be evidence lending an air of reality to both of these elements. Typically, the second element is established through the assertion by the accused or counsel for the accused that he believed the complainant consented although her evidence is to the contrary. It is in relation to the first element — honest belief — that difficulties arise in establishing an air of reality. In order for the belief to be honestly held, the accused cannot have been wilfully blind about whether consent was given: *R. v. Sansregret*, [1985] 1 S.C.R. 570. Furthermore, since recklessness about whether there was consent constitutes one aspect of the mens rea of sexual assault (*Pappajohn*, supra, at p. 146), the accused cannot have been reckless in his belief that there was consent. While the belief need not be reasonable, there must be something in the evidence of the circumstances surrounding the alleged assault which lends an air of reality to an *honest belief* in consent.

In the case at bar, the accused testified that he believed V. consented, contrary to her evidence that she resisted intercourse throughout. The element of mistake is made out. There is no evidence, however, which lends an air of reality to the assertion by the accused that he had an honest belief in V.'s consent to intercourse. The evidence of Livermore was that V. clearly consented. The evidence of V. was that, far from consenting, she resisted and repeatedly said "no". T.'s testimony corroborated V.'s testimony in this regard. The question to be answered is whether there was evidence adduced which would nonetheless lend an air of reality to the creation in the accused's mind of an honest belief that V. was consenting notwithstanding the fact that their testimony on the central issue of consent was so diametrically opposed. In other words, was there a realistic evidentiary basis, upon which the jury could conclude that what really happened was a third version, that is, lack of consent but honest mistake by Livermore that it had been given. In my view, there was none.

The accused's bare assertion that he "believed" that the complainant consented must be supported by something in the circumstances that suggests that he may honestly have held such a belief: *Pappajohn,* supra. Otherwise, the goal of screening out the spurious defence based on nothing but the accused's facile assertion of belief will be thwarted. Examples of such circumstances are well documented in the jurisprudence. For example, sexually aggressive conduct by the complainant, a previous relationship of intimacy coupled with no reason to suspect a change of heart, and the case of the known prostitute are frequently cited as examples of situations in which an honest mistake may be made as to consent. Similarly, as noted in *R. v. Park*, [1995] 2 S.C.R. 836, independent evidence, particularly real evidence, may lend an air of reality to the defence: at pp. 851-52 per L'Heureux-Dubé J. If there is no evidence permitting an inference that the accused honestly believed in consent, then the accused in assuming consent must be taken to have closed his eyes to whether there was real consent, i.e., he must have been wilfully blind or reckless as to whether there was consent. In such a case, the required air of reality on the element of the honesty of the accused's belief will be lacking.

I agree with Abella J.A. that evidence of being out late, drinking beer and switching seats in a car is incapable of providing a foundation for an honest belief in consent to sexual intercourse. Such conduct, being equally consistent with non-consent as with consent, lacks any probative value on the issue. A man who assumes that equivocal acts such as these amount to consent to intercourse is assuming consent not on the basis of the circumstances, but as a result of recklessness or wilful blindness. The fact that the girls had an opportunity to leave the car before there was any indication that the accused had sexual intercourse in mind does not give rise to an inference of consent. The fact that V. did not scream although the car windows were open does not lend an air of reality to the defence: the two men were twice V.'s age. The fact that the accused hugged V. when she left the car (whether initiated by her or not), the fact that he gave T. a slip of paper with his name and phone number on it, the fact that V. and T. did not flee when finally they returned to T.'s apartment, are relevant to V.'s credibility as a witness. However, even if believed, they are insufficient to lend an air of reality to an honest belief in consent.

To put it in the language of Galligan J.A., for the majority, the case was one of consent or no consent. There was nothing in the evidence which supported a third version that V. had not consented but that Livermore honestly believed that she had. We are therefore left with his bare assertion of belief. On the jurisprudence of this court, this is insufficient to lend an air of reality to the defence of honest but mistaken belief. I conclude that the trial judge erred in putting the defence of honest but mistaken belief to the jury. . . .

In this case, we have no way of knowing whether the jury acquitted because it had a reasonable doubt about whether V. consented, or whether it acquitted on the basis of a defence which should not have been left with it. The cumulative effect of the numerous errors in this case is such that the *Morin* test is made out. Absent the significant errors at trial, a reasonable jury properly charged may well have reached a different verdict. I would allow the appeal, set aside the acquittal and direct a new trial.

*Appeal allowed; new trial ordered.*

**Questions/Discussion**
1. The 1983 and 1992 amendments to the Criminal Code dealing with sexual assault will do little to redress the problems which were witnessed under the old rape laws. Address and discuss this statement with reference to both the old and new legislation.
2. Consider the following statement: "Little will or can be done about the problem of sexual assault in Canadian society until there is a re-structuring of the economic and social relationships which underlie these problems". Do you agree or disagree with this statement in the context of sexual assault? Why or why not? What effect does criminal law have on the social problem of sexual assault in Canadian society? Is it of any relevance to the finding of a solution to the problem?
3. Of what value are legal reform and legal responses in regard to the problems faced by women in a nonegalitarian society? Do you think that more women judges will go a long

way toward solving some of the problems inherent in the current legal responses? Why or why not? What other measures are needed to address the problem of sexual assault?
4. One of the recent issues in the area of sexual assault has been the question of the production of a victim's therapeutic records for use by the defence. For a discussion of this subject, see *R. v. O'Connor* (1996), 44 C.R. (4th) 1 (S.C.C.), and the series of articles contained in "A Criminal Reports Forum on *O'Connor* and *B. (A.)*: Abuse of Process, Disclosure and Access to Therapeutic Records" (1996), 44 C.R. (4th) 130-194.
5. What should be the requirements for a defence to sexual assault based on a mistaken belief as to consent? Would you require that the mistake be both honest *and* reasonable. On what grounds would you make your argument?

## Further Reading
- Clark, L., *Evidence of Recent Complaint and Reform of Canadian Sexual Assault Law: Still Searching for Epistemic Equality* (Ottawa: Canadian Advisory Council on the Status of Women, 1993).
- Clark, Lorenne and Armstrong, Susan, *A Rape Bibliography* (Ottawa: Solicitor General of Canada, 1979).
- Clark, Lorenne and Lewis, Debra, *Rape: The Price of Coercive Sexuality* (Toronto: The Women's Press, 1977).
- Dawson, T. Brettell, "Legal Structures: A Feminist Critique of Sexual Assault Reform" (1985), 14 Resources of Feminist Research 40.
- Griffin, Susan, *Rape: The Power of Consciousness* (San Francisco: Harper and Row, 1979).
- Hinch, Ronald, "Inconsistencies and Contradictions in Canada's Sexual Assault Law" (1988), 14 Canadian Public Policy 282.
- Kasinsky, Renee G., "Rape: The Social Control of Women" in W.K. Greenaway and S.K. Brickey, eds., *Law and Social Control in Canada* (Scarborough: Prentice-Hall, 1978).
- Kinnon, Diane, *Report on Sexual Assault in Canada* (Ottawa: Canadian Advisory Council on the Status of Women, 1981).
- Le Bourdais, E., "Rape Victims: Unpopular Patients" (1976), 3 Dimensions in Health Service 53.
- MacDonald, G. and Gallagher, K., "The Myth of Consenting Adults: The New Sexual Assault Provisions" (1993), 42 University of New Brunswick Law Journal 373-380.
- Marshall, P., "Sexual Assault, The Charter and Sentencing Reform" (1988), 63 C.R. (3d) 216.
- Martin, R., "Bill C-49: A Victory for Interest Group Politics" (1993), 42 University of New Brunswick Law Journal 357-372.
- Minch, C., *et al.*, "Attrition in the Processing of Rape Cases" (1987), 29 Cdn. J. of Crim. and Corr. 389.
- Nightingale, M., "Judicial Attitudes and Differential Treatment: Native Women in Sexual Assault Cases" (1991), 23 Ottawa Law Review 71-98.
- Renner, K. Edward, and Sahjpaul, Suresh, "The New Sexual Assault Law: What Has Been Its Effect?" (1986), 28 Canadian Journal of Criminology 407.
- Rioux, Marsha, *When Myths Masquerade As Reality: A Study of Rape* (Ottawa: Advisory Council on the Status of Women, 1981).
- Roberts, J.V., *Criminal Justice Processing of Sexual Assault Cases* (Ottawa: Canadian Centre for Justice Statistics, 1994).
- Roberts, J.V. and Grossman, M., *Sexual Assault: A Bibliography* (Ottawa: Crime and Justice Research Centre, 1991).
- Steed, E., "Reality Check: The Sufficiency Threshold to the Air of Reality Test in Sexual Assault Cases" (1994), 36 Criminal Law Quarterly 448-473.

- Stuart, D., "The Pendulum has been Pushed Too Far: The Effects of Bill C-49" (1993), 42 University of New Brunswick Law Journal 349-356.
- Usprich, S.J., "A New Crime in Old Battles: Definitional Problems with Sexual Assault" (1987), 29 Criminal Law Quarterly 200.
- Usprich, S.J., "Two Problems in Sexual Assault: Attempts and the Intoxication Defence" (1987), 29 Criminal Law Quarterly 296.

## 8.2 RACISM AND THE CRIMINAL JUSTICE SYSTEM

**Introduction**

The issue of racism within the criminal justice system is one which in the past has been largely ignored by a profession and by enforcement mechanisms which insisted on the myth of neutrality. Recently, however, there have been some hopeful signs that the state is willing to attempt to approach the subject and recognize the reality of the problem and its systemic nature within the Canadian criminal justice system. Along with class and gender bias, racism is a problem which has been recognized as endemic to our system of justice, and a matter which must be addressed if we are to achieve a true system of criminal "justice".

One of these attempts at addressing racism in the criminal justice system was the inquiry into the wrongful arrest and conviction of Donald Marshall, Jr., a Micmac Indian from Nova Scotia who spent 11 years in prison for a crime which he did not commit. The events surrounding the matter and their consequences were brought to light by the inquiry in its hearings and in its 1989 report. This section, intended as a brief introduction to the nature and dimensions of the problem of racism, reproduces several excerpts from the inquiry's report which highlight the nature of the problem in Nova Scotia, although the issues and the inquiry's conclusions can be applied across Canada and to other disadvantaged visible minorities. For example, the rates of imprisonment for native people have been criticised as too high in western provinces such as Alberta where natives comprise one-third of the jail population yet make up only one-twentieth of the general population, and the treatment of blacks at the hands of Montreal and Toronto police and judicial agencies have been attacked as racist in recent years. What has been particularly problematic is the unwillingness of the state to effectively address the issue, coupled with the state's often unqualified support for the enforcement and judicial agencies with the criminal law system. The real test will be the government's willingness to meaningfully and substantively address the problems identified by the various inquiries and reports not only within the criminal law system, but also through measures to redress the lack of real opportunity and advancement in society as a whole for those groups disadvantaged by racist structures, practices and attitudes. However, there is little reason to be hopeful in this regard. For example, the latest federal initiative (in March of 1996) on giving more control to the aboriginal peoples appears to offer significantly less control to native communities than proposed in an interim report by the Royal Commission on Aboriginal Peoples which recommended that aboriginal peoples be allowed to establish their own justice systems in light of the devastating effect of the current system. The federal proposal focuses on giving a greater role in the sentencing of offenders to native communities.

---

[1] Several other inquiries and commissions have been mandated in recent years, including the Manitoba Aboriginal Justice Inquiry, 1991; the Alberta Task Force on the Criminal Justice System and its Impact on the Indian and Métis People of Alberta, 1991; the Saskatchewan Indian Justice Review Committee and Métis Justice Review Committee, 1992; and the federal Royal Commission on Aboriginal Peoples, due to deliver its final report in 1996. Several of these initiatives and the government's responses are described in *Aboriginal Peoples and the Justice System: Report of the National Round Table on Aboriginal Justice Issues* published by the Royal Commission on Aboriginal

Peoples in 1993 at pages 15-41. There is also the *Report of the Commission on Systemic Racism in the Ontario Criminal Justice System* (Toronto: Queen's Printer for Ontario, 1995) which discusses the problem of systemic racism within the Ontario justice system. Whether its recommendations will have any effect remains to be seen.

# Royal Commission on the Donald Marshall, Jr., Prosecution*
## Volume One: Commissioners' Report

\* Excerpts from the Royal Commission Report (Halifax: Province of Nova Scotia, 1989).

## VISIBLE MINORITIES AND THE CRIMINAL JUSTICE SYSTEM

Marshall is the typical Indian lad that seems to lose control of his senses while indulging in intoxicating liquors. Apparently he enjoys a good fight while intoxicated.

> Corrections Canada Admission Document
> concerning Donald Marshall, Jr.
> July 21, 1972
> Exhibit 112, Page 3

One reason Donald Marshall, Jr. was convicted of and spent 11 years in jail for a murder he did not commit is because Marshall is an Indian. The statement quoted above is simply one of the more blatant and overt examples of the seemingly unconscious racism and racial stereotyping that influenced what happened to Donald Marshall, Jr.

That racism played a role in Marshall's conviction and imprisonment is one of the most difficult and disturbing findings this Royal Commission has made. But reaching that conclusion was only the first part of our duty as Commissioners. We also had to determine whether such a tragic and unacceptable incident could occur again today and, if it could, to make recommendations to make sure it does not.

Much has changed — and improved — in Nova Scotia in the 18 years since Donald Marshall, Jr. was convicted of murdering Sandy Seale. But as recent events such as the highly publicized incidents involving fights between Black and White students at a high school in Cole Harbour make clear, one should never automatically assume that the racism and discrimination occurred only in the past.

If a Native — or a Black person — were charged with a similar offence today, what effect might their racial origin have on how their case would be handled by the police, by Crown and defence counsel, by the courts, and/or by the corrections system? If a Native or a Black were wrongfully convicted for a crime and later discovered to be innocent, what effect, if any, would race have on the amount of compensation he or she receives? What positive measures can this Royal Commission recommend to ensure that our justice system will not — and cannot — be influenced by the color of a person's skin?

We realized from the beginning of our work that the bald facts of the Marshall case — a Native youth, who is charged with murdering a Black youth, is investigated, tried and convicted by a criminal justice system that is made up only of Whites — could not help but raise questions about the role the race of the accused and/or the victim may have played in the handling and disposition of this particular case.

To help us deal with the specific issues associated with the Marshall case, we granted full standing to both the Union of Nova Scotia Indians and the Black United Front to allow them to appear before the Commission and to question witnesses during our public hearings. Their input was of considerable assistance to us in reaching our conclusions about the Marshall case.

We also realized that, regardless of the outcome of our deliberations on the Marshall case, we would have to examine how Natives and Blacks are treated in the criminal justice system in Nova Scotia today in order to determine whether what happened to Seale and Marshall could also happen to two teenagers in a similar situation in 1990.

Recognizing that the public hearing process was not a suitable forum for a discussion and analysis of complex issues of discrimination and racism, the Commission launched a parallel research program, which included commissioning independent scholars and researchers to take an analytical look at whether — or to what extent — race is a factor in the criminal justice system in Nova Scotia. Two of the five research reports deal specifically with issues facing Natives and Blacks (Volume 3: "The Mi'kmaq and Criminal Justice in Nova Scotia" and Volume 4: "Discrimination Against Blacks in Nova Scotia: The Criminal Justice System").

The Commission also convened a Consultative Conference in November 1988, to which we invited experts from across North America. Over the course of two-and-a-half days, they provided us with a broader perspective on the issues of discrimination and racism in the criminal justice system, and helped us to focus on our own thinking on possible approaches to dealing with these issues. (See Volume 7 for an edited transcript of this Conference.)

What did we learn from this process of research and consultation?

Although there may be some legitimate and important differences of opinion about precise numbers (see Appendix 18 to Volume 2 of our study, "Public Policing in Nova Scotia"), it is sufficient for our purposes here to point out that the Native and Black population in Nova Scotia is relatively small. The 1986 census figures indicated that out of a total population of 873,176, there are 4,610 Natives on-reserve and 9,615 off-reserve, and 12,945 Blacks.

As a group, those Natives and Blacks are poorer, less educated, more dependent on social assistance, more likely to be unemployed and, when employed, more likely to work in low-paying, menial jobs than their White counterparts. We learned that Blacks and Natives are disproportionately represented in our penitentiaries and prisons, but almost totally absent from the public life of the province.

Witnesses at our public hearings, experts at our Consultative Conference, and the researchers who authored our commissioned studies all made the point that — regardless of intention — racial origin is a factor in this second-class status that minority group members endure in Nova Scotia — in other words, Natives and Blacks are disadvantaged because they are Native and Black. Racism, we were told, is alive and well in Canada, and specifically in Nova Scotia. As Dr. Wilson Head, one of the authors of the research study which appears as Volume 4, put it at the Consultative Conference:

> Is there a different law for the poor and for the rich? For the minorities and the rich? Most minority groups are poor. They get it in the neck because they are poor. They get it in the neck because they

are young. They get it in the neck because they are uneducated. They get it in the neck because they are racial minorities.

What does all of that have to do with the criminal justice system and the duty of this Royal Commission to bring forth recommendations to make sure another Marshall case will not happen in the future?

We recognize that the root cause of much of the discrimination Blacks and Natives complain about can be traced to social, political and economic structures, institutions and values that are not specifically part of the criminal justice system. We also recognize that we do not have the mandate — or the expertise — to make recommendations concerning public education or housing or social services or other matters that lie outside the criminal justice system. Nonetheless, we believe it is important to point out that the criminal justice system is simply one part of the broader social order, and that it will be impossible to solve all the problems we have identified within the justice system without also addressing broader issues such as equal access to education.

While the education system *per se* is not within the terms of our mandate, for example, it is clear that without access to a university education, Blacks and Natives cannot participate in the criminal justice system as lawyers, para-professionals and judges.

There are encouraging signs that access is improving. Dalhousie, Nova Scotia's largest university, is attempting to make it easier for Blacks and Natives to take advantage of post-secondary education options. The university's "Transition Year Program" has been providing educational and other support for Black and Native students, who might not otherwise be able to attend university, since 1969. The Micmac Professional Careers Project at Dalhousie University's Henson College and the Micmac Social Work Program at the Maritime School of Social Work are providing assistance and encouragement to Micmacs who wish to pursue certain professional paths. In addition, a 1989 report by the Dalhousie University Task Force on Access for Black and Native People has made recommendations to deal with a variety of problems facing visible minority students at Dalhousie. Finally — and particularly relevant to the work of this Royal Commission — the University launched a new program in September 1989 to encourage indigenous Black and Micmac students to attend Dalhousie Law School.

These developments at Dalhousie, while largely outside our mandate, are significant and we believe will be helpful in changing or eliminating the perception of Blacks and Natives that the criminal justice system is closed to them.

At the moment, Blacks and Natives clearly do feel aggrieved by their treatment at all levels of the justice system: by police, Crown prosecutors, defence lawyers, government officials and judges. Blacks and Natives believe that those working in the system — from top to bottom — lack sensitivity in dealing with members of visible minority groups. They believe they have no stake in what they regard as the "White man's justice system".

Not only does that system not reflect the needs of their people, Black and Native leaders told us, but it also does not even reflect the simple fact of the *existence* of their people. The number of Natives and Blacks who are police officers, prosecutors, defence lawyers, judges and court workers, for example, is disproportionately and unjustifiably low, while the number of Natives and Blacks who are accused persons is disproportionately high.

None of this to suggest that this is the result of any evil intention to discriminate by those in the criminal justice system. But the Supreme Court of Canada itself has recently ruled that it is no longer necessary to prove that someone or some body intended to discriminate in order to find that that person or institution did discriminate. (See *Ontario Human Rights Commission v. Simpson-Sears*, [1985] 2 S.C.R. 536) The highest court has also considered the notion of what is called systemic or "adverse effects" discrimination. Systemic discrimination is what happens when a specific act, policy or structural factor — intended or unintended — results in adverse effects for members of certain specific groups.

Although much of the discrimination that occurs in the criminal justice system is of an unintended sort, it is no less insidious and its impact is no less devastating because of that. What can be done to eliminate this system discrimination and to give Blacks and Natives faith that the criminal justice system will threat them fairly?

Before we attempt to answer those questions, it is important to make the point that although there are clearly some common interests between Blacks and Natives, these two minority groups do not regard the criminal justice system in exactly the same way. Historical, cultural and constitutional factors have placed Natives in a special position in Canada. Without wishing to oversimplify, we can say that Native groups generally want a greater measure of control of their own judicial affairs while Black groups generally want a stronger voice in the existing system. Because of these important cultural and historical differences, we will deal with the specific concerns of Natives and Blacks in the criminal justice system in separate sections of this Chapters.

To begin, however, we will consider some issues of common concern to both Natives and Blacks. These include the need for governments at all levels to devise firm anti-racism policies: training that would lead to better representation of visible minorities in the criminal justice and legal system; improved access to useful legal information for Blacks and Natives; and more inventive options in sentencing of members of visible minorities.

Our challenge is to propose solutions that will attack these problems in a way that will not only improve the lot of visible minorities in this province but also establish a model that can have an impact even beyond the boundaries of Nova Scotia. Some of our suggested solutions will require the cooperation of the Federal Government, which has jurisdiction over several of the matters before us. We believe this is a unique opportunity for Federal and Provincial Governments to work together towards constructive change.

### *Representation of Natives and Blacks*

A tension exists in Canadian society between the original European partners in Confederation who dominate Canadian institutions and the other people who wish to share fully in the institutional life of the country. Inherent in the notion of diversity of Canadian society as a 'mosaic' is the equal participation of the pieces making it up.

Natives and Blacks are still almost invisible in the institutions operated by the majority White society in Nova Scotia, including the criminal justice system. It is time the complexions of those institutions changed.

That is not to suggest that merely increasing the proportional representation of Natives and Blacks will suddenly solve all our racial problems. Increasing the quality of representation — getting minority group members into senior positions — will be just as important. However, this will only ultimately make a difference if the system itself changes to meet the needs of the minority communities.

With these caveats on the record, however, we still believe increasing the number of Blacks and Natives in the criminal justice system is a necessary and overdue first step in making the system more responsive to and representative of visible minorities.

In addition, the presence of more non-White faces in these important and respected institutions will be of value not only to minority group members. It may also help the general population develop increased sensitivity to — and tolerance for — the needs and aspirations of visible minorities. Their presence will remind us on a daily basis that minorities are members of our society too, and that that society is not — and never has been — completely White.

### Anti-Racism Policies

> Racism exists as a demonstrable social factor in social relations in Canada and the justice system is not excepted. . . . A resolute political will must be adopted to acknowledge up front the existence of racism and to set about eliminating it by moving it onto the public policy agenda. Policymakers, legislators and government have an extra responsibility to create a climate which will be more inhospitable for racism.

Our mandate extends to a complete examination of the criminal justice system in Nova Scotia, its administration and the manner in which criminal justice is delivered. The recommendations which follow focus on the criminal justice system but we realize that our recommendations, if implemented, may have wide-ranging effects in other areas of Canadian society and government as well.

The first step must be for the Province of Nova Scotia to make sure its own house is in order so it can provide leadership for private and other public sector policy-makers and decision-makers. Our recommendations concerning the establishment of clear anti-racism policies within the Provincial Government include specific components dealing with improving the number and the quality of visible minority representation in the Departments of Attorney General and Solicitor General, as well as establishing a mechanism to monitor and enforce this employment equity provision.

Monitoring and enforcement will be vital because unless such mechanisms are in place, there will be no way to evaluate the effectiveness of affirmative action programs or to make certain that those responsible live up to the goals of the programs.

### Recommendation 9

*We recommend that the Departments of the Attorney General and Solicitor General adopt and publicize a Policy on Race Relations that has as its basis a commitment to employment equity and the elimination of inequalities, based on race, in these Departments and their agencies and the reduction of racial tensions between these Departments and the communities with which they interact.*

This policy statement should include goals and timetables for recruitment and hiring to achieve employment equity for visible minority groups. By having more minority group members on staff, these departments, which deliver and administer criminal justice, will gain a better understanding of the needs and views of the visible minority groups with which they are in day-to-day contact. They must also not only make a real effort to increase the hiring of visible minorities but must also work to sensitize all their staff to racial problems.

Mechanisms do not now exist in Nova Scotia to monitor and enforce a policy such as we are recommending. The 1987 Annual Report of the Nova Scotia Civil Service Commission, for example, shows that of a total of 10,123 provincial civil servants, 208 are Black, seven are native. But what does that really mean? Such numbers tell us nothing about the quality of representation of Black and Natives within the Province's public service because there is no monitoring mechanism built into that system to ensure that it is achieving its goals.

We believe that the Human Rights Commission is the most effective body to fulfill this critically important role. But we recognize that in order to be effective, the Commission must have adequate resources and be independent of Government.

The concerns of Natives and Blacks must not only be part of the agenda of the Attorney General and Solicitor General's Departments but must also be integrated into general Government policy. Regular meetings between visible minority group representatives and key government officials will provide opportunities for dialogue and understanding in a non-confrontational, non-crisis atmosphere.

**Recommendation 10**

*We recommend that a Cabinet Committee on Race Relations be established which would include the Attorney General and Solicitor General. This Committee should meet regularly with representatives of visible minority groups in order to assure the input of these groups in matters of criminal justice.*

### *Legal Profession*

Visible minorities in the legal profession fare no better than in government. There are currently almost 1,200 lawyers in Nova Scotia who are eligible to appear before the courts. Of these, about a dozen are Black. There are no Micmac lawyers in Nova Scotia. To our knowledge, only one Native has ever graduated from Dalhousie Law School. There is one Black judge in Nova Scotia, at the Family Court level, and no Micmac judges.

It is obvious that visible minorities cannot be represented among the ranks of Crown prosecutors, defence counsel and the judiciary unless they are entering and graduating from law schools in greatly increased numbers, and they cannot do that without a solid educational foundation. Improvements are needed in the educational system to ensure that minority students are given support, both educational and financial, to put them on an equal footing with White students.

The Dalhousie Law School's recently announced minority admission program — which includes special recruitment efforts and a summer program as well as educational and financial support — would appear to include all the elements we have identified as being necessary to a successful initiative, and we are encouraged by its establishment. But Dalhousie's leadership must be accompanied by the financial support of governments and the bar in order to ensure that the increased participation of visible minorities in the legal profession actually occurs.

**Recommendation 11**

*We recommend that the Dalhousie Law School's minority admissions program for Micmacs and indigenous Blacks receive the financial support of the Governments of Canada and Nova Scotia, and the Nova Scotia Bar.*

In order for such programs to achieve the desired end, of course, it will be essential for those in authority to then take advantage of this growing pool of lawyers from the visible minority communities when making appointments.

**Recommendation 12**

*We recommend that Governments consider the needs of visible minorities by appointing qualified visible minority judges and administrative board members whenever possible.*

Although these recommendations promote diversity in the legal profession and the courts, it is clear the legal profession and the courts are still almost entirely — and will continue to be largely — White institutions. Our research shows that many Natives and Blacks feel poorly served by the legal profession, not only because there are so few visible minority lawyers, but also because many lawyers seem ill-equipped to deal with the special problems of minority clients. The profession has a responsibility not only to encourage racial diversity in its ranks but also to assist in sensitizing its members to minority issues. In order to make sure that those who are part of the system have an awareness of and sensitivity to issues facing Natives and Blacks, education and ongoing training will be necessary.

**Recommendation 13**

*We recommend that the Dalhousie Law School, the Nova Scotia Barristers Society and the Judicial Councils support courses and programs dealing with legal issues facing visible minorities, and encourage sensitivity to minority concerns for law students, lawyers and judges.*

Law schools provide lawyers with their basic legal education, emphasizing legal concepts, skills training, and "thinking like a lawyer". Most students graduate from law school with little exposure to the daily reality of the minority population. While Dalhousie Law School now offers a course in Native Law, this is only available to a few students. In addition to such specific courses, the Law School must encourage law students to consider minority concerns in all their courses. This must be done not only in relation to substantive legal issues, but also in terms of sensitizing our future lawyers to the particular needs of visible minorities.

Once they graduate from law school, lawyers' continuing education is dealt with first through the Bar Admission Course and then through the Continuing Legal Education Society of Nova Scotia. To date, there has been little or no emphasis in these courses and programs on minority issues, and we urge those who run them to make this a priority. With so few minority lawyers in the province, all of the practicing bar must accept some responsibility to become attuned to these issues.

Crown prosecutors have a special role in ensuring that the system is perceived to be dealing with individuals on an equal footing, regardless of race. It is therefore important that continuing professional education programs include sessions which introduce Crown prosecutors to the facts of systemic discrimination.

## Recommendation 14

*We recommend that the Attorney General establish continuing professional education programs for Crown prosecutors, which would include:*
*(a) an exposure to materials explaining the nature of systemic discrimination toward Black and Native peoples in Nova Scotia in the criminal justice system; and*
*(b) an exploration of means by which Crown prosecutors can carry out their functions so as to reduce the effects of systemic discrimination in the Nova Scotia criminal justice system.*

Judges must be fair and impartial in dealing with all who appear before them. They must also appear to be fair and impartial. Our research, as well as anecdotal reports, indicate that some individuals from visible minority groups believe that some judges treat them with less respect than White accused. We cannot comment on whether these perceptions are based on fact, but these perceptions do exist and that causes us concern. A fair judiciary is the cornerstone of our legal system. One incident of unfairness on racial grounds holds the entire judiciary open to disrespect.

The role of judicial councils in disciplining judges for improper conduct is not widely known. The judicial councils, which provide the only mechanism through which a citizen can complain about a judge's conduct, should publicize their existence and functions. The public must be able to see that judges are subject to the same, if not higher, standards of behaviour as other participants in the society.

### *Police*

Police/minority relations are a very important part of the work of this Royal Commission. The Chapter on Policing (Chapter 2.6) discusses the organization, training and services provided by the police, as well as their particular responsibilities in dealing with visible minorities.

We heard allegations in our public hearings about tensions between the Native youth of the Membertou Reserve and the Sydney City Police Department in the early 1970s. For example, Native witnesses have suggested that Native youths were picked out as troublemakers, hassled without cause, occasionally roughed up and regularly kicked out of Wentworth Park, their favorite meeting place. We have evidence from non-Native witnesses who dated Indian boys that the police told their parents they should not hang around with Indians. We also heard that members of the Sydney City Police Department in 1971 received little or no training of any kind, and no training at all in dealing with Native people or other visible minorities. Even now, there is little education of police officers in Sydney — or elsewhere in the province — on the special needs of visible minorities.

**Recommendation 15**

*We recommend that training for all police officers, both at the intake level and as continuing education, include content on police minority concerns and sensitivity to visible minority issues.*

We understand there is such a course on the books at the Atlantic Police Academy, but that it is inactive because of low enrollment. This is simply not good enough.

Many Natives and Blacks believe police officers accept negative stereotypes of members of minority groups. Our researcher was told, for example, that many Natives believe police might respond slowly to an incident on a reserve because the police believe that most such incidents are alcohol-related and will resolve themselves if left alone.

A recent study done by Dr. Joseph Fletcher *et al.* at the Centre of Criminology at the University of Toronto confirms that police officers are prone to racial stereotyping of Natives and other visible minorities. While police may stereotype Natives as a group, the study indicates they are less likely to believe Native people as a group have unique rights that must be recognized. They do not favor programs such as affirmative action to give Native people help in "catching up." According to the study, police officers generally believe individuals control their own personal fate. Consequently, if a particular group fares less well in the social or economic order, police officers believe the problem is simply that they have not tried hard enough.

With a continuing lack of training to help them understand the reality of systemic discrimination — and with younger police officers frequently forming their values and methods of operation from more experienced officers — it is not surprising that these attitudes can become self-perpetuating.

It is essential that those responsible for police recruitment and training, whether at the municipal level or the RCMP, recognize not only that those with racial biases should not be permitted to engage in police work, but that recruits as well as veteran officers must be provided with ongoing training in police/minority issues.

### *Legal Information Needs of Natives and Blacks*

We have heard from many sources that Native and Black communities have little access to information about the law and little knowledge about how the justice system operates. Having an educated and sensitive bar can help, but more is needed.

In Nova Scotia, as in most other provinces, the Public Legal Education Society provides information about the law to the public. This organization has great potential for providing programs specific to the needs of minorities. However, experience has shown that unless this information is geared towards the minority group and produced in cooperation with them, it will probably not be effective. Such organizations must be aware of and sensitive to the needs of the communities to which their material and programming is directed and must work with these communities to fill their legal information needs.

**Recommendation 16**

*We recommend that the Public Legal Education Society consult and work with Native and Black groups to develop and provide legal materials and services for minority users. These initiatives cannot be undertaken without specific funding. This should be provided where necessary by Government.*

### *Sentencing Options*

Both of our minority-related research projects, as well as a recent Nova Scotia court decision (See *R. v. Hebb* (1989), 89 N.S.R. (2d) 137), point out that the lack of a fine options program creates special problems for the poor in Nova Scotia. This has particular relevance for Blacks and Natives because so many of them are poor. Fine option programs provide judges with options other than imprisonment for those who cannot pay court-ordered penalties.

The Nova Scotia Government brought forward legislation in the spring of 1989 to permit the establishment of such a fine options program here. We hope the Government quickly proclaims this legislation and that the regulations under the legislation will take into account the special needs of Natives and Blacks.

**Recommendation 17**

*We recommend that the Government immediately proclaim the Alternative Penalty Act, S.N.S. 1989, c. 2, and that regulations which address the particular needs of Native and Black offenders be enacted.*

Diversion programs are another alternative to sending people to jail. If a goal of the criminal justice system is to prevent crime and permit meaningful rehabilitation of the offender rather than simply to impose routine and unthinking incarceration, diversion of alleged offenders away from the system must be explored.

Police and prosecutors now have enormous discretion to "criminalize" behavior that may have been caused by socioeconomic conditions. The criminal justice system has both the challenge and the opportunity of assisting in breaking the vicious and destructive cycle that results in disproportionate numbers of Native and Black offenders being caught up in the system.

At present, diversion programs are used mainly in relation to young offenders. Such programs can be of particular relevance to Native and Black youth because they may require educational, life-skills, and job-related training in order to steer them away from more long-term problems with the law. Programs dealing with Native youth in various parts of the country have attempted to address the range of problems associated with youth involvement with the law, and these initiatives should be encouraged.

However, we believe diversion programs should be broadened to include adult Black and Native offenders. This would require an amendment to the *Criminal Code*.

**Recommendation 18**

*We recommend that the Province, in close cooperation with the Native and Black communities, formulate proposals for the establishment of appropriate diversion programs for Natives and Blacks, and that the Province actively recommend such programs to the Federal Government with proposals for any necessary amendments to the Criminal Code.*

*Corrections*

The research done for the Royal Commission confirms our view that correctional institutions in Canada and in Nova Scotia are populated primarily by the young, the poor, and members of racial minority groups. According to respondents in our survey, the first thing that needs to be done to improve the corrections system is to improve the attitudes and behavior of guards and other correction authorities. The second priority should be to provide programs and services to offenders and ex-offenders.

**Recommendation 19**

*We recommend that the Department of the Solicitor General of Nova Scotia take steps to, and urge the federal correctional authorities to take steps to:*
*(a) immediately implement programs to recruit and hire more Natives and Blacks in professional and non-professional positions in the correctional service;*
*(b) implement ongoing education and training programs designed to sensitize correctional workers at all levels to the particular needs of Native and Black offenders based on their racial and cultural background;*
*(c) indicate to all correctional workers that discriminatory conduct (including racial slurs) against Natives and Blacks will not be tolerated and may result in adverse employment consequences;*
*(d) offer institutional programs emphasizing the educational, cultural and religious needs of Native and Black offenders in institutions where a significant number of Natives and Blacks are incarcerated; and*
*(e) support rehabilitation programs for Native and Black inmates and former inmates which take into account their background and needs.*

The correctional service, like other segments of the criminal justice system, must make a serious effort to achieve an appropriate representation of Natives and Blacks in both professional and non-professional positions.

In addition, everyone who works in a correctional institution or in the correctional service must receive proper training concerning the social, cultural and economic basis for the problems of visible minority offenders, so he or she will be able to deal sensitively with these offenders.

The correctional service administration also has a role to play in making sure that those working in corrections treat all inmates equally, regardless of their race, and must make it clear that prejudicial or racist treatment will be dealt with harshly. Internal procedures are also needed to ensure that racism is not practised or tolerated in the correctional service.

Rehabilitation is particularly important for Native and Black offenders, but most prison programs, according to respondents to our survey and other observers, focus on security and punishment requirements rather than on rehabilitation.

Correctional authorities should attempt to give inmates the confidence and skills to re-enter society as people who can function without resorting to crime. Education and skills training are a crucial part of this process.

For visible minority offenders, however, there is an added dimension. We have earlier concluded that Natives and Blacks are treated differently than White because of their race. Because of this, it is necessary that racial factors be recognized within the walls of the institution. We suggest that, where there are sufficient numbers in an institution to justify them, specific programs for Natives and Blacks should be established, taking into account their education, social and religious needs.

These needs must also be considered when it is time for visible minority inmates to leave the institution. Service agencies such as the John Howard Society should be funded to sponsor programs to help Native and Black offenders integrate themselves into the community after prison. Providing a minority liaison person to assist offenders in making the transition to the outside world, for example, would fill a real need.

Too often, programs of this type are dependent on short-term project funding. The Solicitor General's Department should provide longer term financial assistance to such worthwhile initiatives.

## NOVA SCOTIA MICMACS AND THE CRIMINAL JUSTICE SYSTEM

At the time of the killing of Sandy Seale in 1971, Donald Marshall, Jr., was a 17-year-old Micmac youth living on the Membertou Reserve in Sydney, Nova Scotia. His parents were well-respected members of the reserve community. Donald Marshall, Sr. is the Grand Chief of the Micmac Nation. His son, Donald Jr., (known to his friends and family as Junior) is one of the Marshalls' ten children — six boys and four girls. At home and on the reserve, he spoke Micmac, although not exclusively. When he went to school in Sydney, however, he spoke English. He left school during grade six, and at the time of Seale's murder, was working part time in his father's drywall business.

Sydney is the third largest city in Nova Scotia with a population of 35,000 people. The economy is based mainly on the steel and coal industry. The Membertou Reserve, located within the city of Sydney, is close to the downtown and within about a half-mile of Wentworth Part. About 500 Micmac live on the Reserve. A fair number of Blacks also live in Sydney, primarily in the Whitney Pier area. At the time of his death, Sandy Seale's family had recently moved from Whitney Pier to Westmount on the outskirts of the city.

It is difficult today to determine the existence or extent of racial problems in Sydney in 1971. Some witnesses at the Royal Commission described the city as a "redneck town", but there is no reason to believe Sydney was any more racist or "redneck" than any other small city in the region, or elsewhere in Canada. Although some Native witnesses at the public hearings suggested the relationship between Whites and Natives in Sydney was not a particularly comfortable one, there is little evidence of overt hostility between the White and Native communities, or between the White and Black communities in Sydney, or between the two minority communities.

We have concluded that Donald Marshall, Jr.'s status as a Native contributed to the miscarriage of justice that has plagued him since 1971. We believe that certain persons within the system would have been more rigorous in their duties, more careful, or more conscious of fairness if Marshall had been White.

The discussion and recommendations that follow go beyond merely looking at which might happen if there was a situation similar to the Marshall case in 1989. If Marshall's treatment in this case occurred because he was a Native, then other Natives will have — and have had — similar experiences. We have attempted to look at the ways in which Natives interact with the justice system, to determine where and how the system has failed them.

> ... The overrepresentation of Native peoples in our prisons is the result of a particular and distinctive historical process which had made them poor beyond poverty. And that process is in the process of colonization, whereby we, as a dominant society, have come to North America and have sought to make over Native people in our image. That process has left Native people, in most parts of the country, dispossessed of all but the remnants of what was once their home lands. . . . It's a process which is recognized as having the inevitable consequence of causing immense social and personal demoralization everywhere it has happened in the world. We have recognized the consequences of that in Africa. We have embarked and almost completed, with the exception of South Africa, the process of decolonization. In Canada, we haven't yet recognized that we have that problem. And yet, it is, in my estimation, the central problem which lies at the root of horrendous figures relating to Native people in the criminal justice system.

Having found that Marshall was denied justice because he is an Indian, and that Indians suffer adverse effects from the predominantly White criminal justice system, we need to find ways to change the system. Native Canadians have a right to a justice system they respect and which has respect for them, and which dispenses justice in a manner consistent with and sensitive to their history, culture and language.

Many Natives feel that the criminal justice system — including police, lawyers, judges and courts — is not relevant to their experience, not only in terms of its language and concepts but also in terms of its essential values. Natives rely on resolving disputes through mediation and conciliation, methods which emphasize reconciliation rather than laying blame. Those traditional values frequently clash with our adversarial system. That means that if we are going to change the criminal justice system, either in substance or in its delivery, we must take into account the unique historical and cultural background of Native people.

. . . .

## Framework for our Recommendations

Until recently, it has been assumed that the best thing Natives could do was to assimilate into the mainstream of society because, after all, White society is more "civilized" and affluent. Why would anyone want to preserve a way of life that is so lacking in services, employment and economic prosperity? Why would Native people not want the advantages of full participation in a White society?

To even ask these questions, of course, indicates a not uncommon ignorance of the strength and traditions of Native society, and the pride Natives take in their society.

As aboriginal peoples, Natives lived in what we now call Canada thousands of years before the English and the French colonized it.

They had their own established ways of living and settling disputes. They were not based on our adversarial system — confrontation, determination of guilt and then punishment of the offender by the State — but on mediation between the parties, with restitution to the victim and to the community. There was not just one person sitting in judgment either. Community elders and leaders settled disputes, and they based their decisions on what they believed was best for the whole community. This community-based approach to justice may be different than our method of resolving disputes, but that does not make it any less valid.

The list of Native criticisms of how our judicial process affects them is long. To begin, they argue that it is not relevant to the real lives of Native people. The court is an unfamiliar and intimidating institution, conceptually removed from the indigenous processes of social control based on mediation and restitution. It is usually physically removed as well. Most courts are located some distance from reserves, making it difficult for Natives to attend. In addition, many Natives, especially those from rural reserves, have problems comprehending the English language. When you add to those things the reality that all the faces in the justice system are White, that Natives constitute a small minority of the population and that Natives suffer from stereotyping and other forms of discrimination, you begin to understand why Natives are unhappy with the current system of administering justice.

The Royal Commission has considered many possibilities for dealing effectively with these problems. One approach would be to identify each problem and then deal with each one individually. For example, their problems with language could be solved by having Native interpreters available in court; their lack of familiarity with court procedures and concepts could be tackled by establishing a professional court worker service; their isolation from the court itself could be remedied by having provincial court judges actually hold court on reserves; their concerns about using their own traditional ways of settling disputes could be addressed by making some adaptation to the structure of sentencing. All of these solutions (and others) are important, and will be the subject of discussion and recommendation by the Royal Commission.

But this is a piecemeal approach. It does not address the differences between Native and White societies, or the argument of some Natives that justice for Natives must be on Native terms and according to Native concepts. Having looked at the problems and the options, we believe the time has come to deal with these broader concerns by establishing — on an experimental basis — a Native Criminal Court that will allow Natives some measure of direct control over the administration of justice within their communities.

*Native Criminal Court*

At a conference on Indian justice held in Saskatoon on October 12, 1983, the Minister of Indian Affairs stated that:

> Justice is a basic need in the life of every person. It has confronted, challenged and concerned every society which ever joined together for mutual benefit. . . . The law belongs not to governments, not to bureaucrats, not to lawyers, but to the people. . . . The many alternative means of resolving disputes suggested now — mediation, arbitration, restitution, reconciliation, to name a few — are the very methods which are part of customary law. . . . Native peoples have been deprived of their own traditional laws, concepts of justice and legal procedures. We realize that the Native peoples of Canada expect a system of justice that reflects their own cultural heritage.

We accept these comments of the then Minister. We agree some degree of control should be accorded to Native people in respect of their institutions of justice. A Native Criminal Court is one way to return to them some degree of control over Native justice.

**Recommendation 20**

*We recommend that a community-controlled Native Criminal Court be established in Nova Scotia, initially as a five-year pilot project, incorporating the following elements:*
*(a) a Native Justice of the Peace appointed under Section 107 of the Indian Act with jurisdiction to hear cases involving summary conviction offences committed on a reserve;*
*(b) diversion and mediation services to encourage resolution of disputes without resort to the criminal courts;*
*(c) community work projects on the reserve to provide alternatives to fines and imprisonment;*
*(d) aftercare services on the reserve;*
*(e) community input in sentencing, where appropriate; and*
*(f) court worker services.*

A Native community may choose to opt in our out of the model Native Criminal Court we propose. That is and must be recognized as its right.

The proposal we make is modest and will not completely satisfy the demands of some Native groups. However, we believe the proposal is sound and, while experimental in nature, should either chart the way for future development in Nova Scotia, or result in a recognition that, for whatever reasons, Native Criminal Courts are not appropriate here.

We wish to make it clear that the Native Criminal Court we propose will administer the same law as applies to all other Canadians. We do not propose a separate system of Native law, but rather a different process for administering on the reserve certain aspects of the criminal law. The laws enacted by Parliament and the Legislative Assembly will continue to apply to Natives, and the safeguards for accused persons under the Charter would apply in any Native Criminal Court. In the event that any Native customary law is introduced, it would be only after the period of study noted in our next recommendation.

Any sort of Native court system will no doubt seem threatening to some. There will be those who will say, "Why should the Natives get their own justice system?" The answer: "Because they are Native." As aboriginal people, the Micmacs not only have a history and culture that thrived in Nova Scotia before the province was colonized by Whites but they also had in place their own successful methods for resolving disputes.

As noted in our recommendation, Section 107 of the *Indian Act* already provides a mechanism by which a limited type of Native Criminal Court can operate. Under that section, the Federal Cabinet may appoint persons to be justices of the peace to adjudicate cases arising under the *Indian Act* and summary conviction offences under the *Criminal Code*.

Two reserves in Quebec — Kahnawake and St. Regis — have established courts under this authority. The Court of Kahnawake, which we took the opportunity to visit during our deliberations, is a positive example of how Native people can successfully take some control over their own justice institutions. While limited in the scope of their authority by the terms of their appointment, the Native Justices of the Peace have managed to take account of the particular needs of Native people while still upholding the laws of the larger community. By using Native court personnel and court workers, an informal court process and sentencing with community and individual needs in mind, the Native Justices of the Peace appear to have struck an appropriate balance between the old and the new ways. They are now attempting to obtain funding to include mediation and diversion facilities in the range of services provided. Under the Kahnawake model, the Court has jurisdiction over summary conviction offences committed within the boundaries of the reserve, whether by Natives or non-Natives; appeals are taken either to provincial or federal courts depending on the offence.

Critics of the Court of Kahnawake feel that by simply enforcing 'majority' laws, the Court does not go far enough in recognizing the customary law of the Native people. It is true that courts established under the *Indian Act* authority do not provide an answer to the question of the full acceptance of indigenous Native justice mechanisms. But with the benefit of the services recommended in our proposal (some of which are now provided at Kahnawake), the Kahnawake model provides a good starting point for discussion.

It is wrong to think that Native people who wish to see Native traditions reflected in their justice procedures merely want to turn back the clock to simpler times. Changes in the Native and non-Native way of life have brought changes in our laws that cannot be ignored. An accommodation can be reached between Native traditions, human rights law and the Charter, so that the end result will be relevant to Native people and consistent with the protections provided to all Canadians. The historical and cultural justification for establishing Native justice systems must override the fear of problems which might arise. The Court of Kahnawake, for example, shows it can be done.

Future development of Native Criminal Courts in Nova Scotia will be determined by a number of factors:

- *the will and ability of the Micmac people and their leaders to move in this direction;*
- *the political will of the Federal and Provincial Governments to resolve outstanding issues and to support the development of the proposal;*

- *the establishment of a body to do the required development work; and*
- *the establishment of a tripartite forum (Micmac, Provincial and Federal Government) for the discussion and negotiation of a Micmac justice system.*

The development of a community-based justice system will require a research and information base, and coordination between the bands, the Native political organizations and Government. When the Court is established, training of personnel and legal research will become necessary. Because of the importance of Native justice issues in Nova Scotia, we believe that long-term assistance must be given to Nova Scotia Micmacs in order to facilitate this effort.

**Recommendation 21**

*We recommend that a Native Justice Institute be established with Provincial and Federal Government funding to do, among other things, the following:*
*(a) channel and coordinate community needs and concerns into the Native Criminal Court;*
*(b) undertake research on Native customary law to determine the extent to which it should be incorporated into the criminal and civil law as it applies to Native people;*
*(c) train court workers and other personnel employed by the Native Criminal Court and the regular courts;*
*(d) consult with Government on Native justice issues;*
*(e) work with the Nova Scotia Barristers Society, the Public Legal Education Society and other groups concerned with the legal information needs of Native people; and*
*(f) monitor the existence of discriminatory treatment against Native people in the criminal justice system.*

Differences between Micmac and Government involving the administration of justice could be dealt with in a tripartite forum with representatives from the Micmac, the Provincial and Federal Governments. The Ontario Indian Commission, while not a perfect model, shows that such a mechanism can be extremely effective. Established in 1978 by agreement between representatives of the Governments of Ontario and Canada and Ontario Indian leaders, its purpose was to examine, discuss and set priorities for identifying and negotiating all matters affecting the Indian people of Ontario and their relationship with the Governments. If a similar structure were implemented in Nova Scotia, the parties could also agree that the negotiation of justice issues would be part of the agenda.

**Recommendation 22**

*We recommend that a tripartite forum (Micmac/Provincial/Federal Government) similar to the Ontario Indian Commission be established to mediate and resolve outstanding issues between the Micmac and Government, including Native justice issues.*

### Interpreters

As we pointed out earlier, there are many specific problems relating to the administration of justice that will still need to be dealt with, regardless of whether our recommendation for a pilot Native Criminal Court project is accepted. These include everything from the need for Native court workers to interpreters to assist Native accused in dealing with the criminal justice system.

**Recommendation 23**

*We recommend that all courts in Nova Scotia have the services of an on-call Micmac interpreter for use at the request of Micmac witnesses or accused.*

The Royal Commission has been told about some of the differences between Micmac and White concepts and language. Several Micmac witnesses, including Donald Marshall, Jr., testified before us, so we were able to observe their reaction to the court-like process of the Inquiry. That gave us first-hand knowledge of some of the problems Natives may experience in such a setting.

In addition to our observation of Marshall's testimony before us, we also read the transcript of his testimony at his Supreme Court trial and at the Reference before the Appeal Division of the Nova Scotia Supreme Court. There are obvious differences. Before the Supreme Court and the Appeal Division, the Court asked Marshall on at least 29 occasions to speak up or remove his hand from his face so he could be heard. While Marshall is naturally soft-spoken, the court's numerous interventions probably compounded his discomfort, and may have seemed to Marshall as evidence that officials were harassing him or were at least hostile toward him. The Court, on the other hand, may have regarded Marshall's demeanor as a negative factor and that may have influenced the ultimate disposition of the hearings.

. . . .

It is disturbing to think of a young Native person, such as Donald Marshall, Jr., on trial for a very serious offence, in an environment where, because of his Native background, he is unable to make a full defence based on a variety of factors beyond his control.

If we seek to obtain the best evidence from all witnesses, to assume innocence until guilt is proved and to give all accused the resources to assert their innocence, we must deal seriously with these subtle language problems.

### Native Court Workers

While the use of an interpreter will alleviate some of the language difficulties, the problems go much deeper than mere language comprehension.

## Recommendation 24

*We recommend that the Provincial and Federal Governments, in consultation with Native communities, work together to establish a Native court worker program, as an immediate first step in making the criminal justice system more accessible to Native people.*

The first court worker program in Canada was established in Alberta in 1970 and the program undertaken by Native Counselling Services of Alberta is still the most comprehensive and highly regarded in the country. The percentage of Indians as inmates in provincial institutions, for example, has decreased from 58 percent to 28 percent, and many credit this to the effective work done by the Native Counselling Services. Its Executive Director, Chester Cunningham was one of the experts who attended our Consultation in November 1988.

The benefits of a court worker program are evident in the following comments from judges being interviewed for an assessment of the Alberta program:

> Throughout the extended conversations with the judges, it is apparent that the Bench, for the most part, is aware of the bewilderment that many Natives experience in the legal system, and particularly in the courtroom setting itself. The ritualistic formality and sense of coded behavior, the 'suit and tie' atmosphere, the monotone 'legalese' of the courtroom English, the depersonalized conveyor belt sense of processing ... as the judges face a lengthy docket and limited time — all these would combine to shake the confidence of even a person well seasoned in systems. Within this setting, language and interpretation become pivotal. Often, as the judges themselves are keenly aware — it is difficult to get beyond 'yes' or 'no' responses to the essence of what the Bench needs to know in order to make an informed and sensitive decision. Indeed in the clear words of yet another Native court worker. 'Most Natives don't talk in the grey area of extenuating circumstances.'

> It is easy to see, then, how it is that the Bench has come to identify the Native court worker as a 'communication device,' bridging the interests of both the court and the Native accused. It is to the credit of our court system that so many of the judges who were interviewed could have spoken the words of one of their number: 'Someone who speaks their language or understands their background instills more confidence than I could no matter how well-meaning I am. In this way, the purpose of Native Counselling is all about communication and justice.'

At one time or another, all provinces in Canada have had court worker programs, although several, including Nova Scotia, have discontinued them.

A Native court worker does not give legal advice but acts as a paralegal. A properly trained court worker can bridge the gap between the Native person with little or no knowledge of the criminal justice system and the system itself. The role of the court worker — who would be available to all Native people, on or off the reserve — should include a variety of functions, including:

- *arranging for the provision of legal services, if required;*
- *explaining the charge and plea options, as well as courtroom procedures;*
- *translating for the client and counsel if requested, if a translator has not been provided;*
- *assisting the client in getting to court appearances or meetings with counsel;*
- *explaining the client's rights and obligations in the process;*
- *explaining the role of Crown and defence counsel, and judge and jury; and*

- *other assistance as required.*

An effective court worker can also help sensitize non-Native personnel in the criminal justice system to the needs of Native people.

One of the most frequent criticisms of court worker programs is that the method of providing funding as well as the amount of funding allocated is not sufficient, resulting in inadequate staff training and too few staff to meet the demand. Establishing a Native court worker program will cost money. However, the cost will be more than justified if the program provides — and is seen to provide — much-needed assistance to Native people in the court system.

### *Provincial Courts on Reserves*

### Recommendation 25

*We recommend that the Chief Judge of the Provincial Court take steps to establish regular sittings of the Provincial Courts on Nova Scotia reserves.*

Some Micmac leaders and criminal justice personnel have suggested that establishing Provincial Court hearings on reserves would be another positive way of bridging the physical and conceptual distance between Micmac communities and the Courts. While such a move would be a change in form only, and not in substance, and would not deal in a significant way with the deep-seated feeling of alienation Micmac people have for the criminal justice system as a whole, it would be an important and easily implemented gesture of respect for the special concerns of Natives within the justice system.

For reserves that do not choose to adopt the Native Criminal Court proposal we made earlier — and until our recommendation for the establishment of Native Criminal Courts is implemented — Provincial Court sittings on reserves for on-reserve offences should be supported.

There would undoubtedly be a number of positive side effects from such a move. Native accused would be more likely to show up for court appearances, for example, since distance would not be a problem and since the community would likely monitor court appearances more closely. Micmacs would believe they had a greater stake in the system if they could actually see it operating in their own communities. At the same time, justice system personnel, including judges, would gain a greater understanding of Micmac concerns and reserve conditions if they were required to do a regular reserve circuit.

### *Lawyers' Duty to Native Accused*

Clark's research identified several areas in which Micmacs seem dissatisfied with the treatment they receive from lawyers. These include access to counsel, inadequate explanation of the proceedings and concerns regarding plea bargaining. Many of these concerns can be resolved if some of our other recommendations — "educating" the bar about the problems facing Native clients, directed public legal education programs and implementation of the Native court worker program — are implemented.

On the basis of what we have heard, access to legal counsel was not a problem for Donald Marshall, Jr. in 1971, and it does not appear to be a problem today. Legal aid lawyers are available throughout the province, and the fact that there are no legal aid offices on reserve does not appear to pose a problem for Native clients.

We do get the clear impression, however, that legal aid counsel are overworked. While this has an effect on all Nova Scotians who are eligible for and require legal aid services, it has a particularly negative effect on Native clients who may require more time with their lawyer than a non-Native client because of their fear and lack of knowledge of the justice system. The legal aid lawyer's lack of time, coupled with the natural communication problems Natives may have in dealing with representatives of the legal system, combine to make Native clients feel they are being poorly served.

Some of these problems indicate the different perceptions Natives and legal aid lawyers have of their duties. Clark says many Natives he interviewed believed legal aid lawyers would rather plea bargain for a lesser sentence than pursue the matter forcefully. Says Clark: "This contributes to the belief already held by many Micmacs that all justice system personnel, including defence counsel, are in league against the people being served. Often this is further perceived as discrimination against Indians."

. . . .

There needs to be ongoing liaison between lawyers and Native people. The Nova Scotia Barristers Society should organize such programs in consultation with the Native people.

**Recommendation 27**

*We recommend that a program of ongoing liaison between the bar — prosecutors, private defence and legal aid — and Native people, both on and off reserve, be established through the Nova Scotia Barristers Society. The Society must also educate its members concerning the special needs of Native clients.*

*Juries*

The lack of Natives on juries in Nova Scotia concerns members of the Native community. We know of no evidence that suggests Natives are deliberately excluded from jury duty in Nova Scotia. Nor can we argue definitively that the presence of a Native person on a jury in a case involving a Native accused will result in fairer treatment for the Native. Still, Native concerns are not unreasonable: Would a White person facing a Native prosecutor, defence lawyer, judge and jury, have some apprehension whether he would get as fair a hearing as if everyone were White?

. . . .

*Conclusions*

The recommendations we have made to improve the treatment of Natives and Blacks in the criminal justice system have focussed on specific policies and legislation, as well as education and training. Such initiatives will be doomed to failure, however, without regular and effective monitoring. We have not proposed a separate body be established with responsibility for overseeing implementation of these recommendations. Instead, we suggest that Government, judges, lawyers, the police and others ultimately be responsible for their own area of jurisdiction.

It is easy to blame Governments for all that we might identify as "wrong" in our society, and we have attempted to avoid this temptation. Government, however, must accept that it has a special duty in these matters. As legislator and employer, the role and influence of Government in this province cannot be underestimated.

These recommendations provide a rare opportunity for everyone involved in the system — not only Government — to change patterns of behavior and policies that have been well entrenched but never questioned, and to open doors that have remained closed for much too long to the full participation of minorities.

## ADMINISTRATION OF CRIMINAL JUSTICE

We have found that Donald Marshall, Jr. was wrongfully convicted of murder and deprived of his freedom for 11 years because the justice system broke down. Each component of the system — every check and balance — failed. The Sydney City Police, Crown prosecutors, defence counsel, the courts, the Department of Attorney General and the RCMP all contributed to Marshall's conviction and continued imprisonment by failing to perform to an acceptable standard. In the months that followed Marshall's eventual release and acquittal, there were accusations that racism played a role in Marshall's conviction and that, if he had been White, the process by which he was acquitted and his struggle for compensation may have been handled differently.

If there are differing standards of justice in Nova Scotia, depending on one's race or social standing, it suggests internal control within the system has broken down. It also suggests that the major components of the system are not fulfilling their proper functions and the appropriate interrelationships are not understood or observed.

. . . .

A properly functioning criminal justice system is the bedrock on which society's acceptance of our system of law and the maintenance of order is based. But because of what has happened in the Marshall case and some others we will examine now, many people in Nova Scotia have begun to question the fairness and independence of the province's justice system. This erosion of confidence must be stopped and public confidence restored. This can only be accomplished through the unwavering and visible application of the principles of absolute fairness and independence.

**Questions/Discussion**
1. What role does the criminal justice system have to play in the alleviation of racism in Canada? What are its inherent limitations in fulfilling such a role? In this regard, see McKenna, I., "Canada's Hate Propaganda Laws — A Critique" (1994), 26 Ottawa Law Review 159.
2. What is the best way in which to combat racism within the criminal justice system; for example, is it through the hiring or appointment of more police officers, judges and

prosecutors from minority groups, or in the case of aboriginal peoples through the provision of separate systems of justice?
3. Can the exercise of discretion within the criminal justice system be restrained in order to limit the potential effects of racist biases on the part of the actors and agents within the system? In what sectors of the system might this be possible? If *a priori* restraint remains a problem, then what types of review processes might be useful to control the abusive effects of such attitudes?
4. In 1990, a judge in the Northwest Territories was quoted as saying that rape was different in the North: "The majority of rapes in the Northwest Territories occur when the woman is drunk. The man comes along, sees a pair of hips and helps himself. That contrasts sharply to the cases I dealt with (in southern Canada) of the dainty co-ed who gets jumped from behind" (*Ottawa Citizen*, January 19, 1990). Besides betraying a disturbing ignorance about the nature of rape generally, the comments illustrate a dangerous attitude toward the nature of the problem in the northern communities.
5. For an examination of the problems and issues surrounding racism, criminal justice and the black community in Nova Scotia, see Volume 1 of the Marshall inquiry report at p. 182. For a discussion of the problems and effects of systemic racism in the Ontario criminal law system, see the *Report of the Commission on Systemic Racism in the Ontario Criminal Justice System* (Toronto: Queen's Printer for Ontario, 1995).
6. An interesting footnote to the Marshall inquiry is that the lawyers involved in the process received a total of $2.4 million while Donald Marshall himself received compensation of only $270,000. The total cost of the inquiry was $8.6 million. (*The Lawyer's Weekly*, May 25, 1990).
7. For a discussion of the issues surrounding the collection of crime statistics broken down by the race or ethnic origin of the suspect and/or the victim, see the series of articles in the April, 1994 issue of the Canadian Journal of Criminology (volume 36) pp. 149-185.

## Further Reading
- Baker, D. (ed.), *Reading Racism and the Criminal Justice System*, (Toronto: Canadian Scholar's Press, 1994).
- Barsh, R., "Native Justice in Lethbridge" (1995), 6 Journal of Human Justice 131.
- Birkenmayer, A.C. and S. Jolly, *The Native Inmate in Ontario* (Toronto: Ontario Ministry of Correctional Services, 1984).
- Canada, *Correctional Issues Affecting Native Peoples — Correctional Law Review Working Paper No. 7* (Ottawa: Solicitor General of Canada, 1988).
- Griffiths, C.T., and Verdun-Jones, S., *Canadian Criminal Justice 2nd ed.* (Toronto: Harcourt Brace & Company, Canada, 1994), Chapter 15.
- Hathaway, J., "Native Canadians and the Criminal Justice System: A Critical Examination of the Native Court Worker Program" (1989), 49 Saskatchewan Law Review 201.
- Jackson, M., "Locking Up Natives in Canada" (1989), 23 University of British Columbia Law Review 215.
- LaPrairie, C., "The Role of Sentencing in the Over-representation of Aboriginal People in Correctional Institutions" (1990), 32 Canadian Journal of Criminology 429.
- Mannette, J., *Elusive Justice: Beyond the Marshall Inquiry* (Halifax: Fernwood Publishing, 1992).
- McFarland, J., "Manitoba's 'Aboriginal Justice Inquiry' ", *Canadian Dimension*, June 1989, p. 6.
- Petersen, C., "Institutionalized Racism: The Need for Reform of the Criminal Jury Selection Process" (1993), 38 McGill Law Journal 147.

- Schwartz, B., "A Separate Aboriginal Justice System?" (1990), 19 Manitoba Law Journal 77.
- Silverman, R., and Nielsen, M., *Aboriginal Peoples and the Canadian Justice System* (Toronto: Butterworths, 1992).

## 8.3 CRIME IN THE WORKPLACE

**Introduction**

The issues surrounding the topic of crime in the workplace are many and varied. The two articles presented below are intended only as a brief introduction to selected areas of the topic. Not all types of crimes which occur in the workplace are covered in this section nor are presented all the issues associated with the topic. While there are many types of workplace crime, including administrative and financial or tax violations, environmental violations, labour law offences, and unfair business practices, there is often a similarity as to the nature of the problems associated with this general category of offences. The principal problem is often one of lack of enforcement or at least a lack of success in curbing the activities proscribed in the particular area, and several reasons as to why this is so are examined. Historically, crimes which have been committed by corporations and their executives have rarely been subject to effective intervention by the criminal law, even though the damage which has resulted may have been great. This is particularly true in the areas of environmental crime, illegal merger and monopoly activities, and labour violations (such as unsafe working sites). What is special or different about this type of crime that has led to this lack of enforcement and effectiveness and, furthermore, has led the general public to focus on so-called "street crimes" to the exclusion of corporate crime?

### How Society Whitewashes Corporate Crime*
*M. Cash Mathews*

* (1988), 65 Business and Society Review 48

Each year, more people die from street crime than from corporate crime. But, the economic costs of corporate crime far outweigh the economic costs of street crime. Most people view the threat to their physical and economic well-being as coming from street crimes rather than corporate crimes. Our perceptions (or misperceptions) are based on our culture, and our culture has historically focused on street crime rather than corporate crime.

Different cultures utilize language in similar but also very different ways. For example, Eskimos have dozens of words to describe "snow." Snow is, of course, an integral part of Eskimos' everyday life. An extensive vocabulary enables some social interactions to focus on snow and its properties. Without such a sizable vocabulary, these specific interactions could not take place. Social cohesion in the group might be lessened and could even lead to the group's survival being threatened. Therefore, development of an adequate vocabulary to discuss an integral part of everyday life is a critical aspect of any society.

Crime is an integral part of everyday life in many technologically advanced societies, especially the United States. This includes the fear of crime, actual participation (perpetrator or victim) in a criminal event, and response to criminal activities.

However, our vocabulary pertaining to "crime" is focused on street or ordinary crime, such as robbery, murder, rape, burglary, etc. We have many ways of discussing and writing about such crimes and most members of the society have at least a general conception and understanding of this type of criminal activity. Much of the response to such crimes is based on information from the mass media: newspaper, magazines, television, and radio. Daily newspapers in major cities often have at least one article on the front page dealing with street crime or how society has responded to such a crime. Street crimes are both understood (to varying degrees) and feared, especially in large metropolitan cities.

## FOCUS IN SCHOOLS

The concept of street crime is also a frequent focus of social interaction in primary and secondary groups. Colleges and universities teach many classes about such criminal activity, the theories underlying the behaviour, and the societal reaction, through the criminal justice system, to such activity. More mundanely, parents warn their children to "stay away from strangers." How severe or lenient the treatment of offenders and prisoners currently is, how it was in years past, and how it should be in the near and distant future are often topics of discussion in the average American's daily life.

Our vocabulary in this area is extensive, and our behaviour is shaped accordingly. On the one hand, it is reasonable to conclude that this sizable vocabulary promotes social cohesion and solidarity by clearly identifying the boundaries beyond which an individual may not step for fear of being labelled a deviant or criminal.

On the other hand, our rich vocabulary for street crimes is clearly in contrast to our limited and inadequate vocabulary for corporate criminal activity. The vocabulary focuses our attention on street crime and away from corporate crime. Further, there are at least several terms for corporate crime—"elite deviance," "management fraud," "white-collar crime," "organizational crime," and "economic crime." The resulting confusion over the exact meaning of corporate crime is understandable because no clear-cut meaning or definition is agreed on.

Distinctions can be made between white-collar and corporate crime — corporate crime is illegal activity undertaken on *behalf* of the organization (e.g., bribery, intentional manufacture of unsafe products to increase market share), while white-collar crime is illegal activity taken *against* the corporation (e.g., embezzlement). However, even these two categories can overlap, causing further confusion about the terminology. And the question "Is corporate crime really crime?" is posed again and again.

## WEAK RESPONSE

While corporate crime may be more costly (in terms of economic as well as physical harm) to society than street crime is, most citizens view the threat to their economic and physical well-being as emanating from street crime. The oftentimes weak societal response to corporate crime is undoubtedly due in part to our learned vocabulary pertaining to it. It is easy to understand the importance of attempting to decrease the level of street crime, but for many consumers and the general public it is difficult to understand the necessity of trying to control or decrease corporate crimes. For example, how many consumers understand the importance of organizing against monopolistic practices on the part of corporations, illegal dumping of chemical or toxic wastes (unless it's their specific town which is involved), poor or substandard quality products, or, to a lesser degree, prescription drugs that may have long-term negative health effects?

It is difficult to become concerned about such events when the likelihood of their occurrence is in the distant future. Street crime seems much more real. The public views street crime as happening to anyone, at any time. Corporate crime is not perceived as being a part of our everyday interactional patterns, no matter how incorrect this perception may be.

## PROMULGATION OF MYTH

Criminal justice programs in colleges and universities do little to correct these misperceptions. The curriculum in such programs and departments usually focuses on street crime. If any courses or graduate seminars are offered on the subject of corporate crime, the number is minuscule in comparison to the courses offered on street crime.

When courses relating to nontraditional crimes are offered, the focus is likely to be on white-collar rather than corporate crime (i.e., embezzlement, employee theft, computer crime, and other such individual crimes). Students who enroll in criminal justice programs and departments are likely to come away with the impression that those in the lower economic classes are the threat to citizens' wellbeing, safety, and the social order, rather than the threat's coming as a result of elite deviance.

Further, such an emphasis on street crime in the curriculum overlooks the massive damage done to the social fabric by corporate crime. For example, if top-echelon executives do not adhere to the ethical and legal norms in society, others in the society may believe that they also have no such duty to engage in legal and ethical behaviour. Therefore, a poor teenager who lives in an urban ghetto may conclude that if those at the highest levels of society break the law, why shouldn't he? The only difference may be in the opportunities for lawbreaking. The poor teenager's opportunities for lawbreaking are likely to be limited to burglary, theft, and robbery, while the corporate executive's opportunities are on a more grandiose scale and may adversely affect more people. A corporate executive may be involved in the decision to market an unsafe product so that the corporation for which he works will garner a larger market share as soon as possible. The unsafe product may cause hundreds of injuries and a number of deaths Yet the high-ranking executive is not likely to think of himself as a criminal, and neither will his family, friends, or most other members of the society.

Part of this problem stems from anthropomorphizing the corporation in common speech patterns. In speaking about corporations, terminology is used which makes it appear that "the corporation" is a living, breathing entity. Newspaper and other mass media accounts frequently contain articles that state that "Corporation X made such and such a statement today." We are so accustomed to hearing and reading such accounts that we take the anthropomorphization of corporations for granted. However, "the corporation" is really nothing more than a juristic person. A corporation cannot act on its own and therefore can act only through corporate agents — human beings who comprise the entity known as "the corporation." A corporation does not make statements; rather, specific individuals within the corporation make not only the statements but also the decisions. In speaking of the social responsibility, social responsiveness, or ethics of a "corporation," we mystify and obscure the relationships involved. For example, a corporation cannot be socially responsible or socially responsive — it is the individuals who comprise the corporation whom we expect to be socially responsible and socially responsive. Further, a corporation cannot have ethics — it is the individuals who are the corporate actors who do or do not adhere to ethical and legal norms.

It is not the corporation that is constrained by the corporate culture, or to which social approval or social approbation is meaningful, but rather the individuals within the corporation. The unit of focus in the understanding of behaviour (criminal and noncriminal) within the corporate organization should be at the level of the individual and the small group, not at the level of the corporation. The constraints upon action and behaviour are strongly influenced by the norms and values not only within the corporation but within the small group as well.

The specific vocabulary of motives used by corporate executives and managers essentially "allows" them to engage in illegal activity. By using this vocabulary, a person or group rationalizes the behaviour in *advance* (contrary to the standard usage of the term "rationalization," which refers to explanations or excuses which are made *after* the behaviour occurs) and releases the energy to engage in illegal activity. Perhaps a deadline must be met, and an illegal shortcut such as inadequate product testing is perceived as a way to meet it. The individual or group within the corporation may conclude, "Everybody else is don't it, why shouldn't we?" If such activity is undertaken within a group (e.g., sales or production), it may lead to the group's adhering to deviant or criminal behaviour as the group norm. It may come to a case of "we against they." "They" can be other groups within the corporation, other corporations, or governmental regulatory agencies.

This adherence to deviant or illegal norms is supported by a vocabulary that reinforces and rewards such behaviour. Lack of communication within a corporation must be considered too, for what is not said may be equal in importance to what is said. Lower and middle managers are often afraid of giving bad news to their bosses. Within the corporation, "everybody knows" that bad news is not to be passed up to the higher echelon. Problems are to be solved at the lower levels, which leaves the burden on middle managers, supervisors, and eventually on the individual worker.

## CHANGING FOCUS

Of course, this discussion should not be interpreted as suggesting that the use of vocabulary and anthropomorphizing corporations are the only variables affecting societal reaction to corporate crime. Clearly, vocabulary, shared meanings, and anthropomorphization are only a few facets of this reaction — facets that have often been neglected in the past.

The recent focus on inside trading, defense contractor overcharges, and other such white-collar and corporate crimes helps to publicize the unacceptability of such illegalities. Nonetheless, there is still the traditional question, "How illegal is this behaviour, really?" and verbal rationalization, "Everybody does it" or "If we don't do it, someone else will." For some observers and participants in the corporate sector, the error is in getting caught, not the illegal act itself. Only with the increase in awareness and consciousness about illegal behaviour within corporations will such crime be taken as seriously as street crime.

## Law, Ideology and Corporate Crime: A Critique of Instrumentalism*
### Neil Sargent

* (1989), 4 Canadian Journal of Law and Society, 39.

### INTRODUCTION

Since the ground-breaking work by Sutherland in the 1930s and 1940s, corporate crime research has remained an area of considerable empirical and theoretical importance for criminologists. Studies in Canada and the United States suggest that the cost of economic crime by corporations — for example, business fraud, tax evasion, and illegal trade practices — may far exceed that of conventional street crime. At the same time, the social costs of other forms of illegal corporate behaviour, in injuries to employees, risks to consumers and harm to the environment, are such that failure to utilize criminal sanctions against corporate offenders raises fundamental questions concerning the willingness or ability of the criminal justice system to treat equally all forms of socially deviant behaviour.

Much of the recent research into corporate crime in Canada has tended to adopt a critical conflict or instrumental Marxist perspective to account for the prevalence of corporate crime and the failure of the criminal justice system to respond to it. This approach emphasizes the power and wealth of large corporate offenders and the degree of cultural or class identification between legislators, judges and high-status corporate executives; the low visibility of much corporate crime, resulting from a lack of attention on the part of the mass-media and the criminal justice system; and the lack of resources devoted to the investigation and prosecution of corporate crime, together with the reluctance of law enforcement officials and judges to make use of criminal sanctions, especially imprisonment, against corporate offenders.

According to these analyses, the differential treatment accorded to traditional and corporate crime is largely attributable to the power of dominant economic elites, and their ability to influence the enactment and enforcement of laws which appear to run counter to their economic interests. Legal or organizational impediments to enforcement, such as procedural or evidential difficulties in establishing individual or corporate liability, or the limited range of sanctions available against corporate offenders, tend to be viewed either as a liberal smokescreen, obscuring the class basis of the administration of justice, or as a reflection of the power of economic elites to influence the specific content of legislation — the most important form of power.

The aim of the present study is to explore the limits of such class instrumentalist analyses of law in accounting for the failure of the criminal justice system to control corporate crime. The first part of the paper examines current theoretical perspectives in Canadian corporate crime research, with particular emphasis on the instrumentalist analyses of law which predominate in the literature. The remaining parts of the paper develop a critique of such class instrumentalist analyses of law, and argue for an approach which problematizes the social character of law as an institution which reproduces consent for capitalist social relations. In particular, it is argued that attempts to theorize the failure of the criminal justice system to respond to corporate crime require investigation not only of external factors influencing the enactment and enforcement of legislation designed to control illegal corporate behaviour, but also the ideological discourses underlying the form and content of criminal law, which in turn serve to reinforce consent for the unequal treatment of different classes of offences and offenders by the criminal justice system. Failure to problematize the ideological role of law in legitimating the differential treatment of suite and street crime is thus likely to undermine reforms designed to make corporate offenders more accountable for their illegal behaviour.

## THEORETICAL PERSPECTIVES IN CANADIAN CORPORATE CRIME RESEARCH

What is corporate crime? It is crucial not to restrict the definition of corporate crime to violations of the *Criminal Code* since the vast majority of offences for which corporations can be convicted in Canada are found outside the *Criminal Code* in federal and provincial regulatory statutes. Following Kramer, then, corporate crime is defined as illegal acts (of omission or commission) engaged in by corporate organizations themselves as social or legal entities, or by officials or employees of the corporation acting in accordance with the operative goals, standard operating procedures and cultural norms of the organization, and intended to benefit the corporation itself.

This definition stresses the organizational nature of corporate crime and serves to differentiate corporate crime from what Clinard and Quinney have referred to as "occupational crime," namely, "offenses committed by individuals for themselves in the course of their occupations and the offenses of employees against their employers." As Clinard and Quinney observe, both corporate crime and occupational crime are forms of white-collar crime, but they are different in important respects. Thus, while occupational crime is typically committed by an individual or group of individuals for their own benefit against the economic interests of their employer or the public at large, corporate crime is typically committed within an organizational framework, involving the participation of several individuals acting on behalf of the organization itself. For this reason Braithwaite and Geis have argued that corporate crime should be regarded as a conceptually different phenomenon from traditional or occupational crime and that legal principles and enforcement practices developed in relation to traditional or occupational crime should not automatically be assumed to apply to corporate crime. This point is also made by Goff and Reasons, who argue that this distinction is necessary to avoid the individualist orientation of much white collar crime research, which fails to deal adequately with "the special characteristics of illegal behaviour in organizational settings."

In Canada two main theoretical approaches can be observed in the literature on corporate crime. On the one hand, the liberal-reformist approach deplores the social costs associated with illegal corporate behaviour and seeks to explain the poor enforcement record of legislation governing such things as corporate price fixing, product safety or environmental pollution, in terms of the inadequacy of existing laws. This approach is exemplified by the world of the Law Reform Commission of Canada in its 1976 Working Paper on *Criminal Responsibility for Group Action* and more recently in a series of papers on the enforcement of environmental laws which focus attention on the legal and organizational impediments to the enforcement of criminal sanctions against corporate offenders. Factors such as the complexity of much corporate activity; the costs of investigation and prosecution; procedural and evidential difficulties in establishing corporate or individual liability; and the limited range of sanctions under the *Criminal Code* and many regulatory statutes are all identified as reasons for the inability of the criminal justice system to respond more effectively to the corporate crime "problem." Considerable emphasis is therefore laid upon the need for legal reform to achieve more effective legal and regulatory control over deviant corporate behaviour.

By contrast, the critical conflict/Marxist tradition in Canadian corporate crime research views the failure of the criminal justice system to respond to corporate crime as a transparent reflection of elite or class interests. Starting from the premise that class conflict, rather than consensus, is at the root of social ordering, the focus of much of this research has been to expose the relative immunity accorded to corporate offenders by the criminal justice system, and the challenge this poses for consensus theorists. As a result, the critical conflict literature has emphasized "exposure" studies which focus on the prevalence and social costs of corporate crime under capitalism. Thus Henry argues that "crime is inherent in the capitalist mode of production because maximizing profit is the overwhelmingly important goal of capitalist production and the most effective means of maximizing profit are frequently criminal." Henry lists a catalogue of corporate "criminal" behaviour, ranging from sales of infant formula to third world countries, to automobile safety violations, pollution offences, combine conspiracies and violations of occupational health and safety laws. Along similar lines Goff and Reasons offer a "typology" of corporate crime which is equally ambitious in its attempt to reduce the causes of corporate crime to capitalist relations of production.

Central to these analyses is the rejection of any legal definition of crime, "since it is clear that actions of the powerful are less likely to be defined as crimes." As a result little attention is given to the questions why and under what circumstances laws governing corporate crime are enacted. Nor is any attempt made to explain the contradictory role of the state in enacting legislation designed to control corporate crime. Instead, the state is viewed unproblematically as a captive agent or organ of capitalist interests, despite the authors' concessions that the state may occasionally be responsive to pressures "from below" in enacting or enforcing legislation which inhibits capitalist accumulation, even at times against the express opposition of dominant corporate interests.

The "instrumentalist" analysis of law adopted by Henry and Goff and Reasons is also evident in various studies of the origins and enforcement of federal anti-combines legislation. Thus, Goff and Reasons and Snider attribute many of the well-documented weaknesses of Canada's anti-combines legislation to the influence of large corporate interests (specifically the banking and financial establishment) in the enactment of the legislation, as well as in effectively blocking subsequent attempts to strengthen the enforcement provisions of the legislation and to remove technical obstacles to conviction.

Instrumentalist writers also emphasize the ability of economic elites to define legislation regulating their activities as non-criminal. Comparing sanctions imposed following conviction for traditional property offences under the *Criminal Code* with sanctions imposed under federal regulatory legislation such as the *Food and Drugs Act*, the *Hazardous Products Act,* the *Weights and Measures Act* and the *Combines Investigations Act,* Snider has argued that the "continuing non-criminal status of the latter activities reflects not their lack of harmfulness but, rather, the superior resources of upperworld criminals and corporations. They have been successful in defining their own acquisitive acts as non-criminal and even harmless, despite the reams of data that have documented the heavy dollar losses and the even heavier loss of life and limb they cause."

Similarly, recent Marxist analysis of the enforcement of provincial occupational health and safety laws have focussed on the quasi-criminal status of such legislation in accounting for the differential treatment of violence inside and outside the workplace. Reasons, Ross and Patterson posit that a corporation which knowingly violates health and safety regulations in the workplace is unlikely to be criminally prosecuted for any resulting injuries or deaths and is, at most, likely to be fined a small amount for non-compliance with regulatory standards. These authors argue that the lenient treatment of occupational health and safety laws reflects the class bias of the criminal law. They note that corporate maintenance of unsafe working conditions in violation of mandatory standards usually reflects a "rational, premeditated, conscious choice concerning capital expenses and business profits." Such behaviour is rational, since the likelihood of detection is low, and relatively light penalties are often imposed only after repeated and serious violations. According to these authors, therefore, a corporation which threatens workers' safety for profit should be regarded as equally criminally culpable where death or injury results as an armed robber who also threatens violence in pursuit of economic profit.

Taking the analysis somewhat further, Glasbeek and Rowland have argued that existing *Criminal Code* offences such as criminal negligence and manslaughter could be utilized against corporate employers where employees are injured or killed as a result of their negligent or reckless violation of mandatory safety standards. The situation is analogous, Glasbeek points out, to that of a conviction for dangerous or impaired driving, where the necessary *mens rea* is established by a finding of reckless disregard of risk to human life and limb on the part of the driver. Likewise, if a corporate employer requires employees to continue working in conditions which are known to be unsafe, in violation of mandatory safety standards, the employer should be held criminally liable for manslaughter or criminal negligence if death or injury result from this reckless disregard of risk. Failure to apply criminal sanctions in such circumstances, Glasbeek points out, proves the inherent class bias of the criminal justice system, and its willingness to turn a blind eye to "harm-causing conduct when it is closely related to private profit-making."

## A CRITIQUE OF INSTRUMENTALIST ANALYSES OF CORPORATE CRIME

The critical conflict/Marxist perspective appears to predominate in the literature on corporate crime in Canada. Much of this literature adopts an explicitly instrumentalist analysis of law and the state in accounting for the failure of the criminal justice system to respond to corporate crime. Both power conflict and Marxist class analyses tend to regard the weakness of legislative attempts to control corporate crime and the reluctance of law enforcement agencies to impose severe sanctions, particularly against large corporate enterprises, as a reflection of the ability of dominant economic elites to influence the enactment and enforcement of legislation in accordance with their own interests. State initiatives which appear to diverge from ruling class interests therefore tend to be dismissed as simply part of an elaborate confidence trick perpetrated on a gullible public in order to create the false impression that the state is at times responsive to their interests.

Yet this instrumentalist analysis of law has been subject to considerable criticism from both pluralist and neo-Marxist theorists. According to the critics, instrumentalist analyses are unable to account historically for the enactment of social legislation which is not in the objective interests of the capitalist class. Minimum-wage legislation, occupational health and safety laws, environmental protection legislation and, more recently, federal and municipal initiatives against tobacco advertising, all represent examples of state initiatives which at least at the level of their content have as their apparent objective the protection of employees, consumers and the general public from the social costs of unregulated corporate behaviour. Evidence of the poor enforcement record of such legislative initiatives notwithstanding, their very existence suggests the need for a more historically specific and theoretically grounded analysis of the relationship between law, the state, and class interests than is supplied by the instrumentalist conspiracy framework.

In addition, neo-Marxist scholars have criticized the theoretical and empirical inadequacy of the concepts of class and state used in most instrumentalist analyses. Thus, Smandych notes that the instrumentalist conception of class creates a "false impression" of ruling class unity and is therefore incapable of accounting for intra-class conflict within the capitalist class. Similarly, the instrumentalist conception of the state as a captive agent of the capitalist class fails to account for the legitimation function of the state, which must at times be responsive to pressures "from below" (though in differing degrees at different times) in order to maintain social harmony. Indeed, it is the State's "ability to transcend the particular interests of individual capitalists," according to Smandych, which "is crucial in order for it to be able to protect the long run interests of the capitalist class as a whole."

At the same time, the instrumentalist characterization of law as a fundamentally repressive tool which can be manipulated at will by ruling elites precludes any analysis of the contradictory way in which law mediates class relations within capitalist society. As Bierne and Quinney note: "There is much evidence to demonstrate that dominant social classes are unable to manipulate legal institutions and legal doctrine consistently, without contradiction and without political opposition." As a result, much recent neo-Marxist theorizing on law has tried to explain more precisely the consensual nature of law, particularly the ways in which law functions to reproduce ideologies supporting capitalist relations of production, despite the differential application of law in practice.

This new emphasis in turn has led to increased interest in the concept of ideology on the part of many neo-Marxist theorists, and on the role of law as an institutional site for the production and dissemination of ideologies which serve to sustain or reproduce consent for unequal and exploitative class, race and gender relations within capitalism. Indeed, the pervasive ideological role of law in both defining the way in which social relations are lived and experienced, and the manner in which social and political conflicts are identified and resolved is seen by such theorists as central to understanding how law contributes to the reproduction of "hegemony" within liberal-democratic societies. Gavigan, for example, argues that courts are primarily ideological agents, rather than instrumental or coercive agencies. Further evidence in support of this claim is provided by Hay's celebrated analysis of the relationship between terror and consent in eighteenth century English criminal law, which emphasizes the ideological role of criminal law in reproducing consent for a system of property rights founded on an agrarian oligarchy.

In exploring the concept of ideology, Hunt stresses that ideologies should not be seen simply as a false representation of the "real," or as a mere reflection of economic relations or class position. He observes that this "reflection metaphor" is common in such Marxist theorizing on ideology, and asserts the primacy of material relations in determining the content of ideologies. Thus, for Hunt, the connection between ideologies and material relations should not be assumed *a priori*. Instead, the concept of ideology is useful precisely in order to explore the links "between ideas, attitudes and beliefs, on the one hand, and economic and political interests on the other."

Nor is the concept of an objective social reality "distorted" by ideology more helpful because it assumes a social reality which exists independently of consciousness. It further assumes that ideologies can be evaluated in terms of their truth or falsity, according to how closely they match this objective social reality. Following Althusser, Hunt argues that ideologies should not be seen as externally imposed forms of consciousness, but as being themselves constitutive "of the unconscious in which social relations are lived."

This conception of ideology may have considerable importance for an understanding of the ideological significance of law in mediating class relations within capitalist society. Instead of viewing law simply as a mystifying force or a legitimating device, attention is directed to how law constitutes the way in which social relations are lived and experienced. Law plays an ideological role in individualizing and decontextualizing the experience of social relations under capitalism. "It is by transforming the human subject into a legal subject that law influences the way in which participants experience and perceive their relations with others." Moreover, the recognition that law is both grounded in social reality and shapes the experience of social actors is profoundly important for understanding the contradictory nature of law. In particular it helps explain why exposing the class character of law does not necessarily weaken either law's claim to popular legitimacy or the "moral hegemony" of the concept of legality itself.

At the same time, it is important to be alert to the connections between the ideological functions of law and those of other social institutions. Legal ideology does not operate in a vacuum, isolated from other non-legal ideological bases of legitimation. Rather, as Sumner points out:

> The effectiveness of law as an ideological force, as a means towards ruling class hegemony, depends upon its ideological encapsulation of a consensus constructed outside itself in other economic, political and cultural practices.

Nor should one assume the consistency or coherence of legal ideology. Ideologies are not pre-constructed bodies of ideas, beliefs and attitudes which are fashioned by all-seeing elite groups and transmitted from above through the medium of institutions such as the family, the law, religion or the media. Ideologies themselves operate in a state of disorder, "constantly being communicated, competing, clashing, affecting, drowning, and silencing one another in social processes of communication." Consequently, law should not simply be conceived of as a passive site for the transmission or reflection of ideologies elaborated and articulated elsewhere. Instead, law can itself be viewed as a combination of different institutional sites (the courts, legal education, legal doctrine, legal professionals) in which diverse ideological discourses are in a constant process of articulation and competition.

## IDEOLOGY AND LAW

The use of the concept of ideology to the study of corporate crime permits a more sophisticated analysis of the relationship between law, state and crime than is possible within a class instrumentalist framework. Rather than viewing the legal definition of crime as simply a reflection of elite power over the law-making process, it becomes possible to conceive of the definition of criminality as an arena of struggle over which competing ideologies are in contention. In this respect Carson's research on the emergence of nineteenth century English factory legislation is significant for its investigation of the ideological dimension of the law-making process.

Building upon Gusfeld's concept of "symbolic crusades," Carson argues that the origins and subsequent pattern of enforcement of English factory legislation can only be understood by examining the dynamic interplay between the instrumental and symbolic meanings attached to the proposed legislation by its adherents and opponents. Moreover, he suggests that the symbol of ideological meanings associated with the legislation were not intrinsic to the law-making process, but took significance from the external social and political context in which the debate over enactment occurred.

While useful in drawing attention to the ideological dimension of law as an arena of struggle, Carson's analysis ultimately remains firmly located within a perspective which sees law from without, as a reflection of struggles between competing interest groups. Legal ideology is seen as being shaped by external forces or interests, rather than as being influenced by internal discourses or practices, or in any way constitutive of social experience. For Carson, the ideological significance of law is seen as resulting from the particular outcome of struggles between competing interest groups and ideologies over the form and function of law. Law is assumed to have no identical contours of its own, but to take on ideological shape and colour from the external forces, interests and ideologies which affect it.

A similar point can be made with respect to Snider's recent work on the enactment and enforcement of regulatory legislation. Focussing on the process of struggle and change at the "ideological level," Snider attempts to explain why real improvements in life chances and conditions for working people have resulted over time from such regulatory reforms, despite the fact that "state action has been minimal, obstructive, and more often supportive of corporate crime than the reverse." Departing from her earlier instrumentalist stance, Snider argues that ideological struggles by unions, consumers, environmentalists and other social activists, have succeeded in changing "the key ideological bases which underlie and support the relations of production under capitalism":

> Successful ideological struggles have 'upped the ante' for the corporate sector; that is, they have increased the price of legitimacy for the corporation, by raising the standards of corporate behaviour necessary to secure public acceptance. This has resulted in new definitions of "reasonable" business behaviour, new standards of corporate morality against which transgressions are assessed, and a series of new limits on tactics which are acceptable to maximize profits and risks which are legitimate for employees.

According to Snider, then, it is changes at the ideological level which affect the material relations of production, rather than the reverse. Indeed, she explicitly rejects the determinist explanation that legislative reforms flow from changes in the structural requirements of capitalism, associated with the rise of monopoly capitalism and the need to ensure stable conditions for the reproduction of labour and the maintenance of economic demand.

At the same time, Snider appears to reject the view that law plays a significant role in shaping the potentiality of rights struggles:

> At most law reflects, and rather weakly at that, changes which had already occurred on the ideological level, changes which were necessary because hegemony was threatened. Once in place, law was used to strengthen legitimacy, but was certainly not the vehicle of change. Law's relative autonomy seems to be limited to a symbolic reinforcement of changes which have been made necessary by mechanisms on the ideological level.

Snider's view of law represents an advance upon earlier instrumentalist accounts which typically conceive of law in coercive or repressive terms. Nevertheless, in seeking to separate law from the ideological terrain, Snider limits the potentiality of her analysis exploring the significance of law as an arena or site within which ideological struggle occurs, and which in turn helps to shape the contours of the struggle. Ultimately, Snider appears to view law in functionalist terms as a passive agency, which merely reflects and reinforces ideologies which are formulated and struggled over elsewhere, and which remain external to law. Yet it remains unclear from Snider's analysis where this ideological terrain is situated, and what is the precise nature of the relationship between law, ideology and other social, economic or cultural practices or discourses located outside the law.

By contrast, recent work by Brickey and Cormack emphasizes the social character of law as an historically constituted form of discourse and a set of practices resulting from a social process of struggle and resistance in which real social action are engaged. Rather than viewing law as the object or result of struggles which take place elsewhere in an unspecified ideological zone, Brickey and Comack argue for a theorization of law as an important ideological institution or agency which itself defines and shapes struggle. Citing Weitzer, they note that "law is not simply imposed upon people, but is also a *product and object of* and provides an arena which circumscribes class (and other types of) struggle."

The significance of this perspective is that it problematizes both the form and content of law. Instead of viewing law simply as a tool of elite interests, or as a relatively autonomous agency which functions to legitimate capitalist relations of production, law is viewed in dynamic terms as emerging from a particular historical process, the form and function of which may vary according to the balance of "social forces that struggle around and within the legal order." This in turn has implications for the potential of law as an agent of societal transformation. By emphasizing the social character of law as an arena of struggle in which real people are involved, Brickey and Comack suggest that "rights discourse at the least offers the potential of facilitating the mobilization of political action among subordinate groups."

At the same time, Brickey and Comack recognize that struggles around and within law should not be confined to the specific content of legislation or legal norms, but must also embrace the ideological discourses underlying the form of legal discourse and practice. This insight is also shared by Piciotto, who argues that in order to understand the way in which law mediates class relations it is necessary to theorize the ideological underpinnings of its form, which appear as "an empty vessel that can be filled with whatever content society chooses." This apparently neutral form symbolically transforms social actors into juridically free and equal subjects, and thus individualizes and depoliticizes the experience of social relations. "Relations of power and force" come to "appear as the relations of free and equal individuals." Consequently, Piciotto notes that the discourse of legal rights in itself plays a critical role in limiting the potentiality of "rights struggles" to achieve significant social or political gains for oppressed groups:

A 'right' in bourgeois legal form does not create but fragments class solidarity.... Substantive gains are achieved through collective struggles building up class solidarity; the channelling of such struggles into the form of claims of bourgeois legal right breaks up that movement towards solidarity, through the operation of legal procedures which recognize only the individual subject of rights and duties.

## LEGAL IDEOLOGY AND CRIMINAL LAW

It follows from this analysis that in order to theorize the potentiality of law as an agency of societal transformation it is necessary to explore the social and historical character of its form, as well as its content. In the specific context of corporate crime this requires an investigation not only of external factors influencing the enactment and enforcement of legislation designed to regulate corporate behaviour, but also of the ideological discourses underlying the form and content of criminal law, which in turn operate to reinforce and reproduce ideologies located outside law.

At present, little attention has been paid by critical theorists to the substantive content and form of criminal law, perhaps because of its obviously repressive or instrumental character. With few conspicuous exceptions, critical engagement with the form and content of criminal law has been largely directed towards demystifying the claims of bourgeois jurisprudence in order to reveal the coercive or politically contingent nature of its application.

Yet it is apparent that the ideological discourses underlying the form of trial and legal conceptions of responsibility play a crucial role in legitimizing the use of criminal law as an instrument of social control.

> The criminal justice process is the most explicit coercive apparatus of the state and the idea that police and courts can interfere with the liberties of citizens only under known law and by means of due process of law is thus a crucial element in the ideology of the democratic state.

Nor should this simply be dismissed as a sham or as a way of mystifying the experience of state oppression. As Thompson points out:

> If the law is evidently partial and unjust, then it will mask nothing, legitimate nothing, contribute nothing to any class's hegemony. The essential precondition for the effectiveness of law, its function as ideology, is that it shall display an independence from gross manipulation and shall seem to be just. It cannot seem to be so without upholding its own logic and criterion of equity; indeed, on occasion, by actually being just.

Consequently, it is important for a critical analysis to explore to what extent the ideological discourses underlying the rhetoric of due process and legal conceptions of responsibility in fact operate to legitimate that differentiated treatment of offenders which is characteristic of the criminal justice system in practice.

A useful starting point for such analysis is to explore the ideological assumptions imbricated in the very form of the criminal trial, which appears as an "adversarial contest between competing subjects of right based on formal conventions as to proof of fact and judgement of law." The adversarial nature of the trial process "which today seems in its basics to be the essence of rationality," has the effect of abstracting the legally relevant "facts" from their complex social reality, thereby depoliticizing the issue before the court.

> The case thus takes on its own logic within the framework of the 'facts of the case,' and any other issues mentioned, hinted at or unknown, lose any relevancy to the meaning of the case that they may have had to the meaning of the incident.

Grau puts this still more concretely:

> Courts recognize narrowly defined legal issues that may bear little resemblance to underlying social issues. Cases are tried only between legal parties with defined legal interests that conflict over narrowly drawn legal issues. Collective needs are denied. The specificity of the rights and the narrowness of the legal issues combine to preclude the introduction of broader, though relevant, social questions. This restriction effectively depoliticizes the case. For example, an unemployed black accused of theft is tried on whether or not he took the property of another; he cannot defend himself by demonstrating the structural relationship between his act, racism, and class, nor by arguing that property is theft.

McBarnett further observes that the structure of the trial process — or the "case method" — helps to explain the apparent contradictions between the rhetoric of a legal system apparently geared to protecting the rights of the accused and the selective processing of offenders and the routine manufacture of high conviction rates. This contradiction is possible, according to McBarnett, because the rhetoric of justice and the operationalized requirements of the legal system operate at two quite distinct levels within the law. While legal concepts such as "due process" and the "rights" of the accused are constructed in abstract terms and operate primarily at the level of rhetoric (or ideology), the actual legal procedures and rules by which justice is operationalized are designed for individualized application at the level of a particular case. The open texture of legal rules of procedure and evidence and the particularistic nature of the case method in turn permit magistrates and judges to derogate from the abstract principles of due process on a case by case basis through provisos, exceptions and qualifications.

> Cases can readily accommodate both statements of general principle and the exceptions of particular circumstances. Thus an appeal on the grounds of abuse of a legal right can be rejected because of the circumstances of the particular case, while at the same time a grand statement reiterating that right is made. The conflicting rhetoric of due process and the practical demands for crime control are thus both simultaneously maintained and the gap between rhetoric and practice is managed out of existence.

This two dimensional character of law is important, according to McBarnett, in understanding how the courts are able to manage the gap between the rhetoric of due process and the reality of conviction, without undermining the value of the rhetoric as ideology. This can be seen, for example, in the way in which an accused's right to silence can be constructed at the level of rhetoric as an important procedural safeguard against self-incrimination; while at the same time an accused's failure to give evidence can be construed in appropriate circumstances as some evidence of guilt. Similarly, McBarnett points out that common law and statutory controls on police powers play an important role at the level of rhetoric as a protection against excessive state power; but at the level of operationalized justice such controls do not always translate into real protections for an accused, for example with respect to the admissibility of illegally obtained evidence.

McBarnett's analysis of the different levels at which legal rhetoric and legal practice operate also provides a useful framework for understanding the role of legal conceptions of responsibility in criminal law, particularly the requirement of *mens rea* as an essential element of criminal responsibility. Like the concept of due process it is argued that the concept of *mens rea* operates primarily at the level of rhetoric. At this level, *mens rea* is invariably discussed as one of the two fundamental elements of a crime (the other being the *actus reus*). At the level of practice, however, it is exceedingly difficult to elaborate a clear or precise definition of this elusive concept. For some offences proof of knowledge or intention on the part of an accused person is required. For other offences proof of recklessness is sufficient. For still others, criminal liability may be based on negligence. Moreover, both at common law and by statute, courts and legislators have permitted numerous exceptions to this principle, either in whole, with respect to so-called strict or absolute liability offences, or in part, with respect to offences such as constructive murder, where the requirement of *mens rea* is suspended with regard to a material element of the offence.

As a result, it is clear that at the level of practice, the concept of *mens rea* has little meaning as a requirement of criminal responsibility, or as a real protection for the accused. Nevertheless, at the level of rhetoric the concept of *mens rea* retains its significance as a powerful ideological symbol of the moral strength of the criminal law as an agency of social control. By focussing on the abstract intention of the accused person, divorced from the social, economic or political environment in which the offence was committed, the rhetoric of *mens rea* stresses the values of freedom of choice and individual autonomy, while at the same time reinforcing the appearance of the criminal law as a neutral agency, regardless of its disproportionate impact on certain social or racial groups in reality. In addition, the concept of *mens rea* plays a significant role at the level of rhetoric as an important constraint upon state power, in particular as a way of circumscribing the use of the ultimate coercive power of the state to those offences where the accused has acted culpably.

This latter point is reflected most clearly in the ongoing debate over the proper scope of criminal law. Thus the Law Reform Commission of Canada has argued that the criminal law proper should be restricted to "real crimes" — that is, offences involving seriously harmful conduct which contravenes fundamental social values — and that all other offences should be removed from the *Criminal Code*. In determining what is a real crime, the Law Reform Commission stresses not only that the conduct must be seriously harmful, that it contravene fundamental social values, but also that it must be morally wrong, in the sense that the accused must have acted culpably. This in turn imparts the concept of *mens rea* as an essential precondition of liability for "real crimes."

> Our view . . . is that the criminal law's main contribution is to underline our values by forbidding conduct violating them. Such values, however, are not normally seen as so seriously violated by acts done involuntarily or by mistake as to warrant reprobation by the criminal law. Such reprobation is reserved for more deliberate defiance of social values by conduct involving personal moral fault.

The Law Reform Commission's emphasis on *mens rea* as the cornerstone of criminal law is explicitly framed at the level of rhetoric rather than practice. Consequently, challenges to the relevance or utility of *mens rea* as a determinant of criminal behaviour by psychiatrists, criminologists or even legal academics are dismissed by reference to the overriding values of humanity, justice and individual autonomy associated with the concept of *mens rea*. Likewise, the distinction between "real crimes" and regulatory offences, which is central to the Law Reform Commission's vision of the proper scope of the criminal law, is constructed as the level of rhetoric. In practice, the majority of penal offences found outside the *Criminal Code* in federal, provincial or municipal regulatory statutes do import some requirement of *mens rea*, either in the form of an explicit burden imposed on the prosecution to prove knowledge or negligence on the part of the accused, or whether by legislative fiat or judicial interpretation, by means of allowing an accused to establish a defence based on the exercise of due diligence.

Nevertheless, the significance of this rhetoric in legitimizing and perpetuating the relative immunity accorded to corporate violators of regulatory statutes should not be underestimated. By articulating a distinction between "real crimes," based on the violation of accepted social values, and mere regulatory or public welfare offences, which are conceived of as less morally opprobrious, and therefore involving less social stigma, this rhetoric plays an important ideological role in reinforcing a separate sphere of regulation in which corporate violators continue to be relatively immune from criminal sanctions, notwithstanding the degree of harm which results from their illegal behaviour or the degree of culpability exhibited by individual corporate offenders.

This tension between the rhetoric of justice incorporated in such concepts as due process and *mens rea* and the actual legal rules by which justice is operationalized is also discernible at the point of sentencing. Thus Mandel observes that the shift in sentencing rhetoric away from retribution and just dessert towards more "humanitarian" sentencing rationales based on denunciation, rehabilitation and deterrence has also been accompanied at the level of practice by a shift in emphasis away from the consequences of the offence to the harmfulness or dangerousness of the offender.

Mandel points out that denunciation, rehabilitation and deterrence as sentencing rationales are premised upon the ideals of freedom of choice, individual responsibility and respect for fundamental values. In reality, he argues, such sentencing rationales are less harmful effects of crime, than with disciplining workers for their role in the social relations of production. The use of individualized sentencing models leaves the courts with discretion to hand down differentiated sentences which vary more according to the class background and employment record of the offender, than with the seriousness or harmfulness of the offence committed. This is crucial, according to Mandel, in understanding the "superstructural" role of the sentencing process in reinforcing the social status quo based on capitalist relations of production. Thus, the degree to which the offender exhibits support for capital productive values (through evidence of good "character," prior employment record, social status, etc.) is assumed to be relevant with respect to both the prevention of recidivism and the presumed impact of the sentence on the offender. Consequently, the higher the social status of the offender, the greater the stigma associated with prosecution and conviction for an offence is assumed to be. Additional penalties such as incarceration may be regarded as unnecessary in bringing home to an offender the gravity of the offence. Similarly, if the goal of rehabilitation is to promote voluntary compliance with capitalist social values it follows that most white collar and corporate criminals can be easily rehabilitated, since in most cases they will not have strayed far from the straight and narrow path of profitable capitalist accumulation.

## LEGAL INDIVIDUALISM AND CORPORATE ACCOUNTABILITY: CORPORATIONS AS CRIMINAL ACTORS

The preceding discussion indicates that in order to account for the failure of the criminal justice system to respond to corporate crime it is important to look not only at external factors influencing the attitudes and conduct of legislators, law enforcement officials and judges, but also at the ideological discourses underlying the form of trial and such legal conceptions as responsibility and sanctioning. In particular, it is argued that the individualist orientation of criminal law, both in its trial and sentencing moments, plays a significant ideological role in facilitating and legitimizing the preferential treatment accorded to corporate offenders by the criminal justice system.

At present, corporations have been reluctantly assimilated into the individualist model of criminal responsibility and sanctioning by regarding them as individual moral actors, on the same basis as natural persons. However, this was not always the case. Despite the inclusion of bodies corporate within the definition of "person" under the *Criminal Code*, 1906 (R.S.C. 1906, c. 146, s. 2(13)), it was not until 1941 that a corporation was first held criminally liable for an offence requiring proof of *mens rea*. Prior to this time, corporations in Canada were held to be immune from criminal liability for real crimes requiring proof of *mens rea* on the basis that a corporation could have no guilty mind of its own. Moreover, the range of criminal sanctions available for use against corporations under the *Criminal Code* remains limited, reflecting the individualist orientation of the criminal justice system.

From a legal perspective, then, the "problem" of corporate criminal liability has always centred around the search for a theory of liability and criminal sanctioning which is consistent with the individualist model. Courts and legislators in Canada have tried to fit corporate offenders into this individualist model of liability, rather than attempting to adapt the legal system to accommodate the collective reality of large-scale corporate organization. Thus Canadian courts have remained reluctant to extend the scope of corporate criminal responsibility to include the illegal acts or omissions of a corporation's agents or employees, on the basis that vicarious liability has no place in a system of criminal law based on principles of individual responsibility.

The limits of this individualist model of liability are apparent when it is sought to impose criminal responsibility on a corporation for systemic illegally activity resulting from the collective participation of numerous individuals within the organization. Thus, studies of the Ford Pinto prosecution in the United States point out not only the significant disparity in resources available to the prosecutors on the one side and the corporation's defence lawyers on the other, but also the considerable evidentiary and procedural obstacles involved in successfully prosecuting a large corporate entity, even when the prosecutors had access to a large body of internal corporate information derived from previous civil suits against the corporation. These difficulties are often exacerbated by the complexity of the scientific or technical information involved, and the consequent difficulty of establishing a direct causal link between the alleged illegal corporate activity and the harm which is alleged to result from it.

Consequently, the more anonymous the criminal actor (and a large diversified corporate organization is a paradigm example of an anonymous actor), the more complex the causal link between the illegal activity and the harm which will be held criminally responsible or treated with severity by the criminal justice system.

Equally significant, in terms of the effectiveness of criminal sanctions against corporate offenders may be the internal organizational structure of the corporation itself. Given the elaborate division of management functions within large corporate structures, decisions resulting in illegal corporate behaviour may be made at various levels in the corporate hierarchy, without any one individual being ultimately responsible for the illegal activity. In such circumstances, the decentralization of management and diffusion of responsibilities typical of large corporations may promote illegal corporate behaviour, while at the same time insulating individual participants from criminal responsibility for their actions.

The ideological impact of legal individualism in immunizing corporate offenders from the reach of the criminal law can also be seen in the realm of criminal procedure, particularly in light of the decision of the Supreme Court of Canada in *Hunter v. Southam Inc.* This case arose out of an inquiry under section 8 of the *Combines Investigation Act* into the production, distribution and supply of newspapers in Edmonton, Alberta. Acting under the power conferred by section 10(3) of the *Act*, the Director of Investigation and Research authorized several combines investigation officers to enter and examine documents and other articles held at the business offices of the *Edmonton Journal*. This action was challenged by Southam Inc., the owner of the *Journal*, on the grounds that section 10, which confers wide powers of search and seizure on the Director of Investigation and Research, contravenes section 8 of the *Charter of Rights and Freedoms*, which protects the right to secure against unreasonable search and seizure. After lengthy court proceedings, the Supreme Court of Canada upheld the unanimous decision of the Alberta Court of Appeal, holding that the powers of investigation and search under section 10 of the *Combines Act* were inconsistent with section 8 of the *Charter* and thus of no force and effect.

In reaching this decision the Supreme Court endorsed a broad, purposive interpretation of the *Charter*, stressing that its aim is to guarantee, within reasonable limits, the rights and freedoms of the individual, and to constrain governmental action which is inconsistent with those rights and freedoms. In considering the validity of the powers of investigation and search under section 10 of the *Combines Act*, the courts should therefore focus on the "unreasonable" impact of a search on the individual concerned (and for this purpose "individual" includes legal persons, *i.e.*, corporations) rather than simply looking at the aims of the legislation authorizing a search and seizure in furtherance of some valid government objective. This approach requires a balancing of the individual's right to privacy, against the interests of the State in advancing its goals of law enforcement. Moreover, the Supreme Court held that this act of balancing should occur *prior* to the execution of any power of search and seizure, and that the authorization should be given by a person who is capable of acting in a judicial capacity (*i.e.*, neutral and impartial). Since the power of authorization under section 10 of the *Combines Act* is vested in the Director of Investigation and Research, who is also the official responsible for enforcement of the *Act*, this requirement of neutrality and impartiality was not met.

In addition, the Supreme Court considered that the minimum criterion required to be met before authorization of an investigation and search under section 10 — namely the authorizing officer's reasonable belief that evidence relative to an inquiry carried out under the *Act* may be found at the premises to be searched — was below the minimum standard required to protect the individual's right to freedom from unreasonable state intrusion. In view of the criminal nature of proceedings under the *Combines Act*, the Supreme Court felt that at a minimum, reasonable and probable grounds for belief that an offence under the *Act* has been committed, and that evidence relevant to the offence is likely to be found at the premises to be searched, should be established, upon oath, before such an authorization should be given. In effect, therefore, the Court imposed the same conditions as are required for issuance of a search warrant under section 443 of the *Criminal Code*.

This decision was hailed by civil libertarians as a victory for the rights of accused persons in criminal proceedings. However, the context in which the decision was handed down is crucial to understanding its impact on the control of corporate crime, and more specifically with respect to the *Combines Investigation Act*. The effect of the Supreme Court's decision, as business commentators immediately pointed out, was to negate the pro-active powers of enforcement accorded to the Director of Investigation and Research under the *Combines Act*. This was consistent with previous Supreme Court rulings which have done much to render the previous combines legislation effectively unenforceable, at least with regard to the most serious offences. Given the insistence by the courts on "hard" evidence to support a conviction under section 32 of the *Act*, and the low visibility of most offences under the *Act* (which in turn means that few victims are likely to initiate enforcement proceedings, contrary to most forms of street crime), the need for pro-active investigatory powers on the part of enforcement officials is apparent. In striking down the investigation and search powers of the Director in the name of the "individual's" right to protection from unreasonable search and seizure, the Supreme Court's decision therefore underscores the tension which exists between the individualist orientation of the criminal justice system, and its ability to respond to corporate crime.

The practical difficulties of obtaining convictions against corporations and their directors and officers have led to calls for "a new approach to culpability" stressing the social harm resulting from the illegal corporate activity, rather than the subjective intent of the corporate offender or its directors and officers. Thus, Reasons argues that while manufacturers or construction companies do not necessarily intend to cause harm to consumers or employees by producing defective products or maintaining unsafe places of work, nevertheless their negligent or reckless actions or omissions provide the basis for such harm to occur. As a result, any harm which does occur as a result of violations of regulatory standards governing health and safety in the workplace, product safety, or protection of the environment, should be dealt with severely: "[s]trict liability and/or the use of criminal negligence would provide the impetus to deter such crimes, coupled with better policing and protection."

This combination of lower standards of culpability, coupled with the use of penal sanctions is characteristic to the enforcement provisions of much federal and provincial regulatory legislation. Indeed, it can be argued that the move towards strict liability in criminal law, as with the corresponding shift towards strict liability in tort, has largely occurred in response to the proliferation of the corporate form as the primary actor in many fields of economic activity, and the need to develop appropriate legal mechanisms for regulating socially harmful corporate behaviour. Carson, for example, points out that the enactment of strict liability offences in nineteenth century English factory legislation was intended to facilitate enforcement of regulatory standards by rendering it more difficult for corporate offenders to evade liability through legal defences.

Notwithstanding the proliferation of strict liability and negligence offences, however, numerous studies indicate that little use is made of penal sanctions in enforcing regulatory standards in practice. In part, this appears to reflect the enforcement philosophy of regulatory officials, who may prefer to use the threat of penal sanctions as a lever to ensure compliance, rather than to enforce the law in all cases of non-compliance. This preference, in turn, is related to a view often shared by courts, legislators, regulatory officials, as well as the corporate violators themselves, that the aims of such legislation are essentially administrative rather than penal in nature. The corollary of this view is that even on the rare occasions when enforcement proceedings are taken against corporate violators, conviction for a regulatory offence under federal or provincial legislation carries a lesser social stigma than conviction for a *Criminal Code* offence.

In view of the reluctance of regulatory officials to initiate prosecutions under regulatory statutes, and the absence of social stigma which follows upon conviction, many commentators have emphasized the importance of criminalizing wilful corporate violations of regulatory statutes, in order to attract public notice and raise the social stigma associated with prosecution and conviction.

A recent initiative along these lines is the proposal by the Law Reform Commission of Canada to incorporate a new offence of endangering the environment into a revised *Criminal Code*. The philosophy behind the Commission's proposal is that protection of the environment should be regarded as a fundamental social value; consequently, flagrant violations of emission standards which result in serious harm or danger to the environment, as well as to human life or health, should be treated as criminal and therefore subject to prosecution under the *Criminal Code*. At the same time, however, the Commission recommends against any deviation from traditional criminal standards of culpability, namely intention, recklessness or criminal negligence. Nor will the Commission countenance any infringement upon the procedural and evidentiary protections for the accused, for example through the use of a reverse onus clause, to facilitate obtaining the evidence necessary to prosecute. As the Commission's Working Paper states, "[w]e continue to be of the view that it is preferable to lose cases and free some who are guilty rather than achieve convictions at the risk of compromising basic principles of justice." As a result, it is questionable how many successful prosecutions would be likely to result if such an offence were to be enacted into a revised *Criminal Code*.

The Law Reform Commission's recommendation illustrates the difficulties involved in fashioning appropriate strategies for the control of corporate crime, given the ideological discourses underlying the present form of criminal law. This tension inheres from the premise that the moral stigma associated with prosecution and conviction for "real crimes" is intimately connected with the rhetoric of legal individualism and voluntarism expressed in the requirement of *mens rea* as an essential element of criminal responsibility. Consequently any lowering of the fault standard is assumed to result in a lessening of the social stigma associated with conviction, as observed in relation to strict liability offences under regulatory statutes. Conversely, criminalizing corporate violations of regulatory statutes in order to increase the stigma associated with conviction carries the risk that convictions will become more difficult to obtain, and enforcement efforts therefore less effective. When coupled with the related view of regulatory offences as occupying a realm of conflicting values, and as being primarily concerned with illegal behaviour occurring in the course of otherwise legitimate activities, rather than conduct which is itself morally opprobrious, it is clear that these ideological discourses play a significant role in perpetuating the preferential treatment enjoyed by corporate offenders under the criminal justice system.

The point is not that criminal law cannot be used against corporate offenders. Clearly this is not the case. The point is rather that these ideological discourses intersect in such a way as to reinforce the creation of a legal double standard which insulates most corporate violators of regulatory standards from criminal sanctions, regardless of the harmfulness of their illegal behaviour. As a result, failure to take such ideological discourses into account is likely to undermine attempts to improve the responsiveness of the criminal justice system to corporate crime by further criminalizing corporate violations of regulatory statutes. Indeed, by emphasizing the *symbolic* potential of criminal law in stigmatizing unlawful corporate behaviour critical commentators on corporate crime often unwittingly reaffirm the legitimacy of the very ideological discourses which serve to perpetuate the existence of this legal double standard.

## CONCLUSION

In summary, it is argued that the instrumentalist conception of law, which is common to most class conflict analyses of corporate crime, provides an inadequate theoretical tool for accounting for the apparent inability of the criminal justice system to respond to the corporate crime "problem." While there is considerable evidence in support of the instrumentalist contention that powerful corporate interests are often able to influence the law-making process in such a way as to limit the scope and effectiveness of laws designed to control corporate criminal behaviour, nevertheless, the instrumentalist assumption that law and the state represent tools which can be wielded by the capitalist class in order to maintain their dominant class position appears to be at odds with the historical evidence of struggle and contingency associated with the enactment of such legislation. Nor should the poor enforcement record of such legislation simply be written off as evidence that "[m]embers of the ruling class [are] able to violate laws with impunity while members of the subject classes will be punished." Such an approach ignores the "real improvements in life chance and conditions for working people" which have resulted from such legislation. Moreover, this analysis also appears to preclude any hope that law itself can be utilized for progressive ends. Yet, paradoxically, this is precisely the position of class conflict theorists such as Glasbeek, and Reasons, Ross and Patterson, who advocate the criminalization of corporate violations of regulatory statutes, in order to bring home to the corporate violators, and to the public at large, the unacceptable social costs of unlawful corporate behaviour.

More significantly, perhaps, the instrumentalist characterization of law as an instrument for maintaining class dominance precludes any analysis of the social character of law as both the product of an historical process, and as a set of ideological discourses affecting the way in which social relations are defined and experienced. It has been argued in this paper that the ideological discourses which underly the form of trial and the criminal law conceptions of responsibility and judicial sentencing practices play a crucial role in individualising and depoliticizing the experience of social actors confronted by the criminal justice system. By emphasizing the values of individual responsibility and freedom of choice, these ideological discourses serve to reinforce popular notions of the objectivity and neutrality of law, regardless of evidence of its particularized and unequal application in practice. Rather than seeking to expose law's claims to popular legitimacy as a mere sham, as most class conflict theorists seek to do, it is important to explore its real ideological significance in reproducing consent for a system of social relations based on formal equality and substantive inequality.

Only by taking the ideological significance of the form of law seriously is it possible to develop a "jurisprudence of insurgency" which is capable of challenging the "moral hegemony" of criminal law in supporting and reinforcing the unequal treatment of different classes of offenders and offences by the criminal justice system.

It follows from this that struggles to increase the responsiveness of the criminal justice system to corporate crime should be directed not only at the content and application of regulatory laws governing corporate offences, but also at the ideological assumptions underpinning the particular form of individualized justice enshrined in the present system of criminal law. In particular, it is important to develop strategies which counter the ideological role of criminal law in decontextualizing and depoliticizing the experience of social actors confronted by the criminal justice system. Interestingly, this is a central thrust of recent feminist critiques of the criminal justice system, which are explicitly aimed at making criminal law more responsive to the real experience of women, both as victims and as offenders. Similarly, Goldman points out that pressure by victim's groups for reform of the criminal justice system is premised in part upon concerns that the trial process and the sentencing process are abstracted from the real social context in which crimes are committed. Taken together, these critiques by feminist legal scholars and by victim's groups alike represent a significant challenge to the ideological hegemony of the present form of criminal law, and an attempt to substitute its individualist orientation with a more harm-oriented conception of responsibility. This in turn has clear implications for legal structures aimed at making the criminal law more responsive to the harmfulness of illegal corporate behaviour. Whether such pressures will be translated into real reforms of the form and function of criminal law remains to be seen. Nevertheless, emphasizing the social and historical character of law as an arena of struggle contributes to our understanding of the contradictory character of law as both an instrument for maintaining coercive and ideological domination, and, at the same time, an institution containing the seeds of resistance to its own domination.

**Questions/Discussions**
1. How do you explain the failure of society to adequately address the problem of crime in the workplace and specifically of corporate crime? Why do the media, both entertainment and information, focus so much attention on certain types of crime, particularly violent street crime, to the exclusion of corporate crime?
2. Is criminal law an effective device to use against crime which occurs in the workplace or should we rely on other types of control or of law, for example, administrative law? What inherent problems, for example, in regard to the degree of proof required or the adversarial nature of the system, can one point to which might present impediments to the use of criminal law as an effective weapon in this area?

**Further Reading**
- Casey, J., "Corporate Crime and the Canadian State: Anti-combines Legislation, 1945-1986" (1992), 3 Journal of Human Justice 22-35.
- Glasbeek, H., "Why Corporate Deviance is Not Treated as a Crime — The Need to Make 'Profits' a Dirty Word" (1984), 22 Osgoode Hall Law Journal 393.
- Glasbeek, H. and S. Rowland, "Are Injuring and Killing At Work Crimes?" (1979), 17 Osgoode Hall Law Journal 507.
- Goff, C. and C. Reasons, *Corporate Crime in Canada* (Scarborough: Prentice-Hall, 1978).
- McMullan, J., *Beyond the Limits of the Law: Corporate Crime and Law and Order* (Halifax, N.S.: Fernwood Publishing, 1992).

- Northey, R., "Conflicting Principles of Canadian Environmental Reform: Trubek and Habermas v. Law and Economics and the Law Reform Commission" (1988), 11 Dalhousie Law Journal 639.
- Pearce, F. and L. Snider (eds.), *Corporate Crime: Contemporary Debates* (Toronto: University of Toronto Press, 1995).
- Reasons, C., *et al.*, *Assault on the Worker: Occupational Health and Safety in Canada* (Toronto: Butterworths, 1981).
- Sargent, N.C., "Law, Ideology and Social Change: An Analysis of the Role of the Law in the Construction of Corporate Crime" (1990), 1 Journal of Human Justice 97-116.
- Schrecker, T., "The Political Context and Content of Environmental Law" in T.C. Caputo, *et al.*, eds., *Law and Society: A Criminal Perspective* (Toronto: Harcourt Brace Jovanovich Canada, 1989).
- Snider, L., *Bad Business: Corporate Crime in Canada* (Scarborough, Ont.: Nelson Canada, 1992).
- Webb, K., *Pollution Control in Canada: The Regulatory Approach to the 1980s* (Ottawa: Law Reform Commission of Canada, 1988).

## 8.4 YOUNG OFFENDERS

### Introduction

The problem of how to deal with youthful offenders is not a new one for the criminal justice system; issues such as the cut-off age for differential treatment, what rights and processes to provide to those in this category, how to punish or treat those found guilty, and so on, have been the source of debate for a long period of time. Moreover, the fundamental question of why to treat such offenders differently has been examined from many perspectives.

The article by Bala which is reproduced below examines many of the pertinent issues in the context of Canada and the changes which were brought about by the relatively recent changes in the juvenile justice system in this country. These changes were ushered in with the implementation of the Young Offenders Act in 1982 which was designed to replace the regime under the previous Juvenile Delinquents Act which dated from the beginning of the century. The Y.O.A., the new system, the most recent amendments, and the rationale and goals of the regime are discussed in the article. As you read the article, ask yourself whether these goals and these changes are valid in the general context of the criminal law and its purposes, and address the important issue of *why* should society treat young offenders differently than adult offenders.

If there should be differential treatment, then how should that be accomplished, based on what notions of state and individual responsibility? Furthermore, note the problem of the lack of resources at the provincial level and the difficulties which arise when one level of government has the responsibility to make the law in a particular area while the sometimes costly measures provided for in the legislation (as to treatment, diversion programmes, or alternative sentencing initiatives) depend upon another level of government for their actual formulation and drafting. Of course, "what works" is as questionable in the field of juvenile justice as it is in the adult system.

As you shall see, the theme of changes to the juvenile justice system in recent years has been a "get tough(er)" approach by many governments and lobby groups. This is seen not only in the legislative changes which have occurred, but also in the media and, in particular, in proposals advanced by the government of Ontario in 1996 to set up "strict discipline" jails or "boot camps" for young offenders. The belief is that by getting tougher, the problem of youth crime will somehow be addressed. It is interesting to note that Ontario already has the highest custody rate for young offenders in Canada with a rate of 1 in 71 (versus 1 in 218 in Quebec and 1 in 91 nationally). Youth crime is a serious problem but it cannot be solved by simple-minded, get-tough "solutions" which appeal to the baser instincts and media-driven fears of the wider public. It requires a broad range of social and community initiatives which attack the root causes of both youth and adult crime.

## "The 1995 Young Offenders Act Amendments: Compromise or Confusion?"*
### by Nicolas Bala

* from (1994), 26 Ottawa Law Review 643

### 1. INTRODUCTION

Few, if any pieces of Canadian legislation have been the subject of such sustained public criticism as the *Young Offenders Act (Y.O.A.)*, and the "reform" of the *Act* has been a major priority for the Liberal government. The *Y.O.A.* has been attacked by critics coming from very different perspectives, from the "law & order" right for not being "tough enough", and from the "therapeutic left" for failing to do enough to rehabilitate adolescent offenders. The Liberal government introduced Bill C-37, amendments to the *Y.O.A.*, that are intended to offer a compromise between these two critical perspectives, both of which have support within the Liberal caucus as well as in the broader community. While the dominant public message given by the government is that the *Act* is being "toughened", in particular as a response to violent youth, there are also elements in the Bill intended to strengthen the rehabilitative aspects of the youth justice system.

Merely enacting statutory reforms is unlikely to have a significant impact on levels of youth crime in Canada, at least in the absence of significant changes in the types of services which are actually provided to adolescents in the youth justice system. Even so, there is considerable merit to some of the fundamental objectives of Bill C-37: taking a more retributive approach to the relatively small numbers of youth who commit the most serious offences, in particular murder, while limiting the use of custody for most youths and attempting rehabilitation for all. Unfortunately, it is not clear that Bill C-37 will achieve even these objectives.

This paper offers a discussion of the political and legal context of Bill C-37, and analyzes the most important features of the new law, pointing out some of its limitations and some of the provisions that were amended in the legislative process.

### II. BACKGROUND TO BILL C-37: DECADES OF CONTROVERSY REACH A CRESCENDO

The *Juvenile Delinquents Act (J.D.A.)*, enacted in 1908, created a juvenile justice system separate from the adult system, with a distinctive child welfare oriented philosophy, treating the delinquent youth "in so far as practicable . . . not as a criminal, but as a misguided and misdirected child . . . needing aid, encouragement, help and assistance". The *J.D.A.* created an informal justice system, with little emphasis on legal rights, and very significant discretion for a range of justice officials, including probation officers, judges and correction officials. With its treatment orientation, sentences were indeterminate, to be served until rehabilitation was effected. There was also very substantial interprovincial variation in the implementation of the *J.D.A.*

The process of reforming the *J.D.A.* began in the 1960s and was contentious, but most of the debate was conducted by various professional groups, and between the federal and provincial governments. By the early 1980s, the introduction of the *Charter of Rights and Freedoms* made major juvenile justice reform inevitable. The lack of procedural rights in the *J.D.A.* was inconsistent with the emphasis on due process in the *Charter*. Further, the provincial disparities in treatment of juveniles permitted under the *J.D.A.*, especially in regard to the differing minimum and maximum ages, was considered to be contrary to section 15 of the *Charter* which came into effect in 1985 and guaranteed equality before the law.

There was also a recognition that the exclusively welfare oriented focus of the *J.D.A.* was neither realistic nor appropriate, and indeed did not reflect actual practices under that *Act*. Rehabilitation can be achieved with some youth, but it cannot be the sole focus for legal intervention. Accountability and the protection of the public must also be important considerations.

The *Young Offenders Act* was enacted in 1982, and came into force in 1984. Given the contentious nature of the process of reform prior to 1982, and the present controversy, it is a little surprising, but the *Act* received the unanimous support of Parliament at that time. The *Y.O.A.* gives youths very significant legal rights, and established a uniform age jurisdiction of 12 to 18. The *Act* provides for determinate sentencing, and formal "alternative measures" programs to divert less serious cases from the youth court. The *Act* also contains a "Declaration of Principle" that provides decision-makers with guidance for dealing with young persons in conflict with the criminal law:

3(1) It is hereby recognized and declared that

(a) while young persons should not in all instances be held accountable in the same manner or suffer the same consequences for their behaviour as adults, young persons who commit offences should nonetheless bear responsibility for their contraventions;

(b) society must, although it has the responsibility to take reasonable measures to prevent criminal conduct by young persons, be afforded the necessary protection from illegal behaviour;

(c) young persons who commit offences require supervision, discipline and control, but, because of their state of dependency and level of development and maturity, they also have special needs and require guidance and assistance;

(d) where it is not inconsistent with the protection of society, taking no measure or taking measures other than judicial proceedings under this Act should be considered for dealing with young persons who have committed offences;

(e) young persons have rights and freedoms in their own right, including those stated in the *Canadian Charter of Rights and Freedoms* or in the *Canadian Bill of Rights*, and in particular a right to be heard in the course of, and to participate in, the processes that lead to decisions that affect them, and young persons should have special guarantees of their rights and freedoms;

(f) in the application of this Act, the rights and freedoms of young persons include a right to the least possible interference with freedom that is consistent with the protection of society, having regard to the needs of young persons and the interests of their families;

(g) young persons have the right, in every instance where they have rights or freedoms that may be affected by this Act, to be informed as to what those rights and freedoms are; and

(h) parents have responsibility for the care and supervision of their children, and, for that reason, young persons should be removed from parental supervision either partly or entirely only when measures that provide for continuing parental supervision are inappropriate.

Given Parliament's failure to prioritize these principles, it is not surprising that section 3 has not in practice provided significant direction for decision-makers. Perhaps more accurately, there is sufficient vagueness to each of the principles, and even more in the Declaration as a whole, that judges and others can find support for virtually any decision in them. Decision-makers may feel that their actions are in some sense directed by the Declaration, but in reality, there is substantial discretion. As a result of this lack of guidance, there is substantial variation in how the *Y.O.A.* is applied, with very significant differences in sentencing practices and rates of custody use between the provinces, as well as in the use of such programs as alternative measures.

While the Declaration is therefore not unproblematic, it is nevertheless more realistic to recognize that dealing with a complex problem like juvenile crime will inevitably require a balancing of principles and objectives, rather than having a single simplistic statement of principle like that found in the welfare-oriented *J.D.A.* It must also be appreciated that the "ambivalence" found in the Declaration, and in some of the substantive provisions of the *Act*, reflects a fundamental tension in Canadian society about youth crime, and perhaps even an ambivalence towards adolescents in general. Society is demanding protection from youth, and wants adolescents held accountable for their acts; at the same time, adolescence is recognized as a time of growth, change and making mistakes, and it is recognized that adolescents need to be nurtured to become productive adult citizens.

The *Y.O.A.* came into force in the midst of optimistic hopes that it would usher in a "new era" in juvenile justice. While there have been significant changes, the optimism of the early 1980s has disappeared, as has the political support for the *Y.O.A.*

By far the greatest publicly expressed concern in recent years has been that the *Y.O.A.* is not "tough" enough on youth crime. Some of this reflects a belief that in terms of moral accountability (or punishment or vengeance) sentences in youth court are too short, and transfer to the adult court system, where there is fuller accountability, occurs too rarely. Much of the public concern about the *Y.O.A.* appears to be based on a belief that the *Act* does not provide an adequate deterrent to crime, and has therefore contributed to a significant increase in youthful criminality.

There are a number of problems with this critique of the *Act*. To begin with, although youth crime is a serious social problem with significant costs for victims (many of whom are other adolescents) there is significant controversy among criminologists about whether there has actually been an increase in youthful criminality in recent years in Canada, or whether we simply have awareness of the existence of youth crime.

While there has been a very substantial increase in youths being charged and brought before the courts, criminologists like Tony Daub and Paul Brantingham have argued that this is due to an increased public sensitivity to crime, especially violent crime, and a greater willingness to report youth crime to the police, both by victims and agencies like schools, and to increased charging practices by police. These experts point to the fact that youth homicide, the one offence that is not influenced by public reports or police charging practices, has remained relatively constant for many years and even fell in 1993-94, the last year for which data is available. However, other criminologists, like Raymond Corrado and Alan Markwart, have argued that there has been a significant increase in violent crime by adolescents in Canada; this perception is widely shared by police and professionals who work with adolescents.

The empirical question of whether there has *really* been an increase in youth crime in the past few years in Canada is probably unresolvable, since we have great difficulty in determining present rates of criminality and no way of accurately determining previous rates. There is, however, a clear perception among the public and professionals that in the past few years youths have been committing more violent offences and made greater use of weapons, and this has led to a demand for law reform. It is important to observe that even those criminologists who argue that there has been an increase in youth crime recognize that this is still a less serious problem in Canada than in the United States, and that its causes are complex and cannot be blamed on the Y.O.A.

Criminologists and academic commentators widely acknowledge that there is no evidence that longer sentences or more transfers to adult court actually have an impact on youthful crime. The available social science evidence clearly indicates that youths who are committing crimes lack judgment and foresight, and are not considering the consequences of their acts, let alone weighing the possible sanctions. While improving police enforcement *may* have some impact on offending behaviour by adolescents, a "tougher" law will not. Indeed, there is some evidence that longer custodial sentences and more transfers to adult court may actually increase the likelihood of recidivism.

Another problem with the public perception that the Y.O.A. is not "tough enough" is that there has actually been a very substantial increase in the number of young persons in custody in recent years. One indicator of this is that between 1986-87 and 1992-93 the daily incarceration rate per 10,000 youths in Canada increased from 17.8 to 21.3. Most of the youths who are placed in custody are there for non-violent offences. While it is difficult to get an accurate picture, it would seem that youths charged with more serious offences, including violent offences, actually serve shorter sentences than adults charged with the same offence. However, a very significant number of youths committing less serious offences, in particular violations of court orders for probation or court attendance, as well as property offences, are receiving custodial dispositions, and may actually be serving longer periods in custody than adults charged with the same offences, at least in part because some youth court judges may be using these dispositions out of a desire to achieve social rehabilitative objectives.

At the same time, some critics of the Y.O.A. have argued that the *Act* undermines certain types of rehabilitative efforts, pointing in particular to section 22 which requires the consent of a youth if the judge wants to impose a disposition requiring detention in a mental health facility. Since few offending youths are willing to consent, very few "treatment" orders are made. It should, however, be appreciated that mental health services and other rehabilitative resources can be made available to youths sentenced to custody. Youths in custody can usually be persuaded to participate in rehabilitative efforts with the prospect of sentence review and early release, though, at least in theory, without their tacit consent, they cannot be required to receive such services. In reality, the main blockage in terms of achieving access to rehabilitative services is not the issue of consent, but rather that, while some youth custody facilities (such as Ontario's Syl Apps Centre which deals with youths aged 12-15 convicted of very serious offences) have excellent treatment and educational services, many custodial facilities have very limited rehabilitative resources.

From a legal perspective, the concept of "rehabilitation" applies to young offenders in a very ambiguous fashion. While for adults rehabilitative concerns invariably support non-custodial dispositions, or relatively short custodial sentences, for young persons the concept of rehabilitation may support longer sentences.

This was illustrated and reinforced by the 1993 Supreme Court of Canada decision in *R. v. M(J.J.)*, the first *Y.O.A.* disposition case to reach the Court. The Supreme Court affirmed a sentence of two years in open custody for an aboriginal youth convicted of three counts of break and enter, and one of breach of probation. He came from an abusive home environment, which the Court characterized as "intolerable", and therefore the Court felt that "child welfare considerations" justified the relatively long sentence.

Justice Cory emphasized that youth courts need to make individualized assessments about young offenders' sentencing, balancing the protection of society and the reformation of the youth. He accepted the "proportionality principle" for sentencing young offenders, but indicated that it was less important than for adults, and had to be weighed against child welfare concerns.

> It is true that for both adults and minors the sentence must be proportional to the offence committed. But in the sentencing of adult offenders, the principle of proportionality will have a greater significance than it will in the disposition of young offenders.

The Supreme Court also indicated that general deterrence should have a role in sentencing youths, but less than for adults. The primary aim the Court emphasized was rehabilitation.

> The aim must be both to protect society and at the same time to provide the young offender with the necessary guidance and assistance that he or she may not be getting at home. Those goals are not necessarily mutually exclusive. In the long run, society is best protected by the reformation and rehabilitation of a young offender. In turn, the young offenders are best served when they are provided with the necessary guidance and assistance to enable them to learn the skills required to become fully integrated, useful members of society.

Although *R. v. M.(J.J.)* resolved the relatively abstract controversies about the legitimacy of considering general deterrence and child welfare concerns when sentencing a young offender, it gives judges little specific direction. The Supreme Court emphasizes individualized decision-making and judicial discretion, and gives only a limited sense of priority for different sentencing factors.

The decision also raises concerns that youths may perceive themselves as receiving more severe dispositions because of their difficult family backgrounds. In a dissenting opinion in *R. v. M.(J.J.)* at the Manitoba Court of Appeal level, Madam Justice Helper felt that a sentence of one year was appropriate as a "fit sentence" for the offences, arguing that the "criminal justice system ought not to be used to supplement the lack of resources that exist in the child welfare system". In *R. v. M.(J.J.)* the youth had actually sought assistance from child protection workers before the offences, but failed to receive it. However, the Supreme Court decision accepts that for a variety of reasons, including inadequate funding, child welfare services may not always be available for troubled youths, and that judges may feel that the *Y.O.A.* has to be used to meet the needs of adolescents.

Decisions like *R. v. M.(J.J.)* emphasize the discretionary nature of the *Y.O.A.*, and have contributed to the creation of a youth justice system where there is still very substantial variation in how youths in different parts of the country are treated. Different provincial policies about administrative structures and resources, as well as differences in police charging practices and prosecutorial discretion, have also played a major role in shaping interprovincial variations. As a result of these administrative and judicial factors, there are, for example, very substantial differences of custody use between provinces, with, for example, Saskatchewan having a rate three times higher than Quebec.

In regard to transfers to adult court, where judicial (and prosecutorial) discretion and interpretation play a determinative role, there are also enormous differences between provinces, with Manitoba and Alberta having by far the highest transfer rates in the country.

At the same time as receiving critiques of various aspects of the *Y.O.A.* from different perspectives, the federal government is also acutely aware of mounting fiscal problems for itself and the provinces. While politicians are sometimes loath to publicly emphasize fiscal concerns when dealing with justice issues, there is no doubt that financial considerations are weighing on their minds, especially when faced with enormous increases in the use of expensive custody resources.

## III. AMENDING THE *Y.O.A.*: 1986-1995

The federal Parliament amended the *Y.O.A.* in 1986 and 1992, and in 1994-95 enacted the most ambitious set of amendments to the *Act* since it came into force in 1984. While each of these reform initiatives have been set in a broadly similar context, the heightened public perceptions about the inadequacy of the *Y.O.A.*, as well as increased fiscal concerns, have pushed the new government towards more aggressive responses.

The 1986 amendments were relatively minor and received little public attention. Most of these amendments were intended to facilitate implementation of the *Act*, for example simplifying record keeping provisions. Some were intended to increase the protection of the public, for example by allowing for the police to obtain a court order permitting the publication of identifying information to aid in the apprehension of a potentially dangerous youth who is at large. There were some relatively weak provisions that were intended to signal the courts to reduce unnecessary use of custodial facilities, but they seem to have had no appreciable effect on sentencing practices.

By the late 1980s, public concerns about violent youth crime and the perceived inadequacy of the *Y.O.A.* were increasing. In 1989 the Progressive Conservative government proposed amendments to the *Y.O.A.* to deal with murder sentencing and transfer to adult court. These amendments proceeded slowly through Parliament, in part because of a lack of a sense of urgency at that time, but also because the Liberals and New Democrats were then expressing concerns about the unwarranted "toughening" of the approach of the *Y.O.A.* These amendments were enacted in 1992, with the government emphasizing that they were intended to increase the protection of the public. The maximum sentence that a youth court could impose for murder was increased from three years to five years less a day; the test for transfer was altered to state that the "protection of the public" was to be "paramount", but the test still left great discretion to trial judges. To decrease judicial reluctance to transfer for murder cases, the date of parole eligibility for transferred youth in these cases was reduced from a range of 10 to 25 years to a range of 5 to 10 years, and provisions were added to allow transferred youths to remain in youth custody facilities and avoid immediate placement with adults.

No transfer cases have yet been appealed to the Supreme Court of Canada under the 1992 amendments. Because of the vagueness, or ambiguity, of some of the 1992 transfer provisions, there have been radically different approaches to transfer in different provinces since they came into effect. These disparities are more fully discussed below.

By the election of 1993, public concerns about the *Y.O.A.* were reaching a crescendo, and every party except the Bloc Québécois took a position in effect "running against" the *Y.O.A.* The Reform Party took by far the strongest stance, advocating such measures as lowering of minimum and maximum ages, and automatic transfer to adult court for offences like murder or for a second violent offence. The Liberal platform had to accommodate both the "law and order" and the "progressive" elements within the Party. Parts of the Liberals' election platform *Red Book* emphasized concerns about violent crime, and the recommendations included such measures as increased sentences of violent crimes, the development of a concept of "dangerous youth offender" who would be automatically transferred to adult court, and release of identifying information about violent young offenders. However, reflecting the ambivalence of Canadian society in regard to youth crime, other passages of the *Red Book* put adolescent criminality in a social context, emphasized the need for rehabilitation and even recommended restricting the range of offences for which a youth can be transferred to adult court.

Interestingly, attitudes towards the *Y.O.A.* have been very different in Quebec from the rest of Canada. Public opinion polls indicate that there is much more support for the *Y.O.A.* in Quebec than elsewhere in Canada, and the Bloc Québécois was the only party in the 1993 election to "speak out against law and order rhetoric" during the campaign, and to oppose amending the *Y.O.A.* to "toughen" the law. Quebec has long had a distinctive juvenile justice policy, with a high degree of integration between child welfare and young offenders services, and the lowest rate of custody orders in Canada. It is an interesting question why Quebec has a different attitude towards the *Y.O.A.* The province in general has more supportive policies towards children, reflected in their cash payments to parents after children are born. There may well be distinctive attitudes in that province towards juvenile crime and punishment, as well as towards children and families.

Since the 1993 election Canada has had a new Liberal Minister of Justice, Allan Rock, a man viewed as a skillful new figure on the Canadian political stage, and perhaps a future Prime Minister. Faced with a very broad range of criticism of the *Y.O.A.*, and a host of political, constitutional and fiscal constraints, he introduced Bill C-37 in June 1994. There were House of Commons hearings in the autumn of 1994. The Bill was passed, with amendments, by the House of Commons on February 28, 1995, and is expected to come into force by the end of 1995.

These are by far the most extensive amendments in the *Act*'s history, and deal with:

- longer maximum sentences for murder in youth court;
- transfer to adult court;
- the Declaration of Principle & dispositional guidelines;
- alternatives to custody, levels of custody, and placement in mental health facilities;
- information sharing and records;
- medical and psychological assessments and victim impact statements;
- conditional discharges; and
- youth statements to police.

The Minister of Justice has also asked the House of Commons Committee on Justice and Legal Affairs to undertake a broad review of the *Act* as the "Second Phase" of *Y.O.A.* reform, though it seems that most of the contentious aspects of the *Y.O.A.* are already dealt with in the 1995 reforms, other than the issue of age jurisdiction.

In introducing Bill C-37, the Minister of Justice was clearly playing to the dominant political law and order sentiments in Canada, emphasizing the murder sentencing, transfer and information sharing provisions:

> the government is sending a strong message—we are dedicated to ensuring that Canadians can continue to live . . . in communities that are safe and free from fear. . . . Public protection must be our primary objective in dealing with young offenders.

But the Bill is very much a compromise, containing provisions that are intended to satisfy the progressive wing of the Liberal Party as well as the law and order advocates within the Party. For example, provisions aimed at reducing the use of custody for non-violent offenders are clearly intended to appease the progressives in the Liberal caucus. Even the new transfer provisions are drafted in a balanced fashion, and their ultimate effect on the number of youths who will be transferred is not clear.

The Minister also recognized that changing the legislation will not, by itself, have an impact on youth crime; resources, staffing and facility issues need to be addressed, and there must be at the very least a "retargeting" of spending in this area. However, the reality is that the provinces have the responsibility for spending and resource decisions in this field. While the federal government may influence provincial spending decisions by placing conditions on its cost-sharing programs for youth justice and corrections, it is not clear that federal initiatives alone can have much impact on the provision of youth corrections programs in custody or the community.

## IV. MURDER SENTENCING

Murder is the youth offence that has, perhaps understandably, most captured public attention. Relatively few youths (30 to 60 per year) are charged with this offence, and the majority of those charged with murder are ultimately convicted only of manslaughter, since the Crown cannot prove that these often unpredictable and senseless acts were deliberate.

For youths *not* transferred to adult court, the maximum sentence under Bill C-37 will be ten years for first degree murder, with a maximum six years of custody and the balance on conditional supervision, presumably served in the community. For second degree murder, the maximum sentence in youth court will be seven years, with a maximum initial sentence of four years in custody and the balance on conditional supervision. These are maximum custodial sentences, and in appropriate cases youth courts may impose shorter sentences or release earlier on review. However, it seems likely that most judges will view the amendments as a signal to increase the sentences imposed. The longer periods of community supervision have the potential to help youths, provided that adequate resources are devoted to assist for meaningful supervision, counselling and reintegration into the community. In appropriate cases of apprehended danger, a youth may be detained in custody by a youth court judge during the period of community supervision.

While some of the statements of the Minister of Justice and the Liberal *Red Book* suggest that the longer youth court sentences may be needed for rehabilitative purposes, there is no real evidence that the present provisions were inadequate in this regard. Clearly, the dominant purpose for having longer sentences is to satisfy public demands for greater accountability or punishment, as the Minister acknowledged in introducing Bill C-37.

In the Committee Hearings on Bill C-37, the Minister admitted that it is still too early to draw definite conclusions about the effect of the 1992 transfer amendments; indeed, at the time that Bill C-37 was introduced, few, if any, youth courts had dealt with conditional supervision provisions introduced in 1992. However, this did not prevent him from proposing further amendments to these provisions, as the government believed that the maximum youth court murder penalty was "simply wrong", "as a matter of principle". That is, the issue of accountability is the dominant concern in the increase in the maximum youth court sanction.

It is not clear in what manner long sentences by "young offenders" who will ultimately be in their 20s will be served. Clearly this is an issue that will face correctional officials and youth courts in the future. Presumably most will be released on community supervision before reaching the age of 20, or transferred into adult correctional facilities by youth court order under section 24.5 of the *Y.O.A.* sometime after reaching their eighteenth birthday.

The *Y.O.A.* will provide for youths charged with murder and *not* transferred to be able to elect trial by jury, since the *Charter* guarantees this. If the youth chooses to have a jury trial, it will be conducted by a superior court (*i.e.* federally appointed) judge, albeit sitting as a "youth court" judge pursuant to the *Y.O.A.* with its provisions governing such matters as publicity. These superior court judges will be responsible for sentencing, even if the conviction is for a lesser and included offence; there is a concern that they may not be as aware of the needs and facilities for adolescents as regular youth court judges.

To limit the overlap between the youth system sanction and the adult system sanctions, the minimum periods of parole eligibility for transferred youths who are 16 or 17 at the time of the offence and are convicted of murder in adult court have also been increased to ten and seven years for first degree murder respectively. Transferred youths who are under 16 at the time of the offence and transferred will have parole eligibility dates set at five to seven years.

One would expect that the effect of the longer youth court sentences and longer periods to adult court parole eligibility, considered *alone*, should actually tend to *decrease* the number of youths facing murder charges who are being transferred, as these charges will tend to make youth court sentences seem more appropriate for murder. However, any assessment of the total effect of the 1995 amendments on transfer has to also take account of other conflicting changes in the section 16 transfer test.

## V. TRANSFER TO ADULT COURT

While only a relatively small number of youths commit very violent offences or are considered for transfer to adult court, these are the cases that are the primary focus of media attention and public concern.

The *Y.O.A.*, as originally enacted, stipulated that transfer was to occur if, upon application, invariably by the Crown, a youth court was satisfied that this was "in the interest of society... having regard to the needs of the young person." Not surprisingly there were great differences in the judicial interpretations of this very vague standard, with the result being enormous variation in how youths in different provinces were treated. A youth in Quebec facing a first-degree murder charge was likely to remain in the youth system and receive a maximum three year sentence in a youth custody facility, while one in Alberta or Manitoba would most likely be transferred, and face life imprisonment in an adult penitentiary with no parole eligibility for twenty-five years.

The 1992 amendments to the *Y.O.A.* significantly reduced some of the discrepancies, especially as to the consequences of a decision about transfer. Youths remaining in the youth system and facing murder charges were to receive a maximum sentence of five years less a day, while those transferred and convicted in adult court were to receive life sentences, but have parole eligibility in 5 to 10 years. Further, a transferred youth facing an adult sentence could be confined, at least for some time, in a youth custody facility before going to an adult facility.

The 1992 test for transfer is *somewhat* more structured than the 1984 test. The primary aspect of the 1992 test is the "interest of society" which "*includes*" the protection of the public" and "the rehabilitation of the offender". This provision specifies that if these latter two objectives cannot be reconciled by the youth remaining in the youth system, then "the protection of the public shall be paramount" and the youth transferred. It does not, however, specify what is to occur if both be reconciled, but rather leaves the vague concept of the "interest of society" as the dominant factor.

Until we have a Supreme Court of Canada decision interpreting the 1992 amendments, it is not possible to fully assess the 1992 amendments. The reported case law clearly indicates great variation in the interpretation of section 16(1.1), and that relatively few cases are being transferred. However, in those cases involving murder, and a youth who does not appear amenable to rehabilitation in the youth system, the courts are required to make the protection of the public paramount and have done so by transferring the youth to adult court where a very long sentence may be imposed.

In 1993-94 (the last year for which data is available), there were 94 youths transferred, including 6 of 30 youths charged with murder. Over half of all transfers were in Manitoba and Alberta, where the courts are interpreting section 16(1.1) broadly, and including deterrence, accountability and the value of public trials as aspects of the "interest of society" In dealing with transfer, judges in Alberta and Manitoba have not only been considering the young person before the court and his or her potential future dangerousness, but also broader societal factors.

Other provinces have had lower transfer rates, with most provincial appeal courts interpreting section 16(1.1) as not permitting transfer if the court is satisfied that rehabilitation is sufficiently likely to occur in the youth system and hence the protection of the public can be achieved without transfer. Most judges have therefore not directly assessed accountability, general deterrence or other societal concerns as factors in transfer, but rather have focussed exclusively on the youth before the court, and attempted to assess his or her future danger to the public if not transferred.

The provisions of Bill C-37 which deal with transfer are complex. For youths under 16, there will be an onus under the new section 16(1) for the applicant, invariably the Crown, to apply to the youth court for transfer, and satisfy the court that transfer is necessary. The new section 16(1.1) will apply to youths 16 and 17 years of age and charged with:

- murder (25 in 1992-93);
- attempted murder (45 in 1992-93);
- manslaughter (5 in 1992-93); or
- aggravated sexual assault (4 in 1992-93).

Under section 16(1.01) the case will presumptively be dealt with in adult court, but the youth (or Crown) may seek "transfer down" by applying to youth court.

For all situations, the new test for transfer is:

s.16(1.1) In making the determination . . . [whether to transfer] the youth court shall consider the interest of society, which includes the objectives of affording protection to the public and rehabilitation of the young person, and determine whether those objectives can be reconciled by the youth being under the jurisdiction of the youth court, and

> (a) if the court is of the opinion that those objectives can be so reconciled, the court shall
> (i) in the case of an application under subsection(1), refuse to make an order that the young person be proceeded against in ordinary court, and
> (ii) in the case of an application under subsection (1.01) [reverse onus for 16 and 17 year olds charged with listed offences] order that the young person be proceeded against in youth court; or
> (b) if the court is of the opinion that those objectives cannot be so reconciled, protection of the public shall be paramount and the court shall
> (i) in the case of an application under subsection (1), order that the young person be proceeded against in ordinary court in accordance with the law ordinarily applicable to an adult charged with the offence, and
> (ii) in the case of an application under subsection (1.01), refuse to make an order that the young person be proceeded against in youth court.

(1.11) Where an application is made under subsection (1) or (1.01) [the reverse onus provision for murder, attempted murder, manslaughter and aggravated sexual assault], the onus of satisfying the youth court of the matters referred to in subsection (1.1) rests with the applicant.

The public rhetoric of the Liberal government about the new transfer provisions suggests that they expect substantially more youths charged with the more violent offences, in particular those who are 16 and 17 years of age, to be transferred to adult court, and serve longer sentences. The provision is complex, however, and its overall effect will depend upon how provincial governments, police, prosecutors and judges react.

The new test for transfer would appear to resolve some of the issues that have arisen in the conflicting jurisprudence under the 1992 law.

The new section 16(1.1) indicates that the "interest of society" includes *only* an assessment of rehabilitation of the youth and protection of the public. Factors such as accountability and the value of publicly reported hearings, which have, for example, influenced the Alberta and Manitoba courts to have a relatively high transfer rate, should *not* be taken into account. In this regard, the new provision may actually make if more difficult for the Crown to have youths transferred.

While the new provision does not explicitly resolve the existing controversy over whether general deterrence should be a factor in assessing the "protection of the public", it can be argued that there is an implicit signal for the courts in the new section 16(1.1). The Alberta courts have used general deterrence as a factor in favour of transfer in serious cases, as they believe that this will enhance the "protection of the public". While it might have been desirable for Parliament to explicitly deal with this issue, as it has not, it is submitted that general deterrence should not be a factor under the new section 16(1.1). Otherwise the individualized assessment of the youth contemplated by that section will not occur. If accountability or general deterrence were to be factors one might expect that all very serious charges should be transferred, and the new provisions clearly do not contemplate automatic transfer for any offence. Further, all available social science evidence indicates that increasing the number of youths transferred does *not* have a deterrent effect and enhance the protection of society.

Finally, consideration must be given to the amendment to the Declaration of Principle found in the new section 3(1)(c.1), which provides that "the protection of society ... is best achieved by rehabilitation, wherever possible ... and rehabilitation is best achieved by addressing the needs and circumstances of a young person". This statement of Parliamentary intent also supports the view that the appropriate interpretation of section 16(1.1) should focus on the youth before the Court, and his or her amenability to rehabilitation. If the interpretive approach to the new section 16(1.1) that is advocated here is adopted by the courts, there is the prospect that the substantial interprovincial variation in the application of the transfer provisions will be reduced by Bill C-37.

For 14 and 15-year-olds (12 out of 94 transfers in 1993-94), even those charged with murder, the new test in section 16(1.1) combined with the longer sentences for murder in the youth system as well as the longer period before eligibility in the adult system are very likely to decrease transfers.

The shift in onus under section 16(1.01) for 16 and 17-year-olds will presumably cause some more of these youths to be transferred, though it would seem from the case law under the present transfer provision that relatively few cases would be decided differently because of the change in onus. Already in transfer cases involving very violent offences, many judges have indicated that they will only refuse a transfer application if the prospects of rehabilitation in the youth system are "sufficiently promising". Conversely, in cases where a youth facing a charge like murder is not able to satisfy the court that rehabilitation is "likely" to occur in the youth system, but only is "possible", transfer has been ordered. That is, in practice there has generally already been a tactical onus on the youth to adduce evidence of amenability to rehabilitation within the youth system, and the shift in onus by Bill C-37 *may not* be that significant. Of course, it will ultimately be for the courts to interpret the new reverse onus provision of section 16(1.01), and they may feel that this is intended to dramatically alter the nature of transfer proceedings.

For youths *not* facing murder charges the new provisions do nothing to clarify the complex issues surrounding the length of time in custody actually served by young offenders or the place where sentences are served. Under the 1992 law, very few youths who are *not* transferred and are convicted in youth court of offences other than murder receive the maximum disposition of three years (or two years if the maximum adult sentence is less than life imprisonment). However, any disposition actually imposed by a youth court judge is more likely to be fully served than a sentence imposed by an adult court judge as youth court judges are much more reluctant to permit for early release at *Y.O.A.* review hearings than are adult parole officials dealing with those in the adult system. On the other hand, one can expect that youths who are transferred to adult court will have their age taken into account as a mitigating factor on sentencing, and at a parole hearing, and they will generally serve less time than adults convicted of the same offences.

The *Y.O.A.* sections 16.1 and 16.2 (allowing transferred youths to remain in a youth custody facility by court order) and section 24.5 (allowing a youth court to order a "young person" to serve his sentence in an adult facility, once he has reached the age of 18) will also continue to provide some flexibility over the place where sentences are served. Those youths who are transferred may nevertheless serve a significant portion (or all) of the "adult" sentences in youth facilities, while those who are not transferred to adult court may later be transferred at some point after sentencing in youth court by a youth court judge to an adult correctional facility, provided they have reached the age of 18.

The public pronouncements of the Minister of Justice do not dwell on the issues of his expectations about the actual place of custody or length of sentence, nor is it clear how these confounding factors will affect judges at transfer hearings. However, most transfer decisions compare the "real time" rather than the "paper time", suggesting that judicial consideration of the actual length of sentences likely to be served in the two systems will make judges reluctant to transfer for offences other than murder.

Police and prosecutors may also have a very significant effect on the number of transfers. In many situations involving 16 and 17-year-old youths there will be significant police discretion about whether to lay a charge with a presumption of transfer, like aggravated sexual assault, or some lesser offence, like sexual assault causing bodily harm, where the onus remains on the Crown to satisfy the court of the necessity for transfer. In its original form, Bill C-37 included aggravated assault in the list of offences for which there would an onus on the older youth to justify not having the case in adult court. This would have resulted in many more transfer hearings (there were 212 such charges in 1992-93 for 16 and 17-year-olds, compared to only 69 for murder, manslaughter, attempted murder and aggravated sexual assault). Aggravated assault was removed from the list in section 16(1.01) during the House of Commons Committee hearings because of concerns that there would be a huge and unnecessary increase in the number of transfer hearings.

It is unclear how Crown prosecutors will respond to the new provisions; it is possible that in many cases under section 16(1.01) they will choose not to oppose "transfer down". When challenged by a Bloc Québécois member at the Committee hearings about section 16(1.01), the Minister of Justice suggested that a province could have a policy directive instructing Crown prosecutors to regularly request "transfer down" for certain types of cases. Such a policy may well be implemented in the province of Quebec, which could create very significant interprovincial variation in how the new law is applied. Subsection 16(1.04), added to the Bill in the Committee hearings, provides that if the Crown does not file a notice opposing a youth's request to "transfer down", the case shall be transferred down without a hearing, facilitating provincial action to limit the number of transfer hearings.

In sum, the new transfer provisions are clearly intended to give the *public* the *impression* of a tough new regime for violent youth, especially 16 and 17-year-olds charged with more serious offences. The new provisions raise the corresponding spectre of relatively large numbers of adolescents serving sentences in adult correctional facilities, with their relatively brutal atmosphere and lack of appropriate services. It seems highly likely, especially in the first stages of implementation, that there will be *more transfer hearings* for 16 and 17-year-olds, with their concomitant expense and delay.

It is more difficult to accurately predict effect of the new transfer provisions on the number of youths transferred. It seems likely that the net effect of these changes will be *an increase* in the number of 16 and 17-year-olds being transferred to adult court, but *a decrease* in the number of younger youths being transferred. On balance, one might expect little overall effect on total numbers being transferred as a result of Bill C-37, though it should be appreciated that numbers have fluctuated considerably under the 1992 law, going from 33 in 1992-93 to 94 in 1993-94, despite a drop in the most serious types of charges.

However, if the new provisions were to result in a large number of youths serving time in the potentially abusive and inevitably corrosive adult prison environment, one might actually expect that the 1995 reforms will ultimately *decrease the long term protection* of society. At least some of those sentenced as adolescents to adult correctional facilities and serving lengthy sentences there may well pose a greater threat to the public upon release than if they were not transferred.

Research from the United States demonstrates that amending the law to have more transfers does not have a deterrent effect on youthful offending, and placing youths in adult court actually appears to have a negative impact on their future re-offending behaviour.

As an alternative to having an increase in the number (and hence expense and delay) of pre-trial transfer hearings, Parliament should have given consideration to other changes in the *Y.O.A*. Transfer in its present form could be abolished, and provisions for longer maximum sentences in youth court be provided for a short list of very violent offences.

One of the problems with transfer hearings is that the youth court judge does not have complete information about the offence, but rather is obliged to essentially accept the Crown's evidence, which is usually based on hearsay at this stage, about the offence. For tactical reasons, defence counsel often declines to have the youth testify at the transfer hearing, so the court has an incomplete picture of the situation. It might be preferable to abolish pre-trial transfer hearings altogether, and deal with the issue of length and place of sentence after conviction.

The complexity of the situation created by Bill C-37 is most obvious for murder, where there may be a transfer hearing; a jury trial whether or not there has been a transfer; if transfer has occurred, another hearing under section 16.2 of the *Y.O.A*. to determine whether part of the sentence will be served in a youth facility and if transfer has not occurred a hearing under section 24.5 of the *Y.O.A*. to have a youth serve the last portion of a sentence in an adult facility.

The pre-trial transfer hearing should be abolished. For murder and a few very violent offences, the Crown would be required to indicate before trial whether a sentence of longer than five years less a day will be sought, in which the youth would have the right to elect for a jury trial. The issue of length and place of sentence should be dealt with after conviction. This would be fairer and more efficient.

## VI. DISPOSITIONAL DECISION-MAKING: ASSESSMENT & VICTIM IMPACT STATEMENTS

Bill C-37 includes provisions to ensure that judges receive more information about youths for the disposition or transfer stage of proceedings, in particular in cases involving violence.

Section 13 is amended to make clear that a medical, psychological or psychiatric assessment may be ordered by the court on its own motion, as well as at the request of either of the parties. It will no longer be necessary for the court to believe that the youth is suffering from some emotional disturbance or disability to request an assessment. The judge will be able to order a report if the youth's history "indicates a repeated pattern of criminal conduct" or the youth is charged with "an offence involving serious personal injury".

Section 14 is amended to specify that a provincial director may include a "recommendation" as to disposition in a pre-disposition report, if the director considers this appropriate. It has been a common, but not universal, practice for reports to provide recommendations, and the new section 14(2)(d) clarifies that this is an acceptable practice. The youth workers preparing the reports will also be expected to contact, "where reasonably possible and appropriate", members of the youth's "extended family", and determine whether they can exert "control and influence" on the youth. This will be especially relevant for aboriginal youth, and may allow for more community based dispositions involving members of the extended family.

The *Y.O.A.* is also to be amended to explicitly allow courts to receive victim impact statements under section 735(1.1) of the *Criminal Code*. These statements are already being used in some youth courts. Increased use of these statements may give youth courts more information at the time of sentencing, as well as giving victims a greater degree of satisfaction with the justice system.

These amendments are intended to ensure the courts have more information, in particular for cases involving serious violence. Together with amendments discussed below, they are also intended to ensure a more "efficient" (*i.e.* limited) use of custody facilities, and more use of non-custodial dispositions for youths who do not pose a significant risk to the community.

## VII. THE DECLARATION OF PRINCIPLE & JUDICIAL DISCRETION AT SENTENCING

There are several critical areas where the *Y.O.A.* grants enormous discretion to judges and other decision-makers, and it is scarcely surprising that they have exercised their discretion in very different ways. Bill C-37 attempts to give somewhat more structure to the exercise of discretion.

The present Declaration of Principles (s. 3) reflects the *Act*'s failure, in several crucial areas, to structure the exercise of discretion. While the relatively complex, generalized statements found in section 3 are undoubtedly more realistic than the single, simplistic philosophy of the *J.D.A.*, the lack of prioritization and ambiguity of most of the principles has meant that this statement in practice offers little guidance or constraint to decision-makers. In fairness to the legislators, the Declaration reflects not just a compromise, but also prevailing societal ambivalence and uncertainty about how to deal with problems of youth crime in general. Further, in the effort to ensure that judges meet the needs of the individual youth being dealt with, most pieces of Canadian legislation that govern children before the courts resort to vague statements of principle and highly ambiguous concepts like "the best interests of the child".

The courts have also emphasized the discretionary nature of the *Y.O.A.*, following the lead of the Supreme Court of Canada. In a 1989 transfer decision, the highest court wrote about the importance of respecting the individualized "*viewpoint of the tribunal in question*". The 1993 Supreme Court judgment on youth court sentencing in *R. v. M. (J.J.)* again emphasized the importance of individualized dispositional decisions, rejecting the idea that proportionality in responding to the offence should limit youth court sentences, at least to the extent that it does in adult court.

In significant measure, the *Y.O.A.*, as interpreted by the courts, has created a highly variable system of youth justice, with great differences between provinces, and even between individual judges in the same cities. Some of the generalized criticism of the *Y.O.A.*, for example, that the *Act* is "too soft", may be inaccurate, both for missing variability and placing "blame" on the *Act*, rather than recognizing that the *Y.O.A. permitted* different decision-makers to do very different things. Many of the problems that critics associate with the *Y.O.A.* are not directly *caused* by the *Act*; rather, they have been *permitted* by the *Act*, but have been *caused* by individual decision-makers.

For example, some critics charge that the enactment of the *Y.O.A.* has *caused* a large increase in the use of custody because it has de-emphasized child welfare concerns. In reality, while it is true *most* jurisdictions in Canada have experienced substantial increases in the use of custody since the *Y.O.A.* came into force in 1984, in some places there has been little, if any, increase. Further, at least with some judges, the increase in use of custody may reflect rehabilitative concerns rather than a desire to be punitive. Similarly, critics on the right who argue that sentences are too short, fail to recognize that some judges impose quite lengthy sentences under the *Y.O.A.*

While amending the Declaration of Principle is unlikely to have as much impact as more directly structuring specific decision-making, such as having sentencing grids, the Liberal government is providing some clear signals about its philosophy, in particular by explicitly adding crime prevention and rehabilitation to the Declaration:

> (a) crime prevention is essential to the long-term protection of society and requires addressing the underlying causes of crime by young persons and developing multi-disciplinary approaches to identifying and effectively responding to children and young persons at risk of committing offending behaviour in the future;
>
> . . . . .
>
> (c.1) the protection of society, which is a primary objective of the criminal law applicable to youth, is best served by rehabilitation, wherever possible, of young persons who commit offences, and rehabilitation is best achieved by addressing the needs and circumstances of a young person that are relevant to the young person's offending behaviour.

The importance of crime prevention and rehabilitation were recognized in a 1993 House of Commons Committee Report and in the Liberal campaign policy *Red Book*, though one has to question whether other provisions of Bill C-37, in particular those relating to transfer, reflect that broader understanding. More fundamentally, without the expenditure of resources, the articulation of these goals may not be very significant. Further, as noted above, the concept of "rehabilitation" as a decision-making philosophy for young offenders is quite problematic, and has been used to justify longer custodial dispositions. Some of the proposed amendments to section 24, discussed below, are apparently intended to prevent this interpretative approach to section 3(1)(c.1).

There is a considerable body of research on delinquency prevention, which demonstrates that programs based in preschools, schools and the community, can provide a long term cost effective means of reducing levels of delinquency. These programs are most effective if they are long lasting (two to five years), start early (preferably in the first five years of life), focus on multiple risk families, and are broadly based. They will not provide a "quick fix", but they offer the prospect of long term returns for our present social investment.

## VIII. ALTERNATIVES TO CUSTODY

There is wide variation in how judges sentence young offenders, as well as substantial interprovincial differences in rates of custody use. However, in Canada as a whole, the number of youths receiving custody dispositions has increased significantly since the *Y.O.A.* came into force, though the average time served is less than under the *J.D.A.'s* indefinite sentences.

Parliament enacted some relatively minor amendments to the *Y.O.A.* in 1986 with the apparent objective of ensuring that custody is not overused. For example, section

24(1) was amended to provide that a judge should not make a committal to custody unless it is considered "necessary for the protection of society, having regard to the seriousness of the offence and . . . the needs and circumstances of the young person." While the 1986 amendments were intended to reduce inappropriate use of custody, they have had no appreciable effect. Indeed, the amendment to section 24(1), combined with the 1993 Supreme Court judgment in *R. v. M. (J.J.)*, can be interpreted as endorsing use of longer sentences than the offence itself might merit for "rehabilitative" purposes, in order to achieve the long term protection of society.

Some observers argue that the only way to substantially reduce dispositional disparity for juvenile offenders is to adopt a "sentencing grid", where there is presumption that the offence and prior record will produce a sentence within a particular range. This type of approach has been adopted in some American states for sentencing, for both adults and juveniles. While this type of proposal merits consideration, given the enormous geographical variation in available custodial and correctional resources, such a scheme may not be suitable for dealing with young offenders in Canada. Further, in the present political climate, any grid that would be adopted would likely result in substantial increases in the use of custody without increasing social protection.

One of the major concerns about *Y.O.A* dispositions has been the growing use of custodial dispositions, especially for youths not involved in violent offences. This has been very expensive, both in financial terms and in regard to long term rehabilitation, which is often more likely to be achieved in community based programs. Bill C-37 has a number of provisions intended to reduce inappropriate use of custody, beyond those dealing with assessment reports and the Declaration of Principle which were discussed above.

A new provision is added to section 24, with the obvious intent of avoiding unnecessary use of custody.

> s. 24(1.1) In making a determination under subsection (1), the youth court shall take the following into account:
>> (a) that an order of custody shall not be used as a substitute for appropriate child protection, health and other social measures;
>> (b) that a young person who commits an offence that does not involve serious personal injury should be held accountable to the victim and to society through non-custodial dispositions whenever appropriate; and
>> (c) that custody shall only be imposed when all available alternatives to custody that are reasonable in the circumstances have been considered.

The evident intent of section 24(1.1)(a) is to reduce the inappropriate use of custody. This provision endorses the Ontario Court of Appeal judgment in *R. v. M.B.* where it was held that a youth court sentence for a young offender must be "responsive to the offence", and *not* just a "sensible way of dealing with a youth who had a personality problem and needed a place to go". While not explicitly reversing the Supreme Court of Canada decision in *R. v. M.(J.J.)*, the new provision would at least appear to require some modification of the approach taken in that case, since it seems that the Court did not fully explore the alternatives to custody, especially in the child welfare system. Similarly, taking the authority away from the courts for specifying the level of custody, discussed below, is intended to reduce the tendency of some judges, illustrated in *R.*

*v. M.(J.J.)*, to view open custody as a "therapeutic" sentence that might be longer than justified in terms of accountability.

Youth court judges who impose a custodial disposition will be required under the new section 24(4) to give reasons why a non-custodial disposition would not have been adequate. This is intended to have judges specifically address the appropriateness and availability of non-custodial dispositions. However, in significant measure, the extent to which use is made of non-custodial dispositions will depend on the extent to which provinces make resources available for community based dispositions. The federal government has indicated that it will "re-target" some of its shared cost funding to encourage community based dispositions, though it remains to be seen whether this will occur.

Arguably, section 24(1.1) is expecting youth court judges to take a more activist role in developing non-custodial dispositions for youths. If this was intended, it would have been desirable to also give judges more explicit powers to fashion specific non-custodial dispositions when provincial correctional officials are unwilling to arrange or finance such dispositions. At least, a provision should have been enacted to allow judges sentencing under the *Y.O.A.* to order authorities to provide child welfare services in appropriate cases as an alternative to custody. Such a provision did not, however, appear in Bill C-37.

While judges will continue to determine the length of custodial dispositions, section 24.1 will be amended to allow provincial governments to have the provincial director — a juvenile correctional official — determine the level of custody: open or secure.

A number of provinces, including Ontario, have been seeking this transfer of responsibility from judges to correctional officials. At least in theory this should allow decisions about the level of custody to be made by those with most knowledge of available resources, and the professional background to assess the needs of young offenders. It may also cause judges to be a little more cautious about imposing a custodial disposition, since some judges appear to have been imposing *open* custody when they would not have considered a "purely" custodial disposition, based on the premise that these open facilities are less punitive and more rehabilitative than secure custody. As there are weak statutory distinctions between the two types of facilities and provincial governments have enormous latitude in how facilities are designated, some of the judicial optimism about open custody may be unfounded.

The federal government evidently has some concern about exactly how provincial directors will exercise their discretion over placement in levels of custody. It provides some discretion structuring factors for the exercise of this discretion in section 24.1(4), emphasizing the "least degree of containment and restraint"; and also gives a youth or a parent the right to appeal to a youth court a placement by a provincial director in secure custody. Regrettably, there is no statutory requirement for the appeal to be held within a stated period and there is a concern that a sentence may be largely or totally served before an appeal is heard. It should be noted that under section 24.1(4)(d) a youth court judge shall still be permitted to make a "recommendation" about the appropriate level of custody at the time of original sentencing to the provincial director, and in some cases this may have considerable influence on the initial decision of the director.

The new section 24.1 will also give provincial directors a broader power to transfer youths from one level of custody to another while a sentence is being served. If the director transfers a youth from open to secure custody, there is a right of appeal to the youth court.

One major concern is that decisions about the level of custody by provincial directors may be driven more by administrative and budgetary concerns than by the needs of the youth, or even of society.

## IX. DETENTION FOR TREATMENT

Mental health professionals and others have frequently attacked the provisions of the *Y.O.A.* that require a youth's consent before an order can be made for "detaining the youth for treatment", arguing that "youth, especially those involved in offending, may not be in the position to make ultimate decisions regarding the value of mental health intervention".

Bill C-37 abolishes sections 20(1)(i) and 22, provisions which allowed youth courts to order that a youth could be "detained for treatment" instead of being placed in custody, but only if the youth consented. These types of orders were very rarely made, in part because youths were unwilling to consent to being placed in mental health facilities, but probably more due to lack of suitable facilities. It will, of course, continue to be possible for provinces to provide substantial treatment services in custody facilities, subject only to general provincial laws about imposing medical treatment (*i.e.* drugs, electroshock) on unwilling, competent individuals. However, there remains some scepticism about whether the provinces will actually provide the necessary level of services.

## X. CONDITIONAL DISCHARGE

Under the *Y.O.A.* as originally enacted in 1984, there were no provisions for conditional discharges, premised on the view that the various non-disclosure and deeming provisions meant that all youths who committed only one offence were in effect conditionally discharged. Many judges and youth justice professionals have expressed a desire to have an explicit conditional discharge option, to be able to give a youth receiving a sanction a clearer message that if the terms of the disposition are carried out, the youth will have the "record wiped clean", and will then not be viewed as "an offender".

Bill C-37 adds section 20(1)(a.1) allowing a court to order that a "young person be discharged on such conditions as the court considers appropriate". Conditions might include a donation to charity, undergoing counselling, paying a fine or doing community service work. The new section 45(1)(d.2) will provide that three years after the imposition of a conditional discharge records relating to that offence can no longer be used for any purpose, provided the terms of the discharge are honoured.

## XI. INFORMATION SHARING & RECORDS

The *Y.O.A.* has a number of provisions that are intended to promote the rehabilitation of young offenders by preventing the dissemination of information about them.

These provisions have been controversial, as the media and members of the public have argued that they have a "right to know" about youthful offenders. Amendments were enacted in 1986 to permit police to apply to a youth court to allow publication of identifying information about youths considered dangerous and at large. On the whole, the present scheme has much to commend it, reflecting the potential negative stereotyping and labelling that can result from the dissemination of information, and the reality that in general members of the public can do little to protect themselves as a result of having access to identifying information about young offenders in the media. There are, however, circumstances in which professionals working with or treating young offenders are not always getting access to information that would be helpful to them. In the case of young offenders in the community, some limited dissemination of information may help ensure public safety.

Bill C-37 allows for two new categories of disclosure: administrative disclosure (s. 38(1.13)) and disclosure by youth court order (s. 38(1.5)).

The new section 38(1.13) will allow provincial governments to have regulations to allow police and probation officers to share the information with designated school officials (such as a principal or vice principal), or other professionals, such as child welfare workers. These professionals will be able to disclose the information to other persons if necessary to monitor compliance with a court order or to protect "safety" in the school or other settings. While these officials are required to keep youth court based information separate from other records and destroy it when no longer required, it seems likely that this amendment will result in significantly more access to information about offending behaviour within schools.

A new provision, section 38(1.5), will allow a youth court, after a hearing, to permit disclosure of information to members of the public where the youth is thought to pose a "risk of serious harm" and the disclosure of information is "necessary" to avoid risk. Although the media is still prohibited from publicizing the identity of the youth, it seems likely information will circulate widely in the community if an order is made under section 38(1.5). While section 38(1.5) does not specify whether the court should consider the potential harm to the youth from disclosure, the new section 13(2)(f) provides that the court may order a psychological or psychiatric assessment for a disclosure hearing. This suggests that the court should take account of the effect of disclosure on the youth, as well as the other criteria mentioned in section 38(1.5).

Section 38(1.5) is a response to widespread demands that the public has a "right to know" of offenders released into their community. In particular, it is a response to one highly publicized case in British Columbia involving a young sex offender who was released into the community where he later assaulted and killed a neighbourhood child. Section 38(1.5) could in theory permit neighbours in such situations to be informed and neighbourhood children warned of the potential danger. There were actually many problems with how the British Columbia case was handled under existing law in terms of lack of communication between police and probation services. Furthermore, one can question whether this type of statutory change was necessary to deal with such situations more effectively.

One can appreciate the sentiments behind section 38(1.5), especially the desire to protect children, but its ultimate effects may be very problematic. Unless all children in the community are warned, the protection afforded by this provision may be slight.

Further, once neighbours and fellow students are "warned" about a particular youth, meaningful reintegration into the community will be very difficult, and offenders may be likely to move away from supports and seek anonymity in large urban centres, making rehabilitation much more difficult to achieve. There is no justification for this type of provision only for young offenders; if anything, it is more urgent for adults. The American experience with this type of provision suggests significant problems with implementation, and that it may actually be counterproductive to the objective of increasing community protection.

Various record keeping provisions are also being amended by Bill C-37 to allow longer retention of records, especially where violent offences are involved. For murder, attempted murder, or aggravated sexual assault, records may be kept indefinitely in centralized police records, and for a longer list of less serious, violent and sexual offences, the period will be ten years as opposed to the present five years. On the other hand, for summary conviction offences, records will only be kept for three years from the completion of a disposition, reduced from the present five years, provided that there are no further offences.

These new provisions are obviously intended to address the criticisms of media, politicians, professionals and members of the public that more needs to be known about young offenders so that appropriate protective steps can be taken. While professionals who are treating and counselling youths should have adequate access to information about them, one has to wonder whether public safety will actually be increased if more information is made available in the community. One can expect more negative stereotyping and labelling of young offenders by their communities as a result of these changes. The longer period of retention for records of violent offences for possible use in subsequent adult criminal investigations or sentencing hearings is a justifiable attempt to increase public safety.

## XII. STATEMENTS TO THE POLICE & DUE PROCESS

The *Y.O.A.* adopted a due process model of juvenile justice, which effectively guarantees every youth charged with an offence the right to a lawyer paid by the state, and requires judges to exclude statements made by youths to the police unless detailed cautions are given to the youth. These protections are more extensive than those afforded adults under the *Charter*.

Some critics decry the financial expense of providing such extensive legal services and argue that at least some of these resources might be better spent on providing therapeutic services to youths. However, the youth court process is complex and adolescents are less sophisticated and knowledgeable than adults: special measures to ensure that youths have adequate legal representation may be justified to ensure that they can understand and meaningfully participate in the process. But the unfortunate reality is that while some lawyers involved in this type of work are knowledgeable and have the social skills to communicate effectively with adolescents, others do not. Adolescents are generally not sophisticated consumers of legal services, and may not even know when they are receiving inadequate legal representation. Provincial governments should ensure that lawyers involved in representing youths charged under the *Y.O.A.* have adequate training, just as lawyers in Ontario who represent children in chid welfare cases must undergo specialized training.

Adolescents may be more easily pressured into making statements to police than adults, and may even be coerced by authority figures into making false confessions. They also often lack appreciation of the legal and other consequences of making a statement to the police. This may justify affording them special protections when they are being questioned by the police. However, section 56 of the *Y.O.A.* imposes a very strict standard on the police. A police officer is required to give a youth, who is generally unknown to the officer, an explanation in, "language appropriate to his age and understanding" of relatively complex legal rights. At present even a relatively minor technical defect results in the automatic exclusion of the statement.

A violation of the *Charter* in regard to an adult or youth only gives rise to a situation where the court has a *discretion* to exclude a statement if its "admission would bring the administration of justice into disrepute". While special legal protections for youths are justifiable, arguably there should be some judicial discretion for the admission of statements where there has been a good faith effort by police to comply with the statute. There are situations at present in which youths have confessed their guilt to the police, and cannot understand why they are not being held accountable. Bill C-37 deals with some of the difficulties faced by police, and clarifies some conflicting jurisprudence, though not all of the problems with section 56 are addressed.

Section 56(2) is amended to clarify that police have an obligation to provide a warning to a youth who is arrested or detained, *or* where a youth is being questioned by a police officer who reasonably suspects the youth of having committed an offence. By implication, however, section 56 will not apply to other situations where police are questioning a youth, for example if the young person is a potential witness, but there are *no* reasonable grounds at the time of questioning to believe that the youth committed an offence.

In its original form, Bill C-37 contained a provision to clarify the effect of a 1993 Supreme Court of Canada decision and alert police that a youth who is being questioned must be warned "when applicable", that he or she "may be dealt with as an adult, and if dealt with as an adult, could face the same consequences as an adult". This provision was very broad since under section 16 any youth 14 or older charged with any indictable offence, other than some relatively minor property offences, *may* in theory face a transfer application; the provision therefore appeared to require that for virtually all indictable or hybrid offences the police would have had to provide this warning. This proposal was withdrawn from the final version of the Bill, as it was felt too draconian to statutorily require a police warning about a merely theoretical possibility for transfer in situations where transfer is not a realistic prospect. Unfortunately, in the absence of legislation, the Supreme Court of Canada decision appears to continue to require such a broad caution. A preferable solution would be for legislation to specify that such a statement is only admissible if such caution is given in a case where there is a presumption under section 16(1.01) or where the Crown actually applies to transfer.

Section 56(4) allows a youth to waive the right to consult a parent or lawyer in writing; this is amended to allow a videotaped waiver as well. This amendment is desirable as it should encourage more videotaping, which will provide a much more accurate record of questioning for any later court hearing than the common practice of police notetaking.

A new provision, section 56(5.1), gives courts a relatively narrow jurisdiction to admit statements where the police have not adequately complied with the section 56 warning provisions because the young person has held himself or herself out as being 18 years of age or older at the time of the police questioning, and the officer made reasonable inquiries to establish the youth's age.

These proposed amendments to section 56 are quite narrow, and do not erode the due process rights currently afforded youths under the *Y.O.A.*

The House of Commons Committee studying Bill C-37, the Justice and Legal Affairs Committee, completed its hearings in December 1994 and the Bill received Third Reading in the House of Commons February 28, 1995.

The Committee has also been asked by the Minister of Justice to carry out a Second Phase of its hearings, with a broader inquiry into the youth justice system. This Second Phase is not expected to begin before late in 1995. The issues that the Minister would like explored are:

- the nature and extent of youth crime and criminal behaviour in young adults;
- public knowledge of and attitudes towards youth crime, the *Young Offenders Act* and the youth justice system, including particularly the knowledge and attitudes of young people;
- the *Young Offenders Act*, including the underlying issues governed by the current provisions of the *Act*, including but not limited to: the age range of the *Act*, transfer to adult court, sharing of information and publication of names, records, parental responsibility, statements by young persons, and sentencing provisions;
- alternatives to legislative responses to juvenile crime;
- the inter-relationship of youth services and the legislation; and
- aboriginal youth and the justice system, with an emphasis on culturally appropriate crime prevention and rehabilitation.

In light of the relatively extensive amendments to the *Y.O.A.* in Bill C-37 and the Liberal *Red Book* policy statements, as well as the limited scope for *legislative* reform in this area, one might expect few recommendations for further *statutory* reform after the Second Phase of the hearings, unless the Committee decides to fundamentally reconsider issues or principles.

The only major issue of legislative concern which Bill C-37 did not address is age jurisdiction, a matter of considerable interest, at least to some of the provincial governments. With Bill C-37 creating a new regime for 16 and 17-year-olds charged with the most serious offences, one might expect that the public pressure for lowering the maximum age will be reduced. The issue of minimum age continues to be controversial.

Under the *J.D.A.*, criminal liability began at age 7, though children under 14 could be acquitted if they lacked the capacity to appreciate the consequences of their wrongful conduct (the *doli incapax* defence). In practice relatively few children under 12 were charged under the *J.D.A.*, and even fewer were removed from parental care. The expectation of the drafters of the *Y.O.A.* was that children under 12 who commit offences could be adequately dealt with by their parents or child welfare authorities.

While the problem of children under 12 committing offences since the *Y.O.A.* came into force may be exaggerated in the media, the question of minimum age jurisdiction is a continued cause for concern. For most children in this younger age group who are committing offences, a parental response, with perhaps a police caution and a referral to an appropriate social agency, is sufficient. For more serious situations, however, reliance on child protection agencies has not been totally successful. Although some child welfare agencies have responded with specific programs, offending by children under 12 is not a priority for many child welfare agencies, perhaps understandably given the rising child abuse caseloads and shrinking budgets.

Longer sentences for young offenders may not have any deterrent effect, but effectively announcing to children under 12 that they have *no* legal responsibility can only tend to increase offending behaviour. Furthermore, earlier involuntary court ordered intervention may be desirable with some children in this age group.

The confidence of police, victims and members of the public in the justice system is understandably undermined when ten and 11-year-olds are committing offences without an effective societal response. There have been a few serious offences committed by children in this age group in Canada, but if we ever face a situation such as those which have occurred in Britain and the United States where nine and ten-year-olds have committed homicide, there will understandably be an enormous public outcry. Even without a homicide, confidence in the justice system is being eroded by the apparent lack of response to offending behaviour by children under 12.

While any minimum or maximum age has an element of arbitrariness, ages 12 through 18 have the advantage of roughly coinciding with the adolescent stage of physical, social and psychological development. Children under 12 generally have not reached puberty, and have not achieved the level of moral development of older youths, though most children ten and older can appreciate the differences between right and wrong and understand fundamental legal concepts. Ideally the best approach for offending behaviour by children under 12 might be for provinces to establish regimes that deal with offending behaviour but focus on their welfare, providing for social protection by allowing long term involuntary intervention in appropriate cases.

Unfortunately, such an ideal approach seems unlikely to be adopted in the present fiscal and political climate and it may be necessary to consider a criminal response. If the criminal option is pursued, the minimum age for *Y.O.A.* jurisdiction could be lowered, perhaps to ten, an age that England has adopted, and one that may be consistent with the views of adolescents themselves. For offenders under 12, any youth justice response should be a last resort, with clear restrictions on removal from parental care, and provisions to ensure that these children are not placed with older offenders.

## XIV. CONCLUSION

The history of juvenile justice in Canada is one of successive reform. In the nineteenth century the reformatories for juveniles replaced the adult prisons; in 1908 the *Juvenile Delinquents Act* created the juvenile justice system, and in 1984 the *Young Offenders Act* came into force. Each change brought improvements, but ultimately failed to fully satisfy the objectives of its proponents.

It is difficult to decide whether to be cynical or cautiously optimistic about the 1995 reforms. The cynicism may be easier to understand. In some respects Bill C-37 represents a too common political response, to *appear* to be "solving" the complex problem of youthful crime by enacting a new "tougher" law. In reality this type of new law cannot hope to have the effect of reducing the levels of adolescent offending.

Bill C-37 appears in large measure to be an attempt to respond to the public clamour for "getting tough" with youth crime, and to be seen as a relatively rapid implementation of the 1993 election promises of the Liberal *Red Book*. However, a detailed reading of the Bill suggests that it contains somewhat inconsistent messages, especially in the high profile area of transfer. Of course the different themes found in Bill C-37 reflect conflicting policies found in the *Red Book*, and a divergence of views within the Liberal caucus. Certainly it is *possible* to be cynical, or at very least doubtful, about whether the Bill will increase the long term protection of the Canadian public.

On the other hand, the present Minister of Justice, Allan Rock, appears to be a thoughtful politician, who understands the complex nature of juvenile crime and recognizes the limitations of a "get tough" approach. Before the introduction of Bill C-37, he observed:

> If the answer to crime was simply harsher laws, longer penalties, and bigger prisons, then the United States would be nirvana today ... We are only going to be able to have long-term and effective results if we create a society in which we minimize conditions which breed crime.

Viewed in this light, Bill C-37 may be considered a compromise measure, intended to satisfy the enormous public demands (outside Quebec) for government action while maintaining the fundamental integrity of the youth justice system. Although some measures, especially the presumptive transfer provisions for older youths, will be complex and expensive to implement and seem undesirable, others in the sentencing field may actually tend to produce a more rehabilitative community-based system for young offenders.

At least initially Bill C-37 may result in more transfer hearings, especially for 16 and 17-year-old youths with the very violent offences listed in section 16(1.01). However, it seems possible that once the courts resolve the appropriate interpretation of section 16(1.1), there may be no increase in the number of transfers. Indeed, for 14 and 15-year-olds and for older youths not charged with the designated very violent offences, the Bill holds out the prospect of fewer transfers and more consistent treatment between provinces. It should also be emphasized that relatively few youths are involved in very violent offences, and Bill C-37 holds out the prospect that a relatively large number of less serious offenders will be receiving more appropriate community-based dispositions rather than their present custody-based sentences.

As with all law reform efforts in the juvenile justice field, the ultimate effect of the 1995 Liberal initiative will depend more on judicial interpretation and provincial implementation than on Parliamentary intent. The actual effect of any merely legislative change on juvenile crime in Canada is unlikely to be significant, as even the Minister of Justice himself appeared to recognize.

Reducing the levels of juvenile crime will require more sophisticated educational and social policies, addressing the underlying causes and reality of youthful offending. This will require more effectively addressing such problems as child abuse, neglect and poverty, adolescence substance abuse and youth unemployment. While changes to the youth justice and corrections system can have some effect, reforming the health, education, social service and day care systems will ultimately have much more of an effect on levels of youthful criminality in Canada, and will in the long term be much more likely to result in a safer, more productive society.

**Questions/Discussion**
1. What was the change of philosophy in the treatment of young offenders with the introduction of the Young Offenders Act? Do you agree with this philosophical stance? Why or why not? What degree of responsibility should society take and what should be the level of responsibility of the young offender for his or her actions?
2. Do you agree with age limits placed on the definition of young offenders, both at the lower and at the upper ends of the scale? Why? If so, what should those limits be and why?
3. Is there an argument to be made that the provinces should have a greater say in the formulation of criminal justice policy given the role they play in the enforcement and implementation of the schemes which are adopted at the federal level? What are the arguments against an enhanced involvement by the province at that stage of the production of criminal law?
4. It is important to recognise that, as in most other areas of criminal law, the law pertaining to young offenders, no matter how good it may be or may become, can provide only a very limited "solution" to dealing with the problems and issues surrounding two young people in conflict with the law. Attacks, often costly, on problems such as poor housing, child abuse, lack of opportunity, and inadequate education are necessary as well, though often underfunded or nonexistent.
5. For examples of how the courts deal with requests by the Crown to have a young offender's case transferred to adult court, see *R. v. C. (D.)* (1994), 85 C.C.C. (3d) 547 (Ont. C.A.) and *R. v. L. (M.)* (1994), 89 C.C.C. (3d) 264.

**Further Reading**
- Archambault, O., "Young Offenders Act: Philosophy and Principles" (1980), 7 Provincial Judges Journal 1.
- Corrado, R. *et al.* (eds.), *Juvenile Justice in Canada: A Theoretical and Analytical Assessment* (Toronto: Butterworths, 1992).
- Griffiths, C.T. and S. Verdun-Jones, *Canadian Criminal Justice*, 2nd Ed. (Toronto: Harcourt Brace & Company, Canada, 1994), Chapter 14.
- Hudson, J. *et al.* (eds.), *Justice and the Young Offender in Canada* (Toronto: Wall & Thompson, 1988).
- Jaffe, P., *et al.*, "Youth's Knowledge and Attitudes About the Young Offenders Act: Does Anyone Care What They Think" (1987), 29 Canadian Journal of Criminology 309.
- Reid, S., "The Juvenile Justice Revolution in Canada: The Creation of New Legislation for Young Offenders" (1986), 8 Canadian Criminology Forum 1.
- Reid, S. and M. Reitsma-Street, "Assumptions and Implications of New Canadian Legislation For Young Offenders" (1984), 7 Canadian Criminology Forum 1.
- Riley, P., "Proportionality as a Guiding Principle in Young Offender Dispositions" (1994), 17 Dalhousie Law Journal 560-586.
- West, W.G., *Young Offenders and the State* (Toronto: Butterworths, 1984).